NORTHERN/IRISH FEMINIST JUDGMENTS

The Northern/Irish Feminist Judgments Project inaugurates a fresh dialogue on gender, legal judgment, judicial power and national identity in Ireland and Northern Ireland. Through a process of judicial re-imagining, the project takes account of the peculiarly Northern/Irish concerns in shaping gender through judicial practice. This collection, following on from feminist judgments projects in Canada, England and Australia takes the feminist judging methodology in challenging new directions. This book collects 26 rewritten judgments, covering a range of substantive areas. As well as opinions from appellate courts, the book includes first instance decisions and a fictional review of a Tribunal of Inquiry. Each feminist judgment is accompanied by a commentary putting the case in its social context and explaining the original decision. The book also includes introductory chapters examining the project methodology, constructions of national identity, theoretical and conceptual issues pertaining to feminist judging, and the legal context of both jurisdictions. The book, shines a light on past and future possibilities — and limitations — for judgment on the island of Ireland.

Note on the cover image:
The photograph is from Rose Comiskey's exhibition, 'Against the Tide', which chronicles protests around women's reproductive rights in Ireland in the 1980s and 1990s.

Northern/Irish Feminist Judgments

Judges' Troubles and the Gendered Politics of Identity

Máiréad Enright, Julie McCandless and Aoife O'Donoghue

·HART·
PUBLISHING
OXFORD AND PORTLAND, OREGON
2017

Hart Publishing
An imprint of Bloomsbury Publishing Plc

Hart Publishing Ltd
Kemp House
Chawley Park
Cumnor Hill
Oxford OX2 9PH
UK

Bloomsbury Publishing Plc
50 Bedford Square
London
WC1B 3DP
UK

www.hartpub.co.uk
www.bloomsbury.com

Published in North America (US and Canada) by
Hart Publishing
c/o International Specialized Book Services
920 NE 58th Avenue, Suite 300
Portland, OR 97213-3786
USA

www.isbs.com

First published 2017

British Library Cataloguing-in-Publication Data
A catalogue record for this book is available from the British Library.

ISBN: PB: 978-1-84946-574-8
ePDF: 978-1-50990-893-6
ePub: 978-1-50990-894-3

Library of Congress Cataloging-in-Publication Data

Names: Enright, Máiréad, author. | McCandless, Julie, author. | O'Donoghue, Aoife, 1981– author.

Title: Northern/Irish feminist judgments : judges' troubles and the gendered politics of identity / Máiréad Enright, Julie McCandless, and Aoife O'Donoghue.

Description: Oxford [UK] ; Portland, Oregon : Hart Publishing, 2017. | Includes bibliographical references and index.

Identifiers: LCCN 2016045788 (print) | LCCN 2016046237 (ebook) | ISBN 9781849465748 (pbk. : alk. paper) | ISBN 9781509908943 (Epub)

Subjects: LCSH: Judges—Ireland. | Women judges—Ireland. | Judicial process—Ireland. | Justice, Administration of—Ireland. | Judicial process—Northern Ireland. | Justice, Administration of—Northern Ireland. | Feminist theory.

Classification: LCC KDK1652 .E57 2017 (print) | LCC KDK1652 (ebook) | DDC 347.417/07082—dc23

LC record available at https://lccn.loc.gov/2016045788

Typeset by Compuscript Ltd, Shannon
Printed and bound in Great Britain by Lightning Source UK Ltd

A prayer to St Bridget in her most pagan incarnation

Bridget let us keep our eyes and poke theirs out –
we need another word than justice
for these contests where everyone we care
about almost always loses,
we need new phrases for the way our bodies
are perceived as traps for men
to unsuspectingly get caught in and for how
we are made comply with this.

We need other words than conviction and witness
for the surrender and regrant submission
that even successful prosecutions entail for their victims,
we need to summons a diatribe so savage
that it sounds like our maternal ancestors howling at us
enraged at our obediences
we need to let them shame us into resistance
whenever we are denied jurisdiction
over our own interiors, our own existences.

Yes we need sentences but more than that
we need a whole new language for the damage
that happens when some overseer or other gets to tell us
what the severed parts of our anatomies were worth;
what price a broken pelvis, an unnecessary hysterectomy,
or a decade of forced labour in a laundry
and who gets to be the judge of this?

We need new mouths to make it known
that we won't stand for this—it will take a litany of curses
harsh and vicious enough to make the judge and jury
of public opinion actually listen
we need to expose the concealed weapon
of our intelligence and not apologise for it
no matter how uncomfortable this makes things,
we need to put the power brokers on notice
that if they call our protests hysterical
we will catch them by their gullets.

We need to make it known that the days
of us putting our own eyes out are over
and that as and when it's necessary
we will fix our sights on each and every stuffed shirt
who attempts to discuss the mitigating circumstances
that mean it was okay to hurt us,
we need a daylight court
that we can enter into whole and leave intact,
and we need words for this, women
we have lost our tongues in battle
and we need to take them back.

Sarah Clancy
5 November 2015

FOREWORD

During my career as a scholar and practitioner, human rights commissioner and legislator, I would have yearned for a book like this. I am certain others will feel the same. We have so much to learn from its contents, whether as judges or lawyers, advocates or activists, and its timing could not be better.

What goes on in the higher, law shaping courts, in tribunals or judicial inquiries, affects the lives of all of us. How the story gets told and how it is heard is everything. By showing how a judgment can be rewritten using the evidence and material available at the time of the original judgment, each author illustrates the relevance of context in each of their cases. They demonstrate the lack of inevitability regarding judgments and the alternative perspectives that can be brought to bear when taking a feminist perspective. They alert us to issues of power and control, visible or invisible, public or private, at the individual, household or societal level.

The 26 rewritten judgments and commentaries included here address the issues of gender, legal judgment, judicial power, and national identity following on from feminist judgments projects in other common law jurisdictions such as Canada, England, Australia and the USA. The book's introductory chapters examine national identity, as well as theories and concepts explaining feminist judging and the legal context of the Northern/Irish jurisdictions. In contrast to other feminist judgment projects, the editors have incorporated the fields of art and literature, as well as engaging with legal and non-legal expertise and experience. The methodology is innovative and its multi-form cases and multi-disciplinary approach takes us in important and challenging new directions in legal and judicial thinking. It should stimulate and reinvigorate interest in feminism, and not just a feminist approach to cases, in teaching and training.

I recommend that the next Judicial Studies Board (Northern Ireland) and the Judicial Studies Committee (Ireland), and indeed any other training body related to law making, should distribute a book chapter to each of its participants. A workshop should be organised where each participant is expected to lead a discussion and deliberate with others on what they have learned. I suspect it would be a steep learning curve for all those involved. The editors are aware of this as they themselves note: 'in recognising that judges are not the disinterested and objective tools of the law but rather accepting that judicial impartiality, fairness and independence are not compromised by acknowledging that judges bring their own lived experiences to their decisions *an avenue for alternate judicial voices has been created*'. Having led one of the Judicial Studies Board sessions on domestic violence many years ago I would be delighted to do so again, using the contents of the book to create such an avenue for alternate judicial voices.

The lack of gender diversity amongst the Northern Ireland judiciary needs to be acknowledged as another complicating factor. Since the partition of Ireland in 1922 until 2016, there were no female judges amongst the senior judiciary in Northern Ireland. This was finally addressed when Justice Siobhan Keegan and Justice Denise McBride were recently appointed to the Northern Irish High Court. At a public engagement event in Belfast on the feminist judgments project, for which I acted as chairperson, I extended my best wishes to both judges and took the opportunity to discuss whether being a woman made a difference to their role as judges. At this event, both judges acknowledged the relevance of the Northern/Irish Feminist Judgment project and spoke to the approaches of the feminist judges in a number of cases. Moreover, they addressed the significance of the project in emphasising judicial diversity but also alternative techniques of decision-making. Such engagements augur well for the project and should take place at regular intervals to ascertain the level of institutional change.

We should also be mindful that there are much needed alternatives to judicial law making for political and cultural change to take place in the Northern/Irish jurisdictions. This should come as no surprise to those of us involved in the women's movement and aware of the limitations of litigation. By hearing from activists and other intervenors in the cases, and here I declare my own hand in such a role, the feminist judgments and commentaries in this book pay attention to their interests as well as those of judges. What also makes this such an interesting and inspiring project is the extensive amount of work undertaken, and the editors and authors should be commended for the commitment to seeing their colloboration through to frutition.

As Sarah Clancy argues in her evocative poem at the beginning this book, 'we need to expose the concealed weapon of our collective intelligence and not apologise for it'. This book is no apology; it is full of collective intelligence that has been brought out into the open. I am enthused and excited by the Northern/Irish Feminist Judgments project. It opens up the potential to push for law reform through altering legal discourse at this crucial time of transition, and hopefully transformation, in Northern/Ireland. It is long overdue and I for one hope to be around to see the outcomes, not just at the level of 'judicial reimagining' but in our society and culture more widely.

Professor Monica McWilliams

ACKNOWLEDGEMENTS

The Northern/Irish Feminist Judgments Project and this book have been collaborative enterprises involving the support, energy, assistance and friendship of a large number of people. We owe them all tremendous thanks, and we hope that anyone we have inadvertently forgotten will still accept our gratitude. We would like to thank the plucky Northern/Irish women, too many to name and found in the most unlikely of places, who inspired us to start this project. We would also like to thank the many people who cared for the participants of this project over the past four years, to include those who made our dinners, or otherwise sustained us with cups of tea or coffee. To all the authors of the judgments and commentaries in this collection, as well as Mary Shine Thompson, Sarah Clancy and Monica McWilliams, we thank you for your hard work on this book, your enthusiasm throughout the project, and of course for your patience and generosity during the editorial process.

A project of this size does not happen without considerable organisational support, and we would particularly like to thank the following people for generously hosting drafting workshops and other project events: Mary Donnelly; Claire Murray; Tanya Ní Mhuirthile; Catherine O'Rourke; Liam Thornton; Judy Walsh; and Sally Wheeler. Our thanks also extends to those who provided administrative or other support to our institutional hosts.

We also had considerable financial support from several sources. Durham Law School, Gender and Law at Durham (GLAD) and the Kent Centre for Law, Gender and Sexuality (KCLGS) funded the inaugural workshop in September 2012 and provided seed funding to get the project established. Thanks to those who assisted in the creation of our website, www.feministjudging.ie. Institutional funding and provision of facilities and support were provided during the lifetime of the project from: Department of Law—London School of Economics and Political Science; Durham Law School; GLAD; Faculty of Social Sciences, University of Kent; School of Law—Griffith College Dublin; School of Law—Queen's University Belfast; School of Law—University College Cork; Sutherland School of Law—University College Dublin; Transitional Justice Institute—University of Ulster. Generous funding and encouragement was also provided from the journal *Social and Legal Studies*. The Law Society of Northern Ireland permitted us the use of their facilities for a project event in March 2016.

Many friends and colleagues gave generously of their time and expertise by reading and commenting on project, book and funding proposals, as well as parts of this book itself. We would particularly like to thank: Rosemary Auchmuty; Nicola Barker; Marie Fox; Emily Grabham; Ruth Houghton; Maria Luddy; Linda Mulcahy; Siobhán Mullally; Vanessa Munro; Sinéad Ring; Yvette Russell; Sally Sheldon; Michael Thomson; and Judy Walsh. We owe special gratitude to the co-directors of the English Feminist Judgments Project, Rosemary Hunter, Clare McGlynn and Erika Rackley, who have supported us from the outset and been remarkably generous with their time and expertise. You are three of the plucky women we can name.

Several students provided invaluable research assistance: Zoe Carter, Eleanne Hussey and Ellen Jepson collated materials for the project website; Sandra Duffy undertook (with incredible good grace) the unenviable task of coding our drafting workshop discussions; Emma Wilson conducted a literature review; Sarah Trotter assisted in the preparation of the book manuscript; and Lucy Cowell collated teaching resource materials. Sandra Duffy and Ruth Houghton also wrote reports of our drafting workshops. Many more students contributed to discussions at our drafting workshops, or got in touch about various things along the way. We are glad that you did and hope you continue to do so. Thanks also to the many students who have enthusiastically participated in teaching workshops based around the project.

Thanks to Rose Comiskey for allowing us to use her wonderful photograph from her 'Against the Tide' exhibition on the front cover of this book. We could not have wished for a better image for the project. Artists Sarah Browne, Emma Campbell and Jesse Jones also allowed us to use some of their images on our website. We are, and continue to be, incredibly inspired by their work and creativity and thank them for being so interested in law and our project. Vicky Conway, Colin Murray, Kevin J Brown and others took great photographs during our drafting workshops, many of which are on the website. Thank you for doing so, as they always make us smile.

We had the support and encouragement of several judges during the project, who not only shared their insights with us, but also patiently answered our many questions. We valued your thoughtful and genuine engagement with our project. Particular thanks go to: Judge Sinéad Ní Chúlacháin; Justice Donnell Deeny; Justice Aileen Donnelly; Justice Gerard Hogan; Justice Siobhan Keegan; Justice Denise McBride; Justice Catherine McGuinness and Justice Mary Ellen Ring. We also benefitted from the valuable reflections of several activists, litigants, artists, poets and other professionals during the project. For keeping us inspired, we thank: Rachael Anderson; Sarah Browne; Ronan Burtenshaw; Emma Campbell; Philomena Canning; Sarah Clancy; Kathy D'Arcy; Larne Abse Gogarty; Goretti Horgan; Jesse Jones; John Keanie; Claire McGettrick; Pat Neeson; Marie O'Connor; Katherine O'Donnell; Audrey Simpson; Maeve Taylor; and William Wall.

At our drafting workshops, many academic colleagues shared work and expertise that spoke to the theoretical themes of our project. We know that some of you were baffled, and sometimes a bit anxious, about talking with a room full of feminist lawyers. We thank the following for sticking with our invitations and giving so generously of their time: Emma Campbell; Mark Coen; Marianne Elliott; Elaine Farrell; Mary Gilmartin; Lisa Godson; Maebh Harding; Myrtle Hill; Elizabeth Kiely; Tina Kinsella; Heather Laird; Máire Leane; Maria Luddy; Mary McAuliffe; Sandra McAvoy; Joan McCarthy; Leanne McCormick; Kieran McEvoy; Kathryn McNeilly; Thomas Mohr; Linda Mulcahy; Anne Mulhall; Seamus Mulholland; Sarah Ramshaw; Louise Ryan; Alex Schwartz; Ailbhe Smyth; Lisa Smyth; and Mary Shine Thompson. We would also like specifically to thank Aisling McMahon and Patrick Hanafin for the time and energy they gave to the project.

Also at our drafting workshops, colleagues read and commented on draft judgments and commentaries, and/or chaired presentation panels. In particular, Rosemary Hunter's advice and comments to our judges were always of great insight. We thank the following for their thought-provoking contributions: Fiona Bloomer; Kevin J Brown; Kate Butler; Sorcha Uí Chonnachtaigh; Linda Connolly; Valerie Connor; Ciara Considine Eileen Fegan; Alan Greene; Nikki Godden-Rasul; Robin Hickey; Anna Louise Hinds; Niamh Howlin; Emma Hutchinson; Ursula Kilkelly; Louise Mallinder; Imelda Maher; Sylvia de Mars; Elizabeth Martin; Aisling McMahon; Laura McMahon; Ronagh McQuigg; Monica McWilliams; Lynette Moran; John Morison; Linda Mulcahy; Therese Murphy; Anne Neylon; Patrick O'Callaghan, Rory O'Connell; Katherine O'Donnell; Sinead O'Malley; Charles O'Sullivan; Niamh Purceil; Erika Rackley; Eilish Rooney; Jane Rooney; Claire-Michelle Smyth; Shauna Stanley; Ntina Tzouvala; Ben Warwick; and Sally Wheeler.

Our thanks also go to the editorial, production and marketing team at Hart Publishing; you were terrific and helped make smooth what could have been a very difficult process.

Personal thanks go to Ben Hunter, who had to keep a honey badger secret for longer than he expected, as project deadlines rolled by, to Tara Mulqueen for relentless optimism, and to Colin Murray, for maintaining the '/' in the title as a basis of strength.

Máiréad Enright
Julie McCandless
Aoife O'Donoghue

CONTENTS

THE CONTRIBUTORS

Anna Arstein-Kerslake is a Lecturer at Melbourne Law School, University of Melbourne.

Ivana Bacik is Reid Professor of Criminal Law and Criminology at Trinity College Dublin.

Hilkka Becker is a practising solicitor in Ireland, specialising in migration, nationality, refugee and human rights law, and a current Member of the Refugee Appeals Tribunal.

Christine Bell FBA is Professor of Constitutional Law at Edinburgh Law School and Assistant Principal (Global Justice) and Co-director of the Global Justice Academy, the University of Edinburgh.

Claire Bruton is a practising barrister based in Dublin.

Lucy-Ann Buckley is a Lecturer at the School of Law, National University of Ireland, Galway.

Liz Campbell is a Senior Lecturer at Edinburgh Law School, University of Edinburgh.

David Capper is a Reader at the School of Law, Queen's University Belfast.

Sarah Clancy is a poet based in Galway.

Emilie Cloatre is a Senior Lecturer at Kent Law School, University of Kent.

Donal Coffey is a Lecturer at the School of Law, University of Surrey.

Joanne Conaghan is Professor of Law and Head of the Law School at the University of Bristol.

Vicky Conway is a Lecturer at the School of Law and Government, Dublin City University.

Fiona Cooke is a professional animal behaviourist, with a PhD in animal welfare law, who specialises in animal welfare and dog law.

Louise Crowley is a Senior Lecturer at the School of Law, University College Cork.

Eoin Daly is a Lecturer at the School of Law, National University of Ireland, Galway.

Yvonne Marie Daly is a Senior Lecturer at the School of Law and Government, Dublin City University.

Katie Dawson is a practising barrister based in Dublin.

Mary Donnelly is a Professor at the School of Law, University College Cork.

Marian Duggan is a Lecturer in Criminology at the School of Social Policy, Sociology and Social Research, University of Kent.

Máiréad Enright is a Senior Lecturer at Birmingham Law School, University of Birmingham.

Caroline Fennell is a Professor at the School of Law, University College Cork.

Ruth Fletcher is a Senior Lecturer at the School of Law, Queen Mary University of London.

Marie Fox is Professor of Socio-legal Studies at Birmingham Law School, University of Birmingham.

Lorna Fox O'Mahony is a Professor at Essex Law School, University of Essex.

Eilionóir Flynn is the Deputy Director of the Centre for Disability Law and Policy, and a Senior Lecturer at the School of Law, National University of Ireland, Galway.

Maebh Harding is an Assistant Professor at Warwick Law School, University of Warwick.

Laura Hilly is a Postdoctoral Research Fellow at the Faculty of Law, University of Oxford and the Deputy Director of the Oxford Human Rights Hub.

Ruth Houghton is a Graduate Teaching Assistant and PhD Candidate at Durham Law School, Durham University.

John Kennedy is a Lecturer at the School of Law, Ulster University.

Louise Kennefick is a Lecturer at the Department of Law, Maynooth University, National University of Ireland, Maynooth.

Fiona de Londras is the Chair in Global Legal Studies at Birmingham Law School, University of Birmingham.

Julie McCandless is an Assistant Professor at the Law Department, London School of Economics and Political Science.

Claire McCann is a Senior Lecturer at the School of Law, Northumbria University.

Sheelagh McGuinness is a Senior Lecturer at Bristol Law School, University of Bristol.

Deirdre McGowan is a Lecturer at the School of Languages, Law and Social Sciences at the Dublin Institute of Technology.

Kathryn McNeilly is a Lecturer at the School of Law, Queen's University Belfast.

Tanya Ní Mhuirthile is a Lecturer at the School of Law and Government, Dublin City University.

Siobhán Mullally is Professor of Law and Director of the Centre for Criminal Justice and Human Rights, University College Cork. She is currently a Commissioner on the Irish Human Rights Commission and a member of the Board of the Equality Authority and the Permanent Court of Arbitration, The Hague.

Cliodhna Murphy is a Lecturer at the Department of Law, Maynooth University, National University of Ireland, Maynooth.

Claire Murray is a Lecturer at the School of Law, University College Cork.

Colin Murray is a Senior Lecturer at the School of Law, Newcastle University.

Colm O'Cinneide is Professor of Human Rights Law at University College London.

Cian Ó Concubhair is a DPhil Candidate, University of Oxford.

Aoife O'Donoghue is a Senior Lecturer at Durham Law School, Durham University.

Catherine O'Rourke is a Senior Lecturer at the Transitional Justice Institute and School of Law, Ulster University.

Maeve O'Rourke is a barrister at 33 Bedford Row, London, and a PhD candidate at Birmingham Law School, University of Birmingham.

David Prendergast is an Assistant Professor at the School of Law, Trinity College Dublin.

Sara Ramshaw is a Senior Lecturer at Exeter School of Law and former member of the bar of the Law Society of Upper Canada (2000–2010).

Sinéad Ring is a Lecturer at Kent Law School, University of Kent.

Carmel Roulston is a Senior Lecturer in Politics at the School of Criminology, Politics and Social Policy, Ulster University.

Aideen Ryan is a practising solicitor and Partner at McDowell Purcell, Dublin.

Christine Ryan is a SJD student at Duke University School of Law, USA.

Fergus Ryan is a Lecturer at the Department of Law, Maynooth University, National University of Ireland, Maynooth.

Mary Shine Thompson is Fellow Emeritus of St Patrick's College, Dublin City University.

Olivia Smith is a Lecturer at the School of Law and Government, Dublin City University.

Liam Thornton is a Lecturer at the School of Law, University College Dublin.

Siobhán Wills is Professor of Law at the University of Ulster.

ABBREVIATIONS

AG	Attorney General
DPP	Director of Public Prosecutions
ECHR	European Convention on Human Rights
EU	European Union
Fr	Father (Catholic Priest)
IRA	Irish Republican Army
NIHRC	Northern Ireland Human Rights Commission
NICA	Northern Ireland Court of Appeal
NIHC	Northern Ireland High Court
PSNI	Police Service of Northern Ireland
ROI	Republic of Ireland
RUC	Royal Ulster Constabulary
QC	Queen's Counsel
SC	Senior Counsel
SPUC	Society for the Protection of the Unborn
TD	Teachta Dála (Member of Parliament)
TFEU	Treaty on the Functioning of the EU
UKHL	United Kingdom House of Lords

TABLE OF CASES

Ireland

UK

Australia

Canada

Denmark

New Zealand

USA

European Court of Human Rights

Court of Justice of the European Union

International Court of Justice

TABLE OF STATUTES AND LEGISLATION

Ireland

Legislation

Statutory Instruments

United Kingdom

Primary Legislation

Secondary Legislation

Australia

Canada

South Africa

USA

Council of Europe

European Union

Directives

International Conventions, Treaties, etc

Part I

Introduction

1

Introduction: Troubling Judgment

JULIE McCANDLESS, MÁIRÉAD ENRIGHT AND AOIFE O'DONOGHUE

The Northern/Irish Feminist Judgments Project

The Northern/Irish Feminist Judgments Project inaugurates a fresh dialogue on gender, legal judgment, judicial power and national identity in Ireland and Northern Ireland. It does so by engaging in a collective process of writing 'missing' feminist judgments in a series of legal cases that have been significant in shaping Irish and Northern Irish law. Through this process of judicial re-imagining, the project has taken into account peculiarly Northern/Irish concerns in investigating how gender is shaped through judicial practices, and how the Northern/Irish judiciaries have contributed to the construction of a gendered national identity across the island since the founding of the two jurisdictions almost a century ago. In considering how themes of gender and national identity have cross-cut women's experiences and activism in both jurisdictions, our project—following on from feminist judgments projects in other common law jurisdictions such as Canada,[1] England,[2] Australia[3] and, most recently, the USA[4]—takes the feminist judging methodology in important and challenging new directions.

At the outset of the project a number of key questions, designed to enable an engagement with the project's underpinning themes of gender and national identity, were put to participants, to be explored during the judgments' drafting process. For instance, what different legal outcomes might have been produced through the deployment of feminist legal reasoning and judgment methodologies in leading Northern/Irish case law? As a method, what can feminist judging reveal about the techniques of identity politics as they appear in Northern/Irish case law? How can feminist legal theory contribute to a re-thinking of gendered judicial techniques and legal concepts in Northern/Ireland? How have Northern/Irish women used litigation to challenge the boundaries of membership in gendered, religious, national and other social groupings? What are the obstacles and limitations encountered in the use of litigation for transformative feminist ends? How have Northern/Irish feminist

[1] Special Issue: *Rewriting Equality* (2006) 18(1) *Canadian Journal of Women and the Law*. Some of the rewritten judgments are available here at www.thecourt.ca/ (last accessed 26 March 2015).

[2] Rosemary Hunter, Clare McGlynn and Erika Rackley (eds), *Feminist Judgments: From Theory to Practice* (Oxford, Hart Publishing, 2010).

[3] Heather Douglas, Francesca Bartlett, Trish Luker and Rosemary Hunter (eds), *Australian Feminist Judgments: Righting and Rewriting Law* (Oxford, Hart Publishing, 2015).

[4] Kathryn Stanchi, Linda Berger and Bridget Crawford (eds), *U.S. Feminist Judgments: Rewritten Opinions of the United States Supreme Court* (Cambridge, Cambridge University Press, 2016).

movements conceived of the role of the judge in approving or dissenting from judicial pronouncements? As will be explored in this book, the answers to these questions are both myriad and surprising.

Twenty-six rewritten judgments are collected in this book. Each is accompanied by an introductory commentary, which puts the case in its wider social context and explains the original decision and the approach—and limitations—of the feminist judgment. The book also contains introductory chapters examining constructions of national identity in Northern/Ireland, as well as theoretical and conceptual issues pertaining to the feminist judging methodology and the legal context of both jurisdictions, to include Northern/Irish peculiarities of judicial craft. Any reader who has already skimmed the acknowledgements at the start of the book will be aware that the project involved a large number of participants beyond those who have directly contributed to this publication. In this introductory chapter we detail the form of this extensive collaboration and situate it not only in the wider feminist judging methodology, but also in the particular methodology of the Northern/Ireland Feminist Judgments Project. In contrast to other feminist judgment projects, which have channeled considerable legal expertise, both academic and practitioner-based, we designed our judgment drafting process to further incorporate interventions from feminist (and other) activists, litigants, poets, visual and performance artists, and non-legal academic expertise. This broad collaboration was fundamental to the project's methodology, enabling a richly contextual understanding to the judgments, as well as the wider Northern/Irish social, cultural, historical and political context. As the title of this chapter suggests, by doing so, we have attempted to 'trouble' legal judgment by asking it to listen and engage with non-legal expertise and experience.[5]

Before detailing the project's methodology more fully, we first outline what a feminist judgments project is, and briefly explain feminist judging methodology. We also discuss some of the other unique features of the Northern/Irish Feminist Judgments Project, offering some tentative hopes on the new directions we hope this project may take feminist judging methodology. Towards the end of the chapter we outline the structure of the book and explore how we think it might be used by academics and other researchers, practitioners and litigants, and in teaching contexts.

Feminist Judgments Projects and Feminist Judging Methodology

Feminist Judgments Projects

Feminist judgments projects are a form of 'academic activism' that seeks to intervene in prevailing academic and political discourse around law and its limits.[6] Participants are tasked

[5] Asking law to listen does not, of course, exclude the possibility that sometimes listening will be difficult or impossible, and that protest may be a more effective strategy.

[6] Rosemary Hunter, Clare McGlynn and Erika Rackley, 'Feminist Judgments: An Introduction' in Hunter, McGlynn and Rackley, above n 2, 8.

with imagining themselves as practising judges, bound by the same law, doctrinal strictures, conventions, temporal knowledge and evidence as the original decision-maker(s). In rewriting the judgments, participants put feminist theory, knowledge and critique into action, in order to show how real-life legal cases could have been decided and/or reasoned differently, even within the bounds of the available law and evidence.[7] While feminist legal theory has long warned against over-investment in the law—particularly judge-made law—as a site within which progressive social or political transformation might begin,[8] feminist judgments are increasingly regarded not only as advancing critique of legal judgment, rules and doctrine, but also as uniquely accessible and powerful models of alternative judicial practice.[9] They suggest that other forms of judging, which have the potential to lead to different legal outcomes and potential social orders, are possible. As a legal intervention, therefore, they present a relatively rare opportunity to critique both the standard and its application.

While feminists are not the first to recalibrate the internal mechanics of judicial reasoning by rewriting judgments,[10] feminist judgments projects have been characterised by a distinctively collective ethos, whereby multiple feminist perspectives collaborate in an attempt to shift legal discourse and cultures.[11] Inspired by the Women's Court of Canada, which focused on the application and interpretation of the equality guarantee in the Charter of Human Rights and Freedoms by the Canadian Supreme Court,[12] the English Feminist Judgments Project, which was broader in scope in terms of court jurisdiction and substantive legal areas, did much to establish feminist judging as a new and legitimate critical legal method, and to locate it as a facet of legal practice within particular jurisdictions.[13] This ground-breaking project has been a model for sister projects in other common law jurisdictions.[14]

[7] Rosemary Hunter, 'An Account of Feminist Judging' in Hunter, McGlynn and Rackley, above n 2, 30–43.

[8] Carol Smart, *Feminism and the Power of Law* (London, Routledge, 1989). See also Mary Jane Mossman, 'Feminism and Legal Method: The Difference it Makes' (1987) 3(1) *Wisconsin Women's Law Journal* 147–68; Catharine MacKinnon, *Towards a Feminist Theory of the State* (Boston, MA, Harvard University Press, 1989); Nicola Lacey, *Unspeakable subjects: feminist essays in legal and social theory* (Oxford, Hart Publishing, 1998).

[9] Rosemary Hunter, 'The Power of Feminist Judgments?' (2012) 20(2) *Feminist Legal Studies* 135–48.

[10] Previous efforts have focused on writing multiple judgments for the same case: Lon Fuller, 'The Case of the Speluncean Explorers' (1949) 62(4) *Harvard Law Review* 616–45 and Peter Suber, *The Case of the Speluncean Explorers: Nine New Opinions* (New York, Routledge, 1998); Jack Balkin (ed), *What 'Brown v Board of Education' Should Have Said: The Nation's Top Legal Experts Rewrite America's Landmark Civil Rights Decision* (New York, New York University Press, 2002) and Jack Balkin (ed), *What 'Roe v Wade' Should Have Said: The Nation's Top Legal Experts Rewrite America's Most Controversial Decision* (New York, New York University Press, 2005).

[11] Margaret Davies, 'The Law Becomes Us: Rediscovering Judgment' (2012) 20(2) *Feminist Legal Studies* 167–81.

[12] Above n 1.

[13] Above n 2. See further Erika Rackley, 'Why Feminist Legal Scholars Should Write Judgments: Reflections on the Feminist Judgments Project in England and Wales' (2012) 24(2) *Canadian Journal of Women and Law* 389–413.

[14] Such as Australia, above n 3; the USA, above n 4; and New Zealand/Aotearoa, see further at www.lawsociety.org.nz/lawtalk/lawtalk-archives/issue-875/rewriting-judgments-from-feminist-viewpoint (last accessed 26 March 2016). These jurisdictionally bound feminist judgments projects are happening alongside a number of other judgments projects, focusing on feminism and international law and diversity issues in the European Court of Human Rights, but also other contexts such as children's rights, medical ethics and environmental law, illustrating the range of contexts on which this critical methodology can be brought to bear. See further IntLawGrrls, 'Invitation to Participate in the Feminist Judgments Project' (16 January 2014) at https://ilg2.org/2014/01/16/invitation-to-participate-in-the-feminist-international-judgments-project/ (last accessed 26 March 2016); Eva Brems (ed), *Diversity and European Human Rights: Rewriting Judgments of the ECHR* (Cambridge, Cambridge University Press, 2013); the Children's Rights Judgments Project at www.liverpool.ac.uk/law/research/european-childrens-

These projects have been collaborative enterprises, not just in the sense of involving significant numbers of participants, but in the way that the method of the projects resonates with over three decades of feminist legal scholarship, political activism and law reform, in order to stimulate a socially reflective dimension to judgment that encourages an ethically good, critical and responsible mode of interacting with the law.[15] As a consequence, individual cases are rewritten in the context of a much broader dialogue and critique, whereby multiple feminist approaches, perspectives and concerns jostle together to 'trouble' 'the judgment space',[16] as well as the decision-maker. Feminist judgments projects have not been afraid of 'messy jurisprudence'.[17] For instance, they have made transparent points of contestation and disagreement between feminist approaches,[18] and been clear that the judgments produced in each collection are not the only possible feminist interpretations. Moreover, many feminist judges have adopted the technique of being upfront about the moral and political quandaries of a case in their rewritten judgments,[19] whether by revealing 'the constant strain involved in meshing human lives with abstract principle'[20] or by exposing a struggle between coming to a 'good' decision for a particular woman, without negatively impacting on the lives of other women who may be differently situated or affected by a particular outcome, as well as others who are marginalised by society and legal discourse.[21] In some instances, they have 'called law out' by following its patriarchal impulses to logical conclusions and pointing out the costs to women's personhood, autonomy and bodily integrity, as well as the gendered effects on their lived experience and material lives.[22]

As feminist judgments projects constrain themselves by adapting the strictures of legal method, a cynical characterisation would regard them as futile and as attempting to salvage a space that many see as unreceptive—if not impervious—to feminist method and input.[23]

rights-unit/childrens-rights-judgments/ (last accessed 26 March 2016); Stephen Smith John Coggon, Clark Hobson, Richard Huxtable, Sheelagh McGuinness, Jose Miola and Mary Neal (eds), *Ethical Judgments: Re-Writing Medical Law* (Oxford, Hart Publishing, 2016); and the Australian Wild Law Judgments Project at www.earthlaws.org.au/wp-content/uploads/2015/02/Call-for-Abstracts_Wild-Law-Judgments-Project_4-February-2015.pdf (last accessed 26 March 2016).

[15] Hunter, above n 7, 31; Davies, above n 11, 170; Douglas Bartlett, Luker and Hunter, above n 3, 3–6.

[16] Zenon Bankowski, 'In the judgment space: The judge and the anxiety of the encounter' in Zenon Bankowski and James McLean (eds), *The universal and the particular in legal reasoning* (Aldershot, Ashgate, 2007) ch 2, as cited in Davies, above n 11.

[17] Hunter, above n 7, 43.

[18] This contestation was clear during the drafting process and is revealed to readers in the commentaries that precede each judgment. For the Northern/Irish Feminist Judgments Project, some podcasts of drafting discussions are available on the project website in the 'cases' section at www.feministjudging.ie/?p=29 (last accessed 26 March 2016).

[19] See, eg, the feminist judgments of *AG v X* (this collection, ch 18), *A and B (by C) v A (Health and Social Services Trust)* (this collection, ch 30) and *McKinley v Minister of Defence* (this collection, ch 24).

[20] Davies, above n 11, 176.

[21] See the discussion across the rewritten judgments in the English Feminist Judgments Project: Hunter, McGlynn and Rackley, above n 6, 12–17.

[22] A particularly striking example of this can be found in the Australian Feminist Judgments Projects, whereby the feminist judges refused to reinterpret Australian common law prior to legislative change in 1976 as not providing for spousal immunity in cases of rape, in contrast to the original decision. They instead followed the common law to its conclusions, pointing out the injustice for married women and offering a judicial apology: Wendy Larcombe and Mary Heath, 'Judgment: *PGA v R* [2012] HCA 21' in Douglas, Bartlett, Luker and Hunter, above n 3, ch 16.

[23] See above n 8; see also Gillian Rose, *Broken Middle: Out of Our Ancient Society* (Oxford, Blackwell Publishers, 1992). This criticism resonates with Audre Lorde's famous observation: 'For the master's tools will never dismantle the master's house. They may allow us temporarily to beat him at his own game, but they will never enable us to bring genuine change.' *Sister Outsider: Essays and Speeches* (Berkeley, CA, Crossing Press, 1984) 110–14.

This criticism may be fair for any feminist—or other critically orientated—judgments project that claims to 'rupture' that which it emulates; but we are not aware of any such project. Feminist judgments projects are more likely to characterise themselves as law *reform* projects, which perform the law anew and in so doing, create spaces for subtle, yet meaningful, changes.[24] Like other critical projects that refuse to see law as rigid and determinative as some might claim,[25] they finds spaces, however cramped, for alternative iterations of oppressive legal principles. We could say they 'irritate' rather than 'rupture'. Yet we should not underestimate the collective potential and effect of sustained irritations. As Margaret Davies observed in her review of the English Feminist Judgments Project:

> In the end, the law (as opposed to individual laws) is not going to be changed by theory, it is not going to be changed by specific reforms or by individual judges, and it is not going to be changed by critique. All of these interventions have an influence, of course. But the only way the identity of law—in its ethos, its culture, its fundamental attachments, its boundaries, and its metaphysics—has ever changed, and the only way it ever will change, is through sustained critical-mass practices which bring new meanings, and new directions to legal culture. For this reason it is the collective effect of this book rather than individual pieces or any theoretical rationalisation, which most contributes to legal change.[26]

In addition to the immediate outcomes of a feminist judgments project—usually a book like this—the projects are also stirring a wider body of scholarship that critically engages with the feminist judging methodology, opening up new avenues of exploration and critique.[27] This attests to the wider collaboration and dialogue within which the projects and the methodology are inherently situated.[28]

Lastly, just as some may be uncomfortable with a methodology that demands a certain amount of fidelity to existing legal structure, tradition and form, others may question whether investing time in rewriting legal judgments undeservedly prioritises one aspect of a much wider legal picture and ongoing drama. In response, we would argue that feminist judgments projects, in addition to being a type of legal intervention, are also a type of political intervention, which put juridification and modes of reliance on law itself under the microscope. Just as rewritten judgments can shed light on alternatives that would have been *possible*, they can also shed light on limitations and the *impossible*, provoking further

[24] Douglas, Bartlett, Luker and Hunter, above n 3, 8; Davies, above n 11, 175.

[25] See, eg, Sarah Ramshaw, *Justice as Improvisation: The Law of the Extempore* (Abingdon, Routledge, 2013) and the Translating Improvisation Research Group, particularly the sub-project, 'Into the Key of Law', which considers the role of improvisation in creative and responsive decision making in the particular context of child protection cases in Northern Ireland, at http://translatingimprovisation.com/ahrc (last accessed 26 March 2016).

[26] Davies, above n 11, 180–81.

[27] See, eg, Harriet Samuels, 'Feminizing Human Rights Adjudication: Feminist Method and the Proportionality Principle' (2012) 21(1) *Feminist Legal Studies* 39–60; Kate Fitz-Gibbon and JaneMaree Maher, 'Feminist Challenges to the Constraints of Law: Donning Uncomfortable Robes?' (2015) 23(3) *Feminist Legal Studies* 253–71; Kcasey McLoughlin, 'Judicial fictions and the fictive feminists: re-imagination as feminist critique in PGA v The Queen' (2015) 24(4) *Griffith Law Review* 592–615. See also the 'FLaK Seminar: Mixing Feminism, Legality and Knowledge', organised by the Editorial Board of *Feminist Legal Studies* in anticipation of the journal's 25th Anniversary. The event is intended to encourage reflexive consideration on feminist legacies of praxis, internationalisation and openness, with the methodology of the Northern/Irish Feminist Judgments Project providing the provocation for a panel on 'Making Law Listen'. For further detail, see Ruth Fletcher, 'FlaK: Mixing Feminism, Legality and Knowledge' (2015) 23(3) *Feminist Legal Studies* 251–52 (editorial).

[28] See further, this collection, ch 3.

explorations of 'irritant' spaces, legal or otherwise.[29] In the particular methodology of the Northern/Ireland Feminist Judgments Project, we have deliberately sought a number of interventions that have greatly assisted in enlarging our mentality around legal judgment and the individual cases selected for rewriting. This is discussed in more detail below, but by way of demonstrative example, by hearing from litigants, activists and other intervenors in the cases—when this has been possible—many of our feminist judgments and commentaries give attention to their role as law-makers and in law-making, as much as that of judges.

Feminist Judging Methodology

Feminist judging provides a means of re-imagining the role of the judge. It requires participants to adhere to the rules of precedent and custom that typically bind judges in common law jurisdictions, while demonstrating that it is possible to decide even very difficult cases in ways that take proper account of feminist concerns.

The feminist judging methodology utilises a range of reasoning techniques in order to engage with the diversity of women's lives before the law, as well as other marginalised groups in society.[30] So for example, feminist judgments will often adopt contextual and relational techniques of reasoning, rather than the adversarial and abstract approaches we have come to expect. They may make use of feminist 'common knowledge', as well as feminist scholarship and empirical research. They might ask 'the woman question' and focus on the gendered effects of apparently 'neutral' liberal legal constructs and practices, and/or challenge gender bias in legal doctrine and judicial reasoning. They may be motivated to promote substantive rather than formal equality, or to challenge judicial distinctions between 'public' and 'private'. They may reframe the narrative of the case and retell the facts to make women's lived experiences more visible in legal discourse and the construction of legal rules. In doing so, it is possible to expose the gendered biases present in the original judgments, as well as the contingency of judicial decision-making.

The feminist judging methodology operates on the premise that judges are not disinterested and objective tools of the law.[31] In accepting that judicial impartiality, fairness and independence are not compromised by acknowledging that judges bring their own lived experiences to their decisions, the methodology provides space for alternative judicial

[29] Novel techniques have emerged in existing feminist judgments projects, when participants have been met with 'the impossible'. For example, in the Australian Feminist Judgments Project, feminist judge Nicole Watson wrote a fictional appeal decision based in a future society, where a Treaty Act governs relations between Indigenous and non-Indigenous Australians, and where an Indigenous court, based on Indigenous laws and values rather than the Eurocentric legalist approach, has jurisdiction over Indigenous matters: 'Judgment: In the matter of *Djappari (Re Tuckiar)* [2035] FNCA 1' in Douglas, Bartlett, Luker and Hunter, above n 3, ch 27. Indeed, in the same project, Irene Watson rejected the judicial form altogether, on the basis that it was incapable of hearing Aboriginal women's voices on their own terms: 'First Nations Stories, Grandmother's Law: Too Many Stories to Tell' in Douglas, Bartlett, Luker and Hunter, above n 3, ch 3. That these two novel approaches were taken in the context of a feminist judgments project in which many other feminist judges appealed to legal formalism in order to give proper effect to the progressive political intentions underpinning legislative reform (see Douglas, Bartlett, Luker and Hunter, above n 3, ch 2) attests to the adaptability of the method in the context of a wider collective enterprise.

[30] These tenets of the feminist judging methodology are drawn from Rosemary Hunter's work: Hunter, above n 7 and Rosemary Hunter, 'Can Feminist Judges Make a Difference?' (2008) 15:1–2 *International Journal of the Legal Profession* 7–36.

[31] For an early consideration of this, see John Griffith, *The Politics of the Judiciary* (London, Fontana, 1977).

voices.[32] In doing so, as Hunter has argued, 'A feminist approach must always be subordinated to judicial norms. But this allows considerable scope for feminism.'[33] Hunter goes on to identify several areas in which a feminist approach can impact upon a case.[34] First, in correcting perceived injustices, improving women's lives and promoting substantive equality within the limits of precedent and custom, the case itself can change how a set of facts is perceived and utilised thereafter. Secondly, in exercising discretion within the bounds of existing statutory, constitutional or common law parameters, judges may utilise a feminist approach to come to alternative conclusions regarding the facts or the law itself. Thirdly, in the development of legal doctrine, whilst bound by precedent, constitutional provisions and statute, and thus being bound by key outcomes, the manner in which the doctrine is considered and discussed can have a longer-term impact upon subsequent cases and law reform. In doing so, cases rewritten through the techniques of the feminist judging methodology, as Rackley has argued, aid in loosening the perceived fixed inevitability of the judgments as they have been presented by the courts and the wider legal community.[35]

In assuming a position of authority that feminists are unlikely to hold easily in reality,[36] the feminist judging methodology has been described as an exercise in 'drag', whereby feminists play the role of judges to subversive ends.[37] However, as with all drag performances, where the purpose is to consciously inhabit and perform a set of conventions that are not one's own, the performance must keep faith with the assumed role or else it fails.[38] This project has chosen to remain diligently tied to the rules of judicial function, with all our feminist judges confining themselves to the strict parameters of accepted judicial form. However, as discussed above, we do not see this approach as excluding the possibility of alternative steps, such as rejecting the judicial form altogether.[39] Moreover, just as those of us who have engaged with the feminist judging methodology have reworked existing legal texts, our texts will be used by others—to include practising judges—whether to produce their own theories of judicial practice—alternative or otherwise—or to evaluate the scope and operation of the feminist judging methodology, possibly in light of theories or phenomena that we have not envisioned.[40] Of course, this is true of most academic work that is published or otherwise made public,[41] and none of the cases that have been rewritten in this

[32] Hunter, above n 7, 31.

[33] ibid, 32.

[34] ibid, 32–33.

[35] Erika Rackley, 'Difference in the House of Lords' (2006) 15(2) *Social and Legal Studies* 163–85, 181.

[36] Davies, above n 11, 161.

[37] Hunter, McGlynn and Rackley, above n 6.

[38] Davies, above n 11. Davies takes this claim further by suggesting that all judging is in fact a performance in drag, but that women and feminists may encounter particular issues in making the performance convincing, in relation to how the role fits with their 'outsider' identity. For further critical consideration of this point, see this collection, ch 3.

[39] See Irene Watson, above n 29.

[40] Reg Graycar, 'A Feminist Adjudication Process: Is There Such a Thing?' in Ulrika Schultz and Gisela Shaw (eds), *Gender and Judging* (Oxford, Hart Publishing, 2013) ch 5.4.

[41] As Hanna Arendt observed towards the end of her life, 'Each time you write something and you send it out into the world and it becomes public, obviously everybody is free to do with it as he pleases and this is how it should be. I do not have a quarrel with this. You should not try to hold your hand now on whatever may happen to what you have been thinking for yourself. You should rather try to learn from what other people do with it.' As cited by Margaret Canovan in her introduction to Hannah Arendt, *The Human Condition*, 2nd edn (Chicago, IL, the University of Chicago Press, 1998).

collection are intended as the 'last word' on a particular case, legal or social issue. Just as we have been inspired by work on sister feminist judgments projects, we hope that others will be inspired through this project and our adoption of the feminist judgments methodology to further explore the many significant issues that this book raises in relation to gender, judgment, judicial power, and gendered national identity in Northern/Ireland and beyond. In the next section, we discuss some possible new directions in which we see this project taking the feminist judging methodology.

Possible New Directions

The Northern/Irish Feminist Judgments Project has extended the critical purchase of the feminist judging methodology by examining how it can be deployed as a critical legal and political intervention tool in a Northern/Irish context. We suggest that the Northern/Irish focus has taken the methodology in new directions not only by taking a cross-jurisdictional frame, but also by (i) framing judgment as intimately connected to questions of national identity politics and (ii) considering the relationship between judicial decision-making and local political and cultural struggles and contestations. In doing so, the project considers how judges have enabled cross-cutting religious, ethno-nationalist and gendered governmental politics of identity to mark Northern/Irish life, while also examining how feminist methodologies of dissent, protest and litigation have fostered new conceptions of gender since the founding of the two jurisdictions.

While other feminist judgments projects have explored the gendered political implications of judicial law-making, they have not focused explicitly on judges' political agency, a key dimension of which involves judicial entanglement in governmental projects of collective national identity.[42] Given the difficult political history of Ireland and Northern Ireland, and the approach of various celebrations relating to the founding of the two jurisdictions almost a century ago,[43] our project offered a timely opportunity to focus on the relationships between judging, national identities and the political lives of women, as well as considering how the judicial role can be critically re-imagined in national contexts of partition, transition from conflict, colonialism and religious patriarchy.

In the remainder of this section, we offer further detail on the mixed conception of identity formation adopted in this book, before elaborating on the political role played by judges in the Northern/Irish context.

[42] However, it is important to note that as feminist judgments projects mature, we have seen their parameters more explicitly informed by the political history of the jurisdiction under examination. For example, in the Australian Feminist Judgments Project, the legacy of Australia's settler-colonial history and its devastating and enduring impact on indigenous people, as well as the role of immigration in the development of the Australian national project, underpin some of the most interesting chapters in the collection, provoking Irene Watson and Nicole Watson to work outside the constraints under which the original decision-maker would have operated, on the basis that the patriarchal and colonial history of Australian law—which includes the elevation of written text—makes it impossible to hear or understand Aboriginal women's voices and stories on their own terms, or to account for indigenous perspectives: see above n 29.

[43] See further, this collection, ch 4.

Why Northern/Irish?

For the sake of brevity, many will refer to this project as the 'Irish Feminist Judgments Project'. However, we have chosen a different official name, wherein the two jurisdictions are noted with a solidus/slash. In using Northern/Irish in its name, the project attempts to both draw attention to the two distinct jurisdictions whilst also not setting them as isolated from or in contradistinction to one another. To have adopted 'Irish and Northern Irish'—irrespective of being quite a mouthful—would have suggested a separation that does not reflect the lived history of the two jurisdictions. In our project we wanted to create space to explore the ways in which they have affected and defined themselves in relation to each another over time, and to consider the commonalities of women's experiences before and between the laws of Ireland and Northern Ireland. In doing so, we are not suggesting that legal differences or challenges can be collapsed into one overarching or shared set of rules or values; rather, we take our lead from a long-standing tradition of collaboration between feminists on both sides of the border.[44] The project instigates a feminist approach to understanding the lives of women across the island not delineated by political borders, but rather recognises their individual and shared lived experiences, their significant contributions to all elements of life and the magnitude of their influence on the contemporary role of law and the judiciary on the island. The solidus/slash in our title therefore keeps in mind the contested relationship between the two jurisdictions in a way that is more nuanced than spelling out 'Ireland and Northern Ireland'. We invite readers to see it as representing not a border, but rather a set of adjacent possibilities—an 'either/or'.

Keeping in mind this contested relationship meant that our project provided an opportunity to challenge dominant narratives of the Northern/Irish context, which are hamstrung by a number of entrenched assumptions: that Irish and Northern Irish legal identities are best understood as developing 'in parallel' rather than in relation to one another; that Irish law's exclusions can be reduced to Catholicism and Northern Ireland's to inter-community conflict; that the politics of identity that have had most force in shaping Northern/Irish law are in the past. We argue that these assumptions are ripe for re-evaluation, especially as both jurisdictions encounter the purportedly 'new' challenges of post-national politics[45] and revisit old vexed questions around women's reproductive rights, religious institutional authority and family forms. While the parameters of this aspect of our enquiry were necessarily limited by the number of cases selected and the issues they addressed, examining both jurisdictions in tandem provided the opportunity to explore cross-jurisdictional synergies, particularly in relation to the myriad ways in which women have been excluded and marginalised in political, cultural and legal discourse. This general focus on the contested, rather than separate, relationship between the two jurisdictions is mirrored in the

[44] This collaboration has often pertained to women's reproductive rights. See further Emilie Cloatre and Máiréad Enright's commentary on *McGee v AG*, this collection, ch 5.

[45] Gerard Delanty, 'Beyond the Nation-State: National Identity and Citizenship in a Multicultural Society—A Response to Rex' (1996) 1(3) *Sociological Research Online* at http://socresonline.org.uk/1/3/1.html (last accessed 26 March 2016); Gerard Delanty, 'Habermas and post-national identity: Theoretical perspectives on the conflict in Northern Ireland' (1996) 11(1) *Irish Political Studies* 20–32; Desmond Clarke 'Nationalism, the Irish Constitution, and Multicultural Citizenship' (2000) 51(1) *Northern Ireland Legal Quarterly* 100–19; John Harrington, 'Citizenship and the bio-politics of post-nationalist Ireland' (2005) 32(3) *Journal of Law and Society* 424–49.

organisation of the rewritten cases for this collection. Rather than displaying the feminist judgments by jurisdiction—and then by traditional subject-matter—we have organised them thematically into four identity positions that reflect the main feminist concerns present in the cases: issues to do with mothering, othering, choosing and embodiment.[46] In organising the cases in this way, we hope to provoke further consideration of the relationship between gender, judgment and national identity politics, and the type of gendered subject positions that are simultaneously constructed for and protested against by women, whether in Northern/Ireland or elsewhere.

It would be remiss of us not to mention that rewriting judgments from two separate legal jurisdictions came with its own challenges. These were not only legal[47] and intellectual in nature, due to the typically jurisdictionally bound expertise of our participants, but sometimes also very practical.[48] While there were many shared experiences and commonalities to draw from, the project did sometimes have to tackle a sense of strangeness, unfamiliarity and incommensurability amongst participants, which sometimes led to either overcautious or quite simply confused conversations. But overall, these conversations tended ultimately to be beneficial rather than obstructive.[49] Moreover, these challenges would also likely have occurred in single jurisdiction Irish and Northern Irish feminist judgments projects, given the reality that many Northern/Irish academics—as well as practitioners and activists—often move to other common law jurisdictions, particularly Great Britain, while still engaging with Northern/Ireland.[50] Indeed, at the outset of the project, we were not unconcerned that as co-directors we were all based at English institutions, albeit institutions with a great deal of relevant expertise in feminist legal studies and judicial studies. However, in the end we decided to embrace this diasporadic dimension as bringing a further provocation to the project, given the significance of diaspora for the Northern/Irish context and associated notions of national identity.[51] As is discussed further below, we addressed some of these challenges in our project methodology, by inviting interventions during our drafting process from a wide range of persons, to include activists, litigants and academics with non-legal expertise, to help deepen our understanding of the national and legal context in which judgments are produced.

Extending the scope of the feminist judging methodology to encompass two jurisdictions has not only been a successful intellectual endeavour, but has also established an enduring network of feminist interdisciplinary scholars, activist and legal practitioners, who would otherwise have had little opportunity to come together to share and build knowledge.

[46] For ease of accessibility, the cases are also listed as per traditional subject matter in Table 1 at the end of this chapter.

[47] eg Ireland has a written constitution, Northern Ireland does not; differences in court structure; see further, this collection, ch 4.

[48] eg funding applications for this project were difficult, given the location of the three co-directors at English institutions and the typical need for lead applicants to be based at an Irish institution to be eligible to apply for funding from organisations such as the Irish Research Council. More generally, every drafting workshop involved considerable co-ordination across institutions and borders.

[49] A good example here is the discussions around the concept of the 'marital family' in the Irish Constitution, and associated notions of 'autonomy' and 'privacy'. The concept itself and the form of its protection were quite baffling to participants not familiar with Irish Constitutional Law.

[50] Of the 56 authors of commentaries and judgments in this book, 26 are based outside Northern/Ireland.

[51] Breda Gray, *Women and the Irish Diaspora* (London, Routledge, 2004); Dianne Hall and Elizabeth Malcolm, 'Diaspora, Gender and the Irish' (2009) 8(1) *Australasian Journal of Irish Studies* 3–29.

We are hopeful that the project will lead to exciting work in future studies pertaining to gender, law, judicial studies and national identity in the Northern/Irish context. We also hope that our project will speak to feminists in other jurisdictions that have been marked by partition and/or transition from conflict, colonialism and religious patriarchy.

Judges' Troubles

'Judges' Troubles' is the other part of this book's title that merits further explanation in this section. It draws on the colloquial term—'The Troubles'—for over three decades of sectarian violence pertaining to Northern Ireland's constitutional status, which took place mainly in Northern Ireland, but also in parts of Ireland, England and sometimes mainland Europe.[52] We have used this wording in the title not to prioritise sectarian violence as the defining feature of Northern/Irish identity, but rather to highlight the difficult and important role that judges can have in societies marked by violent conflict and an associated unsettled politics around national identity.[53] Judges play different roles according to their political environment, and given the difficult—and overlapping—political histories of Ireland and Northern Ireland, as marked by partition, post-colonialism, ethno-national conflict and violence, as well as religious conservatism, it is perhaps not unsurprising that the Northern/Irish Feminist Judgments Project has framed judgment as intimately connected to questions of national identity politics.

Over the past century, the stability and authority of the legal orders in both jurisdictions have been subject to considerable contestation.[54] In unsettled times, we argue that judges are crucial, if not always nakedly, political figures, who at times require litigants to perform ideal identities, while at other times reworking them.[55] Judgments then are written texts that reveal a great deal about how judges articulate the role and purpose of law in a particular national context, as well as ideal national futures characterised by certainty, stability and respect for established order, custom and socio-cultural mores.[56] As is explored in depth in the feminist judgments collected in this book, as well as in the following chapter, judicial identity projects directly affect women's lives by defining women's relationship to the state, setting the bounds of political action and sparking or smothering dissent, resistance and reform.[57] While certain gender stereotypes and expectations of women seem familiar across

[52] Whether 'The Troubles' are over is a point of contestation for many in Northern Ireland, particularly in light of continued sectarian attacks and killings. However, the term 'The Troubles' is generally used to refer to the 30-year conflict framed by a civil rights march in Londonderry in 1968 to the adoption of the Good Friday Agreement in 1998.

[53] The use of the term is also a nod to Judith Butler's book: Judith Butler, *Gender Trouble: Feminism and the Subversion of Identity* (New York, Routledge, 1990).

[54] See further, this collection, ch 4.

[55] Patrick Hanafin, 'Same Text, Different Story: Reinterpreting Irish Constitutional Identity' (1998) 4(2) *Bullan: An Irish Studies Journal* 109–20; Patrick Hanafin 'Rewriting Desire: the Construction of Sexual Identity in Literary and Legal Discourse in Postcolonial Ireland' (1998) 7(3) *Social and Legal Studies* 409–29.

[56] Richard Devlin, 'The Rule of Law and the Politics of Fear: Reflections on Northern Ireland' (1993) 4(2) *Law and Critique* 155–85.

[57] See further Linda Connolly, *The Irish Women's Movement: From Revolution to Devolution* (Basingstoke, Palgrave Macmillan, 2002); Siobhán Mullally, *Gender, Culture and Human Rights: Reclaiming Universalism* (Oxford, Hart Publishing, 2006); Carmel Roulston, 'Women on the Margin: The Women's Movement in Northern Ireland, 1973–88' (1988) 53(2) *Science and Society* 219–36.

national boundaries,[58] we hope that readers of this book gain a sense of how Northern/Irish women have become custodians of a particularised gendered national identity, especially as idealised mothers, daughters, wives and victims,[59] and the role of the judiciary in the governmental politics of national identity. In sustaining this national identity, women's roles as active political players, judges, fighters, community leaders and so forth have been repeatedly side-lined in public cultural forums, not the least of which are the published and considerably reproduced texts of appellate judgments. In examining how judges have responded to feminist dissent, protest and litigation, and how they have engaged with the religious, ethno-nationalist and governmental political identities that have dominated Northern/Irish life and law, this project sheds light on the role that judges have played in shaping these collective national identities. That it does so by providing tangible examples of alternative judicial practice provides 'irritating space' not just for 'troubling' judgment, law and the role of the judge, but also for re-imagining dominant notions of national identity, which typically operate to exclude or marginalise women or other dominated groups in society. Law and judgment remain powerful defining discourses in society, which is precisely why they are disputed and engender protests. It is our hope that the feminist judgments collected in this book go some small way to responding to Irish poet and novelist Mary Dorcey's observation (which we would extend to Northern Ireland) that 'while at the institutional level the country [Ireland] is profoundly conservative, it is gradually becoming a pluralist culture. Ideas and debate are far in advance of the public position on just about every issue of national concern'.[60]

Troubling Judgment

> The difficulty is that I have no mouth through which I can speak. I can't make myself understood, not in your world, the world of bodies, of tongues and fingers; and most of the time I have no listeners, not on your side of the river. Those of you who may catch the odd whisper, the odd squeak, so easily mistake my words for breezes rustling the dry reeds, for bats at twilight, for bad dreams.[61]

This quotation comes from Margaret Atwood's retelling of the ancient myth of Penelope and Odysseus, as most famously told in Homer's *Odyssey.* In *The Penelopiad*, Atwood

[58] See Davies, above n 11; Julie McCandless, 'Review: Heather Douglas, Francesca Bartlett, Trish Luker and Rosemary Hunter (eds), *Australian Feminist Judgments: Righting and Rewriting the Law*' (2015) 54 *Irish Jurist* 180–82.

[59] Ruth Fletcher, 'Post-colonial Fragments: Representations of abortion in Irish Law and Politics' (2001) 28(4) *Journal of Law and Society* 568–89.

[60] Mary Dorcey, 'Interview with Mary Dorcey' in Ide O'Carroll and Eoin Collins (eds) *Lesbian and Gay Visions of Ireland: Towards the Twenty-First Century* (London, Cassell, 1995) 43. A very good example here is the issue of abortion, where polls over recent years in both jurisdictions have consistently shown that a majority of the population is in favour of abortion reform; yet successive governments have failed to act. See further Irish Family Planning Association, 'Abortion in Ireland: Public Opinion', at www.ifpa.ie/Hot-Topics/Abortion/Public-Opinion (last accessed 26 March 2016); 'Similar Attitudes towards abortion in North and Republic', *The Irish Times*, 5 November 2015, at www.irishtimes.com/news/social-affairs/similar-attitudes-towards-abortion-in-north-and-republic-1.2417531 (last accessed 26 March 2016); MillwardBrown, 'Attitudes to Abortion' (commissioned by Amnesty International, October 2014), at www.amnesty.org.uk/sites/default/files/milward_brown_poll_results_october_2014_final_0.pdf (last accessed 26 March 2016).

[61] Margaret Atwood, *The Penelopiad: The Myth of Penelope and Odysseus* (Edinburgh, Canongate, 2005).

uses alternative sources to tell a very different version of the story from the perspective of Penelope and her 12 maids, who were hanged by Odysseus upon his return to his kingdom after a 20-year absence. In the quotation, Penelope recounts the difficulty of being heard in the world of the living now that she is dead; but we can easily imagine that Penelope had similar difficulty in relation to being heard when she was alive. Atwood, by retelling the story from a very different perspective from Homer, complicates not only the traditional framing of the myth, but also what counts as 'fact' and 'truth' in how we have hitherto understood the tale. In doing so, Penelope and her maids are 'heard' in a written form of the myth, perhaps for the first time.

The Penelopiad is part of a wider series retelling myths.[62] While myths, as ancient stories with roots in the divine and mystical, may as a genre seem far removed from the case law of more recent decades, both tell stories that reflect and shape our lives and desires. In retelling the myths, the authors have turned 'the familiar on its head to show us ourselves in a new light'.[63] In doing so, they encourage us to question what we think we know and understand, not just about the individual stories, but also about myth as a genre.[64] For instance, what counts as a myth? How does one evolve? What issues get addressed in myths? Who gets to tell the stories that become myths? Why do we need them?

In a similar vein, the Northern/Irish Feminist Judgments Project has sought not only to rework a selected body of case law—ie tell different stories—but to change Northern/Irish feminist political discourse about law. We have done this by engaging with alternative and non-legal modes of judging, crafting texts and deciphering Northern/Irish national identity. When we set out in the project, we were aware of a critical mass of Northern/Irish feminist legal scholars working on discrete substantive areas of law. However, we struggled to find work that advanced broader feminist theories of judgment in the Northern/Irish context. As we delved further, we realised that this reflected a general lack of studies on Northern/Irish judicial craft, in contrast to other common law jurisdictions.[65] In modelling judging as engaged with the constitutive dimension of national identity, we have utilised the feminist judging methodology in such a way as to ask broader questions about feminist engagements with law, and the relationship between local political and cultural struggles, judicial decision-making and collective identities. Given that we had few published resources to draw from, the particular methodology of our project had to be devised to allow participants to 'hear' these struggles and interventions so that they might come to 'trouble' the cases to be rewritten. By incorporating a wide range of interventions in our drafting process, we hope to have laid open the conditions for not only re-imagining the process of judging, but also a re-imagining of the potential of the process and the position it holds in Northern/Irish society. In this section, which should be read alongside the feminist judging methodology section above, we detail the particular form of our drafting process.

[62] See further at www.themyths.co.uk/ (last accessed 26 March 2016).

[63] Publisher's note on Jeanette Winterson's rewriting of *Weight* (Edinburgh, Canongate, 2005), at www.themyths.co.uk/?p=10 (last accessed 26 March 2016).

[64] See further Joanna Overing 'The role of Myth: An Anthroplogical Perspective, or: "The Reality of the Really Made-Up"' in Geoffry Hosking and George Schöpflin (eds) *Myths and Nationhood* (London, Hurst, 1997) ch 1; and Marina Warner, *Monuments And Maidens: The Allegory of the Female Form* (London, Vintage, 1996).

[65] See further, this collection, ch 4. For some notable studies, see Caroline Fennell, 'The Culture of Decision Making: A Case for Judicial Defiance through Evidence and Fact-Finding' (2001) 2(2) *Judicial Studies Institute Journal* 25–65; Mary Kotsonouris, 'Criticising Judges in Ireland' (2001) 2(2) *Judicial Studies Institute Journal*

Drafting Collaboration

As noted above, feminist judgments projects involve significant collaboration. This project utilised this to the utmost. During the drafting process, the project brought together well over 100 academics, students, legal practitioners, judges, activists, litigants, artists and poets, all of whom engaged in deliberating both on the individual cases and on the wider questions of identity that the project brings forth. This process of collaboration was designed to aid the feminist judgment writers in their quest to adopt a feminist judicial voice.

A great deal of this collaboration took place in person over the course of five workshops and a seminar on judicial craft. An inaugural workshop at Durham University in September 2012 established the parameters of the project, to include the core concern of the relationship between gender, judging and national identity. We were very fortunate to have the co-directors of the English Feminist Judgments Project, Rosemary Hunter, Clare McGlynn and Erika Rackley, attend this inaugural workshop and share their experiences with us.[66] As will be evident from the acknowledgements, we have remained in close dialogue with them throughout the lifetime of the project, and indeed with the wider membership of the English Feminist Judgments Project, attesting to the enduring nature of the collaboration amongst and across feminist judgments projects.[67]

After this workshop, participants set about initial written drafts of their feminist judgments and commentaries, all of which were submitted for discussion at one of our four intensive two-day drafting workshops during 2014–15. These workshops were organised thematically around the four main subject positions identified in early readings of the cases, the categorisation of which is reflected in the organisation of this book: mothering subjects; othered subjects; choosing subjects; and embodied subjects.[68] They were held at the University of Ulster, Queen's University Belfast, University College Cork and Griffith College Dublin, respectively. The feminist judges and commentators presented their drafts and discussed the process of judgment writing, both the difficulties faced in adopting a judicial voice and the new insights they had gained in the process. This also gave the judges and commentators the opportunity to discuss the questions they had about their own judgments, such as how they could adopt alternative feminist approaches, or how best to ensure the veracity of their judicial voice. They were also able to consider how their judgments interacted with the others in the project. At each drafting workshop we invited a number of discussants, with both legal and other expertise relevant to the cases in the workshop theme. These discussants also had access to the draft judgments and commentaries in advance of the workshop. Their insights and feedback were invaluable, and went some way

79–97; Kieran McEvoy and Alex Schwartz, 'Judges, Conflict and Past' (2015) 44(4) *Journal of Law and Society* 528–55; The Hon Mr Justice Philip O'Sullivan, 'A Hot Tub for Expert Witnesses' (2004) 4(1) *Judicial Studies Institute Journal* 1–7; Tanya Ward, 'Independence, Accountability and the Irish Judiciary' (2008) 8(1) *Judicial Studies Institute Journal* 1–36.

[66] Note that Rosemary Hunter is also a co-director of the Australian Feminist Judgments Project, which she spoke about at one of our drafting workshops.

[67] We also had some opportunities during the lifetime of the project to meet with participants from other feminist judgments projects at international conferences.

[68] While most cases stayed in their original category, some were reorganised upon a deeper appreciation of the issues at hand.

to recreating the sense of 'audience' that practising judges experience in the courtroom.[69] For participants not able to attend in person, recordings of these drafting discussions—and indeed workshop proceedings generally—were made available via a dedicated member's section on the project website. We also made some short podcasts of judgment discussions publically available on the website, to encourage a wider engagement with the project.[70]

Other Interventions

At each drafting workshop we incorporated a number of panels relating to the project's core theoretical concerns of gender, judgment, national identity, and the relationship between local political and cultural struggles and judicial decision-making.[71] These panels interspersed and informed the discussions of the cases, and we heard from academics from a broad range of disciplines, including history, women's studies, Irish studies, geography, sociology, social anthropology, English, midwifery, politics, law and art. The presentations and discussions that followed brought an importantly contextual understanding to the judgments themselves, as well as the wider Northern/Irish social, cultural, historical and political context. For some cases, we also heard perspectives from litigants, or persons otherwise involved in the case, giving our judgment writers and commentators further insight into what it was like to be directly involved in the case, beyond reading the opinion or opinions from the bench.[72] We were further privileged to hear from several activists during these panels, who discussed their enduring work over many years, giving project participants critical insight into how law works in contesting, litigating and questioning societal and legal norms, while also inspiring all attendees with their commitment and enthusiasm over decades of feminist and other campaigning. All of these interventions were crucial in enlarging the project's mentality around judgment, particularly for the feminist judges, all of whom were academic or practising lawyers.[73] Hearing from this wide array of perspectives led to a very rich environment of collaboration, consideration, reflection and critique, which enabled our feminist judges to 'trouble' their judgments in ways they might not otherwise have considered.

[69] A judicial 'audience' can of course extend to those waiting outside the courtroom, such as media reporters or litigant supporters, who may not have attended the hearing in person.

[70] As noted above, these are available in the 'cases' section of the project website, at www.feministjudging.ie/?p=29 (last accessed 26 March 2016).

[71] Full details available in the 'events' section of our website at www.feministjudging.ie/?p=42 (last accessed 26 March 2016).

[72] It is worth noting that while at least three judges sit on the bench during Northern Ireland Court of Appeal cases, there is typically just one opinion delivered, with which the other judges agree. There are some notable exceptions to this, two of which relate to cases involving abortion that are rewritten in this collection (see chs 21 and 22). We could find no real explanation for this phenomenon, which is in stark contrast to the English Court of Appeal counterpart. One participant did suggest that it may have something to do with the entrenched sectarian divisions in Northern Ireland, and the pressure on judges to be seen as 'above' such divisions by presenting as a united front. Further research would be needed before any categorical conclusions could be reached on the matter. What it did mean for this project was that participants had fewer Northern Irish judicial voices and styles to glean from, which led most of our feminist judges rewriting Northern Irish cases to adopt their own judicial style, rather than model their judicial voice on previous judicial decision-making.

[73] There was more diversity amongst our commentators, to include a political scientist, an academic lawyer active in Irish politics, and an animal behaviouralist with expertise in dog and animal welfare law.

Of particular import to the project was the engagement of poets and visual and performance artists. At one workshop, Kathy D'Arcy[74] and Sarah Clancy[75] performed their poetry, while William Wall read his polemic piece, 'Four Women Who Died for Ireland: On the Concept of Involuntary Patriotism'.[76] Hearing their poetry encouraged us to think about the use of language, rhetoric and form in the drafting process, as well as creative ways in which judgments might tell—or retell—stories, facts, evidence and situations. Emma Campbell presented her work, 'When they put their hands out like scales—Journeys',[77] in which she juxtaposes Northern Irish women's abortion journeys to England with the 'political bluster and suffocating reality of the legal constrictions'[78] in Northern Ireland. Drawing on her own activist experiences, she further reflected with us on the nexus between feminism, law, art and protest. This nexus is also captured on the front cover of this book, with Rose Comiskey's wonderful photograph of a protester jumping out from under a giant papier mâché judicial puppet. The photograph comes from her 'Against the Tide' exhibition, which contains photographs from various campaigns for women's reproductive rights in Ireland in the 1980s and early 1990s.[79] We selected this photograph in order to capture many things about this project, not the least of which is the playfulness with which our feminist judges and commentators, and indeed the wider group of participants, have approached the task of remodelling judgment. So the photograph is less a symbol of us as some sort of judicial 'puppeteer'—which would quite frankly be an insult to the work that judges do—and more an indication of our efforts to embody the role in a way that connects with the wider politics of female dissent and contestation.[80]

At another workshop, we co-hosted an evening event with artists Sarah Browne and Jesse Jones, who are currently engaged in their co-commissioned project *In the Shadow of the State.*[81] This project explores how the female body came to be the focus of repressed histories and political desires under the regulation of the state, particularly through contemporary legal and judicial systems. The co-hosted public performance event, 'The Voice Emerges', took place at the historic Green Street Courthouse in Dublin,[82] and was attended by many project participants during the 'Embodied Subject' workshop. The event examined the conflicted relationship between female body and female voice, exploring different constructions of the plausibility of female testimony. Sarah and Jesse further contributed to all four drafting workshops, and their understanding of law, contestation and dissent challenged much of what we thought we already knew. Along the way, they invited other artists along with them, and we are very grateful for the enthusiasm with which they engaged with us.

[74] www.kathydarcy.com/ (last accessed 26 March 2016).

[75] www.salmonpoetry.com/details.php?ID=256&a=216 (last accessed 26 March 2016). Sarah Clancy also tweets about poetry and politics, @sarahmaintains.

[76] Full text available at https://bogmanscannon.com/2015/03/05/four-women-who-died-for-ireland-on-the-concept-of-involuntary-patriotism/ (last accessed 26 March 2016). Note that the title of this poem informs the title of the following chapter in this collection.

[77] See further http://emmacampbell.co.uk/journeysintro/ (last accessed 26 March 2016).

[78] ibid.

[79] See further www.rosecomiskeyphoto.com/gallery_591983.html (last accessed 26 March 2016).

[80] For a discussion of the role that puppets have played in protest movements, see David Graeber, 'On the Phenomenology of Giant Puppets' in Catherine Flood and Gavin Grindon (eds) *Disobedient Objects* (London, V&A Publishing, 2014) 68–77.

[81] See further at www.create-ireland.ie/current-press/major-new-collaborative-commission-for-2016 (last accessed 26 March 2016).

[82] See further http://archiseek.com/2010/1797-green-street-courthouse-dublin/ (last accessed 26 March 2016).

The final collaborative dimension of the project was with judges from across the island. A number of practising and retired judges contributed to discussions at our drafting workshops, while in April 2015 we held a particularly informative workshop on judicial craft at University College Dublin. Here we benefitted from the insight of practising judges who discussed with us the process of judgment writing and how they perceive their own role with regard to the law. These discussions were particularly useful in understanding both the limits imposed on and, perhaps more critically, the opportunities that judgment writing gives to the judge in setting out the facts, law and outcome of a particular case. It also demonstrated to us how fortunate we were in having the time and opportunity to discuss our own judgments with each other, which is something judges themselves rarely have. As editors of this collection, we are particularly indebted to the judges who participated in this seminar for their patient answering of our many questions and for their review of our 'judicial craft guidance' memo to our feminist judges. In March 2016, as we neared the completion of this manuscript, we were delighted to have Justice Siobhan Keegan and Justice Denise McBride from the Northern Irish High Court attend a public engagement event on the project during the Ulster University Festival of Art and Design.[83] At this event, they spoke to the approaches of our feminist judges in a number of cases, as well as of the significance of the project for the region in terms of placing an emphasis not only on judicial diversity,[84] but also on alternative techniques of decision-making. Their genuine and thoughtful engagement with the project gives us hope that in this book we have produced something of value to practising judges.

An Enduring Dialogue

As discussed above, the feminist judging methodology has been in a wide dialogue from the outset, namely with an extensive corpus of feminist legal theory as well as the law profession. We hope to have extended that dialogue during our project in a creative and vibrant fashion. While entering into a ground of struggle that is already pre-determined in so many ways is challenging, the project has generated effective conditions for thoughtful critique. Our extensive interdisciplinary—and quite public[85]—collaboration, as designed around

[83] This festival was designed to provide space within which different perspectives and intellectual and artistic trajectories could meet, and generate new ideas and new ways of engaging with the world. See further at www.ulster.ac.uk/festivalartdes/about (last accessed 26 March 2016). This event was organised in partnership with the Transitional Justice Institute at the University of Ulster, which hosted the first of our drafting workshops.

[84] See further Dermot Feenan, 'Judicial Appointments in Ireland in Comparative Perspective' (2008) 1(1) *Judicial Studies Institute Journal* 37–66; Dermot Feenan 'Women Judges: Judging Gender, Justifying Diversity' (2008) 35(4) *Journal of Law and Society* 490–519. Ivana Bacik, Cathryn Costello and Eileen Drew interviewed a series of focus groups of women students at King's Inns for *Gender InJustice: Feminising the Legal Professions?* (Dublin, Trinity College, 2003), at http://edepositireland.ie/bitstream/handle/2262/16579/Gender%20In%20Justice.pdf?sequence=1&isAllowed=y (last accessed 26 March 2016).

[85] From the outset of the project we have had significant material on our publicly accessible website, on which we have invited engagement from persons interested in the project. This tactic was successful in reaching out to a number of activists, artists and practitioners who then became involved in the project, as well as academics with whom we were not familiar (such as Mary Shine Thompson, who is the author of ch 3 in this collection). A wide dissemination of our activities on social media—including live tweeting of workshop proceedings—was also used to keep in touch with our wider audience.

our theoretical foci of gender, national identity and feminist political engagement with law, has afforded our participants the opportunity to develop alternative modes of judging, crafting texts, and incorporating occluded, forgotten and plural identities. In this book, as well as on the project website, we have sought to lay open our processes, and see this as a necessary condition for generating an enduring critical dialogue about the project and the feminist judging methodology. Lastly, while it was perhaps not our initial aim, the intensity and scope of our drafting progress has built a vibrant, sustainable and significantly inter-generational community of feminist scholars, practitioners, activists, artists and poets with an interest in Northern/Irish affairs. We are excited to see where their ongoing dialogue leads, and the effect such might have on Northern/Irish life, 'troubling' or otherwise.

The Organisation of the Book

Introductory Chapters

The chapters that follow in this Part of the book cover three discrete areas. The first, written by Máiréad Enright, queries the role of law and the judiciary in the creation of the Northern/Irish female identity, in particular the use of social, historical, socio-economic and political myths alongside patriarchal values and religiosity to establish a fictional ideal of Northern/Irish women. This is followed by a chapter written by Mary Shine Thompson that examines the performance of judging and judgment writing. It considers how knowledge is transposed and used within the judicial structure, and the roles women must play to access this knowledge. The final chapter in Part I, by Aoife O'Donoghue, examines the judiciary, its structure and development in both jurisdictions, how participants have confronted and used these structures within the project, but also the role of women trailblazers in opening up courts to women. These chapters set the scene in moving toward the judgments themselves, as they consider not only where the original judgments came from, but also how the project itself may be transformative.

Judgments

The cases cover a broad range of substantive legal topics, some of which are addressed by the feminist judging methodology for the first time. They include constitutional, contract, human rights, property, international, children, medical, tort, employment, discrimination, animal and criminal matters and equity, amongst others, demonstrating the vast applicability of this critical method to legal judicial reasoning. Of course there are omissions, but this leaves room for others to take the methodology further and continue the critical discussion that is started here. For ease of access we have included a table at the end of this chapter, which places the judgments into more traditional legal categories.

We have selected 26 judgments for examination. These rewritten judgments are subdivided into four categories that mirror the drafting workshop structures discussed above. They tackle traditional legal feminist concerns, such as the law's construction of family forms, reproductive harm and bodily autonomy, as well as legal topics to which feminist perspectives are less often applied: private law, religious freedom, civil liberties, transitional justice and policing.

The project also incorporates a mix of appellate and first instance cases, as well as one Judicial Inquiry Report, pushing the methodology into another direction. Some judges have chosen to sit as 'imagined' appeals, others to sit as concurrences or dissents, or to stand in place of the original judgment. The rationales for these choices are discussed in Chapter 4, but also in the commentaries that precede each judgment.

Commentaries

The commentaries offer an opportunity for reflection on both the rewritten judgments and their original counterparts. The commentators offer both critical reflections and explanations of the choices made by the feminist judgment writers, and in doing so highlight the alternative feminist choices that could have been made. They also offer a contextual understanding of the original judgment, with some reflecting the wider public coverage of the case, the political ramifications of both the case being taken and the decision, and the impact the case had on the cases that followed; while others offer some personal reflections on the importance of the case. These commentaries offer a window into the judicial decision-making process that is unique to this methodology.

Potential Applications and Implications

We see this project as making a number of significant interventions in academic discourse around judging, feminist judging and legal feminism, as well as amongst practitioners and within legal education in Northern/Ireland and beyond.

Academic

In the first instance, this project and book make an important contribution to our understanding of the Northern/Irish judicial role, in relation to both its impact on gender and identity across the jurisdictions and also its distinctive Northern/Irish character. In considering the judicial role across a range of cases, this collection presents a snapshot of the form that Northern/Irish judicial practice takes, locating it as a facet of governmental politics of national identity. In adding to the feminist judgments' literature in an innovative fashion through its cross-jurisdictional approach, its focus on identity and local political and cultural engagements and contestations with law, its multi-disciplinary workshop format and its multi-form case choices, this project makes an important contribution to this growing body of research literature.

Practice

Regarding practitioners, this volume presents some of the alternative interpretations and characterisations of cases, as well as constitutional and statutory interpretation that can be presented to courts, including some of the staple elements of the Northern/Irish legal infrastructure. As became very clear to our feminist judges during the drafting process, judges are dependent on practitioners' presenting innovative arguments that challenge paradigmatic assumptions about law and society. As such, practitioners are also clearly law-makers, given their key role in initially framing and interpreting cases. In this project we have shown the validity of a feminist judicial approach, but in many instances, the scope of that approach was hampered because useful lines of enquiry were not introduced in opening arguments. While this book does not directly engage with wider questions of feminist legal practice,[86] many of the techniques of and approaches to feminist judging that this book explores resonate with general legal method. The book will therefore be a valuable resource not only to practising judges interested in a feminist or critical perspective to law, but also to legal practitioners more generally.

Teaching

Previous feminist judgments projects have already proved themselves to be excellent tools in demonstrating to law students the lack of inevitability regarding judgments, and the alternative perspectives that can be brought to bear when taking a feminist perspective.[87] The broad range of cases included in this collection allows this feminist judgments project to be utilised across a significant number of substantive legal areas, whilst also providing a methodology for application to areas not covered here. This intervention in legal education can be achieved through a number of methods.

In looking at these cases alongside their original variants, students will become aware of the alternative frames that law can take, not just from a feminist perspective but also more broadly, enabling them to question the role of precedent and judicial voice. In exploring how facts, statutes and precedents are presented, students will become aware of the assumptions that are made within the cases and the law itself. The introductory commentaries serve as good indicators to students of how the feminist judge attempted to question the underlying assumptions that were made in the original judgment. In reading a selection of rewritten cases, students will also gain insight into the operation of gender and other inequalities in Northern/Irish society and culture, and the role of law and the judiciary in constructing, changing, and sometimes questioning national and collective identities.

This collection will aid students in interrogating judicial method and to reflect on the choices that are made by the judiciary in writing their judgments. Making students aware of particular judicial voices enables them to consider more closely the differences amongst the judiciary in how they present facts, arguments and their conclusion, but also what they

[86] For a critical appraisal of what conditions would be necessary for such, see Graycar, above n 40.

[87] Jennifer Koshan, Diana Majury, Carissima Mathen, Megan Evans Maxwell and Denise Réaume, 'Rewriting Equality: The Pedagogical Use of Women's Court of Canada Judgments' (2010) 4(1) *Canadian Legal Education Annual Review* 121–48; Special Issue 'The Feminist Judgement Project' (2012) 46(3) *The Law Teacher* 213–80.

choose to omit in doing so. An engagement with this collection offers students a chance to hone their legal reasoning and case analysis skills in a way that deepens their understanding of the role of judgment in law, as well as the power of the judiciary to effect progressive change in society. We hope that a consideration of these issues sparks considerable interest amongst students about not only judicial power, but also the lives and biographies of those who are vested with judicial authority.

This collection also gives students an opportunity to attempt to rewrite judgments themselves. As part of this project, we have undertaken a number of highly successful workshops with diverse groups of students, including large numbers of non-law students. As part of these workshops, students were given the basics of the feminist judging methodology and then worked in groups to read an original judgment, before coming back to discuss what a feminist methodology can add or change, be it asking 'the woman' questions, challenging the linguistic decisions of the original judge or the presentation of cultural or societal assumptions as true or paradigmatic, or exploring how the claimants, victims or defendants are presented and what alternative legal arguments could potentially be made. Students were then asked to rewrite sections of the judgment within groups and individually, to demonstrate both what they could bring to the judgment and also the constraints and difficulties associated with judgment writing. This allowed students to gain skills in case-reading, feminist legal theory, feminist methodology and critical methodology, and in writing a judgment, a deeper understanding of the difficulties faced by judges in coming to conclusions in often difficult legal and factual scenarios.

Lastly, the collection can be used for teaching and other education initiatives that may not be directly focused on judging, judicial method or case analysis. For example, the rewritten cases could be used by students in preparing for mooting competitions, or indeed in devising what form a feminist, or other politically motivated moot may take. The project can also be used as a provocation on postgraduate research methodology courses, for both socio-legal and doctrinal law-focused options. Perhaps most obviously of all, the rewritten cases and their introductory commentaries can be used by students who strive for a critical engagement with substantive areas of law, or who wish to engage with feminist legal theory and the success and limitations of law reform projects, feminist or otherwise. The introductory chapters to this collection, as well as the commentary for each feminist judgment, signpost considerable feminist literature for students interested in further associated reading.

Cases by Subject Area[88]

While we have presented the cases thematically in this collection, to ensure accessibility the cases are listed in Table 1 below as per the traditional subject area, with most judgments appearing repeatedly due to their content.

[88] Note that while many of the feminist judgment citations will be identical to the original case citation, where the feminist judgment is an imaginary appeal, the case citation will differ by signaling the imaginary, rather than the original, court.

Table 1: Cases by Subject Area

Administrative Law	— *In Re White* [2000] NICA 1 — *Re Family Planning Association of Northern Ireland* [2004] NICA 39 — *Zappone and Gilligan v Revenue Commrs* [2006] IEHC 404 — *O'Keeffe v Hickey* [2008] IESC 72 — *Foy v An t-Ard Chláraitheoir & anor* [2009] IR 1 — *Society for the Protection of Unborn Children's Application* [2009] NIQB 92 — *Barnes v Belfast City Council* [2011] NICty 3
Animal Rights	— *Barnes v Belfast City Council* [2011] NICty 3
Children's Rights	— *Attorney-General v X* [1992] IESC 1 — *North Western Health Board v HW and CW (PKU case)* [2001] 3 IR 622 — *O'Keeffe v Hickey* [2008] IESC 72 — *In re E (a child)* [2008] UKHL 66 — *A and B by C (their mother and next friend) v A Health and Social Services Trust* [2011] NICA 28 — *Stokes v Christian Brothers High School Clonmel & anor* [2015] IESC 13
Constitutional/ Public Law	— *McGee v Attorney General* [1974] IR 284 — *Flynn v Power* [1985] IR 648 — *Mhic Mhathúna v Attorney-General* [1989] IR 504 — *McGimpsey v Ireland* [1990] IR 110 — *Attorney-General v X* [1992] IESC 1 — *BJM v CM [1996]* 2 IR 547 — *Lobe v Minister for Justice, Equality and Law Reform* [2003] IESC 3 — *Zappone and Gilligan v Revenue Commrs* [2006] IEHC 404 — *In re E (a child)* [2008] UKHL 66 — *Foy v An t-Ard Chláraitheoir & anor* [2009] IR 1 — *Stokes v Christian Brothers High School Clonmel & anor* [2015] IESC 13
Contract Law	— *National and Provincial Building Society v Lynd* [1996] NI 47
Criminal Law	— *McGee v Attorney General* [1974] IR 284 — *DPP v Tiernan* [1988] 1 IR 250 — *People (DPP) v C* [2001] 3 IR 345 — *CC v Ireland* [2006] IESC 48 — *Barnes v Belfast City Council* [2011] NICty 3 — *Report of the Tribunal of Inquiry into the 'Kerry Babies' Case'* [2015]
Discrimination Law	— *Flynn v Power* [1985] IR 648 — *Zappone and Gilligan v Revenue Commrs* [2006] IEHC 404
Education	— *Flynn v Power* [1985] IR 648 — *In re E (a child)* [2008] UKHL 66 — *O'Keeffe v Hickey* [2008] IESC 72 — *Stokes v Christian Brothers High School Clonmel & anor* [2015] IESC 13
Employment	— *Flynn v Power* [1985] IR 648
Equity	— *In the matter of Article 26 of the Constitution and in the matter of the Matrimonial Homes Bill* [1994] 1 IR 305 — *National and Provincial Building Society v Lynd* [1996] NI 47

(*continued*)

Table 1: ***(Continued)***

Evidence	— *People (DPP) v C* [2001] 3 IR 345 — *Barnes v Belfast City Council* [2011] NICty 3
Family	— *McGee v Attorney General* [1974] IR 284IESC — *Mhic Mhathúna v Attorney-General* [1989] IR 504 — *McKinley v Minister for Defence* [1992] 2 IR 333 — *BJM v CM* [1996] 2 IR 547 — *In the matter of Article 26 of the Constitution and in the matter of the Matrimonial Homes Bill* [1994] 1 IR 305 — *North Western Health Board v HW and CW (PKU case)* [2001] 3 IR 622 — *Lobe v Minister for Justice, Equality and Law Reform* [2003] IESC 3 — *Zappone and Gilligan v Revenue Commrs* [2006] IEHC 404 — *Foy v An t-Ard Chláraitheoir & anor* [2009] IR 1 — *A and B by C (their mother and next friend) v A Health and Social Services Trust* [2011] NICA 28
Human Rights	— *McGee v Attorney General* [1974] IR 284 — *In Re White* [2000] NI 432 — *Re Family Planning Association of Northern Ireland* [2004] NICA 39 — *In re E (a child)* [2008] UKHL 66 — *Foy v An t-Ard Chláraitheoir & anor* [2009] IR 1
Immigration Law	— *Lobe v Minister for Justice, Equality and Law Reform* [2003] IESC 3
International Law	— *McGimpsey v Ireland* [1990] IR 110
Medical Law	— *McGee v Attorney General* [1974] IR 284 — *Attorney General v X* [1992] IESC 1 — *McKinley v Minister for Defence* [1992] 2 IR 333 — *North Western Health Board v HW and CW (PKU case)* [2001] 3 IR 622 — *PM v the Board of Management of St Vincent's Hospital and Justin Geoghegan and the Attorney-General* [2003] IR 1 — *Re Family Planning Association of Northern Ireland* [2004] NICA 39 — *Society for the Protection of Unborn Children's Application* [2009] NIQB 92 — *A and B by C (their mother and next friend) v A Health and Social Services Trust* [2011] NICA 28
Policing	— *In re E (a child)* [2008] UKHL 66 — *Barnes v Belfast City Council* [2011] NICty 3 — *Report of the Tribunal of Inquiry into the 'Kerry Babies' Case'* [2015]
Privacy	— *McGee v Attorney General* [1974] IR 284IESC — *Flynn v Power* [1985] IR 648 — *Attorney-General v X* (1992) IESC 1 — *Foy v An t-Ard Chláraitheoir & anor* [2009] IR 1 — *A and B by C (their mother and next friend) v A Health and Social Services Trust* [2011] NICA 28
Procedure	— *PM v the Board of Management of St Vincent's Hospital and Justin Geoghegan and the Attorney-General* [2003] IR 1 — *Report of the Tribunal of Inquiry into the 'Kerry Babies Case'* [2015]

(*continued*)

Table 1: ***(Continued)***

Reproductive Rights	— *McGee v Attorney General* [1974] IR 284 — *Attorney-General v X* (1992) IESC 1 — *McKinley v Minister for Defence* [1992] 2 IR 333 — *Re Family Planning Association of Northern Ireland* [2003] NICA 39 — *Society for the Protection of Unborn Children's Application* [2009] NIQB 92 — *A and B by C (their mother and next friend) v A Health and Social Services Trust* [2011] NICA 28 — *Report of the Tribunal of Inquiry into the 'Kerry Babies' Case'* [2015]
Sentencing	— *DPP v Tiernan* [1988] 1 IR 250 — *CC v Ireland* [2006] IESC 48
Tort	— *McKinley v Minister for Defence* [1992] 2 IR 333 — *O'Keeffe v Hickey* [2008] IESC 72 — *A and B by C (their mother and next friend) v A Health and Social Services Trust* [2011] NICA 28

2

'Involuntary Patriotism': Judgment, Women and National Identity on the Island of Ireland

MÁIRÉAD ENRIGHT

In this land
where the law is like a public bar
with no toilet –
the men pissing out the back yard …
Ruth Hooley[1]

The only time [the judge] ever felt mastery was when he withdrew to his study to work on his cases, to sit most of the night turning the pages again and again, reading the same dry stuff and suddenly his brain incandescent, agog, some chink, something which his legal mind could latch onto, a loophole, a moment of pure joy, as it might be to a painter discovering a new pigment. Sometimes during these nights he got up and went out into the garden and in the moonlight hit a few balls with a hurly stick and re-imagined himself in the fields, the stony fields of long ago, his mind like the leather ball itself, an acceleration to it, spinning out of moral sight. Some little twist or turn within the labyrinth of the law which he could follow up and this feeling of supremacy and happiness, alone with the moon and the damp grass.
Edna O'Brien[2]

As this chapter was being written, a range of feminist artists were looking anew at the ways in which the law of the independent Irish state has come to shape the lives of its women citizens.[3] The occasion for this flow of work is the centenary of the 1916 Rising; the mythic

[1] Ruth Hooley, 'Parity" (1992) 18(1) *Canadian Journal of Irish Studies* 111.

[2] Edna O'Brien, *Down By The River* (London, Hatchette, 2014) 271.

[3] See, eg, 'In the Shadow of the State', at www.create-ireland.ie/in-the-shadow-of-the-state> (last accessed 18 April 2016); 'Eastrogen Rising: A Rebel Cabaret' *5 Lamps Arts Festival*, at www.fivelampsarts.ie/new/production/eastrogen-rising-a-rebel-cabaret/ (last accessed 18 April 2016); 'Embodied at the GPO', *Dublin Dance Festival*, at www.dublindancefestival.ie/programme/performance/embodied-at-the-GPO (last accessed 18 April 2016); 'GPO Women in Chains Proclaim "ownership of Own Bodies"', at www.irishtimes.com/news/social-affairs/gpo-women-in-chains-proclaim-ownership-of-own-bodies-1.2167670 (last accessed 18 April 2016); 'The Woman Is Present—Women's Stories of 1916', at www.ireland.ie/events/woman-present-womens-stories-1916 (last accessed 18 April 2016).

origin of the post-colonial state in the South[4] and of decades of violent ethno-nationalist struggle over the North. Feminists have been reflecting, in particular, on the role of nationalist women in that foundational conflict,[5] and on the contrasts between their revolutionary activism and the repressive states that they inadvertently helped to birth.[6] In beginning the Northern/Irish Feminist Judgments Project,[7] at the end of the 'Decade of Centenaries', we were conscious of these emerging calls to understand how nationalist struggle and state apparatus have intersected to undermine women's hopes of emancipation, and to impose unwanted identities upon them. In William Wall's words, legal orders have often demanded an 'involuntary patriotism' of women. Re-appropriating the old trope of 'dying for Ireland', Wall argues that the state often requires that women sacrifice themselves for 'the things that make us what we are'.[8] Following these prompts, we wanted to identify ways in which Northern/Irish judgment and judgecraft[9] have been complicit in these processes, or have generated opportunities to resist them.

This chapter presents the results of that inquiry in three stages. First, it discusses how judges in Ireland and Northern Ireland have become associated with national identity projects. Secondly, it explores how the judgments rewritten in this collection speak to the relationships between gender, law, judging and national identity, and in particular, how judges have valorised particular gendered subjectivities at the expense of living women, North and South. Lastly, it locates the Northern/Irish Feminist Judgments as a resistant and creative feminist response to that gendered judicial identity work. This chapter does not advance

[4] On whether Ireland can properly be considered a post-colonial state, see Stephen Howe, 'Questioning the (bad) Question: "Was Ireland a Colony?"' (2008) 36 (142) *Irish Historical Studies* 138–52; David Lloyd, 'Ireland after History' (1999) *A Companion to Postcolonial Studies* 377; David Lloyd, 'Regarding Ireland in a Post-Colonial Frame' (2001) 15(1) *Cultural Studies* 12–32. Begoña Aretxaga, *Shattering Silence: Women, Nationalism, and Political Subjectivity in Northern Ireland* (Princeton, NJ, Princeton University Press, 1997) 15.

[5] For a sample of commentary and artistic and political engagement, see Sadhbh Walshe, 'Eight Women of the Easter Rising', *The New York Times*, at www.nytimes.com/interactive/2016/03/16/opinion/eight-women-of-irelands-1916-easter-rising.html (last accessed 18 April 2016); Tinteán Editorial Team/EMcK, 'The Women of 1916 Mural', at https://tintean.org.au/2016/04/06/the-women-of-1916-mural/ (last accessed 18 April 2016); RF Foster, *Vivid Faces: The Revolutionary Generation in Ireland, 1890–1923* (London, Penguin UK, 2014); Lucy McDiarmid, *At Home in the Revolution: What Women Said and Did in 1916* (Dublin, Royal Irish Academy, 2015); Liz Gillis and Mary McAuliffe (eds), *Richmond Barracks, 1916: 'We Were There': 77 Women of the Easter Rising* (Dublin, Dublin City Public Libraries, 2016); 'Seven Women', at https://1916.rte.ie/risingonrte/seven-women/ (last accessed 18 April 2016); 'Revolutionary Women', at www.storiesfrom1916.com/1916-easter-rising/revolutionary-women/ (last accessed 18 April 2016); 'Mná 1916—Women 1916' (*Ireland 2016*, 13 April 2016), at www.ireland.ie/events/mna-1916-women-1916 (last accessed 18 April 2016); '"Women of the Rising" Campaign Launched on International Women's Day', at www.ria.ie/news/publications-decade-centenaries/women-rising-campaign-launched-international-womens-day (last accessed 18 April 2016).

[6] National Women's Council of Ireland | NWCI.ie, 'Orla O'Connor: 100 Years after 1916, What Are We Celebrating?' (*National Women's Council of Ireland | NWCI.ie*'), at www.nwci.ie/index.php/learn/blog-article/orla_oconnor_100_years_after_1916_what_are_we_celebrating (last accessed 18 April 2016); 'The Women of 1916" by Rita Ann Higgins', at https://poethead.wordpress.com/2015/11/10/the-women-of-1916-by-rita-ann-higgins/ (last accessed 18 April 2016; Office of the President of Ireland, 'Speech by President Michael D. Higgins to Commemorate the Role of Women in the 1916 Easter Rising Royal Hospital Kilmainham, 8 March 2016', at www.president.ie/en/media-library/speeches/speech-by-president-michael-d.-higgins-to-commemorate-the-role-of-women-in (last accessed 18 April 2016).

[7] See ch 1 for an explanation of our choice of the term 'Northern/Irish'.

[8] William Wall, 'Four Women Who Died for Ireland: On the Concept of Involuntary Patriotism', at https://bogmanscannon.com/2015/03/05/four-women-who-died-for-ireland-on-the-concept-of-involuntary-patriotism/ (last accessed 18 April 2016).

[9] Richard Moorhead and Dave Cowan, 'Judgecraft: An Introduction' (2007) 16(3) *Social & Legal Studies* 315–20.

a set of comparative claims about the relative legal positions afforded to women in each jurisdiction; neither space, nor the resources available in the existing literature, nor the spread of judgments rewritten in this project would allow that. This is a broad thematic overview of the project, intended to stimulate debate about the role judges can play as active, if sometimes overlooked, agents in the nationalist policing of women's bodies and lives in 'the state which is not one, but two'.[10]

Projecting Identity: Judges, *Ethnos* and Law

Undoubtedly, some judges have believed that law and its associated techniques of reasoning are largely autonomous from questions of identity. For example, asked whether the Constitution was interpreted in ways that favoured particular classes, Barrington J answered:

> It is not really open to me to answer that question because my job as a judge is to try and interpret what the people have said in their Constitution. I am not concerned as such about whether it is a particular class view.[11]

Barrington J here distinguishes between identity work and judgment. However, from a feminist perspective, judicial identity work is at least partly concealed precisely because the judge's power to impose order on conflict does not reside in his person or his politics. Judith Butler notes that 'the judge does not appear to originate the law or its authority; rather he "cites the law", consults and re-invokes the law'. He dwells amid an 'echo chain'[12] of legal tradition, and merely gives effect to that prior authority.[13] In citing the law, the judge draws on its associations with civilisation, community, justice and right, thereby distancing himself from prevailing divisive social forces. Nevertheless, it is clear that judges in both jurisdictions have projected particular nationally distinct legal identities, whether overtly or integrated with a broader liberal legalist ethos; whether solicitous of or resistant to the demands of the majority.

In 1921, the Irish judiciary and legal professions were split under the Government of Ireland Act. Judges North and South embarked on the projects of creating two separate jurisdictions. Of course, judges in both jurisdictions had a great deal in common. Prior to 1925, barristers from both parts of the country were educated together at the King's Inns, and there was no separate Northern Irish Bar before 1920.[14] The new judiciaries of both states were soon occupied with ensuring the persistence of colonial legal order. When the

[10] Ailbhe Smyth, 'Paying Our Disrespects to the Bloody States We're In: Women, Violence, Culture, and the State' (1995) 7(1) *Journal of Women's History* 190–215, 194.

[11] Gerard Hogan, Donal Barrington and Patrick McEntee, 'The Constitution, Law and Ideology' (1985) 9(2) *The Crane Bag* 104–09, 104.

[12] Writing about the chains of his own judge father's self-restraint, Paul Durcan says that he was a great judge, 'because you were a great clown / In a wig and gown ... a wig and gown festooned with chains / In chains from neck to ankle / You felt attired to deliver/ The balanced verdict; / And you did': Paul Durcan, *Life Is a Dream: 40 Years Reading Poems 1967–2007* (London, Random House, 2011) 266.

[13] Judith Butler, *Bodies That Matter: On the Discursive Limits of 'Sex'* (London, Routledge, 2014) 107.

[14] On the foundation of the Northern Irish Bar, see JAL McLean, 'The Honorable Society of the Inn of Court of Northern Ireland.' (1972) 23 *Northern Ireland Legal Quarterly* 90, 90. Brian Hutton was the first Lord Chief Justice of Northern Ireland to have been called to the Northern Irish Bar on completion of his training.

Four Courts in Dublin burned in 1922, the magazine *Punch* had published a cartoon in which a crowned female 'Spirit of Law' speaks to an 'Irish rebel' and tells him, 'You may have destroyed my courts and my records, but you have not destroyed me!'[15] The courts were to be the embodiment of that resolve.[16] After partition, they were faced with similar issues around armed violence, policing, compensation and imprisonment, in their new disordered jurisdictions.[17] Of course, another point of commonality was the maleness of the courts. Although women had served on the subversive pre-independence Dáil Courts, no woman was appointed to the Free State Courts after partition, and it was many decades before women found a place on the bench in either jurisdiction.[18]

Despite these commonalities, within years of foundation both judiciaries became remarkable for the ways in which their membership, organisation and jurisprudence came to reflect profound identitarian differences. The first Lord Chief Justice of Northern Ireland, Denis Henry, was a former MP, Solicitor General and Attorney General for Ireland, who had frequently been tasked with defending government policy during the War of Independence. In the same period, the first Chief Justice of the Free State, Hugh Kennedy, had been senior legal adviser to the Dáil. In 1921, Henry inaugurated his court with the traditional levee as the Lord Chancellor had done in Dublin for the united Irish courts the previous Easter. Kennedy, by contrast, speaking in English and fluent Irish at Dublin Castle, told the assembly that 'the silence of the Gael was for the first time in hundreds of years broken in the law courts of the Pale'.[19]

In the South, Kennedy's stated ambition was to create a law that departed from its English inheritance.[20] Kennedy called the common law 'an alien structure imposed by statute, an exotic from which a cutting has been artificially fostered in Ireland but which has not taken root or become acclimatised in any real sense'.[21] The point was to create something Irish, in part to overcome colonial representations of the Irish as lawless and deserving of repressive government,[22] and in part to inspire public confidence in the new courts.[23] Speaking

[15] *Punch*, 22 July 1922.

[16] One Northern Irish case indicates the legal and political consequences of the split in arrestingly formalistic terms. In *County Council of Fermanagh v Farrenden* [1923] 2 IR 180, the Northern Ireland Court of Appeal considered whether a soldier shot and maliciously injured in Fermanagh could be compensated for his injury, even though the shot had been fired from Donegal. The council argued that it could not be liable to pay compensation because, while the *actus reus* had taken place in Northern Ireland, the *mens rea* only existed in the Free State. The Court disagreed, insisting that 'the intent is present during every fraction of space and moment of time that is traversed by the bullet'. The split in jurisdictions was not a split in time and space. WN Osborough, 'Law in Ireland 1916–26' (1972) 23 *Northern Ireland Legal Quarterly* 48.

[17] ibid. On women's experience during this time, see Louise Ryan, '"Furies" and "Die-Hards": Women and Irish Republicanism in the Early Twentieth Century' (1999) 11(2) *Gender & History* 256–75.

[18] See further, this collection, ch 4.

[19] Osborough above n 16, 59.

[20] See Gerard Hogan, 'Irish Nationalism as a Legal Ideology' (1986) 75 (300) *Studies: An Irish Quarterly Review* 528–38.

[21] Cited in Thomas Mohr and Jennifer Schweppe, *Thirty Years of Legal Scholarship* (Dublin, Round Hall, 2011). For an account of rural Irish counter-legalities in the colonial period, see Heather Laird, *Subversive Law in Ireland, 1879–1920: From Unwritten Law to Dail Courts* (Dublin, Four Courts, 2005).

[22] On 19th-century characterisations of the Irish as 'lawless', see Sinéad Sturgeon, '"Law of Their Own": Notes on Legal Alterity in Early 19th-century Ireland' (2010) 46(5) *Journal of Postcolonial Writing* 468–78. On the new state's ambitions, see Jason Knirck, *Afterimage of the Revolution: Cumann Na nGaedheal and Irish Politics, 1922–1932* (Madison, WI, University of Wisconsin Press, 2014) 65–66.

[23] In *People v O'Shea* [1982] IR 384, 432, Henchy J refers to 'the bitter Irish race-memory of politically appointed and Executive-oriented judges, of the suspension of jury trial in times of popular revolt, of the substitution

in 1925, WB Yeats, then a senator, explained, 'We want the people to realise that the law is now their own creation, their own instrument … that the judges are their own judges and not imposed on them from without.'[24] At the same time, the state did not desire revolutionary courts; the Dáil courts were abolished in favour of establishing something more suited to 'normal times'.[25] In practice, the law changed little under Kennedy's direction. Early romantic aspirations for a revival of the Brehon law[26] were abandoned, arguably at some cost to feminism.[27] The essential machinery of the courts, a great weight of precedent and the form of legal education were inherited from England.[28] In his efforts to depart from British positivism, Kennedy was in a minority on his own court,[29] clashing in particular with the Anglo-Irish judge Fitzgibbon J.[30] Even judicial costume, despite Kennedy's efforts to change it, remained the same for decades after partition.[31] But the sense of Irish law as something different from English remained important for some judges. McCarthy J, for example, described Irish judicial reliance on English precedent as 'forelock-tugging' and a 'cultural cringe'.[32]

It would be misleading to characterise Irish judge-made law using the single word 'Catholic', since it draws on multiple inherited and new international sources, and Irish judges have been educated in and influenced by traditions of liberal legalism that also hold weight in other jurisdictions. However, the engagement with Catholicism has been an important influence on Irish judicial identity, broadly understood. In the post-colonial state, Catholicism became the defining characteristic of Irishness, understood in opposition to Englishness. In the 1937 Constitution, the Preamble, the Directive Principles of Social Policy and the provisions on fundamental rights all bear the marks of Catholic teaching. The old Article 44 recognised the 'special position' of the Catholic Church, though it never became an established Church. The vast majority of Irish judges appointed since

therefore of summary trial or detention without trial, of cat-and-mouse releases from such detention, of packed juries and sometimes corrupt judges and prosecutors, had long implanted in the consciousness of the people'.

[24] WB Yeats, Seanad, 22 July 1926. On Anti-Treatyite refusal to recognise the courts, see Donnacha Ó Beacháin, *Destiny of the Soldiers—Fianna Fáil, Irish Republicanism and the IRA, 1926–1973: The History of Ireland's Largest and Most Successful Political Party* (Dublin, Gill & Macmillan Ltd, 2010).

[25] Kevin O'Higgins, quoted in Knirck, above n 22, 64. See further Mary Kotsonouris, *The Winding-up of the Dáil Courts, 1922–1925: An Obvious Duty* (Dublin, Four Courts Press Ltd, 2004).

[26] Refusal of the Brehon law was central to early colonisation of Ireland. In ad 1280, King Edward I declared that the Irish laws were 'so contrary to all laws that they ought not to be called laws'. Cited in Richard F Devlin, 'Law, Postmodernism and Resistance: Rethinking the Significance of the Irish Hunger Strike' (1994) 14 *Windsor Yearbook of Access to Justice* 3.

[27] See Margret Fine-Davis, *Gender Roles in Ireland: Three Decades of Attitude Change* (London, Routledge, 2014) 7–8.

[28] Donal Barrington notes that when he was a student in UCD in the late 1940's, the textbook on constitutional law was Dicey's *Law and the Constitution*; Donal Barrington, 'The constitution and the courts' in Frank Litton (ed) The constitution of Ireland 1937–1987 (Dublin, RoundHall, 1987), 110.

[29] For a critical perspective on this issue see Donal K Coffey, 'Judiciary of the Irish Free State, The' (2011) 33 *Dublin University Law Journal* 61, 63–64.

[30] See in particular *In re Westby Minors (No 2)* [1934] IR 311 for a dispute between Kennedy CJ and Fitzgibbon J on whether educating one's children in England could be considered consonant with 'grievous disloyalty' to the new state.

[31] See '"Ocular Demonstration" or "tremendous Treasure"?', at www.historyireland.com/20th-century-contemporary-history/ocular-demonstration-or-tremendous-treasure/ (last accessed 18 April 2016). The Supreme Court adopted new European-style robes in 2012.

[32] Mr Justice Niall McCarthy, Foreword to the First Edition of R Byrne and JP McCutcheon, *The Irish Legal System*, 4th edn (Dublin, Butterworths, 2001) v.

independence have been middle-class Catholics, though many have been publicly associated with positions that would not be approved by the Church hierarchy. In 'Poem not Beginning with a Line by Pindar', Paul Durcan captures the idea of the judge as embodying a relationship between the judiciary and a certain monied Catholic patriarchy. He describes his father, President of the Circuit Court, as a man of 'Faith, chivalry, property, virility … Walk tall to the altar rail in pinstripe suit and silk tie.'[33] George Gavan Duffy stands out for his commitment to Roman Catholic teaching: as a judge, he was willing to take judicial notice of it without need for expert evidence.[34] For Gavan Duffy J, Irish law should be rooted in a Catholic common law, which had been 'temporarily polluted' by English common law during colonisation.[35] In *Cook v Carroll*,[36] he famously upheld a priest's sacerdotal privilege, rejecting the English common law position. In *Tilson*,[37] he held that a Protestant father was bound to abide by the *Ne Temere* doctrine[38] and return his children to their Catholic mother's custody, again rejecting the English law on ante-nuptial agreements. In that case he summarised:

> For religion, for the family and the children, we have laid our own foundations. Much of the resultant polity is both remote from British precedent and alien to the English way of life and, when the powerful torch of transmarine legal authority is flashed across our path to show us the way we should go, that disconformity may point decisively another way.

Perhaps the closest point of contact between Catholicism and judicial law-making was the natural law approach to constitutional interpretation;[39] in particular the assumption that there are certain constitutional rights that are 'natural', 'inalienable', 'imprescriptible' and superior to positive law. Constitutional rights jurisprudence is one of the hallmarks of Irish judicial identity. Beginning in the 1970s, the courts began to develop a constitutional rights jurisprudence that was quite distinct from the inherited British public law tradition, and which installed judges as active watchdogs over state power.[40] In a series of influential cases beginning with *Byrne v Ireland*,[41] judges such as Brian Walsh, Cearbhall Ó Dálaigh and Seamus Henchy began to develop the citizen's right to sue the state. Colm Tóibín summarised:[42]

> The *Byrne* case was the legal equivalent of taking the Union Jack down from the mast in the Castle. The Fluoridation case [*Ryan v AG*] had established the court's ability to define 'rights', the *Byrne*

[33] Durcan, above n 12, 254.

[34] See, eg, *Burke and O'Reilly v Burke and Quail* [1951] IR 216; *Maguire v Attorney General* [1943] IR 238.

[35] *Re Howley* [1940] IR 119.

[36] *Cook v Carroll* [1945] IR 515.

[37] The judgment was upheld by the Supreme Court. Murnaghan J upheld the ruling for what might be considered feminist reasons. He held that 'the absolute dictatorship of the father in matters of his children's religion' was 'derived from the serfdom of women' ([1951] IR 36). The Protestant judge on the bench, Black J, expressed some concern that the High Court judgment appeared to discriminate between Protestants and Catholics.

[38] This Catholic doctrine required partners to a 'mixed marriage' to promise that their children would be baptised and raised as Catholics.

[39] For a fuller discussion see Aileen Kavanagh, 'The Irish Constitution at 75 Years: Natural Law, Christian Values and the Ideal of Justice' (Social Science Research Network 2012), SSRN Scholarly Paper ID 2211457, at http://papers.ssrn.com/abstract=2211457 (last accessed 19 April 2016).

[40] Hogan above n 20, 542.

[41] *Byrne v Ireland* [1972] IR 241.

[42] This approach proved controversial at first. Barrington J says that the High Court judge in *Byrne* admonished him for his arguments, saying that 'by their fortuity [they] had reduced the High Court to the lowest level it had reached at the Bench or at the Bar': 'Peter Ward Meets Donal Barrington', *The Law Makers*, at www.rte.ie/radio1/podcast/podcast_thelawmakers.xml. It seems that the Supreme Court's approach upset the political establishment, and had adverse effects on some judges' careers: Colm Tóibín, 'Inside the Supreme Court', *Magill* (February 1985) 8.

case and the *Haughey* case established that the court's point of departure in defining those rights would be the interests of the individual rather than the state.

This commitment has generated substantial debate about where the line might lie between judges being 'overly reverential'[43] to state projects, on the one hand, and avoiding the sin of 'judicial activism' on the other.[44] For our purposes, the most important issue has been the tension between the demands of constitutional interpretation and the felt need to acknowledge the Catholic commitments of the state. Judges have disagreed over whether the natural law theory underpinning the constitution was religious or secular; whether in mediating between the text of the Constitution and the changing needs of the people, they should be guided by religious teaching. The key cases notably turn on issues of gender and sexuality. In *Ryan v AG*,[45] Kenny J cited the Papal Encyclical *Pacem in Terris* in order to identify an unenumerated constitutional right to bodily integrity. In *Norris v AG*,[46] O'Higgins CJ famously relied on the Constitution's Christian foundations to reject arguments for the unconstitutionality of the criminalisation of homosexuality. He argued that the people who enacted the Constitution were 'proclaiming a deep religious conviction and faith'. Other judges were less committed to Catholic sources. In *McGee v AG*,[47] rewritten in this collection, Walsh J argued that the natural law could found a right of marital privacy that rendered the prohibition on importation of contraception unconstitutional, in clear violation of Catholic teaching. Writing elsewhere, he described the Irish judicial approach not as positivist but as humanist, centred on 'human needs and feelings'.[48] In his dissenting judgment in *Norris*, Henchy J located natural rights in human dignity and human personality. By 1995, the struggle between pluralism and Catholicism in the Constitution was resolved to the satisfaction of the Supreme Court in the *Abortion Information Act* case.[49] Hamilton CJ held that in a pluralist society, Roman Catholic doctrine could no longer determine the scope of fundamental constitutional rights.[50] Nevertheless, as discussed below, Catholic concerns continue to inform Irish cultures of judging, with a variety of serious consequences for women.

In Northern Ireland, there was not the same effort or opportunity to develop a law that broke from its British origins. There are many reasons for this. First, there was no Northern Irish equivalent to the Irish Constitution. In addition, in many respects, the UK legislated for many areas of social activity in Northern Ireland, which in the South were left to the courts.[51] The Northern Ireland courts are also part of the larger British courts system. Their judgments can be appealed to the UK Supreme Court, though in practice only a very small

[43] 'Untangling the Threads of the Supreme Court's Thinking', at www.irishtimes.com/news/crime-and-law/untangling-the-threads-of-the-supreme-court-s-thinking-1.1456003 (last accessed 19 April 2016).

[44] Adrian Hardiman 'The Role of the Supreme Court in our Democracy' in Joe Mulholland (ed), *Political Choice and Democratic Freedom in Ireland: Forty Leading Irish Thinkers* (Dublin, Roundhall, 2004) 42.

[45] *Ryan v AG* [1965] IR 241.

[46] *Norris v AG* [1983] IESC 3.

[47] *McGee v AG* [1974] IR 284.

[48] Donald C Bennett and Brian Walsh, 'Anarchy as Utopia [with Comments]' (1974) 63 (252) *Studies: An Irish Quarterly Review* 323–38, 337.

[49] *Re the Regulation of Information Bill* [1995] 1 IR 1.

[50] Mr Justice Rory O'Hanlon had taken a controversial public position to the contrary: 'Former Judge Whose Stance on Abortion Led to Controversy', *The Irish Times*, at www.irishtimes.com/news/former-judge-whose-stance-on-abortion-led-to-controversy-1.1055657 (last accessed 19 April 2016).

[51] Kay Goodall, 'What Defines the Roles of a Judge—First Steps Towards the Construction of a Comparative Method' (2000) 51 *Northern Ireland Legal Quarterly* 543, 550.

number are.[52] Northern Irish judges can be appointed to the House of Lords/UK Supreme Court, and indeed many have gone on to be influential members of those courts. Goodall also suggests that the politicisation of nationalism in Northern Ireland, and the Unionist desire to maintain links with Britain, dampened down any desire for a distinctively Northern Irish law.[53] At the same time, she notes, at the height of The Troubles, judges were also subject to IRA violence, and this is likely to have undermined any nascent judicial nationalism.[54]

Even if it did not seek to imbue the law with a particular ethno-nationalist character, the Northern Irish judiciary was indelibly associated with the wider Unionist state. Richard Devlin argues that the very construction of the state was 'driven by the fear of being overwhelmed by the Catholic hordes'.[55] From partition, the state and its alliance with Britain were marked by determined sectarian discrimination against Catholics,[56] and government efforts to suppress Catholic opposition to the existence of the new state.[57] Government tactics from early in the life of the new state included manipulation of the electoral system and discrimination in housing and public sector employment. The most obvious expression of Unionist authority, however, was the legal system,[58] which was marked by enforcement of coercive security powers[59] and the maintenance of security forces with deep roots in Protestant communal defence, internment[60] and official tolerance of anti-Catholic violence. In keeping with these broader patterns, the bench was maintained as a Protestant Unionist domain. Into the 1970s, many judges were former Unionist politicians who had held positions in the Northern Ireland government.[61] While the first Lord Chief Justice was a Catholic Unionist, no Catholic succeeded him until John Shiel, almost 25 years after the former's death.[62] By 1976, just eight of 74 judicial appointments in the jurisdiction were held by Catholics.[63] Even then, there was a perception that these judges were right-wing 'establishment Catholics'.[64] Refusal to recognise the Northern Ireland courts was part of a broader Republican ideology. As part of a larger UK courts structure, members of the

[52] See further Brice Dickson and Gavin Drewry, *The Judicial House of Lords: 1876–2009* (Oxford, Oxford University Press, 2009) 309–13; Kieran McEvoy and Alex Schwartz, 'Judges, Conflict, and the Past' (2015) 42(4) *Journal of Law and Society* 528–55, 547.

[53] Goodall above n 51, 548.

[54] ibid, 556.

[55] Richard Devlin, 'The Rule of Law and the Politics of Fear: Reflections on Northern Ireland' (1993) 4(2) *Law and Critique* 155–85, 175.

[56] On how this account is complicated by class, see ibid, 157.

[57] Joseph Ruane and Jennifer Todd, *The Dynamics of Conflict in Northern Ireland: Power, Conflict and Emancipation* (Cambridge, Cambridge University Press 1996) 122.

[58] Devlin, above n 55, 161.

[59] See, eg, the Civil Authorities (Special Powers Act) 1922 and the Emergency Provisions Act 1973.

[60] For a summary of the history and effects of internment in Northern Ireland, see Laura K Donohue, *The Cost of Counterterrorism: Power, Politics, and Liberty* (Cambridge, Cambridge University Press 2008) 37–42.

[61] See, eg, Hillyard, noting in 1990 that 15 out of 20 High Court judges were openly associated with Ulster Unionism: Paddy Hillyard, 'The Political and Social Dimensions of Emergency Law in Northern Ireland' in Anthony Jennings (ed), *Justice Under Fire: The Abuse of Civil Liberties in Northern Ireland* (London, Pluto Press, 1990) 202; Jean Marie McGloin, 'A Historical Consideration of the Police and Prosecution/Courts in Northern Ireland' (2006) 16(2) *International Criminal Justice Review* 77–98, 83.

[62] See further John O'Brien, *Discrimination in Northern Ireland, 1920–1939: Myth or Reality?* (Cambridge, Cambridge Scholars Publishing, 2009) 36.

[63] John Whyte, 'How Much Discrimination Was There under the Unionist Regime, 1921–68' (1983) *Contemporary Irish Studies* 1–35, 9.

[64] McEvoy and Schwartz, above n 52, 542.

Northern Irish judiciary may have been considered players in a wider distrusted colonial system.[65] In criminal justice matters, in particular, an informal paramilitary-run courts system emerged, which replaced the official courts system in some communities.[66] There was also a wider sense that ordinary Catholics did not have confidence in the judicial system.[67] In 1976, Fr Denis Faul explained:

> Our people are afraid of the courts: they believe the judicial system as it operates in the blatantly sectarian conditions of life here is loaded against them. Whether this is based on fact or not is important enough, but the really vital point is: if the common opinion of reasonable men of the minority believes that justice is difficult or impossible to obtain in many cases, especially in those with a sectarian or political tinge, then the law has lost the confidence of a large section of the people where it should be operated for the common good of all the people and it should be seen to operate fairly towards all sections.[68]

In the 1960s, Catholics began to organise to demand the civil rights due to them as British citizens. The civil rights movement was an important identity struggle—a challenge not only to Unionist supremacy, but also to the sectarian division of the Northern Irish working classes.[69] Women were active initiators of many civil rights actions.[70] From the executive's point of view, civil rights campaigns were a threat to the integrity of the state.[71] The aggressive policing of the Derry Civil Rights March and the People's Democracy March from Belfast to Derry in 1968 was evidence of this attitude.[72] Stephen Livingstone calls the Northern Irish judiciary in this period 'at best irrelevant, at worst hostile'[73] to these attempts to protect civil rights during the conflict. However, it should also be said that the absence of activist litigators[74] in Northern Ireland, and the broader failures of British law to provide remedies for discrimination,[75] meant that few human rights claims were brought on behalf of oppressed Catholics in the first place.

[65] These broader perceptions of law often presented stumbling blocks to women's cross-community organising against unjust law. See, eg, Eilish Rooney, 'Political Division, Practical Alliance: Problems for Women in Conflict' (1995) 7(1) *Journal of Women's History* 40–48, 43; Linda Hagan, 'Missing Voices: Women and the Three "Ps": Politics, Prejudice and Paternalism' (2006) 32(1) *The Canadian Journal of Irish Studies* 12–22, 19.

[66] McGloin, above n 61, 87, 89 and 91.

[67] Kieran McEvoy, 'Law, Struggle, and Political Transformation in Northern Ireland' (2000) 27(4) *Journal of Law and Society* 542–71, 547–53.

[68] Quoted in Gianluca De Fazio, 'Legal Opportunity Structure and Social Movement Strategy in Northern Ireland and Southern United States' (2012) 53(1) *International Journal of Comparative Sociology* 3–22, 13.

[69] Simon Prince, 'The Global Revolt of 1968 and Northern Ireland' (2006) 49(3) *Historical Journal* 851.

[70] Rooney, above n 65, 41.

[71] Gianluca De Fazio, 'Civil Rights Mobilization and Repression in Northern Ireland: A Comparison with the US Deep South' (2009) 2 *The Sixties* 163, 171.

[72] Prince, above n 69.

[73] Stephen Livingstone, 'And Justice for All? The Judiciary and the Legal Profession in Transition' in Colin J Harvey (ed), *Human Rights, Equality and Democratic Renewal in Northern Ireland* (Oxford, Hart Publishing, 2001) 143. See Lord Lowry's account of the civil rights movement, which omits any reference to security forces' oppression of Catholics: Lord Lowry, 'National Security and the Rule of Law' (1992) 26 *Israel Law Review* 118, 122–23.

[74] See, eg, Livingstone above n 73, 147. See Eileen V Fegan, 'Northern Ireland's Abortion Law: The Morality of Silence and the Censure of Agency' (2003) 11(3) *Feminist Legal Studies* 221–54; and Kieran McEvoy, 'What Did the Lawyers Do During the "War"? Neutrality, Conflict and the Culture of Quietism' (2011) 74(3) *Modern Law Review* 350–84, 359–60, explaining that while small collectives of radical lawyers emerged at key junctures in The Troubles, they had difficulty maintaining their presence, until the establishment of the Committee on the Administration of Justice.

[75] Kevin Boyle, 'Human Rights and Political Resolution in Northern Ireland' (1982) 9 *Yale Journal of World Public Order* 156, 160; McEvoy, above n 74, 356–58; Fazio, above n 71, 168. For more detail see Fazio, above n 68, 12–14.

When Northern Irish judges have reached for the tools of liberal legalism, it has often been as a means to project a 'studied neutrality', which set them apart from the ethno-nationalist conflict that divided the polity.[76] Judges' claims to neutrality were also designed to address perceptions that they were unduly compliant with executive will.[77] The tensions at play—which, of course, have also had their mirrors in the Republic—were particularly acute after the imposition of direct rule in Northern Ireland.[78] Judges were charged with applying laws that undermined civil liberties in the purported interests of national security, in heavily pressurised circumstances.[79] Prominent judges, such as Lord Lowry[80] and Lord MacDermott,[81] spoke of the Northern Irish judiciary during this period as steadfast defenders of the rule of law. But while they clearly appreciated the threats to the maintenance of order posed by non-state actors' violence, they were insufficiently critical of abuses of state power. Stephen Livingstone wrote that judges displayed 'no sense of any alternative perspective on terrorism and the right of the state to combat it even in such a divided polity'.[82] Judges were, of course, heavily reliant on the security forces because they were themselves targets of terrorist violence,[83] and the smallness of the jurisdiction bred relationships between the forces and the judiciary, and between members of the judiciary themselves, that militated against reflection and critique.[84] These difficulties manifested in two areas. First, judges tended to take the view that, where security forces reasonably suspected that the armed forces were engaged with terrorists, they should not be second-guessed, and this led to a very high level of acquittal in cases of unlawful killing.[85] On occasion, prominent Northern Irish judges made comments openly praising the security forces in cases in which they had used unjustifiable force.[86] Secondly, in trying terrorist suspects, judges did not do enough to uphold basic civil liberties. This was particularly the case in the Diplock courts, in which the protections available to such suspects were significantly reduced.[87] Of course, as Kevin Boyle argues, these non-jury trials were installed by a Westminster Government dissatisfied with earlier judicial insistence that involuntary statements obtained from defendants

[76] McEvoy and Schwartz, above n 52, 542.

[77] David Hayton, *Law's Future(s)* (London, Bloomsbury Publishing, 2000) 77; Livingstone, above n 73, 139.

[78] Angela Hegarty, *Human Rights: 21st Century* (London, Cavendish Publishing, 1999) 95. See also Brice Dickson, 'The Administration of Justice in Northern Ireland' (1986) 75 (297) *Studies: An Irish Quarterly Review* 56–66, 59.

[79] Hannah Quirk, 'Don't Mention the War: The Court of Appeal, the Criminal Cases Review Commission and Dealing with the Past in Northern Ireland' (2013) 76 *MLR* 949, 962.

[80] Lowry, above n 73.

[81] Lord MacDermott, 'The Quality of Judgement' (1970) 21 *Northern Ireland Legal Quarterly* 178.

[82] Livingstone, above n 73, 153.

[83] McEvoy and Schwartz, above n 52, 540.

[84] Quirk, above n 79, 957–59.

[85] Livingstone, above n 73, 151–52.

[86] For instance, in *R v Montgomery* (1984) unreported, Gibson LJ praised the RUC for 'their courage in bringing the three deceased men to justice; in this case the final court of justice': Hillyard, above n 61, 192. In 1980, Lord Lowry handed down suspended sentences to four RUC officers guilty of offences including bombing a Catholic bar in South Armagh and kidnapping a priest. He said, 'All of the accused have admitted their offences and all of them have acted wrongly or emotionally under the same powerful motives, in one case the mortal danger of their service and in the other the feeling that more than ordinary police work was needed and justified to rid the land of the pestilence which has been in existence.' ('A Shameful Part of Our Country's Troubled History', *The Irish Times*, at www.irishtimes.com/culture/books/a-shameful-part-of-our-country-s-troubled-history-1.1578119 (last accessed 3 April 2016)).

[87] On the background to the Commission, see Donohue, above n 60, 43–48. On the operation of the courts, see Quirk, above n 79.

should be inadmissible in court,[88] and which had already shown itself hostile to judicial scrutiny of emergency powers.[89] Nevertheless, judicial resistance to the Diplock regime was muted once it was in place. For 25 years, judges tried individuals alone,[90] convicted them on the basis of confessions obtained by coercive interrogation[91] and committed them to a violent prison regime. While there were instances of judges applying some common law constraints to the interpretation of the state's emergency powers,[92] they were broadly deferential to the claims of national security as articulated by Parliament.[93] In participating in the Diplock process, judges added a normalising veneer of legality[94] to an extraordinary regime of mass imprisonment, surveillance, domestic raids, disruption of private and family life, and sexual harassment and assault including strip-searching,[95] designed to silence the state's nationalist 'Other' and depoliticise republican prisoners.[96] By the time of the Belfast Agreement, as Northern Ireland entered a phase of transition from decades of sectarian conflict, Catholics were more prominent within the judiciary, and judicial independence from politicians more clearly established.[97] Northern Irish judges now have particular responsibilities for managing that transition; in particular under the rubric of human rights adjudication. Judges' involvement in the identity politics of the past has yet to undergo serious public examination.[98]

Judgment, Women and National Identity: Mothers for the Nation

So far, I have shown that Northern/Irish judges have been directly and indirectly associated with national identity projects. In this section, I consider what judicial involvement in national identity projects has meant for women. In elaborating upon this dimension of the judicial role, my aim is not to give a complete treatment of women's lives before Northern/Irish courts, but rather to set the judgments rewritten as part of this project in the context of our broader concern with national identity projects. The nation is often

[88] Boyle, above n 75, 162.

[89] ibid.

[90] 'There was no jury, none at all, / The pig-in-the-wig was right, / And only fools saw fit to stand and challenge him with fight./For this court is a farce, my friends, and justice knows no light': Bobby Sands, *Skylark Sing Your Lonely Song: An Anthology of the Writings of Bobby Sands* (Mercier Press: Cork, 1989) 38–65.

[91] Boyle, above n 75, 165–69; see generally Lisa White, *Transitional Justice and Legacies of State Violence* (London, Routledge, 2015).

[92] Lord Lowry gives an account of Northern Irish judges' approach to the Diplock regime as one of reasonable judicial resistance to the rules imposed from Westminster: see Lowry, above n 75 126–34.

[93] McEvoy and Schwartz, above n 52, 536–39. For Livingstone, the most important example of judicial resistance to the Diplock process—the eventual rejection of uncorroborated 'supergrass' evidence—can be explained not as a direct rejection of Westminster's counter-terrorism agenda, but as a return to legalistic evidentiary standards; ibid, 547–48; Livingstone above n 73, 145–50.

[94] McEvoy and Schwartz, above n 52, 534.

[95] On women's resistance to the prison regime from within, see Theresa O'Keefe, 'Menstrual Blood as a Weapon of Resistance' (2006) 8(4) *International Feminist Journal of Politics* 535–56.

[96] Devlin, above n 55, 37.

[97] See further Graham Gee et al, *The Politics of Judicial Independence in the UK's Changing Constitution* (Cambridge, Cambridge University Press, 2015) 229.

[98] See further McEvoy and Schwartz, above n 52.

imagined as a woman who motivates men to fight over her—in Irish nationalism as the Maid of Erin, Dark Rosaleen, Cathleen ni Houlihan, the Shan Van Vocht, or the Hag of Beare.[99] It is not only that the nation is spoken of as a woman, but that individual women become responsible for performing nationalist feminine ideals in their own lives.[100] In contexts of ethno-nationalist conflict, the struggle to attain or resist state power is simultaneously a conquest of the female body: self-governance means control of the nation's women.[101] Ailbhe Smyth writes that '[w]omen, powerless under patriarchy, are maintained as Other of the ex-Other, colonized of the post-colonized'.[102] As Deniz Kandiyoti writes, the concept of nation is an assertion of control over women; it places 'pressure on women to articulate their gender interests within the terms of reference set by nationalist discourse'.[103] Recall Wall's concept of 'involuntary patriotism'. Women are mothers *for* the nation.

Women find themselves in this position because their very bodies are central to securing a stable communal identity: they produce and raise new members, holding them to the traditions that distinguish the nation from its outside.[104] The mothering subject is central to national identity; her virtue is the nation's virtue. Within Irish nationalist discourse, women's role was to provide the homes where pious Gaelic men could be raised.[105] Post-independence, as Barry Collins and Patrick Hanafin note, the old nationalist iconography of the vulnerable but alluring maiden, who is taken from us by the coloniser and who implores men to fight for her cause, is replaced in the Constitution with that of the suffering mother. The apparent reversal in power relations here is important—woman changes from demanding siren to dutiful mother. Maternal confinement and self-abnegation redeem male loss of life.[106] For Hanafin, in post-colonial Ireland, 'the body of the citizen was to become a martyr of the everyday, a body which following the example of the iconic martyred figures of the anticolonial struggle was to derive satisfaction and redemption through suffering and denial'.[107] Luke Gibbons associates this Irish veneration of resigned maternal

[99] On the centrality of female images to Irish nationalism, see Declan Kiberd, *Inventing Ireland: The Literature of a Modern Nation* (Dublin, Random House, 2009) 362. See further Agata Szczeszak-Brewer, 'Joyce's Vagina Dentata: Irish Nationalism and the Colonial Dilemma of Manhood' (2013) 34(2) *Frontiers: A Journal of Women Studies* 1–24; Patrick Hanafin, 'Defying the Female: The Irish Constitutional Text as Phallocentric Manifesto' (1997) 11(2) *Textual practice* 249–73; Richard Kearney, *Postnationalist Ireland: Politics, Culture, Philosophy* (London, Psychology Press 1997) 117–18.

[100] Heather Ingman, *Twentieth-Century Fiction by Irish Women: Nation and Gender* (London, Ashgate Publishing Ltd, 2007) 144.

[101] Louise Ryan, 'Negotiating Modernity and Tradition: Newspaper Debates on the "Modern Girl" in the Irish Free State' (1998) 7(2) *Journal of Gender Studies* 181–97.

[102] Ailbhe Smyth, 'The Floozie in the Jacuzzi' (1989) 6 *The Irish Review* 7–24.

[103] Deniz Kandiyoti, 'Identity and Its Discontents: Women and the Nation' (1991) 20(3) *Millennium-Journal of International Studies* 429–43.

[104] On women as 'boundary and metaphorical limit' of national identity, see Anne Mcclintock, *Imperial Leather: Race, Gender, and Sexuality in the Colonial Contest* (London, Routledge, 2013) 354; Nira Yuval-Davis, Floya Anthias and Jo Campling, *Woman, Nation, State* (London, Macmillan, 1989) 7.

[105] Angela K Martin, 'The Practice of Identity and an Irish Sense of Place' (1997) 4(1) *Gender, Place & Culture* 89–114, 104.

[106] Barry Collins and Patrick Hanafin, 'Mothers, Maidens and the Myth of Origins in the Irish Constitution' (2001) 12(1) *Law and Critique* 53–73, 67.

[107] Patrick Hanafin, 'D(en)ying Narratives: Death, Identity and the Body Politic' (2000) 20(3) *Legal Studies* 393–408, 395. See further on the abjection of women as the necessary point of origin of the new state, Mary Condren, 'Sacrifice and Political Legitimation: The Production of a Gendered Social Order' (1995) 7(1) *Journal of Women's History* 160–89.

self-sacrifice with Catholic devotion to the Virgin Mary.[108] The relegation of women to the domestic sphere also chimes with a revived Gaelic,[109] but also Victorian, vision of family life.[110] The wife assumed the 'mystical identity of a priestess through whose selfless ministrations the altar of domesticity was supposed to be kept spotless'.[111] Such women should be fixed in the home, surrounded by male domains such as land and the workplace.[112] Similar trends emerge in the North after partition. For many Northern Protestant religious groups, particularly Calvinists, women's role was to be submissive to men,[113] and Unionist parties continue to emphasise that women's primary social role is as wives and mothers.[114] In the context of conflict that public/private split is amplified: warrior men become protectors of the home, while women are encouraged to maintain the family,[115] and their own sexual integrity,[116] through the upheavals of war.[117]

Women in Ireland and Northern Ireland have understood that law is a central tool in the state's efforts to preserve its hegemony over performances of national identity by generating consensus and stability around the enforcement of particular standards of female behaviour.[118] As this collection demonstrates, in Ireland, North and South, women have come—deliberately or reluctantly—before courts and tribunals. In court, women have contested the boundaries of involuntary patriotism, demanded accountability for the harms done to them by past laws and attempted to assert their own subaltern subjectivities.[119] Some women have done this work alone, but more have been part of wider movements that developed tactics to capitalise on progressive decisions,[120] and to support women to protest and cope with[121] the consequences of regressive judgments. Law has always been important to feminist organising in Ireland and Northern Ireland.[122] Engagement with law not only

[108] Luke Gibbons, *Transformations in Irish Culture* (Notre Dame, IN, University of Notre Dame Press, 1996) 108. See also Ingman, above n 100, 143.

[109] Cusack argues that nationalism is split by a desire for progress and a nostalgia for the past. In Irish nationalism, this split was managed along gendered lines, with women consigned to traditional roles while men forged a new path for the nation: Tricia Cusack, 'Janus and Gender: Women and the Nation's Backward Look' (2000) 6(4) *Nations and Nationalism* 541–61.

[110] Gibbons, above n 108, 108.

[111] Tom Inglis, 'Origins and Legacies of Irish Prudery: Sexuality and Social Control in Modern Ireland' (2005) 40(2) *Éire-Ireland* 9–37.

[112] Martin, above n 105, 105.

[113] Linda Racioppi and Katherine O'Sullivan See, '"This We Will Maintain": Gender, Ethno-Nationalism and the Politics of Unionism in Northern Ireland' (2001) 7(1) *Nations and Nationalism* 93–112, 98.

[114] ibid, 104.

[115] Condren, above n 107, 179.

[116] Fidelma Ashe, 'Gendering Ethno-Nationalist Conflict in Northern Ireland: A Comparative Analysis of Nationalist Women's Political Protests' (2007) 30(5) *Ethnic and Racial Studies* 766–86, 770.

[117] ibid, 769.

[118] Devlin, above n 55, 164.

[119] Iris Marion Young and Danielle S Allen, *Justice and the Politics of Difference* (Princeton, NJ, Princeton University Press, 2011) 63.

[120] See, eg, the Women's Law and Research Group, discussed in Eileen Evason, *Against the Grain: The Contemporary Women's Movement in Northern Ireland* (Cork, Attic Press, 1991) 36–38.

[121] See, eg, in the context of abortion litigation, Women's Information Network, the Irish Women's Abortion Support Group, Abortion Support Network and Women on Web.

[122] In both parts of the island the women's movement of the 1970s crystallised around campaigns for legal change. The Northern Irish Women's Rights Movement began with a campaign around the Sex Discrimination Act, while the Irish Women's Liberation Movement made claims for the reform of the laws on housing, marriage and contraception in its manifesto *Chains or Change?* (Dublin, Irish Women's Liberation Movement, 1970). See further June Levine, *Sisters: The Personal Story of an Irish Feminist* (Cork, Attic Press, 2009).

has been the preserve of governmental feminism, but has been driven by grassroots agitation built on feminist critique of the relationship between nationalist patriarchy and the prevailing legal order.[123] In their turn, conservative activists, religious and state agents have also sought to use litigation to more regressive ends—to uphold long-established gendered legal constructions of family, community, religion, propriety and so on.[124] Examples rewritten in this collection include *Mhic Mhathúna v Ireland*[125] and *Society for the Protection of Unborn Children, Re an Application*.[126] Judges have often[127] responded to these efforts with judgments valorising particular jural subjects; attempting to restore order, or re-assert the boundaries of national identity. Their identity work is especially important, because the law they wield is vested with a particular power to quell social struggle. As Patrick Devlin writes, in court, judges determine when contests over identity should cease.[128] Judge-made law is 'a medium for the imposition of order when the incommensurability of social practices can no longer be controlled by other means'.[129] Judges have defended law's preferred performances of identity by denying others, translating women's claims into law's own language, marking them as deviant or deficient, or erasing them altogether.

Mothering in the Rewritten Judgments: Exposing and Undoing Judicial Identity Commitments

Although this collection discusses multiple aspects of women's experience before the law, most of the rewritten judgments are attentive to and contest ways in which judges have enforced the demands of mothering for the nation.[130] Some of the feminist judgments encounter and draw attention to the judicial assumption that motherhood is women's natural state and primary aspiration. In *BJM v CM*,[131] Flood J, in the original judgment, described the wife in a nullity case as 'having reached the zenith of all womanhood' by giving birth to several children within marriage.[132] In *DPP v Tiernan*,[133] in articulating the

[123] Smyth argues that the divide between left radicalism and state-focused reformism was less pronounced in the Irish women's movement than elsewhere: Ailbhe Smyth, 'The Contemporary Women's Movement in the Republic of Ireland' (1988) 11 *Women's Studies International Forum* 331–41, 333. In the North, Unionist and Nationalist women sometimes took different approaches to the validity of engagement with state power, see Ingman, above n 100, 141.

[124] Smyth, above n 123, 339.

[125] This collection ch 7.

[126] This collection, ch 22.

[127] The point here is not to suggest that Irish or Northern Irish judges are or have been a homogeneous unit; Goodall above n 51.

[128] Smyth, above n 123.

[129] Richard F Devlin, 'Law's Centaurs: An Inquiry into the Nature and Relations of Law, State and Violence' (1989) 27 *Osgoode Hall Law Journal* 219, 225.

[130] Many of the techniques deployed here can be read, in part, as iterations of the core techniques of feminist judging outlined by Rosemary Hunter, including 'telling the story differently', 'using contextual materials', 'challenging gender bias' and 'anti-essentialism': Rosemary Hunter, 'An Account of Feminist Judging' in Rosemary Hunter, Clare McGlynn and Erika Rackley (eds), *Feminist Judgments: From Theory to Practice* (London, Bloomsbury Publishing, 2010) 35–42.

[131] *BJM v CM* [1996] 2 IR 574.

[132] This collection, ch 25.

[133] *DPP v Tiernan* [1988] IR 250.

effect of rape on women, the original judgment constructs them as future mothers. Feminist judges Louise Kennefick and Caroline Fennell address this by insisting that women may react to rape in a plurality of ways, not all of which can be contained within the maternal frame.[134]

More of the rewritten judgments deal with the indirect effects of law's tendency to foreground maternity as the primary role women play for the nation. There are three important issues here. First, transgressions of the maternal role are often punished by judgment. Thus, motherhood without marriage may have serious consequences; *Flynn v Power*[135] deals with the exclusion of unmarried mothers from employment by religious schools.[136] Irish judges have at times been happy to rationalise those exclusions: in his Circuit Court judgment in Eileen Flynn's case, Judge Noel Ryan said, 'In other places women are being condemned to death for this sort of offence. … I do not agree with this, of course. Here people take a very serious view of this, and it is idle to shut one's eyes to it.'[137]

The *Report of the Tribunal of Inquiry into the 'Kerry Babies' Case*[138] considers an especially violent episode in the effective criminalisation of unmarried motherhood in Ireland. Vicky Conway, in approaching the Kerry Babies Tribunal, critiques how intrusive judicial processes were manipulated to undermine the credibility of a woman who had transgressed majority sexual mores by having children out of wedlock. Crucially, she highlights Joanne Hayes' position as a grieving mother—restoring a status to her that is largely forgotten in the original report.[139] States may also be reluctant to permit the purported refusal of motherhood that comes with seeking abortion rights.[140] Female agency, in the shape of the choice to terminate a pregnancy, is constructed as a threat to national reproduction.[141] Three judgments rewritten in this collection address that issue: *Attorney General v X*,[142] *Re Family Planning Association of Northern Ireland v Minister for Health*[143] and *Society for the Protection of Unborn Children, Re an Application*.[144]

The feminist judgments that deal with these transgressions show a much richer understanding of how they have been policed than do the original judgments. First, many of the original judgments that concern women's transgression of the precepts of motherhood tend to present each 'offender' as an individual exception, set apart from the broader history of Irish womanhood. Some of the rewritten judgments reverse this move, by narrating counter-histories of women's oppression. In her feminist judgment in *AG v X*, Ruth Fletcher emphasises the historical place of abortion in Irish society, specifically mentioning St Brigid

[134] This collection, ch 23.

[135] *Flynn v Power* [1985] IEHC 1.

[136] This collection, ch 6.

[137] Tom Inglis and Carol MacKeogh, 'The Double Bind: Women, Honour and Sexuality in Contemporary Ireland' (2012) 34(1) *Media, Culture & Society* 68–82, 77.

[138] This collection, ch10.

[139] This collection, ch 10.

[140] Lisa Smyth, 'The Cultural Politics of Sexuality and Reproduction in Northern Ireland' (2006) 40 *Sociology* 663-80, 664.

[141] See further Lisa Smyth, *Abortion and Nation: The Politics of Reproduction in Contemporary Ireland* (London, Ashgate, 2005); Ruth Fletcher, 'Post-Colonial Fragments: Representations of Abortion in Irish Law and Politics' (2001) 28 *Journal of Law and Society* 568–89.

[142] This collection, ch 18.

[143] This collection, ch 21

[144] This collection, ch 22.

as a Catholic saint reputed to have performed abortions.[145] The effect is to make room for an Irish female identity in which abortion is normal and even valued. Other judgments emphasise the state's implication in women's oppression. In both jurisdictions, a complex system of 'coercive confinement' was established to house and punish pregnancy and sexual activity outside the norms of the marital family,[146] including the Magdalene Laundries,[147] the Mother and Baby Homes and their associated industry of illegal adoption, the industrial schools,[148] the reformatories and the psychiatric institutions. This institutional architecture reflected entrenched sexual attitudes that centred on self-denial and self-sacrifice, on 'silencing, hiding and denial of sex and the confinement of talk about sex to the confessional'.[149] In the South, it is known that judges sentenced women to serve terms in the Magdalene Laundries.[150] In her rewriting of *O'Keeffe*,[151] Maeve O'Rourke explicitly counters the historical narrative that Hardiman J constructs in order to undermine state responsibility for child abuse in schools. Hardiman J here exemplifies what Emilie Pine calls a 'social agnosia' about the state's religious past; an inability to recognise what is being seen.[152] O'Rourke, by contrast, faces up to the historical co-constitution of Church and state power in education, and de-exceptionalises child abuse by placing it in the context of the wider institutional oppression of women in Ireland. My judgment in *McGee v AG* also draws attention to the judicial involvement in the institutionalisation of women who became pregnant outside marriage.[153]

Second, many of the feminist judgments point to the subtle harms that women suffer when law and religious patriarchy merge; harms that, in the original judgments, escaped judicial notice. In his feminist judgment in *Flynn v Power*, Eoin Daly writes about the experience of religious disciplinary power in terms of domination, and explores the strategies of self-invigilation and self-censorship expected of Irish women under conditions of religious patriarchy.[154] My feminist judgment in *McGee v AG*[155] similarly identifies harms specific to women in the criminalisation of access to contraception. The original judgment focuses on the largely illusory threat that couples' marriages might be harmed by the prospect of the intrusion of the criminal law. The feminist judgment, by contrast, recounts the everyday humiliation, inconvenience and suffering that the legislation visited on women.

[145] This collection, ch 18.

[146] See further Eoin O'Sullivan and Ian O'Donnell, 'Coercive Confinement in the Republic of Ireland The Waning of a Culture of Control' (2007) 9(1) *Punishment & Society* 27–48.

[147] On the relationship between the state and the Laundries, see Sheila Killian, '"For Lack of Accountability": The Logic of the Price in Ireland's Magdalen Laundries' (2015) 43 *Accounting, Organizations and Society* 17–32. See further: Miriam Haughton, 'From Laundries to Labour Camps: Staging Ireland's "Rule of Silence" in Anu Productions' Laundry' (2014) 57(1) *Modern Drama* 65–93.

[148] See further Kate Kenny, 'Affective Disruption: Walter Benjamin and the "history" of Ireland's Industrial Schools' (2013) 8 *Management & Organizational History* 10.

[149] Inglis above n 111.

[150] Clíona Rattigan, *What Else Could I Do?: Single Mothers and Infanticide, Ireland 1900–1950* (Dublin, Irish Academic Press, 2012) 224.

[151] This collection, ch 16.

[152] Emilie Pine, 'Commemorating Abuse: Gender Politics and Making Space', at http://researchrepository.ucd.ie/handle/10197/6255 (last accessed 9 July 2015); Aine McDonough, 'Lost in Translation: The Legal Appropriation of the Voice of Child Sexual Abuse Victims in Ireland' (PhD, National University of Ireland Maynooth 2010), at http://eprints.maynoothuniversity.ie/2251/ (last accessed 28 June 2015).

[153] This collection, ch 5.

[154] This collection, ch 6.

[155] This collection, ch 5.

Aside from questions of child-rearing and child-bearing, relentless valorisation of married motherhood means that alternative expressions of sexuality may be denigrated or misrecognised. For instance, the refusal to recognise same-sex relationships in law—the subject of the *Zappone* case[156] – speaks to an exclusionary focus on the heteronormative family,[157] and to a determination to associate marriage with particular forms of child-rearing. More generally, the focus on the maternal in law and judgment may bury darker truths about the regulation of sexuality in society. Several of the feminist judgments in this collection upset 'common sense' assumptions about men's entitlement to access women's bodies, both within and outside marriage. In rewriting *BJM v CM*, Aideen Ryan and Katie Dawson reverse the harms recognised by a law of nullity that sees a wife as obliged to present a particular kind of body to her husband. The original judgment legitimates the responses of a man 'destablised' and 'revulsed' by his wife's scars, disappointed not to receive the 'snowy-breasted pearl'[158] that Count John McCormack sang about. Indeed, Flood J himself felt entitled to speculate about the woman's 'aura of sexuality', and noted that she was 'beautifully walked'. The feminist judgment, by contrast, focuses on the financial and social harms to women of an unduly flexible law of nullity in the period immediately surrounding the legalisation of divorce.[159] In addition, where the law's default assumption is that women should behave as essentially passive 'desexualised, quasi-divine mothers',[160] judges may be inhospitable to women whose sexual conduct does not comport with expectations of moral purity.[161] In their feminist judgment in *DPP v C*, for example, Sinéad Ring and Eilionóir Flynn (as Rynn J) address the intersection between 'rape myths' and the idea of 'honest belief' in the context of rape, directly excavating the ways in which it depends on gender hierarchies and patriarchal expectations around women's sexual availability and entitlement to assert sexual agency.[162]

Third, motherhood is often constructed as incompatible with other social and political roles: if women's primary functions lie in the private sphere (the home), opportunities to participate in the public sphere may be foreclosed. In both jurisdictions, men have appropriated the spaces of law-making and nation-making to themselves. In the South, the early years of the new state saw a raft of new legislation designed to remove women from the public sphere.[163] Famously, the 1937 Constitution—which Flann O'Brien wryly

[156] This collection, ch 14.

[157] On homosexuality and Irish identity, see Kathryn Conrad, 'Queer Treasons: Homosexuality and Irish National Identity' (2001) 15(1) *Cultural Studies* 124–37, 127. For a contrasting reading of the relationship between Irishness and queerness, see Joseph Valente, 'Self-Queering Ireland?' (2010) 36(1) *The Canadian Journal of Irish Studies* 25–43. On a history of homosexual law reform in Ireland, see Chrystel Hug, *The Politics of Sexual Morality in Ireland* (London, Springer, 2016) 207–10.

[158] *Snowy Breasted Pearl—John McCormack*, at www.youtube.com/watch?v=rXVwDEPJ7jc (last accessed 23 April 2016).

[159] This collection, ch 25.

[160] Kearney, above n 99, 119.

[161] See further Inglis and MacKeogh, above n 138. Earner-Byrne notes that rape victims were often sent to Magdalene Laundries: Lindsey Earner-Byrne, 'The Rape of Mary M.: A Microhistory of Sexual Violence and Moral Redemption in 1920s Ireland' (2015) 24(1) *Journal of the History of Sexuality* 75–98.

[162] See this collection, ch 26.

[163] See, eg, Civil Service Regulation (Amendment) Act 1926; Local Authorities (Officers and Employees) Act 1926. On the suppression of revolutionary Irish feminism in the new state, see generally Maryann Gialanella Valiulis, 'Power, Gender, and Identity in the Irish Free State' (1995) 7(1) *Journal of Women's History* 117–36. See also Ryan, above n 17.

called 'your ultimate and fundamental statement of your Irish identity and destiny'[164]—exalted the marital family above all positive law, and contemplated that women's proper place was in the home.[165] In the North, ongoing male resistance to women's serving in the legislature[166] meant that female voices remained absent in law. Some of the feminist judgments respond to these problems. In rewriting *McGimpsey*, for instance, Aoife O'Donoghue responds to an original judgment on citizenship and loyalty in which only men people the space of the nation-state. She emphasises that the legal conception of citizenship must be expanded to encompass Northern Irish women's experiences.[167] Similarly, in my own judgment in *McGee v AG*, I was eager to ensure that political arguments from freedom of conscience should be available to women and capable of expression in familial and domestic settings.[168] In contexts of ethno-nationalist conflict, and in subsequent transition,[169] women's concerns may be forgotten altogether, subordinated to the political differences that dominate men's lives.[170] Judges have not been immune from such forgetfulness. Catherine O'Rourke's feminist judgment in *In Re White*[171] points up the judicial assumption that the regulation of controversial parades in Northern Ireland should pay attention to the concerns of 'two communities'—a feat that can be achieved without necessarily including any women. Alternatively, women may be rebuked for performing motherhood in ways that seem to involve their children in conflict;[172] an issue lurking at the margins of the Holy Cross dispute[173] which animates *In re E (a child)*.[174]

Lastly, because it stands for so much more than itself, the power to define motherhood has been kept out of women's hands. It is defined by patriarchal forces along axes of tradition and modernity; belonging and foreignness; stability and anarchy; religiosity and common sense. Thus, when women attempt to make use of motherhood, asserting it as a source of political capital or legal rights, their efforts meet with patriarchal resistance. For example, although the state valorises women's work in home-making in principle, this support is often not matched with secure socio-economic rights.[175] *Mhic Mhathúna*

[164] Flann O'Brien and Kevin O'Nolan, *Further Cuttings: From Cruiskeen Lawn* (Dublin, Dalkey Archive Press, 2000) 137.

[165] Maria Luddy, 'A "Sinister and Retrogressive" Proposal: Irish Women's Opposition to the 1937 Draft Constitution' (2005) 15 *Transactions of the Royal Historical Society* (Sixth Series) 175–95, 188.

[166] Racioppi and O'Sullivan See, above n 113, 96.

[167] This collection, ch 11.

[168] This collection, ch 5.

[169] Kate Fearon and Monica McWilliams, 'Swimming against the Mainstream: The Northern Ireland Women's Coalition' in Carmel Roulston and Celia Davies (eds), *Gender, Democracy and Inclusion in Northern Ireland* (London, Palgrave Macmillan, 2000).

[170] Karyn Stapleton and John Wilson, 'Conflicting Categories? Women, Conflict and Identity in Northern Ireland' (2014) 37(11) *Ethnic and Racial Studies* 2071–91, 2074.

[171] This collection, ch 12.

[172] Of course, women have exploited the family and the home as part of their participation in ethno-nationalist struggles throughout the history of both jurisdictions. Martin J McCleery, *Operation Demetrius and Its Aftermath: A New History of the Use of Internment Without Trial in Northern Ireland, 1971–75* (Oxford, Oxford University Press, 2015) 57. Stapleton and Wilson above n 171, 2075. Carol Coulter, *The Hidden Tradition: Feminism, Women, and Nationalism in Ireland* (Cork, Cork University Press 1993) 10.

[173] Stapleton and Wilson above n 172, 2075.

[174] This collection, ch 15.

[175] On anxieties over maternity in Irish welfare legislation, see Lindsey Earner-Byrne, 'Reinforcing the Family: The Role of Gender, Morality and Sexuality in Irish Welfare Policy, 1922–1944' (2008) 13(4) *The History of the*

v Ireland,[176] *Matrimonial Homes Bill*[177] and *National and Provincial Building Society v Lynd*[178] all consider judicial responses to questions at the intersection of motherhood, family life and socio-economic rights, including the right to housing. In rewriting the immigration case of *Lobe*, Siobhán Mullally and Cliodhna Murphy observe how the original judgment constructs the foreign pregnant woman as an 'opportunistic' mother; they deflate the state argument that migrant child-bearing is an obvious and inherent risk to the state.[179] A number of the feminist judges in this collection—particularly in *McKinley*, *McGee v AG* and the *Matrimonial Homes Bill*[180]—find themselves wrestling with the constitutional protection of the family, a notoriously patriarchal legal concept intended to confine women to the maternal role. All find ways to reorientate 'the family' for feminist purposes, converting it from a private institution that the state, in military language, must defend from attack,[181] into something more concerned with the emergence of gendered relations between men and women. Similarly, in *A, and B (by C)*, Julie McCandless is required to find a feminist approach to one of the oldest patriarchal functions of the family: the preservation, or apparent preservation, of blood relationships.[182] A striking example of radical reinterpretation of a legal concept grounded in the policing of motherhood is Mary Donnelly's repurposing of the concept of standing developed in *SPUC v Coogan*[183] in order to allow legal representation of the interests of the 'unborn child', and counter women's refusal of mandatory motherhood. Donnelly adapts 'standing' so that it can be used to make an incapacitated woman more present in a crucial decision-making process.[184] A legal concept effectively used to undermine women's bodily autonomy in one case is repurposed to better support women's choices in another.

Conclusion: Hesitant Fathers, Rebellious Daughters

The original judgments rewritten in this project clearly disclose traces of judicial engagement with the gendered dimensions of national identity. No more comprehensive research is available on Northern/Irish judicial attitudes to these questions, and so, to a great extent, the task of constructing a feminist judgments project is one of imagination. It is tempting to imagine judges as exercising undisturbed unilateral power as they police the gendered boundaries of Northern/Irish identity. Irish judges have not spoken in detail about these

Family 360–69. See also Lindsey Earner-Byrne, 'Parading Their Poverty: Widows in Twentieth Century Ireland' in Borbála Faragó and Moynagh Sullivan (eds), *Facing the Other: Interdisciplinary Studies on Race, Gender and Social Justice in Ireland* (Cambridge Scholars Publishing, 2008) 87.

[176] This collection, ch 7.
[177] This collection, ch 8.
[178] This collection, ch 9.
[179] This collection, ch 13.
[180] See this collection, chs 5, 8 and 24.
[181] Sophie Cacciaguidi-Fahy, 'Images of the Irish Family' in Anne Wagner and William Pencak (eds), *Images in Law* (London, Ashgate Publishing Ltd, 2006) 237.
[182] This collection, ch 30.
[183] *SPUC v Coogan* [1989] 1 IR 734.
[184] This collection, ch 20.

particular difficulties of judgment, but some literary portrayals provide a place to begin. The excerpt from Edna O'Brien at the beginning of this chapter illustrates this aspect of the judicial imaginary. It presents the Irish judge, Frank, puzzling out a case in terms of confident, playful, Gaelic masculinity. Later in the novel, faced with a difficult abortion case and a recalcitrant religious colleague, he says, 'the law is a labyrinth and clever men learn how to use it'.[185] He believes in the possibility of mastery over the law, even in difficult circumstances. It is a mastery of subject-matter unavailable to him elsewhere; a last refuge of masculine power in a changing world—represented in particular by a young defiant daughter, Molly, who insists he decide in the pregnant girl's favour. When she rages against his refusal to openly empathise with the girl, he speaks to her about conscience, deliberation and 'digesting' the arguments.[186] O'Brien captures something of the terror that law's all-knowing, confident, masculine power holds for the woman about to be judged, in this case a rural girl, walking along the road where she has been raped and made pregnant by her father:

> In the City far away, men of bristling goatee beards, men of serious preoccupied countenances, move through the great halls, corporeal figures of knowledge and gravity, the white of their wigs changing colour as they pass under the rotunda of livid light, ribs of yellow hair, smarting, becoming phosphorescent, powerful men, men with a swagger, a character personified by the spill of the gown or the angle of a coiffed wig, their junior a few paces behind them laden with briefs and ledgers, the whole paraphernalia of the law in motion, some already at the bench, others, walking slowly to the appointed courts, men of principle who know nothing of the road or the road's soggy secret will one day be called to adjudicate upon it, for all is always known, nothing is secret, all is known and scriven upon the tablet of time.[187]

There is, of course, a counter-reading.[188] O'Brien suggests later in her novel that even Frank is less powerful than he wishes himself to be.[189] A more detailed analysis along these lines, with a judge as protagonist, can be found in Colm Tóibín's novel *The Heather Blazing*. Tóibín understands judicial reasoning as something more confused and fragile; not a place of respite and order. The novel charts the judge Eamon Redmond's weary self-examination as he decides a constitutional case about the policing of young women's sexual behaviour, about unmarried motherhood, about transgression of dominant religious norms. Unlike O'Brien's Frank, when he realises that the constitutional text makes no clear provision for this case, Eamon Redmond finds himself unmoored by the realisation that multiple possible readings of the constitutional provisions protecting the family are possible.[190] He becomes deeply uncomfortable with the position of interpreter and mediator,

[185] O'Brien, above n 2, 284.

[186] ibid, 270.

[187] ibid, 6.

[188] Both of these novels spring from the abortion cases of the 1990s. In recent years, judges have begun to reappear as characters in Irish literature, particularly in the context of examinations of religious institutional abuse. On 'tribunal theatre' and the representation of judges as characters in plays based on Irish tribunal proceedings, see Sheila McCormick, 'The Darkest Corner : Documenting Institutional Abuse and Its Consequences at the Abbey Theatre' (2012) 20(2) *Irish Studies Review* 179–91.

[189] It is worth noting that later in the book, the same judge and a colleague are described as 'caricatures of men, arms athwart, groping and gasping for respiration': O'Brien, above n 2, 286.

[190] Cearbhall Ó Dálaigh realised this difficulty, saying, 'We have a Constitution, but nobody knows what it means': Hogan, Barrington and McEntee, above n 11, 106.

participating in an on-going social process at a time of heightened conflict, applying law to 'a world in which opposite values lived so close to each other'.[191] Throughout, the judge meditates on his own family's association with the formation of the new austerely republican state. He dwells on his daughter, Niamh, also an unmarried mother. She insists to him, 'I know what it's like to be a woman in this country'; but he withdraws from confrontation, and simply tells her that she is not a legal expert.[192] Here the judge, as patriarch, insists on making his decision from a 'site of blindness and ignorance'.[193] Judicial authority in this encounter is opposed to women's experience of life in 'this country', even as law is about to shape that shared life. At the same time, the elderly judge is disturbed, unsettled by the indeterminacy of law, and by the young women whose claims to a hearing have touched on his attempts to make sense of it. What Tóibín portrays here is identity in uncertain play with difference. As a judge, Eamon Redmond is saturated by identity discourse, conscious of himself as already constrained by the authority of representation that 'programs and precedes' him.[194] In his re-reading of the Constitution, he seeks some closure from law and finds it lacking. He reaches back for the authority of legal tradition, but it does not dissolve his struggle. He is the embodiment of what, in the title of this collection, we called 'judges' troubles'.[195] In his dilemma about the 'the right of an ethos to prevail over the right of an individual',[196] he is, at times, a model of reflective judging, conscious of his reluctant place in on-going identity struggles.

This collection's feminist engagement with judges' troubles lies somewhere between Frank's creative, strategic confidence in the infinite malleability of law, and Eamon Redmond's struggle to reconcile law with the wider demands of community and identity. Like Redmond, the feminist judgments are acutely conscious of the shortcomings of judicial authority; of the open-endedness of law; of the constraints—however reluctantly borne—of others' expectations of judicial power. What distinguishes them from the judges who people O'Brien's and Tóibín's imaginary, is that they prioritise 'what it's like to be a woman in this country'; that they are attentive to the impact of judicial identity work on women's lives. They are distinguished by an openness to women's knowledge and experience of the demands of 'involuntary patriotism'. They take the daughter's side—the side of Niamh and Molly—rejecting unreflective servitude to the nation's patriarchal law.

[191] Colm Tóibín, *The Heather Blazing: A Novel* (New York, Scribner, 2012) 90. See further, Liam Harte, 'History, Text and Society in Colm Toibin's The Heather Blazing' (2002) 6(4) *New Hibernia Review* 55–67, 61.

[192] Toibin, above n 192, 99.

[193] Hanafin above n 107, 402.

[194] Jacques Derrida, Peter Caws and Mary Ann Caws, 'Sending: On Representation' (1982) 49 *Social Research* 294–326 304.

[195] The title is also a reference to Judith Butler, *Gender Trouble: Feminism and the Subversion of Identity* (London, Routledge, 2011).

[196] Tóibín, above n 191, 90.

3

Doing Feminist Judgments

MARY SHINE THOMPSON[1]

Introduction

The judgments that have been rewritten as part of the Northern/Irish Feminist Judgments Project, and which form the substantive content of this book, range over the period 1973–2015. In 1969, the archetypal Irish Supreme Court judge was 'white, male, upper middle-class, urban, a barrister, with a background in politics'.[2] The same could have been said of his Northern counterparts who, in addition, were exclusively Protestant and Unionist. Forty-six years later, superior court professionals are more heterogeneous in terms of class and gender: the Chief Justice and three of the ordinary members of the Supreme Court are now women, and women comprise a significant number of all legal professionals. Northern Ireland still lags behind other common law jurisdictions in having appointed its first two female High Court judges only in late 2015.[3] Furthermore, as the current Chief Justice of the Irish Supreme Court, Susan Denham, observed, 'What is required of judges is changing.'[4] One aspect of the changing requirement is the necessity to embed experiential, gendered knowledge into juristic practice. The increased number of female judges alone, in the absence of critical reflection, is not likely to effect this significant change, given that the 'liberal orthodoxy underlying modern law stresses the principle of sexual neutrality as the paradigmatic standard for the articulation of legal issues, often even including those traditionally pertaining to sexed bodies and experience'.[5]

This chapter examines how values informing this project can impact positively on the judging process. The first section begins by summarising some key aspects of feminist judgments projects. The second section examines features of feminist subjectivities that

[1] I gratefully acknowledge the invaluable comments of this book's editors, Julie McCandless, Aoife O'Donoghue and especially Máiréad Enright, and of Rosemary Hunter, when writing this chapter.

[2] Paul Charles Bartholomew, *The Irish Judiciary* (Dublin, Institute of Public Administration, 1971).

[3] 'Female judges appointed to NI High Court for first time', *The Irish Times*, 23 October 2015. The *Irish News* reported Baroness Nuala O'Loan's criticism earlier in 2015 that the lack of senior female judges within the Northern Irish judiciary was 'absolutely unacceptable' (24 August 2015). Baroness O'Loan is one of the three female Northern Irish members of the House of Lords, out of a total of 24 members.

[4] Susan Denham, *The 21st Century Judge. The Evolving Role of Judges in the Administration of Courts and the Judiciary, with Special Reference to Ireland*, Oration given to The Australasian Institute of Judicial Administration on 4 November 2010, at www.aija.org.au/Orations/Oration10.pdf (last accessed 6 December 2015).

[5] Kathryn McNeilly, 'The Illusions of Post-feminism, Ghosts of Gender and the Discourses of Law' (2012) 1(2) *feminists@law: an open access journal of feminist legal scholarship* 1–14.

are necessary to feminist judging. These are not presumed to conform to a single feminist model, but they do imply selfhoods that are capable of agency. Another aspect of the implied feminist subjectivity is a willingness to operate within existing legal norms, rather than to dis-identify with them, while judiciously disrupting them. The third section addresses how feminists do feminist judgments. It is centred around the Aristotelian concept of *technē*, the professional technical knowledge and discourse essential to writing judgments, but which present difficulties for feminists torn between their desire to pass as no different from their male counterparts and yet to allow their 'Otherness' to speak. The fourth section suggests how doing that jurisprudence[6] in the course of judgment can draw on experiential knowledge, and highlights the enabling properties of professional practical knowledge.

Feminist Judgments Projects

The feminist legal scholarship that has emerged in the past two decades in Northern/Ireland is one response to the changing environment, and this project is one manifestation of this scholarship. In its approach, the project echoes the wide range of theoretical positions of feminist legal social criticism of its predecessors, the Canadian, English and Australian feminist judgments projects, while speaking in its own unique voices. It has pioneered within the two jurisdictions of this island an innovative mode of re-imagining the given,[7] thereby not only critiquing judgments of the superior courts, but also leading the way in framing alternative decisions imbued with feminist values. This Northern/Irish approach to feminist judgments is structured and reflective: it consists of legal scholars and practitioners, male and female, donning the robes of feminist judges. Its methodology involves delivering judgments that privilege feminist elements heretofore marginalised in normative accounts, and contextualising them politically, socio-culturally and/or historically. It also involves practical reasoning:[8] deploying, for example, 'common knowledge' of female experience so that lived experience[9]—and 'lived law'[10]—is the grounding of argument. It addresses, but does not confine itself to, 'female' topics, such as equal rights, reproduction and children's issues, or domestic and sexual abuse.

To the question 'Who speaks?', this project's answer is that feminism empowers those hitherto voiceless, or who suffer socially constructed prejudices based on pre-existing power structures.[11] It acknowledges the voices of women who were denied consent to sex;[12]

[6] Naveem Thayyil Kamaluddin, 'Feminist jurisprudence and navel gazings: Some reflections' (2008) *UCL Jurisprudence Review* 308–26, 309.

[7] Seamus Heaney, 'whatever is given / can always be reimagined': *Seeing Things* (London, Faber, 1991) 29.

[8] Katharine T Bartlett, 'Feminist Legal Methods' (1990) 103(4) *Harvard Law Review* 829–88.

[9] See Christine Ryan's commentary to *BJM v CM* (this collection, ch 25).

[10] Máiréad Enright, 'Preferring the Stranger? Towards an Irish Approach to Muslim Divorce Practice' (2013) 49(1) *The Irish Jurist* 65–69.

[11] See feminist judgment of *BJM v CM* (this collection, ch 25).

[12] See feminist judgment of *DPP v C* (this collection, ch 26).

adults too ill to represent their case;[13] children;[14] animals;[15] or, less obviously, men from the Northern Unionist community, such as the McGimpsey brothers, who claimed that the Anglo-Irish Agreement violates the Irish Constitution.[16] The project also acknowledges the liberal, autonomous individuals who want to engage private law to achieve their gendered ends.[17] Empowering them implies changing utterances that remain private because they are denied a public forum, into 'a political "common language", one capable of articulating the collective reality and truth of women's lives'.[18]

Characteristics of Feminist Judgments

The emphasis of the project is on the practicalities of the doing of juristic thinking, on the shapemaking, the structuring process that is jurisprudence, and the actual lived experience of jurisprudence, which is knowledge-in-action and which is undertaken by physical, embedded, relational individuals. Feminist judges' revised decisions such as those in this book integrate feminist conceptual and theoretical positions into their various practical methods. The project is premised upon the possibility of specific changes that do not jettison all the continuities of the law: it recognises that legal norms are necessary, not only 'in order to live, and to live well',[19] and to live the good life, but also to apprehend just categories for administering justice. Feminist judges base their decisions on facts governing the original decisions. However, they take into consideration not only the gendered production of those facts, but also the omissions, absences and differences of emphasis in the presentation of the facts that shape a traditional, non-feminist judicial approach. Established legal methodologies and conventions,[20] legal reasoning, constitutional and statutory interpretation, legal classification and the doctrine of *stare decisis* (albeit often applying different precedent sets) are as integral to their approach as to that of any conscientious judge. The judicious adherence to legal norms is reflected in the judgments and commentaries in this book. Legal methodologies restricted, for example, O'Donoghue J, so that she had to depend on international obligations based on formal equality and not on structural inequalities. They prevented McCandless LJ, in her revised appellate decision in *A and B (by C)*,[21] from developing a germane line of argument, because counsel had not introduced

[13] See feminist judgment of *PM, Applicant v The Board of Management of St Vincent's Hospital and Justin Geoghegan and Attorney General, Respondents* (this collection, ch 20).

[14] See feminist judgments of *O'Keeffe v Hickey* (this collection, ch 16); *North Western Health Board v HW and CW* (the PKU case) (this collection, ch 19); *A and B (by C) v A (Health and Social Services Trust)* (this collection, ch 30); and to a lesser extent, *Re E* (the 'Holy Cross' case) (this collection, ch 15).

[15] See feminist judgment of *Barnes v Belfast City Council* (this collection, ch 29).

[16] See feminist judgment of *McGimpsey v Ireland* (this collection, ch 11).

[17] Máiréad Enright attends to feminist aspects of contract law in: 'Dispositional Contracts and Frozen Embryos: Right for Women? (2006) 12(1) *Medico-Legal Journal of Ireland* 31–39. In this collection, see feminist judgments of *National and Provincial Building Society v Lynd* (ch 9); *O'Keeffe v Hickey* (ch 16); and *McKinley v Minister for Defence* (ch 24).

[18] Maria Drakopoulou, 'Revisiting Feminist Jurisprudence: A Rehabilitation' (2013) 3(2) *feminists@law: an open access journal of feminist legal scholarship* 1–29.

[19] Judith Butler, *Bodies That Matter: On the Discursive Limits of Sex* (Abingdon, Routledge, 1993) 232.

[20] Garrett Barden and Tim Murphy perceive conventional law as 'those judgments and choices that in recurrent kinds of circumstances are generally accepted and approved in a particular community': *Law and Justice in Community* (Oxford, Oxford University Press, 2010) 3–4.

[21] This collection, ch 30.

it into the case. Counsel had failed to raise the issue that a clinic supplying donor sperm of a type other than that agreed upon had interfered with the privacy of children conceived with that sperm and with that of their parents.

Feminist judges take full advantage of the rules of fair procedure and constitutional justice. Donnelly J, for example, rewrote *PM's* case,[22] foregrounding an argument on the necessity for legal representation and fair procedures, highlighting how the original hearing had marginalised the applicant, who had been critically ill and absent from the hearing. Fox O'Mahony J adverts specifically to 'fair and proper exercise of the court's discretion' in her rewritten case of the Lynds,[23] defaulting mortgagors who petitioned the Northern Irish High Court to extend time to meet their contractual obligations. Not all feminists are as forthright in condemning the decisions with which they engage as are, for example, the feminist judges in *BJM v CM*,[24] who claim that the 'blatant and vulgar sexism revealed in the original is more than a legal aberration'. Some of the judgments make little—if any—overt reference to feminist legal theory and practice *per se*.[25]

While the project's feminist judges do not advocate judicial activism to resolve complex structural inequalities, they acknowledge the value of, for example, academic activism, and of taking 'judicial notice' of the law and of adjudicative and legislative facts.[26] The project is itself a form of judicial activism.[27] As to taking judicial notice, Rynn J does this overtly in *DPP v C*,[28] where she acknowledges the established literature that shows how victims' responses to rape include dissociation. McCandless LJ[29] recognises feminist critiques of previous conventional awards in cases relating to reproduction, in order to underline the distinction between the award she makes in the case in question and those awards intended to substitute for full damages recoverable 'but for' a policy-based exception.[30] Fox J, confronted with flawed legislation relating to public safety, having assessed the evidence and facts presented in *Barnes v Belfast City Council*,[31] asserted her right to reach conclusions alternative to those reached in the original.

The project's method denaturalises conventionalised categories of gendered authority. It strives to accommodate that flexible, situated knowledge which is inseparable from

[22] A fictional proceeding based on JM, *Applicant v the Board of Management of St Vincent's Hospital and Justin Geoghegan and Attorney General, Respondents*, brought by PM who sought declarations.

[23] This collection, ch 9.

[24] This collection, ch 25.

[25] eg, O'Donoghue J's feminist judgment of *McGimpsey v Ireland* (ch 11).

[26] Colin Tapper, *Cross and Tapper on Evidence* (Oxford, Oxford University Press, 2010) 692: 'Judicial notice may be taken of notorious facts'. Gerard Hogan and Gerry Whyte, *JM Kelly: The Irish Constitution*, 4th edn (Dublin, Tottel, 2003) 2038, paras 7.8.25–26, cite the precedent of *Burke and O'Reilly v Burke and Quail* [1951] IR 216 to support the proposition that 'the Court requires no formal proof of the ordinary obligations of a Catholic'. Irish courts are obliged to take judicial notice under section 4 of the ECHR Act 2003 of any ECtHR declaration, decision, advisory opinion or judgment. In *O'Donnell v Dublin County Council* [2007] IEHC 204, the Supreme Court held that this provision requires courts 'subject to the Constitution, to take "due account" of *clear and consistent* principles laid down in Strasbourg jurisprudence'.

[27] Máiréad Enright, 'Meeting Mrs McGee: Reflecting on Feminist Judgment as Critical Legal Practice', plenary lecture given at the Sibéal Conference, 21–22 November 2014, at www.feministjudging.ie/?p=1002 (last accessed 10 October 2015).

[28] This collection, ch 26.

[29] This collection, ch 30.

[30] McCandless LJ cites Nicolette Priaulx, 'Damages for the "unwanted" child: time for a rethink?' (2005) 73(4) *Medico-Legal Journal* 152–63.

[31] This collection, ch 29.

women's personal experience, knowledge that might be termed 'unruly'.[32] It is the kind of knowledge that can seem anathema to legal textbooks; that is 'marginal', 'subjugated', 'naive' and 'located low down' in most official hierarchies of ideas.[33] In so doing, it exposes their hidden normative logic and their claim to ethical superiority: this is exemplified in, for example, the rewritten case of *CC v Ireland*.[34] The original judgment held that a strict liability offence under section 1(1) of the Criminal Law (Amendment) Act 1935, criminalising a man who had sexual intercourse with a girl under the age of 15, was unconstitutional.[35] Cian Ó Concubhair's commentary on Prendergast J's feminist judgment challenges 'the unsophisticated, 'common-sense' (read 'reasonable', middle-aged, white, male judge) reasoning in Hardiman J's account of responsibility in sexual power dynamics'.[36] Ó Concubhair goes on to point to the limitations in criminal law in confronting deep-seated, patriarchal notions of sexuality and in bringing closure to survivors of sexual crimes. He raises doubts about the efficacy of strict liability in changing attitudes to abuse. One effect of feminist judgments and commentaries is that they identify ways of impeding the forcible citation of the original judgment and, in the process, of interrogating received gendered legal subjectivity as necessarily self-serving, adversarial and individualised.[37] The feminist judgments also recognise how the courts tend to elevate expert knowledge over experiential, less theorisable, concrete and contextualised being-in-the-world.[38] In the original case of *Foy*,[39] for example, McKechnie J relied on a test based on biological indicators because 'transsexualism ... cannot, at least as of now, found its existence in neuro science'.[40] Ní Mhuirthile J, in her feminist rewrite, exposes this.

The revised judgments reflect the incorrigible plurality[41] of women's experience, and the manner in which class, age, ethnicity and sexuality[42] interact with personal experiences.

[32] Marilyn J Boxer, 'Unruly Knowledge: Women's Studies and the Problem of Disciplinarity' (2000) 12(2) *National Women's Studies Association Journal* 119–29.

[33] Michel Foucault, 'Two Lectures' in *Power/Knowledge: Selected Interviews and Other Writings* (London, Harvester Press, 1980) 82–85, 82.

[34] This collection, ch 27.

[35] Prendergast J (this collection, ch 27) exposes the limitations of the 'common-sense' Hardiman J's decision in the original case, with which his fellow judges of the Supreme Court agreed.

[36] Ó Concubhair also cites Anne Cossins, *Masculinities, Sexualities and Child Sexual Abuse* (The Hague, Kluwer Law International, 2000); and Frances Olsen, 'Statutory Rape: A Feminist Critique of Rights Analysis' (1984) 63(3) *Texas Law Review* 387–432.

[37] Rosemary Hunter, 'Feminist judgments as teaching resources' (2012) 2(5) *Oñati Socio-legal Series* 47–62, 50. Hunter cites Jennifer Nedelsky, 'Reconceiving Autonomy' (1989) 1(7) *Yale Journal of Law and Feminism* 7–36; Jennifer Nedelsky, 'Law, boundaries and the bounded self' (1990) 30(1) *Representations* 162–89; Martha Fineman, 'The Autonomy Myth: a Theory of Dependency' (New York, New Press, 2004). On contract law and women, see Enright, above n 17.

[38] Hunter, above n 37, cites Michel Foucault, *The Order of Things: An Archaeology of the Human Sciences.* (London, Tavistock, 1970); Michel Foucault, *Security, Territory, Population: Lectures at the Collège de France* (Basingstoke, Palgrave Macmillan, 2007); Peter Miller and Nikolas Rose (eds), *The Power of Psychiatry* (Cambridge, Polity Press, 1986); Carol Smart, *Feminism and the Power of Law* (London, Routledge, 1989); Katherine O'Donovan, 'Law's knowledge: the judge, the expert, the battered woman and her syndrome' (1993) 20(4) *Journal of Law and Society* 427–37; Nikolas Rose, *Politics of Life Itself: Biomedicine, Power, and Subjectivity in the Twenty-First Century* (Princeton, NJ, Princeton University Press, 2006).

[39] Lydia Foy v An t-Ard Chláraitheoir, Ireland and the Attorney-General [2007] IEHC 470, [2012] 2 IR 1.

[40] ibid, para 121.

[41] Louis MacNeice, 'Snow', *Collected Poems* (London, Faber & Faber, 1979).

[42] Hunter, above n 37, cites Kimberlé Crenshaw, 'Demarginalizing the intersection of race and sex: a black feminist critique of antidiscrimination doctrine, feminist theory and antiracist politics' (1989) 140 *University of Chicago Legal Forum* 139–67; Kimberlé Crenshaw, 'Mapping the Margins: Intersectionality, Identity Politics, and Violence

The judgments refuse to define law exclusively in oppositional terms: as, for example, merely a conflict between the ethic of care and a 'hierarchy of rights',[43] as the judgment of and discussion about the case of *O'Keeffe*[44] highlights; or as conflict only between agency and victimhood,[45] which McNeilly LJ discusses in *FPANI v Minister for Health*;[46] as simply the clash between the 'two communities' of Northern Ireland, a central concern in *McGimpsey*;[47] or as a battle of conflicting rights,[48] constitutional and otherwise, as addressed in *Flynn v Power*,[49] *O'Keeffe*[50] and *Mhic Mhathúna*.[51]

Identity and Feminisms

Inevitably, the diverse ideological positions that feminist judges adopt in relation to personal identity affect how they arrive at their decisions. This chapter proposes two premises of a feminist jurisprudence, both embedded in practice: first, that jurisprudents' concepts of gendered selfhood imply subjects who are capable of agency, that is, of effecting positive change. Agency, or the capacity for some level of self-determination, is necessary to feminist resistance to legal norms, whether that resistance is predicated upon the Foucauldian postmodern concept of identity constituted in and through culture (a concept reconfigured by Judith Butler), or whether it derives from the liberal notion of autonomous subjectivity.

against Women of Color' (1991) 43(6) *Stanford Law Review* 1241–99; Emily Grabham, Davina Cooper, Jane Krishnadas, Didi Herman (eds), *Intersectionality and Beyond: Law, Power and the Politics of Location* (Abingdon, Routledge, 2008); Helma Lutz, Maria-Teresa Herrera Vivar and Linda Supik (eds), *Framing Intersectionality: Debates on a Multi-Faceted Concept in Gender Studies* (Farnham, Ashgate, 2011).

[43] Rosemary Hunter, above n 37, cites Carol Gilligan, *In a Different Voice: Psychological Theory and Women's Development* (Cambridge, MA, Harvard University Press, 1982); Joan C Tronto, *Moral Boundaries: a Political Argument for an Ethic of Care* (New York, Routledge, 1993); Robin West, *Caring for Justice* (New York: New York University Press, 1997); Selma Sevenhuijsen, *Citizenship and the Ethics of Care: Feminist Considerations on Justice, Morality and Politics* (London, Routledge, 1998); Virginia Held, *The Ethics of Care: Personal, Political and Global* (New York, Oxford University Press, 2005).

[44] This collection, ch 16. O'Rourke J's feminist judgment invokes the ethics of care in noting the enormous pressure the state's aggressive stance imposed on Louise O'Keefe, the plaintiff.

[45] Hunter, above n 37, cites Ann C Scales, 'The Emergence of Feminist Jurisprudence: An Essay' (1986) 95 *Yale Law Journal* 1373–1403; Rosemary Hunter, 'Consent in violent relationships' in Rosemary Hunter and Sharon Cowan (eds), *Choice and Consent: Feminist Engagements with Law and Subjectivity* (Abingdon, Routledge, 1992) ch 9; Martha Fineman, 'The Vulnerable Subject: Anchoring Equality in the Human Condition' (2008) 20(1) *Yale Journal of Law and Feminism* 1–23.

[46] This collection, ch 21.

[47] This collection, ch 11. See also Hunter, above n 37, who cites Francis Olsen, 'The Myth of State Intervention in the Family' (1984) 18 *University of Michigan Journal of Law Reform* 835–64; Katherine O'Donovan, *Sexual Divisions in Law* (London, Weidenfeld & Nicolson, 1985); Susan Moller Okin, *Justice, Gender and the Family* (New York, Basic Books, 1989); Martha Fineman and Roxanne Mykitiuk (eds), *The Public Nature of Private Violence: The Discovery of Domestic Abuse* (New York, Routledge, 1994); Margaret Thornton (ed), *Public and Private: Feminist Legal Debates* (Melbourne, Oxford University Press, 1995); Susan Boyd, *Challenging the Public/Private Divide: Feminism, Law and Public Policy* (Toronto, University of Toronto Press, 1997).

[48] Hunter, above n 37, cites Elizabeth Kingdom, *What's Wrong with Rights? Problems for Feminist Politics of Law* (Edinburgh, Edinburgh University Press, 1992); Aileen McColgan, *Women under the Law: The False Promise of Human Rights* (Harlow, Longman, 2000).

[49] This collection, ch 6.

[50] This collection, ch 16.

[51] This collection, ch 7.

The second premise is that feminist judges, wherever positioned on the feminist spectrum and however their ideologies may collide, might pragmatically set aside differences. Taking their lead from Ann Scales,[52] collaboration across schools of thought is possible, in order to promote broader feminist legal values.

Multiple Feminisms[53]

The 'we' of feminism is a contested category: there is no unitary 'we'. If a sisterhood exists, it is no coven of clones. Consensus among and even within its causes is neither desirable nor possible. This project is alive to the fact that categories of feminisms and feminist ideologies are manifold and contradictory: that they range from Marxist, radical, liberal and cultural, but also across anti-binarist, essentialist, dominance-theorist feminists, LGBTQI supporters and late capitalist feminists; they in turn form complex alliances with postcolonial, queer, literary, race, ethnicity and ecology theorists. The woman for whom sex work is 'a fair pay-back for years of capitalist patriarchy ... an aspect of my feminism'[54] (an example perhaps of Naomi Wolf's re-sexualised 'power feminism')[55] is likely to have limited common ground with, for example, the generic 'woman' who, in Catharine MacKinnon's view, is silenced by 'man's' foot on her throat.[56] Notwithstanding even intractable inter-feminist differences, feminist discourses and jurisprudence survive—and even thrive. Thayil Kamaluddin believes that this is in part because they 'avoided the trap of a conversation of exclusion',[57] a conversation that could have led to the exclusion of fellow feminists.

Feminist judgments projects exemplify how a wide range of feminist positions can find ways of working together so as to interrogate the law's substance and structure. They are likely to share a paradigmatic empathy[58]—a consciousness of and an affinity with multiple feminist positions, and an acknowledgement of the value of female experience—that facilites inquiry, agency and reflection. This empathetic stance involves recognising that knowledge is experiential and both contextualised and context-specific. It also implies recognising not only the value of gendered empathy, but also its limitations, which can

[52] Above, n 45.

[53] See Rosemary Hunter, 'The Power of Feminist Judgments?' (2012) 20(2) *Feminist Legal Studies* 135–48, which discusses productive disagreements between feminists in the context of the English project.

[54] Carol Hunt, 'Sex Worker Kate McGrew of new RTE Reality Show "Connected" Talks Feminism in her Field', *Irish Independent*, 21 September 2014.

[55] Naomi Wolf, *Fire with Fire: The New Female Power and How it Will Change the 21st Century* (New York, Random House, 1993); Rebecca Hains, 'Power Feminism, Mediated: Girl Power and the Commercial Politics of Change' (2009) 31(2) *Women's Studies in Communication* 89–113.

[56] Maia Ettinger captured something of the drama of one heated exchange between Carol Gilligan, Catharine MacKinnon, Mary Dunlap and others in 'Color me Queer: an Aesthetic Challenge to Feminist Essentialism' (1993) 8(1) *Berkeley Women's Law Journal* 106–21.

[57] Kamaluddin, above n 6, 319.

[58] Kathleen Ryan and Tara Graban, 'Theorizing Feminist Pragmatic Rhetoric as a Communicative Art for the Composition Practicum' (2009) 61(1) *Critical Contemporary Culture* 277–99, 281. The Canadian Judicial Appointments Advisory Committee, an independent body, which recommends candidates to the Attorney General for judicial appointments, cites 'empathy' among its list of criteria for appointment. Judicial Appointments Advisory Committee, *Policies and Processes* (Toronto, August 2002), at www.ontariocourts.on.ca/judicial_appointments/policies.htm (last accessed 2 December 2015). Ulrike Schultz and Gisela Shaw (eds), *Gender and Judging* (Oxford, Hart Publishing, 2013) 94, also identify empathy as a feature of an ideal judge, who would also be keen to introduce feminist insights into judicial decision-making processes.

be as problematic as its absence: in *BJM v CM*,[59] a High Court judge empathised with a petitioner-husband and declared his 17-year marriage, within which six children were born, void for want of consent and voidable for lack of capacity, leaving the former wife without legal status and no state supports or reliefs. His judgment is a textbook example of how the law can objectify, depersonalise and stereotype a woman. In contrast, the judgment of McKechnie J in *Foy's* cases[60] is notable for its sensitivity towards transgender persons, in particular towards the plaintiff and towards his wife and daughters, notwithstanding McKechnie J's reliance on a biological test for legally recognising gender.

What may be inferred from existing scholarship, including this project, is that the effect and effectiveness of resistance to jurisprudential norms depend largely on the intellectual instruments (including modalities and methodologies) that feminist resistors deploy. Two centrally influential modes of framing feminist subjecthood may appear to be binaries: one is epitomised by the dictum that 'the personal is political'.[61] The other evolves from Michel Foucault's concept that power generates resistance, and that selfhood is merely an *effect* of subjection to discipline and of the normalising thrust of institutions, a concept that Judith Butler developed in discussions on gendered subjectivity. However, even this Butler-Foucauldian approach allows the gendered subject a capacity for self-determination and effective resistance.

Agency versus Determinism

Legal practice is conducted within networks of discourses that articulate that doing. The early Foucault bleakly claimed that the subject was merely the effect of 'power relations which are exerted over me and which I exert over others'.[62] Butler echoed this postmodernist, post-Nietzschean[63] stance when she claimed that 'the doer' is merely a fiction imposed on 'the doing', and that 'the gendered body … has no ontological status apart from the various acts which constitute its reality'.[64]

Both changed their positions, Foucault even going so far as to concede the existence of a 'soul' as something more than 'an illusion, or an ideological effect'.[65] '[T]here is always the

[59] *BJM v CM* [1996] 2 IR 574.

[60] Foy v An t-Ard Chláraitheoir, Ireland and the Attorney-General [2002] IEHC 116; Foy v An t-Ard Chláraitheoir, Ireland and the Attorney-General [2007] IEHC 470, [2012] 2 IR 1.

[61] Carol Hanisch, 'The Personal is Political' in Shulamith Firestone and Anne Koedt (eds), *Notes from the Second Year: Women's Liberation* (New York, New York Radical Feminists, 1970). Hanisch says the phrase had currency in feminist circles before she used it. Kerry Burch discusses the term in *Democratic Transformations: Eight Conflicts in the Negotiation of American Identity* (London, New York, Continuum, 2012) 137–59.

[62] Michel Foucault, Politics Philosophy Culture Interviews and Other Writings 1977–1984 (New York, Routledge, 1990) 39.

[63] Friedrich Nietzsche, *On the Genealogy of Morals (Zur Genealogie der Moral)* (Original 1887; trans Daniel Smith, Oxford, Oxford University Press, 1996) 29.

[64] Judith Butler, *Gender Trouble: Feminism and the Subversion of Identity* (New York, Routledge, 1999) 136: 'The mobilization of identity categories for the purposes of politicization always remain threatened by the prospect of identity becoming an instrument of the power one opposes. That is no reason not to use, and be used, by identity. There is no political position purified of power, and perhaps that impurity is what produces agency as the potential interruption and reversal of regulatory regimes.'

[65] Michel Foucault, *Discipline and Punish* (London, Allen Lane, 1975) 29: 'It would be wrong to say that the soul is an illusion, or an ideological effect. On the contrary, it exists, it has a reality, it is produced permanently around, on, within the body by the functioning of a power.'

possibility of changing', he later wrote; 'resistance comes first ... power relations are obliged to change with the resistance'.[66] Butler, too, modified her stance.[67] Her revised understanding of the performativity of gender includes an essence presumed external to the self, which is repeated, ritualised and thereby naturalised—but also, therefore, capable of being recast, or altered through alternative repetitions and rituals. In this way, she, like Foucault, escapes the net of determinism: 'to claim that the subject is *constituted* is not to claim that it is *determined*'.[68] Rather, she argues,

> our possibilities for action and thought are both constrained and enabled by the discursive frameworks which structure these possibilities, but this is not equivalent to saying that it is the framework itself which determines our choices or how we respond to the range of options that become available within it.[69]

There is agreement, therefore, between Butler and Foucault that the latter's concept of power, while it restricts and limits, does not deny the individual or group the capacity for engendering change. This Foucauldian thinking—which acknowledges the danger implicit in deconstruction of 'effacing political action',[70] and which refuses to take refuge in utopianism—is invaluable in that it facilitates a focus on activity associated with shaping subjectivity. Foucault's self, however constructed, is not without values, whether these are viewed as effects of a truth regime, or as deeply felt. A Foucauldian approach is also helpful because it acknowledges that the complex functioning of power can both fetter and engage; it can ground resistance as well as compliance, in that power is channelled through networks and capillaries—such as feminist judgment projects—that individualise that power and facilitate resistance to it.

Feminist De-normatising or Dis-identification

The woman intelligible as a judge is, at one level, the effect of the roles that she performs[71] within a rigid, regulated power economy that limits available roles and which has naturalised modes of doing over centuries. The judge embodies and performs a stylised, corporeal, linguistic and citational series of acts, repeated within rigidly defined linguistic and epistemological boundaries. Social regulation—of the sort essential to the highly formalised practice of the law—presents a challenge to feminists: how to minimise, or whether to remove entirely, the impact of its normative processes when they fail to acknowledge

[66] Michel Foucault, 'Sex, Power and the Politics of Identity' in Paul Rabinow (ed), *Ethics: Subjectivity and Truth* (trans Robert Hurley) (New York: New York Press, 1997) 167.

[67] Butler, above n 64, xxiv. She wrote that 'this "I" that you read' is *not* 'determined by the language that makes this "I" possible'.

[68] Seyla Benhabib, Judith Butler, Drucilla Cornell and Nancy Fraser, *Feminist Contentions: A Philosophical Exchange* (New York, Routledge, 1995) 46.

[69] Aurelia Armstrong, 'Beyond Resistance: a response to Zizek's critique of Foucault's subject of freedom' (2008) 5 *Parrhesia* 19–31, 25.

[70] Nicola Lacey, 'Violence, Ethics and Law: Feminist Reflections in a Familiar Dilemma' in Susan James and Stephanie Palmer (eds), *Visible Women: Essays on Feminist Legal Theory and Political Philosophy* (Oxford, Hart Publishing, 2002) 123.

[71] Michel Foucault, *The History of Sexuality: Vol 1* (trans Robert Hurley) (London, A Lane, 1979) 94: 'relations of power are not in superstructural positions, with merely a role of prohibition or accompaniment; they have a directly productive role, wherever they come into effect'.

female experience and understanding. Nicola Lacey articulates the problem as follows: 'Should feminism aspire to replace or reconstruct the framework of modern legal thought, or should it resist the desire for foundations in favour of a more resolutely critical stance?'[72] Since not all feminist lawyers want to reject legal conventions and paradigms entirely (and contributors to feminist judgments projects are unequivocally in this camp), not all will agree with Butler that what is needed is '*disidentification* with those regulatory norms by which sexual difference is materialized'.[73] Feminist jurisprudents plot their courses between these poles of modification and disidentification; this project seeks to transfigure, but not dismantle, judicial apparatus.

In their daily practice, judges and other legal practitioners tacitly consent to reiterate traditionally defined roles that differentiate participation along hierarchical lines, not least because those roles—which evolved within a patriarchal dispensation—are elevated to normative practices and are scrupulously policed by the legal professions and the processes of legal education and acculturation.[74] Judges, male and female, the latter as always latecomers to the profession, are expected to reference established norms, codes and texts that draw their power from repetition and citationality, which attribute continuity, authority and disciplinary status to jurisprudents. They perform 'an act that has been going on before one arrived on the scene'.[75] This requires that judges adopt readymade, artificial roles, and incorporate—that is, give physical form to—constructed and naturalised reality, with its complex discourse and highly formalised gestures. In effect, they work within given texts, producing and reproducing them.

In that doing, the self of the judge takes form. One fiction that has currency is that gender is a category irrelevant to practitioners of law, that it is a signifier beyond and barred from the rational, rule-bound and depersonalised domain of legal practice: the ideal to be achieved in this case is that of a 'disembodied neutral judicial officer who is neither male nor female'.[76] This perception is predicated upon the belief that the law is objective, coherent, socially apolitical, despite being, in Máiréad Enright's words, 'littered with the remainders of past cultural practices'.[77] So-called 'neutral' doctrines, including the selectivity of legal doctrine in addressing harm,[78] the normalising effects of law on socio-political movements,[79] the silencing of certain voices and narratives in court-based dialogue, [and]

[72] Nicola Lacey, *Unspeakable Subjects: Feminist Essays in Legal and Social Theory* (Oxford, Hart Publishing, 1998) 167.

[73] Butler, above n 19, 4 (emphasis added).

[74] Alison Blunt and Gillian Rose (eds), *Writing Women and Space: Colonial and Postcolonial Geographies* (New York, Guildford Press, 1994); Peter Goodrich, *Legal Discourse: Studies in Linguistics, Rhetoric, and Legal Analysis* (Basingstoke, Macmillan, 1987).

[75] Judith Butler, 'Performative Acts and Gender Construction: An Essay in Phenomenology and Feminist Theory' in Sue Ellen Case (ed), *Performing Feminisms: Feminist Critical Theory and Theater* (Baltimore, MD, Johns Hopkins University Press, 1990) 270–82, 272.

[76] Kathy Mack and Sharyn Roach Anleu, 'Skills for judicial work: Comparing women judges and women magistrates' in Schultz and Shaw, above n 58, ch 2.5, 227–28.

[77] Enright, above n 10.

[78] For instance, the divergence of opinion in the decisions of Geoghegan J and Hardiman J in *O'Keeffe v Ireland* (2014) 59 EHRR 15, regarding the state's vicarious liability for putting Louise O'Keeffe at risk, as discussed by Laura Hilly in her commentary on the feminist judgment in this book (ch 16).

[79] Margaret Davies, 'Feminism and the Flat Law Theory' (2008) 16(3) *Feminist Legal Studies* 281–304. John Kennedy creates a counter-argument in his commentary on McCann J's feminist revision of *Society for the Protection of Unborn Children's Application for Judicial Review* [2009] NIQB 92.

the gendered nature of legal culture,[80] can all be forms of exclusion. In the Northern Irish context, Kathryn McNeilly has shown that in relation to 'gender neutrality in policy, the legislative presentation of sexual crimes, and the adjudication of gendered issues by judges', gender is presented as 'absent'.[81]

Pragmatic Feminism

What conditions counter the fiction of gender neutrality, and instead nurture modalities of feminist jurisprudence? Fundamental among them is a loosely communitarian attitude that does not baulk at an absence of consensus among feminist judges, or at the divergent forms of their practice: in other words, a pragmatic coalition. This project demands a determination to imagine an alternative judicial community,[82] to collaborate with its members to identify shared criteria for distinguishing rational and desirable feminist jurisprudence. To advocate this pragmatism is not to abjure theory,[83] moral norms or ethics. It is not to endorse either the exclusion of,[84] or the exclusive focus on, methodology; or to prescribe a specific role to men[85] (indeed, men have contributed to this project as feminist judges). It is not either a sceptical 'series of denials rather than affirmations'[86] or a 'helpfully destructive' 'anti-philosophy',[87] nor a fundamental distrust of the capacity of language to represent meaning.

Rather, it might take the form of pragmatic action that Scales envisaged: an action not devoid of values, nor endowed with unrealisable idealism or vacuous cynicism. Scales's pragmatism was integral to her method. She grounded her practical feminism in women's experiential continua as women, rather than in an 'essentialist enterprise'.[88] She conceded

He credits her with normalising abortion by drawing attention to the fact that abortions are performed in Northern Ireland, thereby contradicting the narrative of illegal abortion propounded by SPUC (this collection, ch 22).

[80] Davies, above n 79, fn 4: 'For instance, the use of the partial defence of doctrine of provocation against women, and the unwillingness of judges to apply it to gendered violence except where the masculinity of a killer was under threat by a "homosexual advance"'. Or the lack of recognition of gender-specific harms in areas of international law: Judith Gardam and Michelle Jarvis, *Women, Armed Conflict and International Law* (The Hague, Kluwer Law International, 2001); Hilary Charlesworth and Christine Chinkin, *The Boundaries of International Law: A Feminist Analysis* (Manchester, Manchester University Press, 2000).

[81] McNeilly, above n 5.

[82] See Benedict Anderson's concept of the imagined community in *Imagined Communities* (London, Verso, 1983); and Davina Cooper, *Everyday Utopias: The Conceptual Life of Promising Spaces* (Durham, NC, Duke University Press, 2014).

[83] Margaret Radin, 'The Pragmatist and The Feminist' (1990) 63 *Southern California Law Review* 1699–1726, 1699–1700.

[84] I am indebted to Thayil Kamaluddin, above n 6, at 319, for the summaries in the remainder of this paragraph; and for the five footnotes that follow. Richard Posner, *The Problems of Jurisprudence* (Cambridge, MA, Harvard University Press, 1990) at 19, provocatively advocates a 'helpfully destructive' 'anti-philosophy'.

[85] Christine Littleton, 'Reconstructing Sexual Equality' (1987) 75 *California Law Review* 1279–1337, 1294. Littleton's pragmatism envisages men playing 'an important role in disseminating and implementing feminist ideas'.

[86] Tibor Machan, 'Posner's Rortyite (Pragmatic) Jurisprudence' (1995) 40(1) *American Journal of Jurisprudence* 361–75, 364.

[87] Posner, above n 84, at 19.

[88] Ann Scales, 'Disappearing Medusa: The Fate of Feminist Legal Theory' (1997) 20(1) *Harvard Women's Law Journal* 34–46, 38–39, 8, cited in Lynne Henderson, 'Flexible Feminism and Reproductive Justice: An Essay in Honor of Ann Scales' (2014) *Scholarly Works* Paper 892, 141–69, 145.

the need for 'modesty in matters of knowledge', since '"[k]nowledge" is always open to revision'.[89] Her method included presenting sceptical judges with 'a dejargonized account of why legal theory, and feminist legal theory in particular, should matter to them',[90] expressed in terms intended to disarm them. For her, the law was always provisional: 'Find the best answers for now', she exhorted her readers.[91] Scales actively sought harmonious relationships and worked to inspire the 'solidarity that made transitions from stuckness to not-so-stuckness possible'.[92] She sought to rephrase contentious issues in terms that defused at least some tensions, most notably when she forged an unlikely alliance with queer theorists in her exploration of abortion.[93] The feminist judgments projects exemplify this kind of linking hands across the ideological barricades, enabling jurisprudents to focus on their utterances.

Technical Knowledge and Feminist Judging

In order to explore some of the constraints operating within current judicial practice, and to suggest a framework for a way forward, this chapter draws on the work of Maria Drakopoulou and Martha Nussbaum relating to the Aristotelian frameworks of *technē*, knowledge associated with skills, and *phronēsis*, that is, practical wisdom. The discussion of *technē* shows how the pervasiveness of inherited, legal techniques that are inescapably gendered affects female legal practitioners. However, the thrust of the argument is that feminist judges can integrate technical knowledge into the exercise of feminist practical wisdom.

Drakopoulou's feminist mode of engagement, rather than acting in the name of the law, squares up to it, pitting her thinking against it. She modifies the established feminist concepts of positionality. For her it is a signifier of the identity of the legal scholar orientated towards a particular corpus of knowledge. It also denotes the scholar's self-reflexivity as to her mode of engagement with that knowledge: 'it is through reflexivity that an awareness and assessment of the power relationships present in the encounter of feminist jurisprudence with law, and consequently, of the political nature of this encounter, can be achieved'.[94]

Technē

The law not only assumes the authority of the truth, but also performs its own truth. It constitutes, in Foucault's term, a regime of truth that can absorb and neutralise difference. But that general concept 'is only as good as its role in the correct articulation of the

[89] Ann Scales, *Legal Feminism: Activism, Lawyering, and Legal Theory* (New York, New York University Press, 2006) 87, cited in Kathryn Abrams, 'The Outsider Within: The Radical, Not-So-Scary Feminist Jurisprudence of Ann Scales' (2013) 91(1) *Denver University Law Review* 23–40, 32.

[90] Scales, above n 89, 4.

[91] ibid, 111–12.

[92] Abrams, above n 89, 35.

[93] ibid, 36–37.

[94] Drakopoulou, above n 18, 11.

concrete'.[95] Where the concrete reality remains absent or overlooked in the actual exercise of the law, radical revision is required. Where the rationality underpinning 'the general' is predicated upon a complex set of pre-specified legal objectives, approved forms of evaluation, clear criteria and desired outcomes, there is little scope for experiences that cannot be articulated in those terms.

Specialised, technical knowledge, with its pre-defined objectives, is indispensable to any profession or trade, and is characterised by varying degrees of complexity and differentiated discourses. The more complex it is, the more likely it is to be open to controversy. Legal professional knowledge, an essential and complex intellectual tool of a craftsperson, operates within a confined circuit. It tends not to precipitate socio-political change but rather to react to it, sometimes after a considerable lapse, often only when firmly nudged to do so. The cases of *O'Keeffe*[96] and *Foy*[97] are examples of Irish jurisprudence changing in response to ECHR decisions. Accreted within a long-established tradition, the law as discourse privileges *technē*'s schematic knowledge, in which action can be resolved in analysis, disembedded from its contexts and reframed in its discourse. It has found expression in some practices and procedures that have become calcified, and that claim to adhere to objectivity, but are tainted by what Scales has called 'unexamined certainty'.[98] The law measures its achievements in predictable forms: for example, in results that reflect precedent. In these respects and others to which I allude, its thrust is primarily androcentric.

Aristotle associates *technē* with 'the trained ability of making something under the guidance of rational thought'.[99] Plato concedes that virtue and vice are not the province but rather the object of *technē*.[100] *Technē* is the type of skill that a bricklayer, or a poet—or a judge—acquires with time and effort, which enables the bricklayer to build a straight line of wall, or a poet to create a syncopated line of verse.[101] It is the kind of skill that a criminal might deploy to cover up his tracks: it is not concerned with the good life, or values. It has its own brand of excellence: that of a knower who generates a thing, and who desires that this product take a particular form; for example, the form of a legal product such as a judgment or a statute. A judge's *technē* might be two-fold: an ability to reason along particular

[95] Martha Nussbaum, 'The Discernment of Perception: An Aristotelian Conception of Private and Public Rationality' in *Love's Knowledge: Essays on philosophy and Literature* (Oxford, Oxford University Press, 1991) ch 2.

[96] The state's vicarious liability for the torts committed by Louise O'Keeffe's teacher in the course of his employment and the school manager's failure to report allegations of abuse was not conceded until the Grand Chamber of the European Court of Human Rights (ECtHR) held in favour of O'Keeffe in *O'Keeffe v Ireland* (2014) 59 EHRR 15. See Laura Hilly's commentary on the feminist judgment in this book (ch 16).

[97] The European Convention on Human Rights (ECHR) has had considerable impact on Irish law since the original *Foy* case came before McKechnie J. In *Goodwin v UK* (2002) 35 EHRR 18; *I v UK* (2003) 36 EHRR 53, the ECtHR had held that the UK's failure to recognise a transgender woman was a breach of her rights under Art 8 of the ECHR. Furthermore, the ECHR Act of 2003 had become part of Irish law. In 2007, McKechnie J could only 'apply legal principles which exist at the time of the dispute' (*Foy v An t-Ard Chlárаitheoir, Ireland and the Attorney-General* [2007] IEHC 470, [2012] 2 IR 1, para 38). However, in the second set of proceedings (beginning at para 45), McKechnie J granted Dr Foy the declaration of incompatibility that she had sought under the ECHR Act (para 110). See Ivana Bacik's commentary in this book (ch 28).

[98] Scales, above n 88, 34.

[99] Aristotle, *Nicomachean Ethics* (Loeb Classical Library, Cambridge, MA, Harvard University Press, 1994) 1140a9–10; cited in Drakopoulou, above n 18, 16.

[100] Susan Levin, 'Women's Nature and Role in the Ideal Polis: Republic V Revisited' in Julie Ward (ed), *Feminism and Ancient Philosophy* (New York, Routledge, 1996) ch 2, 18. Plato devotes considerable attention to *technē* in the Gorgias. Available at www.gutenberg.org/files/1672/1672-h/1672-h.htm (last accessed 10 June 2015).

[101] Plato would question this; he claimed poets know no *technē: The Republic*, 5 98d–e.

lines, and an ability to obey the rules and protocols of the practice of the law,[102] the former requiring a capacity for deliberation, the latter adhering to clearly formulated, binding regulation. Once the product is complete, however—once a judge hands down a decision or a statute becomes law—the judgment or statute becomes an object in its own right, no longer connected to the *technēte* (the judge or the drafter). The knowledge implied by *technē* contrasts sharply with Aristotle's other category, *phronēsis*, discussed below, which implies the virtue of practical thinking.

Karl Llewellyn identifies *technē* as 'a significant body of working knowhow'.[103] Some of its limitations are implied in that reductive term 'knowhow', and in the way Aristotle separates it from rational thought, seeing it as 'the *trained* ability of making something' under the guidance of rational thought. The demeanour of detachment that it adopts and its lack of committedness can yield to rigidity, as Antony Anghie illustrates in the application of one example of legal *technē*, analytical positivism, to another, legal definitions:

> The analytical school establishes a definition, adheres to it and applies it rigorously and unyieldingly. Any conflict between the realities disclosed by the historical researchers and the definition must be resolved in favour of the definition, in order to maintain its 'consistency and therefore usefulness.' Language, it would seem, cannot yield to acknowledge empirical reality where this could lead to destabilizing the concepts and categories on which the system is based.[104]

A further tendency associated with *technē* is that its knowledge concerns itself with types rather than individuals; for feminist jurisprudence, on the other hand, the relationship between the general and the particular is paramount: feminists seek to re-member the differentiated experience that cannot be captured adequately within the 'universal'. *Technē* does not, for example, conceptualise the dismissal of one woman, Eileen Flynn,[105] from her teaching post, although it may take a position on the class of women to which she belongs. Furthermore, the logic of *technē* is the logic of ends and means. It is not that ethical practice or the exercise of justice are not central to the practice of law, but rather that they too can become mere objectives to be achieved within the perspective of *technē*. That danger is highlighted in the case of *JM*.[106] The original case concerned a hospitalised, comatose woman, PM, on whose behalf an urgent application to the High Court was made to direct the hospital and her medical consultant to perform a liver transplant and blood transfusion. She had previously refused the treatment. The rewritten feminist judgment discusses PM's right to fair procedures and the need for legal representation, showing how her views had not been adequately taken into account in the original judgment, despite procedures having been followed conscientiously.

[102] Joseph Dunne, *Back to the Rough Ground: 'Phronēsis' and 'Technē' in Modern Philosophy and in Aristotle* (Notre Dame, IN, University of Notre Dame Press, 1993) 260.

[103] Karl Llewellyn, *The Common Law Tradition: Deciding Appeals* (Boston, MA, Little, Brown and Company, 1960), cited in Drakopoulou, above n 18, 16.

[104] Antony Anghie, *Imperialism, Sovereignty and the Making of International Law* (Cambridge, Cambridge University Press, 2005) 60.

[105] *Flynn v Power and the Sisters of the Holy Faith* [1985] ILRM 336, HC, Costello J presiding.

[106] *JM, Applicant v the Board of Management of St Vincent's Hospital and Justin Geoghegan and Attorney General, Respondents and PM, Notice Party* [2003] 1 IR 321.

It is arguable that *Flynn v Power*[107] illustrates how a Circuit Court judge and a High Court judge both based their decisions on a gendered, hierarchical status quo, in which justice as an objective has been administered but has become detached from one set of particulars of the case, as this extract from Costello J's judgment suggests:

> Not only were there complaints relating to the quality of her [Ms Flynn's] work but, *of much more importance*, the principal learnt from formal complaints by parents that an association between the appellant and a married man (whose *wife had recently left him* and who owned a *licensed premises* in the town) had developed. *The principal is a very experienced teacher and administrator and a very balanced and fair-minded person.*[108]

This passage conveys polarised values, of which one set is normalised. The values of a religious institution closely allied to the state (ironically, a community of women) are pitted against those of a woman who cohabited with a publican. The qualities associated with the respondents—'balance' and 'fair-mindedness'—align them with the law. Implied is that these attributes are lacking in the plaintiff. If evidence of the plaintiff's lack of 'balance' and 'fair-mindedness' had been adduced during the hearing then the judgment might have flagged it here, but it did not. The decision evinces no recognition that before the Family Law Acts of 1995 and 1996, it would have been exceedingly difficult to have legally regularised the marital status. Costello J has identified certain objectives, and the law is the instrument by which they can be achieved.

Numerous examples might be adduced of the insidious and invidious nature of instrumentalist legal *technē* when it floats free of humane referents. William Shakespeare's woman lawyer Portia in *The Merchant of Venice*,[109] despite the feminist acclaim she has attracted, arguably embodies technical expertise devoid of heart. Antonio cannot repay his interest-free loan to Shylock, who insists on specific performance, although an alternative remedy is available. Balthazar, *aka* Portia, disguised in male lawyer's attire and adopting an androcentric lawyerly mien, holds that Shylock is entitled to precisely a pound of flesh, but no blood, otherwise he dies and all his 'goods are confiscate'. Shylock wants to settle, but Portia/Balthazar will have none of it. Shylock refused the remedy in court, so he forfeits his bond. Now Portia/Balthazar raises the stakes: she enforces a Venetian law that where an 'alien' attempts to take a citizen's life, half his goods go to the state, and half to his victim. In a show of racist cruelty, she deprives the 'alien' Shylock of his property. Unlike her, the Duke bestows mercy, although only on condition that Shylock converts to Christianity.

Shakespeare here highlights how the law 'is able to present force as consent, authority as participation, hierarchy as paradigmatic order, and control as legitimacy, and thereby shield itself from critique'.[110] What is apparently gender-neutral and classless is gendered and class-specific. Portia, passing in the garb of a male judge and in an ostentatious show of legal technique, presses home the logic of the ends and means, and sets a precedent for future behaviour. She knows the quality of mercy. Yet she hands down a racist judgment devoid of mercy that normatises and legalises racism—and in a *volte face* then eloquently

[107] *Flynn*, above n 105.

[108] ibid (emphasis added).

[109] William Shakespeare, *The Merchant of Venice*, 4.1.58–60. See further Erika Rackley, 'Reassessing Portia: The Iconic Potential of Shakespeare's Woman Lawyer' (2003) 11(1) *Feminist Legal Studies* 25–44.

[110] See further Drakopoulou, above n 18, at 14, and references therein.

pleads for mercy for Antonio.[111] In doing so, she maintains the existing imbalance of power. With her grasp of *technē*—of arcane laws, saving clauses and professional pyrotechnics—she/he (for Portia has adopted a male legal *persona*) turns the merciless *technē* of law on a heartless man. Not only her garb, but also her demeanour marks her as 'passing' as a member of the legal fraternity, and simultaneously as an upholder of the values of a parallel, male institution, the Christian Church. She, and the court, stifle their compassion for the petitioner's plight.[112]

The *technē* of legal principles, methodology and perspectives is inescapably gendered,[113] as is apparent viewlessness, which conveys an illusion of transparency and timelessness, and so claims to articulate and dispense 'objective' justice.[114] Neutrality is 'a position which is culturally enabled to deny its positionality—it is position which is empowered to know'.[115] These principles are incorporated into gendered bodies, 'with the consequence that bodies are produced which signify that law on *and* through the body'.[116] Notwithstanding increasing numbers of women legal practitioners at all levels, the default embodied legal performer is a male who adheres to 'patterns of socialisation, experience and values of a particular group of privileged educated men'.[117] While the authoritative nature of justice dispensed in the law courts is reflected in its adherence to legislation and in binding precedents, when unprecedented legal situations arise, judges depend on their own apprehension of the normative,[118] and their apprehension is never neutral. The 'disinterested, disengaged and distant' judge is a 'myth'.[119]

The mode of acknowledging sources in judicial decisions privileges the judge who creates the precedent as much as the decision—'the authority and the proposition are

[111] By contrast, in sentencing Oscar Pistorius for the culpable homicide of his partner, Reeva Steenkamp, Judge Thokozile Masipa noted the necessity of balancing retribution and clemency, and alluded specifically to the need for mercy: 'a long sentence … would lack the element of mercy'. Press Association, 'Oscar Pistorius Begins Jail Term', *Irish Independent*, 21 October 2014. Lord Lane CJ alluded to the 'quality of mercy' speech in *Attorney General's Reference (No 4 of 1989)* [1990] 1 WLR 41, CA: 'The Court of Appeal referred to an earlier statement "that mercy should season justice" as a proposition as soundly based in law as it is in literature.' Lord Lane has been cited several times, eg, *No 70 of 2008 (sub nom R v BW)* [2009] EWCA Crim 100, [2009] 2 Cr App R (S) 64 (at 454). In *DPP v NY* (CCA, 19 December 2002), 'the trial court is under an obligation to administer justice rather than mercy but very often the reasons given for the plea of mercy are reasons which are relevant to the assessment of a just sentence'.

[112] This phrase comes from *Perdido v INS* 420 F 2d 1179 (1969), a case concerning a citizen-child born to undocumented immigrant parents deemed subject to constructive deportation.

[113] Drakopoulou, above n 18.

[114] eg, in Catharine MacKinnon, 'Method and Politics' in *Toward a Feminist Theory of the State* (Cambridge, MA, Harvard University Press, 1989) 114.

[115] Margaret Davies, *Asking the Law Question* (Sydney, Law Book Co, 1994) 176–77.

[116] Butler, above n 64, 134–35.

[117] Lucinda Finley, 'Breaking Women's Silence in Law: The Dilemma of the Gendered Nature of Legal Reasoning' (1989) 64 *Notre Dame Law Review* 886–910, 893. See also Penny Darbyshire, *Sitting in Judgment: The Working Lives of Judges* (Oxford, Hart Publishing, 2011) *passim*.

[118] Heather Douglas, Francesca Bartlett, Trish Luker and Rosemary Hunter (eds), *Australian Feminist Judgments: Righting and Rewriting Law* (Oxford, Hart Publishing, 2014) 421; Robert Cover, 'Nomos and Narrative' (1983) 97 *Harvard Law Review* 4–68.

[119] Brenda Hale, *Maccabaean lecture in jurisprudence 2007: a minority opinion?* Lecture to the British Academy, London, 13 November 2007. Cited in Rosemary Hunter, 'Can feminist judges make a difference?' (2008) 15(1)–(2) *International Journal of the Legal Profession* 7–36, 16.

intertwined'.[120] Margaret Davies evokes the example of Ronald Dworkin's Hercules,[121] exemplar of judicial wisdom that derives from a model of 'supermasculinity'; he is a violent 'superhero' whose politics are exclusionary.[122] Colm Tóibín[123] cites an example in the Irish context of the exercise of such autocratic politics of exclusion within the judiciary as it arose in the case of *McGlinchey v Wrenn*.[124] O'Higgins CJ decided to omit Walsh J from a three-judge Supreme Court panel intended to hear an appeal from the state against a decision that Irish National Liberation Army (INLA) member Dominic McGlinchey be extradited to Northern Ireland to face charges there. Walsh J had indicated to the Chief Justice that he was willing to sit on the panel, but that he believed McGlinchey should be tried for offences allegedly committed within the Irish jurisdiction and should not be extradited. The Chief Justice favoured immediate extradition. According to Tóibín, had Walsh J not made his disagreement with the process so clear, he would have been invited to sit on the court. In the event, the court that was convened did extradite McGlinchey, thereby reflecting O'Higgins CJ's preference.[125] The decision in *McGlinchey v Wrenn*, which effectively excluded acts of terrorism from the category of political offences,[126] is also notable as another example of 'supermasculine' judicial activism. It led the then chair of the Bar Council, Patrick McEntee SC, to remark that 'the court "had been led into areas of policy-making and legislation" and had "substantially amended the Extradition Act" without reference to the Oireachtas'.[127]

A different and overtly gendered example of such exclusionary judicial tactics may be found in the case of *AB v JB*,[128] in which the plaintiff sought a declaration that she was entitled to a legal right share of her deceased (second) husband's estate. She had left home because the deceased had refused to spend time with her, preferring to eat and sleep regularly at his former family home, and Blayney J found this as fact. Nonetheless, the judge held that the husband's abandonment did not constitute just cause for the plaintiff to leave home. Rather, he held that this attachment to his family was merely a quirk in the husband's character, which the plaintiff, as his wife, had perforce to accept. One outcome of this case is that it is now extremely difficult to establish the kind of behaviour that might give rise to a charge of desertion.

[120] See Rosemary Hunter, Clare McGlynn and Erika Rackley (eds), *Feminist Judgments: From Theory to Practice* (Oxford, Hart Publishing, 2010) 16, for related arguments.

[121] Ronald Dworkin, *Law's Empire* (London, Fontana, 1986), cited in Margaret Davies, 'The Law Becomes Us: Rediscovering Judgment' (2012) 20(2) *Feminist Legal Studies* 167–81, 172.

[122] Davies, above n 121, citing Sandra Berns, 'Integrity and Justice or When is Injustice Mandated by Integrity' (1991) 18 *Melbourne University Law Review* 258–76; Rosemary Hunter, 'Border Protection in Law's Empire: Feminist Explorations of Access to Justice' (2002) 11(2) *Griffith Law Review* 263–85; and Allan Hutchinson, 'Indiana Dworkin and Law's Empire' (1987) 96 *Yale Law Journal* 637–65.

[123] Colm Tóibín, 'A Brush with the Law' (Autumn 2007) 28 *Dublin Review of Books*, at https://thedublinreview.com/a-brush-with-the-law/ (last accessed 31 December 2015).

[124] Although Tóibín, ibid, does not identify the specific case in question, it is *McGlinchey v Wrenn* [1982] IR 154, [1983] ILRM 169. The role of O'Higgins CJ was confirmed in a letter to *The Irish Times* from Larry Power, under the heading 'McGlinchey Extradition Case' (20 April 1998).

[125] The other two judges on that occasion were Henchy J and Griffin J.

[126] Hogan and Whyte, above n 26, para 7.4.285, 1655.

[127] Power, above n 124.

[128] *AB v JB and MB* [1991] 2 IR 501.

As the thrust of this book's judgments underlines, the increasing number of women lawyers in itself is insufficient to turn the tide towards a less masculinist legal culture.[129] Senior judges especially remain a homogeneous group,

> [b]y and large, … upper middle class … the majority educated in fee-paying schools prior to attending University … by the time they are serious candidates for judicial appointment, they must be exceptionally wealthy individuals working in a small professional caste.[130]

The process of acculturation into the legal professions remains scrupulously policed. The few routes into the professions and time-honoured practices ensure high degrees of uniformity, the smooth transmission of traditional mores and a vested interest among professionals in the status quo: the motto of the King's Inns,[131] which train barristers, is '*Nolumus mutari* [We will not change/be changed]'.[132] Anne Boigoel, in writing about the French *Magistrature*, has remarked:

> Even if the ideology of the disembodiment of judges in the service of impartiality is very strong, even if judges are all trained in the same way, even if courts' work is more and more standardised, that does not mean that judges are 'social eunuchs'.[133]

The exclusionary quality of what Tóibín calls 'clubbability' remains a desirable commodity in Irish juristic circles; Tóibín believed that a political (Fine Gael) clique of judges and barristers disliked Walsh J, for example, partly because he lacked that quality.[134] Similarly, in Tóibín's view the same group disapproved of Mary Robinson because 'she tended to bring high-profile cases relating to personal rights rather than get involved in the day-to-day business of the Bar'.[135] One speaker has remarked—as recently as June 2014—that, in relation to the gendered network exclusion surviving within the Irish Bar, 'The idea of "golf course business" is reportedly still evident.'[136] Ivana Bacik, Cathryn Costello and Eileen Drew evinced in 2003 the 'selection procedures which set great store by experience, age and professional networks—all of which criteria are more easily met by male applicants',[137] as a reason for fewer women being appointed judges in common law countries.

[129] Elizabeth Fitzgerald, 'Barrister fee records reveal scale of gender inequality', *The Irish Times*, 20 January 2014: 'Female senior counsel who work for the State are getting paid less for each brief than men'; Conor Gallagher, 'Why are so few women becoming senior counsel?' *The Irish Times*, 9 December 2013: 'Women will soon outnumber men in the law library, but their progress to the "inner bar" has been much slower.'

[130] Oran Doyle, 'Conventional Constitutional Law' (2015) 38(2) *Dublin University Law Journal* 325–26.

[131] Mary Robinson, former President of Ireland, was highly critical of her experience while training as a barrister in the mid-1960s: Mary Bourke, 'The Education of the Irish Barrister' (1966) *Justice—Irish Student Law Review* 16. Ivana Bacik, Cathryn Costello and Eileen Drew interviewed a series of focus groups of women students at King's Inns for *Gender InJustice: Feminising the Legal Professions*? (Dublin, Trinity College, 2003, at http://edepositireland.ie/bitstream/handle/2262/16579/Gender%20In%20Justice.pdf?sequence=1&isAllowed=y (last accessed 2 December 2015). They report no gender bias within the King's Inns institution, but the interviewees expressed dissatisfaction and frustration with the male culture (at 189–91). Women's experience of the Law Society's training courses for solicitors was reportedly more positive (191–95).

[132] Colum Kenny, '*Nolumus Mutari*: Time for Change at King's Inns?' (2005) 1 *The Irish Jurist* 321–46.

[133] Anne Boigeol, 'Feminisation of the French "*Magistrature*": Gender and Judging in a Feminised Context' in Schultz and Shaw, above n 58, ch 2.1.

[134] Tóibín, above n 123.

[135] ibid.

[136] Auditor (E Ryan), 'Women and the Law: Women in the Irish Legal System', The Law Students' Debating Society of Ireland, King's Inns (3 June 2014), at www.kingsinns.ie/news/item/2014/06/women-and-the-law/ (last accessed 12 November 2015).

[137] Bacik, Costello and Drew, above n 131, at 126.

Feminist Knowledge and Drag/Passing

When scholars bypass such traditional networks of clubs and school ties, and lay claim to the discourse of the law, as the feminist judgments projects authors do when they deliver feminist judgments, Rosemary Hunter, Clare McGlynn and Erika Rackley claim that they are engaging in drag performances that are parodic and subversive.[138] Davies takes up their conceit of performance, and argues that the process of judging is always performative, in the sense of performing a role, and drag for female and feminist judges is 'the judicial norm, not the exception'.[139] The cultural tensions between a woman's roles as woman and as judge mean that she must 'code as both a woman and a judge' in order that she may 'pass herself off' as the same as her male counterpart. That strain can create animosity and opprobrium.[140] The woman lawyer 'passing herself off' as male misrepresents herself, but her intention is not to draw attention to her assumed role, as a theatrical drag artist might do. Rather, is it to root herself firmly in a fixed male category or class, to create a voluntarily misrecognition based on identifying with the established professional roles.

Jennifer Drouin's distinction between drag and passing[141] can offer further insight into the distinction between the feminist judge and her colleagues. Drouin's idea of passing involves adopting a convincing exterior form and an earnest desire for authenticity, and is predicated upon adherence to rigidly determined, gendered categories. Passing seeks to minimise and camouflage its not-quite-rightness, rather than highlight it. Drouin[142] has therefore compared passing to Homi Bhabha's[143] concept of mimicry, in which the Other, who is 'the subject of a difference that is almost the same, but not quite',[144] mimics the coloniser, continually repeating rather than re-presenting the illusion. The repetition is integral to sustaining the illusion, and it masks no presence or identity.[145]

The female legal practitioner layers her identities—gendered, professional (and perhaps other, perhaps domestic)—maintaining the male-lawyer role uppermost, discernible when she deploys institutional legal discourse and adopts legal garb, posture, gesture, idiom and rhetoric. This guise exemplifies the 'complex strategy of reform, regulation, and discipline, which "appropriates" the Other as it visualises power'.[146] Bhabha asserts that 'Mimicry is the sign of the inappropriate, a difference or recalcitrance which coheres the dominant function of power, intensifies surveillance, and poses an imminent threat to both "normalized" knowledges and disciplinary powers.'[147]

[138] Rosemary Hunter, Clare McGlynn, and Erika Rackley, 'Feminist judgments: An introduction' in Hunter, McGlynn and Rackley, above n 120, ch 1, 8.

[139] Davies, above n 121, 173.

[140] ibid, citing Carol Menkel-Meadow, 'Feminist legal theory, critical legal studies, and legal education or, the "fem-crits go to law school"' (1988) 38 *Journal of Legal Education* 61–85; Erika Rackley, 'Representations of the (woman) judge: Hercules, the little mermaid, and the vain and naked emperor' (2002) 22(4) *Legal Studies* 602–24; Margaret Thornton, '"Otherness" on the Bench: How Merit is Gendered' (2007) 29(3) *Sydney Law Review* 391–413.

[141] Jennifer Drouin, 'Cross-Dressing, Drag and Passing: Slippages in Shakespearean Comedy' in James Bulman (ed), *Shakespeare Re-dressed: Cross-gender Casting in Contemporary Performance* (Cranbury, NJ, Associated University Press, 2008) 23–56.

[142] Drouin, above n 141, 31.

[143] Homi K Bhabha, *The Location of Culture* (Oxford, Routledge, 2004).

[144] ibid, 122.

[145] ibid, 126. In that respect, Bhabha is seen to parallel Butler's concept of gender roles as performative.

[146] ibid, 11–12.

[147] ibid, 108.

Any feminist judge, then, is in a dilemma. Her professional integrity demands that she keep faith with the normalising *technē*, protocols and wisdom of the law accumulated over millennia. To adhere to its behavioural norms, she is expected to acknowledge its precedents, its authoritative registers, its categories and methodologies of rationalisation, and the bureaucratic 'events' that de-individualise experience. She must conform to its linguistic norms, including codification, idiom and rhetoric, and the re-lexicalisations[148] that the discipline of legal writing imposes. However, the normalising *technē* is not only textual; it also ranges across myriad other forms of semiotic activity, including sociolect, gesture, ritual, hierarchies and etiquette.

Discourse and Legal *Technē*: Acquired Speech

Women judges have proved themselves well capable of adopting the convincing exterior form and an eloquent legal idiolect of the bench. Nonetheless, it is likely that they 'perform and experience the role differently to men'.[149] The 'mimicking' lawyer or judge possesses 'knowledges and disciplinary powers' that are under-utilised and which, when they are deployed, can disrupt the epistemological convictions accreted over centuries. Like the colonial mimic, the feminist judge is 'at once resemblance and menace'.

In a memorable passage from James Joyce's *A Portrait of the Artist as a Young Man*, literary schoolboy Stephen Dedalus realises that the Dean of Studies of his Jesuit school, an English priest, is unfamiliar with the word 'tundish', an Elizabethan term commonly used in Ireland (an alternative term is 'funnel'). The priest's limited vocabulary leads Stephen to realise that

> [t]he language in which we are speaking is his before it is mine. How different are the words home, Christ, ale, master, on his lips and on mine! I cannot speak or write these words without unrest of spirit. His language, so familiar and so foreign, will always be for me an acquired speech. I have not made or accepted its words. My voice holds them at bay. My soul frets in the shadow of his language.[150]

Joyce was referring to the colonial angst of a literary young man conscious that the language he so loves, the English language and its rich literary canon, is an instrument of British imperial power, a power personified in the Dean of Studies, rather than his possession by right. The feminist legal scholar who has neither made nor accepted the discourse of the law, whose soul frets in its shadow, may echo Stephen's *cri de coeur*, and indeed recognise the distinctive import of the words 'home, Christ, ale, master' on the lips of a woman rather than a man. The rewritten judgments of the feminist judgments project constitute an act of recognition of the power relations that are constructed and expressed through a calibrated range of linguistic idioms and discursive formations implied in Joyce's work. How different are the technical vocabularies and rhetorical devices when they are used to

[148] MAK Halliday, *Language as a Social Semiotic: the Social Interpretation of Language and Meaning* (London, Edward Arnold, 1978).

[149] Davies, above n 121, 172, citing Dermot Feenan, 'Editorial introduction: Women and judging' (2009) 17(1) *Feminist Legal Studies* 1–9. Sharon Roach Anleu and Kathy Mack, 'Opportunities for new approaches to judging in a conventional context: Attitudes, skills and practices' (2011) 37(1) *Monash Law Review* 187–215.

[150] James Joyce, *A Portrait of the Artist as a Young Man* (New York, Penguin, 1977 [1916]), 221.

normalise, prohibit and pathologise certain gendered identities and practices, and to affirm and detoxify them![151]

The power of a patriarchal legal discourse is a thread that runs through many of the commentaries and feminist judgments of this book. Thornton J, in the case of *Mhic-Mathúna*,[152] adduces arguments to show that although the text of the Irish Constitution, especially Article 41.2, which privileges women's life within the home, is inescapably gendered, nevertheless it may be possible to explicate it in ways that acknowledge complex feminist approaches. Another judge, Rynn J, refuses to use the term 'complainant' in the case of *DPP v C*[153] concerning consent to sex, opting instead for woman (and 'man' instead of 'accused'), because in her view these words downplay sexual violence and summon the stereotype of the complaining, unreasonable woman. In her commentary on the feminist decision in *FPANI v Minister for Health*,[154] Sara Ramshaw interprets the preference of the original trial judge, Kerr J, for the term 'anti-abortion' over 'anti-choice', as reducing the scope of a pregnant woman, who is already disadvantaged, for self-determination. She also criticises the language of a guidance document on the circumstances in which pregnancy may be terminated in Northern Ireland,[155] which was intended for health and social care professionals. She notes that the feminist activist group Alliance for Choice[156] argued that the guidance document criminalised women who sought abortion, that it tried to create restraints in addition to those already provided for by the law, that it further ingrained the views of the current legal framework, and that it further embedded cultural views of women as mothers and propagators. Feminist judge McNeilly LJ in *FPANI v Minister for Health*[157] comments that the result of the apparently neutral approach of her colleagues on the bench was that the experiences of women at the core of the case were no longer visible. These cases show how 'attempts to state ideas in particular sets of words can alter the ideas as the words change'.[158] The feminist process of altering the linguistic and ideological status quo holds up a mirror to the resistors and to the shortcomings of the legal system, making of it both a menace and a model.

This female mirroring-menace finds acute expression in the character of Aoibheall in *The Midnight Court*, Brian Merriman's eighteenth-century poem. According to Seamus Heaney, the poem blasts volleys of 'surrealistic ridicule'[159] at the repressive socio-political regime

[151] 'Discourse is what transforms our environment into a socially and culturally meaningful one.' Jan Blommaert, *Discourse: A Critical Introduction* (Cambridge, Cambridge University Press, 2005), 4.

[152] This collection, ch 7.

[153] This collection, ch 26.

[154] This collection, ch 21.

[155] *The Limited Circumstances for a Lawful Termination of Pregnancy in Northern Ireland: A Guidance Document for Health and Social Care Professionals on Law and Clinical Practice* (2013). at http://allianceforchoiceni.org/FINAL%20AFC%20Response%20Abortion%20Guidance%20July%202013.pdf (last accessed 26 March 2016).

[156] In its submission to the Committee for the Elimination of Discrimination Against Women (CEDAW): Alliance for Choice, *The Limited Circumstances for a Lawful Termination of Pregnancy in Northern Ireland: A Guidance Document for Health and Social Care Professionals on Law and Clinical Practice* (July 2013), at http://allianceforchoiceni.org/FINAL%20AFC%20Response%20Abortion%20Guidance%20July%202013.pdf (last accessed 26 March 2016).

[157] This collection, ch 21.

[158] John Dyson Heydon, 'Threats to Judicial Independence: The Enemy Within' (2013) 129(2) *Law Quarterly Review* 205–20, fn 16, 220.

[159] Seamus Heaney, *The Redress of Poetry: Oxford Lectures* (London, Faber, 1995) 48.

that governed private and public life in eighteenth-century Ireland,[160] and any appraisal of its reflection of contemporary law must allow due regard for Merriman's consciously satirical excess, and his burlesque of poetic conventions, including the trope of the court of love. Aoibheall, the fairy queen of Munster, is cast in the role of judge during a midnight court that replaces its official British judicial equivalent. In her judgment, she excoriates the male complainant as 'spunkless' and as having failed his 'women, one and all'.[161] She condemns the double standard that castigates women's promiscuity and condones men's; and she approves the need to increase fertility, to address a declining population and to acknowledge guiltless female sexuality: 'If things go on like this, then fuck it! / The men will have to be abducted!'[162] Through her denunciation she constructs an alternative jurisprudence that builds alternative legal capital. Aoibheall's values include impartiality, equality and incorruptibility. Her menace is in its doubleness, in her masculinist lawyerliness and her female Otherness. Her submerged alterity surfaces in her verdict. Unlike her real-world judicial counterparts, she has no need to hide and repudiate a professional identity that is her own but does not seem like hers, and instead to enact a role that is not hers but appears to be just that.[163]

Feminist Knowledge: Practical Wisdom

The mirror-menace of feminist judges who 'perform and experience the role differently to men' disrupts established authority, and 'is always subversive at the moment of its exposure'.[164] This capacity to perceive differently is evident in, for example, some—although by no means all—of the dissenting judgments of Susan Denham, current President of the Supreme Court. In the *Sinnott* case[165] she pithily condemned an instrumentalist view of the Irish Constitution, exposing it as a 'document for the people of Ireland, not an economy or a commercial company'. Later in that decision she forthrightly showed how the breach of the rights of one family member (the plaintiff), could precipitate inordinate repercussions on other family members, especially on the primary carer, in this case, the mother. Denham J was the only judge to dissent in the decision in *Attorney General and SPUC v Open Door Counselling*,[166] in which SPUC (the Society for the Protection of Unborn Children) sought to prevent Open Door Counselling from providing abortion advice. In another judgment,

[160] See also Eugene O'Brien, '"More than a language … no more of a Language": Merriman, Heaney and the Metamorphoses of Translation' (2004) 34(2) *Irish University Review* 277–90.

[161] Seamus Heaney, *The Midnight Verdict* (Dublin, Gallery Books, 1993). This version is an abridged refraction of the original rather than a translation. Brian Merriman, *The Midnight Court/Cúirt an Mheáin Oíche: A Critical Edition* (New York, Syracuse University Press, 2011), Brian Ó Conchubhair (ed and intro), David Marcus (trans) is one of many translations available of the original Irish, *Cúirt an Mheáin Oíche.* There have been numerous other translations of the poem, including by Arland Ussher, Frank O'Connor, Thomas Kinsella and Ciaran Carson.

[162] Heaney, above n 161, 27.

[163] Drouin, above n 141, 32.

[164] ibid, 29.

[165] *Sinnott v Minister for Education* [2001] IESC 63.

[166] *Attorney General and the Society for the Protection of Unborn Children v Open Door Counselling* [1988] IR 593, [1989] ILRM 19.

TD v Minister for Education,[167] Denham J dissented from a majority Supreme Court decision that the High Court had purported to force the state to build and open secure units for vulnerable children. In her view, the circumstances constituted exceptional circumstances that justified a mandatory order against the executive.

Judgments such as these—and indeed, those in this book—do not reject out of hand law as *technē*, but they do raise the issue of alternatives. What kind of knowledge attends experience, gendered and/or otherwise? And what are the characteristics of the doer of jurisprudence, taking account of gendered experience? Feminism must interrogate the principles embedded in the law's technical working knowledge, not least because '[p]rinciples are authoritative only insofar as they are correct; and they are correct only so far as they do not err with regard to the *particulars*'.[168] It is in the particulars that important female concerns are to be found, and it is to particulars that Aristotle attends in his exploration of practical wisdom, *phronēsis*. Experience is integral to the phronetic model of knowledge, and it is therefore sympathetic to the needs of women whose particular situations the law as *technē* fails to discern. It is a knowledge that is not wholly measurable, that privileges the particulars over the universal, and that values a judgement (with a second 'e') and a judgment, not only because of their consequences, but also in themselves.[169] It acknowledges that the same value sets do not inform every judgement individuals make, that the same metric is not appropriate to all situations, and that emotions and imagination can play a part in rational thinking. It is the type of knowledge that informs legal practice, positionality and orientation. Christine Ryan, commentating on Ryson J's rewritten feminist judgment relating to *BJM v CM*, highlights how Ryson J reasons from the lived experiences of the parties.[170]

Practical Knowledge

When practical knowledge animates the law, it insists that a lawyer or judge grasp law's value and not just achieve proficiency in a book-knowledge of it. 'The really rational way to choose', Nussbaum writes, citing Aristotle, 'is to reflect on and acknowledge the special contribution of each item [from which a choice must be made], and to make the understanding of that heterogeneity a central part of the deliberation'.[171] Within this logic, conscious erasing of difference (including gender difference) is not rational, while accepting difference is. Within *phronēsis*, the reasons a decision is taken are important, as are ethical considerations that may affect the decision-making process. A generalised framework of rules and principles, therefore, is not appropriate to every case, especially if that framework is androcentric. The concrete, the individual instantiation, must take precedence over the general. This proposition stands in opposition to the Platonic elevation of abstraction. Aristotle does not propose that there cannot be universally applicable rules, but he holds that the capacity to discern the particulars is a matter of overriding importance.

[167] *TD v Minister for Education* [2001] 4 IR 259.
[168] Nussbaum, above n 95, 69, calls these characteristics metricity, singleness and consequentialism.
[169] ibid, 58.
[170] This collection, ch 25.
[171] Nussbaum, above n 95, 60.

Aristotle anticipates that a discerning legal practitioner may be required to amend or add to general formulations of law:

> When then the law speaks universally, and something comes up that is not covered by the universal, then it is correct, insofar as the legislator has been deficient or gone wrong in speaking simply, to correct his omission, saying what he would have said himself had he been present and would have legislated if he had known.[172]

Gender-related legal subjects expose gaps and non sequiturs, and have most vigorously punctured the generalising nature of the *technē*-informed law—cases relating to surrogacy,[173] transgender issues, under-age sex[174] and abortion[175]—exposing the inadequacy of Irish law on gender. Aristotle's concept of knowledge implies an imperative to correct and supplement both the particulars and the general formulation. This is a pliant concept of the law, at odds with the monolithic, accreting approach to knowledge that characterises *technē*.

Phronēsis: The Rule of Lesbos

In order to make his point about the need for a flexible ethic that overtly disavows objectivity, which is integral to *phronēsis* or practical wisdom, Aristotle[176] deploys a powerfully evocative trope that has a particular resonance in the current argument, and that underlines the applicability of his principles to feminist jurisprudence. He proposes the rule of Lesbos as the means to measure the incommensurability of *phronēsis*. The Lesbian rule 'bends to the shape of the stone and is not fixed'.[177] Nussbaum diametrically opposes it to the technical method expounded by Grandgrind, the heartless grinder of facts and figures in Dickens' novel, *Hard Times*: 'With a rule and a pair of scissors, and the multiplication table always in his pocket, sir, ready to weigh and measure any parcel of human nature, and tell you what it comes to.'[178] The acceptance of indeterminacy and indefinability radically extends the scope and the responsibility of knowledge, and creates an imperative to act ethically and inclusively. Within this dispensation, a wise person cannot automatically take refuge in the safe havens of precedent or convention. While guidelines can continue to play a role in designating good practice, they should not dominate the decision-making process,[179] nor should they be applied without reflection. A practitioner is called upon to

[172] Aristotle, EN1137 bl3ff, cited ibid, 69.

[173] *MR & DR v An tArd Chlaraitheoir, Ireland and the Attorney General* (HC, 5 March 2013).

[174] *MD v Ireland, AG and DPP*, SC Appeal No: 176/2010. The Supreme Court, Denham J presiding, rejected the submission that 'the fact that the female alone can become pregnant is not a ground which justifies an immunity' from prosecution under s 5 of the Criminal Law (Sexual Offences) Act 2006, in circumstances that involved a 14-year-old girl and a 15-year-old boy.

[175] An instance of the implementation of the Protection of Life During Pregnancy Act 2013 led in August 2014 to the refusal to perform an abortion on a young immigrant rape victim and to the delivery of her premature child by caesarian section: *Ms Y v Health Service Executive & Ors* [2016] IEHC 136. For a timeline of what is publicly known about this case until 13 October 2014, see at www.irishtimes.com/news/social-affairs/timeline-of-ms-y-case-1.1951699 (last accessed 26 March 2016).

[176] On the difficulties of using Aristotle for feminist purposes, see Cynthia Freeland (ed), *Feminist Interpretations of Aristotle* (University Park, PA, University of Pennsylvania Press, 2010).

[177] Aristotle, 1137b30–32, cited in Nussbaum, above n 95, 70.

[178] Charles Dickens, *Hard Times* (London, Penguin, 1995; ed by Kate Flint [1854]).

[179] Nussbaum, above n 95, 73.

improvise, to be open and responsive to what is relevant in a complex situation; and gender is *always* relevant. Joseph Dunne summarises the challenge in terms applicable to the legal decision-maker:

> Being virtuous is difficult because it involves finding one's way through … the uncircumscribable range of potentially noticeable features and the consequently unlimited possibilities of action that inhere in each situation—and settling on the one best and most appropriate action.[180]

The imperative is to find what is best and most appropriate, and not just to complete a task: the call is to aspire to excellence. What that may be is 'subject to contingency and directed at beings who are subject to change'. It 'rehabilitates conjectural knowledge and the type of intelligence that proceeds obliquely'.[181] Action merges with striving after, or desire for, excellence. It is not enough just to complete the task, to achieve a competent legal result. This kind of virtuous vocational practice is not therefore morally neutral but orientated towards a good: towards justice, in the case of the law, and one of its integral component is emotion. *Technētes* invest less in an end product, in that they stand back from it dispassionately, having exercised their skills to the best of their ability. *Phronēsis* implies excellent performance, an ethical stance, an orientation towards the good: it has no reality outside of this. *Phronēsis* is not easily practised or described, and is resistant to theorisation. Only the individual in the particular situation can decide what is virtuous action in a particular context. Implicit here is an imperative to forgo established conceptual positions. Aristotle's own statement identifies the priority: 'we do not wish to know what bravery is but to be brave, nor what justice is but to be just'.[182] Aristotle is not so much jettisoning reason as privileging the concrete situation and then attending to reason within it.

While much empirical research remains to be done in the Northern/Irish context to establish how gender differences affect legal judgments, there is some international evidence suggesting that female judges privilege values associated with *phronēsis*.[183] The comments of a female judge whom Maria Rita Bartolomei interviewed underline this:

> I think that the experience of being female is a crucial element of being more willing and able to hear and understand the stories of women litigants and of listening carefully and respectfully about their lives. Our own experience enables us to respond sympathetically and to succeed in putting gendered experiences into legal discourse.[184]

This interviewee's reflection highlights experiential knowledge as a basis for an empathy and respect. It carries no hint of the dangerous essentialism that Judge Sotomayor exemplified in her remark that 'I would hope that a wise Latina woman with the richness of her experiences would more often than not reach a better conclusion than a white male who hasn't lived that life.'[185] Sotomayor here flips the gender binary, privileging the one and handicapping the other on the basis of two fluid characteristics, ethnicity and gender. She

[180] Dunne, above n 102, 311–12.

[181] Marcel Detienne and Jean-Pierre Vernant, *Cunning Intelligence in Greek Culture and Society* (trans Janet Lloyd) (Sussex, Harvester Press, 1978) 317, cited in Dunne, above n 102, 260.

[182] Aristotle, *Eudemian Ethics*, 1216b, cited in Nussbaum, above n 95, 72.

[183] Schultz and Shaw, above n 58, *passim*.

[184] Maria Rita Bartolomei, 'Gender and Judging in Traditional and Modern Societies' in Schultz and Shaw, above n 58, ch 3.3, 292.

[185] Judge Sonia Sotomayor, as cited in Schultz and Shaw, above n 58, 27–28.

does not allow a white male the possibility of a set of enriching experiences from which he might build knowledge, feminist and/or otherwise. In contrast, female judges whom Bartolomei interviewed identified certain experiential values that conform to the rule of Lesbos. These included a determination to

> focus on the concrete situation of participants in the proceedings, to reason from the broader social context on which the legal rules in question operate and to produce a decision that is individualised rather than abstract. Taking everything into consideration, they try to approach legal issues in a way that is not strictly formalistic and goes straight to the point. They do not worry about diverging from precedent and current jurisprudence. Furthermore, they do not indulge in juridical technicalities.[186]

Conclusion

The history and historicity of the law 'is indissociable from relations of discipline, regulation, punishment'.[187] Those regulatory and disciplinary relations have been predicated upon conventions that have made silent presumptions about women judges, lawyers, administrators, litigators, victims of crime and defendants; about classes of women and girls, and about males excluded from patriarchal norms. The process of consciously engendering the law and thereby interrogating those certainties can lead to what Scales called 'not-so-stuckness'. 'Not-so-stuckness' proceeds by way of conjecture and improvisation to shore up a body of experiential knowledge, practice and wisdom that is the best for now, but is ready to accede to the better as soon as it reveals itself. Its feminist knowledge is present- and future-orientated, slanted in the direction of people and particulars. It gives 'tongue its freedom';[188] it cracks the lock on the safes of convention, and its rasping hinge is promise of a space where 'thought might grow'.[189]

There is of course no entitlement at law to have a case tried by either a male or a female judge, or a judge with feminist or indeed masculinist characteristics;[190] nor should there be. Furthermore, feminist judges have no monopoly on justice or wisdom. And, as this book illustrates, there is no unanimity among feminists as to what constitutes a feminist judgment. Judgments written by male judges share many of the characteristics identified in the decisions of the feminist judges in this book.[191] But the values underpinning feminist jurisprudence deserve to 'be celebrated more universally'.[192] This book is such a work of celebration.

[186] Bartolomei, above n 184, 292–93.

[187] Butler, above n 19, 232.

[188] Seamus Heaney, 'The indefatigable hoof-taps, Sylvia Plath', *The Government of the Tongue* (London, Faber, 1988) 166.

[189] Derek Mahon, 'A disused shed in county Wexford', *Collected Poems* (Lough Crew, Meath, Gallery, 1999) 89.

[190] See Judicial Appointments Review Committee, *Preliminary Submission to the Department of Justice and Equality's Public Consultation on the Judicial Appointments Process* (30 January 2014) para 50, at www.supremecourt.ie/SupremeCourt/sclibrary3.nsf/%28WebFiles%29/51E71A71B9961BD680257C70005CCE2D/$FILE/A%20Preliminary%20Submission%20of%20J.A.R.C.%2030.01.2014.pdf (last accessed 26 March 2016).

[191] See in particular, the feminist judgment of *McGee v AG* (this collection ch 5) and *Foy v An t-Ard Chláraitheoir* (this collection ch 28).

[192] Thadd Blizzard, 'Book Review: Gender and Judging' (2014) 25(2) *Hastings Women's Law Journal* 267–304, 303.

4

Judging and the Judgment Writing Process: A Northern/Irish Perspective

AOIFE O'DONOGHUE

When the Brehons deviated from the truth of nature, there appeared blotches on their cheek.[1]

Introduction

The first time a person sits to write a judgment, it is often without guidance or shared knowledge of how exactly to go about that task.[2] Mr Justice Nicholas Kearns has commented that, '[j]udgment writing creates a multitude of challenges for a judge and can at times be a burden of considerable weight'.[3] While the judges in this project did not share the burden of making determinations on persons before them in a courtroom, the weight of maintaining the integrity of judicial writing was a task which all profoundly felt in coming to their conclusions. This solicitude toward judicial writing was not based upon a reverence for the judicial method; rather, in keeping with the methodology of the project, it was essential that the judgments in this collection could sit alongside those of their sistern without any hesitation as to their validity.

This chapter considers the judicial writing process in the context of the two jurisdictions that are at the centre of this collection. It considers the judicial writing process within Ireland; the historical role women have played in the professional development of law and the judiciary in Ireland, as well as the impact that this role had on our judgment writers.

Judgment Writing Within the Project

While this collection draws upon the shared experiences of previous feminist judgments projects, what was evident from the judges who discussed their experiences with us during

[1] W Neilson Hancock, *Ancient Laws of Ireland*, vol 1, Published under Direction of the Commissioners for Publishing the Ancient laws and Institutes of Ireland (London, Printed for HM Stationery Office, 1865) 23.

[2] Erika Rackley, 'The Art and Craft of Writing Judgments: Notes on the Feminist Judgments Project' in Rosemary Hunter, Clare McGlynn and Erika Rackley (eds), *The Feminist Judgments: From Theory to Practice* (Oxford, Hart Publishing, 2010) 44.

[3] Mr Justice Nicholas Kearns, 'Some Thoughts on Judgment Writing', *The Irish Times*, 10 November 2008.

our project workshops, was that the art of judgment writing is not one for which, upon their first appointment, they received much guidance or training.[4] Knowledge of judgment writing was garnered from reading judgments and, in effect, accumulating information on the writing process from what other judges had written before them. This experience is one shared within the project. While the judgment writers looked to the original judgments they chose to rewrite, as well as to the particularised knowledge they garnered as lawyers over years of judgment reading, there was also an additional concern that this project elicited in its participants: What would the feminist judge bring to the particular case and the process of judgment writing?

In contrast to other common law jurisdictions, there is comparatively little study of Irish judicial craft.[5] Whether there is a uniquely 'Northern/Irish' judicial voice has not been a question that this project has been able to answer, albeit the lived experiences of the judges on the island will naturally be unique and particular to the two jurisdictions.[6] Articles that examine the composition or character of the judiciary in Ireland often fail to remark on the lack of women on the bench.[7] For instance, in one article on judicial qualities in Ireland and beyond, only two female judges are mentioned, and the single judge described as a feminist was a male judge, while broader considerations of diversity are not critiqued.[8]

Historical volumes have focused either on the common law tradition, or on Ireland's distinct Brehon past, albeit that the latter has established some critical discussion of women's place within the law, though, at times, through an idealised lens.[9] For instance, Heather Laird discusses how, as the translations of the Brehon law were beginning to be published in the 1860s, the better position of married women under the Brehon law with regard to

[4] Rackley, above n 2, at 44; Heather Douglas, Francesca Bartlett, Trish Luker and Rosemary Hunter, 'Reflections on Rewriting the Law' in Heather Douglas, Francesca Bartlett, Trish Luker, Rosemary Hunter (eds), *Australian Feminist Judgments: Righting and Rewriting Law* (Oxford, Hart Publishing, 2013).

[5] Caroline Fennell, 'The Culture of Decision Making: A Case for Judicial Defiance through Evidence and Fact-Finding' (2001) 2(2) *Judicial Studies Institute Journal* 25–65; Mary Kotsonouris, 'Criticising Judges in Ireland' (2001) 2(2) *Judicial Studies Institute Journal* 79–97; Kieran McEvoy and Alex Schwartz, 'Judges, Conflict and Past' (2015) 44(4) *Journal of Law and Society* 528–55; The Hon Mr Justice Philip O' Sullivan, 'A Hot Tub for Expert Witnesses' (2004) 4(1) *Judicial Studies Institute Journal* 1–7; Tanya Ward, 'Independence, Accountability and the Irish Judiciary' (2008) 8(1) *Judicial Studies Institute Journal* 1–36.

[6] For a discussion of judicial voice, see Sandra Berns, *To Speak as a Judge: Difference, Voice and Power* (Dartmouth, Ashgate, 1999) and Erika Rackley, 'Representations of the (Woman) Judge: Hercules, the Little Mermaid and the Vain and Naked Emperor' (2002) 22(4) *Legal Studies* 602–24.

[7] The Hon Mr Justice John L Murray, 'Judicial Cosmopolitanism' (2008) 8(2) *Judicial Studies Institute Journal* 1–17; The Hon Mr Justice Ronan Keane, 'Judges as Lawmakers: The Irish Experience' (2004) 4(2) *Judicial Studies Institute Journal* 1–18.

[8] Evan Bell, 'Judicial Qualities: Illustrations from Past Lives' Experience' (2008) 8(2) *Judicial Studies Institute Journal* 18–57, 26, 32, 34.

[9] Mary Kotsonouris, *The Winding-up of the Dáil Courts, 1922–1925: An Obvious Duty* (Dublin, Four Courts, 2004); Heather Laird, 'India and the Translation of the Irish Brehon Laws' in Tadhg Foley and Maureen O'Connor (eds), *India and Ireland: Colonies, Culture and Empire* (Dublin, Irish Academic Press, 2006); Fergus Kelly, *A Guide to Early Irish Law* (Dublin, Dublin Institute for Advanced Studies, 2008); Sophie Bryant, *Liberty, order [and] law under native Irish rule: a study in the book of the ancient laws of Ireland* (London, Harding, 1923); F Elrington Ball, *The Judges in Ireland, 1221–1921* (London, John Murray, 1926); Paul Charles Bartholomew, *The Irish Judiciary* (Notre Dame, IN, University of Notre Dame Press, 1971); Thomas F O'Rahilly, 'Irish Poets, Historians, and Judges in English Documents, 1538–1615' (1921–24) 36 *Proceedings of the Royal Irish Academy*, section c, 86–87; Francis Headon Newark, 'Notes on Irish Legal History' (1946–48) 7 *Northern Ireland Legal Quarterly* 121; VTH Delany, 'History of Legal Education in Ireland' (1959-60) 12 *Journal of Legal Education* 396–406.

their property than under the English common law was a significant point of comparison.[10] These tracts also refer to women Brehons or judges such as Brigh.[11] The role of the Dáil and other subversive courts, and particularly the role of women in their administration during the period leading up to partition, demonstrates that the exclusion of women from the law was not inevitable, and was in fact a concerted attempt to confine women to the private sphere.[12]

Mr Justice Kearns, reflecting on Irish judgment writing, suggests that shared amongst common law jurisdictions is a judicial technique that requires judges to set out in sufficient detail the facts and legal principles, and apply these in a coherent manner. However, he argues there remains considerable scope for particular styles of judicial writing. He adds that in Ireland there is perhaps a reluctance to be imaginative:

> Are we as judges too reluctant to express a degree of individualism in our written output, too hide-bound by traditional methods of composition—in a sense too prim to lick the yoghurt from the lid of the container?[13]

During the project it became evident that judicial writing in Northern/Ireland is not as restrained as is perhaps suggested by Kearns J. There are examples of less reserved judicial language that intimate a willingness on the Northern/Irish benches to incorporate prose that may not at first be considered the norm. For instance, in the *Lobe* case, Denham J begins with:

> Over thousands of years waves of people have come ashore on the island of Ireland. However, the island found by those early migrants was very different from the Ireland of today. The differences included those of the landscape, society and governance. Tales of early refugees to Ireland are told in myth and legend.[14]

In *Barnes v Belfast City Council*,[15] Girvan J talks about medication mellowing a dog, personifying the animal; while Kerr J, in *Re Family Planning Association of Northern Ireland*, is very clear in his perception of what this judgment will do for the understanding of abortion in Northern Ireland:

> It has been said that there is a widespread belief that abortion here is always illegal. If there is such a belief, there is no justification for it. It is wrong and after this case there is no reason that it should persist.[16]

[10] W Neilson Hancock, *Ancient Laws of Ireland*, vols 1–5, Published under Direction of the Commissioners for Publishing the Ancient Laws and Institutes of Ireland (London, Printed for HM Stationery Office, 1865–1901), at https://archive.org/details/ancientlawsirel00hancgoog (last accessed 21 March 2015); Heather Laird, *Law, Colonialism and Anti-Colonial Resistance in Ireland*, paper delivered at a project drafting workshop at UCC, 6 February 2015, at www.feministjudging.ie/?page_id=1153 (last accessed 21 March 2016); Sophie Bryant, *Liberty, order [and] law under native Irish rule: a study in the book of the ancient laws of Ireland* (London, Harding, 1923) 94.

[11] Bryant, above n 10, 321.

[12] Heather Laird, *Subversive Law in Ireland: From 'Unwritten Law' to the Dail Courts* (Dublin, Four Courts Press, 2005); Kotsonouris, above n 9.

[13] Kearns, above n 3.

[14] Denham J in *Lobe v Minister for Justice, Equality and Law Reform* [2003] IESC 3, 65.

[15] Girvan J in *Barnes v Belfast City Council* [2012] NICA 19.

[16] Kerry J in *Re Family Planning Association of Northern Ireland* [2003] NIQB 48.

Indeed, extra-judicial writing also demonstrates a similar flair within the Northern/Irish judiciary, as well as indicating that key assumptions about a homogeneous legal audience sharing a particular life position and outlook run through their judicial perspective:

> Many of us here today, if not all, are married. Most of us have children. Those of us who do, I can say without a shred of doubt, love our children dearly and would do nothing which might have any adverse consequences for them. In short, we want the best for 'our kids'.[17]

The judges who shared their experiences with us were clear that they envied the opportunities we had as judgment writers to consider and discuss our own judgments, as well as the lengthy lead-in periods we had to finalise our contributions. The temporal pressures that judges face also form part of the writing process, and while within this project deadlines were not pressing, certainly the prospect of having less time to consider language and tone, as well as outcome as a factor that would inevitably impact upon judgment writers sitting in courts across Northern/Ireland, became clear to our judges.

Just as there is a judicial writing form, there is also an academic style that, as with judicial writing, varies from author to author but also shares core characteristics.[18] For the academic judge, one of the particular issues that became evident during workshops was the nature of the writing process, and the forms and tropes on which academic writing relies for its own legitimacy. Removing volumes of references, finding and adopting a distinctive judicial voice, deciding how much guidance for application of the law to include, how much of the original terminology to utilise, particularly when it is inappropriate, how to present facts and societal norms, as well as the strictures of the methodology channelling your conclusion down a particular route, was not a form that seemed natural to the legal academic.[19]

Whilst the commentators, in considering the context, giving an explanation of some of the decisions made by our judges, as well as discussing the alternative feminist approaches that were not present in the judgment, relieved some of this tension—a practice to which sitting judges have no access—this shift in writing style remained an issue for all in the project. Fox O'Mahony J, during the process of workshopping *NPBS v Lynd*, commented that the judicial writing process forced a form of honesty upon her critique of existing cases.[20] Even when coming to the same conclusion as the original judgment, she had to find firm evidence for her conclusions and, more particularly, her assumptions. Flynn J and Ring J (appearing in this collection as Rynn J)[21] in *DPP v C* observed that attempting to replicate the types of knowledge available to the judiciary at the time of the original judgment, in that instance a consideration of ableism, curtailed what they could achieve while rewriting judgment. This exercise shed light on how academics critique past judgments and what we think judges know or ought to know.[22]

Within the project, each judge had to make some elementary decisions regarding the form of judgment he or she was going to write: whether to make a fictional appeal, to join a majority decision or to make a dissent, to rewrite the Court of Appeal, High or Supreme

[17] Judge McKibbin, 'Round and round the mulberry bush' (2010) 10(1) *Judicial Studies Institute Journal* 1–15, 1.

[18] On academia see, eg, the work of Pierre Bourdieu, *Homo Academicus* (trans P Collier) (Stanford, CA, Polity, 1988).

[19] Douglas et al, above n 4.

[20] *NPBS v Lynd* [1996] NI 47, workshop discussions were recorded and catalogued.

[21] Fling J has promised to appear at a book launch or two.

[22] *DPP v C* [2001] 3 IR 345.

Court decision, or to look to take an entirely different approach such as Tribunal review. Several reasons lay behind the ultimate decisions made, many of which are outlined in the commentaries that accompany the judgments that follow, but some important issues emanate from the decisions made by our judges, which are worth considering as a whole. Further, in the research that the judges conducted, some of our participants found access to state institutions and non-governmental organisations (NGOs) relatively straightforward, even enabling access to skeleton arguments. Others found dealing with institutions within Northern Ireland and Ireland difficult. This, in turn, impacted upon the choices they made in their judgments.

Before discussing these particular questions, it is important to note that in some instances these decisions were curtailed by the legal systems in which they were operating. The Government of Ireland Act 1920 created a separate court structure for the two jurisdictions in Ireland.[23] While the founding of the Free State in 1921 created an entirely new legal structure in Dublin, the initial system created in 1920 in Northern Ireland remains largely intact. The legal context, whether temporally distant or not, provides the space in which each judge had to operate. Each jurisdiction—be it its structure, the presence or absence of women on the bench, or the role of women in the professions—brought a distinct character to the approach of our feminist judges.

Northern Ireland

The 1920 Act established the Supreme Court of Judicature of Northern Ireland, consisting of a High Court and a Court of Appeal. A Court of Criminal Appeal was added in 1930, and below these courts sit the county and magistrates' courts, with the senior courts possessing the ability to sit in divisions. Appeals from the Court of Appeal go directly to the UK Supreme Court (or House of Lords), although only one of our judges—in *In re E (a child)*—chose this option.[24] In only one case, *Re Barnes*, did the judge decide to operate as the county court. Whilst there were some significant changes made, such as the introduction of the Diplock courts in the 1970s, which included juryless trials for scheduled offences, the basic structure of the courts has remained constant.[25]

The 1998 Belfast Agreement impacted upon most governance orders in Northern Ireland but has left little impression upon court structures, albeit that, as this collection demonstrates, the cases coming before it have in some ways been influenced by its content.[26] All but one of the cases from Northern Ireland in the project post-date the Belfast Agreement, although the impact of The Troubles remains clearly evident in both *In re E (a child)* and

[23] Government of Ireland Act 1920.

[24] *In re E (a child)* [2009] 1 AC 536, [2008] UKHL 66. At the time of the original judgment the final UK court of appeal was still the House of Lords, as the decision pre-dated the coming into effect of the Constitutional Reform Act 2005, which established the UK Supreme Court.

[25] The Diplock courts were established under the Northern Ireland (Emergency Provisions) Act 1973, and their most recent reform occurred under the Justice and Security (Northern Ireland) Act 2007.

[26] Criminal Justice Review Group, Northern Ireland Office, Review of the Criminal Justice System in Northern Ireland 2000 (Belfast, HMSO, 2000).

In Re White, as well as cases from the Republic, including *McGimpsey v Ireland* from the Supreme Court in Dublin.[27] As discussed in previous chapters, the effect of the previous years of violence is clearly demonstrated in the choices that women made in regarding the forms of activism and dissent prior to 1998. As Carmel Roulsten commented during discussions of *In re White*, there are intricate problems in resolving competing and intersecting claims for justice, equality and fairness in transitional societies like Northern Ireland.[28] Roulsten continued that this impacted on how the peace process was perceived in building expectations of a new innovative approach to human rights and social justice, and this played out in the choices the judiciary made in these cases. By making alternative choices, the cases in the project often provide a point of rupture from the dominating discourse in Northern Ireland.[29]

The Belfast Agreement's most significant influence upon the courts' deliberations within the project was the establishment of both the Northern Ireland Human Rights Commission (NIHRC) and the Equality Commission under the Northern Ireland Act 1998.[30] The NIHRC is a manifest presence in several cases in the collection. Significantly—and in stark contrast to the irritation with the NIHRC demonstrated by the Northern Irish judiciary—our feminist judges have chosen to understand this body as a new and distinct voice, separate from the binary representations often brought before the Courts. The Northern Irish Court of AppealCourt in *Re White* and the UK Supreme Court in *Re E* are both very critical of and hostile toward the intervention of the NIHRC, and our judges were compelled to respond to this in their rewritten judgments, as were their commentators.[31] Lord Murray of Agherton argued, while workshopping *In re E*, that there is something innately conservative about human rights that the original judges failed to realise in their antagonism toward the NIHRC. Further, in a male-dominated judiciary and legal profession, an alternative state structure, such as the NIHRC, taking the side of an otherwise marginalised or silenced group can potentially make an entirely feminist intervention in how law is conducted in Northern Ireland. The choices made by the feminist judge go against the grain of judicial feeling toward this state institution. The NIHRC is an excellent example of the choices that can be made by a feminist judge within the parameters of the methodology and in the context of a specific jurisdiction where such human rights concerns are considered unnecessary to the law. To utilise an approach dismissed by the original Court—not because it was outside of legal parameters but rather due to an antagonism toward its existence and intervention—and mould this into a feminist judicial insight, was a particularly important example of the contribution this project can make to understanding arguments presented to the Northern Irish courts.

While women make up 51 per cent of the population of Northern Ireland, the number of women holding high legal office is extremely low in comparison to their counterparts in

[27] *McGimpsey v Ireland* [1990] IR 110.

[28] *In re White* [2001] NICA 1.

[29] See the commentaries in this collection in *A and B (by C) v A (Health and Social Services Trust)* [2011] NICA 28 (ch 30) and *Family Planning Association of Northern Ireland v Minister for Health* [2004] NICA 39 (ch 21).

[30] The establishment of the Parades Commission under the Public Processions (NI) Act 1998 has also resulted in several cases before the High Court and Court of Appeal.

[31] *In re White* [2000] NI 432; *In re E (a child)* [2009] 1 AC 536, [2008] UKHL 66.

Dublin, though not as stark when equated to the rest of the UK.[32] The Northern Irish Bar is overwhelmingly male-dominated, and until 2015 there had never been a female judge in the senior judiciary.[33] Indeed, Lord Murray of Agherton, while workshopping *In re E*, noted that whilst Baroness Hale was present in the Supreme Court, knowing there was not a single female voice in the senior judiciary in Northern Ireland made him concerned that he was simply adding another male voice to the discourse. He also noted that the promotion of Lord Carswell as 'the Northern Irish judge' in the Supreme Court had the effect of diminishing the possible impact of Baroness Hale in that decision. In discussing *SPUC*, McCann J found that locating the women in the narrative felt entirely incongruous within the context of the Northern Irish judiciary and within that particular case, where women are all but absent for the court albeit that they are at centre of the proceedings.[34] As Rosemary Hunter has argued:

> [T]he feminist judgment projects ... precisely reverse the usual expectations, encouraging the provision of 'perspectives previously absent'. Such expectations may, indeed, mitigate (if not entirely obviate) the need for bravery on the part of non-traditional judges in coming out as different and adding the substantive value of which they are capable at the points where it matters.[35]

Whilst is clear that the legal profession reflects Northern Irish public structures, where politics and the professions remain largely male-dominated, conservative and ethnically homogeneous, activism and several exceptions to this general picture within the profession demonstrate the alternative possibilities within Northern Ireland for a different picture to emerge, where women are acknowledged as active participants in society and law.[36] A questionnaire of female judges described the legal culture as 'still very much an old boy's network', with a general feeling that, from magistrates level upwards, the higher judiciary is 'still male dominated'. Furthermore, women judges in Northern Ireland felt that informal networks and socialising amongst men influenced judicial appointments and adversely affected women.[37] A further legacy of The Troubles may also be a contributing factor, as Ben Warwick suggested while workshopping *In re White*, as the security detail that comes with a judicial post in Northern Ireland may act as a deterrent for those considering applying for positions at the bench.[38]

[32] The Council of Europe collates data on women in the judiciary across Europe, available from the European Commission for the Efficacy of Justice at www.coe.int/t/dghl/cooperation/cepej/default_en.asp (last accessed 17 March 2016).

[33] Details on the bar in Northern Ireland are available at www.barofni.com/ (last accessed 17 March 2016). See also Erika Rackley, *Women, Judging and the Judiciary: From Difference to Diversity* (Abingdon, Routledge, 2013); Rosemary Hunter, 'Can Feminist Judges Make a Difference?' (2008) 15:1–2 *International Journal of the Legal Profession* 7–36.

[34] *Society for the Protection of Unborn Children, Re an Application for Judicial Review* [2009] NIQB 92.

[35] Rosemary Hunter, 'More than Just a Different Face? Judicial Diversity and Decision-Making' (2015) 68(1) *Current Legal Problems* 119–41, 140. See also Madam Justice Bertha Wilson, 'Will Women Judges Really Make a Difference?' (1990) 28(3) *Osgoode Hall Law Journal* 507–22; Sally J Kenney, *Gender and Justice: Why Women in the Judiciary Really Matter* (Abingdon, Routledge, 2013).

[36] Marie Fox and John Morison, 'Lawyers in a Divided Society: Legal Culture and Legal Services in Northern Ireland' (1992) 19(1) *Journal of Law and Society* 124–45, 137.

[37] Dermot Feenan, 'Women judges: Gendering judging, justifying diversity' (2008) 35(4) *Journal of Law and Society* 490–519, 503.

[38] See also McEvoy and Schwartz, above n 5.

There is no Women's Bar Association in Northern Ireland. The lack of female presence in the professions is noticeable in the sparse numbers of applications for silk. Factors frequently cited as reasons not to apply for silk within Northern Ireland include: childcare factors, uncertainty about the criteria, and the inconvenience of time and travel. These concerns suggest a process that is not open to the needs of the non-traditional members.[39] Moreover, over 40 per cent of female holders of judicial office perceived that informal networks or socialising could adversely affect women's success in applications for judicial office or silk.[40] Fifty per cent of female barristers knew of women who had left private practice for reasons associated with their gender.[41]

Several attempts have been made to ameliorate this problem. For instance, the 2000 Northern Ireland Criminal Justice Review's reforms on judicial appointments appear more radical than their English counterparts in attempting to diversify the profession.[42] A 2000 Report on the reform of Northern Ireland's judicial appointments procedure highlighted serious concerns about the 'unrepresentative nature of the bench in Northern Ireland in terms of community background', as well as the lack of women and ethnic minorities in judicial roles,[43] albeit that, typically, concerns regarding diversity begin with the binary characterisation of the Northern Irish population. The Justice (Northern Ireland) Acts of 2002 and 2004 established the Northern Ireland Judicial Appointments Commission (NIJAC) with a statutory remit to ensure that appointments were based solely on merit.[44] Following the Northern Ireland Act 2009, the NIJAC, in addition to recommendations for Crown and non-Crown appointments, is involved in the consultation process on the appointment of the Lord Chief Justice/Justices of Appeal.[45] These changes were specifically aimed at increasing the number of female appointments to the bench.

Research conducted since these changes has concluded that the reforms introduced over the past decade have increased the transparency of the judicial appointments process by significantly reducing the role of the executive, and, as a result, the NIJAC compares favourably with other similar panels, such as the Republic of Ireland's Judicial Appointments Advisory Board (see 'Republic of Ireland' below) whose role is more limited by the Executive ability to reject a nominee from the panel.[46] Nonetheless, as *In re White* demonstrates and as is clearly articulated in its rewritten form here, attempts to ensure representation on public bodies in Northern Ireland often sacrifice gender representation in favour of ensuring that the two majority communities are primarily represented, even if this, at times, means disregarding some of the administrative steps necessary to ensure representation beyond

[39] Dermot Feenan, 'Applications by Women for Silk and Judicial Office in Northern Ireland' (Belfast, Commissioner for Judicial Appointments for Northern Ireland, 2005) 6.

[40] ibid.

[41] ibid.

[42] John Jackson, 'Shaping the Future of Criminal Justice: Human Rights, Equality and Democratic Renewal in Northern Ireland' in Colin Harvey (ed), *Human Rights, Equality and Democratic Renewal in Northern Ireland* (London, Bloomsbury Publishing, 2001) ch 7.

[43] Ray McCaffrey and Fiona O'Connell, *Judicial appointments in Northern Ireland* (Report for the Northern Ireland Assembly, 2012) 7, at www.niassembly.gov.uk/globalassets/Documents/RaISe/Publications/2012/justice/1912.pdf (last accessed 17 March 2016).

[44] ibid, 3.

[45] ibid, 4.

[46] ibid, 25, details of the Irish Judicial Appointments Advisory Board being available at www.jaab.ie/ (last accessed 17 March 2016).

sectarian lines.[47] Currently, the NIJAC's 12 Commissioners include three women, although no women from the judiciary or the legal professions are represented.[48]

In 2012 the NIHRC's submission to the United Nations Committee on the Elimination of Discrimination against Women noted that the reforms 'did not seem to be bearing fruit' by increasing female recruitment, suggesting that certain cultural barriers remain intact.[49] This is probably most evident at the Bar in Northern Ireland and from the ongoing lack of senior women holding legal office within the jurisdiction, albeit 2015 appointments of Justice Siobhan Keegan and Justice Denise McBride to the High Court are very welcome. One stark statistic that emerged from this project was that of the 17 barristers we could identify in the seven cases from Northern Ireland, only two were women. As noted by McCann J and Lord Murray, this directly impacted upon how our judges perceived their role, both in finding a distinct feminist voice *and* in hearing a female voice at any point within the deliberations. In a context in which women are largely absent from the senior echelons of the legal infrastructure, it would be impossible for their absenteeism to not clearly bear weight on how our judges approached rewriting their cases.

Finding a female judicial voice in Northern Ireland is difficult when a precursor, feminist or otherwise, simply does not exist in the reported cases. The focus on The Troubles when discussing law in Northern Ireland has also meant that there has been relatively little on women's lived experiences of the law, or a feminist analysis of areas of the law unrelated to The Troubles. Whilst this has changed somewhat in recent years, it did make the role of the feminist judge in Northern Ireland of a different quality to other feminist judgments projects, and was a key differential for those engaged with cases from the Republic of Ireland. The recent appointment of Justice Siobhan Keegan and Justice Denise McBride to the High Court of Northern Ireland means that any future project will not face this issue.

Republic of Ireland

Albeit that its core structures remain constant, the court system in the Republic of Ireland (ROI) has undergone various periods of evolution, through two Constitutions and several different Acts, including quite recent reforms. The 1922 Constitution and the Courts of Justice Act 1924 established a legal system aimed at entirely replacing the UK legal structure. Although no longer binding precedent—and in some instances the Constitution, the courts and the legislature have introduced divergences—much of the substantive common law from the pre-independence period remains intact. Until the Statute of Westminster 1931 enabled Ireland to remove it entirely from the legal system, the Privy Council remained

[47] *In re White* [2001] NICA 1.

[48] Details of Commissioners available at www.nijac.gov.uk/index/who-we-are/commissioners.htm (last accessed 17 March 2016).

[49] Submission to the United Nations Committee on the Elimination of Discrimination Against Women on the list of Issues for the United Kingdom of Great Britain and Northern Ireland to be determined by the CEDAW Committee Pre-Session Working Group on 22 October 2012, at www2.ohchr.org/English/bodies/cedaw/docs/ngos/Northern%20Ireland%20NHRI_ForTheSession_UK_CEDAW55.pdf (last accessed 17 March 2016).

as a largely unused point of appeal from the Dublin Supreme Court.[50] The present courts come under the ambit of Article 34 of the 1937 Constitution and the Courts (Establishment and Constitution) Act 1961. While these long processes of reform impacted on what is binding precedent before 1961, none of our cases dates to this period, albeit that the use of precedent, and in particular, a willingness to cite English and other jurisdictions' case law, remains a fixed feature of Irish judicial methodology.[51] Granted, this proclivity is less common in constitutional cases.[52] Our feminist judges make good use of this judicial willingness to look beyond the immediate jurisdictional borders to include case law from Canada, the US and Australia, thus expanding the sight lines of the judiciary.

The ROI's legal system operates around a four-tier structure: the Supreme Court, the High Court, the Circuit Courts and the District Courts, which have been supplemented over time. Some additions, such as the Special Criminal Court, were a direct response to The Troubles in Northern Ireland, albeit that this has now morphed into a wider remit; others, such as the recent introduction of the Court of Appeal, which deals with appeals from the High Court in civil and criminal cases, is a direct result of increased litigation before the courts.[53] All the cases in this collection, bar the *Kerry Babies Tribunal*, are either High Court or Supreme Court cases, though some of the High Court cases are of first instance. The High Court also sits as the Central Criminal Court, and some cases in this collection came through this avenue.

One notable feature of the ROI's judicial system is an Article 26 reference to the Supreme Court. *In the matter of Article 26 of the Constitution and in the matter of the Matrimonial Homes Bill* is an example of this process.[54] This case came about due to a reference by the Irish President to the Supreme Court on the constitutionality of the Matrimonial Homes Bill. Article 26 of the Constitution enables the President to refer a Bill to the Supreme Court, to test its constitutionality before signing it into law. This is of particular import, as once such a reference is made, the constitutionality of the provisions cannot be reconsidered before the courts, thus shutting off an avenue of contestation.

The court structures impacted on some of the choices our judges made regarding whether to focus on an appeal, fictional or otherwise, or to rewrite a case at first instance. Whilst Ní Mhuirthile J decided to write the *Foy* judgment as a fictional appeal to the Supreme Court that, due to the particular circumstances in that case, did not occur, de Londras J chose not to follow this route in *Zappone*, adding to the original High Court judgment instead.[55] In doing so both chose to explore different avenues of debate that the original cases brought forward, and to use the court structure to tackle the issues they faced in each case. This was

[50] Statute of Westminster 1931; Thomas Mohr, 'The Statute of Westminster, 1931—An Irish Perspective' (2013) 31(4) *Law and History Review* 749–91.

[51] Murray, above n 9.

[52] The use of Brehon law, the legal system that preceded the introduction of the common law into Ireland, was also a feature of early jurisprudence: see Thomas Mohr, 'Law in a Gaelic Utopia: Perceptions of Brehon Law in Nineteenth and Early Twentieth Century Ireland' in O Brupbacher, *Remembering and Forgetting: Yearbook of Young Legal History* (Munich, Martin Meidenbauer, 2007) 247–76; Laird, above n 12.

[53] Court of Appeal Act 2014; Offences Against the State Act 1939.

[54] Art 26.1.1° Constitution of Ireland—Bunreacht na hÉireann; *In the matter of Article 26 of the Constitution and in the matter of the Matrimonial Homes Bill* [1994] 1 IR 305.

[55] *Foy v An t-Ard Chláraitheoir & anor* [2007] IEHC 470; *Zappone and Gilligan v Revenue Commrs* [2006] IEHC 404.

also the case for Conway J in the *Kerry Babies* Tribunal Report.[56] In deciding to revisit the original Inquiry as a newly constituted Tribunal to review the earlier findings, Conway J moves away from the court structure. In so doing she remains within the legal structure but brings focus to an event that brings into question the entire edifice of the Irish legal order, including the judiciary and the police and their attitude to women not comporting with the perceived societal norms of 1980s Ireland.

The decision of our judges to choose cases dating from just the past 40 years (*McGee v Attorney General* is the oldest case in this collection)[57] reflects a plethora of rationales. Some, such as the *X* case, *Foy* or *Zappone*, echo the largely conservative character of the state created under both the 1922 and (particularly) the 1937 Constitutions.[58] Both Constitutions reflect an apparent 'traditional' political, religious and social discourse that had dominated the legal culture since the foundation of the state, as well as the economic restraints that most individuals living in the ROI over most of its history since 1921 would have felt.[59] In turn this made it more difficult for those who wished to challenge this discourse to take cases that contested the perceived cultural norms; and certainly while the dominant debate was conservative, at no time did this truly reflect the entirety of the state. This has meant that many cases would simply not have been taken due to socio-economic limitations, or political and social conformity, which silenced some who might otherwise have chosen to challenge their circumstances. Of course, whether litigation was a useful strategy in this context may also have been a strong contributing factor to the forms of litigation taken. As is discussed in Chapter 2, other avenues of dissent were being frequently, and often successfully, utilised.

As Kennefick J while workshopping *Tiernan*, and Thornton J, in *Mhic Mhathúna*, both observed, 1980s Ireland remained a deeply conservative place.[60] This makes the early cases that were taken, such as *McGee* in particular, all the more important, as they stand as critical examples of what was possible within Irish jurisprudence even during this period.[61] Indeed, as Enright J commented while workshopping *McGee*, it remains a critical constitutional case taught in all law schools, and as such this feminist judgment can bring a fresh perspective to students studying this significant decision and the impact of jurisprudential interpretations of the Constitution that date from this period. But what remains striking is that whilst most cases, as with Northern Ireland, date from the 1990s and onwards, with the exceptions of *McGee*, *McGimpsey*, *Mhic Mhathúna*, *Tiernan* and the *Kerry Babies* Tribunal, the nature of the more recent decision-making remains highly problematic, providing a plentiful remit for our judges to make an intervention.

[56] *Report of the Tribunal of Inquiry into the 'Kerry Babies' Case* Official publications. Pl.3514 [1985] Dublin: Stationery Office.

[57] *McGee v Attorney General* [1974] IR 284.

[58] *Attorney General v X* [1992] IESC 1; *Foy v An t-Ard Chláraitheoir & anor* [2007] IEHC 470; *Zappone and Gilligan v Revenue Commrs* [2006] IEHC 404.

[59] See, eg, Sandra McAvoy '"A perpetual nightmare": Women, Fertility Control and the Irish state: the 1935 Ban on Contraceptives' in Margaret Preston and Margaret Ó hÓgartaigh (eds), *Gender and Medicine in Ireland 1700–1950* (Syracuse, NY, Syracuse University Press, 2012) ch 11; Yvonne Scannell, 'The Constitution and the Role of Women' in Brian Farrell (ed), *De Valera's Constitution and Ours* (Dublin, Gill and MacMillan, 1988) ch 9.

[60] *Mhic Mhathúna v Ireland* [1989] IR 504; *DPP v Tiernan* [1988] 1 IR 250.

[61] *McGee v Ireland* [1974] IR 284.

The year 1963 saw the first appointment of a female judge, Justice Eileen Kennedy, at the District Court, which is quite extraordinary given that it was not until 1976 that the procedural bars preventing women from serving on juries were removed following *de Búrca v Attorney General*.[62] The first female judicial appointment to the superior courts was that of Justice Mella Carroll in 1980, and there has been an at first rather slow but swelling number of women on the Irish bench since this period. For instance, the current President of the Supreme Court, Chief Justice Susan Denham, is a woman, as is the sitting President of the District Court.[63] Nonetheless, while our feminist judges in the ROI did not face the issue of a lack of female voice within the court system like their counterparts rewriting cases in Northern Ireland, there remains a question as to whether these voices, male or female, were and are necessarily feminist.[64] Enright J remarked, when workshopping *McGee*, that at the time the case was taken, women had as yet not entered the appeal courts, and thus she could only really have been a man during this period. In workshopping *McGimpsey*, O'Donoghue J perceived a level of homosociality amongst those involved in the case, in that they were all male and from the same social class, with very similar educational backgrounds, which appeared to be an important feature in the judiciary, particularly at the High Court, in identifying with the plaintiffs, albeit that they came from Northern Ireland.

A 2013 Government Report, *Toward Gender Parity in Decision-making in Ireland*, found that women 'are reaching the highest levels in the Judiciary to a much greater extent than in any of the other decision-making areas in Ireland', albeit that this falls short of the 40 per cent target set by the Government for women across decision-making roles within state institutions.[65] Currently 30 per cent of the Supreme Court, the Court of Appeal and High Court, with a slightly higher percentage at the Circuit Court and District Court levels, are women.[66] Rosemary Hunter asks whether a more diverse judiciary results in substantially different decision-makings, and concludes:

> The evidence suggests that this may but will not inevitably occur. And it will only occur under certain conditions. Those conditions are a combination of opportunity (in terms of both subject matter and legal space), plus personal commitment and/or external encouragement. Opportunities for most judges are likely to occur relatively infrequently. That is not, of course, a reason for soft pedalling on judicial diversity ... there are many other good reasons for having a more diverse judiciary—in terms of what the presence of non-traditional judges represents symbolically, how they manage their courtrooms, and the contributions they make behind the scenes and extrajudicially. But if we want a more diverse judiciary to result in fairer decision-making for all members of the community, to achieve 'equal justice for all' the opportunities must be grasped when they do arise.[67]

[62] *de Búrca v Attorney General* [1976] IR 38. This case found that the 1927 Juries Act was unconstitutional.

[63] The current Attorney General and Director of Public Prosecution and the Minister for Justice are also women, though these are more recent achievements, with the first female Attorney General being appointed in 2011.

[64] Hunter above n 35, 119–41.

[65] *Towards Gender Parity in Decision-making in Ireland: An initiative of the National Women's Strategy 2007–2016* (2013) 85, at www.justice.ie/en/JELR/FINALTowards%20Gender%20Parity.pdf/Files/FINALTowards%20Gender%20Parit.pdf (last accessed 17 March 2016).

[66] Details of the members of all courts are available at www.courts.ie (last accessed 17 March 2016).

[67] Hunter, above n 35, 119–41, 140–41.

A new structure for the appointment of judges, the Judicial Appointments Advisory Board (JAAB), was introduced under the Courts and Court Officers Act 1995. This aimed to initiate a more merit-based assessment of judicial appointments, as previous selections, which were controlled by the executive, were regarded as too political.[68] Critically in contrast to Northern Ireland, the Government is not obliged to appoint a person who is on the list of names recommended by the Board, although no Government has, as yet, chosen not to follow the recommendations. Presently, five out of the 12 members of the JAABare women, four of whom are from either the judiciary or the legal professions, with the fifth being an academic.[69]

Regarding the professions, whilst, as in Northern Ireland, there is a significantly higher percentage of women graduating with undergraduate and postgraduate degrees in law, it is taking some time to filter through to the senior levels of the judiciary, Bar and solicitors professions.[70] Remarkably, according to the Law Society of Ireland, Ireland is the first country where 'the number of female practising certificate holders exceeds their male counterparts'.[71] It is reported that this will also be the case at the Bar in the near future, albeit that women currently make up only 39 per cent of barristers.[72]

There have always been trailblazers in this regard.[73] The first woman to graduate in law in either Britain or Ireland was Letitia Alice Walkington, in 1888 from the Royal University of Ireland.[74] In 1901 a Miss Weir Johnston asked if a lady could become a member of the Irish Bar; this request was refused.[75] Frances Kyle and Averill Devrell were the first female barristers in 1921, prior to such appointments in England.[76] Mary Dorothea Heron became the first woman solicitor admitted in Ireland in 1923.[77] Georgina Frost, following a protracted legal battle, was the first woman to hold public office in the UK when she was appointed as a petty sessions clerk in Sixmilebridge, County Clare, in 1920.[78] During the period leading to independence, the operation of the Dáil Courts in parallel to the official state structure included women judges such as Hannah Sheehy Skeffington, Maude Gone

[68] Ward, above n 5; Eoin O'Malley, Stephan Quinlan and Peter Mair, 'Party Patronage in Ireland, Changing Parameters' in Petr Kopecký, Peter Mair, Maria Spirova (eds), *Party Patronage and Party Government in European Democracies* (Oxford, Oxford University Press, 2012) ch 11; Dermot Feenan, 'Judicial Appointments in Ireland in Comparative Perspective' (2008) 1(1) *Judicial Studies Institute Journal* 37–65.

[69] Further details are available at www.jaab.ie/ (last accessed 17 March 2016).

[70] *Towards Gender Parity in Decision-making in Ireland*, above n 65, 86.

[71] Teri Kelly, 'Professions Perfect Parity' Jan/Feb 2015 *Law Society Gazette* 20–21.

[72] Bar Council Annual Report, 2014–2015, 8, at http://issuu.com/scsreview/docs/barcouncilannualreport (last accessed 17 March 2016); Conor Gallagher, 'Why are so few women becoming senior counsel?', *The Irish Times*, 9 December 2008.

[73] Ivana Bacik and Eileen Drew, 'Struggling with juggling: Gender and work/life balance in the legal professions' (2006) 29(2) *Women's Studies International Forum* 136–46; Ivana Bacik, Cathryn Costello and Eileen Drew, *Gender InJustice: Feminising the Legal Professions?* (Dublin, Trinity College Dublin, 2003).

[74] Bacik, Costellow and Drew, above n 73, 53.

[75] ibid, 51.

[76] ibid; Matthew Holmes, *Female Lawyers in Ireland*, at www.first100years.org.uk/female-lawyers-in-ireland/ (last accessed 17 March 2016). Francis Kyle was also the first person called to the Northern Irish Bar on 7 November 1921.

[77] Bacik, Costellow and Drew, above n 73, 55.

[78] *Frost v Rex* [1919] IR 84; Ronan Keane, 'Frost, Georgina (1879–1939)', *Oxford Dictionary of National Biography* (Oxford, Oxford University Press, 2004).

McBride and Kathleen Clarke (who would become Dublin's first woman Lord Mayor).[79] Indeed, David Foxton has remarked that it took the Irish state over 40 years before it could match the number of women who were involved in law's operation during this period.[80] Other significant women writing about politics and law at the time included Sophie Bryant, who wrote about the possibilities of using the Brehon law to create a more equal Ireland upon independence.[81] In her book, *Liberty, order [and] law under native Irish rule: a study in the book of the ancient laws of Ireland*, she considers the need for pay that reflected women's labour and the protection of children, all of which she argued could be grounded in Brehon law.[82] She also clearly felt that women would be involved in creating the new law of the state that followed independence, and that this would be a more just system: '[t]hose fortunate Irish men and women, whose privilegeit will be to devise that system, will find much wisdom to their hand in the Great Ancient Law of the Gael'.[83] Ultimately, the hopes for an Ireland where the law and legal structures would be more open to women were dashed as the Free State was established, and Heather Laird remarks on what a different Ireland might have emerged had these ambitions come to fruition.[84] Hannah Sheehy Skeffington, Maud Gonne MacBride, Dorothy McArdle and Grace Plunkett created an informal group entitled 'The Optimists', which met to discuss the inequities of the new order that followed from so much hope for an Ireland that would be progressive on women's rights; and indeed political women of this period continued to protest as an ever increasing anti-feminist and Catholic doctrinal view of Ireland began to take hold.[85]

Judge Eileen Kennedy was the first woman to be appointed as a judge in 1963 and was 'the first female to sit in a court with her head uncovered', a point of much critique at the time.[86] Professor Frances Moran was the first female Senior Counsel in 1947; this is two years before a similar call in England, albeit that Ms Justice Mella Carroll was the first woman to practise as a Senior Counsel in 1977.[87] Professor Moran also had the distinction of being the first woman to hold a Chair in Law on either island.[88] Upon Professor Moran's death, an obituary was published in the *Dublin University Law Journal* by the then Regis Professor of Law RVF Heuston, the content of which bears remarking upon for the manner in which her professional accomplishments, as well as her private life, are discussed.[89]

[79] Dorothy Macardle, *The Irish Republic: A Documented Chronicle of the Anglo-Irish Conflict and the Partitioning of Ireland, with a Detailed Account of the Period 1916–1923* (California, Corgi Books, 1937).

[80] David Foxton, *Revolutionary Lawyers: Sinn Féin and the Crown Courts in Ireland and Britain 1916–1923* (Dublin, Four Courts Press, 2008).

[81] Sophie Bryant, *Liberty, order [and] law under native Irish rule: a study in the book of the ancient laws of Ireland* (London, Harding, 1923). She was apparently the first woman to own a bicycle: Peter Berresford Ellis, 'Sophie Bryant Part 2' in *Irish Democrat* (Dublin, Connolly Publications, 2008).

[82] Bryant, above n 81.

[83] ibid, 54.

[84] Laird, above n 10.

[85] Roy Foster, *Vivid Faces: The Revolutionary Generation 1890–1923* (London, Allen Lane, 2014) 315–17.

[86] Mary Redmond, 'The Emergence of Women in the Solicitors' Profession in Ireland' in Eamonn Hall and Daire Hogan (eds), *The Law Society of Ireland 1852–2002—Portrait of a Profession* (Dublin, Four Courts Press, 2002); Daire Hogan, *The Legal Profession in Ireland 1789–1922* (Dublin, Incorporated Law Society of Ireland, 1986) 37, 146–47.

[87] Matthew Holmes, *Female Lawyers in Ireland*, at www.first100years.org.uk/female-lawyers-in-ireland/ (last accessed 17 March 2016).

[88] VTH Delany, 'History of Legal Education in Ireland' (1959–60) 12 *Journal of Legal Education* 396–406.

[89] RFV Heuston 'Frances Elizabeth Moran' (1989) 11 *Dublin University Law Journal* 1–9.

First, the author makes some very particular personal comments about Professor Moran, including stating that 'nobody called her Fanny to her face a second time' and that her voice 'never grew shrill', implying that both her insistence on being called as she wished and her voice's not adopting a stereotypical female tone when passionate set her slightly apart from her sex.[90] Secondly, the first two paragraphs are dedicated to Professor Moran's father, with a final pronouncement suggesting that her very public life would have been at odds with her father's political outlook. Thirdly, the author almost immediately questions her professional qualifications. He comments that her doctorate was by publication, immediately suggesting that this was a lesser qualification that would be odd by today's standards, although doctorate by publication remains a possibility and one availed of by legal academics. Yet the author insists that her wish to be addressed as Dr Moran instead of Ms Moran was somehow strange.[91] The author also comments on the form of her lectures at Trinity College Dublin, dismissing their content as merely describing the law to her students. Thus he dismisses her skills as a lecturer, while simultaneously suggesting that this was the norm for lectures at the time.[92]

He goes on to question Professor Moran's qualifications as a SC, commenting that her call 'must have been more as a tribute to the respect in which the profession held her than to her fame as an advocate', as her work was mainly conveyancing and so 'involved paperwork rather than advocacy'.[93] Professor Heuston thus undermines both her academic Chair and her status as SC, commenting that she neither often appeared before the Court nor accepted academic invitations, out of fear of being 'outshone by other people': quite a remarkable statement regarding an SC and Chair of Law.[94] He also questions her nature as a women, commenting that 'Fran never stood in a supermarket queue'—an accusation that certainly would not be made in the obituary of a male academic or SC.[95]

The only area where the author is willing to give Professor Moran credit is with regard to women's education and the furtherance of women's position in society, perhaps because he felt this to be a more fitting role for her intellect.[96] The obituary is quite remarkable in its treatment of Professor Moran almost as a figure of fun, certainly as an oddity. This oddity is not seen as perhaps more common amongst idiosyncratic academics or SCs but as a strange role for a woman to play. The need to undermine both her qualifications and professional abilities, despite her huge accomplishments, seems completely unnecessary and entirely based on conjecture. That such an obituary could be published as late as 1989 is astonishing.

The first female head of the Law Society was Moya Quinlan, in 1980.[97] Fidelma Macken was the first woman Judge of the European Court of Justice in 1999. Justice Macken, who later served on the Supreme Court, was critical of attempts to frame her appointment in terms of her gender, as she felt this made no difference to her judgments, although she did

[90] ibid, 1, 7.
[91] ibid, 1.
[92] ibid, 4–6.
[93] ibid, 2.
[94] ibid.
[95] ibid.
[96] ibid, 6–8.
[97] Redmond, above n 86; Teri Kelly, 'Professions Perfect Parity' Jan/Feb 2015 *Law Society Gazette* 20–21.

describe her parents as feminists.[98] The juxtaposition between the 'firsts' that the Republic managed to have set against the cases in this collection is quite striking, and it suggests just how determined women were to push through the societal and legal constraints that had been put in place to prevent them from emerging within the legal professions.

It is also important to note that these were not the only women in courtrooms. As this project demonstrates, women appeared before and were subject to the decisions of judges on both sides of the border.[99] In taking cases, these women, like May McGee or Finola McKinley, were engaging politically with the legal order, generally in ways that they perhaps would rather not have chosen, but nonetheless they were making important marks on the judiciary. These women were also representative of a much broader part of Irish society that was not part of the political or economic elites, and which was thus much less likely to enter the professions or take the role of judge. It is imperative that these voices are not written out of our understanding of how judgments are considered in their historical context, in the way in which women are often deleted from other aspects of Irish history.[100]

Yet there remain deeply imbedded problems. For example, whilst the state hires women as briefs—and indeed the top-paid barristers were women from 2002–13—overall women are paid significantly less than their male counterparts, in 2012 receiving only 36 per cent of the total distribution of fees from the state.[101] Further, at the Bar, less than a quarter of appointments to Senior Counsel over the past decade have been women, with over 80 per cent of Senior Counsel being men.[102] The Bar Council of Ireland has recently introduced a mentoring system with the aim of ameliorating this issue; nonetheless, there is clearly quite a distance to go before the women who choose the Bar have equal opportunities to secure a place at the top of their profession.[103]

Locating the female legal voice in the Republic, while not as difficult as in Northern Ireland, certainly remains problematic. While the rise of women within the law at a higher rate than in other professions within the Republic suggests that law is not as unwelcoming for the female voice as other areas, this has not necessarily resulted in seniority; and even those voices that would identify as feminist still operate within a legal regime that, as this collection demonstrates, is not sympathetic to questions of gender. Certainly, while the move towards gender parity is to be welcomed and forms part of a broader societal change within the ROI where the dominant discourse is far from homogeneous, it is certainly not time to make a claim that a feminist voice is a clear presence within the law in the ROI.

[98] Sally Jane Kenney, *Gender and Justice: Why Women in the Judiciary Really Matter* (London, Routledge, 2013) 114–15.

[99] See, eg, Mary McAuliffe, '"To Change Society": Irishwomen United and Political Activism 1975–1979' in Mary McAuliffe and Clara Fischer (eds), *Irish Feminisms; Past, Present and Future* (Syracuse, NY, Arlen House, 2014).

[100] See, eg, the project on the 77 women who were detained following the 1916 rising. Details available at www.richmondbarracks.ie/women-1916/women-detainees-list/ (last accessed 17 March 2016).

[101] Elizabeth Fitzgerald, 'Barrister fee records reveal scale of gender inequality', *The Irish Times*, 20 January 2014.

[102] Conor Gallagher, 'Why are so few women becoming senior counsel?', *The Irish Times*, 9 December 2013.

[103] Bar Council Annual Report (2014–2015), 5, at http://issuu.com/scsreview/docs/barcouncilannualreport (last accessed 17 March 2016).

Voice of Women in Northern/Irish Legal Orders

The absence or presence of women within the legal order in Northern/Ireland has been significant to many of the judges involved in this project. For example, the lack of representation at the Senior/Queen's Counsel level has meant that in many of the cases in this collection, even when the litigants were female or the subject matter was intrinsically linked to women's questions, the majority, if not all, of the voices heard in the case will have been male. While this project would be unable to replicate the original hearings for obvious temporal and contextual reasons, the fact that the gender breakdown of the project would have required the same male participants to take on the roles of judges, counsel and solicitor, would have brought into stark relief the reality of the absence of women from the courts in Northern/Ireland.

This factor is important to bear in mind with regard to the types of arguments that counsel will have chosen to bring forward in the cases examined in the project. As the content of the arguments presented to the judges is critical to the choices that the judge can then make in coming to a decision, when all voices are homogeneous it begs the question of whether, for example, the lived experiences of women are ever given space for consideration by the court.

Non-judicial voices were particularly at issue in the *Kerry Babies* Tribunal, where the treatment of Joanne Hayes on the stand was of critical import. They were also present in *JM/PM v St Vincent's Hospital*, where the woman was gravely ill and thus unable to appear in court, and in the original judgment her voice was channelled through her husband. In *Re E* the applicant was a child and was represented by her mother; in *Lobe* the families are represented through the children. In *McGimpsey* the two brothers were considered to stand in the place of over half the population of Northern Ireland and to speak for them. *In the matter of Article 26 of the Constitution and in the matter of the Matrimonial Homes Bill* the issue was considered in the abstract without a particular litigant in mind; whilst in *Mhic Mhathúna* the case revolved around unmarried mothers, yet no unmarried mother was present or represented. In each of these instances the feminist judge has had to work within the strictures of these legal orders to find and assert the female voice, both as a judicial embodiment *and* with regard to the women represented and purported to be represented in the original cases.

The Northern/Irish project learned a tremendous amount from earlier projects in England, Canada and Australia, as well as from the excellent research that has been undertaken into judicial diversity and reasoning. In looking to Northern/Ireland and seeing how these issues played out here, we have been able to consider the particularised contextual issues that have been significant in judgment writing on the island. While both the shared common law and homogeneous character of the judiciary is something we unfortunately share with many other jurisdictions, the nature of the particularised Northern/Irish judicial experience has required specific responses in looking to embodying a Northern/Irish feminist judge and giving voice to that strain of judicial reasoning that has long been absent from the judgment-writing process on the island.

There is not an inevitability to the legal structures and form of judicial writing in Northern/Ireland. As was discussed with regard to the critical role individual women have played in the evolution of law in Ireland, there have been moments—for example the late nineteenth and early twentieth centuries—when women were not kept apart from the judicial role, and were directly engaged in debate as to how Irish law and legal structures ought to develop. It was a political decision to remove the female voice from the law, and for quite a considerable period this attempt to eliminate women from the bounded judicial and professional arenas was largely successful. Yet it is possible to reignite those moments from the past where women pushed for access to the judicial world. Those early pioneers ought to act as catalysts in both re-imagining what might have been and also stressing the import of the feminist judicial voice to ensure that it is never again removed from debates on the future of Northern/Ireland.

Part II

Mothering Subjects

5

Commentary on *McGee v Attorney General*

EMILIE CLOATRE AND MÁIRÉAD ENRIGHT[1]

Hearing Mrs McGee

In *McGee*,[2] the Supreme Court overturned the statutory ban in the Criminal Law Amendment Act 1935 (the 1935 Act) on the importation of contraceptives to Ireland. In her feminist judgment, Máiréad Enright takes the place of a majority judge on that Court, reaching the same conclusions but for different reasons. She adopts an unsettled judicial persona. Women did not sit on the Irish superior courts in 1973; Enright J is, therefore, something of a 'drag act'.[3] To that end, the judgment ventriloquises Irish men who disapproved of the 1935 Act and the regime of social control it represented. It draws in particular on Austin Clarke,[4] Samuel Beckett,[5] George Bernard Shaw,[6] Patrick Belton

1 Our thanks to those interviewed whose stories are incorporated into this commentary. Thanks as well to the people, too many to name, who welcomed us into their homes, shared personal archives and photographs, and provided us with contact details for interviewees. More complete accounts of the family planning movement in Ireland are in progress, but we are happy to hear from anyone who, having read this account, wishes to correct or add to it. This commentary is dedicated to the memory of the wonderful Martina Keogh, who was interviewed for this project and who died in 2015.

2 *McGee v Attorney General* [1974] IR 284. Note that *McGee* is the earliest case in this collection.

3 Rosemary Hunter, Clare McGlynn and Erika Rackley, *Feminist Judgments: From Theory to Practice* (Oxford, Hart Publishing, 2010) 8.

4 The judgment's reference to 'tired obedience' is a nod to Austin Clarke's 1967 poem, 'The Redemptorist', which depicts a woman whose confessor orders her to submit to further pregnancies despite her serious illness: '"No pregnancy. You'll die the next time," / The doctor had said. / Her tiredness obeyed / That Saturday night; her husband's weight / Digging her grave.' *Collected Poems of Austin Clarke* (New York, AMS Press, 1978) 379.

5 The reference to 'our Northern borders' gestures to a line from Samuel Beckett's novel *Watt*. Part of the narrative in *Watt* centres on an aphrodisiac called Bando, banned by a country that closely mimics the Irish Free State: '[Bando] cannot enter our ports, nor cross our northern borders, if not in the form of hazardous and surreptitious dribble. I mean piecemeal in ladies' underclothing, for example, or gentlemen's golfbags or the hollow missal of a broad minded priest, where on discovery it is immediately seized, and confiscated, by some gross customs official half-crazed with seminal intoxication and sold, at ten and even fifteen times its advertised value, to exhausted commercial travellers on their way home after an unprofitable circuit.' The ban on Bando represents the Free State's frequently-circumvented ban on contraception. Samuel Beckett, *Watt* (London, Faber & Faber, 2012) 146.

6 The reference to 'calling our souls our own' references Shaw's characterisation of the Free State, which began to restrict access to contraception, as 'a little grass patch in which a few million moral cowards are not allowed to call their souls their own, by a handful of morbid Catholics'. Cited in Diarmaid Ferriter, *Occasions of Sin: Sex and Society in Modern Ireland* (London, Profile Books, 2009) 188.

TD[7] and Noel Browne TD.[8] The patchwork result is a voice of reflective, but nonetheless male, authority, certain of its own importance.

We interviewed May and Shay McGee as part of a larger project on organised resistance to the 1935 Act. May McGee's voice, heard throughout this commentary, is very different from that assumed by Enright. It is the voice of a young woman who was sitting in the stalls of a room in the Four Courts in Dublin in December 1973, intently writing a list of Christmas toys to buy for her children, as the men around her deliberated on her rights.[9] May McGee's experience was of not being listened to by men in power. Her request to the customs officers to release her package of Staycept jelly was denied: 'I wrote just explaining and they still didn't want to know.'[10] Her case in the High Court was dismissed within, it seemed to her, mere minutes: 'I don't think we even sat down'.[11] Of O'Keeffe J, May McGee says:

> [He] just threw it out, didn't want to know … He didn't even listen, didn't even try five minutes and I couldn't believe it and I said to myself 'Is that the way women are really treated?' sort of thing … I have to say that it was only then I realised just how badly women were really treated in the way we were seen but not heard. Our opinion didn't count.[12]

Enright J's reasoning reflects an attempt to redress that silencing, by honouring women's experiences under the 1935 Act.

The Marital Family in *McGee*

Enright J moves away from the original judgment's status-based reading of marriage as an institution deserving of protection in itself, to a relational reading, which foregrounds the individual agency of the partners. This move reflects a basic feminist critique of family privacy;[13] that if we fail to distinguish between the partners' interests, we may not give

[7] Patrick Belton TD, speaking in the Second Stage Debate on the Control of Importation, Sale and Manufacture of Contraceptives Bill, 11 July 1974: 'Men have been discussing a problem which is 90 per cent a woman's problem. Men have a part in it but a woman lives with it. It is a part of her nature. She has to bear the children. She has a monthly period. She becomes pregnant. She has morning sickness for three months. She carries the child for nine months with all the risk of a miscarriage. She is thinking of the child all the time. The child may be born dead. Consider the sorrow and depression that go with that. She has the pain of childbirth. She has to build up her health before and afterwards. The husband who causes the pregnancy visits her in the nursing home and goes out and gets drunk. He celebrates for a week when a child is born. Women are involved, not men, and men are laying down the law for women.'

[8] Dr Noel Brown speaking on the Commission on the Status of Women on July 25 1973: 'It seems to me that it [sending a child to pre-school while its mother goes to work] represents a very ignorant—and I am using a crude word—misunderstanding of the role of the mother to her children if she thinks that having a baby is just like a cow dropping a calf in a field and going away and leaving it for somebody else to rear.' Dr Browne was supportive of Senator Mary Bourke's contraceptive legislation, attempting to get it read in the Dáil in 1972. His words are put in Enright J's mouth as a nod to the conflicted and often contradictory position of liberal men under patriarchy.

[9] Interview, Mary and Seamus McGee, 25 June 2014.

[10] ibid.

[11] ibid.

[12] ibid.

[13] The judgment pursues a privacy justification rather than an equality justification for reproductive rights. For feminist critiques of privacy-based justifications, see Sara Ahmed, *Differences That Matter: Feminist Theory and Postmodernism* (Cambridge, Cambridge University Press, 1998) 38–40; Lauren Berlant, 'The Subject of True Feeling: Pain, Privacy and Politics' in Jodi Dean (ed), *Cultural Studies and Political Theory* (Cornell, NY, Cornell

enough space to those of the woman. Henchy J, for example, imagined the criminal law violently imposing itself on the marital relationship. This is very much a male lawyer's construction of the relevant harm. Enright J's feminist approach allows us to see more of women's experience. Married couples were not prosecuted under the 1935 Act.[14] The injury most commonly done to married women was that which Enright J takes time to describe: they were deprived of opportunities to control their own fertility; they suffered stress and ill-health; and they were often humiliated and disciplined by those empowered to restrict their access to contraception, particularly doctors, priests, state officials and their own husbands. The men and women we interviewed who became part of the early family planning movement often alluded to these experiences, which intermingled religion, conservative medical practice and uncertainty about the law. One interviewee, who later became a family planning nurse, described her experience in asking her doctor to renew the prescription he had given her for the contraceptive pill (which some doctors prescribed for non-contraceptive purposes) after her first daughter was born:

> He said, 'Do you want that for contraceptive purposes?' I said, 'I suppose I do, yes.' I'd never thought what I wanted. I just knew it stopped you having babies. He said, 'Go to one of your own kind.' And turned his back on me; I didn't know who 'one of my own kind' was.[15]

Another woman, later a leader in the family planning movement in the West of Ireland, told us:

> [My husband] was a student as well and we didn't want to have children immediately so we went looking for contraceptives and we couldn't get condoms in Galway, so I went to a doctor in Galway trying to get the pill and he wouldn't give me the pill. He said not until you have a child. You had to prove first that you had a child ...[16]

An early Irish Family Planning Association (IFPA) volunteer described her sense of the costs of the Church's approach to family planning:

> This little woman, small in stature came in wearing this navy coat. I still see her ... and she said, 'I hope you can help me' and I said, 'I'm sure we can'. When she came out [having seen the doctor] I said, 'Well, were we able to help you?' and she said, 'Oh, not really. I couldn't use any of those things' ... and I naively said to her, 'If I get a priest to talk to you will you come back to us?' The chaplain attached to the primary school I taught in had worked in Birmingham so I thought that we would have a liberal member of the Roman Catholic Church and I very naively spoke to him. But of course that was the end of that. That is one of my strongest memories of that woman being abandoned I suppose is what you could say.[17]

Of course, some women found supportive doctors and others found supportive priests, but the point is that the law at the time of McGee's case reduced many women to

University Press, 2000) 48–55; Catharine A MacKinnon, *Toward a Feminist Theory of the State* (Cambridge, MA, Harvard University Press, 1989) 184–94. For an equality-focused alternative, see Drucilla Cornell, 'Dismembered Selves' in Wendy Brown and Janet Halley (eds), *Left Legalism/Left Critique* (Durham NC, Duke University Press, 2002) 379.

[14] This is not to say that women who illegally obtained contraceptives never encountered legal troubles as a result. Sex workers, in particular, were vulnerable to having condoms confiscated by the gardaí on a variety of pretexts: Interview, MK, 22 July 2015.

[15] Interview, NS, 1 July 2014.

[16] Interview, ES, 26 June 2014.

[17] Interview, FP, 25 June 2014.

dependence on powerful interlocutors who often refused to help them. Enright J is attentive, particularly in the opening narrative, to the precarious situation in which the law placed the McGees; one that they could not remedy despite their best efforts. May McGee referred to their position as 'Russian roulette'.[18]

McGee and Conscience

Here, Enright J develops an argument dismissed in both the High and Supreme Courts. Walsh J held that the protections of Article 44 were confined to religious conscience,[19] whereas May McGee, he said, was making an argument from social conscience. The conscience argument, by contrast, was important to May McGee: 'I felt that we should be able to think for ourselves. We were paying taxes, we were working, we were having kids, we were doing everything and we weren't allowed to think!'[20] The argument was also important to feminists at the time: it was printed on an Irish Women's Liberation Movement leaflet distributed to those who travelled on the 'contraceptive train' to Belfast in Northern Ireland in 1971.[21] The point of the recourse to conscience is to frame some of the burdens of pregnancy, not only as bodily concerns, but also as concerns going to the root of human personality. The overall effect—mirroring Ruth Fletcher's work on *AG v X* in this collection[22]—is to sketch the possibilities as they existed at the time—integrating arguments from the rights to privacy, bodily integrity, freedom of conscience—for an essentially pro-choice constitutional position;[23] one that sees women's 'sacred trust'[24] in terms of personal commitment to conceive and rear children, rather than in terms of overwhelming duty.

Enright J first demonstrates that May McGee's use of contraceptives engaged her freedom of religious conscience. In doing so, she gestures towards the impact of the 1935 Act on minorities whose faiths did not prohibit the use of contraception.[25] Protestant doctors came under intense scrutiny lest they prescribe contraceptives to Catholic women,[26] and the first prosecutions under the legislation were of Quaker[27] and Jewish

[18] Interview, Mary and Seamus McGee, 25 June 2014.

[19] The judgment was only elaborated upon very recently in *AM v Refugee Appeals Tribunal* [2014] IEHC 388, paras 32–34.

[20] Interview, Mary and Seamus McGee, 25 June 2014.

[21] See further June Levine, *Sisters: The Personal Story of an Irish Feminist* (Cork, Attic Press, 2009).

[22] See ch 18.

[23] The *McGee* decision arguably fuelled demands for the Eighth Amendment, which constitutionalises extreme restrictions on abortion. See, eg, Emily O'Reilly, *Masterminds of the Right* (Cork, Attic Press, 1992) 47–48. The feminist judgment does not attempt to address that possibility by disguising the judgment's pro-choice potential.

[24] In *Norris v AG* [1984] IR 36, 103, decided prior to the passage of the Eighth Amendment, McCarthy J describes pregnancy as a 'sacred trust'. In this judgment Enright uses the same language to describe autonomously chosen motherhood.

[25] Sandra McAvoy, 'A Perpetual Nightmare: Women, Fertility Control, the Irish State and the 1935 Ban on Contraceptives' in Margaret Helen Preston (ed), *Gender and Medicine in Ireland, 1700–1950* (New York, Syracuse University Press, 2012) 197–99, discussing the pressures on Protestant doctors in the aftermath of the Papal Encyclical.

[26] Lindsey Earner-Byrne, *Mother and Child: Maternity and Child Welfare in Dublin, 1922–60* (Manchester, Manchester University Press, 2013) 42.

[27] The Quaker firm of Henry Bell Chemists in Waterford was among the first to be prosecuted under the 1935 Act. The firm had ordered contraceptives prescribed by doctors. The District Judge dismissed the defendants under the Probation Act: 'Waterford Firm Charged', *Munster Express*, 16 March 1936. The defendants' counsel

pharmacists.[28] Enright J also sets the decision in the context of contemporary Catholic debates on the permissibility of using artificial contraception. The Church held that even where further pregnancies posed a great threat to the woman's health, contraception could not be used; a married couple in that position were advised to 'live together as brother and sister'.[29]

Enright J gently subverts Article 41, which is typically associated with the reproduction of dominant familial ideology. In this judgment, the family becomes a site for conscientious departure from state-supported religious norms. This reasoning reflects the reality of the time. At the time the McGees were preparing for marriage, many Catholics expected that the Vatican would relax the traditional position on contraception. By the time the 1968 Papal Encyclical *Humanae Vitae* confirmed, to their surprise, that there would be no change, some Irish doctors were already offering contraception to their patients.[30] The contraceptive pill, as the Chief Justice acknowledged in *McGee*, had been available in Ireland since 1963, and thousands of women were taking it on the pretext that it was a 'cycle regulator'.[31] Despite the Irish hierarchy's determined attempts to enforce the reaffirmed teaching, ordinary Catholics were making up their own minds. May McGee recalled that in the course of bringing the case, she and her husband were 'practically condemned from the altar' while at Mass. 'I didn't leave the church, I stayed there ... People were still talking to us; people didn't really seem to mind because they all knew change had to come.'[32] Individual conscientious departures from Catholic social teaching were crucial to the transformations embodied in decisions like *McGee*. The feminist judgment aims to foreground that social shift.

Enright J's focus on conscience is also appropriate given the political underpinnings of the 1935 Act, which go largely unacknowledged in the original judgments. The Act is a product of a period in Irish history in which sexual conduct was a particular focus of state regulation,[33] and nation-building became synonymous with the control of women and the enforcement of conservative Catholic mores. In the newly independent state, contraceptives—by then in reasonably wide use among middle-class women,[34] and readily and legally available by mail order from England[35] and in some shops[36]—were viewed through

was Frederick Budd BL, later Budd J, who was part of the majority in *McGee*. Budd told the court that the Bells were 'ordinary, decent, law-abiding citizens' and, as pharmacists, 'bound to keep every species of drug that might alleviate suffering': 'Prosecution Against Waterford Firm', *Munster Express*, 20 March 1936, 7.

[28] David Glick, a Jewish chemist's assistant and a man of the 'highest character', was fined £100 for importing contraceptives he had bought while on holiday in London: 'Criminal Law Charges', *The Irish Times*, 3 July 1936, 13. Ivor Kronn, a Jewish shopkeeper, was fined over £150 and sentenced to six months' imprisonment for offences under the 1935 Act: 'Prison Sentence to Stand', *Irish Independent*, 23 October 1936, 3.

[29] John Cooney, *John Charles McQuaid: Ruler of Catholic Ireland* (Dublin, The O'Brien Press, 2012) 279. The McGees recalled that counsel in the High Court asked them why they would not live by this advice.

[30] ibid, 393–94.

[31] Michael Solomons, *Pro Life?: The Irish Question* (Dublin, Lilliput Press, 1992) 10.

[32] Interview, Mary and Seamus McGee, 25 June 2014.

[33] Una Crowley and Rob Kitchin, 'Producing Decent Girls' (2008) 15(4) *Gender, Place and Culture* 355–72.

[34] On women's use of birth control in the Free State, see McAvoy, above n 25 at 190–94; Greta Jones, 'Marie Stopes in Ireland—The Mother's Clinic in Belfast, 1936–47' (1992) 5(2) *Social History of Medicine* 255–77, 258.

[35] McAvoy, above n 25, 190, notes that by 1934 the customs authorities had ceased to seize imported contraceptives under the existing law.

[36] See Ferriter, above n 6, at 194. Some pharmacists employed ruses to keep their trade. In 1936, the Dublin manager of a pharmacist's shop, Charles Joseph Brocklebank, was also prosecuted under the Act, for keeping for sale tins of condoms bearing the legend 'for prevention of disease only': 'Criminal Law Charges', *The Irish Times*, 3 July 1936, 13. See also 'Illegal Imports Charge', *The Irish Times*, 29 July 1936, 2.

the lens of public morality rather than of public or maternal health. The Evil Literature Committee of 1927 and the Carrigan Committee of 1931 argued that continued ready access to birth control would 'remove the consequences of sexual indulgence among the unmarried',[37] exacerbate a perceived 'loss of parental control' over young women[38] and expose the fledgling Irish State to new risks of depopulation: so-called 'race suicide'.[39] The influence of these views was soon felt in law. By 1929, it was illegal to advertise contraceptives or to publish printed matter 'advocating the unnatural prevention of conception'.[40] Nevertheless, there was public acknowledgement from the Carrigan Committee, as well as from a minority of politicians and prominent doctors,[41] that some women should be permitted to access contraception on grounds of reproductive health.[42] That in 1935 the new Fianna Fáil Government enacted a total prohibition on importation and sale speaks to a particular kind of religious nationalism.[43] A hard line on contraception distinguished the new Catholic state from its former coloniser.[44] In particular, the total prohibition on sale and importation, with no health exception, was closer to the latest Catholic teaching, embodied in the 1930 Papal Encyclical *Casti Connubii*.[45] It departed from the teaching of the Church of Ireland, which allowed artificial contraception to preserve the woman's health. The 1935 Act was the latest in a long list of Free State initiatives intended to control women's behaviour by regulating cinema,[46] publications,[47] drinking[48] and dancing,[49] and by excluding them from jury service[50] and state employment.[51] At the same time, Church and state co-operated in the construction of carceral regimes intended to punish and 'reform' unmarried mothers, and to deter other women from having sexual intercourse

[37] Sandra McAvoy, 'Regulation of Sexuality in the Irish Free State' in Greta Jones and Elizabeth Malcolm (eds), *Medicine, Disease and the State in Ireland, 1650–1940* (Cork, Cork University Press, 1999) 254.

[38] ibid, 259.

[39] See Jones, above n 34, at 257–58.

[40] Censorship Act 1929, s 16(1). On the history of the Act, see John Horgan, 'Saving Us from Ourselves: Contraception, Censorship and the "Evil Literature" Controversy of 1926' (1995) 5 *Irish Communications Review* 61–67. Pharmacists and booksellers were already open to prosecution under the Obscene Publications Act 1857. See Ferriter, above n 6, at 189. Some years later, in 1957, Alan Simpson, the head of the Pike Theatre Company, was prosecuted for the common law offence of obscene libel: *AG v Simpson* (1959) 93 ILTR 33. Simpson was charged with 'showing for gain an obscene and profane performance'. In his production of Tennessee Williams' *The Rose Tattoo*, the actress Anna Manahan had mimed the action of throwing a condom to the floor. Simpson was eventually acquitted, but the prosecution contributed to the closing of the theatre. See further Lionel Pilkington, *Theatre and the State in Twentieth-Century Ireland: Cultivating the People* (London, Routledge, 2002) 156; Joan FitzPatrick Dean, *Riot and Great Anger: Stage Censorship in Twentieth-Century Ireland* (Madison, WI, University of Wisconsin Press, 2010) 156–59.

[41] See Ferriter, above n 6, at 193; Chrystel Hug, *The Politics of Sexual Morality in Ireland* (London, Palgrave Macmillan, 1998) 82.

[42] McAvoy, above n 37, at 200.

[43] Sandra McAvoy suggests that Fianna Fáil's Sean T O'Kelly—later President of Ireland—played a key role in tipping the balance: ibid, 202. See similarly Ferriter, above n 6, at 193; Mary E Daly, *The Slow Failure: Population Decline and Independent Ireland, 1920–1973* (Madison, WI, University of Wisconsin Press, 2006) 91.

[44] McAvoy, above n 25, at 202. De Valera rejected Archbishop John Charles McQuaid's request for a constitutional ban on contraception: Cooney, above n 29, 98.

[45] See further, Daly, above n 43, at 89–90.

[46] Censorship of Films Act 1923.

[47] Censorship of Publications Act 1929.

[48] Intoxicating Liquor Acts 1924 and 1927.

[49] Dance Halls Act 1935.

[50] Juries Acts 1924 and 1927.

[51] Civil Service Amendment Act 1925; Conditions of Employment Act 1934.

outside of marriage.[52] The marital family was exalted as the foundational unit of Irish society, at the expense of women who transgressed its boundaries.[53] The home was woman's proper place.[54] The accompanying social denigration of unmarried pregnant women was apparent to May McGee as a young woman:

> [M]en made their own rules. But that [having sex outside marriage] was alright for them but never OK for us and we were the ones that had the bun in an oven if we got into trouble and we were the ones that were getting the bad name ... you were afraid to get pregnant years ago because it was such a disgrace wasn't it and it's hard to believe it. We were so, women were treated very bad weren't they? They [men] got away with it.[55]

In her judgment, Enright J takes judicial notice of the difficult position of unmarried pregnant women in Ireland in the 1970s, foreshadowing recent public acknowledgement of the wrongfulness of the state's support for industrial schools, Magdalen Laundries, and Mother and Baby homes. In describing the position of unmarried women, the judgment borrows a great deal from Henchy J's later dissenting judgment in *Norris v AG*;[56] describing women's experiences using some of the sensitive and empathetic language he used to describe a gay male plaintiff's degradation under a hostile criminal law.[57]

Beyond the Judgment: Transformative Illegality

Irish readers will be familiar with stories of individuals importing condoms for their own use, from abroad or over the border with Northern Ireland.[58] The judgment may give the impression that May McGee was one of these lone importers. This is not the whole story. Although she was the first to challenge the law in its own space—the courtroom—two groups were breaking the law in an organised fashion on a daily basis. The Fertility Guidance Company (later the IFPA) and Family Planning Services Ltd (FPS) were both created with a view to making contraceptives available to patients.[59] The IFPA was at its founding in 1968 a 'medical' organisation, which supplied contraceptives to individuals via its clinics, while FPS, officially founded a few months after the 1972 High Court decision in

[52] Local Government (Temporary Provisions) Act 1922; Maternity Homes Act 1934. See further James Smith, *Ireland's Magdalen Laundries and the Nation's Architecture of Containment* (Notre Dame, IN, University of Notre Dame Press, 2007).

[53] Crowley and Kitchin, above n 33.

[54] ibid.

[55] Interview, Mary and Seamus McGee, 25 June 2014.

[56] *Norris v AG* [1984] IR 36.

[57] Henchy J in that judgment describes the transformation of Norris's 'fear into indignation'. He notes that 'denigratory and hurtful treatment [has been] meted out to him' and that 'in a number of subtle but insidiously intrusive and wounding ways he has been restricted in, or thwarted from, engaging in activities which heterosexuals take for granted as aspects of the necessary expression of their human personality and as ordinary incidents of their citizenship'.

[58] Jones, above n 34, documents connections between the family planning movement in the North and women living in the South.

[59] More detail on FPS's activities emerged in a High Court case in 1976, as discussed in the final section of this commentary. The Court heard that FPS provided a postal and personal service to about 30,000 couples in the state in respect of the supply of contraceptives and family planning advice.

McGee, focused exclusively on the wider distribution of non-medical contraceptive devices. These law-breaking groups were established at a time of increased political agitation around access to contraceptives. Late in 1970, the Irish Family Planning Rights Association (IFPRA) had set up to lobby for law reform on contraception. One of its members, Senator Mary Robinson, made the first of seven attempts in 1971 to introduce a family planning bill in Parliament, but could not obtain colleagues' support.[60] The Irish Women's Liberation Movement (IWLM) had also spoken out against the contraceptive legislation in its manifesto *Chains or Change*, and had famously staged the 'contraceptive train' in May 1971, importing contraceptives from Northern Ireland via Connolly Station, and in the process demonstrating that the state would not stop them.[61]

The Ireland of the early 1970s hosted a vibrant cluster of agents and activities concerned with the question of generalised access to contraceptives in Ireland, animated by a shared sense that the 1935 Act was unjust and unviable. To them, contraceptives were an essential aspect of family planning, and family life, and the state's attempts to prevent women from accessing them had unacceptable social and personal consequences.[62] Thus the law had a very obvious—if not necessarily exceptional—dual character: it was highly problematic in political terms, but it had lost practical significance to many because it was so frequently broken. As a feminist activist based in Cork explained to us, 'I thought it was so ridiculous anyway, everybody knew it was ridiculous. Now, if you asked a taxi driver where to get contraceptives, they'd tell you. The whole thing was just so ridiculous.'[63]

The founders of FPS were neither doctors, nor lawyers, nor politicians but ordinary and otherwise law-abiding citizens, many of whom had been members of IFPRA or the IFPA. It started as small-scale project of distribution, mainly of condoms, by mail order. But by the time May McGee's case came to the High Court, this project was starting to grow faster than any of its creators had anticipated. There was a clear demand for contraception across Ireland; FPS's condoms could be supplied without a doctor's intervention, and mail order was an effective tool for mass distribution that matched the few resources the group could assemble. Mail order was private, and was accessible to people living outside Dublin who could not readily travel to the IFPA clinic. The group was largely built through personal connections between its founders and a few friendly supporters. The beginnings were small and simple. A pharmacist in the North of Ireland had agreed to receive the deliveries that FPS placed with the London Rubber Company (now Durex). Frank Crummey, one of the founders of FPS, travelled over the border in a small van, as often as he could, to collect supplies, smuggling the products back in large boxes. Frank, who had worked with An Post, had arranged for orders to be delivered to a post office box in central Dublin, and the address was publicised by the media.[64] Customers wrote from all over the country, often including long descriptions of their personal circumstances, asking for contraceptives and enclosing a donation. A packet of condoms was £1. On Thursdays, a small production line would be

[60] Ferriter, above n 6, at 410.

[61] Angela Bourke, 'June Levine. From Sisters: The Personal Story of an Irish Feminist (1982)' in *The Field Day Anthology of Irish Writing* (New York, New York University Press, 2002) 200–01.

[62] On changing public attitudes to contraception in Ireland, see Yvonne Galligan, *Women and Politics in Contemporary Ireland: From the Margins to the Mainstream* (London, Pinter, 1998) 150.

[63] Interview, GS, 4 July 2014.

[64] Interview, AMcC, 23 June 2014.

started on a member's kitchen table, where orders would be opened and products packaged, stamped and prepared for their imminent postal travel.[65] In time, FPS would enclose an order form and 'price list' of suggested donations with each order, with spare forms for customers to give to friends.[66] The founders were volunteers, balancing this work with demanding day-jobs and with rearing young families.

These activities were illegal under the 1935 Act if you consider that FPS was selling contraceptives and importing them for sale. The IFPA's doctors, including Dr Loughran, gave its own order forms to clients, who used them to purchase condoms, spermicides and diaphragms from the International Planned Parenthood Federation, receiving them in the post from England in small flat packages.[67] The clients here, like May McGee, bore the risk of illegality. Doctors might also supply contraceptives free of charge to those who could not pay, or to tide clients over until their order arrived, and the IFPA used a network of friends and supporters to import small amounts of contraceptives illegally for this purpose.[68] But the founders of FPS decided to try to circumvent the Act's provisions on sale by using a different practice. They saw a 'loophole'; that they could sell contraceptives without admitting that they were selling.[69] To this end, they relied on a system of 'donations'. Instead of asking for 'payment' for the products they distributed, they suggested an amount of money that customers might wish to donate. By converting 'payment' to 'donation', FPS could argue that it was neither selling nor importing for sale. The founders did not wait for lawyers or litigation to confirm their entitlement to operate in this manner; they were confident of their own interpretation. This somewhat thin but important interpretive argument proved sound in practice. It allowed FPS to maintain a veneer of legality about its activities, and by all accounts, the group's right to operate in this way was never directly challenged. The demand for contraceptives was such that, very quickly, FPSs mail order business grew to the point where, by 1973, the company could establish a small staffed office in Leeson Street in Dublin from which condoms were sold, and later a full family planning clinic on Pembroke Road, purely from the income generated by the sales. By the time of May McGee's case, FPS, the IFPA and the IFPRA constituted a small but vibrant network that had already thought about and strategised possibilities to challenge, or break, the contraceptive laws:

> It was just getting bigger and bigger … Now the objective is still to change the law but while the if you like the family planning rights association were going along with meetings and public meetings and we were actually supplying a market for which there was a demand and it kind of grew I mean it went from literally around a kitchen table into premises and our objective was always to actually get the law changed and things were starting to move in the parliament. There was a movement.[70]

Though not associated with those movements in any formal sense, May McGee and her case were closely connected to them. May McGee's doctor, Jim Loughran, who became an important witness in her case, was involved in the IFPRA and was a founder of the IFPA. Dr Loughran was also instrumental in establishing the FPS.[71] He was therefore well aware

[65] Interview, AMcC, 23 June 2014; Interview, DMcC, 12 March 2014; Interview, FC, 19 February 2014.
[66] Interview, DMcC 12 March 2014; Interview, RC, 25 June 2014.
[67] Solomons, above n 31 at 14.
[68] ibid.
[69] Interview, RC, 25 June 2014.
[70] Interview, AMcC, 23 June 2014.
[71] Interview, DMcC, 12 March 2014; Interview, RC, 25 June 2014.

both of the contraceptive dilemma faced by May McGee (and indeed had prescribed her both a diaphragm and the contraceptive jelly she was seeking to import) and of the broader legal and political context in which her difficulties were entangled. Some of his associates in the nascent family planning movement, were also keen to bring a constitutional case challenging the 1935 Act, but needed a 'frontrunner'; a litigant with a compelling personal case.[72] There is little doubt that, from their perspective,[73] May's case, and her specific health difficulties, presented a unique opportunity to bring the challenges to the law they had been pursuing through their own activities into the space of the courtroom. As May McGee's barrister, Donal Barrington, explained to us, Dr Loughran 'had strong views on contraception and … here he had a patient who was in risk of death if she had another pregnancy and so, it was the classic case'.[74]

This relationship placed May McGee in a privileged position to think about her possibilities for challenging the law, and for understanding the complexity of the legal and political landscape surrounding access to contraceptives at the time. Although the support of Dr Loughran and others was important, the case was triggered by her own frustration with the difficulties she had in accessing contraceptives to which she and her doctor felt she should be entitled, and by her own desire to do everything she possibly could to secure access to contraceptives as of right. Her solicitor, Dudley Potter, said Dr Loughran 'may have encouraged her but I think that when she came to me I think she was her own person, she wanted to take this case and she wanted to challenge it'.[75] It is clear too, that while the original judgment repeatedly hints at her fragility and vulnerability, the case was enabled by May's sheer strength and determination:

> She was a strong-minded woman you know and she … had a practical problem. I mean, she was told by her doctor 'if you have another pregnancy, you are in danger of death' and she just went with it, you know?[76]

May McGee herself said of her journey to the Supreme Court, 'I really couldn't believe that you had to do so much fighting to get there and be heard. It was like they didn't want to listen, the rule was made and that was it.'[77] She was intimidated sometimes, by the questioning, by the 'horrible' setting of the Four Courts and by 'those fellows in the big wigs and they looking down at you'.[78] Nevertheless, her commitment was real. She was willing, if she lost in the Supreme Court, to go to Strasbourg. She was willing, if it came to it, to go to prison.[79]

The *McGee* judgment affected the early family planning movement in three ways. First, the *McGee* case did not immediately result in legislation. Fine Gael's Control of Importation, Sale and Manufacture of Contraceptives Bill 1974 did not pass. In the period between the decision and Fianna Fáil's eventual legislation in 1979, the official legal impact of *McGee* was unclear. During this period, FPS was able to rely on its own expansive interpretation of the judgment. It relied on the *McGee* decision to import thousands of condoms

[72] Interview, RC, 25 June 2014.
[73] Interview, FC, 19 February 2014.
[74] Interview, DB, 23 June 2014.
[75] Interview, DP, 24 June 2014.
[76] Interview, DB, 23 June 2014.
[77] Interview, Mary and Seamus McGee, 25 June 2014.
[78] ibid.
[79] ibid.

in bulk, under the ruse that, since section 17(3) of the 1935 Act had been struck down by the Supreme Court, members were entitled to import sufficient condoms for 'their own personal use'. This interpretation was never directly contested in the courts, but it certainly provided a working remedy. Our interviewees seemed agreed that the police were either tolerant of, or indifferent to their activities. A story from the Galway Family Planning Clinic illustrates some of the contradictions at play:

> We did have a burglary in the clinic once and it was after we moved to Merchants Road and it happened on St Patrick's weekend. I think it was, yes and of course the Gardaí had to be called then and it was great sport because they all came up very seriously. The guards were all dead serious back then, they were dusting for fingerprints all over the boxes of Durex. But of course, they knew who did it; the guards knew who were involved. They were youngsters you know and they might have thought there was money on the premises, that sort of thing. It was really nothing more and nothing less but it was just the idea of you know, it was all followed up and all the rest of it by the guards but it was the idea of them being inside all over the clinic dusting with these feathers. But anyway, from that point of view really things really died down quickly enough.[80]

Indeed, it must be borne in mind that the police themselves were often using the services of the family planning movement. Customs seizures and stoppages were also rare, and could be negotiated with a degree of skill and tact. A favourite story of many interviewees involved Frank Crummey's evading seizure at a police checkpoint by citing his interpretation of *McGee*:

> I had to import from London Rubber to import it down, from the North of Ireland, across the border and every second Saturday I would go to Portadown and it was my job to get through the border checkpoints, you see ... and in those days you were stopped at the checkpoints, you are not now. And I noticed they were stopping every third car. And I remember thinking 'Oh fuck, I'm third' and I had to change for another car, I would lift up the bonnet and then I would get through. And the only time I was ever stopped, I was way over the border, just outside Dublin in Balbriggan, you know where that is, it's about 20 miles outside Dublin, and I was stopped at a Garda checkpoint, they were looking for the IRA, they stopped me and I had 40,000 condoms. And the poor Guard didn't know what to do. And he said 'You are not supposed to have them on you' I said 'Excuse me they are in my possession for my own personal use and I will challenge you if you interfere with me'. And he just said 'Have a nice weekend'.[81]

Secondly, the *McGee* case produced a significant backlash from the Catholic right, against the activities of the IFPA and FPS. In June 1973, John O'Reilly placed orders for contraceptives and family planning booklets with both companies by post, making his young daughters sign the letters of request. When the orders were fulfilled, he reported FPS to Pearse Street Garda Station, which began prosecutions for sales offences under the 1935 Act. The case backfired for Mr O'Reilly when the District Court found that there was no evidence of sale.[82] The judgment emboldened FPS to continue with its strategy of supply for donation, and legitimated its efforts to develop new ways of relating to the contraceptive laws.[83]

Thirdly, the *McGee* case contributed to public understanding of access to contraception as a constitutional right. New groups committed to distributing condoms grew up around

[80] Interview, DM, 8 March 2014.
[81] Interview, FC, 19 February 2014.
[82] 'Family plan case', *Irish Independent*, 20 February 1974, 7.
[83] Interview, DMcC, 12 March 2014.

the country: family planning clinics were founded in Cork (1974), Limerick (1975) and Galway (1977), and the Well Woman Clinic was established in Dublin (1978). In 1975, Students' Unions in Trinity College Dublin and University College Dublin began providing condoms to students illegally. And FPS provided supplies, funding and practical support to all of these organisations. For years, FPS and its allies operated very successfully, if not entirely legally. The publicity surrounding the *McGee* case had also lent the issue broader interest and support, amongst the general public.

May McGee's case thus made visible a set of illegal activities, attracting support for and interest in them, as well as some significant backlash from those seeking to stop or disrupt them. Summarising some of the significance of the *McGee* case for the Irish public, Donal Barrington said:

> Oh there was huge interest, but I think the women, by and large, were in the course of changing their mind on the issue of contraception at the time and I think it was a popular win when we won the case, you know? But in conservative quarters it was a cause of concern and the politicians were just frightened.[84]

Legislation to replace the 1935 Act, when it came, in the form of the Health (Family Planning) Act 1979, was much more restrictive than these activists would have wished. Indeed it appeared designed to cripple the emergent family planning movement. It provided that contraceptives could only be supplied to married couples (for *bona fide* family planning purposes), on a doctor's prescription, and could only be sold by a pharmacist. The last two provisions, if obeyed, would have closed the mail order service and required fragile new clinics to obtain expensive medical services. The Bill was firmly resisted by FPS, which joined with the radical feminist Contraceptive Action Programme to sell condoms openly in Dublin and elsewhere for the first time. When the legislation was passed, FPS and its ally clinics set about circumventing it, just as they had done with its predecessor, in the process pursuing their own interpretation of the *McGee* judgment. For a long time after the 1979 Act came into force, the family planning movement retained the lion's share of the market in contraceptives, albeit that it was a black market.

Conclusion

McGee is often taught as a judgment about the mechanisms of official legal change; about how Walsh J's recourse to natural law allowed the Constitution to bend in the direction of justice at a time when the law prohibited access to basic goods. What is forgotten in the process is that the case's social impact was complex; the legislature was both slow in responding to *McGee*, and disloyal to the judgment's underpinning values. The basic services that the McGees required remained essentially illegal for decades after the judgment, even as the judgment became part of a web of aspirations and strategies that facilitated new forms of service provision. In hindsight, May McGee was a central defiant actor in a wider process of social change, built as much on illegal, or barely legal, activity as on official constitutional discourse.

[84] Interview, DB, 23 June 2014.

284 IRISH REPORTS [1974]

MARY MCGEE, PLAINTIFF V THE ATTORNEY GENERAL AND THE REVENUE COMMISSIONERS, DEFENDANTS

[1971 No 2314 P]

ENRIGHT J.:-

Under s. 17 sub-s.3 of the Criminal Law Amendment Act 1935, it is an offence to import a contraceptive into Ireland. As a matter of law, contraception can neither enter our ports nor cross our Northern borders. Of course, there is no criminal prohibition on the use of contraceptives. However, the effect of the Act is that they are very difficult to obtain and, legally at least, impossible to purchase. Some individuals and couples who are able to travel abroad, perhaps to England or Northern Ireland, may resort to importation for their own personal use, and in doing so they commit a crime. The penalty for importation is a fine of up to £50, a period of imprisonment of up to six months, or both.

Mary McGee is the plaintiff in this case. She is 29 years of age. She left school at 16. She lost most of her hearing as a result of a childhood illness. She was married to Seamus in 1968. They live in a mobile home in the garden of her mother's house in Skerries, Co. Dublin with three of their four small children. The McGees are not wealthy. Mr. McGee is a fisherman. It is seasonal work, and he is paid a percentage of the value of each catch. He earns about £20 per week. Repayments on their mobile home are £17.52 per month. As is the case with many families in Dublin at the present time, the McGees' housing does not meet their needs. It has three small rooms, and lacks sewage facilities. Their eldest son must live with his grandmother for want of space. The McGees are, quite reasonably, concerned about their ability to support a growing family.

Despite conscientious efforts at family planning, the McGees had four children in less than two years. Martin was born prematurely in December 1968. During that pregnancy Mrs. McGee suffered from toxaemia; an illness characterised by high blood pressure, which carries a high risk of organ damage and fatality. After the birth she attempted to use the temperature method of natural birth control. This was not successful, and in January 1970 she gave birth to Gerard. In the last month of that pregnancy she had a serious stroke. She almost died, and required several weeks of hospital treatment. For a time she was paralysed down one side of her face and body. After this frightening episode, she and her husband decided to use artificial contraception. However, while being examined by her doctor, Dr. James Loughran—three months after her last birth—she discovered that she was pregnant with twins. Her latest pregnancy was again marked by toxaemia and high blood pressure, and by understandable anxiety and fear. Sylvia and Sharon were born prematurely in November 1970. There were serious complications during the birth, and Mrs. McGee required a blood transfusion afterwards. Dr. Loughran advised Mrs. McGee that further pregnancies would place her at risk of death, or of life-altering disability. On his advice, she was fitted with a watch-spring diaphragm. Because of her medical history, this was the most suitable solution; the oral contraceptive pill was not appropriate. The diaphragm is not reliable unless used in combination with a contraceptive jelly or cream. Dr. Loughran gave Mrs. McGee a small initial supply, together with a prescription for more. He did not, of course, breach the Act in doing so, because he did not sell the jelly. With his prescription, Mrs. McGee ordered "Staycept jelly" by post from England, since it is impossible to purchase it legally in Ireland. Mrs. McGee finds herself before us because this act of importation was caught by the Act. The jelly was seized by the customs authorities in accordance with s. 17 sub-s. 3 of the Act of 1935. Mrs. McGee and Dr. Loughran wrote to them asking for the jelly to be released, but to no avail. She has since been fitted with an intra-uterine device; a contraceptive device also caught within the terms of the Act. She now claims that s. 17 sub-s. 3 of the Act of 1935 is unconstitutional. O'Keeffe P. in the High Court disagreed.

This court is agreed that s. 17 sub-s. 3 of the 1935 Act breaches the constitutional right to marital privacy, and I will not repeat the arguments of the majority at length. The relevant right is, in my view, ancillary to Article 41 of the Constitution, which recognises that the family is a moral institution of particular importance. We are agreed on the interests that the right to marital privacy guarantees to protect: these are interests, *inter alia*, in making decisions as to whether to bear and raise children and interests in making an intimate life together without undue interference from the state or other outsiders. Recent United Nations Declarations on Population and on Social Progress and Development, and Tehran Resolution XVIII on the Human Rights Aspects of Family Planning indicate a growing international consensus on the fundamental nature of this right.

In the course of argument, we were urged towards a very narrow, stunted view of the relationship between the married couple and the state. I note the Chief Justice's contention that marriage is an essentially private institution, and that couples—even if they find themselves in very difficult circumstances—must simply negotiate such troubles as they encounter, as best they can, without any expectation of special consideration or assistance from the state. In my view, the right to marital privacy is not only a right of the couple to be let alone to fend for themselves, but a right to the state's support and consideration: the State in the text of Article 41 guarantees to protect the family. That obligation to protect must be read in the light of the driving obligation of the state, asserted in the preamble and in Article 45.1, to ensure a social order informed by the demands of justice and charity, and by regard for the dignity and freedom of the individual; *Murtagh Properties v. Cleary* [1972] IR 330. Sexual intercourse is an extremely important aspect of a loving marriage, and where the state seeks to criminalise aspects of sexual behaviour it strikes at the very core of individual dignity and freedom.

I wish to say something to elaborate upon and clarify the concept of marital privacy set out in the majority judgments. It is a mistake to attribute the protection afforded by the right to marital privacy to the couple as a blunt unit. The rights attached in my brethren's judgments to the married couple *simpliciter* are better understood as individual rights enjoyed jointly in the context of a co-operative marital relationship; a relationship of "bilateral loyalty", to borrow from *Griswold v. Connecticut* 381 U.S. 479 (1965). In *Eisenstadt v. Baird* 405 U.S. 438 (1972), cited to us in argument, Brennan J. of the United States Supreme Court observes that:-

"the marital couple is not an independent entity with a mind and heart of its own, but an association of two individuals each with a separate intellectual and emotional makeup. If the right of privacy means anything, it is the right of the individual, married or single, to be free from unwarranted governmental intrusion into matters so fundamentally affecting a person as the decision whether to bear or beget a child."

An individual right to privacy, exercised under the protective shield of marriage, is a better fit for the relationships and exchanges which the state endeavors to protect. I will explain why I think this is so.

The Constitution clearly conceives of marriage as a covenant; a deep and lifelong interpersonal relationship in which adults steadfastly commit themselves to one another and take responsibility for one another. But we know that this is not always achieved in practice. It would be quite wrong if the right to marital privacy recognised here today were applied in future cases to shield abuse and domination from state intervention under the bald assumption of partnership. The Constitution protects marriage, the marital family, and the life of women within the home. It does so in acknowledgement of the belief that these institutions provide the context within which our personal lives deepen and flourish, and our integrity is secured. In this case, no particular difficulty is apparent if the court attributes rights to the married couple as a unit, because the McGees have created for themselves a sustaining and mutually considerate marriage. In this instance, husband and wife embarked on the shared marital project of determining the size of their family in the shadow of a serious, but avoidable, threat to the wife's health. They assessed that threat together and they agreed to do something about it. Mary McGee acted on that joint agreement in ordering and importing contraceptive jelly. But if Seamus McGee had not been supportive of his wife's decision, would she have been entitled to, for example, seek out an alternative form of contraception and use it in secret? In my view, she would have. Consider, hypothetically, a law that required a wife to obtain the written permission of her husband before she could be fitted with an intra-uterine device. Surely such a law would violate the Constitution. This is because her right cannot be dependent on her husband's consent and co-operation. It must exist, to some extent, as an independent right to privacy. The men and women who took the Constitution upon themselves knew that, in many marriages, husbands do not act in their wives' best interests. They cannot have intended the state to protect any and all marital projects, whether the wife is a full and free participant in them or not, whether she is harmed by them or not. If it is otherwise, then what the Constitution most often protects in practice is not the authority of the family unit working in concert, but the immovable authority of the husband and father.

It is often difficult to see conflicts of rights within the marital family, and to separate out the distinct and competing interests of family members because we traditionally assume that the members of the family owe duties to one another. It is true that some family members may put their interests aside for the benefit of others. The habitual and voluntary assumption of these duties blurs distinct individual interests into an apparently harmonious whole. But the law cannot require that any familial role, especially that of wife and mother, becomes a position of tired obedience to the arbitrary demands of others. We might regretfully observe that such has often been the lot of mothers in this country, particularly in circumstances of poverty and hardship. Some women have shown a genius for survival in the worst of circumstances. Nevertheless, there can be no constitutional expectation of radical self-sacrifice for the sake of others' preferences. That is why family members must enjoy individual rights in respect of their family life. The Constitution protects the commitment of the married pair, not for its own sake, but for the sake of the individuals joined together by law.

It is especially important that women are empowered to assert this sort of individual autonomy within marriage where pregnancy and childbirth are in issue. My brethren write in their judgments about the shared decision to have children, and the shared decision to use contraception as protected aspects of the right of marital privacy. Certainly, the right to marital privacy protects the joint interests embodied in such decisions. For instance, social honour and good name are matters of concern to both men and women: husband and wife share an interest in keeping aspects of their intimate life to themselves. Henchy J. describes the harm that is done when the right to marital privacy is breached in terms of the glare of publicity. However, it should be obvious that women have additional distinct interests where pregnancy and childbirth are concerned. For wives, sexual relations come with risks much more serious than the potential public exposure of intimacies. In pregnancy, wives are exposed to a set of inevitable bodily, emotional and psychological burdens which a husband, however kind, cannot wholly share and need not alleviate. The woman must become pregnant, and cope with the illnesses that may attend pregnancy. She must carry the pregnancy, and take all the risks of miscarriage. She must bear the children, and take the risks of childbirth, and bears her portion of the sorrow if a wanted child is born dead. As the court has acknowledged, and as this case demonstrates, these burdens may be palpably deleterious to woman's health, and may even impinge upon her right to life. Furthermore, it would be less than honest to suggest that, when children are born, the obligations around their care are distributed equally between husband and wife. Having a child, to borrow a term of art, is not as simple as dropping a calf in a field and walking away. The mother must rear it. All of us will have some appreciation of how these many burdens may multiply, and of how distressed a woman may become, if she does not have the means to control the number of children she has, or to put enough years between their births that she has time to play with them and enjoy their company, teach them, and develop their understanding of the world. In marriages that are not characterised by the mutual support typified by the McGees, a woman's lot may be starkly affected by her husband's choices, and her well-being gravely threatened where the state needlessly restricts the ways in which she may conduct herself within marriage. That being so, the woman's particular interests can only be safeguarded if we recognise that the right to marital privacy is an individual right. It seems to me that the people who gave the Constitution to themselves understood this in accepting Article 41.2, which gives special acknowledgement to the role of women "within the home". That special constitutional position certainly encompasses the care of young children, and the necessary demanding attendant role of sustaining foetal life in pregnancy. The constitution contemplates that women are charged with a sacred trust. Given the paramount importance of this life-giving social function, it seems to me obvious that women must be empowered to make private decisions as to whether and when they will have children, and how many they will have.

In interpreting Article 41, I am bound to consider the Constitution as a whole. In this respect, I am reinforced in my view that an individual right to privacy must exist as part of the constitutional firmament by other constitutional provisions, which my brethren have not elaborated upon but which counsel for Mrs. McGee raised in argument. First, in *Ryan v. AG* [1965] IR 294 this court recognised the unenumerated right to bodily integrity. O'Dálaigh C.J. wrote that:-

"the State is organised for the common welfare of all its citizens and is a society arising from man's nature. Apart from particular expressed limitations contained in the Constitution, the Oireachtas may not enact legislation depriving citizens of their essential rights as human persons or as members of the family. The State has the duty of protecting the citizens from dangers

to health in a manner not incompatible or inconsistent with the rights of those citizens as human persons."

The current law does not meet this standard. It compels a woman in Mrs. McGee's position to make an impossible choice. On the one hand, she may do without contraception, placing her life or health in real peril. On the other, she may commit a crime to obtain an effective means of avoiding that danger. She may need to do this repeatedly, running the risk each time that the contraceptives will be confiscated, and she will be vulnerable to another dangerous pregnancy. Even if she is willing to do so, the effect of s. 17 is that access to contraception may be beyond her knowledge and resources. Perhaps she will be unable to find a sympathetic doctor to assist her in navigating possible medical options, and will be humiliated or taken advantage of. Perhaps she will be unable to access the medical option which is best suited to her health needs, and will be required to take less reliable measures. In sum, s. 17 places women in an essentially oppressive position of profound dependence and uncertainty in matters fundamental to their health. As such, the current law must engage the woman's right to bodily integrity.

Second I would draw, at greater length, on the express constitutional right to freedom of conscience. The plaintiff invoked Article 44.1.2° of the Constitution, which states that "[f]reedom of conscience and the free profession and practice of religion are, subject to public order and morality, guaranteed to every citizen." The court's engagement with this argument so far has been brief and underdeveloped. The Chief Justice states that the freedom of conscience referred to in this section relates to the choice and profession of a religion and to that alone. Walsh J. in his judgment agrees. As they would have it, Mrs. McGee's decision to use contraception cannot attract the protection of Article 44, because it falls under the rubric of social rather than religious conscience. She has no constitutional right, as such, to live her own private life in the way she thinks best. I cannot share this position. In the first place, I do not find the neat distinction between social and religious conscience convincing, particularly in this context. If the McGees had been Protestant, or Jewish, we would have no trouble in recognising that the 1935 prohibition on the sale and importation of contraception engaged questions of religious freedom. Indeed, members of those faiths have vigorously protested and made known the impact of the 1935 prohibition on their family lives. But those same questions are curiously invisible to my brethren. Mrs. McGee is a Mass-going Catholic who has decided to use contraceptives. This is not a purely social decision for her. It should be readily understood that this decision has significance in the context of her religious beliefs. The High Court heard that she delayed in deciding to use artificial contraception because she was then very religious and understood, from the many newspaper reports on the issue of *Humanae Vitae* published in the early years of her marriage, that the Pope had forbidden Catholics to use it. The use of contraceptives is morally wrong according to the official teaching of a church to which 95% of citizens belong. Although that church supports family planning, and thus permits some practices undertaken with contraceptive intent and results, it does not permit contraception by artificial means. Mrs. McGee has since determined that she cannot in good faith accept this social teaching, though she considered it and applied herself to it. I take note of the ongoing recent public debate between Irish Catholics—indeed, between Catholics worldwide—as to the wisdom and authority of the hierarchy's position on contraception. I make no comment on that debate here. It is not the role of the judiciary to adjudicate on the internal theological contests of religious groups. However, I am bound to say that the existence and continuation of these debates demonstrate that the pluralism which Walsh J. acknowledges as a part of the constitutional fabric exists within religious communities as well as between them. The protections of Article 44 cannot logically be confined to those faithful whose lives conform in every aspect to the orthodoxy of their religious community. Freedom is always the freedom of dissenters; those whose life projects might upend the preferences of the majority. The reasons for that protection are precisely the same as those Walsh J. attributes to the protection of religious freedom more generally. We must be entitled to call our souls our own. If it is otherwise, and the disobedient citizen cannot invoke the right of conscience, then the fundamental rights protected under Article 44 are not those of individuals but those of powerful religious institutions.

In any event, I am not convinced that Article 44 excludes matters of social or political conscience. Certainly, as Walsh J. observes, the text of Article 44 deals largely with religious practice. But there is nothing in its text to eliminate the possibility of an independent fundamental right to freedom of conscience. Indeed, I would argue that our constitutional structure depends for its functioning on effective expressions of conscientious dissent from the prevailing order. Our constitution insists that the laws must ultimately comport with justice; that there is no omnipotent parliament that may pass such laws as it pleases, and justify them simply on the basis that they accord with the wishes of the majority. This is what distinguishes the legal system established under our Constitution from that inherited in colonial times. The preamble confirms that the people are the origin of constitutional meaning in our democracy. It is they who are sovereign. As this court held in *Byrne v. Ireland* [1972] IR 241, the state is the creation of the people, and is accountable to them. This means that our courts should be as attentive as we may be to the felt necessities of the present time and to the aspirations of the people. These needs and aspirations are most apparent when individual citizens become indignant and challenge the laws of state on the basis that they are unconstitutional. More broadly, the entire constitutional structure depends on the ability of citizens to make their own informed judgments as to whether to lend the daily support of their obedience to the laws promulgated under the Constitution. Accordingly, it would be curious indeed if the Constitution did not endeavor to protect social and political conscience, whether through Article 44 or independently.

I am happy to find that the Constitution guarantees a right, not only to think for oneself, but to build a private life in accordance with one's conscience. The special protection of the family, under Article 41, and its acknowledgement that the family bears rights which are 'antecedent and superior to all positive law' suggests that, in the sphere of family life in particular, the people may make especially strong claims on state power. I should say that the lives of many families—as the reference to conscience in Article 42, it seems to me alludes to—would lose something of their integrity if there was no acknowledged right to build a life for oneself, together with loved ones and according to one's own designs. Acknowledging the right to freedom of conscience in the context of pregnancy and child-rearing provides women with a layer of constitutional protection beyond that already articulated in this judgment so far. The burdens of pregnancy may, as I have said already, be obvious and tangible. But they may also be more subtle and insidious. Indeed, anticipation of the very prospect of becoming pregnant, it seems to me, may impose intolerable humiliations on a woman in some circumstances. To put it simply, a woman may legitimately wish to avoid or delay pregnancy—even where her health is not at risk—because motherhood is incompatible with her present aspirations and endeavors. Reproductive capacity is a realm in which women may be restricted in, or thwarted from, engaging in activities that men may take for granted as aspects of the necessary expression of their human personality and as ordinary incidents of their citizenship. It is in precisely these sorts of social realm—in which one's pursuit of the freedom and dignity assured by the Constitution appears constricted by one's natural status or condition—that the possibility of conscientious self-determination has its most important role to play. Without that freedom of conscience, the individual can never truly be an end in herself, but only a means to others' ends. My sense is that the argument is made stronger, not weaker, by the fact that pregnancy makes such intimate demands on a woman's life. There can be no clearer example, in my view, of the exercise of constitutionally protected conscience than Mrs. McGee's deliberate breach of a provision of the criminal law that imposes a particular set of moral principles on the citizenry. We may find it easier to identify the value of social conscience when a person acts as part of an organised movement for social change. It was not suggested that Mrs. McGee was part of such a movement. No effort was made to associate her with recent campaigns for law reform in this domain. She was not, it stands to reason, the only person to illegally import a contraceptive into the country in recent years, but even the individual acting entirely alone, and even the individual whose actions scandalise her neighbours and cannot command their support, can attract the protection of the Constitution.

The right to marital privacy cannot be absolute. The rights that I identified as supporting it—to bodily integrity, and to freedom of conscience—are enjoyed subject to the demands of public order and morality. That is not to say that the government may limit these rights to the extent it pleases merely because it can assert some good reason for doing so. That is why it is not enough to argue, as the defendants did, that access to contraception is a matter of social policy, and thus lies within the exclusive jurisdiction of the legislature. The state must show that the costs of such restrictions to the individual are proportionate to the benefit to the broader common good; *Ryan v. Attorney General* [1965] IR 294. In applying this notion of proportionality, we ought to bear in mind that the right to marital privacy is allied to Article 41. That Article itself contemplates that the family's rights are 'antecedent and superior to all positive law'. As such, it seems to me that the state must be required to advance a very significant argument from the common good in order to justify restriction of this right.

The original justifications for the criminalisation of the sale and importation of contraceptives, whatever their merits may have been at the time, cannot avail the state in 1973. The 1935 Act proceeds from the assumption that family planning is properly regulated alongside sexual offences. The Act deals with the supply of contraceptives in the same breath as unlawful carnal knowledge. The sale or importation of contraceptives is one of the most serious crimes for which it provides and attracts one of the most stringent penalties. Even without embarking on an investigation into the historical motivations behind the passage of the Act, it seems clear that this is legislation designed to attach the sanctions of the criminal law to certain purportedly immoral acts. I can find no supplementary justification for maintaining the provision. There is nothing harmful in the contraceptives to which the plaintiff seeks access. Indeed they are of great benefit to her, not only in respect of her health, but in respect of her capacity to build a fulfilling family life. The Attorney General has not sought to suggest that, if contraceptives are legalised, there will be a breakdown in public morality; indeed, the state did not suggest that public morality was at any grave risk in the period prior to 1935, in which contraceptives were subject to some censorship but were by no means illegal.

Is it possible that there is a constitutional right of privacy in matters of reproduction that exists independently of the institution of marriage? It is not necessary to answer that question in order to decide this case. However, I take my lead from the Chief Justice, who in disagreeing with us holds that the plaintiff's claim in this case is as a citizen, so that in holding s. 17 sub-s. 3 of the 1935 Act unconstitutional, we must give the benefit of our decision equally to be enjoyed by every other citizen, be they married or not. I make my argument here without the benefit of direct submissions from counsel. The majority of my brethren avoid the consequences of the Chief Justice's assertion. For them, this is a judgment taken, as Henchy J. notes, in deference to Mrs. McGee's distinct standing as a wife and mother. It is possible, however, to proceed on the basis that Mrs. McGee's case would not have failed had she been a single woman. Of course, she could not have found refuge in Article 41, but would have to rely on her claim to a personal right of privacy under Article 40.1.3°. In legislating on matters of medical or social policy, the state is, of course, entitled to draw distinctions of function between women who are married and unmarried, and between those who are mothers and those who are not, where such distinction is necessary in the interests of the common good. Again, because we seek to safeguard the pluralism necessary for the preservation of the democratic state envisaged by the Constitution, we must be alive to the costs of drawing such distinctions using the resources of the criminal law. Whatever the demands of morality may appear to be, the costs of criminal proscription are often greater.

No member of the Irish judiciary today can pretend ignorance of the hardship that can face the woman or girl who becomes pregnant outside of marriage. Irish courts at every level regularly make orders in respect of the welfare of women who find themselves in this position, as well as orders to provide for their children, who will often come to reside in one of the several private institutions—such as the mother and baby homes, the industrial schools and the Magdalene institutions—which dot our landscape. I heard of several such cases in my years at the Bar, and no doubt my brethren will have seen others. Outside of the courts, it is well known that a great many more families come to their own arrangements, for good or ill. It is only very recently that the state has begun to pay a small allowance to unmarried mothers under the auspices of the Social Welfare Act. I do not imagine that unmarried pregnant women are always able to live happily in the positions this society has designated for them. Certainly, many will face hurtful and denigratory treatment. Others will leave Ireland altogether. The law as it stands may ruin unmarried women's opportunities to realise the good in life. Reflecting on this, it seems to me very clear that the protected interests which I have identified with married women are not only shared by single women, but that where a woman is not married, the personal, social and economic demands of pregnancy are often manifestly amplified. That being the case, a single woman may have a solid constitutional claim to use contraception without state interference, albeit she does not enjoy the special position reserved for married women under the law. I can see no good reason of public policy for restricting this right through distinctions between categories of person who should have access to contraception. In this line of reasoning, I am at one with the approach of the United States Court of Appeals for the First Circuit in *Eisenstadt v. Baird*, 405 U.S. 438 (1972) as approved by Brennan J. in the United States Supreme Court:–

"To say that contraceptives are immoral as such, and are to be forbidden to unmarried persons who will nevertheless persist in having intercourse, means that such persons must risk for themselves an unwanted pregnancy, for the child, illegitimacy, and for society, a possible obligation of support. Such a view of morality is not only the very mirror image of sensible legislation; we consider that it conflicts with fundamental human rights. In the absence of demonstrated harm, we hold it is beyond the competency of the state."

For the reasons I have given, I would grant the plaintiff a declaration that s. 17 sub-s. 3 of the Criminal Law Amendment Act, 1935 is not, and was not at any time material to these proceedings, of full force and effect as part of the laws of the State. While it is not necessary to consider the remainder of s. 17 for the purposes of deciding this case, our reasoning here suggests that it may be that the prohibition on sale, in an appropriate case, would also prove unconstitutional.

6

Commentary on *Flynn v Power*

DEIRDRE McGOWAN

Introduction

The decision in *Flynn v Power*[1] was handed down in 1985, but the facts that precipitated it unfolded in the midst of an ultimately successful political campaign, supported by the Catholic Church and its hierarchy, to insert a ban on abortion in the Irish Constitution.[2] The Pro-Life Amendment Campaign (PLAC), endorsed by the Congress of Catholic Secondary School Parents Associations,[3] launched their campaign in April 1981 and secured extensive newspaper coverage throughout 1982.[4] PLAC downplayed the abortion issue during the November 1982 general election campaign, but the Society for the Protection of the Unborn Child (SPUC), one of its constituent organisations, heavily politicised it in selected constituencies, including County Wexford.[5] On a national level, tiny brass lapel pins, depicting the feet of a foetus of 10 weeks' gestation, were distributed to children attending Catholic secondary schools.[6] A SPUC film depicting a developing foetus and a happy natural childbirth, followed by several full colour slides of an abortion and aborted foetuses at various stages of development, was shown in more than 250 secondary schools.[7] This was a very uncomfortable time to experience an unplanned, extra-marital, pregnancy. Irish society was agreed on the virtues of childbearing and the rights of the unborn child, but remained ambivalent about extra-marital sex and unmarried motherhood. This discomfort emerges clearly from the original High Court judgment in *Flynn v Power*, which refuses to give legal weight to the appellant's pregnancy, condemns its moral context and removes the mother's means to support her child.

[1] *Flynn v Power* [1985] ILRM 336.

[2] This campaign led to the insertion of the Eighth Amendment to the Constitution, which reads, 'The State acknowledges the right to life of the unborn and, with due regard to the life of the mother, guarantees in its laws to respect, and, as far as practicable, by its laws to defend and vindicate that right.'

[3] Tom Heskin, *The Second Partitioning of Ireland: the Abortion Referendum of 1983* (Dun Laoghaire, Brandsma Books, 1990) 12.

[4] ibid, 57.

[5] ibid, 188.

[6] Known as 'Precious Feet', these pins are the international pro-life symbol, reportedly adopted as such at a symposium in Dublin in 1979. They are still distributed free of charge to schools on request via www.familyandlife.org. During the referendum campaign in 1983, they were distributed through Catholic organisations such as the Saint Vincent de Paul. *The Kerryman* of 5 August 1983 carries an advertisement for the pins at p 22.

[7] *Magill Magazine*, July 1982, 20. The film was shown to students over 15 years of age with parental consent.

The Facts of *Flynn v Power*

In 1979, at the age of 24, Eileen Flynn was appointed a permanent teacher of history and Irish at the Our Lady of Lourdes Secondary School in New Ross. On 22 August 1982, the school manager terminated her position with a letter requesting that she not attend at the school when it re-opened in September, 'in the interests of the pupils'.[8] The stated reason for dismissal was Flynn's 'open rejection of the norms of behaviour which our school exists to promote'.[9] The school had received complaints from members of the community early in the school year about her relationship with a man whose wife had recently left him. Her pregnancy confirmed the sexual nature of the relationship and a child was born in June 1982.

The school, like most other Irish secondary schools, was owned by a Roman Catholic religious order, in this case the Holy Faith Sisters.[10] These 'intermediate' schools receive capital funding and running costs, including teachers' salaries, from the state. Nonetheless, responsibility for the recruitment and retention of teachers remains with the school managers.[11]

Following her dismissal, Flynn sought a determination from the Employment Appeals Tribunal that she had been unfairly dismissed. She failed before the Tribunal, the Circuit Court and the High Court.

Social Context

The Irish Constitution recognises the right to freedom of religion,[12] but the dividing line between the Catholic Church and the institutions of the state was far from clear in the 1980s. The education system, although state-funded, was largely denominational. Although the provisions of both the Constitution and the Intermediate Education (Ireland) Act 1878 required provision to be made for children to receive secular education at state-funded denominational schools, the requirement was, in practice, ignored.[13]

During the 1980s, the views of the Catholic Church on issues of sexual morality were accepted without question by the state. Contraception was available only on prescription

[8] *Flynn v Power* [1985] ILRM 336, 339.

[9] ibid, 339.

[10] Alison Mawhinney notes that in 2008, 93% of schools, primary and secondary, were managed by the Roman Catholic Church, just over 5% were Protestant controlled and almost 2% were privately initiated, multi-denominational schools. There are no state-funded secular schools in Ireland. Alison Mawhinney, *Freedom of Religion and Schools: the Case of Ireland* (Saarbrucken, VDM, Verlag Dr Müller, 2009) 1.

[11] Dympna Glendenning, *Education and the Law* (Dublin, Lexis Nexis, 2004) 34.

[12] Art 44.2.1 Constitution of Ireland 1937 provides, 'Freedom of conscience and the free profession of religion are, subject to public order and morality, guaranteed to every citizen.'

[13] Art 44.4 provides, 'Legislation providing State aid for schools shall not discriminate between schools under the management of different religious denominations, nor be such as to affect prejudicially the right of any child to attend a school receiving public money without attending religious instruction at the school.'

to married couples.[14] Divorce was forbidden.[15] Male homosexual practice was a criminal offence.[16] A means-tested, social welfare allowance was available to unmarried mothers, but a woman was disqualified from receiving an allowance if, and so long as, she and any person were 'cohabiting as man and wife'.[17]

Unmarried motherhood was not an acceptable lifestyle choice. Flynn had given evidence at the Employment Appeals Tribunal of the options she considered upon finding she was pregnant; travelling abroad for an abortion or adoption.[18] In the event she chose to keep her child, in the face of social approbation and her effective exclusion from her chosen profession. Her courage was severely tested during the course of the legal proceedings that attracted significant media attention and public discussion. The outcome was condemned by the teachers unions and welcomed by Catholic school managers.[19] Brother Declan Duffy, on behalf of the Council of Managers of Catholic Secondary Schools, welcomed the decision 'with great satisfaction', noting that a contrary decision 'would have threatened the very existence of Catholic schools in this country'.[20] Catholic education survived, but Eileen Flynn paid a terrible personal price, enduring years of media attention and social judgment, the loss of her job and her profession.[21]

The High Court Judgment

Costello J based his decision on the stated reason for dismissal, Eileen Flynn's 'association with a married man',[22] and in particular the concern that parents had expressed with regard to it. He rejected the proposition that her dismissal resulted wholly or mainly from her pregnancy, and focused instead on whether her affair created substantial grounds for dismissal. Referring to English case law, Costello J accepted the principle that an employee's sexual conduct outside the workplace can justify dismissal if it has the capacity to damage the employer's business. He also relied on the Canadian Supreme Court decision

[14] Heath (Family Planning) Act 1979. The 1979 Act refers to contraception being prescribed for '*bona fide*' family planning or medicinal purposes. 'Family' was interpreted as referring to the constitutional, marital family.

[15] Art 41.3.2 of the Constitution provided that 'No law shall be enacted providing for the dissolution of marriage'. The provision was removed following a referendum in 1995.

[16] Offences Against the Person Act 1861, s 61, repealed by Criminal Law (Sexual Offences) Act 1993.

[17] Social Welfare (Social Assistance Allowance) Regulations 1973 (SI 190/1973), reg 7.

[18] Michael O'Regan, 'Sacked teacher says she considered having an abortion', *The Irish Times*, 15 December 1983, 10.

[19] 'The Eileen Flynn Case', *The Irish Times*, 9 March 1985, 19.

[20] 'Flynn ruling widely criticised', *The Irish Times*, 11 March 1985, 13.

[21] Radio Teilifis Eireann, the national broadcaster, has produced two documentaries, one for radio and one for television, on the Eileen Flynn case. In the radio documentary, both Flynn and her employer describe the circumstances leading up to her dismissal: 'Dismissal of Eileen Flynn—New Ross School Teacher' (RTE 1997), at www.rte.ie/radio1/podcast/podcast_documentaryonone.xml (last accessed 25 August 2015). In the television documentary, her partner, Richie Roche, reflects on the choice Eileen had to make between giving up her child and giving up her career. He comments, '[I]n the end she wouldn't swap all the jobs for a hair of his head.' Richie also describes how it took 20 years for Eileen to return to teaching, but that after only two years she died suddenly at the age of 53. Kevin Cummins, 'Scannall—Eileen Flynn' (RTE 2010), summary at www.rte.ie/tv/scannal/eileenflynn.html (last accessed 25 August 2015).

[22] *Flynn v Power* [1985] ILRM 335, 338.

in *Caldwell & anor v Stuart & anor*,[23] in which it was held that religious conformance by teachers was reasonably necessary to assure the provision of a distinctly Catholic education. Applying these authorities to the facts, he found that Flynn's unconcealed affair with a married man, in a small town where such behaviour would soon be common knowledge, violated her obligations to the school because it affected the school's ability to foster in their pupils the religious principles it had been established to promote.[24] It was therefore reasonable in the circumstances for the school to dismiss her. Flynn had argued that her affair was a private matter, and that there had been no 'open' rejection of the school's ethos. This argument was not considered by the court; Costello J simply assumed that institutional religious freedom trumped Flynn's rights to privacy, freedom of conscience and autonomy.

Seven years prior to the decision in *Flynn v Power*, the Supreme Court, in *McGrath & O'Ruairc v Trustees of Maynooth College*,[25] described the primary aim of the constitutional prohibition on religious discrimination as being 'to give vitality, independence and freedom to religion'.[26] It was designed, the Court concluded, to allow religious belief and practice to flourish. The subsequent Employment Equality Act 1998 adopted a similar approach, providing an exemption from the general legislative prohibition on religious discrimination in employment for religious, educational and medical institutions, where such discrimination is reasonable in order to preserve their 'religious ethos' or avoid offending the 'religious sensitivities' of their clients or members.[27] The legislation was referred to the Supreme Court by the then President, Mary Robinson, for a determination as to its constitutionality.[28] Counsel appointed to oppose the Bill argued that it failed to strike a proper balance between the rights of religious denominations to manage their own affairs and the rights of citizens to equality before the law[29] and to earn a livelihood.[30] The Court was not willing to engage in a balancing exercise and, following a cursory analysis, upheld the constitutionality of the relevant sections. Echoing the decision in *McGrath & O'Ruairc v Trustees of Maynooth College*,[31] Hamilton CJ noted that differential treatment based on religion was acceptable in order to 'give life and reality to the constitutional guarantee of free profession and practice of religion'.[32]

Section 37 of the Employment Equality Act 1998 remains in force and, taken together with the authority of *Flynn v Power*, would appear to specifically permit dismissal of a teacher who engages in conduct, within or outside school, that damages the school's ethos.[33] A recent amendment to the section provides that action taken by a state-funded educational or medical institution to prevent an employee from undermining its religious ethos must

[23] *Caldwell & anor v Stuart & anor* [1984] 2 SCR 603.
[24] *Flynn v Power* [1985] ILRM 335, 342.
[25] *McGrath & O'Ruairc v Trustees of Maynooth College* [1979] ILRM 166.
[26] ibid, 187.
[27] Employment Equality Act 1998, s 37.
[28] Pursuant to Art 26 of the Constitution.
[29] Pursuant to Art 40.1 of the Constitution.
[30] An unenumerated right protected by Art 40.3; see *Murtagh Properties Limited v Cleary* [1972] IR 330.
[31] *McGrath & O'Ruairc v Trustees of Maynooth College* [1979] ILRM 166.
[32] *In Re Article 26 and the Employment Equality Bill 1996* [1997] 2 IR 321, 325.
[33] Marguerite Bolger, 'Discrimination on grounds of religion: theory and practice' (2004) *Irish Employment Law Journal* 48.

be capable of objective justification.[34] Such action will be objectively justified if it is 'rationally and strictly related' to the ethos, and is a response to the employee's conduct rather than his or her gender, civil status, family status, sexual orientation, age, disability, race or membership of the travelling community. Further, action taken must be proportionate to the conduct of the employee, having regard to the consequences for the employee, his or her right to privacy and the actual damage caused to the religious ethos.[35] Although such a provision will likely shift the focus of legal argument should a *Flynn*-type case arise again, the outcome may not be significantly different. The threat of dismissal therefore remains for those teachers, doctors and nurses employed in religious-run institutions whose private lives *and practices* conflict with the religious tenets of their employers.[36] This poses a particular difficulty for gay, lesbian and bisexual teachers, as the religious doctrine governing the ethos of 93 per cent of Irish schools prohibits homosexual conduct. Deaglán O'Fathaigh's 2003 research found that non-heterosexual teachers fear discovery and must develop strategies to maintain a strict distinction between their personal and professional lives.[37] It seems fair to assume that other employees with non-conforming personal lives experience similar difficulties. The recent amendment to section 37, in acknowledging that an employess of a state funded religious institution can be disciplined for conduct 'undermining the religious ethos of the institution', is unlikely to make a material difference to the culture of conformity and fear found by O'Fathaigh among teachers in Irish denominational schools.[38]

Crafting a Feminist Judgment

Costello J gave greatest legal weight to the school's institutional right to religious freedom. He did not consider Flynn's right to freedom of conscience or her right to privacy, nor her right to earn a livelihood. His judgment reflected existing Irish legal and political understandings of the hierarchy of constitutional rights. This preferencing of institutional freedom of religion over individual freedom of conscience causes a particular difficulty for feminists, because many gender-specific rights violations are grounded in religious practices.[38] In Ireland, the exclusion of married women from the workforce was based on Roman Catholic social policy and supported by cultural practice. Limitations on the availability of contraception also reflected Church teaching, whilst the Eighth Amendment to the Constitution, effectively banning abortion, endorsed Catholic doctrine.

[34] Employment Equality Act 1988, s 37(1B), as inserted by s 25 of the Equality (Miscellaneous Provisions) Act 2015.

[35] Employment Equality Act 1988, s 37(1C), as inserted by s 25 of the Equality (Miscellaneous Provisions) Act 2015.

[36] Denominational schools remain a major part of the Irish educational system at both primary and secondary level. The Department of Education reported in 2012 that 96% of primary schools in Ireland are under the patronage of religious denominations, 90% of these schools being owned and under the patronage of the Catholic Church. Department of Education, *Report of the Advisory Group to the Forum on Patronage and Pluralism in the Primary Sector* (Department of Education, 2012) 29.

[37] Deaglan O'Fathaigh, *Echoes down the corridor: An examination of gay and lesbian teachers in Ireland*, unpublished M.ed thesis 2003 UCD, as cited at Mawhinney, above n 10, at 177.

[38] Donna Sullivan, 'Gender Equality and Religious Freedom: Toward a Framework for Conflict Resolution' (1991-2) 24 *New York University Journal of International Law and Politics* 795–856, 795.

Conflict between women's rights and religious values sets principles of equality against values of liberty.[39] In his feminist judgment, Eoin Daly attempts to resolve this antagonism by drawing on recent alignments of feminist theory with the republican political tradition.[40] Republicanism, in the form developed by Philip Pettit (and adopted by Daly J), relies on an understanding of freedom as non-domination; exposure to the arbitrary power of another represents the greatest evil in this republican canon.[41] In classical republicanism, domination is the weapon of tyrants, but similar issues arise when men dominate women, or indeed when employers dominate their employees. A characterisation of freedom as non-domination rejects as inadequate liberal notions of freedom as non-interference. A kindly master may not interfere with the actions of his slave, but that does not make the captive free. Likewise the wife of an indulgent husband is not free if social institutions enforce dependency upon her.[42]

From a neo-republican perspective, legal regulation is part of an institutional framework that must promote freedom by guarding against arbitrary interference with individual freedom. Law must not allow men to exercise arbitrary power over women, nor employers to dominate their employees. Situating conflicts between religious freedom and women's equality within this frame moves debate away from liberal concerns with conflicting individual rights toward a broader deliberation of what is right or just. The issue in *Flynn* becomes broader than balancing an employee's right to privacy against an employer's right to free practise of religion. Freedom as non-domination acknowledges social embeddedness and the variety of social and cultural factors, including race, class, gender and religion, that shape identity and individual experience.[43]

The Feminist Judgment

Costello J focused on the specific; the school was Catholic and in a small town, the parents complained, and the teacher was given an opportunity to cease her relationship. It relied upon taken-for-granted notions about what constituted appropriate behaviour for a teacher in a denominational school, taking a cultural shortcut without fully appreciating the nature of the issues at stake. Writing in 1985, Madden doubted the judgment's value as a precedent,[44] and indeed it has not been cited in any subsequent superior court decision. Yet Costello J's decision has had very significant practical effects for the day-to-day lives of individual teachers in denominational schools.

Daly J's first move in re-imagining the judgment, therefore, is to specifically generalise the issues, stripping away the unspoken assumptions to clarify that Flynn's position raises

[39] ibid, 798.

[40] Anne Phillips, 'Feminism and republicanism: is this a plausible alliance?' (2000) 8(2) *Journal of Political Philosophy* 279–93.

[41] ibid, 288.

[42] The role of social institutions and structures in supporting the subordination of women is a central theme of radical and second-wave feminism. See, eg, Christine Delphy and Diana Leonard, *Familiar Exploitation: A New Analysis of Marriage in Contemporary Western Societies* (Cambridge, Polity, 1992).

[43] M Victoria Costa, 'Is Neo-Republicanism Bad for Women' (2013) 28(4) *Hypatia* 921–36, 924.

[44] Declan Madden, 'Flynn v The Sisters of the Holy Faith' (1985) 3 *Irish Law Times* 86.

important legal questions, and that the decision has the potential to adversely affect large numbers of employees of denominational institutions. He states, '[this case] concerns primarily whether a religious employer may dismiss an employee whose private activities it understands as undermining its religious ethos'.

Daly J goes on to reject the school's claim that the dismissal was not related to Flynn's pregnancy. Pregnancy, he finds, cannot be examined in isolation. The purpose of the legislative protection is to give employment security to women made vulnerable to dismissal as a result of the presumed consequences of pregnancy. To allow dismissal motivated by the consequences rather than the pregnancy itself would be to circumvent the purpose of the legislation. In this case, the pregnancy was represented as the 'last straw' in a series of events. As with the consequences of pregnancy, it is not possible to separate the fact of pregnancy from the events leading to it in order to argue that these events, and not the pregnancy itself, were the motivation for dismissal.

Finding in favour of Flynn on this ground, Daly J then considers the question of whether there were 'substantial grounds' for dismissal within the meaning of section (6)(1) of the Unfair Dismissals Act 1977.

The Constitution was not referenced in the original judgment, although an authority based on the Human Rights Code of British Columbia formed part of the Court's reasoning. Flynn's behaviour was, in the eyes of the school, self-evidently a danger to its ethos, and no issue of conflicting constitutional rights arose. Daly J, in broadening the parameters of the case, takes the view that constitutional values are implicated; adjudicating the dispute between the parties requires a weighing of the religious freedom of the school against the privacy and employment rights of Flynn. Arguments based on Articles 42 and 44 of the Constitution are attributed to the school, emphasising the religious freedom of the school and the rights of parents to have their children taught in an authentically denominational environment.

Article 42 of the Constitution deals with Education, and Article 44 with Religion. Reflecting Roman Catholic social teaching, Article 42.1 acknowledges the family as the natural educator of the child, and guarantees the right of parents to provide for 'the religious and moral' education of their children. Article 42.4 obliges the state to provide free primary education and to give aid to private and corporate educational initiative, with due regard to the rights of parents, 'especially in the matter of religious and moral formation'. Denominational schools are given specific support in Article 44.2.4, and religious denominations are guaranteed the right to manage their own affairs under Article 44.2.5.

The school, in the revised judgment, argues that the Constitution requires not only an absence of constraint on religious practice, but also positive State support for the 'institutional and social infrastructure that is necessary to enable its collective exercise'. This includes a guarantee that religious employers are free to deploy an assessment of personal conformity with religious ethos when making decisions to employ or dismiss individual workers. Daly J accepts the proposition that religious institutions can require employees to abide by religious norms in their personal conduct, but only to the extent necessary to uphold their employer's ethos.

Whilst Costello J took a broad view of what was necessary in this context, Daly J focuses on the proximity of employees to the 'core of the religious function'. Religious denominations must have complete discretion in the selection of ministers, but unfettered freedom in relation to administrative and support staff is unwarranted. With regard to teachers in denominational schools, their position relative to the core religious function will determine whether non-conforming private behaviour constitutes 'substantive justification' for dismissal. Particularly relevant in Flynn's case is the social function of the school, which although denominational is almost entirely funded by the state to provide both secular and religious education.

The issues between the parties are thus reformulated in terms of the competing interests of the school and its employees. The school claims that the constitutional guarantee of free profession of religion protects its freedom to manifest and meaningfully exercise the religious beliefs that it was established to promote and protect. The provisions of the Unfair Dismissals Act 1977 must therefore be interpreted in a way that gives life and vitality to that guarantee by allowing the school to discriminate against employees on the basis of private adherence to religious norms.

Daly J, applying Pettit's notion of freedom as non-domination, conceptualises the 1977 Act as part of an institutional framework that must guard against arbitrary interference with individual freedom. The liberal non-interference model of religious freedom suggested by the school is found lacking because it gives the religious order power to dominate its employees in general and Flynn in particular.

A benign, and perhaps truly Christian (or feminist), employer might have embraced Flynn in her difficulty, stood against local gossip and protected her livelihood and profession. The Holy Faith Sisters, however, demonstrated the limitations of an understanding of freedom as non-interference. They could choose to dominate Flynn, to remove her freedom to follow a profession, to live as she wished and to support her child from her own earnings. Further, in dismissing her, they transferred their own arbitrary power to dominate to the father of her child, who in turn could choose whether or not to support and care for mother and child.

As Daly J points out, allowing the objective of the Act to be circumvented in the manner suggested by the school would significantly impinge upon the social and religious freedom of employees of religious institutions. Even those not immediately threatened by dismissal would be required to engage in 'strategies of self-invigilation and self-censorship, checking their own life plans and projects, in order to apprehend potentially ruinous consequences'. Clear parallels can be drawn between the position of teachers in denominational schools and that of Irish women as a whole in the 1980s. Flynn's story reflects that of thousands of her contemporaries, dominated by institutional structures that allowed men, the Catholic Church and other powerful interests to exercise arbitrary power over their lives.

Flynn, and other non-core employees of religious orders, argues Daly J, must be freed from the capricious power of their employer to invoke 'religious freedom' in respect of the private lives of its employees. He concludes that the school does not have the claimed level of discretion in employment policy. Any action taken by it in relation to the private conduct of employees must be proportionate and necessary having regard to the social and religious function of the school, and must take account of an employee's specific role in performing those functions. Flynn was a teacher of Irish and history, and although the school's religious ethos was not confined to religious instruction classes, Flynn's role in the school was not in sufficient proximity to its religious core to allow a complete exemption from the legislation in her case. The appeal is therefore allowed.

Conclusion

Prior to the enactment of the 1977 Act, an employer could dismiss an employee without reason, subject only to providing notice or pay in lieu thereof. Summary dismissals had led to significant industrial unrest during the 1970s, as whole workplaces walked out in support of unfairly dismissed colleagues. The 1977 Act was intended to prevent such strikes by providing an individualised remedy to dismissed employees.[45] The individualised nature of the remedy, in Eileen Flynn's case, allowed the court in the original decision to focus only on the particular individual and to ignore the wider social issues affecting her ability to work as a teacher in Ireland. By drawing on constitutional provisions and a broad understanding of religious freedom, Daly J is able to pull back from the individual, in order to undertake a 'frank appraisal of the competing social and individual claims underlying the dismissal'.

The effect of the original decision was to confer a type of freedom as non-interference on all teachers in denominational schools living outside the tenets of their employer's religion. Like the slave or dependent woman, they are not truly free, being subject to the potential exercise of arbitrary discretion. Schools have the power to determine which 'sins' are sacking offences. This is particularly dangerous both from Flynn's perspective and from a broader feminist standpoint. Women's 'sins', particularly in the sexual domain, manifest themselves physically, through pregnancy and childbirth, in a way that men's do not.

Male domination has been a central concern of feminists, and Pettit's reinterpretation of republicanism as a perspective that opposes domination has much to offer feminist critique.[46] In his own work, Pettit uses the relationship between husbands and wives to illustrate his concept of non-domination, and Daly J demonstrates that it can equally be applied to the workplace. Pettit's work also aligns with feminist perspectives in taking into account broader social contexts that make domination both possible and, on occasion, inevitable. In acknowledging the hegemonic position of the Catholic Church in Irish state education, Daly J recognises the gravity of the school's action. It was simply not an option for Flynn to obtain work in a secular school; none existed in 1980s Ireland.

Had Daly J's approach been taken in the original case, Eileen Flynn would have kept her job and not been excluded from her chosen profession for much of the rest of her working life.[47] The Employment Equality Act 1998 may have included a requirement that discrimination be 'reasonably necessary' to protect religious ethos. Most significantly, non-conforming employees of religious institutions would not have to live in constant fear that their employers might discover, and object to, the content of their private lives.

[45] Purpose as stated by the Minister for Labour, 29 March 1977, Seanad deb vol 86 col 510.

[46] Marilyn Friedman, 'Pettit's Civic Republicanism and Male Domination' in Cécile Laborde and John Maynor (eds), *Republicanism and Political Theory* (Oxford, Blackwell, 2008) ch 10.

[47] Maeve Sheehan, 'Teacher who learned the hardest lesson', *Irish Independent*, 14 September 2008.

High Court

Eileen Flynn, Appellant v Sister Mary Anna Power and The Sisters of the Holy Faith, Respondents

[1985 No. D5310]

High Court 8th March 1985

Daly J.

This ruling is an appeal from a ruling of the Employment Appeals Tribunal. It concerns primarily whether a religious employer may dismiss an employee whose private activities it understands as undermining its religious ethos.

The facts

The basic facts are not in dispute. Eileen Flynn was a teacher in a Catholic denominational secondary convent school at Rabercon, County Wexford, which was managed and controlled by the second respondents.

During 1980/81 the school principal, the first respondent, received complaints from parents of children attending the school, alleging that the appellant was having a relationship with Richard Roche, a man living in the town who was married although separated. In August, 1981, the first respondent informed the appellant of these complaints. She insisted that an extra-marital relationship of this sort was inconsistent with the appellant's responsibilities as a teacher in a Roman Catholic denominational school committed to imparting Roman Catholic values. She warned the appellant that if the relationship continued, her contract of employment would be terminated. The appellant acknowledged the existence of the relationship in question; however, in replying she asserted that she had not openly rejected the school's religous norms and that her personal life was a matter of her own private concern. In November 1981, the appellant began to live with Mr Roche in his home. In April 1982, the school principal, Sister Power, learned that the appellant was pregnant. In a meeting, the manager referred again to the religious character of the school, referred to the "rights" of the parents of children at the school and the concerns expressed by some of them concerning the appellant's relationship. She insisted that if the appellant did not change what she termed her "lifestyle", her position in the school would be untenable. For her part, the appellant frankly acknowledged that she was living with Mr Roche, that she loved him and that she would not leave him.

On 6th August, 1982, the appellant was informed that she would have to resign or be dismissed. She did not resign and her employment with the school was terminated by letter on August 22. In this letter the school manager stated: "I could not allow you to continue teaching in the school, because of your open rejection of the norms and behaviour and the ideals which our school exists to promote", and referred to "scandal" allegedly caused by the appellant's behavior. The appellant brought an appeal to the Employment Appeals Tribunal under the Unfair Dismissals Act, 1977 ("the Act"). The Tribunal ruled that the dismissal had not been unfair. From that decision the appellant appealed to the Circuit Court which upheld the decision of the Tribunal. The appellant appealed to the High Court.

Issues to be determined

This judgment is based primarily on provisions of the Unfair Dismissals Act, 1977. However, an important background consideration that has been raised by the respondents is the question of what weight should be assigned—both constitutionally and in a general sense—to the religious "ethos" of the school. Therefore the provisions of the Act must be read in light of certain provisions of the Constitution.

Section 6, sub-s. 1 of the Unfair Dismissals Act, 1977 ("The Act"), provides:–

> "Subject to the provisions of this section, the dismissal of an employee shall be deemed, for the purposes of this Act, to be an unfair dismissal unless, having regard to all the circumstances, there were substantial grounds justifying the dismissal."

Section 6, sub-s. 2 (f) of the Act provides *inter alia* that a dismissal shall be deemed to be unfair if it results from the pregnancy of the employee.

Article 42 of the Constitution of Ireland, 1937 provides:–

"1. The State acknowledges that the primary and natural educator of the child is the Family and guarantees to respect the inalienable right and duty of parents to provide, according to their means, for the religious and moral, intellectual, physical and social education of their children.

2. Parents shall be free to provide this education in their homes or in private schools or in schools recognised or established by the State.

3. 1° The State shall not oblige parents in violation of their conscience and lawful preference to send their children to schools established by the State, or to any particular type of school designated by the State.

   2° The State shall, however, as guardian of the common good, require in view of actual conditions that the children receive a certain minimum education, moral, intellectual and social.

4. The State shall provide for free primary education and shall endeavour to supplement and give reasonable aid to private and corporate educational initiative, and, when the public good requires it, provide other educational facilities or institutions with due regard, however, for the rights of parents, especially in the matter of religious and moral formation.

5. In exceptional cases, where the parents for physical or moral reasons fail in their duty towards their children, the State as guardian of the common good, by appropriate means shall endeavour to supply the place of the parents, but always with due regard for the natural and imprescriptible rights of the child."

Article 44 provides:–

"1. The State acknowledges that the homage of public worship is due to Almighty God. It shall hold His Name in reverence, and shall respect and honour religion.

2. 1° Freedom of conscience and the free profession and practice of religion are, subject to public order and morality, guaranteed to every citizen.

   2° The State guarantees not to endow any religion.

   3° The State shall not impose any disabilities or make any discrimination on the ground of religious profession, belief or status.

4° Legislation providing State aid for schools shall not discriminate between schools under the management of different religious denominations, nor be such as to affect prejudicially the right of any child to attend a school receiving public money without attending religious instruction at that school.

5° Every religious denomination shall have the right to manage its own affairs, own, acquire and administer property, movable and immovable, and maintain institutions for religious or charitable purposes.

6° The property of any religious denomination or any educational institution shall not be diverted save for necessary works of public utility and on payment of compensation."

Submissions

The appellant contends that her dismissal in August 1982 was "unfair" within the meaning of the Act because it came about a result of her pregnancy, a criterion that is specifically prohibited under Section 6, sub-s. 2 (f) of the Act. She also contends that her dismissal was unlawful because there were no "substantial grounds justifying the dismissal" within the meaning of Section 6, sub-s. 1 of the Act. Additionally she argues that the "substantial grounds" (for dismissal) referred to in the Act cannot be construed as encompassing considerations that have no direct and functional bearing on professional performance, and accordingly, that her dismissal was "unfair" in this additional and distinctive sense.

The respondents contend that the Ms Flynn's dismissal was not "unfair" within the meaning of the Act because, in light of her acknowledged extra-marital relationship in particular, there were "substantial grounds" justifying the dismissal in view of the religious and moral mission of the school in which she was employed. Additionally they contend that the dismissal was not "unfair" within the meaning of Section 6, sub-s. 2 (f) of the Act because it was not directly a result of pregnancy *per se* but rather, a necessary consequence of the allegedly disruptive effects, educational and moral, of her extra-marital relationship generally. The respondents also maintain that the "substantial grounds" referred to in the Act must be constructed broadly as encompassing conduct which, although carried on outside of the workplace, undermines the employers' moral and religious mission.

Application

The main issue in this case is whether it can be said that the respondents had substantial grounds for terminating the appellant's employment in their school. This in turn raises broader questions as to the relationship between the terms of the Unfair Dismissals Act, 1977 on the one hand, and broader constitutional and public-policy considerations on the other.

In reality the Act accords a great deal of latitude to the Employment Appeals Tribunal and in turn, to the Courts, in determining what constitutes sufficient justification for termination of employment under particular circumstances. To some extent, general constitutional principles may be of some assistance in employment disputes involving religious claims. However, this does not relieve the Court of its responsibilities in defining the criteria based on which dismissals may be considered substantially "justified". This cannot be understood as a mechanical application of precedent or of clear statutory rules. Instead, it requires a frank appraisal and weighing-up of the competing social and individual claims underlying a dismissal of this nature. It is irreducible, in effect, to any determinate intention of the legislature that can be discerned solely through the Act itself, even though apparent legislative intentions may be instructive in some respects. The Court, in short, cannot ignore the wider social conflicts that provide the context for employment disputes of this kind. In particular, it has a responsibility to ensure that the provisions of the Act are interpreted and applied in a way that upholds and promotes the social aims that inform and underlie employment legislation. By necessity, the Act leaves a degree of flexibility or discretion to the Courts in addressing diverse contexts and circumstances, but this interpretive latitude should not be used to frustrate the social policies that the legislation embodies.

The appellant relies on a provision of the Act by which a dismissal of an employee shall be deemed to be unfair if it results wholly or mainly from the pregnancy of the employee or matters connected therewith (s. 6, sub-s. 2 (f)). In response, the respondents argue that the dismissal did not result from her pregnancy *per se* but rather the broader problems posed by her extra-marital relationship.

As a preliminary point this contention seems implausible, as it would defeat the clear purpose and intendment of the Act in protecting against dismissal on grounds of pregnancy. Every employer who dismisses an employee as a result of pregnancy does so presumably because of a perceived set of consequences that are assumed to flow from pregnancy—assumptions which are the product of deeply entrenched, sexist stereotypes. If an employer could classify dismissals following upon pregnancy as stemming from related circumstances of the pregnancy, this would circumvent the clear intendment of the Oireachtas in precluding dismissals based on pregnancy, and in counteracting the historical stereotypes on which such assumptions are based (the concept of legislative intent was discussed by the Supreme Court in *Rahill v. Brady* [1971] I.R. 69). If dismissal resulted from a range of factors including a pregnancy, the existence of other such factors does not obviate the fact that dismissal was effectively a "result" of pregnancy, notwithstanding the existence of other such factors. It would lead to absurdity if the existence of other motivations for dismissal could lead to the protections on pregnancy grounds being circumvented in the manner the respondent has argued, if pregnancy was, all things considered, a dominant consideration. In this case, the respondent's pregnancy was portrayed as the "final straw" in a series of events that led to her dismissal and in that sense, her dismissal was a "result" of her pregnancy despite being a result of other, concurrent factors. In order to give meaningful effect to the statutory protection against termination on grounds of pregnancy and to avoid frustrating the social aims of employment legislation, the Court must necessarily reject any argument to the effect that pregnancy can be interpreted as a proxy of other, legitimate criteria for dismissal.

It remains to be determined whether these other factors constitute a substantial justification for dismissal within the meaning of the Act.

The respondents claim that to dismiss a teacher on the grounds of her known, extramarital relationship, conducted within the community that the school shares, is permissible in view of the legitimate aim of upholding the religious ethos of the school. For her part, the appellant contends that her private romantic and sexual activities cannot constitute a substantial justification for dismissal insofar as they have no bearing on the performance of her duties.

In one sense this can be framed as a dispute as to whether non-professional activities and relationships can have a bearing on the reputation and interests of an employer and whether such activities can, accordingly, constitute legitimate grounds for discipline or dismissal.

Effectively the respondents argue that this consideration applies with greater force in the present case because of the importance and weight that is attached to the religious mission of the employer as a denominational school. Effectively, this is to argue that the interest of a denominationally managed body in upholding its ethos, as embodied by its staff and all their public activities, outweighs competing interests of privacy or employment security. They claim that the ambiguities of the Act must be read in light of an overarching principle that recognises the freedom of religious denominations to maintain educational and other charitable institutions in such a manner that permits them to fully and substantially exercise their beliefs in a collective, institutional setting. They argue that if employment legislation were to be interpreted in a manner that restricted the capacity of denominationally managed schools to impart a set of religious messages and doctrines—through lived example, as well as didactically and academically—this would undermine freedom of religion in its broad sense, as religious denominations would then be prevented from exercising and imparting their beliefs in institutional and collective settings. Effectively, they argue that denominational and religious freedom not only requires an absence of legal constraints upon religious practice, but that it also in effect requires the State to respect and protect the institutional and social infrastructure that is necessary to enable its collective exercise. Such guarantees, they argue, are necessary to give "life and reality" to freedom of religious practice, as was established in *McGrath and Ó Ruairc v. Trustees of Maynooth College* [1979] I.L.R.M. 366. And in the present case, they argue this encompasses a guarantee that denominational employers may select employees based not only on functional and occupational requirements, but based also on their capacity and willingness to maintain and observe religious norms in contexts other than the professional environment considered in its narrow sense.

Additionally, the respondents argue that the Court should attach some weight not only to considerations of denominational autonomy, but also to the constitutional and legal protections that are implicitly recognised for denominational education. These principles are derived primarily from the provisions of Article 42 of the Constitution, which deals with the role of the State in the education system (*Crowley v. Ireland* [1980] I.R. 102). The respondents argue that if employment law were interpreted as limiting the ability of religious employers to require employees to uphold religious norms in the community generally rather than the narrow professional environment specifically, this would not only undermine the collective religious rights of denominations and individuals; it would also undermine the right of parents to have their children educated in an authentically religious environment.

I have no doubt but that religious institutions are, in a general sense, entitled, constitutionally and otherwise, to use religious criteria in selecting employees insofar as this is necessary to uphold doctrinal requirements and to the extent that such employees fulfil a religious function. Equally, I am satisfied that that to a limited extent at least, they may require such employees to abide by religious norms in their conduct. But this begs a number of further, specific questions. First, it must be established whether or not this general right entitles religious employers to insist on employees upholding religious norms in private and non-professional contexts as well as in the workplace environment, and how far such demands may extend. Secondly, more specifically, the question arises whether religious employers may insist that employees refrain from entering sexual and romantic relationships that are interpreted as being inconsistent with the religious norms in question, bearing in mind the impact this may have with respect to competing rights and interests. Thirdly, and relatedly, it must be considered whether or not this denominational right to insist on respect for religious norms extends to all categories of denominational employees or only to those whose occupational function is directly connected to religious exercise.

The general right of religious employers to insist on respect for religious norms is, quite obviously, qualified in various respects. I accept that ambiguous statutory provisions must be read subject to a presumption that religious organisations have a general right to manage their own affairs. However, this cannot be allowed to serve as a pretext for such organisations claiming a free hand, so to speak, in exempting themselves from the various social responsibilities that legislation embodies or indeed to subvert the social protections it offers.

The Court must be mindful that to recognise such claims in a more or less unqualified way might inflict considerable social and individual harms, particularly in the context of legislation aimed at giving greater security to women—and particularly pregnant women—in what has traditionally been, and still remains, a vulnerable and precarious position at least from the employment perspective. The Unfair Dismissals Act, 1977 was enacted in order to give effective protections to those at risk from unbridled institutional discretion or managerial caprice in the workplace, and it explicitly gave protections against dismissal on grounds of pregnancy, with a view, presumably, to remedying an historical and ongoing problem of gender discrimination at work, and with a view to promoting and facilitating greater rates of female participation in the workplace. Many thousands of women are employed by denominational or denominationally managed bodies in Ireland—many of whose functions and responsibilities are not directly connected to religion—and if the Court were to adopt the construction of the Act which the respondents advocate, it would effectively deny such pregnant women, and indeed potentially other categories of employees, the important protections that the legislation offers. To circumvent the legislation, the employer would need only to invoke its religious ethos or that of the denomination to which it is connected, even in relation to staff who perform essentially secular functions and duties and who have no occupational function connected to the religious ethos that the employer seeks to embody and reflect. This, in effect, would be to subject women, in particular, to subtle but potent abuses of power and indeed, to arbitrary forms of social hierarchy and social control, all under the pretext of denominational rights.

The respondents argue that it is impossible to separate out the religious and secular functions of different categories of employees, because staff with ostensibly secular responsibilities are expected to uphold and even embody the employer's religious ethos; in effect they argue that their religious ethos cannot be compartmentalized because it pervades the entire mission of the institution. However, while this point may carry some weight, the Court cannot accept that statutory employment protections may be derogated from on religious grounds for all employees of a religiously managed body irrespective of the nature of their function. This would place a very great number of employees in a very precarious position and so seems to run counter to the intendment and purpose of the Act. This is all the more compelling in light of the fact that the tribunal and Courts are not generally well positioned to evaluate the doctrinal substance or the *bona fides* of the religious norms that might form the basis of a dismissal. It is true that in *Quinn's Supermarket v. Attorney General* [1972] I.R. 1, the Supreme Court heard evidence concerning Jewish law in evaluating religious-freedom rights, yet the religious rationale for dimissals or sanctions will likely be amorphous, unclear and contested in many other cases.

With this in mind, I do not exclude the possibility that in some circumstances, concerns of a religious nature may constitute "substantive justification" for dismissals within the meaning of the Act. For instance, this might be the case where an employee occupies a position that is equivalent or tantamount to clergy or a minister of religion, in whatever form. The closer to the core of the religious function that a particular post or occupation will be, the stronger the case to exempt the denomination in question from certain provisions of employment legislation (see Bruce Bagni, "Discrimination in the Name of the Lord: A Critical Evaluation of Discrimination by Religious Organisations" (1979) 79 Columbia Law Review 1514). Certainly, religious denominations must surely be given unfettered power to select their clergy. However, where a denomination or denominationally managed body employs persons in ancillary secular functions such as administration, for example, the Court will necessarily be hesitant to accept such arguments given the very wide powers of invigilation and interference that this may grant to religious employers over a very broad range of employees. In this instance, the appellant is a teacher in a denominationally managed secondary school. This falls somewhere between the two poles mentioned; a clergy member or minister of religion on the one hand, and a secular administrative worker on the other. In this case, the appellant, a secondary teacher, is not a teacher of religion (indeed it is arguable whether or not a teacher of religion may be understood as equivalent to a minister of religion for this purpose).

The Court accepts that the religious ethos of the school in question will not be confined to timetabled religious-instruction classes, and that teachers of subjects other than religion will be looked upon to reflect, to some extent at least, the spiritual and moral values the school aims to represent. But it does not follow from this that a religious denomination or a denominationally managed body can designate any of its employees as having religious functions or religious significance and thus exempt itself from the relevant legislative obligations. Such claims must be appraised in individual cases based on a weighing up of competing considerations: the extent to which the employee or category of employees in question is engaged with the spiritual core or epicentre of the denomination in question, on the one hand, and the concrete effects the claimed exemption will have on those employees, on the other. This does not involve drawing up any rigid distinctions between "public" and "private" spheres; rather it means that any consideration as to whether or not there is "substantive justification" for dismissing or sanctioning employees, for religious-orthodoxy reasons, must account for the specificity of their function and role, taking all relevant circumstances and considerations into account. In this instance, the appellant may have a role as a moral exemplar, in light of the Christian message and doctrine of her employer, rather than simply as an instructor in a narrow secular sense. However, the school is not solely a religious institution and cannot be treated, legally or constitutionally, as being equivalent to a church or a religious denomination per se—notwithstanding that its religious ethos has legal and constitutional significance. It is of considerable relevance that the school in question is, if not public in ownership or management, nonetheless "public" in a variety of other senses. It is responsible for education in the community generally as well as religious instruction specifically, and this is reflected in the fact that its running costs as well as teachers' salaries are paid almost entirely by the State. (The nature of this historical "patronage" model was considered by the Supreme Court in *Crowley v. Ireland* [1980] I.R. 102). Thus in considering whether or not there exists "substantial justification" for dismissing an employee in a case such as this, the Court must be mindful of the social function of the relevant institution, in its broad sense.

There remains the question of whether or not the Court may query the religious-doctrinal basis for a dismissal. There is, of course, a risk that religious norms may serve as a pretext for dismissals that are in reality prompted by other considerations, or considerations that are only nominally or loosely related to religion: social disapproval or obloquy in the community generally, say, or prejudice concerning employees' lifestyles and practices, etc. On the one hand, the Court has no jurisdiction to determine whether or not, or to what extent, a particular sexual practice is inconsistent with the core norms of a religious denomination. A court must generally accept at face value what a religious denomination describes its ethos and doctrines as being, albeit while bearing in mind the diversity of beliefs that exists within all faith communities. And indeed, there is little reason to doubt, in this case, that extra-marital relationships are at odds with Catholic teachings. However, the Court must be mindful that there is no neat division between religious and non-religious motivations for dismissal, and that historically religious doctrines may be used to give expression to the same social prejudices and caprices—those norms of respectability and so on—against which the Act aims to offer some measure of protection. It is not implausible, in turn, that the burden of such caprices and prejudices will fall disportionately on particular sections of the community, especially women. Historically and at present, such norms are manifested as a prerogative of control over women's bodies. For this reason in particular, religious claims to accommodation in this context, while *prima facie* legitimate on constitutional grounds, must be appraised with such risks in mind. An employer cannot be permitted to exempt itself from the provisions of the Act, whether by merely invoking its connection to a religious denomination, or by designating employees' private conduct as being inconsistent with religious doctrines. Such claims are *prima facie* valid but they are not beyond scrutiny.

The second respondents' argument is a discourse about freedom. It contends that to apply the Act with full force to a religiously managed school would represent an interference in its freedom to manifest and meaningfully exercise, both collectively and individually, a set of religious beliefs which it wishes to uphold and express in its employment policies. Moreover it argues that this claim should be ascribed constitutional status. But what of Ms Flynn's countervailing interest in this case? Can hers not equally be understood as a claim about, and an interest in freedom—even one that has, perhaps, its own constitutional grounding? The respondents appeal to a notion of freedom understood as non-interference, that is, the freedom to be left to their own devices insofar as employment is concerned. They insist the State must permit individuals and associations to exercise and express their ideals and beliefs, their values and their doctrines, through their institutional prerogatives and prescriptions. And indeed this is a valid claim *prima facie*; it must have some weight, legally and constitutionally. However, it seems quite arbitrary to accept this as being a constitutional, freedom-based interest and thus as automatically trumping the supposedly lesser interest that the legislation and indeed, Ms Flynn's interest are understood as representing. Whether in the context of religion or otherwise, freedom cannot be understood solely as a claim against coercive interference or regulation by the State. Freedom must be understood in terms of how relationships of power affect individuals' ability to exercise legitimate choices and life plans in a real and concrete sense. Freedom depends on relationships of power, on the disparities of power between different persons and groups, and on how these disparities are regulated and checked. Freedom can be diminished not only by interference imposed by the State, but by various forms of domination that are suffered by virtue of unchecked or capricious private power. It is the kind of freedom that is lost with the constant apprehension and second-guessing of others, in the requirement to keep in others' good stead, to ingratiate oneself so as to keep in others' favour. Understood in this light, the Unfair Dismissals Act is not simply a limitation on the exercise of employers' freedom, imposed for the sake of some separate social goals. If we understand freedom in this subtler way, we can understand that although the legislation in question is a form of coercive state interference—one that affects the pursuit of religious and equivalent goals in some instances—it nonetheless *constitutes* or protects freedom rather than simply limiting it, because it offers some checks against abuses of power.

Thus freedom can be diminished through an absence of, or indeed a derogation from legislation, as much as, or perhaps more than, by legislative interference itself. Therefore, the court must pay heed to the various, often subtle injuries and harms that are inflicted upon those who are denied the protections of legislation of this sort. The court must also be mindful of the fact that, historically and at present, these injuries and harms have disproportionately been suffered by women, given the highly unequal distribution of power and resources between men and women in various spheres of "private" as well as "public" power. Legislation such as the Unfair Dismissals Act can be understood in part as an attempt to redress, albeit in some limited way, these historical forms of domination and oppression. Those who are denied the protection of legislation of this sort will experience domination as a form of arbitrary power—that is, the kind of domination we experience where others, often those with a greater measure of social or official power, may interfere at will in the choices we are positioned to make. Even if they are never dismissed or sanctioned, those whom the respondents would have us place beyond the Act's protection will have to engage in strategies of self-invigilation and self-censorship, checking their own life plans and projects, in order to apprehend potentially ruinous consequences. To deny persons in that position the protection of legislation is to place them under the unchecked power of potentially capricious employers, and thus it is to deny them a measure of their social and political freedom.

Of course, this freedom-based claim might be limited by other considerations, just as the respondents' competing claim is. But the nature of the interference is quite different in each case. The legislation may represent a form of interference in the respondents' freedom to exercise their religious beliefs by giving effect to various denominational prescriptions and classifications. But those institutional prescriptions cannot be effectuated and exercised without the support of the community and the infrastructure of the law and the State in the first instance. They are not merely a matter for the "private sphere"; rather they are buttressed and supported by the State in various direct and indirect ways. Discrimination and oppression inflicted by a private body is, in effect, indirectly upheld and inflicted by the State as well, considering how the State is intertwined with organisations such as denominational schools at various levels and in various ways, financial and otherwise. The interference suffered by institutions such as the respondents' is not an arbitrary interference; rather it is a proportionate restriction imposed by the national parliament that is aimed at enhancing the rights of others. The Court must respect the clear intendment of the legislature in reconciling competing freedom-based claims in this proportionate, non-arbitrary form. The interference suffered by Ms Flynn and her peers, on the other hand, is essentially arbitrary and invidious, as it places them at the more or less unbridled discretion of potentially capricious employers. It makes them vulnerable to a form of social caprice, and it affects their social, sexual and religious freedom in important and concrete ways. With such consequences in mind, the Court must not undermine the social protections the Act offers.

Accordingly, the Court allows the appeal.

7

Commentary on *MhicMathúna v Attorney General*

COLM O'CINNÉIDE

Introduction

MhicMathúna v Ireland is an intriguing case.[1] The identity of the litigants, the ambitious legal arguments they made before the High and Supreme Courts, and the reasoning deployed by the Irish courts in dismissing their claim all provide plenty of fuel for critical feminist analysis. Liam Thornton's feminist judgment engages with the full complexity of the case—in contrast to the Supreme Court's original decision—and provides us with a thought-provoking alternative ruling that is firmly rooted in a feminist perspective and yet alive to the constraints that bind the hands of appellate judges.

Background and Context

This case was commenced in April 1986, when the plaintiffs—Úna Bean MhicMathúna and her husband, Séamus MacMathúna—instituted legal proceedings seeking a declaration that various provisions of tax and social welfare legislation (and regulations made thereunder) were invalid on the basis that they breached Articles 40.1 and 41 of the 1937 Constitution.[2] Their case was based on a set of interconnected arguments, which can be boiled down to three principal contentions, namely that: (i) the lower level of tax and social welfare allowances received by married parents in relation to their dependent children as compared to the level of allowances received by unmarried parents constituted unlawful discrimination contrary to the constitutional equality guarantee set out in Article 40.1; (ii) this less favourable treatment of married mothers also constituted a breach of the state's obligation under Article 41 to protect and support the family based on marriage, on the grounds that it created an 'inducement' for couples not to enter into matrimony, or to separate and live apart if married; and (iii) the payment of below-inflation levels of welfare allowances paid

[1] *MhicMathúna v Ireland* [1995] IR 484.

[2] The plaintiffs also invoked the unenumerated personal rights provisions of Art 40.3 and the directive principles set out in Art 45 in support of their core arguments.

to married parents also breached the state's obligations under Article 41 by failing to ensure that married families enjoyed an adequate standard of living. Thornton J in his alternative judgment has described these lines of argument as the 'equality', 'protection of the marital family' and 'socio-economic' grounds of challenge respectively.

In other words, this was a test case brought by the MacMathúnas to challenge what they saw as the failure by the state to provide adequate support through the tax and social welfare systems for married parents with children. They argued that this failure constituted a violation of the state's duty to protect the traditional institution of marriage set out in Article 41, by making it very difficult for families such as theirs, who were living in impoverished socio-economic circumstances, to sustain their collective family life. They backed up this claim by presenting expert evidence to the effect that social support for married mothers with children had failed to keep pace with the rising rate of inflation in the period 1978–87, making it very difficult for the plaintiffs and other families in a similar situation to manage economically.[3] Furthermore, they contrasted this lack of support with the higher levels of tax and social welfare allowances made available to unmarried mothers—and argued that this differential level of support was not only discriminatory but constituted another line of attack against marriage, as it created an incentive for couples with children to live outside of the conventional bonds of matrimony.[4]

The identity of the plaintiffs in this case is worthy of note. Úna MhicMathúna was a leading figure in the pro-life movement and other Catholic conservative groupings for several decades. She was a founding member of *Mná na hÉireann* ['Women of Ireland'] (c. 1972–late 1970s) and the *Irish Housewives Union* (c. 1980–early 1990s), was very active in other organisations such as the *Council for Family Rights* (1980s), the *Friends of Youth Defence* (1990s) and *Cóir* ['Justice'] (2000s), and played a prominent role in the anti-abortion and anti-divorce campaigns of the 1980s and 1990s.[5] As a co-founder of *Mnáy hÉireann*, MhicMathúna spent much of the 1970s regularly attacking the erosion of traditional moral values by what she viewed as the 'foreign' influence represented by the women's liberation movement. Christina Murphy, Woman's Editor of *The Irish Times*, summed up the group's politics as being against 'obscenity, contraception, abortion, "so called" women's liberation, masturbation and mothers working outside the home'.[6] Úna continued to play a prominent role in the pro-life and anti-divorce movements well into the 2000s, becoming notorious for being caught on camera telling victorious pro-divorce campaigners in the aftermath of the 1995 referendum to 'G'way, ye wife-swapping sodomites'.[7] She married her

[3] This evidence is summarised in the judgment of the Supreme Court: see *MhicMathúna v Ireland* [1995] IR 484, 489–91.

[4] Mothers with children who had separated from their husbands, along with widows, fell into a different category for the purposes of the relevant tax and social welfare legislation: this is why the phrase 'unmarried mothers' is used throughout this commentary, as it was in the original judgments, in preference to the phrase 'single mothers'.

[5] This biographic information has been obtained from research in the online archive of *The Irish Times*, and also from a 2012 profile of Úna MhicMhathúna published on the *Come Here to Me* local history blog: see Sam McGrath, 'Úna Bean Mhic Mhathúna: Over 40 years of reactionary politics', 29 July 2012, at http://comeheretome.com/2012/07/29/Úna-bean-mhic-mhathÚna-40-years-of-reactionary-politics/ (last accessed 2 August 2015).

[6] ibid.

[7] ibid. See also Kathy Sheridan, 'How Wife-swappin' Sodomites Won the Right to Remarry', *The Irish Times*, 19 January 2015.

husband, Séamus MacMathúna, in the late 1960s: he was a leading folk singer who played a prominent role in two of the leading Irish cultural organisations, namely *Conradh na Gaelige* ['Irish League'] and *Comhaltas Ceoltóiri Éireann* ['Society of Musicians of Ireland']. As outlined in the judgments in the case, they had nine children: their daughter, Niamh Nic Mhathúna, was a founding member and leading light of the anti-abortion organisation *Youth Defence*, which was formed in the MacMathúna family home in 1992.[8]

The timing of the action is also worthy of note. It was launched in the run-up to the divorce referendum held two months later in June 1986, at a time when the Catholic Church and various pressure groups (with the organisations in which Úna MhicMhathúna was active) were fighting to reassert the dominance of the traditional concept of marriage. It also took place against the background of the global right-wing political backlash of the early to mid-1980s against the feminist gains and shifting social mores of the previous two decades.[9] Unmarried mothers became a particular focus of this backlash. In right-wing political and media discourse, they were regularly depicted as promiscuous 'welfare mothers' who embodied the social evils unleashed by both feminism and 'welfarism'.[10] In Ireland, Úna MhicMhathúna and members of her family were to the forefront in churning out this rhetoric, with her daughter, Síle, characterising single mothers in a letter published in the *Irish Press* on 18 August 1982 as 'pampered' women who had 'chosen fornication—or perhaps adultery' and grown wealthy on state benefits while married mothers were forced to take their 'place in the queue'.[11]

These views did not receive an exact echo in the legal arguments put forward by the MacMathúnas in this case. In fact, the plaintiffs emphasised that, in challenging the higher level of tax and welfare allowances allocated to unmarried mothers, they were not seeking to have these payments reduced but rather to ensure that state support for married parents was levelled up. However, by arguing that the provision of higher levels of social support to unmarried mothers constituted an inducement for couples to live outside the traditional matrimonial relationship, the plaintiffs' legal claim was essentially framing single mothers as a threat to the constitutionally privileged institution of marriage. In other words, this element of the plaintiffs' case can be viewed as an attempt to give 'neutral' legal expression to the hard-line 'family values' political discourse that was Úna MhicMhathúna's particular calling card: it indirectly pathologised single mothers, by depicting them as a threat to the orthodox social order based on traditional marriage.

Furthermore, as the High and Supreme Courts confirmed in their judgments in this case, if the plaintiffs had succeeded in their claim, the only remedy that the courts could have granted was to invalidate the statutory provisions that granted greater levels of tax and welfare allowances to unmarried mothers. In other words, if their legal action had been successful, it would have produced a levelling down of social protection for

[8] ibid.

[9] See Susan Faludi, *Backlash: he Undeclared War Against American Women* (London, Random House, 1992).

[10] See generally Parvin R Huda, 'Singled Out: A Critique of the Representation of Single Motherhood in Welfare Discourse' (2001) 7(2) *William and Mary Journal of Women and the Law* 341–81. For a recent Irish example of how unmarried mothers continue to be demonised in this way, see Kevin Myers, 'An Irishman's Diary', *The Irish Times*, 8 February 2005, who commented that 'our system of benefits to unmarried mothers is creating a long-term time-bomb. Even as things stand, we are bribing the unmotivated, the confused, the backward, the lazy into making the worst career decision of their young lives, and becoming professional unmarried mothers, living off the State until the grave takes over'.

[11] The original text of this letter as published is reproduced in McGrath, above n 5.

unmarried mothers. This was not the professed intention of the plaintiffs, and this negative result might ultimately have been remedied by the Oireachtas electing to level up benefits for married and unmarried mothers alike. However, as the Irish courts were at pains to emphasise, this 'levelling down' result would have been the immediate outcome of the case had it been successful, which would have seriously disrupted the provision of state support to unmarried mothers—who constituted then and continue to constitute a particularly vulnerable social group, who face especial difficulties in accessing the labour market and escaping poverty,[12] and who have also been the subject of particular demonisation, discrimination and human rights abuses in Ireland over the decades.[13]

As a result, there are key elements of the legal claim brought by the MacMathúnas that, when viewed in context, are clearly ripe for challenge from a feminist perspective. However, perhaps unexpectedly, given the identity and political beliefs of the plaintiffs, some of the legal arguments they advanced in this case also resonate with feminist perspectives on social justice and the value of labour. In fact, it could be argued that one of the central planks of the plaintiffs' case—namely that the state was obliged to ensure that mothers working at home were guaranteed an adequate standard of living—shares plenty of common ground with feminist social thought.

To begin with, the plaintiffs' legal claim highlights the manner in which the work of all mothers within the home remains radically undervalued. Women have historically assumed the bulk of unpaid devalued caregiving work in society, as part of a gendered hierarchy whereby they become dependent on a male 'breadwinner': as Huda puts it, 'differences between the two sexes' work translate into the man's valuable waged labor and the woman's invisible, debased, unpaid domestic labor'.[14] This applies to women living within traditional marriage structures as well as to unmarried mothers.[15] The MacMathúnas, in contesting the failure by the state to ensure that married mothers are guaranteed an adequate standard of living, were by extension challenging this structural undervaluing of the caregiving work of women. In all likelihood, Úna MhicMhathúna in particular would have been horrified to learn that she could be accused of making a feminist legal argument: however, the underlying logic of this aspect of her claim is not very far removed from the feminist critique of labour value.

Furthermore, this 'socio-economic' aspect of the MacMathúnas' case also chimes with some of the wider social justice concerns of the feminist movement. As Fineman has argued, feminist analysis has often failed to recognise the necessary links between transformation of the spheres of personal and family life and wider socio-economic context: however, the 'need for recognition of caregiving can evolve into a general critique of … the ideology of free market capitalism and a claim for the universal provision of social goods'.[16] In other

[12] See Huda, above n 10. See also Mary M Slaughter, 'The Legal Construction of "Mother"' in Martha A Fineman and Isabel Karpin (eds), *Mothers in Law: Feminist Theory and The Legal Regulation of Motherhood* (New York, Columbia University Press, 1995) 73–102.

[13] See generally James M Smith, *Ireland's Magdalen Laundries and the Nation's Architecture of Containment* (Manchester, Manchester University Press, 2012). For a contemporary journalistic perspective, see also Kitty Holland, 'Why Ireland is Not a Welcoming Place for Single Parents', *The Irish Times*, 27 June 2014.

[14] Huda, above n 10, at 354.

[15] The latter group receives additional social support from the state unavailable to the former, but the singling-out of single mothers in this way can enhance their social stigmatisation, as discussed in detail by Huda, above n 10.

[16] Martha A Fineman, *The Autonomy Myth: A Theory of Dependency* (New York, New Press, 2005).

words, feminist critique points towards the need for the state to recognise the existence of certain basic socio-economic rights, such as freedom from poverty.[17] The MacMathúnas, in arguing that this constitutional commitment should be interpreted by the courts as imposing substantive obligations upon the state, were thus in effect arguing that the Constitution should be read as recognising the existence of legally enforceable socio-economic rights—a position that many feminist theorists would endorse, notwithstanding the distinctively anti-feminist orientation of other strands of their claim.

Taking all this background and context into account, the reason why *MhicMathúna* is an intriguing case is apparent. Aspects of the legal claims made by the plaintiffs chime with feminist perspectives, while others are radically at variance—as might be expected, given Úna MhicMhathúna's political views. In turn, the response of the Irish courts to the complexity of this test case is also interesting, not least for what it has to say about the development of Irish constitutional law when viewed through a feminist lens.

The High and Supreme Court Judgments

From a doctrinal point of view, the MacMathúnas' legal arguments were ambitious, to put it mildly.[18] This is particularly true of the first and third grounds of their claim—namely the 'equality' and 'socio-economic' points of challenge. The equality jurisprudence of the Irish courts is radically underdeveloped: Irish judges have been very reluctant to give much substance to the constitutional guarantee of non-discrimination set out in Article 40.1, and have been quick to accept that differences in treatment between different social groups are based on legitimate grounds.[19] Similarly, the courts have also been generally unwilling to recognise that the 1937 Constitution imposes legally enforceable obligations on the state to provide social support to particular social groups, or otherwise gives rise to enforceable socio-economic rights claims.[20]

As a result, the MacMathúnas were always going to struggle to establish the existence of a breach of the non-discrimination right set out in Article 40.1, or the existence of a constitutionally recognised right to a minimum level of income. Furthermore, in judgments such as *Madigan v Attorney General*,[21] the Irish courts have repeatedly emphasised that the legislature and executive enjoyed wide discretion in framing national tax and social welfare policies. As a result, the MacMathúnas were venturing into terrain where the Irish courts have been reluctant to tread. In general, the Irish courts have been allergic to the idea that

[17] See in general Beth Goldblatt, 'Gender, Poverty and the Development of the Right to Social Security' (2014) 10(4) *International Journal of Law in Context* 460–77.

[18] The 'socio-economic' element of their claim was particularly novel: Walsh J, writing extra-judicially at the time their case was commenced, noted his astonishment that Art 41.2.2 had never been invoked by a litigant in support of a claim that the state was under a positive duty to provide adequate social support for mothers with children—see Brain Walsh, 'The Constitution and Constitutional Rights' in Frank Litton, *The Constitution of Ireland 1937–1987* (Dublin, Institute of Public Administration, 1988) 86–109, 98.

[19] See Colm O'Cinnéide, 'Aspirations Unfulfilled: The Equality Right in Irish Law' (2010) 1(1) *Irish Human Rights Law Journal* 1–41; Oran Doyle, *Constitutional Equality Law* (Dublin, Round Hall, 2004).

[20] Gerry Whyte, *Social Inclusion and the Legal System: Public Interest Law in Ireland* (Dublin, IPA, 2002).

[21] *Madigan v Attorney General* [1986] ILRM 136. See also now *Sinnott v Minister for Education* [2001] 2 IR 545.

the 1937 Constitution should be interpreted as having a social dimension.[22] The ideology of liberal individualism has proved to be very potent in Irish constitutional interpretation, notwithstanding the gestures towards a more communitarian/'caregiving' ethos set out in the text of provisions such as Articles 41 and 45.

The one aspect of the MacMathúnas' claim that had some foundation in existing case law was their second ground of challenge, ie the 'protection of the marital family' ground. The Supreme Court had shown previous willingness to strike down tax and social welfare legislation on the basis that it treated married couples less favourably than unmarried couples and thus constituted a threat to the traditional institution of marriage. For example, the Supreme Court ruled in *Murphy v Attorney General* that the imposition of a higher rate of tax on married couples when compared to an unmarried couple living together constituted a breach of Article 41.[23] Similarly, in *Hyland v Minister for Social Welfare*,[24] the Supreme Court held that a limitation on the amount of social welfare that an unemployed married couple could receive, which did not apply to unmarried couples, again breached the positive obligation imposed upon the State by Article 41.3.1 to protect the institution of marriage.

The MacMathúnas could therefore point to Supreme Court decisions that had ruled that less favourable treatment of married couples in the context of the functioning of the tax and social welfare systems had breached Article 41. In other words, their argument that the higher levels of social support received by unmarried mothers potentially threatened the marital family was the only aspect of their claim that rested on a relatively solid basis of precedent. From a feminist perspective, this is striking: the element of the MacMathúnas' claim that was arguably most problematic, on the basis that it valorised marriage while framing state support for unmarried mothers as a threat to its integrity, was also the element with the best foundation in existing case law.

In general, the text of Article 41 and the manner in which it has been interpreted by the Irish courts can be viewed as problematic from a feminist perspective. Article 41.3.1, as interpreted by the Supreme Court in cases such as *Murphy* and *Hyland*, arguably valorises the institution of marriage and establishes a hierarchy of families—with the traditional family based on marriage on top. Other types of family grouping are not necessarily excluded from the scope of Article 41,[25] but they are implicitly framed as enjoying second-class status at best. Furthermore, the language of Article 41.2 in particular places specific emphasis on the work done by women within the home, ensuring that a gendered understanding of family responsibilities and labour value is built into the textual foundation of the Irish constitutional order. However, Article 41 is one of the few elements of the Irish constitutional order

[22] When arguing their case before the High Court, the plaintiffs attempted to bolster their 'socio-economic' claim by invoking the provisions of Art 45.2.1, which provide that the state shall direct its policy towards securing that 'citizens (all of whom, men and women equally, have the right to an adequate means of livelihood) may through their occupations find the means of making reasonable provision for their domestic needs'. However, as Carroll J confirmed in the High Court, the directive principles set out in Art 45.1 cannot be invoked as a basis for a legal challenge against the state.

[23] *Murphy v Attorney General* [1982] I IR 241.

[24] *Hyland v Minister for Social Welfare* [1989] IR 624.

[25] See the comments by McCarthy J in *L v L* [1992] ILRM 115, at 123–24, cited by Thornton J in his rewritten judgment.

that gives rise to legally enforceable positive obligations that, as demonstrated by *Murphy* and *Hyland*, are capable of taking effect in the socio-economic sphere. This is why it became the principal point of attack for the MacMathúnas in this case, which presumably chimed completely with their political convictions: however, from a feminist viewpoint, it sheds a troubling light on the system of values underpinning the Irish constitutional framework.

The MacMathúnas were assisted by counsel in presenting their case before the High Court, where their claim was dismissed by Carroll J in January 1989.[26] Subsequently, they represented themselves before the Supreme Court, demonstrating the extent of their activist commitment. Inevitably, their arguments before the Supreme Court appear to have been less legally-structured than was the case in the court below: however, as the judgment of the Supreme Court makes clear, this was taken into account by the Court in adjudicating their claim. It took five years for their appeal to be heard—in June 1994, reflecting the glacial pace of justice at the highest level of the Irish courts—before the Supreme Court handed down its judgment a month later in July 1994, dismissing their appeal.[27]

Both the High Court and the Supreme Court rejected the claim for broadly similar reasons. In essence, both courts concluded that: (i) the state had legitimate grounds for granting higher levels of state support to unmarried mothers, so no discrimination contrary to Article 40.1 had taken place; (ii) the plaintiffs had not established their case that this differential level of support constituted a threat to the institution of marriage; and (iii) there was no legally enforceable right to an adequate standard of living. Both courts also emphasised that the courts would not intervene in 'political decisions' relating to tax and welfare policy unless a clear breach of constitutional rights was established to exist—which was not the case here.

In other words, the High and Supreme Court judgments affirmed existing constitutional orthodoxy in respect of socio-economic rights. They rejected the argument that Article 41 could be interpreted as giving rise to a legally enforceable right to an adequate standard of living, and concluded that the courts should not interfere with political decisions relating to tax and welfare policy absent a clear violation of established individual rights. Finlay P, in delivering the single judgment of the Supreme Court, left open the possibility that 'under certain circumstances statutory provisions, particularly those removing in its entirety financial support for the family' might violate Article 41.[28] However, the substantial cuts in social support at issue in this case did not pass that hypothetical threshold. The judgments in *MhicMathúna* thus exemplify the highly deferential approach to political decision-making that Whyte has identified as the default mode of Irish constitutional adjudication relating to socio-economic issues.[29]

Furthermore, in the Supreme Court, this deferential approach was also applied to dispose of the MacMathúnas' claims that the higher level of support granted to unmarried mothers constituted both discrimination and a threat to the marital family. Previously, in *Murphy* and *Hyland* as discussed above, the Supreme Court had concluded that the less favourable treatment of married couples within the framework of tax and social welfare legislation did

[26] *MhicMathúna v Ireland* [1989] IR 504.
[27] *MhicMathúna v Ireland* [1995] IR 484.
[28] ibid, 499.
[29] Whyte, above n 20, especially at 158–59.

constitute a threat to the marital family. However, the close review of the legitimacy of the legislation under review in *Murphy* and *Hyland* was not duplicated in *MhicMathúna*, where the Court elected instead to defer to the political branches and concluded without much discussion that the plaintiffs had failed to establish that the legislature had erred in granting higher levels of social support to single mothers.

This meant that the Supreme Court did not discuss in detail the vulnerable status of unmarried mothers, or the question of whether the duty imposed by the state under Article 41 to protect the marital family also extended to cover families not based around the traditional institution of marriage. These issues were glossed over in Finlay P's judgment, which in general fails to engage with the complex legal and social issues thrown up by this case. From a feminist perspective, the Court can be accused of retreating into legal formalism: the Court based its judgment on the need to show deference to political decision-making, rather than fully responding to the legal arguments made by the MacMathúnas.

In contrast, Carroll J in the High Court did engage in detail with the plaintiffs' arguments in relation to unmarried mothers. She began her judgment by noting that the only remedy available to the plaintiffs was to have the relevant legislation declared invalid: as a result, she pointed out that 'the best result the plaintiffs could hope to achieve would be the removal of benefits from unmarried mothers and their children and from the parents of incapacitated children without achieving any benefits for themselves'.[30] She went on to conclude that the Oireachtas was justified in treating unmarried and married mothers differently:

> The parent on his or her own has a more difficult task in bringing the children up single-handedly because two parents living together can give each other mutual support and assistance. I have no doubt that the role of a single parent is more difficult than that of two parents and that in giving a tax-free allowance to a single parent, the Oireachtas recognised that and attempted to alleviate it.[31]

Furthermore, in relation to the argument that higher levels of social support for unmarried mothers constituted an inducement not to enter matrimony, Carroll J held:

> I am completely satisfied that no such inducements not to marry exist ... The burden and responsibility of parenthood is heavier on a single parent than on a married couple living together. The extra support directed by the State to single parents (including unmarried mothers) is child centred and cannot, in my opinion, be designated as an attack on the institution of marriage.[32]

Carroll J's judgment in the High Court thus demonstrated a healthy awareness of the vulnerable status of unmarried mothers. In this regard, it may be worth highlighting that Carroll J was the first female judge appointed to the High Court: her judgment in *MhicMathúna* could perhaps, with due qualification, be cited as an example of how female judges may bring fresh perspectives and different degrees of emphasis to bear on legal problems.[33] In contrast, there is little discussion of this element of the case in the judgment of Finlay P. The Supreme Court endorsed Carroll J's arguments in general terms,

[30] *MhicMathúna v Ireland* [1989] IR 504, 510.
[31] ibid, 512.
[32] ibid, 513–14.
[33] See generally on this point, Erika Rackley, *Women, Judging and Judiciary: From Difference to Diversity* (London, Routledge, 2013).

but for the most part simply tolled the bell of deference. It could be argued that this represented a wasted opportunity to say more about the vulnerability of unmarried mothers, and in general to engage at a deeper level with the complex questions thrown up by *MhicMathúna*. Certainly, 20 years on, the Supreme Court's case law on discrimination, socio-economic rights and the scope of Article 41 has not developed much beyond its conclusions in *MhicMathúna*.[34]

The Feminist Judgment

Thornton J's rewritten judgment adopts a strongly feminist approach in its reasoning. Like Carroll J's judgment in the High Court, it foregrounds the vulnerable status of unmarried mothers, while also acknowledging the positive contribution they make to Irish society. Thus, in rejecting the plaintiffs' discrimination claim, he concludes that the grant of higher levels of social support to unmarried mothers is objectively justified on the basis in particular of the 'social stigma' they continue to face in Irish society. He also affirms that the 'recognised special position' of the family based on marriage under the Constitution 'in no way prevents the Oireachtas protecting other vulnerable categories of individuals or groups', or can justify 'devaluing the important social function played within Irish society of single parents'.

In addition, Thornton J's judgment affirms that the constitutional duty to protect the family set out in Article 41 extends beyond the traditional family based on marriage, to include 'obligations of support' towards unmarried mothers performing caring duties. He also acknowledges the problematic manner in which the gendered wording of Article 41.2 in particular valorises the role of women within the home. Thus, in contrast to the original judgment of the Supreme Court, this revised judgment faces up to the gendered language of the constitutional text, and strives to interpret it in a manner that reflects critical feminist perspectives. In particular, he seeks to read the text in a manner that opens up some room for recognition of the caregiving work undertaken by all mothers.

Furthermore, in relation to the socio-economic rights aspect of the claim, Thornton J's judgment suggests that

> there may be occasions, where, due to the absolute failure of the State to ensure individuals and families have a standard of living appropriate to this society, where human dignity is debased and/or bodily integrity is not respected and/or individuals right to develop as a human person is seriously hampered, that the Courts are constitutionally mandated to intervene.

This goes further than the Supreme Court did in its original judgment, which just flagged up the possibility that, as quoted above, the courts might intervene 'in certain circumstances' to strike down statutory provisions that removed financial support 'in its entirety' from families in need. In contrast, Thornton J indicates that the Irish courts may be

[34] See generally in relation to discrimination, O'Cinnéide, above n 19; in relation to socio-economic rights, *Sinnott v Minister for Education* [2001] 2 IR 545; for the scope of Art 41, see, eg, *Zappone v Revenue Commissioners* [2008] 2 IR 417.

prepared to intervene where the state has failed to provide social support to either individuals or families, where this would result in a denial of their human dignity and/or right to bodily integrity. In other words, he suggests that the Irish constitutional order might be capable of recognising a right to a minimum level of social support in situations where human dignity was on the line, which reflects Fineman's arguments, outlined above, about the need to acknowledge the existence of 'claims for the universal provision of social goods' to all in need.

Nevertheless, Thornton J's judgment recognises that the hands of appellate judges are tied to a large extent, as a result of their limited democratic legitimacy. As a consequence, while he notes the gendered language of Article 41.2, he also acknowledges the fact '[t]hat such language remains in our basic law is something for the political realm to consider', ie that the problematic language of the constitutional text can only be corrected via the political process. He also makes clear that the courts will be slow to interfere with political decision-making in the socio-economic sphere, and concludes that the MacMathúnas had not made out a case for judicial intervention in this regard. A feminist judge less concerned with respecting the parameters of the existing system of separation of powers might have gone further than Thornton J does, in particular by perhaps recognising the existence of a constitutional right to an adequate standard of income. However, Thornton J's judgment is faithful to the constrained role allocated to judicial decision-making within the Irish constitutional order, and recognises the limits that exist in practice to the freedom of appellate judges to re-shape Irish law.

The rewritten judgment therefore engages fully with the complexities of the *MhicMathúna* case, whilst also acknowledging the existence of substantial constraints on the ability of appellate judges to infuse feminist perspectives into their interpretation of law. However, the true value of Thornton J's rewritten judgment lies in the manner in which it illustrates the potency of critical feminist approaches to disentangle the progressive and reactionary elements of a cross-grained set of legal arguments such as those at issue in *MhicMathúna*.

Una MhicMathúna and Seamus MacMathúna, Plaintiffs v Ireland and the Attorney General, Defendants

[S.C. No. 105 of 1989]

Supreme Court 14th July 1994

Thornton J. **14th July 1994**

Introduction

The plaintiffs are challenging the constitutionality of various legislative enactments within the taxation and social welfare field. The sum of the plaintiffs' arguments revolve around the unconstitutionality of certain legislative provisions that treat married couples less favourably for tax and social welfare purposes than certain other family forms.

Una MhicMathúna and Seamus MacMathúna married in February 1969. Mrs. MhicMathúna gave birth to nine children between November 1969 and October 1983. Mr. MacMathúna is employed by Comhaltas Ceoltóiri Éireann as a promoter of Irish music with gross earnings of IR£265 per week, with a net take home pay of IR£193 per week. Mrs. MhicMathúna has not been in paid employment since her marriage, and has worked in the home and cared for their children full time. In addition, Mrs. MhicMathúna spoke of the financial difficulties that the family face, suggesting that she may have to enter paid employment or the family may have to emigrate so as to make ends meet. The trial judge accepted the evidence of the plaintiffs that they are finding it difficult to manage financially, and I too accept this evidence. Ultimately, the plaintiffs' legal challenge was rejected by Ms. Justice Mella Carroll in the High Court, and it is this decision the plaintiffs now appeal. For the reasons outlined below, I too would dismiss the plaintiffs' appeal.

The Legal Challenge in the Supreme Court

While the plaintiffs had the assistance of counsel in the High Court, the plaintiffs represented themselves before the Supreme Court. With that in mind, the Court needs to be mindful that arguments put by the plaintiffs, as lay litigants, may not be as carefully crafted as the arguments presented by the defendants. That said, the precise grounds of appeal from the High Court decision were difficult to pinpoint. However, the duty of a judge is to assist lay litigants in so far as is possible.

Before this court, the plaintiffs emphasised that they do not wish allowances or social assistance payments to any other family form to be denied or reduced. As was held in *Maher v. Attorney General* [1973] I.R. 140, the task of Courts is not to re-write legislation, but simply to decide on its constitutionality. In this Court, the plaintiffs adopted a more limited argument than in the High Court, not wanting a tax-free allowance for disabled children to be impacted by the challenged provisions. If the legislation is to fall, it must do so in its entirety. Carroll J. in the High Court clearly stated this principle, noting at p. 510 of the report that:-

> "In declaring a section of an Act to be unconstitutional the court cannot delete part of a section if to do so would amount to an amendment rather than interpretation."

The plaintiffs argue that legislative reduction and ultimately the withdrawal of child tax-free allowances between 1978/1979 and 1986/1987 for marital parents with children and provision of social assistance allowance for unmarried mothers, which the first plaintiff is not entitled to, is invidious discrimination and a fundamental attack against the marital family, in breach of Article 40.1 and Article 41 of the Irish Constitution.

The taxation statutes challenged by the plaintiffs, as identified by Mella Carroll J. in the High Court, are Section 138A of the Income Tax Act, 1967 (as inserted by Section 4 of the Finance Act, 1979 and as subsequently amended) and section 3 of the Finance Act, 1986. In sum, these provisions amended taxation law, which ultimately withdrew the right of the plaintiffs to benefit from a child tax-free allowance. However, these statutory provisions maintained child tax-free allowances for certain families, namely: separated married parent, widowed parents, single mothers raising children, and couples/persons raising a disabled child. The child tax-free allowances maintained within these statutes ranged from IR£1,500 for widowed persons to IR£2,000 for separated married parent raising a child, single mothers and persons rearing an incapacitated child who suffered from mental or physical infirmity. Section 197 of the Social Welfare (Consolidation) Act, 1981 (re-enacting Section 8 of the Social Welfare Act, 1973) provided for a social assistance payment for unmarried mothers. The first plaintiff is not entitled to this payment, by virtue of her marital status, and claims that this is either unequal treatment and/or an unconstitutional attack on the marital family.

In evidence placed before the High Court the plaintiffs sought to adduce that the reduction in tax-free allowances from the second plaintiff's salary, from IR£240 to nil per annum, and various increases in social welfare payments for their children, amounted to an average 6.8% increase per annum for a nine-year period, from 1978/1979 to 1986/1987. This was far short of the 12.3% per annum Consumer Price Index increase. The plaintiffs also introduced various comparators but, as noted in the High Court, seemed to have a particular interest in the financial allowances and taxation affairs of single mothers. The plaintiffs utilised a comparator; an unmarried single mother with nine children the same age as the plaintiffs' family. This comparator single mother would have received IR£2,197.22 per annum more in social welfare payments than the plaintiffs' total state allowances over the period 1978/1979 to 1986/1987. This was an average rise of 14.4% per annum in social welfare assistance payments, and was 1.9% over the Consumer Price Index increase for this period.

The defendants argue that the State is entitled to take into account the different social functions of unmarried mothers in determining that such persons are in need of greater support under Article 40.1 of the Constitution. Article 41 of the Constitution does not require the State to ensure that the constitutional family, at all times, must be treated better than or equally to an unwed mother, or any other societal group however so categorised. It is, the defendants argue, a matter for the Oireachtas to consider whether social assistance payments and tax-free allowances should or should not be provided to any family form, constitutionally protected families or otherwise.

Issues for Constitutional Consideration

To my mind, there are three core issues of constitutionality that the court must consider.

The constitutional equality protection: Whether the statutory exclusion of the plaintiffs from benefiting from particular child tax-free allowances under the Finance Acts and/or the provision of a social assistance payment for unmarried mothers is contrary to Article 40.1 of the Constitution?

Constitutional marital family protection: If the above does not violate Article 40.1 of the constitution, is it an invidious attack on the marital family, contrary to Article 41 of the Constitution?

The socio-economic rights ground: Apart from both other grounds above, are there any other constitutional obligations upon the State to provide for the plaintiffs, given that they are finding it difficult to live on their limited income?

Before considering each of these claims in turn, it is important to emphasise that decisions on levels of taxation and levels of social welfare payments, are for the Executive and the Oireachtas.

Article 11 of the Constitution provides:-

> "All revenues of the State from whatever source arising shall, subject to such exception as may be provided by law, form one fund, and shall be appropriated for the purposes and in the manner and subject to the charges and liabilities determined and imposed by law."

Article 17.2 of the Constitution provides:-

> "Dáil Éireann shall not pass any vote or resolution, and no law shall be enacted, for the appropriation of revenue or other public moneys unless the purpose of the appropriation shall have been recommended to Dáil Éireann by a message from the Government signed by the Taoiseach."

Article 45 of the Constitution is concerned with "principles of social policy … intended for the general guidance of the Oireachtas" and "shall not be cognisable by any Court". However, as Kenny J. stated in *Ryan v. Attorney General* [1965] I.R. 294 at pp. 335–336, the Court may take into consideration Article 45 "when deciding whether a claimed constitutional right exists." In the same manner, this Court considers that Article 45 also allows organs of State, in particular the Oireachtas, as the democratic expression of the Peoples' will in social and economic policy matters, to be best disposed to ensuring a just social order, subject to the requirements and obligations of the Irish Constitution.

The Oireachtas, as recognised in Article 45.1 of the Constitution:-

> "shall strive to promote the welfare of the whole people by securing and protecting as effectively as it may a social order in which justice and charity shall inform all the institutions of the national life."

Similarly, Article 45.2 of the Constitution obliges the State to:-

> "… direct its policy towards securing–
>
> i. That the citizens (all of whom, men and women equally, have the right to an adequate means of livelihood) may through their occupations find the means of making reasonable provision for their domestic needs.

ii. That the ownership and control of the material resources of the community may be so distributed amongst private individuals and the various classes as best to subserve the common good."

In a similar vein, the State commits itself, through the vehicle of Article 45.4.1 of the Constitution:-

> "... to safeguard with especial care the economic interests of the weaker sections of the community, and, where necessary, to contribute to the support of the infirm, the widow, the orphan, and the aged."

O'Higgins C.J in *Madigan v. Attorney General* [1986] I.L.R.M. 136 at 161 noted that the State is constitutionally empowered to collect taxes and distribute those taxes in "accordance with the principles of social justice and having regard to the exigencies of the common good". In *Madigan v. Attorney General* [1986] I.L.R.M. 136, that plaintiff had challenged the constitutionality of the imposition of a residential property tax in the Finance Act 1983. In the course of that decision O'Hanlon J. noted (at p. 151):-

> "very considerable latitude must be allowed to the legislature in the enormously complex task of organising and directing the financial affairs of the State."

I agree with O'Hanlon J.'s assessment, but would add that while the State has considerable latitude, this could never offend against constitutional rights of individuals or the family as protected in the Constitution. Therefore, in exploring the plaintiffs' Supreme Court arguments, this Court must consider whether any of the legislative provisions that provide differing social assistance payments or taxation allowances to different family formations is permissible.

The Equality Ground

The first limb of the plaintiffs' arguments on taxation invokes Article 40.1 of the Irish Constitution. Article 40.1 states:-

> "All citizens shall, as human persons, be held equal before the law.
>
> This shall not be held to mean that the State shall not in its enactments have due regard to differences of capacity, physical and moral, and of social function."

The plaintiffs, at least in the High Court, utilised single mothers as one example of the preferential differentiation within the tax and social welfare codes in comparison to the marital family. In the High Court they provided detailed statistical analysis of their own economic means, including their entitlement to State welfare payments. One of their core arguments is that State support did not keep pace with the Consumer Price Index (in comparison to a single mother who received State support slightly above the Consumer Price Index). The plaintiffs preferred to receive tax-free allowances, rather than forms of social assistance payments. The Government's policy over the 1980s was to eventually abolish child based tax-free allowances for married couples. The reason provided for this was that this tax-free allowance unduly favoured high earners. Those on lower earnings did not receive the same degree of benefit from child tax-free allowances. However, the Oireachtas did, by virtue of Section 3 of the Finance Act, 1986, maintain a child tax-free allowance for widowed persons (of IR£1,500) and unmarried mothers (IR£2,000). Are such distinctions, between married parents' tax-free allowances and categories of other single parent's tax-free allowances, permissible under Article 40.1?

According to the 1989 Labour Force Survey, there were 44,330 recorded lone parents, with 37,470 recorded lone parent mothers. According to the Census of the Population 1991, Volume 3, there were 44,071 lone parents; 38,235 lone mothers and 5,836 lone fathers. These are the minority of parents. Over 90% of children were reared by marital couples, of which there were 414,560. The Oireachtas, in not treating lone mothers in a similar fashion in the tax or social welfare codes to marital parents, recognises that particular social, economic and societal disadvantages may be faced by a lone parent. The effects of the legislative child-focused taxation and social assistance measures enable (at least in part) a lone parent to gain financial autonomy and secure substantive socio-economic rights for her family.

The taxation and social welfare statutes challenged clearly treat the plaintiffs differently than other family forms. However, the Oireachtas is constitutionally permitted to differentiate. Treating all categories of persons equally, despite differences in capacities or social functions, may in fact result in treating persons unequally. The historical, and in some cases continuing, condemnatory treatment of single parents in and by Irish society continues, notwithstanding legislative developments such as the Finance Act 1986. The introduction of a social assistance allowance for unmarried women with a child emerged after the recommendation of the 1972 Commission on the Status of Women, where the final report (at para. 338) noted:-

> "We consider that there should be some financial support available to an unmarried mother who keeps her child ..."

The Oireachtas could rely on its detailed and significant knowledge, as the elected branch, of the hardships faced by different family forms. In 1989, 18% of lone mothers were in full-time employment, while 7% of lone mothers were in part-time employment (Millar et al., *Lone Parents, Poverty and Public Policy in Ireland* (Combat Poverty Agency), p. 45). It is important to emphasise that one-parent families face particular hardships in this country. The majority of these families live in or at risk of poverty. The provision of either child tax-free allowances or unmarried mothers allowance recognises the many difficulties lone mothers, and lone parents more generally, can face. This may be in accessing the labour market, or where a social assistance payment is provided where a single parent must provide a home life for her children.

In *Dennehy v. Minister for Social Welfare* (unreported judgment, Barron J., 26 July 1983), the High Court held that there had not been a violation of the Constitution by virtue of provision of a deserted wives allowance under the Social Welfare (Consolidation) Act, 1981, where no similar benefit accrued to deserted men. The validity of this decision was recently affirmed by Costello J. in the High Court in *Lowth v. Minister for Social Welfare* [1994] I.L.R.M. 378, where similar constitutional arguments relating to equality under Article 40.1 between deserted wives and deserted husbands were rejected. In the case before this Court, Mrs. MhicMathúna is clearly legislatively barred from receiving the social assistance payment for unmarried mothers. In the High Court, Carroll J. rejected the arguments of the plaintiff that legislative provision of social assistance payments for unmarried mothers constituted an 'inducement' not to marry ([1989] 1 I.R. 504 at 513).

Coupled with this court's analysis of the application of Article 41 of the Constitution below, and recognising the unique hardships that can be faced by a single female parent raising a child or children, the Oireachtas acted in a constitutionally appropriate manner as regards confining this social assistance payment to unmarried mothers.

In this particular case, Mrs. MhicMathúna can point to the fact that she is a stay-at-home carer. Like any other person in a parenting role, her family faces economic challenges. To what extent can the Oireachtas deem Mrs. MhicMathúna's role as a mother to be different to that of a lone female parent? The payment is designed to enable unmarried mothers who have no or very limited other sources of income, to get some assistance from the State. The core purpose of the unmarried mothers allowance is a poverty prevention mechanism. It is not designed to, nor does it in fact, in any way violate the constitutional guarantee of equality. This does not diminish or seek to privilege the significant caring role that mothers, be they married or unmarried, provide our society.

Courts should not trespass on the decisions taken by the Oireachtas, where such decisions do not impact upon the constitutional rights of the more dominant family set-up in the State, that of the marital family. Lone parents have limited political power as a group. Therefore, it is important to my mind that this court recognises this reality in any assessment of constitutional equality arguments. In protecting politically under-represented and minority groupings in the State, the Court needs to be cautious in ensuring it does not further entrench socio-economic disadvantage.

> Legislative provisions will only be struck down where these are:-
>
> "arbitrary, capricious or otherwise not reasonably capable, when objectively viewed in the light of social function involved, of supporting the selection or classification complained of" (*Dillane v. Ireland* [1980] I.L.R.M. 167 at 169).

As was noted by this Court in *Murphy v. Attorney General* [1982] I.R. 241 at p. 284, distinctions between taxation entitlements of married couples and other non-marital family forms do not automatically raise concerns as regards the constitutional protection of equality. As stated by Carroll J. in the High Court at p. 511:-

> "The parent on his or her own has a more difficult task in bringing the children up single-handedly because two parents living together can give each other mutual support and assistance. I have no doubt that the role of a single parent is more difficult than that of two parents and that in giving a tax-free allowance to a single parent, the Oireachtas recognised that and attempted to alleviate it."

That the Oireachtas has decided to differentiate between the taxation benefits of people in situations like the plaintiffs and an unmarried mother who is earning a living, recognises the potential hardship that an unmarried mother can face in Irish society, by having to raise her child or children alone, and engaging in the labour force. This hardship is well documented, with children raised by a single mother more likely to face poverty in Ireland. There continues to be a social stigma attached to a single mother raising her child or children that does not attach to children of a marital union. Approaching the equality protection provided for in Article 40.1, while there is a distinction between the rights of on the one hand marital parents, and on the other an unmarried mother, this distinction is justified.

The Marital Family Ground

Even if the child tax allowance, available to categories of single parents, and unmarried mothers allowance does not violate Article 40.1, is the availability of these advantages a violation of Article 41?

Provisions of Article 41 relied upon by the plaintiffs include–

"1 1° The State recognises the Family as the natural primary and fundamental unit group of Society, and as a moral institution possessing inalienable and imprescriptible rights, antecedent and superior to all positive law.
2° The State, therefore, guarantees to protect the Family in its constitution and authority, as the necessary basis of social order and as indispensable to the welfare of the Nation and the State.
3 1° The State pledges itself to guard with special care the institution of Marriage, on which the Family is founded, and to protect it against attack."

The plaintiffs also made reference to Article 41.2 of the Constitution, which states–

"2 1° In particular, the State recognises that by her life within the home, woman gives to the State a support without which the common good cannot be achieved.
2° The State shall, therefore, endeavour to ensure that mothers shall not be obliged by economic necessity to engage in labour to the neglect of their duties in the home."

Article 41 of the Constitution creates:-

> "... not merely a State interest but a State obligation to protect the family" (*O'B. v. S.* [1984] 1 I.R. 316 at p. 338, per Walsh J.).

There is no definition of family provided for in the Constitution or in any subsequent legislative enactment. Past jurisprudence from this Court and lower Courts has solely interpreted Article 41 as protecting the marital family. Walsh J. in *The State (Nicolaou) v. An Bord Uachtala* [1966] I.R. 567 stated that the family referred to in Article 41 "is the family as founded on the institution of marriage ...". Hamilton J. in the High Court in *Murphy v. Attorney General* [1982] I.R. 241 at p. 276 stated:-

> "Article 41, which deals with the family, relates only to the family based on marriage."

In *Murphy v. Attorney General* [1982] I.R. 241, this Court found that certain provisions of the Income Tax Acts (as amended) violated the State's obligation to protect the family based on marriage. In this case, the plaintiffs, a married couple, were treated less favourably than a co-habiting couple living together. This difference was not "compensated for or justified by [other] such advantages or privileges" (per Kenny J., [1982] I.R. 241 at 287). In *Hyland v. Minister for Social Welfare* [1989] I.R. 624, this Court found provisions of the Social Welfare (No. 2) Act, 1985 to be invalid, where purported changes to social welfare law would result in a marital couple being IR£11.18 worse off per week in comparison with a cohabiting couple. During the course of this decision, this Court noted that changes to taxation or social welfare laws could not act as a defence to an attack on the institution of the marital family. In both *Hyland* and *Murphy*, the core issue that had to be decided was whether differences in taxation and social welfare affecting negatively the marital family, were constitutionally permissible.

An argument that was raised before this Court, but not in the High Court by the plaintiffs must also be considered. The plaintiffs claim that Article 7 of the Social Welfare (Social Assistance Allowance) Regulations, 1973 acts as an inducement for married women to leave their husbands so as to claim unmarried women's social assistance allowance.

Article 7 of the Social Welfare (Social Assistance Allowance) Regulations, 1973 (S.I. No. 190) provides:-

> "A woman shall be disqualified from receiving an allowance if and so long as she and any person are cohabiting as man and wife."

This argument is based on a misunderstanding by the plaintiffs of the effect of this Regulation and a misreading, when read with Section 197 of the Social Welfare (Consolidation) Act, 1981. As Mrs. MhicMathúna is married, even if she were to leave her husband, she would not be entitled to unmarried mother's social assistance payment. Although not mentioned during argument, but so as to cover all bases, the Court wishes to inform the plaintiffs that, even if Mrs. MhicMathúna did gain a judicial separation under the Judicial Separation and Family Law Reform Act, 1989, this does not have the effect of extinguishing the marriage, given as Article 41.3.2 of the Constitution provides:-

> "No law shall be enacted providing for the grant of a dissolution of marriage."

As the primary legislation sets down categorically (amongst other things) in section 197(1)(a) of the Social Welfare (Consolidation) Act, 1981, a woman must be unmarried before entitlement to this social assistance payment can be granted. Section 8 of the Social Welfare Act, 1973 has been re-enacted by Section 197 of the Social Welfare (Consolidation) Act, 1981, with further particulars of entitlement set down in statutory regulations. In summary, these provisions provide for a payment, at rates set by the Oireachtas, for any woman with a child or children, who is (i) unmarried and (ii) not living with a man, as husband and wife and (iii) satisfies a means test as regards entitlement to this social assistance payment.

The constitutional structure on protections of family's needs to be considered as a whole. Not all differences between marital families and other family forms constitute an attack on the marital family.

In L. v. L. [1992] I.L.R.M. 115 at 126-127, Egan J. stated:-

> "[Article 41.2.1] gives a recognition of the support which woman, by her life within the home, gives to the State. [Article 41.2.2] is the one which imposes an obligation on the State (including, of course, the judicial arm thereof) to endeavour to ensure that mothers shall not be obliged by economic necessity to engage in labour to the neglect of their duties in the home."

This notion of women as solely mothers and carers would have been inherent within Irish (and other) societies in 1937. This is reflected in the wording of Article 41.2.1 of the Constitution. As McCarthy J. noted in *L. v. L.* [1992] I.L.R.M. 115 at 123-124:-

> "I am not to be taken as holding that these guarantees are restricted to mothers of families based upon the institution of marriage. It is because of the importance of her life within the home that the State shall endeavour to ensure that mothers shall not be obliged by economic necessity to engage in labour to the neglect of their duties in the home."

This constitutional protection places an obligation on the State to ensure that women engaged in caring duties should receive some level of State recognition. That such language remains in our basic law is something for the political realm to consider. In taking this constitutional protection, as it is, this Court is of the view that McCarthy J.'s interpretation of Article 41.1.2 captures the essence of its protection. It is not limited to the family, but recognition that the State has obligations of support towards women undertaking caring duties. Interpreting Article 41.1.2 in a harmonious manner with other constitutional provisions, in particular Article 41, the Oireachtas is entitled to take the view that caring duties undertaken by unmarried single mothers need support over and above the supports provided to the marital family.

The plaintiffs have not established how the provision of tax-free allowances to family forms other than the marital family, or provision of a social welfare payment to an unmarried mother, is an attack on their family. While the marital family has a recognised special position under the Constitution, this in no way prevents the Oireachtas from protecting other vulnerable categories of individuals, including families that do not accord with the constitutionally envisioned norms. A female care giver will, most likely, head one-parent families. Protecting the marital family, under Article 41.3.1 of the Irish Constitution, should not and cannot result in the devaluing of the important social function played within Irish society of single parents, be they widowed, deserted or unmarried, working or having to rely on social assistance payments. The Court cannot overlook that the majority entitled to these allowances are women and, in the words of Article 41.1.2, their societal contributions are "indispensable to the welfare of the Nation and the State".

The Socio-economic Rights Ground

The final issue this Court has to briefly examine relates to the plaintiffs' arguments that without added financial protection from the State, either the first or second plaintiff, or both, may have to seek employment outside the home and/or the entire family may have to emigrate in order to achieve a reasonable standard of living. This Court has not had an opportunity to consider such a socio-economic rights argument previously. In *O'Reilly v. Limerick Corporation* [1989] I.L.R.M. 181, the plaintiffs, members of the travelling community, argued that Limerick Corporation had failed in their statutory duties under the Housing Act 1966, in not providing serviced halting sites, with hard surfaces on which their caravans could be placed, toilet facilities, running water and a regular refuse collection. Costello J. accepted the following:-

> "The plaintiffs … and their children (of which there are 150 under the age of 16) live in conditions of great poverty and deprivation. They have no running water or toilet facilities; no hard surface on which to place their caravans; no means for storing their domestic refuse and no service for its collection. They are the persons referred to by the city manager in a report to the city council of 4 December 1987 as 'living in totally unacceptable conditions without basic facilities'."

In dismissing the plaintiffs' claims, Costello J. stated that such claims, ones of distributive justice, should be advanced in the Oireachtas and not enter the commutative justice realm of these Courts.

This Court accepts that the other branches of State, the Oireachtas and the Executive, are primarily charged with distributing communal resources on the basis of political judgment. However, such distribution must also be in accordance with the Constitution. While courts will rarely interfere with political decisions relating to societal resource allocation by the elected branch, the constitutional protection of dignity (Preamble), vindication of personal rights (Article 40.3) of individuals and families (Article 41), must be respected and vindicated by these Courts. The plaintiffs' contention that they are unable to make ends meet falls far short of the circumstances wherein this Court, or other Irish Courts, could or should intervene. While not proven in this instance, there may be occasions where, due to the absolute failure of the State to ensure individuals and families have a standard of living appropriate to this society, human dignity is debased and/or bodily integrity is not respected and/or an individual's right to develop as a human person is seriously hampered, the Courts are constitutionally mandated to intervene. As this point was not pursued in detail by the plaintiffs, it would not be appropriate to comment any further.

Conclusion

Unfortunately in this case, the plaintiffs must leave the Court without any remedy for the economic hardships that they face in raising their family.

The plaintiffs appeared in person
Solicitor for the defendants: The Chief State Solicitor

8

Commentary on the *Matrimonial Homes Bill*

LOUISE CROWLEY

Introduction

This case assessed the constitutional validity of the legislative attempt to create an automatic statutory right for a non-owning spouse to acquire a 50 per cent equitable and potentially legal share in the family home.[1] The Bill was drafted 17 years after the enactment of the Family Home Protection Act 1976,[2] and shortly after the Judicial Separation and Family Law Reform Act 1989.[3] The Bill sought to progress the rights of a non-owning spouse in respect of the family home, such rights arising by virtue of his or her status as a spouse, as distinct from any direct or indirect contributions, and applicable on marriage rather than on its breakdown. It is not surprising that the focus of the Bill was on the family home—an especially significant asset in the context of the protection, regulation and (in later years) dissolution of the marital union. The proposal of an automatic 50 per cent property entitlement was novel under Irish family law,[4] which, like most common law jurisdictions, traditionally adopted a discretionary approach to asset distribution, requiring the presiding judge in a contested case to take an equitable rather than equal approach to the fair distribution of the available property, in light of the circumstances of the marriage. By contrast, the radical 1993 Irish proposal sought to apply the 50 per cent entitlement in respect of the family home by virtue of the fact of the marriage, operating outside both the typical scope of matrimonial property (commonly defined in other jurisdictions as assets

[1] Art 26 of the Constitution permits the President of Ireland to refer any Bill to the Supreme Court for a decision as to whether any provision thereof is repugnant to the Constitution. Such referrals are rare, perhaps due to the difficulties of abstract argument, and because, if upheld, the legislation may never again be constitutionally challenged. A single decision of the Supreme Court is delivered, thus the feminist judgment in this collection is a replacement decision. Note, however, that due to word constraints, Buckley CJ's judgment deals only with the Bill's provisions on the family home itself (not the similar provisions on household chattels), and addresses only spousal and familial rights, rather than third-party interests.

[2] The Family Home Protection Act 1976 introduced the statutory necessity for both spouses to consent in advance in writing to any transaction that results in the sale of or securing a charge on the family home, irrespective of the legal ownership of that property.

[3] The 1989 Act was the first legislative response of the Irish state to the issue of marital breakdown, and introduced the limited remedy of judicial separation, which relieved the parties of their obligation to cohabit and permitted applications for ancillary relief orders but did not dissolve the marital union.

[4] Note the automatic legal right share of a surviving spouse under s 111 of the Succession Act 1965.

acquired in the course of the marriage) and the more typical premise of compensatory based asset allocation in light of the respective spousal contributions.

The feminist judgment delivered by Buckley CJ presents a rational re-evaluation of the arguments relied upon in the original judgment, which ultimately defeated the 1993 Bill. In identifying the importance of the rights of the domestic contributor (typically female), and challenging the prioritisation of the rights of the property owner, the feminist judgment repositions the rights of the homemaker and regards the provisions and impact of the Bill as appropriately balancing the competing Constitutional rights.

Marriage as Partnership

The attempted enactment of a statutory based automatic right of equal ownership was justified in light of the protected status of the married family under Article 41 of the Constitution, and an expectation that this elevated status would permit a significant departure from normal rules of property ownership.[5] Of course, this was not to be the case; the original judgment deemed the individual property rights of the owning spouse, protected by Article 43 of the Constitution, as not capable of being eclipsed by the state's express pledge to protect the elevated position of the marital family, and to endeavour to ensure that mothers 'shall not be obliged by economic necessity to engage in labour to the neglect of their duties in the home'.[6] The fact that the same constitutional pledge in respect of the family served to defeat the interests of the female homemaker in the original judgment, demonstrates the antipathy traditionally shown towards the contributions of female homemakers in Ireland and the unwillingness to translate the Article 41.2.2° pledge into meaningful recognition.

By way of contrast and from a feminist perspective, it is interesting to note the express significance of domestic contributions on separation and divorce in the Family Law Act 1995 and the Family Law (Divorce) Act 1996 respectively, and the judicial endorsement of the theory of marital partnership, the same premise that underlined the 1993 Bill. Certainly, the Supreme Court explanation in *T v T*[7] of the concept of 'proper' provision aligns the Irish regulatory approach to asset distribution with the perspective of 'marriage as partnership', with Murray J interpreting the proper provision standard as mandating a fair sharing of the fruits of the marital endeavour.[8] Thus, notwithstanding the absence of a starting point of equal entitlement, the legal framework upon marital breakdown now recognises marriage as a partnership of equals. This judicially enhanced interpretation of the overarching aims of the process is supported by the statutory obligation to have regard to all spousal contributions, irrespective of their nature.

[5] The constitutional obligation on the state to protect the family, especially mothers, was emphasised by the then Minister for Justice, Brian Lenihan, when introducing the Bill to the Seanad; 59 Seanad Debates, col 414 (Second Stage (Committee)). See further Lucy Ann Buckley, '"Proper Provision" and "Property Division": Partnership in Irish Matrimonial Property Law in the Wake of *T v T*' (2004) 3 *Irish Journal of Family Law* 8, 11. Buckley concludes that '[m]arriage is more than simply a legal bond between individuals ...; hence it is appropriate to think of needs and objectives, including financial needs, in joint, rather than individualistic terms'.

[6] Art 41.2.2°.

[7] *T v T* [2002] 3 IR 334.

[8] ibid, at 429.

The Authority of the Family

Article 41.1.2° includes a guarantee by the state to protect the family in its 'constitution and authority', which has been interpreted as according decision-making rights to the family, in a manner that purports to exclude the capacity for state intervention.[9] As correctly noted in the course of the feminist judgment, such authority is not and cannot be absolute in nature; and the state retains the right, and indeed the obligation, to create protective structures in support of vulnerable members of the family unit. This is evidenced, for example, in the context of domestic violence, children in state care, inter-spousal maintenance obligations and the overriding requirement for judicial approval of financial arrangements on the dissolution of a marriage. Against this backdrop the feminist judgment determines that the rights arising from the operation of the Bill are not disproportionate and represent a justifiable exception to the autonomy of the family, and indeed a necessary intervention by the state in order to protect the vulnerable spouse. The ruling supports state intervention that promotes a more balanced approach to the weighting of competing rights; and in this instance resolves the tensions through family ideology by positively acknowledging the need to protect the domestic homemaker from the negative financial consequences arising from her contributions in the home. Diduck and Kaganas have similarly recognised the need for the state, through family law measures, to protect 'both the welfare and the rights of family members, the integrity of the unit and the autonomy of the individuals within it'.[10]

Role of the Woman in the Home

The identification and expectation of married women as domestic contributors and financial dependants reflected certain societal views at the time of the drafting of the Constitution. Hogan and Whyte[11] note that whilst this provision is perhaps the most dated in the Constitution, 'it may have had popular support in 1937'. Citing the views of Lee,[12] it was suggested that 'De Valera's image of woman was widely cherished in Ireland, not least by women themselves'.[13] It is not unreasonable to suppose that women might have welcomed this recognition and protection of their longstanding, unacknowledged contributions within the home. Not surprisingly, however, the provision has, in more recent years, been criticised, with numerous calls for its removal or amendment. In 1993 the Second Commission on the Status of Women called for its deletion,[14] whilst the 1996 Report of the Constitutional Review Group recommended a gender-neutral constitutional provision to

[9] The state's pledge in Art 41.1.2° has been relied upon by the courts, originally in *McGee v the Attorney General* [1974] 1 IR 284 (SC), to develop the concept of familial autonomy.

[10] Alison Diduck and Felicity Kaganas, *Family Law Gender and the State*, 3rd edn (Oxford, Hart Publishing, 2012) 31.

[11] Gerard Hogan and Gerry Whyte, *JM Kelly: The Irish Constitution*, 4th edn (Dublin, Lexis Nexis Butterworths, 2003) at 1866.

[12] Joseph Lee, *Ireland 1912–1985: Politics and Society* (Cambridge, CUP, 1989) at 207.

[13] Hogan and Whyte, above n 11, at 1866.

[14] *Report of the Second Commission on the Status of Women* (Pl 9557, 1993) at 27.

recognise the contributions made by all homemakers.[15] Most recently, at the Convention on the Constitution,[16] a strong majority of the 100 Convention members recommended that the wording of Article 41.2.2° be amended to remove the reference to women as a select group requiring recognition and protection.[17] In the second report of the Convention, published in May 2013, the members of the Convention called for the reference to the role of women in the home to be rephrased in a gender-neutral manner that would include other caring roles.[18]

The meaning and impact of Article 41.2.2° has often been queried. Notwithstanding the opposing views evidenced in the Supreme Court ruling in *Sinnott v Ireland*,[19] the dissenting views of Denham J are worth noting:

> Article 41.2 recognises the significant role played by wives and mothers in the home. This recognition and acknowledgement does not exclude women and mothers from other roles and activities. It is recognition of the work of women in the home. The work is recognised because it has immense benefit for society. This recognition must be construed harmoniously with other Articles of the Constitution when a combination of Articles fall to be analysed.[20]

The apparent pledge to protect the role of women in the home has been relied upon in a limited number of actions taken against the state, but has never given rise to any substantial rights for such women, except perhaps in the context of more favourable treatment than men as regards income maintenance from the state.[21] In *Dennehy v Minster for Social Welfare*, Barron J concluded in favour of such discriminatory treatment by the state, saying:

> Having regard to the provision of Article 41(2), it does not seem to me that as a matter of policy it would be unreasonable, unjust or arbitrary of the Oireachtas to protect financially deserted wives who are mothers who have dependent children residing with them or to recognise that mothers who have had to care for children will have lost out in the labour market and so are likely to need similar protection.[22]

Despite the state's apparent commitment to ensuring that a woman is not forced by economic circumstances to neglect her 'duties' in the home, this express constitutional preference is not supported by any direct or even indirect financial support. This was highlighted

[15] *Report of the Constitution Review Group* (The Constitution Review Group, Dublin, Stationery Office, 1996) at 303–04.

[16] The Convention on the Constitution was a forum of 100 people, representative of Irish society and parliamentarians. It was established in July 2012 to make recommendations on certain topics that may require future amendments to the Constitution; see at www.constitution.ie.

[17] *Voting Results: Women in the Home and the Participation of Women in Politics/Public Life* (17 Feb 2013), at www.constitution.ie/AttachmentDownload.ashx?mid=cee1b183-0b79-e211-a5a0-005056a32ee4.

[18] Notwithstanding this call for gender-neutral laws, Diduck and Kaganas, with reference to Carol Smart, 'Preface' in Richard Collier and Sally Sheldon (eds), *Fathers' Rights Activism and Law Reform in Comparative Perspective* (Oxford, Hart Publishing, 2006) and Richard Collier and Sally Sheldon, *Fragmenting Fatherhood: A Socio Legal Study* (Oxford, Hart Publishing, 2008), observe that the 'debates about the law and the family, which emphasise gender neutrality and equality, are unconnected with the realities of care'; above n 10, at 341.

[19] *Sinnott v Ireland* [2001] 2 IR 545 (SC).

[20] ibid, at 665.

[21] *Dennehy v Minster for Social Welfare* (HC, 26 July 1984) and *Lowth v Minster for Social Welfare* [1998] 4 IR 321 (SC), [1994] 1 ILRM 378 (HC). Art 41.2.2° was successfully relied upon by the state in both cases concerning the provision of financial state support for women who had been deserted by their husbands, where men in similar deserted circumstances were not afforded any such financial support.

[22] *Dennehy v Minster for Social Welfare* (HC, 26 July 1984) at 19.

in the course of parliamentary debates surrounding the drafting and enactment of the Judicial Separation and Family Law Reform Act 1989, where Deputy Barnes asserted, 'The Constitution, with its high sounding words with regard to the value of woman's work in the home and the value of the family unit to society, in legal terms offered nothing.'[23]

Similarly a short-lived attempt by Barr J,[24] referred to in the feminist judgment, to equate the domestic contributions of a married woman to her right to a share in the family home held in her husband's sole name, was ultimately overturned by the Supreme Court in *L v L*.[25] What Hogan and Whyte refer to as a 'laudable attempt to improve the economic situation of the home maker'[26] was regarded by the Supreme Court as a usurping of the legislative role, resulting in the refusal by Finlay CJ to accept that 'the transfer of any particular property right could be a general jurisdiction capable of being exercised in pursuance of … [Article 41.2.2°] … of the Constitution'.[27] This reluctance to act so definitively in favour of the homemaker spouse, although regrettable, is arguably understandable given the social and legal context at that time, and the lack of legislative impetus in this area. The fact of the existing property rights protected by Article 43 and the absence of any legislative direction in favour of the recognition of such rights for the homemaker, discretionary based or otherwise, gave rise to a legitimately conservative approach by the judiciary. Their reluctance to act is in turn somewhat exonerated by the subsequent ruling of the Supreme Court in respect of the 1993 Bill. Interestingly, the scope for such extensive intervention now exists (albeit on a discretionary basis) under the provisions of the Family Law Act 1995 and the Family Law (Divorce) Act 1996, particularly in sections 16 and 20 respectively. These sections require the court to have regard to domestic contributions as well as any career sacrifices that may have been made in the course of the marriage by one of the spouses in order to provide support for the family in the home. The current legislation therefore differs from that proposed under the 1993 Bill, which conferred a share in the property purely because of the *fact* of the marriage, with no reference to the spousal contributions or sacrifices made in the *course* of the marriage. The challenge for feminists in this context is of course the capacity for the approach advocated by the Bill to reinforce stereotypes of traditional family forms and gender role expectations within the home. The argument in favour of supporting the position of the woman who remains in the home and equating her role with that of the breadwinner is in fact a double-edged sword in this regard. In challenging the merits of strictly defining marriage Aylward has noted the difficulties surrounding the traditional presumption that a marriage would result in the man as sole breadwinner and the woman as homemaker.[28] Citing Weitzman's criticisms that such assumptions are 'anachronistic and inappropriate',[29] Aylward agrees that such presumptions deny individual autonomy.[30]

Putting these legitimate queries to one side and in examining the effects of the Bill, it has been argued that the merit of legislatively equating the differing, financial and non-financial

[23] Dáil Debates vol 377 3 Feb 1988—Second Stages (Resumed) of the Judicial Separation and Family Law Reform Bill 1987 at 1143 per Deputy Barnes TD.
[24] *L v L* [1989] ILRM 528 (HC).
[25] *L v L* [1992] 2 IR 77 (SC).
[26] Hogan and Whyte, above n 11, at 1868.
[27] *L v L* [1992] 2 IR 77 (SC), at 108.
[28] Ross Aylward, 'The problem with defining marriage' (2006) 4 *Irish Journal of Family Law* 21.
[29] Lenore Weitzman, *The Marriage Contract: Spouses, Lovers and the Law* (New York, The Free Press, 1981) 135.
[30] Aylward, above n 28, at 22.

contributions of the spouses can easily be defended. Certainly this is view adopted by many: Alicia Kelly has referred to marriage as 'an economic exchange', where 'individual choices and outcomes become joint—a community of interest—and a shared future emerges'.[31] Similarly, Lady Hale has argued that whilst parties may be free to contract into marriage, 'they are not free to write all the terms for themselves'.[32] In the context of the more recent debate about the enforceability of pre-nuptial agreements, Lady Hale has acknowledged the collective interest in 'imposing the sharing principle upon couples who have freely and deliberately renounced it'.[33]

The merits of imposing an automatic 50 per cent ownership on parties, and thereby limiting their capacity for autonomy, represented an insurmountable hurdle in the original judgment. The feminist judgment has relied upon the purpose and impact of marriage to support and approve the 1993 Bill. The equality principles that underlie its provisions reflect the societally beneficial view of marriage as an equal partnership, entered into and maintained for the good of the spouses, their children and society as a whole. Thus in prioritising the rights of the family unit over individual property rights, and thereby recognising the importance of the marriage relationship, the feminist judgment is to be welcomed for promoting the parties' freedom to adopt the roles best suited to their circumstances, and not forcing the domestic contributor and often non-earner to issue proceedings and prove the breakdown of the unit in order to assert a valid legal entitlement to a share in the family home.

From a traditionalist viewpoint, by beginning the marriage as the recipient of a substantial share in the family home, the homemaker spouse is now incentivised to more readily embrace her domestic role, as lauded by Article 41.2.1° of the Constitution, thereby controversially perpetuating the gender-specific spousal roles in modern Ireland. However, a more progressive interpretation is that the right to equal ownership of the property serves to reflect the understanding of spouses as equal participants in a vital social partnership. Whereas feminist literature demonstrates that law was historically utilised to subordinate women,[34] the 1993 Bill operates to eliminate such subordination, at least in respect of ownership of the family home, representing the apex of gradual efforts since the mid-nineteenth century in England/Wales and more recently in Ireland, to reach a position of equality. What is even more interesting in the Irish context is the further step attempted by the 1993 Bill, moving away from what was originally the feminist promotion of liberal theories of individual property ownership, resulting in the recognition of the rights of women to have legal title in the marital home. In a shift from this victory, regarded as egalitarian in aim but eliminating equitable claims in practice and impoverishing the domestic contributor, the 1993 Bill seems to accelerate the position of the non-earner, and accords an automatic interest in anticipation of the community of marriage. In endorsing the provisions of the 1993 Bill, the feminist judgment has properly captured the altruistic motives underpinning the 1993 Bill, sanctioning a law that gives substance to the state's pledge under Article 41.2.2° to support and vindicate the position of a domestic contributor.

[31] Alicia Kelly, 'Rehabilitating Partnership Marriage as a theory of wealth distribution at divorce in recognition of a shared life' (2004) 19 *Wisconsin Women's Law Journal* 141, 142.

[32] Brenda Hale 'Equality and autonomy in family law' (2011) 33 *Journal of Social Welfare and Family Law* 3, 4.

[33] ibid, at 12.

[34] Carol Smart, *Feminism and the Power of Law* (London, Routledge, 1989); CA MacKinnon, *Women's lives, men's laws* (Cambridge, MA, Belknap Press of Harvard University Press, 2005).

In the matter of Article 26 of the Constitution and in the matter of The Matrimonial Home Bill, 1993

[S.C. No. 367 of 1993]

Supreme Court 24th January, 1994

Buckley C.J. 24th January, 1994

This is the decision of the Supreme Court on the reference to it by the President of the Matrimonial Home Bill, 1993, pronounced pursuant to Article 26 of the Constitution of Ireland, 1937.

Assertion of repugnancy to Article 41

The first question which falls to be decided by the Court is whether the provisions contained in the Bill, vesting in each spouse equal rights of ownership in the matrimonial home unless they already have these rights, are repugnant to Article 41 of the Constitution.

Article 41, under the heading "The Family", states, *inter alia*:-

"1.1° The State recognises the Family as the natural primary and fundamental unit group of Society, and as a moral institution possessing inalienable and imprescriptible rights, antecedent and superior to all positive law.

2° The State, therefore, guarantees to protect the Family in its constitution and authority, as the necessary basis of social order and as indispensable to the welfare of the Nation and the State.

2.1° In particular, the State recognises that by her life within the home, woman gives to the State a support without which the common good cannot be achieved.

2° The State shall, therefore, endeavour to ensure that mothers shall not be obliged by economic necessity to engage in labour to the neglect of their duties in the home.

3.1° The State pledges itself to guard with special care the institution of Marriage, on which the Family is founded, and to protect it against attack."

Assertion that the Bill is unnecessary to protect the family or the dependent spouse

Counsel for the Attorney General contended that the Bill enhances the position of the dependent spouse and children with regard to the family home. By protecting the interest of the homemaking spouse, the Bill provides security for spouses and children, thereby strengthening the position of the family. By contrast, counsel assigned to challenge the constitutional validity of the Bill submitted that existing legislation adequately protects the position of the dependent spouse and the family with regard to the family home.

A variety of legislative measures already exist to vindicate spouses' rights in respect of the family home and other property. However, all such measures are limited in their scope and effects.

The Married Women's Status Act, 1957, permits a spouse to apply to the court to determine the spouses' proprietary interests in particular property, including the family home. However, it does not confer a share of that property on either spouse; nor does it provide any mechanism for adjusting the spouses' existing legal and equitable rights in respect of the property. Thus, unless a dependent spouse is able to establish a pre-existing equitable interest in the property (for example, but not limited to, under a resulting trust), the 1957 Act cannot assist her.

The Succession Act, 1965, entitles a surviving spouse to a defined share of the deceased spouse's estate, on either testate or intestate succession. The surviving spouse also has a right to appropriate the family home, in full or partial satisfaction of any share to which he or she is entitled. However, the 1965 Act operates only on death. It does not affect or confer any proprietary interests while both spouses live.

The Family Law (Maintenance of Spouses and Children) Act, 1976, provides for discretionary financial support orders for spouses and children in appropriate circumstances, but does not confer either spouse with any proprietary interest in the family home or other property.

The Family Law (Protection of Spouses and Children) Act, 1981, deals with barring orders and protection orders, along with a very limited provision regarding rights to chattels. It confers no proprietary entitlements in respect of the family home or other property.

The Judicial Separation and Family Law Reform Act, 1989, permits the court to confer, inter alia, a proprietary interest in the family home on a spouse on the granting of a judicial separation order. However, such an order is purely discretionary, and the court must exercise its discretion in the light of specified factors. The Act does not confer any proprietary interest in the family home on either spouse prior to judicial separation and no claims or orders can be made without acknowledging that the marital relationship has broken down.

The sole statutory measure that enhances the legal protection offered to spouses in respect of the family home while both spouses still live and cohabit is the Family Home Protection Act, 1976. This, however, does not confer any proprietary interest in the family home on the non-owning spouse, but merely prevents the transfer of an interest in the family home without the prior written consent of that spouse.

Common law and equitable doctrines also offer some protection to spouses, both during marriage and on marital breakdown. However, the protection afforded by each is restricted. The common law confers on a wife a very limited right of support, effectively restricted to the provision of necessaries, for which an estranged wife may pledge her husband's credit in some circumstances (Shatter, *Family Law in the Republic of Ireland* (Dublin, Wolfhound Press, 3rd edition, 1986), at p.432). It does not confer any power to transfer property between spouses. Equity permits a wife to establish an interest in the family home or other property through the doctrine of the presumed resulting trust. However, only direct and indirect financial contributions are recognized for trusts purposes, and a homemaker spouse, who has not been in a position to make financial contributions either to the acquisition of the family home or to the family budget generally, may be left without any equitable entitlements. This was clearly established by the recent decision of this Court in *L v. L* [1992] 2 I.R. 77. That case also established that the Constitution does not confer any proprietary interest in the family home on a homemaking wife and mother.

It is clear from the foregoing that homemaking spouses, most usually wives, may be left, during marriage, without any economic security or recognition for their labours, other than a right to apply for maintenance on a discretionary basis. However, the most recent evidence demonstrates that the effectiveness of this measure is greatly undermined in practice by enforcement difficulties (see Ward, *The Financial Consequences of Marital Breakdown* (1990, Dublin, Combat Poverty Agency)). The other statutory measures that protect spousal interests either do not confer proprietary rights, or operate only on marital breakdown (again on a discretionary basis) or on death. Common law and equitable doctrines are inadequate to fill this gap, and the Constitution offers no assistance.

It might be argued that a spouse does not require a legal interest in the family home outside of the context of marital breakdown. However, it seems peculiar indeed that the great value of homemaking contributions, which is constitutionally recognised, is vindicated only retrospectively (on death or judicial separation). It is stranger still that, during the spouses' lifetimes, a dependent spouse may only obtain an interest in family property on judicial separation (on a discretionary basis) or under the doctrine of the presumed resulting trust. The first option may encourage discontented spouses to separate, potentially promoting marital breakdown. The second option requires litigation to establish the plaintiff's equitable entitlements, again promoting marital disharmony. Either option may undermine marital stability, contrary to the constitutional protection of marriage contained in Article 41.3.1°. These are real concerns, as evidenced by *L v. L* [1992] 2 I.R. 77. In that case, the wife had endured very significant physical and mental cruelty, including false accusations of adultery, on the part of her husband. She decided to leave him, but the parties were subsequently reconciled. Eventually, the marriage broke down completely. Barr J, in the High Court, found as fact that the wife's concern for her economic security, and the husband's refusal to place the family home into joint names, was one of the key contributing factors in the final breakdown in the marriage (see the comments of Barr J at p.87 of the report).

Assertion that the Bill constitutes a breach of the authority of the family

Counsel assigned to challenge the constitutional validity of the Bill submitted that the Bill undermines the authority of the family in an impermissible way, in breach of Article 41.2°. The right of the spouses to make joint decisions on matters affecting the family was established by the decision of this Court in *McGee v. The Attorney General* [1974] 1 I.R. 284. Consequently, ownership of the family home is for the family to determine. By creating an automatic joint tenancy, with no reference to individual circumstances or to factors such as oppression, need or detriment, the Bill contravenes the authority of the family.

It is clear from Article 41.2° that the authority of the family is particularly to be respected. However, the right of the family to determine matters within its purview necessarily requires that the appropriate family members (in practice, most commonly the spouses) are able to contribute freely to the decision-making process. Respect for family authority and decision-making therefore raises important concerns regarding personal autonomy. These concerns are peculiarly complex, particularly within the intricate and finely-balanced context of family relationships. They must therefore be addressed broadly and within the context of the rights of the family unit as opposed to the rights of individual family members.

It does not necessarily follow, simply because a family home is held in one spouse's sole name, that this represents a mutual, fully autonomous decision by both spouses—that is, a decision to which both spouses consent, having been free, in a meaningful way, and without unfair pressures, to consider the matter and to make an informed choice. Sometimes circumstances may preclude such a choice: one spouse may have acquired the family home prior to marriage, or may have inherited it subsequently. Indeed, the issue of placing the family home into joint names may never have been addressed due to the optimism that naturally arises in the early marital period, or due to a fear by the non-owning party that raising the issue would disturb the equilibrium of the relationship or generate family disputes. At other times, particularly in the past, the force of social assumptions may have been such as to preclude an expectation by either party of joint home ownership. In other words, it may simply have been expected that the husband would be the sole owner of the family home, due to his traditional social and economic role as the family breadwinner. Such expectations were likely to inform the thinking, not only of the spouses themselves, but of legal advisors, banks and other lenders, as well as the wider family. In these circumstances, a wife with a preference for joint ownership of the family home might well have faced strong pressure to comply with prevailing mores. Such pressures might well have affected the wife's willingness or ability to contest the matter.

Other factors may also skew the balance of power between the parties. Domestic violence (which typically affects women), or a disparity in economic power between the earning and the dependent spouse, may restrict the more vulnerable party's ability to negotiate freely within the marriage. The extensive legal, social and financial disadvantages affecting Irish women, including their historical exclusion from the labour market and their lower earning capacity, are amply outlined in the reports of the Commission for the Status of Women (see the *Commission for the Status of Women: Report to the Minister for Finance* (1972), Chapters 2, 3 and 4, and, recently, the Second Commission for the Status of Women, *Report to Government* (1993), Chapter 3). These significant disadvantages may have served in the past to undermine women's ability to contribute to family decision-making, and indeed may still do so.

Social expectations may change over time. Writing in 1972, the Commission on the Status of Women noted that the family home was normally in the husband's sole name, but that this appeared to be gradually changing, and that there was an increased level of joint ownership among younger couples (*Commission for the Status of Women: Report to the Minister for Finance*, 1972, at paragraph 447). While it is not the role of this Court to speculate as to why this might be, it is reasonable to query the extent to which the apparent historical predominance of male home ownership—a trend strongly reflected in the case law in this area—can be attributed purely to personal preference and mutual choice.

This is not to say that decisions on home ownership were never free or mutual, but rather that we cannot assume that they always were, or indeed that the legal position regarding ownership of the family home necessarily results from an agreement at all, or that a vulnerable party should be presumed to be protected by membership of a family unit. The court must therefore proceed with some caution in this area, as there is a danger that automatically upholding family arrangements, or simply the *status quo*, in the name of assumed family authority, might simply support and maintain an imbalance of family power. Indeed it is arguable that the State has a residual protective role in respect of vulnerable spouses, and a duty to address equality concerns, in this context, for the common good.

With this in mind, it is now necessary to consider the decision of this Court in *McGee v. The Attorney General* [1974] 1 I.R. 284. The plaintiff in that case, a married woman, had four children, and was medically advised that another pregnancy would put her life at risk.

The plaintiff and her husband decided not to have any more children, and attempted to import a contraceptive jelly, which was not lawfully available in Ireland. The packet containing the jelly was seized by Customs officers and the plaintiff brought an action challenging the constitutionality of s.17 of the Criminal Law Amendment Act, 1935, which prohibited the sale of contraceptives or the importing of contraceptives into Ireland for sale or any other purpose. On appeal, the majority of this Court held that the provisions of s.17(3) of the 1935 Act were no longer in force as they were not in compliance with the Constitution of 1937 and constituted an unjustified invasion of the plaintiff's right to marital privacy under Article 40.3.1°.

Although *McGee* established the right of spouses to privacy in their personal decision-making, it did not establish that family decisions must necessarily override all social policy concerns, or that the State could never interfere with family choices, even where there appeared to be potentially conflicting interests or power disparities within the family. *McGee* related specifically to issues of sexual privacy and childbearing, concerns which this Court emphasised were peculiarly a matter for the family itself. As Walsh J noted:-

> "The sexual life of a husband and wife is of necessity and by its nature an area of particular privacy. If the husband and wife decide to limit their family or to avoid having children by use of contraceptives, it is a matter peculiarly within the joint decision of the husband and wife and one into which the State cannot intrude unless its intrusion can be justified by the exigencies of the common good" (at p.312 of the report).

Likewise, Budd J emphasised that "the matter of marital relationship must rank as one of the most important of matters in the realm of privacy" (at p.322 of the report), and that the impugned legislation failed to "defend or vindicate the personal rights of the citizen or his or her privacy relative to matters of the procreation of children and the privacy of married life and marital relations" (at p.322). Griffin and Henchy JJ expressed similar views (at p.335 and p.328 respectively).

It is clear from this that the focus of this Court in *McGee* was very much on the unjustified and intrusive interference of the State with the deeply private matter of the marital sexual relationship. This is very different in kind to issues of property or home ownership, where strong principles of marital partnership, fairness and equality may justify state intervention to ensure that both spouses have some measure of economic security and share in the fruits of the marriage, and that the dignity and contributions of each are recognised. The decision in *McGee* did not establish a general right to family authority, applicable to all issues and impervious to all external regulation or scrutiny. This is also clear from previous decisions of this Court: see, e.g., *Ryan v. The Attorney General* [1965] I.R. 294.

Furthermore, it is clear that even the right of marital privacy, and the right to personal choice inherent within that right, was not unbounded. Walsh J commented:-

> "The private morality of its citizens does not justify intervention by the State into the activities of those citizens *unless and until the common good requires it*" (at p.312 of the report (emphasis added)).

It is clear from this that, had a sufficiently serious injury to the common good been established, the State might well have had grounds for some level of intervention. *A fortiori*, the same principle must apply to family issues that do not fall within the ambit of the right to marital privacy established in *McGee*. The principle of family authority, though undoubtedly important, is not absolute, and is subject to the exigencies of the common good. Hence, although the present Bill may interfere with family decision-making in some (though not necessarily all) cases, it does not follow that this interference automatically constitutes a breach of the family's constitutional rights under Article 41. Rather, the question arises as to whether the State's interference with family authority may be justified by the common interest.

In *McGee* itself, no public interest argument was made that could apply to the particular context, a fact emphasised by Walsh J (at p.314 of the report). This is very different to the current situation, where the State has advanced a clear argument based on public policy concerns. Further, although Walsh J made it clear in *McGee* that the State can only interfere with marital privacy where the common good so mandates, as a last resort and where other attempts to deal with the matter are unavailing (at p.314 of the report), it does not follow that the same high standard must necessarily apply to all State interventions in matters affecting the family. Rather, the standard here must be one of proportionality. The proportionality of the Bill as a means of achieving the State's declared policy goals will be discussed further below.

Assertion that the Bill constitutes a breach of the owning spouse's constitutional right to private property

Counsel assigned to challenge the constitutional validity of the Bill contended that the Bill constitutes an impermissible breach of the constitutional right to private property by automatically depriving the owner of the family home of half of his interest, with no reference to the justice of the case and no provision for compensation. Counsel for the Attorney General contended that the Bill does not represent a disproportionate interference with the essential elements of property rights.

It is clear that the Bill represents an interference with the property rights of the owner of a family home subject to the legislation. Section 4 of the Bill provides that any interest in a family home, as defined, to which either or both of the spouses is or are entitled, shall vest in both spouses as joint tenants. This applies unless the spouses are already joint tenants of the matrimonial home, or are tenants in common in equal shares, or unless (as stipulated by s.15), the spouse in whose favour s.4 applies is already bankrupt or an arranging debtor. The Bill stipulates that the interest vesting in both spouses under s.4 shall be an equitable interest only, although this may be converted to a legal interest by means of registration, under s.8. Accordingly, the Bill adjusts the position of the spouses with regard to the ownership of their matrimonial home so as to make them equal equitable co-owners, and ultimately possibly legal co-owners, of an interest previously held by one spouse alone, or by both spouses in unequal shares. The court must therefore consider whether the Bill's interference with spousal property rights amounts to a breach of constitutional rights.

Article 40.3 of the Constitution states:-

> "1° The State guarantees in its laws to respect, and, as far as practicable, by its laws to defend and vindicate the personal rights of the citizen.
>
> 2° The State shall, in particular, by its laws protect as best it may from unjust attack and, in the case of injustice done, vindicate the life, person, good name, and property rights of every citizen."

Article 43 of the Constitution, under the heading "Private Property", states:-

> "1.1° The State acknowledges that man, in virtue of his rational being, has the natural right, antecedent to positive law, to the private ownership of external goods.
>
> 2° The State accordingly guarantees to pass no law attempting to abolish the right of private ownership or the general right to transfer, bequeath, and inherit property.
>
> 2.1° The State recognises, however, that the exercise of the rights mentioned in the foregoing provisions of this Article ought, in civil society, to be regulated by the principles of social justice.
>
> 2° The State, accordingly, may as occasion requires delimit by law the exercise of the said rights with a view to reconciling their exercise with the exigencies of the common good."

The relationship between these articles is complex and difficult. It has been held that Article 43 protects the institution of property ownership from State interference, while breaches of individual citizen's particular property rights are dealt with under Article 40.3.2°: *Blake v. Attorney General* [1982] I.R. 117. However, this Court has long rejected the contention that the purpose of Article 43 is simply to protect the institution of private property from complete abolition within the State: *Buckley and Others v. Attorney General* [1950] I.R. 67. It is clear that private property rights may be restricted where this is required for the common good, and that while the requirements of the common good are primarily for the Oireachtas to determine, the determinations of the Oireachtas may be subject to judicial scrutiny: *Buckley and Others v. Attorney General* [1950] I.R. 67; *Blake v. Attorney General* [1982] I.R. 117. It is also well established that an "unjust attack" on property rights within the meaning of Article 40.3.2° must be interpreted in the light of the values contained in Article 43: *Dreher v. Irish Land Commission* [1984] I.L.R.M. 94. In that case, Walsh J. stated (at p.96) that "any State action that is authorised by Article 43 of the Constitution and conforms to that Article cannot by definition be unjust for the purposes of Article 40.3.2". This statement was followed in several later cases, notably *O'Callaghan v. Commissioners of Public Works* [1985] I.L.R.M. 364 and *Madigan v. Attorney General* [1986] I.L.R.M. 136.

Accordingly, where legislation infringes upon the constitutional property rights of individuals, this infringement must be justified by "the principles of social justice" and "the exigencies of the common good" or it will constitute an "unjust attack" upon the individual's property rights. In pursuing its objectives, the State must continue to protect the constitutional rights of the citizen, as far as possible: *Cox v. Ireland* [1992] 2 I.R. 503. It is for the court to determine whether, objectively speaking, legislation can be regarded as being in the interests of social justice or the common good, and additionally whether the restrictions or delimitations of the property rights of individual citizens are reasonably proportionate to the legislative objective. The State's duty to vindicate and protect the constitutional rights of citizens (including the right to private property) must therefore be balanced against the State's duty to promote social justice and the common good, and the means chosen to achieve the relevant objective must be rationally connected to that objective and must not be excessive or arbitrary. Where the means used are disproportionate to the objective, the intervention will constitute an "unjust attack" on the personal property rights of the citizen, within the meaning of Article 40.3.2°.

The Objective of the Bill

Counsel for the Attorney General submitted that the Bill strengthens the family by equalising the spouses' entitlements in respect of the matrimonial home. The Bill recognizes the connection between family life and the home in which that family life is conducted. Imposing joint ownership of the family home recognizes and vindicates the equal partnership of the spouses and upholds the value of domestic and caring contributions. It protects the non-owning spouse and children by securing the family home for the family. Accordingly, the Bill supports the institution of marriage, and is justified by the exigencies of the common good. Supporting this, counsel particularly relied on the decision of this Court in *L. v. L.* [1992] 2 I.R. 77. Referring to the concept of joint spousal entitlements in respect of ownership of the family home, this Court stated (at p.107):-

> "... anything that would help to encourage that basis of full sharing in property values as well as in every other way between the partners of a marriage must directly contribute to the stability of the marriage, the institution of the family and the common good."

Counsel assigned to challenge the constitutional validity of the Bill did not dispute the legitimacy of the legislative objectives, but submitted that the Bill is an unjust attack on individual property rights. While there is a legitimate social concern to protect vulnerable spouses, recognize marital partnership and vindicate caring contributions, the Bill goes beyond a reasonably proportionate response to these concerns by imposing an automatic joint tenancy in respect of every family home, without reference to the particular family circumstances.

It is clear from Article 41.2 that the constitutional concept of marriage respects and values the contributions of both spouses. The Article contains an important recognition of the value of homemaking contributions, and an acknowledgement that domestic and caring work is predominantly undertaken by mothers—an acknowledgement that continues to hold considerable truth today, notwithstanding significant changes in gender roles since the foundation of the State. This is clearly demonstrated by the most recent census data. An analysis of the 1986 census, published in August 1993 by the Central Statistics Office, states:-

> "The age group with the highest female labour force participation rate was the 15–24 age group. Thereafter the rate declined with older age groups reflecting the effects of marriage and childbearing on women's participation in the labour force. Approximately seven in every ten women in the 35–44 and higher age groups were engaged in home duties in 1986" (CSO Ireland, Census 86 Vol. 6, *Principal Economic Status and Industries* (Stationery Office, Dublin, Pl. 9819), at p.12).

The importance of caring work to the common good is clearly acknowledged by Article 41.2, which provides that the State shall "endeavour to ensure that mothers are not obliged by economic necessity to engage in labour to the neglect of their duties in the home". This is not to denigrate the equally valuable contributions of the breadwinner. Rather, the provision is best read as an important reminder of the value of caring work, and the contributions of mothers, framed at a time when such contributions might tend to be overlooked or taken for granted, or otherwise devalued, in comparison with the more tangible financial contributions of the (usually male) breadwinner. The Constitution thus incorporates values of spousal equality and marital partnership, which have been consistently highlighted in the decisions of this Court, for instance, in relation to parental authority (see *Re Tilson, infants* [1951] I.R. 1, rejecting the common law doctrine of paternal supremacy, and recognising the equal and joint parental authority of both spouses in matters relating to the religious education of the children).

However, a lifetime of caring work comes with a price. A wife and mother who spends her best years caring for others within the home clearly suffers in terms of the economic opportunities available to her, including the opportunity to engage in the paid labour market or to acquire property in her own name. Nor do these disadvantages end when child-rearing and domestic responsibilities may ease, since the loss of earning capacity and career potential is likely to have continuing and profound long-term effects on the economic well-being of the homemaker spouse. By comparison, the breadwinner, commonly the husband, is free to progress in his career and to acquire property, and this freedom is facilitated by, and in a large part derived from, the homemaker's responsibility for family care and domestic duties. As Lord Simon of Glaisdale so memorably expressed it thirty years ago, "The cock bird can feather his nest precisely because he is not required to spend most of his time sitting on it" (Sir J. Simon, *With All My Worldly Goods* (1964, Holdsworth Lecture, Birmingham, at pp.14–15).

For these reasons, and with the support of the Constitution, it is appropriate that the legislature should seek to recognise the partnership of the spouses, and vindicate their equal but different contributions to the family, by ensuring that both spouses share, to some extent, in what may be termed the fruits of the marriage. Having carefully considered the submissions of counsel and the provisions of the Bill and of the Constitution, the Court accepts that the provisions of the Bill are directed to encourage the joint ownership of matrimonial homes (commonly the most significant marital asset) and are rationally connected to this objective. The Court further accepts that this objective is an important element of the common good conducive to the stability of marriage and the general protection of the family, enshrined in Article 41. In this context the Court relies upon the views expressed in its decision in *L. v. L.* [1992] 2 I.R. 77 (given above).

The Proportionality of the Bill

The next question is whether the means used to attain the legitimate objective of the Bill constitute a necessary and proportionate delimitation of the personal property rights of the spouse whose rights are delimited by the Bill. The essential question here is not whether the Bill represents the ideal means of achieving the State's objective, but whether the chosen statutory scheme is within the competence of the Oireachtas.

The Bill provides that spouses shall automatically be constituted joint tenants in equity of any dwelling occupied by them as a married couple on or after the 25th of June 1993, other than dwellings already owned equally by them, irrespective of when that dwelling was acquired. Counsel assigned to challenge the constitutional validity of the Bill contended that the arbitrary use of a particular date for the application of the Bill discriminated against couples who separated prior to the chosen date. However, since the only way to avoid such discrimination would be for the legislation to apply retrospectively, which could cause serious, possibly irremediable, practical difficulties, the Court does not consider the selection of an application date to be invidious. It appears that the purpose behind specifying an application date, which was the date the Bill was introduced before the Oireachtas, was to ensure that spouses standing to lose part of their equitable interest under the legislation would have no incentive to separate before the Bill came into force. The use of the specified date prevents marriage being undermined in this way, and protects spouses who might otherwise be deprived of a benefit under the Bill. While spouses who separated prior to the specified date will not benefit under the Bill, they may well have a remedy under the Judicial Separation and Family Law Reform Act, 1989, or may already have been provided for under a deed of separation. It would be unfeasible for financial arrangements made previously under a separation deed or on judicial separation to be unravelled retrospectively, perhaps years after the event.

The Bill's application is not restricted to matrimonial homes acquired after the legislation comes into force. Again, there are solid reasons for this. Excluding existing matrimonial homes would mean that older wives, who are most likely to need the Bill's protection, would be unlikely to benefit, unless a new family home were to be purchased. As previously noted, patterns of home ownership may be changing, with joint ownership of the family home becoming increasingly common (Commission for the Status of Women, *Report to the Minister for Finance*, 1972, at paragraph 447). If this is correct, restricting the Bill's application to future home acquisitions would protect those least in need of protection, while leaving unprotected those who need it most, and who have spent longest contributing to the family. This would be invidious indeed, and would clearly not be conducive to achieving the legislative objective of promoting and recognizing marital partnership.

The Bill's application does not depend on whether the pre-existing position as to ownership of the home is injurious to the interests of a spouse or other family members, or demonstrates a failure by either spouse to discharge what might fairly be considered as his or her family obligations. The Bill does however contain a right of defeasance. Under s.7, a spouse who would otherwise benefit by virtue of the provisions of s.4, sub-s. 2, by becoming an equal owner of the family home, may, after receiving legal advice, declare in writing that he or she does not wish the section to apply to the home. Furthermore, s.6 permits the owning spouse to seek an order of the court declaring that s.4 shall cease to apply to the interest in the family home, though the court shall not grant such a declaration unless it is satisfied that it would be unjust not to do so, having regard to all the circumstances. The section then lists, non-exhaustively, factors to which the court must have regard in determining whether it would be unjust not to grant the declaration. Accordingly, the constitutional property rights of the owning spouse suffer an initial delimitation, but this may be reversed where the court deems it just, or the spouses so agree.

The Court has already noted that it cannot be assumed that the vesting of the family home in the sole name of one spouse was the result of a decision jointly and freely taken by both spouses, but in some cases such a joint decision may genuinely have been taken. Accordingly, the Bill may disturb not only a genuine decision of both spouses, but also subsequent arrangements regarding the ownership of family assets, which may have been founded on the original decision. Hence, couples may need to review their entire financial situation to determine whether they wish their existing arrangements to continue. If they conclude that they so wish, the spouse in whose favour s.4 operates must register a declaration under s.7 of the Bill. It is entirely possible that a spouse might decline to register such a declaration, on reasonable or unreasonable grounds. The only recourse then available to the other spouse is an action under s.6, effectively compelling the spouses to litigate. However, as this Court has previously noted, current law also requires a spouse who is not the legal owner of the family home to engage in litigation, and potentially to separate legally from the other spouse, in order to obtain an interest in the property. The potential for spousal dispute therefore exists whether or not the Bill is upheld, and it is by no means clear where the greater risk of discord may lie.

It is useful to contrast the approach adopted in the Bill with that originally proposed by the Law Reform Commission in its *First Report on Family Law* (LRC 1—1980). The Commission proposed to grant the Court a broad equitable discretion to determine the spouses' respective beneficial interests in the family home, in line with their contributions to the acquisition, maintenance or improvement of the home. "Contributions" were defined to include both financial contributions and caring work. The proposal therefore resembled, in kind, the model later adopted in the context of judicial separation under the 1989 Act, that is, a discretionary mechanism based on particular factors and the broad justice of the situation.

The Commission's proposal offered greater initial recognition of the particular family circumstances, since a share in the family home would only be conferred on an applicant spouse where this was just and equitable. However, the Commission's approach, in requiring litigation to establish an entitlement, would create the potential for significant marital conflict. Furthermore, greater barriers (financial and psychological) might face the dependent spouse with regard to taking the necessary legal action, bearing in mind the factors previously outlined that might limit the exercise of autonomy. The owning spouse might exert pressure on the dependent spouse to refrain from bringing a claim, and such pressure might be exacerbated in relationships where there was a history of abuse or economic dependency. Such pressure might of course also be applied in the model adopted by the Bill, to dissuade the spouse disadvantaged by s.4 from applying to avoid the legislation, or indeed, to persuade the spouse in whose favour s.4 applies to waive her statutory entitlements, though some procedural safeguards are contained in the Bill to minimize such abuse. However, placing the onus on the non-owning spouse to apply for a share of the family home presents particular difficulties, which arguably exceed the difficulties faced by a spouse who wishes to avoid the application of the Bill. It might well be psychologically more difficult for a dependent spouse to claim a share in an asset to which she had no previous legal entitlement, than for a former sole owner to seek to reclaim the full interest in his property. Consequently, although the model proposed by the Law Commission accords greater weight to the property rights of the owning spouse (as they are not subjected to unnecessary, though reversible, delimitation), it is possible, even probable, that the legislative objective might be less effectively achieved. Accordingly, the approach adopted in the Bill to the ownership of the matrimonial home is not disproportionate to the legislative objective.

Compensation

However, this is not the end of the matter. The Bill does not entitle a spouse who is deprived of part of his interest in the family home, pursuant to the legislation, to compensation. The question therefore arises as to whether this failure invalidates the Bill.

Unlike the "Takings Clause" under the Fifth Amendment to the American Constitution, the Irish Constitution does not explicitly require that State (or other) expropriations of private property must be compensated. Nevertheless, it has generally been recognised that an individual whose property is compulsorily acquired by the State or one of its agencies, for purposes deemed by the Oireachtas to be necessary to the common good, should, broadly speaking, be entitled to compensation. Thus, in *Electricity Supply Board v. Gormley* [1985] I.R. 129, a statutory power of the plaintiff to erect masts to carry power lines across the defendant's lands, without the payment of compensation (though compensation was payable for damage to trees and bushes), was held to be unconstitutional. Several cases have also addressed the issue of the appropriate level of compensation: see *Blake v. Attorney General* [1982] I.R. 117; *In Re Article 26 of the Constitution and the Housing (Private Rented Dwellings) Bill, 1981* [1983] I.R. 181; *Dreher v. The Irish Land Commission* [1984] I.L.R.M. 94. Normally, compensation may be calculated by reference to the market value of the property that has been compulsorily acquired. However, it is clear from the decided cases that the right to compensation is not absolute, and that there may be circumstances where no compensation is required, or where compensation may not equate to market value.

In *Dreher v. The Irish Land Commission* [1984] I.L.R.M. 94, the Land Commission compulsorily acquired lands belonging to the plaintiff. The plaintiff alleged that the relevant compensatory provisions constituted a violation of his constitutional property rights under Articles 40 and 43, as the compensation was paid in land bonds, which fell significantly in value. The plaintiff's claim was unanimously rejected by this Court. In the course of his judgment, Walsh J. noted (at p. 96) that the market value of the land could not always be equated to just compensation, since, depending on the circumstances, the market value might be either excessive or inadequate compensation.

In *Central Dublin Development Association v. The Attorney General* (1975) 108 I.L.T.R. 69, Kenny J. considered the constitutionality of the delimitation of private property rights in the context of the Local Government (Planning and Development) Act, 1963. Kenny J. held that statutory restrictions on the right to compensation did not constitute a breach of Article 43 and did not fail to defend and vindicate the personal rights of property. The restrictions in question did not constitute a confiscation of rights but merely provided that interference with one of the rights of property should not be compensable. Kenny J. further held that the restrictions were not an unjust attack upon property rights as they were reasonable and limited in their scope, and included a mechanism to mitigate any resultant hardship. They therefore represented a reconciliation of the rights of property with the exigencies of the common good.

In *O'Callaghan v. The Commissioners of Public Works in Ireland and Another* [1985] I.L.R.M. 364, the Commissioners for Public Works made a preservation order which prevented the plaintiff from carrying out ploughing operations on land which was partially occupied by a prehistoric promontory fort. The relevant legislation did not provide for the payment of compensation in respect of such an order. The plaintiff alleged that he had suffered an unjust attack on his property rights within the meaning of Article 40.3.2°. Upholding the High Court's decision refusing the plaintiff's claim, O'Higgins C.J. held that the lack of compensation did not render the delimitation of the plaintiff's property rights unconstitutional, as the delimitation was imposed to meet the exigencies of the common good (in that case, the national aspirations set out in the Preamble to and Article 1 of the Constitution).

The decisions in *O'Callaghan* and *Central Dublin Development Association* are not on all fours with the current situation. The plaintiff in *O'Callaghan* was substantially on notice of the preservation requirement when he purchased the land, and of the consequent limitation of the ordinary rights of user on the part of the landowner. This awareness appears to have played at least some part in the ultimate decision of this Court. Nor was the plaintiff in either case deprived of ownership of the land or any part of it, since the preservation order in *O'Callaghan* merely restricted the way in which the land could be used, while the measures in *Central Dublin Development Association* limited the right to compensation for a refusal of planning permission in certain circumstances. By contrast, the present Bill deprives the owning spouse of an actual interest in the family home (presuming that the spouses do not agree otherwise under s.4), and the spouse whose interest is diminished will frequently have had no notice of such a potential deprivation either on marriage or at the time of the home's acquisition, since the Bill applies to all family homes occupied as such by spouses on the relevant date.

There are, however, special considerations applicable to the reallocation of interests as between spouses, imposed by the Bill. It is not the case here that the property of private individuals is being expropriated by the State for its own purposes, or for the benefit of society in general. Were this the case, very exceptional grounds would clearly be required to justify such an uncompensated deprivation. However, the concern of the Oireachtas in the Bill is to reconcile the interests of different family members, specifically spouses, in the family home. This clearly accords with the constitutional reference to "the principles of social justice" contained in Article 43.2.1°, discussed above. It also gives effect to the values enshrined in Article 41, which recognizes that work in the home is indispensable for the welfare of the family, as well as the common good. Under the Bill, the owning spouse is not deprived of an interest in the family home to benefit a stranger, or wider society. Rather, the owning spouse is deprived of the full interest in the family home to benefit the person to whom he or she is married, with whom he or she has an intimate connection, and with whom he or she is forging a lifelong partnership, in circumstances where the contributions of each partner are of equal value and are equally essential to the well-being of the family as a whole.

Conclusion

Marriage is both a civil contract and a social status which contains a life-long commitment. It therefore creates reciprocal obligations as between the spouses, which are designed for their mutual protection and welfare, as well as the welfare of any children of the marriage. It is reasonable, therefore, that the Oireachtas should seek through legislation to balance the interests of the spouses, including their property interests, and to vindicate their differing contributions, both during marriage and in the unhappy event of marital breakdown. Accordingly, following careful consideration, the Court concludes that the rights arising from the Bill are not a disproportionate interference with spousal property rights and are within the ambit of the Constitution.

9

Commentary on *National and Provincial Building Society v Lynd*

DAVID CAPPER

Introduction

This case is concerned with the approach that should be taken to the exercise of the High Court's power under section 36 of the Administration of Justice Act 1970 (as amended by section 8 of the Administration of Justice Act 1973), to give time to a defaulting mortgagor under a mortgage of land consisting of or including a dwelling-house to pay any sums due under the mortgage or otherwise remedy any default in meeting the mortgagor's contractual obligations. The alternative to giving such time to the mortgagor is that the mortgagee's application for possession of the property would be granted. The *Lynd*[1] case is of interest to feminists because it considers the Court's discretion and the role of contractual obligations in the context of the Lynd family home. It essentially asks how the Court should use its powers to balance the rights and needs of both 'commercial' mortgagees and 'residential' mortgagers. In doing so, the judge must consider the traditionally excluded private sphere in reaching a decision about the terms of a contract.[2]

As Lisa Whitehouse has pointed out,[3] a mortgagee seeking possession of a mortgaged property with a view to its sale need not show grounds why possession should be granted. On the contrary, the mortgagee is entitled to go into possession 'before the ink is dry on the mortgage' (*per* Harman J in *Four Maids Ltd* v *Dudley Marshall (Properties) Ltd*).[4] While most mortgages contain provision that the mortgagee cannot go into possession without default by the mortgagor, the effect of default was graphically illustrated by *Birmingham Citizens Building Society* v *Caunt*,[5] where Russell J held, in effect, that if the mortgagor

[1] *National and Provincial Building Society v Lynd* [1996] NI 47.

[2] For feminist analyses of contract and land law, see respectively Linda Mulcahy and Sally Wheeler (eds), *Feminist Perspectives on Contract Law* (London, Routledge-Cavendish, 2005); and Hilary Lim and Anne Bottomley (eds), *Feminist Perspectives on Land Law* (London, Glasshouse Press, 2007). On the family home see Lorna Fox, *Conceptualising Home: Theories, Laws and Policies* (Oxford, Hart Publishing, 2006).

[3] Lisa Whitehouse, 'A Longitudinal Analysis of the Mortgage Repossession Process 1995–2010: Stability, Regulation and Reform' in S Bright (ed), *Modern Studies in Property Law*, vol 6 (Oxford, Hart Publishing, 2011) 151.

[4] *Four Maids Ltd v Dudley Marshall (Properties) Ltd* [1957] 1 Ch 317, 320.

[5] *Birmingham Citizens Building Society v Caunt* [1962] Ch 883.

committed any breach of the mortgage contract, typically by failing to pay an instalment, the mortgagee was entitled to possession of the mortgaged property as a matter of course. The court's power to adjourn proceedings was limited to a very short time to allow the mortgagor the opportunity to raise funds and pay off *the entire mortgage debt*. Section 36 operates as a graft upon the mortgagee's common law right, but mainly as a defence. The mortgagee need not in terms demonstrate that it is entitled to possession; on the contrary, the mortgagor must, in effect, show that possession should *not* be granted immediately.

Section 36 provided that the court could adjourn proceedings, stay or suspend execution of an order for possession, or postpone the date for delivery of possession if it appeared that the mortgagor was likely to be able, within a reasonable period, to pay any sums due under the mortgage, or to remedy a default consisting of a breach of any other obligation arising under the mortgage. The section 8 amendment was introduced to deal with the problem that arose in *Halifax Building Society* v *Clark*[6] and other cases. There it had been held that if the mortgage involved payment by instalments, and it was provided in the mortgage contract that in the event of one breach, typically one missed payment, the entire loan became immediately payable, the sums due under the mortgage were the entire outstanding mortgaged loan. This clearly had the consequence that possession had to be given to the mortgagee even if the mortgagor were able to clear arrears and resume regular payments fairly quickly. Section 8 provides that the court is to decide whether the mortgagor is likely to be able to pay only those sums that she would have been expected to have paid by the time of default within a further reasonable time. If so, the court could exercise the section 36 power in the mortgagor's favour.

Case Context

The particular context in which the *Lynd* case fell to be decided was that occasioned by the decision of the Court of Appeal in England and Wales in *Cheltenham and Gloucester Building Society v Norgan*.[7] In that case it was held that the remaining term of the mortgage could be taken into consideration when determining the 'reasonable period' within which a mortgagor could pay off arrears. Prior to *Norgan* the practice had been to require the payment of arrears and/or the remedying of any default within four or five years. *Lynd*, as decided by Girvan J, declined to follow *Norgan* so far as it held that the starting point was the outstanding period of the mortgage. The judge accepted that the outstanding mortgage period *could* be a 'reasonable period' for the purposes of section 36, but did not make particularly clear whether this should generally continue to be a relatively short period or whether the court had an unfettered discretion as to the time the mortgagor should be given. It is one of the strengths of the feminist judgment that it makes clear that the court has an unfettered discretion to be exercised in light of all the relevant circumstances of the case. To the extent that the feminist judgment reaches the same outcome as, and is in accord with, Girvan J's approach, the commentator would say that it better understands *Norgan*. Fox O'Mahony J

[6] *Halifax Building Society v Clark* [1973] Ch 307 (Pennycuick V-C).
[7] *Cheltenham and Gloucester Building Society v Norgan* [1996] 1 All ER 449.

is clear about her discretionary power, and uses it to respond to the specific context of the case in a way that is sensitive to the needs and vulnerabilities of both the Lynds and the building society.

The Feminist Judgment

The feminist judgment displays a much wider, deeper and holistic sense of what the relevant circumstances of the case are than does Girvan J's judgment in the *Lynd* case itself.[8] The feminist judgment bases its reasoning more securely on the *Report of the Committee on the Enforcement of Judgment Debts*,[9] chaired by Payne J (the Payne Report). The terms of reference of the Payne Report included consideration of whether the operation of an order for possession of mortgaged property should be postponed. It was not limited to enforcing judgments; and in relation to both judgments' enforcement and mortgagee possession applications the Payne Report recommended not just greater efficiency, but also an even-handed approach to the rights of both parties—creditor and debtor in the enforcement of judgments, and mortgagee and mortgagor in possession proceedings. This was a time of radical reform of the system of judgment enforcement in Northern Ireland, with the setting up of the Enforcement of Judgments Office in 1971 following on from the Judgments (Enforcement) (NI) Act 1969. The Payne Report recommended an enforcement office for England and Wales, although it would have operated differently from the one in place in Northern Ireland since 1971, in the sense that the office would have processed creditors' applications for enforcement rather than undertaking most of the enforcement work itself. No new enforcement system was introduced to England and Wales, and thus the main contributions the Payne Report made to the development of the civil law came in the form of attachment of earnings orders and section 36 of the Administration of Justice Act 1970.

The feminist judgment recognises that one cannot make sense of section 36 without a clear understanding of the growth in home ownership in all parts of the United Kingdom throughout the twentieth century. Mortgages of dwelling-houses are not for the security of needy persons desperate for a loan of money or for commercial and industrial development.[10] They are the means by which people today (and in 1996) acquire a place to live, a place that is their *home* and of which they are trying to become the *owner*. This most relational of contracts requires considerable weight to be given to the commitment by lender and borrower to the achievement of the borrower's ambition to become a home owner.[11] The lender's commitment to this is seen in statements by the Council

[8] Reasoning from context and lived experience, as opposed to categorical or abstract decision-making, is defined by Rosemary Hunter as one of the techniques of feminist judging: Rosemary Hunter, 'Can *Feminist* Judges Make a Difference?' (2008) 15 *International Journal of the Legal Profession* 7.

[9] *Report of the Committee on the Enforcement of Judgment Debts* (1969, Cmnd 3909).

[10] Business loans secured against domestic property and policed through the formula laid down in *Royal Bank of Scotland v Etridge (No 2)* [2001] UKHL 44 are a modern example of this phenomenon but a different issue from the one being examined here.

[11] On relational contract theory, see David Campbell (ed), *The Relational Theory of Contract: Selected Works of Ian MacNeil* (London, Sweet & Maxwell, 2001). MacNeil believed that all contracts were to a degree 'relational' because they were made in a network of relationships between persons in society. Some contracts are more

of Mortgage Lenders to the effect that repossession is a last resort, and that every effort will be made by lenders to ensure that borrowers are given the chance to clear arrears and get the mortgage paid in the end. Issue may thus be taken with Girvan J's suggestion that section 36 was meant to ensure a steady stream of interest payments for mortgagees, and that this made capitalisation of interest arrears, another form of spreading arrears over the remaining mortgage period, inappropriate.[12] True, the Payne Report emphasises the need to respect the interests of mortgagees as well as those of mortgagors, but this statement somewhat misses the point that section 36 says that mortgage contracts are about acquiring homes rather than financial assets.

There are two further aspects of 'all the circumstances of the case' that the feminist judgment emphasises. Girvan J's judgment did not acknowledge the needs of the borrower's family in determining how the creditor's application for possession should be decided. This is ironic, since Mrs Lynd represented her husband throughout the negotiations with the creditor and in the litigation. More importantly, it fails to understand that the fundamental purpose of the Payne Report was to find a way to assist the borrower to purchase a *home*.[13] A home is not just bricks and mortar—it is a place where someone lives and where, typically, that person's spouse or partner and children live too. The voices of Mrs Lynd and the couple's children were never heard in Girvan J's judgment.[14] This was not just anti-feminist; it treated Mrs Lynd and the children as 'property outsiders'.[15] Now the commentator would have to confess to having a problem with the suggestion (if that suggestion is being made) that judges should as a matter of distributive justice confer rights on people to whom the substantive law has not given rights. However, that is not the point made by the feminist judgment. On the contrary, the feminist judgment says that section 36 properly understood requires that the interests of others living in the mortgaged property as their home must be taken into account when deciding whether to suspend a possession order.

Secondly, there is the very interesting implicit suggestion that account should be taken of developments in the housing market. The feminist judgment observes that average house prices had risen by about 150 per cent since the Lynds bought their property. One

relational than others, and any kind of long-term contract where the parties are working together to achieve common objectives is the most relational of all. The feminist judgment does not explicitly use relational contract theory.

[12] See *National and Provincial Building Society v Lynd* [1996] NI 47, 59–60. In passing, note the judgment of Master Ellison in *Bank of Scotland Plc v Rea* [2014] NIMaster 11, where the bank relied on a contractual right to capitalise interest arrears without actually wiping out the arrears!

[13] On the importance of recognising that it is the debtor's *home* that is being repossessed, see Fox, above n 2.

[14] On the importance of ensuring that the interests of other members of the borrower's family are taken into account, see Elizabeth Warren, 'Bankrupt Children' (2002) 86 *Minnesota Law Review* 1003; and Lorna Fox, 'Re-possessing "Home": A Re-analysis of Gender, Homeownership and Debtor Default for Feminist Legal Theory' (2007-08) 14 *William and Mary Journal of Women and Law* 423.

[15] See Lorna Fox O'Mahony, 'Property Outsiders and the Hidden Politics of Doctrinalism' (2014) 62 *Current Legal Problems* 409. See also Rosemary Auchmuty's feminist judgment of *Royal Bank of Scotland v Etridge (No 2)* [2001] UKHL 44 (in Rosemary Hunter, Clare McGlynn and Erika Rackley, *Feminist Judgments: From Theory to Practice* (Oxford, Hart Publishing, 2010) ch 9), which involved undue influence in the context of mortgages. Auchmuty rejects the traditional 'balancing of interests' framing of disputes between mortgagors and mortgagees—or other parties living in the home, as was the case in *Royal Bank of Scotland v Etridge (No 2)*—and frames her feminist perspective in terms of power. In doing so, she teases out the particular significance of the home to housewives, for whom the home represents their primary domain of influence. A podcast discussion of the case can be accessed at http://podacademy.org/podcasts/legal-judgments-rewritten-from-a-feminist-perspective/.

consequence of a rise in house prices is that mortgagees are often well secured against mortgagor default, and consequently may find it easier to accept flexible rearrangements in the repayment of loans. That, however, is not the case where house prices are falling, negative equity stalks the market and mortgagees are likely to be left with large unsecured debts where they succeed in getting possession of mortgaged properties. To what extent and in what way would matters like these affect the exercise of the section 36 power? In both *Norgan* and *Lynd* it was emphasised that the time given to the mortgagor to remedy the default should take account of whether the mortgagee's security is at risk. Since it was not at risk in *Norgan*, the remaining term of the mortgage was more of a 'reasonable period' than in *Lynd*, where the value of the mortgaged property appeared to be just about sufficient to pay off the loan.

Nearly 20 years on from these cases, we are dealing with a different problem in the housing market: the large number of houses sold at prices that were unaffordable, and the accompanying mortgages that stretched mortgagors' ability to pay beyond breaking point. To this may be added another problem—the crash in the property market that consigned much of the real estate in Northern Ireland into negative equity. Where a mortgagor falls into arrears, it would seem that the mortgagee's security will be routinely at risk. However, it cannot be right that where a mortgagor produces a realistic plan to pay off arrears, she is denied this chance because the mortgagee's security is at risk.

It is also worth observing the much-increased incidence of people buying dwelling-houses, particularly apartments, as investments and not as homes. It would seem that in the event of someone's purchasing a property like this and afterwards experiencing difficulty in paying the mortgage, not much reason would exist for giving the mortgagor time to clear arrears. Sale and cutting one's losses might have to be the order of the day, especially in the negative equity context noted above.[16]

When it came to the precise terms of the court's order in the original *Lynd* case, the difference (or lack of difference) between that decision and *Norgan* can clearly be seen. Basing herself on the unfettered discretion of the court to do the best it could in all the circumstances of the case to allow the mortgagor to get the mortgage paid in the end, the feminist judge decided that as mortgagee and mortgagor were agreed on the monthly payments that should be made, these were the sums to be paid. So far this was the same as Girvan J. Over what period of time were they to be paid? No term was specified in either the original judgment or the feminist judgment, but Girvan J attached a rider to his order that the mortgagor's performance would be reviewed in six months' time to see how the mortgagor was managing. This seems unnecessary, as the mortgagee was happy to accept the mortgagor's proposals and would have been entitled to seek a possession order in the event of default under those new arrangements. It is not apparent from either judgment how long the monthly payments the Lynds were to make would take to pay off the mortgage, whether the outstanding period of the mortgage or some other time. The feminist judgment avoids having to state whether this is the outstanding period, and to this extent it relies more on the judgment of Evans LJ in *Norgan* than that of Waite LJ. This is wise,

[16] See, however, *Titanic Quarter Ltd* v *Rowe* [2010] NICh10, which focused on the purchase of property as a home and the reliance on a contract of purchase with no 'subject to credit' clause. The case addressed how the risk should be spread between the property developer and the purchaser, Neil Rowe, who became unable to pay the purchase price following the crash in the Northern Ireland property market.

because the circumstances in which the section 36 discretion falls to be exercised vary so much that rigid rules, presumptions and starting points are all best avoided.

When the two principal judgments in *Norgan* (Waite LJ and Evans LJ) are read together, it becomes clear, as the feminist judgment understands, that this decision does not establish any strong presumption that the remaining term of the mortgage should be the 'reasonable period' for the mortgagor to remedy the default. *Norgan* was concerned with getting away from the commitment to 'reasonable periods' of two to five years. The remaining term was suitable in *Norgan* because the mortgagee's security was firm, but it was unsuitable in *Lynd* because the mortgagee's security was not firm. In *Lynd*, Girvan J pointed out that spreading arrears over the remaining life of the mortgage increased the amount of interest the mortgagor had to pay, so would not automatically be for the mortgagor's benefit. Lisa Whitehouse's research referred to above[17] provides evidence that district judges have declined to suspend possession orders for the full term for this reason. So, in the end, one wonders if the difference between *Norgan* and *Lynd* is more a matter of rhetoric than anything else.

Conclusion

The feminist judgment and the original judgment in *Lynd* came to the same conclusion. The reasoning, however, was very different, and in a way that potentially could make for profound differences were the feminist judgment to be applied as a precedent. The feminist judgment insists on a faithful application of the legislative intention behind section 36 of the Administration of Justice Act 1970. That legislative intention recognised that the strict terms of contracts entered into to enable people to purchase a *home* for themselves and their families to live in could not always be followed rigidly. Flexibility would be required to fulfil the objective of these contracts, and this in turn would require the voices of all persons living in the home, men and women, adults and children, to be sufficiently taken into account.

[17] See Whitehouse, above n 3, at 163.

National and Provincial Building Society v Lynd and another

CHANCERY DIVISION

FOX O'MAHONY J

3, 28 June 1996. The following judgment was delivered.

On 28 January 1988, John and Sharon Lynd bought their home at 34 Hillview Park, Glengormley, Co Antrim. The purchase was funded by a loan of £24,800 from the National and Provincial Building Society, and the property was secured by sub-demise by an instalment mortgage. The mortgage terms required Mr and Mrs Lynd to pay monthly instalments for just under 17 years, a small part of which went towards reduction of capital, with the rest paid towards interest.

Since 1988, the Lynds have struggled to meet their monthly instalments. Miss Johnston, the solicitor who represented the Lynds in a previous hearing on this matter has indicated that Mr Lynd was employed by several companies and businesses which had experienced financial difficulties and which were forced to close, leaving him without employment and so without an income for significant periods. By 29 August 1991, the Lynds had fallen into arrears on their mortgage, and National and Provincial Building Society sought possession of their home by originating summons.

Between 1991 and the date of this hearing, Mr and Mrs Lynd have continued to struggle financially. By July 1992, they had accrued arrears of 44 unpaid instalments. Following ongoing delays in payment, the matter was brought before the court when the Building Society sought possession of the property. An order for possession made on 14 January 1994, suspended on the condition that the Lynds paid off the arrears at a rate of £180 per month, while also meeting new payments as they fell due. On 12 October 1994, the Master, presumably satisfied of the good faith of the defendants and their ability to pay off the arrears, discharged the previous order, and made a fresh order for possession, suspended on condition that the Lynds discharged the arrears at a rate of £90 per month, while also meeting repayments as they fell due. The Lynds struggled under the pressure to discharge the arrears at this level while continuing to make repayments, and by a summons dated 28 November 1995, the Building Society sought an order for leave to issue execution of the suspended order for possession.

By 12 December 1995, the accumulated arrears amounted to £9,385.66, and the Building Society requested execution of the suspended possession order. The Master considered the Building Society's petition under the court's discretion, as set out in section 36 of the Administration of Justice Act 1970, and applied in the recent English Court of Appeal decision of *Cheltenham & Gloucester Building Society v Norgan* [1996] 1 All ER 449; 26 HLR 703 (CA). The *Norgan* approach indicated that the court could start from a strong presumption that, when determining whether the borrower was likely to be able to pay the sums due under the mortgage within a reasonable period, the residue of the length of the term represented the reasonable period which should be given to the defaulting mortgagor. On that basis, the Master made an order suspending possession on the condition that the Lynds paid £100 per month of the arrears while continuing to meet instalments as they fell due. The Building Society appealed.

This court's power to determine the appeal is based in section 36 of the Administration of Justice Act, 1970. In reviewing the Master's decision, I am cognisant of the role of the section 36 discretion in empowering the court to determine an appropriate balance of consideration for the rights of creditors in the event of mortgage default, on the one hand, and the needs and interests of debtors and their families, on the other. The intended effect of section 36 in possession proceedings involving mortgaged homes is fundamental to the determination of this appeal. In the period leading up to the 1970 Act, it was widely recognised that the roles and functions of the mortgage had evolved, from the last refuge of the necessitous borrower under the shadow of usury laws, to the enabler of capital investment to support industry and commerce from the Industrial Revolution, and then to the emergence of the domestic mortgage as a routine instrument by which building societies enabled the growth of owner-occupation in the UK. As policies promoting widespread owner-occupation have anchored the mortgage more firmly within the domestic realm, it has been transformed from a specialised instrument of industrialisation and capital investment, to become the primary vehicle through which the majority of the population, people like John and Sharon Lynd, access housing in the form of an 'owner-occupied'—subject to a mortgage to the building society—home. In enacting section 36, Parliament clearly directed the court to distinguish its approach to cases involving dwelling houses, from that applied to other mortgaged properties, in light of the specific social context of the mortgaged family home as the foundation for modern housing policies.

National and Provincial Building Society's action to recover this debt should also be understood against the backdrop of the building society's responsibilities as a membership-based, special statutory creature with the object purpose (set out in section 1(1) of the Building Society Act 1962) of raising a stock or fund through the subscriptions of members for making advances to members upon security by way of mortgage. The Lynds' mortgage was not the classical investment mortgage of the nineteenth century, or a short-term loan arrangement; the 'instalment mortgage' executed by John and Sharon Lynd for the benefit of National and Provincial Building Society was designed to enable the Lynds to repay the cost of their housing, the acquisition debt that funded the purchase of their home at 34 Hillview Park, according to a schedule that spreads the repayment of principal and interest by instalments over a period of almost 17 years, eight of which have now passed.

At common law, no distinction is drawn between the rights of the mortgagee according to the nature or purpose of the mortgage. A legal mortgagee is entitled to go into possession immediately upon the execution of the contract by virtue of his estate in the mortgaged property unless that right to possession is excluded by the terms of the mortgage. In *Four-Maids Ltd v Dudley Marshall (Properties) Ltd* Harman J noted that '[t]he mortgagee may go into possession before the ink is dry on the mortgage' ([1957] 1 Ch 317 at 320). While this common law principle applies across the gamut of secured transactions, in a typical residential mortgage—in recognition of both the purpose of the mortgage in enabling the acquisition of a home to live in, and the reality of the long-term, ongoing relationship between borrower and lender—the right to enter into possession is usually excluded unless and until the borrower defaults on repayments or otherwise breaches a term of the mortgage. Although this underlying common law principle remains extant, as mortgage practice and use has evolved over the last century-and-a-half, it has also been overlaid by a series of provisions that have sought to better enable courts to strike an appropriate balance between the rights of the creditor and the needs and interests of debtors and their families.

Until the mid-nineteenth century, the procedure by which a mortgagee was required to issue proceedings for possession was borrowed from the old procedure for recovery of land following wrongful dispossession. The development of processes specific to mortgage possession proceedings can be traced to sections 168–221 of the Common Law Procedure Act 1852, which established the procedure for a writ of ejectment, including the service of notice to defend possession proceedings on any occupier of the mortgaged property (*Longborne v Fisher* (1878) 47 LJ Ch 379). In 1934, the Supreme Court Rule Committee amended the Rules of Supreme Court with the Ordinance 55, rule 5A. These revisions adopted a balanced approach to the procedure for recovery of land: on the one hand, by enhancing the mortgagee's right to possession by enabling an order to be made against the debtor and 'any other person in, or alleged to be in possession of the property'; while also conferring on the court a discretion to adjourn possession proceedings if the Master thought fit, and a power to require notice of the proceedings to be served on such persons as the court might think fit (Ord 55, r6). Together, the rules balanced the court's powers to order recovery of land with protections for the debtor and for others who were in possession of the property; for example, by allowing any other person in, or alleged to be in, possession of the property to appear before the court and to be heard.

On its face, Rules of Supreme Court Ordinance 55 appeared to construct a framework for the court to balance the needs and circumstances of mortgagors—and others in possession of the mortgaged property—and the strict legal rights of mortgagees. Yet Ordinance 55 was not effectively applied to achieve this end, not least because many wives' claims in this period were based in occupation without shared ownership, and so were regarded as personal against their husbands only. The difficulties in applying this general principle concerning 'others in possession' to cases involving spouses (usually wives) at risk of possession proceedings following default by the debtor (usually the husband), were delineated in a line of cases from *Temperance Permanent Building Society v Nevitt* [1940] 3 All ER 237; *Alliance Building Society v Varma* [1949] 1 Ch 724; *Leicester Permanent Building Society v Shearley* [1951] Ch 90. In *Brighton and Shoreham Building Society v Hollingdale* [1965] 1 WLR 376 the court held that it was not necessary for a person in occupation of the property who was the wife of the mortgagor to be joined as a defendant, since she could not claim an independent right to remain in occupation as against the mortgagor.

In the same period, the decision of the Court of Appeal in *Birmingham Citizens Building Society v Caunt* [1962] Ch 883 marked a broader, and significant, turning-point, when the Court rejected the claim that it had any jurisdiction under RSC Ord 55, r5A, or otherwise, to decline a possession order to adjourn a hearing regardless of the circumstances of the case. The Court of Appeal re-asserted an absolute version of the mortgagee's automatic right to possession, stating that:

> "Equity was never and should never be in the hands of the judges a sword to attack any part of the security itself, and the right to possession was an important part of that security, more particularly in association with the ability to give vacant possession on the exercise of the power of sale." (896, per Russell LJ)

In departing from "the then current wind of change in favour of the benevolent treatment of mortgagors in possession of their homes" (*Caunt*, 897), Russell LJ clearly shifted the focus of the court's considerations away from the context of the modern instalment mortgage and its role in enabling access to owned housing for debtors and their families, and towards concern for the security of the creditor's rights.

These decisions strictly limited the court's power to delay possession proceedings beyond the very limited scope of the common law. The strictness of the common law approach was based in the structure of the mortgage instrument, and most particularly, in the legal mortgagee's automatic right to possession. As Sir William Grant MR stated in *Cholmondeley (Marquis) v Clinton (Lord)* (1817) 2 Mer 171, 359, at common law, the legal mortgagee's automatic right to possession meant that: "... a mortgagee may assume possession whenever he pleases, and ... a court of equity never interferes to prevent the mortgagee from assuming the possession." In addition, the procedure under Ordinance 55 was not in fact designed or intended for use by mortgagees, but rather to enable an owner who had been wrongfully dispossessed to reclaim land (*Temperance Permanent Building Society v Nevitt* [1940] 3 All ER 237).

Section 36 of the Administration of Justice Act 1970 was enacted to expand the court's discretionary power to delay possession proceedings—and so, in effect, defer the premature determination of the mortgage through forced sale as a response to default. I therefore turn to consider the nature and extent of the discretion conferred on this court under section 36 of the 1970 Act, and the responsibilities conferred upon this court to strike an appropriate balance between the Building Society's rights, on the one hand, and the needs and interests of the Lynds, on the other. From the reasoning of the House of Lords in *Black-Clawson International Ltd v Papierwerke Waldhof-Aschaffenburg AG* [1975] AC 591 it seems clear that, in doing so, I am entitled to consider the Report of the Committee on Enforcement of Judgment Debts' (1969) (Cmnd 3909) (the Payne Committee), which set out the aims and purpose of the provision. At its heart, section 36 was enacted to address the Payne Committee's concern that the common law approach, as reflected by the Court of Appeal in *Caunt*, was too severe: that it failed to take account of the court's responsibility to protect mortgagors against hardship where appropriate; that it failed to ensure that justice is done by the court in every class of case, including those where the lender is not as responsible, tolerant and understanding as National and Provincial Building Society have been in this case; and that it failed to recognise the crucial role of the modern residential instalment mortgage in facilitating access to housing, and the precariousness of the present day economic difficulties in leaving some debtors at the mercy of the mortgagee or the court to keep the roof over their families' heads. As such, I understand that in applying section 36 I must draw a line under that absolute approach and seek to follow the logic and spirit of section 36 as it was articulated by the Payne Committee.

Section 36 provides that:

> (1) Where the mortgagee under a mortgage of land which consists of or includes a dwelling house brings an action in which he claims possession of the mortgaged property, not being an action for foreclosure in which a claim for possession of the mortgaged property is also made, the court may exercise any of the powers conferred on it by subsection (2) below if it appears to the court that in the event of its exercising the power the mortgagor is likely to be able within a reasonable period, to pay sums due under the mortgage ...

(2) The court—
  (a) may adjourn proceedings, or
  (b) on giving judgment, or making an order for delivery of possession of the mortgaged property, or at any time before the execution of such judgment or order, may (i) stay or suspend execution of the judgment or order, or (ii) postpone the date for delivery of possession, for such period as the court thinks reasonable.

The purpose of section 36, as set out by the Payne Committee, was to adopt a balanced approach to the rights of creditors and the needs of debtors and their families. The Committee sought to ensure that, just as the role of mortgage debt in everyday life has changed from medieval times to become "as indispensible to the economy of ordinary families as it was to the development of industrialism", so too "the legal machinery [to ensure the repayment of legally binding debts] must [evolve to ensure that it is] efficient, capable of reaching out to all the assets of a debtor and yet sensitive to both the needs and social circumstances of debtors and to the rights of creditors" (Payne Report, para 46). In another section of the Report, the observation is made again, that while "[e]nforcement is predominately a matter of legal rights ... it would be foolish to ignore its crucial effects not only upon the individual debtor but also upon his family..." [para 76]. I therefore approach the case before me, mindful that the fair and proper exercise of the court's discretion under section 36 turns upon the necessity to have regard to the needs of the Lynds while seeking to achieve an outcome that respects the legal rights of the Building Society.

In seeking to strike an appropriate balance between the rights of the Building Society, on the one hand, and the needs and social circumstances of the Lynds, on the other, I also recognise that there is no suggestion of wrongful conduct on either side of this case. When faced with actions for the recovery of debts, this court is sometimes called upon to determine cases in which borrowers who acquire goods and services have done so in circumstances where they are not in a position to exercise a true freedom of contract; or where borrowers have behaved wrongfully in their failure to meet obligations that are lawfully due. Neither proposition has been advanced in this case. No suggestion has been made to the court that the terms of the Lynds' mortgage were unfair. In contrast, the evidence before the court indicates that the Building Society has endeavoured to exercise forbearance in light of the debtor's difficult financial circumstances. Equally, there is no suggestion that the Lynds have been profligate, nor that they have not made every effort to meet their obligations, notwithstanding their financial difficulties, which have resulted from Mr Lynd being made redundant by several companies and businesses which themselves experienced financial difficulties and are now closed. Mrs Lynd, who appeared in person to represent the interests of her family in this action and who has worked with the Building Society to negotiate repayments and to defend her family home, indicated in a previous heading that she would prefer to discharge her arrears sooner rather than later, and that she felt confident that she could pay £100 per month of the arrears, while meeting new instalments as they fall due.

The wording of section 36 of the 1970 Act sets out the court's discretion to adjourn proceedings or to stay execution or postpone an order for possession, and is to be read in conjunction with section 8 of the Administration of Justice Act 1973, which was enacted to remedy an unintended effect of accelerated liability clauses which threatened to make the protection conferred by Parliament illusory; section 8 clarified that 'any sums due' referred to only those sums in arrears and not the whole mortgage debt. The court's discretion is bounded by the terms of section 36: in order for the discretion to arise, it must appear to the court that in the event of the court exercising the power, the mortgagor is likely to be able to pay the sums due under the mortgage or to remedy a default consisting of a breach of any other obligations under the mortgage within a reasonable period. In *Alliance and Leicester Building Society v Carlisle* (8 Sept 1995, unreported), Campbell J set out principles of application then emerging from available authorities:

1. It is the intention of both sections to give a measure of relief to those people who find themselves in temporary financial difficulties, unable to meet their commitments under their mortgage and in danger of losing their homes. (*Bank of Scotland v Grimes* [1985] 2 All ER 254, per Griffiths LJ at 259)
2. 'Likelihood' is a question of fact, to be determined by the judge on evidence before him. (*Royal Trust Co of Canada v Markham* [1975] 1 WLR 1416 at 1422, Sir John Pennycuick)
3. Adjournment or suspension or postponement must be for a defined or ascertainable period. (*Royal Trust Co of Canada v Markham* [1975] 1 WLR 1416)
4. A court might if it thought reasonable to do so keep control of the matter by holding it in abeyance for a specific period with liberty to apply in the meantime, and reconsider the situation at the end of that period or upon an earlier application by either party. In a suitable case the specified period might even be the whole remaining prospective life of the mortgage. (*Western Bank Ltd v Schindler* [1977] Ch 1)
5. It is not wrong for a judge to act on the basis merely of information given to him informally by those representing the mortgagor especially where the mortgagor is present in Court and available to be questioned. (*Cheltenham & Gloucester BS v Grant* [1994] TLR 255 per Nourse LJ).

In *Bank of Scotland v Grimes*, Griffiths LJ made reference to "temporary financial difficulties" ([1985] 2 All ER 254, per Griffiths LJ) affecting the borrower's ability to pay, and I am conscious that "temporary financial difficulties" can encompass a range of circumstances, and that both the nature of the difficulties, and the way in which the parties respond to them, is likely to affect ability to pay in the longer term of the life of the mortgage. In some cases, the mortgage may have been agreed on the basis of a given or prospective income which thereafter, due to temporary circumstances, the mortgagor becomes unable to discharge as repayments fall due. In other cases, unforeseen but more than temporary circumstances might mean that the restructuring of the financial relationship between the mortgagor and the mortgage is necessary if repayment of the mortgage is to remain viable within the mortgage period. In either case, the circumstances that give rise to inability to pay can result from factors on the borrower's side (for example, difficulties in securing employment following redundancy, as in the case of John Lynd), or on the creditor's side (for example, rising interest rates on a variable rate mortgage).

The 1970 Act was explicit in its aim to bring the law of mortgage possession actions into the new era of widespread home ownership, reflecting the Payne Committee's concern that "[t]here has come into existence a very large class of owner/occupiers, who might suddenly find themselves financially embarrassed and at the mercy of their mortgagees and of the courts" [para 1373]. I also understand the orientation of section 36 around the status of the property as a "dwelling house" as directing the court towards consideration of the particular dynamics of the building society mortgage in enabling access to housing in the late twentieth century. It is important to recognise that lenders—and particularly building societies—do not as a matter of practice seek to take possession as a remedy of first resort; and, indeed, National and Provincial Building Society has engaged in a long process of forbearance with the Lynds since they began to encounter difficulties in repayment. In many cases, as in the case before me, the debtor and the mortgagee are likely to have already engaged in attempts to restructure the repayment of the debt. At the same time, I am conscious that judgments of this court in applying section 36 provide an important frame within which practices of informal mediation, restructuring and forbearance evolve.

The crucial test for establishing scope for the exercise of discretion has four limbs: (a) that the mortgagor is likely to be able (b) within a reasonable period (c) to pay (d) any sums due under the mortgage. In its recommendation, the Payne Committee indicated (see para 1390) that the discretion should be exercised judicially and with due regard to the interests of the mortgagee as well as mortgagor and with due regard to the mortgage deed. I now proceed to consider the scope of the court's discretion in the present case in light of the proper interpretation of these qualifying factors.

The meaning of (d) 'any sums due' was clarified by section 8 of the Administration of Justice Act 1973, as only the amount which the mortgagor would ordinarily have had to pay if the mortgage had run in the normal way. Section 8 was enacted to correct the potentially punitive approach adopted in *Halifax BS v Clark* [1973] Ch 307, when Pennycuick V-C concluded that the defendants had no prospect of paying the due sums (including the entire capital, which because due on default) within a reasonable period, and that the discretion could not therefore be exercised. Lord Hailsham, introducing the amending legislation, indicated that its object was to enable the intention of the Payne Committee—that courts have proper scope to balance the needs and circumstances of the debtor against the rights of the creditor—to be carried into effect.

Clauses (a) and (c) together relate to the mortgagor's likely ability to pay, although it should be noted that, in balancing the creditor's rights against the debtor's needs and circumstances, the court should approach this question from two perspectives. Firstly, from the creditor's perspective: is the debtor—if the court exercises its discretion—likely to be able to pay, such that the debt obligation can be fulfilled; and, secondly, from the debtor's perspective: is a court-sanctioned delay likely to enhance the affordability of those obligations, taking account of the needs and circumstances of the debtor. The outcome that the court should seek is one in which the terms of the court's order require the debtor to repay what they can afford by way of remedying default, while also ensuring that the creditor is paid what is due under the terms of the mortgage. The ethos of the Payne Report was clear in directing the court to consider both questions, and to balance these against one another: one relating to payment, and the impact of any delay on the creditor; and another relating to affordability and the impact of any delay in enhancing the debtor's ability to discharge their obligations.

Finally, the interpretation of a 'reasonable' period should also be understood in the context of the court's obligation to act judicially and with due regard to the interests of the mortgagee as well as mortgagor, and with due regard to the mortgage deed. This means that in interpreting what is meant by the 'reasonable period' of section 36, the court must consider not only the needs of creditors but also the needs of debtors and their families. I do not consider an interpretation of the 'reasonable period' which takes account only of the needs of the creditor to be adequate or consistent with the court's obligation to act judicially and with due regard to the interests of both parties. This is also consistent with the court's obligation, where a statute uses the term 'reasonable', to consider the whole statutory context; in this instance, the aims and purpose of section 36. In applying the criteria of section 36 to the present case, I am therefore obliged to make my judgment based on the 'reasonableness' of the period within which the Lynds can, affordably, discharge their arrears and the remaining mortgage debt, as well as the reasonableness of the period in which the creditor is required to wait for repayment. In approaching this in general terms I am guided by the reasoning in *Monkland v Jack Barclay Ltd* [1951] 2 KB 252, that "Reason varies in its conclusions according to the idiosyncrasies of the individual and the times and circumstances in which he thinks. Thus when a contract provides that a contractual obligation is to be performed within a reasonable time all the circumstances must be taken into account in deciding what is a reasonable time." Similarly, when legislation refers to a reasonable time, all the circumstances relating to the aim of the provision must be taken into account when determining a "reasonable time".

In the case of section 36, I come back to the stated intentions of the Payne Committee: to empower the court to strike an appropriate balance between the strict legal rights of the creditor and the needs and circumstances of debtors and their families, taking account of the effects of delay on the creditor and the effects of repossession on the debtor, and sensitive to the context of the modern domestic residential mortgage in securing access to a family home. My duty in applying section 36 in this regard is greatly aided by the recent decision of the Court of Appeal in *Cheltenham and Gloucester Building Society v Norgan* [1996] 1 All ER 449; 26 HLR 703 (CA), which offers a clear framework within which courts can consider the application of section 36. Prior to *Norgan*, this court's practice was to assume that a "reasonable period" was a relatively limited period with an outer limit of around four to five years (*Alliance and Leicester Building Society v Carlisle*; *National and Provincial Building Society v Williamson* [1995] NI 366).

The decision in the *Norgan* case was delivered on 5 December 1995 and appears to have heralded a quite different approach. To understand the decision it is necessary to state some of the relevant facts to put the case in its context. In that case the relevant property was worth £225,000. Christina Norgan, who occupied the property with her husband and five sons aged between 6 and 18, had lived there since 1974 and, like Sharon Lynd, was the lead litigant in the appeal. In November 1986, in order to raise capital to finance his business activities, Mr Norgan had transferred his interest to Christina who became sole owner, paying £90,000 for the transfer. This sum was borrowed from the Cheltenham and Gloucester's predecessor, the Guardian Building Society. The property was mortgaged to the building society and the term was for 22 years with interest at 11.25% (variable). The monies due to the building society were guaranteed by Mr Norgan and secured by reference to his pension funds. He fell into difficulties and arrears of interest built up. By May 1990 the arrears were at £14,744.

Unsuccessful attempts to refinance were made. Mrs Norgan applied for suspension of the order for possession and the district judge ordered payment of arrears at £454 per month which would have taken some three years to discharge the arrears. No further payments were made though promises to do so were made. A further suspension was obtained on terms that arrears were paid at the rate of £551 per month. There was a temporary improvement for a period and then arrears developed again. In September 1993 the district judge refused to make any further order for suspension. This was appealed to Judge O'Malley. At this stage arrears were £20,000. Judge O'Malley exercised his discretion and considered that a period of four years to discharge the arrears was appropriate. The matter went on appeal to the Court of Appeal, which held that, for the purposes of section 36 of the 1970 Act and section 8 of the 1973 Act, when assessing a reasonable period for the payment of arrears by a defaulting mortgagor the court should take into account the whole of the remaining part of the original term of the mortgage and the existing practice of imposing a shorter fixed period of two or more years should no longer be followed. The Court of Appeal concluded that the judge at first instance had erred in adopting a period of payment (four years) unrelated to the remaining term of the mortgage (13 years). Waite LJ stated (at 458)—

> "... it does seem to me that the logic and spirit of the legislation require, especially in cases where the parties are proceeding under arrangements such as those reflected in the [Council of Mortgage Lenders'] statement, that the court should take as its starting point the full term of the mortgage and pose at the outset the question: would it be possible for the mortgagor to maintain payment off of the arrears by instalments over that period?"

In the circumstances the matter was remitted to the county court judge with directions, *inter alia*, to make a determination of the question whether in the light of the court's findings as to the current and prospective ability of the mortgagor to discharge the instalments there were any unusual circumstances justifying a departure from the principle that the remaining term of the mortgage is *prima facie* a "reasonable period" for the purposes of section 36 and section 8.

The decision in *Norgan* is to be welcomed for its approach of seeking to strike an appropriate balance between the needs and circumstances of the debtor and her family, and the rights of the creditor in recovering the debt that is owed. Since the emergence of widespread domestic mortgages in the middle of this century, UK courts have repeatedly curtailed their own powers, when asked by a mortgagee to order possession of a domestic residential property, to balance the needs and circumstances of debtors and their families with the commercial imperatives of the lenders. Even in the light of the clear guidance offered by the Payne Committee, courts have held to their previous practices in requiring that the debtor make good on arrears with the shorter period of 2–4 years. In doing so, we have failed to give due regard to the legislative intentions of section 36 (read in conjunction with section 8). The decision in *Norgan* has provided helpful clarity on this point and is to be welcomed for its emphasis on the court's responsibility to balance the competing interests of the parties, as intended by the Payne Committee, and cognisant of the context of section 36 with respect to modern residential mortgage transactions.

Nevertheless, I am also cognisant that it is not the function of the Court of Appeal to lay down rigid rules (*Cheltenham & Gloucester Building Society v Grant* (1994) 26 HLR 703). In that regard, I am grateful for the additional guidance offered by Evans LJ (*Norgan*, at 463), setting out the wider range of considerations which are relevant to establishing a 'reasonable period' for the purposes of section 36:

a) How much can the borrower reasonably afford to pay, both now and in the future?
b) If the borrower has a temporary difficulty in meeting his obligations, how long is the difficulty is likely to last?

c) What was the reason for the arrears which have accumulated?
d) How much remained of the original term?
e) What are the relevant contractual terms, and what type of mortgage is it, ie when is the principal due to be repaid?
f) Is it a case where the court should exercise its power to disregard accelerated payment provisions (s 8 of the 1973 Act)?
g) Is it reasonable to expect the lender, in the particular circumstances of the case, to recoup the arrears of interest (1) over the whole of the original term; (2) within a shorter period; or even (3) within a longer period, ie by extending the repayment period? Is it reasonable to expect the lender to capitalise the interest, or not?
h) Are there any other reasons affecting the security which should influence the length of the period for repayment?

I respectfully agree with Evans LJ's enunciation of the considerations which are likely to be relevant when a "reasonable period" has to be established for the purposes of section 36 of the 1970 Act. What is or is not a reasonable period must be answered by reference to the circumstances of the individual case, and Evans LJ's statement of relevant considerations—which include, but are not restricted to, the whole remaining term of the mortgage—correctly in my view, impresses on the court the need to look at all the circumstances of the case. By stressing that the balance of the term should be kept in mind as a potentially relevant "reasonable period" the Court of Appeal was correcting an established practice which had inappropriately fettered the court's discretion under section 36. I prefer Evans LJ's longer list of factors to Waite LJ's *prima facie* presumption because it reflects more fully the legislative intentions of section 36 (and section 8), which I understand to be intended to empower the court to balance the needs and circumstances of debtors and their families with the rights of creditors, with reference to the mortgage terms and in the context of the domestic mortgage attached to a home. In cases such as the present case, in which the relevant mortgage was by instalments, I am persuaded by the logic advanced by Scarman LJ in *First Middleborough Trading and Mortgage Co Ltd v Cunningham* ((1974) 28 P & CR 69), and quoted by Evans LJ in *Norgan*, that:

> "Since the object of the instalment mortgage was, with the consent of the mortgagee, to give the mortgagor the period of the mortgage to repay the capital sum and interest, one begins with a powerful presumption of fact in favour of the period of the mortgage being the 'reasonable period'." (at 75)

It is beyond the scope of my judgment to consider what an appropriate approach might be in a case involving a repayment mortgage. That would be a matter for the relevant court to consider, taking account of the factors set out by Evans LJ, which helpfully structure the questions that the court should consider in the balancing of the respective parties' interests. I understand that commercial lenders often purport to seek, from the law, certainty in outcomes. In that regard, I also understand the pragmatic attractiveness of the pre-*Norgan* approach in enabling courts to dispose of cases. But Parliament was not seeking, through section 36, to create a route for the pragmatic disposal of mortgage repossession cases in the interests of the commercial lender. Quite the opposite. Parliament was seeking to achieve a more balanced approach to the thorny problem of domestic mortgage default, which allows appropriate scope for consideration of the needs and circumstances of debtors, as well as the rights of creditors to recover monies due. Mortgages for the acquisition of domestic property are long term relationships, often lasting twenty years or more. Inevitably, much may change during the period of the mortgagee, both in the financial and personal circumstances of borrowers and in the financial and economic climate in which lenders conduct their businesses. Borrowers marry, and sometimes separate; they bear and raise children, to adulthood and beyond, while gradually, progressively, repaying by monthly instalments the mortgage that has funded the roof overhead. Sometimes, they face financial difficulties that require a re-negotiation of the scheduled repayments. In these cases, it is often the wife and mother of the family who shoulders the burden—as Mrs Lynd has—of negotiating with lenders, hanging on to the family home to keep the roof overhead as far as she can. Indeed, the financial impact of child-rearing means that it is often families with children, and particularly women living alone with children, who are at greatest risk of debtor default, and for whom the court's faithful application of the Payne Committee's intended approach is likely to be critical.

Although Northern Irish lenders and borrowers have been mercifully saved the worst impacts of the recent recession and housing market crisis in England and elsewhere, experiences across the water in the late 1980s and early 1990s have highlighted the impact of external shocks on the sustainability of home ownership, and the significance of section 36 in framing the long-term relationships between borrowers and lenders in the modern era of widespread home ownership. For lenders who follow the guidance of the Council of Mortgage Lenders, like the National and Provincial Building Society, mortgage repossession is the remedy of last resort. Indeed, I read the history of the litigation before me as one of lender forbearance and flexibility, through the significant difficulties that the Lynds have faced, from John's misfortunes in employment to their persistent difficulties in discharging arrears due while continuing to meet payments under the mortgage. National and Provincial Building Society have demonstrated their commitment to working with the Lynds to find an affordable solution to their mortgage debt, and to avoid the last resort of repossessing their family home. The ability of a building society to sustain this forbearance against default is supported by the strength of the Northern Ireland housing market, where average prices, which have risen by about 150% since the Lynds bought 34 Hillview Park in 1988, currently stand at an historic high. While this court was not offered evidence relating to the current market value of the property, it is relevant to consider the scale of the accumulated arrears in the context of the likely increased value of the lender's security.

I also note, with reference to the longer list of *Norgan* factors enumerated by Evans LJ, that the difficulties that led to default on repayments were not the fault of John and Sharon Lynd, and that John is now in employment and making repayments. The instalment mortgage agreed between the parties envisaged that only a small amount of the capital would be repaid by instalments, which were mostly payments of interest, which is charged at a variable rate to protect the Building Society against changing economic conditions.

The checklist set out by Evans LJ in *Norgan* permits me to consider whether it is reasonable to expect the lender, in the particular circumstances of the case, to recoup the arrears of interest (1) over the whole of the original term; (2) within a shorter period; or even (3) within a longer period, ie by extending the repayment period; or to capitalise the interest, or not. Mrs Lynd has not asked the court to make an order adjusting the term of the mortgage, or to capitalise accumulated interest. Rather, she asks the court to uphold the order made by the Master suspending possession on the condition that the defendants pay

£100 per month of the arrears while continuing to meet payments as they fall due, a sum which she agreed would be affordable and which the Master was satisfied would adequately protect the Building Society's interest in receiving a steady flow of interest payments while awaiting capital repayment according to the terms of the mortgage.

Finally, in deciding the outcome of this appeal, I noted above that I have taken account of Nourse LJ's statement, in *Cheltenham & Gloucester Building Society v Grant* (1994) 26 HLR 703, that it is not the function of the Court of Appeal to lay down rigid rules as to how busy district and county court judges should satisfy themselves for the purposes of section 36. In considering whether a decision should be upheld, the test that Nourse LJ applied was whether he was able to say that the decision was plainly wrong. He said:

> "It may well be the case that another judge would have taken the opposite view. But the discretion in this case was entrusted to this judge, and in the light of the comparatively slight information we have as to what went on before him at the end of the day I am unable to say that his decision was plainly wrong." (708)

Mr Toner on behalf of the Building Society indicated that the Building Society at this juncture would regard execution of an order for possession as a matter of last resort. The Building Society's preferred option is to significantly increase the monthly payments which the Master directed should be paid if the defendants were to avoid execution of the order for possession. Mr Toner argued that the defendants should be directed to pay something of the order of £190 per month by way of reduction of the arrears on top of the ongoing obligation to pay instalments at the current rates. The arrears themselves will of course continue to accrue interest, and I am mindful that it is in the financial interests of both parties that these are discharged as soon as is both feasible and affordable for the Lynds.

Mrs Lynd gave evidence which purposed to show that Mr Lynd was now in full employment by a haulage contractor and was in receipt of earnings of £380 per week nett. In her affidavit sworn on 19 April 1996, Mrs Lynd gave evidence of monthly outgoings of just under £1,088. Mrs Lynd indicated a readiness and ability on the part of the Lynds to pay off the arrears at around £180 to £190 per month. Mr Toner indicated on behalf of the Building Society that it would not object to an order suspending execution of the order for possession provided that such monthly payments were made.

In determining whether or not and if so how the court should exercise its discretion under section 36 the court should take into account and give proper weight to the views expressed by the mortgagor concerning affordability and the ability to pay, and the mortgagee who has a legitimate claim to recover arrears due. In this case, both the Building Society and the borrower have acted wisely and with an appropriate degree of responsibility, to avoid a forced sale of the property which would be unlikely to obtain the best price for the Building Society and would have major adverse consequences for the Lynd family. Since the Lynds have indicated a willingness and ability to pay at the rate of £190 per month towards the discharge of arrears I consider that it is proper in this case for the court to exercise its discretion to stay execution of the order for possession provided that instalments as they currently fall due are paid and provided that the £190 per month is paid by the defendants towards the discharge of arrears. Provided that these arrears are paid off at that rate the arrears should be paid well before the end of the term of the mortgage.

Order accordingly.

10

Commentary on *The Report of the Tribunal of Inquiry into the 'Kerry Babies Case'*

YVONNE MARIE DALY

Introduction

Most judgments examined in this book come from appellate cases. There has been a long-acknowledged imbalance in the attention devoted to questions of law in appellate courts and disputed questions of fact in courts of first instance.[1] In the specific context of feminist judging, the conduct or management of the first instance trial or hearing process has also gained little attention.[2] The 'judgment' delivered by Vicky Conway here is unique within the Northern/Irish Feminist Judgments Project, as it reviews a report from a Tribunal of Inquiry. A Tribunal of Inquiry is a unique legal process, which is first instance in the sense that it hears directly from witnesses, but it is not the same as a trial. A Tribunal is an inquisitorial, as opposed to adversarial, process aimed at making findings of fact, not law, and no criminal consequences attach to any findings made. Nonetheless it is a powerful tool, which produces an official 'truth', and individual reputations can be significantly impacted by its findings.

The Tribunal under examination here was established to inquire into the facts and circumstances leading to the preferment of criminal charges against Joanne Hayes and her family members in connection with the death of an unnamed male infant, and the subsequent withdrawal of those charges; related allegations surrounding garda questioning of Joanne Hayes and her family and the taking of statements from them; and any matters

[1] See Jerome Frank, *Law and the Modern Mind* (New York, Brentano's, Inc, c1930); Jerome Frank, 'Why not a Clinical-Lawyer School?' (1933) 81(8) *University of Pennsylvania Law Review* 907–23; Jerome Frank, *Fate and Freedom* (New York, Simon and Schuster, 1945). See also William Twining, 'Taking Facts Seriously' in *Rethinking Evidence: Exploratory Essays*, 2nd edn (Cambridge, Cambridge University Press, 2006).

[2] See Rosemary Hunter, 'Can feminist judges make a difference?' (2008) 15:1–2 *International Journal of the Legal Profession* 7–36, 17. See, however, Marie Fox's feminist judgment in this collection, ch 29. Fox rewrote a Northern Ireland county court judgment rather than the appellate level judgment. One of her motivations was to conduct a re-evaluation of the expert evidence.

connected therewith.[3] However, in the course of the Tribunal its Chairman, High Court judge Mr Justice Kevin Lynch, suggested that the process could be seen as analogous to a claim for damages by Joanne Hayes and her family against An Garda Síochána.[4] This conflicts with the exceptional nature of a Tribunal of Inquiry, equating it with a traditional adversarial contest between two parties. This binary combative conception of the process was clear in the manner in which witnesses before the Tribunal, specifically Joanne and her family, were allowed to be questioned by lawyers. This impacted on the eventual outcome of the process wherein, basically, the gardaí were exonerated and members of the Hayes family were found to be liars. Given the approach adopted by the Chairman, it could not be otherwise: if the gardaí were to be exonerated then Joanne and her family had to be liars.

Within this commentary I first set out briefly the social and factual context of the case. I then consider the feminist features of Conway J's 'judgment' (hereinafter 'the review') before going on to examine Joanne's experience at the Tribunal, linking this to issues of female credibility in courtroom proceedings. I conclude by highlighting the public outpouring of support for Joanne Hayes and her family, which is interesting from both a socio-legal and a feminist perspective.

Social Context

In his exploration of the Kerry Babies story, Inglis provides the social context of the times, highlighting matters such as the economic recession of the 1980s, attitudes towards sexual morality, the death of Ann Lovett and her baby, the rising number of single mothers in the state and claims of moving statues, amongst other things.[5] He points to the collision between Catholic Ireland and the rise of individualism: 'On the one side was traditional, conservative, Catholic teaching emphasising purity, chastity and self-denial. On the other was modern, liberal, individualism emphasising self-expression, eroticism and sexual experience.'[6] While there was a move towards an 'á la carte Catholicism' in Irish life at the time,[7] the Catholic Church still had a strong hold over society.[8]

In October 1983, Joanne Hayes discovered that she was pregnant by a married man, Jeremiah Locke. She already had one child, Yvonne, as a result of their long-term affair and, like a growing number of single mothers in Ireland at the time, had kept and was raising her child.[9]

[3] See Appendix A to the Tribunal Report, at http://opac.oireachtas.ie/AWData/Library3/Library2/DL035878.pdf (last accessed 2 February 2016).

[4] Tribunal Transcript, 15/2.

[5] Tom Inglis, *Truth, Power and Lies: Irish Society and the Case of the Kerry Babies* (Dublin, University College Dublin Press, 2003) ch 8, 'The Context', and ch 9, 'Long-term processes of change'.

[6] ibid, 124.

[7] ibid, 129.

[8] ibid, 126.

[9] Inglis, above n 5, notes a study from June 1984, which suggested that the number of single mothers who were keeping their babies had increased; he states that this was part of a sea change (referencing *The Irish Times*, 12 June 1984).

This second pregnancy was a worry to her, however,[10] and it was about to give rise to police interrogation, murder charges and the Tribunal of Inquiry under examination here.

The Facts

The facts are more fully detailed in Conway J's review, but in extremely truncated form they are as follows: Joanne Hayes was charged with the murder of a baby boy found dead on a beach at Cahirciveen, Co Kerry, and members of her family were charged with concealment of birth.[11] Joanne, as noted above, had been pregnant as a result of her long-term affair with a married man, and she had given birth around the time that the baby was discovered on the beach. Joanne and her family were questioned by gardaí, including three senior members of the 'murder squad' (known in other circles as 'the heavy gang'),[12] and gave confession statements detailing the stabbing of the 'Cahirciveen baby' and his disposal over the cliffs near Slea Head. However, the body of the baby to whom Joanne gave birth (the 'Tralee baby') was found on her family farm, and all charges against her and her family were eventually dropped when it was found that her blood type was different from that of the Cahirciveen baby. A Tribunal of Inquiry was set up in the wake of media and public concern as to how the clearly false confessions could have come about.

The Feminist 'Judgment'

Much of Conway J's review of the Tribunal and its ultimate Report relates to the manner in which witnesses were examined, the weight placed on certain evidence and the conclusions reached as a result. She seeks to assert Joanne's voice within the review, and is critical of the Tribunal for allowing irrelevant personal questions to be asked of Joanne, who, during five days of aggressive cross-examination, was understandably emotional and upset. Conway J notes the lack of sympathy shown to Joanne by the Chairman, and ultimately issues an apology to Joanne on behalf of the judiciary for the ordeal she experienced before the Tribunal.[13] This is a very bold step to take, and one that seeks to redress the hurt caused to Joanne by the extremely personal questions she was asked, the

[10] Joanne Hayes, *My Story* (London, Brandon/Mount Eagle Publications, 1985) 34, 'I felt I could not expect my family to accept a second child by this married man of whom they did not approve'.

[11] It remains unclear why a charge of murder was preferred against Joanne rather than the more appropriate charge of infanticide. Even if Joanne had been the mother of the Cahirciveen baby and had stabbed that baby to death, the offence of infanticide specifically exists to be applied in such circumstances: see s 1(3) of the Infanticide Act 1949 (since amended in part by the Criminal Law (Insanity) Act 2006).

[12] Inglis, above n 5, at 192.

[13] The importance of official apology from a feminist perspective is examined in Reg Graycar, 'A Feminist Adjudication Process: Is there such a Thing?' in Ulrike Schultz and Gisela Shaw (eds), *Gender and Judging* (Oxford, Hart Publishing, Oñati International Series in Law and Society, 2003) 435–57.

insensitive attitude towards her display of raw emotion, and the fact that counsel acting on behalf of individual members of An Garda Síochána were allowed to question her as aggressively as an accused in a criminal trial, if not more so. Joanne felt this very strongly. In her book she states that one of the things that struck her most about her experience under cross-examination was

> that there seemed to be no humanity in the relentless way in which I was pursued by my legal interrogators. The process of the law allowed for me to be torn asunder and every part of me examined in such a way as to denigrate and degrade me.[14]

Conway J also concludes that the evidence before the Tribunal does not substantiate a number of the findings of fact, including the finding that Joanne killed the baby born to her. This conclusion by Conway J is extremely important. Joanne was very hurt by the original findings of the Tribunal in this regard,[15] which ignored the expert testimonies of forensic pathologist Dr John Harbison and forensic scientist Dr Louise McKenna in favour of the testimonies of Joanne's aunt, Bridie Fuller, and her brother, Mike, both of whom ought to have been regarded as unreliable witnesses. Dr Harbison's evidence was that he had failed to establish that the baby had achieved an existence separate from Joanne, and Dr McKenna found no evidence of a birth in Joanne's bedroom (in contrast to the testimony of Bridie and Mike) but did find vegetation on Joanne's clothes, which substantiated Joanne's account of giving birth in a field on the farm:

> To me this attitude of the judge to two state witnesses is the most hurtful of all, because it leads him to the conclusion that I killed my baby and that I beat it with a bath brush. This really shattered me. Everything I suffered during the course of the Tribunal, everything else said about me in the report, pales into insignificance beside that.[16]

As explained in her review, Conway J comes to the conclusion that no new inquiry into the matter ought to be established, given what Joanne and her family suffered during the Tribunal, the passage of time since the events and Joanne's refusal to discuss the case in the intervening years. She accords priority to the interests of Joanne and the Hayes family, whom she deems the 'victims of this whole saga'.

Conway J's review of the Tribunal process and its ultimate Report is informed by a feminist approach and seeks to illustrate how the Tribunal failed Joanne as a woman. In her Foreword to *Feminist Judgments: From Theory to Practice*, UK Supreme Court Judge, Lady Brenda Hale, observed the importance of how a story is told in a judgment: 'Feminist judges will take different facts from the mass of detail to tell the story in a different way, to bring out features which others discard, and to explain the features which others find difficult to understand.'[17] This is certainly true of the review of this Tribunal. I hesitate to refer to the Tribunal by the title bequeathed upon it in the official report, ie the *Report of the Tribunal of Inquiry into 'The Kerry Babies Case'*, because it was not an inquiry into the 'Kerry Babies': the terms of reference related to the garda conduct of the investigation and prosecution,

[14] Hayes, above n 10, at 166.
[15] ibid, 171–72.
[16] ibid, 172.
[17] Brenda Hale, 'Foreword' in Rosemary Hunter, Clare McGlynn, and Erika Rackley (eds), *Feminist Judgments: From Theory to Practice* (Oxford, Hart Publishing, 2010) v.

rather than to the facts surrounding the actual deaths of either the Cahirciveen baby or Joanne's baby. Indeed, Joanne and her family preferred to refer to it as 'The Kerry Garda case'.[18] This indeed seems a more accurate reflection of the terms of reference, though not of Joanne or her family's experiences before the Tribunal.

The Tribunal of Inquiry

Mr Justice Kevin Lynch was among 43 male officials in the Tribunal who engaged in a 'public probe of the private life of Joanne Hayes':[19] all of the lawyers were men, all of the gardaí were men, all but one of the medical/scientific experts were men.[20] And indeed, the Tribunal involved itself in the very public questioning of the very private details of Joanne's life. Rather than focusing on how the gardaí elicited false confessions from members of the Hayes family, the focus seemed to be on Joanne herself: her sexual life, her menstrual cycle, her contraceptive use and the events on the night she gave birth to the 'Tralee baby'.

Joanne felt this deeply and was very aware of the gendered nature of the Tribunal proceedings: 'I felt I was some kind of prey pursued by hunters, who were men and who invaded the privacy of my body and my emotions in their dragging out of all the details about me.'[21]

Smart has noted that women

> go to law as mothers, wives, sexual objects, pregnant women, deserted mothers, single mothers and so on ... In going to law women carry with them cultural meanings about pregnancy, heterosexuality, sexual bodies ... [L]aws that deal with the private sphere operate on fully gendered subjects.[22]

Not only does the law view women in this categorised manner, the media seizes upon this branding of women too, with certain headline-grabbing classifications being more commercially lucrative.[23] Joanne Hayes was an unmarried mother of an 'illegitimate' child, and a woman who had conducted a long-term affair with a married man. She was suspected of killing her own child. The media was certain to make the most of this story,[24] and it seems clear from the conduct of the Tribunal and its final report, that the legal system viewed her in a certain light also.

[18] Hayes, above n 10, at 172.

[19] Nell McCafferty, *A Woman to Blame: The Kerry Babies Case* (Cork, Attic Press, 1985) 'Prologue', xv. McCafferty's book provides a fascinating feminist analysis of the entire affair, drawing on her contemporaneous coverage of the Tribunal in the *Irish Press*. For other accounts of the case see, amongst others, Gene Kerrigan, 'The Kerry Babies Case' (1985) *Magill* 16–51; Moira J Maguire, 'The changing face of Catholic Ireland: Conservatism and liberalism in the Ann Lovett and Kerry Babies scandals' (2001) 27(2) *Feminist Studies* 335–58; Tom Inglis, 'Sexual transgression and scapegoats: a case study from modern Ireland' (2002) 5(1) *Sexualities* 5–24.

[20] In the mid-1980s the sole female member of the Irish superior courts was Ms Justice Mella Carroll. Although it is not required by law that Tribunals of Inquiry should be chaired by a judge, the convention in this jurisdiction is to that effect. Given the significant imbalance of gender on the judicial benches, the majority of Tribunals established to date have, unsurprisingly, been chaired by a male judge.

[21] Hayes, above n 10, at 167–68.

[22] Carol Smart, 'Law's Truth/Women's Experience' in Reg Graycar (ed), *Dissenting Opinions: Feminist Explorations in Law and Society* (Sydney, Allen and Unwin, 1990) 7–9.

[23] On the media portrayal of female criminal offenders, Jewkes argues that they are constructed around a narrow range of stereotypes relating to sexuality, physical attractiveness, maternity, monsterisation and victimhood: Yvonne Jewkes, *Media and Crime*, 2nd edn (London, Sage, 2011).

[24] See Inglis, above n 5, ch 13, 'The Media'.

Joanne expressed clearly in her book her feelings of insecurity within the legal processes, and her realisation of the power imbalance therein:

> In approaching the Tribunal I knew almost nothing about the way in which courts, let alone tribunals, operated, and I was utterly unprepared for what happened.
>
> As the Tribunal began to settle into its probing concentration on my personal and sexual life I felt bewildered and horrified. What had been announced as an inquiry into the behaviour of the gardaí had already become, even before I gave evidence, an inquisition into my life and character.
>
> … I had never really considered questions of power and how it is structured; I had never considered the law as such and how it operated within society. But as I looked at many of the lawyers and heard their accents and tones of voice, I felt as if they were some kind of alien force—alien, that is, to the society in which I had lived. In their manners and in the ways they spoke they seemed to be expressing some kind of code which I had never encountered before and as the Tribunal progressed I grew to hate that code.[25]

This sense of power imbalance is not unique to Joanne's experience: as discussed below, the alienating effect of the law and legal discourse can disadvantage female witnesses, plaintiffs and complainants more than their male counterparts.

Female Credibility in Courtroom Proceedings

Beginning his analysis of the complaints raised by Joanne and the Hayes family against the gardaí, which included allegations of physical assault, Mr Justice Lynch said:

> If the Gardaí were prosecuted before a Jury for the matters alleged against them by the Hayes family, the Jury would have no hesitation in throwing out all such charges because of the broad unreliability so far as truthfulness is concerned of the Hayes family.[26]

On the other hand, when discussing the creditworthiness of the gardaí, the Tribunal Report refers to a tendency 'to elevate honest beliefs or suspicions into positive truth'[27] or a 'gilding of the lily'.[28] While this, again, illustrates the Chairman's traditional adversarial approach to what was supposed to be a fact-finding Tribunal of Inquiry, it also raises questions around the performance, as such, of Joanne and her family in testifying before the Tribunal as compared with the performance of experienced gardaí in delivering their version of events. The latter spoke a language the Chairman understood; the language of the law, the language of those experienced in giving testimony before a court, the language of middle-aged men. Joanne and her family did not speak this language.

Graycar and others have noted the difficulties for women and other 'outsiders' in having their stories believed or taken seriously in the courtroom: 'there are enormous obstacles

[25] Hayes, above n 10, at 165.
[26] Tribunal Report, 63.
[27] ibid, 60.
[28] ibid, 61.

to women's stories and outsiders' stories occupying the same space and doing so with the same authority as the stock stories that underpin the common sense of deeply gendered and racialised legal discourses'.[29]

Joanne Hayes was not only a woman, but an outsider too. She was an outsider because she had had an affair with a married man and had a child with him. It seems inevitable that Joanne's story would not be believed, while the Garda story would find favour. Hunter has observed that

> [t]he fact that a witness is a woman does appear to trigger a set of moral judgments for determining credibility that is not applied to men. In other words, fact finders tie the worth of a woman's testimony to her moral worth. Women judged to be 'bad,' and therefore unreliable, include prostitutes, lesbians, women who leave their children or whose children are in foster care, women who abuse alcohol or drugs, and women perceived to be angry.[30]

Examining research on cases involving sexual violence, Hunter has also observed the informal mechanisms by which women's credibility is undermined or devalued in court proceedings. She has noted a consistent finding in (US) research on gender bias in the courts, to the effect that

> women litigants and witnesses are frequently subjected to inappropriate and demeaning conduct that affects their credibility. This conduct includes informal modes of address, the use of endearments, comments on a woman's appearance, sexual innuendo, sexist remarks or jokes, patronizing behavior, physical and verbal bullying, intimidation, and badgering. The studies identify instances of judges and opposing counsel making an issue of a woman's title, name, or marital status and of counsel questioning female witnesses in a snide, condescending tone or deliberately asking embarrassing questions.[31]

Interestingly, in this context, beyond the obvious questioning of Joanne on extremely private matters in the extremely public setting of the Tribunal, Joanne asked her own lawyers, during the course of the Tribunal, to request that the lawyer representing three of the Superintendents refer to her by her correct name—Joanne—rather than Joanna/Johanna as he had been doing, whether by design or otherwise.[32]

[29] Reg Graycar, 'The Gender of Judgments: Some Reflections on "Bias"' (1998) 32(1) *University of British Columbia Law Review* 1–21, 19. See also Richard Delgado, 'Storytelling for Oppositionists and Others: A Plea for Narrative' (1989) 87(8) *Michigan Law Review* 2411–41.

[30] Rosemary Hunter, 'Gender in Evidence: Masculine Norms v Feminist Reforms' (1996) 19(1) *Harvard Women's Law Journal* 127–67, 165, referencing Helena Kennedy, 'Eve Was Framed: Women And British Justice' (London, Vintage, 1992) 124–27 and Morrison Torrey, 'When Will We Be Believed? Rape Myths and the Idea of a Fair Trial in Rape Prosecutions' (1990–1991) 24(4) *University of California Davis Law Review* 1013–46. See also Rosemary Hunter, 'Evidentiary Harassment' in Mary Childs and Louise Ellison (eds), *Feminist Perspectives on Evidence* (London, Cavendish, 2000) ch 6.

[31] Hunter, 'Gender in Evidence', above n 30, at 162, referencing the Report of the Florida Supreme Court Gender Bias Study Commission 122 (1990); Report of the Illinois Task Force on Gender Bias in the Courts 113 (1990); Final Report of the Michigan Supreme Court Task Force on Gender Issues in the Courts 37–38 (1989); Final Report of the Washington State Task Force on Gender and Justice in the Courts 41 (1989).

[32] Hayes, above n 10, at 88.

Community Support

One of the most striking aspects of the 'Kerry Babies' case, from a socio-legal and feminist perspective, is the level and nature of the public support that Joanne and the Hayes family received. Even those who believed that Joanne might have had a hand in the death of her own son, were sympathetic to her plight before the Tribunal, where she was questioned intensely on intimate private details before a Chairman who seemed to become frustrated with her increasing upset on the stand. At this 30-year remove it is extraordinarily moving to read about the way in which different groups came together and organised various ways of showing support to Joanne and her family.[33] Without the modern advantages of social media or mobile phones, persons and groups took it upon themselves to reach out to the Hayes family, to travel to Tralee (where the Tribunal was hearing evidence), to send letters, cards and a succession of hundreds of single yellow roses. One hundred and forty-two Mass cards were also sent. The triumph of individual empathy over the constraints of 1980s Catholic Ireland this evokes is powerful. Women, and men, had specifically arranged for Masses to be said on behalf of Joanne Hayes, the unmarried mother who had been having a long-term affair with a married man, because of the ordeal she was suffering before the Tribunal. Maguire suggests that Joanne's indiscretions, as such, were viewed as 'irrelevant in the face of what many people regarded as a gross abuse of power on the part of the state'.[34]

Support for Joanne and the Hayes family came from many quarters, and was expressed at parliamentary level too, with the Oireachtas Committee on Women's Rights characterising the questioning of Joanne as 'insensitive', 'frightening', 'harrowing and quite horrific', and as 'mental torture'.[35]

Almost the entire village of Abbeydorney, the nearest place to the Hayes family's farm, arranged to come to Tralee on one of the days the Tribunal was sitting. The men and women of this small Irish village held placards declaring 'Abbeydorney supports Joanne', and for two hours they walked silently up and down outside the council building that housed the Tribunal. On the following day, the villagers' silent protest was replaced by a demonstration co-ordinated by a number of feminist groups, including the Tralee Women's Action Group. This brought hundreds of people, mainly women but men too, from all around the country to Tralee. This was certainly a livelier protest than that of the previous day, and this led the Tribunal Chairman to describe the feminist protestors as 'raucous, ignorant, urban dwellers', and to threaten them with contempt of court and imprisonment for any insult to or obstruction of the Tribunal.[36] There seems to have been an implicit suggestion that those who had come from Dublin, Cork and Belfast, and perhaps even those from the urban town of Tralee itself, had no right to be interested in or to take up the cause of a single mother

[33] McCafferty provides a profound account of these matters: McCafferty, above n 19, at 107–27.

[34] Maguire, above n 19, at 348.

[35] Renagh Holohan, 'Deputies demand action by Noonan on Kerry tribunal', *The Irish Times*, 23 January 1985.

[36] McCafferty, above n 19, at 128. Protests also occurred outside the Department of Justice in Dublin, with representatives of Sinn Féin, the Women's Community Press, the Union of Students of Ireland, the Socialist Workers' Movement, and the Dublin Lesbian/Gay Collective. A group of women also protested outside the Irish Embassy in London. See Hayes, above n 10, at 103.

from a farm in rural Ireland. What did the feminists of urban Ireland know about what goes on in small-town Ireland?[37]

Conclusion

The 'Cahirciveen baby' was laid to rest in a grave with a simple wooden cross inscribed 'I am the Kerry Baby … named John, and I forgive'.[38] Whether or not Joanne Hayes has forgiven the legal system for its brutal treatment of her at her lowest ebb is not known.

[37] On urban-rural feminism generally see Janice McCabe, 'What's in a Label? The Relationship between Feminist Self-Identification and "Feminist" Attitudes among U.S. Women and Men' (2005) 19(4) *Gender and Society* 480–505; Marvin L Anderson, 'Reluctant Feminists: Rural Women and the Myth of the Modern Family' in Anne E Carr, Mary Stewart Van Leeuwen, (eds) *Religion, Feminism and the Family* (Kentucky, Westminster/ John Knox Press, 1996), ch 12; and Elizabeth Kenworthy Teather, 'The Double Bind: Being Female and Being Rural: A Comparative Study of Australia, New Zealand and Canada' (1998) 8(3) *Rural Society* 209–21.

[38] The wooden cross was replaced in February 2004 by a marble headstone which was vandalised, apparently with a sledgehammer, in July of the same year: 'Slab on grave of the 'Kerry Baby' is smashed', *The Irish Times*, 9 July 2004.

REPORT
OF THE
INDEPENDENT EXAMINATION
BY MS JUSTICE VICKY CONWAY
OF THE CASE
FOR A REOPENED INQUIRY
INTO THE 'KERRY BABIES' CASE

INDEX

I OVERVIEW AND INTRODUCTION

1. In October 1985, Mr Justice Kevin Lynch submitted his report of a Tribunal of Inquiry to the Minister for Justice. The Tribunal was established in 1984 to examine the facts surrounding the "Kerry Babies" case. The facts, widely known, concern the deaths of two new-born babies in County Kerry in April 1984. In the weeks following these deaths Ms Joanne Hayes and several of her family members gave statements to members of An Garda Síochána, implicating themselves in killing and disposing of one, if not both babies. It has since been established that the family had no connection to, or contact with, the second child. Their statements to the Gardaí were false.
2. Following a failed internal investigation, and with somewhat surprising speed, a Tribunal was established on December 13th 1984 to examine the circumstances in which these false statements were given. The Hayes family alleged that gardaí had physically abused them. The Tribunal sat for 77 days in both Tralee and Dublin, hearing from 109 witnesses who were asked 61,000 questions. The Tribunal's report is 160 pages, with 100 pages in appendices. The Tribunal was empowered to inquire into three definite matters of urgent public importance:

    1. **"the facts and circumstances leading to the preferment ... of criminal charges against [Ms Hayes and others] ... and the subsequent events which led to the withdrawal of those charges;**
    2. **related allegations made by [Ms Hayes and others] concerning the circumstances surrounding the questioning and the taking of statements from those persons ...;**
    3. **any matters connected with or relevant to the matters aforesaid which the tribunal considers it necessary to investigate in connection with their inquiries [into] (1) and (2)."**

3. Many criticisms could be levelled at these terms of reference: they do not directly focus attention on garda behaviour. They do not require the Tribunal to make recommendations, which was unusual at the time.
4. Ultimately the Tribunal found limited fault with the actions of the gardaí involved but seriously questioned the Hayes' credibility and determined Ms Hayes was responsible for one child's death.
5. Although welcomed by An Garda Síochána, the Tribunal's findings have been critiqued since their publication.[1] The coincidence of the Tribunal's 30th 'anniversary' and ongoing concern surrounding garda conduct has seen renewed questioning of the findings. This is the context of my review of the Tribunal's documents, to assess whether a new inquiry into these facts should be held.

[1] For instance, Tom Inglis, *Truth Power and Lies: Irish Society and the Case of the Kerry Babies* (2003) UCD Press; Moira Maguire, "The Changing Face of Catholic Ireland: Conservatism and Liberalism in the Ann Lovett and Kerry Babies Scandals" *Feminist Studies,* Vol. 27, No. 2 (Summer, 2001), pp. 335–358.

II REVIEWING PREVIOUS INQUIRIES

6. Reviews of older cases are not uncommon: one such review led to the establishment of the Morris Tribunal, which examined allegations of police corruption in Donegal, and a number of barristers were recently tasked with reviewing some 300 garda investigations to see whether inquiries were warranted. Some years ago, British and Irish governments invited Mr Justice Peter Cory to examine allegations of state collusion, generating six further inquiries. The re-examining of a tribunal report is not without precedent in Ireland: in 2006 Mr Paul Coffey SC was appointed to review whether a further inquiry into the Stardust Fire, in which 48 persons died at a nightclub, was warranted. Recently the Planning Tribunal, which is examining corrupt payments to politicians, revised its own findings. Such reviews have also occurred in the UK; the Hillsborough Disaster, questioning the police's role in the deaths of 96 football fans during a crush at a stadium, and Bloody Sunday, when the British Army killed 14 persons who had been attending a civil rights march in Northern Ireland, being prime examples.
7. There are valid reasons for conducting such reviews. While Tribunal findings are not legally actionable, they are not free of consequence. Careers and family lives can be damaged; governments could conceivably fall. They can prompt an organisation to reform, or enable defence of existing practices. And in Ireland, where there is something of a national fascination with ongoing tribunal proceedings, even the line of questioning adopted can influence the court of public opinion. Even where done in good faith, a review can easily reopen old wounds. Tribunals are lengthy and costly mechanisms, not just for the State, and can involve the dissection of personal matters by judges, lawyers, the media and the public.
8. Therefore, any decision to hold a fresh inquiry should only be taken where the government can be confident that the benefit to society outweighs any impact for all those concerned. The subject matter must also be considered a matter of 'urgent public importance', as per the *Tribunals of Inquiry (Evidence) Act 1921*. Unfortunately, the standard I should apply in conducting the review is unclear.
9. Addressing this issue in conducting the review of the Stardust Inquiry, Mr Coffey SC considered the following points. Neither the terms of reference nor the *Tribunals of Inquiry (Evidence) Act, 1921-2004* provide guidance on the standard to be applied. However, he noted that both the *Railway Safety Act, 2005* and the *Merchant Shipping (Investigation of Marine Casualty) Act, 2000* provide for the reopening of inquiries where the Minister is satisfied that there is "new evidence available which could materially alter the findings of the Inquiry and that the purpose of the Inquiry would be served by reopening it". Under the *Criminal Procedure Act 1993* "newly discovered facts" are required in order to reopen a case in which a miscarriage of justice is alleged.
10. It is clearly accepted in relation to a range of matters that where new evidence brings the original findings into doubt, a new review can be recommended. I, however, have a limited role and have not been empowered to hold hearings or compel witnesses. I have not, resultantly, been able to identify new evidence. The question I have encountered is whether I am empowered to recommend a new review where I have determined that the findings are in question based on the evidence existing at the time

of the original Tribunal. Mr Coffey SC commented that he was instructed by government to consider "all the issues", leading him to conclude that:

> *"As not all of the issues so raised are based on new evidence, it must follow that I am entitled to assess the case not merely by reference to new evidence but also by reference to any other issues raised which disclose that a further inquiry should be established."*[2]

11. I concur with Mr Coffey SC in concluding that I am entitled to recommend a new review based on the pre-existing evidence. My task, therefore, is to evaluate the Tribunal's findings of fact and assess whether, in consideration of all relevant materials, these are now sufficiently in question that as a matter of urgent public importance, a new inquiry is warranted. In *Maguire v Ardagh*[3] Hardiman J defined a finding of fact as one "susceptible of rigorous, objectively justifiable, demonstration." This is the standard I will apply in evaluating the original findings of the Tribunal report: are those findings susceptible to rigorous, objectively justifiable demonstration in light of all the evidence?

III FACT FINDING

12. The Report I am considering stems from the judge's role in making findings of fact, rather than of law. Judges daily perform this role in the summary trials of the District Court. However, the District Court operates within the parameters of an adversarial system, while a Tribunal of Inquiry is inquisitorial. An inquisitorial inquiry shifts the focus from determining which of two competing accounts to accept, to examining what happened in a broader sense. As Denham J outlined in *Boyhan v Beef Tribunal*,[4] "[a] tribunal is not a court of law—either civil or criminal. It is a body—unusual in our legal system—an inquisitorial tribunal. It has not an adversary format".
13. Further, unlike the findings of fact made in the District Court, the findings of a Tribunal do not have legal consequences. This means that Tribunals are not, as per Article 34 of our Constitution, involved in the administration of justice. The constitutional provisions concerning judicial independence do not, therefore, apply to the performance of this role.
14. The law makes few stipulations about the conduct of Tribunals. The ordinary rules of evidence do not apply. The Chair of the Tribunal is afforded significant discretion in conducting proceedings. To enable fact-finding, Tribunals are given statutory powers, similar to the High Court, to compel witnesses to attend, to examine witnesses under oath and to compel the production of documents. They are also permitted under section 4 of the 1979 Act to make whatever orders are necessary to perform their functions, mirroring a High Court judge's powers. Failure to comply with an order of a Tribunal attracts sanctions. These substantive and enforcement powers are what set Tribunals of Inquiry apart from any other form of government-initiated investigation, such as non-statutory inquiries. In many instances these inquisitorial powers provide the only means of ascertaining the facts of a complex event.

[2] Paragraph 1.19.
[3] [2002] 1 IR 385 at 668.
[4] [1993] 1 IR 210 at 222.

15. Therefore, I must bear in mind that, although Mr Justice Lynch was performing a function quite different to those normally within the perimeters of judicial office, he was well equipped with statutory powers to do so.
16. In undertaking this review, I have accessed the Tribunal report and the transcripts of the hearings. This review is not conducted under the *Tribunal of Inquiries Acts* and so I do not have the power to call witnesses or hold public hearings.

IV ESTABLISHMENT OF THE LYNCH TRIBUNAL

17. On 14 April 1984 the body of a male newborn, who had been stabbed 28 times, was found on a beach in Cahirciveen, Co Kerry. Gardaí, appropriately, began looking for a local woman who had recently given birth, and whose baby appeared to be missing. Ms Joanne Hayes, who had been in a relationship with a married man, Jeremiah Locke, gave birth at home on the night of 12 April 1984 to a boy who died during or immediately following his birth.[5] She wrapped this boy in plastic and hid the body on the farm. Ms Hayes lived on the farm with her sister Kathleen, her brothers Ned and Mike, her mother, Mrs Mary Hayes and her aunt, Bridie Fuller. Two days later she presented at the local hospital, claiming to have suffered a miscarriage. She spent a week there. In hospital a nurse suggested after an initial examination that she had been 16 weeks pregnant. Ms Hayes did not correct her as Dr Daly had said "the Guards would have to be involved" if the pregnancy were more advanced.[6] Concealment of birth is an offence under section 60 of the *Offences Against the Person Act, 1861*. Scans revealed the pregnancy was closer to full term.
18. As the garda investigation progressed, the team was joined by a number of Dublin gardaí, members of what was known as "the Murder Squad". These were specialist interrogators, against whom allegations of oppressive questioning and brutality had been made, though never substantiated, in a number of high-profile cases. On 1 May 1984, now aware of Ms Hayes' stay in hospital, gardaí asked her and other family members to attend Tralee garda station for interview, without explaining the purpose. The family were not arrested. These events took place before gardaí were empowered to arrest an individual without charge under section 4 of the *Criminal Justice Act 1984*. Thus, the range of safeguards associated with that legislation, which are now perhaps taken for granted, such as the recording of interviews, the maintenance of a custody record and the right of access to legal advice did not apply. Nevertheless, Mr Justice Lynch noted that the valid grounds for suspecting Ms Hayes' involvement, based on the available evidence, could have justified an arrest, rather than an invitation to attend the station. Instead, the Hayes family attended voluntarily, meaning that existing safe-guarding procedures did not apply. Lay citizens often did not understand this key distinction and may not have understood that they were free to leave at any point.
19. Ms Hayes, fearing that she was being investigated for concealing a birth, initially told gardaí that she had miscarried. Once she realised the detention concerned another baby's death she told gardaí that she gave birth on the farm, alone and that the baby was

[5] The Tribunal in fact found that Ms Hayes killed this child, but, as shall be maintained in this report, that finding cannot be substantiated.

[6] Tribunal Transcript 8/70.

buried in a pond in a field. Her family all denied knowledge of her pregnancy and birth when questioned. Within hours, however, gardaí were in possession of very different confessions admitting involvement in killing and disposing of a baby by throwing it into the sea. As per the regulations of the times, the garda written record of the interviews is the sole documented account of these confessions. Ms Hayes was charged with murder and her family with concealment of birth.

20. Gardaí sent a search party on 1 May 1984 to a location on the farm Ms Hayes had indicated. They did not find the body. They refused her repeated offers to show them its location. It was only then, on 2 May 1984, that Ms Hayes disclosed to her family that the body was on the farm. They searched and found it, and called the gardaí, who removed it.
21. Gardaí were now dealing with the deaths of two newborns. The investigators determined, to the exclusion of alternative possibilities, that Ms Hayes had borne twins and killed both and that all charges should stand. However, initial blood tests determined that the children had different blood types and so could not have the same father. Again, instead of considering alternatives, investigating gardaí decided that two different men had impregnated Ms Hayes; a phenomenon known as super-fecundation. Later blood tests would show she could not have been the Cahirciveen baby's mother. The case proceeded until 10 October 1984 when it was struck out by the State Solicitor for Kerry. No further legal proceedings were ever initiated in relation to either death. The Cahirciveen baby's identity has never been established.
22. Immediately following the striking out of the case the Hayes family made numerous allegations of ill-treatment during garda custody. Media coverage raised questions about garda conduct and in mid-October 1984 calls were made in the Dáil for an inquiry.[7] In December the government determined the case involved a matter of urgent public importance and asked Mr Justice Lynch to chair the Tribunal.
23. Presented with conflicting accounts of the same incidents, Mr Justice Lynch was tasked with determining what did in fact occur and where the truth lay between the differing accounts provided by the Hayes family and the investigating gardaí. Once satisfied with what did happen, Mr Justice Lynch was also tasked with determining whether what did happen is what should have happened, i.e. whether the actions of those involved were within the parameters of the law.
24. I determine that two aspects of the Tribunal are problematic: the procedure adopted and the findings of facts made.

V TRIBUNAL PROCEDURE

25. With respect to my colleague, and being conscious not to apply current standards, I have identified five problematic features of the approach and procedure adopted in the course of the hearings.
26. First, in his opening address to the Tribunal Mr Justice Lynch stated: "insofar as one can seek an analogy with a trial it has some similarity to a civil action by the Hayes family

[7] 16 October 1984, Dáil Eireann, Vol 352, No 10.

for damages against the Guards".[8] This is a direct and inappropriate comparison to an adversarial system, and I am concerned that this statement may have prompted parties to the proceedings to adapt their presentation of evidence and their general approach to proceedings accordingly. In other instances, adversarial language is used: in the Report, Mr Justice Lynch refers to Ms Hayes as the "wrongdoer".[9] I have an overarching concern that the Tribunal deviated from a strictly inquisitorial approach and can only be described as, at least on occasion, adversarial. Were Mr Justice Lynch applying accusatorial standards this would substantially affect decisions as regards the procedure of the Tribunal as well as his findings. I will now address other procedural concerns which are problematic in themselves but also substantiate my conclusion that Mr Justice Lynch applied an inappropriately accusatorial standard.

27. Second, the Tribunal spent substantial time on the theory of superfecundation. This was the theory that if Ms Hayes had sexual intercourse with two men in a short space of time she could, in theory, have become pregnant by both and borne twins of different fathers. This was the basis for the gardaí's continued pursuit of the Hayes family after it had been established that the two babies had different blood types (from May to October 1984).

28. This theory was first raised as early as day three of the Tribunal[10] but was not dismissed until day 72. Dr Patrick Lincoln showed that Ms Hayes could not have carried a child with the Caharciveen baby's bloodgroup. In the meantime the issue was repeatedly discussed, almost as if the Tribunal's task was to establish whether it could have occurred, despite the fact that the Director of Public Prosecutions (DPP) had discounted it. The question focused on was whether Ms Hayes had had sex with two men,[11] and not, as the terms of reference required, why the gardaí clung to such an improbable theory, to the point that they failed to explore other avenues. Mr Justice Morris, when considering police misconduct in Donegal, discussed this as "tunnel vision" which "can fuel a drive to suspect certain individuals while ignoring evidence that has the potential to exonerate them".[12]

29. The approach Mr Justice Lynch adopted and permitted in relation to this particular issue was adversarial: gardaí sought to justify it as a valid line of inquiry while Ms Hayes' credibility was repeatedly questioned. There was substantial discussion of who the second father might be, even though the man the gardaí suggested, Tom Flynn, was not in the jurisdiction at the relevant time. This speculation was raised in the initial days of the Tribunal but not accurately eliminated until the 32nd day, by which time the theory that Ms Hayes had another partner had become a valid line of inquiry.

30. I accept a certain amount of relevance to this evidence; it established suspicion on the part of gardaí that justified the initial questioning of Ms Hayes and her family. However, prior to the Tribunal's establishment, the DPP had accepted that Ms Hayes had not killed the Cahirciveen baby. Why Mr Justice Lynch allowed this line of questioning

[8] Tribunal Transcript, 15/2.
[9] Tribunal Report, p.146
[10] Tribunal Transcript, 3/89.
[11] Tribunal Transcript, 3/89
[12] Morris, F. (2008) *Report on the Detention of 'Suspects' Following the Death of the Late Richard Barron*, page 1181, para 15.09

to feature so prominently throughout the Tribunal is difficult to understand. The relevance warranted this issue being raised, but it should have been addressed in full early on in proceedings and dismissed. In the inquisitorial system the gathering of evidence and the calling of witnesses is the Tribunal's responsibility. It must therefore bear the responsibility for these delays which diverted the Tribunal's attention away from the central concern of the terms of reference: why gardaí continued this line of inquiry despite an abundance of evidence indicating otherwise. Instead we see statements from Mr Justice Lynch: "there were times when we all thought she had twins". Not only did this approach divert attention from what should have been the Tribunal's focus, but it also directed unnecessary attention to private matters of Ms Hayes' sexual history.

31. My third concern centres on the nature of questioning of Ms Hayes. She was questioned for 5 days, the longest that anyone had spent on the stand in Ireland up to that point. She was asked over 2000 questions. She was quizzed at length about intrinsically private issues: a previous miscarriage, about the size of blood clots, about previous sexual partners, about her menstruation, about her contraceptive practices. The impact on her was clear: she was visibly upset throughout this questioning and broke down on several occasions. Others were questioned at length about her private life: a gynaecologist was questioned about the size of her uterus and her breasts. The relevance of this level of detail to the terms of reference is not clear.
32. The Tribunal's response when Ms Hayes experienced difficulties merits consideration. One morning she left the stand hyperventilating, vomiting and shaking in what her doctor described as a state of "acute anxiety". She had to be sedated. Nevertheless, she was required to return to the stand that afternoon and answered questions with closed eyes and a slurred voice. Friends were concerned she would take her own life that evening. Proceedings were suspended twice; however, Justice Lynch stated on one occasion where he refused to suspend proceedings: "If I rise now I'll be rising every five minutes. Which is better, sooner or later?" Mr Justice Lynch did not reflect on Ms Hayes' difficulties at all. Indeed the only mention of Ms Hayes' questioning in the report is to comment that she was asked about her garda interrogation "in a quiet and sympathetic way".[13]
33. Ms Hayes was not fit to be questioned at this time. For reasons of credibility of the evidence presented to the Tribunal, she should not have been questioned in this way. Such private details were not relevant and the form of the questioning was inappropriate.
34. I reiterate that Ms Hayes was a witness, assisting the Tribunal in inquiring into whether garda misconduct contributed to her making a false confession. At no point does the Tribunal recognise that the matter at issue was the death of Ms Hayes' child. She was not on trial for this and so a certain degree of sensitivity should have been shown toward her as she discussed her loss.
35. The Tribunal expressed sympathy to the wife of a garda who was at the centre of proceedings who miscarried during the course of the Tribunal, describing her as "far more gravely wronged than any member of the Hayes family".[14] When protestors gathered to

[13] Tribunal Report p.54.
[14] Tribunal Report, p.147.

display their support for Ms Hayes, Mr Justice Lynch determined that this constituted "serious and unwarranted harassment" of gardaí,[15] and that the protests were "grossly improper".[16] This expression of compassion to professional police officers, in the face of what Ms Hayes endured, was inappropriate.

36. I conclude that the nature of the questioning of Ms Hayes was inappropriate and indicative of a broader problem with the focus and orientation of the Tribunal. I apologise to Ms Hayes on behalf of the judiciary for the ordeal she experienced over the course of that week.

37. Fourth, proceedings focused to an inordinate degree on whether Ms Hayes had a propensity to lie. Again, given that the truth of her testimony needed to be determined, some questioning as to her credibility was permissible. But this is not what happened. Lawyers for gardaí asked her work colleagues if they expected such lies from Ms Hayes, had they "reckoned how cunning she could be"? This questioning did not aim to establish whether Ms Hayes was credible, but whether others realised the extent of her lying. When asked to intervene Mr Justice Lynch replied that he would not "limit unduly the bounds of language used". Psychological evidence was presented that Ms Hayes was a liar, though no such efforts were made against those she accused of lying; the investigating gardaí. These questions as to her creditworthiness contribute to a palpable sense that Ms Hayes was on trial and that this was an accusatorial format.

38. A final point concerning procedure is that the Tribunal report is surprisingly free from legal detail. Indeed the Report does not consider the standards against which garda conduct was being evaluated. To some extent this is a product of the time. Legislation regulating the garda conduct in cases of infanticide and concealment of birth or the treatment of suspects in custody was negligible, nor was case law well developed. That said, the Garda Code of 1966, in operation at the time, says this about the offence of concealment of birth, which was heavily connected to the current case:

> *"A case of concealment of birth requires very delicate handling, otherwise much cruelty may be inflicted upon an unfortunate woman who may have secretly given birth to a child and yet may not have committed an offence against the law. A garda should, therefore, act with extreme caution in such a case, so as not to cruelly outrage the feelings of a person innocent of a criminal offence who may, however, in other respects be unfortunate: and he should also be careful not to do or say anything which might be the cause of serious injury to the woman's health."*[17]

39. While not statutory in nature this was the advice presented to gardaí investigating this particular offence. The gardaí involved should have been judged against these standards of sensitivity, established for 20 years at the time. Mr Justice Lynch did not do so.

40. In conclusion, I find that in respect of the issues identified herein the Tribunal adopted inappropriate, at times defective, and accusatorial procedure. Not only did this cause unnecessary distress and hardship to Ms Hayes and her family but it may have altered the totality of the evidence presented to the Tribunal. At the very least, it calls into question the 'objective justifiability' of the evidence forming the basis of the Tribunal's conclusions.

[15] Tribunal Report, p.7.
[16] Tribunal Report, p.144.
[17] Garda Code 1966, p.111.

VI FINDINGS OF FACTS

41. I now move to the Tribunal's findings. I shall assess whether these are objectively justifiable. Some of the findings I will highlight are relatively minor; however, I concern myself with the cumulative nature of these findings, particularly as regards Ms Hayes' credibility. Certain early findings of the Tribunal made it easier to reach later ones.
42. Early in his report Mr Justice Lynch commented on the relationship between Ms Hayes and Mr Locke. He levels much criticism at Ms Hayes as he deems her to be the "main or dominant force in the liaison". Mr Justice Lynch makes numerous judgments as to her character; she was "well aware" he was married but "allowed herself and indeed, encouraged herself to develop an over-riding infatuation … entertained foolish dreams".[18] He stated that she was "anxious to become pregnant by him". No evidence was presented to substantiate this conclusion. Ms Hayes' testimony was that she "just happened to fall in love with him" and Mr Locke confirmed that he too was in love with her. Rather than simply accepting the existence of an extra-marital relationship, Mr Justice Lynch constructed Ms Hayes as calculating. This finding as to her character is unsubstantiated.
43. What overshadows the Tribunal's main findings is the credibility of Ms Hayes and her family. This determined what was found in relation to both what happened to the babies but also how gardaí treated the family. They had admitted that they made false confessions: the Tribunal should have been concerned with why that had happened. This is not substantially examined. Before even investigating the family's allegations, Mr Justice Lynch determined that following the birth "The whole family embarked on a planned deception of the neighbourhood".[19] The wording is laden with culpability. Rather than recognising that something terribly distressing had occurred in the family home, that their failure to reveal the truth may have been motivated by a wish to retain privacy, and fear of a prosecution for concealment of birth, Mr Justice Lynch presents them as devious and conniving. He barely acknowledges that Ms Hayes claimed that gardaí threatened that her child would be placed for adoption, the family farm would be sold and her mother would be prosecuted for murder.
44. Part IV of the report is concerned with the Hayes family's allegations. This section begins with a chapter on the "creditworthiness" of the Hayes family[20] with a particular emphasis on the female members. The findings within this chapter are unreflective of the complexity of the situation and are problematic when contrasted with the Chairman's sympathetic analysis of the credibility of the garda witnesses.
45. The statements and testimony of the Hayes family are inconsistent. It was appropriate for Mr Justice Lynch to attempt to find the truth between these accounts. However, in his efforts to find that truth, Mr Justice Lynch reaches unsubstantiated findings to corroborate his overarching conclusions. For instance, when considering the conflicting accounts presented by Mrs Hayes (Joanne Hayes' mother) to the gardaí, he concludes: "Mrs Hayes invented this new evidence to try to corroborate the case that Joanne Hayes had gone outside and had had the baby outside in the field."[21] A motive that fits with his

[18] Tribunal Report, p.15.
[19] Tribunal Report, p.25.
[20] Tribunal Report, p.51 and Chapter 17.
[21] Tribunal Report, p.114.

analysis is presented without reference to any supporting evidence for this conclusion or the conditions of the detention.

46. By contrast, when Mrs Hayes alleges that investigating gardaí did not read her statements back to her, Mr Justice Lynch describes this as a "totally unnecessary, totally useless and totally obvious lie".[22] His reason for concluding that this was such an outlandish lie was that: "Whatever the gardaí might do, they would not be so ridiculously stupid as not to read over a statement before getting the interviewee to sign it."[23] Again, there is no basis for making such a judgement of the gardaí concerned.
47. Ms Hayes is described as lying on the witness stand, but again no allowance is made for her mental and physical state during this questioning, that it related to the child's death, and that she may still have feared prosecution for concealment of birth, if not infanticide. The context of the evidence is not made relevant, as would be proper in an inquisitorial Tribunal of Inquiry.
48. Similarly we find contradictory determinations concerning the witnesses' suggestibility. Bridie Fuller, Ms Hayes' aunt, was deemed to be suggestible and so her evidence had to be approached with caution, while Mike Hayes, Ms Hayes' brother, was also suggestible and "anything which he said which is manifestly not in accordance with the truth was said by him under the influence of the female members of the Hayes family and is far less blameworthy in his case".[24] It is difficult to see how such inconsistent conclusions as to the suggestibility of witnesses, that Ms Fuller is suggestible by nature but Mr Hayes is suggestible because of the Hayes women, could be justified.
49. The Tribunal Report then assessed the credibility of the gardaí but concerned itself not with whether gardaí perjured themselves, but whether they had elevated "honest beliefs or suspicions into positive facts". This appears a more sympathetic analysis. Acknowledging that gardaí made problematic statements, Justice Lynch concluded: "They are not barefaced lies on the part of the gardaí (as regrettably is the case with members of the Hayes family) but they are an exaggeration over and above the true position, or a gilding of the lily, or wishful thinking elevated to the status of hard fact."[25] Why this differentiation between forms of untruth for gardaí but not for others?
50. On the basis of these two chapters and the conclusions reached therein, Justice Lynch proceeded to consider the family's allegations of ill-treatment. As already noted, this time, interrogations in garda stations were not recorded and so Mr Justice Lynch was faced with the difficult task of deciding between conflicting accounts. Mr Justice Lynch concluded that the family were lying while the gardaí were guilty only of wishful thinking, and dismissed the allegations. I can see no credible basis for aspects of these findings: Mr Justice Lynch construed Ms Hayes' account of a garda sitting her in his lap as the garda endeavouring "to comfort her because she was in an extremely hysterical state".[26] Mr Justice Lynch should have expressed concern at a garda attempting to comfort a suspect in this way.

[22] Tribunal Report, p.53.
[23] Tribunal Report, p.54.
[24] Tribunal Report, p.57.
[25] Tribunal Report, p.61
[26] Tribunal Report, p.65.

51. Kathleen Hayes' allegations were dismissed because she did not mention them to others immediately. Ned Hayes' allegations were dismissed because he gave somewhat conflicting accounts and nobody corroborated that he was screaming in the station—after all he has a "fertile literary and dramatic imagination".[27] Discussions of Mike Hayes' allegations became bogged down in what he was wearing at the time. The judge accepted that a description of his clothing, which was "not part of the original narrative of the notes and were squeezed in on the right hand side" afterwards, was accurate. That the gardaí may have added this to counter Mike's allegations was not countenanced. Instead Mr Justice Lynch finds that Mike's story was concocted for him by his sisters. Further, Mr Justice Lynch appears to accept that gardaí may have altered statements following signing, but neither pursued the impropriety of this nor considered whether it occurred on other occasions. At no point did he inquire as to what motivated these alterations.
52. A matter consuming a great deal of the Tribunal's time was the manner of the baby's death on the farm. Mr Justice Lynch determined that the reason the Hayes family lied about the Cahirciveen baby was to cover up for the wrongdoing on the farm. Mr Justice Lynch determines that Ms Hayes killed the baby, stating that she choked him to stop him crying and hit him on the head with a bath brush. Not only are these conclusions unsupported by specific evidence but the available evidence is contradictory: the State Pathologist specifically stated that the baby was not hit on the head with the bath brush. To find that Ms Hayes was responsible for her child's death was insupportable and will unquestionably have been most hurtful for Ms Hayes.
53. What is not disputed is that many members of the Hayes family made a false confession. However, because the Tribunal found that the Hayes family had and continued to lie, and that the motive for this was to cover up wrongdoing on the farm, it did not examine garda methods adopted in these interrogations in depth. The family alleged that the garda interrogators threatened that children would be taken into care; that the dead children would haunt them; that they would lose their home and farm; that they would be charged with murder; that they were physically abused and told to pray; and that they were never told they were not under arrest and could leave at any time. With hindsight and knowledge of more recent instances of Garda misconduct, it is perhaps easy to say that the allegations made do not sound particularly incredible. Justice Morris documented very similar misconduct by gardaí in the Donegal division in his inquiries.
54. But even without hindsight, there were valid reasons to be cautious of the garda testimony. In 1977 *The Irish Times* ran a series of articles concerning the operations of the so-called Heavy Gang which was alleged to use abusive techniques to secure confessions. Nicky Kelly had made allegations of a similar nature following his arrest for the Sallins Mail Train Robbery the previous year. Also in 1977, Amnesty International conducted a visit to Ireland and found significant evidence of ill-treatment in custody. The Irish Council for Civil Liberties were vocal on this issue. I mention these not to draw any conclusions, but to show that it would have been appropriate for Mr Justice Lynch to be more rigorous in the investigation of what happened in these interrogations,

[27] Tribunal Report, p.70.

particularly given that many of the gardaí against whom allegations had been made in other instances were involved in this investigation.

55. The terms of reference necessitated exploration of why gardaí did not examine other possible explanations. The Tribunal should have asked why, once the blood test results were known, gardaí continued to pursue Ms Hayes, rather than re-examining the case and exploring other possibilities. This tunnel vision continued to be evident at trial where gardaí giving evidence continued to maintain that Ms Hayes had twins, despite all the scientific and forensic evidence that disproved these theories. This tunnel vision and unwillingness to explore other possibilities should have been a more substantial area of focus for the Tribunal.
56. I find that Mr Justice Lynch made unsupported findings of facts regarding the credibility of the Hayes family, the credibility of the gardaí, the cause of death of the baby on the farm and the treatment of the Hayes family during interrogation among other things. The significance and impact of these findings for those involved must not be under-estimated. I am alarmed that for over 30 years the official public record has stated that Ms Hayes caused the death of her child and lied deviously afterwards. I recommend therefore that it be recognised that these findings cannot be substantiated and should not be considered to have lawful authority. I add a further apology to Ms Hayes on behalf of the judiciary that these findings were made: at a time when she should have been supported through her grief she was labelled responsible. I can only imagine the hurt this caused.

VII CONCLUSION

57. I conclude that the Tribunal's procedure was inappropriate and that Ms Hayes deserves a state apology for her treatment at the time. I have gone to great pains to ensure I am not unduly critical of Mr Justice Lynch, given the landscape of Ireland at the time, but the insensitivity displayed is difficult to justify even in that context.
58. I conclude that many of Mr Justice Lynch's findings lacked substantiation and, as far as it is within my power to recommend it, should no longer be considered to have lawful authority.
59. Greater attention should have been paid to more critical examination of the appropriateness of garda actions. A number of events in Ireland and Amnesty International's 1977 Report had given reason for caution. Legislation was being passed while the Tribunal was sitting, which provided for the recording interviews; evidence of knowledge that this mattered. The 1978 O'Briain Report had highlighted many deficiencies in practice and procedure, and given that this was a Tribunal and not a court of law it may have had more leeway to be critical in that respect.
60. Returning to Mr Justice Hardiman's language in *Maguire v Ardagh*,[28] I cannot conclude that the findings of the Lynch Tribunal are "susceptible of rigorous, objectively justifiable, demonstration". I conclude, therefore, that a case for a new inquiry can be made.

[28] [2002] 1 IR 385 at 668

61. I do not however recommend that a fresh inquiry be held. I make this finding for two reasons:

    (1) Thirty years have passed. The principal probative evidence at the Tribunal was the testimony of the Hayes family and of the gardaí. The Tribunal's role was to determine what had occurred, bearing in mind both sets of evidence. Mr Justice Lynch attempted to do so, but not, as I have found, in a way that can stand the test of time. While the passage of time does not prevent the issue being revisited, I am slow to recommend such action in this particular case as I see no basis for believing the evidence would be different. Should some of those involved decide to change their story, and be in a position to justify and explain that change satisfactorily, then it might be possible, but, for the second reason I shall now turn to, I fear that it is an unjustifiable risk.
    (2) I do not find that this is a matter of *urgent* public importance. There is an issue of public importance in knowing whether and how the gardaí involved abused their powers. That may be relevant to other cases from that time. There is unquestionably a public value and interest in holding the gardaí to account for their actions, even when such time has passed.
        i. However, in concluding that this is not urgent, I take the victim's perception into consideration. What is perhaps most striking in re-reading the Report, Transcripts, media coverage and subsequent statements, is the extent to which Ms Joanne Hayes was not listened to at the original Tribunal. Whether she had any involvement in the death, Ms Hayes was still a recently bereaved mother. She had requested that allegations of garda abuse be investigated, but the law at the time did not provide a mechanism for that beyond internal inquiries. She had not sought a tribunal in the first place. She was clearly significantly traumatised by her experience of giving evidence at the Tribunal. The report brands her a liar for reasons that are not evidenced. Since its publication she has repeatedly refused to discuss the case and has actively sought to prevent any dramatization of the events in film.
        ii. Unless witnesses voluntarily recant their evidence from the original Tribunal, the evidence that would be examined by a new Tribunal would likely not be very different. We can hope that a new inquiry would apply proper procedures and would be more sensitive and focused in its approach. That is not to say however, that it would not be traumatising for those concerned, or that it would reach any more satisfactory conclusions. Were the Hayes family adding their voice to calls for a review I might conclude differently.

62. To conclude, while I find that there is a case for a new inquiry to be held and that there is a public interest in establishing the truth, I am unconvinced as to urgency and insufficiently satisfied that a preferable outcome could be reached as to warrant putting the Hayes family, and in particular Ms Hayes, through such an ordeal again.

Part III

Othered Subjects

11

Commentary on *McGimpsey v Ireland*

RUTH ALICE HOUGHTON

Introduction

McGimpsey v Ireland[1] concerns two men, the Irish Constitution and the law of treaties in international law; it is not an obvious choice for a feminist judgments project. Yet the case raises questions about how the courts in Ireland construct citizenship, how they use ideas of community and the importance they place on the public life of litigants. In 1987, Christopher and Michael McGimpsey, who were members of the Official Unionist Party of Northern Ireland and public figures, challenged the constitutionality of the Anglo-Irish Agreement 1985. The approach taken by the Irish Supreme Court in *McGimpsey v Ireland* provoked Aoife O'Donoghue to question if a Northern Irish housewife, as a metaphor for other marginalised groups and individuals, could bring a similar constitutional challenge in the late 1980s.

This commentary will explore why women or other minority groups might have been dissuaded from bringing a constitutional challenge. First, the commentary will situate *McGimpsey v Ireland* in the political landscape. Secondly, the issue of *locus standi* will be explored, emphasising the way in which the court used ideas of citizenship and the weight that was placed on the public standing of Christopher and Michael McGimpsey, to show the hurdles faced by a potential female litigant. Thirdly, the commentary focuses on the issue of community within the judgment, in particular highlighting how O'Donoghue J uses human rights law to obviate the damage of community.

Understanding *McGimpsey v Ireland*

The Anglo-Irish Agreement 1985, between Ireland and the United Kingdom, provided for an intergovernmental conference and secretariat that would facilitate discussion on the status of Northern Ireland. Unionists, who want Northern Ireland to remain part of the United Kingdom, rejected the involvement of the Irish Government in the governance of Northern Ireland.

[1] *McGimpsey v Ireland* [1990] IR 110.

Christopher and Michael McGimpsey were Unionists. They rejected the territorial claim in Article 2 of the Irish Constitution that the national territory consisted of the whole island of Ireland, and argued that Article 3 did not facilitate the making of laws for Northern Ireland by the Irish Government. The McGimpseys brought a case challenging the constitutionality of the Anglo-Irish Agreement. They argued that the Anglo-Irish Agreement was unconstitutional because it was contrary to the claim of the whole island, it fettered the Irish Government's foreign powers and it prioritised the situation of one community above another. The Supreme Court in 1990 rejected the argument that the Anglo-Irish Agreement was unconstitutional, but decided that Articles 2 and 3 of the Irish Constitution were a 'legal claim of right' by Ireland over Northern Ireland. This finding of the Court played an important part in the amendment of the Irish Constitution in 1998,[2] which removed the territorial claim and modified the jurisdictional claim in Articles 2 and 3 of the Irish Constitution.

Political Context

> If the McGimpseys were correct in their 'legal claim' thesis, Unionist fears of being subsumed within a politically united Ireland would be justified, but at least the hated agreement which was inevitably going to trundle us there more quickly should be deemed unconstitutional and would, we reasoned, have to be abandoned. (Mr Ken Maginnis, Fermanagh and South Tyrone MP)[3]

The Anglo-Irish Agreement was strongly protested against by Unionists, who felt that it had been imposed on them undemocratically. There were rallies protesting against the Agreement, including a rally with 100,000 people at Belfast City Hall.[4] For years, there were political boycotts and demonstrations.[5] The Unionists were angered because Unionist leaders were not consulted on the Agreement,[6] and many felt that they were powerless in its implementation.[7]

The Supreme Court judgment largely ignores the political contestation that had taken place. The courtroom was not the 'place' for political concerns, and strict rules on *locus standi* meant that *actio popularis* were excluded.[8] In contrast, O'Donoghue J, in her concurring opinion, places the particular protests and unrest at the forefront of her decision. In so doing, she signals the importance of this political debate within a legal framework that seeks to temper political disputes. Whilst protests and political disputes are conceptualised as

[2] House of Commons, Research Paper 98/57, 'Northern Ireland: Political Development Since 1972' (11 May 1998).

[3] HC Deb 14 March 1990, vol 169 cols 641–48.

[4] David McKittrick and David McVea, *Making Sense of the Troubles* (London, Viking, 2012) 192.

[5] ibid, 193.

[6] ibid, 191.

[7] Cathal McCall, 'From Barrier to Bridge: Reconfiguring the Irish Border after the Belfast Agreement' (2002) 53(4) *Northern Ireland Legal Quarterly* 476, 487.

[8] *Cahill v Sutton* [1980] IR 269. See Ann Sherlock, 'Understanding Standing: Locus Standi in Irish Constitutional Law' (1987) *Public Law* 245, 247, 251.

being outside of the courtroom, taking a legal challenge can feed into the political process. This is because the case acts as the initiation of dialogue between the court and political elites.[9] The role of the feminist judge adopted by O'Donoghue J is not only to facilitate that dialogue, but also to alert political elites to the importance of democracy.

Throughout her judgment, O'Donoghue J stresses the importance of listening to all the people in Northern Ireland. Christopher and Michael McGimpsey were not necessarily representative of the people in Northern Ireland; their Official Unionist Party of Northern Ireland membership, as well as their professions as company directors, meant that they did not speak for women, people outside of the party or people from a different socio-economic background. However, O'Donoghue J creates a space for the disempowered. Democracy is built into the Irish Constitution in Article 5 and into the Anglo-Irish Agreement in Article 4(c) and Article 5(c), so that the status of Northern Ireland cannot change without the consent of the majority of Northern Irish people. O'Donoghue J uses these articles to highlight that the Anglo-Irish Agreement will devolve power so that decision-making happens at a more local level. This more localised decision-making would enable the participation of those who had been restricted from visiting Dublin or London, ensuring the increased engagement of women and minority groups.

The *McGimpsey* case is seemingly dominated by men: two male plaintiffs, five male counsel, one male High Court judge and five male judges in the Supreme Court. In the proceedings of the High Court and in the Supreme Court, it would seem that the only woman present in the courtroom was the reporter, Nuala Butler. Such a depiction is an incorrect representation of the political situation in Northern Ireland at the time, as there were grassroots women's movements, support groups and campaigns.[10] To rectify the skewed political landscape within the judgment, O'Donoghue J highlights the role of women within the peace process. The Noble Peace Prize winners and activists, Betty Williams and Mairéad Corrigan Maguire, are mentioned for their work on cross-community campaigning. Williams and Maguire argued that 'the voice of women has a special role and a special soul-force in the struggle for a nonviolent world'.[11] The place of women in the peace process was a role that was ignored by the Supreme Court in *McGimpsey.*

Placing women within the *McGimpsey* judgment redraws the political battle lines. Noting the cross-community work of Williams and McGuire counters the binary distinction drawn between majority and minority communities in the original judgment and the Agreement. By placing women within the judgment, O'Donoghue J highlights the important role women had in the peace process, and the broader impact of this decision on society as a whole.

[9] See Margaret Davies, 'The Law Becomes Us: Rediscovering Judgment' (2012) 20 *Feminist Legal Studies* 167, 171; Kieran McEvoy, 'Law, Struggle and Political Transformation in Northern Ireland' (2000) 27(4) *Journal of Law and Society* 542.

[10] Monica McWilliams, 'Struggling for Peace and Justice: Reflections on Women's Activism in Northern Ireland' (1995) 6(4) *Journal of Women's History* 13.

[11] Betty Williams gave this 1976 Nobel Peace Prize Acceptance Speech on behalf of herself and Máiréad Corrigan Maguire.

Questions of Citizenship and Standing

One of the questions in *McGimpsey v Ireland* was whether a plaintiff needed citizenship to bring a case about Ireland's external relations. In 1988, the general rule for standing in *Cahill v Sutton* was that standing was not restricted to citizenship, but the individual had to show that his or her interests had been adversely affected.[12] In cases concerning the external relations of Ireland, *Crotty v An Taoiseach* provided for an exception to the rule in *Cahill*, such that where a law would affect the community at large, it was not necessary to show any particular effect or impact on the citizen.[13] However, it was not clear whether *Crotty* restricted this exception to citizens.

This question remained open after *McGimpsey*, because in the High Court Barrington J found that the brothers were Irish citizens as they were born in Ireland.[14] In the Supreme Court, although they briefly considered whether a non-citizen could bring a claim, the majority assumed that the McGimpsey brothers had citizenship, leaving open the possibility for a person without citizenship to bring a claim. However, in his concurring opinion, Carthy J argued that the brothers did not have *locus standi* because they were not citizens. He argued that it is 'unlikely that a non-citizen would have been allowed' to bring an external relations claim.[15] As the question remained open, O'Donoghue J is able to provide an alternative decision. As a feminist judge, O'Donoghue J argues that citizenship was not a requirement for standing. She then unpacks how citizenship could be claimed in the 1980s and 1990s, highlighting problems that would be faced by women and people from poorer socio-economic backgrounds.

In the Irish Nationality and Citizenship Act 1956 under section 7(1), individuals born in Northern Ireland were entitled to Irish citizenship if they declared themselves Irish citizens. However, the Act did not state how individuals were supposed to declare themselves citizens. The application for a passport, which involved coming forward to the authorities, is a public act and evidence of citizenship. In acknowledging that Christopher McGimpsey had a passport, the Court used visible and public acts when deciding whether someone has citizenship. However, Michael McGimpsey did not have a passport, and had not made a public declaration. O'Donoghue J notes there was no formula for a citizenship declaration, which means that she can consider private acts. She highlights those people who do not or cannot travel and would therefore find it difficult to demonstrate that they had claimed citizenship. O'Donoghue J challenges the public/private divide underlying the Irish Supreme Court's approach to citizenship, making it easier for women and disadvantaged groups of people to claim citizenship.

Even if women, minority groups and people from lower socio-economic backgrounds could overcome the barriers to claiming citizenship, they would be faced with a further barrier: *locus standi*. There is a suggestion in *Cahill v Sutton* that a citizen challenging the constitutionality of an Act has to meet a threshold requirement.[16] The citizen wishing to

[12] *Cahill v Sutton* [1980] IR 269.
[13] *Crotty v An Taoiseach* [1987] IR 713.
[14] *McGimpsey v Ireland* [1988] IR 567, 570 (Barrington J).
[15] *McGimpsey v Ireland* [1990] 1 IR 124 (McCarthy J).
[16] *Cahill v Sutton* [1980] IR 269, 284.

challenge the Act cannot be a 'litigious person, the crack, the obstructionist, the meddlesome, the perverse, the officious man of straw and many others'.[17] In other words, the court must decide whether the plaintiff is a serious person with a serious case. In contrast, when the case concerns external relations, *Crotty v An Taoiseach* provides an exception. In deciding on standing for the McGimpsey brothers, Barrington J conflates the two tests in *Cahill* and *Crotty* when he states, 'the plaintiffs are patently sincere and serious people who have raised an important constitutional issue which affects them and thousands of others … [I]t would be inappropriate for this court to refuse to listen to their complaints'.[18] It is not clear what makes it inappropriate to refuse the case. The question of sincerity and seriousness seems to fall within the *Cahill* test of meeting the threshold of seriousness, and the constitutional issue affecting thousands meets the *Crotty* requirement.

The effect of the conflation by Barrington J is that the courts in external relations cases can continue to construct an idea of the ideal litigant for the purposes of *locus standi*. There are two ways in which the ideal litigant is constructed in *McGimpsey*: first, the ideal litigant is a good citizen who is loyal to the state; and, secondly, the litigant has a public life or good public standing within the community.

The loyalty of the good Irish citizen is derived from Article 9, section 3 of the Irish Constitution 1937. It provides that citizens should show 'fidelity to the nation and loyalty to the State'.[19] However, this loyalty is magnified by the majority in *McGimpsey*, who considered citizens to be no more than 'servants' for the state.[20] The servitude of the citizens effectively removes potential political disagreement. Defence counsel in *McGimpsey* argued that the brothers were not loyal citizens, and therefore lacked standing, because they disagreed with Ireland's national territory claim in Article 2 of the Constitution. McCarthy J agreed that citizens of Ireland were bound by Article 9, section 3 to show fidelity and loyalty. However, even McCarthy J acknowledges that this political duty of fidelity and loyalty did not prohibit disagreement with the content of the Constitution. The McGimpsey brothers could disagree with the Constitution and still be loyal to the state.

For the feminist judge, the idea that a citizen's loyalty to the state effectively amounts to servitude is problematic. O'Donoghue J highlights how Article 46 of the Constitution, which provides for changes to the Constitution via referenda, allows for disagreement with the content of the Constitution. In pointing to Article 46, O'Donoghue J facilitates views and opinions that challenge the Constitution, without there being any repercussion for the individual's *locus standi* claim. Whilst this reemphasises the importance of contestation and evolution within the Constitution, referenda offer limited and marshalled space for disagreement. Moreover, direct forms of democracy have the potential to remove the protection of minority rights in favour of a majority.[21]

The Court's idea of the ideal litigant and the good citizen includes public standing within the community. The public life of the McGimpsey brothers is discussed at length in the High Court and Supreme Court. Although to some extent these comments are *obiter dicta*, the facts of the brothers' public lives were influential in the decision of the Court to grant

17 *Cahill v Sutton* [1980] IR 269, 284.
18 *McGimpsey v Ireland* [1988] IR 567, 580 (Barrington J).
19 Art 9, s 3 of the Irish Constitution 1937.
20 *McGimpsey v Ireland* [1990] 1 IR 110, 122 (Findlay CJ).
21 Anne Phillips, *Engendering Democracy* (University Park, PA, Penn State Press, 1991) 144.

standing. The decision of the High Court was premised in the finding that 'the plaintiffs are patently sincere and serious people'.[22] This focus on seriousness, sincerity and public life raises concerns for marginalised individuals in the 1980s and early 1990s if they attempted to bring a case.

The importance of public life would have made establishing *locus standi* difficult for women. Women did have public lives in the 1980s and 1990s, in particular there were grass-roots women's movements.[23] However, there were few female representatives: only 60 out of 566 councillors were women following the 1989 elections in Northern Ireland,[24] and there were no female representatives for Northern Ireland in the Houses of Parliament in Westminster.[25] The McGimpseys' public life in politics was evidence to suggest that their claim was serious, but in the 1980s the women's movement was marginalised in national politics; women's concerns were deprioritised and not taken seriously during the disagreements following the Anglo-Irish Agreement.[26] Women in the public sphere would find it difficult to show they were 'sincere and serious' when the popular depiction of 'politicised' women was of the hysterical or emotional female.[27] As late as 1996, women in politics were still 'treated with derision'.[28] This attitude towards women and women's movements would make it difficult to demonstrate seriousness or sincerity. This might have made it difficult for women to get standing in the court.

In deciding that citizenship is not a requirement for *locus standi* in external relations cases, O'Donoghue J implicitly rejects the construction of the ideal litigant. Given that the majority decision in the Supreme Court does not challenge the use of seriousness and public standing by the High Court, the role of the feminist judge would have been to expose the dangers of the approach taken by the court.

From One or Other Community

> They say that am not I
>
> but some kind of we, that I do not know
>
> where I end—sometimes there is no one
>
> to ask ...[29]

The Anglo-Irish Agreement 1985 had a profound effect on the identity of people within Northern Ireland. The Ulster Unionist Party MP Harold McCusker stated that his

[22] *McGimpsey v Ireland* [1988] IR 567, 580, cited *McGimpsey v Ireland* [1990] 1 IR 110, 114.

[23] McWilliams, above n 10.

[24] Rick Wilford, Robert Miller, Yolanda Bell, Freda Donoghue, 'In Their Own Voices: Women Councillors in Northern Ireland' (1993) 71(3) *Public Administration* 341, 342.

[25] McWilliams, above n 10, at 30.

[26] ibid, 30–31.

[27] Bill Rolston, 'Mothers, Whores and Villains: images of women in novels of the Northern Ireland Conflict' (1989) 31(1) *Race and Class* 41, 50.

[28] Mark Simpson, 'Women Treated with Derision', *Belfast Telegraph*, 2 August 1996, cited in Cornelia Albert, *The Peacebuilding Elements of the Belfast Agreement and Transformation of the Northern Ireland Conflict* (Frankfurt am Main, Peter Lang, 2009) 66.

[29] Medbh McGuckian, 'The Appropriate Moments', *Captain Lavender* (Co Meath, Gallery Press, 1994).

constituents had become 'Irish-British hybrids'.[30] The construction of a hybrid identity is mirrored in the words of Medbh McGuckian's poem. Here the words indicate that the individual's identity was both lost and then reconstructed in The Troubles in Northern Ireland as the conflict was shaped by community divides.[31] Individuals were placed within a community, irrespective of whether they chose to be part of that community. Medbh McGuckian is a Northern Irish Catholic whose work comments on the 'Northern [Ireland] political situation'.[32] Her invocation of the obliterated yet reconstructed self within the poem acts as a reminder of the role of the judge in the construction of identities and communities in the *McGimpsey* judgment.

The Anglo-Irish Agreement and the majority of judges in *McGimpsey* do not focus on individuality. Within the judgment, there is a merging of identity into citizenship and ideas of community. In the Supreme Court judgment, 'citizens' are treated by McCarthy J as a homogeneous 'People', which obfuscates any individual identities or concerns.[33] O'Donoghue J's decision that citizenship is not a requisite for standing allows Michael McGimpsey, in particular, to maintain his identity.

Within this 'People', citizens are assigned to either the majority or minority community as defined in ethno-national (sectarian) terms.[34] The binary distinction between the majority and the minority communities excluded other minority groups that did not align with either side of the political debate, or which were excluded from participating in the debate by these communities. For example, some Unionists excluded the LGBTQ community. In response to the 1978 draft Homosexual Offences (Northern Ireland) Order, which sought to decriminalise homosexual acts between consenting adults, the Democratic Unionist Party, led by Ian Paisley, started a petition to 'Save Ulster from Sodomy'.[35] This petition collected nearly 70,000 signatures, showing the extent of the exclusion supported by Unionists and others.[36]

In response to the binary distinction drawn between the majority and the minority in the judgment and the Agreement, O'Donoghue J adopts a liberal feminist approach and repositions the discussion in human rights and anti-discrimination law. She uses Ireland's international human rights obligations, in particular those obligations under the European Convention on Human Rights, to focus on the individual and show that people cannot be discriminated against. To some extent this facilitates the protection of individual identity in a political environment dominated by sectarian divides.

However, the focus on human rights has limitations for women and minorities,[37] not least because it isolates individuals from their particular social context.[38] Restricted by

[30] McKittrick and McVea, above n 4, at 192.

[31] Elmer Kennedy-Andrews, Writing Home: Poetry and Place in Northern Ireland 1968–2008 (Cambridge, Boydell and Brewer Ltd, 2008) 228; Jonathan Hufstader, Tongue of Water, Teeth of Stones: Northern Irish Poetry and Social Violence (Lexington, KY, University Press of Kentucky, 2015) 271.

[32] Kathy Cremin, 'Book Review' (1996) 4(14) *Irish Studies Review* 40, 49.

[33] *McGimpsey v Ireland* [1990] 1 IR 110, 124 (McCarthy J).

[34] ibid, 122.

[35] *Dudgeon v The United Kingdom* [1981] 4 EHRR 149, para 25.

[36] ibid.

[37] Celia Romany, 'Women as Aliens: A Feminist Critique of the Public/Private Distinction in International Human Rights' (1993) 6 *Harvard Human Rights Journal* 87.

[38] Reg Graycar and Jenny Morgan, 'Equality Rights: What's Wrong?' in Rosemary Hunter (ed), *Rethinking Equality Projects in Law: Feminist Challenges* (Oxford, Hart Publishing, 2008) 109.

legal methodology, O'Donoghue J had to rely on international obligations that are premised on formal equality. This formal equality does not appreciate structural inequalities.[39] Alternatively, O'Donoghue J could have reinterpreted the legislation to achieve substantive rather than formal equality. However, this is not always possible,[40] and it has been suggested that some political methods can be a better mechanism for discussing 'concerns about substantive inequality'.[41] Reg Graycar and Jenny Morgan have explored whether it is possible to 'engage with the notion of equality for women without necessarily doing so via a constitutional/statutory provision'.[42] Whilst O'Donoghue J could have discussed equality more broadly, a court judgment is constructed using legal authority (such as legislation and cases) so as to be persuasive,[43] coercing her to rely on the formalistic notions of equality found in human rights law.

O'Donoghue J's use of human rights and anti-discrimination law is also constrained by the role of the judge. O'Donoghue J cannot ensure that minority rights are actually protected outside of the courtroom; rather, she can only comment *obiter* on the need to bring legal cases to protect rights: 'the presumption of constitutional compliance in Government action ought to, as the plaintiffs have done here, be vigorously contested'. Yet, as explored above, there are financial and legal hurdles for women and other marginalised groups when bringing such cases.[44] In these respects, focusing on human rights and anti-discrimination law has limitations when protecting minority groups.

Concluding Remarks

In rewriting *McGimpsey v Ireland*, O'Donoghue J asked whether it would have been possible for an Irish or Northern Irish housewife, as a metaphor for marginalised and excluded individuals, to bring a similar constitutional claim in Ireland in the 1980s and early 1990s. This commentary has highlighted issues with the judgments of the High Court and the Supreme Court, to show that it would have been difficult for a woman or a person from a minority group to bring the sort of constitutional claim that the McGimpseys did in 1988. The comments on citizenship and *locus standi*, as well as the failure of the Supreme Court to challenge the remarks of Barrington J in the High Court in relation to the public standing of the McGimpsey brothers, could have disadvantaged women and other minority groups, who might have been dissuaded or even prevented from bringing a case.

[39] Rosemary Hunter, Clare McGlynn and Erika Rackley, 'Feminist Judgments: An Introduction' in Rosemary Hunter, Clare McGlynn and Erika Rackley (eds), *Feminist Judgments: From Theory to Practice* (Oxford, Hart Publishing, 2008) 24.

[40] ibid, 15.

[41] Graycar and Morgan, above n 38, at 124.

[42] ibid.

[43] Hunter, McGlynn and Rackley, above n 39, at 16.

[44] Graycar and Morgan, above n 38, at 109.

Christopher McGimpsey and Michael McGimpsey, Plaintiffs v Ireland, An Taoiseach and Others, Defendants

[S.C. No. 314 of 1988]

Supreme Court 1st March, 1990

O'Donoghue J. 1st March, 1990

The issues raised in this appeal are of fundamental import to all those living on this island and in Great Britain. The significance of the Anglo-Irish Agreement is evident in its Preamble in which both the Irish and UK Governments reaffirm:-

> "their commitment to a society in Northern Ireland in which all may live in peace, free from discrimination and intolerance."

Both Governments in attempting to resolve the conflict in Northern Ireland have negotiated an agreement that will impact upon all individual lives on both islands. The Agreement aims to establish good governance on a non-discriminatory basis in Northern Ireland. Whether the Agreement will have the impact sought remains unknown, however, the immediate impact of the Agreement upon all those living in Northern Ireland is evident. The repeated public demonstrations and the various opinions that have been put forth, both pro and anti the negotiations, demonstrate the ongoing importance that these matters have in Northern Ireland and the level of disquiet amongst the population regarding the settlement. In taking this case Christopher and Michael McGimpsey demonstrate the concerns shared by many in Northern Ireland that this international treaty will have a negative impact upon their daily lives and their sincerely held view that its implementation will ultimately be negative. Christopher and Michael McGimpsey claim that in concluding the Anglo-Irish Agreement the Irish Government is in violation of the Constitution.

Christopher and Michael McGimpsey were both born and are resident in Northern Ireland and bring their appeal as individuals who believe that they will be affected by the terms of the Anglo-Irish Agreement. Both complain, as was well summarised by Barrington J in his judgment in the High Court:-

> "that the Irish government, in entering into the Anglo-Irish Agreement, neglected its duty to the majority community in Northern Ireland and violated the provisions of its own Constitution."

In their appeal from the High Court Christopher and Michael McGimpsey argue that the Anglo-Irish Agreement, specifically Articles 2, 3, 29 and 40 are contrary to Articles 2, 3, 29 and 40 of the Constitution. Their complaint may be further broken into three parts: first, the Anglo-Irish Agreement is inconsistent with the Constitutional claim to state territory extending to the entire island, second, it fetters Governmental external powers, third, and significantly, that the Agreement requires the Irish Government to consider the situation of one community above others. The defence contest these claims while also raising the issue of the plaintiffs' *locus standi*.

Locus Standi

In the High Court, Barrington J. found that both plaintiffs, having been born on the island, were citizens and the defence has not sought to challenge this here. My colleague Finlay C.J., for the majority, following the High Court, has also assumed that both plaintiffs are citizens albeit my colleague McCarthy J. disagrees on this point. The nature of how citizenship was attained and the substantive claims of the plaintiffs are linked and, as such, it is necessity to consider whether, in this instance, citizenship is a requirement of *locus standi*, whether the plaintiffs are in fact citizens and, if so, how this was attained.

The ability of non-citizens to make constitutional claims was affirmed in *Kostan v. Ireland* [1978] I.L.R.M. 12, while in *Cahill v. Sutton* [1980] I.R. 269 this Court stated that to claim *locus standi* persons must be able to assert that their interests have been adversely affected again not restricting standing to citizens:-

> "standing in constitutional matters is that the person challenging the constitutionality of the statute or some other for whom he is deemed by that court to be entitled to speak, must be able to assert that because of the alleged unconstitutionality, his or the other person's interests have been adversely affected, or stand in real or imminent danger of being adversely affected … subject to expansion, exception or qualification when the justice of the case so requires."

Under *Crotty v. An Taoiseach* [1987] I.R. 713 citizenship provides a basis for *locus standi*. The question is whether *Crotty v. An Taoiseach* [1987] I.R. 713 restricts external relations claims to citizens or, in circumstances where the impact is upon all on the island, notwithstanding a failure to prove the threat of any special injury or prejudice, the claimants have *locus standi* irrespective of citizenship. It could be argued that the nature of this appeal requires the plaintiffs to be citizens. In *Boland v. An Taoiseach* [1974] I.R. 338 and *Crotty v. An Taoiseach* [1987] I.R. 713 this Court accepted that a constitutional claim regarding Governmental external powers was justiciable. In the latter case this Court stated that it was satisfied:-

> "in accordance with the principles laid down by the Court in *Cahill v. Sutton* [1980] I.R. 269, that in the particular circumstances of this case where the impugned legislation, namely the Act of 1986, will if made operative affect every citizen, the plaintiff has a *locus standi* to challenge the Act notwithstanding his failure to prove the threat of any special injury or prejudice to him, as distinct from any other citizen, arising from the Act."

It is with specific regard to Northern Ireland that the Agreement is said to have an adverse effect or be in real or imminent danger of adversely effecting, the plaintiffs and the majority community. My colleague McCarthy J. argues that those from Britain would not be allowed to take this case and that is correct. Nonetheless, Articles 2 and 3 of the Constitution, the statutory entitlement to citizenship for those born in Northern Ireland, as well as the Anglo-Irish Agreement's focus on Northern Ireland, places the plaintiffs, like Mr Crotty, in a position where the impugned treaty affects all those living on the island, including the plaintiffs, and enables them to hold *locus standi* irrespective of their citizenship. As such, citizenship is not a prerequisite for *locus standi*. The defence argued that neither plaintiff would suffer injury or prejudice, however, as per the reasoning in *Crotty v. An Taoiseach* [1987] I.R. 713, the Anglo Irish Agreement will, like the Single European Act, impact upon all those living in Northern Ireland in a substantive fashion thus entitling the plaintiffs to standing even if they cannot show special injury or prejudice.

Citizenship arises under Articles 2 and 9 of the Constitution and has been implemented under ss. 6(1) and 7(1) of the Irish Nationality and Citizenship Act, 1956. Under the Act, citizenship is accorded to individuals born on the island of Ireland before 6 December 1922, in the territory which currently comprises the Republic of Ireland, or in Northern Ireland on or after 6 December 1922 with a parent who was an Irish citizen at the time of birth. In the alternative, under s. 7(1), individuals are entitled to Irish citizenship if born in Northern Ireland albeit they are not automatically an Irish citizen and no formula has been prescribed for a declaration taking up this citizenship entitlement. Neither plaintiff has declared that he is a citizen, and they have not presented evidence that due to their birth dates or that of their parents they are automatically entitled to citizenship under s. 6(1) of the Act.

The State (K.M.) v. Minister for Foreign Affairs Unreported Judgment of High Court, 29 May 1978 stated that all citizens are entitled to a passport and, as such, the right to travel outside the State. Thus, the possession of the passport corresponds with citizenship. The first plaintiff, Christopher McGimpsey, holds an Irish passport and since no formula for a declaration under s. 7(1) has been prescribed under the Act, it can be assumed that the first plaintiff, in undertaking a positive act by claiming citizenship in seeking a passport, has taken up his entitlement. As has already been demonstrated in *Kostan v. Ireland* [1978] I.L.R.M. 12, citizenship is not a prerequisite of a successful constitutional claim thus the act of making the claim by Michael McGimpsey does not necessarily mean a form of citizenship has been made in undertaking a constitutional claim. While my learned colleague McCarthy J. in concurrence argues that Mr. Crotty was an 'undoubted citizen' this is largely irrelevant when the circumstances do not require the plaintiffs to be citizens to have standing.

The lack of prescription as to the necessary elements of the declaration under s. 7(1) of the Irish Nationality and Citizenship Act, 1956 places those entitled to citizenship at a unique disadvantage as to how to attain their citizenship without either seeking a passport, or making a declaration of citizenship before a Court within Ireland or before the authorities of a foreign jurisdiction. For the individual that does not embark on foreign travel nor possesses the resource or reason to come to the attention of the authorities in the Republic it would seem difficult to claim citizenship if it remains entirely within the personal and private claim of the individual. As such, the second plaintiff could have taken up his entitlement to citizenship, albeit there is no such claim here, and it be an entirely private act. Further, precluding persons who have not had an opportunity to make a declaration under s. 7 of the Irish Nationality and Citizenship Act, 1956 from making constitutional claims would disadvantage a group that has not previously sought or had the opportunity to make a public claim of citizenship.

Christopher McGimpsey, in claiming a passport, has made a declaration of Irish citizenship though this does not preclude other citizenship entitlements that the first plaintiff may have or seek to claim in the alternative or in combination. The second plaintiff has not sought to make a declaration in this case however nor has the state prescribed how the entitlement to citizenship is transformed into actual citizenship. As such, Michael McGimpsey's legal entitlement to citizenship stands. In combination with the territorial claim made under Articles 2 and 3 of the Constitution and s. 7(1) of the Irish Nationality and Citizenship Act, 1956 the Court can assume that the entitlement to citizenship as an element of these Constitutional claims, if not actual citizenship, would give the second plaintiff an additional claim to *locus standi*. To find otherwise would be to automatically disadvantage those living in Northern Ireland that have not made active public steps towards declaring citizenship and further, would make the character of citizenship itself of an entirely public character excluding those whose lives are largely lived in what the law regards as the private sphere. Further, decoupling this claim from citizenship enables Michael McGimpsey to maintain his identity, a key element of the Anglo-Irish Agreement's recognition of the communities of Northern Ireland.

The defence suggest that neither plaintiff believes that the national territory includes Northern Ireland as per Article 2 of the Constitution and that this affects their *locus standi*. The Constitutional claim extends an entitlement to citizenship for those born in Northern Ireland irrespective of political belief and allows the possibility to contest treaties as unconstitutional without requiring individuals subject to these claims to openly avow their belief or otherwise in the veracity or correctness of Constitutional content. The defence's claim would prevent challenges to constitutional provisions or interpretations which individuals regard as fundamentally negatively affecting their lives. Indeed such a claim would preclude the potential for debate as part of referenda under Article 46 of the Constitution or to challenge the creation of unenumerated rights as per *Ryan v. Attorney General* [1965] I.R. 29 both of which prevent the calcification of the Constitution in 1937. It is even possible that at some future date Article 2 or other Articles of the Constitution may be amended in line with the plaintiffs', or others', beliefs. Thus to exclude the plaintiffs due to an impugned belief of theirs would be contrary to the spirit of the potential for Constitutional debate and evolution.

Whilst in *Attorney General (at the relation of the Society for the Protection of Unborn Children) v. Open Door Counselling Ltd.* [1988] I.R. 593 the Court was satisfied that the Attorney General had a 'bona fide concern and interest for the protection of the constitutionally guaranteed right' the fact that both plaintiffs are elected representatives of the Unionist Community does not in itself mean that they embody the interests of everyone that either identifies as Unionist or in the alternative does seek to be identified as Nationalist although they have demonstrated that the Anglo-Irish Agreement will, in line with *Crotty v. An Taoiseach* [1987] I.R. 713, affect all individuals on the island and most particularly those in Northern Ireland.

It is also critical that both individuals' chosen political identities as Unionists and, as such, part of the majority community, as it is assumed to be under the Anglo-Irish Agreement, be respected and acknowledged. In *Boland v. An Taoiseach* [1974] I.R. 338, a case taken to challenge the Sunningdale Agreement, a precursor to the Anglo-Irish Agreement, the claim was taken by an individual who identified as both a Nationalist and citizen. The mere fact that in this case the plaintiffs take the opposite view ought not raise any questions as to loyalty to the Constitution nor require them to be citizens if this status is unnecessary for the case to proceed or if the plaintiffs do not seek to be citizens. Under the Constitution individuals are entitled to the freedom and autonomy to express their convictions and opinions and, as such, whether Christopher and Michael McGimpsey agree with the content of the Constitution, or consider it to be fundamentally contradictory to their [aspirations] or the political aspirations of the state, ought not be a bar to making a claim of unconstitutionality.

My colleague McCarthy J. raises the question of Article 9.3 of the Constitution which states that:-

> "[f]idelity to the nation and loyalty to the State are fundamental political duties of all citizens"

and links this to the question of the plaintiffs' citizenship and their *locus standi*. Relying on *Crotty v. An Taoiseach* [1987] I.R. 713 and *The State (Nicolaou) v. An Bord Uchtála* [1966] I.R. 567, my colleague suggests that the matters before the Court are such that they require citizenship and finds that neither the first nor the second plaintiff is, in fact, a citizen. Very few citizens make declarations to uphold the Constitution and indeed some may aver to be unsupportive of some of its content whilst a non-citizen could also surely claim to wish to uphold the Constitution. Even in such an instance where a declaration of loyalty was made this would not preclude challenges as to the substantive implementation or debate of constitutional provisions. In sum, the Anglo-Irish Agreement has the potential to impact upon all those on this island but, in particular, those living in Northern Ireland and the facts are such that no special injury as distinct from other individuals in Northern Ireland needs to be demonstrated. As such, citizenship is not a prerequisite for *locus standi.*

The Merits

The plaintiffs argue that the Anglo-Irish Agreement is contrary to Articles 2 and 3 of the Constitution; that the establishment of an intergovernmental conference and secretariat fetters the powers of the Government under Articles 28 and 29 of the Constitution; and finally that the State may not enter into a treaty whereby it commits itself to have regard to one section of the Irish society to the disregard of another. Each of these will be dealt with in turn.

Regarding Articles 2 and 3 of the Constitution, I have read the majority judgment and I am satisfied with the interpretation put forth therein that both Articles 2 and 3 of the Constitution are legal claims. This is firmly asserted by this Court in *Re Art 26 and the Criminal Law (Jurisdiction) Bill, 1975* [1977] I.R. 129, when this Court stated that Article 3:-

> "expressed not only legal norms but basic doctrines of political and social theory."

However, I would disagree that Article 3 prohibits the enactment of laws applicable in Northern Ireland; rather Article 3 prohibits their enforcement. To this extent I agree with the submissions of both parties and their interpretation of the dictum of O'Keeffe P. in *Boland v. An Taoiseach* [1974] I.R. 338 and O'Byrne J. in *The People v. Rutledge* [1978] I.R. 376. In *Re Art 26 and the Criminal Law (Jurisdiction) Bill, 1975* [1977] I.R. 129 this Court looked at the historical and international legal issues related to the extra-territorial effect of legislation introduced which related to Northern Ireland and found that the particular legislation was not in violation of international law or the Constitution. The Irish Nationality and Citizenship Act, 1956, as discussed previously, is one example of an Act which is applicable in Northern Ireland but is not enforceable without the voluntary consent of other governments to the uptake of the entitlement to citizenship.

Article 5 of the Constitution commits Ireland to democracy and this is reaffirmed in *de Búrca v. Attorney General* [1976] I.R. 294 where the Court also asserted that lack of representativeness, in that case regarding property qualifications and gender on juries, was a violation of Articles 38 and 40 of the Constitution. In *Russell v. Fanning* [1988] I.R. 505 concerning Article 6 of the Constitution this Court made clear that only through democratic means should decisions as to policy in line with the common good, including with regard to re-integration of Northern Ireland, be made. The democratic character of enacting laws that are applicable to though not enforceable on individuals that have no part in the democratic process is problematic, especially for those, who unlike the plaintiffs do not have either the political voice or resource to object to such laws, the Constitution and its subsequent interpretation. The fact that enforcement of the law cannot take place ameliorates the difficulty in reconciling Article 3 with Article 5, however the disenfranchisement that takes place of whole portions of Northern Irish society who are not part of vocal political processes ought to be taken into consideration when the State enacts laws which impact upon Northern Ireland. Nowhere in the Irish Constitution is there a claim to extra-territorial jurisdiction although certain matters, all or part of which take place outside the State, may still be subject to this jurisdiction.

In *Russell v. Fanning* [1988] I.R. 505 this Court stated that re-integration of Northern Ireland under Articles 2 and 3 is a Constitutional imperative. Ireland's Constitutional commitment to democracy under Article 5, as well as its international legal commitments to substantive democracy within the European Convention on Human Rights and the International Covenant on Civil and Political Rights, as well as the right to self-determination which forms part of customary international law, forms part of the Government's legal considerations on how it fulfils this Constitutional imperative.

With regard to the terms of the Anglo-Irish Agreement and specifically Article 1, I agree with my colleague Finlay C.J. and with Barrington J. in the High Court that this recognises the political situation in Northern Ireland but further is in line with the democratic imperative set out in Article 5 of the Constitution that commits the Government to democratic means of consultation. Articles 1 and 2 of the Anglo-Irish Agreement, particularly the assertion of sovereignty and the recognition of current jurisdictional operations of the UK and Ireland, can be read in line with Articles 2, 3 and 5 of the Constitution. The claim to the territory of the entire island stands but the democratic character of both the UK and Ireland, as well as the right of all those living in Northern Ireland to be engaged with processes that determine their futures, is made clear under the Anglo-Irish Agreement. Finally, the Agreement does not state what the ultimate status of Northern Ireland will be and does not change the current claims of either the UK or Ireland; rather it sets the terms of democratic engagement for those living in Northern Ireland.

The plaintiffs have claimed that the Anglo-Irish Agreement will create an estoppel claim within international law and specifically relying on the cases of the *Temple of Preah Vihear* [1962] I.C.J. Rep 6 and *Eastern Greenland* 1933 P.C.I.J. (ser.A/B) No.53. In both cases, the International Courts found that statements as to territorial claims could be used to estop governments from subsequently altering their position. In the particular circumstances here, the Government has not recognised nor acquiesced to a change to the Constitutional territorial claim. Rather, the Anglo-Irish Agreement recognises the *de facto* situation in Northern Ireland while maintaining both Governments' respective territorial claims. In such circumstances international law will not estop Ireland from continuing with its territorial claim under Articles 2 and 3 of the Constitution. If Ireland's treaty or state practice were to change this may cause estoppel under international law to come into effect whatever the domestic Constitutional status were to be and this ought to be borne in mind in future negotiations on the status of Northern Ireland.

The plaintiffs argue that, in breach of Article 29 of the Constitution, the Anglo-Irish Agreement fetters the Government's ability to conduct its external relations. Here I would disagree with my colleague for the majority in distinguishing *Crotty v. An Taoiseach* [1987] I.R. 713 on the grounds that the Anglo-Irish Agreement is a bilateral treaty while the Single European Act is multilateral in form. There is no basis in international law for differentiating between a bilateral and multilateral treaty or the manner in which either may or may not fetter a Government's conduct of its external relations. Where I would agree with the majority is to distinguish the character of fettering involved in both instances. Within international relations it is common for international secretariats and permanent fora to be established and this was anticipated by Ireland's membership of the League of Nations as the Constitution came into force. Indeed Article 29 of the Constitution's commitment to the pacific settlement of disputes and to peace and friendly relations based upon international justice and morality makes it incumbent upon the Government to seek such solutions and does not constitute the transfer of any power to conduct foreign relations. Ireland's continued membership of the IMF, World Bank and UN follows that pattern. The degree of integration and the forms of decision-making at the European level introduced by the Single European Act are of an entirely different character both to that proposed in the Anglo-Irish Agreement and Ireland's other current international commitments and thus it is possible to distinguish *Crotty v. An Taoiseach* [1987] I.R. 713.

The commitments in Articles 4 and 5 of the Anglo-Irish Agreement to human rights, co-operation against terrorism and the development of economic, social and cultural co-operation are in line with Article 29 of the Constitution and to Ireland's international legal commitments in both treaty and customary international law. Articles 4(c) and 5(c) of the Anglo-Irish Agreement regarding devolution are in line with the Constitution's Article 5 commitment to democracy. Indeed enshrining consent into the Anglo-Irish Agreement underpins the Constitutional commitment. Devolution, properly undertaken, would lead to decision-making at a more local level and enable a wider array of those living in Northern Ireland to be engaged in the political process without the necessary resource implications of travelling and engaging with either Dublin or London. None of these commitments to human rights, including democracy, or to co-operation with another state to attain peace are new to the Irish Government and are entirely in line with Articles 5 and 29 of the Constitution and in particular the Preamble orientation toward:-

> "the dignity and freedom of the individual [which] may be assured, true social order attained, the unity of our country restored, and concord established with other nations."

Articles 4 and 5 of the Anglo-Irish Agreement do not bind the Irish Government in the manner in which or as to the substantive outcome in which it negotiates with the UK Government. However if, under the auspices of the Anglo-Irish Agreement, the Government were to introduce legislation contrary to its constitutional and international human rights obligations, for example, with regard to equality, then this would be challengeable in the prescribed manner. Indeed, in negotiating with the UK to find a peaceful solution to the territorial claim in Articles 2 and 3 in line with international law the Irish Government is working under the terms of Article 29 of the Constitution.

The third basis on which the plaintiffs challenge the constitutionality of the Agreement is more problematic. The plaintiffs argue that the Anglo-Irish Agreement permits the Irish Government to disregard the interests of the majority community in favour of the minority community in Northern Ireland. As an international treaty the Agreement must be interpreted in line with the Vienna Convention on the Law of Treaties. Ireland has not ratified the Convention; however as it codifies customary international law it is binding within international law. Article 31 of the Vienna Convention requires treaties to be interpreted in good faith in accordance with the ordinary meaning in their context and in light of their object and purpose. To decipher the object and purpose under Article 31 of the Convention parties are to look to the preamble:-

> "2. The context for the purpose of the interpretation of a treaty shall comprise, in addition to the text, including its preamble and annexes ..."

The terms of the Anglo-Irish Agreement are not solely couched in the language of community but refer to a plethora of other terms which together are construed to identify two distinct interests in Northern Ireland. With regard to the status of Northern Ireland these interests are designated as the "two traditions" or:-

> "those who wish for no change in the present status of Northern Ireland and on the other hand by those who aspire to a sovereign united Ireland achieved by peaceful means and through agreement;"

The Agreement further references Unionists and Nationalists, while also alluding to the majority of the people of Northern Ireland. At no point in the Agreement is the minority or majority community specifically identified. Binary descriptions are put forward, such as Unionist and Nationalist or the two traditions that when combined with thestatistical break-down of the population of Northern Ireland into two specific groups, Catholic and Protestant, it can be assumed that these are the communities referenced by both Governments.

With regard to community under the Agreement, it is used with specific reference to the notion of identity utilised in the Preamble:-

> "Recognising and respecting the identities of the two communities in Northern Ireland, and the right of each to pursue its aspirations by peaceful and constitutional means;"

The Anglo-Irish Agreement does not differentiate between any particular groups regarding its commitment to peace, stability, reconciliation, human rights and economic, social and cultural co-operation. As such these Articles, including Article 4, may be understood to mean everyone living in Northern Ireland irrespective of their political, religious or other affiliation.

After the reference to community in the Preamble it is the Anglo-Irish Agreement's use of community in Articles 4(c) and Article 5(c) that Christopher and Michael McGimpsey find problematic. They argue that these articles are in breach of Article 40.1 and Article 40.3. 1° of the Constitution and its protection of equality:-

> "The Conference shall be a framework within which the Irish Government may put forward views and proposals on the modalities of bringing about devolution in Northern Ireland, in so far as they relate to the interests of the minority community."

The approach taken by the two Governments assumes that the "interests" of the population of Northern Ireland may be subdivided into two groups. What is evident in the Agreement is that only one interest will have Irish Governmental representation as it appears to be assumed that either the British Government's view will coincide with the other interest or in the alternative that this other interest is already fully represented and will be engaged in devolution negotiations or other processes that follow from the Agreement. The existence of political parties and Noble Peace Prize winning activists such as Betty Williams and Mairéad Maguire that are cross-community indicates that the binary description chosen by the Governments does not necessarily provide a sufficient description of the interests or indeed the identities of all those in Northern Ireland.

The assumption of two interests is problematic in that it assumes that the two traditions and communities can and do represent the views of all those living in Northern Ireland, even those that choose not to self-identify with these groups, individuals when the two traditions or communities would not wish to represent or those whose voices, which often is the result of community dynamics, are drowned out or not given volume. This binary division may leave portions of the community from participating in any new political and legal structures that emerge under the Anglo-Irish Agreement. This is particularly problematic for those individuals in the population that due to reasons of gender or socio-economic structures have been unable to participate in the political structures dominated by two distinct viewpoints to the exclusion of others

Barrington J. in the High Court is correct that *East Donegal Co-op Livestock Mart Ltd. v. Attorney General* [1970] 1 I.R. 317 cannot be used in the interpretation of treaties and thus the text of the Agreement. Rather in line with the Vienna Convention the subsequent articles of the Treaty ought to be interpreted with the object and purpose as set out in the Preamble of ensuring, amongst other claims, that all will live without discrimination. Article 40.1 has been interpreted by this Court in *East Donegal Co-op Livestock Mart Ltd. v. Attorney General* [1970] 1 I.R. 317 as meaning that unless discriminatory action could be shown it should not be readily assumed, instead it ought to be assumed that the Government will act within the purview of constitutional, administrative and in this instance, human rights law. While that case is not directly applicable here it will dictate how any implementing legislation will be examined. The extent to which legal structures and protection emerge from the Agreement ought to be set against its object and purpose as well as Article 4 which states that both respect for human rights and the identities of the two traditions are co-equal under Articles 4 a (i), (ii) and 5. In addition Article 53 of the Vienna Convention specifically voids any treaty concluded in violation of peremptory norms. The Vienna Convention does not specify the content of these norms, however it can be assumed that the basic human rights protection which they offer will be maintained under the Anglo-Irish Agreement.

Further should the Government introduce domestic legislation following the Anglo-Irish Agreement it can be assumed that the actions the Government may take in the implementation of law will be in line with the Constitution as per *East Donegal Co-op Livestock Mart Ltd. v. Attorney General* [1970] 1 I.R. 317 and *Boland v. An Taoiseach* [1974] I.R. 338 though as with all of these situations the presumption of constitutional compliance in Government action ought to, as the plaintiffs have done here, be vigorously contested. The question is whether the references to the dignity of the individual are enough to assume that if the Government were to go beyond advice or the suggestion of proposals that would become enforced law on behalf of one group it would be in compliance with

Ireland's Constitutional and international equality obligations. Under Article 40 of the Constitution:-

> "1 All citizens shall, as human persons, be held equal before the law.
>
> This shall not be held to mean that the State shall not in its enactments have due regard to differences of capacity, physical and moral, and of social function.
>
> ...
>
> 3 1° The State guarantees in its laws to respect, and, as far as practicable, by its laws to defend and vindicate the personal rights of the citizen."

This Court stated in *Quinn's Supermarket v. Attorney General* [1972] I.R. 1:-

> "this provision is not a guarantee of absolute equality for all citizens in all circumstances but it is a guarantee of equality as human persons and (as the Irish text of the Constitution makes quite clear) is a guarantee related to their dignity as human beings and a guarantee against any inequalities grounded upon an assumption, or indeed a belief, that some individual or individuals or classes of individuals, by reason of their human attributes or their ethnic or racial, social or religious background, are to be treated as the inferior or superior of other individuals in the community. This list does not pretend to be complete; but it is merely intended to illustrate the view that this guarantee refers to human persons for what they are in themselves rather than to any lawful activities, trades or pursuits which they may engage in or follow."

Ireland's international obligations provide a firm grounding of equality protection all of which are also aspects of UK law within Northern Ireland and as this Court demonstrated in *Bourke v. Attorney General* [1971] I.R. 316 international human rights obligations are considerations when examining the application of law in Ireland. They also impact in examining Ireland's international legal obligations under the Anglo-Irish Agreement. As this case does not relate to the domestic legislative action of the Irish Government and its constitutionality the case of *Re Ó Laighléis* [1960] I.R. 93 and the issue of Ireland's implementation of its human rights obligations are not relevant. Nonetheless, in *Ireland v. United Kingdom* (1978) 2 E.H.R.R. 25, the state relied on the European Convention on Human Rights with regard to Northern Ireland and therefore recognises its applicability in holding the UK and itself to account for actions in Northern Ireland.

Ireland is bound to equality before the law under Article 14 of the European Convention on Human Rights and Article 26 of the International Convention on Civil and Political Rights both of which the Government have signed albeit the latter currently remains unratified though the international legal commitment remains. Article 14 of the European Convention ensures that rights under the Convention are not to be subject to discrimination on grounds of 'sex, race, colour, language, religion, political or other opinion, national or social origin, association with a national minority, property, birth or other status' albeit this is in reference to rights under the Treaty. The multiple references to rights in the Anglo-Irish Agreement and particularly the potential introduction of a Bill of Rights within Northern Ireland, and the fact both the UK and Ireland are signatories of the Convention would probably mean that any such Bill of Rights would be under the Convention's rubric and thus the intention of both Governments that these rights form the basis of rights under the agreement.

Under the International Convention on Civil and Political Right, equality is extended thus to:

> "All persons are equal before the law and are entitled without any discrimination to the equal protection of the law. In this respect, the law shall prohibit any discrimination and guarantee to all persons equal and effective protection against discrimination on any ground such as race, colour, sex, language, religion, political or other opinion, national or social origin, property, birth or other status."

The EEC also has significant equality legislation, Article 119 EEC stating that:-

> "[e]ach Member State shall during the first stage ensure and subsequently maintain the application of the principle that men and women should receive equal pay for equal work."

This has since been interpreted by the European Court of Justice in Case 149/77 *Defrenne v. Sabena* [1978] E.C.R. 1365 as directly applicable within states and being further refined in Case 69/80 *Worringham and Humphreys v. Lloyds Bank* [1981] E.C.R. 767.

The majority decision has found that the Anglo-Irish Agreement is not "law" as intended by Article 40.1. The capacity of the Government to put forward views and proposals as to the bringing about of devolution or re-integration is not holding any person equal or unequal before the law. In *The State (Nicolaou) v. An Bord Uchtála* [1966] I.R. 567 the Court makes direct reference to the laws of the State which places the Agreement, as an international treaty, outside Constitutional parameters in this respect. Nonetheless as has already been discussed, such a treaty cannot be in violation of the Vienna Convention of the Law of Treaties and in line with Article 29 of the Constitution there is nothing to suggest that it would be in violation if the rights of all individuals within Northern Ireland are protected and vindicated in line with Ireland and the UK's international and domestic human rights commitments.

The plaintiffs also argued that the provisions of Article 40.3. 1° were violated; the majority found that the mere fact of expressing views and proposals as they relate to the interests of the minority community did not constitute an abandonment of the majority. This follows the reasoning of this Court in *Crowley v. Ireland* Unreported; Judgment of Supreme Court, 1 November 1979 where the Court emphasised that this provision related only to the State's legislative activity. As with Article 40.1 the Anglo-Irish Agreement as a whole commits itself to the human rights of all individuals in Northern Ireland separate to its binary use of community or tradition. As such the rights of all individuals within Northern Ireland ought to be protected and vindicated under the Agreement. Should, as is envisaged by Article 40.1 or Article 40.3.1, the Agreement lead to law clearly intended to differentiate between the parties, the test as set out in *de Búrca v. Attorney General* [1976] I.R. 294 would be applicable. The invidious or arbitrary character of the discrimination and following *O'B. v. S.* [1984] I.R. 316 the object and purpose of the legislation is critical in interpreting discrimination. If legislation following the Agreement maintained its commitments to human rights provisions and to democracy for all individuals the recognition of the two interests and the Irish Government's advocacy for the minority community would be balanced by the recognition of rights protection no matter the political interests which the individual may lay claim to or the multiple communities the individual may identify with in Northern Ireland.

In finding that the Anglo-Irish Agreement is constitutional this Court is clearly stating that while Articles 2 and 3 of the Constitution are both legal and political claims, any change to the status of Northern Ireland must be through democratic means in line with the other Articles of the Constitution and this may be the ultimate protection of all interests in Northern Ireland including those who are either not citizens or do wish to claim to be so. This judgment also finds that the guarantee of good governance in the absence of discrimination and the introduction of human rights protection in a peaceful and secure environment under the terms of the Anglo-Irish Agreement aims to aid in enabling all individuals with their multitude of interests to take part in deciding the future of Northern Ireland.

12

Commentary on *In Re White*

CARMEL ROULSTON

Introduction

The feminist judgment by Catherine O'Rourke in this fictional appeal to *In re White*,[1] which reverses the original Northern Ireland High Court decision by Carswell LCJ, provides a welcome example of an innovative judicial approach that accords due respect to and recognises the constitutional importance of the central principles of the Belfast/Good Friday Agreement (the Agreement). These principles were intended to underpin and shape the creation of political institutions and public law in Northern Ireland. Within the context of a commitment to equal political and civil rights, the Agreement recognised 'the right of women to full and equal political participation'; however, during the extended, contentious and contested processes of implementing the Agreement, the continued foregrounding of ethno-national/religious differences resulted in the establishment of practices whereby women's rights became considered relevant primarily (or in some views only) to a discrete set of issues that concern discrimination against women.[2] This marginalisation of women's roles appeared to demonstrate the validity of the conclusion drawn by several feminist researchers that the restoration of 'peace is invariably conceptualized as a return to the gender status quo, irrespective of the non-traditional roles assumed by women during conflict'.[3]

Ms Evelyn White applied in May 2000 for judicial review of appointments to the Parades Commission, arguing that the failure to appoint any female members was discriminatory. Carswell LCJ ruled that the Secretary of State had discretion to appoint an exclusively male membership to a significant public body (the Parades Commission), and that gender was not relevant to the issues with which the Parades Commission would be concerned. The ruling ignored the substantial contribution by women's organisations to the achievement of the Agreement, reinforced the false separation between gender and ethno-national identities, entrenched the marginalisation of women in public life and undermined the legitimate

[1] *In re White* [2000] NI 432.

[2] Bernadette C Hayes and Ian McAllister, 'Gender and consociational power-sharing in Northern Ireland' (2013) *International Political Science Review* 34(2) 123–39; and Katherine Side, 'Women's Civil and Political Citizenship in the Post-Good Friday Agreement Period in Northern Ireland' (2009) 24(1) *Irish Political Studies* 67–87 for discussions of marginalisation of gender equality issues.

[3] Sheila Meintjes, Anu Pillay and Meredeth Turshen (eds), *The Aftermath: Women in Post-conflict Transformation* (London and New York, Zed Books, 2001).

expectation that the numbers of women appointed to public bodies would increase. O'Rourke LJ has reinstated the important principle that gender relations are not discrete and separate from other social and political relationships in Northern Ireland.

Women in Politics during the 'Troubles'

From 1969 until the ceasefires in the 1990s, the armed conflict in Northern Ireland (euphemistically referred to as the 'Troubles') meant that national identity and associated questions of statehood dominated the political scene and were the focus of mainstream electoral politics. The focus on the 'national question' and the associated violence meant that other political matters, in particular those that were of most interest to women, were given a low priority.

While never completely absent from formal politics in that era, there were relatively few women in mainstream electoral politics. At no time in its history were more than four women elected to the Northern Ireland Parliament at Stormont (suspended in 1972 due to the violent conflict); even fewer women were elected from Northern Ireland constituencies to Westminster (in 1997, there were none among the 18 MPs at Westminster). All of the three Members of the European Parliament were male. In local government, by 1999, 14.6 per cent of council members were female. Women were, however, active, and did participate in political campaigning, most notably in complex networks of community-based or non-governmental organisations, which were a striking feature of political life in Northern Ireland for more than 20 years.[4] In these networks, women not only campaigned for women's rights, but also engaged in cross-community peace-building initiatives and with policy-makers on a broad range of social and political issues during the period of 'direct rule' from Westminster.

However, women's engagement in campaigning and support work was seldom recognised through the process of appointments to public bodies that became increasingly influential in policy-making during direct rule. Given the male-centred character of political structures, it comes as little surprise to find that appointments not only did not reflect the proportions of men and women in the population, but also in no way reflected the commitment of women to their community organisations. A Commissioner for Public Appointments was created in 1995 to regulate, monitor and report on ministerial public appointments. In 1997/98, 65 per cent of members of public bodies were male, 35 per cent

[4] There is an extensive literature documenting and analysing women's movements in Northern Ireland: see, eg, Linda Connolly, *The Irish Women's Movement: from Revolution to Devolution* (Basingstoke, Palgrave Macmillan, 2001); Kate Fearon, *Women's Work: The Story of the Northern Ireland Women's Coalition* (Belfast, Blackstaff Press, 1999); Kate Fearon and Rachel Rebouche, 'What happened to the women? Promises, reality and the Northern Ireland Women's Coalition' in M Cox, A Guelke and F Stephen (eds), *Farewell to Arms? Beyond the Good Friday Agreement*, 2nd edn (Manchester, Manchester University Press, 2006) 280–301; Yvonne Galligan, Eilis Ward and Rick Wilford (eds), *Contesting Politics: Women in Ireland North and South* (Boulder, CO, Westview Press, 1998); Yvonne Galligan, 'Women in Northern Ireland politics: Feminising an armed patriarchy' in M Sawer, M Tremblay and L Trimble (eds), *Representing Women in Parliament: A Comparative Study* (Abingdon, Routledge, 2006) 204–20; Eilish Rooney, 'Women in Northern Irish Politics: Difference Matters' in Carmel Roulston and Celia Davies (eds), *Gender, Democracy and Inclusion in Northern Ireland* (Macmillan, Basingstoke, 2000) 164–86; and Rosemary Sales, *Women Divided: Gender, Religion and Politics in Northern Ireland* (London and New York, Routledge, 1997).

female. Men dominated the Chair positions (70 per cent and 30 per cent respectively). By the time of Carswell LCJ's ruling on Evelyn White's application, the numbers of women appointed to and holding Chair positions had in fact declined, so that 32 per cent of appointments and approximately 27 per cent of Chair positions were held by women. At the time of the original judgment, there were no women in the senior judiciary (High Court and above), a situation that continues at the time of writing. The fictional O'Rourke LJ is therefore the first senior female judge in Northern Ireland. A feminist judge might have pondered whether these facts demonstrated that there was a broader problem in public life to which this case was relevant, as O'Rourke LJ has done in her feminist judgment.

The feminist judgment highlights the extent to which and the diverse ways in which women's experiences are affected by and participate in the conflicted politics of Northern Ireland. Women's civil society activism, work in community groups and 'transversal' dialogue made a significant contribution to the creation of conditions for the commencement of peace negotiations, and to the success of those negotiations. In 1992, the Opsahl Commission of Inquiry on Northern Ireland was established; a panel of independent experts invited, documented and reviewed submissions from the people of Northern Ireland (and others interested in finding a resolution to the conflict) on possible ways to break the political deadlock. The report of the Commission, which documented and drew attention to the unrealised potential of civil society activism[5]—with particular focus on women's organisations—was one factor in the decision to draw a wider spectrum of political opinion into the processes of negotiating and agreeing an enduring political settlement. At the same time, co-ordinated by the Northern Ireland Women's European Platform, women's sector campaigners were developing plans to ensure that women's and other civil society perspectives would be represented in the forthcoming political talks. Drawing on their experience of working at the international as well as the local level (most notably in creation by a broad and diverse set of organisations of a shared perspective for the UN Beijing Platform for Action in 1995), women's groups came together in a series of conferences to identify common visions for the future should the talks prove to be successful.[6] The importance of women's presence at peace negotiations was subsequently confirmed at the international level by United Nations Security Council Resolution (UNSCR) 1325 on Women, Peace and Security, adopted in October 2000, which also advocated women's participation in political life more generally. Regrettably, the Resolution was adopted after the High Court decision in *Re White*. Nevertheless, Carswell LCJ's withering dismissal of the Northern Ireland Human Rights Commission's (NIHRC) written intervention signalled the Court's clear lack of interest in the UK's international obligations to advance women's equality, including in public life:

> I do not consider that any of the provisions of the several conventions cited by the Human Rights Commission adds anything of consequence to those of domestic law. The International Covenant on Civil and Political Rights, the Convention on the Elimination of Discrimination Against Women and the Convention on the Political Rights of Women each contain provisions for the elimination of discrimination ... To dilate further on these conventions would be an unnecessary elaboration and lengthen this judgment unnecessarily, and I do not propose to spend further time on them.

[5] Marianne Elliot, 'The Role of Civil Society in Conflict Resolution: The Opsahl Commission in Northern Ireland, 1992–93' (2013) 17(2) *New Hibernia Review* 86–102.

[6] Niamh Reilly, 'The UN "Beijing Platform for Action" 1995–2005: Local Global Political Spaces, NGO Advocacy, and Governmental Responses in the Republic of Ireland' (2005) 20(2) *Irish Political Studies* 187–200.

The Court's posture towards the NIHRC intervention also shaped the feminist judgment, in discouraging extensive attention to relevant international commitments, including UNSCR 1325.[7] Nevertheless, in line with Colin Murray's feminist judgment in *Re E*[8] in this volume, O'Rourke LJ robustly articulates the importance of NIHRC interventions and the Commission's authority to make such interventions.

The Northern Ireland Multi-Party Peace Negotiations

The Belfast/Good Friday Agreement was signed—after many setbacks and obstacles—at the conclusion of a lengthy (6+ years) 'peace talks' process. This success, compared to prior attempts to reach a negotiated settlement in Northern Ireland, was achieved to a large extent because a much broader range of political opinions was represented in the negotiations. A novel feature of the negotiations that commenced in 1996 was the presence of parties who aimed to speak for a much wider spectrum of ideologies and identities than in prior negotiations; among these was the Northern Ireland Women's Coalition (NIWC), whose participation had been achieved as a result of pressure by women's organisations to ensure that women's voices would be heard in the process. During the elections to the Forum for Peace and Reconciliation (which were the gateway to participation in the negotiations), in the Forum's deliberations and during the months preceding the opening of formal peace negotiations, the NIWC faced continual (often overtly hostile and aggressive) challenges over the legitimacy of making claims to represent women.[9] In their resistance to such attacks and through their policy proposals, the NIWC acted as a catalyst for the inclusion in the agenda for the negotiations concerns about the under-representation of women in public life, and as a result achieved the important commitment to women's full and equal political participation in the Agreement. In a broader sense, during the negotiations, the NIWC connected with what has been described as a 'parallel peace process'[10] focused on achieving a commitment to human rights, social justice, fairness and equality in the Agreement. One of the notable achievements of the NIWC was to ensure that a commitment to recognition of the harms suffered by victims was specifically included in the Agreement.

Women in Politics after the Good Friday Agreement

As previously noted, the Agreement did contain a strong equal rights dimension and a commitment to 'equality proofing' of legislation. However, at its heart the Agreement

[7] For an interesting critique of the UK Government's stance on UNSCR 1325 and Northern Ireland, see Elizabeth Law and Ann Marie Gray, 'The politics of defining "armed conflict" in Northern Ireland' (2014) *Open Democracy*, at www.opendemocracy.net/5050/elizabeth-law-ann-marie-gray/politics-of-defining-armed-conflict-in-northern-ireland.

[8] *In re E (a child)* [2008] UKHL 66; see ch 15.

[9] Kate Fearon, *Women's Work: The Story of the Northern Ireland Women's Coalition* (Belfast, Blackstaff Press, 1999).

[10] Colin Harvey, *Human Rights, Equality and Democratic Renewal in Northern Ireland* (Oxford, Hart Publishing, 2001) 87.

centered upon power-sharing, and its proposed political institutions would be based on 'consociational' principles. Critics of such systems note that they tend to privilege the leaders of the most militant protagonists, reinforce a limited and essentialist version of their community identity, and sideline political identities and ideologies other than those which have ethno-nationalism as their basis. O'Leary notes that 'the terms of reference of the Belfast Agreement specify two communities only. The text of that Agreement suggests that these communities should be construed as Irish nationalist and British unionist'.[11] O'Leary accepts that this raises an issue with regard to those whose primary identification is with neither of those communities, but argues that the provisions for equality along multiple axes in section 75 of the Northern Ireland Act 1998, the human rights provisions and the provision for a consultative Civic Forum all provide opportunities for these 'others' to achieve representation. We can conclude, therefore, that the Belfast/Good Friday Agreement did not intend there to be exclusive focus on the two 'ethno-national' communities but contained provisions for the protection and promotion of the rights of women.

The peace process was in fact far from complete with the signing and ratification of the Agreement, and even with the subsequent creation of the Assembly. Lengthy, bitter and protracted negotiations and stand-offs followed until 2006, when the St Andrew's Agreement brought about the restoration of devolved government. Those negotiations were neither transparent nor inclusive, but they were extremely significant in the (re)design of devolved government for Northern Ireland. During that protracted period of negotiation, parties not associated with ethno-national identities did not 'count' in many of the critical votes, as a key feature of the structure of the Assembly was the requirement that support from parties identified with the two major ethno-national blocs was required for votes on matters they considered central. Thus sectarian divisions about the constitutional position, and not broader social justice or welfare issues, dominated the political agenda. Indeed, the new Assembly was marked by hostility and sexism towards certain women Members of the Legislative Assembly, particularly, though not exclusively, when they were introducing issues relating to gender equality.[12]

With hindsight, a weakness of the Belfast/Good Friday Agreement has been the absence of any process for monitoring implementation. Without clear targets to which all parties signed up—requiring accountability for subsequent defections and departures—the Northern Ireland parties could and did 'cherry-pick' the sections that were more acceptable to their voters and discard the 'uncomfortable' elements. As the next section indicates, the Northern Ireland courts became a venue for airing and potentially resolving disputes over how the Agreement should be implemented. In relation to the promises not delivered for women, the Carswell LCJ ruling on Evelyn White's application can be seen as a major opportunity missed. We can note that in relation to public appointments, the percentages of women appointed and women holding Chair positions have remained static in the years

[11] Brendan O'Leary, 'The Protection of Human Rights under the Belfast Agreement' (2001) 72(3) *The Political Quarterly* 353–65, 358.

[12] See among others Cera Murtagh, 'A Transient Transition: The Cultural and Institutional Obstacles Impeding the Northern Ireland Women's Coalition in its Progression from Informal to Formal Politics' (2008) 23(1) *Irish Political Studies* 21–24; and Bernadette C Hayes and Ian McAllister, 'Gender and consociational power-sharing in Northern Ireland' (2013) 34(2) *International Political Science Review* 123–39.

since the Agreement. By 2013, only 35 per cent of all public appointments and 22 per cent of Chairs of public bodies were held by women.[13]

The Interface Between Law and Politics in Northern Ireland

In the absence of agreed and/or functioning political institutions in Northern Ireland, particularly after the suspension of the Northern Ireland Parliament in 1972, the courts and the law became a forum for resolving disputes over public policy, and as such can be viewed as 'a crucial tool in the transformation' of Northern Irish society.[14] While the Agreement provided a framework for the creation of inclusive political institutions, continued political divisions and disputes over its implementation meant that there were frequent interruptions to the process, leading to the suspension of the Northern Ireland Assembly for lengthy periods. As a result, the courts continued to be the venue where difficult and contested issues of public law were resolved.[15] The decision of the Northern Ireland High Court in Evelyn White's application may be appropriately contextualised within two related lines of jurisprudence of the post-Belfast/Good Friday Agreement Northern Irish courts. First, there was a series of challenges to public appointments dealing with contentious conflict-related issues, such as the Parades Commission, the Victims Commission and the Police Service of Northern Ireland. Secondly, there was a body of litigation addressing the legal and constitutional significance of the Belfast/Good Friday Agreement and its appropriate interpretation, in terms of the Agreement itself and the Northern Ireland Act 1998 that gave legislative effect to the Agreement.

Although Carswell LCJ's interpretation of 'representative of the community' in *Re White* was intended to be *obiter*, it was in fact relied on by the Northern Ireland High Court and Court of Appeal in subsequent challenges to the representativeness of the Commission. For example, *In re Duffy*[16] concerned the Secretary of State's decision to write only to the leaders of the Loyal Orders to encourage their application to the Parades Commission, but not to write likewise to the Nationalist residents groups, and also the failure of his officials to appropriately consider in the appointment process the conflict of interest that membership of the Loyal Orders would present for the Commission members. It was averred that the Secretary of State had failed to comply with his statutory obligation to secure, so far as is practicable, a Commission that was representative of the community in Northern Ireland. It was also claimed that the Secretary of State failed to take account of a number of relevant considerations and that in writing only to the leaders of the Loyal Orders to encourage their application to the Parades Commission, but not writing to the Nationalist

[13] Michael Potter, *Women and Public Appointments Northern Ireland* (12 November 2014), Northern Ireland Assembly Research and Information Service Briefing Paper, at www.niassembly.gov.uk/globalassets/documents/raise/publications/2014/assembly_exec_review/11914.pdf).

[14] Kieran McEvoy, 'Law, Struggle and Political Transformation in Northern Ireland' (2000) 27(4) *Journal of Law and Society* 542–71, 568.

[15] See Gordon Anthony 'Public Law Litigation and the Belfast Agreement' (2002) 3(3) *European Public Law* 401–22; and Christopher McCrudden, 'Equality and the Good Friday Agreement: Fifteen Years On', UK Constitutional Law Blog (29 March 2013), at http://ukconstitutionallaw.org for discussions.

[16] *In re Duffy* [2006] NIQB 29.

residents groups, he discriminated, contrary to section 76 of the Northern Ireland Act 1998. Section 76(1) provides:

> It shall be unlawful for a public authority carrying out functions relating to Northern Ireland to discriminate, or to aid or incite another person to discriminate, against a person or class of person on the ground of religious belief or political opinion.

The application was allowed by the Northern Ireland High Court, on grounds that

> the notion of a body which is representative of the community in Northern Ireland encompasses not just diversity but also the concept of balance. That applies not just to the decision-making of the Secretary of State when he is presented with the appointable pool but also to the process by which the appointable pool is formed.[17]

Morgan J's judgment furthered the interpretation of 'representative of the community' to mean sectarian 'balance', an argument that was first advanced by Carswell LCJ in the High Court decision in *Re White.*

The Northern Ireland Court of Appeal, however, reversed the decision of the High Court in *Re Duffy*,[18] largely on the basis of the Secretary of State's broad discretion to make such appointments. Nevertheless, in the Court of Appeal, Nicholson J made a robust dissent, finding the Secretary of State in breach of section 76(1) of the Northern Ireland Act 1998. As a result of this breach, according to Nicholson J, the Secretary of State was 'unable' to comply with the requirement to exercise his powers of appointment so as to secure that as far as practicable, the membership of the Commission was representative of the community in Northern Ireland (para 19).

The feminist judgment in *Re White* relies heavily on the dissenting judgment of Nicholson J in the Northern Ireland Court of Appeal's decision in *Re Duffy* (paras 17–19), in particular in his framing of what constituted relevant considerations for the purpose of the Secretary of State's exercising his discretion to appoint the Parades Commission. In making this leap, however, the important distinctions in the protection afforded to groups defined by religious identity or political opinion and the broader equality agenda in Northern Ireland must be noted. While the statutory equality duty on public bodies to promote equality of opportunity, introduced to the jurisdiction by the Northern Ireland Act 1998, section 75, identified multiple axes of discrimination, including gender, the section 76(1) prohibition on discrimination referred only to religious belief or political opinion. Evelyn White's efforts to invoke section 76(1) in her application were rejected by Carswell LCJ, who held:

> I do not consider that the applicant has established that the Secretary of State was guilty of any discrimination against any persons on the ground of political opinion. He was scrupulous in his attempt to achieve a community balance, which reflects broadly not only religious but political differences.

It is only through supposing a bright-line distinction between gender-based and political and religious discrimination in Northern Ireland that such a conclusion was possible. It is this very distinction that the intersectional approach of the feminist judgment attempts to redress.

[17] ibid, Morgan J, para 18.
[18] *In re Duffy* [2006] NICA 28.

The House of Lords in *Re Duffy*[19] concurred with Nicholson J and reversed the majority decision of the Northern Ireland Court of Appeal, on the grounds that the Secretary of State had acted unreasonably in his approach to soliciting and considering applications from the Loyal Orders. Notable also is that the Law Lords reached this conclusion without giving any weight to section 76(1) of the Northern Ireland Act. Given the acknowledged discretion afforded to the Secretary of State in conducting public appointments, the House of Lords' concurrence on this matter is notable. *In re Duffy* is therefore significant in two respects: first, the facts of the case illustrate the lengths to which the Secretary of State was willing to go in order to achieve legitimacy for the Parades Commission in the view of the Loyal Orders (these lengths are tellingly contrasted with the absence of any particular initiatives to encourage female applicants, even after the challenge *In re White* to the failure to appoint any women); secondly, *In re Duffy* is significant in demonstrating the limits of the Secretary of State's discretion to appoint the Parades Commission. The courts were not willing to affirm the Secretary of State's unfettered discretion to appoint, and they arrived at this conclusion in a set of facts arguably no more perverse than those of *In re White*.

Conclusion

The courts in Northern Ireland may have been prepared to ensure the implementation of certain key principles of the Agreement, but they have not been capable of challenging the situation whereby ethno-national or religious identities are given priority over others. The judgment of Carswell LCJ entirely lacks the feminist awareness that one cannot mechanistically separate and oppose ethno-national identities and politics to gendered identities and politics. Feminist research and practice has demonstrated that political and social identities are always premised upon gendered hierarchies, and that it is impossible to separate 'normal' societal violence from violence arising from political conflict.[20] These feminist insights have become influential at the international level through the UN Women Peace and Security Agenda, but in Northern Ireland security continues to be understood simplistically as a matter for mainstream politics only:

> The bluntness of the language of the two communities, certainly does not cope with the feminist argument concerning the essentially 'manmade' nature of cultures and identities, which, to date, do not adequately represent the perspectives and influences of women in their more public manifestations.[21]

By imposing a rigid divide between the requirements of parity of gender representation and ethno-national representation, the judgment not only constructed an apparently

[19] *In re Duffy* [2008] UKHL 4.

[20] See, eg, the work of Cynthia Cockburn, *The Space Between Us. Negotiating Gender and National Identities in Conflict* (London, New York, Zed Books, 2001); and Laura Shepherd, *Gender Matters in Global Politics: A Feminist Introduction to International Relations* (London, Routledge, 2010) ch 1.

[21] Women into Politics: Preliminary Submission to the Northern Ireland Human Rights Commission on A Bill of Rights for Northern Ireland, cited in Siobhan Byrne, *Beyond the Ethnonational Divide: Identity Politics and Women in Northern Ireland and Israel/Palestine* (2009), PhD thesis, Queen's University, Kingston, Ontario, at https://qspace.library.queensu.ca/bitstream/1974/1671/1/Byrne_Siobhan_C_200901_PhD.pdf, 198.

gender-free image of 'the two communities', but also prioritised ethno-national identity over gender. These positions are now so entrenched that in recent times we find that peace-building 'is still considered to be a man's business, and accounts of negotiations in Northern Ireland tend to tell of political parties and paramilitaries, not of the actions of civil society and the women's movement'.[22]

In 2001, the Northern Ireland Affairs Select Committee inquired into the Parades Commission and, *inter alia*, appointments to the Commission. Referring to the circumstances and outcomes of the *In re White* case, the Committee concluded that, while 'unfortunate', it 'simply demonstrate[d] the acute shortage of suitably qualified women candidates' (para 22). More recently, the Commission for Public Appointments undertook a review of ministerial public appointments. The 2014 report confirmed that there was under-representation and a lack of diversity (in terms of gender as well as age, ethnicity and disability), and made 26 separate recommendations on how the selection process could be improved. Very little progress has been made in ameliorating the situation, as the Chief Commissioner noted.[23]

The O'Rourke LJ judgment, in contrast, understands that the Parades Commission is a public body of central importance in the processes of creating a society where citizens can be as secure as possible. O'Rourke LJ recognises that security is complex, incorporating physical and ontological dimensions that are likely to be experienced differently depending on the social location of individuals and communities. She displays awareness of the highly gendered and aggressive resistance to women who have attempted to introduce women-centered perspectives into the ethno-national negotiation and bargaining processes that have characterised Northern Irish politics throughout its history.

It is intriguing to speculate whether progress towards a genuinely inclusive appointments process would have been possible had O'Rourke LJ's judgment applied.

[22] Niki Seth-Smith, 'Why are the hopes of the Good Friday Peace Agreement still unfulfilled?' (2014) *Open Democracy*, at www.opendemocracy.net/5050/niki-sethsmith/why-are-hopes-of-good-friday-peace-agreement-still-unfulfilled.

[23] 'One year on I see no evidence of a concerted effort from the Office of First and Deputy First Minister to begin implementing this report.': John Manlie, 'Watchdog hits out at leaders over failure to reform system', *Irish News*, 16 March 2015, at www.irishnews.com/business/watchdog-hits-over-failure-to-banks-not-doing-enough-to-help-north-s-r-1419583.

In the Matter of an Application by Evelyn White for Judicial Review

[2000] NI 432, [2004] NICA 1

QUEEN'S BENCH DIVISION (CROWN SIDE)

CARSWELL LCJ

18 May 2000

COURT OF APPEAL

20 April 2001

O'ROURKE LJ. (delivering the judgment of the court)

INTRODUCTION

[**1**] The appellant in this case, Evelyn White, is an elderly woman. In her lifetime, she has seen remarkable change in Northern Ireland. As a resident of the Garvaghy Road in Portadown, a site of some of the most entrenched and robust sectarian clashes in the jurisdiction, she has perhaps seen more than most of the darker side of life in Northern Ireland, even since the Belfast/Good Friday Agreement. Indeed, the clashes at the Garvaghy Road seem hopelessly immune to the broader more positive political developments in the jurisdiction. Evelyn White, given her position at the coalface of sectarian hostility in Northern Ireland at the time of this application, might reasonably have wondered 'what peace process?'

[**2**] Evelyn White is, of course, at the centre of this case, although it is very easy to lose sight of her in more abstract discussions about 'the community' and what it means to be representative of that community and the symbolism and significance of parading to 'the community'. For parading did not have only symbolic significance to Evelyn White; it had the material power to dictate her daily movements and the movements of her family. Her daily experiences must have contrasted painfully with television images of landmark handshakes between formerly bitterly opposed political leaders, and media-friendly shots of international leaders and music stars celebrating the success of the peace agreement. Evelyn White's daily life, by contrast, consisted of helicopters constantly overhead, impeding her ability to sleep. Frequent blockades of her street meant that even accessing the most basic of foodstuffs was a challenge, not to mention the daily battles to keep younger family members indoors and away from clashes with police and protestors.

[**3**] The contrast between the high-profile political events of Northern Ireland's public life, with the ongoing disruption to the constrained private life of the appellant, is a contrast that is lived by many people—and perhaps in particular by many women on the Garvaghy Road—in this jurisdiction. The depth of the disappointment, even despair, felt by the people of Portadown, the Garvaghy Road residents and members of the Loyal Orders, that the achievement of a cross-party political agreement endorsed by popular referendum had done so little to dissipate the tension and violence of annual parading in Portadown, must have been acute.

PROCEEDINGS TO DATE

[**4**] On 19 May 2000, Carswell LCJ delivered judgment in a judicial review application by Evelyn White. Ms White had challenged the validity of the appointment by the Secretary of State for Northern Ireland of the members of the Parades Commission for Northern Ireland (the Commission). She sought a declaration that their appointment was unlawful, because the eventually constituted Commission contained no women members, which she claimed was a breach of the terms of the Public Processions (Northern Ireland) Act 1998 (the 1998 Act). Ms White is a resident of the Garvaghy Road area of Portadown.

[**5**] Ms White challenged the validity of the appointments on a number of grounds. It was averred that the Secretary of State had failed to comply with his statutory obligation under paragraph 2(3) of Schedule 1, which provides that:

> 'The Secretary of State shall so exercise his powers of appointment under
>
> this paragraph as to secure that as far as is practicable the membership of the Commission is representative of the community in Northern Ireland.'

It was also claimed that the Secretary of State had failed to take into account a number of relevant considerations and that the failure to appoint a woman constituted discrimination contrary to s 75 or 76 of the Northern Ireland Act 1998.

[**6**] At the High Court, Carswell LCJ indicated, obiter, that the obligation on the Secretary of State to appoint a Commission 'representative of the community in Northern Ireland' referred, in the context of parading, to the two sectarian blocks and not to the gender composition of the Commission. Further, on the practicability issue, because of the practical difficulties encountered and the need to appoint on merit and avoid religious imbalance, the Court held that the Minister took all steps open to him to make the Commission representative. In the circumstances, to appoint a Commission that included at least one woman would have required the appointment of a less qualified women ahead of a better qualified man, which would have been unlawful. Finally, Carswell LCJ rejected the argument that public commitments made by the Secretary of State that appointments to the Parades Commission would be consistent with the Guidance published by the Commissioner for Public Appointments gave rise to a legitimate expectation that this would be done.

[**7**] The appellant appeals against that decision on a number of grounds. The principal arguments advanced by the appellant on the hearing of the appeal may be broadly summarised as follows:-

1. The judge erred in law by interpreting the obligation to be 'representative of the community' as referring only to the sectarian blocks.
2. The judge further erred in finding that the Secretary of State did everything 'as far as practicable' to ensure that the appointments were representative of the community.
3. The judge erred in holding that the Secretary of State had acted within his scope of discretion in approaching a man from outside of the appointable pool to fill the last seat of the all-male Commission.

DOES 'REPRESENTATIVE OF THE COMMUNITY' IN THE CONTEXT OF PARADING REFER ONLY TO THE TWO SECTARIAN BLOCKS?

[**8**] Although this question was dealt with only in obiter comments by the High Court, because of its relevance to the assessment of the practicability question, I will deal with this question first.

[**9**] It is often remarked that, of the approximately 3,000 parades that take place in Northern Ireland each year, it is only a small group which give rise to dispute. Notwithstanding the relatively small number of disputed parades, the scale of the dispute can be very serious. Consequently, the Parades Commission of Northern Ireland was established in 1997 and given statutory basis in 1998.

[**10**] In the High Court, my honourable colleague Carswell LCJ expressed the view that the term 'representative of the community' referred, in the context of parading, to the two main sectarian blocks. Regrettably, the basis for this belief was given little elaboration by the Court, but appeared to rely on select sections of the North Report, published in January 1997, which led to the enactment of the Parades Commission. The North Report was commissioned by the then Secretary of State to review the current arrangements for handling public processions and open-air public meetings and associated public order issues in Northern Ireland and to make recommendations. Chapter 12 of the North Report set out a series of recommendations to the Secretary of State:

Recommended the creation of an independent body that would:

- (a) allow interested parties to put their views forward about proposed parades;
- (b) encourage them to settle difficulties locally, and where that proved impossible,
- (c) itself come to a view on what, if any, conditions should be imposed on contentiouss parades after an appropriately transparent process of examination of all the relevant issues against the background of reformed legal provisions.

The composition of the proposed commission was accepted to be of critical importance to its success (para 12.31): it would need widespread acceptance, self-confidence and an ability in its members to work together. The report went on to state:

> The Parades Commission would need to have a geographical spread and both cross-community and gender balance.

[**11**] The review body's recommendation was accepted, and a commission was established on an informal basis in March 1997. In that year the police allowed the parade to process down the Garvaghy Road, but the area was effectively sealed off and residents were confined to their homes for a number of hours. Steps were then taken to give the commission formal recognition, and in February 1998 the Public Processions (Northern Ireland) Act 1998 was enacted. This established the commission as a body with a chair (or 'chairman', as the legislation stipulates) and up to 6 members. Its duties, expressed in section 2, were in part educational and advisory but included the promotion and facilitation of mediation as a means of resolving disputes about public processions. It was empowered under the same section to facilitate mediation between parties to particular disputes, to take such other steps as might be appropriate to resolve such disputes and to issue determinations in respect of particular proposed public processions. It was to issue a code of conduct for those organising or taking part in public processions or public meetings and to issue procedural

rules and guidelines. Under section 8 it had power to impose conditions on those organising or taking part in proposed public processions, prescribing among other things the route to be followed. Criminal penalties attached to wilful breach of conditions imposed by the commission. Relevant for present purposes is paragraph 2(3) of Schedule 1 to the Act:

> The Secretary of State shall so exercise his powers of appointment under this paragraph as to secure that as far as is practicable the membership of the Commission is representative of the community in Northern Ireland.

[**12**] In the lower court, Carswell LCJ indicated at page 440 that he was:

> not altogether persuaded that the phrase 'representative of the community' in paragraph 2(3) of Schedule 1 to the 1998 Act was intended to mean that there should be gender balance, or at least some representation … The phrase in question does not refer to gender or to the make-up of the population of the Province. It refers specifically to 'the community', which in the context of parades is constantly used to denote the different sectarian blocks—see, for example, the reference in paragraph 1.15 and 1.16 of the North Report to 'another part of our community' and 'the other part of the community', which are plainly references to the sectarian divide.

Carswell LCJ's interpretation of the meaning attached to the term 'community' in the North Report is based on a partial and selective reading of said report. Contrary to the assertion that community refers in the report to the sectarian blocks, 'community' is given many and varied meanings throughout the report. While there is indeed reference to 'the two parts of the community', 'communities' is also used in a plural sense to refer to the communities living in the various areas of contested marches in Northern Ireland (para 1.17), 'the various parts of the community' referring to more than two sides (para 1.38). Moreover, the Report recognizes internal diversity within different parts of the community ('some sections of the Nationalist part of the community have felt excluded from those discussions over their future', para 1.41). Throughout the Report, 'community' is frequently used to refer all individuals living in Northern Ireland, that is one single community ('the community', passim). I do not agree, therefore, with my honourable colleague's reliance on the North Report to ground a belief that the reference to the community in the legislation refers only to the sectarian blocks. This is a question that merits further interrogation and reflection.

[**13**] The appointments to the first Parades Commission were also the subject of judicial review on the grounds of 'representativeness'. *In the Matter of an Application for Judicial Review by Jane Elizabeth Armstrong* (Unreported. Belfast High Court, 3rd and 29th April 1998), it was argued on behalf of the applicant that two of the Catholic appointments were 'non-nationalist Catholics' and thus failed to provide an adequate counter-balance to the two Loyalist appointees and thus the two Catholic appointees were not 'representative' of the community which they appeared to have been selected to represent. The application was ultimately unsuccessful, but the case raised the vital question of whether the term 'representative' implied that the Commission should be an exact mirror-image of society on political, religious, gender or geographical grounds. The judge held (in relation to the two Catholic appointees) that 'representative of the community' was not necessarily achieved by choosing candidates to be pitted against one another. Rather, candidates should be representative of 'a wide spectrum and broad diversity'. Of further significance in this regard is the recognition by the North Report of the diversity of parades conducted each year in

Northern Ireland. Relying on Royal Ulster Constabulary statistics, the Report notes that of the 1996 parades, 2,404 were held by organisations identified as Loyalist, 230 by Nationalist organisations, and 526 by 'others', the last designation referred to, for example, marches by guides and scouts and trade unions (para 3.1). The Report itself noted that 'there would be merit in there being a rather fuller breakdown of these categories, to reflect more fully the diversity of organisations and parades' (para 3.47). The North Report also dedicated extensive discussion to 'the views of other interested parties', recognizing that not just marching groups and residents had a stake in the issue and were impacted by parading disputes, for example peace constituencies and business people (6.18–6.30).

[**14**] Contrary to High Court's determination that parading in Northern Ireland 'referred to the two Sectarian blocks', therefore, it is clear that there is much greater diversity evident in parading in the jurisdiction. While parading in Northern Ireland is typically regarded as a male activity, parades routinely include women. For example, a distinct women's organisation grew up out of the Orange Order. Called the Association of Loyal Orangewomen of Ireland, this organisation was revived in December 1911 having been dormant since the late 1880s. They have risen in prominence in recent years, largely due to protests in Drumcree. The women's order is parallel to the male order, and participates in its parades as much as the males apart from 'all male' parades and 'all ladies' parades respectively. The contribution of women to the Orange Order is recognised in the song 'Ladies Orange Lodges O!' There is considerable evidence of the operation of flourishing of the Association since the early 1900s. *Laws and ordnances [*sic*] of the Association of Loyal Orange women of Ireland* was published in 1888. Having become somewhat dormant thereafter, the organisation experienced a revival in 1911 and has been active ever since. In addition to the Association of Loyal Orange Women of Ireland, there is also a Junior Orange Women's Association of Ireland. By the Orange Order's own figures, there are over 100 lodges of the Association of Loyal Orange Women, with over 2,500 members. Information on the gender profile of other groups and organisations engaged in parades (e.g. nationalist organisations commemorating the Easter Rising, or trade union marches to mark May Day) is unfortunately not as readily available, but a Ladies Ancient Order of Hibernians and a female auxiliary to the Ancient Order, known as the Daughters of Erin, are documented. There is little reason to believe that women are not present in significant numbers within those groups and organisations also.

[**15**] Moreover, it is clear that women as well as men are impacted by decisions of the Parades Commission. Unlike my distinguished colleague in the High Court, I have had the advantage of seeing the exhaustive report of the Rosemary Nelson Inquiry before arriving at my determination in this decision. The report is instructive for several reasons, not least in capturing the exigent circumstances that form the backdrop to this judicial review, that is the profound disturbance to daily life posed by the contentious parades to all residents of Portadown, the extreme—often violent—hostility faced by the marchers, and the impact of this apparently local disturbance on political and public life throughout the jurisdiction. Indeed, the Rosemary Nelson Inquiry Report noted that:

> There were fears that Drumcree had the potential to derail the Peace Process. One senior Northern Ireland Office official told us: 'Drumcree had become a microcosm for political and other issues in Northern Ireland. Ifwe were unable to resolve this issue, then a lot of other things could fall apart. Drumcree had shown its potential to act like a septic sore, poisoning Northern Ireland and damaging the political settlement process, with the risk

of de-stabilising the Good Friday Agreement'. The Prime Minister was advised on 25 June 1998 that it was 'not impossible that Drumcree could lead to the collapse of the whole [Good Friday] Agreement' (para 7.6).

[**16**] That the stakes were high in Drumcree in 1998 is a matter of public record. From these brief, though revealing, comments, it is surely clear that the subject matter of the Parades Commission is anything but a narrow sectarian matter. Rather, parading stands at the centre of the process to end Northern Ireland's three decades of violence and to secure a peaceful, democratic and inclusive political dispensation for the benefit of the entire community. Women are regular participants in parades. Moreover, women's daily lives, in particular in sites of contentious parades, are heavily shaped by decisions to permit, deny or re-route parades. Women have a fundamental interest in the operation, deliberation and effectiveness of the Parades Commission.

[**17**] I conclude, therefore, that the judge erred in law in determining that, in the context of parading, 'representative of the community' referred only to the sectarian blocks. This question is not, however, determinative of the merits of the appeal. The Court must further consider whether the Secretary of State operated within the scope of his discretion in failing to appoint any women to the Commission and whether he acted 'as far as practicable' to ensure the representativeness of the Commission.

WHAT IS THE SCOPE OF THE SECRETARY OF STATE'S DISCRETION TO APPOINT?

[**18**] It was stated by the lower court, and is affirmed here, that the Secretary of State is afforded wide discretion by the Parades Commission Act Schedule 2(3) in making appointments to the Commission. It is in my view clear that the statutory discretion given to the Secretary of State to secure that as far as is practicable the membership of the Commission is representative of the community in Northern Ireland gives him a wide discretion in relation to the interests which he can take into account. This demonstrates the diversity of interests which the Secretary of State is entitled to take into account and is consistent with the respondent's position that his decision is an evaluative judgment. I accept the respondent's argument that appointments to the Commission belong to a category of decisions where the threshold for judicial intervention is high. A large area of discretion is available to the decision-maker particularly because of the political content of the decision. It is the court's function only to ascertain whether the decider has taken into account the correct considerations and made the decision within the proper parameters by correct application of the law. The proper parameters of the Secretary of State's discretion are set out by the legislation:

> The Secretary of State shall so exercise his powers of appointment under this paragraph as to secure that as far as is practicable the membership of the Commission is representative of the community in Northern Ireland.

[**19**] It is evident, however, that the proper parameters of the Secretary of State's discretion were altered by the Secretary of State and erroneously affirmed by the High Court. Whereas the legislation refers to the qualified requirement for the appointments to be 'representative of the community', this was in fact interpreted to mean the achievement of 'religious balance' in the composition of the Commission. In both the submissions to the

Court, and in the High Court's presentation of the legal issues to be addressed in the case, this altering of the terms of the Secretary of State's discretion is apparent. To draw on the High Court's dealing with this issue, when the recruitment process resulted in an uneven number of Catholic and Protestant members and no female members:

> The Secretary of State was then faced with the necessity to adopt one of several possible courses of action, none of which was ideal. He considered and rejected the following as undesirable, for the reasons set out against each:
>
> (a) to go to the reserve list—as the persons on this list were all Protestants, the appointment of one of them would have meant an undesirable *religious imbalance* in the membership of the Commission;
> (b) to appoint a Catholic female who did not get on to the reserve list—he considered that it would be contrary to the requirements of the general law prohibiting discrimination on grounds of sex or religion to appoint a woman who was not as well qualified as those on the reserve list (and did not reach the merit threshold for the post) in order to maintain a *religious balance*;
> (c) to put back the date on which the new Commission was to take up office—there would then have been a period of indeterminate length when no Commission was in operation;
> (d) to let the new Commission commence its work without filling the vacancy—it would then have operated for a period with a *religious imbalance* until a suitable appointment could be made.

[**20**] From the submissions to Court and the reasoning of the lower court, it is clear that the Secretary of State and the High Court had substituted the qualified requirement of community representativeness with a requirement of 'religious balance'. The scope of the Secretary of State's discretion is wide, but he or she is not free to alter the terms (or proper parameters) of the statutory discretion. There is no judicial authority for so interpreting 'representative of the community'. Indeed, the authority that does exist is directly contrary to this narrowing of the 'representativeness' standard and instead interprets representative of the community to mean 'a wide spectrum and broad diversity' (*In re Armstrong*). The question remains as to whether the Secretary of State acted 'as far as practicable' to ensure that the Commission was representative of the community, where 'representativeness' is not reduced to meaning 'sectarian balance'.

DID THE SECRETARY OF STATE ACT 'AS FAR AS PRACTICABLE' TO ENSURE REPRESENTATIVENESS?

[**21**] The under-representation of women is a stark fact of Northern Irish public life. Indeed, it was an issue specifically identified for redress in the Belfast/Good Friday Agreement, which guaranteed 'the right of women to full and equal political participation' (6.1), although this provision was not included in the Northern Ireland Act 1998 which gave legislative effect to the peace agreement. The irony is not lost on this member of the bench of this Court, as its first female appointment, to adjudicate on the lawfulness of the failure to appoint any women to the Parades Commission. While the recent years of the peace process and new institutions established by the Belfast Agreement have offered promise in many respects, the seeming immutability of the under-representation of women within public

appointments in the jurisdiction persists. Indeed, the percentage of women in overall public appointments has in fact fallen since the signing of the Belfast Agreement. In 1998, 35% of the membership of public boards in Northern Ireland was made up of women; in 2000, that percentage had reduced to 32%.

[**22**] Even compared to this unsatisfactorily low percentage of women in public appointments in the jurisdiction generally, the number of female applicants to the Parades Commission was particularly low. The term of office of the first chair and members of the Commission was due to expire on 18 February 2000. In October 1999 the Secretary of State put in train the process of appointment of a fresh set of members, to take up office on 19 February 2000 for a two-year term. Advertisements inviting applications for appointment were placed in the press in early October 1999, setting out the function of the Commission and the terms of appointment of the members. The advertisement described the skills required for membership of the Commission as: assessing/evaluating; decision-making; team working; and presentation. A total of 82 persons applied for membership of the Commission, of which 46, or 83%, were male and only 14, or 17%, were female. An interview panel considered the applications against the advertised criteria for appointment and shortlisted 23 candidates for interview, of whom three (13%), were female, thus further reducing the proportion of women under consideration. Further to interview, 16 candidates were deemed appointable, consisting of 13 Protestant males, one Catholic male, one Protestant female and one Catholic female, thus further reducing the proportion of women eligible for appointment to 12.5%. These 16 persons were ranked by merit, and the Secretary of State was recommended to appoint the first six. Those six persons consisted of four Protestant males, one Catholic male and one Catholic female. The reserve list, being the remainder of the 16 ranked persons, then consisted of one Protestant female and the rest were Protestant males.

[**23**] The Secretary of State accepted the panel's advice and the Northern Ireland Office (NIO) approached the six persons selected. Initially all of them indicated their willingness to accept appointment, and arrangements were made to announce the composition of the new Commission. Three days before the announcement, the female appointee informed the NIO that she would not accept an offer of appointment. In the event, as established by the High Court, the Secretary of State decided that in the exceptional circumstances which had arisen that the NIO should approach a person directly who they judged met the necessary competences. On this basis, an existing male Catholic member of the Commission who had not applied for membership was approached but he declined to consider appointment. An approach was then made to Mr Peter Quinn, who had considerable experience in the context of the parades issue and had been a facilitator in talks concerning the Drumcree parade in 1998 and 1999. The Secretary of State met Mr Quinn personally on 7 February 2000 and Mr Quinn indicated that he would accept appointment.

[**24**] The Secretary of State is enjoined by paragraph 2(3) of Schedule 1 to the 1998 Act to ensure that the membership of the Commission is representative of the community 'as far as practicable'. I concur with the interpretation of this requirement adopted by my honourable colleague Lord Chief Justice Carswell in the High Court. 'Practicable' is a more stringent standard than 'reasonably practicable', see, e.g., *Gregson v. Hick Hargreaves & Co Ltd* [1955] 3 All ER 507, at 516, per Parker LJ. I concur with Carswell LCJ's assessment that 'practicable' in many contexts 'means feasible, which is probably the nearest to a synonym

for the term'. In line with Carswell LCJ, I take notice of the judgment of Boreham J in *Brookes v J & P Coats Ltd* [1984] 1 All ER 702 at 719, where he was dealing with a factory occupier's statutory duty under section 121 of the Factories Act 1961 to make effective and suitable provision to render harmless, so far as practicable, all such fumes, dust etc as might be injurious to health. He stated in the course of his judgment:

> I take practicable in this context to mean a precaution which could be taken or undertaken without practical difficulty.

[**25**] In the present context, the obligation placed upon the Secretary of State to ensure the representative nature of the membership of the Commission is qualified by the provision that it is to be representative of the community as far as is practicable. Certain practical limits are placed by the small size of the Commission upon his ability to make the membership representative. The need to observe the merit principle in appointments constitutes another very important practical constraint.

[**26**] The lower court's formulation of the Secretary of State's options as to appoint either 'a less qualified woman' or 'a better qualified man' is wrong on the facts and flawed on the law. The lower court erred in interpreting that the appointment of a less qualified candidate than those on the reserve list was the only option open to the Secretary of State if he wished to appoint a woman. In fact, when the public appointments process failed to deliver an equal 'balance' of Catholic and Protestant representatives, the Secretary of State and his officials chose to move entirely outside that process and to directly approach an individual, Mr Quinn, whom they considered desirable for the position and whose appointment would secure the desired sectarian 'balance' of the Commission. The respondents failed, however, to consider whether approaching a Catholic woman would be appropriate, in light of the absence of any women on the Commission. Once the Secretary of State moved outside of the appointable pool identified through independent assessment and the normal procedures of the Office of the Commissioner for Public Appointments (OCPA), he was not limited to choosing between only 'a less qualified woman' or 'a better qualified man' and the High Court erred in accepting this formulation of the respondent's options. Rather, the respondent was free to approach anyone judged to meet the necessary competences and furtherethe objective of appointing a Commission that was 'representative of the community, as far as practicable'. Based on an erroneous interpretation of what constitutes 'the community' in the context of parading, and based on a flawed formulation of the options open to the Secretary of State, the respondents failed to consider approaching a Catholic woman to fill the sixth seat on the Commission.

[**27**] No reasonable person, knowing of the importance of parading decision-making and the recognized value of including women in this decision-making, could have failed to consider approaching a woman in these circumstances in order to secure a Commission that is 'representative of the community'. The respondents do not appear to have considered whether a suitably qualified woman could have been identified and approached for the sixth position. They do not appear to have considered whether the activities and decisions of a body including no women would command widespread acceptance among the general public. Had these matters been addressed, as in my opinion they plainly should have been, the conclusion would have been reached (and certainly should have been reached) that appropriate efforts were necessary to consider a suitably qualified woman for the final

position on the Commission. It was one thing to ensure that the sectarian balance was maintained within the Commission, but quite another to fail to consider approaching a suitably qualified female candidate in the circumstances.

[**28**] I consider therefore that the appointment process of the sixth member of the Commission was unlawful in that the Secretary of State's officials failed to take into account a material consideration as a result of which they failed to secure as far as was practicable that member of the Commission was representative of the community in Northern Ireland. It is not enough that a consideration is one that may properly be taken into account, nor even that it is one which many people, including the court itself, would have taken into account if they had to make the decision. If there are matters so obviously material to a decision that anything short of direct consideration of them by a minister would not be in accordance with the intention of the Act they would constitute relevant considerations to be taken into account. I am satisfied that the decision of the Secretary of State was flawed because he relied on the absence of an appropriately qualified woman in the reserve pool as sufficient evidence to ground a belief that no such woman was available anywhere in the jurisdiction. A similar conclusion was not drawn from the absence of an appropriately qualified Catholic man in the reserve list. This was a matter so obviously material to the decision which was taken to appoint Mr Quinn that failure to take it into consideration was not in accordance with the content of the 1998 Act. As a result, the Secretary of State was unable to comply with paragraph 2(3) of Schedule 1 to the 1998 Act whereby he was required to exercise his powers of appointment so as to secure that as far as was practicable the membership of the Commission was representative of the community in Northern Ireland.

[**29**] In the context of appointments to the Parades Commission, the choice of six men and no women upsets the balance to such an extent as to render the membership of the Commission unrepresentative of the community. I cannot accept the proposition that if one appoints no women, yet nevertheless maintains a sectarian balance, one is securing as far as practicable a Commission which is representative of the community in Northern Ireland. I feel bound to conclude that the decision to appoint Mr Quinn, without giving due consideration to the appointment of a suitably qualified woman, was one which a reasonable Secretary of State could not have made if properly directing himself on the law, if seized of the relevant facts and inaking account of considerations which, in this context, he was bound to take into account. The appointment was therefore unlawful.

[**30**] It is clear that the difficulty in appointing a suitably qualified female is linked to the small number of female applicants to the Commission. It seems reasonable to conclude that it was this particularly low number of female applicants to the Parades Commission that likely contributed to the perception that there were few appropriately qualified women and the Secretary of State's judgment that his only option was to appoint 'a less qualified woman' or a 'better qualified man'. That the Secretary of State found it plausible that no suitably-qualified Catholic woman was available in Northern Ireland also raises profound questions about the qualification criteria attached to these appointments. While women are under-represented across public appointments in the jurisdiction (32%), the dearth of female applicants to the Parades Commission is striking (17%). In dealing with the police, the Loyal Orders, the Parades Commission, the Secretary of State and, indeed, this Court, the belief that all relevant decision-making is undertaken by men must have been powerful for the applicant and her associates. The High Court's determination that parading engages

'the sectarian blocks' and that the obligation on the Secretary of State is therefore to ensure 'sectarian balance' in appointments to the Commission no doubt further compounded a view of decision-making in parading as an exclusively male activity. The good work of non-governmental organisations in the jurisdiction such as Democratic Dialogue demonstrates that, while women are no less likely than men to be politically active, such as in the community and voluntary sector, women have much less access to political activities associated with power (Democratic Dialogue, *Power, Politics and Positionings*, 1996). The participation of women in parading throughout the jurisdiction and the impact of parading on the lives of women, at the same time as their exclusion from relevant decision-making is judged to be lawful, is another example of this dynamic. The murder of Rosemary Nelson, a lawyer prominent in legal action concerning parading, was a chilling and powerful message to women who sought to challenge this status quo of exclusively male decision-making. The applicant and her associates were no doubt constantly aware of robust, often violent, resistance to efforts by women to influence parading decision-making. This court cannot collude in the further marginalization of half of the population from the decision-making that shapes their lives by judging the respondent's behaviour in this appointment process to be 'reasonable'.

[**31**] The Code of Practice for Ministerial Appointments sets out that 'All public appointments should be governed by the overriding principle of selection based on merit' (2.2). Further, 'no one who has not been reviewed by an Independent Assessor should be listed' within the appointable pool (2.3). The principle of independent scrutiny is the second of the seven principles underpinning the Code of Practice. Merit is indeed the correct and fitting touchstone for all public appointments, but this Court cannot endorse an understanding of merit that permits the exclusion of the skills, knowledge and perspectives of women. Merit is not the antithesis of diversity, rather the principle of diversity is critical for securing a meritorious Commission. The Guidance further provides that, where circumstances arrive that are not covered by the Guidance, the Commissioner's Office should be consulted (1.6). In the High Court, Carswell LCJ at page 440 appeared to give considerable weight to the fact that the Commissioner for Public Appointments gave her approval:

> She gave her approval to the method of appointment, stating that she was satisfied that the NIO had made every effort to ensure both that the Commission was representative of the community, as far as was practicable, and had been appointed on merit.

Having defended his actions on the basis that the appointments to the Parades Commission is not governed by the Commissioner for Public Appointments, the Secretary of State cannot now seek validation in having relied on the advice of that Office. It is the Court's view that it was due only to the erroneous interpretation of 'representative of the community' identified above that the Commissioner for Public Appointments arrived at this conclusion.

[**32**] For the reasons elaborated above, the Secretary of State failed to ensure that the appointments to the Parades Commission were representative of the community, as far as practicable.

THE INTERVENTION OF THE NORTHERN IRELAND HUMAN RIGHTS COMMISSION

[**33**] The intervention by the Northern Ireland Human Rights Commission (NIHRC) on behalf of the appellant has been the subject of some contention. While not the specific subject of appeal in this case, given the fledgling nature of the NIHRC and its nascent role in making interventions in judicial proceedings, I feel it necessary to comment on the High Court's treatment of the NIHRC written intervention. It is clear from his judgment that Carswell LCJ did not consider the NIHRC's written submission, with its discussion of the relevant international treaties to which the UK is party, to add anything of consequence to address the specific issues before the court. In this case, the NIHRC's written submissions identified provisions of the International Covenant on Civil and Political Rights, the Convention on the Elimination of All Forms of Discrimination Against Women and the Convention on the Political Rights of Women, relevant to the rights of women to political participation. This particular issue remains of considerable importance to society in Northern Ireland as a whole.

[**34**] Even if the NIHRC's intervention does not affirm the position of one of the parties, such a role will have been adjudged by the Commissioners as important for securing the role of human rights in Northern Ireland. For the appellant in this action in particular, challenging as she is the exclusion of women from public decision-making, the fact of the NIHRC's intervention provides a powerful reassurance that official bodies take these claims seriously. However frustrating some of my colleagues might find an element of generality in submissions before the Court, this is a small price to pay for the societal benefits thereby secured. I would therefore disagree with, and indeed deplore, any effort to disparage the role of the NIHRC in bringing the Court's attention to the international legal commitments of the UK in this regard.

13

Commentary on *Lobe v Minister for Justice, Equality and Law Reform*

HILKKA BECKER

Social, Policy and Legal Context

In the 1990 Supreme Court decision in the case of *Fajujonu v Minister for Justice and Another*,[1] Keane CJ clarified that

> whereas the parents who are not citizens and who are aliens cannot, by reason of their having as members of their family children born in Ireland who are citizens, claim any constitutional right of a particular kind to remain in Ireland, they are entitled to assert a choice of residence on behalf of their infant children, in the interest of those infant children.

The Court further determined that any reason justifying the removal from the state of the Fajujonu family, three of whom were Irish citizens, would have to be 'grave and substantial' and 'associated with the common good'.

Walsh J, in his ruling in *Fajujonu*, highlighted that 'it is abundantly clear that citizens of this state may not be deported' and that

> if the … parents of the infant children are deported, the effect must be that their children who are Irish citizens are faced with the choice of remaining within this state as they are entitled to do so and therefore in effect being compulsorily separated from their parents, or having to leave the state with their parents and thus ceasing to have the benefit of all the protection afforded by the laws and the Constitution of this state.

Following the *Fajujonu* decision, parents of children born in Ireland were routinely granted permission to remain in the state, without families necessarily having resided in Ireland for a long period or an offer of employment being in place. However, as the numbers of immigrants into the state grew and more parents lodged applications for permission to remain on the basis of their parentage of an Irish citizen child, the Government began to refuse residence permit applications.

[1] *Fajujonu v Minister for Justice and Another* [1990] 2 IR 151.

This change of policy occurred in the context of a sharp rise in applications for refugee status, from 424 in 1995 to 11,634 in 2002.[2] Moreover, a significant number of asylum applications were being withdrawn due to applicants' having children born in the state who were entitled to Irish citizenship under the *jus soli* principle, then enshrined in Article 2 of the Irish Constitution. From 1996 to 23 January 2003, 10,584 persons were granted permission to remain on the basis of their parentage of an Irish citizen child.[3] As at 19 February 2003, 11,493 applications were pending. Of these, 996 applications were returned as parents had an alternative legal basis to remain in the state.[4] According to a statement made by the Minister for Justice, Equality and Law Reform in November 2003, it was 'likely that the majority of the remaining applicants will be issued with letters under the terms of section 3(3) of the Immigration Act 1999, as amended, informing them of the Minister's intention to deport'.[5]

Prior to this, in December 2001, following the separate initiation of High Court proceedings in the *Lobe* and *Osayande* cases,[6] *The Irish Times* reported that, 'faced with a surge in births to asylum-seekers—running at about 3,000 a year—the Department of Justice is seeking to break the link that up to now has given residency to the parents of an Irish-born child, no matter where they come from'. The report further stated that 'short of a constitutional amendment, there is nothing the Department can do about the automatic entitlement of a child born here to Irish citizenship'. The issue was described as a 'political hot potato', leading to a situation where 'now, for the first time, the Department is seeking to deport some parents of Irish born children', concentrating initially on recent arrivals.[7]

Lobe and Osayande—the Supreme Court Decision

The *Lobe* and *Osayande* cases arose from a refusal of the Refugee Applications Commissioner (ORAC), affirmed by the Refugee Appeals Tribunal (RAT), which determined that both sets of applicants' asylum claims should be processed in other Member States pursuant to the Dublin Convention[8] and that the applicants should be removed to those countries.

The applicants challenged these decisions by way of judicial review. Both families had Irish children, and they argued that, pursuant to Article 2 and Article 40.3.1 of the Constitution, those children (Kevin Lobe and Osaze Osayande) had a right to reside in Ireland with their parents, and that the families had rights under Articles 41.1.1, 41.2 and 42 of the

[2] Emma Quinn, *Handbook on Immigration and Asylum in Ireland 2007* (Economic and Social Research Institute, Research Series Number 5, Dublin 2008), 12.

[3] Dáil Debates, vol 575, no 3, 25 November 2003.

[4] ibid.

[5] ibid.

[6] *Lobe and Osayande v Minister for Justice, Equality and Law Reform* (High Court, 8 April 2002).

[7] 'Surge in births leads to Department move', *The Irish Times*, 1 December 2001, at www.irishtimes.com/news/surge-in-births-leads-to-department-move-1.339973 (last accessed 11 September 2015).

[8] Convention determining the State responsible for examining applications for asylum lodged in one of the Member States of the European Communities [1997] OJ C254/1 (now replaced by Regulation (EU) No 604/2013, establishing the criteria and mechanisms for determining the Member State responsible for examining an application for international protection lodged in one of the Member States by a third-country national or a stateless person (recast)).

Constitution. The circumstances of the families are explored in some detail in the feminist judgment, although the cases were treated by the state and by the Supreme Court as test cases, with little attention given to the families' lived experiences. In the High Court, Smyth J referred to the cases as 'a random sample of a large number of cases'.[9] The High Court refused judicial review, and held that there were grave and substantial reasons associated with the common good that required that the residence of the parents within the state should be terminated, even though, in order to remain a family unit, their children would also have to leave the state.

The seven-judge Supreme Court was split 5:2, with the majority judges (in particular Keane CJ, Murray J and Hardiman J) emphasising the wide powers of the state to maintain the integrity of the asylum and immigration system in the light of the 'major changes in Ireland'[10] that had occurred since the decision in *Fajujonu*.

In contrast, the two dissenting judges centre their judgments on the children's citizenship and the rights flowing therefrom. As McGuinness J put it, 'some import and meaning must be given to the concept of the birthright of the Irish born person and to the declaration that such a person is part of the Irish nation; it is not a mere shibboleth'.[11] Fennelly J agreed that Article 2 of the Constitution, enshrining this birthright, represented 'a particularly strong and solemn declaration made very deliberately by the people in referendum'.[12] Both disagreed with the proposition that the decision in *Fajujonu* was 'a type of sympathetic aberration'[13] that could be easily distinguished on the basis of the length of time the family had spent in the state. McGuinness J opined that there would need to be specific evidence of a clear danger to the common good, related to the parents concerned, before the parents of an Irish child could be deported;[14] and Fennelly J was of the view that 'the need to preserve the asylum and immigration system is an abstract, open-ended administrative reason that could not satisfy the test proposed in *Fajujonu*'.[15]

The Aftermath

In the aftermath of the Supreme Court's decision in *Lobe and Osayande* in January 2003, the Government suspended its practice of granting residency to parents of Irish citizen children, leaving a total of 10,497 persons in limbo with pending applications for permission to remain. In July of that year, the Department of Justice, Equality and Law Reform began issuing notifications of intention to deport parents who had no legal basis for remaining in the state other than their Irish citizen child(ren). By late 2003, up to 700 such notifications had been issued, and by late 2004, 37 parents had been deported from the state.[16] The Irish Human Rights Commission expressed concern that 'the issue of deportation letters and

[9] Smyth J in *Lobe and Osayande v Minister for Justice, Equality and Law Reform* (High Court, 8 April 2002).
[10] Keane CJ in *Lobe and Osayande v Minister for Justice, Equality and Law Reform* [2003] 1 IR 1, at 25.
[11] McGuinness J, ibid, at 99.
[12] Fennelly J, ibid, at 181.
[13] McGuinness J, ibid, at 120.
[14] McGuinness J, ibid, at 122.
[15] Fennelly J, ibid, at 102.
[16] Dáil Debates, vol 593, no 2, 24 November 2004.

the resulting uncertainty about their future has caused alarm and distress not only to the actual recipients but also among the wider community of non-national parents in similar situations'.[17]

In November 2003, the Minister had voiced concern

> at the abuse of Irish citizenship law by persons with no connection to the State arriving in Ireland with the sole objective of giving birth to a child who will, as a result of being born in Ireland, be entitled to Irish citizenship.

He highlighted that

> Ireland is the only member state of the European Union which grants citizenship to a child based solely on its birth on the national territory. In all other member states the citizenship of a child is dependent on the citizenship of the parents and/or the status and duration of residence in the member state concerned.

Against this background, a referendum on the 27th Amendment of the Constitution, designed to effectively dilute the pure form of birthright citizenship contained in Article 2, took place in June 2004. During the referendum campaign, a number of prominent legal academics expressed deep concern that the amendment would leave Irish citizen children of non-Irish national parents in a precarious position regarding constitutional rights.[18] The Irish Human Rights Commission also expressed concern about the implications of the proposed amendment.[19] The speed of the whole process and lack of public consultation prior to the announcement of the referendum was also criticised.[20]

In spite of the considerable controversy engendered by the proposed amendment, the referendum was passed by a 3:1 majority in June 2004, and Article 9 of the Constitution was amended, with paragraph 2.1 now providing:

> [N]otwithstanding any other provision of this Constitution, a person born in the island of Ireland, which includes its islands and seas, who does not have, at the time of the birth of that person, at least one parent who is an Irish citizen or entitled to be an Irish citizen is not entitled to Irish citizenship or nationality, unless provided for by law.

A subsequent change in the Irish Nationality and Citizenship Act 1956 then limited access to citizenship for children born in Ireland to non-Irish national parents only to those children with a parent who had, during the period of four years immediately preceding the child's birth, been resident in the island of Ireland for a period of not less than three years or periods the aggregate of which was not less than three years.[21]

In order to deal with the backlog of pending applications as well as with new applications from parents of Irish citizen children who were born in the state prior to the amendment of the citizenship legislation coming into force on 1 January 2005, the Government

[17] Irish Human Rights Commission, *Position of Non-National Parents and their Irish-Born Children* (21 October 2003), at: www.ihrec.ie/download/pdf/sub_nonnational_parents_200310.pdf (last accessed 11 September 2015).

[18] See the proceedings of a conference hosted by Trinity College Law School, 'The Citizenship Referendum: Implications for the Constitution and Human Rights' (Trinity College Dublin, May 2004), available to order at www.tcd.ie/Law/events/past-conferences.php (last accessed 11 September 2015).

[19] 'Commission "concerned" over citizenship referendum', *The Irish Times*, 25 May 2004, at www.irishtimes.com/news/commission-concerned-over-citizenship-referendum-1.980255 (last accessed 11 September 2015).

[20] Lorna Siggins, 'Referendum a Railroading Affair', *The Irish Times*, 15 May 2004, at http://www.irishtimes.com/news/referendum-a-railroading-affair-1.1140540 (last accessed 11 September 2015).

[21] Irish Nationality and Citizenship Act 1956, s 6A(1) (as amended).

introduced the so-called IBC/05 Scheme. Under this administrative scheme, 17,917 applications for permission to remain in the state were made, 16,993 parents were granted residence permits, while the remaining 1,119 applications were refused.[22] Reasons for refusal included failure to prove continuous residence in the state since the child's birth, failure to prove identity, criminality and a parent not actually having a role in the upbringing of the child.[23]

The Feminist Judgment

In their feminist judgment, Siobhán Mullally and Cliodhna Murphy refuse to yield to the 'appalling floodgates vista' presented by the respondents in these cases, and find in favour of the appellants on the basis of their rights as families as protected by the Constitution and, in line with Ireland's obligations under international law, Article 8 of the European Convention on Human Rights and Fundamental Freedoms. With reference to the *Sinnott* case, in which the Supreme Court, in 2001, overturned a High Court ruling that an autistic man had an entitlement to education for as long as it was beneficial, irrespective of age,[24] they highlight that

> a breach by the State of the rights of one member of the family unit could have a disproportionately negative impact upon the family, and particularly on the person [or persons] charged with the primary care of the family.

Unlike the Supreme Court's decision in *Lobe and Osayande*, the feminist judgment in this chapter not only assesses the rights of the Irish citizen children involved in these cases from a viewpoint of their Irish citizenship, but also evaluates their rights as citizens of the European Union (EU) under then Article 17 TEC (now Article 20 TFEU). The judgment finds that in order to ensure that the children can effectively vindicate their rights as citizens of the EU within their own country of nationality, it is necessary to recognise a derivative right of residence of their parents who are primary carers.

From a feminist perspective, the rewritten judgment aims directly to critique the gendered nature of the legal reasoning put forward by the state and reflected in the majority judgments. The implicit characterisation of the asylum-seeking woman as 'opportunistic reproducer'[25] is particularly troubling, and tackling this narrative is a central element of the feminist judgment.

The key finding of the majority of the Supreme Court is its endorsement of the decision in *Fajujonu* that a compelling reason is required to deport the parents of an Irish child, and the Court's acceptance that a general need to protect the integrity of the asylum and immigration systems constitutes a sufficiently compelling reason. In turn, finding that such a general need is raised by the circumstances of these cases effectively requires the Court to

[22] Figures as reproduced in *Bode v Minister for Justice, Equality and Law Reform & Anor* [2007] IESC 62, para 7, based on cases completed by 31 January 2006.

[23] ibid.

[24] *Sinnott v Minister for Education* [2001] IESC 63.

[25] John A Harrington, 'Citizenship and the Biopolitics of Post-Nationalist Ireland' (2005) 32(3) *Journal of Law and Society* 424–49, 442.

accept that pregnant asylum-seekers are a threat to the common good and the integrity of the asylum and immigration system, simply by virtue of the fact that they could give birth to a citizen child. This argument of the state was a sleight of hand: the suggestions as to exactly how these families undermine the integrity of the system were vague. Fennelly J, in his judgment, draws attention to this problem, reminding us that the respondent Minister did not provide any concrete information or statistics on the impact of asylum-seekers on the state, or any form of cost–benefit analysis in this regard.[26]

Both dissenting judges reject the state's reasoning (as well as that of the majority) but do not address the gendered aspects head on. Drawing on feminist critiques of legal liberalism, the feminist judgment seeks to fill that gap.

As Hunter explains, the concept of legal liberalism refers to 'a set of assumptions found within law in societies and regimes in which liberalism is the dominant political philosophy'.[27] These assumptions broadly concern both the nature of the legal person and the role of law.[28] Feminist critiques of the liberal legal person have drawn attention to its intrinsic masculinity, with Finley observing that these masculine features can be seen in the rational, self-interested actor of contract law and the unencumbered worker of labour law, for example.[29] These persons operate autonomously and freely in the public sphere. This applies here to the figure of the asylum-seeker, who seems to be expected or required to arrive across the border unencumbered, objective and autonomous—and certainly not pregnant. Here, women, along with their partners and children, are punished because, as Naffine points out, 'women's bodies are not susceptible to the sort of self-mastery required of a self-proprietor'.[30] The failure of pregnant women to fit liberal law's construction of the asylum-seeker resulted in their characterisation as a threat, and the *de facto* deportation of their citizen child born in these circumstances.

The approach in the judgment also draws on literature that situates the *Lobe and Osayande* case and the subsequent citizenship referendum within the broader project of Irish nation-building in the post-nationalist era.[31] Harrington, in particular, draws attention to the role that 'biopolitics' has played in this project, and the way in which the state seeks to further developmental goals through regulating women's fertility. This can be done by, among other things, 'variously encouraging smaller or larger families, encouraging or otherwise non-natives and dependants, and determining which families are legitimate and

[26] Fennelly J in *Lobe and Osayande*, above n 10, at 202. As he also states in this paragraph of the judgment, 'The Court is left to assume that the presence in the State of the parents of the two children involved in these cases is ipso facto and self-evidently inimical to the common good, simply because they are failed asylum seekers.'

[27] Rosemary Hunter, 'Contesting the Dominant Paradigm: Feminist Critiques of Liberal Legalism' in Margaret Davies and Vanessa Munro (eds), *The Ashgate Research Companion to Feminist Legal Theory* (Farnham, Ashgate, 2013) ch 1.

[28] ibid.

[29] Lucinda M Finley, 'Breaking women's silence in law: The dilemma of the gendered nature of legal reasoning' (1989) 64(5) *Notre Dame Law Review* 886–910, 896. See also Ngaire Naffine, 'Who are Law's Persons? From Cheshire Cats to Responsible Subjects' (2003) 66(3) *Modern Law Review* 346–67.

[30] Ngaire Naffine, 'The legal structure of self-ownership: Or the self-possessed man and the woman possessed' (1998) 25(2) *Journal of Law and Society* 193–212, 193.

[31] See Siobhán Mullally, 'Citizenship and Family Life in Ireland: Asking the Question "Who Belongs?"' (2005) 25(4) *Legal Studies* 578–600, 578; Steve Garner, 'Babies, Bodies and Entitlement: Gendered Aspects of Access to Citizenship in the Republic of Ireland' (2007) 60(3) *Parliamentary Affairs* 437–51; and Bryan Fanning and Fidèle Mutwarasibo, 'Nationals/Non-Nationals: Immigration, Citizenship and Politics in the Republic of Ireland' (2007) 30(3) *Ethnic and Racial Studies* 439–60.

illegitimate'.[32] The *Lobe and Osayande* case is a clear illustration of this point. Here, the children of asylum-seekers are denied equal access to the benefits of citizenship to which they are legally entitled—these families (and citizens) are rendered illegitimate because of the circumstances of the child's birth. Thus, the case demonstrates that the border that matters is no longer that which divides the North of Ireland from the South, but that which separates Europe from its others, 'which runs through the ports and the airports, right into the maternity wards of the state'.[33]

The Future Situation of Irish Citizen Children and Their Non-Irish National Family Members in Ireland

The feminist judgment pre-empts and foresees a number of issues that have, in the years following the judgment of the Supreme Court in 2003, changed the landscape for Irish citizen children and their family members. First, the judgment of the Court of Justice of the EU (CJEU) in the *Zambrano* case,[34] concerning a Columbian national couple and their two Belgian national children resident in Belgium, delivered in March 2011, has now significantly altered the position of Irish citizen children with regard to the recognition of their rights as EU citizens resident in their own state of nationality. The CJEU established in this case that

> [a] refusal to grant a right of residence to a third country national with dependent minor children in the Member State where those children are nationals and reside, and also the refusal to grant such a person a work permit[35] has the effect of depriving those children of the genuine enjoyment of the substance of the rights attaching to the status of European citizen.[36]

Following the *Zambrano* judgment, the Irish Naturalisation and Immigration Service (INIS) introduced a specific application procedure for parents of Irish citizen children. However, the INIS announced that the terms of the *Zambrano* judgment will not be applied to a non-EU national parent of an Irish citizen child, where the parent has been convicted of serious and/or persistent criminal offences. Furthermore—and this is probably an issue that may ultimately need to be clarified by the courts, at national or EU level—parents who have left Ireland of their own volition are currently excluded from the making of a *Zambrano*-type application in Ireland. One question that clearly arises here is whether Irish citizen children who are currently residing outside the state can be held liable for a decision made by their parents some time ago, which was then or now is contrary to their own best interest, and whether the children, on that basis, can now be deprived from re-entering the state with their family members on whom they are dependent.[37]

[32] Harrington, above n 25, at 429. He cites in turn Nira Yuval-Davies, *Gender and Nation* (London, Sage, 1997) at 22.

[33] Harrington, above n 25, at 439.

[34] Case C-34/09 *Gerardo Ruiz Zambrano v Office National de l'Emploi (ONEm)* [2011] ECR I-01177.

[35] ibid, paras 42–43.

[36] ibid, para 45.

[37] See further Hilkka Becker, 'The Law on Family Reunification in Ireland' (2014) 17(1) *Irish Journal of European Law* 103–10.

The High Court has since applied the rules established by the CJEU in *Zambrano* in a number of judgments, such as the cases of *AO v Minister for Justice, Equality and Law Reform & Ors (No 2)*[38] and *EA & Anor v Minister for Justice & Anor*.[39]

The High Court clarified that 'Ruiz-Zambrano turns on factors ... such as dependency, residence in the territory of the Member State in question and the right of European citizens to enjoy one of the real benefits of that citizenship, namely, the right to reside within the territory of the Union'.[40] In the latter case, Hogan J found that in a situation where the parents of an Irish citizen child were separated and, with the mother having been granted refugee status, it was not to be expected that the deportation of the father would in fact lead to a situation where the child would effectively be forced to leave Ireland and the wider EU, 'there are no grounds for contending that [the father] is entitled to an interlocutory injunction restraining his deportation on Zambrano grounds'.[41]

Interestingly, when Hogan J went on to assess the child's right to the care and company of his father under the Irish Constitution, he found himself coerced to the conclusion that 'there [are] abundant grounds for suggesting that the substance of [the child's] constitutional right to the care and company of his father would be denied were his father to be deported' and that '[t]his would ordinarily be sufficient in itself to justify the grant of an interlocutory injunction restraining the deportation of [the father], his disreputable and egregious conduct notwithstanding'.[42] He concluded that 'the court must [...] approach this application not from the perspective of the father, but rather from that of the child'.[43]

It seems, therefore, that the rights of minor Irish citizens to remain in their country of nationality, and with that in the territory of the EU, as well as to the care and company of both their parents, are best protected when courts and governments consider the situation of these children and their families based on a combination of national and international, as well as EU, human rights and citizenship law.[44]

[38] *AO v Minister for Justice, Equality and Law Reform, Ireland and the Attorney General (No 2)* [2012] IEHC 79.
[39] *EA & Anor v Minister for Justice & Anor* [2012] IEHC 371.
[40] *AO v Minister for Justice*, above n 38, para 18.
[41] *EA v Minister for Justice*, above n 39, para 14.
[42] ibid, para 17.
[43] ibid, para 40.
[44] See further Becker, above n 37.

THE SUPREME COURT

109/02 AND 108/02

BETWEEN

DAVID LOBE, JANA LOVEOVA, ALADAR LOBE (A MINOR SUING BY HIS FATHER AND NEXT FRIEND, DAVID LOBE), JANA LOBE (A MINOR SUING BY HIS FATHER AND NEXT FRIEND, DAVID LOBE) AND KEVIN LOBE (A MINOR SUING BY HIS MOTHER AND NEXT FRIEND, JANA LOVEOVA)

AND

THE MINISTER FOR JUSTICE, EQUALITY AND LAW REFORM

AND

BETWEEN

ANDREW OSAYANDE AND OSAZE JOSHUA OSAYANDE (A MINOR APPLICANT SUING BY HIS MOTHER AND NEXT FRIEND, FLORA OSAYANDE)

AND

THE MINISTER FOR JUSTICE, EQUALITY AND LAW REFORM

Judgment DELIVERED THE 23RD Day of January by Murphy J (Mullally J concurring).

Facts

The facts of the cases are not in dispute before this Court. The two cases, both of which were heard together in the High Court, were also heard together before this Court.

The first case concerns the Lobe family, who are of Czech Roma origin. When the first named applicants, Jana and David Lobe, arrived in Ireland with their three children on March 31st 2001, Mrs Lobe was in advanced stages of pregnancy. They sought asylum in Ireland, but it was decided, pursuant to Article 8 of the Dublin Convention, that their asylum applications would be transferred to the United Kingdom. An appeal against this decision before the Refugee Appeals Tribunal was rejected.

Further representations were made on behalf of the applicants to the respondent in this case, the Minister for Justice, Equality and Law Reform, arguing that given Mrs Lobe's advanced state of pregnancy and related health concerns, she and her family should not be removed to the United Kingdom.

The present proceedings were commenced on 5th October 2001. Kevin Lobe was born on November 2nd 2001, in Galway. Mr Lobe's parents, brother and sister are in Ireland, although there is no evidence presented before this Court as to their status in the State. While the present proceedings are mainly concerned with Kevin Lobe's position as an Irish citizen, it was also submitted in representations to the Minister that the applicants' other children (Aladar aged ten, Jana aged four and Lukas aged two) are settled in Clifden and that removal would not be in their best interests. Aladar attends school and has made friends in the local community, and the children have become very attached to the support of their paternal grandparents, whom they see regularly.

The second case before this Court concerns the Osayande family. The first named applicant, Andrew Osayande, is a Nigerian national who had previously claimed asylum in the United Kingdom, unsuccessfully. On his arrival in Ireland, with his wife Flora (next friend in this case) and daughter Emmanuella, he stated that he had not previously sought asylum elsewhere. In fact, as noted above, he had sought asylum unsuccessfully in the United Kingdom. After enquiries were made, the UK authorities provided information on his asylum application to the Department of Justice, Equality and Law Reform and agreed to accept responsibility for his application under Article 8 of the Dublin Convention. An appeal by Mr Osayande against this decision to the Refugee Appeals Tribunal failed.

A deportation order was issued in respect of Mr Osayande but not in respect of Mrs Osayande (who was heavily pregnant at the time that the deportation order issued against her husband) or Emmanuella. Mrs Osayande has claimed refugee status in the State and she has said that she will reside here until she is compelled to leave. Evidence presented to the High Court suggests that Emmanuella, who is aged three-and-a-half years, is settled and integrated into everyday life in Ireland, and is attending play school in Castlebar. In correspondence with the Minister, the family observed that she had already experienced upheaval through forced displacement, and to uproot her further would not be in her best interests.

Judicial review proceedings were commenced by the applicant, when notice of the deportation order was received. Mr and Mrs Osayande's son, Osaze Joshua Osayande, was born on 4 October 2001 in Castlebar and is an Irish citizen. These proceedings were commenced on 5 October 2001.

On the specific question of the citizenship and birth of the Irish children in each case, the Minister invited further representations from the families, each of which sent a letter of reply to the Minister. Mr John Lohan of the Department of Justice, Equality and Law Reform, then prepared a report for the Minister in each case. In December 2001, the Minister confirmed the deportation orders in both cases, enclosing a copy of the Lohan memorandum to explain his decision.

The Lohan memorandum and its reasoning are central to the case. The report accepted that the children were Irish citizens and that they had a *prima facie* right to reside in Ireland. The children also had the protection of the Constitution, specifically through the right to the company, care and parentage of their parents within a family unit. The memorandum recognises that the circumstances surrounding both cases and the issuing of deportation orders could be interpreted as 'a constructive deportation' of the citizen children affected.

Against those factors, the relevant criteria, which were determinative of the case were, in brief:

1. *the length of time the family had been in the State—only nine months,*
2. *the application of the Dublin Convention to which Ireland is a party,*
3. *the overriding need to preserve respect for and the integrity of the asylum and immigration systems.*

In addition, the Lohan memorandum further states that: "*the Lobe family and Kevin Lobe can adapt to the family's return to the United Kingdom and the Czech Republic and that their lives or well being would not be endangered*".

According to the memorandum, the Minister was entitled to take into account the manner in which the family entered the State, and specifically that the "*actions of the applicants in the proceedings were designed to circumvent the operation of the Dublin Convention.*"

As can be seen from this brief description, the two cases are very similar: they have taken a similar legal route and the legal reasons given for initiating deportation proceedings are almost identical. The only meaningful distinctions between the two, from the perspective of the present proceedings, are the following:

1. Mr Osayande had made a false statement that he had not made an asylum application in any other state.
2. The additional reason given by the Minister in respect of the Lobe case concerned the adaptability of the family to life in the UK and the Czech Republic, and the absence of a threat to the lives or well-being of the family.

The cases before us are similar to many other pending cases, and to the situations in which many families and Irish citizen children now find themselves. The judgment of this Court will have significant consequences not only for the applicants before us, but also for those children and their families.

The High Court Judgment

The learned High Court judge, Smyth J. was satisfied that the Minister in both cases was entitled as a matter of law to reach the conclusion that he did and to make the deportation orders in question.

He considered the findings of this Court in *Fajujonu v Minister for Justice and another* [1990] 2 IR 151 in some detail and agreed with the applicants that this case establishes that a citizen child has a right to reside in the State, and also has a right to the company and care of his or her parents.

He concluded, however, that *Fajujonu* was distinguishable from the instant cases, in that the family in that case had been resident in the State for what Finlay C.J. had described as "an appreciable time", and that in the instant cases, unlike *Fajujonu*, there was evidence that the Minister had given careful consideration to all the relevant factors in the case, including the period of time spent living in Ireland.

Having refused the reliefs sought by the applicants in both cases, pursuant to s. 5(3)(a) of the Illegal Immigrants (Trafficking) Act, 2000, the High Court certified that its decision involved points of law of exceptional public importance and that it was desirable in the public interest that an appeal should be taken to this Court. As has been noted, these cases raise concerns as to the best interests of the children involved, the right to family life and the meaning and significance of Irish citizenship. It would be difficult to identify matters of greater public importance than these.

Issues

It is agreed by the parties that the children were entitled to Irish citizenship. It is also agreed that as such, and on the basis of the decision of this Court in *Fajujonu v Minister for Justice*, the children have a right to reside in the State and to the company and care of their parents. Being of tender age, the choice to reside in the State must be exercised by the parents on behalf of the Irish citizen children. In *Fajujonu*, this Court confirmed that, given the State's obligations to vindicate the constitutional rights of the child and of the family, and absent compelling reasons, the non-Irish citizen parents of a citizen child should not be deported. The main legal issue thus becomes whether the present case can be distinguished from *Fajujonu v Minister for Justice and another* [1990] 2 IR 151. Both sides accept that *Fajujonu* was correctly decided, as do I.

It was conceded by the applicants that the parents had no right of residence in the State, absent their citizen child. The legal issues raised thus boil down to the question of whether the deportation of the parents and siblings in these circumstances constitutes a violation of the rights of the citizen child and of the family.

In summary, while there are 26 grounds of appeal from the High Court, the main issue for determination is whether the Minister may, in the general interests of maintaining the integrity of the asylum and immigration system, deport the parents of an Irish citizen child. This Court is essentially required to consider two important constitutional claims: the right of a citizen child to reside in the State and enjoy the company and care of his or her parents and siblings, on the one hand, and the power of the State to control the entry and residence of immigrants in Ireland, on the other.

Birthright citizenship

Article 2 of the Constitution, as amended in 1998, states:

> *"It is the entitlement and birthright of every person born in the island of Ireland, which includes its islands and seas, to be part of the Irish Nation. That is also the entitlement of all persons otherwise qualified in accordance with law to be citizens of Ireland. Furthermore, the Irish nation cherishes its special affinity with people of Irish ancestry living abroad who share its cultural identity and heritage."*

This amendment essentially constitutionalises the legislative provision for birthright citizenship contained in s. 6(1) of the Nationality Act 1956, which reads: "Every person born in Ireland is an Irish citizen from birth."

Birth on the island of Ireland is the only precondition to the entitlement to birthright citizenship stated in Article 2, which does not provide for any exceptions. Indeed, it is agreed by all concerned that there is no doubt that the children in the present case are Irish citizens.

The parties are also agreed that Article 2 does not operate to confer a higher status on citizens born on the island of Ireland than is conferred by s. 6(1) of the 1956 Act. I cannot accept, however, that there is no significance or 'added value' in constitutional rights terms, to placing the *ius soli* principle on a constitutional footing as opposed to leaving it as a legislative provision only. Enshrining this right within the Constitution removes it from the vagaries of legislative change, and prevailing political concerns. This pure form of *ius soli,* protected by the Constitution, cannot be altered other than by referendum.

It is also notable that Articles 2 and 3 of the Constitution were just recently amended in 1998, following a difficult and fragile peace negotiation process in Northern Ireland, brought to conclusion by a multi-party agreement. That process and the constitutional settlement that followed, is one that should be given the highest respect and deference by this Court, especially given the troubled history of this violent conflict on this island, and the lengthy multi-party negotiations in Northern Ireland that led to a referendum and constitutional change. It was open to the State, when enshrining just 5 years ago, the principle of *jus soli*, in the constitutional text for the first time, to limit the claims that might be brought by parents of citizen children or to limit birthright citizenship for those who parents had not been in the State for an appreciable period. The State did not choose to do so even though, given the important fundamental rights jurisprudence in the U.S. on this point, and significant legislative changes on birthright citizenship in jurisdictions such as the U.K. and Australia, it cannot (or should not) have been unaware of the claims that can arise from a citizen child.

It is a fundamental principle of constitutional and international law, that a State may not expel its own citizens. Counsel on behalf of the State concedes that the circumstances of the removals of the Lobe and Osayande families amounts to "constructive deportation" of Kevin Lobe and Osaze Osayande: the State has expressly advised the families that the best interests of the child as residing within the family unit necessitate that they accompany the family members who are being deported. This is, as noted, constructive deportation by the State of its own citizens; it constitutes deportation by stealth.

The child is either a citizen or not. The cardinal value of citizenship is the right to reside in the country of which one is a national. On this point, I must respectfully disagree with the views of the majority of this Court, and of my learned colleague Keane C.J., that the rights of a citizen child to reside in the State do not vest in the child until she is capable of exercising this right. The value and significance of citizenship for a child would, if this view were to hold sway, be stripped of its very essence.

The State wishes us to accept that the right of the citizen children to reside in the State is not breached, but merely postponed until they are old enough to make the choice to reside in the State themselves and thereby exercise that right. This is a mere fiction, as such postponement would deprive the children concerned of the opportunity to enjoy their constitutional rights in the State in their formative years. In particular, this includes the right to education provided for under Article 42, but also the rich body of rights both enumerated and un-enumerated in the constitutional text, that have enjoyed the protection of this Court. It is also pertinent to note the rights granted protection by the UN Convention on the Rights of the Child, to which the State is a party, which include not only education, but also rights pertaining to health and participation in decision-making. In the case of a child, the presence of his or her primary carer(s) is required in order to vindicate the right to reside in the country of nationality. Once the right to citizenship by birth is recognised, the quality of a child's right as a citizen should not be affected by the 'fortuity' or otherwise of her or his birth to undocumented immigrant parents.

As has been noted in arguments presented to this Court, in the U.S., and elsewhere, while the *ius soli* principle continues to apply, citizen children born to undocumented immigrant parents are subject to constructive deportations, their right to membership of the nation-state 'postponed' because of the legal status of their parents. A citizen child in the United States cannot confer what the U.S. courts have referred to in *Perdido v I.N.S.* (1969) 420 F.2d 1179 as an "immigration benefit" on her parents (at p.1181), as she has not made a deliberate decision to make the U.S. her place of residence. Her birth in the U.S. is seen as merely fortuitous. This argument is not binding on this Court, but has been cited by Counsel for the respondents. It should be noted of course, that none of us, citizens or not of this State, make a deliberate decision as to the place of our birth. The absence of such deliberation is not a consequence of the immigration or citizenship status of a child's parents, and cannot logically therefore be considered relevant to this argument.

In *Perdido*, the Court concluded that the constructive deportation of a citizen child does not produce a "constitutional infirmity" (at para. 10). Further, they also concluded that it was necessary to "resist the eloquence of petitioners' counsel and stifle our compassion for petitioners' plight." I would respectfully disagree with this conclusion. To exercise compassion is essential to our role as judges in the adjudication of fundamental rights. In challenges to deportation proceedings involving U.S. citizen children, such as *Perdido*, the perspective of the citizen child as a bearer of rights is too often marginalized, with disputes turning largely on the balancing of states' interests in immigration control against the residence claims made by immigrant parents. As is well recognised, the Irish Constitution differs in that, in Article 41, it specifically recognises and gives protection to the family relationships within which the child is situated and on which she is dependent. The significance of family life to the vindication of personal rights, including the personal rights of the child as safeguarded by Article 40.3 distinguishes the Irish Constitution and its protection of fundamental rights from constitutional jurisprudence of U.S. courts, such as the oft-cited *Perdido* case. The rights attaching to citizenship, and the limits of the State's power to deport, must be read in light of the protections afforded by the Irish Constitution. Moreover, it should be recognised that in the more recent case of *Beharry v Reno* (98 CV 5381 US District Court for the Eastern District of New York, 2002 U.S. Dist. Lexis 757), U.S. courts recognised the necessity of considering a child's future well-being and interests when assessing constructive deportation, rather than simply focusing on parental behaviour and past affiliations.

I will return to the question of the State's power to deport, and the limits arising from constitutional recognition of the personal rights of the child and the protection of family life. Before addressing these issues, I will address the significance of citizenship of the European Union to the proceedings before this Court.

Citizenship of the European Union

It should not be forgotten that, deriving from their status as Irish citizens, Kevin Lobe and Osaze Osayande are also citizens of the European Union (EU). Enabling a young child to exercise her or his citizenship rights effectively thus engages EU law, as well as the fundamental rights protected by the Irish Constitution.

The status of citizen of the European Union cannot have been intended to be an empty concept, established as it was by Member States of the Union through the adoption of the *Treaty of the European Union* (the *Maastricht* Treaty) Official Journal C 191, 29/07/1992. Article 8 provides that every person holding the nationality of a Member State shall be a citizen of the Union. As is the case with a child's Irish citizenship, it is necessary to recognise a derivative right of residence to their parents, as their primary carers, to ensure that citizen children can also effectively vindicate their rights as citizens of the EU, including their rights of residence and of free movement. Further, the rights attaching to the concept of citizenship of the EU cannot be dependent on an EU citizen having moved from one Member State to another, without producing arbitrary and unsatisfactory results.

The rights of the child and family life: Irish constitutional law

Much of the argument before the Court has centred on the interpretation of *Fajujonu v Minister for Justice*. I do not propose to go through the facts and details of this case as they are outlined succinctly in the judgments of my learned colleagues, which I have had the opportunity to read.

In my view, *Fajujonu* establishes quite a simple principle: if it is proposed to deport the parents of Irish citizen children, and thus effectively expel the Irish citizen themselves, the State must offer a "grave and substantial reason" for doing so. It also confirms that there is a presumption in favour of permitting the citizen child to reside in the State, with the benefit of the company and care of their parents, unless the Executive can show a compelling reason why this should not be so. I see nothing in the judgment of either Walsh J or Finlay C.J. to suggest that their findings are confined to a very specific and narrow set of facts involving families who have been in the State for an appreciable period. Citizenship status does not turn on the passage of time; it turns on birthright, by virtue of Article 2. This has consequences also for the constitutional protection of the child's personal rights and the protection of family life in Article 41. While the greater part of the arguments in this case have concerned the rights of the citizen child, it should be noted that family life, so carefully protected by Article 41 of the Constitution and by this Court in cases such as *North Western Health Board v HW and CW* [2001] 3 IR 622, is potentially undermined by the State's exercise of its powers to control entry and residence in the State. Although it was not argued before this Court, it is self-evident that the Article 41 rights of parents to make decisions on behalf of and in the interests of their children are severely circumscribed by the decision to deport.

In *Northants Co. Council v. ABF* [1982] ILRM 164, p.166, a case involving an adoption order, Hamilton J. drew upon a natural law-based argument, finding that the universality of the rights protected under Article 41 means that all human persons, be they citizens of the State or not, are entitled to the vindication of such rights. Furthermore, it is clear from the case-law of this Court, and the constitutional text itself, that the Constitution does not presume the human person to be an isolated, atomistic unit. The protection of family life, and of necessity the intimate relationships of which we form a part, requires the State to vindicate the imprescriptible and inalienable rights of the family, as stated in Article 41 of the Constitution. In this case, these rights must be vindicated through recognition by the State of the rights of the immigrant parents of an Irish citizen child, to remain in the State in the company of their child.

In relation to the rights of the citizen children here, Kevin and Osaze, it is timely to recall the significance of the statement by my learned colleague Finlay C.J. giving the judgment of the court in *The Adoption No.2 Bill 1987* [1989] IR 656, where he held that: "The rights of a child who is a member of a family are not confined to those identified in Articles 41 and 42 but are also rights referred to in Article 40, 43 and 44." A refusal to allow the parent, who is the primary carer of a child, to reside with that child in Ireland, would deprive the child's right of residence of any useful effect. It is clear that enjoyment by a young child of a right of residence necessarily implies that the child is entitled to be accompanied by the person who is his or her primary carer. The derivative right of residence that arises for the parents in these cases, as the children's primary carers, turns on the significance of their children's citizenship status, as already stated above, and also on the constitutional protections afforded to the rights of the child. As noted by Finlay C.J. such rights are recognised in several constitutional provisions, Articles 40, 41, 42, 43, and 44.

It is timely to recall the dissenting judgment of our learned colleague, Denham J., in the case of *Sinnott v Minister for Education* [2001] IESC 63, where she drew upon a relational understanding of rights and responsibilities within the family. Denham J., in a strongly worded dissent, noted that Kathy Sinnott had rights and duties as a parent within the family unit. A breach by the State of the rights of one member of the family unit could have a disproportionately negative impact upon the family, and particularly on the person charged with the primary care of the family—in that case, Kathy Sinnott.

This recognition afforded by Denham J. in *Sinnott*, to the relationships within which citizen children seek to vindicate their rights, is evident also in the case of *Fajujonu*. In *Fajujonu*, Walsh J, while concurring with the majority judgment, placed greater emphasis on the rights of the family as a constitutionally protected unit and specifically on the rights of the children within that unit. The children in this case, he said, were of tender age, requiring the society of their parents. Walsh J also noted that deportation proceedings could not be taken against a family that included citizen children, simply because of a family's limited financial resources, particularly where that situation of poverty could be attributed to the absence of a work permit. The rights of the citizen child, acted as trumps against utilitarian arguments such as those presented before this Court.

In summary, it is for the State to regulate and control immigration, but it must do so in accordance with the law and with respect for the fundamental rights protected by the Constitution.

The right to family life and EU law

In *Carpenter*, Case C-60/00 [2002] ECR I-6279, the ECJ recognised the right to family life of a UK national, Mr Carpenter, who resided in the Member State of his nationality, but provided occasional services to recipients located in other Member States. The Court concluded that deportation of his wife—a third country national—would be a disproportionate interference with Mr Carpenter's right to family life, which enabled him to exercise a fundamental freedom. The right to residence of Mr Carpenter's spouse could be inferred from the principles and rules of Community law. The freedom to provide services could not be "fully effective", the Court held, if obstacles to the entry and residence of his spouse in his country of origin were not removed.

The rights to family life of Kevin and Osaze, essential to their potential exercise of fundamental freedoms, can be considered no less deserving of protection. As such, the State is required to remove obstacles to the residence of their parents within the State.

I will now turn to the very rich case law of the European Court of Human Rights, on Article 8 ECHR, and specifically on the permissible restrictions on the right to family life recognised in Article 8(2).

The right to family life and international law

The ECHR, though not forming part of our domestic law, is nonetheless persuasive, and has been cited in many cases by judges of this Court.

In *O'Domhnaill v Merrick* [1984] IR 151 Henchy J. (speaking for the majority), expressed the view that a statute should be construed and applied "in consonance with the State's obligations under international law, including any relevant treaty obligations." He was commenting on the relevance of Article 6 ECHR to the process of statutory interpretation. More recently, in *Doyle v Commissioner of An Garda Síochána* [1999] 1 IR 249, the ECHR was specifically cited by the Supreme Court as a potentially useful source to draw upon in attempting to identify unenumerated personal rights safeguarded by Article 40.3. This point was subsequently cited with approval by Hardiman J. in *Gooden v Waterford Regional Hospital* (unrept.d Judgment 21 February 2001). I could continue to cite the now rich body of jurisprudence of this Court, upholding the State's obligations under international law.

The Courts have on a number of occasions shown a willingness to consider the terms of international human rights treaties to which the State is a Party. In *MV Toledo: ACT Shipping Ltd. v Minister for Marine* [1995] 2 ILRM 30, Barr J. at p. 45 held that "the general position in Irish law would appear to be that the established principles of international law may be part of Irish municipal law, provided they are not contrary to the Constitution, statute law or the common law".

Article 29 recognises Ireland's commitment to international law, not presuming a strict delineation between the domestic and international, particularly in the protection of individual rights. We can therefore usefully look to the provisions of Article 8 ECHR and to the UN Convention on the Rights of the Child, recognising their limits, and noting the absolute protections afforded to family life in the Irish Constitution.

Article 8 ECHR states that any interference with the right to respect for family life must be "in accordance with the law" and "necessary in a democratic society in the interests of national security, public safety or the economic wellbeing of the country, for the prevention of disorder or crime, for the protection of health or morals, or for the protection of the rights and freedoms of others". Of particular significance to this case, and cited by Counsel for the respondent on behalf of the Minister, is the judgment of Lord Philips in *Mahmood* [2001] WLR 840, in which he opined that "[r]emoval or exclusion of one family member from a state where other members of the family are lawfully resident will not necessarily infringe Article 8 provided that there are no insurmountable obstacles to the family living together in the country of origin of the family member excluded, even where this involves a degree of hardship for some or all members of the family" (at 861).

In my view, Article 8 does not and is not intended to import an "insurmountable obstacles" test, such that it applies an exceptionality rule in the determination of the rights of citizen children to family life, and to the attendant right to reside in the State. The search for a hard-edged or bright line rule to apply in the generality of cases is, in my view, incompatible with the difficult evaluative exercise required by the terms of Article 8, and in particular by Article 8(2).

In undertaking the proportionality test required by this exercise, the best interests of the child must be a primary consideration. This means that they must be considered first. The UN Convention on the Rights of the Child is a useful guide to the Court in the appeals before us. The interests of the child have often been absent from the case-law of the European Court of Human Rights. It should be noted, however, that a failure to recognise the child's right to the company, care and parentage of her parents in the State of which she is a national, would impair the very essence of her right to private and to family life protected by Article 8 ECHR. It is not disputed that the citizen children in these cases have the right to respect for their family life. Of necessity, this requires respect also for the rights of those, both siblings and parents, with whom family life is enjoyed.

In *Mahmood,* Lord Phillips MR concluded that the ordinary hardship endured in any deportation or expulsion proceedings was not enough, in his view, to engage the protection of Article 8. I would, however, respectfully disagree with this conclusion. The hardship that comes with exile is not an ordinary one. It is a hardship that is very well understood by the people on this island. The 'unhealable rift', the essential sadness that comes with exile, to borrow from Edward Said, is also one of terminable loss. The rights denied to the citizen child and her family, through a forced exile from her native place, result in lasting damage, and an 'unhealable rift' with the Nation of which she has a right to be part.

To return to the text of the law, and to the legal imperatives here engaged, the case of *Boultif v Switzerland* [2001 33 EHRR 50] 1179 is of particular interest, although it is not one of the cases relied upon by Counsel for respondent. Nonetheless, as a case that sought to state "guiding principles" (at paragraph 48), it should be considered here. There, the Court found that a State seeking to justify expulsion even of a person convicted of a crime must be able to point to "a pressing social need" and identified relevant criteria, including the length of the applicant's stay in the country from which he is going to be expelled, the nationalities of the various persons concerned, and the seriousness of the difficulties which family members are likely to encounter in the country of origin. In both *Abdulaziz v UK* (1985) 7 EHRR 471 and *Gül v Switzerland* (1996) 22 EHRR 93, the Court emphasised that the State has the right to control the entry of non-nationals into its territory. None of the cited cases here, however, exhibits the common features of the present appeals—that the children are Irish citizens and have constitutional family rights under the Constitution.

It should also be noted of that the Convention does not prevent Contracting States from putting in place higher standards for the protection of fundamental rights and freedoms in domestic law. In this case, compliance with the standards laid down by the Convention itself, will not necessarily satisfy the constitutional safeguards provided in Irish law. A failure to consider the citizen child's personal rights, protected by Article 40.1 of the Constitution, and her right to family life, protected by Article 8 ECHR, is a failure to comply with the positive obligations imposed by Article 8 to ensure that the citizen child's rights are 'practical and effective', not merely theoretical or illusory.

It is incumbent upon the Court to consider the child's right to family life, and to consider in light of *Sen v The Netherlands* (application no. 31465/96, 21 December 2001), what is the 'most suitable way' for the families here before us to continue their life together (*le moyen le plus adéquat*). This requires us to consider the full panoply of rights protected by the Convention, and also by the Constitution. Given the tender age of the citizen children in the cases before the Court, their inherent vulnerability and dependency on their family to exercise their rights, the State has a positive obligation to recognise the right of their parents to reside in the State.

The sovereign power of the State to regulate the entry and expulsion of non-Irish citizens

Against the rights of the child and of the family, it has been accepted by the courts on many occasions that the Executive branch of the State has the power to control the entry, residence and expulsion of non-Irish citizens. This power derives from the sovereign nature of the State, as stated in *Osheku v Ireland* [1986] IR 733; *Pok Sun Shun v Ireland* [1986] ILRM 593; and *The State (Bouzagou) v Station Sergeant Fitzgibbon Street* [1985] IR 426. The findings of the Superior Courts in these cases are clear: "it is in the interests of the common good of a State that it should have control of the entry of aliens, their departure, and their activities and duration of stay within the State is and has been recognised universally and from earliest times" (*per* Gannon J. in *Osheku*).

The sovereign claims of the State are more correctly designated, not as rights of the State as such, but as 'powers', which must be exercised in a manner that respects the constitutional rights of the individuals concerned. The common good must also serve to vindicate such rights. I must respectfully disagree with the unduly narrow characterisation of the common good in the judgments of my colleagues in this Court, which focus on the State's obligation to maintain the integrity of the asylum and immigration systems, rather than its duty to vindicate the dignity of the individual.

In terms of Ireland's obligations under EU law, it must be recognised that the Dublin Convention (*Convention Determining the State Responsible for Examining Applications for Asylum lodged in one of the Member States of the European Communities* 15 June 1990, Official Journal C 254, 19/08/1997 p. 0001–0012) does not oblige the State to transfer an individual to another convention country for the purpose of having an application for asylum determined. It merely sets out a mechanism for such a possibility, and it sets minimum standards only. The rights of the citizen child must be fully and effectively vindicated and cannot be set aside by the possibilities presented to the State in the Dublin Convention, the purpose of which is to allocate responsibility for the determination of asylum applications, rather than to determine the rights of citizen children or their parents.

It has been argued on behalf of the Minister that if non-Irish national parents who came to this country for purpose of seeking asylum could claim an automatic right to remain in the State by reason of the 'fortuity' that a child was born to them while awaiting a final decision on their application, the immigration and asylum system could be distorted.

The respondents are also suggesting that in such a situation a substantial number of non-Irish nationals could come to the State to seek asylum with the intent of circumventing the controls that the State has imposed on immigration in the interest of the common good. This suggestion has been vague and almost unspoken in the submissions for the State. Although Mr Lohan swore an affidavit in these proceedings and referred to certain matters including the increase in the numbers of asylum claims in recent years, no statistical evidence has been presented to the Court to substantiate these claims, in relation to either (a) the evolution in the numbers of applications for asylum since the 1980s, or (b) the extent to which affording residence rights to parents of Irish citizen children is a 'pull factor' for asylum seekers.

Moreover, there was no evidence presented to support the argument that the families in these particular cases were in fact attempting to manipulate the asylum system or abuse it through ensuring that their children, Kevin Lobe and Osaze Osayande, were born in Ireland. The Lohan memo simply states that "the actions of the applicants were designed to circumvent the Dublin Convention" without giving any further detail on the individual experiences of the families or any evidence to support the contention that there was an intention to abuse the asylum and immigration systems of the State. Indeed, it would be very difficult for the State to go about proving such a contention, given the diverse and often traumatic circumstances that asylum seeking families endure.

In presenting such generalised policy arguments, the Minister is in effect asking the Court to support the assumption that a girl or woman who seeks asylum or arrives as an irregular migrant in Ireland, and who is of child-bearing age, is a potential threat to the integrity of the asylum and immigration system, simply by virtue of the fact that she may give birth to a child in the State. I am deeply unimpressed by this reasoning, which is so central to the State's case. If taken to its logical conclusion, this would mean classifying many migrant women as a potential threat to the integrity of our sovereignty.

I cannot accept, in a State that has prided itself on the constitutional protection of the child and the family, that pregnancy and the birth of a child can ever be classified as a threat to the common good. Moreover, women ought not to be regarded simply as bodies of reproduction. I certainly do not find that these vague, unsupported and potentially discriminatory policy choices constitute the sufficiently "compelling" or "grave and substantial" reason (required by the *Fajujonu* decision) to negate the strong presumption in favour of the citizen being permitted to enjoy their constitutional right to reside in the State, and to the company and care of their parents.

It should be noted that it is not disputed by any party to this case that the acquisition of citizenship by the children in these cases is lawful. There is nothing reprehensible about taking advantage of a possibility conferred by Irish law. The 'floodgates' argument presented by the respondents isare beyond the proper scope of judgment for this Court. It is for the legislature to make the law. Once made, the Court must properly apply the law to the cases that come before it. Where the law to be applied is the Constitution itself, expressing the will of the people, in this case in a recently held referendum, it is not for this Court to subvert the clear meaning of the constitutional provision and the applicable law.

If the Executive branch of government is of the opinion that this position results in a distortion of the asylum and immigration systems, and wishes to change the law, they should propose a constitutional amendment to limit *ius soli*, rather than limit the rights of citizens who have validly obtained citizenship in accordance with Article 2 of the Constitution.

The Constitution requires the State to vindicate and protect the family life of the citizen children before us, and their rights to the care, company and parentage of their parents/family. Yielding to the appalling and unsubstantiated floodgates vista presented to us here, would require us to ignore the Constitution and the law. It would render the protection of fundamental rights vulnerable to the whims of populist sentiment and political panic.

The rights protected by the Constitution, it must be remembered, are trumps. They trump the conception of the common good that is presented by the respondents in these appeals. It is a conception of the common good that would infringe, rather than vindicate as it should, the rights of the Irish citizen children, Kevin Lobe and Osaze Osyande and their families.

Conclusion

For the reasons outlined above, I would allow the appellants' appeal.

14

Commentary on *Zappone and Gilligan v The Revenue Commissioners, Ireland and the Attorney General*

SIOBHÁN WILLS AND MÁIRÉAD ENRIGHT

Introduction

This request by two well-known women, domiciled in Ireland but married in Canada, to have their marriage legally recognised in Ireland, attracted a great deal of attention. Arguably the case kick-started the campaign that culminated in the referendum to amend the Constitution's provisions on marriage, passed with overwhelming popular support on 22 May 2015. The attempt to write a feminist judgment in this case is illustrative of the profound challenges of using litigation to secure same-sex couples' access to marriage. We may want to ask whether cases like *Zappone*[1] are part of a feminist political project at all. As Louise Crowley notes elsewhere in this collection,[2] marriage is a deeply gendered institution, especially in Ireland, endowed with deep significance for the persistence of the nation. Marriage is intrinsic to the state's efforts to discipline and control sexual and familial life. It is a public institution, not a purely private relation.[3] Historically, marriage has been used to exclude those considered sexually 'deviant'; not only gay people, but also unmarried mothers, sex workers, those in non-monogamous relationships and couples who have separated. In Irish nationalist discourse, gay people have often been entirely invisible, or outsiders whose coupling represents a dangerous deviation from the (constitutional) heterosexual ideal.[4] On this reading, gay people, in seeking access to marriage now, are asking for little more than assimilation to an oppressive traditional norm; and that norm may constrain the radical possibilities of demands for marriage equality. First, as Michael Warner points out, many gay activists have historically valorised non-normative forms of kinship and commonality, and the concern is that a new focus on marriage will go hand in hand with a

[1] *Zappone & Anor v Revenue Commissioners & Ors* [2006] IEHC 404.

[2] These issues are discussed more fully in ch 8 of this collection, by Louise Crowley in her commentary on Lucy-Ann Buckley's feminist judgment of the *Matrimonial Homes Bill* case.

[3] Michael Warner, *The Trouble with Normal: Sex, Politics, and the Ethics of Queer Life* (Boston, MA, Harvard University Press, 2000) 108.

[4] Kathryn A Conrad, *Locked in the Family Cell: Gender, Sexuality, and Political Agency in Irish National Discourse* (Madison, WI, University of Wisconsin Press, 2004) 65.

denigration of those alternative structures.[5] It would, in his words 'make for good gays—the kind who would not flaunt sexuality and who would not insist on living differently from ordinary folk'.[6] Secondly, a focus on marriage equality as the gay rights issue of our time may privilege some forms of political recognition at the expense of others. Writing about the marriage equality referendum, the poet Sarah Clancy described her anger that

> in the place of say redress and maybe a state apology for all those who this state has hurt with its puritan catholo-capitalist policing of our personal lives ... a seeming trinket such as access to marriage might now become a fig leaf behind which any further grievances might be concealed.[7]

Along these lines, campaigns for state recognition of same-sex relationships are sometimes vulnerable to the criticism that they have tended to select 'good' figureheads who appeal strongly to the popular mainstream, and whose relationships easily fit with traditional ideas of marriage. Anne Mulhall advances this critique of the 2015 marriage equality referendum:

> The official campaign for 'marriage equality' in Ireland did not diverge in any substantial way from the familiar white middle-class neoliberal register. Once the heavily and cleverly strategized referendum campaign proper got under way a few months before the vote (involving many LGBT and other organizations and advisers beyond the core Yes Equality coalition), the pitch shifted. The focus was on the personal, on family ties and friendship circles, on the 'positive story', on self-revelation and emotional truth. And the address was, of course, to the straight population. The straight citizen-public had to be persuaded not primarily of the economic logic involved in welding queer couples together with 'commitment devices' and 'forever love' ... but of the 'sameness' of lesbian and gay love and family-making. From a particular perspective, this normativizing drive is a corollary of the argument for marriage as neoliberal devolution of State and collective social responsibilities to the family, both being held in position by the marriage contract. If lesbian and gay people are 'just like us' (the 'B', the 'T' and needless to say the 'Q' were consigned to unspeakability for the duration), then they deserve what 'we' have—equality granted on the basis of sameness, on a shared humanity—but a humanity that does not diverge in any alarming way from what 'we' recognise as 'just like us', a fellow 'citizen' who does not disturb the established image the nation has of itself, but makes of it, as Burton had it, the 'rainbow nation' ...[8]

To some extent, similar threads are in evidence in public representations of *Zappone*. Katherine Zappone, now a senator, and Ann Louise Gilligan, a theologian, were considered 'perfect as a test-case couple': they were 'ideal poster girls ... able to speak to Middle Ireland', and 'able to speak in quite religious language as well, and spiritual language'.[9] The two plaintiffs, 'radiating confidence and competence', not only provided the journalists with 'a well-drafted press release', but also thanked their family, supporters and solicitors,

[5] Warner, above n 3, 89; Katherine Franke, *Wedlocked: The Perils of Marriage Equality* (New York, New York University Press, 2015).

[6] Warner, above n 3, 113.

[7] Sarah Clancy, 'Mixed Emotions One Month On—Campaigner Sarah Clancy Reflects on the Marriage Referendum' (20 June 2015), at http://bogmanscannon.com/2015/06/20/mixed-emotions-one-month-on-campaigner-sarah-clancy-reflects-on-the-marriage-referendum/ (last accessed 18 December 2015).

[8] Anne Mulhall, 'The Republic of Love' (20 June 2015), at https://bullybloggers.wordpress.com/2015/06/20/the-republic-of-love/ (last accessed 18 December 2015). For a contrasting oral history of the campaign, see Una Mullally, *In the Name of Love: The Movement for Marriage Equality in Ireland* (Stroud, The History Press, 2014).

[9] 'The KAL Case Kickstarted a Decade of Debate on Marriage Equality', *thejournal.ie* (12 December 2014), at www.thejournal.ie/readme/katherine-zappone-ann-louise-gilligan-marriage-case-1827118-Dec2014/ (last accessed 18 December 2015). See further the couple's memoir, Ann Louise Gilligan and Katherine Zappone, *Our Lives Out Loud: In Pursuit of Justice and Equality* (Dublin, The O'Brien Press, 2012).

and mentioned that they had recently celebrated their third wedding anniversary and the 25th year of their 'life partnership together'.[10] Kathy Sheridan, reporting the case in *The Irish Times*, commented that the 'aura of goodwill almost dazzled journalists—more accustomed to snarls from the usual denizens of the courts'.[11] The emphasis here is on the couple's proven fitness for marriage, their respectability (by comparison to the 'usual denizens' of the courts) and their sameness with straight married couples. At the same time, there is no doubting the significance of *Zappone* as the first case in which Irish law was made to reckon with the reality of long-term, committed same-sex relationships.

Bearing in mind these tensions within the politics of same-sex marriage, feminists may wish to ask whether law can be used to secure access to legal rights in ways that do not automatically entail gay people's assimilation to oppressive norms. There are, after all, strong transformative possibilities in the lived experience of marriage. Didi Herman has written that the legal recognition of gay families may be less about 'mimicking' the heterosexual norm and more about 'troubling' the norm itself.[12] Same-sex couples may live married life in ways that reflect alternative experiences of kinship and family-making. But if law is to assist rather than retard these efforts, we need feminist legal arguments that create space for them. It is significant, from this perspective, that Fiona de Londras in her feminist judgment ultimately comes to the same conclusion as Dunne J in the original judgment: that the Constitution did not require recognition of same-sex marriage. Her difficulty in justifying a different outcome speaks to in-built limits in Irish constitutional law, many of which are of general relevance to efforts to reshape law in response to profound social change. At the same time, however, de Londras J is able to write a judgment that successfully excavates some difficult assumptions about the relation between marriage and sexuality, in the process producing a judgment very different from the original.

Dynamic Constitutional Interpretation

Like the original judgment, the feminist judgment concentrates on the Constitution rather than on the European Convention on Human Rights.[13] Under Irish law the Constitution takes precedence over the Convention, and therefore Zappone and Gilligan would have had to show that same-sex marriage was compatible with the Constitution, which at that time did not explicitly recognise same-sex marriage. The state argued that the Constitution's provisions on marriage clearly envisaged a union between a man and a woman. Given that this was a first instance hearing by a judge sitting alone, de Londras J would have needed substantial evidence that there was an overwhelming consensus, or at the very least a majority view, in favour of same-sex marriage domestically or regionally, in order to justify a dynamic interpretation of the Constitution in her feminist judgment; which in 2006 there was not.

[10] Kathy Sheridan, 'Love Was in the Air but Not All Around', *The Irish Times*, 4 October 2006, at www.irishtimes.com/news/love-was-in-the-air-but-not-all-around-1.1010967 (last accessed 18 December 2015).

[11] ibid.

[12] Didi Herman, *Rights of Passage: Struggles for Lesbian and Gay Legal Equality* (Toronto, University of Toronto Press, 1994) 147.

[13] Contrast Rosie Harding's feminist judgment of *Wilson v Kitzinger* in Rosemary Hunter, Clare McGlynn and Erika Rackley (eds), *Feminist Judgments: From Theory to Practice* (Oxford, Hart Publihsing, 2010) ch 25.

Had de Londras J been hearing the case in 2015 the situation would have been very different, even without the referendum. In 2006 three European states provided for same-sex marriage, the Netherlands, Belgium and Spain (since 2001, 2003 and 2005 respectively). Outside of Europe same-sex couples could marry in Canada and Massachusetts, and from November 2006 in South Africa. Today 13 states in Europe recognise same-sex marriage (plus Malta, which provides for same-sex partnerships on a par with marriage and recognises same-sex marriages contracted abroad). On 26 June 2015, *in Obergefell*, the US Supreme Court held that same-sex marriage is legal in all 50 States[14] (immediately prior to the judgment, same-sex marriage had been recognised in 37 US States plus British Columbia).

Since the Constitution does not explicitly exclude the possibility of same-sex marriage, and bearing in mind that her judgment was a first instance one, de Londras wanted to leave open the opportunity of different judgment to a judge in a future same-sex marriage case. Hence she explains that her judgment is simply based on the fact that insufficient evidence has been put before her to reach a more dynamic interpretation of the Constitution. She is thus inviting a superior court to reach a different conclusion. In taking this position, it was important to give a judgment that recognised that society's views on marriage, and indeed on same-sex relationships, can evolve, and that the legal position may also change accordingly.

Discrimination and the Role of Parliament

Both the applicants and the defence focused on differential treatment of married and unmarried persons. The applicants argued that they were being discriminated against as compared with opposite-sex married couples; and the defence argued that the applicants were being treated no differently from opposite-sex unmarried couples, and hence no discrimination arose. For de Londras J the core discrimination (and one that it was important to state in view of the possibility of this coming before a court again, either on appeal or at a future date) is not between married and married, married and unmarried, or unmarried and unmarried, but between persons in same-sex and opposite-sex relationships: people in opposite-sex relationships have the option of marrying; people in same-sex relationships do not. Thus de Londras J holds that non-recognition of same-sex marriages is undoubtedly discrimination. However, she adopts a firmly deferential approach, holding that it is up to the Supreme Court, or a future court, or the Dáil, or indeed the People in a referendum, to rectify this.

Child-rearing as a Locus of Prejudice

Very few Irish cases consider the question of gay rights. *Zappone* was the first significant such case to do so since *Norris*.[15] It is tempting simply to assert that the law's attitude to

[14] *Obergefell v Hodges* 576 US 26 (2015).
[15] *Norris v AG* [1983] IESC 3, [1984] IR 36 (22 April 1983).

intimate relationships between same-sex partners has changed appreciably in the intervening years. Recall that O'Higgins CJ in 1983 held that homosexuality was considered an affront to nature, viewed with deep revulsion by all religions. Moreover:

> Public order and morality; the protection of the young, of the weak-willed, of those who may readily be subject to undue influence, and of others who should be deemed to be in need of protection; the maintenance inviolate of the family as the natural primary and fundamental unit of society; the upholding of the institution of marriage; the requirements of public health; these and other aspects of the common good require that homosexual acts be made criminal in many circumstances.[16]

Dunne J's tone in the original *Zappone* judgment is devoid of any equivalent assertions. Nevertheless the original judgment's long and repetitive discussion of the potential effects of gay marriage on children, and the effort that counsel for the applicants put into preempting any concerns of this nature, suggest the persistence of homophobic prejudice despite the shift in tone. This focus on children reappeared as a strong theme in the 2015 marriage equality referendum campaign—those resisting the amendment suggested repeatedly that recognition of gay marriage represented a constitutionalisation of family forms that were demonstrably harmful for children. In Ireland, as elsewhere, 'the figure of the child of non-heterosexual parents becomes a cathected site for anxieties over cultural purity and cultural transmission'.[17] There are various routes to addressing that discourse. In *Obergefell v Hodges*, Kennedy J held that protection of children's rights was in fact a reason for *granting* same-sex couples the legal right to marry, since marriage allows children 'to understand the integrity and closeness of their own family and its concord with other families in their community and in their daily lives', and that it also 'affords the permanency and stability important to children's best interests'.[18] For Kennedy J, that most states allow gays and lesbians to adopt 'provides powerful confirmation from the law itself that gays and lesbians can create loving, supportive families'.[19] De Londras wanted to minimise discussion of the welfare of children, both because this couple are childless and because all of the evidence produced to the Court on the welfare outcomes for children of same-sex couples and children of single-parent families was inconclusive.[20] She also wanted to draw attention to the fact that the courts have long ago recognised, in *Murray* in particular,[21] that marriage is not necessarily linked to having children. In doing so, de Londras' judgment makes more space for a vision of marriage that is not exclusively tied to child-rearing.[22]

[16] ibid, judgment of O'Higgins CJ.

[17] Judith Butler, *Undoing Gender* (New York, Routledge, 2004) 112.

[18] *Obergefell v Hodges*, above n 14, 15.

[19] ibid.

[20] The stigmatisation of single mothers in Ireland is discussed in this collection by Liam Thornton and Colm O'Cinnéide in the feminist judgment and commentary to *Mhic Mathúna v Ireland* in ch 7.

[21] *Murray v Ireland* [1985] IR 532.

[22] On contestations of legal relationships between 'the child' and homosexuality, see Daniel Monk, 'Sexuality and Children Post-Equality' in Robert Leckey (ed), *After Legal Equality: Family, Sex and Kinship* (Abingdon, Routledge, 2015) ch 12.

Neutral Citation Number: [2006] IEHC 404

THE HIGH COURT

[2004 No. 19616 P.]

BETWEEN

KATHERINE ZAPPONE AND ANN LOUISE GILLIGAN

PLAINTIFFS

AND

REVENUE COMMISSIONERS, IRELAND AND THE ATTORNEY GENERAL

DEFENDANTS

AND

THE HUMAN RIGHTS COMMISSION

NOTICE PARTY

Judgment of Ms. Justice de Londras delivered on the 14th day of December 2006

1. The plaintiffs in this case have known and loved one another for over twenty years. Having met in 1981, they made a lifelong commitment to one another in 1983, although they did not marry until 13 September 2003. Their wedding took place in British Columbia, Canada. They now seek recognition of that marriage in Ireland. For reasons that I will shortly address, the case primarily revolved around the meaning of marriage in the Constitution. The plaintiffs in this case—Katherine Zappone and Ann Louise Gilligan—are both women.

Factual Background

2. I am satisfied as to the validity of the plaintiffs' marriage under Canadian law and do not intend to consider arguments relating to that.

3. Having returned from Vancouver, the plaintiffs' solicitors wrote to both Oifig an Ard-Chláraitheora (on 26 April 2004) and the Revenue Commissioners (on 26 April 2004) asking for the marriage to be recognised (in the former case) and for their taxes to be dealt with as a married couple under the Taxes Consolidation Act 1997 (in the latter case). This case concerns the response of the Revenue Commissioners. They replied by letter on 1 July 2004 as follows:

> "Section 1017 TCA 1997 provides for a husband being assessed on his and his wife's total income. Section 1019 provides for a wife being assessed on her and her husband's total

income. The Taxes Act do not define husband or wife. The Oxford English Dictionary offers the following:

- — Husband—a married man especially in relation to his wife.
- — Wife—a married woman especially in relation to her husband.

Revenue's interpretation of tax law is that the provisions relating to married couples relate only to a husband and a wife. Therefore I cannot allow your clients for allowances as a married couple."

The plaintiffs sought leave for judicial review in respect of that decision and the matter came on for hearing before the High Court by way of plenary proceedings on 3rd October, 2006.

4. The plaintiffs claim they would benefit financially under the Tax Code if recognised as a married couple. They further plead that the words "married persons", "spouses", "husband and wife" as used in tax legislation can be interpreted to include spouses of the same sex. It is pleaded that in their interpretation of tax law and the refusal to treat the plaintiffs as a married couple, the defendants acted without lawful authority, subjected the plaintiffs to unjust and invidious discrimination and acted in breach of the constitutional rights of the plaintiffs under Articles 40 and 41 of the Constitution with particular reference to the provisions of Article 40.1, Article 40.3.1°, Article 40.3.2°, Article 41.1, Article 41.3.1° and Article 43. If the relevant provisions of the Tax Code cannot be interpreted to include spouses of the same sex, the plaintiffs seek to have them deemed invalid having regard to the Constitution. Alternatively reliance is placed on Articles 8, 12 and 14 of the European Convention on Human Rights. The key claim is that the unenumerated right to marry under Irish constitutional law includes a right to marry a person of the same biological sex, so that a refusal to recognise their marriage is unconstitutional. Should the plaintiffs successfully establish this, the Revenue Commissioners ought to recognise their marriage as they do other Canadian marriages. Should they fail to establish this, the constitutional discrimination claim cannot stand. Thus, while the core claim relates to the decision of the Revenue Commissioners, this case is primarily about the meaning of the right to marry under the Constitution. Arguments as to the ECHR are relevant to legislative interpretation *per se* but failure to establish the constitutional claim essentially settles the ECHR claim under the ECHR Act 2003 and so this judgment deals primarily with the constitutional questions raised. It is for this reason that much of the evidence heard during this case, and which I summarise below, relates to broader issues than that of taxation and rather traverses general arguments as to the constitutional meaning of "marriage" such as the welfare of children.

The Evidence

5. A large volume of evidence was produced to the court in the course of these proceedings. Dr. Zappone outlined her background, meeting Dr. Gilligan, the commencement of their relationship in 1981, and her concerns about the tax implications of them not being married in respect of sale of property, inheritance, and a gift to her of a recently-matured SSIA from Dr. Gilligan. Dr. Zappone said that marriage brings diverse rights, responsibilities, benefits and obligations but within that highlighted the obligation to care for Dr. Gilligan in sickness or in health, to be faithful to her for the rest of her days, and to live

together as a couple. Although she said that at this point in their lives issues of taxation and financial security had become more important, they were secondary to the desire to make a life commitment and marry Dr Gilligan. Hence, they travelled to Vancouver and married there. The law did not require them to be resident in British Columbia. At all times they were domiciled in Ireland.

6. Dr. Zappone testified that she experienced a great sense of discrimination because of the Revenue Commissioners' refusal to recognise her marriage. She conceded that she had not sought legal advice in Ireland before getting married, but she had looked at a document online entitled "How to get married in British Columbia". She saw the part of that document which advised that it was not necessary to be a British Columbia resident in order to be married there. She noted that the licence to marry was only valid in British Columbia. She did not see the part of the document that advised people to "contact the appropriate authorities in the jurisdiction where you are a resident to determine whether your marriage will be recognised". She confirmed that she became aware of the Civil Registration Act 2004 during the course of these proceedings.

7. While Dr. Zappone acknowledged that the situation of gay people in Ireland had improved as a result of the abolition of the offence of "buggery" and equalization of the age of consent by the Criminal Law (Sexual Offences) Act 1993, and introduction of non-discrimination law, she noted that these laws did not protect the plaintiffs in respect of this action. They did not allow them to marry or have their marriage recognised in Ireland.

8. Dr. Zappone's evidence was mirrored by Dr. Gilligan, who was not cross-examined by the State.

9. I then heard substantial amounts of expert evidence, which I summarise briefly below inasmuch as it is relevant to the particular arguments made to the Court. A substantial amount of the evidence to the Court that was of a more general manner (relating to homosexuality and same-sex parenting *per se*) is not summarised below. Much of this was not germane to the legal matter before me. Indeed, it is not clear that much of the expert evidence heard by me was necessary at all. If the plaintiffs have a constitutional right to marry that is because they are constitutional subjects who are not distinguished, within the Constitution, from other constitutional subjects who wish to marry persons of the opposite birth gender; it is not because same-sex parents can or cannot raise healthy, happy well-adjusted children, or because marriage between persons of the same sex does or does not bring the same benefits (and disadvantages) as marriage between persons of the opposite sex.

10. As to the evidence before me: a witness statement noting differential tax treatment of the plaintiffs from couples whose marriages were recognised in Irish law from Mr. Cremins of Price Waterhouse Coopers was handed in to the court by agreement. Professor Henry Kennedy testified that the social stigma and discrimination attached to homosexuality can give rise to mental illnesses in those subject to them. He also noted that stigma and discrimination can lead to material adversity in careers and other aspects of citizenship and social inclusion.

11. A statement of evidence from Dr. Evelyn Mahon was submitted to the court. This statement concerned census and demographic information and also included an appendix setting out the position in other EU countries relating to same-sex marriage and civil partnership.

12. Professor Richard Green, a psychiatrist and lawyer, then gave evidence on whether children of or raised by same-sex couples are any worse off than those raised by opposite-sex couples. His evidence traversed a large number of studies and his own published research. Professor Green's summation was that that there was great consistency in the findings from several studies conducted in the U.S., England and Continental Europe spanning at least two decades that children raised by gender or sexually atypical parents do not experience adverse impacts. It is, he said, the quality of the parent/child relationship that is essential for effective parenting and the best interest of the child.

13. Professor Green was vigorously cross-examined, mostly on the methodological approach taken in the studies considered in his evidence. It was put to him that there was some controversy in the literature about whether any meaningful conclusions could be drawn from these studies given their sizes and natures. Professor Green did not agree that there was such a degree of controversy, but accepted that some who wrote in this field thought it was too early to draw conclusions as to the welfare of children brought up in families headed by same-sex couples. However, he reiterated his view that there was sufficient consistency across the studies to make his conclusions reliable. This concluded the evidence for the plaintiffs.

14. Professor Patricia Casey then gave evidence on behalf of the defendants. As she has not done any research into the particular questions relating to outcomes for children of being raised in same-sex headed families, I focus on her evidence relating to research methodology. Professor Casey explained the importance of controls in research such as that relied on by Professor Green and opined that in her view the studies he cited do not meet the criteria expected of good epidemiological research. As a result, in her view the only conclusion one could reasonably draw was that we do not yet know whether children suffer adverse outcomes from being raised in same-sex headed families and that more studies were required.

15. The final witness called for the defendants was Professor Linda Waite of the University of Chicago. Professor Waite has studied marriage in the context of cohabitation, divorce, working families, and ageing families. She testified that the research indicates that marriage changes the choices and behaviour of individuals and those around them in ways that make them better off, improves their physical and emotional health, and improves outcomes for children. Although there is continuing debate as to some of the benefits she described, Professor Waite testified that there was a general consensus that spouses in opposite-sex marriages do benefit in these ways. When asked whether the 'complimentarity of the sexes' was relevant to these benefits, including the benefits for children, she testified that some studies indicate that mothers and fathers help to develop different skills in children and that their different forms of interaction with children can benefit those children in different ways. She said that there was no analogous research in the context of same-sex headed families. Research on opposite-sex marriage had been ongoing for many years and was based on large-scale survey research with a more persuasive methodology than that used in studies of same-sex parenting. She also made the point that if the situation in which families are operating has changed very fundamentally (e.g. if attitudes, the economy, or the legal structure has changed), something that mattered in the past may not matter now and this needed to be taken into consideration in drawing conclusions.

16. Asked about Professor Green's evidence, which she had considered, Professor Waite said that in her view the methodology employed in the studies he cited was such that they could only be suggestive.

17. Professor Waite was then cross-examined, particularly about *The Case for Marriage*, a book she coauthored with Margaret Gallagher. Professor Waite expressed the view in the book that she was either neutral or in favour of same-sex marriage. She explained that this was because she felt there was insufficient evidence one way or another as to the consequences of same-sex marriage. In response to direct questioning on whether there any reliable scientific evidence that children are worse off if their same-sex parents are married as opposed to unmarried, she indicated that she knew of no evidence on that point. She indicated that she could not comment on whether the benefits of marriage she had outlined could be enhanced for same-sex couples if they were recognised by the State as entitled to marry. Her view was that it may or may not be the case; there is simply insufficient evidence one way or another.

Recognition of the Plaintiffs' Marriage

18. At the opening of the case on behalf of the defendants Mr O'Donnell SC handed the court a report on 'Private International Law Affect of British Columbian Law', authored by Professor Joost Blom. Based on this, counsel for the defendants submitted that when capacity to marry was at issue, validity and recognition of a marriage was a matter to be determined by a court in accordance with the law of domicile, i.e., in this case, by reference to Irish law. In response, Mr. Collins SC for the plaintiffs accepted that, should the plaintiffs not have capacity to marry in Ireland, Irish law would not recognise their British Columbian marriage even if it were valid in British Columbia.

19. As already stated, I accept the validity of the marriage as a matter of Canadian law. Section 2(2)(e) of the Civil Registration Act 2004 provides:

> "(2) For the purposes of this Act there is an impediment to a marriage if –
>
> ...
>
> (e) both parties are of the same sex."

20. It is clear that the 2004 Act introduces an impediment to marriage between the plaintiffs on the basis of capacity. As Ireland was their country of domicile at the time of marriage, there is no independent ground upon which the plaintiffs' marriage can be recognised by this Court. We must, then, move to the constitutional matters arising.

A Right to Marry in Constitutional Law

21. The plaintiffs argued that for the unenumerated constitutional right to marry (*Donovan v Minister for Justice* [1951] 85 I.L.T.R. 134; *Ryan v Attorney General* [1965] I.R. 294; and a passage from the dissenting judgment of Fitzgerald C.J. in *McGee v Attorney General* [1974] I.R. 284, at 301) to be meaningful, it must encompass a right to marry the person one loves, regardless of sex, and that any bar on doing so is a *prima facie* infringement of that right, which must be justified. While some capacity restrictions (e.g. within prohibited degrees of relationship) could be justified, Mr. Collins SC submitted that a prohibition on

same-sex marriage was not justifiable as it constituted discrimination on the basis of sexual orientation and sex. The right to marry is so strong, it was argued, that any definitional exclusion must be clearly justified, citing cases including *Loving v Virginia* 388 U.S. 1 (1967) in which the US Supreme Court struck down bans on interracial marriage. Mr. Collins SC submitted that distinctions on these grounds were 'suspect', i.e. shift the burden to the State to justify the exclusion of a class of persons from exercising a constitutional right.

22. On the basis that it was not clear from the defence filed what justifications for this exclusion would be advanced by the State, counsel for the plaintiffs analysed the essence of the right to marry and the justifications for limiting marriage to opposite-sex couples that had been proffered by State authorities elsewhere. Four such potential justifications were identified.

1. That marriage is related to procreation and that the biological ability to procreate is an essential feature of marriage. As same-sex couples lack this essential feature they can be justifiably excluded from the constitutional right to marry.
2. That the welfare of potential children is better protected in opposite-sex headed families, so that same-sex couples can be justifiably excluded from marriage.
3. That marriage is and always has been between a man and a woman and, thus, that marriage under the Constitution is definitionally limited to the right of one man to marry one woman and vice versa.
4. That there is an assumption that a majority in society disapprove either of homosexuality or of homosexual conduct for religious, philosophical or other reasons and that the State is entitled to act on foot of that presumed majority to prohibit same-sex marriage.

The State did not base its justification on potential justifications 1 or 4. Thus, I will not consider the arguments put to me in relation to these potential justifications.

23. Submissions on the welfare of children largely focused on the evidence outlined above. Mr. Collins SC for the plaintiffs argued that, even if one accepted that the State had a legitimate interest in regulating marriage by reference to the welfare of children, and even if one accepted that the state might have a preference that children be raised in opposite-sex headed households, it could not be established that excluding same-sex couples was reasonably related to that purpose in a manner that treated each class fairly. If the justification invoked by the state is the welfare of children, then the real question is whether children raised by same-sex parents would be better off if their parents could marry. The effect of the prohibition, he submitted, was to deny these children the benefits of being raised in a household where their parents had the constitutional protections associated with marriage.

24. In response, Mr. O'Donnell SC for the defendants noted that the concept of marriage was located within the constitutional provision dealing with the family, but did not deal at length with the arguments relating to the welfare of children *per se*. Rather, counsel for the defence argued that the State was entitled as a matter of public police, and obliged as a matter of constitutional law, to treat the institution of marriage with special consideration, that the definition of marriage in Irish constitutional jurisprudence is limited to marriage between a biological man and a biological woman, and that this Court may not apply a dynamic interpretation to the concept in the manner requested by the plaintiffs.

25. Counsel for the plaintiffs extensively examined Irish, ECHR and comparative case law on the definition of marriage. It was submitted that the Constitution, the ECHR and the Taxes Consolidation Act 1997 mention but do not define 'marriage'. The common law definition of marriage was classically stated by Lord Penzance in *Hyde v Hyde* (1866) L.R. 1 P and D 130, 133:

> "The voluntary union of one man and one woman, to the exclusion of all others."

26. In *Murray v Ireland* [1985] I.R. 532 Costello J. considered the meaning of marriage in the Constitution and held, at p. 536:

> "The concept and nature of marriage, was derived from the Christian notion of a partnership based on an irrevocable personal consent given by both spouses which establishes a unique and very special life-long relationship."

27. Costello J. went on to make clear that a married couple without children could be defined as a constitutional family. This definition was adopted by the Supreme Court in *TF v Ireland* [1995] I.E. 321. In *DT v CT* [2003] 1 I.L.R.M. 321, Murray J. held that marriage is:

> "A solemn contract of partnership entered into between man and woman with a special status recognised by the Constitution and that it was in principle for life."

28. Reference was also made to the judgment of McKechnie J. in *Foy v an tArd Chlarath-eoir* (Unreported, 2002, High Court, 9 July 2002) in which he held:

> "Marriage as understood by the Constitution, by statute and by case law refers to a union by a biological man with a biological woman."

29. *Foy* predates the decision of the European Court of Human Rights in *Goodwin v United Kingdom* (2002) 35 E.H.R.R. 18, which came to a different conclusion. However, while decisions of the European Court of Human Rights can be taken into account in constitutional interpretation in this jurisdiction, they are not binding in respect of the meaning of the Constitution. Thus, in interpreting the Constitution this Court is not required to follow the decisions of the European Court of Human Rights: indeed, if it were required by the Constitution, an Irish Court could grant far more extensive rights under the Constitution than those recognised under the ECHR.

30. The plaintiffs accepted that there is a long-standing common law and statutory prohibition on same-sex marriage, but argued that there has been a shift in the understanding of marriage so that the longevity of same-sex couples' exclusion is not determinative of the issue. The essence of their argument was that the constitutional understanding of marriage should be subject to dynamic interpretation. In support they cited the decision of the Ontario Court of Appeal in *Halpern and Others v Attorney General of Canada* (2003) 65 O.R. (4) 161. In that case the Court reformulated the definition of marriage having regard to the equality rights of same-sex couples under s. 15(1) of the Canadian Charter of Rights and Freedoms as "the voluntary union for life of two persons to the exclusion of all others". That decision was followed by other courts in Canada and ultimately led to the acknowledgement of the right to marry for same-sex couples in the Supreme Court of Canada case of *Reference re Same Sex Marriage* [2004] 3 SCR 698. The plaintiffs referred to further comparative cases in arguing that the constitutional concept of marriage was capable of dynamic interpretation so that same-sex marriage was not excluded by reference to the

definition of marriage *per se*. Counsel for the plaintiffs pointed to the judgment of Walsh J. in *McGee v. Attorney General* [1974] I.R. 284 where he stated, at 319:

> "According to the preamble, the people gave themselves the Constitution to promote the common good with due observance of prudence, justice and charity so that the dignity and freedom of the individual might be assured. The judges must, therefore, as best they can from their training and their experience interpret these rights in accordance with their ideas of prudence, justice and charity. It is but natural that from time to time the prevailing ideas of these virtues may be conditioned by the passage of time; no interpretation of the Constitution is intended to be final for all time. It is given in the light of prevailing ideas and concepts."

31. In further support of the possibility of dynamic interpretation, counsel for the plaintiffs pointed to *Sinnott v. Minister for Education and Science* [2001] 2 I.R. 545.

32. In response Mr. Gallagher SC for the defendants argued that the plaintiffs had not offered any legal basis for the dynamic interpretation they sought; rather they had simply argued that the Constitution is not limited to its meaning in 1937. He argued that the Court was being asked to rewrite the plain meaning of Article 41 of the Constitution, notwithstanding the fact that the Oireachtas made clear that the concept of marriage in Irish law does not include marriage between same-sex couples as recently as 2004. It was noted that in Ireland recognition has been given to marriage in the context of the family under Article 41. The parties did not dispute that in 1937 there was no doubt that the constitutionally contemplated family was that founded on opposite-sex marriage. Mr. O'Donnell SC for the defendants argued that the institution of marriage, as protected by the Constitution, is not simply about the private relationship between two people. Rather, it relates to the role of marriage in society, its relationship to the family, and the family's relationship to the social order posited by the Constitution. By reference to the same authorities opened to this court by the plaintiffs, the defence argued that marriage in Irish constitutional law is understood as the monogamous union of biological man with biological woman and that, in that, there was nothing unusual when compared to other jurisdictions. While the original understanding of marriage as indissoluble had been changed by the introduction of divorce, that was effected by a referendum and not by judicial interpretation. It was submitted that the definition of marriage within the Constitution was so clear, and so fundamental to traditional constitutional values, that it was not possible to alter it without a referendum. In other words, what the enacting electorate had decided in relation to a fundamental concept could only be changed by the enacting electorate, i.e. in a referendum. Thus, it was argued that dynamic interpretation was not possible here.

33. Counsel for the state further argued that the English case of *Wilkinson and Kitzinger v. Attorney General* (High Court, Unreported, 31st July, 2006), which related to the attempt to have a British Columbian marriage recognised by reference to the ECHR, had been unsuccessful and showed that non-recognition was not incompatible with the Convention. The relevance of *Wilkinson* is, however, limited: there is no equivalent constitutional protection of marriage in the UK and at the time the case was heard that jurisdiction provided for civil unions under the Civil Partnership Act 2004, which are not available to same-sex couples in this jurisdiction.

Conclusion on the Right to Marry

34. Although the Irish jurisprudence opened to the Court refers to marriage as being between a man and a woman, I must consider whether this limitation in those cases was material to the nature of constitutionally recognised marriage, or a product of social convention. The plaintiffs claim that the right to marry is about the right to marry the person that you love. Certainly, marriage brings certain financial and other advantages with it, particularly where the couple has sufficient means that matters such as capital gains tax are germane, as is the case here, but the essence of their argument is that we ought to have the right to marry the person whom we love. That marriage would be about love is, of course, the ideal from a personal perspective. It is also consistent with the notion that, for many people (although not for everyone), the institution of marriage is a means of recognising, supporting and protecting a particular, dear, and dignity-enhancing interpersonal relationship between two adults. However, the legal and the social understandings of marriage are not always congruent.

35. The law recognises that one need not love someone to have a valid marriage with her, and that one may love someone but be legally precluded from marrying her. Furthermore, the legal regulation of marriage historically has more to do with property and control than with love: indeed, up to relatively recent times people for whom the maintenance and acquisition of land was culturally and familialy important often married in the hope of love but the certainty of financial stability. While societal realities have, thankfully, moved on from this and we generally recognise that legal institutions such as marriage may help to maintain the bonds of love and inter-dependence between spouses, the historical aspect is significant in understanding the legal right to marry. While a marriage is ideally about love, love itself may be beyond the legal definition of marriage. Indeed, this case itself is about both love (the plaintiffs' love for one another, which they have chosen to given a marital form) *and* finances (recognition as spouses in the context of tax). Furthermore, it is an unfortunately common truth that rather than nurture and enhance spouses as individuals, marriage can constrain and expose people to exploitation, unhappiness and in some cases abuse. In reality, no two marriages are the same; in law, however, we apply a single definition regardless of the health, happiness and longevity of the particular marriage in question.

36. Notwithstanding the fact that marriage is an unhappy state for some, Irish constitutional jurisprudence holds that marriage has a social function of some importance as to entitle the State in its enactments to treat married couples differently from other types of relationship for the purpose of Article 40.1: *The State (Nicolau) v An Bord Uchtála* [1966] I.R. 567, *G v An Bord Uchtála* [1984] I.R. 316, and *Murphy v Attorney General* [1982] I.R. 241. Our Constitution treats marriage as an important social institution that brings welfare and stability to the family and, through the family, to society. That constitutional protection means that marriage stands at the pinnacle of a hierarchy of familial relationships; no other form of relationship can be treated more favourably than marriage (*Murphy v Attorney General* [1982] I.R. 241) and no other form of intimate adult relationship enjoys legal recognition in Ireland. Arguments advanced by counsel for the plaintiffs suggest that this is because we believe marriage brings stability and better welfare outcomes for children. Indeed, although the plaintiffs in this case do not raise children together, I heard plentiful evidence on the welfare of children raised by same-sex parents. In this respect,

and notwithstanding the fact that of course many married couples do not have and/or raise children together, three observations are germane.

37. First, it was not established in evidence that children raised by same-sex parents have better or equally good welfare outcomes to those raised by opposite-sex parents; nor was it established that their welfare outcomes are worse. Until relatively recently it was rare for same-sex couples to live together as openly romantic partners, and to raise children together. Opposite-sex couples have done both since the foundation of the State, and of course before. Thus, it is to be expected that sample sizes in studies relating to same-sex headed families might be smaller than those relating to opposite-sex headed families and, indeed, that there might be fewer longitudinal studies on which to rely. As a result it is unsurprising that such studies were not opened to this court. Given this, the simple contrasting of research about opposite- and same-sex headed families is unhelpful. Second, while the protection of marriage within Article 41 suggests that the welfare of children is relevant to the constitutional definition of marriage, the constitutional concept of marriage is not dependent on whether or not a couple has, can have, or wants to have children. As held in *Murray v Ireland* [1985] I.R. 532, the constitutional protection of marriage applies with or without children or the opportunity to conceive. Thus, matters relating to children cannot be determinative. Third, social reality is relevant. Throughout the country same-sex couples raise children together. This has always been the case. This will always be the case. For those children, the fact that their parents cannot marry has constitutional implications: their families do not enjoy constitutional protection. While I did not hear conclusive evidence on the welfare outcomes for children of being raised by same-sex parents, we do know that children raised in non-marital families bear legal implications of the current understanding of the Constitution and that these are to their disadvantage when compared to children whose parents are married.

38. Thus, I am not convinced that the relationship between marriage and children is such that it must exclude same-sex couples from the status of marriage under the Constitution.

39. Given the social understanding of marriage outlined above, there would appear to be no innate reason why same-sex couples ought not to have the choice to marry should they wish to do so. However, the fact remains that the Supreme Court, by whose decisions I am bound, has defined marriage in opposite-sex terms. So too, although not in a manner that is binding upon this Court, has the European Court of Human Rights. The plaintiffs have asked me to focus on the character of marriage and to apply a dynamic interpretation to the Constitution so as to recognise a right on their behalf to marry one another regardless of the fact that they are both women. The implication of such a finding would be the invalidation of s. 2(2)(e) of the Civil Registration Act 2004, even though this remedy was not expressly requested. In response, the State argues that the understanding of marriage in Article 41 is so long-standing and central to public policy that it should not be 'distorted' by judicial intervention.

40. There is nothing about the concept of marriage *per se* that means it is not amenable to dynamic interpretation, the acceptability of which has been established since *McGee v Attorney General* [1974] 1 I.R. 284. Marriage is such a fundamental social institution in Ireland that it would be nonsensical to immunise it from social change since 1937. All constitutional concepts must keep abreast of social realities to the extent possible within the confines of the judicial role. That, as noted by Walsh J. in *McGee*, is how the preambular commitment to prudence, justice and charity effectively informs the Constitution.

41. However, this does not mean that dynamic interpretation can be undertaken on the basis of slender legal materials. The original understanding of marriage in the Constitution would not have included same-sex marriage: for most people, such a thing would have been unthinkable in 1937 when there was no protection from discrimination on the basis of sexual orientation, many forms of male homosexual sex were criminalized, and homosexuality was considered a disorder rather than a simple fact of life. At that time, homosexuality was a matter of stigma and shame; thankfully both society and the legal system have moved on from that time. For example, one could not imagine our contemporary Supreme Court handing down a judgment condemning homosexual citizens today as it did in *Norris v Attorney General* [1984] I.R. 36. However, this alone does not demonstrate a movement of sufficient weight and velocity to underpin the plaintiffs' claim, most particularly as the Oireachtas reaffirmed the common law understanding of marriage as being between a man and a woman as recently as 2004. Furthermore, very few countries permit persons of the same sex to marry, the European Court of Human Rights has confirmed that Article 12 protects 'traditional', i.e. opposite-sex, marriage (e.g. *Parry v. the United Kingdom* (dec.), no. 42971/05, ECHR 2006-XV, and *R. and F. v. the United Kingdom* (dec.), no. 35748/05, 28 November 2006). There is no evidence of a widespread social endorsement of same-sex marriage at this time, although a number of jurisdictions seem to be considering introducing marriage equality. In addition, increasing numbers of jurisdictions are introducing other means of recognising and providing legal protection short of marriage to same-sex relationships, such as civil unions and registered partnerships. Although falling short of marriage, such an innovation might bring relief as to taxation, for example, for the plaintiffs if it were made available in this jurisdiction.

42. Bearing all of this in mind, I must reluctantly conclude that sufficient materials to support the dynamic interpretation of the right to marry have not been opened to this Court. This does not mean, of course, that the Supreme Court might not find otherwise, that the Oireachtas could not repeal s. 2(2)(e) of the Civil Registration Act 2004 thus indicting a political will to extend marriage to same-sex couples, that a social and comparative legal consensus in favour of such marriages might not emerge in the future, or that the Constitution definitively precludes same-sex marriage. It simply means that insufficient evidence was presented to me to support a dynamic interpretation of the Constitution so as to assert a positive constitutional right to marry the person one loves, even if that person is of the same biological sex.

43. Given my finding that the Constitution does not protect a right to marry at this time, I deal very briefly with the claim relating to Article 12 ECHR as, even if successful, this cannot require the defendants to change their position (although it might inspire them to do so). To date, the European Court of Human Rights has held that contracting parties may limit marriage to opposite-sex couples without violating Article 12, i.e. that whether or not to allow same-sex marriage is within the States' margin of appreciation (*Parry v. the United Kingdom* (dec.), no. 42971/05, ECHR 2006-XV, and *R. and F. v. the United Kingdom* (dec.), no. 35748/05, 28 November 2006). Thus, there is no violation of Article 12, or basis in Article 12 for this Court to interpret taxation legislation as applying the benefits of marriage to the plaintiffs under s. 2 of the ECHR Act 2003. I note, however, that the fact that marriage is within the States' margin of appreciation means that same-sex marriage does not violate Article 12: the ECHR is no impediment to legal change to create marriage equality in this jurisdiction.

The Claim of Discrimination

44. Mr. Collins SC for the plaintiffs argued that, in respect of marriage, two distinct classes have been created: those who have the capacity to marry and those who lack the capacity to marry by virtue of the fact that they are of the same sex. In creating different classes, Mr. Collins SC argued the State must adhere to the test outlined in *Brennan v Attorney General* [1993] I.L.R.M. 449, at 480 to the effect that a classification must be:

> "For a legitimate legislative purpose ... It must be relevant to that purpose, and ... each class must be treated fairly."

45. The plaintiffs argued that by excluding same-sex couples from marriage a distinction is made based on sexual orientation, and that this should give rise to a presumption that there is a breach of constitutional rights and, accordingly, that the burden shifts to the State to justify this distinction. While the plaintiffs accepted that there was no concept of 'suspect category' such as applies under U.S. constitutional law, there was nevertheless a basis in Irish law for shifting the burden of proof in this way. This was based on the decision of the Supreme Court in *Re Article 26 and the Employment Equality Bill* [1997] 2 I.R. 321 at p. 347:

> "The forms of discrimination which are, presumptively at least, proscribed by Article 40.1 are not particularised: manifestly, they would extend to classifications based on sex, race, language, religious or political opinions."

46. Counsel for the plaintiffs argued that none of the four presumptive justifications outlined above was sufficient to justify the differentiation in treatment. Counsel referred to the decision of the European Court of Human Rights in *Karner v Austria* (2003) 38 EHRR 528 to the effect that

> "A difference in treatment is discriminatory if it has not an objective and reasonable justification, that is, if it does not pursue a legitimate aim or if there is not a reasonable relationship of proportionality between the means employed and the aim sought to be realised ... just like differences based on sex, differences based on sexual orientation require particularly serious reasons by way of justification."

In this case, the protection of 'traditional' family forms was found to be insufficient:

> "The court can accept that protection of the family in the traditional sense is, in principle, a weighty and legitimate reason which might justify a difference in treatment ... The aim of protecting the family in the traditional sense is rather abstract and a broad variety of concrete measures may be used to implement it. In cases in which the margin of appreciation afforded to Member States is narrow, as the position where there is a difference in treatment based on sex or sexual orientation, the principle of proportionality does not merely require that the measure chosen is in principle suited for realising the aim sought. It must also be shown that it was necessary to exclude persons living in a homosexual relationship from the scope of application of [the relevant law]."

The English Court of Appeal reached a similar conclusion in *Ghaidan v. Mendoza* [2004] 4 All E.R. 1162.

47. The State argued that the plaintiffs' marriage was not recognised in Irish law, that they were treated in the same way as all other unmarried couples in Ireland, and thus that no discrimination had been established. Accordingly it was argued that the plaintiffs' claim

should fail *ad limine*. Any argument that unmarried couples are treated differently to married couples in Irish law could not sustain a claim of discrimination on the basis of the particular constitutional position of marriage. Thus, the classification in this case—which it was argued was that of married persons as against unmarried persons—was not only contemplated but authorised by the Constitution, made for a legitimate constitutional purpose, and justifiable by Article 40.1 of the Constitution.

Conclusions

48. There can be no question that in Irish constitutional law, such differential treatment is permitted. As noted in *Murphy v Attorney General* [1982] I.R. 241 the institution of marriage is deserving of special constitutional protection, and that remains the case. The plaintiffs argued that the classes that were created, and which had to be justified, were between heterosexual persons who could marry and homosexual persons who could not. In response, the defence argued that the classification was between married and unmarried persons.

49. It seems to me that the classification requiring consideration is, in fact, between homosexual and heterosexual persons.

50. In the case of heterosexual persons, or those in opposite-sex relationships, one has the option to marry and thus to acquire the constitutional and other legal privileges and obligations of marriage. In the case of homosexual persons, or those in same-sex relationships, no such option is available in Ireland. While Mr. O'Donnell SC is right to note that there is no suspect category or similar in Irish constitutional law, it is nevertheless the case that a classification of this kind is *prima facie* discriminatory and requires justification by reference to *Brennan v Attorney General* [1993] I.L.R.M. 449.

51. The provision creating the classification in this case is s. 2(2)(e) of the Civil Registration Act 2004. That provision was enacted in order to make clear who has capacity to enter into a marriage in the State: i.e. for a legitimate legislative purpose. It is clearly relevant to that purpose. The question that remains is whether each class is treated fairly. Those excluded from the possibility of marriage by virtue of a capacity rule are treated less favourably than those who marry, not least in the tax code as outlined above and under consideration in this case. In addition to this, such persons do not have any possibility to enter into a marriage with the person with whom they love and want to form a lifelong relationship of love, commitment and interdependence. This inability to marry a partner of one's choice has negative impacts on those who fall into the excluded class, including those in same-sex relationships.

52. In order for that difference in treatment to be 'fair' it must be related to the nature of marriage and the nature of the exclusion itself. As outlined above, the inability to conceive children does not exclude persons from marriage under Article 41: *Murphy v Attorney General* [1982] I.R. 241. Thus, that cannot be a justifying basis for excluding same-sex couples. There is no question but that same-sex couples can and do provide love, commitment, monogamy, care and support to one another in the same way as many opposite-sex couples do; however, unlike with opposite-sex couples who can marry, the State neither recognises nor supports this in any way whatsoever. This not only means that such couples are

treated differently to others, but that the love, affection, commitment, caregiving, and support within those relationships are implicitly relegated to a lesser position to that between opposite-sex partners who, with few exceptions, can marry if they wish to do so. The State did not address these differences in treatment between the appropriate comparators: i.e. heterosexual married couples, and same-sex couples who cannot marry but who wish to marry in Irish law.

53. Thus, when compared to those persons who are married and in a marriage recognised by Irish law, the plaintiffs suffer a disadvantage that has not been justified by the State. The only remaining possible justification would be that the Constitution does not permit recognition of same-sex marriage. This is a qualitatively different claim to that considered above, namely that the Constitution positively guarantees a right to enter into a same-sex marriage for those who wish to do so. Should the Constitution permit recognition of same-sex marriage but not positively guarantee such a right to marriage the State could, for example, recognise a foreign marriage such as that of the plaintiffs but not be required to permit such marriages domestically, although such a distinction would be intellectually incongruous in many ways.

54. However, in order to hold that the Constitution does not prohibit recognition of foreign same-sex marriages I would have to apply a dynamic interpretation to the Constitution. For the reasons outlined above, this is not something I find myself able to do in this case. Thus, although there are clear differences in treatment between homosexual and heterosexual couples in respect of marriage in the State which constitute a *prima facie* discrimination, the constitutional conception of marriage as being a union of a man and a woman offers a clear and compelling legal justification for such discrimination. The justice and fairness of that is another question, and it seems to me that this case demonstrates the need for the Oireachtas to revisit the matter of the Civil Registration Act 2004 and engage in rigorous and fair-minded debate as to whether one should be precluded from marrying someone simply because she or he is of the same biological sex.

Discrimination under the European Convention on Human Rights

55. The plaintiffs argued that the refusal to recognise their marriage, or to permit them to marry in Ireland, was a violation of Article 8 combined with Article 14, i.e. discrimination in violation of the ECHR. As I have already found that Article 12 does not require the State to permit the plaintiffs to marry the remaining ECHR claims can be dealt with in brief. The European Court of Human Rights allows a significant margin of appreciation to States in respect of recognition of different family forms although, as established in *Karner v Austria* (2003) 38 EHRR 528 considered above, protection of "traditional" family forms is not always sufficient justification. While the failure to provide any recognition in law to the plaintiffs' relationship might be said to violate Article 8 *per se*, this argument was not made before the Court. Rather, the plaintiffs focused on the claim that failure to recognise their marriage or allow them to marry was an unjustifiable discrimination by reference to their Article 8 rights. However, it is clear that Article 8 does not require States to permit persons to marry, not least because Article 12 is currently interpreted as applying to traditional marriage. Limited attention was paid to the Convention arguments before the Court, thus I am

reluctant to embark upon a speculative assessment of whether there was an Article 8 breach, bearing in mind the meaning of Article 12. However, especially given the introduction into law of the ECHR Act 2003, this may merit further consideration in the future. That said, on the basis of the arguments before me relating to the ECHR I cannot find any violation of Article 8, 12 and 14.

Conclusions

56. For the reasons outlined above I find:

1. That the plaintiffs' British Columbian marriage cannot be recognised by this Court.
2. The constitutional right to marry in Ireland does not extend to a right to marry a person of the same biological sex.
3. Given the lack of such constitutional right, the relevant tax legislation cannot be interpreted in a manner that would result in the plaintiffs being treated as a married couple.
4. That the limitation of constitutional marriage to opposite-sex couples provides sufficient legal justification for the *prima facie* discriminatory exclusion of the plaintiffs from the possibility of marriage.
5. That as Article 12 of the ECHR has not been interpreted to include a right to marry persons of the same biological sex there is no violation of the ECHR.

57. Having reached these conclusions, I must reluctantly conclude that the Plaintiffs' claim for recognition of their Canadian marriage must fail, as must the challenge to the relevant provisions of the Taxes Consolidation Act 1997.

58. In their evidence to this Court and in their lives together the plaintiffs have amply demonstrated their love and commitment for one another and eloquently explained the importance, for them, of having their marriage recognized by law at home in Ireland. Although the strict result of this case is that the plaintiffs cannot require the State to treat them as a married couple for the purposes of tax, it is of greater significance than mere taxation. My judgment means that the State may—although not that it *must*—treat their relationship as something lesser than marriage, and their love as one that cannot be contained within the institution of marriage as recognised by the Constitution. It is to be hoped that the Oireachtas will return to this matter and consider seriously whether such an outcome is truly just, and in keeping with our constitutional values of prudence, justice and charity.

15

Commentary on *In Re E (a child)* (the 'Holy Cross' case)

CHRISTINE BELL FBA

Introduction

Feminists used to say that 'the personal is political', but responding to this case, the political and legal feel very personal. It is from a personal as well as a legal engagement with the case that I comment on the House of Lords judgments and Colin Murray's alternative feminist judgment.

I was a member of the Northern Ireland Human Rights Commission (NIHRC) when it was first established under the terms of the Belfast/Good Friday Agreement (the Agreement). As a member of the Commission I was involved in the decision to support the 'Holy Cross' case that ultimately resulted in the ruling that Murray's feminist judgment addresses.

Taking the Case: The Importance of Strategic Litigation to Women

The case underlines for me the importance of strategic litigation to women. There was no attempt to take a 'feminist' approach to the NIHRC case-work strategy, or indeed focus on gender equality. Rather there was a focus on trying to bring international human rights standards to bear on how the European Convention on Human Rights (ECHR) was interpreted and applied in Northern Ireland, and a case selection focus, born of limited resources, on the most serious of the ECHR standards—Articles 2 and 3. Despite the lack of focus on women as such, this strategy was to see the Commission become critical to two of the feminist judgments in this book: the *In re White* case,[1] which challenged the lack of balance (including under-representation of women) on the Parades Commission, which makes decisions on lawful parades, and the above case. The ECHR is notoriously weak on women, with no stand-alone anti-discrimination clause in its main text, and

[1] *In re White* [2000] NI 432. See ch 12.

no specific gender equality emphasis.[2] It is vital that it is interpreted and applied in a way that aligns it with specialist conventions on women—and in this case, children. In these cases and in its investigations, the NIHRC's record on women was significant and important.

However, the going was not easy and should give rise to feminist concern. In *Re White*, Lord Carswell (the author of the majority judgment in the House of Lords in this case), then as Lord Chief Justice in Northern Ireland, began a line of attack that he was later to take to its conclusion in a case involving the NIHRC's articulation of international standards in the Coroner's hearings on the Omagh bomb. There he decided that the NIHRC had no third-party intervention power.[3] This decision was ultimately to be overruled by the (then) House of Lords, which made short shrift of this reasoning, but to the cost of the NIHRC's losing valuable early-year interventions, and of course to the cost of well over £100,000 of taxpayer money (£60,000 or so on the NIRHC side).[4] In the House of Lords' judgment in *In re E*,[5] Lord Hoffman reprises the idea that the NIHRC's role should be judicially limited, criticising the NIHRC third-party intervention for not 'adding anything' to the submissions of the parties, something that Colin Murray's feminist judgment takes care to rebut. However, Lord Hoffman's reprisal misunderstands the role of the NIHRC, and the ways in which its gradual mounting of arguments based on international human rights standards comes to shape the arguments of legal teams more widely.

Moreover, while the NIHRC clearly should not be exempted from judicial criticism, those criticisms should be made in the knowledge that they feed into a wider political context. Without exaggerating the point, from its inception the NIHRC and its Commissioners came under sustained political attack. For many of us this was new, and certainly not a standard part of membership of all public bodies, although perhaps paralleled in those perceived to touch the political situation. My time on the NIHRC saw me and others being the subject of untruthful, loathsome and damaging accusations in public and in our workplaces, experiencing threats to our physical safety and to our families, and being abusively attacked verbally at meetings, with some physical safety concerns there too. So, at the starkest level, the most malevolent and personally worrying attacks come from those same 'sinister forces' who have the capacity for killing that the judges agreed the police were right to capitulate to in this case.

The bottom line was that without the NIHRC's support, the case would not have existed in the first place, and many lawyers who now use international standards in support of their clients would not do so. While the case was lost at every level of court, in my view it importantly clarified the law's limits (and importantly what is and is not 'free speech'). More than that, in particular through the Northern Ireland Court of Appeal level, it left a legal record of important moral and political contribution, by articulating an official, unequivocal

[2] See ECHR as amended by Protocols 11 and 14 and supplemented by Protocols 1, 4, 6, 7, 12, and 13, at www.echr.coe.int/Documents/Convention_ENG.pdf/. On gender and the ECHR, see Council of Europe Factsheet, 'European Human Rights Court—Gender Equality', at www.coe.int/t/dc/files/source/equality_factsheet_en.doc; and Ivana Radacic, 'Gender Equality Juripsrudence of the European Court of Human Rights' (2008) 19(4) *European Journal of International Law* 841–57.

[3] *In Re Northern Ireland Human Rights Commission* [2001] NI 271.

[4] *In Re Northern Ireland Human Rights Commission* [2002] HL 25.

[5] *In re E* [2008] UKHL 66.

condemnation of the protests in a way the wider Northern Irish political establishment had not been able to manage at the time.

Taking the Case

Every morning I would turn on my television in Derry over breakfast and see the Holy Cross dispute featured (unusually for Northern Ireland) nationally, and even more unusually on *Lorraine Kelly*—the popular breakfast time TV show. Lorraine Kelly and her viewers watched small girls, aged between 4 and 11, walking through violent protests to get to school, flanked by policemen in full riot gear, and saw Alabama in the 1960s, with a small African American girl being escorted to school by the National Guard in the face of an ugly white racist mob. In Northern Ireland, however, opinions were much more mixed.

When the Holy Cross protest recommenced in the new school year, September 2001, my second daughter, then aged 4 (just), was also starting school. I left her, and a baby I was nursing, to travel from Derry to Belfast, to witness, as a Commissioner, the journey to the school with parents and their daughters, and to accompany them. A blast bomb had been thrown at the children just shortly before, and I remember well the feelings of paranoia and stress as I travelled to the area. My reading of the judgments in this case is unavoidably coloured by the automatic 'compare and contrast' I exercise with conditions for the girls on the road. Colin Murray has written a feminist judgment that captures many of the dynamics of the events. I also feel that the House of Lords' judgments on the case include a feminist judgment among them. The judgment of Baroness Brenda Hale captured and articulated many of the concerns I witnessed. Although I disagree with her conclusion, nonetheless I would commend the judgment for the humanity of its approach.

Ultimately, however, I question the capacity of legal reasoning to address the reality of the girls' experience in those days. The following issues were very tangibly present on the road, and structured police and judicial decision-making relating to how girls should walk to school, but are only casually noted in the official case judgments, if at all.

The Invisibility of the Children: How the Girls Went Missing

The most striking contrast between the road and the decision-making that surrounded it is how the girls went missing. Somehow, the fact that this whole dispute had at its centre tiny girls, many as young as 4 years old and in their first week at school, was forgotten as people debated and made decisions focused on the dispute between adults. The decisions of the police balanced rights to protest against what these girls were experiencing. I still find it hard to understand how this happened. To me it takes on an additional symbolism that the girl at the centre of the case literally also went missing, and the case became about the mother (a matter both Murray and Hale deplore).

In the middle of what was a mass of adults on the road, the tiny girls were just too small to be seen. The broader context of their day was never seen or discussed. When I visited the school, I realised that this was not a conflict about a journey to school that stopped at the school door. This was a conflict about the very existence of the school that had entered the school gates and grasped each tiny girl in a grip of fear throughout every aspect of her school day. The day before our visit, when metal shutters were being fitted to the school windows for protection (given the urgency, while the girls were in class), workmen dropped a shutter, and around half the girls in the class had wet themselves in panic that the school was being attacked. The Head showed us the many cards of support the school had received from around the world, and some of the thank-you letters written back by the girls. Many of the thank-you letters thanked their supporters for 'helping them not feel that they were so bad'. I remember first wondering how children could see themselves at fault for this very adult protest, before quickly remembering how children always do view commotions around them as somehow their fault. In all of this, the idea that the rights of the child were being adequately protected is difficult to accept.

Bring in the Men: Turning a Daily Journey into a March

A part of the dynamic of the girls' invisibility was the way in which the policing of the walk itself fed a dynamic in which it was responded to as a battle between men. The drama and dynamics of the walk down the road itself were very curious—a matter noted by Baroness Hale. The policing of the situation meant that the only degree of any security that could be offered to those coming and going from school was if they arrived and left at the same time in a group. As I experienced, this meant that parents and their children would be kept together at either end of the journey, and marshalled into a group to walk down the road. The daily walk to school was turned into almost a 'march' (with all of the connotations in Northern Ireland), which took place almost as a 'march' against the backdrop of the jeers and abuse. While for the most part women take their children to school, as the protests continued men also accompanied the walk in increasing numbers. On one hand this was a reaction of protection, but from the point of view of the protestors the sight of Republican men 'marching' through their community was a provocation, and reinforced decisions to treat it as an 'inter-communal conflict public order dispute'. The walk to school was forced into the very territorial claiming and counter-claiming of streets that fed the escalation of the situation.

The Sexualised Nature of the Abuse

Appearing in the judgments, and much more overtly in our feminist one, but inevitably in a way that does little to convey exactly how hostile it felt in real life, was the sexualised nature of the abuse to which the girls and their mothers were subjected. Accompanying the girls along the road that day, women holding the hands of small girls were called 'whores' all the way along the road, and a women next to me with darker skin, 'Paki whore'. Urine was thrown, and most notably there were pictures all along the road held by Protestors of the Priest who walked with the children, saying 'Paedophile priest'.

The sexualised and racialised nature of abuse against what was essentially a completely white population of parents, spoke to the deep sectarian 'othering' of ethnic conflict as mixed with misogyny. Yet I was also struck by women protestors abusing the children, often in vile ways, using sexualised language. I remember even noting a disabled woman in a wheelchair, holding a poster and shouting very close to me.

'Intersectionality'

Another identity dynamic, however, was much less visible but much more structuring of the official decision-making in the case. This is the question of class. This was a school with largely working-class parents from a Catholic working-class area, walking through a Protestant working-class area. It is inconceivable to me that had this been a protest that disrupted children from attending one of Northern Ireland's prestigious grammar schools, which educate the middle-classes in nice districts of Belfast, it would have been allowed to last two minutes. Also inconceivable to me, is that parents in those schools would have accepted a level of physical threat against their children that included the throwing of a blast bomb, insecurity against the school building, and sexualised abuse on entry and leaving as a situation in which their children could be adequately educated. I also severely doubt whether they would have felt that scurrying in through a back door would somehow be safer or consistent with their child's educational equality, any more than did the parents in Ardoyne, or indeed in Alabama in the early 1960s. And had this situation arisen in leafy South Belfast, I suspect that 'the great and the good' would have found a louder moral voice with which to condemn it.

In fact, because of the physical infrastructure of the city and class and sectarian geographies, a similar situation of Loyalist protest around a middle-class Catholic or Protestant school almost certainly would not and could not happen. This seems to me to be an important equality issue, but how would it ever be proved and litigated in a court of law? With difficulty, I imagine.

Torture from the Eyes of a Child

The official judgments and Colin Murray's feminist judgment carefully cite how torture is to be evaluated differently when children are concerned. Again, this was graphically brought home to me on visiting the school. Looking through their work, in the children's drawings for their daily diaries they depicted themselves as surrounded by space-age monsters with masks—these were the police. As they walked down the road each day, on either side a line of police stood in full riot gear—a highly militarised get-up, including visors, heavy boots, huge helmets, truncheons, guns and body-length shields. Having monitored the policing of protests for many years, I have noticed that police tend to face in the direction from which they see the threat as coming. As police protected Orange Order marchers from Catholic/Republican protests, they always stood with their backs to the marchers, riot gear and plastic bullet guns pointed down the streets towards the protesting Catholic community. This was the community from which violence against the police was deemed most likely to come. In the Holy Cross protest, the police faced inwards towards the girls, backs to the baying protestors. Perhaps there was some policing reason for this? Perhaps faces, even behind visors, were viewed as more 'friendly' than backs? However, I remember thinking that normality in policing public protest would for me be achieved when the religion and background of the respective groups did not determine the direction the police faced—for whatever reason. For the girls, however, they saw lines of armed men facing them with guns, riot shields and riot gear, and close behind more lines of jeering crowds. The police direction meant that in the girls' eyes, the police were just part of one threatening mass of people flanking their walk to school.

Did the Police Breach Article 3?

It was clear to all, and judges repeatedly affirmed that the children's Article 3 rights were violated. The difficult question was whether the state was involved: had the police failed to adequately protect them or not? The courts found that they had done all they could. In essence, they found that the state could not have been expected to do anything else to protect the Article 3 rights of girls aged 4, on their first days at school.

If I had to write my own judgment, its critical focus would be the policing decision to allow the protests to build, with some free speech protection when the school term recommenced in the September. Whatever immediate pressures the police faced to police a developing situation in June, the school summer holidays are two months long in Northern Ireland. As Colin Murray's judgment significantly notes, this had been a summer with a build-up of crises, and it was clear that the protests would re-start with the new school year and against a backdrop of greater instability and crisis for the peace process than before. During that time, police and other authorities knew what the situation foretold: they knew that the protests were likely, that they would be violent and that, once commenced, they would be difficult to disband and would be underwritten by the threat of lethal violence. Yet basing the decision in part on a commitment to the protestors' freedom of speech, they let this situation develop again. For me, this decision, rather than the daily policing decisions or the ways in which police reacted to contain the initial phase of the protest, was the critical decision that prejudiced the rights of the children.

Baroness Hale, alone of the official judges, picked up and powerfully articulated many of the factors above, pushing back on the police reasons for why they policed as they did. Colin Murray has also written a judgment that articulates them. Crucially, however, they reach different results. Why?

While Colin Murray found room to disagree with the policing decisions, in contrast Baroness Hale agreed with them. She did so because she took seriously the police argument that had they stopped the protest by arresting ring leaders (something, as she points out, they eventually did successfully), 'sinister forces' on the Loyalist side would exploit the situation and perhaps use 'more serious violence' elsewhere in Belfast. However, aware perhaps that this argument can always be made by police without challenge, she decided on her own part:

> I do not think that it has been demonstrated that, had the police behaved at the outset in the way in which it is now said that they should have behaved, the children's experience would have been any better. Indeed, it could have been a great deal worse. They were in very real physical danger at the beginning. On 5 September an explosive device was thrown into the road where they were walking but thankfully injured no-one. The difficulties and dangers to them in doing what it is now suggested should have been done cannot be ignored.[6]

[6] *In re E*, above n 5, para 14.

The 'hindsight' argument played heavily, as I think it always must. Judicial review structures the decision to favour the authority of the decision maker. Judges proceed cautiously when they review 'the judgment of a person with responsibility for a given subject matter and access to special sources of knowledge and advice'[7]—in this case the police.

Transcendental Legal Nonsense?

I find it hard to accept that the state had through the police fulfilled its duty to protect the girls from torture. It sits too uneasily with the facts as experienced, against a backdrop of very troubling public order policing decisions. These decisions were taken by a police force resisting institutional change, that was in that same period—as Murray notes—being challenged and re-worked by the Agreement's implementation.

I find it impossible to imagine how any judicial ruling based on this level of deference could ever lead to any ruling against police in public order situations based on their positive obligations, rather than their primary violation of rights.[8] If this is the only reasoning possible, then perhaps we are just saying that judicial review is not appropriate to these sort of policing decisions, because judges are not competent to second-guess policing decisions in such a finely-tuned way: they cannot better define the nature of Article 3's positive obligation than the police. If so, it might be better to just say that straight from the outset, rather than have lengthy court cases and appeals.

Instead we have transcendental legal reasoning that rationalises this decision in legal terms.[9] This reasoning constructs unknown risks communicated by those under scrutiny (the police), and uses proportionality tests to balance them against real blast bombs. It worries about judicial use of hindsight in holding to account the police's refusal to prevent or disperse the protests, without factoring in the certainties that the police knew would proceed from a decision for which they had two months to prepare.[10] The judgment endorses a capitulation to the threat of uncontainable Loyalist violence that can always be made: in just previous years it had been used to justify the reversal of a police decision to refuse to let a Loyalist march through a nationalist area of Portadown, culminating in the beating of nationalist protestors by the police and widescale riots.[11] The reasoning accepts the decision not to arrest, while noting that an arrest policy was ultimately successful in ending the protests. It breaks down decision-making into tiny discrete decisions, each of which appears

[7] per Baroness Hale, citing Lord Bingham in *In re E* [2008] UKHL 66, para 13.

[8] *See DB's Application* [2014] NICA 56, where the Northern Ireland Court of Appeal, relying on *In re E*, overruled a High Court ruling that policing of a 'loyalist flags' protest had facilitated illegal and sometimes violent parade, in breach of the Public Processions (Northern Ireland Act 1998 and section 32 of the Police (Northern Ireland) Act 2000 (http://www.courtsni.gov.uk/en-GB/Judicial%20Decisions/PublishedByYear/Documents/2014/[2014]%20NICA%2056/j_j_MOR9344Final.htm).

[9] Felix Cohen, 'Transcendental Nonsense and the Functional Approach' (1935) 35 *Columbia Law Review* 809, 814-817.

[10] See Lord Hoffman, para 22 et seq (for description of the pre summer and post summer periods of the protests).

[11] See chronology of events and Chief Constable's response at http://cain.ulst.ac.uk/issues/parade/develop.htm.

justifiable, and so avoids questioning the big decision to let protests develop in a context where the very urban geography of the city has seen Republican public protest largely containable in Republican neighbourhoods, but Loyalist public protest much less so.[12]

As a lawyer I can follow the rationality of this legal reasoning, and understand it and debate it on its own terms. Colin Murray's judgment does a good job of showing how these terms could have led to a different result. But as a mother and a feminist, I want to reject more categorically what this legal reasoning does to the facts.

Against dusty case law citations and rationalising legal reasoning: we had 4-year-old girls attacked and damaged; lines of police who talked about how protecting the girls 'stripped' police resources elsewhere in Belfast; who made decisions based on a need to protect protestors' 'right of free speech'; and who justified serious actual violence against the girls, in terms of the 'more serious violence' that could be caused to possible others elsewhere. The police accidentally named the anonymous applicant in the early stages of the case when her life was already at risk. The Chief Constable put illegitimate pressure on the NIHRC to withdraw funding from the case, essentially threatening the Chief Commissioner with public embarrassment over a letter he had privately written doubting the funding of the case.[13] The majority House of Lords opinion was given to a judge to write who viewed the Convention on the Elimination of All Forms of Discrimination against Women (CEDAW) as having little to add to British law, and who had played a less than constructive role with regard to the development of the post-Agreement rights structures, without questioning his standpoint.[14] I would want to firmly reject this as human rights-compliant policing that listened to and took seriously the rights of girl children.

It is difficult not to conclude that if this is the best the state and its legal system can do to protect our daughters when violence threatens, then all those lovely human right commitments on paper are not worth very much at all, even in our relatively 'good' western liberal democracy. As a lawyer and as a mother, it seems to me that that essentially is what the courts told us in this case.

[12] The sectarian geography of Belfast is well documented (see, eg, Frederick Boal, 'Northern Ireland: Geographical perspectives on an Ethnically Polarized Society' (1987) 13(2) *Canadian Journal of Irish Studies* 33–42) and, as the judgment itself indicates, Loyalist public protests frequently have a city-wide implication and capacity, while past public order protests within West Belfast were largely containable there.

[13] For an account of the exchange, see Joint Parliamentary Committee on Human Rights, Fourteenth Report of Session 2002–03, Work of the Northern Ireland Human Rights Commission, HL Paper 132, HC 142, p 16.

[14] Space does not permit a comprehensive review of Carswell's approach to human rights, but his judgments in *In re White* (above n 1and ch 12 of this collection) (where he rejected consideration of CEDAW and questioned the NIHRC's right to intervene) and *In re NIHRC* (above n 3) (where he found that the NIHRC had no power to act as a third-party intervener, despite Parliamentary statements to the contrary, and was overruled by the House of Lords), and his dissent in *Robinson v Secretary of State for Northern Ireland and Others* [2002] UKHL 32 (which would in practice have collapsed the Agreement), indicate a legalistic positivist approach that aligned in outcome with a conservative Unionist approach to the implementation of the Agreement and its human rights provisions, often in contrast to his fellow judges in both the NICA and House of Lords, whether this is his own political position or not. However, his actions as LCJ of Northern Ireland, in opposing a neutral form of oath to replace the one to the Queen required of Senior Council, apparently misrepresenting the views of the judges of the Supreme Court of Northern Ireland to the Lord Chancellor (*In the matter of an Application by Seamus Treacy and Barry MacDonald for Judicial Review* [2000] NIHC 2075), and his published concern that a 'compulsory focus on human rights and international conventions' might lead to an increased focus on the public record of judges on the Bench or the 'actions and statements of candidates for appointment', indicate a conservative outlook and political approach more generally (see Robert Carswell, 'Human Rights and the Rule of Law' (1999) 6(4) *Journal of Forensic Medicine* 249–55; and Brice Dickson and Brian Gormally, *Human Rights in Northern Ireland* (Belfast, Committee on the Administration of Justice, 2015) 643.

HOUSE OF LORDS

OPINIONS OF THE LORDS OF APPEAL FOR JUDGMENT IN THE CAUSE

In re E (a child) (AP) (Appellant) (Northern Ireland)

[2008] UKHL 66

LORD MURRAY OF AGHERTON

My Lords,

70. "Let justice be done even if the sky should fall" has a venerable common law lineage. It was invoked by Lord Mansfield when, in freeing the radical politician John Wilkes, he maintained that judges "must not regard political consequences; how formidable soever they might be"; see *R v Wilkes* (1770) 4 Burr 2527, 2562. It is a comforting maxim for lawyers, serving as useful shorthand for the duty imposed on all those tasked with upholding the law to serve the populace as a whole without sectional favour. But it also requires that the authorities take steps to protect the vulnerable in exercising their powers, even when it appears politically expedient not to do so. The facts before us concern whether the failure by the police to prevent the very real trauma suffered by the appellant and her daughter as a result of a known criminal threat amounted to a breach of this duty.

158 Days in North Belfast

71. The school run is a matter of daily routine for many families across the United Kingdom. For most of these families there is a comfortable regularity to the hubbub of planning for the day, for the minor crises of forgotten lunchboxes and misplaced books. For the 230 pupils of Holy Cross Girls' Primary School on the Ardoyne Road, however, the school run takes them along one of the most prominent sectarian fault lines in North Belfast. Decades of violent displacement of people during the Troubles left this Catholic school bordering the predominantly Loyalist Glenbryn estate, with the result that the main entrance to the school faced this estate and could only be accessed by travelling through part of it.

72. The febrile summer of 2001 shattered whatever normality the journey to school can have in such circumstances. The spark for events outside Holy Cross remains disputed, but the tensions that had been rising within North Belfast for much of the month of June exploded into attacks by stone throwers on pupils and parents outside the Holy Cross School on 19 June. In any event the cause of the events is a matter only relevant to the adults involved. It does not help girls aged between 3 and 11 to comprehend the violence and abuse that they faced. Thereafter, until the school holidays commenced on 28 June, Loyalists blockaded the main entrance to the school.

73. The police did not attempt to lift this blockade, as Assistant Chief Constable McQuillan has explained in his affidavit. Tensions were high. Resources were stretched. The marching season was fast approaching. A direct police response might have been used

as a pretext for more widespread violence. The violence spread anyway; rioting swirled around Holy Cross on successive nights. On several days some children and family members, including the appellant and her daughter, were able to reach Holy Cross via the adjoining grounds of St Gabriel's Secondary School, but for the last week and a half of term the school was all but besieged.

74. Tensions in the area did not abate over the course of the school holidays. If anything, they worsened in the course of a summer of political upheavals which saw the resignation of David Trimble as First Minister and the temporary suspension of Northern Ireland Assembly. On the ground, protracted rioting in North Belfast accompanied the 12 July Orange Order parades. The police became aware that Loyalists would make another effort to block access to Holy Cross along the Ardoyne Road. In response, the police formed a cordon in an effort to permit safe passage for the girls and their families when school resumed on 3 September. That day the Red Hand Defenders, a terrorist group proscribed under schedule 2 to the Terrorism Act 2000, threatened the Holy Cross families, and the police cordon, if further attempts were made to use the Ardoyne Road. In the course of the blockade, this group would on multiple occasions issue direct threats against the appellant's life.

75. The blockade entered its most brutal phase in the first week of September. As the Holy Cross families walked to and from school between a cordon of police officers they were subjected to a barrage of sectarian abuse and death threats, accompanied by a hail of bricks, stones, rubbish, excrement and urine-filled balloons. All of this took place against a cacophony of sirens and whistles. Many of the Loyalists involved in the blockade wore masks. On 5 September, a blast bomb was thrown by Loyalists as the Holy Cross families walked this gauntlet. Four police officers in the cordon were injured, and one woman hospitalised as a result of shock. Thereafter fireworks would be thrown at the families to induce the same terror. The Loyalists' methods did not simply target the Holy Cross pupils for their religion, it targeted them as very young girls. Pornographic posters were brandished and highly-sexualised abusive language yelled at the girls to put their parents off using the main entrance to the school. This conduct was intended to traumatise its young victims and even to rob them of their childhoods.

76. In responding to the situation, the police (with the support of the army) sought to contain the groups of Loyalists and prevent them from blockading the Ardoyne Road entrance rather than seeking to disperse the protesters and arrest those suspected of criminal behaviour. These efforts at containment evolved during the course of the blockade. On the first day of the school year, an effort was made to assemble crash barriers enclosed by a two-metre-high Perspex screen to provide a safe corridor for the children and their families. But the barriers took too long to erect and the Perspex screens proved too flimsy to withstand the missiles hurled at them, and on subsequent days police in riot gear carrying shields accompanied the families directly as they walked between a cordon of armoured police vehicles. Despite police filming of events in early September, by the end of October only 13 arrests had been made in response to the blockade.

77. Over the next two months the Holy Cross families refused to abandon their ordinary route or to see their children ferried to school in an armoured bus. There is a quiet dignity in the appellant's desire to perform life's run-of-the-mill tasks, like walking her child to

school, in the face of such extreme intimidation. Many parents spent entire school days on the premises to be near their children. Through it all the principal, Anne Tanney, and her staff did their utmost to maintain the normal routines of school life and alleviate the visible distress of many of their pupils. The thrice-daily cycle (at morning, lunchtime and the end of the school day) involving the deployment of 700 soldiers and police officers continued until, following protracted negotiations, the protests scaled back from late-October onwards and ultimately suspended on 23 November. Only after the blockade ended was a prosecution strategy actively pursued, with 37 individuals being prosecuted in total over the next year.

Proceedings to Date

78. The appellant challenges the adequacy of policing approaches adopted in response to the blockade under the Human Rights Act 1998. Her challenge focuses in particular upon the second phase of blockade, from September to November 2001, when a threat that she and her daughter would be subject to inhuman and degrading treatment was known to the police who did not, she asserts, take sufficient steps to bring this threat to an end. As a corollary of this assertion, the appellant further submits that the police failure to effectively implement the criminal law discriminated against her as a Roman Catholic. Put simply, she claims that the police approach would have been much more proactive had Protestant primary school children and their families been subject to such violence. To date, the courts hearing this case have accepted the arguments of the Chief Constable, as respondent, maintaining that all duties owed to the appellant during the period in question were fulfilled and that a more robust response to the blockade could have spawned more widespread violence. Kerr LCJ dismissed E's application on 16 June 2004, [2004] NIQB 35, and the Court of Appeal, in which Campbell LJ gave the judgment of the Court, dismissed the resultant appeal on 19 October 2006, [2006] NICA 37.

79. It follows from the above summary of the events that the appellant's daughter is a central figure in these proceedings. The Court of Appeal accepted, at para 77, that the appellant "is entitled to bring proceedings on her own behalf and on behalf of her daughter, who was a young child at the time of the incidents and therefore vulnerable". This decision was reached on the basis that both the mother and daughter met the test laid down in Article 43 ECHR and incorporated into Section 7(1) of the Human Rights Act 1998. Even though the child was very young when this judicial review commenced, no barrier prevented her from being joined as a party, and as her interests are at issue as separate from those of her mother, it would have been preferable to have done so. I agree with Baroness Hale of Richmond that it would have been preferable to have separated out the interests of the mother and daughter, but this omission does not mean that this action was improperly founded.

The Relevant Law

80. The ECHR is often characterised as a treaty which protects individuals against particular encroachments into their lives by public authorities in signatory states. Article 3 ECHR provides that "No one shall be subjected to torture or to inhuman or degrading

treatment or punishment." The negative obligations upon public authorities inherent in this right are evident upon its terms; signatory states undertake not to subject individuals to these forms of treatment. As the European Court explained in *Pretty v United Kingdom* (2002) 35 EHRR 1, at para 52, courts adjudicating upon this right are required to assess whether the treatment an individual has suffered was sufficiently severe to trigger Article 3 ECHR. The classification of treatment as inhuman is determined by factors including whether it was premeditated, its duration and whether it caused "either actual bodily injury or intense physical and mental suffering", whilst the classification of treatment as degrading depends upon whether it "was such as to arouse in its victims feelings of fear, anguish and inferiority capable of humiliating and debasing them"; see *T v United Kingdom* (2000) 30 EHRR 121, at para 69. Conduct of such a nature can satisfy the threshold for degrading treatment even if the victims' humiliation is in their own eyes; see *Smith and Grady v United Kingdom* (2000) 29 EHRR 493, at para 120.

81. Refraining from engaging in such treatment is not, of itself, sufficient for a state to satisfy this obligation. Societies which claim to be organised along liberal and democratic principles (the principles which underpin the ECHR) recognise the inherent dignity of their members. This recognition counts for little if a private individual, or group, within a society is known by the authorities to subject other individuals to degrading treatment without consequence. This much was acknowledged by the European Court of Human Rights in cases such as *Z v United Kingdom* (2001) 34 EHRR 97, a decision which recognised, at para 73, that positive obligations extended to protecting both the right to life under Article 2 ECHR and preventing torture or inhuman and degrading treatment contrary to Article 3 ECHR. Under the test set out in *Osman v United Kingdom* (2000) 29 EHRR 245, at para 116, for a positive obligation to arise:

> "[I]t must be established ... that the authorities knew or ought to have known at the time of the existence of a real and immediate risk to the life of an identified individual or individuals from the criminal acts of a third party and that they failed to take measures within the scope of their powers which, judged reasonably, might have been expected to avoid that risk."

These obligations can be triggered where the infringement of Article 3 ECHR interests by other private actors is facilitated by a public authority's administrative action or inaction.

82. The general vulnerability of certain individuals or groups is relevant alongside the specific threat for the purpose of assessing whether there has been effective protection of Article 3 ECHR in a given case; see *Moldovan v Romania (No. 2)* (2007) 44 EHRR 16, at para 100. In this regard, the European Court has taken account of specialised international instruments, such as the Convention on the Elimination of all Forms of Discrimination against Women (CEDAW) 1979 and the United Nations Convention on the Rights of the Child (UNCRC) 1989, in developing the reach of positive obligations. These instruments are therefore of significance in this case even though the United Kingdom has ratified both but not incorporated their provisions into domestic law. Two provisions of the UNCRC are of particular relevance in highlighting the duties owed by public authorities towards children. First, under Article 3(1) UNCRC, one of the key principles of the Convention is that "the best interests of the child shall be a primary consideration" when public authorities act with regard to children. Second, under Article 19 UNCRC, states are expected to take steps

"to protect the child from all forms of physical or mental violence, injury or abuse". To these provisions must be added the positive obligation in Article 2(e) CEDAW, which enjoins signatory states to undertake "all appropriate measures to eliminate discrimination against women by any person, organization or enterprise".

83. As the European Court has affirmed, these instruments have influenced its approach to the obligations under Article 3 ECHR, and principles derived from them therefore form an important element of the authorities' assessments of this right where children are at issue; see *A v United Kingdom* (1999) 27 EHRR 611, at para 22. One of the most important elements of a positive obligations claim is the basis for establishing that the authorities' failure to adequately respond to inhuman or degrading treatment affected the claimants' rights, thereby engaging the state's responsibility. My learned colleague Baroness Hale of Richmond has expressed her concern with the European Court's rejection of a "but for" test for causation in favour of an approach whereby the claimant must establish that had the state taken adequate steps there would be "a real prospect of altering the outcome or mitigating the harm"; see *E v United Kingdom* (2002) 36 EHRR 519, at para 99. In light of the aim of positive obligations under Article 3 ECHR to protect vulnerable groups in society from the indifference of the authorities, I am not similarly troubled by the European Court's approach. The flexibility of state action is adequately protected by the permitted exceptions to the duty, to which I will return.

84. This Court must, under section 2(1) of the Human Rights Act, take account of the relevant European Court case law in assessing the content of the Article 3 ECHR right. In his opinion in *R (Ullah) v Special Adjudicator* [2004] UKHL 26, at para 20, Lord Bingham of Cornhill interpreted this provision as requiring the domestic courts of the United Kingdom to approach the incorporated ECHR provisions in line with the European Court's jurisprudence, and thereby "keep pace with the Strasbourg jurisprudence as it evolves". This approach prevents this Court from adopting the appellant's suggestion (supported by the intervention of the Northern Ireland Human Rights Commission (NIHRC)) that because the right contained in Article 3 ECHR is couched in unqualified terms, the obligation upon the authorities to secure these interests is absolute. The European Court's jurisprudence, from *Osman* onwards, requires "reasonable steps" by authorities in response to threats of inhuman and degrading treatment, not that the authorities absolutely extinguish all such threats; see *Osman*, [116]. Nothing in the Court's subsequent jurisprudence indicates that there is a likelihood of this standard being displaced; see *Kontrová v Slovakia*, App.7510/04 (31 May 2007), at para 50.

85. The *Ullah* principle, however, does not mandate unquestioning adherence to the letter of the European Court's jurisprudence. As no case decided by the European Court is directly analogous to the facts before us, we must therefore extrapolate the application of the principles laid down in its case law. As Baroness Hale of Richmond has maintained, judges cannot hold up our hands and refuse to engage with the ECHR when the European Court's approach is opaque, where we can make a "good prediction" as to the direction of travel; see *R (Countryside Alliance & Others) v Attorney-General* [2007] UKHL 52, at para 125. The test laid down in *Osman* is clear and objective, as Lord Hope of Craighead recognised in *Hertfordshire Police v Van Colle* [2008] UKHL 50, at para 66, but it has hitherto been applied in cases where the course of action open to the authorities to address the threat is

clear. The instant case requires us to assess the adequacy of a particular response, chosen over other alternative options.

86. The Convention rights must be enjoyed without discrimination against the individual characteristics protected under Article 14 ECHR. The appellants assert that the policing approach adopted in response to the blockade was demonstrably less robust than the policing of nationalist demonstrations at Loyalist parades. In this regard, the European Court has maintained that "a difference in treatment is discriminatory if it has no objective and reasonable justification, i.e. if it does not pursue a legitimate aim or if there is not a reasonable relationship of proportionality between the means employed and the aim sought to be realised"; see *Moldovan v Romania (No. 2)* (2007) 44 EHRR 16, at para 137. It follows that if Article 3 ECHR is found to be engaged, this Court must also consider these claims.

87. At issue when assessing whether the police fulfilled these obligations in the duty imposed on public authorities by section 6(1) of the Human Rights Act 1998 to not act in a manner incompatible with an ECHR right. In the present case the relevant duties which must be fulfilled in a rights-compatible manner are set out in section 32(1) of the Police (Northern Ireland) Act 2000:

(a) to protect life and property;
(b) to preserve order;
(c) to prevent the commission of offences;
(d) where an offence has been committed, to take measures to bring the offender to justice;

Under section 32(5) the Act requires that "Police officers shall, so far as practicable, carry out their functions in co-operation with, and with the aim of securing the support of, the local community". These duties codify, in statutory form, the first of Sir Robert Peel's principles of policing; "the basic mission for which the police exist is to prevent crime and disorder". That this foundational principle needed such codification, however, speaks to the experience of policing in Northern Ireland during the Troubles, and of the dangers which result when large sections of the community no longer trust the police to fulfil this function impartially. Having been promised impartial and effective policing as part of the dividend of the Northern Ireland peace process, the appellant and her daughter were entitled to expect this duty to be fulfilled.

88 Notwithstanding the expectations generated by the peace process, the duty contained within the 2000 Act is not a rigid encumbrance upon policing practice. It must be read in light of the operational discretion the European Court has identified in cases like *Kontrová v Slovakia*, App.7510/04 (31 May 2007), at para 50:

> "Bearing in mind the difficulties in policing modern societies, the unpredictability of human conduct and the operational choices which must be made in terms of priorities and resources, the scope of the positive obligation must be interpreted in a way which does not impose an impossible or disproportionate burden on the authorities."

Efforts by the police to justify, on operational grounds, a course of action which would appear, at first sight, to be a derogation of duty are, however, subject to judicial review.

Such Judicial oversight of police practice is essential to establishing and maintaining trust in policing in Northern Ireland. The role of this Court is to assess whether, even within the context of a measure of operational discretion, the policing response to the Holy Cross blockade adequately protected the rights of the appellant and her daughter.

The Standard of Review

89. The Court of Appeal, at para 89, assessed whether the policing operation was irrational on the basis of the approach laid down in *R v Ministry of Defence, Ex parte Smith* [1996] QB 517, concerning the ban on gay people serving in the armed forces, at 556. This decision urged a cautious approach to review where security concerns were at issue, and relying upon this formula it is unsurprising that Campbell LJ reached the following conclusion:

> "Applying the *Smith* test we consider that taking account of the nature and size of the operation that was mounted over a considerable period of time and the perceived risk if other measures were adopted the police did all that was reasonably open to them to protect the rights of the child."

90. When the European Court ultimately found that the ban breached the rights of gay military personnel it explicitly recognised that the approach to evaluating the irrationality of a decision adopted by the Court of Appeal in *Smith* did not provide for adequate rights protection; *Smith and Grady v United Kingdom* (1999) 29 EHRR 493, at para 138. The Human Rights Act 1998 now obliges the courts to give effect to the incorporated Convention rights in cases in which they are engaged, and a series of decisions have established the inadequacy of the *Smith* approach in this regard; see *R (Daly) v Secretary of State for the Home Department* [2001] UKHL 26, at paras 26–28 (Lord Steyn), and most recently (in an opinion issued after the Court of Appeal decision in the instant case) *Huang v Secretary of State for the Home Department* [2007] UKHL 11, at para 13 (Lord Bingham of Cornhill). The approach of the Court of Appeal to the standard of review was therefore flawed.

91. Where positive obligations under Article 3 ECHR are at issue, the court must make an objective assessment of the appropriateness of the public authority's response to the threat to this right on the basis of the proportionality test. Proportionality requires the court to evaluate the balance of competing interests struck by the public authority, and not simply to identify whether there was some reasonable basis upon which the authority proceeded; see *R (Daly) v Secretary of State for the Home Department* [2001] UKHL 26, at para 27. Whereas the traditional test for irrationality sidelines the rights of the individual in question, requiring judges to concentrate on the actions of the public authority, the application of the proportionality test requires us to keep the interests of the appellant and her daughter at the forefront of the our minds.

The Blockade of the School and Freedom of Protest

92. Before I turn to assess the appellant's submissions regarding Article 3 ECHR one countervailing factor must be considered; the impact of the freedom of expression and assembly enjoyed by the Loyalists conducting the blockade of the Holy Cross School under Articles 10 and 11 ECHR. Assistant Chief Constable McQuillan's affidavit establishes that

the policing approach adopted at Holy Cross in September 2001 was intended to "provide some greater protection for the parents and children and at the same time minimal interference with the rights of the loyalist residents to lawfully protest and make use of the public highway".

93. On one level, a consideration of such interests shows a necessary concern for human rights in the police decision-making process. Articles 10 and 11 ECHR, however, are qualified rights. They can be subject to lawful restriction in line with the ECHR provided the restrictions are in accordance with law and are employed in a proportionate manner to address concerns including the rights of others, public safety, and the prevention of disorder or crime. Restrictions to the ability to protest exist under common law powers of police officers to prevent breaches of the peace and under Article 20 of the Public Order (NI) Order 1987 (SI 1987/463 (NI 7)), which covers obstruction of a highway in such a manner as to prevent lawful users from going about their business. When a group amasses on a public highway for the purpose, evidenced over an extended period, of intimidating other members of the community, the limits of freedom of protest are far exceeded, and the police are within their powers to take proportionate steps to quell such disturbances and arrest individuals involved in unlawful conduct.

94. I am therefore in full agreement with my learned friend Lord Carswell that the terms protest, demonstration and dispute add an unwarranted veneer of legitimacy to efforts by Loyalists outside Holy Cross Girls' Primary School to terrorise children and their families. I will not, however, employ these terms for the sake of convenience within my judgment, as my noble friend has chosen to do.

95. Given the conduct of Loyalists during the June blockade of the school, the police were well aware that the limits of lawful assembly were highly likely to be exceeded with the resumption of the blockade in September. There will undoubtedly be situations where the police will find it difficult to calibrate their response to take account of both the positive obligations owed to one group under Articles 2 and 3 ECHR and the rights involved in freedom of protest under Articles 10 and 11 ECHR. A violent and sectarian mob threatening and attacking children and their parents on their way to and from school is not, however, a difficult case. The appellant and her daughter found themselves at the centre of this maelstrom. The failure by the senior officers responsible for conducting the policing operation at Holy Cross to recognise the limitations to the Loyalists' rights under Articles 10 and 11 ECHR is a factor which militates against this Court finding that the police made appropriate use of their operational discretion in this case.

Positive Obligations under Article 3 ECHR

96. As Lord Carswell has observed the respondents have accepted that, taken as a whole, the conduct of the Loyalists attempting to blockade Holy Cross amounted to degrading treatment under Article 3 ECHR. Whilst this concession alleviates the need for an exhaustive application of the relevant European Court case law to the facts of this case, I must emphasise that the ordeal to which the Holy Cross families were subjected between September and October 2001 was both inhuman and degrading. The conduct of the

blockading Loyalists was tightly orchestrated, extended over a period of months, was intended to induce a state of inferiority and extreme fear, and indeed caused considerable anguish.

97. The European Court's jurisprudence on the Article 3 ECHR threshold also requires an evaluation of the vulnerability of the victim. Consideration of this requirement may have induced the Court of Appeal's assertion, at para 88, that:

> "The fact that she persisted in bringing her daughter to school by Ardoyne Road, in the face of the behaviour towards her of the protesters suggests that so far as she was concerned personally it may not have reached the threshold. In the case of her daughter the minimum level was more easily attained."

The proposition that the threshold for inhuman and degrading treatment applicable to the appellant is higher as a result of her choice to stand up, by entirely lawful means, to intimidation directed at her is tantamount to blaming her for the criminal activity to which she was subjected. The Holy Cross families did not seek "martyrdom" before the world's media by their entirely lawful use of the main entrance to the school. Rather, the police decision to mount a cordoning operation placed the families in the position of either walking the Ardoyne Road under these conditions or succumbing to intimidation. Nothing in the appellant's behaviour should colour this Court's decision as to whether her Article 3 ECHR right, and that of her daughter, was adequately protected.

98. An evaluation of the vulnerability of the appellant and her daughter in the context of Article 3 ECHR should start not with the appellant's behaviour but with a consideration of the impact of the blockade upon the Holy Cross families. Anne Tanney, Holy Cross's principal, has provided moving evidence of the impact of the protracted blockade upon the pupils in her care. Little teaching was possible during the months of the blockade. Dr Tan, general practitioner for many of the families involved, has recounted the range of nervous symptoms displayed by the school children. Many children continued to receive counselling long after the disturbances had ended. Under Article 28(1) UNCRC, the United Kingdom accepts that children's education is to be achieved 'on the basis of equal opportunity'. The importance of the girls' education explains the lengths to which the Holy Cross families went to secure regular access to the school by its ordinary entrance.

99. Whilst it is not in dispute that Article 3 ECHR has been engaged in the case at hand, the scope of the state's positive obligations under this right has proved more controversial. The facts do not indicate that the authorities failed to identify the threat to the appellant or that they took no meaningful steps to respond to it. The threat to the appellant's Article 3 ECHR right, even if it was not discussed in those terms, was evident to the respondent Chief Constable and his officers. Throughout September, October and November, against a backdrop of inter-community tension and strained political processes in Northern Ireland, steps were taken to shield the pupils and their families from the Loyalist blockade. Nor is the dedication to duty of the individual police officers providing that cordon in doubt; 41 of them were injured in the course of the policing operation, some seriously. At issue in this case is the adequacy of the police response, especially in terms of the strategy adopted to policing the blockade.

100. As the written intervention by the Northern Ireland Commissioner for Children and Young People and the Children's Law Centre notes, in assessing whether the police response fulfilled the requirements of Article 3 ECHR this Court must give consideration to the United Kingdom's other relevant international obligations. As noted above, CEDAW and the UNCRC impose duties upon signatory states to take active steps to prevent women and children from discrimination and violence even when it is perpetrated by non-state actors. Positive obligations under Article 3 ECHR may well be a developing area of the European Court's jurisprudence, but *Moldovan v Romania (No. 2)* (2007) 44 EHRR 16 makes it clear that we must take these obligations into account in a case in which the nature of the abuse directed at the school children singled them out as girls even if it was directed at them for religious and ethno-nationalist reasons. In such circumstances these instruments clearly require the authorities to establish the adequacy of the steps taken to fulfil their positive obligations.

101. In the High Court, Kerr LCJ noted (at para 26) that the Royal Ulster Constabulary (RUC) Chief Constable, Sir Ronnie Flanagan, had recognised during the disturbances that the "the rights of the children are to the forefront of our thinking". Kerr LCJ concluded (at para 53) that it had not been established that the police had failed to act in accordance with the "best interests of the child" principle articulated in Article 3 UNCRC. Stating a concern for this principle, however, is not the same as actively engaging with its requirements. At meetings from 6 September onwards NIHRC members raised serious concerns over the impact of the cordon operation upon the children. Dr Tan's evidence before the High Court illustrated how these concerns were borne out. At the time, however, they did not prompt any discernible change in police practice.

102. Protecting all members of the community from harm without prejudice is a vital part of a police officer's duty. But effective policing requires that the community as a whole must also have confidence that law breaking by particular groups will not be tolerated. In 1996 Sir Ronnie Flanagan decided to re-route an Orange Order parade away from the Garvaghy Road in Portadown. Following days of Loyalist disorder which spread far from the area around Drumcree Church, the Chief Constable felt compelled to reverse his decision and permit the march. These events not only provoked reform of the legislative arrangements for policing in Northern Ireland but also adversely affected subsequent policing practice.

103. The police's justification for instituting a cordon between September to November 2001, rather than preventing or dispersing the blockade, lay in the risk that disorder might spread, as it had done in 1996 following policing operations at Drumcree, if more pro-active measures were undertaken. My colleagues have emphasised the experience of the RUC under Sir Ronnie Flanagan's leadership in assessing the reaction to their operations as a significant factor in reviewing the adequacy of this response. But in the aftermath of Drumcree, the Public Processions (Northern Ireland) Act 1998 was enacted in the light of the defects exposed in policing practice. Furthermore, section 32(1) of the Police (Northern Ireland) Act 2000 imposed positive obligations on the police to fulfil their responsibilities for upholding law and order for all sections of the community in Northern Ireland specifically as a response to the legacy of distrust over police even-handedness from both before and during the Troubles. In such circumstances my learned colleagues' readiness to defer to

decision-maker expertise hollows out this Court's independent assessment of the adequacy of the police response.

104. Under the test set out in *E v United Kingdom* (2002) 36 EHRR 519, at para 99, the appellant must establish the real prospect that a police strategy based on ending the blockade as opposed to cordoning the pupils and their families could have prevented them from suffering inhuman and degrading treatment. By herding the appellant and her daughter through a violent sectarian gauntlet, the police perpetuated their isolation and abuse. The state of terror the events inspired in the very young girls going to school was exacerbated, not diminished, by having to walk between dense lines of heavily armed soldiers and police in riot gear. The day-to-day lives of the affected families became dependent upon the timetable of police efforts to establish a cordon. The police's failure to act proactively to prevent the disturbances and arrest those involved in suspected criminality risked sending out a message that the behaviours in question were being tolerated because their victims were working-class Catholic families. It is easy to see how the Holy Cross families could come to interpret the violence as being condoned by the authorities.

105. Taken as a whole, the strategy adopted by the police cannot be characterised as the product of special experience on the part of the police, but of long-standing concerns over the possible spread of Loyalist disorder dominating the decision-making process. The new statutory duties upon the police under the 2000 Act and the positive obligations under Article 3 ECHR, which should have been at the forefront of senior officers' minds, were consequently marginalised. Even accepting that the police enjoyed a degree of operational discretion in the choice of response to the disturbances around Holy Cross, its ambit became considerably more restricted once the protracted and violent nature of the unlawful blockade, and the harm to the vulnerable children and their families, became evident at the start of the new school year in September 2001.

106. Positive obligations under Article 3 ECHR do not require the police to address every instance of violent disorder in a particular way. The operational discretion the police enjoyed in the present case was restricted by the operation of two factors. First, the police were aware that a particular vulnerable group was subject to violence and intimidation which amounted to inhuman and degrading treatment and, second, the manner in which the situation developed gave the police considerable time to prepare their response. The obligations upon the police were not breached in the June phase of the disturbances, when officers were forced to react to a sudden outbreak of public disorder around the Holy Cross School. The intervening time period (in this case more than two months during the school vacation) and the consequent opportunity for the police to assess the situation on the ground transformed the situation. The police had the opportunity to calibrate their response and to prepare contingency measures to take effect as soon as it became evident that a cordoning operation could not effectively prevent intimidation and violence. Every day the police had to plan was a day in which the Holy Cross families' concerns over the coming school year intensified. September saw those fears realised. By allowing the disturbances to continue to terrorise the children, disrupt their education and ruin their home lives for a further two months, such a long period in their short lives, the police response to the Holy Cross disturbances fell far short of being adequate.

107. For these reasons I must depart from the position adopted by my colleagues. The appellant has established that there was a real prospect that a more proactive policing approach, undertaken in the early stages of the blockade of September to November 2001, would have alleviated the abuse of her Article 3 ECHR right and that of her daughter.

Non-Discrimination under Article 14 ECHR

108. Although the police response was inadequate, it does not necessarily follow that this inadequacy was the result of discrimination against the Holy Cross families as nationalists or Catholics. Policing a situation such as the disturbances around Holy Cross school is undoubtedly complex, and the evidence before this Court establishes that the shortcomings in the police response resulted from operational miscalculations and not sectarianism.

109. The policing operation around Holy Cross Girls' Primary School took place at a time when the officers of the RUC were preparing for the Patten Reforms (*The Report of the Independent Commission on Policing for Northern Ireland*, Chaired by Christopher Patten (September 1999)) to come into full effect on 4 November. Indeed, lines of police officers protecting Catholic school girls and their families from attack by a violent mob, day-in, day-out, may indeed have helped to assuage long-held suspicions over whether the incoming Police Service of Northern Ireland would risk their safety on behalf of the community as a whole. The police officers and soldiers on duty outside Holy Cross put their lives in peril to protect the families and the children and the failings exposed in this case relate to the manner in which they were deployed, not their performance on the cordon. Article 14 ECHR is not engaged.

The Northern Ireland Human Rights Commission's Intervention

110. The intervention by the NIHRC on behalf of the appellant has caused some concern amongst my colleagues. Lord Hoffmann and Lord Brown of Eaton-under-Heywood consider that the NIHRC has duplicated the appellant's arguments and that its intervention has thereby added nothing of value to these proceedings. Section 68 of the Northern Ireland Act 1998 established the NIHRC as a successor to the Standing Advisory Commission on Human Rights. The Belfast Agreement envisaged the Commission as having "an extended and enhanced role" over the body it replaced. The statutory terms under which the NIHRC was created, however, were unfortunately unclear. For much of its early existence, its efforts were in large part devoted to defending the bounds of its mandate, including the power to intervene as a third party in cases, a power only affirmed through an appeal to this Court: see *In re Northern Ireland Human Rights Commission* [2002] UKHL 25.

111. The NIHRC has the difficult task of building faith in the institutions and governance arrangements within a still divided society (see C. Bell, *Peace Agreements and Human Rights* (Oxford: Oxford University Press, 2000) at 229–232). In this context, the NIHRC's exercise of its hard-won power to intervene in this case should not lightly be criticised. The events at Holy Cross remain the source of much dispute, even at more than seven years' remove, within society in Northern Ireland. The NIHRC's oral submissions addressed issues such as the limits to freedom of assembly which are of general importance to the people of Northern Ireland.

112. Even if the NIHRC's intervention does affirm the position of one of the parties, the Commissioners will have adjudged such involvement to be important for securing the protection of human rights in Northern Ireland. For the appellant in this action, challenging as she is the adequacy of the authorities' response to sectarian violence, the mere fact of the NIHRC's intervention at her side provides a powerful reassurance that official bodies take such claims seriously. However frustrating some of my colleagues might find a degree of repetition in the submissions before this Committee, this is a small price to pay for the societal benefits thereby secured. I would therefore disagree with, and indeed deplore, any effort to constrain the ability of the NIHRC to intervene in such a case.

Outcome

113. Even the youngest of the children affected by the clashes around Holy Cross will soon be teenagers. The traumatic events of the summer of 2001 will have cast a long shadow over their childhoods and shaken their faith in the capacity and willingness of the authorities tasked with upholding the law to protect them in the course of their day-to-day lives. No judicial decision can erase the memory of those events. The best that this Court can do is to affirm that the police owed a positive duty to protect these children when they were at their most vulnerable, a duty which was not adequately fulfilled in this instance.

114. I would therefore depart from the position adopted by my colleagues and allow the appeal, issuing a declaration that the Holy Cross cordon operation was illegal in its failure to fulfil the duties imposed upon the police under section 32(1) of the Police (Northern Ireland) Act 2000 in such a way as to secure the Article 3 ECHR right of the appellant and her daughter.

16

Commentary on *O'Keeffe v Hickey*

LAURA HILLY

Introduction

The majority decision of the Irish Supreme Court in *O'Keeffe v Hickey*[1] can be seen as one of several blocks in a wall of resistance erected by the state against Louise O'Keeffe in her search for public accountability for sexual abuse committed in Irish National Schools. In 1973, Louise O'Keeffe was the victim of a series of sexual assaults by Leo Hickey, principal in a school managed by the local Catholic parish priest, Fr Ó Ceallaigh. Leo Hickey was a serial sex predator: in 1998, he was charged with 386 charges relating to the sexual abuse of 21 girls. He pleaded guilty to 21 sample charges and was sentenced to three years in prison. Louise O'Keeffe was awarded €67,310 by the Criminal Injuries Compensation Tribunal. Having been awarded a €305,104 default judgment against him in a civil claim in 1999,[2] she continues to struggle to enforce judgment.

What is exceptional in Louise O'Keeffe's story is her dissatisfaction with responsibility for this crime being placed solely on the shoulders of Leo Hickey. Rather than this act being viewed as the exceptional criminality of one, she wanted responsibility to be taken by those who had the power to prevent this systematic abuse, and the obligation to protect vulnerable children at school. Louise O'Keeffe fought for greater accountability by instituting civil proceedings against the state both for vicarious liability in respect of the torts committed by Leo Hickey in the course of his employment, and for the failure of the school Manager, Fr Ó Ceallaigh, to report and act upon reports of sexual abuse made to him by parents of other children subject to the abuse.

After failing to establish state liability at all stages of the domestic proceedings, Louise O'Keeffe pursued this matter to the European Court of Human Rights (ECtHR). The Grand Chamber of the ECtHR ultimately gave judgment in favour of Louise O'Keeffe.[3] Following the announcement of this decision, Louise O'Keeffe spoke of her motivations to pursue this lengthy and difficult litigation campaign:

> It was hard going, but I still felt a wrong had been done. And while Leo Hickey had been called to account for that, I also felt that the Department had a responsibility, the State had responsibility

[1] *O'Keeffe v Hickey* [2008] IESC 72.
[2] *O'Keeffe v Ireland* (2014) 59 EHRR 15, paras 21–23.
[3] ibid.

> with regard to the protection of children in the schools. My worry really was, and I suppose this is why I did take the case, what happened to me in 1973 and the lack of protection that was in place at that time, was still the case in Ireland, really, today, and that's simply wrong. Children must be protected. They're innocent, they must be protected, and they must be protected from possible abuse in schools. They are really so vulnerable in that position, and that is really what kept me going. That is why I took the case in the first place.[4]

The provision of primary public education in Ireland is both complicated and particular. The difficulties of attributing legal responsibility for the misdeeds of teachers in the course of their employment in this case are attributable to the 'triangular pact' between the state (represented by the Minister for Education and Children), the Manager (usually a representative of the Church) and the school teacher.[5] This 'triangular pact' is provided for by the 1937 Constitution in detailing the Irish state's obligations in respect of primary education. Unlike other jurisdictions,[6] including under international law,[7] which provide the 'right to' education, Article 42.4 of the Constitution requires that '[t]he State shall *provide for* free primary education' [emphasis added], with the focus being upon the duty bearer rather than the right recipients.[8] The obligation to 'provide for' free primary education means that the Constitution endorses the outsourcing of educational obligation, an endorsement specifically crafted to match the *status quo* arrangements at the time of drafting (and indeed, pre-dating the drafting) whereby, in practice, almost all primary education was managed by the Church but 'provided for' by the State. Teachers in National Schools under this arrangement are in a contractual relationship with the Manager of the school and not the state. As Conor O'Mahony puts it, '[t]he State, quite simply, is not in the business of primary education provision—it has entirely outsourced its primary education function'.[9]

However, the state is not altogether passive in the context of the provision of education. The state funds the management of schools, pays for teachers appointed by the religious officials running the schools, lays down the academic syllabus (save for religious instruction) and has powers to inspect the secular instruction given.[10]

It is within the context of this complicated structure that Louise O'Keeffe attempted to assign vicarious liability to the state for the criminal acts of Leo Hickey, undertaken in the

[4] Brian Dobson, Interview with Louise O'Keeffe, *RTE News* (28 January 2014), at www.rte.ie/news/player/2014/0128/20514480-interview-with-louise-okeeffe/ (last accessed 25 May 2015).

[5] See *O'Keeffe v Hickey* [2009] 2 IR 302, paras 143–44.

[6] eg, the Constitution of the Republic of South Africa, s 29 provides: 'Everyone has the right to a basic education …'; Art 2 of Protocol 1 to the European Convention on Human Rights (ECHR) provides: 'No person shall be denied the right to education. …'

[7] The Universal Declaration of Human Rights, Art 26(1) provides: 'Everyone has the right to education. …'; The International Covenant on Economic, Social and Cultural Rights, Art 13(1) provides: 'The States Parties to the present Covenant recognize the right of everyone to education. …'

[8] A similar focus upon the duty bearer rather than the right recipient can be seen in the Constitution of the State of New York, Art XI, § 1, which provides that 'The Legislature shall provide for the maintenance and support of a system of free common schools, wherein all the children of this state may be educated.'

[9] Conor O'Mahony, 'State Liability for Abuse in Primary Schools: Systemic Failure and *O'Keeffe v Hickey*' (2009) 28(3) *Irish Educational Studies* 315–31, 316. See also Gerard Quinn, 'Rethinking the nature of economic, social and cultural rights in the Irish legal order' in Cathryn Costello (ed) *Fundamental Social Rights: Current European Legal Protection and the Challenge of the EU Charter on Fundamental Rights* (Dublin, Irish Centre for European Law, 2000) ch 4.

[10] *O'Keeffe v Hickey* [2009] 2 IR 302, para 5.

course of his employment with the Manager, and the omissions of the Manager in reporting the misconduct of Leo Hickey.

The Action

Louise O'Keeffe brought an action for damages for personal injuries arising from Leo Hickey's sexual assault. She claimed that the state was liable for the tortious acts of Leo Hickey. While Louise O'Keeffe's claims at first instance fell under three headings,[11] the sole matter on appeal was whether the state was vicariously liable for the acts of Leo Hickey or, alternatively, the failures of the Manager, Fr Ó Ceallaigh. The Supreme Court delivered three opinions: Hardiman J (with whom Murray CJ agreed) and Fennelly J (with whom Denhan J agreed) formed the majority; Geoghegan J wrote in dissent.

The majority (Murray CJ, Denham, Hardiman and Fennelly JJ) dismissed Louise O'Keeffe's appeal, holding that the state was not liable for the actionable wrongs committed against her because there was no direct employment relationship between the state and Leo Hickey. They held that Hickey was not a state employee; rather he was employed by the patron of the school and was under the direction and control of the school's Manager. While the state, via the Minister, laid down rules for National Schools, the majority characterised these as being general in nature. They did not allow the Minister to govern detailed activities of any individual teacher. The majority also dismissed the claim of vicarious liability of the state attaching to the omissions of the Manager. Central to this determination was that the Manager was the nominee of the patron, and therefore the agent of the Catholic Church, not the state.[12]

Geoghegan J dissented, holding that in the circumstances of the relationship between the Church and state in relation to the school, it would not be just for the state to be exempt from vicarious liability. He held that there was a sufficient connection between the state and the creation of risk that put Louise O'Keeffe in harm's way, to render the state liable.[13]

The major point of difference between the majority decision of Hardiman J, the concurring decision of Fennelly J and the dissenting decision of Geoghegan J, was the characterisation of the test for vicarious liability, and of the relationship between the state, the Manager and teachers in a National School. Hardiman J, taking a conservative approach to these matters, was particularly concerned about the use of 'policy arguments' to expand the reach of vicarious liability beyond the traditional limits set down in the 'Salmond test',[14] which required, in his opinion, a level of control between the state and both Leo Hickey or the Manager. Due to the lack of a direct employment relationship or sufficient direction

[11] ibid, para 19. See the feminist judgment for an articulation of the grounds at first instance.

[12] ibid, para 128.

[13] ibid, para 180.

[14] This test was expressed by Hardiman J, ibid, para 39 as: 'An employee's wrongful conduct must, to render the employer liable, fall within the course and scope of his or her employment. It will do this where it consists of either:- (i) acts authorised by the employer; or (ii) unauthorised acts that are so connected to the acts that the employer has authorised that they may rightly be regarded as modes—although improper modes—of doing what has been authorised.'

from the Minister, that level of control was absent in this case. Geoghegan J was more liberal with his interpretation of the relationship between the state, the Manager and the teacher. He emphasised that the 'tripartite pact'[15] between the three, while distinguished from the traditional 'employer–employee' formulation of control, was sufficient to attach liability to the state where there was 'sufficient connection between the State and the creation of the risk to render the State liable'.[16] In coming to this conclusion, Geoghegan J supported a 'modern theory' of vicarious liability, articulated by Justice McLachlin (as she then was) in Canada, whereby 'first and foremost is the concern to provide a just and practical remedy to people who suffer'.[17] Hardiman J did not feel the same enthusiasm for such an approach.[18] Although Hardiman J was suspicious of the 'modern theory' of vicarious liability, stating that '[i]mposing liability on an individual or entity on the basis of "broader policy rationales" smacks, with great respect, of political or social engineering rather than the administration of commutative justice',[19] he himself invoked 'policy reasons' for resisting the expansion of vicarious liability beyond the confines of the Salmond test.[20]

A constitutional claim, made by Louise O'Keeffe at first instance, was given little consideration by any of the decisions in the domestic proceedings, and perhaps one of the frustrating aspects of the appeal before the Supreme Court was the narrow scope of the case pleaded. It focuses primarily upon the vicarious liability of the state. As Conor O'Mahony notes, the more compelling argument may have been that

> the State was negligent in failing to put in place appropriate measures to prevent and detect child abuse in schools, and that the State's constitutional obligations in the field of education require the attribution of State responsibility, and indeed liability, where this does not occur.[21]

Indeed, this argument focusing upon the direct liability of the state and the obligation to protect was born out in the reasons of the Grand Chamber of the ECtHR.

The Decision of the European Court of Human Rights in *O'Keeffe v Ireland*

Following her failure at the domestic level, Louise O'Keeffe took her case to Strasbourg, where she was ultimately successful. The framing of the case before the ECtHR was distinct

[15] ibid, paras 143–44.
[16] ibid, para 180.
[17] ibid, para 174, citing *Bazley v Curry* [1999] 174 DLR (4th) 45, per McLachlin J.
[18] ibid, para 41.
[19] ibid, para 123.
[20] ibid, para 42: 'A finding of liability for perhaps very serious or gross injuries is not a light thing and has an effect quite separate from its consequences in damages. The fact or risk of such a finding may have a "chilling effect", even on State, private or charitable initiatives and will certainly have an effect on the cost of insurance. Nor can public funds, contributed originally by individual taxpayers, be regarded as a separate type of fund, infinite in extent and invulnerable to an extension of the grounds of liability. First, these funds are in fact finite, secondly, justice surely demands that they, like private charitably held funds, should be paid out only in response to a genuine claim and not have to meet a situation in which the very existence of the funds is a factor tending to expose them to a new species of liability.'
[21] O'Mahony, above n 9, 321.

from that at the domestic level, and it serves as an interesting example of the difference that a human rights framework can provide. The Grand Chamber's decision is marked in the way it characterises Louise O'Keeffe's claim, the harm done to her, and the obligation of the State to take positive steps to respect, protect and fulfil human rights obligations.

So what difference did a human rights framework bring to Louise O'Keeffe's case? Based on the decision of the majority decision of the Grand Chamber, it appears a great deal.[22] Her claim in Strasbourg lay primarily[23] under Articles 3 and 13 of the ECHR; that the system of primary education in Ireland failed to protect her from sexual abuse, and that she did not have an effective domestic remedy in that respect. It is well established in ECtHR jurisprudence that sexual abuse falls within the absolute prohibition of torture or inhuman or degrading treatment or punishment contained in Article 3 of the ECHR.[24] What is also well established, as emphasised by the Grand Chamber, is that Article 3 extends a positive obligation onto the state to take measures designed to ensure that individuals within its jurisdiction are not subject to inhuman or degrading treatment or punishment.[25] While the positive obligation to protect does not 'impose an excessive burden on the authorities, bearing in mind, in particular, the unpredictability of human conduct and operational choices which must be made in terms of priorities and resources',[26] it does require that 'measures, should at least, provide effective protection in particular of children and other vulnerable persons and should include reasonable steps to prevent ill-treatment of which the authorities had, or ought to have had knowledge'.[27] This positive obligation, the Grand Chamber emphasised, 'assumes particular importance in the context of the provision of public services such as primary education'.[28] In contrast to the Supreme Court's interpretation of domestic law, such an obligation remains with the state notwithstanding the 'contracting out' or delegation of the provision of services to other parties: 'a State cannot absolve itself from its obligation to minors in primary schools by delegating those duties to private bodies or individuals'.[29]

Within this framework, the majority of the Grand Chamber characterised the question of state liability to rest on

> whether the State's framework of laws, and notably its mechanisms of detection and reporting, provided effective protection for the children attending a National School against the risk of sexual abuse, of which risk it could be said that the authorities had, or ought to have had knowledge in 1973.[30]

The majority held that the state was, in 1973, on notice of the levels of sexual abuse against minors. This was evidenced though the enforcement of criminal laws on the subject,[31]

[22] See also James Gallen, '*O'Keeffe v Ireland*: The Liability of States for Failure to Provide an Effective System for the Detection and Prevention of Sexual Abuse in Education' (2015) 78(1) *Modern Law Review* 140–63, 162.

[23] It is also interesting to note she also made a claim in respect of the length of her civil proceedings under Art 6 ECHR. Friendly settlement led to this claim's being struck out.

[24] *O'Keeffe v Ireland* (2014) 59 EHRR 15, para 148 and the cases cited therein.

[25] ibid, paras 144–48 and the cases cited therein.

[26] ibid, para 144.

[27] ibid.

[28] ibid, para 145.

[29] ibid, para 150.

[30] ibid, para 152.

[31] ibid, paras 159–60.

a 'steady level of prosecutions of sexual offences against children prior to the 1970s',[32] and various reports prior to and during the 1970s drawing public attention to the sexual abuse of children by adults.[33] In light of this, the majority of the Grand Chamber held that

> when relinquishing the control of the vast majority of young children to non-State actors, the State should also have been aware, given its inherent obligation to protect children in this context, of the potential risks to their safety if there were no appropriate framework of protection.[34]

Rather than putting in place appropriate frameworks for protection, the Grand Chamber found that potential complainants of sexual abuse were directed away from state authorities and instead towards the non-state denominational Managers, such as Fr Ó Ceallaigh.[35] The majority found that this was a breach of the state's positive obligation to protect children such as Louise O'Keeffe from sexual abuse, and consequently was a violation of Convention obligations.

The majority decision of the Grand Chamber, and the framework established by European human rights law, saw state responsibility in a markedly different light from that established under tort law as interpreted by the majority of the Irish Supreme Court. By extending the conception of responsibility beyond an individualised, relational and fault-based system of responsibility, to one that recognises the state's obligation to protect where it has the power to do so, provides greater protection to Louise O'Keeffe and others who are searching for justice in relation to institutionalised sexual abuse.

The Feminist Judgment

Maeve O'Rourke provides a part concurring, part dissenting feminist judgment in the Supreme Court in *O'Keeffe v Hickey*. She concurs, albeit 'troubled by the implications', with Fennelly J (with whom Murray CJ and Denham J also agree) that vicarious liability cannot be attached to the state for the actions of Leo Hickey, in that 'no employment relationship existed between Mr Hickey and the Minister for Education'. O'Rourke J notes *obiter* that had submissions been received on Louise O'Keeffe's constitutional right to be free from torture or cruel, inhuman or degrading treatment, the outcome might have been different. She highlights the explicit responsibility on the state under international law in this regard.[36] She differs from the majority in her conclusions on the state's vicarious liability for the inaction of Fr Ó Ceallaigh, the Manager of the school. The legal arrangements of Managers of National Schools, in conjunction with the state's constitutional obligations under Article 42, lead her to conclude that there was a relationship of 'sufficient control' between the state and Managers so as to render the state vicariously liable for the negligent omissions of Fr Ó Ceallaigh.

[32] ibid, para 161.
[33] ibid.
[34] ibid, para 162.
[35] ibid, para 168.
[36] Citing General Comment 2, UN Committee Against Torture (23 November 2007) CAT/C/GC/2/CRP.1/Rev.4.

O'Rourke J's decision reflects the complex and technical nature of the legal principles at play in this case. She engages with an ongoing transatlantic debate over the appropriate common law test for vicarious liability in cases of institutional abuse.[37] In distinction to the lead decision by Hardiman J, O'Rourke J prefers a wider, and arguably more flexible 'modern' interpretation, whereby vicarious liability is viewed in the light of fundamental concerns of (i) provision of a just and practical remedy for the harm; and (ii) deterrence of future harms.[38] She also engages, in stark contrast with all of the other judgments of the Supreme Court, with the constitutional obligations arising in this case. In line with arguments articulated by other academic commentators on this case,[39] O'Rourke J's decision highlights that more could have been made of the constitutional role and responsibility of the state in the obligation to protect individuals from institutionalised sexual abuse, both by the Court and, arguably, by the parties in submissions. In the midst of this technicality, a clear feminist voice emerges. Three main areas highlight this feminist commitment.

First, O'Rourke J's narration of the facts in this case brings to the fore the experience of Louise O'Keeffe. Rather than seeing her as a faceless claimant, the judgment both contextualises and particularises the harm done to Louise O'Keeffe at the hands of Leo Hickey. In the factual background, O'Rourke J highlights that it is an 'eight year-old girl at the centre of this case'. The harm done to Louise O'Keeffe occurred at a time when she was 'extremely vulnerable'. The factual background focuses on both the impact at the time of abuse—creating fear, anxiety, watchfulness, and withdrawal in eight-year-old Louise to the effect of fundamentally disrupting her schooling—and the 'long-term effects of the abuse … right into adulthood, causing harm to her well-being, relationships and family life'. The 'devastating consequences' upon Louise O'Keeffe are the central narrative of O'Rourke J's decision.

Secondly, O'Rourke J's feminist judgment situates Louise O'Keeffe's story in a narrative broader than that of one woman seeking justice for one woman. As the facts above note, Louise O'Keeffe stood as the public face for a larger class of women subject to Leo Hickey's torment facilitated by state neglect. Louise O'Keeffe has herself described the sense of community and collective redress that motivated her action:

> When a wall is being built it's one block at a time. I would see myself as one block on the wall. The girl who made the first complaint in my case, she was a block on the wall. The other people who have taken cases, whether they've dropped them or whether they are still proceeding, each and every one of them is a block on the wall. And with all the blocks on the wall we are stronger and we are together.[40]

This broader context is not lost on O'Rourke J. She sees Louise O'Keeffe as the representative of a broader group of women. This is a case about one woman, but also about more

[37] For further analysis of this debate, see Desmond Ryan, 'Connections Without Consensus: Recent Approaches to Vicarious Liability in the Irish Supreme Court (2009) 31(1) *Dublin University Law Journal* 457–72; Frank Burton, 'Limitation, vicarious liability and historical actions for abuse: a changing legal landscape' (2013) 2 *Journal of Personal Injury Law* 95.

[38] See *Bazley v Curry* (1999) 174 DLR (4th) 45 per McLachlin J.

[39] O'Mahony, above n 9.

[40] Miriam O'Callaghan, Interview with Louise O'Keeffe on 'Sunday with Miriam', *RTE Radio* 1 (2 February 2014), at www.rte.ie/radio/radioplayer/rteradioweb.html#!rii=9%3A10247011%3A15946%3A02%2D02%2D2014%3A (last accessed 25 May 2015).

than one woman—a case that is symbolic of wider social structures and power relations.[41] O'Rourke J characterises Louise O'Keeffe's claim as a 'test case', and in her final remarks is scathing of the fact that Louise O'Keeffe, having undertaken proceedings in the pursuit of justice 'not just for oneself but for others past and future', was not afforded a protective costs order at the outset. It was not until the very last moment, at conclusion of proceedings before the Supreme Court, that this litigation was formally recognised as test case litigation and relief from general costs principles afforded to Louise O'Keeffe.[42] O'Rourke J's judgment also gives due recognition to the immense toll that the long and aggressively state-pursued litigation has had upon Louise O'Keeffe. As a feminist, O'Rourke J embraces an 'ethics of care' approach to litigation procedure, and in the final section of the judgment focuses concern on the vulnerability of individuals litigating against the state. She emphasises that 'Our system must do better for litigants who may have suffered grave injustices and who decide to undertake the emotionally and financial difficult step of pursuing their case, as it their right, through the courts.' This stands in stark contrast to the context in which Hardiman J situates Louise O'Keeffe's claim. His decision, from the outset, focuses upon the financial implication of her claim for the 'taxpayer'.[43] This is also accompanied by several references to what Hardiman J referred to as Louise O'Keeffe's dissatisfaction with the financial compensation received, imputing to her primarily pecuniary motives for bringing the action against the state and, impliedly, painting the picture of an opportunistic litigant in search of 'deep pockets' for compensation instead of, as Louise O'Keeffe has framed her motivations, a litigant looking for state responsibility for its part in the wrongs perpetrated against her, and against others.

Thirdly, O'Rourke J connects the claims of Louise O'Keeffe and the others who have suffered abuse in National Schools, with other pursuits for justice for violence perpetrated against women, children and those placed in positions of vulnerability in state care. For example, she interrogates the harm that unchecked state power has proved to have upon women and others in Ireland by reference to the ongoing battle for state accountability for the atrocities committed in the nation's Magdalene Laundries: 'It is not difficult to think of systems which have enjoyed official and widespread societal approval … while trampling the constitutional rights of vulnerable individuals caught up in them. The nation's Magdalene Laundries are one such example.' In this way, O'Rourke J explicitly calls out the state for its responsibility for systematic abuse. She highlights violence and abuse as the consequence of structural inequality, rather than the exceptional criminality of isolated individuals. The broader context of institutionalised sexual abuse was highlighted in the decision of Fennelly J, when he notes:

> Cases of sexual abuse have preoccupied our criminal courts and this court for many years. It is surprising that here for the first time this court is confronted with questions relating to the liability of institutions, extending to the State itself, for sexual abuse perpetrated, as in this case, on schoolchildren in a national school, by a teacher.[44]

[41] See Marie Keenan, *Child Sexual Abuse and the Catholic Church: Gender, Power, and Organizational Culture* (Oxford, Oxford University Press, 2011) ch 6 and the literature cited therein.

[42] On 6 May 2009, the Supreme Court refused the state's application for costs, departing, due to the exceptional circumstances of the case, from the general principle that costs should follow the event: *O'Keeffe v Hickey* [2009] IESC 39.

[43] See *O'Keeffe v Hickey* [2009] 2 IR 302, paras 3, 7, 42 and 49.

[44] ibid, para 182.

However, Hardiman J's decision saw the actions of Leo Hickey in quite a different light—one disconnected from any broader structural deficit. He characterised Leo Hickey's criminality as exceptional, 'an unusual act, little discussed, and certainly not regarded as an ordinary foreseeable risk of attending at a school'.[45] He continues later in his reasons to reinforce that

> such actions are, even today, deviant, uncommon and attract the condemnation and disgust of the huge majority of the members of the teaching profession, who would never behave in this way. This is an important point, if the present case and others like it are to be approached in anything resembling a realistic fashion.[46]

This version of 'reality' promoted by Hardiman J reads as completely disconnected from the findings of the Commission to Inquire into Child Abuse, commonly known as the Ryan Commission.[47] Although the final report was published in 2009, after the decision was written, it was the end result of a far-reaching and highly publicised commission commencing in 2000 to inquire into the abuse of children in institutions, including schools and 'any other place where children are cared for other than as members of their families', between 1940 and 1999. It is clear that institutionalised sexual abuse was anything but 'exceptional' in Ireland. The Ryan Report was damning, for both the Church and the state, and pointed to the occurrence of widespread and systematic institutional abuse of children in Ireland.

O'Rourke J's decision to connect Louise O'Keeffe's case to this broader context of seeking to redress injustice, and her refusal to view this as a case only about the exceptional criminality of one man, clearly marks it as feminist.

[45] ibid, para 78.

[46] ibid, paras 121–22.

[47] As established by the Commission to Inquire into Child Abuse Act 2000. The Ryan Report was published in five volumes on 20 May 2009. It contains 43 conclusions and 20 recommendations. Available at www.childabusecommission.ie/rpt/pdfs/ (last accessed 25 May 2015). For a succinct summary of the key findings, see O'Mahony, above n 9, at 319.

Louise O'Keeffe

Plaintiff

v

Leo Hickey

The Minister for Education and Science

Ireland

The Attorney General

Defendants

SUPREME COURT

[2008] IESC 72

(19 December 2008)

Judgment of Ms. Justice O'Rourke delivered the 19th day of December 2008

Introduction

This case concerns the repeated sexual assault of an eight-year-old girl, Louise O'Keeffe, by her primary school Principal, Leo Hickey, while attending Dunderrow National School in 1973.

The issue which Ms O'Keeffe appeals to this court is whether the State can be held vicariously liable for either the actions of Mr Hickey or the inaction of the acting Manager of the National School, a Fr O'Ceallaigh, who failed to respond to a prior complaint of sexual assault by Mr Hickey in 1971.

The relationship between Church and State in Ireland since the 19th century has assumed critical importance in this case. My learned colleagues in the majority find that the State's historical arrangement of outsourcing the provision of primary education to the Catholic Church and some other private organisations, which persists to this day, prevents vicarious liability from attaching to the State for the behaviour of either Mr Hickey or Fr O'Ceallaigh. The majority holds that, because the State decided to pay the Church to manage and provide primary education to the nation's children, and because this was approved by Article 42 of the Constitution, no relationship of employment or sufficient control exists between the State and National School teachers or Managers to enable a finding of vicarious liability. Thus, the vicarious liability claims fall at the first hurdle (the second hurdle being the relationship between the tortious act and the nature of the employment).

In effect, the majority judgments say, the less control the State chooses to take over the provision of primary education in Ireland, the less responsibility the State will shoulder for criminal and/or tortious maltreatment of children in National Schools.

I cannot accept that the State has absolutely no relationship of sufficient control over either teachers or Managers of National Schools for the purpose of imposing vicarious liability. I find that vicarious liability should be imposed upon the State defendants for the inaction of Fr O'Ceallaigh. The legal arrangements regarding Managers of National Schools and the wording of the 1965 Rules for National Schools support this finding. So too, surely, does the State's obligation under Article 42.3.2° of the Constitution, "as guardian of the common good, [to] require in view of actual conditions that the children receive a certain minimum education, moral, intellectual and social".

I am unable to attach vicarious liability to the State for the actions of Mr Hickey, however. This has been a difficult decision. I find that the common law doctrine of vicarious liability in its current form does not stretch to cover the circumstances at hand, where there is no employment relationship between the State and Mr Hickey and the State has deliberately renounced a great deal of control over teachers in National Schools. It may be arguable that the law of tort has failed to provide an effective remedy to Ms O'Keeffe for violations of her constitutional rights (particularly her right to freedom from torture and ill-treatment). I would have welcomed further engagement with the Constitution in the arguing of this appeal.

Factual background

The eight-year-old girl at the centre of this case, Louise O'Keeffe, began to have one-to-one music lessons with the Principal of her National School, Mr Hickey, in January 1973. The lessons took place during play-breaks or after school. During the second lesson, Mr Hickey began to rub Ms O'Keeffe's stomach. By the fifth lesson, Mr Hickey had progressed to digitally assaulting Ms O'Keeffe. The abuse continued until the end of the academic year in 1973, on approximately 20 occasions.

As an eight-year-old pupil, Ms O'Keeffe was extremely vulnerable. She lacked control over whether or not she would attend school each day. She was confined within the school premises between specified times. She was unable to escape to a place where Mr Hickey would not be able to find her. She was visible to Mr Hickey while at school. She lacked the knowledge which would have enabled her to recognise what was happening and to seek help. She had no power whatsoever to stop the abuse.

Mr Hickey, as the Principal of a two-teacher National School, held enormous power over Ms O'Keeffe and the other children in the school, including the power to keep them under surveillance and confined to the school premises during specific times. Mr Hickey's music lessons gave him further power to confine a child alone, which allowed him the opportunity to perpetrate sexual abuse.

Ms O'Keeffe's schooling was disrupted at the time that she was being abused by Mr Hickey. She became fearful, watchful and anxious, and she withdrew from playing with her friends as she sought places to hide from Mr Hickey during break times. The long-term effects of the abuse impacted Ms O'Keeffe right into adulthood, causing harm to her well-being, relationships and family life.

It transpires that eight-year-old Louise O'Keeffe was far from Mr Hickey's only victim. In September 1973, Ms O'Keeffe's parents were approached by a group of other parents in the school who were concerned about allegations of sexual abuse by Mr Hickey. The parents met with the Manager of Dunderrow National School, Fr O'Ceallaigh, following which Mr Hickey went on sick leave. Fr O'Ceallaigh never reported the allegations against Mr Hickey to any State authority, and Mr Hickey went on to teach at a different National School until retirement.

The allegations concerning Mr Hickey in 1973 were not the first to have been made to Fr O'Ceallaigh. Fr O'Ceallaigh had received and failed to take any action in response to a complaint of sexual abuse by Mr Hickey in 1971, from the mother of another child in Dunderrow National School.

In 1998, Mr Hickey was charged with 386 counts of sexual abuse over a 10-year period at Dunderrow National School. He pled guilty to sample charges relating to 21 girls and received a three-year prison sentence.

The present appeal

Following the conclusion of criminal proceedings against Mr Hickey in 1998, Ms O'Keeffe initiated civil proceedings against Mr Hickey and the Minister for Education, Ireland and the Attorney General ('the State').

Mr Hickey having failed to enter a defence, Ms O'Keeffe obtained judgment in default against him in 1999 and an award of damages in 2006. She has encountered great difficulties in enforcing this judgment.

The High Court trial in Ms O'Keeffe's case against the State defendants took place in March 2004. As my learned colleague Hardiman J sets out, Ms O'Keeffe's claim against the State fell under the following headings:

(1) Negligence on the part of the State arising out of the failure of the State defendants to put in place appropriate measures and procedures to protect from and to cease the systematic abuse which the first-named defendant had on the evidence embarked on from 1962 in Dunderrow National School of which she was very much one of the latter victims;
(2) Vicarious liability in relation, not merely to the first-named defendant but also in relation to the curate Fr O'Ceallaigh who was the *de facto* acting Manager, to whom the evidence established that a complaint of sexual abuse of a pupil by that girl's mother was made in or about 1971 on foot of which Fr O'Ceallaigh took no action; and
(3) The constitutional role and responsibility of the State defendants in the provision of primary education arising under Article 42 of the Constitution and the measures which the second-named defendant, the Minister, had adopted and the steps put in place to discharge those responsibilities.

I note from the High Court judgment of de Valera J that Ms O'Keeffe also claimed damages from the State arising from an interference with her constitutional rights to bodily integrity and privacy.

During the March 2004 trial, de Valera J non-suited Ms O'Keeffe's claim in negligence. Ms O'Keeffe did not appeal this order. The learned judge declined the State's application for non-suit regarding the vicarious liability and constitutional issues, however, and the court heard legal argument on those issues.

On 20 January 2006, de Valera J delivered judgment dismissing Ms O'Keeffe's remaining claims against the State. The judge held that vicarious liability did not attach to the State for the tortious acts of Mr Hickey, applying the reasoning of O'Higgins J in *Delahunty v South Eastern Health Board and Others* (High Court, 30/07/03), where it was held that the State did not exercise sufficient (or any) management functions with respect to an industrial school for vicarious liability to attach. I do not find *Delahunty* relevant to the case at hand because it was not concerned with, nor did it consider in detail, the legal arrangements regarding National Schools. The judgment of O'Higgins J is curious, perhaps, in light of the State apology in May 1999 to victims of childhood abuse in industrial schools and the government's decision in 2002 to indemnify the Church past the sum of €128 million in relation to Residential Institutions Redress Board claims.

Mr Justice de Valera did not address the question of vicarious liability for the inaction of Fr O'Ceallaigh in 1971. Nor did de Valera J address the issue of the State's constitutional obligations regarding education under Article 42. De Valera J dismissed Ms O'Keeffe's claim for damages for interference with her constitutional rights to bodily integrity and privacy on the basis that the law of tort applied to Ms O'Keeffe's claim. De Valera J applied the judgment of Costello P in *W (No 2) v The Attorney General* [1997] 2 IR 141 to find that "no action lies for breach of a guaranteed constitutional right where, as in this matter, existing laws protect that right". I set out my views on *W (No 2) v The Attorney General* and the Supreme Court decision that preceded it, *Hanrahan v Merck Sharp and Dohme* [1988] ILRM 629, at some length below.

Mr Justice de Valera having given judgment on 20 January 2006, the order of the High Court was perfected on 24 October 2006. It is this order that Ms O'Keeffe appeals against. As my learned colleague Hardiman J puts it at paragraph 37 of his judgment, Ms O'Keeffe's only remaining claim relates to vicarious liability "alleged to exist for the criminal and plainly unauthorized acts of the first defendant, but also for the alleged negligence of the curate Fr O Ceallaigh who was the *de facto* acting Manager in respect of his alleged failure to take any step on foot of a complaint made to him of a similar nature, in relation to another child, in 1971."

Legal arrangements regarding National Schools

The legal structure of Dunderrow National School was typical of National Schools in Ireland to this day. It was owned by the trustees of the Catholic diocese of Cork and Ross. The Patron of the school was the Bishop of Cork and Ross. The Manager of the school was an Archdeacon Stritch P.P. Archdeacon Stritch being elderly, however, the actual functions of management were carried out by Fr O'Ceallaigh at all material times. The salaries of the teachers in Dunderrow National School were paid by the State. However, the teachers, of which Mr Hickey was one, were employed under contracts with Fr O'Ceallaigh, rather than the State. Fr O'Ceallaigh did not receive a salary from the State.

This tripartite arrangement for the funding, management and ownership of National Schools in Ireland was permitted by Article 42.4 of the Constitution, which was worded so that the State would be obliged not to educate children itself but instead to "provide for" free primary education. This wording was designed to allow for the continuation of a practice, in place since 1833, whereby the government funded a system of national primary education that was managed and delivered by private (mainly religious) institutions who wanted to run schools according to their own ethos.

The Catholic Church was determined to have control over the appointment of teachers in its National Schools. In evidence before the High Court, Professor Coolahan, who is the author of the standard work on the history of the Irish educational system, described the debate between the Church and State authorities after the inception of the Irish Free State thus:

> "... It had to be Catholic Schools under Catholic management, Catholic teachers, Catholic children ..."

Professor Coolahan went on to discuss a dispute which arose in the early 1950s, when the Irish National Teachers' Organisation sought the establishment of local committees to take responsibility for the maintenance and repair of school buildings and similar management functions. The attitude of the Catholic Church was described as follows:

> "Eventually Cardinal Dalton took a very strong view on this issue and said there should be no interference whatever with the inherited tradition of managerial rights of schooling and it did not matter, because it was the thin edge of the wedge in his view, if local authorities [only] took control of the maintenance of schools. In due course, he said, *it might intrude into other aspects of the Manager's authority vis-à-vis the appointment and dismissal of teachers which was of course the key concern that had been fought for and won over the years.*" (My emphasis)

Despite the great degree of control given to religious institutions to manage and deliver national primary education, however, their power was not absolute. The Constitution gave a right to children, through Article 42.3.2°, to "receive a certain minimum education, moral, intellectual and social". Indeed, Kenny J held this to be the case in *Crowley v Ireland* [1980] IR 102 at 126.

The 1965 Rules for National Schools and a great body of Department of Education Circular Letters laid down extensive minimum standards, presumably designed to meet this constitutional entitlement of children. Rule 30 of the 1965 Rules for National Schools provided for the withdrawal of recognition from a National School for non-compliance with the Rules. An inspection regime was also established, which, according to Professor Coolahan, always formed a crucially important part of the system of State oversight and maintenance of standards.

Vicarious liability for Fr O'Ceallaigh's inaction

As set out above, I am of the opinion that the legal relationship between the State and Fr O'Ceallaigh is sufficient for the imposition of vicarious liability. This finding chimes with Article 42.3.2° of the Constitution.

McMahon and Binchy introduce the doctrine of vicarious liability as follows (in Chapter 43 of the *Law of Torts*, 3rd Edition (Dublin, 2000) at p 1091):

> "The law is sometimes prepared to hold one person liable for the wrong committed by another person even though the person held liable is not at fault in the accepted sense of the word. Thus, the law may hold the employer liable for the wrongs of an employee, the principal liable for the wrongs of an agent or the firm liable for the wrongs of its partner in spite of the fact that the employer, the principal or the firm may not have been at fault in any way. When the law imposes liability in these circumstances we speak of an employer, principal or firm being 'vicariously liable'."

I accept that the Manager of a National School is not in an employment relationship with the State. It is not so easy to dismiss the existence of a relationship of agency between the State and Fr O'Ceallaigh, however.

The relationship of agency in its orthodox sense is a creature of contract law; it is concerned with circumstances in which one party may enter into a binding contract with another. Insofar as remuneration of National School teachers is concerned, the Manager of a

National School is in a position akin to an agent of the State (if not an agent in the ordinary contract law sense): once the Manager enters into a contract of employment with a teacher, the State is obliged to pay that teacher's salary. According to Rule 18(1)(a) of the 1965 Rules for National Schools, the Manager must obtain Departmental approval before appointing his or her chosen teacher. Rule 18(2) then requires the Manager, on appointment of the teacher, to "enter into an agreement with the teacher on one of the official forms provided for the purpose" whereupon the State will be liable to pay the teacher's salary.

In addition to the orthodox contractual relationship of agency, however, there have been cases, including *Moynihan v Moynihan* [1951] 1 IR 192 in this court and *Scarsbrook v Mason* [1961] 3 All ER 767 in the Queen's Bench Division of the English High Court, where a more general form of agency was found sufficient for the imposition of vicarious liability.

In *Moynihan*, this court held a grandmother vicariously liable for the negligence of her daughter in pouring tea in the grandmother's house. In *Scarsbrook*, a passenger in a car was held liable for the driver's negligence, having contributed money towards petrol.

As McMahon and Binchy note of the *Moynihan* case, at p.1094:

> "The decision is important because it clearly indicates that the control concept is used, not as a justification for vicarious liability, but rather as a test to determine the persons for whose actions liability will be imposed on the defendant. In other words *if the control element is high then even in the absence of other features the subordinate may be considered a de facto employee and provided the 'controlled person's' acts relate to the 'controller's' business the latter will be vicariously liable for injury caused to third persons by such acts.*" (My emphasis)

Evidence of sufficient control

I turn now to the evidence of the State's control over National School Managers.

In *McEneaney v Minister for Education* [1941] IR 430, Murnaghan J acknowledged that, in the period before the 1965 Rules for National Schools, "the duties and functions of the manager were *minutely* provided for in Rules and Regulations made by the Board." (My emphasis) The 1965 Rules continued this trend: the Rules prescribe the Manager's duties in relation to teachers' conduct; school time-tables; school hours, school meetings and roll-call; the prescribed period of secular instruction per day; maximum permitted vacation time and school closing days; the age of enrolment of children; choice of school books; and the conditions of repair, heating, cleaning and painting of schools (amongst other things).

The wording of Rule 15(1) is striking: "The manager of a national school *is charged with* the direct government of the school, the appointment of teachers, subject to the Minister's approval, their removal and the conducting of the necessary correspondence." (My emphasis) Furthermore, each Manager is required by Rule 15(4) to give to the State "an undertaking in writing that the Rules for National Schools shall be complied with."

Rule 16 dictates that "Managers should visit their schools frequently, and should satisfy themselves that the Rules for National Schools are being complied with." According to Rule 15(9), "The minister may withdraw recognition from a manager for failure to observe the Rules or if it should appear that the educational interests of the district require it".

It is clear that the Manager's primary function, for which he is recognised as Manager by the State, is to implement the constitutionally required minimum education on the State's behalf rather than to act primarily in the interests of the religious institution that owns the National School.

Under the 1965 Rules, Managers have the authority and obligation to ensure that teachers comply with minimum standards of conduct set out in the Rules. Each of the functions which under Rule 15(1) the Manager of a National School "is charged with" (the direct government of the school; the appointment of teachers, subject to the Minister's approval; their removal; and the conducting of necessary correspondence) applies to teachers' conduct as much as anything else under the Rules.

Regarding the conduct of teachers, Rule 121(1) requires that "Teachers should act in a spirit of obedience to the law and loyalty to the State". Other relevant requirements under Rule 121 are as follows:

> "(2) Teachers should pay the strictest attention to the morals and general conduct of their pupils, to the development of a patriotic spirit and outlook and lose no opportunity of inculcating the principles of truth, temperance, unselfishness and politeness, and regard for property, whether public or private.
>
> (3) Teachers should promote both by precept and example, cleanliness, neatness and decency …
>
> (4) Teachers are required to take all reasonable precautions to ensure the safety of the pupils, and to this end shall carry out all lawful instructions issued by the manager …"

A Guidance Note of 6 May 1970 concerning complaints against teachers shows that the State relied upon the Manager to convey to it the information required to set in motion the State's own disciplinary functions under the Rules. According to the 1970 Guidance Note, a person wishing to complain about a teacher was to be informed that the matter was one for the Manager, in the first instance, and asked to clarify whether the complaint had been notified to the Manager. The Manager had to obtain observations from the relevant teacher and forward those observations, together with the Manager's own views, to the Department. The deputy chief inspector within the Department would then identify whether an investigation was required. If so, the inspector was to interview the Manager, the teacher and parents. If an inquiry led to relevant findings against the teacher, Rule 108 could be set in motion, whereby the Minister could discipline a teacher (including through prosecution, withdrawal of recognition, or withdrawal of salary).

Fr O'Ceallaigh's conduct

Once a relationship of agency has been established, the next question is whether Fr O'Ceallaigh's conduct was tortious. If it was, we must ask whether the tortious conduct was within the scope of what Fr O'Ceallaigh was authorised to do by the State, or sufficiently closely connected to it, to attract vicarious liability.

In order to determine whether Fr O'Ceallaigh's failure to take any action in response to an allegation of sexual abuse by Mr Hickey in 1971 was tortious, I turn first to the question of whether Fr O'Ceallaigh owed a duty of care to Ms O'Keeffe. As McMahon and Binchy note (at p. 441), and I agree:

> "Clearly teachers and those involved in the management of schools have a duty of care in relation to pupils who attend the school. The elements of proximity of relationship and foreseeability of potential injury could scarcely be more pronounced."

The standard of care owed by school authorities is to take such care of pupils as a careful parent would take of their children. This was recognised by O'Dalaigh CJ in *Lennon v McCarthy & Anor*, an unreported judgment of this court of 13th July 1966 and, more recently, approved by this court in *Murphy v County Wexford VEC* [2004] 4 IR 202.

Fr O'Ceallaigh's failure to respond in any way to the 1971 complaint was as far from the behaviour of a careful parent as one can imagine. A careful parent would have listened to the complaint that was coming from a young child (in this case through her mother) and recognised its seriousness, both in terms of the need to investigate and the need to minimise the risk of further abuse.

In acting as he did, Fr O'Ceallaigh failed to comply with his explicit obligations under the Department of Education Guidance Note of 6 May 1970 and the 1965 Rules for National Schools more generally. Therefore, I also find that the tortious conduct was within the scope of what Fr O'Ceallaigh was authorised to do—and was "charged with" doing—by the State.

The rationale behind the doctrine of vicarious liability

The doctrine of vicarious liability goes against the general scheme of the common law, whereby liability for a wrong is imposed upon the wrongdoer only. In *Majrowski v Guy's and St Thomas' NHS Trust* [2006] UKHL 34, Lord Nicholls explored the rationale behind the continuation of the doctrine as follows:

> "9. Whatever its historical origin, this common law principle of strict liability for another person's wrongs finds its rationale today in a combination of policy factors. They are summarised in Professor Fleming's *Law of Torts*, 9th ed, (1998) pages 409–410. Stated shortly, these factors are that *all forms of economic activity carry a risk of harm to others, and fairness requires that those responsible for such activities should be liable to persons suffering loss from wrongs committed in the conduct of the enterprise.* This is 'fair', because it means injured persons can look for recompense to a source better placed financially than individual wrongdoing employees. It means also that the financial loss arising from the wrongs can be spread more widely, by liability insurance and higher prices. *In addition, and importantly, imposing strict liability on employers encourages them to maintain standards of 'good practice' by their employees.* For these reasons employers are to be held liable for wrongs committed by their employees in the course of their employment." (My emphasis)

McLachlin J, of the Supreme Court of Canada, gave a similar description of the rationale in *Bazley v Curry* (1999) 174 DLR (4th) 45:

> "Fleming [*The Law of Torts* (9th edn, 1998)] has identified [the] policies lying at the heart of vicarious liability. In his view two fundamental concerns underlie the imposition of vicarious liability: *(1) provision of a just and practical remedy for the harm; and (2) deterrence of future harm.* While different formulations of the policy interests at stake may be made (for example, loss internalization is a hybrid of the two), I believe that these two ideas usefully embrace the main policy considerations that have been advanced." (My emphasis)

In this case, the imposition of vicarious liability upon the State defendants for Fr O'Ceallaigh's negligence satisfies the policy concerns which underpin the modern doctrine. It is just and fair because the State holds an obligation towards children under Article 42.3.2° to ensure that they "receive a certain minimum education", and the State's own Rules for National Schools envisage teachers behaving lawfully and with regard for the safety of children as part of the minimum required educational standards. In addition, the State is constitutionally obliged under Article 42.4 to respect the rights of parents with regard to the "religious *and moral* formation" of their children. The plaintiff's parents—and all parents of children in National Schools—had and have a right to expect that the State will exercise sufficient control over the treatment of their children in National Schools so as to ensure that they are not suffering criminal abuse which a manager knows or should know about.

In addition, it seems to me that the State created a risk when it allowed religious or other private institutions and groups to deliver national primary education, and in particular when it gave those institutions the power to appoint teachers of their own choosing. I commented earlier on the insistence of the Catholic Church that it should retain control over the appointment of teachers. The more importance the Church attached to that power, the more likely it became that situations which may have called into question the Church's abilities in this regard would be suppressed, or covered up, by the institution.

It is a common feature of institutions in general that the desire to self-preserve and individual members' loyalties can sometimes take precedence, whether people are conscious of it or not, over conflicting duties and responsibilities. We need look no further than the Ferns Report and the testimonies that prompted the State apology to industrial and reformatory school survivors and the creation of the Commission to Inquire into Child Abuse for evidence of institutional cover-up of widespread child abuse in Ireland. When Fr O'Ceallaigh was made aware of an allegation of child sexual abuse against Mr Hickey in 1971—and again when he was informed of numerous similar allegations in 1973—he was faced with a conflict of interest. Reporting the allegations, which he was obliged to do under the Rules and 1970 Guidance Note, would reflect negatively, at however slight a level, upon his and his superiors' employment and supervision of Mr Hickey and general ability to run Dunderrow National School.

The remaining policy concern behind the principle of vicarious liability—the encouragement of good practice amongst employees or agents—also applies to the case at hand. Through its ability to create legislation and policy, the State is in a position and should be encouraged to ameliorate standards and behaviours which constitute a threat to the well-being of children and the realisation of their constitutional right to receive a minimum education.

Vicarious liability for Mr Hickey's actions

I turn now to the claim against the State for the actions of Mr Hickey.

Although I am troubled by the implications, I am unable to find that vicarious liability attaches to the State for the actions of Mr Hickey on the basis of the pleaded case. I agree with the judgment of Fennelly J, with whom Murray CJ and Denham J concur, where they find that no employment relationship existed between Mr Hickey and the Minister for Education. As my learned colleagues note, although Mr Hickey's salary was paid by the State, and Mr Hickey was licensed to teach by the State and the State held the power to revoke his licence at the end of a lengthy disciplinary process, Mr Hickey was not employed by the State. Mr Hickey was hired by the Manager of the National School, and the State did not have the power to dismiss him. On a day-to-day basis, the power to direct Mr Hickey's behaviour and the responsibility for ensuring that Mr Hickey complied with the Rules for National Schools lay with the Manager. In general, I am persuaded by the approach adopted in the recent Australian, Canadian and English cases where vicarious liability has been imposed (more flexibly than before) in relation to acts with a sufficiently "close connection" to the employer's work. However, I accept that in all of these cases an employment relationship has still been present.

Had the court received submissions on Louise O'Keeffe's constitutional right to be free from torture or cruel, inhuman or degrading treatment, the outcome might have been different. The court may have found itself grappling with the question of whether the law of tort offered an effective remedy to Louise O'Keeffe. I am aware of the General Comment No 2 issued by the United Nations Committee Against Torture earlier this year, which highlights the particular responsibility of States to prevent torture and ill-treatment by agents, private contractors and others acting on behalf of or in conjunction with the State in all contexts of custody or control, including schools.

Constitutional rights arguments in tort cases

There seems to be a general reluctance on the part of litigants and the judiciary to engage with the Constitution when arguing or deciding claims based on tort law, which derives perhaps from the decision of this court 20 years ago in *Hanrahan v Merck Sharp and Dohme* [1988] ILRM 629.

In *Hanrahan*, Henchy J laid down the principle that a plaintiff will not be allowed to argue or base a claim on breach of a constitutional right if there exists a statutory or common law cause of action which can be said to protect that right. This court in *Hanrahan* held that where there is an existing tort upon which the plaintiff can base her claim, she "is normally confined to the limitations of that tort" (at 636). An exception would only arise "if it could be shown that the tort in question is basically ineffective to protect [her] constitutional right" (at 636).

Hanrahan was applied by Costello P in *W v Ireland (No 2)* [1997] 2 IR 141, and it was the *W v Ireland (No 2)* judgment which de Valera J relied upon in dismissing Ms O'Keeffe's claim in the High Court for interference with her constitutional rights to bodily integrity and privacy. There has been no discussion in this court as to whether the existing law of tort, including its doctrine of vicarious liability, provides effective protection for Ms O'Keeffe's constitutional rights.

I am of the opinion that this court in *Hanrahan* misinterpreted the constitutional role of the courts in holding that they should not consider constitutional rights arguments save where existing statutory or common law causes of action are "basically ineffective" or "plainly inadequate to effectuate the constitutional guarantee in question" (*Hanrahan* at 636). This approach surely fails to ensure full protection for the constitutional rights of the individual.

The *Hanrahan* judgment appears to fly in the face of the judgment of this court in *Meskell v CIE* [1973] IR 121, which held that the existence of a constitutional right implies a right to a remedy for its breach:

> "… if a person has suffered damage by virtue of a breach of a constitutional right or the infringement of a constitutional right that person is entitled to seek redress against the person or persons who have infringed that right." (at 133)

If there is any gap between the rights protection afforded by existing causes of action and the rights protection demanded by the Constitution, I do not see why the courts should not intervene to fill that gap. Indeed, I think it a constitutional imperative that they do.

Reluctance to litigate constitutional rights may have a disproportionately negative impact on the most vulnerable, or marginalised, in our society. The Constitution is their bulwark, where necessary, against the tide of popular opinion or belief. It is not difficult to think of systems which have enjoyed official and widespread societal approval, as well as some degree of legislative authority, while trampling the constitutional rights of vulnerable individuals caught up in them. The nation's Magdalene Laundries are one such example.

Procedure

Before concluding, I wish to acknowledge the toll that these proceedings have, no doubt, taken upon Ms O'Keeffe. It is not easy to litigate against the State knowing that the full force of the State's resources will be brought to bear in defence of one's claim. It takes a deep sense of being wronged and an even deeper desire to see justice done—often not just for oneself but for others in the past and future—to pursue an action to this stage of appeal. Even if I were not to find in Ms O'Keeffe's favour, as the majority has not, I would recognise that she has clearly pursued an issue of immense public and constitutional importance. Hers is a test case on the question of State liability for abuse of pupils by National School teachers, and there are over 100 similar cases awaiting the outcome of this appeal.

I find it regrettable that these proceedings have taken over 10 years to reach this court. Our system must do better for litigants who may have suffered grave injustices and who decide to undertake the emotionally and financially difficult step of pursuing their case, as is their right, through the courts. Litigants in Ms O'Keeffe's position deserve to have their actions dealt with expeditiously. If the judicial system can be resourced so that commercial claims are managed efficiently, the same should apply to claims such as Ms O'Keeffe's.

It is more regrettable still that Ms O'Keeffe has had to bear the enormous psychological burden of not knowing whether or not she will be held liable for the State's costs until she reaches the very end of proceedings. At the conclusion of the High Court proceedings, Ms O'Keeffe was ordered to pay the State's costs, which amounted to €500,000. It has not escaped my notice that this court is now delivering its substantive judgment less than a week before Christmas, to a survivor of inhuman and degrading treatment (if not torture) and a mother of two small children, without making any judgment on the issue of costs. The State intends to apply for an order for costs. Ms O'Keeffe will have to wait until well into next year to discover whether or not she will be held liable.

I am of the view that in a case against the State such as this, which is not merely a personal injury claim but also involves important constitutional questions and is a test case, a protective costs order should, in principle, be available to the plaintiff from the outset.

17

Commentary on *Christian Brothers High School Clonmel v Mary Stokes and the Equality Authority*

CLAIRE BRUTON

Introduction

Christian Brothers High School Clonmel v Mary Stokes[1] came before the Supreme Court in 2014 following an interesting journey from a statutory tribunal through the civil courts, some of which occurred during the lifetime of the Northern/Irish Feminist Judgments Project. The case involved alleged indirect discrimination on grounds of membership of the Traveller community on the basis of the application of a parental rule in the context of a secondary school's admissions policy. The school operated a policy that gave preference to children whose siblings attended the school (the sibling rule), or whose father had previously attended the school (the parental rule) or who had a close connection with the school. John Stokes was the oldest child in his family. He was a Traveller and his father had not attended the school, or indeed any other secondary school. In fact none of John's father's siblings had attended school beyond primary school. His mother, Mary, had completed secondary school. She wanted her son to have the best possible education and to continue to the local boys' secondary school like many of his peers from the feeder national school John attended. John's father's limited education was unsurprising. That Travellers experienced education disadvantage is an inescapable assertion relative to the general population, particularly in the 1980s.

As John's father had not attended the Christian Brothers High School in Clonmel and he had no siblings in the school, John could not meet the parental rule or the sibling rule. He was unsuccessful in obtaining one of the remaining places, which were determined by way of lottery. Legacy parental rules of this kind had been highlighted by the Department of Education as being problematic for minority groups. The Irish Labour Party, while in government, made non-discrimination in admissions policies within schools a policy priority, and in 2015 published the Education (Admission to Schools) Bill 2015.[2]

[1] *Christian Brothers High School Clonmel v Mary Stokes and the Equality Authority* [2015] IESC 13.

[2] Number 35 of 2015, at www.oireachtas.ie/viewdoc.asp?fn=/documents/bills28/bills/2015/3515/document1.htm (last accessed 2 February 2016).

It is unusual for an equality case to receive such extensive judicial consideration: it was heard on appeal from the Equality Tribunal[3] by the Circuit Court,[4] High Court[5] and Supreme Court. The absence of legal aid for equality cases in this jurisdiction, coupled with high costs and low awards of compensation even for successful claims, tends to deter appeals. All the judges overturned the decision of the Equality Tribunal that the parental rule was indirectly discriminatory as it placed members of the Traveller community at a particular disadvantage as compared with non-Travellers, which could not be objectively justified. Only the Circuit Court considered objective justification. The High and Supreme Courts found no discrimination arose, such that there was no necessity to consider objective justification.

Concept of Indirect Discrimination

The concept of indirect discrimination focuses on a wider and more sophisticated understanding of inequality as embedded in institutional and structural norms and policies. It is designed to eradicate structural inequality.[6] It has been predominantly used in gender discrimination cases to undermine rigid and unyielding practices within the workplace, such as the requirement to work full-time or anti-social hours, which cause a disproportionate disadvantage for working mothers.[7] Indirect discrimination occurs when rules providing for apparently neutral distinctions between individuals have a disproportionately negative impact upon members of particular groups. Members of the affected group then experience particular disadvantage as compared to non-members of the group. Where indirect discrimination is established, the respondent must demonstrate that the rule is necessary and justified in the circumstances. The concept represents a fundamental recognition that discrimination is about more than deliberate or overt action, and that inequality has endemic and institutional dimensions that derive from structural practices within important societal institutions.[8] Section 3(1)(c) of the Equal Status Acts 2000–2008 prohibits indirect discrimination on any of the protected grounds, and such discrimination must be inferred by way of demonstrating that the impugned practice or rule places members of a particular protected class at a 'particular disadvantage' as compared to non-members of the protected class.

The Oireachtas has prohibited discrimination (to include direct and indirect discrimination) on grounds of membership of the Traveller community since 1998 under the Employment Equality Act and since 2000 under the Equal Status Act. Aside from cases of exclusion from licensed premises, there has been little in the way of litigation under this protected

[3] DEC-S2010-056.

[4] *Christian Brothers High School Clonmel v Stokes* Circuit Court Record Number 12/2011 (25 July 2011).

[5] *Stokes v Christian Brothers' High School Clonmel* [2011] IEHC, no number assigned.

[6] Christa Tobler, *Indirect Discrimination: A Case Study into the Development of the Legal Concept of Indirect Discrimination under EC Law* (Antwerp, Intersentia, 2005).

[7] *Inoue v NBK Designs* [2003] ELR 98 and *London Underground v Edwards (No 2)* [1999] ICR 194. See also Nicholas Bamforth, Maleiha Malik and Colm O'Cinnéide, *Discrimination Law: Theory and Context* (London, Thomson Sweet & Maxwell, 2008) 310–29; and Aileen McColgan, *Discrimination Law*, 2nd edn (Oxford, Hart Publishing, 2005) 92–97.

[8] Olivia Smith, 'Perpetuating Traveller children's educational disadvantage in Ireland: Legacy rules and the limits of indirect discrimination' (2014) 14(3) *International Journal of Discrimination and the Law* 145–67, 146.

ground or class under both pieces of legislation.[9] The Equal Status Acts 2000–2004 are radical in terms of requiring educational institutions, to include primary, secondary and third level, to put in place admissions policies that do not discriminate in respect of admission or conditions of admission of a person as a student to such an establishment. The Equal Status Act 2000 extends beyond the requirements of EU law in its application to education outside of the protected ground of race. Discrimination in respect of education is prohibited by the Race Directive[10] only on grounds of race or ethnic status, but the Equal Status Acts guarantee such protection to the other eight protected grounds, including that of gender and membership of the Traveller community.[11]

Particular Disadvantage

The origin of the requirement to demonstrate 'a particular disadvantage' within the EU Directives was designed to obviate the need for statistical proof.[12] Indeed, the EU Equality Directives moved away from the requirement to demonstrate 'substantially more disadvantage' to the lower standard of 'particular disadvantage' in the context of meeting the burden of proof for indirect discrimination. The requirement of a 'particular disadvantage' requires a member of a group of the protected class (the Traveller community) to demonstrate that he or she too would be similarly disadvantaged (like other members of the Traveller community) as compared to persons who were not members of the Traveller community. This could be demonstrated having regard to the historically low levels of attendance of members of the Traveller community at second level education as compared to the general population, which personally affected the particular applicant/claimant.

The High Court judgment, which was an appeal on a point of law, adopted an unusual approach to the concept of 'particular disadvantage'. Mr Justice McCarthy held that where a particular provision or measure placed persons generally at a disadvantage *vis-à-vis* others, no sustainable finding of particular disadvantage for a person who was a member of a protected group could be made out. McCarthy J expressed the view that on a comparison of all other applicants apart from John Stokes, 'everyone who is not the son of a past pupil is at a disadvantage by virtue of the rule'.[13] Therefore, McCarthy J ruled that John Stokes had failed to demonstrate that the parental policy placed him at a particular disadvantage as compared to other persons. His decision ignored the well-accepted reality that there is a very low level of attendance by members of the Traveller community at second level school

[9] On the Equal Status Acts, see generally Judy Walsh, *Equal Status Acts 2000–2011: Discrimination in the Provisions of Goods and Services* (Dublin, Blackhall Publishing, 2012).

[10] Council Directive 2000/43/EC.

[11] The eight protected grounds are gender, marital status, family status, sexual orientation, religion, age, disability, race and membership of the Traveller community. The issue of expanding the protection of non-discrimination provisions in EU law beyond the traditional remit of employment and occupation has been controversial, with the Gender Goods and Services Directive expressly excluding education from its preserve (Council Directive 2004/113/EC) and the proposed EU Directive on equality in goods and services, social protection, and education on the grounds of disability, religion or belief, sexual orientation and age not progressing to implementation by reason of the objections of member states to extending its provisions to education.

[12] Case C-237/94 *O'Flynn v Adjudication Officer* [1996] 3 CMLR 103.

[13] McCarthy J, *Stokes v Christian Brothers' High School Clonmel*, above n 5, at para 26.

(accepted both by the Equality Tribunal and Circuit Court), such that the parental rule policy affected members of the Traveller community in a disproportionate way. It was this judgment that was appealed by Mary Stokes on behalf of her son to the Supreme Court.

Mr Justice Clarke's judgment in the Supreme Court began on a positive note. He held that

> the fact that similar discrimination, or disadvantageous treatment, might also apply to others in an unprotected category does not affect the question of whether that same treatment, applying to members of the Travelling Community, might not, after proper analysis, be properly regarded as giving rise to a finding of indirect discrimination.[14]

This is a correct analysis of the position regarding particular disadvantage, which focuses on the disadvantage caused to members of a particular protected group as compared to others on the basis of the application of a particular rule or criterion. Olivia Smith, in her dissenting feminist judgment, agrees with this position and posits that McCarthy J fell into an error of law by conflating direct and indirect discrimination. Indeed, Smith J's point here reflects the feminist concern with the limitations of formal equality (as promoted by the prohibition on direct discrimination) embedded in the concept of consistent treatment, which disregards inequality of outcomes and the contributing role of structural factors.[15] It is also reflective of the desired outcome of indirect discrimination, to focus an emphasis on the proportions of groups that are actually disadvantaged as opposed to interrogating different groups that can comply with the relevant provision or criteria.[16]

However, the remainder of the judgment of the Supreme Court strikes a damning blow for equality and protection from non-discrimination. It determined that in order to establish a particular disadvantage: (i) the extent of the disadvantage must be significant or appreciable and determined by statistical methods; and (ii) it is necessary to examine the totality of the alternative measures available, such as the alternative criteria or qualifications that would allow admission to the school. This statement constitutes a fundamental misunderstanding of indirect discrimination. How the disadvantage, which is *prima facie* potentially indirectly discriminatory, is lessened or changed by the application of other rules and criteria is not relevant to deciding whether this provision is discriminatory, and cannot be utilised to deviate away from the focus of whether the impugned criterion is indirectly discriminatory. The focus must be on whether a protected group, even a small section, suffers a particular disadvantage. The UK House of Lords, in *R v Secretary for State for Employment, ex parte Seymour-Smith and another*,[17] held that a situation, over a seven-year period, in which men and women qualified for protection against unfair dismissal in the ratio 10:9 was enough to establish (subject to justification) the presence of indirect discrimination. Their Lordships were more concerned with the fact that this inequality demonstrated a 'persistent and constant disparity of the order just mentioned in respect of the entire male and female labour forces of the country over a period of seven years'.[18] In adopting a perceptive approach

[14] *Christian Brothers High School Clonmel v Mary Stokes and the Equality Authority*, above n1, 41.

[15] Catherine Barnard and Bob Hepple, 'Substantive Equality' (2000) 59(3) *Cambridge Law Journal* 562–85; and Sandra Fredman, *Discrimination Law*, 2nd edn (Oxford, Oxford University Press, 2011).

[16] McColgan, above n 7, 92–97.

[17] *R v Secretary for State for Employment, ex parte Seymour-Smith and another* [2000] IRLR 263.

[18] For an analysis of this judgment, see McColgan, above n 7, 95–97; and Fredman, above n 15, at 185–86.

to the issue of disadvantage in this case, the House of Lords was not prepared to allow a relatively modest difference in impact between men and women to be overlooked, as it was a 'persistent disadvantage' that could not 'be brushed aside and dismissed as insignificant or inconsiderable'. By contrast, the Supreme Court's approach in requiring a significant or appreciable disadvantage between members of a particular group and other non-members, means that an historical and persistent difference in treatment, even if less than significant in statistical terms, will be acceptable and lawful.

The import of the Supreme Court judgment is therefore a return to a statistical focus of a significant and appreciable extent, to meet the threshold of particular disadvantage that is the gatekeeper to establishing indirect discrimination for a particular group. It ignores historical disadvantage as faced by members of the Traveller community in gaining access to secondary education. If this approach is adopted by the statutory employment tribunals, it is likely to constitute a departure from commonsense assumptions about how one group may be disadvantaged or adversely affected by a particular group. By requiring that indirect discrimination must be established on a statistical basis, the Supreme Court has placed an inordinate burden on claimants, and thus defeats the purpose of the Equality Directives and the desire to move away from statistical proof.

The commonsense approach to indirect discrimination, which does not require an examination of whether disadvantage can be established through the prism of statistics where the disadvantage is plain to see, has been of particular utility in cases involving endemic discrimination against women, particularly those with caring roles. It has been accepted by the Labour Court in *Inoue v NBK Designs*[19] to recognise the reality and commonsense assumption that women are less able to work full-time hours, and would in the ordinary course be placed at a disadvantage if required to work these hours. Rather, by reason of the Supreme Court judgment in *Stokes*, considerable effort and costs will be incurred in requiring claimants to demonstrate the disadvantage faced by females or females with caring responsibilities, as compared to others who are not of this class or group, on the basis of statistical evidence. It is only where the difference is appreciable that indirect discrimination will potentially be made out; and even if the disadvantage or inability to comply with a relevant provision or criterion exists and had existed for a considerable period of time, it is likely the threshold of a particular disadvantage will not be made out. The Supreme Court's approach has side-stepped the Court of Justice's approach to indirect discrimination, which focuses on the risk that a disadvantage will arise, rather than requiring that the impact has in fact occurred. The latter approach allows for the attention of the adjudicator to turn to whether the indirect discrimination can be objectively justified and avoids the necessity for preliminary consideration of whether a disparate impact has been demonstrated. It allows for a stronger interrogation of practices or provisions that have been assumed by employers to be non-discriminatory, by reason of the employer's being required to justify its requirements in the workplace. In this regard, this approach considers the eradication of discrimination as its goal, and focuses instead on the actions of the employer-actor in justifying its practices. This approach is likely to allow women in the workplace to attack with vigour policies and practices that adversely affect them as a group, rather than being locked into complex preliminary issues such as whether a particular disadvantage has been established.

[19] *Inoue v NBK Designs* [2003] ELR 98.

On the basis that the totality of the admissions policy had to be examined in order to determine whether indirect discrimination arose, the Supreme Court posited that the starting point of examination was the differential effects of a combination of the sibling and parental rule on potential applicants to the school who were members of the Traveller community and those who were not. As this had not been addressed by the Director of the Equality Tribunal, because no account had been taken of the ability of applicant members of the Traveller community to qualify for admission by reason of having a sibling in the school, or whether this caused a particular disadvantage for them, no particular disadvantage was established.

The Feminist Judgment

Strikingly, the Supreme Court judgment excludes any reference to the Race Directive and how indirect discrimination has developed at an EU law level. The ability of John Stokes to place reliance on the Race Directive would have been present if the Supreme Court had found, as had been argued before it, that the Irish Traveller Community was an ethnic group. This is rectified, quite correctly, in the dissenting feminist judgment of Smith J. She recognises that the concept of 'particular disadvantage' was introduced in EU law within the Race Directive as a threshold to establish indirect discrimination from the previous definition of a 'substantially higher proportion of the members of one group', and that John Stokes was entitled to rely on the Race Directive as a member of an ethnic group. That provides a stable platform for a simplification in approach to establishing particular disadvantage without recourse to statistics, as was the intention of the introduction of the threshold of particular disadvantage in order to achieve substantive equality. The Race Directive provides that statistical evidence is just one basis on which particular disadvantage may be demonstrated.[20] In adopting this view, Smith J is squarely within a feminist approach, as it allows for social facts to be sufficient to establish particular disadvantage in the absence of the need for laborious, sophisticated and unnecessary statistics, when the disadvantage or impact caused by a particular rule can be established from the knowledge and experience of tribunal members. Smith J's judgment's focus on the social facts approach, as approved in *O'Flynn*,[21] reflects a contextual approach to legal interpretation that has also been applied in Canadian equality jurisprudence.[22] It is feminist in its approach because it expressly links the individual experience of inequality with the wider societal and group-based realities. It provides a workable means of questioning the assumed neutrality of the governing norm, thereby refusing to legitimate obtuse and abstract statistical methods as the sole means of uncovering structural inequality and exclusion of disadvantaged groups. It is focused on outcomes and the preventative and wider remedial function of indirect discrimination provisions in reducing inequalities.[23]

[20] Recital 15.

[21] Case C-237/94, above n 12.

[22] See Colleen Sheppard, *Inclusive Equality, The Relational Dimensions of Systemic Discrimination in Canada* (Montreal, McGill-Queen's University Press, 2010); and Fredman, above n 15.

[23] Sheppard, above n 22.

This approach also correlates with the clear desire in EU law to move away from statistical proof as the prism through which indirect discrimination is established. In general terms, many requirements within the workplace, such as working full time[24] or being required to travel extensively,[25] impact more heavily on female employees with family responsibilities than on other employees, and there is no requirement for extensive statistics to establish the detrimental impact of such requirements on such female employees as it is almost self-evident from social facts. The benefit of this approach to the establishment of particular disadvantage to John Stokes through the admissions policy is demonstrated convincingly by Smith J, who accepts that the systemic nature of educational disadvantage of the Traveller community at the post-primary level, particularly in the 1980s (when John Stokes' father would have been of a post-primary school age), based on accepted social facts, is sufficient to demonstrate that application of the parental rule *prima facie* amounted to indirect discrimination. This is precisely the approach indirect discrimination requires in order to address the unequal treatment that it is designed to eradicate: covert practices that are established within societal arrangements, but which have a greater impact on protected classes or minority groups when examined more closely.[26] This approach is also consistent with the views expressed by the Court of Justice in *O'Flynn*,[27] that a rule is indirectly discriminatory if it is 'intrinsically liable' to affect a particular protected class more than persons who are not members of this class once it is liable to have this effect. It was not necessary to prove that the provision in practice affected a substantially higher proportion of persons in the protected class, as long it was liable to have that effect. In other words, the point of indirect discrimination lies in the risk of the disadvantage and not in the provision of statistics to demonstrate a significant number of the protected class being adversely affected by the rule or unable to comply with the impugned rule. What is required by indirect discrimination is the ability on the part of a complainant to prove that a provision is intrinsically liable to affect his group more than others, and that there is a consequent risk it will place his group at a particular disadvantage. That aim would be defeated by the requirement for extensive statistics required by the Supreme Court.

Smith J also rejects the Supreme Court's insistence that it is necessary to examine the totality of the alternative measures available, such as the alternative criteria or qualifications that would allow admission to the school. She adopts the approach of the Equality Authority, that any disadvantage is not lessened by the consideration of other rules. This is the correct approach, and indeed is reflected in the Gender 'Recast' Directive,[28] the Race Directive and the Framework Directive (the Equality Directives),[29] albeit that only the Race Directive applies to education. These Directives expressly provide that there shall be no direct or indirect discrimination whatsoever against any of the relevant protected groups, and that all discrimination on the prohibited grounds is to be prohibited. Therefore if a particular provision is indirectly discriminatory, it cannot be ameliorated by the effects of any other rule. Clearly the approach of Smith J is feminist, as it attends to a more substantive,

[24] *Inoue v NBK Designs*, above n 19.
[25] *Long v Hanley Group* DEC-E2010-015.
[26] See also Bamforth et al, above n 7, 310–29; and McColgan, above n 7, 92–97.
[27] Case C-237/94, above n 12.
[28] 2006/54/EC.
[29] 2000/78/EC.

contextualised conception of equality in its refusal to allow an indirectly discriminatory sub-provision to be justified by reference to an alternative measure. It will be recalled that indirect discrimination was utilised by the Court of Justice to attack as discriminatory rules that provided less favourable terms and conditions of employment to part-time employees, the majority of whom were female. To suggest that this effect could have been lessened by the application of other provisions, when the very core of the rule was focused on less favourable terms and conditions of employment for part-time employees, is simply a side issue and does not detract from the primary indirect discriminatory nature of the application of terms and conditions to part-time employees.

The Supreme Court

In the matter of section 28 of the Equal Status Acts 2000–2008

Between

Christian Brothers High School Clonmel Circuit Court Appellants/ Respondents to the Appeal

and

Mary Stokes (on behalf of John Stokes a minor)

Circuit Court Respondents/Appellants on the Appeal

and

The Equality Authority

Amicus Curiae

<u>Judgment of Justice Smith delivered 24th February, 2015</u>

1.Introduction

I have had the benefit of reading my colleague Mr Justice Clarke's judgment on behalf of the majority wherein he deals with the important preliminary question as to whether an appeal from the High Court to this court lies under s. 28 of the Equal Status Acts 2000–2008. On this point only I find myself in full agreement with the majority and I do not propose to add any further observations in order that I might move to consider the divergence in my views on the substantive questions of law arising in this case.

This case concerns the prohibition on indirect discrimination that has long been at the heart of domestic and European anti-discrimination legislation. Indirect discrimination is concerned with what has been variously described as structural or systemic forms of discrimination, that is, how the everyday, ordinary rules and practices of institutions that may not be overtly discriminatory on their face, may nevertheless give rise to a prima facie case of indirect discrimination on members of protected groups. Unlike direct discrimination, practices that give rise to indirect discrimination may still be upheld where the respondent meets the test of objective justification. This case concerns a challenge to the admissions policy of a secondary school and the question of its impact on the appellant, as a member of a minority group, namely, the Traveller community.

This case is taken by Mary Stokes, on behalf of her son, John Stokes, a minor, and concerns alleged discrimination in access to education. John, the oldest child in his family, is a member of Ireland's Traveller community. Irish Travellers, as defined in s.2 of the Equal

Status Acts 2000–2008, are a discrete group of people identified both by themselves and by the wider community as possessing a distinct history, culture and traditions, which historically focused around the practice of nomadism. The Traveller community has experienced a long and virulent history of disadvantage, exclusion and discrimination across an array of indicators of well-being in Ireland, including educational disadvantage (see Report of the Task Force on the Traveller Community (1995) Dublin: Government Stationery Office; Central Statistics Office, *Census 2011: Religion, Ethnicity and Irish Travellers* (2012)). The Task Force pointed out that the 'forms of prejudice and discrimination experienced by the Traveller community equate with racism in the international context' (p.79) and recommended the introduction of legal mechanisms to deal with the endemic forms of direct and indirect discrimination endured by Travellers as a group. The legislature subsequently included membership of the Traveller community as one of the nine protected grounds within the state's statutory equality framework, both the Employment Equality Acts 1998–2008 and the Equal Status Acts 2000–2008. These provisions contain, therefore, an important protection through a guarantee of law, that there shall be no direct or indirect discrimination on grounds of membership of the Traveller community in access to and enjoyment of employment opportunities and goods and services respectively. Interestingly, the legislature chose to include a separate ground for the Traveller community, apart from the race ground, which raises the question of the status of Travellers vis-à-vis the EU Race Directive, Council Directive 2000/43/EC, a question to which I will return below.

As this case concerns an application to a post-primary school it falls under the rubric of the Equal Status Acts [the Acts]. This is a case of alleged indirect discrimination, and in the particular case, there is no question regarding any discriminatory purpose or intention of the school in adopting the suspect provision.

Background to the appeal

An application for admission to the Christian Brothers High School, Clonmel, a Roman Catholic voluntary school for boys, was made on behalf of John by his mother, Mary Stokes. This school is one of only two secondary schools for boys in the town of Clonmel, a town with a population of 24,000. The other school is a vocational school.

For entry in the academic year 2010–2011, the school was oversubscribed, receiving 174 applications in respect of 140 places. The school's admission policy set out the following criteria in respect of which a potential applicant would be attributed "maximum eligibility" for admission in the case of oversubscription. These were where the application is made on behalf of a boy:

- whose parents are seeking to submit their son to a Roman Catholic education in accordance with the mission statement and Christian ethos of the school;
- who already has a brother who attended or is in attendance at the school, or is the child of a past pupil, or has close family ties with the school;
- who attended for his primary education one of the feeder schools listed in Schedule Two, these being schools within the locality and demographic area of the school.

It should also be noted that under the admissions policy a number of places were allocated under an "exceptional circumstances" procedure, which according to the school was construed narrowly to cover the loss of a parent, ill-health, relocation to Clonmel through work and students with special needs. This avenue of access has not been challenged in this appeal.

The school's admissions policy operated by way of application rounds in cases of oversubscription: round one would deal with the applications of those with maximum eligibility, that is, those who meet the criteria as set out above. Ninety places were awarded to those applicants fulfilling these criteria. Thirty-six students were admitted under the parental rule, that is, were sons of past pupils and did not have a brother in the school. Three boys were awarded places under the "exceptional circumstances rule", specifically the loss of parent/ill-health criteria. The remaining applications were then placed in the next round's lottery selection—thus 84 names were in the draw in respect of 47 places. John's name was entered into the second round lottery, but he was unsuccessful following the draw.

Mary Stokes appealed the decision to the school and was unsuccessful. An appeal pursuant to s.29 of the Education Act 1998 was subsequently lodged with the Department of Education and Skills Appeals Committee, which disallowed the appeal, determining that the Board had been "fair and reasonable in the application of the school's admission policy in a situation where the numbers of applicants greatly exceeded the places available". This case is concerned not with the question of the fair and reasonable application of the school's admission policy, but rather with very different questions on the legitimacy and impact of its design and operation as regards the Equal Status Acts.

Mary Stokes then lodged a complaint with the Equality Tribunal under the Equal Status Acts, asserting that both the parental and the sibling preference provisions within the school's admission policy were indirectly discriminatory on the grounds of John's membership of the Traveller community. Following its hearing, the Equality Tribunal ruled that the parental legacy rule gave rise to unlawful indirect discrimination on the grounds of John's membership of the Traveller community, which the school could not justify. The Equality Tribunal also found that the sibling rule did not raise a prima facie case of indirect discrimination on the grounds of membership of the Traveller community, and that element of the case does not form part of this appeal. Thus, the concern of all further appeals has been the parental preference element to the admissions policy.

The Circuit Court, overturning the decision of the Equality Tribunal, noted that while there was a prima facie case of indirect discrimination, the school had objectively justified the adoption of the parental rule as a proportionate means of achieving a legitimate aim. The appellant's appeal to the High Court was dismissed, following its holding that the school's use of the "father rule" did not give rise to a particular disadvantage on the appellant as a member of the Traveller community. The appellant argues that the High Court judgment contains an error in law as regards the method relied upon by that Court in dismissing the prima facie case of indirect discrimination.

The main issue that arises from the case is the correct approach to the question as to whether the school's reliance on the "father rule" within its admissions policy, such as to bestow sons of past pupils with maximum eligibility in cases of oversubscription, amounts to unlawful indirect discrimination on the grounds of John's membership of the Traveller community within the meaning the Equal Status Acts.

2. Submissions of the parties

The argument of the appellant is that the school's practice of granting priority to the sons of former pupils puts members of the Traveller community at a particular disadvantage as compared with non-Travellers, as Travellers of his father's generation were unlikely to have attended post-primary school. The appellant relied on figures obtained from the Department of Education that show that in 1988 less than 100 Travellers in the entire country were enrolled in post-primary schools. Further no Traveller had attended the school in the 1980s.

The respondents deny the appellant's claims of discrimination. On the question of indirect discrimination, the High School submitted that the criterion applied is not that a family member has attended second level education but that a family member is attending or has attended the High School. This, according to the school, is a standard admission policy and it is entirely justifiable that the school adopts a clear procedure to follow in cases of oversubscription. The school points to its excellent record of working with students who are members of the Traveller community. There were 5 members of the Traveller community enrolled in the school in 2010 and all Travellers who applied for admission in both 2007 and 2008 were accepted.

In the course of argument before this court, an issue arose about the appropriateness of looking at the discriminatory effect of the parental rule in isolation and whether it was necessary to look at the cumulative effect of the overall admission policy of Clonmel High School on Travellers and non-Travellers respectively. Indeed, Clarke J devoted significant attention to this point, to which I will return shortly.

3. Application

There are then two main issues for determination in this appeal:

This first question in essence is concerned with whether there is a prima facie case of indirect discrimination, and, in particular, the correct approach as a matter of law for determining this question under s.3(1)(c) of the Acts.

Second, where this question is answered in the affirmative, whether the school can objectively justify the use of the policy by reference to a legitimate aim, the means of achieving which were both appropriate and necessary.

S.3(1)(c) of the Equal Status Acts 2000–2008 provides that discrimination shall be taken to occur:

> Where an apparently neutral provision puts a person referred to in any paragraph of s.3(2) at a particular disadvantage compared with other persons, unless the provision is objectively justified by a legitimate aim and the means of achieving that aim are appropriate and necessary.

S.3A provides that "In any proceedings statistics are admissible for the purpose of determining whether discrimination has occurred by virtue of subsection (1)c)."

S.3(2) sets out the protected grounds under the Acts and provides that as between any two persons, the discriminatory grounds and the descriptions of those grounds for the purposes of this Act) are:

> ...
>
> (i) that one is a member of the Traveller community and the other is not (the "Traveller community") ground.

The burden of proving that the provision in question gives rise to indirect discrimination on a protected ground lies with the appellant. If he is successful in making out a prima facie case on the balance of probabilities, then the burden shifts to the respondent school to justify the use of the parental rule within the admissions policy within the meaning of s.3(1)(c) of the Equal Status Acts.

I propose first to outline the error of law taken by the High Court in its interpretation of the governing statutory provision. Thereafter, I discuss my view of the correct approach to the question of proof of indirect discrimination.

The High Court's error.

The High Court's approach to the term "particular disadvantage" involved a reliance on the meaning of the word "particular" as derived from the Oxford English Dictionary, which includes reference to terms such as "restricted to, belonging only to a specified person or thing, distinguished in some way among others of the kind". On this reading, the disadvantage caused by the policy in question according to McCarthy J was not "particular" to Travellers because "it is not restricted to Travellers, does not distinguish among others of the kind, namely 'applicants for admission' because there are others in the same position as they are. In other words, since all those who are not the sons of past pupils are also at a disadvantage, there is no distinction between the extent of the disadvantage suffered by Travellers and others."

This reasoning is problematic as a matter of law because it appears to confuse indirect discrimination with direct discrimination. The mischief with which the former concept is concerned is whether the challenged provision creates "particular disadvantage" for the complainant group as compared with the comparator group, such that it weighs or impacts more heavily on the complainant group. It is not concerned with whether there has been a difference in treatment between the complainant and the comparator, which is the provenance of direct discrimination. The fact that the policy in question disadvantages others who are not members of the Traveller community does not tell us whether Travellers are more likely to be "particularly disadvantaged" by the policy in question than non-Travellers, nor the rate or extent of that disadvantage, if that is the case. Therefore, the High Court judge fell into an error of law.

The provision in question.

At the outset, I must refer to an issue arising from the approach to the identification of the challenged provision in question adopted by my colleagues in the majority.

The statutory provision on indirect discrimination in s.3 of the Equal Status Acts refers to "an apparently neutral provision" that operates to produce "particular disadvantage" for the individual as a member of a protected group as compared with other persons. The term "provision" is not defined in the statute. The suspect provision that is under challenge in this case is an element of the second prong of the school's admission policy through which maximum eligibility may be gained: namely, to be a son of a past pupil. Clarke J, on behalf of the majority, has taken the view that the "provision" in question cannot simply be the "father preference" rule, but must also include the alternative means of qualifying under the second prong of the school's admissions scheme, namely, the "sibling rule", arguing that

> "At the level of principle, where a number of alternative means are provided for complying with a qualifying measure, and where it is only necessary to qualify under one

> heading, then 'the provision' must mean the totality of the alternative measures available. Where there are alternative means of qualification it does not seem that one can sever one possible means of qualification without having regard to all the others" (at para 10.8)

According to Clarke J's finding then, the proper basis of analysis should have involved a consideration as to whether "the second leg as a whole placed persons from the Travelling [*sic*] community at a disadvantage."

I must depart from this approach to the term "provision" undertaken by my colleague for the reasons that follow. I find myself persuaded by counsel for the amicus curiae who argued that a prima facie discriminatory provision cannot be saved by virtue of the fact that there may be another measure which, to a greater or lesser extent, ameliorates the effect of the discriminatory measure. This seems to me to be especially persuasive in the instant case. If, as is discussed below, one element of the provision—the father rule—can be shown to give rise to a prima facie case of indirect discrimination, on the grounds of membership of the Traveller community, that is a sufficiently grave finding in and of itself, which cannot be diluted by the presence of an alternative provision, such as the sibling rule which has no disparate impact by protected group status (as determined by the Equality Tribunal's para 10 of its determination, DEC-S2010-056), particularly where this alternative provision is not designed specifically to offset this disadvantage. This is particularly important in light of the dissuasive impact that facially neutral yet indirectly discriminatory provisions may have in terms of screening out of otherwise qualified candidates or applicants, that is, such provisions can erect barriers to applications from minority groups from the outset. The fact remains that the father preference rule is an avenue of access open to applicants notwithstanding its impact on minority groups.

I find further support for my holding on this point from the EU Race Equality Directive, which the Equal Status Act is required to transpose. National courts are bound to interpret their national laws in light of the wording and purpose of the relevant EU Directive: *Marleasing v La Commercial Internationale de Alimentacion SA* [1990] ECR 4135. I take the view, relying on the UK House of Lords test in *Mandla v Dowell Lee* [1983] 2 AC 548 and supported by the recognition of Irish Travellers as an ethnic group in the UK (see *O'Leary v Allied Domecq* (unreported, 2000)), that the Irish Traveller community are an ethnic group within the meaning of the Race Directive. Article 2(1) states that "For the purposes of this Directive, the principle of equal treatment shall mean that there shall be no direct or indirect discrimination based on racial or ethnic origin". Further, Article 2(2)(b) of the Race Equality Directive refers to indirect discrimination as arising "where an apparently neutral provision, criterion or practice" would put persons of a racial or ethnic origin at a particular disadvantage compared with other persons, thereby utilizing much wider terms that the Irish term of "provision". The reality remains that under the school admissions policy the opportunity to access a scarce resource (a place in the school) was predicated on a provision with two alternative elements, one of which included a practice of rewarding applicants on the basis of the educational patterns of their fathers. In the year in question, the application of that alleged neutral practice meant that 36 boys, none of whom were Travellers, were admitted under this route. I would conclude, therefore, that this practice remains challengeable as being an indirectly discriminatory provision on the Traveller community ground, notwithstanding that an alternative method of qualification—the sibling rule—exists. To find otherwise is akin to justifying the retention of an ethnically indirectly discriminatory practice on the basis of the availability of an alternative, separate admissions route and is contrary to the EU dictum that the principle of equal treatment demands that there be "no discrimination whatsoever" on a protected ground: see *P v S and Cornwall County Council* [1996] All ER 397. This commitment to the primacy of the principle of equal treatment could surely be diminished if a provision, which bestows privilege on certain applicants, and which can simultaneously be shown to particularly disadvantage a protected minority group, was to be "excused" by an alternative means of qualification. I am also extremely conscious of the implications of the findings of Clarke J on this point on the burden of proof for complainants raising complaints of indirect discrimination, particularly given the majority's holding in this decision that a statistical method is the sole means of demonstrating a prima facie case of indirect discrimination, an issue to which I now turn. In effect, the majority's restrictive reading of the term "practice" in this case, coupled with its insistence on statistical methods in this context, operates to erect significant burdens to proof of particular disadvantage for the appellant. In my view, such an approach can seriously restrict the ability of the indirect discrimination provision to tackle more subtle and systemic forms of discrimination.

Proof of 'particular disadvantage'

Moving on from the question of delineating the suspect provision in question, the approach to the first issue requires some exploration of the nature of the evidential burden on the appellant under the terms of the Acts, with respect to how such indirect discrimination can be demonstrated and what type of evidence the courts and tribunals will require in this regard. Indeed, the question of assessing how "particular disadvantage" is to be made out is a matter of law, and this is the first time that this Court has had the opportunity to clarify the required approach. In setting out the correct approach to proof of "particular disadvantage" it is important again to be mindful of the developments and amendments that have taken place in this area of law.

While it is litigated on the individual level, indirect discrimination is concerned with group disadvantage. The essence of indirect discrimination is that the impugned provision must be shown to work to the "particular disadvantage" of the complainant group as compared with the comparator group. There are two issues that arise, therefore: The first concerns what methods of proof are allowable in showing "particular disadvantage" and the second is the extent of the disadvantage that makes it one that has been "particularly" endured by the complainant group. As a matter of logic, the provision in question must create a stronger negative effect on the complainant group than on the comparator group, although the extent of this effect has not been quantified by the legislature.

The definition of indirect discrimination has undergone considerable legislative amendment and refinement since it was first adopted judicially in the European context by the European Court of Justice in the context of sex discrimination in employment in *Bilka Kaufhaus v Weber Von Hartz* C-170/84 [1986] ECR 911. It was placed on a legislative footing in the Burden of Proof Directive, Council Directive 97/80/EC applicable to sex discrimination and was subsequently reconfigured in the Equal Treatment Directive (Recast), Council Directive 2006/54/EC, the Framework Employment Equality Directive, Council Directive 2000/78/EC and the Race Directive, Council Directive 2000/43/EC. These reconfigurations were effected in national law with the amendment of s.3(1)(c) of the Equal Status Act by the Equality Act 2004.

The background to these legislative developments is referenced here because it provides necessary context in determining the correct approaches to proof of indirect discrimination. The first point of note is that this Court should be mindful of the fact that the bulk of superior court decisions, including a considerable body of CJEU decisions regarding proof of a prima facie case of indirect discrimination, were decided in respect of statutory language that differs considerably from the current governing provisions. In addition, the vast majority of these decisions have concerned indirect discrimination in employment. The context to these legislative amendments is that they were prompted by the European legislature in response to the well-noted difficulties associated with proof of a prima face case of indirect discrimination. What may appear to be a simple concept—the recognition that facially neutral practices may have disparate impact or create particular disadvantage for particular groups that share a particular identity and experience—became extraordinarily complicated because of the nature of the burden of proof placed upon complainants as a result of a requirement for statistical forms of proof of indirect discrimination. Contrary to my colleague Mr Justice Hardiman's view in this case, this history of indirect discrimination litigation shows us that it has been far from a "relatively simple matter". In particular, given the expansion of the protected discrimination grounds and the reality that, for historical reasons, statistical information in relation to certain grounds such as the race ground and the sexual orientation ground is not collated in many Member States, there was a legislative shift in how a prima facie indirect discrimination could be evidenced. Indeed, it is possible to see this development with the change of statutory language in the amended definition to indirect discrimination prompted by the need to transpose a range of European equality directives that this court is charged with considering. For example, under the previous formulation of s.3 of the Acts, the court would have been charged with considering whether the neutral provision at issue impacted 'a substantially higher proportion of the members of one group', as compared with the comparator group, which the authorities had held to be a statistical enquiry, see C-400/93 *Specialiarbejederforbundet i Danmark v Dansk Industri acting for Royal Copenhagen* [1995] ECR I-01275. The previous language of this section demanded a comparison between the proportions of the respective groups impacted by the suspect provision in question, which was held to be a statistical enquiry. However, the Race and other EU Equality Directives welcomed a simplification in statutory language away from a consideration of the proportions of members of the respective groups disadvantaged or advantaged by the provision, along with a recognition that indirect discrimination may be demonstrated otherwise than by statistical evidence: see Recital 15 of the Race Directive, which states that national rules "may provide in particular for indirect discrimination to be established by any means including on the basis of statistical evidence".

These developments in indirect discrimination law are important to recognize because they move the provision away from a sole reliance on statistical methods. This widening of the possible means of demonstrating indirect discrimination has been included in domestic law. S.3A of the Equal Status Acts states that "in any proceedings statistics are admissible for the purpose of determining whether discrimination has occurred by virtue of subsection (1)(c)". Therefore, it is clear that while disparate group impact or effect still remains at the heart of indirect discrimination's operative term "particular disadvantage", it appears to me that, as a matter of law, it is no longer the case that statistical evidence will always be mandatory to its proof. However, the majority judgment has entirely overlooked these statutory provisions and the context from which they emerged. For example, Clarke J states, at paras 8.6 and 9.4, that the court when carrying out a "proper analysis" of the extent of any disadvantage at which a protected group has been placed by reason of an ostensibly neutral measure, "necessarily requires some statistical consideration".

Of course it remains the case that the most direct, and in some types of cases, certainly, perhaps the most persuasive and even the only means of demonstrating the disadvantageous effect will be by way of statistical evidence. However, this is not the same as saying that statistical evidence of "particular disadvantage" will always be necessary. The statutory language in s.3(A) provides an avenue beyond statistical methods from which to make out proof of "particular disadvantage".

It has fallen to the tribunals and courts, then, to determine what methods are sufficient in this context. The majority judgment in this case focuses entirely on issues related to a statistical assessment of indirect discrimination, both generally and in the context of the instant case, which, in my view, is not without its problems. Before commenting briefly on these, I find it entirely proper and necessary to elaborate further on what other appropriate ways a prima facie case of indirect discrimination may be made out in the context of the instant case.

To this end, the expert tribunals have already taken the view that reliance on accepted social facts can be sufficient in certain cases to support the establishment of a prima facie case of indirect discrimination. For example, in *Inoue v NBK Designs* [2003] Employment Law Reports 98, which concerned a claim of indirect gender discrimination in employment, the Labour Court held that as an expert tribunal, it could take into account, even in the absence of strict statistical evidence, matters such as the risk of indirect discrimination on a protected ground under the Act which "are obvious to the members of the court ... drawing on their own knowledge and experience from its specialist experience." Similarly, in *McDonagh v Navan Hire Limited* DEC-S2004-017, a decision under the Equal Status Acts, the Equality Tribunal, expressly relying on *Inoue*, found that elaborate statistical evidence to prove the disadvantageous impact of the condition in question (which was a requirement to have a permanent address that was not a halting site and landline phone number) was not required, holding that

> "[i]t would be reasonable therefore to infer from this rationale that an expert tribunal such as the Equality Tribunal, can similarly take account of matters such as the number of Travellers living on halting sites in comparison to the number of non-Travellers, matters which are obvious from the Tribunal's specialist experience".

This is the first time this Court has been called upon to consider the issue of proof of a prima facie case of indirect discrimination under the amended definition of this concept. In appropriate cases, as a matter of law, I can see nothing problematic with this approach to proof of indirect discrimination under s.3 that was taken by both the Labour Court and the Equality Tribunal following their careful examination. This is not to suggest that a social facts or common knowledge approach to proof of "particular disadvantage" would suffice in every case, nor does it suggest that a social facts approach equates with unfettered forms of judicial or tribunal discretion. This is because a proper analysis based on a social facts approach would not permit as acceptable forms of evidence deriving from knowledge of social circumstances that are predicated on unsubstantiated personal opinion or belief.

Rather it is an understanding based on general and accepted social facts deriving from and grounded in available and continuingly relevant research findings, both quantitative and qualitative, that the tribunal or deciding court finds relevant, credible and continuing. In such circumstances the existence and persistence of such social facts, such as, for example, those evinced in the above cases—the understanding that the overwhelming majority of halting site residents are Travellers, or that the vast majority of lone parents are women, or indeed, utilizing my colleague Clarke J's own example, that the average height of women is lower than the average height of men—can obviate the need to undertake strict statistical enquiry at the individual case level. Further, the failure to acknowledge this alternative means of showing particular disadvantage in appropriate cases would not only be to deny the impact of these express legislative amendments introduced by the legislature, but it would also present a fundamental challenge to the underlying purpose of the prohibition within s.3(1)(c), which is to root out structural and systemic forms of discrimination in order to achieve more substantive forms of equality.

It is important to underline that there will certainly be cases of indirect discrimination where the social facts approach will simply not suffice to show the "particular disadvantage" endured by the complainant group relevant to the comparator group. Indeed, on this point, the Labour Court in *Inoue* was careful to point out that there may be cases where the claimant may not be able to meet her evidential burden in the absence of statistics. In such cases statistical evidence retains an important role in unearthing indirect discrimination, particularly where the impact of the indirectly discriminatory provision may not be immediately obvious or is unclear. Therefore, statistical evidence remains frequently key, to rooting out more subtle forms of indirect discrimination. I am not convinced, however, for the reasons developed below that this is one such case.

The Circuit Court in its judgment relied on the social facts approach that is predicated on the well-documented general evidence regarding Traveller educational disadvantage presented before the Tribunal and the Court as sufficient to raise a prima facie case of indirect discrimination in this case. This evidence included national figures obtained from the Department of Education that at the time when John Stokes's father was of secondary school going age, namely, the 1980s, there were only 100 members of the Traveller community in secondary school across the entire state. Extrapolating from these general national figures, the Circuit Court was satisfied, therefore, that a provision that predicates access to educational opportunities upon the historical educational patterns of one's parents, works to "particularly disadvantage" children from the Traveller community as compared with non-Traveller children. This is in my view an unimpeachable application of the social facts approach to the "particular disadvantage" created by an educational institution's reliance on parental legacy rules for members of a minority group, in this case, the Traveller community, whose legacy of educational disadvantage has been well documented in state sponsored commissions and academic research reports. See, for example, the Central Statistics Office, *Equality in Ireland* (2006) report, that shows that non-Travellers were approximately 3.7 times more likely to have attended secondary school than non-Traveller Irish children. This context and history of the endemic levels of Traveller educational disadvantage are critical, therefore, to the consideration of the "particular disadvantage" caused by this type of parental legacy rules. In my view this Court cannot simply ignore this reality or push it to one side given the role that indirect discrimination plays in challenging the discriminatory impact of ostensibly "neutral" practices. Therefore, I take the view that the evidence provided on behalf of the appellant points to the systemic nature of educational disadvantage of the Traveller community at the national level, particularly at post-primary level, and particularly in the relevant era, the 1980s. Further the school has not been able to produce any evidence to suggest that any Travellers attended the school when the appellant's father was of school going age. Therefore, the school's continued reliance on the parental legacy rule raises, on an accepted social facts basis, a prima facie case of indirect discrimination against John Stokes as a member of the Traveller community.

More generally, it is also important to recognize that a reliance on historical patterns of educational participation among parents creates real risks of indirect discrimination for children of other minority groups. For example, it should be noted that such a policy risks creating similar issues of "particular disadvantage" for children of parents of different nationalities who are unlikely to have been educated in Irish schools. Similarly, in the context of the continuing prevalence of single-sex schools in this jurisdiction, such legacy rules may similarly impact children of parents in same-sex families who are being raised by two fathers or two mothers, as the case may be.

While I have taken the view that a statistical enquiry is unnecessary to proof of particular disadvantage in this case, for the reasons set out above, I wish to make some observations about the approach taken by the majority judgment to the statistical means of demonstrating "particular disadvantage", specifically, as regards the legitimacy of relying on national statistics regarding Traveller participation in secondary education in the country as a whole in the instant case. In essence the majority discussion on this point—to utilise the term generally referenced in indirect discrimination litigation—is concerned with the "pool" from which the members of the complainant and the comparator group are selected in order to consider the provision's impact on the respective groups. The selection of the pool is normally a matter for the tribunal or the Circuit Court as the case may be and one with which the appeal court should be slow to intervene. The choosing of the pool of comparators may differ depending on the nature of the suspect provision in question and there has been very little discussion of the choice of the pool in access to employment cases (although I would find persuasive the approach taken in the English Court of Appeal decision in *Jones v University of Manchester* [1992] ICR 52), nor in goods and services cases.

According to Clarke J, there may be circumstances in which it is both possible and appropriate to draw an inference from national figures for the effect of a measure on a protected category in a local area, and he relied on the often used explanatory device around gender height differentials in this context. Of course, this is because there is nothing in gender height differentials that suggest it varies by reference to locality. On my reading, this is precisely what the social facts approach to indirect discrimination entails, but is an approach which the majority has rejected in this context in favour of a statistical enquiry.

The majority judgment asserts that where the effect of the provision is necessarily confined and local, it remains open to the possibility than an identical measure may place a protected group at a particular disadvantage in one part of the country, but not in another. This may be so simply because the effect of the measure on the group in question may itself vary from one part of the country to another owing to relevant characteristics of the group not being identical in those different parts. However, extrapolating from the national figures on Traveller educational disadvantage that such a situation applied in the context of Clonmel High School was an inappropriate analysis, according to my colleague Clarke J.

It was necessary, rather, that some attempt should have been made to apply the national figures to the context of Clonmel and in particular to the context of Clonmel High School and its history of previous Traveller pupils. In other words, the majority was unpersuaded that the national figures could be legitimately applied to the local, Clonmel context, but its reasons on this point are not clear. Of course, another way of reading the majority judgment on this point, is as a rejection of the social facts approach, an approach which I, in turn, reject for the reasons given above.

In any event, I wish to comment on the difficulty I see with this reasoning in the specific context of Traveller educational disadvantage, as I do not see any pressing reason why it would be inappropriate to draw an inference from national figures for the effect of the measure in the local area, which is precisely what the social facts approach does. Indeed, I find the conjecture within the majority judgment on this point to be highly abstract and devoid of any recognition of the stark realities of Traveller educational disadvantage, particularly in the governing era, which is the 1980s. Such abstract approaches to equality are, in my view, unhelpful because of the reality that the failure to see, recognize and remedy inequality, limits the underlying principle of equal treatment, which impacts on the opportunities of real people, particularly disadvantaged groups. Recall that at this time, the state had yet to adopt or implement a culturally appropriate Traveller inclusive educational policy, nor were there any anti-discrimination law precepts applicable to educational institutions in operation to protect minority applicants. Moreover, application to most secondary schools in this period was by way of competitive written examination, which would have particularly impacted on Traveller children given their history and experience of educational disadvantage. Again, there is nothing to suggest in the available research reports that at the relevant time, which is the 1980s, the nature of Traveller educational disadvantage relative to the settled population varied from locality to locality. Nor is there anything to suggest that the experience of Clonmel as a locality, and the Clonmel High School as a specific educational institution, was any different from the starkness of the national picture. Adopting my colleague Clarke J's own formula therefore, there seems no reason to believe that there was a significant difference in the educational participation rates of Travellers in different parts of the country, or put another way, there was no reason to believe that the national figures from the 1980s were inapplicable to the Clonmel area. Indeed, this is supported by the evidence placed before the Equality Tribunal and the courts that not a single member of the Traveller community had attended the school in the 1980s. In light of this evidence, therefore, it strikes me that it is entirely appropriate to draw the inference from the national figures that, at the local level, Traveller educational disadvantage was similarly acute.

Objective Justification

Given my findings on the first issue, I proceed to move on to consider the question of objective justification. The burden of proof now shifts to the respondent school to demonstrate that the policy of granting priority to sons of former students is objectively justified within the meaning of s.3(1)(c) of the Acts. It should be noted here that the school is required to make out each element of the defence, namely legitimacy of aim, appropriateness and necessity.

The aim of the criterion adopted by the school is set out in its admissions policy as follows:

> "On the basis of supporting the family ethos within education by providing education services for the children of families who have or have recently had, a brother of the applicant attend the School for his post primary education".

This provision makes direct reference to the sibling rule, but not the father rule.

In oral evidence before the Equality Tribunal and the Circuit Court, the headmaster of the school, in setting out the appropriateness and necessity of the policy, noted the historical backdrop to the school's admissions policy and the reality of oversubscription in applications to the school. Previously, priority had been awarded in "exceptional circumstances" but the application of this category had become so wide, such that a large proportion of applicants applied on this ground. Prior to that, the application process was by means of written assessment, which was also extremely unsatisfactory. The current policy, which is reviewed on an annual basis, was, therefore, argued to be an "appropriate" compromise between these two former approaches. In support of the necessity test, the school gave evidence of the links between the school and the community, the activities of the past pupils' union that incentivizes high achievement and supports the school through mentoring, bursaries and financial assistance for sons of impoverished parents, and how the activities of such former students help to bridge the shortfall in funds provided by the Department of Education.

While the aim of supporting and strengthening the family ethos within education may be construed as a legitimate aim and appears to be legitimately furthered by the sibling preference rule, I am unconvinced that the means adopted by the school in this instance—the father preference rule—is a proportionate and necessary means of achieving this aim. In terms of the rule's necessity, this also requires demonstration of whether alternative measures without the discriminatory impact could have been put in place in order to achieve the same objective. Thus, while the school's evidence on the appropriateness limb was to emphasise the policy as a response to the problems associated with the previous admissions policy, again, I am not convinced that the adoption of the father preference rule amounts to a response to those problems outlined. Indeed, given the impact which a written examination test would have had on Traveller applications due to low levels of Traveller educational achievement in the past, its necessary replacement with another rule that similarly gives rise to a prima facie case of indirect discrimination would seem rather incongruous.

The school's further argument was that the important role played by the past pupils' union, including mentoring and contributions to funding shortfall, justified the use of the father preference rule, because without it the "outgoings of the school would probably be considerably less". In considering the justifications forwarded by respondents in cases of indirect discrimination, it is important that the Court carefully considers whether the assertions made in support of the policy have its claimed effects. The school argued that its aim of achieving strong bonds with parents in furtherance of a family ethos, that included reliance on contributions from families to plug its funding shortfall, would "probably" be compromised were such parents not guaranteed preferential treatment for their sons in return. This claim, however, would assume that familial financial donations to the school are made in return for the father priority rule. Leaving to one side the worrying implications of such a policy type for wider social and economic equalities, the policy's bestowal of maximum eligibility deriving from the father rule did not depend on parental financial contributions, but on the mere fact of attendance at the school. The priority in question is, therefore, a blanket priority that applies regardless of the level of the engagement of a father with the school. In this context, the means adopted are overbroad, as in many cases, they would not achieve their aim. Therefore, the means adopted by the school are disproportionate to the aim of promoting a family ethos in education. The school policy did not consider what other methods were available to them for promoting parental involvement as part of its aim of supporting a family ethos that had a less discriminatory effect on Traveller children.

Accordingly, I would allow the appeal for the reasons stated above and uphold the finding of indirect discrimination and the remedy as determined by the Equality Tribunal.

Part IV

Choosing Subjects

18

Commentary on *Attorney General v X*

SHEELAGH MCGUINNESS

Introduction

This commentary reflects on the feminist judgment of Ruth Fletcher in the landmark case of *Attorney General v X*.[1] This case involved an attempt to prevent a 14-year-old girl, who was pregnant as a result of being raped, from travelling to England in order to access abortion care.

It is impossible to engage with this decision without a broader consideration of the harm that is wrought on the lives of women in Ireland by the Eighth Amendment to the Irish Constitution: Article 40.3.3. The content of my commentary uses two frames of analysis developed in the work of academic Robin West.[2] First, I consider West's concept of 'gendered harms' in the spheres of reproduction and pregnancy. Joanne Conaghan summarises the concept of 'gendered harms' as 'but one way of recognising that injury has a social as well as an individual dimension' and an acknowledgement of the way in which harms can impact particular group members.[3] Legal systems can compound and legitimate harms that are experienced disproportionately or solely by women, especially in the sphere of reproduction.[4] This harm plays out differently depending on how gender interacts with other social dynamics such as ethnicity in the regulation of reproduction.[5] As is detailed by Fletcher J in her analysis, Article 40.3.3 is a clear instance of law's ability to be an instrument of harm. Secondly, I illustrate the way in which Fletcher J's decision is an example of what West describes as 'progressive constitutionalism', which contrasts with the 'conservative constitutionalism' evident in much of the legal discussion of Article 40.3.3. West suggests that it is '[o]nly by reconceptualising the Constitution as a source of inspiration and

[1] *Attorney General v X* [1992] 1 IR 1.

[2] Robin West, *Caring for Justice* (New York, New York University Press, 1997) ('gendered harm'); Robin West, 'Progressive and Conservative Constitutionalism' (1989–1990) 88 *Michigan Law Review* 641–721 ('progressive constitutionalism').

[3] Joanne Conaghan '*Gendered Harms* and the Law of Tort: Remedying (Sexual) Harassment' (1996) 16(3) *Oxford Journal of Legal Studies* 407–31.

[4] West, above n 2 ('gendered harm').

[5] See Dorothy Roberts, *Killing the Black Body: Race, Reproduction, and the Meaning of Liberty* (New York, Vintage, 19970); Jael Silliman, Marlene Gerber Fried, Loretta Ross and Elena Gutierrez, *Undivided Rights: Women of Color Organize for Reproductive Justice* (Cambridge, MA, South End Press, 2004); Ruth Fletcher, 'Reproducing Irishness: Race, Gender, and Abortion Law' (2005) 17(3) *Canadian Journal of Women and the Law* 365–404.

guidance for legislation, rather than a superstructural constraint on adjudication, [that we] can we make good on its richly progressive promise'.[6] Fletcher J, in keeping with the aims of the feminist judgment endeavour, confines herself to a realistic adjudicative role that remains faithful to the impartial and neutral role of the judge. In doing so she accepts the legal form of the judge, but her judicial craft is an instance of 'controlled creativity' that 'views law as an open set of possibilities, and thus a vehicle for change, growth, and authenticity, rather than the static product of an unambiguous past historical process, and thus a vehicle for obedience'.[7]

In her re-visioning of the decision, Fletcher J harnesses the disruptive potential of the Constitution to address the power imbalances perpetuated by Article 40.3.3. Contrasting her judgment to the original 'expose[s] the contingency and biases of existing decisions and disrupt[s] the unique authority of the courts and legal decision-making'.[8] In my commentary I bring together the work of Fletcher J, the feminist judge, and Ruth Fletcher, the feminist academic, to critique the existence and impact of Article 40.3.3. Reading the judgment in light of Fletcher's academic work merges aspects of critique and law reform that are central to the feminist judging methodology.

The Emergence of Article 40.3.3

In order to understand the decision in *Attorney General v X* it is necessary to consider the historical and jurisprudential context within which the case arose. At that time abortion in Ireland was regulated within a web of constitutional, legislative and common law provisions originating with the Offences Against the Person Act 1861 (OAPA), sections 58 and 59, which prohibit procuring or attempting to procure a miscarriage.[9] Sections 58 and 59 of the OAPA were reaffirmed in the Health (Family Planning) Act 1979.[10] In England, the OAPA was interpreted to allow for an exception to the general prohibition when the life or health (physical or mental) of the pregnant woman was likely to be severely impacted.[11] However, it is clear that even prior to the insertion of Article 40.3.3 into the Irish Constitution, such an interpretation was unlikely to be permissible in Ireland.[12] Evidence for this proposition can be traced through the statements of Kenny J in *Ryan v Attorney General*[13] to its clearest exposition in the judgment of Walsh J in *G v An Bord Uchtála*, when he held

[6] West, above n 2 ('progressive constitutionalism') 651. Although West is speaking here in the US context, this framing applies well to Fletcher J's engagement with the Irish Constitution.

[7] ibid, 688.

[8] Rosemary Hunter 'The Power of Feminist Judgments' (2012) 20(2) *Feminist Legal Studies* 137–48.

[9] James Kingston, Anthony Whelan and Ivana Bacik, *Abortion and the Law* (Dublin, Round Hall Sweet & Maxwell, 1997) ch 1. It should be noted that the Protection of Life During Pregnancy Act 2013 repealed ss 58 and 59 of the Offences against the Person Act 1861; however, s 22 of this latter statute recriminalises the destruction of unborn human life.

[10] Health (Family Planning) Act 1979, s 10.

[11] *R v Bourne* [1939] 1 KB 687.

[12] See Kingston, Whelan and Bacik, above n 9.

[13] *Ryan v Attorney General* [1965] IR 294.

that a child 'has the right to life itself and the right to be guarded against all threats directed to its existence whether before or after birth. The right to life necessarily implies the right to be born'.[14]

Notwithstanding the prevailing jurisprudence, a concern emerged that the Constitution could provide an avenue through which abortion would become permissible in Ireland.[15] Unease grew at the prospect that abortion might fall within the sphere of constitutional privacy rights, as happened in the USA in *Roe v Wade*.[16] In 1974, the Irish Supreme Court, in the decision in *McGee v Attorney General*, had found that the right to marital privacy was implicit in the Constitution, and as such married couples should be allowed to import contraception for personal use.[17] Conservative lawyer William Binchy stated that 'the concept of privacy espoused by that decision is a time bomb which, with changing attitudes, may yet explode in a manner which most of our citizens … would deeply regret'.[18] Here Binchy espouses the sort of constitutional conservatism that West places in opposition to the constitutional progressivism of which I suggest Fletcher J offers an example. Binchy is concerned that the '"majority" carries the danger of being or becoming an irresponsible and excessively egalitarian, or "leveling," mechanism bent on the redistribution of social wealth, power, and prestige'.[19] In order to fend off the possibility of abortion as a personal right, Binchy and others established the Pro-Life Amendment Campaign, which successfully lobbied for a constitutional clause that guaranteed specific and explicit protection for unborn foetal life: the Eighth Amendment to the Irish Constitution.

The Harm of Article 40.3.3

Carol Smart warns of the juridogenic potential of law. She characterises the 'term *juridogenic* to apply to law as a way of conceptualising the harm that law may generate as a consequence of its operations'.[20] Article 40.3.3, and its subsequent interpretation in the courts, is a clear example of what Smart is here referring to. Fletcher summarises the situation as follows:

> Through constitutionalisation, the right to life of the 'unborn' had been legally recognised as an important interest of Irish society. … [T]hrough the judicial interpretation of Article 40.3.3, that right had acquired a status that rendered it more important to Irish society than other constitutionally endorsed interests.[21]

[14] *G v An Bord Uchtála* [1980] IR 32; see also the *obiter dicta* of Keane J in the case of *Society for the Protection of the Unborn Child (Ireland) Ltd (SPUC) v Grogan and Ors* [1989] IR 753.

[15] Kingston, Whelan and Bacik, above n 9; see also Ivana Bacik, 'Legislating for Article 40.3.3' (2013) 3(1) *Irish Journal of Legal Studies* 18–35.

[16] *Roe v Wade* 410 US 113 (1973).

[17] On *McGee*, see further this collection, ch 5.

[18] William Binchy, 'Marital Privacy and Family Law: A Reply to Mr. O'Reilly' (1977) 66 *Studies: An Irish Quarterly Review* 330–35, 333.

[19] West, above n 2 ('progressive constitutionalism') 645.

[20] Carol Smart, *Feminism and the Power of Law* (New York, Routledge, 1989) 12.

[21] Ruth Fletcher '"Pro-Life" Absolutes, Feminist Challenges: The Fundamentalist Narrative of Irish Abortion Law 1986–1992' (1998) 36(1) *Osgoode Hall Law Journal* 1–62.

This amendment, and the interpretation of it, have served to perpetuate and assure harms to women; it is an instance of law purporting to legitimate gendered harm.

In claiming to find legitimacy, Article 40.3.3 rests on an antagonistic framing, meaning the Constitution creates a conflict model of maternal/foetal relations. It gives rise to a legal culture in Ireland that has attributed subjectivity to the foetus. Susan Bordo presents the effect of such framing as follows:

> The essence of the pregnant woman ... is her biological, purely mechanical role in preserving the life of another. In her case, *this* is the given value, against which her claims to subjectivity must be rigorously evaluated, and they will usually be found wanting insofar as they conflict with her life-support function. In the face of such conflict, her valuations, choices, consciousness are expendable.[22]

Through the attribution of subjectivity, the status of the foetus is elevated to that of a separate and distinct individual of equal moral worth to the woman. That this conflict model of maternal/foetal relations was the impetus for the litigation in *X v AG* is evident in the following statement from Harry Whelehan—the Attorney General who initiated the proceedings. During an interview for the *Scannal* programme, Whelan was asked about his perspective on the decision, looking back to which he said:

> I don't want this to sound harsh but where the mother of the child, who is entitled to have its life protected, decides to seek an abortion the only mechanism in our system is for the attorney general to intervene and make a case for the child to be born alive.[23]

Here Whelehan is advocating for an approach that affords protection to the foetus through the constitutionalisation of foetal rights.[24] Constructions of maternal/foetal conflict acknowledge the embodied nature of pregnancy only to the extent that the pregnant woman is viewed as a threat to the foetus. This framing leads to the position of the woman as an aggressor and the foetus as an innocent party rather than a dependant, such as was evident in the approach of some of the original judgments in *X*. As Bordo summarises, 'as the personhood of the pregnant woman has been drained from her and her function as fetal incubator activated, the subjectivity of the fetus has been elevated'.[25] Indeed it is interesting to note that one of the key legitimating narratives associated with the decision in *X v AG* is that of her innocence. This is vividly summarised by Fletcher as follows:

> A famous cartoon in the *Irish Times* in February 1992 clearly depicts the enforcement of the Eighth amendment in nationalist terms. It represents X, who was stopped by injunction from travelling to England for an abortion, as a young girl with a teddy bear on a fenced-in map of the Republic of Ireland. The cartoon clearly plays with Irish nationalist iconography by describing the child as being interned in the twenty-six counties of Ireland as a result of the High Court decision in the *X* case. By depicting the *X* case decision in terms of Ireland's virtual imprisonment of a young

[22] Susan Bordo, *Unbearable Weight Feminism: Feminism, Western Culture, and the Body* (Berkeley, CA, University of California Press, 1993) 79.

[23] *Scannal* programme, at www.rte.ie/tv/scannal/xcase.html (last accessed 27 March 2016); as detailed in 'X case judge Harry Whelehan: I was only doing my duty', *The Sunday Times*, 21 February 2010, at www.timesonline.co.uk/tol/news/world/ireland/article7035006.ece (last accessed 27 March 2016).

[24] Fletcher, above n 21; Fiona de Londras, 'Constitutionalizing Fetal Rights: A Salutary Tale from Ireland' (2015) 22(2) *Michigan Journal of Gender and Law* 243–89.

[25] Bordo, above n 22, 85.

> vulnerable child, the cartoon criticises the Irish state in terms that used to be reserved for the British state when it imprisoned Northern Irish republicans without trial.[26]

I shall return to the linkage between Irish nationalism and reproductive politics below.[27] For now, I wish to focus on how the acceptability of letting X travel to have a termination is reliant on a framing that reduces the 'threat' that X is seen to pose. She is depicted as another 'innocent'. The outcome of this case cannot be understood as 'empowering'; rather, the justifications invoked legitimate and reproduce structural subordination of women in being reliant on X's diminished agency.

Attorney General v X Re-imagined

Article 40.3.3 therefore serves as a tool of subjugation and oppression. Furthermore, it is not just pregnant women who are impacted by this provision, but rather all those with the capacity to become pregnant. Article 40.3.3 ensures that this group lives with the spectre of the unborn; their agency is contingent on a state (pregnancy) that they may never enter. As Drucilla Cornell tells us:

> The very constitution of selfhood cannot be separated from the protection of the future projections of the woman's self as a whole body. The threat takes effect before any woman actually has to face an unwanted pregnancy. Here we have an important example of how the symbolisation of a woman's 'sex' has a constitutive effect on what we have come to think of as selfhood. Not only is a woman's individuality not just given, it is limited in its very definition by certain symbolisations of her 'sex' in the law.[28]

As is clear in the decision of Fletcher J, and the range of abortion and maternity care cases that have arisen since its insertion in the Constitution, Article 40.3.3 is an instrument of law with serious juridogenic effect: it 'poses an impracticable burden on the woman's rightful life', and as such limits her capacity to act as a full citizen. The absence of access to safe and legal abortion services means the absence of full recognition of the bodily integrity of the pregnant woman. Again, in the words of Cornell:

> Understood through the rubric of bodily integrity, the wrong in denying a right to abortion is not a wrong to the 'self,' but a wrong that prevents the achievement of the minimum conditions of individuation necessary for any meaningful concept of selfhood.[29]

The first challenge, then, for Fletcher J's feminist re-imagining is to respond to the limiting impact of Article 40.3.3. She does this by highlighting that even if women cannot ground a claim to access abortion based in dignity, it is possible to limit the impact of Article 40.3.3 through the invocation of a range of other constitutionally protected rights. Specifically,

[26] Fletcher, above n 5, 384.

[27] See also Eithne Luibheid, 'Sexual Regimes and Migration Controls: Reproducing the Irish Nation-State in Transnational Contexts' (2006) 83(1) *Feminist Review* 60–78; Siobhán Mulally, 'Debating Reproductive Rights in Ireland' (2005) 27(1) *Human Rights Quarterly* 78–104.

[28] Drucilla Cornell, *The Imaginary Domain: Abortion, Pornography and Sexual Harrassment* (New York, Routledge 1995) 52.

[29] ibid, 33.

Fletcher J rejects the 'bright line' distinction that has been drawn between 'life' and 'health' in Irish pregnancy and abortion jurisprudence. Here the feminist judge attempts to limit the juridogenic potential of Article 40.3.3 not just with regard to access to abortion care, but also as to the detrimental effect that the Article has had on maternity services generally.[30] In keeping with West's account of progressive constitutionalism, Fletcher J here is interpreting the Constitution to ensure the minimum conditions for a flourishing, or in Fletcher's words 'rightful', life.[31]

Since its insertion in 1983, Article 40.3.3 has been interpreted in a range of cases relating to access to abortion and maternity care, as a mechanism through which the status of the foetus has been elevated to that of 'super subject'. This elevation of the status of the foetus robs the pregnant woman of her own subjectivity and reduces her to the physicality of her role as foetal incubator.[32] Again our feminist judge is both creative and subversive in her approach. She rejects the construction of the foetus as 'super subject' and emphasises the 'life in being' of the pregnant woman:

> The unborn's right to life is to 'bare' biological life. That right may impose an obligation on others to support it, but when there is a conflict, the woman's fuller, rightful life may merit more legal weight than the unborn's bare life.

Fletcher J restores the subjectivity of the pregnant woman and emphasises the contingent and dependent status of the foetus, rejecting the hitherto 'fundamentalist' approach to valuing foetal life.[33] This construction is not an attempt to denigrate the status of the foetus but rather demonstrates the reality that, separated from the body of the pregnant woman, the foetus has no possibility for selfhood; and in doing so it emphasises that the well-being of the foetus cannot be disentangled from the well-being of the pregnant woman 'of whose body it is part'.[34]

'One Step Forward ...'[35]

In considering the progressive judgment of Fletcher J, it is worth asking whether such a decision in 1992 would have prevented the series of terrible decisions that followed in its wake. Probably it would not have done, because to be successful it needs to be part of a broader socio-legal consensus that pregnant women's right to life entitles them to more

[30] For further detail on this see Máiréad Enright and Fiona de Londras, '"Empty Without and Empty Within": the Unworkability of the Eighth Amendment after Savita Halappanavar and Miss Y' (2014) 20(2) *Medico-Legal Journal of Ireland* 85–92.

[31] West, above n 2 ('progressive constitutionalism') 697.

[32] A particularly egregious example of this is the case of *PP v HSE* [2014] IEHC 622, discussed in Máiréad Enright, '*PP v HSE*: Practicability, Dignity and the Best Interests of the Unborn Child' (26 December 2014) *Human Rights In Ireland*, at http://humanrights.ie/gender-sexuality-and-the-law/pp-v-hse-futility-dignity-and-the-best-interests-of-the-unborn-child/ (last accessed 27 March 2016).

[33] Fletcher, above n 21.

[34] Cornell, above n 28, 32.

[35] Mulally, above n 27.

than bare existence.[36] It is not just the existence of Article 40.3.3 that diminishes the status of women, but also the way in which it is interpreted. In 1998 Fletcher published a detailed consideration of how the protection of the foetus as a fundamental value within the Irish legal system and within Irish society had created the conditions for such a case occurring. Fletcher sees the potential impact of *X* as drawing a line under the sort of 'fundamentalist' narratives that had defined litigation (and societal discourse) on Article 40.3.3 until this point. Fundamentalist narratives in this context are simply the absolutist expression of the ideal of protecting foetal life as a constitutional value above and beyond the protection of other values. She summarises the impact of this fundamentalist approach as follows:

> When the fundamentalist narrative assumed legal authority and became a legal narrative as well as a social narrative, the legal conditions were created that would give rise to the X case.... By bringing 'pro-life' absolutism to a climax, and thus exposing the actual consequences of legal endorsement of a fundamentalist narrative for women's lives, the X case also brought that legal narrative to a close and stripped fundamentalism of legal authority.[37]

As has been discussed in this commentary, the maternal/foetal conflict model of understanding the relationship between the foetus and the pregnant woman has the effect of foreclosing the possibility of equal consideration; when understood as being in opposition to each other, the value of respecting one trumps the value of respecting the other. In conceptualising the pregnant woman and the foetus as separate and with the potential of competing interests, we accept the fiction that in cases of conflict we are simply 'balancing' two sides equally. *X v AG* brought all of this to our attention: 'The violation of women's rights through the prioritisation of fetal life became tangible for the Irish public as it took shape in Irish law's victimisation of a particular young woman.'[38]

However, *X v AG* signifies only the possibility of a more progressive approach to understanding the relationship between the rights of the pregnant woman and the rights of the foetus in the context of Article 40.3.3. In a later article, published in 2005, Fletcher picks up on this analysis with a consideration of the circumstances and conditions that made the outcome in *X v AG* possible, and she contrasts these with two other cases: the *C* case[39] and the *O* case.[40] I shall focus primarily on the *C* case. The decisions in *C* and *O* evidence how the legacy of *X v AG* is not a legal and societal awakening about the value of equal citizenship and consequent limitations on the interpretation of Article 40.3.3. Rather, the decisions (and the associated societal discourse) continue to diminish the subjectivity of the pregnant women involved, and also that of migrant women and those from minority ethnic groups. In her article, Fletcher describes the extent to which discourses that provided a legitimating narrative in *X v AG* were not applicable in *C* and *O*. Her analysis describes a failure of progressive thinking, not just within the legal system but in society generally.

The *C* case involved a 13-year-old who was pregnant as a result of rape. C was a member of the Traveller community. C also wished to travel to England to have a termination, but

[36] See further Reva Siegel, 'The Constitutionalization of Abortion' in Rebecca Cook, Joanna Erdman and Bernard Dickens (eds), *Abortion Law in Transnational Perspective: Cases and Controversies* (Philadelphia, PA, University of Pennsylvania Press, 2014) ch 1.

[37] Fletcher, above n 21, 8.

[38] ibid, 58.

[39] *A and B v Eastern Health Board & C* [1997] IEHC 176.

[40] *Baby O (Suing by Mother and Next Friend IAO) v Minister for Justice, Equality and Law Reform* [2002] IESC 53.

one of the features distinguishing her situation from that of X was that C had been taken into care following the rape. This meant that the Court did not just have to decide to let her travel to access abortion care; rather, it had to positively assist her to do so, which it did. It may be imagined at this point that the outcome marks a progressive extension of *X v AG*. Although, as Fletcher details, there are progressive aspects to the judgment that could be co-opted in this way, this is ultimately not the driver for the outcome reached. As mentioned above, the discursive justifications for the outcome in *X v AG* were reliant on a depiction of X as a diminished subject, an innocent, and as such less of a threat to her foetus. While the discursive justifications for C are consistent in reproducing structures that diminish the subjectivity of women and girls, they do so in a different way. For C, she was not capable of constituting a threat—she was 'unfit'. As Fletcher summarises, 'While X was to be spared motherhood because of her innocence, C was to be spared motherhood because she was unfit for it.'[41]

Pervasive in the consideration of the prospects for C and her 'unborn child' if the pregnancy were to continue is the undesirability of the Traveller lifestyle and C's consequent inability to control reproductive decision-making: '[A] young Traveller woman was represented as a less worthy bearer of Irishness in circumstances that celebrated the modernity of the settled Irish population by contrasting it with the backwardness and excessive fertility of Irish Travellers.'[42]

In this case, concerns about the protection of foetal life are hierarchised through the lens of ethnicity and its contribution to Irishness. The facts of *C* highlight the increased burden experienced by women and girls of limited financial means and for whom travelling to access abortion is not straightforward. The case also illustrates the complex and heightened possibilities for individuals who are marginalised in multiple ways to experience harm. These interactions culminate in the case of Miss Y.[43] Miss Y's story evidences the extent of the harm that can be experienced as a result of Article 40.3.3 in a societal context that is suspicious of women, asylum seekers and maternal decision-making. Y was an asylum seeker who was pregnant as a result of rape in her country of origin; she found out that she was pregnant at a health check upon arriving into Ireland. She was deeply distressed by the pregnancy and wished to have a termination. She was informed that this would not be possible in Ireland and that she would need to travel to England, which Y had neither the financial nor the legal means to do.[44] It is beyond the scope of this chapter to discuss this case in detail; suffice it to note that Y is transformed from a woman who is harmed through the refusal of care consequent to Article 40.3.3, to a woman who is harmed by enforced medical care in the interests of the foetus consequent to Article 40.3.3. Y is violated and harmed first through rape, then through enforced pregnancy, and finally through enforced medical treatment.

41 Fletcher, above n 5, 390.

42 ibid.

43 *Ms Y v Health Service Executive & Ors* [2016] IEHC 136. See further Ruth Fletcher, 'Contesting the cruel treatment of abortion-seeking women' (2014) 22(44) *Reproductive Health Matters* 10–21.

44 Notwithstanding these barriers, in circumstances that still remain unclear, Miss Y manages to get a ferry to Liverpool, only to be returned to Ireland upon her arrival there due to her lack of documentation; see 'Report on Ms Y case to include journey to Liverpool to seek abortion', *The Irish Times*, 7 November 2014, at www.irishtimes.com/news/social-affairs/report-on-ms-y-case-to-include-journey-to-liverpool-to-seek-abortion-1.1991580 (last accessed 25 March 2016).

Concluding Remarks

West describes the experience of rape and unwanted pregnancy as 'defining harmful experiences for women'.[45] X, C and Y experienced both; the harm that X experienced under intense media and legal scrutiny is unimaginable. Subsequent to the reversal of the High Court injunction prohibiting her to leave Ireland, X travelled with her parents to England in order to have the termination she had first requested two months earlier. However, after undergoing chorionic villus sampling, in order to obtain genetic material that could be used in the prosecution of X's rapist, X experienced a miscarriage.[46] C did go on to have a termination.[47] In sentencing her rapist, Quirke J emphasised the grave harm he had caused not just in his violation of C, but also in causing the death of a child by abortion.[48] He thereby provided an example of the way in which abortion continues to be cast as an independent harm to a foetal subject, rather than as necessary medical care for a pregnant woman.

In his judgment in *X v AG*, McCarthy J stated that '[t]he failure of the Legislature to enact the appropriate legislation is no longer just unfortunate; it is inexcusable'.[49] Notwithstanding this declaration, it was not until the passing of the Protection of Life During Pregnancy Act (PDLPA) 2013 that the Irish Government 'legislated for *X*'. Therefore, although in the wake of *X v AG* it was accepted that abortion was permissible when the life of the pregnant woman was threatened (including when the threat to life is from suicide), government inertia and unwillingness to confront the issue of abortion meant that how and when women were able to access abortion remained unclear.[50] The failure to provide clarity to the law in this area has been emphasised over the years through a series of high-profile cases including (but not limited to) the *C* case,[51] Miss D's case,[52] *D v Ireland*[53] and *ABC v Ireland*;[54] the death of Savita Halappanavar; and most recently the treatment of Ms Y.[55] During this time McCarthy J's sentiments have been echoed by many judges—most famously by Geoghegan J, who expressed dissatisfaction that that the courts should be considered as 'some kind of licensing authority for abortions'.[56] However, as Marie Fox and Therese Murphy caution:

> Around the world, political careers lurch precariously, and 'passing the buck' becomes the solution when the personal becomes political, especially if the personal in question is abortion. It seems that

45 West, above n 2 ('gendered harm') ch 4.

46 'Whelehan "regrets" hurt caused in X case', *Irish Independent*, 21 February 2010, at www.independent.ie/irish-news/whelehan-regrets-hurt-caused-in-x-case-26634293.html (last accessed 27 March 2016).

47 'C-Case mum: I grieve for my lost baby every day', *Irish Independent*, 5 May 2013, at www.independent.ie/lifestyle/health/ccase-mum-i-grieve-for-my-lost-baby-every-day-29241584.html (last accessed 27 March 2016).

48 'Judge jails C case rapist for "dreadful evil act"', *Irish Independent*, 18 December 1998, at www.independent.ie/irish-news/judge-jails-c-case-rapist-for-dreadful-evil-act-26165826.html (last accessed 27 March 2016).

49 *Attorney General v X* [1992] 1 IR 1, 147.

50 For a full discussion of the journey from *X* to the PDLPA, see Bacik, above n 15.

51 Above n 39.

52 For details, see 'Miss D: my story', *Irish News*, 12 May 2007, at www.independent.ie/irish-news/miss-d-my-story-26288744.html (last accessed 27 March 2016).

53 *D v Ireland*, App No 26499/02 ECtHR (28 June 2006).

54 *A, B and C v Ireland* (2011) 53 EHRR 13.

55 For a discussion of these cases, see Fletcher, above n 43.

56 *A and B v Eastern Health Board* [1998] 1 IR IR 464, per Geoghegan J.

> there is nothing quite like it to bring out depoliticisation by delegation strategies or the seeking of 'refuge in a jurisprudence of doubt'.[57]

It is becoming increasingly clear that the PDLPA does not provide the clarity that is necessary to ensure that women in Ireland receive safe and appropriate maternal and reproductive health care. Some 33 years after the insertion of Article 40.3.3, there is hope that the Irish people may finally get an opportunity to vote to remove this clause from our Constitution, and in doing so remove a key stumbling block to the achievement of full emancipation for Irish women, thus ending a 'struggle ... equivalent to the "heroic and unremitting struggle to regain the rightful independence of our Nation"'.[58]

[57] Marie Fox and Therese Murphy, 'Irish Abortion: Seeking Refuge in a Jurisprudence of Doubt and Delegation' (1992) 19(4) *Journal of Law and Society* 454–66.

[58] per Fletcher J, below.

THE SUPREME COURT

The Attorney General

(Plaintiff)

v

X and Others

(Defendants)

1992 No. 846P

[5th March, 1992]

Status: Reported at [1992] 1 IR 1

Fletcher J.

The facts and issues

The facts of this case are well known. The parents of a fourteen-year-old rape victim sought information from the Gardaí in an effort to support their daughter through the prosecution of the man who had assaulted her. In good faith, they asked if the DNA from an aborted foetus could be used as evidence in a rape trial. This question was referred to the Director of Public Prosecutions and then to the Attorney General. The Attorney General interpreted the question in a different way. He asked if he had a duty to try and stop the planned abortion given the obligations imposed by Article 40.3.3° of the Irish Constitution. The High Court held that there is such an obligation and that it extends to an injunction stopping Ms X and her parents travelling abroad for the purposes of securing abortion care. It falls to this Court to consider on appeal whether this is a sound legal interpretation.

Finlay C.J. has helpfully outlined the 22 grounds of appeal in this case and classified them as concerning four distinct legal issues, namely whether the trial judge erred in law and in fact because:

1. The court does not have jurisdiction to enforce Article 40.3.3° in the absence of legislation
2. Due regard to the pregnant woman's life under Article 40.3.3° means that abortion is permissible in these circumstances
3. Ms X's right to liberty would be unjustifiably infringed
4. Her right to receive services abroad under EC law makes an injunction unlawful

Interpreting Article 40.3.3°

In a sense, we are being asked whether the Attorney General's belief that he was constitutionally obliged to seek an injunction against Ms X and her parents was a reasonable interpretation of Article 40.3.3°. That article, as adopted by the Eighth Amendment to the Constitution, provides:

> "The State acknowledges the right to life of the unborn and, with due regard to the equal right to life of the mother, guarantees in its laws to respect, and, as far as practicable, by its laws to defend and vindicate that right."

The terms of Article 40.3.3° have not been implemented by legislation. The courts, state officials, healthcare providers and pregnant women have received no legislative statement from the Oireachtas as to how the constitutional balance between the right to life of the "unborn" and the right to life of the pregnant woman, referred to in the Constitution as the "mother", is to be drawn.

Nonetheless the Supreme Court has twice declared that the right to life of the unborn in Article 40.3.3° is self-executing (*The Attorney General (SPUC) v. Open Door Counselling* [1988] IR 593, hereinafter *Open Door*, and *SPUC v. Grogan* [1989] IR 753, hereinafter *Grogan*) drawing on *The State (Quinn) v. Ryan* [1965] IR 70 and *The People v. Shaw* [1982] IR 1 in so doing. This means that Article 40.3.3° is directly enforceable without the benefit of legislation. However, it does not tell us how exactly Article 40.3.3° should be enforced. That will have to be decided on a case-by-case basis in light of the particular facts and legal issues raised.

In *Open Door* and *Grogan* the Supreme Court decided that it was justifiable to stop pregnancy counselling agencies and student unions from providing information on abortion services abroad. The courts were not asked to consider the legal issues in relation to any particular pregnancy. In this instance Ms X's right to life, as protected by Article 40.3.3° in harmony with other provisions in the Constitution, is directly engaged. As Mr Rogers argued on behalf of Ms X and her parents, given the absence of legislation on how to balance these rights, which are in conflict in this instance, the court has to "make law on this point". HLA Hart would have said this is one of those occasions when law "runs out" and judges are required to exercise discretion in making a decision (Hart, *The Concept of Law*, 1961, pp. 123–124).

Impartiality

In exercising judicial discretion, we are required to act with objectivity and impartiality in service of the people. O'Higgins C.J. said in *Norris v. The Attorney General* [1984] IR 36 (hereinafter *Norris*) at p. 53:-

> "The sole function of this Court, in a case of this nature, is to interpret the Constitution and the law and to declare with objectivity and impartiality the result of that interpretation on the claim being considered."

Judges are not automatically objective and impartial by virtue of being appointed judges. These are qualities of adjudication that we aspire towards and develop over time. One lesson I have learned along the way is that objectivity is more likely to be achieved by recognising the limits of judicial knowledge. I may have a great deal of legal expertise on human rights and principles of consent, but that does not mean I am expert in the significance of a particular rights protection for a person or group of persons. Ignoring certain life experiences, which may be unfamiliar to us, is likely to produce a rather partial account of law and life. Being objective and impartial about interpreting Article 40.3.3° presents a particular challenge because there is so much silence and stigma about abortion experiences and decisions. In aiming for impartiality and objectivity we have to navigate uneven and obscured terrain as we come up against the partiality of our expertise and experience of legal rules and human life. We have to be wary of the potential for injustice, or legal hypocrisy as McCarthy J. might say (*Norris*, at p. 102), if we develop and apply the law as if ordinary women did not make abortion decisions every day.

In order to become impartial—to rise above our partiality—we draw on a diversity of human experience and expertise. This is what the Court does when it calls on personal and expert evidence in seeking knowledge which is vital to legal, including constitutional, interpretation. But "rising above our partiality" ought not to mean that we stay above legal process somehow, or that we adopt a bird's eye view. Rather rising above our partiality has to be reflective. We try and imagine ourselves in the position of the litigant, and yet take a long view of the problem. In short, we judges regularly have to put ourselves "in other people's shoes" as we adjudicate and come to a legal ruling, often in haste and under pressure. We need to "assess the actual and potential effects" of this injunction on this appellant, as Henchy J. said *obiter* in *Norris* at p. 69.

Sometimes judicial empathy is helped along by the familiarity of certain experiences. In this context, abortion seems such an unfamiliar experience that it is difficult for judges to put themselves in the shoes of Ms X or of other women who decide that abortion is the best resolution for them. And yet, we know that many thousands of Irish women have had abortions before and after the Eighth Amendment. Indeed folklorists and historians tell us that St Brigid herself performed an abortion at a time when restoring a woman's menses and preventing the development of a pregnancy was not seen as a moral or legal sin. We know that unsafe abortion has been a feature of Irish women's lives, particularly during World War II as the traditional escape path to England became difficult to access (Jackson, 'Outside the Jurisdiction: Irish Women Seeking Abortion Abroad' in *Gender in Irish Society*, Galway University Press, 1987), and including the 1939, 1945 and 1956 convictions of midwife and abortionist Mamie Cadden.

The courts have been saved the experience of dealing with unlawful abortion practice since then because women have travelled to safe and legal services elsewhere. More stories are surfacing every day about the ways in which pregnant women have been mistreated and undervalued as some were sent away to Magdalene laundries and had their children taken from them. We do not have the benefit of solid research evidence on women's experiences of and reasons for pregnancy and abortion. But objectivity and impartiality cannot be achieved by ignoring this common knowledge of women's struggle to gain reproductive self-determination and full citizenship, a struggle which I believe will one day be seen as equivalent to the "heroic and unremitting struggle to regain the rightful independence of our Nation", as acknowledged in the Preamble.

Another feature of this case, which makes the terrain uneven and difficult in the search for impartiality, is the different public roles and responsibilities of the parties in this case. I cannot fail but to observe that this case comes before us because one family called on the Guards for help in their time of need. They did not receive the help they asked for but instead the full power of the state through the Attorney General's request for an injunction was brought to bear on their situation. As a result, although their anonymity has been maintained, they have had to endure this threatening disruption to their care plan for

Ms X while the international and national media pore over the details of her case. I for one find it extremely troubling that the effect, whatever the intention, of the Attorney General's actions as guardian of the Constitution has been to expose ordinary people to coercive scrutiny and disruption, when surely our first intuition is that a prudent, just and charitable Constitution requires the opposite.

I am also conscious that this particular family has endured this response while showing remarkable faith in and openness with the legal system. Given what we now know about the past treatment of women such as Joanne Hayes by the authorities, I am mindful of the possibility that Article 40.3.3° could be used to license invasive treatment of women and their loved ones, some of whom may have good reason to be less trusting of the legal system. As we judges strive for objectivity and impartiality in our constitutional interpretation we have an obligation to address gaps in our knowledge, and to consider the effects of uneven legal power on the parties before us.

Harmony

In exercising my judicial discretion to interpret Article 40.3.3° I will apply the doctrine of harmonious interpretation (*Quinn's Supermarket Ltd v. Attorney General* [1972] IR 1). Henchy J. explained the doctrine in these terms in *The People v. O'Shea* [1982] IR 384 at p. 426:-

> "Any single constitutional right or power is but a component in an ensemble of interconnected and interacting provisions which must be brought into play as part of a larger composition, and which must be given such an integrated interpretation as will fit it harmoniously into the general constitutional order and modulation. It may be said of a constitution, more than of any other legal instrument, that 'the letter killeth, but the spirit giveth life'."

The requirement that the state defend and vindicate the right to life of the unborn with due regard to the equal right to life of the mother, needs to be interpreted firstly, in light of the commitments in the constitutional Preamble (see Walsh J. in *McGee v. The Attorney General* [1974] IR 284 (hereinafter *McGee*); O'Higgins C.J. in *State (Healy) v. Donoghue* [1976] IR 325), and secondly in light of the other provisions of the Constitution, including women's fundamental rights under Article 40 (see Budd J. in *McGee* at p. 322).

The Preamble, in language which is similar to many other constitutional and human rights documents across the world, commits to promotion of "the common good, with due observance of Prudence, Justice and Charity, so that the dignity and freedom of the individual may be assured". The difficulty of course lies in deciding the proper legal meaning of "the common good", "prudence" "justice", "charity" "dignity", and "freedom", among other constitutional matters, how to weigh them when they come into conflict with each other, and which mechanisms and standards are appropriate in achieving these constitutional values. Although working out the detail falls to the legislature and the courts, it is clear that the Constitution envisages a people with dignified, free and just lives. Dignity, freedom and justice require that individuals be enabled to make their own lives, apart and together, subject to an obligation not to harm others. As Thompson saw, communities of shared power are vital to remedying the uneven distribution of happiness and enabling everyone to become "fabricators of [their] own destiny" (*Labour Rewarded*, Hunt and Clarke, 1827, at p. 118).

It is true of course that the Preamble also makes reference to the existence of God and acknowledges the people's obligation to "our Divine Lord, Jesus Christ". This constitutional language has been drawn on, most notably in *Norris* at p. 64, to declare the people's intention to "adopt a Constitution consistent with that conviction and with Christian beliefs". In *Norris*, the Supreme Court found that the impugned buggery and indecent assault offences were constitutional because they conformed with long established laws "which had existed for hundreds of years prohibiting unnatural sexual conduct which Christian teaching held to be gravely sinful".

However, coherence with Christian teaching was not sufficient to save the legislation prohibiting the importation of contraceptives in *McGee*. Therefore, conformity with Christian teaching is not, in itself, sufficient to find legislation or legal actions constitutional. In other words, the truth of the matter is that the Preamble lends itself to a variety of possible ways of harmonising these commitments to the dignity and freedom of the individual, to the common good, and to the Christian and democratic nature of the state. Therefore, I shall attempt to do justice to objectivity and impartiality by explaining how I approach the different legal pathways which harmonious interpretation provides.

Text

Precedent and practice tell us that there are three key elements to constitutional interpretation: text, evidence and craft. Each element will be in play as a judge considers the constitutional text, assesses evidence and crafts her judgment as a contribution to living law. Depending on the circumstances, some elements will be more emphasised or obvious than others in particular cases. For example, although constitutional scholars usually emphasise the innovative textual interpretation in *Ryan v. Attorney General* [1965] IR 294 (hereinafter *Ryan*) most of the judgment itself is actually concerned with the evidence on fluoridation in weighing whether there was any infringement of bodily integrity. Each element contributes to the ebb and flow of constitutional interpretation and to the judicial carving out of a legal pathway along the constitutional shoreline.

The doctrine of harmonious interpretation is one kind of textual approach. Harmonious interpretation reflects a coherence approach to textual meaning in holding that it is impossible to derive the meaning of one piece of text without considering how it coheres with the whole. In the process, the meanings of some words are so popularly accepted that they become common sense and are taken as the plain meaning of words. This is what the literal rule of interpretation captures. It is not that the words speak for themselves. Rather the audience is so familiar with the words and there is such a degree of consensus that the meaning becomes plain. But as authors such as Joyce have shown us, plain meanings become less plain when words are re-arranged and their usual pattern disrupted. In a sense, the adoption of the Eighth Amendment was a significant moment in the disruption of the plain meaning of key constitutional terms. The generation of this new constitutional term the unborn has re-arranged and disrupted the plain meaning of birth as the moment when legal personhood and rights normally begin. It falls to the courts to respond to this legal innovation and determine the constitutional meaning of the unborn as a new kind of rights-bearer, even as it is still a piece of the constitutional ensemble.

Evidence

The second element of constitutional interpretation is an evidence-based approach. In *Ryan* O'Dálaigh J., in the Supreme Court (affirming Kenny J. in the High Court), held that there would be times when constitutional meaning cannot be determined in the absence of evidence-based knowledge. He was referring not just to the material factual evidence, which gives rise to the legal issues in every case before a court, but also to the research-based evidence, which may be necessary for determining whether an action is integrity-violating and unconstitutional. *Ryan* then is authority for the role of evidence-based interpretation in assisting a court to decide where the threshold for a constitutional violation is and whether it has been met.

The evidence considered included evidence of Mrs Ryan's views and wishes in relation to her and her children's ingestion of fluoridated water and evidence of scientific research into the question of whether fluoridation could be harmful. In circumstances where there was a conflict between Mrs Ryan's evidence and that of the scientific establishment on the question of the harmfulness of fluoridation and related violation of bodily integrity, the Court relied on the scientific evidence and found that there was no violation of bodily integrity because there was no objective evidence that fluoridation caused any harm (beyond some discoloration of teeth some cases).

Just as the court in *Ryan* had to rely on public health evidence in order to answer the question as to whether fluoridation was dangerous, so a court may rely on public health evidence, among other things, in determining whether pregnancy can be dangerous. Many pregnancies in modern times will be harmless and indeed beneficial to the women that carry them. They may not even require medical attention. But some pregnancies may be harmful for women because they threaten their health, dignity and well-being.

Furthermore, evidence of pregnancy's effects is likely to distinguish it from fluoridation in at least two ways. Pregnancy asks a lot of a woman's body and is therefore a greater incursion on bodily integrity than the ingestion of fluoride. Secondly, the pregnant woman's subjective experience of pregnancy has a known impact on the objective question of whether a pregnancy is harmful or not. Therefore a court may be entitled to give more weight to the wishes and concerns of a pregnant person vis-à-vis the general scientific evidence about pregnancy, than it would to the wishes and concerns of a woman who feels her body to be violated by the ingestion of fluoride, vis-à-vis the general scientific evidence about the effects of fluorides.

In this case before us, the High Court has appropriately relied on personal, parental and professional evidence of an individual risk of self-destruction as that goes to the primary legal issue before us. Here I am making the broader legal point that there are likely to be occasions when more general evidence about pregnancy, or other constitutional matters, will be helpful and even necessary for interpretative purposes. While *Ryan* emphasized the need for scientific public health evidence, as well as personal evidence, in evaluating the question of bodily harm, *Norris* required the submission of many different kinds of evidence in order to consider the question as to whether continued criminalisation of buggery and indecent assault could be constitutionally justifiable in the common good. The *Norris* court, whose judgment that continued criminalisation was justified is on its way to the European Court of Human Rights, heard from sociological, theological and psychiatric experts as well as from Mr. Norris himself.

As Henchy and McCarthy J.J. point out in dissent, a majority of the *Norris* court went against all of the evidence, as this evidence was uniformly of the view that criminalisation was not in the common good. Rather the majority found that criminalisation was justified on grounds of conformity with Christian teaching and given the Christian nature of the state. The aspect of *Norris* which concerns me here, however, is not the decision on criminalisation, but the interpretative rule which was relied on in producing that decision. A wide range of social, moral, medical and personal evidence may well be relevant in deciding whether a particular form of criminalisation is constitutional. I would add that evidence from the person affected is particularly important when fundamental personal rights are at issue.

Craft

The third key aspect of constitutional interpretation is the need for judicial craft itself, particularly given the status of our Constitution as a "living document". McCarthy J. expressed the point eloquently in *Norris* at 96 when he said:

> "I find it philosophically impossible to carry out the necessary exercise of applying what I might believe to be the thinking of 1937 to the demands of 1983 … Suffice it to say that the Constitution is a living document; its life depends not merely upon itself but upon the people from whom it came and to whom it gives varying rights and duties."

McCarthy J. made these comments in dissent but they capture an approach to constitutional interpretation, which is supported by significant constitutional precedent (cf O'Higgins C.J. in *The State (Healy) v. O'Donoghue* at p. 347 and Kenny J. in *Ryan* at pp. 312–3).

The metaphorical depiction of the Constitution as a living document draws our attention to the subtleties involved in reading the tone and texture of law. This can be particularly demanding of judicial attentiveness when there are significant silences in relation to constitutional matters. In short, judicial craft has to be attentive to the fact that we know very little about pregnant women's decision-making and that significant stigma and stereotyping attach to women's practices of determining their own reproductive lives. It may take considerable experience of drawing out the significance of silences and discordant tones in order for constitutional interpretation to be crafted in a way that preserves democratic values and promotes public trust. We would do well to remember that our constitution, indeed our legal system, has been brought into being with joy and with pain. When judges are tasked with the job of giving life to law, of caring for its intricacies and deciding what to do with its rough edges, they must tread gently on the people's dreams.

Article 40.3.3° limits reproductive choices and denies abortion as a personal right

I turn now to the evaluation of Costello J.'s test—whether there is a real and imminent danger to unborn life justifying the injunction and whether the risk that the girl might take her own life is of the same order as the risk of abortion to the unborn—and the clarification of the rules by which such an evaluation will be done, in light of the above. The text of Article 40.3.3° does not refer to abortion specifically. Rather Article 40.3.3° identifies the unborn as the bearer of a right to life. It imposes a positive obligation on the state to defend and vindicate that right "as far as practicable". It imposes an obligation on the state to have "due regard to the equal right to life of the mother" when defending and vindicating the unborn's right.

The language of Article 40.3.3° raises several questions. The unborn is a new constitutional term, whose plain meaning is not yet clear. For example, it is not clear at which point exactly in the development of pregnancy the unborn comes into being and has a constitutional right to life. Is implantation enough? Secondly, the language of Article 40.3.3° implies that the positive obligation to defend and vindicate the unborn's right to life is not an absolute one. This position is consistent with the other fundamental rights in the Constitution, which are generally regarded as being non-absolute and capable of limitation in the common good and given the rights of others (cf *Ryan*). It is also consistent with the common law position on the right to life, which does not normally protect life absolutely, and recognises that there may be circumstances in which the ending of human life is justifiable.

Does the particularity of Article 40.3.3° imply any other particular legal considerations? When will it be impracticable to defend and vindicate the unborn? If an unborn has a significant anomaly, e.g. anencephaly, and is unlikely to survive past birth, do such circumstances make it impracticable to defend and vindicate the unborn? Finally, the text raises questions about the appropriate threshold for due regard to the equal right to life of the mother. When is "due regard" shown to the pregnant woman's life? Does a threshold which requires a risk to a woman's health to become a risk to her life before action is taken violate due regard? What difference do the particular circumstances of pregnancy make to the evaluation of due regard?

In order to answer these questions we need to consider how the other provisions of the Constitution may help in providing a harmonious interpretation of Article 40.3.3°, we need to consider the personal, social, medical, and philosophical evidence which is necessary for determining its meaning, and we need to come to a prudent, just and charitable judgment about which interpretation is best in light of living law. Before we do so, I think it worth noting that this case presents an interesting example of an occasion when the purpose of the amendment will be particularly helpful in defining constitutional meaning (cf Costello J. *The Attorney General v. Paperlink* [1984] ILRM 373, at p. 385). Abortion was a criminal offence under the Offences against the Person Act 1861 s. 58 when the Eighth Amendment was adopted. The amendment did not change the legal landscape by making abortion unlawful. There was also significant obiter commentary implying that abortion was unconstitutional (Budd J. in *McGee* at p. 335; Walsh J. in *G. v. An Bord Uchtála* [1980] IR 32 at p. 69; O'Higgins C.J. in *Norris* at p. 64). The Eighth Amendment made constitutional protection of unborn life explicit, but such protection was implicit before 1983.

That is not to say that this constitutional protection had ever been tested in such a way as to require the elaboration of its specific remit, nor to doubt that whatever constitutional protection existed would of course always have to be weighed with other constitutional interests, including women's fundamental rights and the pursuit of the common good. The addition of the right to life of the unborn to the constitutional ensemble means that any court would have to take that protection into consideration when faced with a particular question about the permissibility of abortion. As a result, it would be impossible, or at least highly improbable, for a court to find that abortion was available to women as of right. Abortion, as such, certainly abortion on request, is not something that can be legalised in this jurisdiction under Article 40.3.3°. Therefore, Ms X does not have legal permission to have an abortion on grounds of a right to abortion simpliciter because this is exactly what Article 40.3.3° prevents.

Article 40.3.3° permits abortion where this vindicates a woman's right to life

Nonetheless, as both counsel accepted, Article 40.3.3° does anticipate that a woman may have an abortion in some circumstances, notably when her right to life is at risk. Counsel differ however, as to the test that should be applied, with the Attorney General upholding the test that Costello J. applied, where the woman's life is in imminent and inevitable danger of death. Mr Murray argues, on behalf of the appellants, for a test of real and substantial risk to the woman's life.

One of the difficulties in determining the meaning of Article 40.3.3° according to the doctrine of harmonious interpretation is that we have a conflict in constitutional rights. One approach to the question of how to determine the balance between the conflicting rights of woman and unborn is the hierarchical approach, or the "hierarchy of constitutional norms" per McCarthy J. in *Murray v. Ireland* [1991] ILRM 465, at p. 476, with the abstract right to life at the top of the hierarchy. Precedent seems to favour such a hierarchical approach to a conflict between a right to life and another constitutional right, but only when a harmonious interpretation is not possible (see *McGee*, *The State (Healy) v. Donoghue* [1976] IR 325 and *The People v. Shaw* [1982] IR 1).

But I do not believe that precedent *requires* the hierarchical approach, for the following reasons. Although the majority in *Shaw* claimed to be taking a hierarchical approach, the judgment actually involved a *reconciliation* of conflicting rights. The Court of Criminal Appeal (O'Higgins C.J., Finlay P. and McMahon J.) was satisfied

> "that, if it needs to be excused, the interference with the applicant's right to liberty is amply excused by the circumstance that the paramount and primary purpose for continuing his detention was the hope of saving the life of the woman from imminent peril" (at p. 23).

In other words, the violation of liberty was justified in concrete circumstances where that violation had a reasonable chance of saving the life of a woman who was in danger. In circumstances where there seems to be a conflict between what a court says and what it does, we are entitled to follow what it does i.e. reconcile rights which conflict in particular concrete circumstances, rather than apply an abstract hierarchy of rights.

Secondly, the judgment in *Shaw* cannot be taken to mean that an immutable list of precedence of rights can be formulated. The right to life of one person (as in *Shaw's* case) was held to be superior to the right to liberty of another but, quite clearly, the right to life might not be the paramount right in every circumstance. If, for instance, it were necessary for a mother to defend her daughter by attacking a person who was assaulting that daughter, and if she killed that person in the process, I have no doubt but that the right of the girl to bodily integrity would rank higher than the right to life of the person assaulting her. It may be justifiable or excusable for one person to kill another when that act is done in defence of another, subject to proportionate use of violence. In other words, it will not always be the case that a right to life takes precedence over another constitutional right, such as the right to liberty, or to bodily integrity. The reconciliation approach is a better fit with what the majority actually reasoned in *Shaw*. It also has the merit of enabling a fact-specific case-by-case approach to rights conflict.

Before elaborating how the various interests at stake in Article 40.3.3° should be reconciled, I need to address another preliminary issue of interpretation. How should the court approach Article 40.3.3°'s reference to "equality" between the "life" of the unborn and the "life" of the pregnant woman? Are there any significant differences between each form of life that should be taken into consideration when determining equal treatment? Clearly, as I have already stated, the purpose of Article 40.3.3° was to make any implicit commitment to protecting a foetal right to life explicit. But I find it difficult to countenance that the purpose of Article 40.3.3° could have been to devalue the life that sustains the unborn, much less to put it in danger. There is a substantive difference, one that has been long recognized by law, between the two lives. The right of Ms X here is a right to a life in being. The right of the unborn is to a life contingent, contingent on survival in the womb until successful delivery. It is not a question of setting one above the other but rather of vindicating, as far as practicable, the right to life of the pregnant woman, whilst vindicating, as far as practicable, the right to life of the unborn.

Why does this matter? It matters because we need to take the value of constitutional life into account when deciding how to treat the unborn and the pregnant woman as bearers of a right to life (in harmony with the other commitments in the Constitution). For the pregnant woman this means that we need to take her needs seriously as a human being who requires the basics of life to survive—oxygen, food, shelter, rest. But it also means that we need to take into account her life interests as a creative, cultural human being. Moreover, if we value the creative role which women's bodies play in bringing new people into being, then we need to show legal respect for that role.

For the unborn, the situation is different. The unborn is a biological human and a social being, but not yet creative, sentient and conscious. Foetal dependence on the pregnant woman for the basics of life—oxygen, food, shelter and rest—in order for it to become creative, sentient, conscious and capable of independent interaction with others, is unique and vital. To compel a pregnant woman to provide that sustenance to a foetus within her body devalues the significance of pregnancy. To treat the unborn and the pregnant woman as if they were the same forms of life would be disrespectful and dignity-violating because it misrecognises each kind of life.

The equality guarantee in Article 40.1 recognises that differences in capacity, physical, moral and social function matter. As philosophers since Aristotle have recognised, equality is not achieved by treating different entities as if they are the same. Given the substantive differences between an unborn life and a pregnant woman's life and given the need to treat the bearer of a right to life with dignity and freedom and in light of the Christian and democratic nature of the state, it is permissible in principle to authorise the ending of unborn life in order to respect the pregnant woman's life.

Further support for this differentiation between the conflicting rights to life may be found in the constitutional text's explicit recognition of a pregnant woman's personal rights as distinct from the unborn's right to life. Ms X has a right to bodily integrity, a right to liberty, a right to privacy, a right to be free of inhuman and degrading treatment and a right to equality, among other interests. In short, her right to life is to a 'rightful' life that is to a life whose specific texture and tone is protected and enabled by these other rights. The unborn's right to life is to 'bare' biological life. That right may impose an obligation on others to support it, but when there is a conflict, the woman's fuller, rightful life may merit more legal weight than the unborn's bare life.

Ms X's right to life ought to be interpreted in light of the principle established in *The State (C) v. Frawley* [1976] IR 365, at p. 372, that the Executive "may not, without justification or necessity, expose the health of that person to risk or danger". For this reason, I find it impossible to draw sharp lines between life and health. Indeed Kenny J. himself did not make any bright line distinctions between life and bodily integrity, or between life and health, when he was considering whether a violation of bodily integrity had taken place in *Ryan*. Rather he asked whether the plea that fluoridation was dangerous amounted to a plea that the Oireachtas had failed to respect the rights to life *and* bodily integrity (emphasis added).

McGee established a right to marital privacy, and the Eighth Amendment was adopted in part to prevent that right to marital privacy grounding an explicit right to abortion, as happened in the U.S. case of *Roe v. Wade* 410 U.S. 113 (1973). The right to marital privacy is not relevant to Ms X given she is not married. However, the right to marital privacy is one particular instance of a more general right to privacy in one's intimate life. She has a right to be free from unnecessary and excessive scrutiny in her intimate life, including her reproductive life. This is a not an absolute right (cf *Ryan*), but it is a right which certainly needs to be weighed in the balance when deciding the extent of any duty to sustain foetal life under Article 40.3.3°.

Ms X also has a constitutional right to liberty. One of the issues before the Court is whether stopping Ms X from travelling for an abortion is a disproportionate violation of her constitutional right to liberty. Counsel maintained that the right to travel, as recognised in *The State (M) v. The Attorney General* [1979] IR 73 at p. 80 and in *Ryan* at p. 311, was an aspect of the right to liberty. I find it difficult to see why the right to liberty is only being considered in relation to the issue of travel out of the jurisdiction and not in relation to the issue of continuing or ending a pregnancy. It's as if counsel cannot imagine liberty applying to pregnancy as distinct from travel. If her legal right to travel to another jurisdiction and have an abortion is being contemplated as an aspect of her right to liberty, then why not a legal right to have a pregnancy terminated on Irish soil? If the state cannot, without just cause, use its coercive power to stop her from leaving its territory, then surely the state cannot use its coercive power to stop her from leaving pregnancy, without just cause. Preserving the bare biological life of the unborn against the will of a pregnant woman who sustains that unborn with her conscious and sentient life, may not always be just cause, particularly when the woman's life is at risk.

Ms X has a right to be held equal as a person before the law under Article 40.1°. To deny women a say in their own reproductive futures treats them as if their views, wishes and feelings do not matter. Telling someone that her views, wishes and feelings about her own life do not matter is a denial of the very essence of personhood, a denial which men, who also contribute to reproduction, are not required to accept. It is 167 years since Irish philosophers Thompson and Wheeler criticised society for encouraging women to repress their sexuality and for denying women civil rights on the basis of their capacity to bear children (*Appeal of One-half of the Human Race, Women, Against the Pretensions of the Other Half, Men, to Retain Them in Political, and Thence in Civil and Domestic Slavery*, Longman, Hurst, Rees, Orme, Brown and Green, 1825). Surely as this court considers how to balance the right to life of the unborn against the right to life of the pregnant woman, it cannot allow the right to life of the unborn to become the means by which women's equal personhood is denied? Such an outcome would be unjust and unreasonable, if not necessarily arbitrary, and therefore a violation of the equality guarantee (see *O'B v. S* [1984] IR 316).

Given the implications of women's constitutional rights, the social value of their voluntary reproductive contributions, and their status as persons of equal value and individuals bearing dignity and freedom, I cannot accept that there is a clear hierarchy of rights with "bare biological life" at the top. Rather I would say that the first part of the test for lawful abortion is whether there is a risk to the pregnant woman's rightful life that is, to a life lived with bodily integrity, privacy, liberty and equality. The evidence presented to the court by Ms X's mother, by the Garda and by the clinical psychologist was clear and unchallenged in finding that there was a risk of self-destruction. While it was not possible to hear from Ms X directly in this instance, the evidence provided the Court with a clear account of her views, wishes and feelings in relation to this pregnancy. Assessments of the violation of fundamental personal rights should give significant weight to the person most affected. The grounds for a lawful abortion on this first element of the Article 40.3.3° test are more than made out.

Article 40.3.3° permits abortion when vindicating the right to life of the unborn is an impracticable burden on a woman's life

The next question for the Court is when does the right to life of the unborn justify the state in acting to prevent abortion even if a woman's right to life is engaged. Our common and constitutional law recognizes that there are circumstances in which the ordinary right to life is justifiably infringed, notably in self-defence. Secondly, the value of life does not usually justify compelling people to take extraordinary measures to sustain someone else's life against their own will (*McFall v. Shimp* 10 Pa D & C 3d 90; July 26, 1978), or against their own interest where their will cannot be expressed. The legal protection of the ordinary right to life acknowledges that life may be justifiably taken in self-defence, or denied the sustenance of involuntarily donated organs, blood and tissue. Therefore, the starting point for determining the scope of an unborn's right to life is that it at least has similar limits.

Article 40.3.3° refers to the right to life of the unborn, it does not refer to all the rights which a born person has. The text seems to imply a distinction between the unborn as the bearer of right to life as far as practicable, and the born as the bearer of a rightful life, a life of rights to bodily integrity etc. Secondly, there are good evidence-based reasons why the unborn's right to life ought to be recognised as more limited that the ordinary right to life. Unborn life has particular characteristics—non-viable, non-sentient, developmental—which differentiate it from the ordinary right to life and the obligations such a right can impose on others. Unborn life is notoriously fragile and contingent, with one in five pregnancies ending in spontaneous miscarriage. Nature itself decides that a significant number of unborns will not survive pregnancy.

There is extensive medical evidence that before viability (approx. 24 weeks gestation), the foetus could not be capable of sustaining life without the support of the pregnant woman because its lungs are not developed to the point of being capable of resuscitation. The only one who can assist this life in sustaining it to viability is the pregnant woman. This is not the same as born life, which can be assisted by anyone. There are times when an unborn has significant developmental anomalies, such an anencephaly, literally 'without a brain', which mean that even if a child is born alive and capable of drawing its own breath, it will not be able to survive long. In such circumstances, it would simply be futile to recognise unborn life, which cannot sustain itself or cannot be technologically sustained, as imposing obligations of sustenance on a pregnant woman.

Unborn human life is in the process of becoming a legal person, an important legal and social process, which ought to be supported. But to treat the process of becoming a person as if becoming has already been achieved misrecognises the nature of becoming. Women's contributions in pregnancy are necessary for the process of becoming a legal and social person. Women have undertaken them voluntarily with joy and happiness, as well as sometimes with fear and anxiety. To compel these contributions by law is to do a terrible disservice to the history and future of voluntary reproduction.

In summary, where the unborn is unlikely to be born alive, implementing the right to life of the unborn and stopping a woman from having an abortion is likely to be an impracticable burden on a woman's rightful life. Where the unborn is non-viable or non-sentient, preventing an abortion, which would reduce harm to the viable, sentient pregnant woman, is likely to be an impracticable and disproportionate burden on a woman's rightful life. Preventing an abortion, which would implement the reproductive wishes of a pregnant woman, *could* logically be seen as an impracticable burden on a rightful life of dignity and freedom. Who but she can judge whether pregnancy and motherhood fit her life plan, and all the dreams and hopes for the future that fill that plan? My conscience tells me that this life's voluntary contribution to the common good ought to be respected. But I accept that the effect of the Eighth Amendment is to limit women's reproductive choices, qualify their constitutional dignity and freedom, and deny them access to abortion as of personal right.

There was no evidence presented to the court on the material scope of the unborn's right to life. Therefore, the extent to which it is practicable to implement a right to life of the unborn in light of foetal anomalies, viability or sentience, was not tested or proved fully. It remains for the Legislature, or another case before another court, to debate or test those issues and establish binding rules thereon. Although the issues of viability and sentience were not argued fully before the court, this was because the legal assumption was that the unborn was neither viable nor sentient given the early stage of pregnancy. Therefore, the second stage of the test for lawful and constitutional abortion has been made out on the evidence in this case. Ms X is clearly distressed, suffering and being harmed by the continuation of the pregnancy, whereas there is no evidence that the unborn's life is one of distress and suffering since it is incapable of feeling. In these circumstances, sustaining the right to life of the unborn imposes an impracticable burden on the woman's rightful life and she is legally entitled to withdraw her sustenance of the unborn and to any necessary assistance in doing so.

Article 40.3.3° permits consideration of the particular circumstances of pregnancy e.g. maturity, vulnerability, experience of rape or assault, when deciding whether a particular pregnancy has become too burdensome

The test adopted by Costello J. is too narrow for another reason. It is insufficiently attentive to life circumstances that may contribute to a pregnancy becoming too burdensome. Circumstances or conditions, which make the pregnancy more difficult to bear, are relevant to the 'impracticable burden' test. Indeed, youth or experience of sexual assault, are circumstances which *prima facie* may make a particular pregnancy burdensome enough to justify an abortion. They are likely to make a pregnancy harmful for that woman in the sense of causing her pain and suffering. In some circumstances such pain and suffering may amount to inhuman and degrading treatment, and be in breach of her constitutional right to be free of such treatment, as established in *The State (C) v. Frawley* [1976] IR 365 at p. 374. The woman's views as to her experience of pregnancy will be pivotal in such instances however. Some women would rather continue a pregnancy even if young and distressed, or if pregnant as a result of non-consensual sex. This is another example of how the subjective experience of human conditions such as pregnancy, has a material bearing on objective assessment, including assessment as to whether someone is being degraded.

Kenny J.'s obiter comments in *Ryan*, as approved by the Supreme Court, provide support for taking the particular circumstances of the pregnant woman into account with a view to deciding whether a pregnancy is too burdensome on her life. When he was assessing whether the effect of fluoridation was a possible infringement of bodily integrity, he specifically mentioned different groups of people, namely the old, the young, the sick and the healthy. There was no reason on the evidence in that case to find that the young or the sick were in danger, even if the healthy were not. But Kenny J. clearly contemplated a situation where the bodily integrity of the young and sick could be violated even though that of the healthy was not. Similarly, if a pregnant woman is vulnerable or distressed because of her immaturity, ill health, or experience of assault or violence, carrying a pregnancy may be more burdensome for her and more likely to violate her rights to life and to bodily integrity, as compared with a woman who is mature, healthy and free from experiences of violence. In this instance, it is clear that Ms X's youth, suicidal feelings and experience of rape contribute to her pregnancy being impracticably burdensome and mean that her right to life would be violated if she was denied access to abortion.

This Court is aware that rape victims are often reticent to report their experiences to the police partly as a result of the trauma usually caused by rape itself, and partly because of a fear that they will not be believed. The Court has a responsibility to develop its legal rules in a way which supports rape victims in accessing justice. For the purposes of assessing whether a particular pregnancy may be terminated because it imposes an impracticable burden on a woman's rightful life, any claim that the pregnancy resulted from non-consensual sex ought to be assumed to be truthful, unless evidence rebutting such an assumption is presented in court.

Article 40.3.3° imposes public duties to support pregnant life

This Court has focused on the obligations which Article 40.3.3° imposes on the pregnant woman in relation to the sustenance of unborn life, and the circumstances in which those obligations may legitimately end. Article 40.3.3° raises another set of obligations however, as it envisages a positive role for the state in the vindication of the right to life of the unborn through the provision of the necessary agencies to help, counsel and encourage pregnant women in making a decision in accordance with the Constitution and the law. In *Norris* at p. 103, McCarthy J. spoke of the right to life of the unborn as "a sacred trust to which all the organs of government must lend their support". If the Eighth Amendment had not been adopted, it is certainly arguable that compelling a woman to bear all the responsibility of that public trust would be a breach of the constitutional values of dignity and freedom.

Since the Eighth Amendment was adopted, a woman bears the lion's share of that responsibility since her reproductive choices are curtailed. In these circumstances, it is all the more necessary for the state to play a positive role in sharing some reproductive responsibility and supporting women. To do otherwise would be to completely privatise the public duty to defend and vindicate the right to life of the unborn, by locating all responsibility on the individual pregnant woman.

Decision

I have not addressed the issue of E.U. law because I do not consider it necessary, since the issues can be resolved in a manner that is consistent with freedom of movement on the basis of domestic law. But for the sake of clarity I agree with McCarthy J. on that issue.

The injunction is unjustified and the Attorney General was not constitutionally required to act in the way that he did. Ms X has a right to abortion in the Irish health care system on the ground that her pregnancy imposes an impracticable burden on her rightful life. This is a practicable and proportionate interference with the right to life of the unborn, given the distinction between a life contingent and a life in being and given the aggravating circumstances which make Ms X's pregnancy particularly burdensome. The state has a positive duty to support her in accessing that abortion care, in terms that respond attentively to her situation as a woman who is pregnant through non-consensual sex and as a young person whose welfare may require added support, subject to her consent.

19

Commentary on *North Western Health Board v HW and CW* (the PKU case)

DONAL COFFEY

Should the state administer a medical screening test on a child against the wishes of the family? The parents in this case refused to allow a test that would have involved taking a pinprick of blood from the child in order to test for certain metabolic disorders—phenylketonuria, homocystinuria and hypothyroidism (the PKU test). The parents objected on religious grounds, that 'nobody is allowed to injure anyone else'.[1] Based on this conviction, they objected to pricking the skin of their child. The Supreme Court upheld the wishes of the family and refused to order the administration of the test.

The case raises certain questions that are not well addressed in the original judgments. For example, if the implications of the judgment are that a child is at risk of a potentially debilitating illness as a result of the parents' decision, should the parents' wishes be adhered to? If untreated, the conditions covered by the test in *North Western Health Board* can give rise, *inter alia*, to epilepsy, behavioural difficulties, learning disabilities, brain damage, liver dysfunction and sepsis. If the outcome of adherence to familial wishes is to lead to a brain-damaged child, is that a decision that can lawfully be made? This is an unspoken assumption of the majority judgments. Moreover, without much considered discussion, the majority judgment reinforced the powers of parents within the marital family, relegating the consideration of the individual child's interest to extreme cases. It also elided the issues of mandatory medical services and a child's individual best interests. The legal background to both issues is discussed in turn, before considering Maebh Harding's suggested approach in her feminist judgment to protecting individual rights within the constitutional family structure, as contrasted with the general propensity of the Supreme Court towards protecting the unit at all costs.

The Power Structures of the Irish Constitutional Family

Feminist legal theory has always confronted the embeddedness of power structures in society.[2] The feminist legal model—and feminism generally—is concerned not simply with

[1] *North Western Health Board v HW and CW* [2001] 3 IR 622, at 628.

[2] See, eg, Margaret Davies, 'Feminism and the Idea of Law' (2011) 1(1) *Feminists@Law*, at http://journals.kent.ac.uk/index.php/feministsatlaw/article/view/9/66 (last accessed 8 October 2015). Indeed, this focus has been

relations between the state and women, but also with the relationships *within* family models. As a matter of history, the locus has tended to be in areas of traditional male power differentials, eg domestic violence and marital rape.[3]

In Ireland, the constitutional model that was ostensibly favoured by the superior courts was based on a theoretical equality between the sexes. One finds this in the early jurisprudence of the Supreme Court on the operation of Article 42.[4] In practice, this equality did not exist. The operation of social mores, and indeed law, dictated that equality was rarely possible within the family. Unmarried women and children were treated less favourably still. Moreover, the focus on the 'traditional' family meant that alternative views of familial arrangements were systematically disregarded.[5]

Moves towards equality in the family sphere have tended to obscure, at least in the minds of liberal commentators, the still-existing power differential within the family itself. The clearest example of this, and the one which this case confronts, is the case of the child within the family. The monolithic 'family' protected by the constitutional model in *North Western Health Board v HW and CW* admits of only limited possibilities whereby the law can intercede on the child's behalf. The issue with which the majority opinion struggles, is the failure to see children as possessors of equal rights within the family unit and instead to prioritise the family unit.

The position of the family within the Constitution, and the relationship of the various parents, spouses and children of the family to each other, is a key question that Harding J addresses in her dissenting feminist judgment.

Mandatory Medical Services?

The provision of compulsory medical treatment has been a perennial question involving ethics, the limits of state power and the freedom of action of the individual. Contrary to the opinion of the majority of judges in the *North Western Health Board* case,[6] the mandatory provision of the PKU test is widespread. The first statute-based PKU test was pioneered in Massachusetts in 1963, with the vast majority of States in the USA dictating a mandatory test by the time of the *North Western Health Board* case.

However, even where a mandatory test was present, there was normally an exception for the religious belief of the parents. This was not universal, and in seven States there was no exception to the test.[7] West Virginia appears to be alone in failing to provide an exception for the religious belief of parents but still imposing a misdemeanour penalty on those who failed to comply with the test.[8]

directed against 'essentialism' in feminist legal theory itself; see Angela P Harris, 'Race and Essentialism in Feminist Legal Theory' (1990) 42 *Stanford Law Review* 581.

[3] See Jill Hasday, 'Contest and Consent: A Legal History of Marital Rape' (2000) 88 *California Law Review* 1373.

[4] *In the matter of Tilson, Infants* [1951] 1 IR 1, 33–34, 37–38 (Black J dissenting).

[5] *Norris v Attorney General* [1984] 1 IR 36, 58, 91.

[6] See *North Western Health Board v HW and CW* [2001] 3 IR 622, 717 (Denham J) and 742 (Hardiman J).

[7] See table 3.1 in *Genetic Screening: Programs, Principles and Research* (National Academy of Sciences, Washington D.C., 1975).

[8] This penalty is now contained in s 16-22-4 of ch 16 of the West Virginia Code.

The debate about the wisdom of compulsory versus mandatory screening was one that exercised a good deal of people in the medical community in the 1970s and 1980s.[9] At the time the focus was primarily on the ethical, rather than legal, importance of parental consent in such mandatory programmes. One might imagine that the debate broke down along libertarian/communitarian lines. However, one of the most powerful arguments in favour of the necessity for mandatory screening was explicitly based on John Stuart Mill's harm principle, and concluded that there was no reasonable justification that overrode the risk of harm to the child.[10] It is important, however, to bear in mind that the scientific community was divided on the issue of mandatory screening.

It is also important to recognise the importance of value judgements in understanding and applying scientific findings.[11] Recently, the debate about the human-papillomavirus vaccine in the USA has demonstrated the situatedness of ostensibly value-free debates about science.[12] The question of how to interpret purportedly neutral 'facts' is therefore one that pre-eminently concerns feminist theory; as Hawkesworth states, 'epistemological assumptions have political implications'.[13] In this light, the question posed in the *North Western Health Board* case provides an excellent example for the implementation of feminist legal theory. It demonstrates how a change in positional perspective can lead to a different result. As Alcoff notes:

> This difference in positional perspective does not necessitate a change in what are taken to be facts, although new facts may come into view from the new position, but it does necessitate a political change in perspective since the point of departure, the point from which all things are measured, has changed.[14]

The majority in *North Western Health Board* were concerned with the provision of a mandatory test by the state, which focuses on a nationwide test. It is important to distinguish between this approach and that ultimately adopted by Harding J, which focuses on the individual case, and individual child, before the court. The question of the relationship between parental consent and state action in medical cases does, however, feature strongly in the feminist judgment.

The Judgment

Harding J concludes that there is a common law jurisdiction wielded by the courts that can be invoked in this case. This is based on the inherent jurisdiction of the court to protect the

[9] See, eg, Ruth Faden, Judith Chwalow, Neil Holtzman and Susan Horn, 'A Survey to Evaluate Parental Consent as Public Policy for Neonatal Screening' (1982) 72 *American Journal of Public Health* 1347; George J Annas, 'Mandatory PKU Screening: The Other Side of the Looking Glass' (1982) 72 *American Journal of Public Health* 1401.

[10] Faden et al, above n 9.

[11] See, eg, Sharon Crasnow, 'Feminist Philosophy of Science: Values and Objectivity' (2013) 8 *Philosophy Compass* 413; Kristina Rolin, 'Standpoint theory as a methodology for the study of power relations' (2009) 24 *Hypatia: A Journal of Feminist Philosophy* 218.

[12] Dan Kahan, Donald Braman, Geoffrey Cohen, John Gastil and Paul Slovic, 'Who Fears the HPV Vaccine, Who Doesn't, and Why? An Experimental Study of the Mechanisms of Cultural Cognition' (2010) 34 *Law and Human Behavior* 501.

[13] Mary E Hawkesworth, 'Knowers, Knowing, Known: Feminist Theory and Claims of Truth' (1989) 14(3) *Signs* 533, 534.

[14] Linda Alcoff, 'Cultural Feminism versus Post-Structuralism: The Identity Crisis in Feminist Thought' (1988) 13(3) *Signs* 405, 434–35.

welfare of the child. The other potential statute-based mechanisms only apply where either the guardians of the child disagree as to the substance of a decision,[15] or there is a more lasting substituted decision-maker, eg in relation to wardship. This inherent jurisdiction allows a third party with an appropriate personal connection, in this instance the North Western Health Board, to seek to review the decision.

The major point of divergence between the decision of Harding J and the other judges in the case relates to the correct test to be applied when the court is asked to intervene in the family unit on behalf of a child. The understanding of the family as the means by which the welfare of the child is secured, the test proposed by Harding J, re-directs the enquiry under the Constitution. In the view of the majority, the correct decision-maker in almost all circumstances is the family as a unit. However, a feminist approach to judgment means that the assumed institutional structures must be considered, as Harding J argues: 'Making the marital family unit an inviolable space until parents abandon their constitutional duties shields abuse within the family.'

Harding J's test is not an oppositional one whereby the welfare of the child must be weighed against the rights of the family—it is the outcome to be secured by the exercise of those rights. This allows Harding J to reconceptualise the relationship between family members as secured by the Article 42.5. This shift in positional perspective may be seen clearly when Harding J notes, 'The Court has been wary to ensure that the state does not tread on the rights of parents. There has been less emphasis in case law on ensuring that the overarching duty of realising children rights is satisfied.' The shift towards a purposive approach to Article 42.5 means that familial rights do not become an unsustainably high barrier to the vindication of the rights of the child. It is on the basis of this shift in positional perspective that the other judgments of the court are criticised. The disjunction between the institutional family approach of the majority, which does not account for the vulnerable members of the institution, and the purposive approach of Harding J, which does account for those members, exemplifies the feminist approach to power balances.

When applying the principles to the facts of the case, Harding J draws attention to the outcome of failing to treat the disease and the probabilities involved. The question of probability was the subject of a bizarre exchange in oral argument, where counsel for the defendants sought to argue that it was the severity of outcome alone, rather than the possibility of the risk, that was important:

> *Murray J*: Is the level of risk of relevance?
>
> *Mr. O'Donnell SC*: I do not balance the medical risk.[16]

This argument is one that cannot be justified and is rightfully avoided in Harding J's opinion. Both the severity of outcome and the possibility of that outcome's occurring must surely play a role in the determination of whether to intervene in a particular case. It is noteworthy in this regard that the probability of PKU in Ireland stands at 1/4,500, while the probability in the USA (where mandatory screening exists in almost all States) is over three times lower, at approximately 1/15,000. In the USA, this lower probability was sufficient to set in train a movement to screen children across the country. The higher probability in

[15] See, eg, *C.O'S v Doyle* [2013] IESC 60.
[16] *North Western Health Board v HW and CW* [2001] 3 IR 622, 653.

Ireland should therefore indicate that the outcome is more threatening still. If the judgement call is a difficult one, then the court will stand over the decision of the parents. If the call is not difficult, then the court will not stand over the decision, for this would conflict with the purposive rationale behind Harding J's interpretation of Article 42.5.

Moreover, Harding J draws attention to what is assumed *sotto voce* in the decision itself: the child in question would have already presented symptoms of several of the conditions before the case was completed if, in fact, he suffered from the disease. This is a particularly problematic form of abductive reasoning. It raises the question of whether the majority's reasoning would have been the same if, in fact, Paul had presented with brain damage. In that case, the individual consequences would be demonstrably, terribly obvious. Moreover, if the outcome would be different in such a case, it follows that the test to be deployed should be one that obviates the need for a child to present with such a disease. Therefore, the test that should be used is one which concentrates on the rights of an individual child, the child before the Court, rather than on a general familial right. In the words of Harding J, 'To turn away from such a child would amount to state protection of objectively harmful decisions at the expense of that individual child in order to protect the principle that most parents do the right thing.'

Implications

The decision of the Supreme Court was one of a series of cases in the early 2000s where the judiciary was unwilling to decide cases in which it was felt another institution was a more appropriate decision-maker.[17] These decisions were based on an interpretation of the Constitution that strictly cabined the powers of the judiciary. The same judicial deference is evinced in *North Western Health Board*. Moreover, Paul Ward has drawn attention to the difference between the current case and the decision of the Supreme Court in *The Western Health Board v Karen M*, where the wishes of a mother that her child not be placed for foster care outside the jurisdiction were overridden.[18] This was based on the fact that in *Karen M* there was a legislative basis for the order, and that the mother was not constitutionally protected to the same degree as she was not part of the marital family. In 2006, the Ombudsman for Children pointed out that this judicial reticence left a 'lacuna in the current legislative framework where children's rights are concerned'.[19]

It also shares with those other cases a certain tendency towards histrionics, which undermines the quality of legal reasoning in the decision. For example, in *North Western Health Board*, the trial judge made reference to Aldous Huxley's novel *Brave New World* in the following manner:

> If the State were entitled to intervene in every case where professional opinion differed from that of the parents, or where the State considered that the parents were wrong in a decision, we would be

[17] See, eg, *TD v Minister for Education* [2001] 4 IR 259; *Sinnott v The Minister for Education* [2001] 2 IR 545.

[18] Paul Ward, 'The Child and the State' (2003) *International Survey of Family Law* 217, 237.

[19] The All-Party Oireachtas Committee on the Constitution, *10th Progress Report: The Family* (Dublin, Stationery Office, 2006) A215.

> rapidly stepping towards the 'Brave New World' in which the State always knows best. In my view that situation would be totally at variance with both the spirit and the word of the Constitution.[20]

The attempt by the judiciary to treat as equivalents the dystopian nightmare of Huxley's vision and a heel-prick test, without which a child may suffer brain damage, is wildly overblown. Nonetheless, the equivalence is based on the positional perspective, where any attempt to ameliorate parental control over individual children is on a spectrum with the very worst attempts to obliterate parental control. This does not sound judicial reasoning make. The test proposed by Harding J preserves the presumption that the best decision-makers are the child's parents, but allows for the presumption to be rebutted where such is in the best interests of the child. The feminist approach does not automatically privilege the wishes of the familial unit, focusing instead on the best interests of the weakest member of that unit.

The question of the weight to be given to the parents' views is also one to which feminist theory must give weight. The debate about whether and how multiculturalism and feminism are compatible is an involved one.[21] This becomes more complicated when dealing with the rights of parents over the child's medical treatment.[22] Harding J deals with this issue by stressing that in most circumstances, the decision of the parent will be determinative; it is only where it conflicts with the best interests of the child that it will not be adhered to.

Moreover, later developments demonstrate a real failure by the judiciary to understand what the *North Western Health Board* case was about at a factual level. In *C.O'S v Doyle*, MacMenamin J presented the case as follows, 'both the parents objected to the State vaccination scheme'.[23] Of course, *North Western* was not a vaccination case; it was a diagnostics case. That is, the PKU test would only reveal whether or not the child had one of the conditions; it was not designed to prevent the child from getting the disease. This is a very obvious scientific mistake, and leads to the suspicion that the courts are simply uncomfortable trying to understand the science underlying the decision. In light of such discomfiture, they defer to the parents' decision. This allows the judiciary to stand over a constitutional principle: judicial deference. Deference obscures the role that the judiciary should play: the vindication of the rights of the child. Harding J's opinion forces the judge to consider what is, as a matter of fact, in the child's best interest, and refuses to rely on judicial deference. It requires the judge to perform an evaluative role.

The test proposed by Harding J may have obviated the need to restate this test in the 31st Amendment to the Constitution.[24] The new Article 42A.2.1° provides:

> In exceptional cases, where the parents, regardless of their marital status, fail in their duty towards their children to such extent that the safety or welfare of any of their children is likely to be prejudicially affected, the State as guardian of the common good shall, by proportionate means as

[20] This quotation was approved by Hardiman J in *North Western Health Board v HW and CW* [2001] 3 IR 622, 757.

[21] See, eg, Oonagh Reitman, 'Multiculturalism and Feminism: Incompatibility, compatibility or synonymity?' (2005) 5(2) *Ethnicities* 216; Monica Mookherjee, 'Autonomy, Force and Cultural Plurality' (2008) 14 *Res Publica* 147.

[22] See Caroline Bridge, 'Religion, Culture and Conviction' (1999) 11 *Child and Family Law Quarterly* 1.

[23] *C.O'S v Doyle* [2013] IESC 60, [23].

[24] Thirty-First Amendment of the Constitution (Children) Act 2012.

> provided by law, endeavour to supply the place of the parents, but always with due regard for the natural and imprescriptible rights of the child.

The refashioning of the Constitution so that it protects the 'safety and welfare' of children as against parental failure was a recognition that the jurisprudence of the Irish courts meant that the welfare of the child was treated as being subsidiary to the integrity of the family unit, rather than the family unit's being treated as the means by which the welfare of the child was to be accomplished. Furthermore, a failure to re-examine the judicial outlook underlying *North Western Health Board* presents a potential future difficulty in the development of constitutional law in this area. If the fundamental position is not considered anew, ideally on the basis of feminist jurisprudence, there exists the possibility that the interpretation of Article 42.A.2.1° will proceed from the same familial unit perspective, and repeat the errors of *North Western Health Board*.

The North Western Health Board, Plaintiff v H.W. and C.W., Defendants

[2000 No. 6348 P.; S.C. No. 321 of 2000]

High Court	27th October, 2000
Supreme Court	8th November, 2001

Harding J 8th November, 2001

How far should the Irish state go to protect children from the damaging effects of poor parental choices? Failure by the court to take action leaves Paul, a vulnerable baby, at risk of developing life threatening metabolic conditions. The damage caused by these conditions cannot be reversed but can be easily prevented with timely, appropriate, medical treatment. What degree of freedom should Irish law give parents to make irrational decisions where the evidence before the court shows that the individual interests and rights of a particular child are being adversely affected?

Paul is 14 months old. He lives with his parents and his four brothers and sisters in Donegal. There is no question raised about Paul's parents' abilities to care for the children in the long term and it seems that their home is warm and loving.

The North Western Health Board provides a free screening programme for new-born children in the area to detect biochemical and metabolic disorders. This test, known as the PKU, or Guthrie test, detects the presence of five conditions; phenylketonuria, galactosaemia, homocystinuria, maple syrup urine disease and hypothyroidism. These conditions are detected by means of a 'heel prick' where blood is taken from the child's heel and sent to Dublin for analysis. All five conditions are caused by the body's inability to break down amino acids or produce essential hormones. Over time, the effects of these metabolic disorders cause mental disabilities and life threatening illness. All are treatable but any damage caused before treatment commences is irreversible.

Paul was born at home. Paul's parents have objected to the PKU test being carried out. The parents made similar objections to the testing of Paul's older sister, Mary. Mary had the PKU test several years ago against the wishes of her parents under the terms of an interim care order granted to the North Western Health Board by the District Court. Paul's parents feel that the PKU test is invasive and offends their religious belief that nobody is allowed to injure anyone else. Moreover, the parents assert that Mary became very unsettled for a long period after the test was carried out. On balance they have decided that it is not something that they want for their child. Should the court interfere with this decision?

This case raises three legal issues for the determination of the court. 1) In what circumstances does the court have the power to intervene in parental decision-making to uphold the individual rights of the child? 2) Is the exercise of the court's inherent jurisdiction appropriate where the child remains within the family or is intervention limited to existing statutory mechanisms? 3) Is the test for exercising inherent jurisdiction satisfied in Paul's case?

Protecting the Individual Rights of the Child

The individual rights of children are not given an adequate level of recognition in Irish constitutional law. Although the rights of children are recognised in the text of the Constitution itself, they are inevitably constructed in Irish jurisprudence as being consistent with the wishes and desires of their parents, except in the most extreme circumstances. This tendency is partially attributable to the structure of the constitutional protections that attach to the marital family and its members.

The personal rights of children are given the same protection under Article 40.3.1° as those of any other citizen although they may be differently realised (*State (Nicolau) v. An Bord Uchtála* [1966] I.R. 591). These rights include 'the right to be fed and to live, to be reared and educated, to have the opportunity of working and of realising his or her full personality and dignity as a human being' (*G v. An Bord Uchtála* [1980] 1 I.R. 32, 56). In order to ensure that children reach their full potential as individuals, Article 42 expressly guarantees children a religious moral, intellectual, physical and social education and Article 42.4 obliges the state to provide children with free primary education.

Article 42 places a duty on parents to provide such an education according to their means, but where they fail in their duties the onus falls on the State 'as guardian of the common good'.

Parents could not fulfil their duties towards their children without legal rights to make decisions about the upbringing of their children. Families are deeply personal, private places. Parents must have the freedom and authority to create their own family dynamic without undue outside interference. The Irish constitutional structure retains an outdated distinction between marital and non-marital families. Article 42 imposes an inalienable right and duty on married parents to provide for the religious and moral, intellectual, physical and social education of their children. The courts have additionally recognised several constitutional parental rights attaching to the mothers of non-marital children under Article 40.3 including the right of custody (*G v. An Bord Uchtála* [1980] 1 I.R. 32, 85). Such rights are accorded in so far as they are necessary for the parent to promote their children's constitutional rights. They are not standalone rights.

The message of the courts and the Constitution is clear; parental rights are accorded to parents in order to allow them to fulfil their parental duties towards their children. Upholding parental rights to make decisions about their children's upbringing is not an inherent good in and of itself. Parental rights are instrumental to ensuring that children's rights are upheld. That is the reason for their existence. The rights of parents are inalienable only when being exercised within their protected scope—to fulfil that parent's constitutional duty towards their child. O'Higgins C.J. warns that the State may have an obligation to protect a child even against its mother, 'if her natural rights are used in such a way as to endanger the health or life of the child or to deprive him of his rights' (*G v. An Bord Uchtála* [1980] 1 I.R. 32, 56).

However, Irish constitutional protection of the family is more complicated than merely considering the conflicting personal rights of parents and children. Article 41 of the Irish Constitution protects the institution of the marital family itself as the fundamental unit of Irish society. By making the marital family a specially protected space, both parents and children are accorded further rights as part of this collective family unit, such as the right to a family life together. However, family members must retain their individual rights within the confines of the marital family unit.

Sometimes vindicating the rights of the individuals within a marital family does not align with maintaining the integrity of the family unit itself. The court must grapple with the relative importance of preserving the structure of the marital family at the expense of its component parts. As a nation we have historically ignored the individual rights of family members in favour of the greater goal of preserving the family structure even where that structure is an empty shell. Let us not forget that the right to leave the structure of the marital family through divorce required a number of divisive constitutional referenda. The individual rights of the spouses for whom the reality of marriage was intolerable, such as victims of violent abuse, were secondary to preserving the ideal of the marital family. We must be cautious not to forge a similar approach to protecting the individual rights of children.

Parents are the decision makers of the marital family. An interference with their decisions not only interferes with their individual rights as parents but also interferes with the marital family as a protected and private space for child rearing. In general, parents are the best people to care for their children and make all day to day decisions. The natural bonds of love and affection between parent and child mean that parents will usually want what is best for their child and often make considerable sacrifices to make this happen. Parents grapple with difficult and multifaceted decisions in the upbringing of the child. It is not easy to predict the future, to know, for example, what school would be best for a child or the consequences of a decision to let the child take up a potentially dangerous sporting activity. Short term detriment or discomfort must be balanced against the potential future benefits of any decision. Parents do their best; they know their children and they have to live with the consequences of their decisions. This is the reason why Irish law accords a general autonomy to parents in their decision making, but this cannot always be guaranteed. Unfettered parental rights may be abused. If a society simply defers to parental care within individual families it must have a realistic mechanism for insuring that the child's need for safety and rights to realise his or her full potential are protected within the confines of the family; marital or otherwise.

My colleagues on the bench are unanimous in holding that parental rights are not absolute; that the state can intervene to protect children. The question is when it is appropriate to do so and whether any appropriate legal mechanism for doing so exists.

Article 42.5 places an express duty on the state 'to supply the place of the parents' in certain circumstances:-

> "In exceptional cases, where the parents for physical or moral reasons fail in their duty towards their children, the State as guardian of the common good, by appropriate means shall endeavour to supply the place of the parents, but always with due regard for the natural and imprescriptible rights of the child."

The duty placed on the state is to ensure that the rights of children are upheld. However, the state is not the primary body tasked with this duty; parents are. Within Article 42.5 is assumption that a life in state care or an adoptive family is second to life in a loving functional family. There a clear duty on the State to step in as a substitute permanent carer where the child has no parents and Article 42.5 has been invoked to justify state care in cases where no parent could be found to care for a child (*F.N. v. Minister for Education* [1995] 1 I.R. 409 and *D.G. v. Eastern Health Board* [1997] 3 I.R. 511).

The appropriate scope of the State's duty to step in where parents have *failed* in their constitutional duty toward the child is much more difficult. The issue has been scrutinised by this court in the context of involuntary adoption; the most permanent substitution of all. The state must use a liberal standard before removing a child from its birth family and replacing the parents with adoptive parents or other permanent care givers. Permanent intervention into the family unit is the most draconian form of state intervention and must be a proportionate response. This type of parental failure occurs only in exceptional cases. A child's right to be protected must be given due regard but their right to be part of an intact marital family must also be considered. The court must consider not only whether intervention is appropriate but also whether the proposed course of action of substitute care is one that will best realise the child's right to realise his or her full potential, in the circumstances of the case before them.

The Court has been wary to ensure that the state does not tread on the rights of parents. There has been less emphasis in case law on ensuring that the overarching duty of realising children's rights is satisfied. In *Re Article 26 and the Adoption (No. 2) Bill 1987* ([1989] 1 I.R. 656, 665–666) the court held that in order for adoption to be a proportionate interference with parental rights, *both* a failure in duty *and* clear abandonment of parental rights was required. In practice, we have seen that the twin criteria of failure and abandonment are very difficult to satisfy even where it is clear that the child's rights have been infringed and adoption seems to be the best solution.

In *Re J.H. v. An Bord Uchtála* ([1985] I.R. 375) this undue emphasis on the rights of parents when applying the Article 42.5 test, developed in the context of involuntary adoption, was extended to the less interventionist issue of custody. In that case, unmarried parents had placed their daughter for adoption and later married. As a result of their marriage the adoption order was quashed and the parents then sought custody of their then two year old daughter child from the would-be adoptive parents. Expert evidence was submitted that the child would be at risk of long-term harm if custody was transferred to the natural parents.

In the Supreme Court, Finlay C.J. was clear. The state cannot supplant the parents by making custody orders unless the Article 42.5 test is satisfied. When the case was returned to the High Court, Lynch J. ordered the transfer of custody with concern about the consequences for the child who had spent 3 years with her foster parents. He reasoned that the change would be no more traumatic than a parent dying which many children would unfortunately have to deal with. This approach, which prioritises parental rights as a goal in and of themselves, is hardly consistent with the court's overarching constitutional duty to uphold the child's right to self-realisation and dignity.

I have serious concerns about the extension of this interpretation of the Article 42.5 test to the issue of custody. A custody order is a much lesser interference with parental rights than an adoption order. In all cases prior to *Re J.H.*, the issue before the court had been a permanent end to the child's education by his or her parents. The parents had either died or permanently abandoned the exercise of their parental duties. On the facts of *Re J.H.*, a custody order would have meant an end to the meaningful exercise of the rights of the parents and could be distinguished on that basis. However, some of my fellow judges on the bench endorse the ruling and see fit to extend the same interpretation of the Article 42.5 test, developed in the context of involuntary adoption, to all situations where the court is asked to vindicate the individual rights of a child in defiance of parental wishes. The high standard that must be met before the court can order an involuntary adoption is not appropriate for cases such as Paul's case before us, where the ongoing exercise of parental rights is not in question and the proposed state intervention is not as extreme.

The structure of Articles 41 and 42 of the Constitution has led some of my colleagues to the rather lazy assumption that the individual rights of the child are inevitably best protected by upholding the integrity of the marital family unit. This approach, most expressly stated by my colleague, Hardiman J. (*North Western Health Board v. H.W. & C.W.* [2001] 3 I.R. 622, 765), replaces the overarching duty of the court to uphold the individual rights of the child with a duty to uphold parental rights and maintain the family unit, on the assumption that this will achieve the same end. Yet for many unfortunate children the marital family unit is the most dangerous place of all. To limit the court's ability to uphold the individual rights of the child to 'exceptional circumstances' narrowly defined, falls very short of the court's duty to uphold the rights of the child to realise full personality and dignity. My sister, Denham J., would limit questioning of parental decisions to surgical decisions in relation to an imminent threat to life or serious injury. My other colleagues make the duty even narrower, finding it difficult to come up with even one practical example of when such a duty would arise. Murray J. limits it to immediate and fundamental threats to the capacity of the child to continue to function as a human person, physically, morally or socially, deriving from an exceptional dereliction of duty on the part of parents to justify such an intervention. With respect, these theoretical situations would surely satisfy the current test for involuntary adoption. A nearly irrebuttable presumption that the decisions of married parents always uphold the best interests of their children cannot be what was intended by the framers of the Constitution and is inconsistent with the court's duty to uphold the personal rights of children as individuals under Article 40.3.1°.

Making the marital family unit an inviolable space until parents completely abandon their constitutional duties shields abuse within the family. In doing so the state abdicates responsibility for the welfare of children who do not live in a loving family. We ignore these vulnerable children for the sake of children living in the ideal marital family which must remain unimpeachable. This 'all or nothing' approach to intervention allows more invasive types of intervention in the very worst situations but allows the state to do very little before the family reaches this stage. There is no scale for proportionate intervention. To limit the development of the law in this way turns our back on the children for whom the paradigm marital family is not a reality, ignoring their personal rights in the day to day reality of their lives.

I agreed with the concerns raised by Keane C.J. that such a parental-rights-focused interpretation of Article 42.5 extends a test, designed to justify the most permanent and invasive type of state intervention, to all types of cases which impact in any way on parental freedom to make decisions. This is disproportionate and would gravely endanger not only Paul but the interests of all children. There is a distinction to be made between the state's duty to take over from parents where they have failed and the state's duty to ensure that children's rights are preserved within their birth family. Adapting the metaphor used by my colleague, Hardiman J., the state should act, not as a super-parent, but as a watchdog to vindicate children's rights.

A better approach is to distinguish between different levels of intervention and ask whether the intervention proposed can be justified in the circumstances to uphold the child's rights or, to use the traditional words of statute, 'further the best interests or welfare of the child'. For example, in *P.W. v. A.W.*, (Unreported High Court Ellis J., 21 April 1979), Ellis J. held that the assumption of parental custody was only a pragmatic starting point.

Under Article 42 a child's rights must be vindicated by leaving her in the custody of her aunt, the solution that furthered her best interests. Parental rights were respected as far as possible because her parents retained guardianship.

There is space for a purely child-centred jurisdiction within our constitutional rights framework when dealing with the ongoing exercise of parental authority. Most parental decisions are entirely unquestioned. Where an issue is brought to the attention of the court respect for the rights of parents is preserved within the structure of the legal system and the way in which evidence is assessed by the court. Parents can take legal action to uphold their own rights and they can respond to court proceedings. Children cannot. Irish law contains no statutory mechanism by which a child can directly seek the adjudication of the courts in a question relating to their own upbringing. Either their guardian or the Health Board must bring such proceedings on their behalf. The way in which evidence is assessed when a case comes to court is also deferential to parental decision making. Parents have ample opportunity to explain their decisions and their plans to further the long term interest of the child. The court must consider, not only the evidence that the child's rights are infringed but also evidence relating to the disadvantages of intervention and the need to promote the stability of a particular family unit. Where the evidence suggests that parents are making a difficult judgment call, with similar risks on both sides, the court will stand over such decisions.

As members of the judiciary we are under an obligation to ensure that the most vulnerable in our society receive the same protection as the strongest. This requires us to take the individual interests of children seriously, not merely agree with parents where serious questions are raised that their choice of action will have a long term detrimental impact on the child.

The Place of Inherent Jurisdiction

Different mechanisms exist in statute law to allow varying levels of intervention into the family. Historically the statutory test for balancing the interests of parents and children is the welfare principle. The principle is one which predates the 1937 Constitution and is commonly used in wardship proceedings. The duty on the court is the same as that imposed by Article 40.3.1°. The court is asked to consider whether the intervention proposed can be justified in the circumstances to further the child's best interests; upholding the child's rights to realise their full personality and dignity as a human being.

There are three statutory mechanisms by which the court can question parental autonomy. This is the first case in which the court finds itself asked to overrule a single parental decision made jointly by two parents because its legitimacy has been questioned by a third party. The statutory mechanisms do not apply to this situation but they must be examined to see if they are sufficient to vindicate the rights of children or whether it is necessary for the court to invoke inherent jurisdiction to provide a suitable mechanism by which to fulfil its constitutional duty to uphold Paul's rights.

Under section 11 of the Guardianship of Infants Act 1964, the guardians of an infant may apply to the court for a direction on any question affecting the welfare of a child and the court may make such order as it thinks proper. This mechanism is only open to the guardians of children and is used when parents disagree. It provides no solution where the joint decision of both guardians is under scrutiny. The legitimacy of the court's decision where parents disagree comes from the fact that the parents have invited the court in. In such circumstances the welfare of the child is to be the court's *first and paramount concern* in matters relating to the upbringing of children (section 3 of The Guardianship of Infants Act 1964). The welfare test requires the court, when balancing all the competing interests, to choose the result which maximises the child's best interest. The maximisation of the child's welfare is not something that is balanced against interference with parental rights. It is what is achieved when competing interests are balanced correctly. Within the welfare test is the understanding that parental rights exist for the benefit of children and that the welfare of the child is factually linked to a continuing relationship with the child's parents. The wishes and interests of the parents are taken into account as a matter of evidence in establishing what is in the best interests of the child but are not weighed against the child's interest. The test places the responsibility on the court to find the best solution for the particular child in each individual case.

The statutory basis for formal state intervention into the family is the Child Care Act 1991. Section 3 places a duty on the Health Board to promote the welfare of children in their area. Section 15 of this Act places a duty on Health Boards to apply to the District Court for a care or supervision order if a child in their area requires care or protection which he is unlikely to receive without the making of the care order. A care order is a highly interventionist measure which hands over wholescale decision-making power to the Health Board for a limited period of time. The Health Board must have regard to the rights and duties of parents and the principle that it is generally in the best interest of a child to be brought up in his own family. The structure of the Act promotes the long-term upbringing of children within the family unit which is appropriate when considering this level of intervention.

Under s.18(1) of the Child Care Act 1991, the court will not make a care order unless it is satisfied that:-

> (a) the child has been or is being assaulted, ill-treated, neglected or sexually abused, or
> (b) the child's health, development or welfare has been or is being avoidably impaired or neglected, or
> (c) the child's health, development or welfare is likely to be avoidably impaired or neglected,
>
> *and* that the child requires care or protection which he is unlikely to receive unless the court makes an order under this section.

Once a child is the subject of a care order, parental objections to medical treatment can be overridden by the court (*A. and B. v Eastern Health Board* [1998] 1 I.R. 464). The question arises whether a care order can be made for the purpose of overriding parental objections to a diagnostic test where there are no other concerns about the parent's ability to care for the child. Under s. 18(1) (c) of the Child Care Act 1991 the District Court may make a care order where it considers the child's health, development and welfare likely to be 'avoidably impaired or neglected' and the child requires care which he is unlikely to receive unless the court makes an order. Such an order was obtained from the District Court to ensure that Paul's sister, Mary received the PKU test. The District Court refused to make a similar order in this case. On appeal, the Circuit Court has suggested that, due to the emphasis in the Child Care Act 1991 on promoting the long-term upbringing of children within the family, care orders are appropriate only where the parents provide a generally inadequate level of care; they are not an appropriate mechanism for considering one decision in isolation. I do not wish to comment on whether a care order should have been used in this case. The Health Board has not appealed this decision but has sought to fulfil its statutory duty to promote Paul's welfare by other means. The assessment of whether or not section 18 is satisfied is a factual decision to be made by the District Court. Consistency can be difficult to achieve. However, the focus of section 18 of the Child Care Act 1991 is on the detriment to the child rather than the actions of the parents and this should not be forgotten when promoting long term care within the family.

The ward of court mechanism has previously been used by this court to protect children from the decisions of their parents. The origin of wardship lies in the idea that the Sovereign as *parens patriae* had a duty to protect his subjects, particularly children or those who were unable to protect themselves. This duty passed to the Lord Chancellor, the Court of Chancery and to the Lord Chief Justice of Ireland under the Government of Ireland Act 1920. The continuation of the duty is reflected today in the role imposed on the state by Article 42 as 'guardian of the common good'. Wardship now vests in the Irish High Court and has statutory basis under section 9 of the Courts (Supplemental Provisions) Act 1961 which reads—'there shall be vested in the High court the jurisdiction in lunacy and minor matters which was formerly exercised by the Lord Chancellor of Ireland'.

The original function of wardship was to protect the property of a minor whose parents were dead or unavailable. A petition for the court to consider making an individual a ward of court can be made by any individual. When a child is made a ward of court both the ward's person and property are subject to the court's control and parental rights of decision-making are superseded for all matters. Wardship continues until it is discharged. When deciding to exercise its wardship jurisdiction the High Court must be satisfied that a child is at serious risk *and* that it is appropriate that the child should be brought into wardship (*Eastern Health Board v. M.K. and M.K.* [1999] 1 J.I.C. 2902). Paul's circumstances may indeed warrant wardship but the powers of the court under wardship are broader than necessary to resolve the issue before the court.

As can be seen, the statutory mechanisms for questioning parental decision-making in Irish law are very limited. None are open to the child. Only guardians may ask for a determination on a particular question. All other mechanisms are for a short or long term substitution for all parental decision making.

Yet the formal wardship mechanism is only one part of the inherent jurisdiction of the High Court. The inherent jurisdiction of the High Court is a flexible protective jurisdiction based on a duty to protect vulnerable individuals, including children, from harm. It can be used for the narrower purpose of reviewing a single decision unless abrogated by statute or the constitution itself.

I agree with Keane J. that an inherent jurisdiction to examine parental decisions to protect the individual rights of the child still exists in Irish law. Children cannot easily bring actions to court to protect their own interests, they are not an active part of the legislature and they cannot advocate their own rights. A legal mechanism is required to protect their rights where they are threatened by the decisions of others. The need for such a jurisdiction was recognised at a point in history where individual rights were accorded less value than they are now. In the absence of a express statutory mechanism by which to review parental decisions made by an intact family unit the existence of such a jurisdiction to protect vulnerable children from harm caused by decisions which may adversely impact the child's constitutional rights is surely constitutionally mandated.

Inherent jurisdiction allows any third party with an appropriate personal connection to the child to invoke the jurisdiction of the High Court to protect that child's rights. Here the refusal of Paul's parents to allow the PKU test puts him at risk of potential harm. The Health Board has a statutory duty to provide for Paul's welfare. It has brought this matter to the High Court's attention for determination of what should happen to Paul. Statutory measures to deal with this type of situation have not been enacted. It has been determined by the District Court that a care order is not an appropriate way of considering the issue on the facts. Inherent jurisdiction is the only mechanism that exists for Paul's individual interests to be formally considered.

Without such a jurisdiction, potential violations of children's rights could only be challenged in the most extreme cases. This would ignore the entire tradition of wardship and inherent jurisdiction which recognised the vulnerability of individuals and sentence the most at risk children to invisibility in the eyes of the state. With no one but their parents to promote their interests they would simply never be heard.

Should the Court Override the Decision of Paul's Parents?

When making a decision under protective inherent jurisdiction the High Court must weigh up all the evidence available and make a decision that furthers the best interests of the child. It is important to assess the potential harm by looking at both the nature of the risk (high or low) and the remoteness of that harm (i.e. the likelihood of it happening). The court must also review the impact of the type of measure needed to obviate the risk when determining whether intervention is justified in the circumstances or, to use the traditional language of inherent jurisdiction, furthers the best interests of the child in the particular circumstances.

The potential harm:-

1. Paul remains at risk of developing any one of three conditions; phenylketonuria, homocystinuria and hypothyroidism. The risk posed by these conditions is substantial. The Health Board describe consequences of failing to treat these disorders as catastrophic.
2. Phenylketonuria is a genetic condition where the body is unable to break down a substance called phenylanine which builds up in the blood. High levels of phenylanine cause damage to the brain. Without early treatment children with this condition develop severe mental disabilities rendering the child unable to lead an independent life. It also heightens the risk of death by strokes or embolism. If a PKU test is not done, Phenylketonuria will not be detected until the child's brain damage exhibits in behaviour difficulties or epilepsy. By this time the damage is irreversible.
3. Homocystinuria is an inability to break down a different amino acid—homocysteine. This causes skeletal abnormalities, vision problems, brain damage and an increased risk of blood clots. Again the only diagnosis is the detection of the damage done: delayed development, mental disability and vision problems. It is treated by taking vitamin supplements.

4. Congenital hypothyroidism is caused by an undeveloped thyroid gland. Again it is easily treated with supplements but there is no way of reversing the serious disabilities a child will develop if they do not receive early treatment.
5. We are told that the rate of phenylketonuria in Ireland is 1 in 4,500 births. The risk of homocystinuria is 1 in 49,000. Congenital hypothyroidism is present in 1 in 3,500 births. The risk is not highly probable, it is remote, but it remains a real possibility.

The risk of damage to Paul's health if he does have one of these metabolic disorders is great if it goes undetected but the probability of such a situation is remote. Is this a risk we are happy to let a 1 year old take? Are we to hope that Paul is lucky? My fellow judges have declared the risk to Paul to be minimal, relying on the low level of probability. They agree that where the outcome of death or serious disability was a clear one, then the court could certainly exercise jurisdiction. If the probability of the damage was higher but the level of risk slightly lower they also admit that they may have felt otherwise. Where the level of risk is high but it is a real possibility the court should look in addition at the impact of intervention before deciding whether or not overruling parental decisions would be the best course of action to further the interests of the child.

Counsel argued that this case could be distinguished from situations in which there was an immediate threat to life but this is a false distinction which focuses on the immediacy of risk over the probability of harm and the level of harm. Paul is no longer at risk of developing galactosaemia or maple syrup urine disease as symptoms of these conditions would by now have presented. However, galactosaemia is a rapidly fatal disorder and maple syrup urine disease causes rapid brain damage and eventual death. The risk to Paul's life if he had had one of the metabolic disorders which are now ruled out would have been immediate. If Paul had had these conditions which had gone untreated, he would by now be dead or severely disabled. The question of whether or not a PKU test should be carried out may indeed involve an immediate threat to life.

The impact of intervention:-

1. Treatment for all three conditions is simple and relatively non–invasive. If phenylketonuria is detected the child will be put on a low-protein diet and will have to take an amino acid supplement. Similar preventive measures are taken with the other conditions. But what of the consequences of interference with the wishes of Paul's parents? How will this level of intervention impact on long term family life? What weight should be given to the desirability of upholding the wishes of Paul's parents?
2. In wardship cases where the goal of the court is to further the best interests of the child, parental rights are given evidential weight (*In Re A. Ward of Court* [1996] 2 I.R. 79. 117). This requires the court to listen to the parents' objections and understand why they are objecting. Here, the parent's objections to the test are based partially on a false understanding of the risks involved. None of Paul's four brothers and sisters had any of the conditions. However, four negative tests does not rule out the possibility that the parents are carriers. Paul's level of risk is not less than any of his older siblings. If both parents are carriers there is a risk of one in four that any child will inherit one of the conditions.
3. It was raised in the High Court that Pauls' parents are objecting to the test on the basis of religious belief. They stated 'It is our strong religious belief that nobody is

allowed to injure anyone else.' The point was not taken any further and it is difficult to give weight to the right to religious freedom when it is not clear whether this is part of set of religious principles or merely a personal belief. If it is merely a personal belief, its rationality should be questioned. The injury caused to Paul by denying him the test and letting him run the risk of severe brain damage is far greater than the injury done to him by the heel prick. When refusal is based on adherence to a set of religious beliefs the court may balance the benefit of religious compliance against the risk to the physical wellbeing of the child when deciding what is in the child's best interest.

4. The only foreseeable detriment to Paul of having such a test would be the potential upheaval to the family unit. Paul will remain in the care of his parents and this is not questioned by either side but their relationship with Paul may be damaged by this court intervention. In contrast, failure to have the test carries a small but very serious risk of long term damage to Paul's health and quality of life.
5. The intervention amounts to a once off event, not a severance of parental authority but a temporary limitation. The stigma of the test will not affect the nature of Paul's upbringing in the same way that medical treatment in contravention of religious tenets might alienate a family from their religious community.
6. Counsel have argued that a decision to intervene in this case would have an impact, not only on Paul's family but on all families. They argued that if the PKU test is determined to be in Paul's best interests it would be rendered compulsory for all children in all circumstances. This black and white thinking ignores the adjudicative function of the court to ascertain when intervention is proportionate on the evidence presented to the court in any particular case. Here, the court must weigh up not only the medical evidence but Paul's particular circumstances and the evidence of the effect ordering such a test would have on the integrity of Paul's family. For another child, in slightly different circumstances the decision may be different. By refusing to question a decision because we cannot be certain it will be questionable for all families, we ignore children in cases where the evidence demonstrates that parents have made a decision that materially and detrimentally affects a child's rights. When making legislation, the Oireachtas balances public interest but cannot tailor to the reality of individual cases. This is why the welfare principle leaves space for the courts to make tailored decisions to promote the best outcome in the circumstances.
7. Some of my colleagues fear that making the declaration that the decision of Paul's parents can be overridden in these circumstances would have a potentially 'chilling effect' on parents everywhere, undermining the family and issuing in a 'brave new world' of state interference. I fear that declaring that a court has no power to interfere with parental decisions, however damaging, except in Article 42.5 circumstances has a rather bleaker chilling effect. It sends a message that no one can intervene. That there is no mechanism in Irish law for a third party to question parental autonomy. If we accept that the care and protection of children is the responsibility of society as a whole we cannot stand over this message. The health worker who inspected the family would have no basis on which to question parental decisions and probe further unless she felt there was reason to suspect that the Article 42.5 would be satisfied.

The Constitution gives rights to the marital family as an entity to prevent unwarranted state interference because we as society believe in general that parents make the best decisions for children. Where we have evidence in an individual case that this assumption is patently untrue, why should the rights of the marital family, created to protect children *in general*, hamper the indication of an individual child's rights? To turn away from such a child would amount to state protection of objectively harmful decisions at the expense of that individual child in order to protect the principle that most parents do the right thing.

Conclusion

On balance, the best interests of Paul and the court's constitutional duty to uphold his right to realise his full potential as a human being require a declaration for the test to be carried out. I would make a declaration to this effect.

20

Commentary on *PM v The Board of Management of St Vincent's Hospital and Justin Geoghegan and the Attorney General*

CLAIRE MURRAY

Introduction

The original case, *JM, Applicant v The Board of Management of St Vincent's Hospital and Justin Geoghegan and Attorney General, Respondents and PM, Notice Party,*[1] involved an urgent application to the High Court seeking an order directing the respondent hospital and consultant medical practitioner to administer appropriate treatment, including a liver transplant and a blood transfusion, to a woman, PM, who at the time of the hearing was in a coma and who had previously refused to accept the treatment. One of the reasons for the refusal was that PM had converted to the Jehovah's Witness faith upon her marriage. Treatment refusal cases involving Jehovah's Witnesses are not uncommon, and there is relevant case law from other jurisdictions.[2] The applicant in the original case, JM, was PM's husband. PM was a notice party to the original hearing, but for obvious reasons was not present at the hearing and she was also not legally represented. The judgment was delivered by Finnegan P in the High Court, and he made an order admitting PM to wardship and, exercising the inherent *parens patriae* jurisdiction of the court, directing the respondents to provide the necessary treatment.

The feminist judgment arises from fictional new proceedings brought by PM in the High Court seeking a number of declarations from the court in light of the outcome of the original case. This approach was adopted by the feminist judge, Mary Donnelly, for a number of reasons. First, because the original case was heard by the High Court in urgent circumstances with one judge sitting alone, a dissenting judgment would not have been possible.

[1] *JM, Applicant v The Board of Management of St Vincent's Hospital and Justin Geoghegan and Attorney General, Respondents and PM, Notice Party* [2003] 1 IR 321.

[2] In England and Wales see *Re T (Adult: Refusal of Medical Treatment)* [1992] 3 WLR 782; from Canada see *Malette v Shulman et al* (1990) 67 DLR (4th) 321 (Ont CA).

Secondly, given that the treatment ordered was described as urgent and life-saving, any appeal would also have been decided in urgent circumstances. The decision not to provide a replacement judgment was based on the fact that a feminist judge would have elicited information from the hearing different from that provided. These limitations would also apply to an appeal. By re-opening the matter as a set of new proceedings seeking declarations in relation to the conduct of the original hearing, the feminist judgment is able to engage with the reasoning in that judgment, to acknowledge the constraints within which Finnegan P was operating, but also to illustrate that another approach might have been possible had greater emphasis been placed on recognising and understanding PM as an autonomous individual situated within a relational context. A broadly similar approach was adopted in *Fitzpatrick v K*,[3] which post-dates JM but which also involved an urgent application to court seeking an order to provide a blood transfusion without consent.

The feminist judgment also identifies specific declarations sought in order to delimit the scope of the matters before the court to those at issue in the original decision. Thus, a decision was made to exclude a claim for damages.

Placing PM at the Centre of the Judgment

A key objective of the project of feminist judging is to tell the story of the case in as full a manner as possible, and to provide the context in which the decision took place. One aspect of doing this is to place the individual most affected by the decision at the centre of the judgment. In the original judgment PM was not a party to the case. She was not legally represented, and one consequence of this was that her voice was not heard, or at the very least there was nobody to put her perspective before the court and to test the medical evidence presented to the court. Throughout the judgment by Finnegan P there are multiple references to PM's husband, and to the extent that we hear the perspective of PM it is related first through her husband and then through Finnegan P. This silencing of PM is a matter of significant concern in the feminist judgment. The ongoing failure of the courts to address this issue is evident in the more recent High Court decision of *PP v HSE*,[4] discussed below.

The final sentence of the original judgment is '[i]n those circumstances it is an easy decision'. The characterisation of the decision in this case as easy is perplexing, as the court was called upon to make a decision about whether to uphold a refusal of treatment when the refusal to sign the consent form occurred in difficult circumstances, and at the time of the hearing PM was in a coma and her husband was seeking to have the treatment refusal set aside. However, the two sentences preceding the final sentence are, 'She has a child and a loving husband. The medical evidence is that she has a 60% chance of survival.' The reasoning, therefore, seems to be that because she has a husband and child she has something to live for, and so should not be permitted to die. This appears to accord limited, if any, weight to PM's own views regarding the refusal of treatment. It also echoes case law in England and

[3] *Fitzpatrick v K* [2008] IEHC 104.
[4] *PP v HSE* [2014] IEHC 622.

Wales in relation to the refusal by women of caesarean sections. In *Re S (Adult: Refusal of Treatment)*,[5] following an *ex parte* hearing the declaration to carry out a caesarean section was granted on the basis that it was in the best interests of S and the unborn child. The judgment in *Re S* was not well received, and subsequent cases moved away from a reliance on the best interests of the foetus and instead restated the importance of the autonomy of the individual woman. However, notwithstanding the more pro-autonomy rhetoric, in practice courts have tended to find that the women seeking to refuse the caesarean section lack capacity. In many of these cases the autonomy and agency rights of the woman involved are blurred and undermined, usually through a finding that the women lacked capacity to refuse treatment, in order to vindicate what are perceived to be the rights or interests of the foetus. For example, in *Re MB (An Adult: Medical Treatment)*,[6] the Court of Appeal found that MB lacked capacity to make the decision regarding the caesarean section because of her needle phobia—the reasoning was that the fear of needles dominated her thinking and rendered her temporarily lacking in capacity.[7] In contrast to the judgment of Finnegan P, the feminist judgment by Donnelly J emphasises that this is a difficult and challenging decision for the judge. On the one hand there is the need to respect the agency and autonomous choice of the individual woman; and on the other there is the need to recognise the situated position of PM within her family context.

Hunter outlines a number of features of feminist approaches to judgment-writing, and notes that several of these relate to the procedures of decision-making, among them '"including women" both in terms of writing women's experiences into legal discourse (as individual litigants and collectively, drawing on relevant research evidence) and in the construction of legal rules'.[8] One of the core objectives in this feminist approach to the case was to make PM visible within the judgment to the greatest extent possible. The feminist judgment places PM front and centre. Not only does it begin by setting out the available facts relating to PM, thus making her real and a key actor within the case, but it also highlights, through a discussion of the right to fair procedures and the requirement for legal representation, the manner in which she was silenced and rendered invisible in the original judgment. While reliance on fair procedures and constitutional justice is perhaps not an evident feminist methodology in itself, this approach is one that could plausibly have been adopted by a court in Ireland at that time, and it allows for an articulation of the significant feminist concerns at the heart of the case. This approach reflects Nedelsky's argument, from a feminist perspective, about the importance of due process not just as an end in itself, but also as a means to an end, and as a way to ensure and support the exercise of autonomy.[9] The importance of participating in decisions that affect a person is neatly captured by Nedelsky, who states that '[t]he right to a hearing declares their views to be significant,

[5] *Re S (Adult: Refusal of Treatment)* [1992] 4 All ER 671.

[6] *Re MB (An Adult: Medical Treatment)* [1997] 2 FCR 541.

[7] A similar approach was adopted in *Tameside and Glossop Acute Services v CH* [1996] 1 FLR 76; *Norfolk and Norwich Healthcare NHS Trust v W* [1996] 2 FLR 6; and *Bolton Hospitals NHS Trust v O* [2002] EWHC 2871. See also Katherine Wade, 'Refusal of Emergency Caesarean Section in Ireland: A Relational Approach' (2013) 22(1) *Medical Law Review* 1.

[8] Rosemary Hunter, Clare McGlynn and Erika Rackley (eds), *Feminist Judgments: From Theory to Practice* (Oxford, Hart Publishing, 2010) 35.

[9] Jennifer Nedelsky, 'Reconceiving Autonomy: Sources, Thoughts and Possibilities' (1989) 1 *Yale Journal of Law and Feminism* 7.

their contribution to be relevant. In principle, a hearing designates recipients as part of the process of collective decision-making rather than as passive, external objects of judgment'.[10]

PM was denied that right to participate in the original hearing of this case, and was certainly a passive object of the judgment of Finnegan P. Undoubtedly, the fact that she was in a coma at the time of the hearing in the High Court did provide a barrier to participation, but not an insurmountable one. By way of illustration, in the case of *PP v HSE*,[11] a woman, NP, who had suffered a brain injury resulting in brain-stem death, was artificially maintained alive on life support in order to preserve the life of her foetus.[12] As in *JM*, a family member, NP's father, was obliged to apply to the High Court to seek a declaration to have life support withdrawn. NP was assigned legal representation, as was the foetus. This was with the agreement of the High Court during a case directions hearing prior to the hearing of the substantive matter. No further details of the arguments presented to the High Court at that prior hearing are available. The issue at the core of that particular case was whether switching off the life-support machine would violate the constitutionally protected right to life of the unborn. Clearly the *PP* case post-dates *JM*, but the principles of constitutional justice/fair procedures that gave rise to the appointment of representation were well established at the time of the decision in *JM*. This is illustrated in the feminist judgment when Donnelly J uses the decision in *SPUC v Coogan*[13] to show the importance afforded by the Irish courts to ensuring that the rights of those who could not represent themselves (in *Coogan*, the 'unborn') are protected.

It is, however, important to recognise the difficulties with allocating legal representation to a person in PM's circumstances—this is to say in a coma and unable to provide any instructions to her legal representatives. There exists the very real risk that not the voice of the individual and her wishes, but rather what the appointed legal representative considers to be in her best interests will necessarily be presented to the court. Nevertheless, the reasoning behind the approach adopted by Donnelly J is that by appointing legal representation to PM in these circumstances, the court would at least increase the chances of her voice being heard in the proceedings. It would also be possible for the legal representative to, at a very minimum, challenge the medical evidence put before the court as to why a blood transfusion and liver transplant was necessary, and to explore the possibility of alternative courses of action open to the court rather than imposing invasive treatment on PM in the absence of her consent. While this may be less than ideal, it is an improvement on the alternative course of action that was adopted in the original case.

Agency

There are a number of layers to PM's case. On a surface level it concerns the right to refuse life-sustaining medical treatment, and the associated rights of autonomy and bodily

[10] ibid, 27.

[11] Above n 4.

[12] There appears to be some disagreement in the judgment on the precise age of the foetus, but somewhere between 13 and 15 weeks was generally agreed.

[13] *SPUC v Coogan* [1989] IR 734.

integrity. These are significant issues of feminist concern. However, it also draws attention to the importance of agency. The failure to recognise and respect the agency of women has been identified in similar projects. Hunter, McGlynn and Rackley note that 'women often find that when they attempt to exercise agency, such as in the context of refusing to consent to sexual activity or medical treatment, they are not taken seriously'.[14]

There is certainly a sense in the original judgment in *JM* that PM's decision to refuse treatment is not given the due consideration and respect that it deserves. It is characterised as a decision that was taken merely to please her husband. The assumption is that this means that it was not her decision. There are two difficulties with this approach. First, it discounts the possibility that as a result of her studies to join the Jehovah's Witness faith, PM had in fact adopted those beliefs and would not wish to accept a blood transfusion for her own deeply held religious reasons. It also presumes that PM only adopted a new system of religious belief because of her cultural background, rather than allowing for the possibility that PM had given some level of thought to the decision to convert to the Jehovah's Witness faith. The reference to culture in the original judgment is striking. In 2003 Ireland was experiencing an increase in immigration, and as a result was dealing with relatively new cultural challenges around accommodating a wider variety of cultural narratives within the state. At that time African women in particular were coming to the attention of the State during pregnancy, amid claims that they were having children in Ireland in order to gain a right to residency by having a citizen-child.[15] Following on from this there was the Supreme Court decision in *Lobe and Osayande*,[16] which found that migrant parents could no longer be permitted to remain in Ireland to bring up their children. The feminist rewriting of this judgment by Siobhán Mullally and Cliodhna Murphy can be found in this collection.[17] This developing discourse ultimately resulted in what was known as the citizenship referendum in 2004, which removed the automatic right to citizenship from all children born in the state and limited it to those children who had at least one parent who was an Irish citizen or entitled to Irish citizenship.[18] References to culture at this time therefore were often shorthand for an ongoing and complex debate around Irishness, citizenship and the state. By way of contrast, in the feminist judgment Donnelly J emphasises the dangers associated with cultural stereotyping. The original judgment also assumes that PM's religious conversion took place without a full appreciation of the consequences of taking on that faith. This latter assumption is undermined by the evidence that PM was aware of the importance of refusing or accepting the blood transfusion, and as a result wished to discuss it with her husband and to have his input into the decision.

Secondly, the approach adopted by Finnegan P suggests that making a decision because PM believed that is what her husband wanted, and that his opinion was an important consideration for her, indicates that it is not a valid exercise of her autonomy and right to

[14] Hunter, McGlynn and Rackley, above n 8, at 22.

[15] For further discussion see Ronit Lentin, 'Migrant women's networking: New articulations of transnational ethnicity' in Gargi Bhattacharyya (ed), *Ethnicities and Values in a Changing World* (Fanham and Burlington VT, Ashgate, 2009); and Siobhán Mullally, 'Citizenship and Family Life in Ireland: Asking the Question "Who Belongs"?' (2005) 25(4) *Legal Studies* 341–.

[16] *Lobe and Osayande v Minister for Justice, Equality and Law Reform.* [2003] 1 IR 1.

[17] See ch 13.

[18] This was the 27th amendment to the Constitution and the referendum was passed by a significant majority—1,427,520 votes in favour and 375,695 votes against.

make decisions about how she conducts her life. This reflects an individualistic approach to decision-making that does not necessarily accord with the reality of decision-making for many people. From the evidence that PM asked her husband 'what he would do in the situation', it appears that PM was attempting to engage in a more relational decision-making process, which recognised her situated nature as a wife and mother, and understood that her decision had implications for those around her. However, it seems that PM's husband did not engage with her in this process, as he advised her that it was her decision to make. It appears that this left PM feeling uncertain and confused. As noted by Donnelly J in the feminist judgment, it is unclear whether PM received any other support from those in the hospital charged with her care and treatment. This failure to engage with PM at a difficult time when she was seeking support to clarify and communicate her wishes is deeply troubling. While the law cannot compel family members to participate in relational decision-making, it can, and should, ensure that where a situation such as that of PM arises, those professionally caring for the person fill the vacuum left by the family and provide the necessary support.

The complexity of the situation is also evident in the contradictory approach adopted by the court: on the one hand, not accepting PM's refusal of treatment on the basis that she was refusing because she was doing what her husband wanted; and on the other, justifying the decision to provide treatment without consent in part on the basis that it is what her husband wanted and that this fact would comfort PM. As Donnelly notes, the judgment of the High Court in the original decision in JM 'shows both the dangers of taking a social or relational approach to agency and the dangers of not doing so'.[19]

The Importance of a Relational Approach to Autonomy

Feminist theory has used the concept of relational autonomy to address issues around agency. This is subject to varied definitions.[20] However, it often draws on critical feminist theories and, as Nedelsky notes, 'one of the contributions of feminism to relational theory is that it is particularly unlikely to make the mistake of romanticising community or relationship'.[21] Theories of relational autonomy therefore emphasise the individual in context, whilst also retaining the importance of autonomy. Elements of this approach are evident in the feminist judgment. Nedelsky sees the aim of relational autonomy as 'transforming a traditionally individual conception of the self into a relational one without subsuming the individual into the collective'.[22] The conception of autonomy within a relational approach is different from that set out in the traditional liberal understanding. According

[19] Mary Donnelly, *Healthcare Decision-Making and the Law: Autonomy, Capacity and the Limits of Liberalism* (Cambridge, Cambridge University Press, 2010) 62.

[20] Catriona McKenzie and Natalie Stoljar (eds), *Relational Autonomy: Feminist Perspectives on Autonomy, Agency and the Social Self* (Oxford, Oxford University Press, 2000); Jonathan Herring, *Caring and the Law* (Oxford, Hart Publishing, 2009); Shelley Day Sclater, Fatemeh Ebtehaj, Emily Jackson and Martin Richards (eds), *Regulating Autonomy: Sex, Reproduction and Family* (Oxford, Hart Publishing, 2009).

[21] Jennifer Nedelsky, *Law's Relations: A Relational Theory of Self, Autonomy and Law* (Oxford, Oxford University Press, 2011) 32.

[22] ibid, 13.

to Nedelsky, under a relational approach autonomy is not equated with independence, but rather 'autonomy is made possible by constructive relationships'.[23] Therefore it is through the existence of positive relationships and supports, including relationships of care, that individuals are in a position to exercise autonomy. One of the strengths of relational autonomy from a feminist perspective is that it does not assume that all relationships are beneficial, and it does not seek to maintain them in all circumstances.[24] A functioning relational approach to law therefore should operate to balance the rights and needs of both parties, and allow individuals to extricate themselves from bad relationships and enhance positive relationships that support the exercise of autonomy.

The concept of a constructive relationship working to strengthen and enhance autonomy resonates in the context of the *PM* case. To the extent that we get a picture of PM from the original judgment, what we see is a woman reaching out to her husband for support and guidance in making a difficult decision in challenging circumstances. She was seeking to rely on what she appeared to understand to be a mutually supportive and presumably constructive relationship, to assist her in making an autonomous choice. She did not, it appears, conceive of the decision to be made as a purely independent one that she alone was responsible for making. That does not mean, however, that she was giving up the right to make her decision, or that her wishes and needs should cede priority to those of others within the family group or relationship. This is where the judgment of Finnegan P runs into difficulty from a feminist and a relational autonomy perspective. He recognises the importance of relationships, highlighting that PM has a loving husband and child, but in doing so he privileges the wishes of JM and attributes those to PM without giving sufficient consideration to whether the evidence in fact supports that conclusion. It may well be the case that had JM expressed his wish that PM take the blood products at the time when PM was seeking to discuss the issue with him, she would have weighed that heavily in her decision-making process. Clearly JM's input was important to her. However, that moment had passed, and PM was no longer in a position to factor that information into her autonomous decision. Finnegan P's relational approach in this case, which had the effect of placing PM at the periphery of this case rather than at the centre, did not enhance the autonomy or agency of PM.

Conclusion

As this feminist judgment is not a first instance judgment, Donnelly J was not faced with the difficult decision about whether to make an order directing the hospital to provide treatment, or upholding the right to refuse treatment with the consequence that PM would die. However, it was also the situation that no new evidence was put before the court, and so in reviewing the original decision of the High Court, Donnelly J was required to determine if, given the facts that were before the court at the time the original decision was made, the

[23] ibid, 118.

[24] Mary Donnelly and Claire Murray, 'The Role of Family in Mental Health Law: A Framework for Transformation' (2013) 25(4) *Child and Family Law Quarterly* 380, 399.

High Court adopted the correct approach. Ultimately the feminist judgment finds that the procedure adopted by Finnegan P in the High Court was inadequate and breached PM's constitutional right to fair procedures. This failure to adhere to fair procedures and to permit PM to participate in the decision-making process may well have had an impact on the evidence that was before the court, as PM's position was not fully articulated and discussed before the court. Nor was the evidence of the other parties to the case tested. In identifying these procedural shortcomings, this feminist judgment also highlights that feminist judging is about more than just the act of writing judgments that draw on feminist theories or feminist teachings. It emphasises that a feminist judge would have approached the case in a fundamentally different manner: a feminist judge hearing this case in urgent circumstances would most likely have asked different questions; he or she would have identified different material as relevant to making the decision; and had such an approach been taken at that point, it may have been the case that the judgment delivered would have been different.

Based on the evidence that was before the court, Donnelly J determined that it was not possible to find that PM had exercised a fully autonomous choice to refuse treatment, and therefore Finnegan P in the High Court did not violate her rights in ordering the provision of the necessary treatment. This conclusion could be seen as falling into the same pattern as existing case law on treatment refusal outlined above, of strongly upholding the right to refuse in principle but not following through in practice. However, the strength of this feminist judgment lies in the manner in which it illustrates the importance of proper and fair procedures, both as an end in and of themselves *and* as a means to an end. In this case the procedural shortcomings that resulted in PM's voice being silenced had a very direct and significant impact on the ability of the court to adequately vindicate the substantive right to autonomy. Participation as a means to enhance and secure autonomy is therefore at the centre of this case, and the contribution of the feminist judgment to discussion in this field is to illustrate this within the context of treatment refusal.

PM, Applicant v The Board of Management of St Vincent's Hospital and Justin Geoghegan and the Attorney General, Respondents

High Court 18th June, 2003

Donnelly J. 18th June, 2003

[1] PM has applied to this Court for declaratory relief in respect of medical treatment which was administered to her, notwithstanding her prior refusal to sign a consent form, following an order of Finnegan P., dated 24th October 2002 (reported in *JM, Applicant v the Board of Management of St Vincent's Hospital and Justin Geoghegan, Respondents and PM, Notice Party* [2003] 1 I.R. 321). This order authorised the respondents to provide to PM appropriate medical treatment, including a liver transplant and blood transfusion. This is not a rehearing of the case and no new evidence is introduced. Rather, the court proceeds on the basis of the evidence which was before the court at the time the matter was heard.

[2] PM requests the court to make the following declarations:-

(a) A declaration that her right to constitutional justice and fair procedures under Article 40.3.1° of the Constitution was breached by the order of the High Court for the administration of treatment to her without her consent which was made without independent legal representation

(b) A declaration that the order of the High Court to authorise the administration of treatment to her in the absence of her consent failed to respect her rights to autonomy and bodily integrity under Article 40.3.1° of the Constitution.

The Facts

[3] On 24th October 2002, JM, the husband of PM, made an application to the High Court for an order to authorise the administration of appropriate medical treatment, including a liver transplant and the administration of blood transfusion(s) to PM, notwithstanding that on 20th October PM had refused to sign a consent form in respect of this treatment. PM's decision to refuse treatment derived from her religious beliefs as a Jehovah's Witness. Abstention from blood represents a fundamental tenet of this religious faith.

[4] At the time of the application PM was on medication and on a ventilator. She was in a coma and was unable to communicate her present views regarding the proposed treatment. The medical evidence provided to the Court was that, although there was a possibility that PM could recover consciousness, this was unlikely to occur in sufficient time to allow the necessary treatment to be provided. It was also asserted that it was unlikely that PM would be able to make a decision for herself during any period of recovery. The matter came before the Court in circumstances of considerable urgency due to the serious medical condition of PM. Medical evidence was provided that PM was critically ill and that she required immediate blood transfusions and a liver transplant. The medical experts stated that, if the treatments sought under the application were carried out, PM had a 60% chance of survival.

[**5**] JM provided evidence to the Court. He stated that PM had become a Jehovah's Witness on her marriage to him some months previously, having commenced studying to become a Jehovah's Witness in March 2002. JM also attested that, on 19th October, JM and PM had discussed the proposed treatment and JM 'spoke to her and told her that the decision was important and that she shouldn't feel obliged to refuse because of him as it was her decision'. PM asked him what he would do in her situation but he said that he left the decision to her. She then said that she would think about the decision to be made. JM's evidence is that PM was lucid at the time of this conversation. JM attested that the following day, PM's condition had deteriorated. She was physically weaker; her speech was less clear and she also appeared to be less clear in her mind. When he spoke with her, she cried and said that she would take blood. He communicated this to the liver transplant team. However, ten minutes later, when a member of the liver transplant team came to PM and asked her to complete a consent form, she refused to do so.

[**6**] Finnegan P. found that the Court's authority to consider the matter derived from the *parens patriae* jurisdiction, the application of which in Ireland had been confirmed by Hamilton C.J. in *In re a Ward of Court (withholding medical treatment) (No. 2)* [1996] 2 I.R. 79, 103. He recognised, as stated by Hamilton C.J. in *Re Ward of Court*, the right of the competent adult who is a terminally ill patient to forego ongoing treatment and found that PM was terminally ill. However, he found that PM had not made 'a clear final decision to have or not have the treatment.'

Conduct of the Hearing

[**7**] The manner in which the hearing was conducted is significant in respect of both declarations sought. Due to the medical circumstances, the hearing took place in urgent circumstances. For this reason, Finnegan P. proceeded on foot of a draft plenary summons and took evidence on oath. The application was brought by JM, PM's husband. The first respondent was the Board of Management of the hospital in which PM was a patient and the second respondent, Mr Geoghegan, was the consultant surgeon who was responsible for the medical care of PM. PM was a notice party. The applicant was legally represented, as was Mr Geoghegan. Neither the first respondent nor PM was represented.

Fair Procedures

[**8**] The decision before the Court concerned one of the most serious matters which can come before a court of law: the resolution of a conflict between an individual's life and her right to make fundamental decisions regarding how her life should be lived. The resolution of the application would result either in PM's death or in a potentially profound bodily intrusion and, as PM may see it, a risk of her eternal damnation for failing to accord with the tenets of her religious faith.

[**9**] The right to fair procedures derives from the common law and from the principle of constitutional justice which, as recognised first by Walsh J. in *McDonald v Bord na gCon* [1965] I.R. 217 is enshrined in Article 40.3.2° of the Constitution. As has been recognised by the Supreme Court on many occasions, including *In re Haughey* [1971] I.R. 217 and *The State (Gleeson) v Minister for Defence* [1976] I.R. 280, the obligation to hear the other side—*audi alteram partem*—is core to the principle of constitutional justice. At the time

of the hearing, PM was clearly not in a position to speak for herself and defend her rights. Moreover, she was not legally represented.

[10] While it is not the case that respect for the principle of *audi alteram partem* requires that an affected party be afforded a right to independent legal representation in all instances, it has, on several occasions in the context of access to legal aid, been recognised that the protection of the constitutional right to fair procedures requires the provision of legal representation (see *Stevenson v Landy & others*, unrep High Court, 10 February 1993 and *Kirwan v Minister for Justice, Ireland and the Attorney General* [1994] 2 I.R. 417). In *Kirwan*, in upholding a right to legal aid for a hearing of an application for release of a person who had been detained in the Central Mental Hospital, Lardner J found that, whether or not a right to legal aid existed depended on several factors: the seriousness of the charge; the nature of the penalty faced: and the capacity of the person to speak for himself and defend himself. While clearly arising in a different context, the factors identified by Lardner J in *Kirwan* are relevant in this case. Applying these to the facts of this case, it is clear that the issue before the Court was very serious; the consequences of a decision either way were profound; and PM could not speak for herself and defend her own interests.

[11] I note also the decision of *The Society for the Protection of Unborn Children Ltd v Coogan and Others* [1989] I.R. 734 where the Supreme Court recognised the importance of ensuring the vindication of personal rights when the holder of rights is not in a position to vindicate his or her own rights. Although the circumstances were different—in *Coogan*, the party unable to vindicate his or her rights was the 'unborn' within the meaning of Article 40.3.3° of the Constitution—the principle that in certain circumstances special procedures may be required to vindicate constitutional rights is applicable in this case.

[12] There are also instrumental reasons why the lack of independent legal representation for PM was problematic. Within an adversarial system, such as ours, the lack of independent representation rendered it very difficult to reach even approximate conclusions regarding what PM would wish to happen. All information was mediated through JM who, inevitably, had his own distinct position on the matter to be determined and which may well have coloured the evidence presented. PM was at the centre of this case yet the Court was afforded limited opportunity to make determinations regarding her preferences or views. Although those preferences would not necessarily be determinative, they must constitute a key aspect of judicial consideration.

[13] The absence of legal representation for PM also restricted the capacity of the Court to engage in the necessary evaluation of the medical evidence. Medical evidence played a crucial role in this case. The urgent nature of the case was determined on the basis of medical evidence, as was the need for the blood transfusions and liver transplant. However, medical evidence was also important in other respects. Important questions to be considered by the Court included the mental state of PM on the day on which she refused to sign the consent form and the extent to which medical staff engaged with PM in discussing the implications of her decision to refuse the proposed treatment and ensuring that she was fully informed of the consequences of the decision. Given the centrality of the medical evidence in this case, it was important for the Court to have an opportunity to evaluate the evidence provided through the process of cross-examination, which is at the core of our adversarial system of justice. Cross-examination would have afforded the Court an opportunity to evaluate the necessity of proposed actions and to consider whether there were alternatives to the treatment sought which might have been more respectful of PM's wishes.

[14] It is of course relevant that this case came before the Court in urgent circumstances. Where such circumstances arise, in the interests of the administration of justice, the court must respond. Certain procedural inadequacies may be overlooked and a more informal approach may be adopted. Steps such as proceeding on the basis of a draft plenary summons and taking evidence on oath, which were adopted in this case, may be justified on the basis of the constitutional obligation of the court to administer justice within the necessary time. However, there are fundamental elements of the process which cannot be set aside on the basis of the urgent circumstances. The function of the court is to administer justice and some procedural inadequacies are so fundamental as to limit the capacity of the court to do this. In the circumstances of this case, for the reasons outlined above, I am of the view that justice could not be administered without some form of representation of the person whose fundamental rights were at stake.

[15] I am, of course, aware that independent legal representation does not, of itself, guarantee that the views of the individual whose rights are at issue will be represented adequately. For this reason, where possible, the services of a guardian *ad litem* should be utilised, as they were in the application for the withdrawal of treatment in *Re a Ward of Court (withholding medical treatment) (No 2)* [1996] 2 I.R. 79. I recognise that circumstances may arise where such services may not be possible and accept that the emergency nature of this case was one. Nonetheless, it is important to emphasise the strong principle that in a case such as this, which concerns fundamental constitutional rights, every effort should be made to ascertain and adequately represent the views of the person who is not able to represent herself or himself and to ensure that legal representatives and guardians are held to account regarding their performance of this function by the court.

[16] The importance of ensuring adequate representation of the person whose rights are at issue, requires that, insofar as is possible, the practice of making applications of this kind in urgent circumstances must be avoided. In this case, PM declined to consent to treatment some four days prior to the hearing. It may well be the case that the urgency of the matter only became apparent with the passage of time. However, it may also be the case that an application could have been made at an earlier point and that, had this occurred, more attention could have been given to ensuring adequate representation of PM.

[17] The application in this case was made by JM, PM's husband. Having to make the application must have added considerably to JM's emotional distress at a very difficult time. A question arises as regards what would have happened if JM had not brought this application. Would the respondent have sought the involvement of the court or would PM's lack of consent have been considered determinative, notwithstanding that there may have been reasons to question the validity of her refusal? The involvement of the court in a matter of fundamental rights should not be dependent on whether or not a spouse or family member decides to refer the matter for judicial consideration. In this respect, I agree with Lord Donaldson M.R. who, in broadly similar circumstances, in *Re T Adult: Refusal of Medical Treatment* [1992] 3 W.L.R. 782 at page 798, stated that the step of seeking court involvement 'should not be left to the patient's family, who will probably not know of the facility and may be inhibited by questions of expense'. This accords with the 'public interest in the vindication of [a] private right which has been guaranteed by the Constitution', which was identified by Walsh J in *The Society for the Protection of Unborn Children Ltd v Coogan and Others* [1989] I.R. 734 at page 743.

The Requirement for Consent to Medical Treatment

[18] At the hearing of this matter, the Court was informed that on 20th October, PM refused to sign a consent form given to her by a member of the liver transplant team. The importance of consent to medical treatment was described by Denham J. in *In re a Ward of Court (withholding medical treatment) (No. 2)* [1996] 2 I.R. 79 at page 156 as follows:

> Medical treatment may not be given to an adult person of full capacity without his or her consent. There are a few rare exceptions to this e.g., in regard to contagious diseases or in a medical emergency where the patient is unable to communicate. This right arises out of civil, criminal and constitutional law. If medical treatment is given without consent it may be trespass against the person in civil law, a battery in criminal law, and a breach of the individual's constitutional rights.

[19] Although it is common practice for hospitals to require patients to complete consent forms, the completion of such forms should not be confused with the actuality of consent. The existence of a form certainly makes life easier for medical professionals and indeed for the court. However, a consent form is no more than evidence of consent. The reason this case arises is not because PM did not complete a consent form but because by refusing to complete the consent form, she indicated that she did not consent to the treatment. Thus, the court's concern is not with the absence of a signed consent form but with what this absence means about PM's wishes.

[20] In *In re a Ward of Court*, the Supreme Court upheld the right to refuse treatment (in this case artificial nutrition and hydration) of a woman who, as a result of a medical catastrophe which had occurred some 23 years previously, was in a 'near PVS state'. The right was derived from the constitutionally protected rights to autonomy and self-determination and the right to privacy, protected under Article 40.3.1° of the Constitution. Hamilton C.J. at page 125 accepted the view which had been put forward by the former President of the High Court, writing extra-judicially, that '[a] competent adult if terminally ill has the right to forgo or discontinue life-saving treatment'. He further found at page 126 that the Ward was terminally (rather than chronically) ill on the basis that, without the nourishment being provided to her by the treatment in question, she would die. The right to refuse treatment was also recognised by Denham J. who found at page 156 that 'If medical treatment is given without consent it may be trespass against the person in civil law, a battery in criminal law, and a breach of the individual's constitutional rights.' Although Hamilton C.J. identified a right to refuse treatment only in circumstances of terminal illness, it is clear from his finding that the Ward was terminally ill that Hamilton C.J. did not regard terminal illness as arising only in circumstances in which the trajectory of a disease will lead to inevitable death. On the basis of Hamilton C.J.'s understanding, PM would also be considered to be terminally ill. This was also the approach taken by Finnegan P. in respect of the original application.

[21] Moreover, even if one were to adopt a less expansive understanding of terminal illness, there is nothing in the judgment of the Supreme Court in *Re a Ward of Court* to indicate that a right to refuse treatment should not extend to a patient who is not terminally ill. In her extensive judgment, Denham J does not refer to the nature of the patient's illness and states the right to refuse treatment in terms which indicate that it applies to all patients of full age and capacity on an equal basis regardless of the nature of their illness.

[22] An important aspect of the right to refuse treatment as identified by Denham J. is that the right does not depend on the court's assessment of the rationality of the reasons for the refusal. Denham J. stated at page 156 that 'The consent which is given by an adult of full capacity is a matter of choice. It is not necessarily a decision based on medical considerations. Thus, medical treatment may be refused for other than medical reasons, or reasons most citizens would regard as rational, but the person of full age and capacity may make the decision for their own reasons.' Thus, it is not for this Court to determine whether or not PM's decision to refuse treatment is appropriate or reasonable. Rather, the function of the Court is to determine whether, in the circumstances of this case, PM's constitutionally protected right to refuse treatment should be upheld.

Status of Advance Refusals in Irish Law

[23] In the passage referred to above, Denham J. identified as an exception to the requirement for consent, the situation of a medical emergency where the patient is unable to communicate. This case is different from that envisaged by Denham J., because although PM was unable to communicate her consent or refusal contemporaneously, she had in advance indicated a refusal of treatment. The matter of a non-contemporaneous refusal of treatment has not to date been considered by the courts in this jurisdiction. However, courts in other jurisdictions have on several occasions upheld a right to refuse treatment, including life-saving treatment, in circumstances in which the refusal had been stated in advance and the patient was unable to communicate current wishes. In several of these cases, the refusal has derived from the patient's religious belief as a Jehovah's Witness. In the Canadian case of *Malette v Shulman et al* (1990) 67 D.L.R. (4th) 321, 330 Robins J.A., found that 'A doctor is not free to disregard a patient's advance instructions any more than he would be free to disregard instructions given at the time of the emergency.' A similar approach to advance instructions may be found in decisions from England and Wales including the decision of the Court of Appeal in *Re T (Adult: Refusal of Medical Treatment* [1992] 3 W.L.R. 782 and the High Court in *Re C (Adult: Refusal of Medical Treatment)* [1994] 1 W.L.R. 290.

[24] It is difficult to see any reason in principle why the constitutionally protected right to refuse treatment should not apply, solely on the basis that the refusal is communicated in advance. In upholding the right to refuse treatment in *Re a Ward of Court*, the Supreme Court was clear that an individual's constitutional rights are not lost because of insentience or incapacity. As described by Denham J. at page 163, 'Simply it means that the right [to privacy] may be exercised by a different process.' There may, however, be differences at an evidentiary level in determining whether, in the circumstances of an individual case, an advance refusal should be upheld. I will return to this matter below.

Other Relevant Constitutional Rights

[25] The right to refuse medical treatment is not the only right implicated in this case. Other relevant constitutional rights, which were also recognised in *In re a Ward of Court*, are the right to life and the right to bodily integrity. It should also be noted that PM has a constitutionally protected right under Article 44.2.1° to the free profession and practice of religion. As was recognised in *Quinn's Supermarket Ltd v Attorney General* [1972] I.R. 1, this right is not restricted in its application to specified or designated religions and therefore would encompass PM's faith as a Jehovah's Witness. However, this right is not central to the determination of the matters at hand because the right to refuse treatment as recognised in *In re a Ward of Court* is not restricted to refusal on religious grounds only.

[26] The right to life is of particular relevance in the circumstances of this case given the medical evidence that, in the absence of the treatment which the respondent seeks to have authorised, PM's life is at risk. The constitutional significance afforded to the right to life is described by Denham J. in *Re a Ward of Court* at page 160 in the following terms:

> The right to life is the pre-eminent personal right. The State has guaranteed in its laws to respect this right. The respect is absolute. This right refers to all lives—all lives are respected for the benefit of the individual and for the common good.

However, Denham J. continued at page 160 by stating that 'The State's respect for the life of the individual encompasses the right of the individual to, for example, refuse a blood transfusion for religious reasons. In the recognition of the individual's autonomy, life is respected.' Thus, it is clear that respect for the right to life does not require that treatment, such as a blood transfusion, be imposed on a patient against his or her will in order to preserve the patient's life and indeed, such imposition would fail to respect the individual's right to life.

[27] The right to bodily integrity, recognised by the Supreme Court in *Ryan v Attorney General* [1965] I.R. 284 protects the individual from violation and mutilation of his or her body. The treatment at issue in this case (blood transfusion/s and a liver transplant) would constitute a very grave infringement of the right to bodily integrity if imposed without the consent of PM. On the basis of the legal interpretation of the right to life as set out by Denham J. in *Re a Ward of Court*, the fact that treatment may save PM's life would not justify the imposition of this treatment if it is imposed contrary to PM's wishes.

[28] Thus, PM clearly had a right to refuse the treatment. The question to be determined is whether she had exercised this right.

Presumptions

[29] Given that the right to life is 'the pre-eminent personal right', a question arises as to whether the Court should adopt a presumption in favour of life so that in cases of uncertainty, any uncertainty will be resolved in favour of the action which saves the person's life. In this case, this approach would have placed the burden of proof on PM. Given that PM did not have any form of representation, this would have effectively pre-determined the case.

[**30**] I am not convinced that the application of a presumption on the basis of protection of life is desirable in a case such as this. Applied in a general manner, it seems to me to unduly undermine the rights to autonomy and bodily integrity. I note also Lord Donaldson M.R.'s refusal to impose a presumption in favour of life in broadly similar circumstances in the English case *Re T (Adult: Refusal of Medical Treatment)* [1992] 3 W.L.R. 782 at page 792, citing his instinctive dislike of introducing presumptions in 'reaching a decision of fact as crucial as this'. Thus, the burden of showing that treatment should be provided must fall on JM. Having said this, I am conscious of the seriousness of the decision which had to be made and of the irreversible consequences of upholding the decision to refuse potentially life-saving treatment. It is appropriate that a court would proceed with great care and would scrupulously examine the evidence in such circumstances.

The Evidence Provided

[**31**] In reaching the decision to order the administration of treatment, Finnegan P. identified as relevant two aspects of JM's evidence. The first related to the kind of person which PM was; the second related to the circumstances in which PM's refusal of treatment took place.

[**32**] In respect of the kind of person PM was, Finnegan P. stated at page 324 that he took account of the fact that PM was African and that it was part of her culture to adopt her husband's religion on marriage. He found at page 325 that her decision to refuse treatment was because of her cultural background and her desire to please her husband and not offend his sensibilities: '[s]he was pre-occupied with her husband and his religion as a Jehovah's Witness rather than with whether to have the treatment and her own welfare'. He considered at page 325 that, if PM was aware of her husband's decision to seek the intervention of the Court, she would agree to have the treatment and would be comforted by her husband's attitude.

[**33**] As Irish society becomes more culturally diverse, the Irish courts must be increasingly careful to avoid the risks of cultural stereotyping. Clearly, not all African women (or indeed women from any other ethnic background) share the same cultural traits. Therefore, a more accurate summation of the evidence presented to Finnegan P. is that PM's particular cultural heritage predisposed her to adopt her husband's religion on marriage; that, as a matter of fact, she did convert on her marriage and that, accordingly, her decision to refuse treatment was found to derive not from her own inherent beliefs but from those of her husband.

[**34**] Those who hold religious beliefs may do so for different reasons. Some beliefs derive from the religion of birth. In other instances, a person may convert to a religion at some point in their lives. It is feasible that a reason for conversion may be the assumption of the religion of one's spouse. It is also feasible that a person's religious belief may derive not from an inherent personal commitment but from an allegiance to a spousal, or indeed a parental, belief. Many religious beliefs or, indeed the rejection of such beliefs, may derive from the cultural and social context within which the person lives. This is not to cast doubt on the sincerity of individual beliefs nor to indicate that individual beliefs should not be respected by the law. Rather, it indicates that any court should be very

cautious before undertaking an attempt to evaluate the sincerity or depth of any individual's religious belief.

[35] As has been noted throughout, an unfortunate element of this case was that very little was known about PM. We do know however, that she was an adult. There is no indication that she encountered any cognitive difficulties or that she was unusually vulnerable or susceptible to undue influence. There is also no indication that she was subjected to such influence. Indeed, JM's evidence is that when she asked him what he would do in her circumstances, he responded that it was her decision. Thus, there are no specific factors which might cause concern to the Court. Rather, the Court is being asked to evaluate the impact of (possible) cultural influences on a decision made. It is very difficult to see how a court can do this—especially in the absence of any evidence beyond that of JM, whose evidence, as already noted, must be viewed with some caution given the inevitable pressures of the unfortunate situation in which he finds himself. On this basis, I find that PM's broader motivations in becoming a Jehovah's Witness and the nature of her beliefs are factors which are beyond the purview of this Court.

[36] The second relevant aspect of JM's evidence related to the circumstances in which PM refused the treatment. From JM's evidence, it appears that, on 19th October, the day before PM refused to complete the consent form, she attempted to discuss the proposed treatment with JM, asking him what he would do, and that he responded that this was her decision. It seems from this that PM envisaged that the decision should be made following consultation within her family unit. In this, she was no different from to many, perhaps most, people who make important decisions not in a solely self-regarding or individual way but in the context of their relationships with others. It may reasonably be expected that, especially when a person is under physical and mental stress, as PM undoubtedly was, he or she will look for some form of help or support in making difficult decisions and that family members will be the most likely source of support. However, it would appear from his evidence that JM did not engage in discussion of the matter, stating that it was PM's own decision and leaving PM to think about the matter. Thus, it would appear that PM was left without any opportunity to discuss the decision to be made and without information about something which was clearly important to her—her husband's views on the matter.

[37] In light of this, it is perhaps no surprise that, on the following day, when her physical condition had deteriorated, PM vacillated between consent and refusal of the treatment, first agreeing to the treatment and then, apparently changing her mind when presented with the consent form by a member of the transplant team. PM was seriously ill and vulnerable. She asked for her husband's advice. Clearly, it is not for this Court to direct how spouses should respond to requests for advice. However, it is a source of concern that in these circumstances, there is no indication that the medical staff attempted to provide support to PM in reaching a decision. Thus, we find PM struggling to make a decision with very significant consequences for her life and the way she wished to live it. She vacillated and appeared to be uncertain although she ultimately refused to sign a consent form.

[38] By identifying the absence of decision-making support in this case, I do not intend to suggest that an individual's decision should be respected only where she or he has been provided with such support. Such a suggestion would inappropriately undermine the importance of the individual's right to make decisions about how to live his or her own life. I emphasise the lack of support in the unique circumstances of this case because one factor which is clear within the very limited amount of information this court has about the way in which PM's decision was reached, is that she asked her husband what he would do and he responded to her that it was her decision.

[**39**] As I have mentioned, this Court is not concerned with the absence of a consent form—this is merely a form of evidence of PM's wishes. Rather, the concern of the Court is with whether or not PM consented to the treatment. On the basis of the evidence before the Court at the time the order was made, I cannot conclude that PM's refusal to sign the consent form represented a considered decision to refuse treatment.

Decision

[**40**] PM has raised two issues in respect of the decision to authorise the administration of appropriate medical treatment. In respect of the first, the absence of fair procedures, I find that there was a breach of PM's constitutional rights which in turn had implications for the way in which the court considered the substantive question. I am conscious in making this finding of the urgency of the matter and the significant time pressures on the Court at the time the order was made. This was in no way the fault of the Court which facilitated the application in every way possible. Nonetheless, I am of the view that the absence of any form of representation for PM meant that the Court was unable to give sufficient consideration to the core element of the application, the perspective of PM.

[**41**] In respect of the decision to order treatment, I have reached the same conclusion as Finnegan P, although for a different reason. I consider that, in the absence of clear evidence of undue influence, a court should be very slow to reach conclusions regarding the nature of an individual's religious belief. Given that relationships are infinitely variable, it is possible that PM's refusal emerged from her pre-occupation with her husband and his religion rather than from her own beliefs. It is also possible that it did not. Bearing in mind that the burden of proof lay on JM, I do not consider that the evidence justified that conclusion that this was in fact the case.

[**42**] However, I am persuaded that the circumstances in which the refusal to sign the consent form took place do not indicate a considered decision to refuse the treatment. Through no fault of PM, it would appear that she was not given the support and information needed to reach a decision which can fairly be assumed to represent her views. In such circumstances, I cannot find the order to authorise the administration of treatment to constitute a breach of PM's constitutional rights to autonomy and bodily integrity. In so finding, I would like to stress my concerns regarding the lack of decision-making support provided to PM by her medical advisors and to note the importance of ensuing that such support is made available to patients who find themselves in the difficult and distressing position of having to make a momentous decision of the kind faced by PM. Such cases are likely to be rare but when they arise in the future, I would expect that the court should be provided with evidence of what forms of decision-making support were provided.

21

Commentary on *Re Family Planning Association of Northern Ireland v The Minister for Health, Social Services and Public Safety*

SARA RAMSHAW

Background to Judgment

Northern Ireland is the only part of the United Kingdom (UK) in which the Abortion Act 1967 does not apply. As Karen Brennan explains:

> The law on abortion in Northern Ireland is governed by the relevant provisions of the Offences Against the Persons Act 1861 and the Criminal Justice (NI) Act 1945, and relevant case-law, including the English case of *Bourne* (1939) and more recent Northern Irish cases decided in the 1990s. The key legislative provision relating to abortion is section 58 of the 1861 Act which provides for the offence of 'unlawfully' procuring a miscarriage. This section criminalises any person who intentionally and unlawfully procures the miscarriage of any woman, whether or not she is in fact pregnant; it similarly criminalises pregnant women who intentionally and unlawfully procure their own miscarriage. Anyone found guilty of an offence under section 58 is liable to the most severe penalty available in law: life imprisonment.[1]

On 13 June 2001, leave was granted for a judicial review in the High Court of Northern Ireland, applied for by the Family Planning Association of Northern Ireland (FPANI) against the Minister for Health, concerning abortion law and the medical practices and provision of abortion services in Northern Ireland. The FPANI sought to secure clearer guidelines for women and practitioners in relation to the legality of abortion in the jurisdiction. The hearing took place on 21–22 March 2002, and Kerr J (as he then was; he would later become Lord Chief Justice of Northern Ireland and is presently The Right Honourable Lord Kerr of Tonaghmore, Justice of the Supreme Court of the United Kingdom) gave judgment on 7 July 2003. As Kathryn McNeilly highlights in her feminist judgment, Kerr J rightly pointed out that abortion *is* legal in Northern Ireland—*in certain situations*. However, Barbara

[1] Karen Brennan, 'The State of Abortion Law in Northern Ireland' in J Schweppe (ed), *The Unborn Child, Article 40.3.3 and Abortion in Ireland: Twenty-Five Years of Protection?* (Dublin, The Liffey Press, 2008) 248–49.

Hewson remarks that, as a result of his judgment, the conditions for lawful abortion were defined much more restrictively than those applicable in other parts of the UK: 'abortions for foetal abnormality (a service previously available in Northern Ireland), or for rape or incest appear to be unlawful'.[2]

The FPANI appealed Kerr J's ruling, which concluded that the Department of Health, Social Services and Public Safety (DHSSPS) did not fail in its statutory duty to: (a) issue advice and/or guidance to women and clinicians in Northern Ireland on the availability and provision of termination of pregnancy services; or (b) investigate whether women in Northern Ireland are receiving satisfactory services in respect of actual or potential terminations of pregnancy in Northern Ireland; or (c) make, or secure the making of, arrangements necessary to ensure that women in Northern Ireland receive satisfactory services in respect of actual or potential terminations of pregnancy in Northern Ireland. It is for this appeal that Kathryn McNeilly contributes her feminist judgment. The other justices, namely Nicholson LJ, Campbell LJ and Sheil LJ, allowed the appeal and declaratory relief was granted, holding that guidelines must be provided.[3] It is of note that McNeilly LJ's is an additional, as opposed to a substitute, written judgment, which concurs with the other justices but for other reasons.

Further Legal Developments

Five years (!) after the Court of Appeal decision, on 13 March 2009, the DHSSPS published a document entitled, *Guidance on the Termination of Pregnancy: The Law and Clinical Practice in Northern Ireland* (the Guidance). This publication was later challenged in the High Court of Northern Ireland by the Society for the Protection of the Unborn Children, which is the subject of a feminist judgment by Claire McCann (with commentary by John Kennedy).[4] In *Society for the Protection of Unborn Children, Re an Application for Judicial Review*,[5] Girvan LJ found in favour of the DHSSPS in respect to five of the seven grounds, namely that the Guidance had not misrepresented or misinterpreted the law on the termination of pregnancy in Northern Ireland. However, it was held that those aspects of the publication dealing with counselling and conscientious objection failed to provide clear and accurate guidance, and the withdrawal of the DHSSPS Guidance was ordered, with a view to its being reconsidered.

The DHSSPS then revised its guidance in relation to those sections on counselling and conscientious objection, and issued them for consultation, beginning on 27 June 2010 and ending on 22 October 2010. No revised guidance resulted from this consultation, and the FPANI brought a fresh legal challenge to force the Minister of Health to comply with the 2004 Court of Appeal order. The FPANI was granted leave to apply for judicial review, with a full

[2] Barbara Hewson, 'The Law of Abortion in Northern Ireland' (2004 Summer) *Public Law* 234, 235.

[3] For academic commentary on this appeal, see Ruth Fletcher, 'Abortion Needs or Abortion Rights? Claiming State Accountability for Women's Reproductive Welfare: *Family Planning Association of Northern Ireland v. Minister -For Health, Social Services and Public Safety*' (2005) 13 *Feminist Legal Studies* 123.

[4] See ch 22.

[5] *Society for the Protection of Unborn Children, Re an Application for Judicial Review* [2009] NIQB 92.

hearing taking place in January 2013. In *Family Planning Association of Northern Ireland's Application*,[6] Treacy J acceded to the application, and revised guidance—*The Limited Circumstances for a Lawful Termination of Pregnancy in Northern Ireland: A Guidance Document for Health and Social Care Professionals on Law and Clinical Practice*—was considered by the Northern Ireland Executive on 28 March 2013. Another public consultation was advised, taking place between 8 April and 29 July 2013.

At this time, no new guidance has been issued.

Further Social/Cultural Developments

In the years that followed the 2003 decision in *Family Planning Association of Northern Ireland, Re an Application for Judicial Review*, there were many social and/or cultural developments that influenced the current political and legal climate surrounding abortion in Northern Ireland. The most recent developments include:

— The opening of the Marie Stopes Centre, Northern Ireland's first private abortion clinic, in Belfast in mid-October 2012.
— The death of Savita Halappanavar in Galway, Ireland on 28 October 2012.
— The latest guidance document, *The Limited Circumstances for a Lawful Termination of Pregnancy in Northern Ireland: A Guidance Document for Health and Social Care Professionals on Law and Clinical Practice* (2013), was highly criticised by feminist activists, for example in the Alliance For Choice (AFC) submission to the Committee for the Elimination of Discrimination Against Women (CEDAW): 'AFC expresses serious concerns about these guidelines including the language used which reinforces the criminalisation of women who seek abortion, the attempts to add restrictions beyond the scope of the current legal framework and further entrenchment of cultural views of women as mothers and reproducers.'
— In October 2013, senior health officials in Northern Ireland considered the cases of Sarah Ewart and another woman known only as 'Laura', who were both forced to travel to England because foetal abnormality is not a ground for lawful termination in Northern Ireland.
— A consultation was conducted by the Northern Ireland Department of Justice on the issue of abortion in instances of foetal abnormality and rape in Northern Ireland (closing date of 17 January 2015). The description from the Department of Justice website states: 'Firstly, [this consultation] looks at whether the law should enable abortion in cases where there is a diagnosis in pregnancy that the foetus has a lethal abnormality. Secondly, it addresses the issue of whether abortion should be available to women who have become pregnant as a result of sexual crime. It is not a debate on the wider issues of abortion law—issues often labelled as "pro-choice" and "pro-life".'
— On 7 May 2014, the High Court in London held that Northern Ireland women are not entitled to free NHS abortions in England.

[6] *Family Planning Association of Northern Ireland's Application* [2013] NIQB 1.

- On 23 September 2014, Jim Wells, who opposes abortion, even for victims of rape, is appointed Minister of Health in Northern Ireland.
- On 19 November 2014, anti-choice protester, Bernadette Smyth, is found guilty of harassing Dawn Purvis, then the Clinic Director of Marie Stopes Northern Ireland.
- On 28 November 2014, the British Pregnancy Advisory Service (BPAS) calls for new law to move anti-choice protesters from the doorstep of its clinics.
- On 2 February 2015, the Northern Irish Human Rights Commission was granted leave to pursue a judicial review of abortion law in Northern Ireland by the High Court in Belfast.
- On 12 April 2015, the Department of Justice in Northern Ireland recommends a change to Northern Ireland's abortion law, allowing for terminations in cases of fatal foetal abnormality.
- On 27 April 2015, Jim Wells resigns as Northern Ireland Health Minister over anti-gay remarks.
- On 15 June 2015, an application by the Northern Ireland Human Rights Commission (NIHRC) for judicial review of the current abortion law in NI is heard in the Queen's Bench Division, Belfast (see below for judgment).
- On 26 June 2015, an open letter is sent to the Northern Ireland public prosecution service, signed by 215 Northern Irish women, confessing to either having taken abortion pills themselves, or having helped women procure them, which is illegal under Northern Ireland's abortion laws. The letter is in response to an ongoing court case, which began in Belfast on 19 June 2015, in which a mother, who cannot be named to protect the identity of her daughter, is charged with unlawfully procuring 'poison' (abortion pills Mifepristone and Misoprostol) for her daughter to have a miscarriage.
- On 29 June 2015, Bernadette Smyth's appeal is successful and her guilty verdict is quashed, the judge finding there was insufficient evidence that she harassed former Clinic Director of Marie Stopes Northern Ireland, Dawn Purvis.
- On 22 July 2015, a mother and her teenage daughter lost an appeal against the UK Government's refusal to allow women in Northern Ireland to have abortions on the NHS. The women are granted permission to appeal their case to the Supreme Court on 23 December 2015, which is scheduled to be heard in November 2016.
- On 30 November 2015, the High Court finds in favour of NIHRC, holding that the current abortion legislation in NI is incompatible with the UK's obligations under the HRA 1998 in cases where women are pregnant and there is a fatal foetal abnormality or where the pregnancy is the result of rape and/or incest. A formal Declaration of Incompatibility is granted by Mr Justice Horner on 16 December 2015.
- On 10 February 2016, a proposal in the NI Assembly to reform legislation and allow abortion in cases of fatal foetal abnormality (FFA) was defeated by 59 votes to 40. The amendment to allow abortion in instances where a woman has become pregnant as a result of a sexual crime was voted down by 64 votes to 32. Voting against the amendments, the Democratic Unionist Party (DUP) asked the Health Minister, Simon Hamilton, to set up a working group to examine issues raised by FFA. This working group, initially scheduled to be formed in February 2016 and due to report back in June 2016, was not formed until July 2016 (see below for further details).

— On 24 March 2016, the NI Executive releases Guidance for Health and Social Care Professionals on the Termination of Pregnancy in Northern Ireland. These guidelines do not take into consideration the ruling by the High Court that NI abortion laws are in breach of human rights.
— On 4 April 2016, the first prosecution under the Offences Against the Person Act 1861 is taken against a 21-year old woman who received a suspended sentence over a self-induced abortion.
— On 20 June 2016, an appeal against the ruling that abortion law in NI is 'incompatible' with human rights law, jointly brought by the Department of Justice and NI Attorney General, John Larkin, begins in Belfast. The appeal lasted four days and judgment has been deferred.
— On 14 July 2016, the working group on FFA has its first meeting, the Chair being the Chief Medical Officer, Michael McBride. The group is expected to report to the Justice Minister, Claire Sugden, and the Health Minister, Michelle O'Neill, by the end of September 2016.

Limitations of Legal Judgment

In light of the limitations on the structure and content of legal judgment, including feminist judgment, this commentary will focus on some key theoretical issues that underlie McNeilly LJ's decision.

Indeterminacy of Legal Judgment

In paragraph 19 of her judgment, McNeilly LJ comments on the 'ineradicable indeterminacy of the law':

> An inherent indeterminacy exists within our common law tradition. Legal principles can never completely eradicate uncertainty and legal practice is never a straightforward application of legal rules in a fully predictable manner. This indeterminacy is what allows our common law adversarial system to operate; parties compete regarding the 'correct' interpretation of a particular legal provision in a particular context. All law is indeterminate.

This is a very brave assertion coming from a judge. Not least because it can be interpreted as undermining the very legitimacy of the law and, thus, that of the judges themselves tasked with enunciating its content. Purportedly, the very purpose of common law precedent or *stare decisis*—that is, the principle that like cases should be decided alike—is to 'restrain the discretion that legal indeterminacy would otherwise give judges'.[7] Yet McNeilly J, albeit daring in her addressing of the issue so openly and directly, is not really saying any more

[7] Caleb Nelson, 'Stare Decisis and Demonstrably Erroneous Precedents' (2001) 87 *Virginia Law Review* 1, 8.

than what legal philosophers and theorists have been expressing for years.[8] Some more recent examples include Peter Fitzpatrick's writings on the necessary 'responsiveness' of law in relation to its supposed determinate nature.[9] I myself have extensively detailed the 'fundamentally improvisational' nature of law,[10] which, put quite simply, is the necessary *negotiation* that takes place between the general (determinate) rules already in place and the singularity of the facts or case/question to be decided. As no two legal actions can be *exactly* the same, law can never completely void itself of indeterminacy, and judges must improvise on the law already in place in every instance of legal judgment.[11] This is not a controversial statement. However, by explicitly acknowledging the indeterminacy at the heart of legal judgment, McNeilly J opens up the possibility of more creative discussions of and solutions to the role of law in relation to women's equality.

Limitations/Gendered Nature of Judicial Review

In Melina Buckley's 'Author's Note' to her feminist judgment for the Women's Court of Canada in *Symes v Canada*,[12] she writes of the importance of judicial review to women's equality:

> Constitutional review[13] is one important, but by no means the only, avenue both for uncovering the structures of inequality as they manifest themselves in government actions, laws, and policies and for initiating steps towards the creation of equality. In this reconsideration of *Symes*, I highlight two features of transformative human rights practices in constitutional litigation: the need for judges to employ a substantive rather than an abstract conception of equality and the need to pay attention to the narrative and voices of women.[14]

Despite Buckley's optimism in relation to the possibility of such review, the issue as to whether judges, as opposed to legislatures, are better placed to ensure equality for and/or the advancement of women is extremely controversial, and the question of whether there is 'a distinctly feminist approach to theorising the legitimacy of judicial review' is nowhere

[8] Legal indeterminacy, first articulated by American Legal Realists in the 1930s, is perhaps most well known as a critique made by prominent Critical Legal Studies (CLS) scholars, such as David Kennedy. However, as Gunther Teubner explains, 'The critics vary in their analysis of legal indeterminacy. They ascribe indeterminacy of law to quite different complexes of causes: individual case decisions, legal institutions, the logic of legal argumentation, legal doctrine, social interests, or policies': '"And God laughed …" Indeterminacy, self-reference and paradox in law' (2011) 12 *German Law Journal* 376, 382.

[9] See, eg, Peter Fitzpatrick, *Modernism and the Grounds of Law* (Cambridge, Cambridge University Press, 2001); and Peter Fitzpatrick, *The Mythology of Modern Law* (London and New York, Routledge, 1992).

[10] Sara Ramshaw, *Justice as Improvisation: The Law of the Extempore* (London, Routledge, 2013) 4.

[11] Sara Ramshaw, 'Deconstructin(g) Jazz Improvisation: Derrida and the Law of the Singular Event' (2006) 2(1) *Critical Studies in Improvisation* 4.

[12] Melina Buckley, 'Author's Note. The Women's Court of Canada: *Symes v Canada*' (2006) 18(1) *Canadian Journal of Women and the Law* 27.

[13] Unlike Canada, under the English doctrine of parliamentary sovereignty, primary legislation (Acts of Parliament) cannot be subject to judicial review, except in limited cases where the primary legislation is contrary to the laws of the European Union. For a recent critical study of the constitutional context of judicial review in the UK (under parliamentary sovereignty), see Amy Street, *Judicial Review and the Rule of Law: Who's in Control?* (London, The Constitutional Society, 2013).

[14] Buckley, above n 12, 28.

near settled.[15] While there is not room in either this commentary or McNeilly J's judgment for a discussion of the advantages and/or limitations of judicial review in relation to women (especially in a jurisdiction such as Northern Ireland, which still does not have even a female High Court judge, let alone a Court of Appeal one), it is an issue that feminist judgments have the potential to explore or address.[16]

Power and Limitations of the Legal Voice

Over a quarter of a century ago, Lucinda Finlay wrote about the importance of thinking about the power and limitations of the legal voice:

> Language, and the thoughts that it expresses, is socially constructed and socially constituting. Rather than being neutral or naturally ordained, it reflects the world views and chosen meanings of those who have had power to affect definitions and create terms. The selected terms and meanings then shape our understandings of what things are, of the way the world is. Careful attention to the language we use can reveal hidden but powerful assumptions framing the way people think about the world. The persistence of the language then entrenches the way of thinking that it expresses.[17]

The power of legal language is evident in the terminology used by the relevant legislation in the FPANI case, such as section 58 of the Offences against the Person Act 1861 and section 25(1) of the Criminal Justice Act (Northern Ireland) 1945, which speak of the foetus as a 'child' or 'unborn child'. Moreover, Kerr J's judgment frames the issue in terms of 'anti-abortion' (para 15) instead of anti-choice. This seemingly neutral language actually reflects a particular world view, which already places a pregnant woman in a disadvantaged position in relation to personal autonomy and decision-making capacity. Moreover, it expresses and entrenches a preference for viewing the situation as one of protecting the foetus from harm as opposed to the pregnant woman's right to choose.

Attentive to the importance of language in relation to the law, in her judgment McNeilly LJ is careful to place 'concern for women's lives at the centre of [the law]' (para 34) and to emphasise that the 'right to life includes protection from more than just deprivation of physical life. Increasingly the right is read as also relevant to the protection of the conditions which sustain life—social, economic and political conditions which enable a human being to thrive and live a viable life' (para 34). This modification in focus and language directs attention back to women as decision-makers and to the problems inherent in forcing determinations with insufficient information, as is the case with the law surrounding abortion in Northern Ireland.

[15] This was an issue addressed at the Feminist Constitutional Theory Workshop at Edinburgh Law School on 28 May 2014. For more information, see www.legaltheorygroup.law.ed.ac.uk/spring-workshops/programme/feminist-constitutional-theory/ (last accessed 27 July 2015).

[16] See, eg, Jo Bridgeman's feminist judgment of *R v Portsmouth Hospitals NHS Trust, ex parte Glass*: '*R v Portsmouth Hospitals NHS Trust, ex parte Glass*' in Rosemary Hunter, Clare McGlynn and Erika Rackley (eds), *Feminist Judgments: From Theory to Practice* (Oxford and Portland, OR, Hart Publishing, 2010). According to Rosemary Hunter, Jo Bridgeman's feminist judgment identified 'the incapacity of judicial review proceedings to regulate potential future conflicts, as opposed to adjudicating retrospectively on past events': 'Feminist judgments as a teaching resource' (2012) 2(5) *Oñati Socio-Legal Series* 47, at https://kar.kent.ac.uk/35676/1/OSLS%20article.pdf (last accessed 27 July 2015).

[17] Lucinda Finlay, 'Breaking Women's Silence in Law: The Dilemma of the Gendered Nature of Legal Reasoning' (1989) 64 *Notre Dame Law Review* 886, 887.

Feminist Judgment—What Difference It Might Have Made?

While it is ultimately unclear how a feminist judgment would have influenced the legal, political and social landscape that followed the 2003 decision, it is beyond doubt that a feminist judgment would have shifted the focus of the debate to women as those who are most affected by the law, and would have marked a significantly different framing of the issues, with feminist-informed guidelines possibly preventing additional litigation and (ongoing) disputes. Alternatively, a feminist judgment might have warned of and alerted others to the potential danger of calling for further guidance that would lead to a narrowing of the scope of legal abortion. This possibility, forecasted by feminists Fegan and Rebouche,[18] is actually what happened in the draft documents to follow the 2004 appeal. The articulation of a feminist judgment in relation to the issue of abortion may have led to abortion being made legal in many more instances, if not all, in Northern Ireland, and Sarah Ewart, 'Laura' and countless unnamed others would have been saved the trauma and expense associated with travelling to England for abortions. Lastly, a feminist judgment in this instance might have opened up discussion on the gendered nature of and potentially limited/widened/reframed the doctrine of judicial review in Northern Ireland and the UK more generally.

[18] Eileen Fegan and Rachel Rebouche, 'Northern Ireland's Abortion Law: The Morality of Silence and the Censure of Agency' (2003) 11 *Feminist Legal Studies* 221, 235.

Family Planning Association of Northern Ireland v Minister for Health, Social Services and Public Safety (SPUC NI and others intervening)

[2004] NICA 39

QUEEN'S BENCH DIVISION

KERR J

21, 22 MARCH, 7 JULY 2003

COURT OF APPEAL

NICHOLSON LJ, CAMPBELL LJ, SHEIL LJ AND McNEILLY LJ

24–26 MAY, 8 OCTOBER 2004

McNEILLY LJ

INTRODUCTION

[**1**] Crisis or unplanned pregnancy is an issue which hundreds of women face and substantial numbers of medical practitioners and other health professionals come into contact with every year in Northern Ireland. It is undoubtedly very often a difficult, stressful and time-sensitive experience both for the woman and the range of professionals who are there to help, advise and support her. In such circumstances it is essential that both patients and professionals have prompt access to clear, accurate and complete information as to all the options which are potentially available, including lawful termination of pregnancy.

[**2**] The appellant in this case, the Family Planning Association of Northern Ireland ('FPANI'), an organisation that provides a range of sexual health services, including assistance for women in such situations, is concerned that this is not always so in Northern Ireland. This case is an appeal to the decision of Kerr J (as he then was) in the Northern Ireland High Court to dismiss an application for judicial review of the alleged failure of the Department of Health, Social Services and Public Safety ('the Department') to fulfil its statutory duty under the Health and Personal Social Services (NI) Order 1972 ('the 1972 Order') and the common law principles of administrative law. The appellant alleges that the Department has unlawfully failed to:

(a) issue advice and or guidance to women and clinicians in Northern Ireland on the availability and provision of termination of pregnancy services; or
(b) investigate whether women in Northern Ireland are receiving satisfactory services in respect of actual or potential terminations of pregnancy in Northern Ireland; or

(c) make, or secure the making of, arrangements necessary to ensure that women in Northern Ireland receive satisfactory services in respect of actual or potential terminations of pregnancy in Northern Ireland.

[**3**] The appellant sought a declaration from the High Court that the respondent had acted unlawfully in failing to fulfil its statutory duty in these three regards as well as an order of mandamus requiring the Minister to cure such unlawfulness. Kerr J dismissed the application based on the conclusion that, in his view, the law on termination of pregnancy in Northern Ireland is clear; no evidence could be found indicating significant uncertainty amongst medical professionals as to the law; nor that women who were entitled to lawful termination services in Northern Ireland were being denied them, leading there to be no need for the Department to investigate whether women were receiving satisfactory services. The declarations outlined above are still being sought by the appellant in the present appeal, although the order of mandamus is not.

[**4**] While I cannot agree with all of his judgment, it is to be welcomed that Kerr J clearly affirmed that termination of pregnancy is legal in Northern Ireland in certain circumstances and that the law is somewhat difficult in its practical application. This in itself marks significant progress in dispelling myths on the legal status of abortion in Northern Ireland and moving towards dealing with the issues surrounding it in a more open and productive way. It is also important to note the necessary limitations of judicial review which judicial comment in this case must operate within. Judicial review is not intended to function as an appeal of the actions of a public body. It must remain focused on review of statutory duty and the legality of decision-making processes and outcomes as opposed to their merits (*R v Secretary of State for Northern Ireland, ex parte Finlay* [1983] 9 NIJB1; *Re Glor Na nGael's Application* [1991] NI 117). In this respect, as has been noted by my learned colleagues, judgment in this case cannot compel any particular action from the Department nor speak to the wider issue of reform of abortion law in Northern Ireland. Although perhaps the questions raised in this case point towards the need to place the law in this area on a legislative footing, if not to overhaul it altogether.

[**5**] My learned colleagues Nicholson LJ, Campbell LJ and Sheil LJ have delivered their judgments, which I have had the advantage of reading in draft. I intend to agree with their final conclusions that the appeal should be allowed, but wish to respectfully differ in reasoning in a number of respects which I will make clear presently. In particular, given the public interest imperatives which drive the doctrine of judicial review, I seek to return to, and ground my decision in, the experiences of those who are affected by the actions, or inactions, of the Department in question in this appeal. My learned colleagues are correct in their remarks that abortion is a sensitive and politically charged issue in Northern Ireland. However, it is my concern that in the judgments which have been made in this case attempts at a 'neutral' approach to the issue have had the effect of rendering invisible the experiences of women who are at the centre of the duties and services in question.

THE DEPARTMENT'S STATUTORY DUTY

[**6**] The Department of Health, Social Services and Public Safety is responsible for the provision of health services and personal social services in Northern Ireland. The respondent is the Minister for Health, Social Services and Public Safety, although given the recent reinstatement of Direct Rule, the Secretary of State will answer as the respondent in this appeal. The Health and Personal Social Services (NI) Order 1972 provides for the duties and powers of the Department. The appellant has outlined Articles 4(a), 4(b), 7, 14 and 51 as they appear in Part II of the 1972 Order as the provisions the Department is failing to lawfully comply with. The relevant extracts from these Articles provide as follows:

> *General Duty of the Ministry*
>
> **4.** It shall be the duty of the Ministry –
>
> (a) to provide or secure the provision of integrated health services in Northern Ireland designed to promote the physical and mental health of the people of Northern Ireland through the prevention, diagnosis and treatment of illness;
> (b) to provide or secure the provision of Personal Social Services in Northern Ireland designed to promote the welfare of people in Northern Ireland

and the Ministry shall so discharge its duty as to secure the effective co-ordination of Health and Personal Social Services.

> *Prevention of Illness, Care and Aftercare*
>
> **7.**–(1) The Ministry shall make arrangements, to such extent as it considers necessary, for the purposes of the prevention of illness, the care of persons suffering from illness, or the aftercare of such persons.
>
> *Health Education*
>
> **14.** The Ministry may disseminate, by whatever means it thinks fit, information relating to the promotion and maintenance of health and the prevention of illness.
>
> *General Social Welfare*
>
> **15.**–(1) In the exercise of its functions under Article 4(b) the Ministry shall make available advice, guidance and assistance, to such extent as it considers necessary and for that purpose shall make such arrangements and provide and secure the provision of such facilities ... as it considers suitable and adequate.

The appellants submit that the Department is also failing to comply with Article 51 contained in Part V of the 1972 Order which provides:

> *Powers of Ministry where services are inadequate*

51. If the Ministry is satisfied, after such investigation as it thinks fit, that any list prepared under this Order –

(a) of medical practitioners undertaking to provide general medical services; or
(b) ...; or
(c) ...; or
(d) ...; or
(e) of persons undertaking to provide any other services;

is not such as to secure the adequate provision of the services in question, or that for any other reason any considerable number of persons are not receiving satisfactory services under the arrangements in force under this Order the Ministry may authorise a Health and Social Services Board to make such other arrangements as the Ministry may approve, or may itself make such other arrangements as appears to the Ministry to be necessary.

[**7**] It is submitted by Lord Lester on behalf of the appellant that

Article 4 imposes a general duty on the respondent to secure the adequate provision of health and personal social services including termination of pregnancy services in Northern Ireland. Article 14 empowers the respondent to disseminate health information. Article 15 imposes a positive duty on the respondent, to such an extent as it considers necessary to make guidance available in the discharge of the general duty under Article 4(b). Article 51 empowers the respondent to make alternative arrangements where satisfied, after such investigation as he thinks fit, that services provided pursuant to the Order are inadequate or unsatisfactory.' In addition, it is submitted that 'the respondent cannot properly discharge the duties imposed on him by the Order or exercise the powers granted to him, unless he has sufficient knowledge and information as to whether an adequate service is in fact being provided in respect of terminations of pregnancy in Northern Ireland.

[**8**] In contrast, the respondent asserts that the Article 4 duty is a target duty which has 'a degree of elasticity and allow[s] a considerable degree of tolerance to the public authority concerned in determining how the appropriate provision should be effected.' In relation to Article 15 the respondent accepts that it does have power to publish and issue guidelines, but that there is no legal duty to do so and it does not 'believe that any purpose of sufficient value would or could be served by issuing guidance to practitioners on the law relating to termination of pregnancies in Northern Ireland.' Article 51, in turn, is asserted as 'no more than an aspect of the target duty imposed by Article 4(a).'

[**9**] It is not disputed by any party, nor was it questioned by Kerr J in the High Court, that the broad Article 4 'target duty' (*R v Inner London Education Authority, ex parte Ali* (1990) 2 Admin LR 822) imposed upon the respondent covers the provision of services relating to the termination of pregnancy and attendance to the physical and mental health and well-being of women facing crisis or unplanned pregnancies. It is also accepted by the Department, as outlined above, that the issuing of guidelines to women and medical practitioners does potentially fall within the duties outlined in the 1972 Order. Mrs Maureen McCartney, a principal Civil Servant in the Department, has given details in her affidavit of when the Department has issued information and guidelines in other areas 'where it has considered that some purpose of sufficient value to warrant publication would be served

by doing so.' What is disputed is, firstly, whether the law on abortion in Northern Ireland is sufficiently unclear as to compel the Department to issue guidelines and, secondly, whether evidence exists to warrant investigation into whether women are receiving satisfactory services in relation to termination in Northern Ireland.

CLARITY OF THE LAW RELATING TO ABORTION IN NORTHERN IRELAND

[**10**] The law relating to abortion in Northern Ireland is contained in sections 58 and 59 of the Offences Against the Person Act 1861, section 25(1) of the Criminal Justice Act (NI) 1945 and a body of case law. Section 58 of the Act of 1861 states:

> Every woman, being with child, who, with intent to procure her own miscarriage, shall unlawfully administer to herself any poison or other noxious thing, or shall unlawfully use any instrument or other means whatsoever with the like intent, and whosoever, with intent to procure the miscarriage of any woman, whether she be or be not with child, shall unlawfully administer to her or cause to be taken by her any poison or other noxious thing, or shall unlawfully use any instrument or other means whatsoever with the like intent, shall be guilty of felony, and being convicted thereof shall be liable …

Section 59 of the same Act provides:

> Whosoever shall unlawfully supply or procure any poison or other noxious thing, or any instrument or thing whatsoever, knowing that the same is intended to be unlawfully used or employed with intent to procure the miscarriage of any woman, whether she be or be not with child, shall be guilty of a misdemeanour, and being convicted thereof shall be liable …

Section 25(1) of the Criminal Justice Act (NI) 1945 provides:

> … Any person who, with intent to destroy the life of a child incapable of being born alive, by any wilful act causes a child to die before it has an existence independent of its mother, shall be guilty of felony, to wit, of child destruction, and shall be liable on conviction thereof on indictment to penal servitude for life. Provided that no person shall be found guilty of an offence under this section unless it is proved that the act which caused the death of a child was no done in good faith for the purpose only of preserving the life of the mother.

[**11**] My learned colleagues have examined in great detail the case law supplementing this legislative framework. Accordingly, I shall not dwell upon the details of this body of case law extensively. To provide a brief overview, *R v Bourne* [1939] 1 KB 687 is the leading case in this area. In this case MacNaughton J read the legislative proviso contained in section 1(1) of the Infant Life (Preservation) Act 1929 (later mirrored in section 25(1) of the Criminal Justice Act (NI) 1945) that 'a person shall not be guilty of an offence if acting in good faith to preserve the mother's life' as also relevant to section 58 of the Offences Against the Person Act. The result was to hold that a person who procures an abortion in good faith for the purposes of preserving the life of the mother—preventing her becoming a 'physical or mental wreck'—shall not be guilty of an offence.

[**12**] The 1990s witnessed a spate of case law engaging the interpretation of this provision. To plot the significant points of this body of case law, in *Northern Health and Social*

Services Board v F and G [1993] NI 268 preserving the life and health of the woman was read as encompassing both her physical and mental health and well-being. This case involved a minor whose mental well-being necessitated a termination. In this case even though the termination was determined as lawful the minor was still required to travel to England for the procedure due to what Sheil J (as he then was) described in his judgment as 'the reluctance of obstetricians in Northern Ireland to carry out the operation.' The case of *Northern Health and Social Services Board v A and Others* [1994] NIJBI, which involved a mentally handicapped woman pregnant as a result of rape, interpreted preserving the life of the woman to entail avoiding an adverse effect which is 'real and serious.' This was further elaborated in *Western Health and Social Services Board v CMB and the Official Solicitor* [1995] (unreported), a case involving a mentally handicapped minor, to be 'permanent or at least long-term.'

[**13**] From this legislative and common law framework, a statement of the law appears to be that termination is permitted where there is a serious and long-term risk to the woman's mental or physical health or well-being. However, while legal practitioners may find clarity in this statement and how it should be applied, the appellant's case raises concerns that much uncertainty greets women and medical practitioners not fortunate enough to possess years of legal experience and knowledge. Kerr J in his judgment spent much time considering the distinction between what the law is and its practical application. His conclusion was that 'the legal principles are … clear and easily absorbed. It might well be difficult in some circumstances to decide whether the facts of an individual case can be accommodated within the principles as outlined but this is not due to a lack of clarity in the principles themselves.' The law, for Kerr J, is not unclear but merely difficult to apply and these difficulties are matters of clinical judgment which the issuing of guidelines could do nothing to alleviate. I wish to make three comments on this issue, the first two relating to medical professionals' understanding and application of the law, the third relating to the certainty of the law itself.

[**14**] Firstly, like my learned colleagues Nicholson LJ, Campbell LJ and Sheil LJ, I am also unconvinced, following evidence submitted by a range of medical professionals, that there exists no uncertainty as to what the law in this area is. An understanding of what the law is must be a prerequisite for the exercise of clinical discretion as to application of the law. Dr James Dornan, Director of Fetal Medicine at the Royal Jubilee Maternity Hospital, pointed in his affidavit towards uncertainty amongst himself and his colleagues as to the legal position of termination in cases of foetal abnormality. It is highly significant that in 2001 Dr Dornan wrote to the Department requesting guidance. I cannot accept, as Kerr J did, that the Department's response of referring Dr Dornan to Mrs McCartney's affidavit submitted to the High Court in the present case constitutes adequate guidance as to the current legal framework governing this area. Ms Breedagh Hughes, the Northern Ireland Board Secretary of the Royal College of Midwives, also expressed concern in her affidavit regarding the absence of guidance for midwives as to their role in termination procedures. Not only does this suggest that lack of open and readily accessible guidance on the law is making the role of professionals difficult, but it is also placing practitioners and ancillary staff in the very serious position of potential criminal liability, a potentiality which will no doubt impact upon their readiness to provide such services. While Kerr J appeared to dismiss such evidence, I do not find it possible to do so.

[**15**] Secondly, even if there was clear evidence of consensus as to what the law is, I do not feel that the issue would be fully resolved. In this regard it is worth spending some time considering Kerr J's comments. While his distinction between what the law is and how it is applied is no doubt accurate, and a chasm which women have indeed struggled with for decades, I do not feel that it can be used to justify inaction in this case. Not only does it sit uncomfortably for judicial comment to state what the law is and then abandon all responsibility for its practical application, deeming it a matter of clinical judgement for non-legal professionals, but this distinction leads to problematic outcomes when we return to the experiences of women. Declaring application of the law to be entirely within the domain of medicine further solidifies the power and legitimacy of the medical profession to make decisions about the lives of women. In contrast, the issuing of guidelines making the legal framework and women's position under it explicit would enhance the position of women to access information and make decisions concerning their own reproductive capacity. This is particularly important in a context where, as the appellant has submitted, conservative attitudes are prevalent amongst the still male-dominated medical profession in Northern Ireland, especially in rural areas, a point I will return to later. Guidance in this respect would enhance not only the understanding of medical practitioners but also the ability of women to access coherent information about termination and its legal availability.

[**16**] Thus, I follow my colleagues in this court in respectfully disagreeing with Kerr J's decision that no relevant uncertainty exists amongst the medical community as to what the law is. I also agree that the issuing of guidance would not, as the Department suggests, merely serve to 'summarise the law relating to abortion as explained by the High Court.' As my colleagues have highlighted, questions of aftercare, the rights and roles of ancillary staff and issues such as clarifying how a referral for a termination is made and where such services are provided would also be of great benefit to women and professionals. Evidence suggests this information is at the least difficult to access, if not completely unavailable. However, a distinction must be drawn between my reasoning here and that of my colleagues, Nicholson LJ in particular. While throughout his judgment the learned judge advances the utility of guidelines for both medical practitioners and women, I find problematic his view that 'it would be wrong to give that guidance to pregnant women unless they request it or in the opinion of the medical profession need it. Otherwise it could be regarded as an encouragement to seek abortion.' Of course, if a patient expresses that a pregnancy is planned there will usually be no need to consider the option of lawful termination, but I must express concern with the paternalistic sentiment which I fear underpins this comment, if unconsciously, climaxing in his concluding comment that 'this judgment is written in the hope that the department will seek to … encourage those seeking an abortion in Northern Ireland to make a different choice.'

[**17**] Just as it is not the position of the court to take the decision of a public body in these proceedings, so too the court has no jurisdiction in advocating, or seeking to dissuade women from taking, a particular course of action. The concern here is whether medical professionals and women can be aided in deciding whether a termination may be lawful in particular circumstances, not reducing the number of lawful terminations which are carried out. Basing a perception that a need for guidance exists on paternalistic concerns such as the need to ensure women know they are consenting to a procedure that 'can have damaging effects on the physical and mental health of the mother' (Nicholson LJ) or to 'protect

the interests of the unborn child' (Sheil LJ) muddies the water of the crux of this case—that evidence suggests guidance may be needed to make the law clearer to those who use it.

[**18**] A further distinction must be made between my reasoning and that of my learned colleagues on the third point which I wish to discuss; whether the law itself is clear in this area. Much consideration has been dedicated to the summary of the law proposed by Mr Hanna for the respondent and approved by Lord Lester for the appellant. Kerr J and Sheil LJ accepted this summary as a clear statement of the law, while Nicholson LJ rejected the summary mainly because the principles 'are not expressed in language appropriate to a criminal trial which is what the medical practitioner would be facing.' Nicholson LJ then goes on to highlight a number of indeterminacies which the principles contain. I agree that Mr Hanna's summary does indeed contain such indeterminacies. However, I must disagree with the frame of illegality which Nicholson LJ's comments place abortion within, further solidifying myths regarding the legality of abortion in Northern Ireland.

[**19**] I also believe that debate surrounding this summary of the law veils a more fundamental issue that the judiciary and all working with the practical application of the law need to embrace—the ineradicable indeterminacy of the law. An inherent indeterminacy exists within our common law tradition. Legal principles can never completely eradicate uncertainty and legal practice is never a straightforward application of legal rules in a fully predictable manner. This indeterminacy is what allows our common law adversarial system to operate; parties compete regarding the 'correct' interpretation of a particular legal provision in a particular context. All law is indeterminate. The law relating to termination of pregnancy in Northern Ireland is indeterminate. This fact is added to by the somewhat ad hoc way in which the law has developed and the sensitivity of the issues involved which has led to a general reluctance to deal with this topic openly and substantively. In an area of law so frequently engaged by non-legal practitioners, guidance would undoubtedly be of use in helping to work through the particular indeterminacy of law in this area. Judicial declarations of clarity or technical fumbling will not be of use to those who need to work with the law in every day, time-sensitive situations. Thus, the best option appears to be to accept the inherent indeterminacy of law and seek to establish mechanisms, such as guidance, which make the law as accessible and workable as possible.

INVESTIGATION

[**20**] The second question in this appeal is whether the Department failed to comply with its statutory duty under Article 4 of the 1972 Order in refraining from carrying out investigation as to whether women are receiving satisfactory services in respect of actual or potential terminations of pregnancy. It is not disputed that no investigation has been undertaken by the Department in relation to the extent and nature of termination services being provided. Mr Hanna for the respondent asserts that there is no evidence that any woman has been deterred from having a lawful termination performed in Northern Ireland and that the appellant's case is based on mere assertions by an interest group. Furthermore, the Department asserts that there is no need to carry out investigation into the extent and nature of termination services because 'all lawful termination will be provided, if required, under the Health and Personal Social Services.' The appellant argues, in contrast, that the Department cannot effectively discharge the duties imposed on it unless it is informed of the adequacy of the services currently being provided.

[**21**] In Kerr J's view, since the law is clear 'there is no evidence to suggest that there is any lack of "satisfactory services" and the case for investigation falls away.' His analysis of this aspect of the appellant's case, therefore, was restricted. Having rejected that the law, and understanding of the law, is as clear as Kerr J proposed it to be, it is necessary to spend some time considering the issues surrounding investigation. Kerr J appears to suggest that because there is no evidence of unsatisfactory service provision in this area no investigation is warranted. In my view, however, positive evidence of satisfactory service provision should be required to successfully argue that no investigation is warranted. Otherwise the Department is permitted to rely on its own lack of investigation to justify that there is no need for investigation. It is here, on the question of investigation, that the Department has a chance to centre its work on the experiences of women as its service users.

[**22**] I concur with Nicholson LJ that from the 1993 case of *Northern Health and Social Services Board v F and G* [1993] NI 268 highlighted above the Department should have been alerted to the fact that there may be a number of women entitled to abortion services who are unable to access them in Northern Ireland. On the contrary, the Department appears to have closed its ears to case law developments and has demonstrated a sustained lack of information collection on abortion services, for example, the grounds on which lawful terminations are carried out. Similarly, the Department was also aware of Dr Colin Francome's 1994 study which found that 11% of Northern Ireland GPs had treated patients suffering from the consequences of amateur abortions. The current legal framework governing termination of pregnancy in Northern Ireland combined with the costly alternative option of travelling to Britain to obtain a lawful termination unfortunately makes it more likely that women may be at risk from 'backstreet abortion' operators. The seriousness of this situation combined with the Department's awareness of research relating to it raises further questions as to why no investigation into whether women are receiving satisfactory services in respect of actual or potential terminations of pregnancy in Northern Ireland has been carried out.

[**23**] The vacuum of quantitative data on termination service provision in Northern Ireland is not the only issue relevant to the question of investigation. In his judgment Kerr J also notes—although dismisses—a significant point advanced by the appellant which, keeping the experiences of women central, warrants consideration. This point relates to the imbrication of socio-cultural values and the practical working of law on abortion. Every judgment in this case has acknowledged the particularly conservative social and religious context of Northern Ireland and the impact this has had in rendering abortion, to say the least, a 'sensitive' issue. As part of this context views on gender, reproduction and family life in Northern Ireland have maintained traditional perspectives on women and motherhood. In my view, the present case must be placed in this context and these issues also point towards a role for the Department in investigation.

[**24**] Mr Hanna on behalf of the respondent raises the concern that the number of health professionals who object to abortion on moral and/or religious grounds may be higher in Northern Ireland than in the rest of the UK. It is quite possible that local socio-cultural attitudes combined with discomfort, uncertainty and misinformation surrounding the law governing abortion may influence application of the law in cautious, conservative ways. Perhaps even in ways which deny access to termination services when such would fall within the law. I regret that I cannot accept Kerr J's conclusion that the current vacuum

of evidence regarding such practices, combined with a medical practitioner's general duty to make sure his/her personal beliefs do not prejudice patients' care, is enough to confirm that such imbrication between law and socio-cultural views does not exist or is not impacting application of the law in this area. FPANI is an organisation that for over two decades has been working with women facing unplanned or crisis pregnancies and has had significant contact with medical practitioners and other health professionals in this area. Given this experience I believe it would be wrong to merely dismiss their concerns as entirely unfounded, and would suggest that such concerns again may indicate the need for thorough investigation by the Department as to the extent and nature of services being provided to women.

[**25**] It is also concerning that, as Ms Audrey Simpson of FPANI asserts in her affidavit, there is currently only one hospital in Belfast which carries out most terminations in Northern Ireland. This assertion remains unchallenged and unexplained by the Department and suggests an unsatisfactory spread of service provision across the province, given that termination of pregnancy is generally not a complex or highly specialised procedure. It is essential that women receive parity of access to impartial information and services wherever they live. The concentration of abortion provision in Belfast raises serious concerns about how widespread the service provision the Department offers currently is. I would also suggest that this information is gathered with attention to the particular socio-cultural context of Northern Ireland and the Department is assured that conservative and religious approaches to gender and reproduction, particularly in more rural areas outside Belfast, are not hindering fulfilment of its statutory duty under Article 4 of the 1972 Order.

[**26**] Informing itself of the situation in respect to services it is providing, or potentially providing, without doubt forms part of the target duty laid down for the Department in Article 4 of the 1972 Order. The Department appears to have fallen down in this duty by taking too few steps to inform itself of the adequacy, or otherwise, of services being provided to women across Northern Ireland. The Department's establishment of a working group to consider whether the issuing of guidance is necessary is a welcome move which, perhaps, could be accompanied by the setting up of an investigative committee to inform both the provision of services in relation to termination of pregnancy and consideration of whether, and on what issues, guidance is required.

HUMAN RIGHTS

[**27**] Lord Lester for the appellant argues that the Department, as a public authority, has a duty under section 6 of the Human Rights Act 1998 not to act in a way which is incompatible with rights under the European Convention of Human Rights. It is submitted that the court is under the same section 6 duty and, moreover, section 3 of the same Act reinforces this duty by outlining a need to read and give effect to primary and subordinate legislation in a way which is compatible with Convention rights. Thus, the appellant asserts that Convention rights, and their domestic enshrinement in the Human Rights Act, are fundamental to the Department's fulfilment of its duties under the 1972 Order and the court's interpretation of it. The particular rights which are alleged as in violation by the Department's current position are Article 2, the right to life, and Article 8, the right to private and family life.

[**28**] Kerr J in his judgment and my learned colleagues in this court are of the opinion that human rights in no way assist the appellant's case. Where an application for judicial review is made wholly or, as in the present case, partly with reference to human rights the applicant must satisfy the test laid out in section 7 of the Human Rights Act 1998. This test mirrors the test for standing before the European Court of Human Rights provided in Article 34 of the Convention and requires that the applicant is a victim of the alleged human rights violation in question. The appellant does not argue that it fulfils such a test, but makes a rights-based argument under the Human Rights Act nonetheless. The question appears to be whether the court can or must consider the 1972 Order and the Department's actions/inactions through the lens of human rights nevertheless. I regret that I cannot so easily agree with the view of my learned colleagues in answering this question in the negative.

[**29**] The case law surrounding Article 34 of the Convention and section 7 of the Human Rights Act has indeed been quite restrictive. In relation to the former, Kerr J and Nicholson LJ rightly cite the authority of *Klass and others v Germany* (1978) 2 EHRR 214 where it was affirmed that an applicant should claim to have been actually affected by the violation in question, rejecting that individuals could complain against a law *in abstracto* or in a kind of *actio poplarius*. However, it is important to note that some case law in the European Court of Human Rights does appear to suggest that abstract review of state action/inaction is possible. For example, *Open Door and Dublin Well Women* (1992) 15 EHRR 244, *Kjeldsen, Busk and Madsen v Denmark* (1980) 1 EHRR 711 and *Brüggemann and Scheuten v Germany* (1977) 3 EHRR 244 point towards a wider interpretation of the Article 34 rule. Domestic case law under the Human Rights Act has also generally taken a strict approach to section 7 standing, although here too the recent case of *R (Rusbrudger) v Attorney General* [2003] UKHL 38 took a wider approach.

[**30**] On first blush, it appears that at both the domestic and European level only by relying on reasonably obscure case law can the appellant be considered to have standing to make human rights arguments. However, I believe it is relevant that while not a victim in the strict sense, the appellant dedicates significant amounts of time and resources to advising women and health professionals on the remit of termination services in Northern Ireland. There is a close imbrication between the interests of the women the appellant alleges are facing potential rights violations and the work that the appellant carries out. The lack of guidance in this area is also hindering the appellant from carrying out its work in the most effective and expedient manner. These facts lead me to conclude that the human rights argument made by the appellant is relevant to review in this case.

[**31**] In addition, there is an increasing importance of human rights in the UK legal system which obliges courts to place their work within a broader human rights frame. This is surely what the duty outlined in section 3 reflects. This increasing importance of human rights appears to me to be particularly important in cases of judicial review. While the section 7 test remains in place, the close relationship between human rights and the public interest, the latter forming the epicentre of the doctrine of judicial review, surely means that human rights concerns can no longer be swiftly dismissed in cases such as the present, even if only considered *obiter*. Thus, in carrying out the function of reviewing public power and the performance of public duties it would be amiss in the contemporary legal landscape for the court to ignore the wider human rights context which its powers of review are located within. I fear that in dismissing any human rights argument as relevant in the present case

my learned colleagues may have taken a rather restrictive approach to the contemporary doctrine of judicial review and its relation to human rights concerns.

[**32**] With this in mind, attention should be paid to the appellant's assertion that the current position in relation to services for the termination of pregnancy in Northern Ireland impacts women's enjoyment of human rights. In particular, Article 2 of the Convention appears to have important resonances. I am not asserting that this is the only right which is relevant. Article 2 does, however, powerfully illustrate how attention to rights may shed further light on the issues raised in this case. This Article provides that:

1. Everyone's right to life shall be protected by law. No one shall be deprived of his life intentionally save in the execution of a sentence of a court following his conviction of a crime for which this penalty is provided by law.
2. Deprivation of life shall not be regarded as inflicted in contravention of this Article when it results from the use of force which is no more than absolutely necessary:
   (a) in defence of any person from unlawful violence;
   (b) in order to effect a lawful arrest or to prevent the escape of a person lawfully detained;
   (c) in action lawfully taken for the purpose of quelling a riot or insurrection.

[**33**] Evidence presented to this court raises concern that practice surrounding the provision of termination services in Northern Ireland may be leading to potential violations of this Article which the Department should be attentive to. Evidence from medical practitioners that there is uncertainty, or at least a lack of clarity, amongst professionals as to when abortion may be lawfully carried out in Northern Ireland indicates that women's physical lives may be placed at risk unnecessarily by lawful termination which is refused or delayed. This refusal or delay may also lead women to turn to illegal 'backstreet' abortion providers, further risking their lives and physical well-being. Anxiety surrounding possible criminal prosecution which may lead practitioners to apply the law conservatively could, as I have suggested above, be aided by the issuing of guidelines leading, in turn, to a more robust protection under Article 2 for women experiencing unplanned or crisis pregnancy.

[**34**] In addition, however, placing concern for women's lives at the centre of statutory duties in relation to lawful services for the termination of pregnancy involves more. The right to life includes protection from more than just deprivation of physical life. Increasingly the right is read as also relevant to the protection of the conditions which sustain life—social, economic and political conditions which enable a human being to thrive and live a viable life. In this sense further concerns are raised as to the Department's current inaction under the 1972 Order. This approach to Article 2 suggests the need for action to ensure, for example, effective aftercare services for all women resident in Northern Ireland who undergo termination, whether in Northern Ireland or elsewhere. It also suggests a role for investigation into women's experiences of termination services. Are current arrangements across the province sufficient to ensure women's lives are being promoted and protected in the widest possible sense? The statutory duties imposed on the Department read in this way require it to attend to the conditions under its control which make the lives of women who face crisis or unplanned pregnancies viable, flourishing, or otherwise. While

this is a reading which may appear *prima facia* unorthodox, it suggests what an approach which values and takes seriously the lives of women may look like.

[**35**] It is also significant to note that Article 2 is a non-derogable right; it cannot be withdrawn or compromised in any circumstance. In the case of *Bugdaycay v Secretary of State for the Home Department* [1987] AC 514 it was held that where non-derogable rights are at issue in a case of judicial review, as I have argued Article 2 is in the present case, 'anxious scrutiny' of the powers and decision-making in question should be undertaken. In light of this, I must respectfully disagree with my learned colleagues and take the Article 2 concerns raised by the current case very seriously. Article 2 is relevant to review of the Department's action/inaction under the 1972 Order and indeed strengthens the need for a reassessment of its current position in relation to the issues raised in this appeal.

CONCLUSION

[**36**] From the above I conclude that the appeal should be allowed and the appropriate declarations made. I reiterate that this conclusion is not directing the Department to issue guidelines on the law governing abortion in Northern Ireland. Such a direction would overstep the function of review and make decisions reserved for elective representatives. What this conclusion is directing, however, is that the Department look again at issues such as clarity about and application of the law amongst medical professionals, availability of information on lawful termination for women facing crisis or unplanned pregnancies, and at the considerable gaps in its own knowledge as to the termination services that are, or are not, currently being provided on the ground.

[**37**] Kerr J is no doubt correct in his assessment that the issuing of guidance, if the Department does come to this conclusion, is not the answer to all the problems in this area of law nor to all the problems experienced by women facing crisis or unplanned pregnancies in Northern Ireland. Nevertheless, some of the difficulties encountered by women and professionals may be alleviated by taking action such as issuing guidance and investigating the nuances of current service provision. This must begin by placing the needs and experiences of those most directly affected by this issue at the heart of the Department's actions. While this case cannot speak to the wider state of the law governing termination of pregnancy in Northern Ireland, it can ensure that the Department is approaching its statutory duties with a mind-set which is committed to providing the best possible service and the most complete information within the current law for those who need it.

22

Commentary on *Society for the Protection of Unborn Children's Application for Judicial Review*

JOHN KENNEDY

The Facts

In March 2009, the Department of Health, Social Services and Public Safety (DHSSPS) published a guidance document setting out the legal principles governing abortion in Northern Ireland, *Guidance on the Termination of Pregnancy: The Law and Clinical Practice in Northern Ireland* (the Guidance). The Guidance was published in response to a 2004 Court of Appeal judgment[1] that held the Department had failed to perform its statutory duty[2] to provide integrated services to women seeking lawful termination of pregnancy in Northern Ireland. The DHSSPS emphasised that the Guidance did not make any changes to the law of Northern Ireland;[3] the purpose of the document was to explain the existing law, with particular reference to the issues of informed consent, conscientious objection and the provision of aftercare services. Reaction to the Guidance was both predictable and revealing. While the Family Planning Association of Northern Ireland (FPANI) cautiously welcomed the development as a 'first step', members of the Democratic Unionist Party (DUP)—in particular Jeffrey Donaldson MP—expressed concern over certain 'unresolved' issues.[4] Carmel Hanna of the Social Democratic and Labour Party (SDLP) expressed her support for the Guidance, 'on the understanding that the absolute legal ban on abortion [remained] unchanged',[5] while Bernadette Smyth of the anti-abortion group Precious Life criticised the move as an attempt to legalise abortion by 'the back door';[6] neither appeared to be familiar

[1] *The Family Planning Association of Northern Ireland v Minister for Health, Social Services and Public Safety and Ors* [2004] NICA 37. See ch 16 of this collection.

[2] Under Art 4 of the Health and Personal Social Services (Northern Ireland) Order 1972 (SI 1265/72).

[3] Department of Health, Social Services and Public Safety, *Guidance on the Termination of Pregnancy: The Law and Clinical Practice in Northern Ireland* (March 2009) para 2.2, 'It is important to emphasise that this guidance cannot, and does not make any change to the law of Northern Ireland. In the event of any conflict between this guidance and decisions of the courts, the latter will always prevail.'.

[4] http://news.bbc.co.uk/1/hi/northern_ireland/7954077.stm.

[5] www.irishtimes.com/news/guidelines-clarify-when-abortion-is-legal-in-north-1.727206.

[6] ibid.

with the considerable canon of common law indicating the legality of abortion in Northern Ireland in narrowly defined circumstances.[7] The Society for the Protection of Unborn Children (SPUC) criticised the Guidance as 'fundamentally flawed'[8] and threatened legal action unless the DHSSPS withdrew the document.[9] Some 10 weeks later, SPUC sought a High Court order of certiorari to quash the publication of the Guidance.[10] In the original judgment, Girvan LJ rejected six of the eight concerns[11] raised by SPUC, but he held those sections of the Guidance dealing with counselling and conscientious objection failed to give accurate direction and should be withdrawn by the Department. Claire McCann's feminist judgment is a substitute judgment that reaches some of the same conclusions as Girvan LJ, albeit on different grounds.

Injecting a Feminist Approach and Reconsidering Medicalisation

McCann J's judgment begins by acknowledging the legality of abortion in Northern Ireland. Unlike Justice Kerr's 2003 judgment,[12] the tone employed by McCann J is subtle and less forceful. The choice of language 'normalises' abortion, and by drawing attention to the fact that abortions are performed in Northern Ireland, the judgment refutes the 'abortion is illegal' narrative propagated by SPUC.[13] McCann J's opening paragraph also invokes the language of self-determination in a way that brings to the fore the uneasy tensions that currently exist between autonomy, paternalism and the medicalisation of abortion. By noting that clinicians ultimately control access to abortion, McCann J draws attention to the (unequal) power relations that exist between the patient and her physician. It is often claimed the medicalisation of abortion helped depoliticise the abortion issue in Britain,[14]

[7] 'Abortion is legal in Northern Ireland—in certain circumstances. It has been said that there is a widespread belief that abortion here is always illegal. If there is such a belief, there is no justification for it. It is wrong and after this case there is no reason that it should persist.' *In the Matter of an Application by the Family Planning Association of Northern Ireland for Judicial Review* [2003] NIQB 48, Kerr J, para 1. See also *Northern Health and Social Services Board v A and Others* [1994] NIJB 1 and *Re SJB*, Family Division, 28 September 1995.

[8] www.spuc.org.uk/news/releases/2009/march23.

[9] 'We don't believe the Executive has been presented with all the facts of this matter so we are hoping that Mr McGimpsey will give his fellow ministers the opportunity to examine our concerns and the legal advice we have been given. I hope he will be reasonable and seek to avoid the unnecessary delay and expense of a judicial review. He should, however, be in no doubt of how serious this situation is. Women deserve better than abortion and we will do whatever is necessary to maintain Northern Ireland's legal protection for women and unborn children.' See www.spuc.org.uk/news/releases/2009/april22.

[10] See www.spuc.org.uk/news/releases/2009/june5.

[11] Eight concerns were summarised in para 24 of Liam Gibson's affidavit, but not all of these were directly addressed by Girvan LJ's judgment. Claire McCann's feminist judgment restricts itself to the six points examined in the original decision.

[12] See above n 7.

[13] For instance, in a 2001 press release, SPUC described the FPANI's initial judicial review as a 'move to bring abortion to Northern Ireland', thereby implying that abortions were not performed in Northern Ireland prior to the litigation; see www.spuc.org.uk/news/releases/2001/may8.

[14] As Eileen Fegan and Rachel Rebouche point out, some politicians find it expedient to contextualise abortion in terms of 'health', thereby avoiding the more politically sensitive language of 'abortion rights': 'Northern Ireland's Abortion Law: The Morality of Silence and the Censure of Agency' (2003) 11 *Feminist Legal Studies* 221–54, 233.

but the medicalisation process was itself the result of competing factions striving to exert control over David Steel's abortion bill (1966).[15] The eventual removal of the bill's 'social clause' reinforced the professionalisation of medicine and positioned physicians as the gatekeepers of abortion services.[16] Abortion law in Britain therefore betrays an odd reality. While the physician's position of privilege remains firmly enshrined in the 1967 Act,[17] the liberal approach adopted by doctors means that women in Britain typically make their own abortion decisions without interference.[18]

The Northern Ireland Context

A very different reality exists in Northern Ireland, a point poignantly demonstrated by the case of *Northern Health and Social Services Board v F & G*, also known as *Re K*.[19] In *Re K*, a 14-year-old girl became pregnant whilst in care under a Fit Person Order. K indicated she did not wish to continue with the pregnancy. She inflicted lacerations on her wrists with broken glass and threatened suicide. The Northern Health Board sought an order that would allow K to leave Northern Ireland and obtain a termination of pregnancy in Britain, but Sheil J (as he then was) took it upon himself to consider whether or not K qualified for an abortion in Northern Ireland. A psychiatrist gave evidence that K would 'either kill herself or the baby',[20] irrespective of the supervision arrangements put in place; two other doctors were satisfied there was a real threat to K's life. Sheil J concluded that K satisfied the legal test set out in *R v Bourne*,[21] but he was informed by a senior consultant that no physician would be prepared to carry out the procedure. One of the reasons cited for this reluctance was concern over the 'perceived uncertainty' of Northern Ireland's abortion law.[22] As a consequence, K—who was already in hospital recovering from appendicitis—had to leave Northern Ireland and seek a termination in Liverpool. Sheil J described the situation as 'most regrettable', but the surgeon's assertion that no physician would be prepared to carry out the abortion went unchallenged.[23] *Re K* brings into focus one of the key problems with

[15] The British Medical Association was determined to oversee the medicalisation of the bill, while the Abortion Law Reform Association was keen to frame the availability of abortion in terms of wider socio-economic considerations. See Malcolm Potts, Petter Diggory and John Peel, *Abortion* (Cambridge, Cambridge University Press, 1977) 283–96.

[16] See, eg, Sally Sheldon, 'The Law of Abortion and the Politics of Medicalisation' in Jo Bridgeman and Sue Millns (eds), *Law and Body Politics: Regulating the Female Body* (Aldershot, Dartmouth, 1995) 105–24; Potts et al, above n 15; and John Keown, *Abortion, Doctors and the Law* (Cambridge, Cambridge University Press, 1988).

[17] 'Subject to the provisions of this section a person shall not be guilty of an offence under the law relating to abortion when a pregnancy is terminated by a registered medical practitioner if two registered medical practitioners are of the option, formed in good faith …' (Abortion Act 1967, s 1(1) (as amended)).

[18] Emily Jackson, *Medical Law: Text, Cases and Materials* (Oxford, Oxford University Press, 2013) 722.

[19] *Re K* [1993] NI 268.

[20] Tony McGleenan, 'Bourne Again? Abortion Law in Northern Ireland After *Re K* and *Re A*' (1994) 45(4) *Northern Ireland Legal Quarterly* 389, 390.

[21] *R v Bourne* [1939] 1 KB 687. *Bourne* confirmed that a doctor, acting in good faith, could lawfully terminate a pregnancy where the continuance of the pregnancy would render the woman a 'physical or mental wreck'.

[22] McGleenan, above n 20, 392.

[23] ibid.

the medicalisation of abortion; once abortion is contextualised as a technical medical issue, 'doctors are free to be as liberal—or as illiberal—as they choose'.[24]

McCann J's judgment also references the conservative character of Northern Ireland, and the litigation in 2003[25] and 2004[26] confirms the view that such conservatism is not confined to the political arena.[27] Nicholson LJ's 2004 judgment, in particular, calls to mind Graycar's *The Gender of Judgments*,[28] which explores stereotyped sexual assumptions in judicial decision-making, and Smart's *The Woman of Legal Discourse*,[29] which traces the crystallisation of gendered roles in nineteenth-century Britain. The link between discourse and subject roles is a familiar one, but while Foucault, for example, focuses on those discourses that lead to the emergence of 'the deviant',[30] Smart explores how legal discourse spawns the 'good mother/bad mother' dichotomy.[31] Nicholson LJ's judgment betrays a similar narrative: the two parent, heterosexual family[32] is advanced as the standard against which others (specifically, pregnant teenagers, single mothers, and divorcees) are measured.[33] Despite emphasising early on that judges 'should not express their personal opinions or beliefs but should approach a case ... objectively', Nicholson LJ concluded his judgment by expressing the hope that the DHSSPS would 'encourage those seeking an abortion in Northern Ireland to make a different choice'.[34] McCann J's feminist judgment tackles this point directly and argues that it would be a 'worrying development' if a woman facing a risk to life or serious/long-term harm, was subjected to counselling designed to dissuade her from obtaining the necessary medical treatment.

The 2003 and 2004 judgments reveal a second limitation of the adjudication model—that the heavy reliance placed on the application of abstract rules often leaves little space for the consideration of more nuanced concerns such as gender, class and race. The works

[24] Sheldon, above n 16, 119-120.

[25] *In the Matter of an Application by the Family Planning Association of Northern Ireland for Judicial Review* [2003] NIQB 48.

[26] *The Family Planning Association of Northern Ireland v Minister for Health, Social Services and Public Safety and Ors* [2004] NICA 37.

[27] 'With the exception of Dáil Éireann, the Northern Ireland Assembly has the lowest female representation of devolved and national legislatures in these islands ... In a European context, with the exception of Italian regional legislatures, the Northern Ireland Assembly has the lowest female representation of comparable devolved institutions in Western Europe.' Michael Potter, 'Women in the Northern Ireland Assembly', Northern Ireland Assembly Research and Information Service, Research Paper 108/13 (September 2013), 3, at www.niassembly.gov.uk/globalassets/documents/raise/publications/2013/ofmdfm/10813.pdf.

[28] Reg Graycar, 'The Gender of Judgments: Some Reflections on Bias' (1998) 32(1) *University of British Columbia Law Review* 1-21.

[29] Carol Smart, 'The Woman of Legal Discourse' (1992) 1 *Social and Legal Studies* 29-44.

[30] Pamela Major-Poetzl, *Michel Foucault's Archaeology of Western Culture* (Brighton, Harvester Press Limited, 1983) 105–48.

[31] Smart, above n 29, 37–39.

[32] 'I consider that it is the duty of the department to give guidance as to all choices open to these women, most of whom will be young single adults or teenagers. On the available evidence there may well be financial assistance if they give birth and keep the child. There are a number of married couples looking to adopt children.' *The Family Planning Association of Northern Ireland v Minister for Health, Social Services and Public Safety and Ors* [2004] NICA 37, para 86.

[33] 'Out of 419 cases known to the appellant in 1999, 337 were single mothers, 19 were separated and 21 were divorced; of the same 419, 9 were under 16, 75 were between 16 and 19, 140 were between 20 and 24 and 93 were between 25–29.': ibid, para 105D.

[34] ibid, para 117.

of Gilligan[35] and Minow and Spelman[36] argue that the experiences and relationships of individuals should play a more prominent role in the judicial decision-making process. The 2003 and 2004 judgments are notable for the absence of a 'female voice'. Kerr J's analysis of *Re K* contained some striking omissions, not least K's inability to obtain a (lawful) termination in Northern Ireland. In fact, his judgment dismissed as 'inconsequentially small' the number of women entitled to abortion in Northern Ireland who travel to Britain to have a termination.[37] By the same token, Nicholson LJ's judgment largely ignored the autonomous rights of pregnant women, not least when he contended that it would be wrong to circulate the Guidance to pregnant women unless they specifically requested it or, in the opinion of the medical profession, needed it.[38] This replicates the construct of the selfish, immature woman who cannot be trusted to make healthcare decisions for herself.[39] McCann J's judgment addresses these issues, most notably at paragraph 29, when she challenges the view that pregnancy diminishes the pregnant woman's ability to make autonomous decisions, and at paragraph 35, when she points out that the stated purpose of the Guidance was to clarify the law and not to discourage women from seeking abortions.

Deciding on SPUC's Challenge

One of the central tenets of SPUC's legal action was the assertion that the Guidance would 'radically alter (ie liberalise) clinical practice' in Northern Ireland.[40] It seemed less concerned that the document might in fact result in the law's being applied more restrictively. It is a measure of SPUC's effectiveness at propagating the 'abortion is illegal' narrative that the more permissive aspects of abortion law in Northern Ireland tend to go unnoticed; there are no *explicit* time limits similar to that found in section 1(1)(a) of the Abortion Act 1967, nor is there a *legal* requirement to the effect that two doctors must certify that the woman's circumstances satisfy the grounds for abortion. As McGleenan points out, the restrictiveness of abortion practice in Northern Ireland stems in no small part from the manner in which the law is *interpreted*:

> Many opponents of abortion in Northern Ireland seem to assume that we already have restrictive legislation. The argument presented here is that our formal legal framework is as liberal as that which applies elsewhere in Europe while our informal mechanisms for termination of pregnancy are opaque and impose a significant degree of hardship upon pregnant women.[41]

[35] Carol Gilligan, *In a Different Voice: Psychological Theory and Women's Development* (Cambridge, MA, and London, Harvard University Press, 1982).
[36] Martha Minow and Elizabeth Spelman, 'In Context' (1990) 63 *Southern California Law Review* 1597.
[37] *In the Matter of an Application by the Family Planning Association of Northern Ireland for Judicial Review* [2003] NIQB 48, para 55.
[38] *The Family Planning Association of Northern Ireland v Minister for Health, Social Services and Public Safety and Ors* [2004] NICA 37, para 84.
[39] Sally Sheldon, 'Who is the Mother to Make the Judgment?: The Constructions of Women in English Abortion Law' (1993) 1 *Feminist Legal Studies* 3-22.
[40] See www.spuc.org.uk/news/releases/2009/april22.
[41] Tony McGleenan, 'Abortion Law in Northern Ireland: Options for Reform' (2000) 1/2 *The Northern Ireland Forum for Ethics in Medicine and Health Care* 59-89.

It is notable that when discussing the issue of abortion law reform in the Republic of Ireland, the former Taoiseach, Bertie Ahern, claimed the 'ethical consensus in the medical profession' constituted the 'only real defence against widespread use of the *X* case as a basis of "social abortion" in Ireland'.[42] In other words, the medical profession proved more effective at keeping abortion 'in check' than legal provisions such as Article 40.3.3 of the Constitution. Northern Ireland arguably finds itself trapped in a similar paradigm.

The DHSSPS's Guidance would have brought certain aspects of clinical practice in Northern Ireland into line with practice in Britain, but, as already noted, this development might have inadvertently added to the restrictiveness of clinical practice in Northern Ireland. While clinical practice in Britain has a legislative framework in the form of the 1967 Act, neither the conscientious objection clause[43] nor the clinical assessment clause[44] set out in the DHSSPS's 2009 Guidance can be traced to common law or legislative principles.[45]

Perhaps the most contentious feature of Girvan LJ's judgment was the section pertaining to counselling, which focused, *inter alia*, on the lawfulness of counselling services that provide advice as to the availability of abortion services outside Northern Ireland. Girvan LJ held:

> Section 5.9 [of the Guidance] is thus unclear in what guidance the Department is intending to give and is actually giving. Unless it is clarified the Guidance as currently expressed could lead to the adoption of counselling procedures which are arguably unlawful even though it is capable of being applied in a perfectly lawful manner.[46]

Girvan LJ expressed concern that the giving of such advice might 'constitute an offence of counselling or procuring an abortion',[47] but in forming this view he apparently failed to consider *Open Door Counselling and Dublin Well Woman v Ireland*,[48] which confirmed that the provision of non-directive counselling is in fact protected under Article 10 ECHR. Commentators have described this aspect of Girvan LJ's judgment as 'inaccurate and misleading';[49] Fegan goes even further and argues that Girvan LJ's failure was so striking as to call into question his ability to carry out his public function.[50] McCann J's judgment

[42] Lisa Smyth, *Abortion and Nation: The Politics of Reproduction in Contemporary Ireland* (Aldershot, Ashgate Publishing, 2005) 129. Ruth Fletcher and Sheelagh McGuinness have written a feminist judgment and commentary for the *X* case in this collection; see ch 18.

[43] DHSSPS, *Guidance on the Termination of Pregnancy: The Law and Clinical Practice in Northern Ireland* (March 2009), para 4.1, 'Although there is no legal right to refuse to take part in the termination of pregnancy some staff may have a conscientious objection to termination of pregnancy on moral and/or religious grounds. No-one should compel staff to actively participate in the assessment or in performing a termination or handling of fetal remains.'

[44] ibid, para 3.1, 'Although not required by law in Northern Ireland two doctors, where practicable, who share prior knowledge of the woman and her clinical circumstances, should undertake the clinical assessment. However, in exceptional circumstances, such as an emergency, it may be sufficient for a single doctor to assess whether a termination of pregnancy is indicated.'

[45] Fiona Bloomer and Eileen Fegan, 'Critiquing Recent Abortion Law and Policy in Northern Ireland' (2013) 34(1) *Critical Social Policy* 109-20.

[46] *Re Society for the Protection of Unborn Children's Application for Judicial Review* [2009] NIQB 92, para 37.

[47] ibid.

[48] *Open Door Counselling and Dublin Well Woman v Ireland* [1992] ECHR 68. It should be noted that this case was not raised by counsel for the Department.

[49] Bloomer and Fegan, above n 45, 114.

[50] Eileen Fegan, 'Abortion Law in Northern Ireland: The Need to Inform Women' (Winter 2011) *Social Justice Review* 18–20, 19.

adopts a more nuanced position, noting at paragraph 38 that the criminal law in this area remains 'untested'. While the Serious Crime Act 2007 makes clear that it is an offence to encourage or assist an extra-territorial offence even when it is not an offence in the jurisdiction in which it is committed,[51] section 3(1) of the Human Rights Act 1998,[52] coupled with the Strasbourg Court's ruling in *Open Door*, would most likely persuade the courts to adopt a flexible approach when determining what constitutes 'encouragement'. Non-directive counselling that neither encourages nor assists the procurement of an abortion is therefore unlikely to prove problematic. In light of this conclusion, McCann J's judgment is forthright in challenging the Department's assertion that section 5.9 did not apply to those Northern Ireland women seeking abortions in Britain. Whereas Girvan LJ restricted his conclusion to the observation that section 5.9 was 'unclear'[53] and further clarification was needed, McCann J's judgment goes further and argues amendment is necessary so as to ensure that non-directed counselling services are not withheld from Northern Ireland women seeking abortion services in Britain.

In the final section of his judgment, Girvan LJ held the guidance document's advice on conscientious objection was unclear and should be withdrawn and amended by the Department. Section 4.1 of the Guidance stated that the right to object on grounds of conscience was recognised, except in circumstances where the woman's life was in immediate danger and emergency action was necessary. Girvan LJ felt it was unclear whether section 4.1 related only to cases where the mother's life was at stake, or whether it extended to cases where there was a permanent or long-term risk to the mother's physical or mental health. Confronted with this apparent uncertainty, Girvan LJ appeared to favour a regime that restricted the conscientious objection exception to those situations where the mother's *life* was at risk:

> Restricting the conscientious objection exception to a situation where the mother's actual life is at stake would protect the right of conscientious objection in relation to an abortion causing the death of the unborn baby where the mother's long term health is in danger, but not her life.[54]

However, Girvan LJ's position became less clear when he elaborated:

> Clearly if a patient presents with a medical problem that indicates a risk to life or long term health from continued pregnancy, a general practitioner who objects to abortion on conscientious grounds remains obliged to take steps to ensure that her medical condition is properly catered for. It would appear obviously necessary for her to be referred to the appropriate clinicians.[55]

McCann J's judgment is assertive on this point, noting at paragraph 33 that the clinician's right of non-participation should not be used to 'obstruct or frustrate the rights of the woman to access appropriate medical services'. Rejecting the charge of uncertainty, McCann J argues the Guidance introduces good practice guidelines that allow for medical professionals to object on grounds of conscience where the woman's life is not in immediate danger. Her judgment (unlike Girvan LJ's) also emphasises at paragraph 31 that in such

[51] See, eg, pt 2 and sch 4.

[52] Under s 3(1), 'So far as it is possible to do so, primary legislation and subordinate legislation must be read and given effect in a way which is compatible with the Convention rights.'

[53] *Re Society for the Protection of Unborn Children's Application for Judicial Review* [2009] NIQB 92, para 37.

[54] ibid, para 45.

[55] ibid.

cases, Trusts should have measures in place to accommodate such requests, so as to ensure that access to abortion services is not further constrained. It should be noted, however, that even if such measures are put in place, further difficulties might arise from the fact that physicians are not legally required to publicise their conscientious objections to abortion.[56] Consequently, there remains the risk that a woman may misconstrue a doctor's reluctance to assist as evidence that she fails to satisfy the legal test for abortion when, in fact, it might be an expression of the physician's conscientious objection.

Envoi

The High Court decision in 2009 was a blow for the FPANI. Eight years after leave had been granted for a judicial review against the Minister for Health, healthcare professionals once again found themselves 'in a vacuum'.[57] SPUC indicated that it was 'very pleased' with the judgment and in a subsequent press release it elaborated:

> Lord Justice Girvan ruled in favour of SPUC's challenge on two grounds. SPUC argued that because *abortion remains illegal in Northern Ireland*, it was wrong to expect medical providers to give non-directive counselling to women who might be considering abortion … The judge ruled in favour of SPUC on these points.[58]

A spokesperson for the DHSSPS stated that it would give 'careful consideration to the two adverse findings'.[59] Revised draft guidance, published in July 2010, was never formally adopted and a further application for judicial review by the FPANI in February 2013 was halted when the DHSSPS promised to publish draft advice within a week.[60] In March 2013, *The Limited Circumstances for a Lawful Termination of Pregnancy in Northern Ireland* was circulated; a 16-week consultation process followed[61] and revised guidance was eventually published in March 2016.[62]

The current guidance is less emotive in tone; it acknowledges *Open Door*[63] and it reiterates that post termination of pregnancy follow-up care should be made available to any woman who seeks it, irrespective of where the termination of pregnancy was performed.[64] The guidance confirms that there is no legal requirement that two doctors must certify that the woman's circumstances satisfy the grounds for abortion;[65] indeed paragraph 3.5

[56] Jackson, above n 18, 693.
[57] Audrey Simpson, Director of the FPANI; quoted from http://news.bbc.co.uk/1/hi/northern_ireland/8385404.stm.
[58] See www.spuc.org.uk/news/releases/2009/november30 (emphasis added). For subsequent examples of the 'abortion is illegal' narrative, see www.spuc.org.uk/news/releases/2010/may27; www.spuc.org.uk/news/releases/2011/november23a; and www.spuc.org.uk/news/releases/2012/january19.
[59] See www.bbc.co.uk/1/hi/northern_ireland/8385404.stm.
[60] See www.bbc.co.uk/news/health-21712388.
[61] See www.health-ni.gov.uk/consultations/guidance-termination-pregnancy-northern-ireland.
[62] Department of Health, Social Services and Public Safety, *Guidance For Health and Social Care Professionals on Termination of Pregnancy in Northern Ireland* (March 2016).
[63] ibid, para 5.12.
[64] ibid, para 5.15.
[65] ibid, para 3.3.

appears cognisant of those cases where a practitioner with the 'necessary competence, knowledge and experience' performs an abortion without the input of a second doctor. Notwithstanding these developments, the revised guidance is no substitute for legislative reform and in this regard, the document points to the battles that no doubt lie in wait. It is, for example, with an air of trepidation that the guidance addresses the issue of abortifacient drugs purchased from the internet, noting that whilst their use is 'likely to be an offence' under the Offences Against the Person Act 1861, ultimately, a doctor is 'unlikely to be able to tell whether a miscarriage has occurred naturally or has been caused by an abortifacient drug'.[66] Whatever the pragmatic benefits of this 'don't ask, don't tell' approach,[67] the fact remains that it offers little in the way of guidance where the practitioner, aware of illegal abortifacient drug use, has the difficult task of reconciling the duty to report a criminal offence with the patient's right to confidentiality.

[66] ibid, para 6.7 and para 6.8. For wider developments in Northern Ireland on prosecutions relating to the use of abortifacient drugs, as well as other legal developments pertaining to abortion, see Sarah Ramshaw's commentary on the *FPANI* case, ch 21 (this collection).

[67] As described by Dr Fiona Bloomer; see www.bbc.co.uk/news/uk-northern-ireland-35904498.

Society for the Protection of Unborn Children's Application for Judicial Review

[2009] NIQB 92

QUEEN'S BENCH DIVISION

30 November 2009. The following judgment was delivered.

McCann J.

Introduction

[1] It is now well established that women can have lawful abortions in Northern Ireland. However, the recent history of litigation on abortion in this jurisdiction indicates that even when they meet the legal criteria, many women are still unable to access this medical service. Clinicians continue to be guardians of access to abortion and in a morally conservative jurisdiction such as Northern Ireland, this places women in a particularly vulnerable position. The Guidance, which is the subject of this litigation, was designed to clarify the law on when abortions can be performed without fear of prosecution and ensure that women can access abortion services within this jurisdiction when lawful to do so. The current legal framework surrounding abortion in Northern Ireland is deferential to the medical judgement of the doctor in the decision-making process, which makes it a difficult task for the drafters of guidance to reflect the principle of patient autonomy in line with the modern trend in healthcare provision. Nevertheless, it is incumbent on the Department to ensure that, insofar as is possible within this legal framework, the contemporary principle of patient autonomy is embedded within the Guidance in relation to consent, counselling and other services and support. This Guidance cannot change the law and where a woman's particular circumstances do not meet the conditions for a lawful abortion in Northern Ireland, she will need to make alternative arrangements to access abortion services lawfully elsewhere at her own expense.

[2] This application for judicial review has been brought by the applicant to seek an order of *certiorari* to quash the publication of the Guidance on the Termination of Pregnancy (the 'Guidance') by the Department of Health, Social Services and Public Safety (the 'Department'). The applicant is the Society for the Protection of Unborn Children ('SPUC'). The aims of SPUC include 'defending the existence of life from the moment of conception'. The court recognises SPUC is permitted to challenge the legality of the Guidance, however, as a pressure group seeking vindication of their values in this case, the court must treat with caution any arguments presented on their behalf.

[3] In 2004, the Court of Appeal in *Family Planning Association of Northern Ireland v Minister for Health, Social Services and Public Safety* [2005] NICA 39 ('*FPA*') ordered the Department to produce clearer guidance on when abortion can be lawfully carried out in Northern Ireland and to clarify the law on referrals, consent, aftercare

and conscientious objection for clinicians. The Court declared that the Minister had failed in his duty under Article 4 of the Health and Personal Social Services (Northern Ireland) Order 1972 ('1972 Order') to secure the provision of integrated health and personal social services to women seeking lawful abortions by, *inter alia*, 'failing to investigate and issue guidance to members of the medical profession and ancillary staff involved in the provision of termination of pregnancy services (including after-care) to those working for concerned organisations and to women in Northern Ireland seeking a termination of pregnancy'.

[4] As a result of this case, the Department engaged in a lengthy consultation process and eventually issued the Guidance in March of this year. The stated purpose of the Guidance is 'to explain the existing law relating to the termination of pregnancy and how it relates to good clinical practice' and to ensure that, within the scope of the law in Northern Ireland, each Health and Social Care Trust ('Trust') secures access to abortion services for its patients. The Guidance cannot go beyond the terms of the existing legal principles, nor can it replace the need for statutory clarification, where there is legal uncertainty.

Grounds of Review

[5] Counsel on behalf of SPUC contended that where there is a risk of an error of law in the Guidance this court should exercise heightened scrutiny. Moreover where an extraneous purpose had infected the Guidance or relevant considerations had not been taken into account, then the court could intervene on grounds of *Wednesbury* unreasonableness. Counsel relied on the decision in *R (Association of British Travel Agents Limited) v Civil Aviation Authority* [2006] EWCA 1356 in which Chadwick LJ found that:

> if the judge was correct in his view that the Guidance Note contains an interpretation of the requirements in the ATOL Regulations which was wrong or misleading, then it is clearly in the public interest that the Guidance Note be amended or withdrawn.

In that case the Court of Appeal directed that the guidance on the sale of air package arrangements and consumer protection be withdrawn as it was likely 'to give the uninformed reader a misleading impression'.

[6] The concerns raised by SPUC about the guidance are summarised as follows:

i. Failure to acknowledge the presumptive illegality of abortion in Northern Ireland and is therefore based on a misleading premise;
ii. Failure to properly recognise foetal rights;
iii. Failure to provide guidance on whether a child is capable of being born alive;
iv. Failure to make adequate provision in relation to the information which ought to be provided to women considering abortion to ensure valid consent is obtained;
v. Failure to properly recognise the right of health care practitioners to decline to participate in abortion procedures; and
vi. Wrongly provides for non-directive counselling.

[7] Counsel for the Department argued that it would be appropriate for a wide degree of latitude and discretion to be given to the Department regarding the content and tone of the Guidance.

[8] It is a serious matter if Guidance issued by the Department is likely to mislead clinicians and women it is designed to help. While the Department should be given some degree of discretion in relation to how it designs this Guidance it should not misstate the correct legal principles, nor should it be wrong or misleading in how it states the law. The issue for this court to consider is whether the Guidance misunderstands the law on abortion or has the potential to mislead medical practitioners in their clinical practice.

[9] If the court finds that the Guidance does not properly reflect the current law or that it misleads clinicians or the public as to the nature of the law on abortion, it is in the public interest to ensure that the Guidance is withdrawn until such time as the error of law can be rectified.

[10] While this Guidance is directed at medical practitioners, it will also have a direct impact on women seeking access to abortion services. The Guidance should ensure that no additional impediments are put in place which might further limit women's access to a lawful medical service. Abortion is governed by incremental development of the common law interpreting the Offences against the Person Act 1861. The Guidance, and indeed this court, cannot go beyond the statutory framework currently in place.

Failure to acknowledge the presumptive illegality of abortion

[11] At this juncture it would be useful to review the current state of the law on abortion in Northern Ireland. Unlawful abortion is criminalised in the Offences Against the Person Act 1861. Section 58 of that Act makes it clear that it is an offence for any pregnant woman to unlawfully administer to herself any poison or use any instrument with the intent to procure her own miscarriage. Similarly, it is an offence for any other person to unlawfully administer any poison or use any instrument with the intent to procure the miscarriage, whether or not the woman is pregnant. Section 59 provides that it is an offence for any person to supply a poison or anything else with the knowledge that it will be used with the unlawful intent to procure a miscarriage. In 1945, section 25 of the Criminal Justice Act (Northern Ireland) made it an offence to destroy a foetus 'capable of being born alive' unless the act was done in good faith and to preserve the 'life of the mother' and incorporated the terms of the English Infant Life (Preservation) Act 1929 into the law of Northern Ireland.

[12] The criminalisation of abortion in the 1861 Act was interpreted in the English case of *R v Bourne* [1939] 1 KB 687. This case distinguished the circumstances in which an abortion can be *lawfully* performed. In this harrowing case, a doctor performed an abortion on a young girl of 15 after she was brutally assaulted and raped and subsequently became pregnant. When the doctor was charged with procuring an abortion under section 58 of the 1861 Act, he raised the defence that the abortion was lawful as he had acted in good faith to preserve the girl's life. Illegal backstreet abortions were

commonplace at this time, filling the void left by the prohibition on abortion, and were usually performed by women. Macnaughten J is at pains to distinguish what he considers the grasping professional woman abortionist from the benevolent paternalism of the male doctor in this case. The direction to the jury interpreted section 58 of the 1861 Act in light of the Infant Life (Preservation) Act 1929:

> if the doctor is of opinion, on reasonable grounds and with adequate knowledge, that the probable consequence of the continuance of the pregnancy will be to make the woman a physical or mental wreck, the jury are quite entitled to take the view that the doctor who, under those circumstances and in that honest belief, operates, is operating for the purpose of preserving the life of the mother.

This case institutionalises abortion as a clinical decision of the paternalistic, male-dominated medical profession.

[13] In 1967 the Abortion Act was introduced in England, Scotland and Wales as a response to the risk to life and health caused by women accessing illegal backstreet abortions. It sought to bring abortion provision firmly within the domain of the medical profession with a stated intent to improve safety and reduce the risk to women. While it has had the effect of liberalising access to abortion, it is also steeped in the paternalism of 1960s medicine. This Act was never extended to Northern Ireland.

[14] The principles of the test in *Bourne* were refined in a series of Northern Irish cases in the 1990s where vulnerable women and girls had to go to court to have their right of access to a lawful abortion vindicated. It is unsurprising that the decision from 1939 is so deferential to the doctor in the case and, as the litigation demonstrates, this deference to medical power still frames abortion access in 2009.

[15] In *FPA* the Court of Appeal confirmed that the test in *Bourne*, as developed through case law, was a good basis for the Guidance. This is accurately stated and summarised in paragraphs 1.3 and 1.4 of the Guidance as follows:

> 1.3 The law governing the termination of pregnancy in Northern Ireland at present and in the cases where that legislation has been interpreted by the court can be summarised in the following principles:
> (i) operations in Northern Ireland for the termination of pregnancies are unlawful unless performed in good faith only for the purpose of preserving the life of the woman;
> (ii) the 'life' of the woman in this context has been interpreted by the courts as including her physical and mental health;
> (iii) a termination will therefore be lawful where the continuance of the pregnancy threatens the life of the woman, or would adversely affect her physical or mental health. The adverse effect on her physical or mental health must be a 'real and serious' one, and must also be 'permanent or long term'. In most cases the risk of the adverse effect occurring would need to be more likely than not. However, in certain circumstances the possibility of an adverse effect may be sufficient if, for example, the imminent death of the woman was the potential adverse effect.

(iv) it will always be a question of fact and degree whether the perceived effect of non-termination is sufficiently grave to warrant terminating the pregnancy in a particular case.

1.4 In summary, it is lawful to perform an operation in Northern Ireland for the termination of a pregnancy, where:

- it is necessary to preserve the life of the woman, or
- there is a risk of real and serious adverse effect on her physical or mental health, which is either long term or permanent.

In any other circumstance it would be unlawful to perform such an operation.

[16] In light of the foregoing, SPUC's argument that the Guidance should affirm the presumptive illegality of abortion must fail. The suggestion that the summary paragraph 1.4 of the Guidance could lead to a situation where this medical procedure was easier to obtain than heretofore must also be rejected. If there is an increase in the number of abortions performed in this jurisdiction, this will be worrying evidence that women have been unable to access to basic health care services which should have been available before now and will confirm the need for this Guidance.

[17] The Applicant further took issue with the language used by the Guidance in paragraph 2.3 which states:

> Within the scope of this Guidance and the law in Northern Ireland, each Health & Social Care Trust must ensure that its patients have access to termination of pregnancy services.

Counsel contended that the use of 'termination of pregnancy services' is an inaccurate euphemism for abortion which fails to accurately reflect the law. These arguments must be rejected. The language of 'termination of pregnancy' is not an inaccurate euphemism. It is a straightforward means of describing an induced miscarriage. 'Abortion' is not without its own ambiguity and can be used to describe both a medically or surgically induced miscarriage and a spontaneous abortion or non-induced miscarriage. The suggestion by the applicant that 'abortion' is more accurate is misguided. The use of language within the Guidance is therefore not misleading or wrong.

[18] SPUC objected to the phrase 'termination of pregnancy services' and argued that 'operation aimed at the prevention of an illness' more accurately reflects the law. However, the word 'operation' is inaccurate as abortions can be performed medically and surgically. Moreover, this guidance is directed to all medical professionals and counsellors who will support women before, during and after an abortion. Changing the language, as suggested by SPUC, would unnecessarily limit the scope of the Guidance and could cause confusion. All Trusts must ensure that women have access to the full range of lawful abortion services.

[19] The applicant's argument that the language risks being interpreted as a right to an abortion on demand is astonishing in light of the foregoing discussion on the current law reflected in the Guidance. Section 3 of the Guidance confirms a woman's access to abortion services is subject to the clinical assessment of her doctor(s) and

is, therefore, clearly not available 'on demand'. As discussed above, abortion law in this jurisdiction is grounded in a paternalistic ethos. It is essential that through the gatekeeping function the doctor does not constrain women accessing abortion services. As evident from the case law, women who meet the legal criteria for abortion are not always able to access the procedure. In *Northern Health and Social Services Board v F & G* [1993] NI 268, K (a minor) was made a ward of court and had to travel to England to access an abortion which should have been available here, but no obstetrician was willing to carry out the procedure. This undoubtedly added to her distress. The risk is not whether abortion is available on demand, but whether it is available *at all*. In *Tysiac v Poland* (2007) 45 EHRR 42 the European Court of Human Rights emphasised the importance of procedural safeguards where the risk of incurring criminal responsibility could have a chilling effect on doctors when deciding whether the requirements of legal abortion are met in an individual case. Where a disagreement arises as to whether the preconditions for a legal abortion are satisfied in a given case, either between the pregnant woman and her doctors, or between the doctors themselves, the Court decided that a review process should be established to ensure swift resolution to the dispute without recourse to the courts. The omission of this review procedure does not render the Guidance misleading or wrong; however, it raises the possibility of future challenge and the Department should carefully consider the inclusion of an independent review or appeals mechanism in the Guidance.

Failure to recognise foetal rights

[20] SPUC argued there is a presumption that neither the legislature nor the executive will act in a manner that is inconsistent with its international law obligations and that the failure of the Guidance to recognise the rights of the unborn child is unlawful. For example, Counsel relied on the preamble to the UN Convention on the Rights of the Child ('UNCRC') which identifies that the child, 'by reason of his physical and mental immaturity, needs special safeguards and care, including appropriate legal protection, before as well as after birth' as evidence that the foetus has an independent right to survival. However this interpretation obfuscates the experience and rights of the pregnant woman or girl and does not stand up to scrutiny. In General Comment 4, the supervising Committee of the UNCRC urged states to provide safe abortion services, adequate and comprehensive obstetric care and counselling where abortion was lawfully available. In providing this Guidance, the Department is in fact reflecting this responsibility to ensure that women and girls will be able to obtain comprehensive health care from clinicians, including proper guidance on abortion, where they meet the legal criteria. It is not necessary for this court to systematically go through each of the arguments presented by Counsel as international treaties do not form part of UK domestic law without incorporating legislation (*Re McCallion's Application* [2009] NICA 55), but it must be noted that the manner in which the various provisions have been selected and presented by the applicant do not accurately reflect the current state of international law.

[21] Unlike the other international law provisions relied on by SPUC, the European Convention of Human Rights ('ECHR') has been incorporated into domestic law by the

Human Rights Act 1998, which creates an obligation on all public bodies to comply with the ECHR. The Applicant argued that article 2 ECHR protects an independent right to life for the foetus. However, in *Paton v UK* (1981) 3 EHRR 408, the Commission made it clear that foetal rights cannot take precedence over the life and health of the pregnant woman and where an abortion is performed to protect the physical and mental health of a pregnant woman, there is no violation of article 2. Furthermore, the Court in *Vo v France* (2005) 40 EHRR 12 recognised that the issue of when life begins comes within the margin of appreciation of states, as there is no European consensus on the scientific and legal definition of the beginning of life, but it rejected the concept of foetal personhood:

> [A]t best, it may be regarded as common ground between States that the embryo/foetus belongs to the human race. The potentiality of that being and its capacity to become a person … require protection in the name of human dignity, without making it a 'person' with the 'right to life' for the purposes of Article 2.

The European Court defers to our domestic law on the matter of how the rights of the foetus should be balanced against that of the pregnant woman, provided that where abortion is permitted, the state 'must not structure its legal framework in a way which would limit real possibilities to obtain it' (*Tysiac v Poland* (2007) 45 EHRR 42).

[22] While it is possible that the current pending case taken by three women challenging the very restrictive law in Ireland may give further clarification on these issues, until there is a judgment of the European Court, it is not appropriate for this court to pre-empt that decision. The current state of Strasbourg jurisprudence clarifies that the State can legislate to provide for abortion services and where such services are provided for by law, a woman's right to life and health will necessarily override whatever interest the foetus may have, as to do otherwise would be to subordinate the women's right to life to that of the foetus.

[23] As a matter of common law, foetal rights do not prevail over the rights of the pregnant women. In *Re MB (An Adult: Medical Treatment)* [1997] EWCA Civ 3093 Butler-Sloss LJ made it clear that '[a] competent woman who has capacity to decide may, … for rational or irrational reasons or for no reason at all, choose not to have medical intervention, even though the consequences may be the death or serious handicap of the child she bears, or her own death'. Until the moment of birth the interests of the unborn foetus cannot be used to override the interests of the pregnant woman who refuses consent to medical intervention. This particular relational status of pregnant women was reiterated by Judge LJ in *St George's Healthcare NHS Trust v S* [1998] 3 WLR 936 who clarified that '[a]lthough human and protected by the law in a number of ways … an unborn child is not a separate person from its mother' and that '[i]ts need for medical assistance will not prevail over her rights'.

[24] As the foregoing review of the international and domestic law makes clear, the foetus does not hold rights independent of and separate to those of the pregnant woman. Pregnancy is a unique experience in medicine and law and it is important that the rights of the pregnant woman are not overridden by an overly invasive medical and legal regulatory system to protect foetal rights. The restrictive nature of law governing

access to abortion in this jurisdiction is such that the pregnant woman's autonomy is already very limited, particularly in relation to other parts of the UK. The Guidance accurately reflects this limited access to abortion services and correctly prioritises women's physical and mental health in the balance of interests.

Failure to give adequate guidance on when a child was capable of being born alive

[25] The vast majority of abortions happen in the very early stages of pregnancy with the most recent figures from the NHS in England and Wales for 2008 confirming that 90% of abortions take place prior to 13 weeks' gestation. In 2008, only 26 of the 1,173 women who travelled from Northern Ireland to England and Wales to have an abortion were at 20 weeks' gestation or more. It clear that these are exceptional cases and should be treated sensitively by medical professionals. The law governing abortion in Northern Ireland does not have a gestational limit on when abortion can be carried out; rather, the focus is on the physical and mental health of the woman seeking the abortion.

[26] Counsel for SPUC argued that the failure to 'provide guidance on, or require investigation into, whether a child is capable of being born alive' was irrational as it did not properly explain whether section 25 Criminal Justice (Northern Ireland) Act 1945 applies. This was linked to the issue of consent as, according to SPUC, the decision to terminate a pregnancy where a child was capable of being born alive was 'materially different' from a decision to abort before this point. It is not clear to this Court that a decision to have an abortion at a later stage is *prima facie* materially different to one that is performed at an earlier stage of gestation. If this is, in fact, the case, the decision is for the woman to make with the appropriate advice and support from her medical team balanced against the risks to her life or health. As confirmed above, the Guidance properly prioritises the physical and mental health of the woman in this balance of interests.

Failure to give adequate guidance on obtaining informed consent

[27] Guidance on consent is available in paragraphs 5.2 to 5.5 and identifies a range of good practice guides for practitioners based on patient autonomy and the right of individuals to determine what happens to their own bodies. The Guidance relies on good practice guides from the General Medical Council ('GMC') on consent, including specific guidance for dealing with children and young people up to the age of 18 (*Consent: Patients and Doctors Making Decisions Together* and *0–18 Years: Guidance for All Doctors*) and from the Department (*Reference Guide to Consent for Examination, Treatment or Care*).

[28] Counsel for SPUC argued that paragraph 5.3, in particular, was inadequate. Paragraph 5.3 states:

> With consent to termination of pregnancy, as with consent for other medical procedures, there are certain criteria which must be met in order for the consent to be valid. The woman must have sufficient competence to understand the procedure and its alternatives in broad terms and to make a decision. It is also important that

> consent must be voluntary and the decision must be made on the basis of sufficient, accurate information. In those cases, where a termination is advised and taking account of the urgency of the procedure, where possible, the woman should be afforded the time to consider the decision to have a termination.

The applicant's Counsel argued that this is a freestanding breach of Article 4 of the 1972 Order, as the Guidance did not include a discussion of alternatives to abortion; a requirement to advise women of the mental and physical health risks of abortion; and a failure to give specific advice to young women and girls who were panicking about their pregnancy.

[29] The arguments presented by SPUC appear to be based on an implicit assumption that women are incapable of making autonomous decisions about consent to medical treatment while pregnant. The Court cannot accept this assumption. Best practice guidance on consent to medical treatment during pregnancy is the same whether this is consent to abortion or another medical procedure. A woman who is considering an abortion can only access that service when it is necessary to save the woman's life or to prevent real and serious long term or permanent harm to her physical or mental health. The decision for the woman in question is to consent to the procedure or to accept the risk to her life or health of continuing with the pregnancy. The Guidance must be read as a whole and alongside the other good practice guides identified in paragraphs 5.2, 5.3 and 5.4. The Guidance is clear that all appropriate information must be made available to the patient to ensure she can make an informed and voluntary decision. The nature of this information will change depending on the individual circumstances. It is not clear from the submissions to this court on what basis the list identified by SPUC should be prioritised over the serious mental and or physical health risks the pregnant woman in facing. The general guidance on consent, including specific guidance for dealing with patients below the age of 18, when read with the Guidance on the Termination of Pregnancy, is sufficient to ensure that clinicians properly understand their responsibility to obtain consent for abortion. There is no breach of the 1972 Order.

Failure to adequately recognise the right of non-participation

[30] There is no common law or statutory right to refuse to participate in an abortion in Northern Ireland similar to section 4 of the Abortion Act 1967. Similarly, as a matter of contract, an employee cannot unreasonably refuse to obey a lawful instruction. While a legal protection for non-participation could be included as an express term in the contract of employment, this is subject to negotiation between employers and the appropriate professional body. The Guidance identifies good practice guidelines for conscientious objection in section 4:

> 4.1 Although there is no legal right to refuse to take part in the termination of pregnancy some staff may have a conscientious objection to termination of pregnancy on moral and/or religious grounds. No-one should compel staff to actively participate in the assessment or in performing a termination or handling of fetal remains. The right to object on grounds of conscience

should be recognised and respected—except in circumstances where the woman's life is in immediate danger and emergency action needs to be taken. Health and Social Care Trusts should have appropriate arrangements in place to accommodate such requests from staff. However, staff with a conscientious objection cannot opt out of providing general care for women undergoing a termination of pregnancy. The personal beliefs of staff should not prejudice general patient care.

4.2 Where a woman presents herself to her GP for advice or assessment in relation to a termination of pregnancy and that GP has a conscientious objection, he/she should have in place arrangements with; practice colleagues, another GP practice, or a Health Social Care Trust to whom the woman can be referred.

This section also references guidance from the GMC, *Good Medical Practice Guide* and the Nursing and Midwifery Council's professional code of conduct which address the matter of referral for medical practitioners who, for religious or moral reasons, do not wish to give advice about or participate in a particular procedure.

[31] The claim by SPUC that the Guidance was contradictory for stating that there is no legal right to refuse to participate, while simultaneously referring to a right to conscientious objection must be rejected. The Guidance does not change the law, but clarifies good practice guidelines to allow for medical professionals to object on grounds of conscience. There is an obligation to provide all care and assistance where the woman's life is in immediate danger and emergency action is required. In all other circumstances, where the risk to life or health meets the legal criteria for abortion but does not require immediate and emergency intervention, the right to conscientious objection should be protected, where possible. As a matter of good practice, Trusts should have appropriate measures in place to accommodate such requests, while ensuring that women's access to abortion is not further constrained.

[32] On the matter of freedom of conscience under Article 9 ECHR, Counsel for the Department identified *Copsey v WWB Devon Clays Ltd* [2005] EWCA Civ 932 which accords with Strasbourg jurisprudence. There is no interference with Article 9 where an employee has voluntarily accepted the terms of contract and is free to resign. Until an employee is successful in arguing that this interpretation does interfere with her/his Article 9 right, the Guidance does not misrepresent the law. Notwithstanding this clarification, the Guidance seeks to mitigate this through good practice guidelines on non-participation.

[33] Counsel for SPUC argued that the right not to participate in an abortion is limited both when a woman's life is in immediate danger and when a conscientious objector must refer the woman to another practitioner who will facilitate the abortion. He claimed that it is wholly unacceptable for the Guidance to require any doctor to put in place arrangements for the 'intentional killing' of what s/he perceives as a child through abortion. This interpretation of the conscientious objector argument presumes that the moral values of the objector prevail over the health of a woman seeking abortion, even where that woman's life is in immediate danger. This argument by

SPUC appears to suggest that this court should create an absolute common law right to conscientious objection, which cannot be accepted. As has already been stated, the circumstances in which a woman can access abortion are already very limited and any woman who qualifies for an abortion in Northern Ireland is facing long term and serious mental and physical health risks. Where a woman's life is in immediate danger, it is imperative that clinicians treat the patient in front of them, regardless of personal moral concerns. Moreover, the obligation to refer is not an onerous one. It requires (1) telling the patient that she has a right to see another doctor, and (2) giving the patient enough information to be able to exercise that right. This court cannot allow a clinician's right of non-participation to obstruct or frustrate the rights of the woman to prompt access to appropriate medical services. The gatekeeping role of clinicians in facilitating or impeding access to abortion services is substantial, as is evident throughout this judgment, and places women who meet the legal criteria for accessing abortion in a particularly vulnerable position. It is vital that access to an essential medical service should not be constrained by the moral values of individual practitioners. This Guidance is designed to ensure mechanisms are established to clarify that situation does not arise. The obligation for medical practitioners to refer does not amount to facilitation of an abortion and is reflective of the general obligation in the GMC's *Guidance on Good Medical Practice*.

The requirement of non-directive counselling

[34] Paragraphs 5.7–5.11 of the Guidance address the matter of counselling. Counsel for SPUC argued that the provision in paragraph 5.9 which provides for non-directive counselling misrepresents the law:

> In terms of best practice, the purpose of counselling for women considering termination of pregnancy is to offer support in a non-judgmental and non-directive way to enable them to make an informed choice about termination or its alternatives. The counsellor or psychotherapist will therefore need to be aware of the choices available including medical interventions, adoption services and support available for continuing with the pregnancy.

The applicant argued that the requirement for non-directive counselling cannot be reconciled with the purpose of Guidance as set out in the Nicholson LJ in the *FPA* case, namely, that it should not encourage women to seek abortions and should instead try to dissuade women travelling to other parts of the UK and Europe to access abortions and encourage women to make a different choice.

[35] The argument on behalf of SPUC that the Guidance cannot provide for non-directive counselling as this will not meet the suggested purpose of reducing the number of women seeking and obtaining abortions in this jurisdiction and elsewhere cannot be accepted. It is not the purpose of the Guidance to discourage women from seeking abortions, either in Northern Ireland or elsewhere, or to deter medical practitioners from making the clinical judgement that they may be necessary. The Guidance is designed to clarify the law and clinical good practice for practitioners.

[36] It is clear from the Guidance that abortion is only available in limited circumstances and a woman's access to abortion in Northern Ireland is based on the clinical judgement of the medical practitioner. It would be a very worrying development if, having identified a risk to life or serious and long-term harm, a woman who was making a decision about whether to have an abortion was subjected to counselling designed to dissuade her from accessing this necessary medical procedure. Similarly, in circumstances where abortion might be lawful but the woman would rather accept the risk presented to her life and health and to continue with the pregnancy, any counselling should be non-directive and non-judgemental. The law in this area is clear that a pregnant woman maintains her status as autonomous being and should not have her will overborne by an argument about her own best interests or the best interests of the foetus. This decision-making process should be informed by appropriate non-directive counselling. To do otherwise would risk undermining the principle of self-determination of the patient, which is fundamental to the principle of consent.

[37] It is not just women who qualify for abortion in Northern Ireland who should have access to non-directive counselling services, but also 'women who are considering or who have undergone a termination of pregnancy, regardless of where it was carried out' (paragraph 5.8). This Court has already referred to NHS statistics identifying that 1,173 women from this jurisdiction travelled to England and Wales last year to have an abortion. These women must organise travel and accommodation, arrange appointments at reputable clinics and pay for the procedure, all within a very tight timeframe. While the Guidance can do very little to ameliorate this situation, it is correct that this category of women should also receive counselling and advice. However, in his submission for the Department, Counsel appeared to suggest that this section of the Guidance should be read in light of paragraph 5.7 which focuses on when termination is lawful in Northern Ireland. This confusion between the plain reading of the Guidance and the argument from Counsel creates a real risk that the Guidance could mislead practitioners.

[38] The criminal law in this area is untested and the Guidance should reassure practitioners that where women do not meet the legal criteria for abortion in Northern Ireland, providing information about lawful abortion services outside of this jurisdiction in a non-directive counselling session would not normally be considered an offence, provided there is no intention to encourage or assist the procurement of an abortion. Moreover, the provision of such information which neither advocates nor encourages an abortion is protected under Article 10 of the ECHR (*Open Door Counselling v Ireland* (1993) 15 EHRR 34). It is important that this Guidance which is designed to clarify the law should not create confusion or have the potential to mislead practitioners as to how the criminal law applies.

Conclusion

[39] The purpose of the Guidance is to clarify the law on abortion within this jurisdiction; to clarify good practice for medical practitioners in how to advise, assess and care for women who are seeking access to abortion; and to ensure that a woman

is adequately supported in any decision about the continuation of her pregnancy. In general, the Guidance achieves this aim, however the information in paragraph 5.9 concerning women who do not meet the legal criteria for abortion in Northern Ireland lacks clarity and has the potential to mislead. This could have the effect of wrongly excluding those women from the scope of this guidance. It is important that this is rectified to ensure that Counsellors properly understand how the criminal law applies and do not inadvertently commit an offence. Moreover, to prevent future legal challenges, the Department should give serious consideration to the inclusion of a review mechanism for women who disagree with the clinical assessment of their doctor or where there is a disagreement between doctors. The potential for the current Guidance to mislead practitioners is a serious one and the court concludes that it is in the public interest for the Guidance to be withdrawn and reconsidered by the Department in a timely manner taking account the contents of this judgment.

Part V

Embodied Subjects

23

Commentary on *DPP v Tiernan*

LIZ CAMPBELL

The Decision

The decision of the Supreme Court in *Director of Public Prosecutions v Tiernan*[1] reviewed the approach of the Irish courts in imposing a sentence for the crime of rape, and rejected the possibility of handing down general sentencing guidelines. The appeal against conviction was heard in 1986, while the Supreme Court decision was handed down in 1988. For their feminist judgment, Louise Kennefick and Caroline Fennell have rewritten the Supreme Court judgment.

To set this case in context, the extant law on definition of rape was Criminal Law (Rape) Act 1981, section 2 of which provides that a man commits rape if he has unlawful sexual intercourse with a woman who does not consent to it and he knows that she does not consent to the intercourse, or he is reckless as to whether she does or does not consent. This is a subjective standard, in that it looks at the actor's knowledge or recklessness, rather than considering a generic objective standard or expectation. To mitigate this somewhat, subsection 2 imposes a 'reasonable grounds' standard in assessing his belief in consent. In other words, the jury must have regard to whether his belief was reasonable or not. Moreover, the definition of rape did not include married parties, as the abolition of marital exemption in relation to rape did not arrive until the Criminal Law (Rape) (Amendment) Act 1990 (section 5). Furthermore, the provision of a corroboration warning was mandatory in all sexual offence trials. Subsequent to the case, section 7 of the Criminal Law (Rape) Act 1990 provided that whether or not a warning was necessary should be left to the discretion of the trial judge.

Nonetheless, there were some movements towards reform. The Rape Crisis Centre in Dublin (endorsed by equivalent centres in Clonmel, Cork, Galway, Limerick and Waterford) made submissions to the Oireachtas Joint Committee on Women's Rights on *Rape Legislation and Investigation Procedures* in May 1986, calling for, *inter alia*, a broader definition of rape, criminalisation of rape within marriage, inadmissibility of past sexual history and separate legal representation of complainants. Indeed, in their subsequent fourth report on *Sexual Violence*, the Joint Committee on Women's Rights largely accepted and

[1] *Director of Public Prosecutions v Tiernan* [1988] IR 250.

endorsed those recommendations, including that of a broader concept of 'rape', stating, 'the definition of Rape to be broadened to include oral sex, anal sex and the use of objects to violate the vagina'.[2]

As noted in the feminist judgment, this case involved a violent, multiple rape, for which Edward Tiernan was sentenced to 21 years' imprisonment. The complainant in this case was raped by numerous men, and was subjected to what the court described as acts of 'sexual perversion'. Without belittling the gravity of the harm inflicted on the complainant, the choice of words by the Court is dubious. The notion of 'sexual perversion' is seen in contrast to the 'norm' or the 'natural' in sex, but of course this is loaded with negative normative content.[3] The idea of acts themselves being 'perverted' is problematic, and this appraisal generally is hetero-normative, homophobic and ambiguous. It often conveys the particular idea of women's sexuality as being perverse, and works to stigmatise those whose sexual practices or desires diverge from the socially constructed conception of normality. Furthermore, it demarcates certain sexual acts as not just different but deviant.[4] The wrong in rape lies in the lack of consent and the sheer objectification of the victim;[5] describing some of the harms committed as perversions is superfluous and maintains a patriarchal view of the sexual *status quo*.

The rather brief judgment of the Supreme Court underlined the gravity of the offence of rape and described both mitigating and aggravating factors that should be considered in sentencing. Finlay CJ rightly stated, 'The crime of rape must always be viewed as one of the most serious offences contained in our criminal law even when committed without violence beyond that constituting the act of rape itself.'[6] Various factors were highlighted to emphasise this gravity: 'The act of forcible rape not only causes bodily harm but is also inevitably followed by emotional, psychological and psychiatric damage to the victim which can often be of long term, and sometimes of lifelong duration.'[7] While the recognition of the multiplicity of harms is to be welcomed, this statement is questionable in a number of respects. First it distinguishes between 'types' of rape, classifying and arguably ranking these, with 'forcible rape' at the apex. Indeed, at one time force or threat of force was necessary to the crime of rape.[8] Though this has changed, it seems that a *de facto* hierarchy remains.[9] Furthermore, the perceived inevitability of subsequent damage leaves little room for the agency of the victim.[10] A similar concern may be raised about the Court's view

[2] Joint Committee on Women's Rights, *Sexual Violence: Fourth Report of the Joint Committee on Women's Rights* (1987) 40.

[3] Linda LeMoncheck, *Loose Women, Lecherous Men: A Feminist Philosophy of Sex* (Oxford, Oxford University Press, 1997) 70 et seq.

[4] ibid. Also see Lauren Rosewarne, *Part-time Perverts: Sex, Pop Culture, and Kink Management* (Westport, CT, Praeger Publishers, 2011).

[5] John Gardner and Stephen Shute, 'The Wrongness of Rape' in Jeremy Horder (ed), *Oxford Essays in Jurisprudence* (Oxford, Oxford University Press, 2000) ch 10.

[6] *DPP v Tiernan*, above n 1, at 253.

[7] ibid.

[8] cf *R v Camplin* (1845) 1 Cox 220.

[9] Indeed it has been shown that juries have similar views of what constitutes rape (and what is part of seduction): Louise Ellison and Vanessa Munro, 'Of "Normal Sex" and "Real Rape": Exploring the Use of Socio-sexual Scripts in (Mock) Jury Deliberation' (2009) 18(3) *Social and Legal Studies* 291–312.

[10] See Janet Halley, *Split Decisions: How and Why to Take a Break from Feminism* (Princeton, NJ, Princeton University Press, 2008) 346.

that 'rape can distort the victim's approach to her own sexuality'.[11] All this underlines the presumptions made about the victim, and the side-lining of her capacity and autonomy.[12]

Moreover, rape was seen by the Court as imposing on 'the victim a deeply distressing fear of sexually transmitted disease and the possibility of a pregnancy and of a birth, whose innocent issue could inspire a distress and even a loathing utterly alien to motherhood'.[13] This observation emphasises the normative interpretation of maternity and the qualities of the ideal mother, linked to the notion of an ideal woman. As Betty Friedan observed, the dominant understanding was that 'women could find fulfilment only in sexual passivity, male domination, and nurturing maternal love'.[14] In addition, this observation of the Court underlines the absolute innocence of any subsequent birth. This is particularly noteworthy, given the absence of a general right to abortion in Ireland, which limits the ability of the raped woman to control or end her pregnancy.[15]

Despite the recognition that rape constitutes 'a gross attack upon the human dignity and the bodily integrity of a woman and a violation of her human and constitutional rights',[16] and so must attract very severe legal sanctions, the Supreme Court declined to impose any sentencing guidelines. This was predicated on the imperative that sentencing judges impose a sentence that 'in their discretion' meets the particular circumstances of the case and of the accused. Thus Finlay CJ doubted that it would be 'appropriate for an appellate court to appear to be laying down any standardisation or tariff of penalty for cases'.[17]

It is positive to see the Supreme Court noting that mitigating circumstances in rape are limited.[18] The guilty plea was deemed to be the only such circumstance in the current case, but it was regarded as a 'significant mitigating factor' due to its preventing the 'ordeal' of cross-examination. Certainly, there is an argument to be made that a degree of mitigation should be based on an early plea. This is due to the plea possibly denoting acceptance of responsibility, and so as ensuring accountability, which is a key function of the criminal trial. Moreover, victims do not necessarily experience a sense of catharsis from a full, contested criminal trial.[19] Nonetheless, the judgment presupposes that the complainant will regard questioning in a negative manner, and does not assess whether a trial, the hearing of evidence and its findings of fact may in fact be valuable, affirming or cathartic for some complainants.

[11] *DPP v Tiernan*, above n 1, at 253.

[12] See Dorothy Roberts, 'Rape, Violence, and Women's Autonomy' (1993) 69(2) *Chicago-Kent Law Review* 359–88; Carine Mardorossian, *Framing the Rape Victim: Gender and Agency Reconsidered* (New Brunswick, NJ, Rutgers University Press, 2014).

[13] *DPP v Tiernan*, above n 1, at 254.

[14] See Betty Friedan, *The Feminine Mystique* (New York, Penguin, 1965).

[15] A recent example of the impact of this concerned Ms Y, a teenage asylum-seeker who had been raped and who discovered she was pregnant on her arrival in Ireland. Though suicidal, her pregnancy was not terminated immediately; rather, her baby was delivered by caesarean section in the third trimester and is in the care of the state.

[16] *DPP v Tiernan*, above n 1, at 253.

[17] ibid, at 254.

[18] ibid, at 255.

[19] See Lee Madigan and Nancy Gamble, *The Second Rape: Society's Continued Betrayal of the Victim* (Michigan, Lexington Books, 1991); Jennifer Temkin, *Rape and the Legal Process* (Oxford, Oxford University Press, 2002) 156.

The Court stated that a lack of premeditation is not a mitigating circumstance and should be described more aptly as 'the absence of aggravating circumstance'. Furthermore, the Court emphasised that neither the victim's previous sexual experience nor her imprudent self-exposure to the danger of rape could be considered a mitigating circumstance. That this even needs to be said is regrettable. Moreover, the choice of the words 'imprudence' and 'self-exposure' casts judgement on the woman, and undermines the culpability and choice of the offender. Referring to 'the danger of rape' reframes the issue as one that seems inexorably occurring, rather than as actions chosen and perpetrated by autonomous men. In seeking to ensure that sexual experience and behaviour do not mitigate, the Court's unfortunate choice of words still reproaches the victim.

Crucially, the Court in *Tiernan* examined the possibility of a non-custodial sentence for rape conviction. The Chief Justice stated that while a judge must impose a sentence that meets the particular circumstances of the case and of the accused person, 'it is not easy to imagine the circumstance which would justify departure from a substantial immediate custodial sentence for rape'.[20] He stressed that it would be 'wholly exceptional'. So, a non-custodial sentence is not precluded, though it should be wholly exceptional.

Throughout the judgment a clear retributive leaning is evident, though there is also some rehabilitative rhetoric. Moreover, the underpinning constitutional principle of proportionality requires the sentence to be cognisant of the offence, but also of the offender's personal circumstances.[21] This permeates the judgment and informs its conclusion.

Application of *Tiernan*

Subsequent cases indicate the implications of this decision, in particular the viewing of a guilty plea as a 'significant mitigating factor'. For instance, in *DPP v G*,[22] the accused pleaded guilty to rape and was sentenced to 12 concurrent sentences of life imprisonment. The Supreme Court reduced the sentence to one of 15 years' of imprisonment, referring to *Tiernan* in so doing. *Tiernan* was also applied in *DPP v WC*,[23] where WC pleaded guilty to the rape of the complainant with whom he had a pre-existing relationship. *Tiernan* ultimately permitted the handing down of a suspended sentence in this instance.

It is worth noting that section 29 of the Criminal Justice Act 1999 now provides that a court, in determining what sentence to pass on a person who has pleaded guilty, shall take into account, if it considers it appropriate to do so, the stage at which and the circumstances in which he indicated an intention to plead guilty. This section overturns suggestions in the aforementioned case law that as a matter of principle a discount must be given for an early plea of guilty.

[20] *DPP v Tiernan*, above n 1, at 253.
[21] *State (Healy) v Donoghue* [1976] IR 325.
[22] *DPP v G* [1994] 1 IR 587.
[23] *DPP v WC* [1994] ILRM 321.

The Feminist Judgment

The contributions of the feminist judgment are manifold, not least as it would guard against decisions such as *WC*. As is explored more fully below, the key aspects are the foregrounding of the victim and the development of sentencing guidelines. Throughout, the feminist judgment grapples with the tensions that exist between judicial independence and consistency. Indeed, it has been argued that the notion of independence in fact may be a façade for male bias.[24] This issue resonates widely, not just in the Irish context, or in the context of sentencing of sexual offences; but it is particularly pressing in this jurisdiction given the extent to which judicial discretion is protected. Indeed, the Irish system of sentencing has been described as one of the most unstructured in the common-law world.[25] The fact that this is not just a feminist issue but a broader ideological one underlines the resistance to sentencing guidelines, though this is slowly beginning to change. More recently, in *People (DPP) v Drought*[26] the High Court assessed and categorised rape sentences, looking at 'lenient', 'ordinary' and 'severe' punishments. In considering 'ordinary punishments', which were seen to range from three to eight years, Charleton J noted that 'In attempting to discover whether there is a normal sentence for rape, my view on this matter is one based on research and is not the establishment of, much less the declaration of, a norm.'[27] Moreover, the Court of Criminal Appeal in *People (DPP) v Ryan* interpreted *Tiernan* to permit guidance to be given on appropriate sentence ranges for certain offences, with due allowance made for any exceptional circumstances.[28]

The underpinning value in the feminist judgment is that of the autonomy of the complainant. This foregrounding of autonomy is crucial, as the trial process and in particular a guilty plea can be disempowering. Moreover, the feminist judgment stresses that victims should not be viewed as an homogeneous class or categorisation, and that their experiences, reactions and interests are not uniform or necessarily consistent.[29] A more recent related development is the introduction of separate legal representation for the complainant,[30] which goes some way to meeting these concerns.

The nature and dimensions of harm are explained, with pregnancy and disease not going to the gravity of harm. The feminist judgment highlights that there is no distinction between stranger/non-stranger rape, and highlights the paradox that while stranger rapes

[24] Judith Resnik, 'On the Bias: Feminist Reconsiderations of the Aspirations for Our Judges' (1988) 61 *South California Law Review* 1877–1944.

[25] Tom O'Malley, *Sentencing Law and Practice*, 2nd edn (London, Round Hall Ltd, 2000) 8. The Law Reform Commission sees sentencing policy in Ireland as 'incoherent', and argues that this results in inconsistency and public mistrust of the system: Law Reform Commission, *Consultation Paper on Sentencing* (Law Reform Commission, 1993) 61–62.

[26] *People (DPP) v Drought* [2007] IEHC 310.

[27] ibid, para 27.

[28] *People (DPP) v Ryan* [2014] IECCA 11. *In Z* [2014] IECCA 13, the Court of Criminal Appeal held that 'there is now an obligation on the prosecution to draw to the attention of a sentencing judge any guidance … which touches on the ranges or bands of sentences which may be considered appropriate to any offence under consideration and the factors which are properly, at least in ordinary cases, to be taken into account'.

[29] See Amanda Burgess-Proctor, 'Intersections of race, class, gender, and crime: Future directions for feminist criminology' (2006) 1 *Feminist Criminology* 2747.

[30] See Criminal Law (Rape) Act 1981, s 4A, as inserted by Sex Offenders Act 2001, s 34.

are statistically less common cases, they are seen as stereotypical. The Rape Crisis Network Ireland notes that of the people who attended Rape Crisis Centres for counselling and support in 2014, 93 per cent of the perpetrators were known to the victim/survivor.[31]

The most radical component of the feminist judgment is the introduction of sentencing guidelines for rape cases, and the pronouncement that a sentencing court is not precluded from imposing the maximum sentence in respect of a guilty plea. Strict sentencing guidelines would not be constitutional in Ireland, given that the principle of proportionality in sentencing is 'a well-established tenet of Irish constitutional law'.[32] Instead, a scheme of principled discretion is advocated in the judgment. The delineation of some guidelines and the affirmation that imprisonment is the norm are hugely significant, given the communicative function and capacity of the criminal trial and sentencing.[33] This prompts us to reflect on the audience and recipient of the judgment, and also of guidelines. Guidelines are a statement to judges in future sentencing contexts, but also to the community, and to victims. And guidelines in this context represent a statement *about* all of these, in so far as they indicate (how) judges need to be guided; they illustrate how we constitute our community's rules; they recognise this (and other) victim's experiences; and they acknowledge the harm caused to women.

Nonetheless, if feminism is to be true to its critical and radical roots, it needs to be sceptical about what the criminal justice system can deliver to victims in terms of accountability. Though the criminal law and the overall process is of great practical and symbolic significance, it is just one component in the societal treatment of victims. The role of and possible interventions from victims are limited, and of course much harmful and criminal sexual violence is never detected, least of all prosecuted.[34]

Lastly, it is striking that the feminist desire for recognition of the harms inherent in and caused by rape through robust punishment sometimes maps onto retributive inclinations. This leads to the co-opting or the compromising of feminism for punitive purposes, in what can be regarded as 'carceral feminism'.[35] A careful path must be navigated in addressing this tension, lest the progressive and positive aspects of feminism become associated with punitive law and order policies that demand lengthy imprisonment in inappropriate cases. The feminist judgment addresses this concern adeptly, in providing a comprehensive and detailed account to guide the application of principled discretion. And the feminist judgment still imposes a sentence that is longer than average life term. The sentencing guidelines maintain the capacity to mitigate due to the particular circumstances of the offender, and the expression of real remorse with a desire for rehabilitation.

[31] Rape Crisis Network Ireland, *National Rape Crisis Statistics 2014* (RCNI, 2014) 20.

[32] Hamilton J in *Rock* v *Ireland* [1997] 3 IR 484, at 500.

[33] See Antony Duff, *Punishment, Communication, and Community* (Oxford, Oxford University Press, 2001).

[34] Conor Hanly, Deirdre Healy and Stacey Scriver, *Rape and Justice in Ireland* (Dublin, Liffey Press, 2009). On the limits of criminal law and carceral feminism, see further Cian Ó Concubhair's commentary on David Prendergast's feminist judgment of *CC v Ireland* in this collection, ch 27.

[35] See, eg, Elizabeth Bernstein, 'Militarized Humanitarianism Meets Carceral Feminism: The Politics of Sex, Rights, and Freedom in Contemporary Antitrafficking Campaigns' (2010) 36(1) *Journal of Women in Culture and Society* 45–71.

The People (at the suit of the Director of Public Prosecutions) v Edward Tiernan
[S.C. No. 190 of 1987]

Supreme Court 13th May, 1988

Kennefick-Fennell C.J. 13th May, 1988

The victim in this case was in a car with her boyfriend when three men attacked them. The men forcibly entered the car, locked the victim's boyfriend in the boot, and drove them some distance to a nearby field. There, two of the men repeatedly raped the victim and subjected her to violence and acts of sexual degradation. Later that day, the two men, including the appellant, were interviewed by the Gardaí, and admitted the crime. The appellant pleaded guilty to rape and was sentenced to serve twenty-one years. He appealed to the Court of Criminal Appeal and his sentence was affirmed. The Attorney General issued a certificate pursuant to section 29 of the Courts of Justice Act, 1924, certifying a point of law of exceptional public importance was involved i.e. the guidelines courts should apply in relation to sentences for the crime of rape. Hence the issue is now before us in the Supreme Court as an appeal against sentence.

The offence of rape is complex, value-laden and emotive. The wrongness of rape is manifold. Each victim experiences the offence on an individual basis. Rape sentencing is all too frequently influenced by stereotypical constructs of victims which can distort and even replace that true experience. Let me be clear on this point: it is not the function of the criminal law to put words in the mouth of a person who has been raped or to seek to ascertain or replicate her wishes. The function of the law is to act as a conduit of justice whereby all such persons, and society, are represented adequately and appropriately, and the rights of the offender are protected and vindicated in accordance with the Constitution. It is the opinion of this Court that the most effective means of achieving justice in cases of rape is through the issuance of sentencing guidelines.

Justification for sentencing guidelines

It is not the function of the sentencing court to presuppose the response of the victim of rape, nor to assume the degree of culpability of the offender. Its function is to take account of the nuanced and wide-ranging effects of a particular offence of rape on the victim, and society at large, in addition to the personal circumstances of the offender at the time of sentence. The sentencing judge must fulfil this mandate while staying faithful to the proper administration of justice in order to maintain the public's trust in the criminal justice system. To be just, the sentence must have regard to the principle of proportionality, inherent in which is the exercise of judicial discretion in light of the circumstances of a particular case, and the principle of consistency, by which we mean the consistent application of sentencing principles, recognising that such application may result in disparate outcomes, and justifiably so.

Having regard to its appellate jurisdiction, it is the duty of the Court to ensure the optimal delivery of justice at all levels. Within that remit, the function of the Court is twofold: it is required to review specific sentencing decisions, in addition to elaborating on the general principles applicable to sentencing. The latter function includes the advancement of sentencing guidelines for use at trial court level. Indeed, we need only look as far as our nearest neighbour to view the superior court practice of delivering guideline judgments; *R v. Billam* (1986) 82 Cr. App. R. 347, where the Court of Appeal (Criminal Division) indicates various benchmarks for sentencing rape offences.

Thus, the issuing of sentencing guidelines in respect of the offence of rape is necessary in the interests of justice, in order to: reaffirm societal values in terms of bodily integrity and sexual autonomy; preserve public confidence in the judicial process via the proposal of general principles and prevent intuitive reactions based on past cases. In an ideal world, the approach advanced in this judgment would be based upon reliable data on previous sentencing practice in the area of sexual offences. That said, the lack of such data at the present time does not inhibit the Court from issuing guidelines based upon its knowledge and experience of such cases. Indeed, the Court envisages this guideline judgment to be but the beginning of a process of evolution which requires time, effort, commitment and resources.

In this judgment, the Court seeks to advance and apply a policy of principled discretion via the elaboration of a working collection of sentencing guidelines for trial courts. In summary, it proposes a system of appropriate sentence ranges for rape offences, with an indication of key mitigating and aggravating factors. Departure from settled principle as manifested in the guidelines would be permissible in exceptional circumstances as required by a particular case. Thus, the proposed system is best suited to respond to our present needs, in that it shall be authoritative but flexible: authoritative, in the sense that the guidelines must be brought to the attention of, and considered by, the sentencing court in all relevant cases by the Director of Public Prosecutions; and flexible, in the sense that the court will not be obliged to follow them where a different approach is justified by the facts of the case.

In general terms, the purpose of this judgment is to instigate the practice of issuing guidance where a suitable case arises, and in accordance with the principles summarised herein. A suitable case for the issuing of guidelines is one where a superior court identifies that it is a priority that the application of the general principles in respect of a particular area be clarified in the interests of justice.

There exists no single unifying aim that sentencing judges in this jurisdiction must prioritise when passing sentence. In fact, the Irish courts have expressly favoured three sentencing aims from which a judge, through the exercise of his discretion, may choose: retribution, deterrence and rehabilitation: *The State (Stanbridge) v. Mahon* [1979] I.R. 214. There are, however, certain constitutional principles which bind judicial discretion in this context.

A primary purpose of this guideline judgment is to assist sentencing judges in discharging their constitutional duty to fix sentences underpinned by the principle of proportionality. It is settled law that a sentencing judge must impose a sentence appropriate to the degree of guilt taking into account all relevant circumstances which may arise in that case: *Deaton v. Attorney General* [1963] I.R. 170; *State (Healy) v. Donoghue* [1976] I.R. 325 applied. Furthermore, the sentence so imposed must be appropriate not only to the offence committed but also to the particular offender: *People (Attorney General) v. O'Driscoll* (1972) 1 Frewen 351 *People (Attorney General) v. Poyning* [1972] I.R. 402; *State (Stanbridge) v. McMahon* [1979] I.R. 214; *State (Healy) v. Donoghue* [1976] I.R. 325.

Thus, a court must impose a sentence proportionate to the gravity of the offence but is obliged to mitigate or aggravate that sentence if required by virtue of the circumstances of the particular offender at the time of sentencing. And while the Legislature has the power to set a maximum sentence in respect of a particular offence (for present purposes, the maximum sentence for rape is penal servitude for life under section 48 of the Offences Against the Person Act, 1861), the actual sentence to be imposed on an offender is a matter for a sentencing judge upon the exercise of his discretionary power: *Costello v. Director of Public Prosecutions* [1984] I.R. 436.

Judicial discretion is an exercise in the application of judgment in accordance with legal principle, to the exclusion of personal or political influence. In terms of judicial discretion at sentencing, it is important to emphasise the constitutional imperative whereby no person should endure imprisonment for a moment longer than is necessary; *Murray v. Ireland* [1985] I.R. 532. Thus, this Court is obliged to ensure the optimal operation of the principle of proportionality. It is in recognition of this obligation that I advance sentencing guidelines as a method of calculating proportionate judgments according to legal principle, and to the exclusion of partiality and bias, while simultaneously permitting flexibility of sentence where the justice of a particular case so demands.

The delivery of individualised justice is a variable endeavour, be that by virtue of judicial discretion or divergent sentencing aims, and so the principle of consistency cannot and, indeed, should not be applied in absolute terms. Nevertheless, some mechanism for structuring the approach of the sentencing courts is required so that the method by which judges arrive at sentences is consistent. In this way, any undue disparity may be reduced without enforcing excessive standardisation.

Plea in mitigation

Before considering the content of sentencing guidelines in general, one matter requires detailed consideration. It is often argued that a guilty plea in rape cases should attract a reduction in sentence. If successful, this argument would mean that the offender would gain from an early plea of guilty; as the latter could be taken to indicate potential for rehabilitation on sentencing. A potential lottery or bonus effect of a guilty plea then benefits the offender by allowing him extra credit for sparing the victim from the particular humiliation pertaining to a rape trial. But it should be understood that the 'ordeal' of the rape trial largely results from the law itself; in particular from the narrow definition of the *actus reus* of the offence, combined with the effect of corroboration rules, and the admissibility of past sexual history evidence.

First, the offence of rape remains very restrictively defined, despite the reforms introduced by the Criminal Law (Rape) Act, 1981. Section 2(1) of the Act provides:-

> "A man commits rape if:
>
> (*a*) he has unlawful sexual intercourse with a woman who at the time of the intercourse does not consent to it, and
>
> (*b*) at that time he knows that she does not consent to the intercourse or he is reckless as to whether she does or does not consent to it ..."

The narrowness of this definition may have implications both for the trial and for matters of evidence and proof. The extent to which the prosecution may find it difficult to establish the *actus reus* should not, however, prove a windfall for the offender.

Second, the court must take account of the impact of the corroboration rule, and of those various provisions in relation to admissibility of sexual history evidence on the particular victim's experience as a witness in a rape trial. The law in relation to the admissibility of past sexual history of the victim is germane to the victim's experience under cross-examination in court. The old common law position deemed all such evidence admissible at trial, so that a complainant could be questioned about her past sexual history with the accused and third parties. Following much lobbying and commentary, the rules in relation to past sexual history of victims in rape trials were reformed by the 1981 Act. The current position is that the complainant's past sexual history with the accused remains admissible, but there is now a measure of judicial discretion with regard to the admissibility of past sexual history with third parties. This means that such evidence is excluded, except to the extent that the Judge grants leave on application made to him or her in the absence of the jury by or on behalf of the accused. The criteria used to determine whether leave should be granted by the Judge are set out in subsection 2(b) of section 3 of the 1981 Act:-

> "The Judge shall give leave if, and only if, he is satisfied that it would be unfair to the accused person to refuse to allow the evidence to be adduced or the question to be asked, that is to say, if he is satisfied that, on the assumption that if the evidence or question was not allowed the jury might reasonably be satisfied beyond reasonable doubt that the accused person is guilty, the effect of allowing the evidence or question might reasonably be that they would not be so satisfied."

The actual difference this change or reform in relation to third party history makes to the complainant's experience in the witness box is questionable. Zsuzsanna Adler found that judges overwhelmingly used their discretion under the English equivalent of this sub-section, 2(2) of the Sexual Offences (Amendment) Act 1976 to admit such evidence (Z. Adler, "The relevance of sexual history evidence in rape: problems of subjective interpretation" [1985] Crim L.R. 769, 770–80). The assumption that evidence of past consent to sexual experiences with the offender is relevant to the issue of the existence or non-existence of consent on the occasion in question is clear in the legislation. However, questions as to such past sexual experiences rarely provide insight into the victim's account of the offence, and usually have the undesired result of distracting the jury from the pertinent facts of the case in question.

Third, issues arise in relation to the very particular treatment of the credibility of the testimony of a woman at a rape trial. The general rule regarding witness testimony is that 'the court may act upon the uncorroborated testimony of one witness, and such requirements as there are concerning a plurality of witnesses, or some other confirmation of individual testimony, are exceptional' (Rupert Cross, *Cross on Evidence*, 6th edn (1985) 207). However certain types of evidence are regarded as being inherently weak or suspect, and so deemed to require additional supportive or corroborative evidence. This rule of practice has the effect of a rule of law (*People (Attorney General) v. Michael Cradden* [1955] I.R. 130). Instances requiring corroboration include accomplice evidence, children's evidence given on oath, and victims' evidence in sexual offences cases. The rationale of the requirement in relation to sexual offence victims is particularly relevant.

In *Hester's Case* [1972] 3 All E.R. 1056, 1059–1060, Lord Morris located the overall rationale here in the untrustworthiness of this category of evidence. Hale, in the context of rape, phrases it as follows: "It is an accusation easily to be made and hard to be proved; and harder to be defended by the party accused tho' never so innocent," (*Pleas of the Crown* 1, 635–6). Glanville Williams located the reason for the corroboration requirement in the fact that: "sexual cases are peculiarly subject to the danger of deliberately false charges, resulting from sexual neurosis, fantasy, jealousy, spite or simply a girl's refusal to admit that she consented to an act of which she is now ashamed". ("Corroboration—Sexual Cases" [1962] Crim L.R. 662).

The arguments in favour of the corroboration requirement in regard to evidence of complainants in sexual cases are variously put as follows: the confusion or hysteria of the victim may lead to a wrong identification; sexual crimes are usually alleged to have occurred in private and may leave no outward traces; there is a danger of the jury feeling excessive sympathy for the victim; and a woman may feel jilted and wish to repudiate what she is ashamed of—the 'hell hath no fury' school of thought.

It is interesting to note that there seems to be a hierarchy of trustworthiness within the categories of case requiring corroboration as a matter of practice. In *R v. Cracker* (1922) 17 Cr. App. R. 46, Lord Hewart C.J. suggests that the testimony of a sexual complainant is more reliable than that of an accomplice. Similarly, in *People (Attorney General) v. Williams* [1940] I.R. 195 at 200, Sullivan C.J. seemed to rank the trustworthiness of the prosecutrix in a rape case higher than that of an accomplice: "In cases of rape the prosecutrix is not *prima facie* a discredited witness, as is an accomplice, nevertheless it has been recognised since the time of Hale that the jury should consider her evidence with particular care and should look for some confirmation of it in the circumstances." In *R v. Jenkins* (1980) 72 Cr. App. R. 354, however, the suggestion is made that in the event of the trial judge's failure to give a warning, the proviso (section 5(1)(a) of Courts of Justice Act, 1928 (that there has been no miscarriage of justice)) is less likely to be applied in sex cases than in others. Cross (R. Cross, *Cross on Evidence*, 6th edn (1985) 222) seems to support this, by saying that the requirement in the case of sexual complainants is a peremptory one.

In addition to this factor, the evidence of rape complainants themselves seems to have been treated in a way which reveals a hierarchy in terms of trustworthiness. In *R v. Zielinski* (1950) 34 Cr. App. R. 93 which concerned an indecent assault on a 73 year old woman, Byrne J. commented that a woman of 73 years is less likely to be suffering from hysteria or exaggeration from which younger women or children might suffer in similar circumstances. Similarly, in *R v. Gammon* (1959) 43 Cr. App. R. 115 it has been postulated that the evidence of boys is more reliable than that of girls. In *People (Attorney General) v. Ward* (1944) 78 I.L.T.R. 64, 65, Sullivan C.J. queries the application of this corroboration requirement to adult male complainants in sexual offences. The inherent incredibility that such rules of corroboration lend to the testimony of sexual complainants clearly benefits the defence.

The major question, of course, when considering a corroboration requirement, is as to what kind of evidence is corroborative. The authority here is *R v. Baskerville* [1916] 2 K.B. 658, where Lord Reading L.C.J. defined corroboration as:-

> "... independent testimony which affects the accused by connecting or tending to connect him with the crime. In other words it must be evidence which implicates him, that

> is, which confirms in some material particular not only the evidence that the crime has been committed, but also that the prisoner committed it."

In *People (Attorney General) v. Williams* [1940] I.R. 195, 200, confirmed in *People (Attorney General) v. Trayers* [1956] I.R. 110, 114, Sullivan C.J. formulated corroborative evidence as: "independent evidence of material circumstances tending to implicate the accused in the commission of the crime with which he was charged".

An important qualification here is the fact that a witness cannot corroborate himself/herself. So, for example, a witness cannot corroborate herself by early complaint of a rape case (*R v. Christie* [1914] A.C. 557). The trial judge's direction as to the finding of corroborative evidence presents difficulty here. Admission of all actions up to the act of the intercourse itself undermines the potential corroborative value of evidence of a struggle, for example torn clothing, etc. This is because the defendant, by alleging last-minute consent on the part of the victim, can force corroboration as to the issue of consent itself. Hence, evidence of an earlier struggle, which would have had corroborative value, had the defence put forward been one of alibi or a denial of the act of intercourse, is of no avail. The defence can, therefore, use the corroboration requirement to make the prosecution's task extremely difficult. This, in turn, further complicates the roles of the judge and jury at trial, and may create a fertile source of appeals.

This discussion should make it abundantly clear that the effective presentation and prosecution of an allegation of rape presents considerable challenges. Two conclusions may be drawn. First, the definition of the offence of rape, and the rules on corroboration and past sexual history evidence have a direct bearing on the victim's experience of a rape as witness, in terms of elicitation of testimony, cross examination, and ultimate reception as credible. Thus, if the avoidance of a trial presents a benefit to the victim, that benefit is so great only because the territory of evidence elicitation and proof is so fraught with potential pitfalls for the prosecution. The benefit is not primarily rooted in anything that the offender has done for the victim. Second, an assumption that the offender should receive an automatic reduction in sentence because he has pleaded guilty early, only compounds the existing benefits to the defence generated by the narrow definition of the offence and by operation of the law of evidence.

Thus, a guilty plea should not always merit a term of mitigation when proffered by the defence. Moreover, there must be occasions where even if there is a guilty plea, the court is not precluded from imposing the maximum sentence.

Sentencing guidelines for rape

The case at hand is extremely serious. The victim was subject to a gang rape by strangers. In what follows, it is in no way the intention of this Court to detract from the victim's experience in this case, or any case of this nature. However, the guidelines set out below will not pit the impact of stranger rape against that of non-stranger, or acquaintance, rape. Whether or not the offender is known to the victim, each category has the capacity to add aggravating factors at sentencing. For, in terms of the harm caused by the offence, it is impossible to weigh the fear a victim of spousal rape may experience, against that of a victim of stranger rape. In principle, therefore, both stranger and non-stranger rape must be put on an even footing in terms of assessing sentence range.

It shall be the responsibility of counsel to draw the sentencing judge's attention to the existence of a relevant guideline judgment, and the responsibility of the sentencing judge to follow the guidelines in so far as it is in the interests of justice to do so.

At this juncture, the Court wishes to make clear the fact that the behaviour of the victim, including past sexual experience, is in no way relevant to the sentencing process. Victims of rape, just as with victims of any other crime, are not responsible for what has happened to them. The guidelines, therefore, focus on the circumstances of the case, and the offender's actions and behaviour towards the victim in this context. The sentencing court may consider the circumstances of the victim, in particular, whether or not she has testified at trial, as per the guidelines.

The Court proposes the following three-step approach as a means of assisting the sentencing judge in the exercise of principled discretion:-

Step 1: Identify the appropriate sentencing range to be applied taking into account the gravity of the offence.

Recommended range	Circumstances owing to the gravity of the offence
0–2 years	— A non-custodial sentence is wholly exceptional; however, the court must not deprive itself of the possibility of identifying the exceptional case where a custodial sentence may not be appropriate.
	— Where the offender displays a realistic capacity for rehabilitation through treatment or education it may be open to a sentencing judge to take such factors into account by imposing a sentence with the prospect of a suspension/partial suspension, conditional on the offender engaging satisfactorily with the relevant services. However, how such a sentence is to be constructed in an appropriate case is a matter to be addressed in some detail by the sentencing judge; *People (Attorney General) v. Poyning* [1972] I.R 402; *State (Stanbridge) v. McMahon* [1979] I.R. 214.
3–7 years	— The court should consider as a guideline an approximate starting point of 5 years in respect of a single offence of rape on an adult victim by a single offender of previous good character who was convicted after trial; *R v. Billam* (1986) 82 Cr. App. R. 347; *R v. Puru* [1984] 1 N.Z.L.R. 248.
8–14 years	— This range is appropriate where the offender displays no realistic attitude or appropriate insight into the repellent and harmful nature of rape.
	— This range is appropriate where the offender uses a weapon to intimidate or injure the victim.
	— This range is appropriate where the offender commits multiple counts of rape.

15 years to life imprisonment	—	This range is appropriate where the offence is committed against child victim(s).
	—	This range is appropriate where the victim is the subject of abduction or prolonged detention at the hands of the offender.

Step 2: Adjust upwards the figure arrived at under Step 1 in the event of the presence of aggravating factors, including but not limited to the following:

a. Rape is premeditated (including where there is evidence of planning).
b. Use of drugs, alcohol or other substances by the offender to facilitate the offence.
c. The offender is aware that he is suffering from a venereal disease.
d. The offender has a high risk of reoffending.
e. The offender subjects the victim to threats in order to prevent the victim reporting the incident.
f. The offender is the subject of previous convictions for rape or other serious offences of a violent or sexual kind.

   Previous convictions should not be held against the offender interminably. The court should have regard to the nature of the offence, its relevance to the offence at hand, and the time that has elapsed since the conviction.
g. Particular circumstances of the victim (e.g. age, evident vulnerability, presence of disability).
h. The sentencing judge may increase the sentence as she or he deems appropriate, on the basis of the physical, psychological and/or emotional impact of the rape on the victim.

Step 3: Consider the culpability of the offender at the time of sentencing, and adjust downwards the figure arrived at under Step 2 in the event of the presence of any mitigating factors, including but not limited to the following:

a. The offender displays real and convincing remorse and co-operates fully with the relevant authorities from the moment of commission or investigation of the offence onwards, together with a manifest intention to seek to rehabilitate himself into society.

   Note that co-operation with the relevant authorities does not entitle the offender to mitigation of sentence. The court must have regard to the genuine nature of the plea and any other relevant circumstances.

   With regards to a guilty plea in particular, the acceptance of such a plea in mitigation may be justified largely on the grounds of the efficient administration of justice in the public interest, rather than because the plea is an automatic indicator of remorse, for example. Furthermore, the assumption that the offender, on pleading guilty, is in some way saving the victim from additional suffering via testifying at trial shall not be accepted outright by the court, as the response of the victim is her own. One victim may wish to avoid a trial, another may wish to confront her attacker in a formal setting, and give voice to her experience. It is for the sentencing judge to decide on the matter in light of the particular circumstances of the case.

b. Particular circumstances of the offender (e.g. old age, youth, disability, mental health condition, etc.).

The prescribed sentencing range may be departed from where a case presents exceptional and compelling circumstances.

Where a factor is an ingredient of an offence or is used to identify a sentencing range, it cannot also be an aggravating factor: the court must take all reasonable steps to ensure that double counting of any factor will not occur at the sentencing stage.

For the avoidance of doubt, the absence of aggravating factors shall not be a reason to mitigate sentence, for example, where the rape is of a short duration.

Application of the sentencing guidelines to the case at hand

Step 1: The following circumstances are present to warrant the application of the 8–14 years sentence range:

— The victim was raped on more than one occasion.

In addition, the following circumstances are present which warrant an increase to the 15 years–life imprisonment sentence range:

— The victim was abducted in the sense that she was forcibly removed from the car she was occupying with her boyfriend.

The Court sets the starting point, prior to the application of aggravating and mitigating factors, at 18 years, owing to the number of circumstances which go to the gravity of the offence.

Step 2: On the basis of the aggravating factors listed below, the Court deems that the starting point be increased to 22 years. Those factors are as follows:

— The offender is the subject of four previous convictions; of particular relevance to the case at hand are those offences of a violent and indecent nature: (a) assault occasioning actual bodily harm, (b) aggravated burglary associated with a wounding, (c) gross indecency, and (d) burglary.

Step 3: On the basis that the offender demonstrated some cooperation with the authorities from the point of investigation, the Court deems that the appropriate sentence to be imposed on the offender is 21 years.

The Court is not satisfied that there is sufficient evidence to show that the offender displays a manifest intention to seek to rehabilitate himself into society. Furthermore, the Court, albeit reluctantly, questions the possibility of rehabilitation in the given case, in light of the lengthy prison sentence necessitated by the gravity of the offence. For, it is the experience of this Court that the longer an offender remains in prison, the more difficult it can be for that person to be the subject of meaningful rehabilitation.

24

Commentary on *McKinley v Minister for Defence*

FERGUS RYAN

Introduction

There is a saying in Irish, 'ar scáth a chéile a mhaireann na daoine'. Loosely translated, this means that people depend on each other to survive and thrive.[1] The sentiment resonates particularly strongly with some feminist approaches to law, most notably with the seminal work of Martha Fineman on dependency and vulnerability.[2] This philosophy challenges traditional liberal assumptions of the individual as an atomised entity, entirely self-dependent and self-sufficient. It instead emphasises that a person's wellbeing depends to a significant extent on the social and interpersonal supports available to her or him.

One implication of this philosophy is that a wrongful act causing injury to a person may reverberate beyond the person immediately and directly injured. This is recognised, for instance, in laws that allow family members to sue for the wrongful death of a relative.[3] It is now well established, also, that a person who suffers psychiatric injury as a result of injury or death negligently inflicted upon a close relative may seek damages, provided she or he can establish a sufficient degree of proximity.[4]

Nonetheless, as Kingsmill Moore J observed in *Spaight v Dundon*, the law of torts tends as a matter of general policy to lean against extending 'liability for a tort beyond the injuries to the person against whom the tort is directly committed'.[5] While acknowledging that human interconnectedness is such that 'an injury to one person nearly always involves injury of some kind or another to other people', he concludes that, with narrow exceptions, the common law typically regards such injuries as too remote to merit relief.[6] It is, as

[1] Literally it means 'people live in each other's shadows' (author's translation).

[2] Martha Fineman, *The Autonomy Myth: A Theory of Dependency* (New York, New Press, 2004); and Martha Fineman, 'The Vulnerable Subject: Anchoring Equality in the Human Condition' (2008) 20(1) *Yale Journal of Law and Feminism* 1.

[3] See Civil Liability Act 1961, s 48(1). See further Bryan McMahon and William Binchy, *Law of Torts*, 4th edn (London, Bloomsbury Professional, 2013) ch 42.

[4] *Kelly v Hennessy* [1995] 3 IR 253. Cf *McLoughlin v O'Brian* [1983] 1 AC 410; *Alcock v Chief Constable of Yorkshire Police* [1992] 1 AC 310.

[5] *Spaight v Dundon* [1961] IR 201, 215.

[6] ibid, 214.

Joanne Conaghan observes in her feminist judgment, unusual to confer 'a right of action on someone other than the primary victim of a tort'.[7]

To this general principle there is, however, an important exception. A husband has long been permitted in Irish law to sue for loss of *consortium* and *servitium* arising from injuries caused to his wife as a result of another's wrongful act.[8] Originally, the remedy was restricted to husbands, though, as discussed below, in the 1992 Supreme Court decision in *McKinley v Minister for Defence*,[9] it was extended to wives in respect of injuries caused to their husbands. The tort addresses the loss to a person of the company and care of that person's husband or wife, and of various domestic services provided by the latter.[10] The precise entitlements for which the remedy offers compensation seem vague and amorphous. Bromley has spoken of consortium as 'the sharing of a common home and common domestic life'.[11] In *McKinley*, O'Flaherty J observed that consortium entailed 'companionship, the rendering of services, sexual intercourse and affectionate relations between the spouses'.[12] How one precisely quantifies the impact of the loss of such nebulous entitlements remains a distinct challenge.

Particular difficulties arise in relation to elements of the tort addressing the loss of spousal and domestic services. Happily, the legal status of marriage no longer guarantees, still less confers, a definitive right to such services as are envisaged by the tort. Given the abolition of the marital rape exemption[13] and of the right to sue for restitution of conjugal rights,[14] a husband, by 1992, could no longer legally require his wife to live with him in a common house, still less compel her to render services, of a sexual nature or otherwise. The tort thus appears to offer compensation for services that the husband is (and was in 1992) no longer entitled to demand as of right, independently of his wife's consent.

The Original Supreme Court Judgments in *McKinley*

Historically, relief was confined to husbands. In England and Wales, in *Best v Samuel Fox and Co Ltd*, the House of Lords declined to extend the remedy to wives.[15] Their Lordships reasoned that the remedy was anomalous to begin with, and ruled against exacerbating this

[7] Conaghan J, below.

[8] See McMahon and Binchy, above n 3, ch 33. This right of a husband to sue for loss of consortium was confirmed as a settled part of Irish law in *Spaight v Dundon* [1961] IR 201 and *O'Haran v Devine* (1964) 100 ILTR 53. The Civil Liability Act 1961, s 35 also refers to an 'action brought for the loss of the *consortium* or services of a wife or for the loss of the services of a child or servant'.

[9] *McKinley v Minister for Defence* [1992] 2 IR 333.

[10] Originally *total* loss of consortium was required, but the Irish courts have more recently accepted that partial loss may also be compensated. See McCarthy and O'Flaherty JJ in *McKinley* [1992] 2 IR 333, 354–55 and 358; and Carney J in *McKinley v Minister for Defence (No 2)* [1997] 2 IR 176.

[11] *Bromley on Family Law*, 5th edn (London, Butterworths, 1976) 111. See also *Kungl v Schiefer* (1960) 25 DLR (2d) 344 (Schroeder JA).

[12] *McKinley v Minister for Defence* [1992] 2 IR 333, 355.

[13] Criminal Law (Rape) (Amendment) Act 1990, s 5.

[14] Family Law Act 1988. See also the Family Law Act 1981.

[15] *Best v Samuel Fox and Co Ltd* [1952] AC 716 (HL). For a thorough analysis of this case, see Joanne Conaghan, *Law and Gender* (Oxford, Oxford University Press, 2013) 29ff.

anomaly by extending it to wives. As Lord Goddard commented, 'English law is free neither of some anomalies nor of everything illogical, but this is no reason for extending them'.[16]

In England and Wales, as well as in Northern Ireland, the favoured solution was abolition.[17] In Ireland, by contrast, the remedy has been not only retained but also expanded in its application. In *McKinley* the Supreme Court by a majority extended the tort to wives in respect of injuries suffered by their husbands.[18] In this case, Séamus McKinley was seriously injured in an explosion while serving in the defence forces. His injuries allegedly were caused by the defendants' negligence and breach of duty in relation to the care, control and handling of explosive substances.[19] Mr McKinley's wife, Finola, sued for loss of and impairment to *consortium* and *servitium* arising from the injuries caused to her husband. In response, the state claimed, *inter alia*, that the tort in question could only be invoked by a husband in respect of injuries to his wife, and not vice versa.

In the High Court, on the preliminary point as to whether the wife had any cause of action, Johnson J allowed the claim to proceed.[20] On appeal to the Supreme Court, a majority agreed that Mrs McKinley could sue for loss of consortium.[21] In the Supreme Court, all of the judges readily accepted that there was no constitutionally-compliant prospect of retaining the tort if it was to continue to be confined only to husbands. Indeed the defendants (including the Ministers for Defence and Justice, and the state) not only conceded this point; they argued that the common law tort was in fact unconstitutional (and hence of no legal effect) due to the unequal treatment of wives. They thus claimed it had not been carried over into Irish law by the provisions of Article 50 of the 1937 Constitution.[22]

The two options facing the Supreme Court were facially egalitarian—extend the tort to wives, or abolish it entirely. A majority (Hederman, McCarthy and O'Flaherty JJ) concluded that it was within the Court's power to extend the remit of the common law tort, thus allowing Mrs McKinley to sue.[23] They relied heavily on the equality guarantee in Article 40.1 of the Constitution, coupled with the provisions of Article 41 affording special protection for and recognition of the family based on marriage.

In his judgment, Hederman J emphasised the organic nature of the common law and its responsiveness to social change.[24] While citing the constitutional equality guarantee in conjunction with the special constitutional status afforded to marriage, Hederman J emphasised, in particular, the terms of Article 41.2 of the Constitution, recognising the special

[16] *Best*, above n 15, 733.

[17] Administration of Justice Act 1982, s 2.

[18] *McKinley v Minister for Defence* [1992] 2 IR 333. For further analysis see Gerard Hogan (1992) 14 *Dublin University Law Journal* 115.

[19] The relevant facts and particulars of the case are set out in *McKinley*, above n 18, 339–40, and in the judgment of Conaghan J.

[20] ibid, 336–37.

[21] When the case returned to the High Court in *McKinley v Minister for Defence (No 2)* [1997] 2 IR 176, Carney J found in favour of the plaintiff and awarded damages. He also determined that the tort provided a remedy for partial as well as total loss of consortium.

[22] See also *McKinley v Minister for Defence* [1992] 2 IR 333, 336, where Johnson J noted that the defendants had conceded 'that to accord such a right to a husband only is discriminatory in the extreme and unconstitutional. It is only proper that they should do so.' See also the argument of counsel for the defendants, ibid, 337–38.

[23] For more recent examples of where women have successfully sued for loss of consortium, see *Coppinger v Waterford County Council* [1998] 4 IR 243 and *Andaloc v Irish Rail* [2014] IEHC 637.

[24] *McKinley v Minister for Defence* [1992] 2 IR 333, 347.

position and contribution of women in the home. He noted, moreover, that Articles 41 and 42 should be read in light of the Preamble to the Constitution, and in particular the objective of assuring 'the dignity and freedom of the individual', concluding that 'the dignity and freedom to which the plaintiff is entitled is assured only by the dismissal of this appeal'.[25]

Concurring, McCarthy J observed 'where a common law rule offends against the principle of equality in a marriage relationship, the solution is to identify and declare the equality by positive rather than negative action'.[26] Regardless of the history of the common law right, 'equality amongst equals', he said, demanded that the Court remedy the discrimination not through abolition but rather by extending this firmly established common law principle.[27] The Court should, he said, bring Irish common law into line with constitutional requirements by affirming the husband's 'established right' and ruling that the denial of a similar right for wives would be unconstitutional.[28] In so doing, McCarthy J maintained, the Court would not be legislating social policy, but rather would simply be removing discrimination.

O'Flaherty J likewise favoured extending the tort, noting that declaring the remedy unconstitutional would be an 'extreme step', negating the Supreme Court's prior reliance on this cause of action.[29] While acknowledging the tort's anomalous nature, O'Flaherty J concluded that both the anomaly and the discrimination could be remedied in 'one fell swoop' by extending the tort to wives.[30] He too relied on both Articles 40.1 and 41 of the Constitution, highlighting 'the need to afford equal rights to both spouses'.[31] Notably, he alludes to the then extant constitutional ban on divorce in support of this conclusion.[32]

From this verdict Finlay CJ and Egan J dissented. Both agreed that the confinement of the remedy to husbands clearly infringed the constitutional guarantee of equality. The Chief Justice, however, reasoned that the right to damages arose from the fact that the husband historically had a quasi-proprietary right to the services of his wife. Observing that this was an integral element of the tort, he concluded that it was not possible to sever the right to damages from the rule confining relief to husbands. As the tort had originally sought to provide redress for the loss of a quasi-proprietary right, any extension of this legal remedy to wives would 'remove … the entire reasoning upon which it was originally based'.[33] Egan J agreed, noting that the tort 'was based on the historical concept of a wife being obliged to render services and in a sense to be regarded as her husband's property'.[34] Noting that this was an 'anathema' in modern times, Egan J asserted that the appropriate approach was to eradicate the tort in its entirety given that it infringed the equality guarantee.

Both the majority and minority agreed that the confinement of the tort to husbands was constitutionally unacceptable, but they differed in their willingness to regard this limitation as being integral to the tort. The majority clearly regarded the restriction of relief to

[25] ibid, 349–50.
[26] ibid, 350. For a critique of this approach, see Hogan, above n 18.
[27] *McKinley*, above n 24, 350.
[28] ibid, 352.
[29] ibid. 356.
[30] ibid.
[31] ibid. 358.
[32] As originally enacted, Art 41.3.2° of the Constitution prevented legislation being enacted permitting a married couple to divorce. The ban was lifted by the Fifteenth Amendment to the Constitution, which came into force in 1996.
[33] *McKinley v Minister for Defence* [1992] 2 IR 333, 344.
[34] ibid, 361.

husbands as severable. The minority, by contrast, saw this element as integral to the tort, as a fundamental basis for its existence. In short, the majority felt willing and able to re-clothe the tort in modern garb; the minority felt unable to decouple the tort from its dubious origins.

A Dilemma for the Feminist Judge

From a feminist point of view, the original decision of the Supreme Court majority may appear, at first glance, to be a very satisfactory one. After all, a remedy that formerly was foreclosed to women was opened up to wives. The decision, indeed, was then the latest in a series of superior court verdicts emphasising the constitutional equality of men and women and, in particular, of husbands and wives.[35] It was thus inevitable that the Supreme Court would not be able to ignore the tort's gender dimension.

On a closer review, however, even in its apparently egalitarian reformulation the tort gives some cause for concern.[36] The remedy it provides was originally founded on the medieval assumption that a husband had a quasi-proprietary right in respect of his wife, such that a loss of consortium and *servitium* equated to damage to this right.[37] The challenge for a feminist judge revisiting *McKinley* is therefore significant, and one that Conaghan J readily acknowledges as 'undoubtedly a difficult issue, yielding no ready resolution'.[38] On the one hand, the logic of extending the tort, formerly confined to husbands, seems compelling. Wives have traditionally been excluded from relief; a logical solution to the conundrum is to extend the ground also to wives, on the same basis as it applies to husbands. Denying the remedy to men as a means of resolving inequality is not especially helpful and, on the face of things, hardly advances the practical position of a woman deprived of the companionship of her husband.[39] Extending the tort appears, also, to enhance the protection of a traditionally vulnerable category of person, such vulnerability being a prime concern of feminist discourse. Arguably, the financial impact of an injury to a spouse in 1992 would generally have weighed much more heavily on the injured party's wife than the injured party's husband, given that wives were much more likely to be financially dependent on their husbands than vice versa.[40]

[35] See, eg, *State (DPP) v Walsh and Conneely* [1981] IR 412; and *CM v TM (No 2)* [1990] 2 IR 52. See also *De Búrca and Anderson v Attorney General* [1976] IR 38.

[36] See Margaret Thornton, 'Loss of Consortium: Inequality Before the Law' (1984) 10(2) *Sydney Law Review* 259.

[37] See Lord Wensleydale in *Lynch v Knight* (1861) 9 HLC 577, 598; and Lord Goddard in *Best v Samuel Fox* [1952] AC 716, 731–32.

[38] Conaghan J, below.

[39] The outcome might usefully be compared with that in *Somjee v Minister for Justice* [1981] ILRM 324, where Keane J upheld as constitutional a legislative measure that made it easier for women married to Irish nationals to acquire Irish citizenship than men married to Irish nationals. Keane J observed that it was not within the judicial power to extend this legislative measure to men. The only solution would be to deny the privilege to women, which would be of no benefit to the male plaintiff in that case. This factor seemed to weigh heavily on the judge in upholding the confinement of this facility to women (though the judge also upheld the measure on other grounds).

[40] See, eg, *Lowth v Minister for Social Welfare* [1998] 4 IR 321. The case concerned measures that differentiated between deserted husbands and deserted wives, in favour of the latter. The discriminatory measures in question,

In certain respects the tort is welcome in recognising the highly dependent nature of human relations. The tort arguably highlights that an injury to an individual has implications, both affective and financial, for those in dependent or co-dependent relationships with him or her. In doing so, it implicitly rejects the concept of the individual as autonomous and self-contained, recognising instead the inter-connectedness of husband and wife. In this regard, Martha Fineman's work on dependency and vulnerability readily springs to mind (though Fineman, of course, would have rejected the exclusive focus on spouses).[41] As Fineman has observed:

> We must begin to think of the state's commitment to equality as one rooted in an understanding of vulnerability and dependency, recognizing that autonomy is not a naturally occurring characteristic of the human condition, but a product of social policy.[42]

Yet, on the other hand, it is difficult for a feminist judge to avoid the shadowy historical rationale lurking behind this tort, one that envisioned the wife as a provider of various services—domestic and sexual—to the husband, and saw injury to her as an attack on the husband's quasi-proprietary right. The tort presupposes (at least in part) that a man is entitled to certain services from his wife, and that when deprived of these services he is entitled to compensation. It is no surprise then that some feminist commentators, such as Margaret Thornton, have advocated the tort's outright abolition.[43]

Some of the justifications for retaining the tort in the original majority judgments in *McKinley* seem to gloss over this history, suggesting that the tort's origins should no longer affect or concern its modern development. The implication is that the patriarchal underpinnings of the tort were no longer at work in the law, and therefore were not worthy of further scrutiny. McCarthy J says as much when he declares that 'the origin of the right of action is of historical interest only'.[44] O'Flaherty J, by contrast, acknowledges more willingly the tort's 'discredited and anomalous ancestry', and speaks of its 'dark past … which not only involved a clear discrimination against wives but consigned them to an inferior status'.[45] Yet he too feels unburdened by the tort's origins, preferring instead to rationalise that 'experience goes to show that many matters that started out as anomalies in the course of time and by a process of refinement were brought into alignment so as to ensure that a just solution was evolved'.[46] It is ironic that the impact of patriarchy could so breezily be dismissed by members of a court then exclusively consisting of five male judges (though, notably, the first female judge was appointed to the Supreme Court in that same year).

The Supreme Court majority judgments, while sympathetic to the plaintiff's plight, seem in some respects just as concerned to preserve this entitlement for husbands as to do right by wives. Indeed, a discourse of male entitlement seems to emerge in places. McCarthy J,

however, were upheld as constitutional on the basis that (*per* Hamilton CJ in the Supreme Court at 341–42): 'there were ample grounds for the Oireachtas to conclude that deserted wives were in general likely to have greater needs than deserted husbands so as to justify legislation providing for social welfare whether in the form of benefits or grants or a combination of both to meet such needs'.

[41] Martha Fineman, *The Neutered Mother, The Sexual Family and Other Twentieth Century Tragedies* (Abingdon, Routledge, 1995).
[42] Fineman (2008), above n 2, 23.
[43] Thornton, above n 36.
[44] *McKinley v Minister for Defence* [1992] 2 IR 333, 354.
[45] ibid, 356 and 355.
[46] ibid, 357.

for instance, claimed that to abolish the tort 'would be judicial legislation by denying such a claim to the husband'.[47] In his concluding remarks, he again noted the potential injustice to husbands that would have arisen had the remedy been abolished, an injustice made more potent by the fact that the case did not expressly address the rights of a husband and in which no husband would have been heard to defend his entitlements.[48] Hederman J too dismissed as 'surreal the argument of the Attorney General in this case that our appropriate answer should be that because of the equality provisions of the Constitution a husband who loses the *consortium* of his wife because of injury to her by a wrongful act should be denied his claim for this loss'.[49] Implicitly, both judges appear to be just as concerned—and possibly more so—that the tort might be made unavailable to men as they are that it had previously been denied to women. Such concern for the plight of men in a position similar to that of Mrs McKinley is not necessarily unworthy. Nonetheless, the implication undermines somewhat the veneer of feminism that one might superficially have thought to have cloaked the original majority verdicts.[50]

Elsewhere Hederman J invokes Article 41.2 of the Constitution (emphasising the special position of the woman in the home and of mothers) in support of his verdict, arguing that the particular status attaching to marriage applies to women perhaps even 'to a greater extent than it attaches to men'.[51] Given that marriage requires the union of both parties and is meant, ostensibly, to be a union of equals,[52] the implication that the status of marriage is more significant for women than for men seems instinctively peculiar, and not in keeping with the concept of spousal equality. Ironically, that status at one point in time resulted in the loss of the legal personality of wives, with the laws of coverture subsuming a wife's legal person into that of her husband. While such laws have since been abolished, the suggestion that marital status weighs more heavily on the shoulders of the wife implies that the spirit of marital equality had yet to bed down in the mind of the particular judge. Thus, the shiny new 'marriage of equals' shopfront crumbles, only to display the same old patronising merchandise as before.

The Feminist Judgment

Conaghan J's contribution squarely addresses the conundrum at the heart of this case, combining learned rigour with appropriate empathy (notably the plaintiff is 'centre-staged' in the initial discussion of facts). In doing so she fashions a solution that strikes at the quasi-

[47] ibid, 350. Later, at 350, he adds, 'the solution is not to deny the husband's right but, pursuant to Article 40, to enforce the wife's right'.

[48] ibid, 354.

[49] ibid, 357.

[50] In *Spaight v Dundon* [1961] IR 201, Kingsmill Moore J, discussing the tort of consortium, offers an illuminating example of male entitlement. He speaks of 'a woman of great beauty', whose face is 'hideously' disfigured in an accident. Her husband too has been 'adversely affected' by being denied her company at dances (as she shuns public appearances), and by being 'deprived of the aesthetic pleasure of contemplating her beauty'. Though he ultimately concludes that the husband should not be entitled to relief in this scenario, the narrative has some parallels with *BJM v CM* [1996] 2 IR 574, also discussed in this volume in ch 25.

[51] *McKinley v Minister for Defence* [1992] 2 IR 333, 349.

[52] See *In re Tilson; Tilson v Attorney General* [1951] IR 1.

proprietary aspects of the tort, and particularly the notion of *servitium*, while retaining some recognition of and relief for relational harm within marriage.

While concurring with the Supreme Court majority as regards the outcome, her decision differs from that of the other majority judges in certain important respects. In line with the majority, Conaghan J opts to retain the tort, while requiring that it be available to wives as well as husbands. In doing so, she relies primarily on the equality guarantee in Article 40.1 of the Constitution, eschewing reliance on Article 41. Notably, she singles out the aspects of the tort relating to *servitium*, the services provided by a wife to her husband, concluding that such elements have 'no place within [the] modern conception of the consortium action'.[53] In this way, Conaghan J makes a notable departure from the judgments of her fellow majority judges, one that incisively rejects the proposition that the 'notion of service' had any 'place in the modern marital relationship, whether at the behest of the husband or the wife'.[54] What remains is a tort primarily addressing the affective or relational aspects of marriage, a remedy more in keeping with the 'modern conception of what the marital bond entails'.[55] The tort is thus retained, but reconceptualised as one addressing solely the impact on the relational elements of the marriage bond.

Conaghan J's approach is confidently and artfully explained and supported in the judgment. It would have been tempting simply to abolish the ground given its dubious origins. Nonetheless, it would have been equally troubling to leave the wife without any remedy given the loss she has undoubtedly sustained. Given that women in 1992 were less likely to have had an independent income than men, and more likely to have been affected financially by injury to their husbands, there was, pragmatically speaking, some considerable merit in fashioning a solution that favoured Mrs McKinley.[56] Equally, however, a judgment that failed to address the troubling roots (and indeed the service-related branches) of the tort would have been deficient. The judgment refashions the tort in the context of evolved understandings of the institution of marriage as a partnership of equals, in line, indeed, with contemporary judicial pronouncements about the nature of marriage as 'a unique and very special life-long relationship'.[57]

In this regard, Conaghan J's surgical removal of the aspects of the tort based on *servitium* does the art of feminist judging some considerable service. Whether it is possible to separate out the elements of what is, after all, a single tort, saving some but ditching others, is nonetheless an interesting question. Certainly, a judge could not constitutionally sever from legislation a provision without which the relevant legislation would not represent the will of the legislature that enacted it.[58] Judges, however, arguably have more leeway to shape the common law, which is, after all, a judge-made body of jurisprudence.[59] As Conaghan J rightly notes, 'the action is a creature of the common law' and it is thus 'open to the Court to recraft it in such a way as to ensure it is fit for purpose in modern times'.[60]

[53] Conaghan J, below.
[54] ibid.
[55] ibid.
[56] cf the rationale of the Supreme Court in *Lowth v Minister for Social Welfare* [1998] 4 IR 321.
[57] Costello J in *Murray v Ireland* [1985] IR 532, 536.
[58] See, eg, *Maher v Attorney General* [1973] IR 140; and *Somjee v Minister for Justice* [1981] ILRM 324.
[59] Though, arguably, they must restrain themselves from creating brand new rights where none existed before, as this may amount to legislating: see *BL v ML* [1992] 2 IR 77.
[60] Conaghan J, below.

Conaghan J uses Article 50 as a filter through which the constitutionally acceptable aspects of the tort can pass but that captures and sieves out the more dubious elements. The judgment favours continuity and avoids abolishing a well-established legal action in the absence of legislative action. What is left, however, is something quite different in focus and purpose from the original tort, and more in keeping with the spirit underpinning the constitutional guarantee of equality and modern understandings of marriage. The outcome closely complements the recommendations of the Law Reform Commission that had recommended retaining the tort shorn of the service element of the action.[61] The Commission concluded that '[t]he social policy served by the action is not the protection of some supposed proprietary interest in a spouse but rather that of protecting family solidarity and the continuity of family relationships'.[62]

A Broader Vista?

Constitutional lawyers may well be cautious of such judicial activism, though it is submitted that Conaghan J has admirably balanced judicial creativity and restraint. It would be naive to think that judges cannot or do not craft the law in various respects, bending it to serve purposes that may be different from those originally conceived by the creators of those laws. Judges regularly refashion the common law and equity in various ways, with a view to addressing contemporary social problems.[63] Nonetheless, in declining to extend the tort further than the particular circumstances of the case demands, Conaghan J appropriately recognises the limitations of judicial creativity.

It would have been tempting for a feminist judge to declare that the tort extends beyond married couples to other family relationships. The privileging of marriage to the exclusion of other relationships certainly appears invidious, though the Constitution's provisions on the special position of marriage broadly underpin and permit this privilege.[64] The question nonetheless remains as to the fairness of the exclusion of other categories of relationship from the tort's remit. Indeed, while prudently leaning against forcing a more expansive approach through judicial action, Conaghan J cautions against 'any impulse to cling to fossilised notions of social organisation'.[65]

Given that modern domestic relations exhibit much greater diversity than was formerly evident, should the risk of a consortium claim really hinge on the fact that the victim happened to be married? Is it not conceivable and foreseeable that a victim would equally be likely to have a cohabitant or civil partner, who would suffer no less from loss

[61] *Report No 1—Family Law* (Law Reform Commission, 1980).

[62] *The Law Relating to Consortium and the Loss of Services of a Child*, Working Paper No 7 (Law Reform Commission, 1979) 37.

[63] One sees this, eg, in *Cawley v Lillis* [2011] IEHC 515, where Laffoy J cleverly employed the device of a constructive trust to blunt the effects of the rules of survivorship in respect of joint tenancies.

[64] *O'B v S* [1984] IR 316.

[65] Conaghan J, below.

of companionship and support?[66] A defendant who wrongfully causes injury to a husband faces the prospect of a consortium claim but is freed of such risk where the victim is unmarried. A tortfeasor would therefore be liable to the wife of a man, married recently after a brief whirlwind romance, but not to the partner of a man in a 20-year-long cohabitation. The effects seem more invidious still when one considers that the spouses may have been estranged: where a woman leaves her husband, only to be knocked down by a bus following her departure, should the husband be able to seek a remedy for loss of consortium?

Likewise, it is not possible for children to make a similar claim in respect of a parent, even though a child is likely to suffer just as profoundly (if not more so) from being deprived of the parent's care. In *PH and Others v John Murphy and Sons*, Costello J rejected a claim for damages by an injured man's children for the loss of non-pecuniary benefits flowing from the relationship with their injured father.[67] In *McKinley*, McCarthy J confirmed that the consortium remedy was ring-fenced such that it did not extend to children in respect of their parents, or to parents in respect of their children.[68] The relationships involved admittedly are very different in character, but they are no less profound. The fact of dependence arises and, indeed, is usually more pronounced in the case of children than spouses.

An Alternative Approach

Nonetheless, it is arguable that such changes, if they are to be made, must be made by the Oireachtas (Parliament), not by the courts. As Conaghan J wisely observes, 'extending the consortium action beyond the confines of the marital relation by judicial fiat alone would, in my opinion, be somewhat bolder than the occasion requires'.[69] In 1992, legislative recognition of relationships outside of marriage was virtually non-existent; it would have been a very bold move indeed for the courts to push the remedy beyond the confines of the marital bond, particularly given that the point was moot in the instant case. Notably, the Oireachtas declined to extend the tort when introducing the concept of civil partnership in 2010: neither civil partners nor cohabitants may claim for loss of consortium (though married same-sex couples will, presumably, be able to avail of this tort).[70] Nor has Parliament followed the Law Reform Commission's recommendation that the tort be extended to children in respect of their parents.[71]

Such reticence may well be prudent. Injury to a person may prompt a knock-on effect for a great variety of others who depend on the injured party—other dependent relatives,

[66] See, eg, *Bulloch v US* 487 F Supp 1078 (1980), where the US District Court for New Jersey accepted that a couple who had been married and divorced, but then reconciled and recommenced cohabitation, could rely on the tort of consortium notwithstanding the fact that they were no longer married to each other.

[67] *PH and Others v John Murphy and Sons* [1987] IR 621.

[68] *McKinley v Minister for Defence* [1992] 2 IR 333, 355.

[69] Conaghan J, below.

[70] Fergus Ryan, 'The Differences Between Civil Partnership and Marriage', *The Outmost*, May 2015, at http://theoutmost.com/opinion/civil-partnership-marriage/ (last accessed 30 June 2015).

[71] See *The Law Relating to Consortium and the Loss of Services of a Child*, above n 62; and *Report No 1—Family Law*, above n 61.

for instance, as well as employees, employers and clients. The consequential losses in some such cases are arguably too remote to require compensation, and may stretch too extensively the realm of foreseeability. It may be unwise, therefore, to extend the tort to what may ultimately become a potentially infinite range of third parties. Shorn of its current confines, it may be difficult to restrain the tort's reach: many vague claims could be made based on relational damage and third-party consequential loss.

Addressing Mrs McKinley's claim for specific losses under headings 6 and 7 in her statement of claim, Conaghan J prudently suggests that a more appropriate approach to some aspects of a claim of this nature may be to ensure that the negative impact of the injury on a victim's dependants and carers is more effectively reflected in the damages secured *directly by the victim himself or herself*:

> [T]he need for additional care and support which injury occasions and similarly the constraints that injury places on one's ability to contribute as one once did to family and domestic life, can also be conceived as a loss directly consequent upon the injury and therefore within the scope of damages recoverable by the injured spouse.[72]

The precise needs of the wronged party may differ from case to case, but in the wake of serious injury, victims are likely to need inter-personal support and care regardless of gender or civil or marital status. Likewise, third-party harm is likely to arise in a wide variety of contexts, whether the injured party is married or not, and particularly where there are children. The most prudent means of addressing some of these impacts, therefore, may well be to provide a remedy for such harm *directly to the injured party*. As Conaghan J acknowledges, this does not necessarily guarantee that the dependent party or carer will receive the allotted compensation, though it does hold out the prospect that the impact of an injury on dependent relationships beyond marriage will be more readily recognised and acknowledged than is the case under the currently formulated tort of consortium, albeit in the more manageable context of providing relief directly to the injured party.

Conaghan J thus concludes a judgment that in equal measure is bold yet appropriately restrained. She surpasses her fellow majority judges in expressly extracting the long outdated 'services' element of the tort, while prudently acknowledging the boundaries of the judicial role. In doing so, Conaghan J ably navigates the feminist dilemmas at the heart of the case, offering an empathetic judgment yielding forensic insights and a more thorough and satisfactory reformulation of the tort.

[72] Conaghan J, below.

Finola McKinley, Plaintiff v The Minister for Defence, The Minister for Justice, Daniel Green, Ireland and The Attorney General, Defendants

[1984 1268P: S.C. No 48 of 1989]

High Court	15th November, 1989
Supreme Court	27th July, 1992

Conaghan J. 27th July, 1992

Does a wife have a cause of action for loss of consortium following an injury to her husband which renders him permanently sterile and impotent and unable to render services to her which previously he could perform? This is in essence the question we are asked to address.

The Facts

The case comes before us as an appeal from a trial of a preliminary issue, namely whether the plaintiff's statement of claim discloses any cause of action. The assumed facts, in so far as they can be ascertained from the statement of claim and reply to a request for particulars, are as follows: In 1981, Finola McKinley's husband, Séamus, a member of the armed forces, was severely injured in an explosion allegedly caused by the negligence and breach of the duty of the first and second defendants. The injuries sustained were serious and included permanent damage to the scrotum which rendered Séamus McKinley sterile and impotent. Séamus spent some time in hospital being treated for his injuries during which period Finola was understandably anxious and distressed. Deprived of her husband's society and companionship, she had to cope alone with domestic and child-care responsibilities. When Séamus eventually returned home, McKinley family life was very different. Séamus and Finola could no longer engage in normal sexual relations and all prospects of having further children had effectively been eliminated. Séamus became depressed and irritable after the accident, placing further strain on marital accord. He could no longer help Finola with many of the normal household chores he had hitherto undertaken. For example, Finola had to learn to drive, a responsibility which Séamus has previously shouldered alone. In sum, and as stated in reply to the request for particulars, 'the continuity, stability and quality of the plaintiff's relationship with her husband and family has been, and continues to be, impaired.'

The Action

At common law there has long existed an action *per quod consortium amisit* by virtue of which a husband can sue another for loss of his wife's consortium. The action is unusual for at least two reasons. First, it is unusual in conferring a right of action on someone other than the primary victim of a tort. In this sense, loss of consortium is a parasitic claim dependent upon injury to a person with whom the plaintiff has a particular relational connection. The nearest analogy here would be a claim for nervous shock which allows someone to sue, albeit within closely circumscribed circumstances, for the psychiatric harm they sustain after witnessing a serious accident to a loved one (*McLoughlin v O'Brian* [1983] AC 520; [1982] 2 WLR 982; [1982] 2 All ER 298). The action for loss of consortium is unusual for yet another reason. Relationally-based in marriage, it is traditionally a one-sided action which vests a claim in the husband with respect to injury to the wife but not a claim in the wife with respect to injury to the husband. The peculiarity of this position can only be understood historically. The action for loss of consortium was part of a package of common law rights, which also included actions for enticement, harbouring and criminal conversation, all of which were premised upon, and lent support to, a medieval notion of the family based upon the *potestas* of the husband/father. In *Best v Samuel Fox & Co Ltd* [1952] AC 716; [1952] 2 All ER 394, in which the English House of Lords, in circumstances similar to those before us today, declined to extend the action for loss of consortium to a wife, Lord Goddard observed:-

> The passages cited to us from Bracton's *De Legibus Angliae*, edited by Sir Travers Twiss, vol II, p 547 [Rolls Series, vol 70], Blackstone's *Commentaries* (1768) Book III, Chapter 8, and Holdsworth's *History of English Law*, vol VIII, p 430—and there are no books of higher authority—all show that the action which the law gives to the husband for loss of consortium is founded on the proprietary right which from ancient times it was considered the husband had in his wife' (at 731; see also the comments of Lord Morton at 735).

The idea that a husband has any proprietary or quasi-proprietary right in relation to his wife is of course anathematic to modern conceptions of the marital relationship as a partnership of equals. For this reason, many common law jurisdictions have eschewed the action for loss of consortium. In England and Wales, for example, the action was abolished by the Administration of Justice Act 1982, s 2(2). Similarly, New South Wales abolished the action in the Law Reform (Marital Consortium) Act 1984. Other jurisdictions have retained the action but extended it to wives, thus eliminating the *de jure* discrimination which so offends modern mores. The State of South Australia and the Province of Alberta, Canada, have enacted legislation to this effect (see respectively Wrongs Act 1936 (SA) s 33; Domestic Relations Act RSA, 1970 c 113 as amended by SA 1973 c 61). Similarly, in the United States, the majority of states now allow wives to bring a claim for loss of consortium (Law Reform Commission, *The law relating to loss of consortium and loss of services of a child*, Working Paper No 7, 1979 ch 4 p 22). Considering the common law position overall then, jurisdictions have tended to go down one of two routes, either to reject the consortium action as a relic of times past with no place in a modern, egalitarian legal system or to rehabilitate it by making it gender-neutral and in some cases, extending the right to sue to family members other than spouses.

As a legal concept, consortium is frustratingly vague and not susceptible to precise definition. In general terms it is thought to encompass the society and services—*consortium* and *servitium*—which one spouse might be expected to render to another but inevitably, the nature of those spousal expectations varies over time and space, depending on how the marital relation itself is legally and socially conceived. According to my learned colleague, Hederman J 'consortium means living together as husband and wife with all the incidents that flow from that relationship'. A fuller elaboration is offered by Schroeder J A in the Canadian case of *Kungl v Schiefer* (1960 25 DLR 2d 344) who states that 'broadly speaking companionship, love, affection, comfort, mutual services, sexual intercourse—all belonging to the marriage state—taken together make up what we refer to as consortium' (at para 11). Note that a number of these features of consortium are affective in character and not easily reduced to monetary value. By contrast the notion of services—and particularly the traditional domestic services which a wife was expected to perform for her husband and family—can be formulated in monetary terms drawing upon the value of purchasing such services in the open market. For this reason, among others, the services element of the consortium action and the material consequences of the loss of consortium more generally tend to be the main focus of damages quantification and assessment (*Toohey v Hollier* (1955) 92 CLR 618).

Against this general background summarising the state of the consortium action in modern common law jurisdictions, I turn directly to the question before this Court: does Finola McKinley have a right to sue for the loss of consortium following an accident to her husband caused by the negligence and breach of duty of the defendants?

The presumed legal position to date has been that the claim vests in the husband only. This position is reflected in the judgments of this Court in *Spaight v Dundon* [1961] IR 201; (1961) 96 ILTR 69 and *O'Haran v Devine* (1964) 100 ILTR 53 and is at least implicit in the text of the Civil Liability Act 1961, s 35(2)(b). The Law Reform Commission, reviewing the law of consortium in 1979, offer a more circumspect position, observing that 'the question whether a wife may sue in respect of loss of consortium resulting from injury to her husband has not so far been determined in this country' (LRC Working Paper No 7 1979 p 3).

The Arguments

It is not contested by either party that the confinement of the right of action to a husband only violates the constitutional principle of equality enshrined in Article 40, s 1 of the Constitution of Ireland, the first sentence of which states: 'All citizens shall, as human persons, be held equal before the law.' The gender-specificity of the traditional consortium action clearly offends this unequivocal guarantee. Nor has it been argued before the Court that the second sentence of Article 40, s 1, which states that '[the principle of equality] shall not be held to mean that the State shall not in its enactments have due regard to differences of capacity, physical and moral, and of social functions', serves as a justification for limiting the right to sue to husbands only. Indeed it is difficult to see how any such argument could be mounted without relying on problematic and now wholly discredited assumptions about the nature of marriage as a hierarchical relation of male dominion and female subjection.

What then is the constitutional position? According to Article 50, s 1: 'Subject to the Constitution and to the extent to which they are not inconsistent therewith, the laws in force in Saorstát Éireann immediately prior to the date of the coming into operation of this Constitution shall continue to be of full force and effect …' If, as has been agreed, the action for loss of consortium in its traditional gender-specific form is indeed inconsistent with the constitutional guarantee of equality under Article 40, s 1, does the application of Article 50, s 1 render that action invalid in its entirety, on grounds of constitutional frailty, or does Article 50, s 1 allow the action to survive except 'to the extent to which [it] is inconsistent' with the equality provision? In other words, is the effect of the Constitution to extinguish the husband's right to bring a consortium claim or does the guarantee of equality require the extension of the right to wives on the same terms as husbands?

According to the defendants, the action for loss of consortium did not survive the enactment of the Constitution of Ireland. They further contend that because the basis of the right derives from a medieval conception of wives as the property of their husbands, it cannot be 'evolved' into modern times because its whole evolution was based on an inequality of status. In short, without that inequality of status, there is no base upon which the consortium action might comfortably rest.

Counsel for the plaintiff argue that the effect of the relevant Constitutional provisions is to extend the right to claim for loss of consortium to wives. They contend that from a constitutional position, there is nothing intrinsically objectionable in the right and that the correct constitutional solution is therefore to sever the discriminatory element but retain the substance of the claim. They further maintain that the Court should seek to place a constitutional construction upon the common law, to encourage its evolution along lines which allow common law and constitutional principles to cohere.

The parties are also in disagreement over the question of whether the action for loss of consortium lies for partial as opposed to total loss of consortium. This issue was argued at the preliminary issue hearing in the High Court, Johnson J ruling that the plaintiff should be allowed to continue her claim whether or not it is based on total loss of consortium or mere impairment. I will return to this issue after I address the Constitutional question to which I now turn.

The Constitutional Issue

This is undoubtedly a difficult issue, yielding no ready resolution. It is no surprise therefore that my judicial colleagues are divided as to the correct outcome. The situation lends itself to conflicting interpretations, as the arguments before the Court reflect.

With this in mind, I turn first to consider the question of whether or not the action for loss of consortium can survive the taint of constitutional frailty. If it is established that it can, it will then be necessary to determine in what form and upon what basis a constitutionally rehabilitated action for loss of consortium might stand.

Confronting the question of whether it is possible to sever the substance of the consortium right from its discriminatory restriction to husbands only, Finlay CJ takes the view that severance is not possible because the discriminatory element underpins the whole basis of the consortium right and is therefore an inherent element of it. I respectfully disagree. Historically this was the case, but more recent common law experience in those jurisdictions where the action has taken a gender-neutral form suggests that the action for loss of consortium adapts quite easily to the loss of the discriminatory element. As Article 50, s 1 states clearly that the laws in force should continue *except to the extent to which they are inconsistent* with the Constitution, we should pause before declaring that a particular legal right, already firmly entrenched in the common law, cannot survive in an adapted form. Taking the clear wording of Article 50, s 1 expressly into account, along with the experience of common law jurisdictions where the right has successfully shed its discriminatory form, I therefore conclude that the action for loss of consortium *can* survive the enactment of the Constitution by discarding that element which directly infringes upon the constitutional guarantee of equality.

It might be suggested that discarding the discriminatory element of the old consortium claim, while surmounting the constitutional problem, leaves the action without any clear or principled foundation. This should not of itself present a problem. As the action is a creature of the common law, it is open to the Court to recraft it in such a way as to ensure it is fit for purpose in modern times. Whether we would wish to do this is another matter. It is tempting to succumb to the trend in many jurisdictions simply to discard the action as a relic of times past with no place in a modern legal system. However, once it has been determined that the action for loss of consortium survives constitutional challenge, albeit in an attenuated form, it is not open to the Court to declare that an action so well entrenched in the common law no longer stands. Abolition, if that is considered the wisest course of action from a social policy perspective, is a step which in these circumstances must be taken by legislation.

I thus turn to the question of how the action for loss of consortium should now be conceived and articulated, drawing upon the inherent power of the Court to develop the common law to ensure its fitness for purpose in the context of social change.

My learned colleague, Hederman J, suggests that modern articulation of the right might be based on Article 41 of the Constitution which emphasises the primary status of marriage as the necessary basis of social order and the special protection of and respect given to women as mothers and homemakers. He observes that 'the case therefore is not based on a question of discrimination in favour of men predating the Constitution but rather, in my view, it is based on the status which the Constitution gave to marriage and to married women in particular'. With respect, reliance on Article 41 cannot be correct here as it leads us back to a consideration of consortium in gender-specific terms which, all parties agree, is not consistent with the constitutional guarantee of equality in Article 40. It is certainly the case that historically the action for loss of consortium has resided exclusively in the marriage relationship. It is thus distinct from the parallel action *per quod servitium amisit* which allowed a master to sue for injuries sustained by his servant. That the actions are historically related is undoubtedly the case, Lord Goddard in *Best v Samuel Fox & Co Ltd* observing that the action for loss of consortium 'was in fact based on the same ground as gave a master a right to sue for an injury to his servant if the latter were unable to perform his duties' ([1952] AC 716 at 732). It is also true that a significant element of the action for loss of consortium as traditionally conceived, was the loss of the wife's services, the notion of consortium encompassing both the affective and material dimensions of wifely duty. Certainly, if the action for loss of consortium is to continue to inhere in the marital relation, as Hederman J suggests, then it must reflect a modern conception of what the marital bond entails. In this respect I consider the notion of service, etymologically derived from the Latin *servitium*, understood as a condition of slavery or servitude, to have no place in the modern marital relationship, whether at the behest of the husband or the wife.

An alternative base for the action of consortium is the family. This is the proposed basis put forward by the Law Reform Commission who suggest that the social policy concern to which the action for loss of consortium should be properly directed is 'protecting family solidarity and the continuity of family relationships' (LRC Working Paper No 7 1979 p 36). The LRC propose that the relevant law be amended in such a way as to expand the current action for loss of consortium to members of the family of the injured person (where family is understood to comprise parents and their children) and to create a 'single family action' which can be brought on behalf of all family members. A not dissimilar approach has already been enacted in Ontario where the action has been aligned with the right of dependants to sue in relation to fatal accidents. Under the Ontario Family Law Reform Act s 61(1), the right of dependants to sue where a person is injured or killed as a consequence of the fault or neglect of another encompasses a wider range of potential claimants than is proposed by the Law Reform Commission with the right to sue vested in individual claimants and not in the family as a single unit.

The idea of extending the action for loss of consortium to family members is not without its attractions and clearly resonates with the special recognition of the family enshrined in Article 41 of the Constitution. At the same time, such a radical reworking of the consortium action raises a range of policy and other considerations which properly require the attention afforded by democratic decision-making processes. While it is open to the Court, indeed incumbent upon it, to develop the common law incrementally to keep step with modern times, and while this may sometimes require, as my learned colleague Hederman J aptly puts it, that we rise to the challenge and 'boldly lay down new principles to meet new social problems', extending the consortium action beyond the confines of the marital relation by judicial fiat alone would, in my opinion, be somewhat bolder than the occasion requires; indeed would stray too close to what my colleague McCarthy J describes as 'judicial legislation'.

Thus far I have determined that the action for loss of consortium has survived the enactment of the Constitution of Ireland but only in so far as it extends to both spouses, that is, is gender-inclusive in its exercise. I have also determined that it is beyond the power of this Court to extend the right beyond the marital relation so that *ipso facto* recognition and respect for the close and intimate bond which marriage creates becomes the basis for and justification of the action for loss of consortium as currently conceived. I have further determined that there is no place within such modern conception of the consortium action for the notion of *servitium*. It remains to be determined what, in practical terms, is comprised in the action for loss of consortium. For what kinds of loss does it provide redress?

The Loss

At this point it is helpful to turn again to the facts of the case before us. The losses averred by Finola McKinley in her statement of claim and reply to a request for particulars can be itemised as follows:-

1. Serious personal anguish, shock, anxiety, distress and trauma consequent upon the injuries to her husband.
2. Deprivation of normal sexual relations by virtue of her husband's impotency.
3. Inability to have further children by virtue of her husband's sterility, placing further strain upon the marriage.
4. Deprivation of her husband's society and company while he was in hospital being treated plus loss of 'all the amenities of family and marriage for the aforesaid period'.
5. Impairment of the comfort and companionship ordinarily associated with the marriage relationship by virtue of the injuries occasioned her husband, which tend to make him depressed and irritable.
6. Inability and incapacity of her husband to perform those services (especially domestic) that he formerly performed on her behalf.
7. Financial losses sustained by Finola from travelling to and from hospital, paying for babysitters and temporary accommodation during hospital visits.

To what extent do these losses fall within the scope of appropriate recovery for loss of consortium understood in terms of recognition and respect for the close and intimate bond of marriage? Thus expressed, consortium is concerned primarily with redressing relational harm, the harm to the quality of the relationship between the spouses prior to the accident. It could be argued that the first loss itemised is not relational, that is, it is expressive not of a harm to the marital relation but rather a harm to Finola McKinley consequent upon her attachment to her husband Séamus. It appears not dissimilar to the kind of bystander harm which is to a limited extent encompassed within the modern law of nervous shock (*McLouglin v O'Brian* [1983] AC 520; [1982] 2 WLR 982; [1982] 2 All ER 298). Should this fall within the scope of the consortium claim? Such authorities as there are tend to suggest not (*Markellos v Wakefield* (1974) 7 SASR 436 per Hogarth J at 437) and on balance, and bearing in mind the need to provide a coherent basis for the consortium claim in the marital relation itself, I would agree, while acknowledging it may on occasion lead to the drawing of fine distinctions between distress consequent upon seeing one's husband suffering and distress consequent upon experiencing a diminution in the quality of the marital relationship.

It seems to me that the second and third items are clear and distinct expressions of relational harm which constitute a loss both to the wife and the husband: the quality of sexual relations is inevitably affected while the husband's sterility presents a significant constraint upon the couple's exercise of reproductive choice. The fourth and fifth items are expressive of the affective dimensions of the harm suffered and commonly recur in consortium actions particularly in the United States, where as the action has expanded to include both spouses, the focus has shifted away from the traditional concept of loss in terms of wifely services towards greater recognition of the emotional distress occasioned (Margaret Thornton, 'Loss of Consortium: Inequality before the Law' 10 *Sydney L Rev* 259 (1983-85) at 270). In the past, some judges have been chary of recognising and recompensing the affective aspects of a consortium claim, most notably Lord Wensleydale in *Lynch v Knight* who maintained that a wife should not recover for loss of consortium precisely because, unlike the husband, who suffered material, calculable loss as a consequence of the deprivation of wifely services, 'the wife sustains only the loss of the comfort of her husband's society and affectionate attention, which the law cannot estimate or remedy' ((1861) 9 HLC 577 at 599). However, if this was ever the position in law, it is much less so now when tort claims based on emotional distress, whether intentionally or negligently inflicted, have become much more commonplace. Therefore, I see no reason why the fourth and the fifth items listed above should not fall squarely within the scope of a consortium claim.

We come now to the sixth and seventh itemized losses encompassing a claim for loss of services and financial losses incurred directly by Finola McKinley consequent upon her husband's injury. I have already expressed the view that a claim for loss of services should not constitute a part of any modern action for loss of consortium. Some might suggest that a primary virtue of the consortium action, at least as a matter of practice, is to allow those who suffer concrete, material losses (whether conceived as services or benefits) as a consequence of injuries to a spouse, to bring a claim. However, the need for additional care and support which injury occasions and similarly the constraints that injury places upon one's ability to contribute as one once did to family and domestic life, can also be conceived as a loss directly consequent upon the injury and therefore within the scope of damages recoverable by the injured spouse. In some jurisdictions, this is the direction the common law is taking (*Donnelly v Joyce* [1974] QB 454; *Griffiths v Kerkemeyer* (1977) 139 CLR 161). This solution is not without its difficulties as there is no formal guarantee that the injured spouse will share the benefits of the compensation he or she receives with the spouse who now provides additional care and performs additional household tasks. However, on balance this is the solution I prefer, certainly in so far as the issue falls to be resolved within the scope of judicial development of the common law. There are jurisdictions which have enacted legislation allowing a family member who provides voluntary caregiving support to another injured member of the family to claim directly. The Ontario provision, for example, allows dependants to claim damages for pecuniary loss (actual and travel expenses) as well as an allowance where the claimant provides nursing, housekeeping or other services (Ontario Family Law Reform Act 1986, s 61(2)). While such provisions may well have much to recommend them, the distributive implications are considerable and, it seems to me, raise issues best left to be determined by the legislative rather than the judicial process.

Conclusion

I conclude, then, that the action for loss of consortium in its modern gender-inclusive form is best understood as a way of recognizing and redressing relational harm, specifically conceived in terms of a diminution in the quality of the marital relationship (understood broadly to include all the incidents that ordinarily flow from the close and intimate bond that marriage occasions) consequent upon a tortiously inflicted injury to a spouse. Such a conception is consistent with the spirit and intent of the Constitution, aligns well with judicially engendered developments of the consortium claim in other common law jurisdictions, and offers a sounder basis for the action than has historically been the case.

It follows too that the action thus conceived clearly encompasses claims for impairment as opposed to total loss of consortium.

It is possible that changes in social norms and practices, in particular, changes in the nature and social significance of marriage and newly evolving conceptions of family, may give rise to a need further to develop this cause of action. The common law should resist any impulse to cling to fossilised notions of social organisation and be open to the possibility of reshaping legal norms to accord with social expectations and practices; in the area of intimate human relationships, more than any other, this is particularly so. There is also a case for following the lead in other jurisdictions and turning the difficult questions which the consortium action presents around the nature of the loss and the scope and bases of recovery over to the legislature for thorough and considered deliberation.

I would dismiss the appeal and allow the plaintiff's claim to proceed.

25

Commentary on *BJM v CM*

CHRISTINE RYAN

Introduction

In the case of *BJM v CM*,[1] the High Court granted a petition of nullity where it was found that at the time of marriage, the petitioner was unaware of his wife's 'physical disfigurement'. That is, before the marriage ceremony, the petitioner had not seen the white scar tissue across his wife's torso that had been caused by a childhood accident. Seventeen years and six children later, the marriage broke down when the respondent learned of her husband's relationship with another woman.[2] The Court found that this union could be invalidated under Irish family law upon consideration of the husband's reaction to his wife's appearance; his claim of 'revulsion'. The union was deemed *void* on the ground of want of consent, and *voidable* on grounds that the parties lacked the capacity to 'enter into and sustain normal marital relations'.[3] Katie Dawson and Aideen Ryan's feminist judgment takes the form of an imaginary appeal to the Supreme Court, where the respondent succeeds in having the declaration of nullity overturned. The appeal also considers the respondent's claim that the High Court took into account irrelevant, gender-biased considerations when determining this case.

While the reasoning and outcome of the feminist judgment depart significantly from the decision of the High Court, it is important to note that the decision is based on the same facts and legal principles that applied to the original. However, the appeal makes clear that the High Court judge was emphatic in endorsing and reasoning from a standpoint of patriarchy, where the female respondent is objectified, stereotyped and discriminated against. This judgment, by contrast, engages in feminist practical reasoning[4] that uncovers the voicelessness of the female respondent and examines her lived reality.

Probing the equality arguments raised in the appeal, I examine how the social and political mores revealed by the High Court judge manifest in contemporary society. It will become clear that the blatant and vulgar sexism revealed in the case of *BJM v CM* is more

[1] *BJM v CM* [1996] 2 IR 574.

[2] ibid, 574–75.

[3] ibid.

[4] Defined by Katherine Bartlett as a method that expands traditional notions of legal relevance to make legal decision-making more sensitive to the features of the case not already reflected in legal doctrine: Katherine Bartlett, 'Feminist Legal Methods' (1990) 103(4) *Harvard Law Review* 829–88, 837.

than a legal aberration. It is a pervasive structural problem that permeates and characterises our legal and social institutions.[5]

The High Court Decision

Nullity of marriage is a legal declaration by the court. It states that although two people went through a marriage ceremony, their marriage never actually existed in the eyes of the law or the state. Under Irish law, there are two types of marriages that may be annulled—*void* marriages and *voidable* marriages.[6] A void marriage is considered never to have taken place. A voidable marriage is considered to be a valid marriage until a decree of annulment is made. The main grounds on which a nullity can be sought include want of capacity to marry, where, for example, one of the parties was already married; lack of consent to the marriage;[7] non-observance of the necessary formalities;[8] refusal or failure to consummate the marriage by 'ordinary and complete' sexual intercourse; and inability to enter and sustain a 'normal marital' (both sexual[9] and emotional)[10] relationship.[11]

In the High Court petition, as heard by Flood J, the respondent sought a decree of nullity on three grounds: (i) that his wife, the respondent, lacked the capacity to fulfil the fundamental terms of the marriage contract at the time of the marriage ceremony; (ii) that consent to the said marriage was apparent rather than real, in that it was not a full, free and informed consent; and (iii) that the petitioner and the respondent lacked the capacity to enter into and sustain a normal functional relationship with each other by reasons of their respective states of mind, psychological conditions, physical conditions and level of emotional development.[12]

Flood J reasoned that the husband's consent to the marriage was not a full and free consent as it was based on an illusion of his wife's physical appearance.[13] The consent was apparent rather than real as he had been deceived; his wife's concealment of her disfigurement deprived him of a necessary 'election'.[14] Would he have accepted a wife with scars

[5] For more, see Catherine MacKinnon, *Toward a Feminist Theory of the State* (Cambridge, MA, and London, Harvard University, 2005); Catherine MacKinnon, *Women's Lives; Men's Laws* (Cambridge, MA, and London: Harvard University Press, 2005); Simone De Beauvoir, *The Second Sex* (London, Vintage, 1997); Iris Young, *Justice and the Politics of Difference* (Princeton, NJ, Princeton University Press, 1990); Drucilla Cornell, *At the Heart of Freedom: Feminism, Sex and Equality* (Princeton, NJ, Princeton University Press, 1998).

[6] See, Geoffrey Shannan, *Family Law* (Dublin, Round Hall, 2011) ch 2; Paul Ward, 'Republic of Ireland: Defective Knowledge, A New Ground for Nullity' in Andrew Bainham (ed), *The International Survey of Family Law* (Leiden, Brill, 1996) 215–35, 218.

[7] Consent must be a 'fully free exercise of the independent will of the parties': see *N (orse K) v K* [1986] ILRM 75 (nullity on grounds of duress); *DB (orse O'R) v N O'R* [1991] 1 IR 289.

[8] *IE v WE* [1985] ILRM 691; *DC v NM* [1997] 2 IR 218.

[9] *S v S* (Supreme Court, July 1976).

[10] *D v C* [1984] ILRM 173, 189, as referenced in *BJM v CM*, above n 1, 579.

[11] *UF v JC* [1991] 2 IR 330. If it could be shown that, at the date of the marriage, the petitioner—through illness—lacked the capacity to form a caring or considerate relationship with his wife, the marriage could be annulled.

[12] *BJM v CM*, above n 1, at 576.

[13] ibid, 577–78.

[14] ibid, 580.

on her body or not? The judge accepted the respondent's assertion that if he had seen the scars before the marriage ceremony, he would never have consented to marry her, as the disfigurement 'in the sensual province gave rise in his mind not to desire but to revulsion'.[15] Accordingly, the marriage was null and void. The Court further accepted the husband's assertion that the disfigurement caused great 'emotional turmoil'[16] and 'psychological revulsion'[17] affecting his capacity to enter into and maintain a normal marital relationship. The Court held that this rendered the marriage voidable. That the marriage had in fact been sustained for 17 years was not deemed relevant in this assessment.

Irish Law on Marital Breakdown

To place this judgment in its proper context, it is necessary to reflect on the distinct background to the law on marital breakdown. As explained in the feminist judgment, in 1991 divorce was not yet legal in Ireland. From the enactment of the Irish Constitution in 1937 until a narrowly-passed referendum in 1995, Irish law rejected any attempts to dissolve the unity of marriage. The ban on divorce was enshrined in Article 41.3.2 such that 'No law shall be enacted providing for the grant of a dissolution of marriage.' Ireland was the only Western European country to maintain a constitutional prohibition on divorce.[18] Prior to the successful 1995 referendum, the ban was enshrined in Article 41 of the Constitution, the provision that set out the state's protection and recognition of the family as the 'natural primary and fundamental unit in Irish society'.[19] As is discussed elsewhere in this volume,[20] constitutional emphasis on family unity and family centrality to national order was a direct consequence of the Constitution's adherence to the values of the Roman Catholic Church.[21]

15 ibid, 576.

16 ibid, 578.

17 ibid, 574.

18 William Duncan, 'Ireland: Waiting for Divorce' (1986-87) 25(1) *Journal of Family Law* 155–67.

19 Before the successful divorce referendum of 1995, Art 41 of the Irish Constitution read as follows:

> 1.1 The State recognises the Family as the natural primary and fundamental unit group of Society, and as a moral institution possessing inalienable and imprescriptible rights, antecedent and superior to all positive law.
> 2.0 The State, therefore, guarantees to protect the Family in its constitution and authority, as the necessary basis of social order and as indispensable to the welfare of the Nation and the State.
> 2.1 In particular, the State recognises that by her life within the home, woman gives to the State a support without which the common good cannot be achieved.
> 3.0 The State shall, therefore, endeavour to ensure that mothers shall not be obliged by economic necessity to engage in labour to the neglect of their duties in the home.
> 3.1 The State pledges itself to guard with special care the institution of Marriage, on which the Family is founded, and to protect it against attack.
> 3.2 No law shall be enacted providing for the grant of a dissolution of marriage.
> 3.3 No person whose marriage has been dissolved under the civil law of any other State but is a subsisting valid marriage under the law for the time being in force within the jurisdiction of the Government and Parliament established by this constitution shall be capable of contracting a valid marriage within that jurisdiction during the lifetime of the other party to the marriage so dissolved.

20 See Máiréad Enright, ch 2, and Louise Crawley, ch 8.

21 Christine James, 'Céad Míle Fáilte? Ireland Welcomes Divorce: The 1995 Irish Divorce Referendum and the Family (Divorce) Act of 1996' (1997) 8(1) *Duke Journal of International and Comparative Law* 175–228.

The 1937 Constitution was drafted to codify an ideal Ireland that articulated the country's Catholic identity after independence from England.[22] This restrictive regime did succeed in ensuring that Irish law was unique, in that it diverged from the more liberal trends in the rest of Europe at that time.[23] However, it failed, of course, to preclude marital breakdown altogether. Accordingly, Irish law provided two means for dissolution of some marriages by judicial declaration. A limited form of separation could be granted if adultery, cruelty, or unnatural practices could be proven over the defences of condonation, collusion and recrimination under section 7 of the Matrimonial Causes (Ireland) Act of 1870. This practice was rarely used however, as the high burden of proof required placed this remedy out of reach for most couples, and certainly for most women.[24] The only other legal mechanism available to couples seeking a solution to their marital breakdown was to petition the High Court for a grant of nullity.

In the 1970s and 1980s, applications for nullity increased significantly and consistently.[25] Jurisprudence evolved and developed in line with the perceived need for the remedy. The law on nullity underwent significant judicial liberalisation as judges sought to make the best of the constitutional ban on divorce.[26] For example, in *N (otherwise K) v K*, the High Court ruled that pressure to marry from the pregnant petitioner's parents amounted to duress such that her marriage was void.[27] In *D v C*, the court found that the husband's manic depression before, during and after marriage severely impaired his capacity to form and sustain a normal marriage by precluding the 'creation of an emotional and psychological relationship between the spouses', and accordingly the marriage was voidable.[28] Commenting at the time, Shatter stated that '[n]ullity law, more than any other area of law is today a juridical monument to the powerful impact of a dynamic judicial creativity'.[29] In particular, judges were broadening the application of nullity in cases where they were assured that a financial package existed such that the wife and children would be provided for.[30] Motivated by compassion, the courts appeared to be expanding the limited remedy of nullity as a compromise and humanitarian solution for families in marital straits.[31] Crucially,

[22] See further Angela Clifford, *The Constitutional History of Ireland* (Belfast, Athol Books, 1985) 313; Maebh Harding, 'Religion and Family law in Ireland' in Jane Mair and Esin Örücü (eds), *The Place of Religion in Family Law: A Comparative Search* (Cambridge, Intersentia, 2011) ch 30.

[23] Masha Antokolskaia, *Harmonisation of Family Law in Europe: A Historical Perspective* (Antwerp, European Family Law Series, Intersentia, 2006) 253.

[24] Harding, above n 22, 162.

[25] William Duncan, *The Case for Divorce in the Irish Republic*, 2nd edn (Dublin, Irish Council for Civil Liberties, 1982).

[26] Tony Fahey and Maureen Lyons, *Marital Breakdown and Family Law in Ireland* (Dublin, Oak Tree Press, 1995) table 6.1, 100.

[27] *N (otherwise K) v K* [1986] ILRM 82.

[28] *D v C* [1984] ILRM 173, 189. However, the characterisation of psychological illnesses as an 'incapacity' to the maintenance of a marriage can be criticised as judicial pathologisation of men's and women's shortcomings.

[29] Alan Shatter, *Family Law*, 4th edn (Dublin, Butterworths, 1997) 181. See further Paul O'Connor, 'Ireland: Nullity and the Judiciary' (1992) 16 *Journal of Family Law* 345; and Paul O'Connor, *Key Issues in Irish Family Law* (Dublin, Round Hall Press, 1988).

[30] Interview with family law practitioner, 20 May 2015, on file with author. It should be noted that the judicial practice of assuring financial packages for spouses was followed on an *ad hoc* basis. In fact, Irish courts had no powers to rectify or make marriage settlements in cases of nullity or judicial separation. Shatter, above n 29, chs 6 and 7.

[31] See Harding, above n 22, 178: 'In many cases, it was in the common good that spouses should be separated, and separation merely recognised the breakdown in the marriage and did not constitute an attack on the institution of marriage.' See also Kathleen Dillon, 'Divorce and Remarriage as Human Rights: The Irish Constitution and

this direction was in line with Catholic canon law. The ecclesiastical courts of the Roman Catholic Church too had become flexible with regard to nullity, and in many cases Irish courts relied directly on such decisions.[32]

While the case of *BJM v CM* was decided along this clear line of judicial activism on nullity, it cannot be said that Flood J's judgment belies compassion for the wife and children in this case. There is no mention of amelioration, despite the fact that upon dissolution of the marriage the respondent was not entitled to claim maintenance, her children were rendered illegitimate and the home that she shared with her former partner could be sold without her consent. The concrete circumstances of her life are subsumed by the judge's empathy for the petitioner's supposed psychological turmoil owing to his wife's appearance and alleged lack of sexual appetite. The respondent is voiceless in this case. She is treated not as a party before the Court in her own right but as a character in her husband's tale of woe.

The Feminist Judgment

The feminist judgment is based on three grounds. The first ground of appeal relates to the inappropriate considerations affixed by the judge to the respondent when evaluating the case. This ground was not determinative, but the judgment takes the opportunity to demonstrate that the High Court judge's treatment of the respondent is discriminatory.[33] The considerations applied to her—her attractiveness, her sexuality and her role in bearing children—are held to be irrelevant to the legal questions to be answered. The blatantly objectifying language of the judge speaks for itself: 'she has a very attractive face, a very slim and well-proportioned figure and is beautifully walked'.[34] The High Court judge focuses expressly on the needs of the male petitioner, to the exclusion of the circumstances of the female respondent. The marginalisation of the female experience and identity is endemic to law, and in particular to family law.[35] Until the twentieth century, the common law observed the system of coverture: when a woman married, her personage merged with that of her husband.[36] Similarly, it was not until the late twentieth century that a husband could be convicted of raping his wife.[37] Before this, a wife's sexual identity was not recognised by the law, which conferred the right to, and control of, marital intercourse on her husband.

the European Convention on Human Rights at Odds in Johnston v Ireland' (1989) 22(1) *Cornell International Law Journal* 63–90, commenting that the critical element in the divorce referendum debate was compassion; voters were called upon to recognise the humanitarian need for support for people 'in trouble'.

[32] eg in *MK (Otherwise McC) v McC* [1982] ILRM 277, the court noted the broader approach of a Roman Catholic Tribunal which had granted nullity owing to duress based on merely moral pressure. See Harding, above n 22, 173; O'Connor (1988), above n 29, 49.

[33] Ryson J's judgment, below.

[34] *BJM v CM*, above n 1, 576.

[35] For more, see Frances Olsen, 'The Family and the Market: A Study of Ideology and Legal Reform' in Patricia Smith (ed), *Feminist Jurisprudence* (Oxford, Oxford University Press, 1993) 335–53; Alison Diduck and Katherine O'Donovan (eds), *Feminist Perspectives on Family Law* (Abingdon, Routledge-Cavendish, 2007); Katharine T Bartlett, 'Feminism and Family Law' (1999) 33(3) *Family Law Quarterly* 475–500.

[36] See William Blackstone, *Commentaries on the Laws of England* (Oxford, Clarendon Press, 1765–69) 271: 'By marriage, the husband and wife are one person in law: (l) that is, the very being or legal existence of the woman is suspended during the marriage, or at least is incorporated and consolidated into that of the husband.'

[37] Re Ireland, see Criminal Law (Rape) (Amendment) Act 1990.

As will be described below, the feminist appeal seeks to redress this exclusion of the female experience and to treat the respondent as a subject in her own right.

The second ground of appeal is that the judge was incorrect in both fact and law in finding want of consent. The marriage was declared void as the judge reasoned that the husband had been deceived and deprived of 'informed consent' as his agreement to marry was based on an 'illusion' of his fiancée's appearance. The appeal makes clear that the petitioner's conduct during the relationship was at significant variance with his assertions before the Court. As the judgment establishes, the fact that the petitioner lived with the respondent for a period of some 17 years in a marriage that enjoyed sexual relations and raised a family, is sufficient evidence of acceptance by the husband of the physical reality of his wife. The epistemic shift between the High Court and feminist judgment is evident here, as the feminist judge reasons from the lived experiences of the parties. Feminist legal methods emphasise contextualised reasoning to allow for greater understanding of the material condition of women's lives and the injustice encountered.[38] Through engaging in this practical reasoning, the feminist judge disregards the husband's claim to lack of informed consent and affords respect to the respondent's experience as a wife and mother for the past 17 years.

The third ground of appeal challenges the High Court's acceptance of the petitioner's claim that his 'psychological revulsion' rendered him incapable of entering into and maintaining a normal functional marital relationship. The feminist appeal dismisses this argument entirely, as the parties had in fact sustained a 17-year marriage that bore six children. Furthermore, as the alleged revulsion only became apparent sometime after the marriage ceremony, the petitioner was not unable to enter into the marriage at the time of the ceremony owing to this revulsion. Despite this, Flood J determined that the law must recognise the petitioner's dissatisfaction with his wife's appearance. The feminist judgment, by contrast, adjudicates based on the reality of the situation. The severe bias of the High Court judge in favour of the husband is succinctly exposed as the feminist judge points to the most basic facts of the case to dismiss the claim that the husband could not maintain a normal marital relationship.[39] The feminist judgment exposes how the female subject has been excluded based on the flimsiest of evidence and the resulting gendered disadvantage suffered. Her life is (mis)shaped[40] by a legal system that values male perspectives over her lived reality.

The Embodied Subject

> 'Whatever else she [a woman] may become, she is importantly a body designed to please or to excite.'[41]

The respondent is overtly objectified throughout the High Court case, marking this judgment as a manifest example of the interconnection between 'sex object culture' and

[38] See Bartlett, above n 4.

[39] Ryson J's judgment, below.

[40] Martha Minnow, *Making All the Difference: Inclusion, Exclusion, and American Law* (Ithaca, NY, Cornell University Press, 1990).

[41] Sandra-Lee Bartky, *Femininity and Domination: Studies in the Phenomenology of Oppression* (New York, Routledge, 1990) 80.

discrimination against women.[42] Flood J openly refers to the respondent's appearance—'she has a very attractive face, a very slim and well-proportioned figure and is beautifully walked'—and, when describing how she did not match the husband's illusory ideal, he too condemns her: 'He is confronted not with "a snowy breasted pearl" but with a partner for life who is seriously disfigured and in the sensual province gives rise in his mind not to desire but to revulsion.'[43] In order to gain social acceptability, women are under constant pressure to correct their bodies and appearance more generally, and to make them conform to the ideals of feminine appearance.[44] In order to be valued in her marriage, the respondent had to live up to this ideal, and similarly to be treated fairly by the Court: 'I would think that in her early 20s she would have been a very physically attractive young woman with quite an aura of sexuality.'[45]

The feminist appeal criticises the High Court's consideration of the wife's sexuality and points to the deeply gendered nature of its discussion.[46] The construction of the wife's sexuality in *BJM v CM* further reveals the Madonna/whore dichotomy inflicted on women. She is praised for being modest pre-marriage,[47] but later condemned for an alleged lack of sexual appetite; the judge takes pity on the petitioner owing to the claim that his wife did not engage in sexual relations 'on an *ad lib* basis but after much persuasion'.[48] Impossible and contradictory expectations dominate women's sexuality in relation to men and deny women autonomy.[49] Indeed, though marital rape was not criminalised in Ireland until 1990, it is difficult to process such endorsement of the dangerous notion that women are supposed to submit to sex.

While it would certainly cause outrage for a judge to employ such objectifying language in a decision today (and one wonders why it did not do so in 1996),[50] both the idealised concept of femininity and the incidental discrimination remain powerful and pervasive tools of female subordination. The sexual objectification of the female body is perhaps the most prevalent and obvious, yet subtle, form through which patriarchy and sexism are sustained.[51] We live in a culture that demands relentlessly high standards of female beauty, the obsessive pursuit of which has become central to our lives. As Naomi Wolf argues, the more legal and social barriers that women have overcome, 'the more strictly and heavily and cruelly images of female beauty have come to weigh upon us'.[52]

[42] See, ibid; Martha Nussbaum, 'Objectification' (1995) 24(4) *Philosophy and Public Affairs* 249–91; Catherine MacKinnon, 'Sexuality, Pornography, and Method: Pleasure under Patriarchy' (1989) 99(2) *Ethics* 314–46.

[43] *BJM v CM*, above n 1, 577. The phrase 'snowy breasted pearl' presumably relates to a song of this name by the band *Wolfe Tones*, see www.youtube.com/watch?v=hLU8pGAzOjM (last accessed 5 August 2015).

[44] eg, as Deborah Rhode highlights, in contexts extending from the workplace, dating and education, appearance is more important for women's success as compared to men: Deborah Rhode, *The Beauty Bias* (New York, Oxford University Press, 2010) 30–32 and 93.

[45] *BJM v CM*, above n 1, 576.

[46] Ryson J's judgment, below.

[47] *BJM v CM*, above n 1, 577, 'she behave[d] with great modesty consistent with her manifest religious and moral beliefs'.

[48] ibid, 579.

[49] Joan Forbes, 'Disciplining women in contemporary discourses of sexuality' (1996) 5(2) *Journal of Gender Studies* 177–89.

[50] There is no newspaper coverage of this case to suggest any public outcry. Informal interviews with lawyers involved in the case described the case as 'a product of its time'. On file with author.

[51] For more, see Susan Bordo, *Unbearable weight* (Berkeley, CA, University of California Press, 1993); Naomi Wolf, *The Beauty Myth: How Images of Beauty are Used Against Women* (New York, Harper, 2002).

[52] Wolf, ibid at10.

Every generation may seem more intensely obsessed with appearance than the last, but my generation, dominated as it is by the #selfie #thinspiration #thighgap presence online, seems to demand an ideal that is without a terminus. Female bodies remain objects to be gazed at, but in contemporary society the embodied subject, now more than ever, must be active and relentless in pursuit of perfection. Such is the ever growing 'thinspiration' presence online, where blogs, Twitter accounts, Tumblr posts, Instagram accounts, Pinterest boards, Facebook pages and chat rooms use words and pictures to encourage followers to obtain perfect bodies—they 'inspire to be thin'. Entire lifestyles are proposed to attain the goal spanning one's entire material existence, dictating what food is (or is not) consumed; what exercise routines should be followed; the products to be purchased; the mental attitudes to be adopted.[53] Varying from stark pro-anorexia and pro-bulimia websites to the ubiquitous #fitfam #cleaneating social media accounts, thin (mostly female, mostly white)[54] bodies are glorified and viewers are instructed to follow suit. As with female sexuality, the dissension between societal expectations of women is reaffirmed. 'Thin' is the pinnacle of female success, yet at the same time society stigmatises anorexia and bulimia.[55] Moreover, even when these 'lifestyle' pursuits do not cause physical harm, they demand time and resources that could be devoted to a myriad of other pursuits that could benefit women's personal development or wellbeing.[56]

The fashion and beauty industries are the usual targets for blame when we critique the tyranny of beauty standards for women. However, the pressure to conform is omnipresent. As Wolf writes, the 'beauty myth' extends into all areas of human functioning.[57] *BJM v CM* reminds us that a woman's body is worth at once so much and so little in law. In the case, the law is expanded to validate sexualised appearance requirements for women. Yet in contemporary society, the law has failed to tackle appearance-related bias or related societal norms that oppress women.[58] Law has been slow to recognise the discrimination inherent in the objectification of the female body. Assessing employment case law in the United States, Bartlett notes that very few courts have recognised standards of attractiveness as a form of sex stereotyping, and that overall courts have avoided finding that sex-specific grooming codes constitute discrimination.[59] Similarly, law has thus far ignored the

[53] See, Tina Hassannia, 'Waging war on web "thinspiration"', *Guardian*, 8 February 2013, at www.theguardian.com/commentisfree/2013/feb/08/waging-war-web-thinspiration (last accessed 5 August 2015); Carolyn Gregoire, 'The secret world of teenage "thinspiration"', *Huffington Post*, 9 February 2012, at www.huffingtonpost.com/2012/02/08/thinspiration-blogs_n_1264459.html (last accessed 5 August 2015).

[54] Our *beauty bias* has traditionally preferred Anglo-European features (see Rhode, above n 44, 30), and this is being reproduced by contemporary technological and media forces.

[55] Kristy Zwickert and Elizabeth Rieger, 'Stigmatizing attitudes towards individuals with anorexia nervosa: an investigation of attribution theory' (2013) 1(1) *Journal of Eating Disorders* 5–15.

[56] Rhode, above n 44, 10 and 30. It can be noted that the successful pursuit of the 'ideal' image can reap benefits; see Rebecca Nash and George Fieldman, 'Cosmetics: They Influence More Than Caucasian Female Facial Attractiveness' (2006) 36(2) *Journal of Applied Social Psychology* 493–504. However, the point is that it is women who overwhelmingly experience this pressure and are penalised to a greater extent for not living up to the ideal. See again Rhode, above n 44, 30; Bonnie Berry, *Beauty Bias: Discrimination and Social Power* (New York, Prager, 2007) 49; Nancy Etcoff, *Survival of the Prettiest: The Science of Beauty* (New York, Doubleday, 1999).

[57] Wolf, above n 51, 17–18, 20, 86, 131, 179 and 218.

[58] Rhode, above n 44, ch 6.

[59] Katherine T Bartlett, Deborah L Rhode, Joanna L Grossman (eds), *Gender and Law: Theory, Doctrine, and Commentary*, 6th edn (New York, Wolters Kluwer Law, 2013) 106. For a contrary example, see *Lewis v Heartland Inns of American* 591 F 3d 1033 (2010), where a plaintiff established a *prima facie* case of sex discrimination based on allegations that she had lost her position as a front desk hotel clerk because she was not 'pretty'.

'thinspiration' epidemic, despite the dangers and inequality perpetuated.[60] The use of 'thinspiration' language could be restricted online;[61] marketing practices that dangerously encourage unhealthy beauty standards could be eliminated; modelling agencies could be prohibited from using models whose weight falls below healthy levels. Law remains silent, the epidemic entirely unregulated.

Marriage

The feminist judgment reminds us that under Irish law, 'the institution of marriage is not simply a contractual legal arrangement between the two parties. Article 41.3 explicitly affords the institution of marriage constitutional protection'.[62] In keeping with the Constitution's foundations in Catholic mores, the institution of marriage that is protected is deeply traditional, based on heteronormative gender roles. As referenced above,[63] Article 41.2 provides:

> 1° [T]he State recognises that by her life within the home, woman gives to the State a support without which the common good cannot be achieved.
>
> 2° The State shall, therefore, endeavour to ensure that mothers shall not be obliged by economic necessity to engage in labour to the neglect of their duties in the home.

The rhetoric of the High Court judgment overtly endorses this traditional view of a woman's role in marriage. The only positive recognition afforded to the respondent is that she had obtained the 'zenith of all womanhood to give birth to children whom she has reared with care and consideration'. The language used by the judge is again crude, and reveals his view of woman as one and the same as mother. Such a strong endorsement of gender stereotypes is consistent with Irish constitutional law. The family home is deemed the appropriate place for women under the Irish Constitution, and it has indeed been the family home that has been the principal site of women's social and economic vulnerability. As Mullally highlights, the state persistently fails to value the care work performed by women in the home.[64] Women's roles as caregivers and mothers have persistently marginalised

[60] A study performed in 2010 found that 'thinspiration' websites lead to higher body dissatisfaction, decreased quality of life and a longer struggle with eating disorders: Dina LG Borzekowski, Summer Schenk, Jenny L Wilson and Rebecka Peebles, 'E-Ana and e-Mia: A Content Analysis of Pro-Eating Disorder Web Sites' (2010) 100(8) *American Journal of Public Health* 1526–34.

[61] For more, see Ashley Fetters, '"An Epidemic, Basically": A Conflicted Weight-Loss Blogger on #Thinspo', *The Atlantic*, at www.theatlantic.com/sexes/archive/2013/05/an-epidemic-basically-a-conflicted-weight-loss-blogger-on-thinspo/275671/ (last accessed 5 August 2015).

[62] Ryson J's judgment, below.

[63] See above n 18-20 and accompanying text.

[64] Siobhán Mullally, Second Report of the Convention on the Constitution (May 2013), s 4.2, at www.constitution.ie/AttachmentDownload.ashx?mid=268d9308-c9b7-e211-a5a0-005056a32ee4 (last accessed 5 August 2015). Care work in the home is mostly unpaid and is awarded little official recognition for its significance to the everyday functioning of society. This is exemplified in the case of *L v L* [1992] 2 IR 77, where the Supreme Court refused to grant a woman a 50% interest in the family home even though she had worked exclusively within the home throughout her marriage. Art 41.2 could not support her claim.

women, cutting them off from most of the social roles that offer responsibility, control and authority.[65]

We may think that times have moved on: Article 41.2 is rarely expressly relied upon in modern judgments, and the model of woman as exclusively wife and mother is no longer preferred to the model of woman as both a wage earner and parent. Yet equality in the family remains elusive. Women shoulder hugely disproportionate caretaking burdens. In Ireland, women perform 66 per cent of all care hours and 86 per cent of childcare.[66] The dominant ideology and practice of female domesticity retains its hold, and does so to the detriment of women. According to the National Women's Council of Ireland, the first step to increasing women's participation is to remove the 'women in the home clause'.[67]

Conclusion

In reflecting on whether this judgment was possibly a 'product of its time',[68] it struck me that the timings both of the judgment by Flood J in *BJM v CM* and of this project—and the resulting feminist judgment—coincide with events that mark significant liberalisation of family law in Ireland. On 24 November 1995, the citizens of Ireland voted in favour of a referendum allowing divorce for the first time since the country gained independence. On 22 May 2015, the Irish people voted to amend the Constitution to enable couples of the same sex to marry in the state. Both represent the most significant changes in family law in the history of the state, and mark dramatic social progress. Yet for women, the foundations need to shift further. As a country, we should be actively engaged in a process of re-examining the extents to which our legal, political and social structures are gendered and thus contribute to the subordination of half the population.

[65] eg 52% of women with children are in paid employment compared with upwards of men with children. Ireland is 24th out of the 27 EU countries for the number of women in politics. Women fill just 20% of boardroom positions: National Women's Council of Ireland, *Submission to the Constitutional Convention* (2013) 6.

[66] ibid.

[67] ibid, 4.

[68] See above n 50.

B.J.M., Petitioner v C.M., Respondent
[1991 No. 43M]

Supreme Court 31st July, 1998

Ryson J.

The contract on which marriage is based was historically a contract of unequal partnership. A husband and wife became one legal identity through the marriage, but it was the husband who could assert that legal identity. The doctrine of Coverture meant that for several centuries, upon marriage, a woman's legal rights and obligations were subsumed by those of her husband. A woman entering marriage even had to contract to obey her husband. Any property the wife brought into the marriage was transferred to the sole ownership of the husband, while any property owned or acquired by the husband remained vested in his ownership. This inequality was further compounded by the rules of primogeniture, which passed property through the male line only.

In the past 100 years, significant progress has been made in seeking to redress this imbalance. However, even in 1974 when the parties in this case were married, a woman entering into a marriage was not fully equal to a man in rights. A wife, for example, could not assert a legal domicile distinct from that of her husband. Indeed, when the parties first met in 1973, a woman could not continue to hold a public sector job after she married, and women had only just been permitted to sit on a jury on same terms as a man. A woman could not claim children's allowance, which was paid to the father only, nor could she claim social welfare payments if she, or any dependent children, were deserted by her husband. The family home of the parties could be sold by the husband without the knowledge or consent of his wife. A woman was unable to obtain a barring/safety order in a case of domestic violence and there was no criminal offence of marital rape. In socio-economic terms, the reality was that women were, in the main, expected to take care of children while men were viewed as the breadwinners of the family.

It is important for this Court to make these observations at the outset as it is the Husband's case that he felt he had no choice but to continue the marriage after he learnt of his wife's scarring which he says left him physically 'revulsed'. It was his case that he believed that he had no way out, that once he had been married there was really no going back and he adjusted to this the best he could. However this Court must consider this assertion in light of the respective legal, and socio-economic rights the respective parties could avail of in 1974. This Court must, considering all the above, conclude that the Husband was, in law and in fact, far more protected than the wife if he had chosen to leave the marriage at the outset.

For a woman, such as the wife in this case, who has borne the primary responsibility for raising children and has made personal and career sacrifices to do so, the consequences of nullity can be particularly punitive and distressing. In declaring a marriage null and void, the Court is saying that the marriage never existed to begin with. Where a Court at the end of a marriage cannot recognise the contributions made by the parties, the ending of that marriage can leave a party entirely without recompense for the investment they have made. There is consequently a heavy burden on any Court in determining whether to grant a decree of nullity. It is not a decision a Court can ever make flippantly or without due consideration.

The wife's case is that this is a marital breakdown. She honoured her marriage vows for 17 years and was, in her mind, repaid with adultery. To then have her husband successfully argue that their marriage never existed because of a physical scar she had disclosed before the parties wed makes a lie of that 17 year marriage. The wife in this case has argued before this Court that the decision of the High Court is wrong in law and fundamentally unfair to her and to the parties' six children. Her husband stepped outside their marriage with another woman and then successfully argued that she was the one to blame.

In 1991, when the petition for the nullity was brought by the husband, there was no constitutional or legal remedy available to address the breakdown of the parties' marriage. His application predated the passage of the Family Law Act of 1995 and the Family Law (Divorce) Act of 1996. However, by the time the hearing of this case concluded on the 18th July 1996, the legal landscape had changed significantly. It was by that stage possible for the husband to have sought a Judicial Separation. Indeed, by July 1996, the final Supreme Court challenge to Divorce Referendum had been rejected by the Court and the Divorce Act of 1996 was anticipated within months.

This Court wishes to make it clear from the outset that the breakdown of a marriage is not, and never has been, grounds upon which a decree of nullity should be sought, or granted. One of the most substantive reasons for this is public policy. In circumstances where parties may have been in a relationship for a number of years, may have children, and may share financial assets including a family home, there is a material difference in the outcome for the parties in obtaining a judicial separation as opposed to a decree of nullity. On granting a decree of judicial separation (or divorce) a Court has the power to grant certain ancillary financial reliefs to either party, for the benefit of that party or any dependent children. In the case of a nullity, the Court has no power to grant orders which might constitute proper provision for both parties.

FACTUAL BACKGROUND

The appellant wife (hereinafter referred to as the wife) and the petitioner (hereinafter referred to as the husband) were married on 28 September 1974 having met in May 1973. When they met the wife was 20 years old and working as a cook in Jervis Street Hospital. The husband was 21 years old and a member of An Garda Síochána. They both came from a rural background and from strict Catholic homes with strong morals and religious beliefs. They did not therefore, engage in pre-marital relations and were married relatively soon after meeting. Given societal norms at this time, this would not have been unusual.

The parties had six children during their 17 year marriage. The relationship between the parties irretrievably broke down in or around 1990/1991 when the wife learned of the husband's relationship with another woman.

The husband based his claim on his wife's scarring following an accident she had when she was a three year old child, and on the effect discovering the scars had on him. It is the husband's case that while she told him about the accident before they were married in 1974, she had not told him about the extent of the scarring.

The wife said that while she had spent a number of months in hospital recovering from her injuries, thereafter, she learned to live with the scar tissue. It never caused her any concern or inhibited her in any way.

The essence of the husband's case is that when he ultimately saw the scarring, it created in him a revulsion which now forms the basis for his petition for a decree of nullity.

THE PETITION

By petition dated the 30 July, 1991, the husband sought an order of the nullity of his marriage to the wife. On the 29 March, 1995, the Master of the High Court directed that the issues to be tried were:

a) Whether the wife lacked the capacity to fulfil the fundamental terms of the marriage contract at the time for the marriage ceremony?
b) Whether the husband's consent to the said marriage was apparent rather than real in that it was not a full, free and informed consent?
c) Whether the husband and the wife had the capacity to enter into and sustain a normal functional relationship with each other by reasons of their respective states of mind, psychological conditions, physical conditions and level of emotional development prior to and at them of the said marriage?

The petition was heard by the High Court (Flood J.) on the 5 July, 1995, and the 17 and 18 July, 1996. The judgment of the High Court was delivered on 31 July 1996 and orders were made in favour of the husband in the terms of paragraphs b) and c) above.

GROUNDS OF APPEAL

The Grounds of Appeal can be summarised as follows:

a) The first ground of appeal is that the learned High Court judge took into account irrelevant considerations when reaching his determination.
b) The second ground of appeal is that the High Court erred in fact and law in making the declaration that the marriage is null and void for lack of full, free and informed consent.
c) The third ground of appeal is that High Court erred in fact and law in making a declaration that the marriage is voidable on the grounds of incapacity to enter into and sustain a normal functional marital relationship.

THE LAW

Marriage

The institution of marriage is not simply a contractual legal arrangement between the two parties. Article 41.3 explicitly affords the institution of marriage Constitutional protection and this Court is bound by the provision of the Constitution.

Article 41.3.1°

"The State pledges itself to guard with special care the institution of Marriage, on which the Family is founded, and to protect it against attack."

Article 41.3.2°

"No law shall be enacted providing for the grant of a dissolution of marriage".

It is noted by the Court that since the date of the original petition Article 41.3.2° was amended, in 1996 with the introduction of divorce, to read as follows:

Article 41.3.2°

"A Court designated by law may grant a dissolution of marriage where, but only where, it is satisfied that

(i) *at the date of the institution of the proceedings, the spouses have lived apart from one another for a period of, or periods amounting to, at least four years during the previous five years,*
(ii) *there is no reasonable prospect of a reconciliation between the spouses,*
(iii) *such provision as the Court considers proper having regard to the circumstances exists or will be made for the spouses, any children of either or both of them and any other person prescribed by law, and iv any further conditions prescribed by law are complied with."*

The contract of marriage is therefore no longer absolutely irrevocable.

Marriage is not statutorily defined. However, the Irish Courts have considered the definition of marriage as set out in the cases of **Hyde v Hyde[L.R.] 1 P & D 130, Murray v Ireland [1985] I.R. 532** and **B v R [1995] 1 ILRM 491.**

In the case of **TF v Ireland [1995] 1 I.R. 321**, the Supreme Court set out the four principles of a valid marriage, namely:

a) The marriage must be entered into freely and without force;
b) It must potentially be for life;
c) It must be monogamous;
d) It must be between parties of a different sex.

Even with the enactment of legislation permitting the dissolution of marriage it is clear that the institution of marriage is afforded significant Constitutional and legal protection This Court must attach substantial weight to these protections in considering any petition for nullity.

Nullity

A marriage which is properly solemnised is presumed valid until the contrary is shown. The common law distinguishes between marriages which are *void ab initio* and voidable marriages.

The grounds upon which a marriage can be declared void are:

a) There is an existing valid marriage;
b) One of the parties was under 18 and had not obtained a judicial exemption;
c) There was a substantial failure to observe formalities;
d) There was absence of consent (on the grounds of duress, undue influence, fraud, misrepresentation and/or mental illness);

e) The parties are within the forbidden degrees of blood relationship; or
f) The parties are the same sex.

If a marriage is void for one of the above reasons, then the marriage was *void ab initio* and never legally existed at all.

A decree can be sought in respect of a voidable marriage on the basis of either:

a) Impotence; or
b) Inability to enter into and sustain a normal relationship.

A voidable marriage is legally valid until one of the parties to the marriage makes an application for a decree to that effect.

JUDGMENT

First Ground of Appeal

The first ground of appeal is that the learned High Court judge took into account irrelevant considerations when reaching his determination.

In particular, the Appellant points to the following observations in Flood J.'s judgment about the Appellant which she asserts are not relevant considerations to the petition for nullity:

a) *"She is now a woman of forty odd years. She has a very attractive face, a very slim and well-proportioned figure and is beautifully walked. I would think that in her early 20's she would have been a very physically attractive young woman with quite an aura of sexuality."* [Page 3 of the judgment]
b) *"He [the husband] spent a courtship with a very attractive person, both outwardly physical and in personality. She behaves with great modesty consistent with her manifest religious and moral beliefs, and on his honeymoon where all inhibitions no longer exist, he is confronted not with 'a snowy breasted pearl' but with a partner for life who is seriously disfigured and in the sensual province gives rise in his mind not to desire but to revulsion."* [Pages 3 and 4 of the judgment]
c) *"She has attained perhaps the zenith of all womanhood to give birth to children whom she has reared with care and consideration. She has attempted to provide the material side of marriage in a very formal, fine and proper manner and she presently feels that all her efforts have been in vain as she has been rewarded by infidelity."* [Page 7 of the judgment]

In summary, the Appellant's argument is that the High Court gave weight to irrelevant issues relating to her gender, including her attractiveness, her sexuality and her achievement in bearing children.

Counsel for the Appellant in her submissions asks the following series of questions: would the learned judge have considered the attractiveness of the husband's face; his proportioned figure; his aura of sensuality? Would the learned judge have used equivalent language to "snowy breasted pearl", in quantifying the wife's expectations on her honeymoon? Would the learned judge both have considered and opined that the pinnacle of the husband's life achievements was having fathered children?

The key question for the Court in this case is whether the husband gave full, free and informed consent to the marriage. In answering that question, the Court must be guided by the actions of both parties and not an assessment of the objective attractiveness of the wife. No view is offered as to the attractiveness of the husband by the High Court Judge.

Article 40.1 of the Constitution provides that *"All citizens shall as human persons, be held equal before the law"*. As Walsh J. summarised in **De Burca and Anderson v Attorney General [1976] IR 38**, at page 76, *"Article 40 does not require identical treatment of all persons without recognition of differences in relevant circumstances but it forbids arbitrary discrimination. It imports the Aristotelian concept that justice demands that we treat equals equally and unequals unequally."*

In answering the key question as to whether full free and informed consent has been given by the party seeking the nullity, on identical facts, there should be no difference in the factors to be considered and the standards applied if the gender of the parties was reversed. This is a central tenant of Justice. To quote Shylock, the husband and wife are both *"fed with the same food, hurt with the same weapons, subject to the same diseases, heal'd by the same means, warm'd and cool'd by the same winter and summer."* The wife in this case should be judged by the same standards that would have been applied to her husband.

This Court is entirely satisfied that the observations pointed to by the Appellant wife are not relevant considerations. The wife's attractiveness, her sexuality, or her achievement in bearing children have absolutely no connection to the key question to be answered. Not only have they no connection to the question to be answered, they have, in the view of this Court, no place in a High Court decision. The language used by the judge is highly unfortunate, unnecessary and regrettable. The legal questions to be determined in this case require no consideration of the attractiveness of wife's face and figure or the aura of her sexuality.

The judge places emphasis on the fact that the the husband "*... spent a courtship with a very attractive person, both outwardly physical and in personality*", but that on his honeymoon where "*... all inhibitions no longer exist, he is confronted not with 'a snowy breasted pearl' but with a partner for life who is seriously disfigured and in the sensual province gives rise in his mind not to desire but to revulsion.*" To this Court's mind the reference to a *"snowy breasted pearl"*, reduces or equates the wife to a possession or ornament of her husband; the discovery of scarring rendering her no longer of *"merchantable quality"* in the contractual sense of the term. The wife is not a jewel or adornment. She is a person in her own right.

Furthermore, there are other connotations of ownership in the judge's comments. *"Beautifully walked"* is a phrase to this Court's mind more commonly used to describe prize animals and is undoubtedly inappropriate, even where no insult was intended.

This Court must also be clear that there is no basis in law for asserting or opining that the *"zenith of all womanhood"* is the achievement of giving birth to children. As such, the view expressed was entirely irrelevant to the legal issue to be determined in this case.

However, notwithstanding the above, this Court is not satisfied, reading the decision of the learned judge in its entirety, that the judge based his decision solely on these considerations, or indeed as to the weight he attached to these considerations. Therefore, this Court is unable to uphold this ground of appeal and now moves on to consider the substantive grounds upon which the nullity was granted.

SECOND AND THIRD GROUNDS OF APPEAL

This Court must then move on to consider whether:

a) The husband's consent to the said marriage was apparent rather than real in that it was not a full, free and informed consent? If so, then the marriage was void ab initio.
b) The husband and the wife had the capacity to enter into and sustain a normal functional relationship with each other by reasons of their respective states of mind, psychological conditions, physical conditions and level of emotional development prior to and at the time of the said marriage? If so, then the marriage is voidable upon the application before this Court.

Onus of Proof

The position in relation to the onus of proof in nullity proceedings has been usefully restated in the case of **PM v TR [1998] IEHC 235**, in which Lavan J., on consideration of the Supreme Court and High Court authorities sets out that the onus of establishing a lack of consent lies with the husband.

The Second Ground of Appeal

This Court has been asked to consider whether the husband's consent to the said marriage was apparent rather than real in that it was not a full, free and informed consent.

Historically, the Courts applied a restrictive approach to a nullity being sought on the grounds of misrepresentation or mistake.

In the case **of Swift v Kelly (1835) 3 Knapp 257**, it was stated that:

> *"No marriage shall be held to be void merely upon proof that it had been contracted upon false representations and that but for such contrivances, consent never would have been obtained. Unless the party opposed upon has been deceived as to the person and thus, has given no consent at all, there is no degree of deception which can avail to set aside a contract of marriage validly made."*

The law has developed in this jurisdiction and has adopted a less restrictive approach to the grounds on which a nullity can be obtained on the issue of "full, free and informed consent to a marriage".

The law as it relates to informed consent has been considered by this Court most recently in the case of **MO'M v BO'C [1996] 1 IR 208.**

Blaney J., on the facts of the case in **MO'M v BO'C** set out the relevant test as follows:

> *"What has to be determined, accordingly is whether the consent of the wife was an informed consent, a consent based upon adequate knowledge, and the test is a subjective one, that is to say, the test is whether this spouse, marrying this particular man, could be said to have had adequate knowledge of every circumstance relevant to the decision she was making, so that her consent could truly be said to be an informed one."*

This Court in applying this test, recognises that there are significant differences between the facts of both cases. A key consideration in the MO'M case was the fact that, the husband in that case had withheld all information relating to the fact that he attended a psychiatrist and this Court noted, that the issue of "...a person's mental health or mental stability" was a matter of great importance and anything that which might throw doubt upon it called for serious consideration.

In this case, the husband was aware that the wife was in an accident. His evidence to the High Court was that wife had told the husband of her accident as a child, but that she had not told the husband the extent of the burns or that she was scarred or disfigured.

The essence of the husband's contention, as summarised in the High Court judgment, is that when he ultimately did see the physical reality in 1974 it created in him a 'revulsion'.

This is the husband's contention, but he is advancing it for the first time in 1991. The husband did not at any point prior to the breakdown in the parties' marriage, indicate to either his wife, or any third party, that he was so physically revulsed by her scarring that he could not sustain a normal functional relationship. Certainly, if he did no such evidence is recorded in the High Court judgment.

Indeed the psychological report of Dr. Fahy states the husband was:

> *"destabilized by what appeared to be his wife's total aversion to any sexual relationship or indeed any display of affection ... [and] underwent stages of emotional turmoil which were added to by his wife's attitude, as ascribed by him, to his need for physical affection and sexual contact".*

The husband claims that he was destablised by the wife's apparent aversion to having a sexual relationship with him and that he suffered emotional turmoil by her response to his need for physical affection and sexual contact. This seems to directly contradict the husband's central assertion that he was so physically revulsed by the wife that his consent to the marriage should now be considered apparent, rather than real. It suggests that notwithstanding her scarring the husband sought a level of physical affection and sexual contact which he believes was not reciprocated by his wife.

It is also clear from the agreed facts that the parties did not consummate the marriage until 8 weeks after they married. The husband had time to reflect upon his position for two months before the marriage was consummated.

It cannot be said he was put under any duress or pressure from the wife. Indeed it seems that it was the husband and not the wife who sought to consummate the marriage because of his *"need for physical affection and sexual contact"*. This Court must consider that the husband exercised his free and informed choice in consummating the marriage and that his desire to consummate the marriage was in the full knowledge of his wife's physical disfigurement. Thus, his consent was real and not apparent.

What this Court can also be certain of is that the parties continued to live together as man and wife for 17 years. They clearly sustained a sexual relationship, to a greater or lesser degree, over a number of years as they have six children together. What this Court can also be certain of is that the husband only sought a nullity after his wife learnt of his extra marital affair.

This leads the Court to have to consider a very distinct alternative possibility, which seems far more probable on any objective consideration of the facts of this case; namely that the parties did sustain a real and bona fide marriage for 17 years and that it was upon the wife's learning of the husband's adultery that the relationship between the parties irretrievably broke down.

On the facts and the law, this Court is satisfied the husband's consent was full, free and informed. The husband, has not, in the view of this court, advanced evidence which rebuts the presumption that this was a valid marriage. For this reason the Court upholds Ground 2 of the Appellant's appeal.

Third Ground of Appeal

Given this Court does not accept that the marriage is void *ab initio*, this Court must now consider whether the marriage is still voidable on grounds of incapacity.

The husband asserts that he did not have the capacity to enter into and sustain a normal functional relationship with the wife.

Again, it a matter of uncontested fact that the husband did not leave the wife after learning about her scarring and that the husband sought to consummate the marriage because of his "*need for physical affection and sexual contact*".

The High Court, following the *ratio* in **D v C [1984] ILRM 173**, decided that the husband's psychological revulsion is something to which the Courts must have regard and recognise. It was also the view of the learned Judge in this case that

> "... *the psychological revulsion of the husband is such, as expressed by him, as to render it improbable that he could maintain an emotional and psychological relationship such as is required to support a marriage and so for this further reason this marriage is flawed.*"

The question for this Court to consider is firstly, whether the husband's psychological revulsion is something this Court should recognise and secondly, whether any such revulsion rendered the husband incapable of forming and sustaining a normal life long marital relationship.

There may be factual circumstances, in which the assertion of a psychological revulsion would be such as to meet the threshold to render a marriage voidable. However, on the facts of this case, the Court is satisfied that the psychological revulsion of the husband is not, and was not, to such a degree so as to render this marriage voidable.

This Court is satisfied as a matter of fact and law that the parties did sustain a marriage for 17 years. The parties lived together and raised six children. The relationship finally broke down because of the husband's infidelity.

CONCLUSION

This court has considered all three ground of appeal and has upheld the second and third ground, thereby striking down the declaration of nullity for the reasons set out above.

It is the view of this court that the husband's marriage to the wife was not *void ab initio*, as the husband has sought to assert, nor voidable upon application to this court. The marriage was not void due to lack of consent and the marriage is not voidable on the grounds of incapacity to form and sustain a normal marital relationship.

The marriage the husband has sought to render void, will not be erased at the stroke of this Court's pen. It stands as a subsisting marriage, and the husband will have to consider what legal steps he may wish to take to address the breakdown of his marriage, as is his legal right.

26

Commentary on *DPP v C*

ANNA ARSTEIN-KERSLAKE

Introduction

Consent, in all areas of the law, is fraught with problems of indeterminacy. This is because an assessment of consent is reliant on internal cognitive processing, decision-making, communication and the perception of communication by outside actors. Each of these is largely unquantifiable and dependent upon subjective factors; as are all judgments that are related to the inner workings of the human mind. The Court of Criminal Appeal tackles these issues in *DPP v C*,[1] and places some parameters around what consent to sex means in Ireland.

The decision of the Court of Criminal Appeal in *DPP v C* contains the only existing definition of consent in Irish law of the offence of rape. The Oireachtas has failed to enact a definition, despite the recommendations of the Law Reform Commission to this effect in 1988.[2] Therefore, *DPP v C* is an important judgment in the context of imagining a feminist approach to rape law. However, the case presented a number of challenges to the goals of the project. First, the appeal itself was argued on the facts and the points of law considered by the Court of Criminal Appeal, relating to the admissibility of admissions made by the defendant and the circumstances of his interrogation and detention. The defendant's appeal was dismissed by the Court of Criminal Appeal and the defendant did not appeal against this decision. Therefore, there is no Supreme Court decision in this case. The judgment writers' decision to imagine the Supreme Court as having heard an appeal on a point of law of exceptional public importance allowed them to consider the definition of consent in isolation. If they had rewritten the appeal, they would have had to deal with the issues raised by the defendant on appeal, none of which explicitly dealt with consent. There is a degree of artificiality in placing the judgment in the Supreme Court, particularly given that the definition of consent in the Court of Criminal Appeal could perhaps be seen as *obiter*, and therefore might not be likely to be appealed by the defendant. However, it enabled them to isolate the issue of consent in order to re-imagine the definition of consent from a feminist perspective.

[1] *DPP v C* [2001] 3 IR 345.
[2] Law Reform Commission, *Report on Rape and Allied Offences*, LRC 24-1988, Recommendation 3, 9 and 29.

Due to the subjective nature of determinations of consent, they are vulnerable to the influence of socially constructed prejudices based on pre-existing power structures. Consent to sex, in particular, is vulnerable to such influences because of its emotion-laden nature and deeply ingrained gender hierarchies[3] and heteronormativity.[4] The feminist judgment writers have used *DPP v C* to illuminate the gaps that remain in the definition of consent, and provide an analysis of the social and legal implications. This commentary examines the specific facts of *DPP v C* to provide context to the judgment's analysis. It then examines the human right to sexual agency and the effect of the victimisation of sexual assault and rape survivors.

DPP v C

The facts of *DPP v C* help provide a background to the specific issues with which the court was grappling and the context in which it made its determination. This, in turn, led to the findings upon which the feminist judgment writers have expanded. In describing the facts of the case, the term 'woman', as opposed to 'complainant', is used in order to avoid the dehumanising effects of the latter term, as discussed in the judgment.[5]

On 4 January 1997, the woman and her boyfriend met several friends in a Dublin pub in order to celebrate the birthday of a friend. At around 1.00 am the group left the pub and went to a friend's house to continue the party. The woman and her boyfriend had arranged to spend the night at this house. The accused man did not go to the pub but joined the group back at the house. The woman did not drink any alcohol after arriving at the house. Between 3 am and 4 am the woman decided to go to bed, and her boyfriend went upstairs with her to their designated bedroom. The woman and her boyfriend had sexual intercourse and chatted for a while, until the woman decided to go to sleep because she had to work the next day. Her boyfriend then went back downstairs to re-join the party.

The woman and the accused man had not met one another prior to this evening. After drinking a significant amount of vodka, the accused man decided to go upstairs to look for cigarettes. He did not find cigarettes, but he did see a bedroom door open. He went into the bedroom with the intention of resting on the bed. He discovered that the woman was in the bed and had sexual intercourse with her after having believed that she had responded to

[3] For a feminist analysis of the language of sexual consent, see generally, Susan Lynn Ehrlich, *Representing Rape: Language and Sexual Consent* (London, Routledge, 2001). For an examination of sexual consent in modern culture, see generally Melissa Burkett and Karine Hamilton, 'Postfeminist Sexual Agency: Young Women's Negotiations of Sexual Consent' (2012) 15(7) *Sexualities* 815–33. For an analysis of the need for rape reform, see generally Susan Estrich, *Real Rape* (Boston, MA, Harvard University Press, 1987).

[4] For a discussion of heteronormativity, see generally Adrienne Rich, 'Compulsory Heterosexuality and Lesbian Existence' (1980) 5(4) *Signs* 631–60. For a discussion of heteronormativity and gender inequality in sexual relationships, see generally Donna Chung, 'Violence, Control, Romance and Gender Equality: Young Women and Heterosexual Relationships' (2005) 28(6) *Women's Studies International Forum* 445–55; and Melanie A Beres, '"Spontaneous" Sexual Consent: An Analysis of Sexual Consent Literature' (2007) 17(1) *Feminism & Psychology* 93–108.

[5] See Diana Majury, 'Seaboyer and Gayme: A Study Inequality' in Julian Roberts and Renate Mohr (eds), *Confronting Sexual Assault: A Decade of Social and Legal Change* (Toronto, University of Toronto Press, 1994) 268, 275.

his advances. There was no conversation that took place between the accused man and the woman. There was some discrepancy in the statements of the woman regarding when she became aware that the sexual intercourse was occurring. At a certain point she indicated that she woke up to find a man on top of her. At another point she stated that she had woken up when someone opened the door to the bedroom and she understood that person to be her boyfriend, and she then acquiesced to sexual intercourse with the man whom she believed to be her boyfriend. However, there was no evidence that the woman ever consented to sexual intercourse with the accused man. There was also no evidence that the accused man was impersonating the woman's boyfriend. Because of this series of events, a dispute ensued between the accused man and the boyfriend of the woman, and the gardaí were called.

The following day, the accused man was arrested and indicated to the gardaí that he felt remorseful because he did not ask permission to have sexual intercourse with the woman. The accused man also stated that he thought that the woman thought he was her boyfriend at the time of the sexual intercourse. The admissibility of these statements was disputed on the grounds that the accused man had had very little sleep and had consumed a significant amount of alcohol the previous night. The accused man was charged with rape of the woman and was convicted on 26 April 1999. He was sentenced to four years' imprisonment, suspended unconditionally on his paying compensation of £7,000 to the woman. The accused man appealed the conviction and the Court of Criminal Appeal heard the matter on 16 October 2000.

The Court of Criminal Appeal made the following finding:

> Consent means voluntary agreement or acquiescence to sexual intercourse by a person of the age of consent with the requisite mental capacity. Knowledge or understanding of facts material to the act being consented to is necessary for the consent to be voluntary or constitute acquiescence. In stating that a person who has sex with one person believing it to be another person, that person is not consenting to sexual intercourse with the former, the court is satisfied that the trial judge made a correct statement of the law.

The Court held that there were no grounds for interfering with the verdict of the trial judge and the accused man's application for leave for appeal was rejected. The facts of *DPP v C* and the findings of the Court of Criminal Appeal raise significant issues regarding the concept of 'voluntary agreement or acquiescence', 'requisite mental capacity' and 'knowledge or understanding of facts material to the act being consented to'. The feminist judgment addresses these issues and also considers the questions of (i) when, if at all, a defendant can raise a defence of mistaken belief in consent, and (ii) the role of corroboration in rape trials. It provides a reframing of consent that takes into account the influence of gender hierarchies and heteronormativity, and attempts to provide better protection for the right to sexual agency of women.

The relevance of such a reframing of consent is beyond merely the application of the criminal law. It also has the potential to infiltrate the broader social consciousness.[6] It sends a message regarding what is and what is not deemed appropriate behaviour. Rape law,

[6] For a discussion of the social impact of law, see Eric A Posner, *Law and Social Norms* (Boston, MA, Harvard University Press, 2000).

in particular, may have such an impact. It can set the tone for sexual activity that society accepts or rejects.[7] As such, where rape law denies the sexual agency of certain individuals, such as women or people with disabilities, this has the potential to trickle into the social consciousness and foster behaviour that similarly denies such agency. In order to prevent this, there is a need to reframe rape law, as this feminist judgment begins to do, to recognise female sexual agency and dispel misogynistic sexual norms, while still robustly criminalising non-consensual sex.

The Right to Sexual Agency

The right to sexual agency is a consistent theme throughout the judgment. Although not specifically mentioned in the judgment, the 2006 Convention on the Rights of Persons with Disabilities (CRPD) provides a right to legal capacity that is directly relevant. Article 12 of the CRPD states that people with disabilities have a right to legal capacity on an equal basis to others in all areas of life. This includes the right both to be a holder of rights and an actor under the law.[8] It includes the right to exercise legal agency in sexual decision-making. This means that the law cannot deny sexual agency on the basis of disability.

In case law that followed *DPP v C*, in both Ireland and England, a functional test of mental capacity to consent to sex has been applied to women with disabilities, in both sexual offence cases and in determinations of mental capacity within the civil law.[9] The feminist judgment has attempted to disrupt the case law that followed *DPP v C* by developing a nuanced understanding of consent, seeking to remove discrimination based on women's perceived 'mental capacity'. The feminist judgment is conscious of this impact, and for this reason it emphasises the discriminatory nature of mental capacity assessments in the context of sexual offence law.

It highlights the hypocrisy in approach, since the criminal law does not routinely check if all complainants have 'capacity' to consent but rather tests only the capacity of those with certain disabilities. The result is the imposition of a higher standard on women with disabilities, in terms of the level of understanding of sex we expect them to have in order to give valid consent, compared with the non-disabled population. Since many people with disabilities need support from family or caregivers to enter sexual relationships, imposing a functional test of mental capacity to consent to sex also creates barriers for them in accessing the support they need in order to exercise sexual agency.

While the CRPD is directed at the rights of people with disabilities, it is only aimed at reinterpreting rights that are already applicable to all.[10] These are the rights in the

[7] For a discussion of the effects of rape law and other social phenomena on the status of women, see Edwin M Schur, *Labelling Women Deviant: Gender, Stigma, and Social Control* (Philadelphia, PA, Temple University Press, 1984). For a discussion of rape law as a 'disability' for women, see Camille E LeGrand, 'Rape and Rape Laws: Sexism in Society and Law' (1973) 61 *California Law Review* 919–41.

[8] General Comment No 1, *The Right to Equal Recognition Before the Law*, Paragraph 12, UN Doc. CRPD/C/GC/1.

[9] See, eg, *IM v LM* [2014] EWCA Civ 37.

[10] Rosemary Kayess and Phillip French, 'Out of Darkness into Light? Introducing the Convention on the Rights of Persons with Disabilities' (2008) 8 *Human Rights Law Review* 1–34.

International Covenant of Civil and Political Rights (ICCPR), the International Covenant of Social, Economic, and Cultural Rights (ICESCR) and the Universal Declaration of Human Rights (UDHR). In this way, it could be said that the rights within the CRPD, while written to highlight the specific needs of people with disabilities, are rights that are potentially applicable to all.

The Convention on the Elimination of Discrimination Against Women (CEDAW) states in Article 15(2), that:

> States Parties shall accord to women, in civil matters, a legal capacity identical to that of men and the same opportunities to exercise that capacity. In particular, they shall give women equal rights to conclude contracts and to administer property and shall treat them equally in all stages of procedure in courts and tribunals.

This is evidence that the right to legal capacity on an equal basis in all areas of life is also applicable to women. It may also be argued that an interpretation of the right for people with disabilities cannot create special rights for people with disabilities. Therefore an interpretation of the right to legal capacity must also be applicable to the right as applied to women. While Article 15(2) of CEDAW does not include the language 'in all areas of life', it may be presumed that if people with disabilities have the right to legal capacity on an equal basis in all areas of life, then so do women.

The scholarship around the right to equal recognition before the law has been reinvigorated by Article 12 of the CRPD and, as such, is opening up new areas of inquiry.[11] As this feminist judgment highlights, the right to legal agency in sexual matters is essential for rebalancing the power relationships that rape law, heteronormativity and gender hierarchies have created.

Victimisation

In discussing rape law, it is critical also to discuss the victimisation of the survivor of rape. The impact of rape should not be down-played; however, it is equally important to recognise the individual who experiences rape as a survivor, and not to diminish her personhood and agency by explicitly or implicitly expressing that the effect of rape presents insurmountable challenges for the individual and that she deserves pity and charity. This type of victimisation can often disempower and objectify the individual.[12]

Violence against women is a powerful tool of marginalisation. This has been true throughout human history. Rape is an assertion of male dominance in the home and other

[11] See, eg, Tina Minkowitz, 'The United Nations Convention on the Rights of Persons with Disabilities and the Right to Be Free from Non–consensual Psychiatric Interventions' (2006–2007) 34 *Syracuse Journal of International Law and Commerce* 405–28; Amita Dhanda, 'Legal Capacity in the Disability Rights Convention: Stranglehold of the Past or Lodestar for the Future?' (2006–2007) 34(2) *Syracuse Journal of International Law and Commerce* 429–62; and Eilionóir Flynn and Anna Arstein-Kerslake, 'Legislating Personhood: Realizing the Right to Support in Exercising Legal Capacity' (2014) 10(1) *International Journal of Law in Context* 81–104.

[12] For a discussion, see Monica Thompson, 'Life After Rape: A Chance to Speak?' (2000) 15(4) *Sexual and Relationship Therapy* 325–43.

settings, including warfare.[13] However, the paternalistic protection of the female body can also be a powerful form of marginalisation and oppression. This can be seen in images of the female as meek and mild and as requiring protection and rescue. This, in turn, leads to women who have survived sexual assault or rape being framed as powerless victims of male dominance. There are several negative consequences of such portrayals. The first is the denial of sexual agency of women. It is important to recognise that a perpetrator of sexual violence is disregarding and disrespecting the agency of the woman. However, it is equally important for the law to recognise the sexual agency of women, and to empower them to recognise it within themselves.

The paternalistic protection of the female body has also led to fear-mongering throughout media and other communication outlets. Women are sometimes encouraged to stay at home, not to walk alone at night, to be wary of strangers and generally live their lives defensively.[14] This may be the most powerful form of marginalisation precipitating from rape law and the victimisation of women who survive sexual assault and rape.[15] It constructs the role of women as constantly subservient to male dominance, and the impending possibility of victimisation.

Conclusion

The facts of *DPP v C* highlight the fraught issues in rape law and in defining consent. The holding establishes that consent does not exist where a man engages in sexual intercourse with a woman who believes him to be another person. The feminist judgment further elaborates on this point of law, finding that consent requires the communication of both agreement and understanding—broadly construed—of the material facts of the sexual act.

The patriarchal domination of the legal system has prevented rape law from developing in a way that provides respect for the sexual autonomy of women while criminalising abhorrent behaviour of men. Of course, these issues do not always fall easily on gender lines. However, it continues to be important to discuss them in these terms, because it is the exclusion of women from the echelons of power that has precipitated such power imbalances in rape law.

Human rights law may provide an additional tool for reform in line with the goals set out in the feminist judgment. It can provide grounding for the claim that sexual agency is due to all people on an equal basis, and that rape law should reflect this. Our societal treatment

[13] For a discussion of the effect of intimate violence and the role of the law, see Rhonda Copelon, 'International Human Rights Dimensions of Intimate Violence: Another Strand in the Dialectic of Feminist Lawmaking' (2002–2003) 11 *American University Journal of Gender, Society, Policy and Law* 865–76.

[14] See, eg, Dara Adeeyo, '21 Potentially Life-Saving Safety Tips That Every Woman Should Know', *Cosmopolitan*, 9 May 2013; and Marissa Calligeros, 'Parks not safe for women, says homicide squad boss', *The Age Victoria*, 20 March 2015.

[15] For a discussion of the role of feminism in law relating to violence against women, see Elizabeth M Schneider, *Battered Women and Feminist Lawmaking* (New Haven, CT, Yale University Press, 2000).

of survivors of rape and sexual assault will also play an important part in instigating reform. Woman can be empowered to act as sexual agents, to assert themselves when wronged and to openly engage with the community without living in fear of sexual violence.

There is a long road ahead to achieve a reframing of rape that does not marginalise women. It will require respect for the sexual agency of women that is balanced with the appropriate criminalisation of non-consensual sexual activity. The reframing of consent in this judgment is a step toward this goal.

The People (Director of Public Prosecutions), Prosecutor v C., Accused

[C.A.A. No.156 of 1999; S.C. 2001]

Court of Criminal Appeal 31st July, 2001

Supreme Court 18th January, 2002

Rynn J. 18th January, 2002

This is an appeal from a conviction for rape contrary to s.4 of the *Offences Against the Person Act, 1861* and s.2 of the *Criminal Law Rape Amendment Act, 1981*, as amended by s.21 of the *Criminal Law Rape (Amendment) Act, 1990.* At the request of the applicant, following the decision of the Court of Criminal Appeal (reported at [2001] 3 I.R. 345), the Director of Public Prosecutions has certified under s.29 of the *Courts of Justice Act 1924* the following point of law of exceptional public importance for this Court's consideration:

> In a trial for rape should the following definition of consent be used:-
>
> "Voluntary agreement or acquiescence to sexual intercourse by a person of the age of consent with the requisite mental capacity.
>
> Knowledge or understanding of facts material to the act being consented to is necessary for the consent to be voluntary or to constitute acquiescence."

This is the definition of consent that was provided by the Court of Criminal Appeal (Murray J.) in this case. Other points argued before the CCA (admissibility of certain inculpatory statements made in custody; that the judge did not direct the jury on conflicting statements in the woman's evidence; the judge's decision not to withdraw the case from the jury, and the judge's decision not to give a corroboration warning) will not be re-examined by this Court. I agree with the view of the DPP that the CCA's definition of consent requires further consideration to give legal certainty to prosecutors, defendants and victims in sexual offence cases. The three features that merit further scrutiny are: the concept of 'voluntary agreement or acquiescence'; 'requisite mental capacity'; and 'knowledge or understanding of facts material to the act being consented to.' In considering the definition of consent I also consider the closely related question of when, if at all, a defendant can raise a defence of mistaken belief in consent. Counsel for the applicant argues that he should have been permitted to raise a defence of reasonable belief in consent. Another ground of appeal, which was rejected by the CCA was that once a woman has given a valid consent to sexual intercourse with A, if she mistakenly has sexual intercourse with B, no rape is committed. Thus, as with the majority of rape cases, the meaning of consent is at the heart of this case.

This Court agrees with the decision of the CCA to uphold the applicant's conviction for rape. While I consider the definition of consent provided by the Court is in need of clarification, I am of the view that this does not affect the soundness of the applicant's conviction. As I explain, there is more than adequate evidence on which the jury could base their decision to convict.

The crime of rape denies the victim's agency to make decisions about one of the most important aspects of human existence: a person's sexual life. Consent goes to the heart of this wrong. As of yet the Oireachtas has not seen fit to set out in statute what constitutes sexual consent. This is disappointing, given the importance of the interests at stake in a rape trial. However the Oireachtas' inaction does not prohibit this Court from providing guidance to trial judges when directing the jury on this important element of sexual offence prosecutions. In this judgment, I will provide guidance for trial judges directing juries on how the question of consent should be approached. I consider that in a trial for rape, the question of whether a woman consented to sexual intercourse should involve a consideration of the circumstances and broader context in which intercourse took place. Through these model directions, I also set clear boundaries on the availability of the 'mistaken belief' defence.

In this judgment I refrain from using the word 'complainant'. This term trivialises sexual violence and invokes the stereotype of the whining and irrational woman. Instead I use the word 'woman' to denote the alleged victim and 'man' to denote the accused in rape trials. I am alert to the reality that attacks of a sexual nature are not only perpetrated on women, and indeed not all perpetrators are men. However, I am confining myself to describing the victim as a woman and the accused as a man, because under s.2(2) of the 1981 Act rape can only be perpetrated by a man against a woman. However, I note that s.4 of the 1990 Act expressly allows for women to be convicted of rape under that section. Similarly, sexual assault and other sexual offences can be perpetrated by women against women or men. Therefore, the guidance provided to judges on how to direct juries as to consent is intended to be used in all sexual offences trials where consent is a defence.

The Crime of Rape

The crime of rape attracts a maximum sentence of life imprisonment. This sentence reflects the grave harms that experienced judges know may follow from rape, including: physical harm, feelings of isolation and psychological harm, such as post-traumatic stress disorder, which may cause a victim to withdraw from full social life and employment. The victim may continue to feel these effects for a long time after the rape, sometimes for decades.

Rape is a crime that affects a significant number of Irish women. The precise figures are difficult to quantify because of the problems of attrition and underreporting. Regrettably, both of these phenomena are related to the legal process itself; victims feel unable to report because of the intrusive questioning and disbelief they may face by some members of An Garda Síochána and when giving evidence in the courtroom. A recent study by the Dublin Rape Crisis Centre (*The Legal Process and Victims of Rape* (The Dublin Rape Crisis Centre: 1998)) refers to the following statistics:

Rapes reported to the Gardaí:

1993. 143

1994. 184

1995. 191

1996. 180

Number of prosecutions for rape commenced:

1993. 40

1994. 78

1995. 66

1996. 67

Convictions for rape recorded:

1993. 7

1994. 4

1995. 2

1996. 2

While the number of rape allegations being made to police is increasing in Ireland, according to the Central Statistics Office, the number of prosecutions commenced and convictions recorded is declining (based on an analysis of the recorded statistics from 1993–1996). These statistics serve to underline the importance of providing legal clarity on the offence of rape, and particularly, on the applicable standard of consent which forms part of the *actus reus* of the offence.

The criminal law has historically exhibited a deep mistrust of victims in sexual offences cases. The stereotypes of the lying, mendacious woman underpinned discriminatory legal doctrines such as the requirement of corroboration and the doctrine of recent complaint. Experienced criminal practitioners and judges are well aware of the existence of rape myths that continue to influence how defence counsel construct their arguments in trials. These discriminatory assumptions include: that women lie about having been raped; that certain people cannot be raped (e.g. sex workers or gay men or women) who have had many sexual partners (with what constitutes 'many' being judged according to out-dated standards); that women who wear revealing clothes or who drink large amounts of alcohol with men are sexually available. These rape myths continue to have the capacity to distort the criminal trial's purpose of finding out the truth of what happened. Therefore these unfounded generalisations must be strongly deprecated by the courts.

The Court of Criminal Appeal's definition of consent in this case

In my view the Court of Criminal Appeal's definition of consent fails to adequately protect the complainant's right to bodily integrity and autonomy, particularly a person's right to choose with whom she wishes to be sexually intimate. In this context, I have regard to the State's duty under Article 40.1 of the Constitution to guarantee equality before the law, as well as the State's duty to protect the personal rights of the citizen under Articles 40.3.1 and 40.3.2°. This duty is further underscored by Article 8 of the European Convention on Human Rights, ratified by the Irish State. Article 8 protects the victim's right to respect for his or her private and family life, home and correspondence. The concept of 'private life' "covers the physical and moral integrity of the person, including his or her sexual life" as held in *X and Y v. Netherlands* (1986) 8 E.H.R.R. 235.

In *X. and Y. v. The Netherlands*, the European Court found that Article 8 also places positive obligations on States to provide rape survivors with 'practical and effective protection' within the criminal law, in order to protect the victim's right to private life. I consider that such positive obligations must include clarity on the definition of consent and the delineation of specific circumstances in which consent should not be presumed, as described further below.

The State's duty to protect the autonomy, dignity and privacy of women mandates a robust approach to consent that focuses on the defendant's state of mind and the actions taken by the defendant to ascertain the woman's consent. In the case of *S.W. v. U.K.* (1996) 21 E.H.R.R. 363 the European Court of Human Rights upheld the decision of the House of Lords, which refused an appeal by S.W. against his conviction for marital rape. In finding that S.W.'s due process rights were not violated, the Court held:-

> "However clearly drafted a legal provision may be, in any system of law, including criminal law, there is an inevitable element of judicial interpretation. There will always be a need for elucidation of doubtful points and for adaptation to changing circumstances."

In light of this principle, as well as changing social norms regarding sexual offences in Ireland, I find it necessary to provide legal clarity on the nature of consent in rape trials.

It seems clear from the jurisprudence of the European Court that the use of the criminal law to prosecute alleged offenders for rape is a proportionate interference with the private life of the accused, once such prosecutions are undertaken 'in accordance with the law' and are 'necessary in a democratic society in the interests of … public safety … for the prevention of disorder or crime' and for 'the protection of the rights and freedoms of others.' Applying this standard to the present case, I find that the elaboration of guidelines for trial judges regarding the presence of consent, and recklessness as to consent, meets the required standard of proportionality to conform with Article 8 of the European Convention on Human Rights.

I now set out my reasons, focusing on the two ingredients of the offence of rape: lack of consent and the defendant's knowledge or recklessness regarding the lack of consent.

A. Was there a Lack of Consent?

Under s.2 of the 1981 Act in order to prove the offence of rape, the DPP must establish that the woman did not consent to sexual intercourse. Voluntary agreement is key to the question of consent. I will address the question of agreement first, and then I will turn to the question of voluntariness.

Agreement

In my view agreement to sexual intercourse is comprised of two elements: understanding and communication.

Understanding

The presence of voluntary agreement to engage in sexual intercourse inevitably requires some level of understanding of the act agreed to. The criteria for understanding were set out by the Court of Criminal Appeal as the possession of 'mental capacity' and sufficient 'knowledge or understanding of facts material to the act being consented to.' The presence or absence of 'mental capacity' in general is only considered where a person has a particular diagnosis of disability or impairment in cognitive functioning. However, there is a wide range of situations, where an individual's mental state might impact on the ability to give voluntary agreement to sexual intercourse—including where he or she is intoxicated. While the mental capacity, knowledge or understanding of the woman in the present case is not at issue, the point is of such exceptional public importance that this Court must provide clarification on this issue.

The only definition of 'mental capacity' in case law to date stems from case law on consent to medical treatment. While this is clearly a very different context from consent to sexual intercourse, it is worth setting out this definition to determine whether it could be applied in the context of rape. The seminal definition of mental capacity to consent to medical treatment is set out in the English case of *Re C.* [1994] W.L.R. 290, which requires the patient to demonstrate that he or she could (a) understand and retain the treatment information (b) believe it (c) weigh it in the balance to arrive at a decision and (d) communicate her or his decision to the treating physician. This standard is now well-established in English case law, having been applied in *Re M.B.* [1997] 2 F.L.R. 426 and *St George's Healthcare Trust NHS v. S.* [1999] Fam 26; but has not yet been applied in an Irish case. *Re C.* arose in a very different context from the present case, and the plaintiff's mental capacity was assessed using a civil law standard.

First, I must consider whether the requirement to understand the reasonably foreseeable consequences of one's decision, is an appropriate standard to impose on women in the context of sexual intercourse. Unlike a course of medical treatment, there is no universal consensus on what might be considered reasonably foreseeable consequences of the decision to consent to sexual intercourse. The risk of pregnancy or contraction of sexually transmitted diseases are certainly possible consequences of unprotected sexual intercourse, but would not be 'reasonably foreseeable' consequences of sexual intercourse in all situations.

The law recognises that adults exercise legal agency in making decisions with legal effect—including the decision to consent to sexual intercourse. A certain level of knowledge and understanding is necessary for many legal decisions, such as the provision of informed consent to medical treatment, or acceptance of a contractual obligation. However, the level of knowledge required for an exercise of legal agency will vary depending on the specific action and the context in which it takes place. It is also important to remember that an action can be legally binding even if the reason behind the specific exercise of legal agency does not appear to be rational, as in *Re C.* [1994] W.L.R. 290. For example, an exercise of legal agency in the casting of a vote, or in entering into a marriage, is an inherently personal decision, and the manner in which this legal agency is exercised may seem unwise or ill-founded to others—but this perception does not diminish its legal effect.

The exercise of legal agency in the context of sexual intercourse involves a particularly intimate and personal decision-making process. For that reason, it is not appropriate to expect women to perform a calculated rational decision-making analysis, whereby they weigh the advantages and disadvantages of consenting to sexual intercourse, consider alternatives, and have regard to the reasonably foreseeable consequences of providing consent. This would result in legal absurdity, creating a standard of proof for consent which is wholly removed from the reality of how decisions to engage in sexual intercourse are made. Therefore, I find that it would be unrealistic to require that in order for the prosecution to prove the *actus reus* of rape, women would have to demonstrate either that they had undergone such a reasoning process and decided to refuse consent, or that they were incapable of weighing up the options with regard to the decision to consent.

This last point is underscored by the particular problems that could arise in cases involving people with disabilities. If an assessment of mental capacity were to be employed in order to make clear that consent was absent, this could give rise to the perpetration of existing stigma and discrimination against people with disabilities. Assessments of mental capacity are typically only undertaken in cases where the individual whose consent is at issue has a recognised impairment in cognitive functioning. Women with such disabilities already face significant barriers in rape cases, including in instructing legal representation, establishing competence to testify, and availing of reasonable accommodation to participate effectively in the trial process. The imposition of an additional barrier in the form of an assessment of the complainant's mental capacity would, in my view, result in indirect discrimination against persons with disabilities, contrary to s.3 of the *Equal Status Act 2000*. Moreover, even if all women, regardless of disability, were asked to undergo an assessment of their mental capacity to consent to sexual intercourse, the women who would be most disadvantaged by this practice would clearly be those with disabilities.

Finally, in my considered view, it would be too onerous a standard to require the court to engage in an assessment of mental capacity in every rape trial. Such assessments may undermine the woman's ability to give an account of whether or not she consented. It also usurps the role of the jury assessing whether the woman's account is credible and reliable. The question of whether there was consent is ultimately a question of fact for the jury to decide, having heard all of the evidence. I consider that the introduction of a formal test of mental capacity to consent to sex would therefore be unnecessarily restrictive and could adversely affect the task of the jury.

Therefore, this Court considers that the applicable standard for voluntary agreement to sexual intercourse is 'knowledge or understanding of facts material to the sexual act.' In my considered opinion, any additional requirement on the woman to demonstrate 'mental capacity' would be superfluous, as a proper consideration of the free and informed nature of the consent provided can be reached by a means which is less stigmatising to the woman and does not constitute indirect discrimination on the basis of disability. The key consideration to determine 'voluntary agreement' to sexual intercourse will be the woman's understanding of the sexual act in question. I apply the standard of understanding set out by Scarman LJ in *R v. Lang* (1976) 62 Cr App R 50: 'the critical question is … whether she understood her situation and was capable of making up her mind'.

I consider that understanding regarding 'the facts material to the sexual act' excludes situations where consent was obtained by fraud as to the nature or purpose of the act as held in *R v Flattery* (1877) 2 Q.B.D. 410 and *R v. Williams* [1923] 1 K.B. 340. If the court finds that the woman was deceived or misunderstood the nature or purpose of the sexual act—believing it to be a medical examination (*R v. Flattery* (1877) 2 Q.B.D. 410), or an exercise to improve her singing voice (*R v Williams* [1923] 1 KB 340), then the fact that the woman gave her agreement to the act on that basis cannot constitute valid consent to sexual intercourse.

The Irish courts have been clear that a fraudulently obtained consent affords no defence to the charge of rape (*R v. Dee* (1884) 15 Cox C.C. 57). The *Criminal Law Amendment Act 1885*, s.4 clearly established that a man who impersonated a woman's husband would be guilty of rape. In its 1988 *Report on Rape* the Law Reform Commission excluded from its definition of free and voluntary consent any consent obtained by, *inter alia*, deception or fraudulent means (p.9). Similarly, it is well established that where a defendant misleads a woman as to his identity in order to secure agreement to sexual intercourse, this constitutes rape since '[a]n essential ingredient of the offence of rape is the proof that the woman did not consent to the actual act of sexual intercourse with the particular man who penetrated her.' (*R v. Linekar* [1995] Q.B. 250). Therefore I am of the view that fraud as to identity means that the person does not understand the 'facts material to the sexual act' and therefore the woman does not consent to sexual intercourse. One of the most objectionable lines of argument pursued in this case was the contention that a woman has given consent to sexual intercourse if she has consented to sex with A, but mistakenly has sex with B. This argument must be deprecated in the strongest of terms. It harks back to conceptions of women as lacking in full moral agency and as being incapable of deciding with whom she wishes to have sexual intercourse. Moreover, if the woman consented to sexual intercourse under certain conditions—for example, requiring her partner to wear a condom—and these conditions were not fulfilled—then this would be sufficient to negate her voluntary agreement.

Clarifying the definition of consent means that the Court must also give life to the woman's sphere of autonomy in deciding to have sexual intercourse. Therefore, notwithstanding what I have already said about fraud and consent, I consider that if the jury is satisfied that the woman understood the physiological nature of sexual intercourse, that is sufficient knowledge upon which to find consent. Given that the decision to engage in sexual intercourse is such a personal and intimate one, this court finds that it is inappropriate to further interrogate the woman's understanding of sexual intercourse beyond a general knowledge and agreement to the physical act. Many people understand the physical nature of sexual intercourse, but for a variety of reasons, including poverty, lack of education, and other factors, may not appreciate the risks of pregnancy or sexually transmitted infections. None of these factors are 'facts material to the sexual act' and therefore lack of knowledge of these facts is not a misunderstanding sufficient to render the woman's consent to sex invalid. Furthermore, the imposition of the requirement to understand all the possible consequences of sex is a disproportionate interference with individual autonomy, and, if strictly applied, would bring many instances of consensual sexual intercourse within the realm of criminal activity. In addition, since there can be no consensus on the 'foreseeable consequences' of sexual intercourse applicable to all situations, then the use of such a standard for knowledge or understanding on which to ground consent is unworkable. Therefore, the 'facts material to the sexual act' should be narrowly construed.

I now turn to the second part of agreement to sexual intercourse: communication.

Communication

The clearest way to establish communication of agreement to sexual intercourse in a situation of first contact between two individuals is for the man to verbally ascertain the woman's agreement prior to sexual intercourse. Since the presence or absence of consent is so central to the very concept of what constitutes a sexual offence involving adults, it is reasonable to require the man to take steps to ascertain whether consent is present.

Agreement to sexual intercourse is generally established through verbal communication; however, communication does not necessarily need to be verbal and can include situations where non-verbal communication—such as actions and gestures—constitutes implied or inferred consent.

While each case will inevitably turn on its specific facts, it is prudent for this court to set out some illustrative examples of situations where voluntary agreement to sexual intercourse might be inferred from non-verbal actions, as well as the non-verbal actions or factors which should not be used to infer voluntary agreement. For example, where the parties know each other well and regularly have consensual sexual intercourse, they may establish an agreed, non-verbal form of communication which constitutes voluntary agreement to sexual penetration.

As a matter of law of exceptional public importance, it is vital for this Court to set out the factors that should never be used to imply communication of consent to sexual intercourse. First, an individual's choice of clothing should never be used to infer voluntary agreement to sexual intercourse. Similarly, the fact that an individual consents to acts such as kissing or sexual touching, cannot be used to infer subsequent agreement to sexual penetration. An invitation to enter an individual's home can also not lead to an inference of communication of agreement to sexual intercourse. Importantly, the mere fact that the parties have previously had consensual sexual intercourse cannot be used to imply or infer voluntary agreement to a specific instance of sexual penetration. This list is not closed and may develop in line with the experience of the courts.

A Voluntary Agreement

The 'voluntary' nature of agreement to sexual intercourse is crucial to distinguish criminal offences from consensual sex. An individual might agree to sexual intercourse, but where this agreement is obtained by use of threats, coercion, intimidation, or in situations where the person fears for his or her life, wellbeing or safety, it should not be regarded as 'voluntary.' Situations where an individual abuses a position or power or trust in order to secure agreement to sexual intercourse should also not be regarded as meeting the standard of voluntariness. For example, a person may only agree to sexual intercourse with a paid carer or employer out of fear of reprisals arising from a refusal. Such an agreement should similarly not be regarded as 'voluntary.'

I consider that the concept of 'voluntary agreement' in the Court of Criminal Appeal's judgment, while helpful, fails to provide the requisite clarity on the applicable legal standard for valid consent.

The CCA's definition of consent seems to equate 'voluntary agreement' with 'acquiescence'. In my view, such an approach would unduly undermine a woman's autonomy and sexual agency. If a woman's consent is to be truly voluntary, then mere acquiescence should not be taken by the jury to mean consent. The common law has long held that it was rape to have intercourse with a woman without her consent, even when there was no force threatened or used (*R v. Camplin* (1845) 1 Cox C.C. 220) for example where the woman was asleep (*R v. Mayers* (1872) 12 Cox C.C. 311). In cases where the woman is not aware of what is taking place because she was asleep or otherwise unconscious, including through intoxication, the common law has also established that it is not appropriate to infer consent. I also take judicial notice of the established body of knowledge that explains that rape victims may respond to unwanted advances by 'freezing' or 'dissociating'. They may not offer any kind of resistance, or even indication that the sexual contact is unwelcome (A.W. Burgess and L.L. Holstrom, "Rape Trauma Syndrome" (1974) 131(9) *Am. J. Psychiatry* 981–6). Furthermore, the Oireachtas has set down in s.9 of the 1990 Act that a woman's failure to offer to resistance is not to be taken as indicative of consent. In my view, 'acquiescence' could easily be conflated with a 'failure to offer resistance' which raises the risk that juries will automatically reason from acquiescence to consent. This would be in contradiction of the clear intent expressed in s.9 of the 1990 Act. For these reasons I consider that the jury should be directed not to infer consent from the lack of physical resistance alone, and that acquiescence should not form part of the law on rape.

The voluntary nature of the agreement can also be called into question in circumstances where a woman's judgement may be affected by the consumption of alcohol or drugs—especially in situations where an individual is so intoxicated that she is unaware of what is happening and therefore unable to give voluntary consent (*R v. Malone* [1998] 2 Cr App R 447; *R v. Camplin* (1845) 1 Cox C.C. 220). However, the mere consumption of alcohol or drugs is not definitive in determining voluntary agreement to sexual intercourse in a specific situation. It is open to the prosecution to demonstrate that the woman did not give free agreement to sexual intercourse on the occasion in question.

In determining whether there was consent, the jury should be directed to consider the specific circumstances which may lead to the absence of voluntary agreement to sexual intercourse in the individual case—including coercion, duress, undue influence, false imprisonment, fear for one's life, safety or wellbeing resulting from a refusal (including unreasonable fear), or a lack of understanding of the physical nature of the sexual act agreed to, or whether the agreement has been given for them by a third party.

Naturally, each case remains to be decided on its own unique facts, and therefore these examples are merely illustrative, and should serve to guide future courts in determining the presence or absence of voluntary agreement to sexual intercourse.

I consider that the rule of law requirement of certainty and predictability of the law requires that some guidance should be given on when consent should be presumed to be absent. Furthermore, the jury's consideration of whether the *actus reus* of rape—non-consensual intercourse—has been proved by the prosecution, should involve a consideration of the context in which the intercourse took place. The most effective way of achieving this objective is to provide guidance to trial judges when directing the jury on how to approach the issue of consent in rape.

Guidelines for trial courts regarding the lack of consent

I hold that where the prosecution has established that one of the following situations pertained at the time of the alleged offence, the jury should be directed to scrutinise very carefully any claim by the defence that the woman gave consent to sexual intercourse. These directions should apply where:-

a. The agreement is expressed by the words or conduct of a third party to the activity;

b. The woman does not understand the physical nature of sexual intercourse;
c. The defendant induces the woman to engage in the activity by abusing a position of trust, power or authority;
d. The woman expresses, by words or conduct, a lack of agreement in the activity;
e. The woman, having initially consented to engage in sexual activity, expresses by words or conduct a lack of agreement to continue to engage in the activity.

However, this does not alter the defendant's entitlement to the presumption of innocence under Article 38.1 of the Constitution. The Irish Constitution guarantees each accused person the right to a trial 'in due course of law', which embraces a range of procedural and substantive rights that flow from the rule of law. In *State (Healy) v. Donoghue* the Supreme Court confirmed that this phrase mandates '[that] every criminal trial shall be conducted in accordance with concepts of justice, that the procedures applied shall be fair, and that the person accused will be afforded every opportunity to defend himself.' In particular the courts have also confirmed that the right to a fair trial ranks superior to other rights and interests, including the community's right to have crimes prosecuted (*State (Healy) v. Donoghue* [1975] I.R. 325, 349 per O' Higgins C.J. citing with approval Gannon J.). This Court has recognised that fairness to the accused has a particularly strong constitutional foundation that means that even respected common law rules must satisfy the requirements of constitutional fairness (*People (DPP) v. McGrail* [1990] 2 I.R. 38, 51 *per* Hederman J.; *Re Haughey* [1971] I.R. 217; *People (A.G.) v. O'Brien* [1965] I.R. 142; *People (D.P.P.) v. Kenny* [1990] 2 I.R. 110). The defendant is also entitled to the robust protection of the presumption of innocence under Article 6(2) of the European Convention on Human Rights as established in *Saunders v. U.K.* (1996) 23 E.H.R.R. 313 and *Van Mechelen v. The Netherlands* (1998) 25 E.H.R.R. 647.

Applying the foregoing analysis to the instant case

In this case the woman was asleep in bed, with her back to the door, when the appellant entered. No evidence was presented at trial that a conversation between the two occurred prior to sexual penetration, and the woman and appellant had not met each other prior to that evening. The appellant stated in evidence that he lay down on the bed to get some rest, began snuggling the woman and then had consensual sexual intercourse with her. The woman testified that she awoke to find someone having sex with her, whom she thought for an instant to be her boyfriend, but quickly realised it was not. Since no explicit verbal agreement to have sexual intercourse existed between the parties, the defence has at trial relied on the woman's silence, bodily gestures and lack of resistance to demonstrate implied consent. However, statements made by the appellant at the time of his questioning by Gardaí after the incident suggest that he did not interpret her silence as consent, or thought that she may have consented thinking that he was her boyfriend, stating:-

> "I think she thought I was her boyfriend. I did not ask her for permission to have sex with her and I know what I did was wrong, I shouldn't have done this."

On the evidence presented it was open to the jury to find that the woman did not consent to sexual intercourse with the applicant. Indeed I consider such a finding to be an appropriate rejection of the applicant's attempt to appeal to the popular rape myth that women who do not actively resist can be taken as consenting to sex. This is one of the most offensive rape myths in existence and it redounds to the jury's credit that they rejected the argument. Thus, I do not find any reason to overturn the jury's finding.

B. Did the Defendant have a Guilty Mind?

The decision of the CCA also requires further clarification in respect of that Court's treatment of the issue of *mens rea* in rape, specifically the issue of honest belief in consent. While the point of law referred to this court by the DPP did not explicitly involve the consideration of the defence of honest belief, this Court holds that the two issues are inextricably linked.

In this case the appellant got into bed alongside the woman and pulled her pyjama bottoms down and had intercourse with her. He did not speak with her, nor did he gain any communication from her. It was a darkened room. *Prima facie* this would seem to constitute recklessness as to consent, which is a sufficient *mens rea* for the offence of rape under s.4 of the 1981 Act. However the appellant claimed that he had a mistaken belief in consent; that he was not reckless, but (mistakenly) believed the woman was consenting.

The Supreme Court in *People (D.P.P.) v. McDonagh* [1996] 1 I.R. 565 has confirmed that s.2(2) of the 1981 Act codifies the law relating to mistaken belief by providing that if a jury has to consider whether a man believed that a woman was consenting to intercourse it has to take into account all relevant matters including the presence or absence of reasonable grounds for the belief. As the Supreme Court noted in *McDonagh*, the jury should only receive an instruction in line with s.2(2) where the facts of the case require such an instruction. This Court considers that in such cases trial juries should be provided with guidance on what constitutes reasonable grounds. This guidance will help minimise the pernicious and distorting influence of rape myths on the trial process.

The trial courts must be vigilant to ensure that stereotypes and discriminatory assumptions about women do not enter into the jury's consideration of what constitutes 'reasonable grounds' under s. 2(2) of the 1981 Act. There are two aspects to this: reasonableness of belief may help juries to evaluate whether or not they wish to accept the defendant's assertion of a belief in consent. If a belief is based on wholly unfounded generalisations about women, then the jury may decide that the belief did not in fact exist. If an honest belief is asserted in a case where the woman repeatedly shouted 'Stop!' and screamed, then the jury is entitled to take the unreasonable nature of the belief into account. The second, related, way in which stereotypes about women need to be considered is in relation to whether the law is willing to give the defendant the benefit of holding discriminatory beliefs which lead to the commission of a crime.

A man who argues an honest but unreasonable belief in consent is often appealing, directly or indirectly, to a number of ideas about female or male sexuality that are manifestly unfounded. These include beliefs that women who say no to sexual intercourse are merely playing sexual games and their 'no' means 'yes'; that because a woman has said yes to sexual intercourse before, with the defendant or another man, she must be consenting to intercourse on this occasion; and that women who wear revealing clothes are available for sexual intercourse. In my view, 'honest beliefs' based on these kinds of discriminatory reasoning about women cannot be said to mean that the defendant was not reckless. Indeed, the holding of such beliefs as justifications for actions are more properly analysed as indicative of recklessness. Therefore I note with approval the English Court of Appeal's interpretation of recklessness in cases such as *R v. Satnam; R v. Kewal* (1984) 78 Cr App R 149 to mean that the accused 'could not care less' whether the woman was consenting or not. I gain support for this view from the English Law Commission's Consultation on Consent which states that a failure to addresses one's mind to the question of whether a woman is consenting or not is 'a violation of her rights, in that it fails to give proper value to her existence as a human being and thereby to accord her full human status' (Law Commission CP No 139, 95) and see Home Office, *Setting the Boundaries*, vol I (2000)). I consider that the 'could not care less' formulation of recklessness should cover situations where the defendant has failed to give any thought to whether the victim is consenting or not.

I agree with L'Heureux-Dubé J.'s statement in *R v. Park* [1995] 2 S.C.R. 836 where she stressed the role of the courts in ensuring that the criminal law is responsive to women's realities rather than 'a vehicle for the perpetuation of historic repression and disadvantage' (at para 51). In raising the defence of honest belief the defendant will have to give evidence that he believed that the woman consented; he will have to adduce some evidence from which the jury can find that he honestly and reasonably believed that she consented. This evidence may include testimony by the defendant, which can be evaluated by the jury as all oral testimony is evaluated. However, I note that the defendant's mere assertion of his belief is not evidence of its honesty, as *per* McLachlin J. in the Supreme Court of Canada Case of *Osolin*:-

> "A belief which is totally unsupported is not an honestly held belief. A person who honestly believes something is a person who has looked at the circumstances and has drawn an honest inference from them. Therefore, for a belief to be honest there must be some support for it in the circumstances. A person who commits a sexual assault without some support in the circumstances for inferring the consent of the woman has, at the very least, been wilfully blind as to consent." (*R v Osolin* [1993] 4 SCR 595 at 649–50).

Furthermore, the jury should be directed that evidence of lack of resistance alone, or absence of such words or conduct, should not be enough of itself, to constitute support for an honest belief. In evaluating belief in consent the jury should be told that there is an important difference between situations where the defendant believed that the woman *would* consent and those where he believed she *did* consent (*R v. Osolin* [1993] 5 S.C.R. 595). This is particularly important given that the Oireachtas has not yet seen fit to restrict the circumstances in which a defendant may adduce the previous sexual history of the woman, including the previous sexual history between the woman and the defendant.

I am of the view that there are certain situations in which it would be a violation of the woman's constitutional right to equality and bodily integrity to allow the defendant to claim a belief in consent. Therefore, where the prosecution has established that one of the following situations arises, I am of the view that the jury should be directed in the strongest terms to be particularly sceptical of the defence of honest belief. This is not an exhaustive list. This direction should be given where:-

a. The agreement is expressed by the words of conduct of a third party.
b. Where, because of his self-induced intoxication, the defendant is incapable of assessing whether the woman is giving consent.

However, this does not affect the defendant's entitlement to the presumption of innocence under Article 38.1 of the Constitution and Article 6 of the European Convention on Human Rights. Indeed, as is the case in all criminal trials, the prosecution will be required to prove its case beyond a reasonable doubt, including negating any defence raised by the defendant.

I consider that in the following situations, the jury at trial should be directed to consider particularly carefully the following factors when evaluating claims of honest belief:-

a. Whether there was violence or the threat of violence. This violence could be directed at the victim or at another person.
b. Whether the victim was in fear for her safety or wellbeing, whether that was a reasonable fear or not.
c. Whether the defendant impersonated another.
d. Whether the woman was falsely imprisoned.
e. Whether the woman was asleep or otherwise unconscious.
f. Whether the defendant was in a position of power over the woman.
g. Whether the woman was in a relationship of dependence with the defendant. (A relationship of dependence includes economic dependence or reliance on the defendant for personal care.)
h. Whether no communication between the victim and defendant takes place immediately prior to the sexual activity.
i. Whether intercourse takes place in the commission of another serious offence.

Application to the instant case

In the circumstances of the present case, the defendant must be able to point to at least some objectively reasonable grounds for his alleged belief in consent. But the evidence reveals no such grounds. Indeed I have a series of pre-trial admissions pointing in the opposite direction. He claims that he and the woman 'snuggled' prior to intercourse. However in claims of reasonable belief in consent the law imposes a higher standard than merely some indication of affection, possibly for a different person.

Furthermore, it is not logically consistent to claim both that the appellant had an honest but mistaken belief in consent and to also say that there was a valid consent. Either the appellant is saying that there was consent or he is saying that there was no consent but that he honestly believed there was. A defendant cannot lead the two logically inconsistent defences (*D.P.P. v. McDonagh* [1996] 1 I.R. 565).

Finally, the guidance we have provided to trial judges on how to direct the jury on consent would be incomplete without an element of education. Research regarding discriminatory attitudes towards women who have experienced sexual violence should be explained to the jury. In particular jurors should be exposed to the vast body of research that explains how women react to sexual violence. This could be done by the judge by way of directions to the jury regarding the pernicious and harmful effects of unfounded generalisations about women who are raped, and by explaining to jurors that academic research has explained that many victims of rape are silent during or after an attack and may not react in the stereotypical way. Psychologists have exposed some of the most common misconceptions about how survivors of sexual assault and rape 'should' behave. For example, while it is commonly supposed that in the hours and days after the assault, the woman will be visibly upset, in fact many women have a controlled response in which they mask their feelings and appear calm and composed (Burgess and Holmstrom, *Rape—Crisis and Recovery* (Bowie, Md., Prentice–Hall, Brady and London: 1979 at p.36). Directions to the jury on the distorting effects of stereotypes about how women should behave as well as on actual responses to sexual violence would further reinforce the effectiveness of the trial judge's directions on consent outlined in this judgment.

I am satisfied that in this case the applicant's conviction for rape should be upheld. The trial judge directed the jury properly and there was ample evidence supporting the jury's finding of guilt. Accordingly I uphold the conviction.

27

Commentary on *CC v Ireland*

CIAN Ó CONCUBHAIR

Introduction

In *CC v Ireland*,[1] the Irish Supreme Court found section 1(1) of the Criminal Law (Amendment) Act 1935, which criminalised a man who had sexual intercourse with a girl under the age of 15, unconstitutional.[2] Section 1(1) was an offence of what is commonly referred to as 'strict liability': a criminal offence that does not require proof of fault in relation to some, or all, of the conduct in question. The *CC* court found the absence of any proof of fault in relation to the girl's age, or the absence of a defence of honest and reasonable mistake about the age of the girl, created the possibility that a 'mentally innocent'[3] man could be convicted of a sexual offence. That a 'mentally innocent' person could be labelled a sex offender, placed on the sex offender's register and face possible life imprisonment, was found to be inconsistent with Article 40 of Bunreacht na hÉireann. The immediate political response to the judgment was a rush to plug the new legislative gap in the child protection legal framework. The result was the enactment of the Criminal Law (Sexual Offences) Act 2006, which provided for a defence of honest mistake under sections 2 (defilement of a child under 15) and 3 (defilement of a child under 17), and removed the gender-specificity of the 1935 Act.

In the original *CC* case, Hardiman J gave a judgment with which all the members of the Court agreed. David Prendergast's feminist judgment in this volume aims to provide the missing dissent in *CC*. Prendergast J's judgment challenges this assertion of 'mental innocence' in the *CC* decision, by arguing that sexual intercourse is inherently risky.[4] Because of this ever-present risk that the act is potentially very wrongful—even when the man believes the woman to be within the age of consent—the claim that the applicant is 'mentally innocent' in having sex with a 13-year-old girl is incorrect. For Prendergast J, the facts as they are

[1] *CC v Ireland* [2006] IESC 33.

[2] The question of consent, while irrelevant to the structure of these offences as the girl is under the age at which she can legally consent to have sexual intercourse (17 years old after s 3 of the Criminal Law (Sexual Offences) Act 2006), is relevant to the context in which the law was challenged. Non-consensual sexual intercourse with a girl aged under 15, or 17, is still prosecutable as rape (Criminal Law (Rape) Act 1981, s 2), regardless of whether the attacker believed she had reached the age of consent or not.

[3] *CC v Ireland* [2006] IESC 33, para 36.

[4] On this point, see further Michelle Oberman, 'Regulating Consensual Sex with Minors: Defining a Role for Statutory Rape' (2000) 48 *Buffalo Law Review* 703-84.

in *CC* shows that there is a degree of objective fault on the part of the appellant, meaning that section 1(1) is not criminalising 'morally innocent' conduct and is therefore constitutionally permissible.

Though I disagree with some of his conceptual claims, Prendergast J's judgment is a valuable critical contribution to the discourse on appropriate legal responses to sexual violence in Irish society. In challenging the unsophisticated, 'commonsense' (read 'reasonable', middle-aged, white, male judge) reasoning in Hardiman J's account of responsibility in sexual power dynamics, Prendergast J invites us to reflect on the complex interrelationship between culturally-informed conceptions of the sexual availability of young women, sexual vulnerability in an environment of ongoing patriarchal structural inequality and the role of the state in addressing these issues.[5]

This Commentary

While Prendergast J's dissent, like others in this volume, is constrained in its scope by the existing legal structures of the criminal justice system, my commentary offers a broader critical review of that system and how it addresses sexual violence. It does not support the majority's views in *CC*, particularly Hardiman J's claims of 'mental innocence'. Instead, it adopts a generally sceptical position regarding the ethical or material appropriateness of deploying the criminal justice system to address complex structural inequalities—be they patriarchal, ethno-cultural or class-based.[6] In this way, while it does challenge some of his dissenting arguments, my commentary should be seen as providing additional critical depth beyond what Prendergast J is permitted, in his dissent, to do.

Hardiman J's judgment in *CC* represents one of the handful[7] of cases in which the Irish Supreme Court questioned the constitutional validity, as well as the ethical legitimacy, of crimes of constructive liability. Constructive liability takes various forms. On one end of the spectrum there are crimes of absolute strict liability, where the actors in question need have no *mens rea* regarding any element of the *actus reus* of the offence, ie they can be held criminally liable for consequences where they were not cognitively aware that the causative actions were occurring. On the other end of the spectrum are examples of constructive liability such as murder under section 4(1) of the Criminal Justice Act 1964. Under this approach, a person who, without justification or excuse, causes the death of another, is guilty of murder if that person intended to kill *or* commit serious injury. The constructive element of this criminal measure lies in the latter form of *mens rea*, as by holding someone

[5] See further ibid; Anne Cossins, *Masculinities, Sexualities and Child Sexual Abuse* (The Hague, Kluwer Law International, 2000); and Frances Olsen, 'Statutory Rape: A Feminist Critique of Rights Analysis' (1984) 63 *Texas Law Review* 387-432.

[6] This critical approach bears some resemblance to feminist literature such as Carol Smart, *Feminism and the Power of Law* (London, Routledge, 1989) and Elena Loizidou, 'The Trouble With Rape: Gender Matters and Legal "Transformations"' (1999) 7(3) *Feminist Legal Studies* 275-97. Of more significance to this appraisal of our criminal justice system is the work of critical theorists such as Barbara Hudson, 'Beyond White Man's Justice: Race, Gender and Justice in Late Modernity' (2006) 10(1) *Theoretical Criminology* 29-47.

[7] Another example is *The People (DPP) v Noel and Marie Murray* [1977] IR 360, where Henchy J spent some time reflecting on the constitutional implications of constructive criminal liability.

liable for intending to kill (which is what murder is generally understood to mean)[8] when that person might only have intended to commit serious injury, we are constructing an enhanced form of culpability (blameworthiness) based on the unfortunate outcome of that person's actual culpable conduct.

The statutory rape offence under section 1(1) of the Criminal Law (Amendment) Act 1935 is a form of constructive, or strict, liability that lies somewhere between these two ends of the spectrum. As explained in the 'Introduction', this offence is strict (ie it has no correlative *mens rea* ingredient) in relation to one component of its *actus reus*: the victim is aged under 15. The offence does not provide for a due diligence defence, a mechanism that establishes an objective standard for recklessness in the form of a positive obligation, that is, that someone in the defendant's position ought to have taken reasonable steps to verify the age of the victim.

In my commentary, I do not challenge Prendergast J's principal legal contention that section 1(1) of the Criminal Law (Amendment) Act 1935 is constitutionally permissible. Instead, I take issue with some of the conceptual and empirical assertions in his judgment, and, as stated above, provide additional critical reflection on the criminal justice system generally.

From experience researching sexual violence in Ireland,[9] and engaging with survivors, offenders and other stakeholders in the criminal justice system and support and advocacy systems, I have serious reservations about the appropriateness or effectiveness of relying on the criminal law to confront and transform pervasive and oppressive patriarchal sexual norms in our society.[10] I believe the criminal law is often not a good, let alone an ideal, mechanism for achieving individual accountability and closure for victims and survivors of sexual violence—even when convictions are achieved.[11] I also have doubts about whether an expansive sphere of criminal liability, epitomised in strict liability offences, is a good way of changing pervasive cultural norms around sexual exploitation and abuse.[12]

Along with these particular instrumental concerns thrown up by his feminist dissent in *CC*, my commentary questions Prendergast J's account of moral culpability. I briefly outline an account of moral responsibility that differentiates between culpability (actions worthy of blame) in the private and public senses, and other ways individuals can be ethically implicated in wrongs and harm. These are views not just about the moral contours of responsibility for the wrongs of sexual violence, but also the ethical limitations of punitive coercive state power.

[8] Barry Mitchell and Julian Roberts, *Public Opinion and Sentencing for Murder* (London, Nuffield Foundation, 2010).

[9] I worked as a researcher on Dr Marie Keenan's qualitative research project, Sexual Trauma and Abuse: Restorative and Transformative Possibilities? (University College Dublin, 2013-2014). See http://researchrepository.ucd.ie/handle/10197/6247.

[10] For a reflection on the deployment of law—particularly criminal, public and anti-discrimination law—as a means of furthering feminist ethical and political values, see Nicola Lacey, *Unspeakable Subjects* (Oxford, Hart Publishing, 1998).

[11] See further Jennifer Temkin, *Rape and the Legal Process* (Oxford, Oxford University Press, 2002); and Sue Lees, *Carnal Knowledge: Rape on Trial*, 2nd edn (London, The Women's Press Ltd, 2002).

[12] On pervasive cultural norms around sexual exploitation and assault, see Cossins, above n 5; and Yvette Russell, 'Thinking Sexual Difference Through the Law of Rape' (2013) 24(3) *Law and Critique* 255-75. For an analysis of the cultural significance of the intersection of sex and race in the sexual assault trial, see Ann Cossins, 'Saints, Sluts and Sexual Assault: Rethinking the Relationship between Sex, Race and Gender' (2003) 12(1) *Social and Legal Studies* 77-103.

Context and the Age of Consent

One last point I want to make before I begin the substantive critique relates to the particular facts of the *CC* case. Though neither the Supreme Court, nor Prendergast J, takes much issue with this, CC's admission that he believed the girl to be 16 years old means that he was 'mentally guilty' of another statutory rape offence under the 1935 Act, namely, section 2(1)—defilement of a girl aged 15 or 16 years old.

This admission by the appellant, and the undisputed reason for that belief (the girl told him she was 16), struck me as relevant to broader questions about the sexualisation of young people in contemporary Irish society; a concern on which Prendergast J's instrumental rationale is based. I think it is relevant to bear in mind, when assessing this particular aspect of the evidence in *CC*, that the age of consent for sexual relations in our nearest neighbour, the United Kingdom, is 16 years old.[13]

It is not, I think, wild speculation to suggest that many Irish teenagers (indeed probably a great many Irish adults) wrongly believe, due to heavy exposure to British media, that the age of consent in Ireland is also 16.

This possibility begs questions about the legitimacy of our current laws on consent, and about the influence of extra-territorial cultures and value systems,[14] with their own patriarchal hierarchies, which our criminal laws have no hope of influencing.[15] Perhaps most significantly, it also raises doubts about the communicative value of the criminal law, and its ability to establish nuanced and targeted criminal laws in the consciousness of the Irish public.

Responsibility for Wrongs and Culpability

Prendergast J's judgment offers an account of culpability in both morality and criminal responsibility, in which the consequences of actions are relevant to the blameworthiness of an individual's conduct.

Let me first deal with Prendergast J's claim regarding criminal culpability:

> [E]mbedded in the criminal law is the idea that the results of action matter for moral responsibility. Other things (especially *mens rea*) being equal, a murderer is more culpable than a person who attempted murder; the drunk-driver who caused death more culpable than the drunk-driver who didn't; the puncher whose victim suffered a broken jaw more culpable than the puncher who left only a bruise. In all these instances *mens rea* is only part of the explanation of the offender's criminal culpability.[16]

[13] The age of consent in Northern Ireland was lowered from 17 to 16 by the Sexual Offences (Northern Ireland) Order 2008 (SI 1769/08).

[14] I would like to thank Stephanie Lord and Andrea Mulligan for pointing out the influence of non-Irish media on popular teenage views of the age of consent in early drafts.

[15] See Catherine O'Sullivan's article, which also touches on this concern, 'Protecting Young People from Themselves: Reform of the Age of Consent Law in Ireland' (2009) 31 *Dublin University Law Journal* 386-411.

[16] Prendergast J's judgment, below, para 16.

On purely descriptive terms, it is beyond doubt that the criminal law holds people liable for consequences that they may not have intended, or even foreseen as a possibility. According to some, such as Gardner,[17] the normative content of *criminal* culpability, under the principle *actus non facit reum nisi sit rea* is as follows: once there is some cognitive fault or guilt accompanying an action, most, if not all, of the subsequent consequences from that initial 'guilty' act are tainted with culpability. As we see from constructive liability offences such as murder, unlawful act manslaughter and dangerous driving causing death, the criminal law can and does blame you, by holding you criminally liable for consequences, and punishing in relation to those consequences.

But just because the criminal law has evolved to blame you for these kinds of consequences, it does not follow, as might be read from Prendergast J's judgment,[18] that you are also morally blameworthy—and therefore deserving of retributive punishment (how the criminal law blames)—for those kinds of consequences. Though limited in space here, many ethical accounts[19] on the principle of retribution (whether carried out by the state, the community or, indeed, the victim) focus on the cognitive awareness of the wrongdoers in their actions, and the consequences of those actions. Under these accounts, to punish wrongdoers for consequences beyond what they anticipated is ethically illegitimate as it is fails to respect their agency, is disproportionate and undermines the communicative value in the criminal law.

Alternatively, others[20] argue that to blame and punish someone for unintended or unforeseen consequences is ethically illegitimate as it makes that blame and punishment dependent on outcome luck.[21] On these accounts, the murderer and the failed attempted murderer are identical in terms of culpability and their deserving blame. Both intended to kill; one was just unlucky in failing to achieve their shared aim (though their intended victim might not consider it bad luck).

For both these ethical understandings of culpability, intention and awareness are central to the kind of moral responsibility that leads to a legitimate response of public blame and punishment.

Yet even accepting this account of moral culpability, there is still a powerful intuitive sense that consequences do matter. In *CC*, a wrong has been committed against the 13-year-old girl. Even though she may not see it as a wrong, we have good reasons for viewing a 13-year-old child's having sex as wrong.[22] CC is responsible for this wrong, even if he did

[17] John Gardner, 'Rationality and the Rule of Law in Offences Against the Person' in John Gardner, *Offences and Defences: Selected Essays in the Philosophy of Criminal Law* (Oxford, Oxford University Press, 2007) 41.

[18] Prendergast has clarified—similarly to Gardner's 'Response to Critics' in *Offences and Defences* (above n 17)—that his argument is not that strict criminal liability reflects true morality but that it is, however, morally defensible to have strict liability. This point, I believe, represents a much broader dispute on the ethics and goals of the criminal law, which this commentary could not hope to address.

[19] See, eg, Andrew Ashworth, 'Criminal Justice and Deserved Sentences' [1989] *Criminal LawReview* 340; Andrew von Hirsch and Andrew Ashworth, *Proportionate Sentencing: Exploring the Principles* (Oxford, Oxford University Press, 2005); and, to a certain extent, Antony Duff, *Answering for Crime* (Oxford, Hart Publishing, 2009).

[20] Andrew Ashworth, 'Taking the Consequences' in Stephen Shute, John Gardner and Jeremy Horder (eds), *Action and Value in Criminal Law* (Oxford, Clarendon Press, 1993).

[21] For a different perspective on outcome luck, or moral luck, see Anthony Honoré, 'Responsibility and Luck' (1988) 104 *Law Quarterly Review* 530.

[22] Oberman, above n 4.

not think he was committing the wrong of having sexual intercourse with someone who was too young. Though, as I argue, CC is not *culpable* with regard to this wrong, he is still ethically implicated in the wrong; CC is still a *wrongdoer*, and a moral response is called for.

Take Prendergast J's account of culpability in relation to *CC*: 'A man in these circumstances ought to have appreciated the risk that the person was too young to consent to sex.'[23] This introduces an objective fault standard: what CC should have known, or should have known he was risking. But fault and the kind of moral responsibility involved in public blaming and punishment are not necessarily one and the same. Not all breaches of standards of behaviour (fault standards) are deserving of blame and punishment.

Take the offence of rape under section 2 of the Criminal Law (Rape) Act 1981:

> (1) A man commits rape if—
> (a) he has unlawful sexual intercourse with a woman who at the time of the intercourse does not consent to it, and
> (b) at that time he knows that she does not consent to the intercourse or he is reckless as to whether she does or does not consent to it.

Under this approach, a man may have engaged in sexual intercourse with a woman, where that woman was not consenting; but if that man believed she was consenting, and did not foresee that she was possibly not consenting, he is not guilty of rape.

It is important to recognise the inadequacies of our current criminal laws on sexual violence and concede, as Prendergast J's dissent implies we should, that section 2 rape is under-inclusive in terms of the conduct that it deems wrongful. Offences such as section 2 allow sexual wrongdoers to defend themselves with subjective beliefs regarding consent that may be objectively unreasonable. Or, more problematically, such offences allow in conceptions of consent that are the result of overarching and pervasive patriarchal conceptions about the sexual availability of women to men.

But even if the man had good objective grounds for believing that the woman was consenting (eg he asked at the outset, and she expressly consented, in circumstances that both he and she would not normally have considered oppressive), the woman in this case is still the victim of a wrong—a very serious wrong.

Now we can begin to see some of the moral contours of sexual violence. There may be cases of sexual violence where, due to a genuine and reasonable[24] mistake by the man, the woman is wronged. Alternatively, as was part of the case in *CC*, that wrongful mistake might be due to overarching patriarchal structural inequalities, resulting in the sexualisation and objectification of young women, which in turn inform societal understandings of consent and the sexual availability of young women.[25] Lastly, there are the most serious cases where the man knows, or is aware of, the risk that the woman is not consenting to the sexual intercourse.[26] In all these cases, the woman is wronged, and the man is ethically implicated in that wrong—he is *morally responsible* for the wrong. But the question we then need to ask

[23] Prendergast J's judgment, below, para 22.

[24] Where the reasonable standard reflects an understanding of the structural inequalities of a patriarchal society.

[25] See further Oberman, above n 4; and Cossins, above n 5.

[26] To be clear, this is not to say that sexual assault and rape that occurs in this context is somehow more 'real'. See further Louise Ellison and Vanessa Munro, 'Of "Normal Sex" and "Real Rape": Exploring The Use of Socio-Sexual Scripts in (Mock) Jury Deliberation' (2009) 18 *Social & Legal Studies* 291-312.

is how we, as a society and moral community, respond to each of these wrongs. Should we blame and punish an individual wrongdoer in these cases, or might we be laying all blame for societal failures on one person?

The wronged woman has, in all cases, a personal claim for accountability[27] against that man, for that wrong. She may also expect that we, as a society and a moral community, will facilitate her in seeking and achieving accountability for that wrong. For example, the common law provides a civil action under the law of tort. However, the typical remedial response of our private laws to sexual violence is problematic, as it conceptualises all wrongs as remediable through financial compensation—something that may demean or degrade the quality of the wrong suffered by that victim.[28] The law of tort does, however, have the benefit of being a public forum, through which the victim can achieve a form of accountability in full public view, which may help her sense of community vindication that she has indeed suffered a wrong that the community recognises. Alternatively, she might expect the state to support her in achieving personal accountability through a number of other, possibly more discrete means—such as a mediation process, or restorative justice.[29] Lastly, in some cases, a wronged woman might demand that the community itself holds the wrongdoer accountable through something like the criminal justice system, and relieve her of the burden of seeking personal accountability.[30]

What these examples show us is that there are different ways in which sexual wrongdoers can be held accountable. My intuition is that the desire to push the scope of criminal liability for wrongdoing beyond wrongdoing that was due to subjectively culpable behaviour, is premised on an assumption that the criminal law is the *only* mechanism for holding sexual wrongdoing to account. But is it morally legitimate, or instrumentally valuable, to pursue accountability for these different qualities of sexual wrongdoing through the criminal justice system?

Responses to Sexual Violence: The Efficacy and Legitimacy of the Punitive State

Regarding the moral legitimacy of using the criminal law, which publicly blames and punishes wrongdoing, to hold all these varying forms of wrongdoing to account, I am sceptical. In cases like *CC*, I do not believe it is fair to blame, punish and label as a sex offender, wrongdoers like CC, when their wrongdoing is the result of societal injustices and failures.

[27] My thinking on this has been influenced by Stephen Darwall's work on Moral Accountability, particularly *The Second-person Standpoint: Morality, Respect, and Accountability* (Cambridge, MA, Harvard University Press, 2006).

[28] See Nikki Godden, 'Claims in Tort for Rape: A Valuable Remedy or Damaging Strategy?' (2011) 22(2) *King's Law Journal* 157-82. Though some victims derive therapeutic value in pursuing civil claims, regardless of the quantum of compensation: see Bruce Feldthusen, 'The Civil Action for Sexual Battery: Therapeutic Jurisprudence' (1993) 25(2) *Ottawa Law Review* 203-35.

[29] Kathleen Daly, 'Different Ways of Conceptualizing Sex/Gender in Feminist Theory and their Implications for Criminology' (1997) 1 *Theoretical Criminology* 25-51.

[30] For a compelling normative account of why we should, as a society, help facilitate accountability for wrongdoing through the criminal justice system, see Sandra Marshall and Antony Duff, 'Criminalisation and Sharing Wrongs' (1998) 11 *Canadian Journal of Law and Jurisprudence* 7-22.

While CC did wrong, and contrary to Hardiman J's claims of 'mental innocence', due to those structural social injustices, may have been at fault in that wrongdoing, I believe that blaming and punishing him is a disproportionate (and arguably hypocritical) response by the state.

But I am also sceptical about the instrumental arguments offered by Prendergast J. He and others[31] rationalise these criminal offences as preventing older men from engaging in sexual intercourse with girls who are deemed vulnerable to sexual exploitation. So the core rationale for this offence is the prevention of sexual exploitation of a girl who is vulnerable to such exploitation by reason of her age. First, I would question the implicit assumption that a law including an honest and reasonable belief *mens rea* component would not achieve the same deterrent effect. It is also not beyond the capability of the Oireachtas to draft criminal offences, containing subjective fault components, to target the specific kinds of sexual exploitation of most concern[32]—such as grooming, or where the abuser is in a position of authority over the child. Such fault components are an essential means of controlling illegitimate use of the criminal justice system as a means of accountability for wrongdoing. Though Prendergast J's dissent is tightly constrained in its scope for structural change to the criminal law, dispensing with such controls on punitive state power will do little to benefit victims and survivors of sexual violence, while at the same time increasing the potential for counterproductive and even destructive deployment of the criminal justice system.

At its rare best, the criminal law reflects, and aims to protect, commonly-held core social values.[33] At worst, it is often an instrument for oppression, marginalisation and disempowerment of vulnerable minorities.[34] In the context of sexual violence, our criminal justice system can provide state and public vindication for the survivor (though such vindication might be achieved more easily by other, non-punitive means). It can protect the public by controlling the offender, and ideally rehabilitating him. But, far more frequently, it fails victims and survivors by effectively monopolising accountability in a manner that alienates victims from the process, while confining that accountability to a limited number of cases.[35]

Though well beyond the capacity of Prendergast J's dissent or the jurisdiction of the Irish courts, it is also possible for the Oireachtas to provide structures, and a more caring culture among all criminal justice agencies, that minimise the retraumatisation of victims of child exploitation in the criminal justice system.

Empirical evidence showing that creating criminal law in any of its guises—ideal, flawed or perverse—ushers in dramatic social and cultural value changes, is hard to come by. Leaving open the question of whether instrumental justifications for the criminal law generally are morally desirable, I argue it is particularly morally dubious to use punitive state power

[31] See McLachlin J's judgment in *Hess and Nguyen v The Queen* [1990] 2 SCR 906.

[32] See the Rape Crisis Network of Ireland's 2006 submissions to the Oireachtas Joint Committee on Child Protection, at www.oireachtas.ie/documents/committees29thdail/child_protection_submissions/Rape_Crisis_Network_Ireland.pdf.

[33] For an idealised vision of criminal justice, see John Brathwaite and Philip Pettit, *Not Just Deserts: A Republican Theory of Criminal Justice* (Oxford, Clarendon, 1990); or more recently Antony Duff, *Answering for Crime* (Oxford, Hart Publishing, 2007).

[34] For one of many examples of this, see Michelle Alexander's outstanding *The New Jim Crow: Mass Incarceration in the Age of Colourblindness* (New York, The New Press, 2010).

[35] See, eg, attrition rates for prosecutions of sexual offending in Hannah McGee, Rebecca Garavan, Mairead de Barra, Joanne Byrne and Ronán Conroy et al, *The SAVI Report: Sexual Abuse and Violence in Ireland* (Dublin, Liffey Press, 2002).

in the form of strict liability for serious criminal offences, unless there are very strong empirical arguments to support its efficacy. If, like Prendergast J, you want to invite an instrumental justification for serious criminal liability without proof of subjective fault, I suggest the empirical burden is on you to show it works better than offences that require proof of subjective fault.

Conclusion

If we are concerned about moral accountability for sexual wrongdoing, I have argued that there are ways of holding wrongdoing to account that reflect the nature of that wrongdoing but which are also sceptical of the capacity of punitive state power to address complex structural inequalities (patriarchal, ethno-cultural and class-based)—inequalities the same punitive state entrenches and exacerbates. I have also argued that the criminal law, which has included strict liability sexual offences for decades, does not appear to be very good, or better than the alternative ways of structuring criminal offences, at achieving the kind of protection it claims to be aiming for. I argue that not only are these strict offences disproportionate in that they criminalise and punish those who possess little or no culpability, but they are also disproportionate in their instrumental inadequacy.

While Prendergast J's dissent was necessarily limited in scope, this broader critical appraisal has sought to demonstrate how removing our criminal law's important, if flawed, fault-based constraints on punitive state power in pursuit of a better feminist outcome, may lead to greater structural inequalities and injustices.

As the protest slogan goes, we would do far better to concentrate our efforts on teaching men about patriarchal inequality, respecting sexual power dynamics from a young age, and not to be rapists. The criminal law has a role to play in this—but it is limited, and it should be limited. To rely so heavily on the patriarchal coercive state is to fall into the same, and I believe flawed, thinking of carceral feminism.

C.C., Applicant v Ireland, The Attorney General and The Director of Public Prosecutions, Respondents

[2005] IESC 48 & [2006] IESC 33, [S.C. Nos. 357 and 358 of 2004]

Supreme Court	12th July, 2005
Supreme Court	23rd May, 2006

Prendergast J. 23rd May, 2006

1 The applicant challenges the constitutionality of the offence of unlawful carnal knowledge in section 1(1) of the Criminal Law (Amendment) Act 1935. This offence is commonly known as statutory rape and is committed by a male who has sex with a child who is female and under the age of 15. A separate offence applies where the female is under 17. The applicant has been charged with the first offence after allegedly having sex with a 13 year old on a number of occasions. The applicant asked the court to interpret section 1(1) of the 1935 Act as providing scope for a mistaken belief in the child's age to exculpate. A majority of this Court held on 12 July 2005 that the statute does not permit this interpretation. Given this holding, the applicant's alternative case now applies: he submits that the offence is unconstitutional because it is a strict liability offence that criminalises a male who had sex with an underage female where he did not know her true age and believed she was older.

2 A majority of this Court concludes that the applicant's challenge must succeed. I dissent. Hardiman J, for the majority, says that section 1(1) of the 1935 Act criminalises the innocent, that it uses one group (men such as the applicant) purely as a means to an end of protecting another group (young females) from harms associated with underage sex. This is an incorrect characterisation of the offence. Section 1(1) of the 1935 Act, while clearly far from perfect in a number of respects, is not unconstitutional. The offence does not stray outside the constitutionally permissible scope for the legislature to choose and set the mental elements in a criminal offence where the offence can plausibly be said to help protect vulnerable people and where the offence does not capture morally innocent persons.

The factual and procedural background

3 The applicant was charged with four counts contrary to section 1(1) of the Criminal Law (Amendment) Act 1935. The alleged offending took place between 20 July and 16 August 2001 and involved the same child. At the time this child was aged 13 and the applicant was aged 18. The applicant admitted to gardaí that he had sex with the child on several occasions but said he believed she was aged 16, that she had told him this was her age, and that she had, by sending him a text message, initiated the meeting which led to the first occasion of sex.

4 Prior to facing trial at the Circuit Criminal Court, the applicant obtained leave to seek a declaration that section 1(1) was inconsistent with the Constitution. The High Court refused to grant this declaration ([2004] I.E.H.C. 288). On appeal to the Supreme Court, as noted, this Court refused to declare that an offence of mistake of age was available for

the offence ([2005] I.E.S.C. 48). A majority of this Court held that the presumption of *mens rea* was rebutted by the clear intention of the legislature that the offence be one for which mistake of age would not exculpate. This intention was clear from the legislative choice in reconstituting offences from the Criminal Law (Amendment) Act 1885 not to include provision for mistake of age for this offence in the 1935 Act while it did for another offence in section 4 of the same Act.

The applicant's standing

5 Irish constitutional law practice requires applicants to have standing in order to impugn the constitutionality of a law and the facts of the applicant's case must supply the factual premises in the argument establishing the law's unconstitutionality (the *jus tertii* principle; *Cahill v. Sutton* [1980] I.R. 269, 280). An applicant is not entitled to rely on the circumstances of a hypothetical third party against whom the law works an injustice.

6 The applicant in the present case has standing because he faces trial for the offence contrary to the statutory provision that he impugns. The facts in this case—which have not been proven in the context of a criminal trial but which were averred in the applicant's affidavit grounding judicial review proceedings in the High Court—suggest that he would still be guilty of another offence even if the impugned offence is invalid: that in section 2 of the 1935 Act, as amended, since, on the supposed facts, he had sex with a child under 17 and he believed the person he had sex with was under 17. This is a different offence, carrying a lesser maximum penalty. If section 1(1) is inconsistent with the Constitution, section 2(1) may also be an invalid law but the applicant would face a *jus tertii* problem in making the case against section 2(1). Even in respect of section 1(1), the applicant's factual scenario is not the strongest scenario for showing how the offence constitutes an unjust criminalisation. The applicant asserts that his mistake of fact was both honest and reasonable. Even if genuine, a question remains whether the mistake was reasonable in the circumstances and, given the offence, this would be a matter for a jury to decide. Be that as it may, the Court has committed to assessing the constitutionality of section 1(1) of the 1935 Act and my dissenting opinion will address the substance of the arguments against it.

The impugned offence

7 Section 1(1) of the 1935 Act reads:-

> "Any person who unlawfully and carnally knows any girl under the age of fifteen years shall be guilty of a felony, and shall be liable on conviction thereof to penal servitude for life or for any term not less than three years or to imprisonment for any term not exceeding two years."

The elements of this offence for the prosecution to prove beyond a reasonable doubt are that the defendant engaged in sexual intercourse with a girl and that this girl was under 15 years. Lack of consent on the part of the victim is not a required proof for this offence. The young age of the victim operates as a proxy for a lack of capacity to consent in the way needed for lawfully permissible sexual relations. Accordingly, the offence is appropriately called statutory *rape*. This Court confirmed in *C.C. v. Ireland* [2005] I.E.S.C. 48 that the prosecution does not have to prove that the defendant knew the true age of the victim, or believed that she was any particular age, and that there is no mistake of age defence. For this offence the defendant's belief, or lack of belief, in respect of the victim's age is irrelevant in establishing his criminal liability.

8 The offence is seen as one of strict liability, that is, having no mental elements. It is inaccurate, however, to say it has no *mens rea* elements whatsoever because there is an implicit *mens rea* of sorts in respect of the conduct of sexual intercourse: such conduct must be done at least knowingly in order for liability to apply. This observation is not simply based on the archaic language of the statute in describing sexual intercourse with the phrase 'carnally knows'. It is an observation that, given the nature of sexual intercourse, it is implicit that it was engaged in intentionally or knowingly by the male in order for liability to apply. There *is* a *mens rea* element corresponding to the *actus reus* element of the conduct of sexual intercourse. But there is no *mens rea* element corresponding to the *actus reus* element of the child's age. Liability in respect of the age element is strict. Accordingly, the offence may be called one of strict liability and it would be misleading to say that it is a strict liability offence only in a technical or trivial sense of lacking full correspondence between *actus reus* and *mens rea*. The age element of the offence is of key moral importance and it is highly significant that it has no corresponding *mens rea* proof.

9 The applicant submits that the unlawful carnal knowledge offence criminalises the 'mentally innocent' and as such offends the constitutional protections of the liberty and dignity of individuals. It is also contended that a criminal trial for this offence is not a trial in due course of law. The crime offends these constitutional principles, the applicant submits, because a defendant, on the basis of circumstances as he believed them to be, may have acted entirely lawfully and yet be found guilty of this offence. His state of belief as to the age of the girl is irrelevant to proof and there is no scope for him to avail of exculpation, no matter how plausible or understandable it was for him to have thought that he was engaging in permissible sexual relations with a partner over the age of consent. The impugned offence carries very high potential penalties and it is an extremely stigmatic offence.

The Constitution's control of substantive criminal law

10 Article 38.1 requires trial in due course of law. The courts of Ireland have long insisted on a robust set of procedural protections for accused persons. The Constitution additionally protects a range of specific rights and freedoms and this means that the criminalisation of certain types of conduct and certain forms of criminal offence are off limits to the Oireachtas. *King v. Attorney General* [1981] I.R. 233 established that offences must not be vague and uncertain in their ambit and that criminalisation must not lend itself to arbitrary enforcement. The form and substance of criminal offences, as well as criminal processes, are subject to constitutional review. The constitutional protections are not absolute: in pursuit of a legitimate legislative aim, a constitutional right or protection may be proportionately restricted and some constitutional concepts, such as trial in due course of law, contain reasonable compromise and limitation within them.

11 The impugned offence in the present case restricts sexual conduct. The applicant faces difficulty in identifying a specific right in the Constitution that is being infringed. In the present case, in identifying the impugned offence's inconsistency with the Constitution, Hardiman J says:-

> "I cannot regard a provision which criminalises and exposes to a maximum sentence of life imprisonment a person without mental guilt as respecting the liberty or the dignity of the individual or as meeting the obligation imposed on the State by Article 40.3.1° of the Constitution:- 'The State shall, in particular, by its laws protect as best it may from unjust attack and, in the case of injustice done, vindicate the life, person, good name, and property rights of every citizen.'"

This characterises the offence as capturing 'a person without mental guilt'—elsewhere referred to as the 'mentally innocent'—which means that an *innocent* person may be convicted of this offence, such is its definition. Imprisoning the innocent—that is, a person who did not in fact commit a crime—is undeniably offensive to the constitutional principles of dignity and liberty, holding trials only in due course of law, and some of the rights under Article 40.3. I will explain later in my judgment why saying that the offence criminalises an innocent, in the sense of person who is morally blameless, is a mischaracterisation, but first I make an observation about the majority judgment. The majority judgment elides the distinction between, on the one hand, a person who is imprisoned for an offence which the person did not actually commit and, on the other hand, a person imprisoned for committing an offence (where there is no reasonable doubt that person's conduct has matched the offence definition) that ought not, constitutionally speaking, be an offence in the first place. With this elision Hardiman J avoids the burden of explaining how it is that the Constitution controls the scope of criminalisation and the substance of offences apart from the areas of specific rights such as freedom of expression. The majority in the present case take a huge step in Irish constitutional law in striking down an offence for being a strict liability offence but do not show or explain how the Constitution permits this development. In the following passages I will take on the burden that the majority avoided in explaining how the Constitution controls the substance of offences. My aim is not to shore up the majority conclusion that the impugned offence is inconsistent with the Constitution—which I dissent from—but to contribute towards establishing a consistent framework for constitutional review of offences in Irish law. I will mention three constitutional values—liberty, privacy, and the presumption of innocence—as potential bases for constitutionally reviewing the impugned offence.

12 *A general liberty protection*: From provisions such as Article 40.3, a broad view of the Constitution, and cases such as *King v. Attorney General* there emerges a general constitutional liberty value that includes sexual autonomy and liberty to engage in sexual relations. The Oireachtas does not have unrestricted discretion to criminalise acts or activities simply because they are not directly covered by specific enumerated or unenumerated constitutional rights. It is notoriously difficult to formulate principles of legitimate criminalisation to uphold this general liberty value. Irish constitutional law does, however, contain the principle that people cannot—absent emergency conditions or specific textual basis in the Constitution—be kept in custody solely as a means

of preventing a future crime. This was the holding in *O'Callaghan v. Attorney General* [1966] I.R. 502. When criminal punishment includes imprisonment, it therefore must be, in part, desert-based: only those who are morally deserving of it may be imprisoned and punishment must be proportionate to wrongdoing. Again, it is difficult to identify a general principle explaining moral desert for punishment but modern criminal law expresses the idea that criminal liability must reflect culpability. This idea undergirds one of the holdings in *Re Article 26 and Employment Equality Bill 1996* [1997] 2 I.R. 321, a case I will discuss later. I will return to this culpability principle in reviewing the impugned offence after first mentioning two other potential ways of explaining how the Irish Constitution limits the content of the impugned offence.

13 *The right to privacy*: In *McGee v. Attorney General* [1974] I.R. 284 the Supreme Court struck down an offence that prohibited the importation of certain contraceptive items. The Court in *McGee* concluded that the offence breached the right to marital privacy, which was held to be protected by the Constitution despite not being expressly listed in the Constitution's text. In *Norris v. Attorney General* [1984] I.R. 36 the plaintiff was unsuccessful in challenging the constitutionality of the criminalisation of certain sexual conduct between consenting male adults. The dissenting judgments of Henchy and McCarthy JJ provided accounts of how such criminalisation encroached on the plaintiff's right to privacy. *McGee* and the dissents in *Norris* provide the grounds for articulating a constitutional right to privacy that includes the freedom to engage in consensual sexual practices. Hence, the Oireachtas must respect individuals' right to privacy when enacting offences, such as those impugned in *McGee*, *Norris*, and the present case, that serve to criminalise or inhibit sexual conduct. These cases relate to the right to privacy in different ways. The impugned offence in *Norris* directly criminalised consensual sexual activity among adults; in *McGee* the criminalisation, as shown in the circumstances of the case, had a powerful inhibition on consensual sexual activity between adults; while the present case, unlike *Norris* but like *McGee*, does not criminalise consensual sexual activity (on the understanding, which is not questioned, that underage sex is, by its nature, not consensual) but may inhibit consensual sexual activity between persons over the age of consent; in the present case, where there is uncertainty as to age.

14 *The presumption of innocence*: An alternative route to open up the impugned offence to constitutional review is to develop the presumption of innocence, which is, according to *O'Leary v. Attorney General* [1993] 1 I.R. 102; [1995] 1 I.R. 254 and other cases, located in Article 38.1 of the Constitution. The presumption of innocence is a procedural protection; its most apparent practical embodiment is that the onus is on the prosecution to prove all the ingredients of an offence beyond a reasonable doubt in order for a defendant to be found guilty of the offence. There is, however, judicial and academic opinion in favour of expanding the presumption of innocence to limit the substance of criminal offences as well as criminal procedures. On this view, a strict liability offence is potentially unconstitutional for the reason that it offends the presumption of innocence. Strict liability is the absence of culpability requirements and without culpability a person is arguably innocent.

15 These three potential routes to explaining the Constitution's control of the substance of an offence are neither exhaustive nor mutually exclusive. The three I have mentioned are (1) a general liberty protection, (2) the right to privacy, and (3) a substantive presumption of innocence protection. The first has the advantage of being the simplest; of the three it needs the fewest concepts and steps to get from Irish constitutional law history to reviewing the present offence. The remaining analysis, conducted though the culpability principle, applies regardless of which starting point is taken.

Culpability and mens rea

16 A manifestation of the culpability principle is the featuring of *mens rea* elements in criminal offences. It is said that *actus non facit reum nisi mens sit rea* (the act is not guilty unless the mind also be guilty) and the expectation is that an offence definition will have *actus reus* and *mens rea* elements. The offence definition will specify mental states possessed by the offender to accompany the acts or conduct proscribed. It is a mistake, however, to see *mens rea* requirements as exhausting the requirements of the culpability principle. First, an offence may specify a full set of *mens rea* elements yet it may still be an unacceptable criminalisation for the reason that it renders criminally liable a person lacking culpability. The offence definition may fail to reflect any real moral wrong. Second, certain conditions, as specified in the range of criminal defences such as self-defence and duress that are not negations of *mens rea*, make a defendant less culpable independent of *mens rea*. Third, the *actus reus* elements of an offence may, on their own, reflect culpability. For instance, embedded in the criminal law is the idea that the results of action matter for moral responsibility. Other things (especially *mens rea*) being equal, a murderer is more culpable than a person who attempted murder; the drunk-driver who caused death more culpable than the drunk-driver who didn't; the puncher whose victim suffered a broken jaw more culpable than the puncher who left only a bruise. In all these instances *mens rea* is only part of the explanation of the offender's criminal culpability. The traditional *mens rea* elements—that is, the cognitive states of intention, knowledge and recklessness—do not have a monopoly on the law's reflection of moral desert. These cognitive states are best seen as proxies for a deeper moral culpability or as partial constituents of culpability. The *actus reus* and *mens rea* elements are useful analytical tools in the playing out of a criminal trial. They help coordinate the prosecution proofs, the defence's strategy, the judge deciding whether there is a case to answer and charging the jury. But, again, criminal culpability—attempting to suitably reflect moral culpability—is not constituted exclusively by *mens rea* elements.

17 In assessing the constitutionality of an offence by reference to the culpability principle, the conclusion cannot be based purely on the presence or absence of *mens rea* elements. In particular, a correspondence principle that looks for *mens rea* elements to line up and match *actus reus* elements is not a constitutionally entrenched principle notwithstanding that it may in effect guide the interpretation of offences, as in *People (DPP) v. Murray* [1977] I.R. 360. The correspondence principle is not maintained at many points in criminal law. Murder, all types of manslaughter, various assault and driving offences, among other offences, lack full correspondence between *actus reus*

and *mens rea* elements. Doctrines of intoxication and secondary liability depart from correspondence. We must look at the overall moral culpability—or lack of it—represented in the offence. Some things are serious moral wrongs even when the author did not mean to do them. That they did not mean it is another way of expressing their lack of intention or advertent recklessness or knowledge of wrongdoing. Some mistakes, because of the context, are morally blameworthy and suitable for criminalisation.

Strict liability, constructive liability, statutory rape, and mistakes

18 Strict liability may mean simply departure from correspondence between *actus reus* and *mens rea*. Alternatively, strict liability refers to an offence for which there is apparently no *mens rea* whatsoever. It is difficult to find such an offence. As noted above, unlawful carnal knowledge carries an implicit *mens rea* element in respect of the conduct of sexual intercourse. The specific conduct must have been engaged in knowingly or intentionally. However, liability is strict in respect of the crucial circumstance of the victim's age. There is a missing *mens rea* element to correspond to the *actus reus* element of the victim's young age; on the first meaning of strict liability above, unlawful carnal knowledge is a strict liability offence.

19 Strict liability in the sense of a missing *mens rea* element might or might not take the description of constructive liability. The common law offence of unlawful and dangerous act manslaughter—also known as constructive manslaughter—illustrates constructive liability and is also an offence of strict liability in this sense. For unlawful act manslaughter the defendant needs no *mens rea* corresponding to the causing of death element of the offence, he or she only needs the *mens rea* for the underlying offence, such as an assault. Liability for manslaughter is constructed on the basis of the less serious unlawful act that led to death. Unlawful act manslaughter facilitates very harsh attributions of criminal liability, for example, in cases of single punches leading to death (for example, *R v. Holzer* [1968] V.R. 481). The defendant's low culpability in such a case can be reflected at sentencing stage but the label of manslaughter remains. Notice, however, that in this instance, while the labelling is harsh, it does not disregard the culpability principle as I have described it above; that is, as a principle sensitive to the overall culpability and not simply equating *mens rea* elements with culpability. The defendant intentionally or recklessly engaged in activity that carried the risk of the harm that eventuated. All that is missing in terms of *mens rea* elements is the specific foresight or advertence on the part of the defendant to the risk of this harm. He or she did not realise what might or ought to have been realised. Such a defendant may attract sympathy but is not faultless; he or she had fair opportunity to avoid the wrongdoing and can be said to possess moral culpability for failing to do so.

20 The impugned unlawful carnal knowledge offence in the present case is of the same structure as unlawful act manslaughter in that one of its main elements carries strict liability. The question is whether it also has the feature of constructive liability, for if it does, this goes some distance to showing that unlawful carnal knowledge criminalises culpable conduct and not—as the applicant submits—innocent conduct. This is an important question because, as the applicant would contend, the *mens rea* element that is present—knowingly engaging in sexual intercourse with a female—is not truly a *mens rea* element because such activity is *prima facie* lawful. This contrasts—the

applicant argues—with the underlying activity in a case of unlawful act manslaughter: the underlying activity may be a punch or kick or shove, something that is by itself *prima facie* unlawful.

21 Sexual intercourse, as legally defined, can be understood in the abstract. The common law defines it as penetration of a woman's vagina by a man with his penis. This definition persisted in statutory codification of the relevant offences in Ireland. To morally evaluate an instance of sexual intercourse, however, more information is needed than simply that sexual intercourse, in the abstract sense, took place. Sexual intercourse may be consented to, in which case it is entirely lawful and permissible. Alternatively, sexual intercourse may have occurred but it was not consented to, in which case a violation has occurred, a violation that is a grave wrong in itself and is known to bring serious harms. Before it can be said whether engaging in sexual intercourse in a certain instance was morally acceptable or morally blameworthy it is essential to know about the circumstances and the most important circumstance is the presence or absence of consent. In this way, consent is morally and legally transformative. Powerful critiques of consent in this transformative role have been made: theorists worry about consent being inauthentic due to societal pressures and culture and about instances of consensual but unwelcome sexual relations that go unregulated and unrecognised. A workable legal regime must draw a line between permissible and impermissible sex and consent remains a leading concept available for this.

22 Unlawful carnal knowledge is a rape offence on the understanding that the young age of the victim means she does not have the capacity to consent in the way needed for permissible sexual intercourse. That the child under the age of consent apparently willingly engaged in sexual intercourse, or that her own report on the matter might be that she agreed to the conduct or encouraged it, does not change its classification as criminal; it was not in law an instance of consensual sexual intercourse. This legal classification tracks a moral assessment of the situation albeit highly imperfectly since the law changes completely from impermissible sex to permissible sex suddenly on the occasion of a particular birthday. A moral assessment would be more hazy and graduated, taking into account the young person's actual maturity, among other aspects. The law operates a bright line rule of age and people can in advance know where they stand in law and structure their activity in light of it. The law may be criticised that it draws the line at an inappropriate age and that it ought to have more grades of liability—the impugned law is part of a scheme that has only two grades: victim under 15 and victim under 17. The scheme also makes no adjustment in liability depending on the defendant's age, how close he might have been in maturity to the victim, the absence of exploitation, and so on. These are serious shortcomings in the impugned law. Nevertheless, the law, in criminalising sex with children below a certain age, reflects a strong moral norm against such conduct on a par with that against rape of adults. Sex with children and sex with adults who do not consent or who lack capacity to consent, whether through extreme intoxication or mental disability, are in morality, as reflected in law, seriously wrongful events. For this reason alone sex is inherently risky: on the sole basis of whether one party is truly consenting, sex can be either morally acceptable (and, potentially, an intrinsically valuable and positive experience for all parties) or a grave moral wrong. The risk will vary greatly depending on the circumstances. The applicant's case involved him, aged 18, engaging in sex with a female child aged 13 but

he did not know that she was only 13. He believed she was 16. She told him this was her age. Apart from the fact that this age is still under the age of consent (and therefore legally non-consensual sex on the applicant's view of circumstances) these facts reveal the risk that was run in the circumstances. A man in these circumstances ought to have appreciated the risk that the person was too young to consent to sex.

23 The analogies with unlawful act manslaughter in showing the constructive liability aspect of the impugned offence are clear. In each case the defendant embraces acts or activities that carry within them the risk of the harm or wrong that eventuates. It was a culpable choice even if the defendant did not appreciate the risk. Assuming no special cognitive deficiencies, the defendant had capacity to appreciate and avoid the risk and the non-exercise of this capacity is culpable. For both manslaughter and unlawful carnal knowledge there is generally fair opportunity to avoid the wrongdoing.

24 The applicant characterises his case as one of mistake where the mistake was honest and reasonable. As noted, these claims are untested in the appropriate context of a jury trial, but I will assume that the applicant truly believed the person was 16 and therefore was mistaken—a mistake by definition being honest—about her age. It is said that the mistake was a reasonable one. In this type of scenario the factors suggesting the mistake was reasonable—as endorsed in Hardiman J's judgment—include the idea that the female child may have looked older than she was, that she was at a venue where only adults socialise, that she confidently asserted her age as higher than her true age. Such analysis leaves out countervailing reasons to believe the person was younger; there may, for instance, arise in conversation warning signs that the person is younger than she says. I leave this observation aside to make the more important general point that simply because the man in this scenario had multiple uncontradicted reasons for believing the person was a certain age does not make his acting on this belief reasonable in the relevant sense to show a lack of moral blameworthiness in having sex with an underage person. Focusing on the victim's age, there may have been a reasonable basis for a false belief, but this does not establish that it was reasonable for the man to proceed with sexual intercourse. The thing he is answerable for is having sex with a 13 year old, not just that a certain belief as to her age formed in his mind. Hardiman J's comments on the scenario proceed as if it is just the latter question and in doing so mischaracterises the applicant's scenario. It is one thing to sell an 18-rated DVD or even tobacco to an underage child, mistaken as to age; it is another to have sex with the child. Given the significance of the conduct one should, morally speaking, proceed with caution and refrain from proceeding if uncertainties cannot be addressed. This is why I reject the contention, which the majority accepts, that the applicant's prosecution amounts to criminalising 'a person without mental guilt'. It has thus not been established that the offence breaches the culpability principle.

The balancing of interests

25 Constitutional review of legislative provisions typically proceeds in a two-step process to potentially reach a declaration of unconstitutionality. First, the plaintiff must establish that the impugned law *prima facie* breaches a constitutional right or imperative. If successful at this first step, the plaintiff must then establish that the breach is not

justified. In recent decades this second step is conducted with reference to a proportionality test. It means that only disproportionate encroachments on constitutional rights, measured against the legislative aim behind the encroaching law, will render the legislation constitutionally invalid. This reflects the idea that constitutional protections are not absolute. In effect, the Irish courts ask whether the impugned law can be rationalised. The Court does not undertake wholesale evaluation of the true effectiveness of the legislation. That would require empirical research and it is the responsibility ultimately of the legislature to reform sub-optimal or ineffective laws. The Court's job as in the present case is to assess for constitutionality.

26 The majority in the present case see the applicant as passing both of the two steps. I explained above why Hardiman J's majority judgment in this case does not convincingly show that the first step is satisfied. Assuming, however, that the first step is indeed satisfied I will now show why the majority's conclusion at the second step is unconvincing. Hardiman J says the impugned offence contains no balance, that it wholly instrumentalises young men in pursuit of the protection of female children. He calls McLachlin J's rationalisation in *R v. Hess; R v. Nguyen* [1990] 2 S.C.R. 906 of the equivalent statutory rape offence in Canada 'utilitarian' by which he means to denigrate it.

27 McLachlin J's account proceeds: female children need protection from men and boys who would seek to have sex with them. Female children also need protection from themselves in the sense that they—because of their immaturity—may not make the best choices in their interactions with men and in their activities in growing up. If men are relieved of the responsibility to make sure that a female is over the age of consent before engaging in sex—and having a *mens rea* as to age proof for unlawful carnal knowledge would, to an extent, relieve them of this responsibility and motivate them to 'ask no questions' about age—then the instances of underage sex might be higher compared to a strict liability regime where men are put on notice that they may pay the price in terms of criminal punishment for their mistakes as to a female's age. McLachlin J refers to the term 'jailbait' as evidence of a culture that learns from a strict liability regime. The use of strict liability aims to deter instances of underage sex specifically by demanding of men not simply that they avoid having sex with female children who they know or suspect to be underage but that they simply avoid having sex with underage females full stop. Trial and punishment of men who fail in this regard reinforces the deterrent effect the more so when such punishment seems harsh.

29 Some features of this rationale: it involves a balancing of interests in that there is conceivably a chilling effect on potential sexual relations between persons who are not underage. This is regrettable but may also be an acceptable cost next to the harms and wrongs of underage sex. Assuming the criminal processes work soundly, no criminal punishment is applied to a man who has not a serious case to answer in morality: namely, that he had sex with an underage female. While such punishment in large part aims to have the effect of preventing future wrongs through deterrence, no innocent person is merely instrumentalised in pursuit of this aim. A theory of negative retributivism is respected in that the punishment is desert-based as well as deterrent-seeking.

30 Nonetheless, it should be recognised that the impugned offence sweeps more broadly than it should in terms of moral desert. It lumps boyfriends of underage

females—boyfriends who may be the same age as or younger than the victim—with sexual predators who target children. It is not a satisfactory answer to this problem to say that flexibility in sentencing allows for different punishments or that prosecutorial discretion can avoid harshness. Clearly the criminalisation could be more precise in reflecting culpability. The merits and demerits of peer exemptions and gender neutral criminalisation are subject to ongoing debate but a lack of consensus about what the substantive law ought to ideally be is no reason to valorise the existing law. I make two observations. First, the culpability principle is a flexible principle. There is no agreed metric for culpability and criminal law would face practical difficulties with an ever-increasing multiplicity of offence gradations in search of precisely reflecting moral culpability. Laws must draw lines. Second, I repeat that under the Constitution of Ireland the courts require right-encroaching legislation to be merely rationally related and proportionate to legitimate legislative aims in order to pass constitutional muster. This is so notwithstanding references to 'minimal impairment' of a right in Irish cases such as *Heaney v. Ireland* [1994] 3 I.R. 593, which quote the proportionality test from Canadian case law—principally *R v. Chalk* [1990] 3 S.C.R. 1303. The key observation is that under the Constitution the Oireachtas has a range of options in the criminalisation of underage sex that manage to respect the culpability principle. The impugned strict liability offence manages to respect the culpability principle in a minimal way. Alternative schemes of full *mens rea* and/or mistake of fact defences respect the culpability principle in greater degree. But the judicially enforced constitutional control of criminal law is not about the optimisation of criminal liability—that is the task for the Oireachtas—but about upholding side constraints or limits on criminalisation. Furthermore, the culpability principle is not the only important consideration in criminal law.

More on the impugned offence's place in Irish criminal law

31 *Analogies from driving offences*: Counsel for the respondents claim that the impugned offence is not anomalous in Irish law, citing an example of a driver of a vehicle who causes a death as a result of his or her vehicle's brakes failing. Suppose a person is driving in an objectively dangerous manner but the person honestly believes his or her driving is not dangerous. Such a person may be guilty of the offence of dangerous driving and if the driving causes a death he or she may be liable for the offence of causing death by dangerous driving. That the driver honestly believed he or she was driving in an acceptable or non-dangerous manner is irrelevant to the question of his or her criminal liability. This is the central holding of *R v. Spurge* [1961] 2 Q.B. 205, which is the case cited in the majority judgment in an apparent effort to gloss over the very thing that the case held. The driver's belief may have relevance for sentencing, just as a defendant's belief that an underage child was the age of consent or older may be relevant to sentence. The reference to dangerous driving joins my comments about unlawful act manslaughter above in showing the featuring of strict liability in the impugned offence is not unique among serious offences in Irish law.

32 *Serious offences and regulatory offences*: The High and Supreme Courts, in *Maguire v. Shannon Regional Fisheries Board* [1994] 3 I.R. 580 and *Shannon Regional Fisheries Board v. Cavan Co Council* [1996] 3 I.R. 267, upheld convictions for strict liability

water pollution offences. It has been argued that strict liability offences are tolerable for regulatory offences such as water pollution that are, as such, not truly criminal, but the same strict liability is not permissible for serious offences that carry high stigma such as statutory rape. Hardiman J's judgment in the present case makes clear it applies to serious offences only. I make two comments.

33 First, as already shown, there are numerous serious offences that feature centrally in Irish criminal law that involve strict liability like that of the impugned offence. In addition to explaining why the applicant's case does not imply that the courts were incorrect in the water pollution cases, the majority's position must also account for why offences such as manslaughter are not unconstitutional or else recognise that *prima facie* unconstitutionality features at quite a number of points in Irish criminal law. Second, the position of the majority would need a principled explanation why strict liability—if not constitutionally acceptable in serious offences—is acceptable for regulatory offences. If strict liability really does criminalise the mentally innocent, how can the Constitution tolerate this for regulatory offences simply because the punishments carry lesser maximum prison sentences but are still of the same kind (that is, fines and imprisonment)? It is convenient to draw this distinction between serious and regulatory offences because it minimises the implications of granting the applicant's declaration in the present case.

34 *The Employment Equality Bill case's application to the present case*: The Supreme Court in *Re Article 26 and Employment Equality Bill 1996* [1997] 2 I.R. 321 in effect recognised a culpability principle restraining the substance of criminal law in Ireland. The case helps show why the present applicant's case is arguable. In the *Employment Equality Bill case* the Court said an offence of vicarious liability that made an employer liable to criminal punishment on the basis of certain proscribed behaviour of his or her employees would not be compatible with the Constitution. Like strict liability, vicarious liability gives rise to concern because it apparently facilitates a person's criminal guilt in the absence of culpability. The *Employment Equality Bill case*, however, is of limited additional relevance to the applicant's case. Notably, the very thing that is missing from the present impugned offence, which the applicant says should be present—a mistake defence—was present in the vicarious liability offence in the *Employment Equality Bill case*. The Court in the *Employment Equality Bill case* did not explain why the availability of this defence could not save the offence but the result shows vicarious liability to be different in a crucial respect from the kind of strict liability in the present case. The conclusion is that strict liability offences (of the kind in issue in the present case) can be more readily defended in constitutional terms than vicarious liability offences such as in the *Employment Equality Bill case* because a mistake defence will not save a vicarious liability offence but it will, by the applicant's own lights, save a strict liability offence.

Conclusion

35 Constitutional review of legislation is not about assessing laws' optimality, all things considered. It is about assessing whether laws fall outside constitutionally permissible bounds. The impugned offence in this case is clearly imperfect in reflecting moral desert

and in pursuing a rationalised aim of protecting children from having sex before they are mature enough to choose to do so. Compelling arguments can be mustered in support of legislative reform. But the arguments as to the offence's inconsistency with the Constitution do not succeed. The Irish Constitution does not rule out strict liability in serious offences per se, though strict liability does open an offence up to scrutiny by reference to the idea that criminal liability must not be attributed in the absence of suitable moral culpability. I called this the culpability principle and it requires that an offence—viewed in the whole—must not capture persons or acts that are wholly nonculpable. This cannot be said about the impugned offence.

28

Commentary on *Foy v An t-Ard Chláraitheoir*

IVANA BACIK

Background to the Case[1]

> I was told that I was a sexual deviant, and I was upsetting society. All hell broke loose …[2]

> There was something of the trailblazer about Lydia. [She was] a very courageous person, prepared to go ahead because she was passionate about this and wanted to help others in her situation.[3]

Dr Lydia Foy is a transgender woman, whose legal case seeking recognition of her female gender was the first transgender rights action taken in Ireland. Significant Irish political and legislative developments have taken place as a direct result of her litigation. These developments are discussed below; but the litigation itself had a long and protracted history. In March 1993, Dr Foy first wrote to the Registrar General of Births, Deaths and Marriages requesting a new birth certificate in her acquired female gender. After corresponding for four years with the Registrar General, in April 1997 she issued her first set of legal proceedings, represented by the Free Legal Advice Centres (FLAC), seeking to change her original birth entry in the Register of Births from 'male' to 'female'.

The 2002 Foy Judgment

McKechnie J gave judgment in the High Court on 9 July 2002 (referred to here as 'the first *Foy* judgment'), refusing this application on the basis that Dr Foy had been a male at

[1] For feminist commentary on transgender issues, see, eg, Judith Butler, *Gender Trouble: Feminism and the Subversion of Identity* (New York, Routledge, 1990); Andrew Sharpe, *Transgender Jurisprudence: Dysphoric Bodies of Law* (London, Cavendish, 2002); Stephen Whittle, *Respect and Equality: Transsexual and Transgender Rights* (London, Cavendish, 2002); Susan Stryker and Stephen Whittle, *The Transgender Studies Reader* (New York, Routledge, 2006). For an overview of transgender issues and activism in Ireland, see publications by the leading Irish transgender rights advocacy group TENI (Transgender Equality Network Ireland) at www.teni.ie, in particular *Equality & Identity: Transgender and Intersex Experience in Ireland* (Dublin, TENI, 2013).

[2] Dr Lydia Foy, speaking in an RTE Radio 1 documentary about initiating her legal case, 'My Name is Lydia Foy', first broadcast on 2 July 2011, at www.rte.ie/radio1/doconone/2011/0620/646740-radio-documentary-my-name-is-lydia-foy-transgender-transsexual/.

[3] ibid, Bill Shipsey SC, Senior Counsel for Dr Lydia Foy.

birth and that the Registrar General accordingly had no power to change the entry in the Register.[4] He did however point out that the Oireachtas should deal with this matter, as the proceedings involved 'complex social, ethical, medical and legal issues'.[5] Dr Foy appealed against this decision to the Supreme Court.

By the time the appeal came on for hearing in November 2005, there had been three significant legal developments. First, the European Court of Human Rights had given judgment in the landmark *Goodwin* case, recognising that the failure by the UK authorities to recognise transgender woman Christine Goodwin as female was a breach of her rights under Article 8 of the European Convention on Human Rights, protecting private and family life.[6] Secondly, the European Convention had become part of Irish law through the European Convention on Human Rights Act 2003 (the ECHR Act). Thirdly, a new system of civil registration of births, deaths and marriages had been introduced in the Civil Registration Act 2004. These developments could not have been dealt with by McKechnie J in the original proceedings, so the Supreme Court remitted the case back to him. However, in the meantime Dr Foy had initiated a second set of proceedings, seeking a declaration of incompatibility against Ireland under the ECHR Act.

The 2007 Foy Judgment

McKechnie J gave his judgment in both proceedings on 19 October 2007 (together referred to here as 'the second *Foy* judgment').[7] In ruling on the first set of proceedings, he held that the post-July 2002 developments could have no impact, since 'a court, when adjudicating on any issue, must be in a position to apply legal principles which exist at the time of the dispute'.[8] However, in the second set of proceedings,[9] McKechnie J found in favour of Dr Foy on the European Convention issue, granting the declaration of incompatibility that she had sought under the ECHR Act.[10]

In coming to this decision, he applied the judgment of the European Court in *Goodwin*,[11] noting that the UK Government had responded by enacting gender recognition law within two years. By contrast, he pointed out that the Irish State had

> failed or declined to produce evidence of any movement, even at an initiating, debating or investigative level, on the plight of transsexual persons in this country ... In this regard, Ireland as of now is very much isolated within the Member States of the Council of Europe.[12]

[4] *Lydia Foy v An t-Ard Chláraitheoir, Ireland and the Attorney-General* [2002] IEHC 116. Note that the first Respondent, while correctly and officially described as An t-Ard Chláraitheoir in the title of the case, is referred to throughout the legal proceedings in the English language as the Registrar General.

[5] ibid, para 177.

[6] *Goodwin v UK* (2002) 35 EHRR 18; *I v UK* (2003) 36 EHRR 53.

[7] *Lydia Foy v An t-Ard Chláraitheoir, Ireland and the Attorney-General* [2007] IEHC 470; also reported at [2012] 2 IR 1.

[8] ibid, para 38.

[9] Judgment in the second set of proceedings begins at para 45.

[10] ibid, para 110.

[11] ibid, para 96.

[12] ibid, para 100.

Concluding his judgment, McKechnie J provided some insightful comments about gender identity disorder.[13] He stated finally, and powerfully, that:

> Everyone as a member of society has the right to human dignity, and with individual personalities, has the right to develop his being as he sees fit… Together with human freedom, a person, subject to the acquired rights of others, should be free to shape his personality in the way best suited to his person and to his life.[14]

Political and Legislative Developments Post-2007

The Government appealed this decision to the Supreme Court, but withdrew the appeal in June 2010 so that the declaration of incompatibility became final. However, by then there was at last some political movement, as a Gender Recognition Advisory Group (GRAG) had been set up to advise on the provision of legal recognition for transgender persons. The Group's report was published in June 2011, and a government working group was then set up to draft legislation.[15]

However, frustrated by the slow progress, Dr Foy issued new legal proceedings in January 2013. The Government then at last published the General Scheme of the Gender Recognition Bill in July 2013.[16] The Joint Oireachtas Committee on Education and Social Protection reported on this Scheme in January 2014, recommending some progressive changes; in particular that the gender recognition process should be open to those aged between 16 and 18, not just to adults.[17]

Meanwhile, a date in November 2014 had been set for Dr Foy's new proceedings to be heard by the High Court. However, Dr Foy settled the case in October 2014, because the Government undertook that the Bill would become law in 2015.

The Gender Recognition Bill 2014

In December 2014, the revised Gender Recognition Bill 2014 was published, providing for the process for granting gender recognition certificates, and requiring medical certification

[13] ibid, paras 116–18. McKechnie J had similarly spoken with compassion in the first *Foy* judgment of the difficulties faced by those with gender identity disorder; see, eg, paras 26–27.

[14] ibid, para 118.

[15] For a critique of the Government delays in addressing the *Foy* case, see, eg, Irish Human Rights Commission, *Submission to Government concerning the protection of the rights of transgendered persons* (Dublin, IHRC, 2008); and Equality Authority, *Submission to the GRAG* (Dublin, Equality Authority, 2010), at www.ihrec.ie/…/equality_authority_submission_to_the_gender_recognition.

[16] The 2013 Scheme had made no provision for those under 18 to apply for gender recognition. The full text of the Report is available at www.welfare.ie/en/downloads/Gender-Recognition-Bill-2013.pdf. The Committee recommended that non-legislative measures should be put in place to support transgender persons under 16, particularly the adoption of guidelines supporting inclusion of transgender young people in schools.

[17] Available at www.oireachtas.ie/parliament/media/committees/educationandsocialprotection/Report-on-Gender-Recognition-Bill.pdf.

to accompany the application.[18] Both Senators and TDs[19] generally welcomed the Bill, and emphasised the impact of Dr Foy's litigation in bringing about its introduction. Indeed, many referred specifically to the presence of Dr Foy, along with her solicitor, Michael Farrell, and other supporters, in the public gallery of both Seanad and Dáil. During the debates, briefings were organised by the Transgender Equality Network Ireland (TENI) and other groups with Oireachtas members. These briefings clearly informed the tone of the debate, in which reference was made by many speakers to the accounts that they had heard directly about the lived experiences of transgender persons in Ireland. In particular, many legislators spoke about their realisation of the suffering caused, especially to young transgender persons, by a lack of understanding in society. For many, including this author, the legislative process represented a real learning curve in transgender rights issues. Expert views on appropriate models for gender recognition laws were extensively and robustly debated, but the language used was respectful and sensitive; any criticisms voiced about the Bill were aimed at making it more progressive. In the course of the debates, three key progressive changes were sought. The first related to age. The Bill provided that young persons aged 16 or 17 could apply to court for an exemption to the normal rule that 18 is the minimum age for a gender recognition certificate. However, some legislators questioned whether there should be an additional statutory process for legal recognition of transgender persons under 16; ultimately this was not included, but the Bill was amended to ensure that its application will be reviewed after two years, and the issue of those under 16 will be specifically addressed in that review.

The second change sought during debates was to the so-called 'forced divorce' clause; the provisions requiring persons applying for gender recognition certificates to be single. These were generally acknowledged to be hugely problematic, but it was noted that the passage of the marriage equality referendum in May 2015 would resolve the issue.[20]

The third change sought was to the pathologisation of transgender persons. Many legislators questioned whether, instead of requiring a medical intervention, the Bill should instead make provision for a self-declaration model, similar that introduced in Denmark subsequent to the Oireachtas Committee's 2014 report. As a result of the forceful arguments made during the debates on this particular issue, based both on expert evidence and on lived experience of transgender persons, the Bill was amended to ensure that applicants over 18 may apply for a gender recognition certificate on a self-declaration basis, thus removing the requirement for a doctor's statement. This represented a highly progressive breakthrough. Effectively, it meant that Ireland has become only the fourth jurisdiction in the world to introduce a self-declaration model for gender recognition legislation. It was truly remarkable to see how much more progressive the Bill became as it proceeded through the Oireachtas. Its final passage in July 2015 was warmly welcomed by TENI in

[18] For the full legislative history of the Bill, including its original text and the debates in both Seanad and Dáil, see www.oireachtas.ie/viewdoc.asp?fn=/documents/bills28/bills/2014/11614/document1.htm.

[19] Teachta Dála (Member of Irish Parliament).

[20] The marriage equality referendum, inserting the Thirty-fourth Amendment to the Constitution, was passed on 22 May 2015, so that Art 41 now includes the following text: 'Marriage may be contracted in accordance with law by two persons without distinction as to their sex.' For more see http://refcom2015.ie/marriage/. Despite the referendum result, the implementation of the amendment was delayed pending court challenges to the referendum process, until the end of July 2015.

the following words, 'This is a momentous occasion for the trans community in Ireland. Dr Lydia Foy's twenty-two year journey is finally coming to an end.'[21]

Feminist Judgment of Ms Justice Ní Mhuirthile

The Foy litigation is remarkable in many respects. It has had a clear and tangible effect in changing the law, and has generated extensive public debate and real legal change for transgender persons in Ireland. This commentary has thus considered in some detail both the actual two judgments of McKechnie J in the litigation, and the significant legal and political developments that have taken place subsequently.

However, Tanya Ní Mhuirthile's feminist judgment is written as if handed down by the Supreme Court on 19 November 2009, on the supposed basis that the first Foy case was lost on the remitted points, and that the appeal had then proceeded to the Supreme Court. In short, the Ní Mhuirthile J judgment is based on the fiction that the second Foy case never happened. This approach enables her to explore an alternative to the *Corbett v Corbett*[22] test for legal gender recognition used by McKechnie J in his first judgment, and discussed below. Ní Mhuirthile J essentially seeks to question or disrupt the primacy of that test within the jurisprudence applicable in 2002.

In fact, the language used by McKechnie J in the second Foy judgment is notably progressive, displaying a clear understanding of the concerns of transgender persons. Even in the first Foy judgment in 2002, while he refused the relief sought, McKechnie J showed compassion both for the applicant, Dr Foy, and for those others most directly affected by the litigation, namely Dr Foy's wife and daughters. Indeed, he expressly stated that Mrs Foy was 'an impressive witness who had a good recall of the main events' and for whom the facts giving rise to the litigation had clearly amounted to a 'very traumatic period'.[23]

However, from a feminist perspective his 2002 judgment may be criticised for its reliance on the biological test for determination of legal gender as set out in the English case of *Corbett*.[24] That was a nullity application: the husband had petitioned the court to annul his marriage on the basis that the woman he had married had been registered as a male at birth. In granting the annulment, Ormrod J ruled that biological factors (the 'chromosomal, gonadal and genital tests'), rather than any 'operative intervention', should determine gender for the purpose of marriage.[25]

In the first Foy judgment, McKechnie J concluded, relying on *Corbett*, that

> biological indicators should continue to act as the governance in the determination of sex for the purposes of this case and that, although transsexualism is undoubtedly a recognised psychiatric disorder, it cannot, at least as of now, found its existence in neuro science.[26]

[21] TENI (Trans-Gender Equality Network Ireland), press release, 14 July 2015, available at www.teni.ie/event.aspx?contentid=1407.

[22] *Corbett v Corbett (otherwise Ashley)* [1970] 2 WLR 1306.

[23] *Lydia Foy v An t-Ard Chláraitheoir, Ireland and the Attorney-General* [2002] IEHC 116, para 18.

[24] For feminist critique of this case, see, eg, Katherine O'Donovan, *Sexual Divisions in Law* (London, Weidenfeld & Nicolson, 1985); Sharpe, above n 1; Whittle, above n 1.

[25] *Corbett v Corbett (otherwise Ashley)* [1970] 2 WLR 1306, paras 1324–25.

[26] *Lydia Foy v An t-Ard Chláraitheoir, Ireland and the Attorney-General* [2002] IEHC 116, para 121.

Accordingly, he found that 'it seems to me that logically, it must follow that in my opinion Dr Foy, at birth, was a male with conforming biological structures'.[27] Thus the Registrar General's entry in the register was correct, and Dr Foy's application to change it was refused.

Clearly, as Ní Mhuirthile J is giving judgment in 2009, she has the benefit of the post-2002 legal developments both at European and domestic level. Moreover, she takes a different approach from that taken by McKechnie J in his second judgment in the first proceedings on the issue of non-retrospectivity. Rather than ruling that the post-2002 changes cannot affect her decision at all, she decides to rebut the presumption that the sex recorded on Dr Foy's register of births represents her self-identified gender—but to make this rebuttal prospective only. She points out that this ruling ensures that the interests of Dr Foy's wife and daughters are protected.

A particular feminist strength of Ní Mhuirthile J's judgment is her emphasis that even in 2002, *Corbett* represented only one possible test for legal gender recognition, and that an alternative test could have been adopted by McKechnie J in his first judgment.[28] She bases this argument on the tests adopted by different US courts in *Re Anonymous* and *MT v JT*,[29] that of a 'harmonisation' approach to the determination of legal sex.[30] Even this approach, she suggests, is not the best model; rather, she asserts a test based on the principle of human dignity, derived from the European Convention on Human Rights and from some Irish constitutional case law. She concludes that the rights-based approach, grounded in respect for the self-determination and dignity of the person, is the correct one to adopt in recognising Dr Foy's acquired gender.

Analysis of the Feminist Judgment

This conclusion, and Ní Mhuirthile J's judgment generally, gives rise to two particular considerations. First, her application of the principle of dignity is interesting and unexpected in a feminist judgment context. It might have been more obvious either to apply equality-based arguments in reaching her decision, or to use the privacy right that grounded the *Goodwin* decision, which has had a more extensive application in feminist jurisprudence. The ambit of the privacy right in the context of women's reproductive choices, for example, was famously articulated by Blackmun J of the US Supreme Court in *Roe v Wade*;[31] although, writing about that case, Catherine McKinnon offers a powerful feminist critique

[27] ibid, para 125.

[28] Ní Mhuirthile J's judgment, below, para 29.

[29] *Re Anonymous* 293 NYS 2d 834 (1968); *MT v JT* 140 NJ Super 77 (1976).

[30] Ní Mhuirthile J's judgment, below, paras 30–31.

[31] *Roe v Wade* 410 US 113 (1973), per Blackmun J at para 153: 'This right of privacy, whether it be founded in the Fourteenth Amendment's concept of personal liberty and restrictions upon state action, as we feel it is, or, as the District Court determined, in the Ninth Amendment's reservation of rights to the people, is broad enough to encompass a woman's decision whether or not to terminate her pregnancy.' This judgment was referenced in the Irish case of *McGee v Attorney General* [1974] IR 284; see the feminist judgment by Máiréad Enright in this collection, ch 5.

of privacy rights, expressing her preference for an equality-based model.[32] Other feminist writers have challenged the traditional liberal distinction between the public and private spheres, on which the right to privacy is grounded.[33]

By contrast, the concept of 'dignity' relied upon by Ní Mhuirthile J has in the past been used in a way that may be seen as antithetical to feminism, particularly in an Irish context where the phrase 'human dignity' is frequently invoked to refer to 'the right to life of the unborn'.[34] The concept of dignity is explicitly referenced in the Preamble to the Constitution, as Ní Mhuirthile J notes. However, its clearest Irish judicial articulation derives from the 'right to die' cases: both the 1996 *Ward of Court* case cited by Ní Mhuirthile J in her judgment;[35] and also the more recent case of *PP v HSE*, a decision deeply troubling from a feminist perspective.[36] The use of 'dignity' is often framed in theological or ethical terms; it is a right that seems a somewhat uneasy fit within feminist discourse.

Despite this inauspicious history, the concept of dignity is arguably highly appropriate to the assertion of transgender rights by a claimant such as Dr Foy; and indeed there are indications that the concept may be 'reclaimed' by feminist lawyers. Millns, for example, has written that, deriving inspiration from European Convention jurisprudence, 'the clarity of the appeal for the need to respect human dignity has much to recommend it to feminist analysis'.[37]

Apart from the theoretical grounding given by Ní Mhuirthile J for her decision, the second consideration arising from her judgment is that of practical impact or legal strategy. It is noteworthy that, despite her use of a feminist-inspired test for legal gender determination, Ní Mhuirthile J remains bound by procedural strictures into giving the same remedy that McKechnie J in fact granted in his 2007 judgment; that of the declaration of incompatibility under the 2003 Act. As a judge, she cannot apply her test retrospectively by finding that the Registrar General should not have recorded Dr Foy's birth as male, just as McKechnie J could not apply post-2002 legal developments retrospectively in his 2007 judgment.

In noting this restriction, Ní Mhuirthile J appears regretful, as a feminist judge would be in the circumstances, stating 'I find myself with very limited options by which to affect a meaningful resolution for the appellant resulting from my findings', and concluding her

[32] Catherine MacKinnon, 'Privacy v Equality: Beyond *Roe v Wade*' in *Feminism Unmodified: Discourses on Life and Law* (Cambridge, MA, Harvard University Press, 1987) 96–97. For discussion of this issue, see Jo Bridgeman and Susan Millns, *Feminist Perspectives on Law: Law's Engagement with the Female Body* (London, Sweet & Maxwell, 1998) 302–05.

[33] See, eg, Carole Pateman, *The Sexual Contract* (Stanford, CA, Stanford University Press, 1988); Susan Moller Okin, *Women in Western Political Thought* (Princeton, NJ, Princeton University Press, 1978); Martha Fineman, 'Feminist Legal Theory' (2005) 13:1 *Journal of Gender, Social Policy and the Law* 13–23.

[34] See, eg, William Binchy, 'Human Dignity and the Unborn Child—a Comment' (2014) 20:2 *Medico-Legal Journal of Ireland* 82–84.

[35] *Re a Ward of Court* [1996] 2 IR 79.

[36] *PP v HSE* [2014] IEHC 622. For commentary see Máiréad Enright, '*PP v HSE*: Practicability, Dignity and the Best Interests of the Unborn Child', at http://humanrights.ie/gender-sexuality-and-the-law/pp-v-hse-futility-dignity-and-the-best-interests-of-the-unborn-child/.

[37] Susan Millns, 'Bringing Rights Home: Feminism and the Human Rights Act 1998' in Susan Millns and Noel Whitty (eds), *Feminist Perspectives on Public Law* (London, Cavendish, 1999) 200. For a feminist analysis of 'dignity' in the context of surrogacy and prostitution, see Carolyn McLeod, 'For Dignity or Money: Feminists on the Commodification of Women's Reproductive Labour' in Bonnie Steinbock (ed), *Oxford Handbook of Bioethics* (Oxford, Oxford University Press, 2007).

judgment by reiterating the call made by McKechnie J in 2002, urging the Oireachtas to review the matter urgently.[38]

This procedural restriction on judicial action demonstrates what amounts to perhaps the most important lesson from the *Foy* case: that judicial action can only represent one part of any campaign for legal change. Dr Foy's case became, as public interest litigation often becomes, a powerful tool for advocates seeking legal change; and her initiation of legal proceedings each time the process was delayed undoubtedly pushed the state into legislating sooner than it might otherwise have done. But ultimately, apart from the litigation, it took extensive lobbying, activism and advocacy by groups like TENI, along with enormous amounts of time spent in political decision-making and legislative drafting and re-drafting, to change the law through the democratic process, so that transgender persons in Ireland may now achieve legal recognition through a highly progressive statutory framework. McColgan has written previously about the limits of rights discourse and judicial action for feminist activists, and the dangers of fetishising the court process, at the expense of carrying out ground-level advocacy and activism to win over public opinion.[39] Both strategies are valuable; legal cases may have more impact when accompanied by activist campaigns. Clearly, public interest litigation such as that so bravely initiated more than 20 years ago by Dr Lydia Foy represents only one aspect of the greater political and social campaign for equality.

[38] Ní Mhuirthile J's judgment, below, paras 55–56.

[39] Aileen McColgan, *Women Under the Law: the false promise of human rights* (Harlow, Pearson, 2000).

Lydia Foy, Plaintiff v An t-Ard Chláraitheoir, Defendants; Jennifer and Claire Foy, Notice Parties

[2007] IEHC 470, [2006 No. 33 S.P.]; [2009] IESC 1

High Court	19th October, 2007
Supreme Court	19th November, 2009

Ní Mhuirthile J. 19th November, 2009

Introduction

[1] Labour wards all over the world reverberate to joyous exclamations of 'it's a boy!' or 'it's a girl!' A seemingly simple statement: one that lies at the very heart of this case. At its core, this case revolves around the question of how legal gender is constructed. How does one become a man or a woman for the purposes of becoming *sui juris*? Is the exclamation in the birthing chamber and the consequent recording of sex on the birth certificate a definitive determination on a point of law, or is it merely, as Mr Justice McKechnie noted in the 2002 High Court judgment on this matter, "a 'snap shot' of matters on a particular day and does not purport to be otherwise"? If the latter, how then is legal gender determined? This is the question which the appellant asks this Court to resolve.

[2] The appellant was born on Monday 23rd June, 1947 in Athlone, Co. Westmeath. As required by law, the appellant's mother registered the birth of her baby, naming her child "Donal Mark" and noting her baby's sex as male. The case arises as the appellant asserts that as he grew he developed a female gender identity. The appellant contends that she has a congenital disability, known as gender identity disorder. This results from a lack of congruence between the physical sex of her body and her internal sense of self as a gendered person. Consequently, in adulthood, and as the married father of two children, the appellant began living as a woman. She applied to the Registrar General to have the sex marker on the register of births amended to note "female" and the names changed to read "Lydia Annice". Throughout this judgment, I will refer to the appellant using female pronouns, apart from where it makes no sense, such as in the historical context

[3] The application to amend the register was refused and the case came before the High Court by way of judicial review proceedings. The appellant sought an order requiring the desired amendment to the birth register or, in the alternative, a finding that the absence of an ability to achieve legal recognition in her gender of preference infringed the appellant's constitutional rights to privacy, dignity, equality and the right to marry a man. In advancing these arguments, the appellant also relied upon the European Convention on Human Rights.

[4] Each of these claims was strongly contested by both the respondents: the Registrar General, Ireland and the Attorney General and the notice parties: Dr. Foy's children.

[5] The High Court ruled that the register of births records the information available at the time of registration and operates primarily as a document of historical record. It is, as

noted in the quotation from McKechnie J. at paragraph 1 above, not intended to serve any other purpose. McKechnie J. also ruled that the appropriate legal test for gender determination was that laid down in *Corbett v. Corbett* [1970] 2 All E.R. 33: namely that the congruence of the chromosomes, gonads and genitals at birth is determinative of the legal gender of an individual.

[6] Dr. Foy appealed that judgment. However, between the time of the filing of the notice of appeal and the initial hearing in the Supreme Court on 8th November, 2005, the legal landscape had altered in three significant aspects. First, two days after the High Court judgment in these proceedings, the European Court of Human Rights in *Goodwin v. United Kingdom* (2002) 35 E.H.R.R. 18 and *I v. United Kingdom* (2003) 40 E.H.R.R. 53, reversing two decades of jurisprudence, found that the continued failure of the UK state to recognise the preferred gender identity of the applicants amounted to a breach of their rights under Articles 8 and 12 of the Convention. Secondly, the Convention itself became part of the domestic legal framework by virtue of the European Convention on Human Rights Act, 2003. Finally, the system of civil registration was repealed in its entirety and replaced by a new system under the Civil Registration Act, 2004, which included provisions in sections 63, 64 and 65 to amend errors in the recording of a birth.

[7] As these matters had not, and could not have, formed part of the legal reasoning in the High Court judgment of 2002, they were remitted back to the High Court for consideration at first instance. Unusually, and by agreement between the parties, the remitted action was again heard by my esteemed colleague McKechnie J. He ruled that as the *Goodwin* judgment was prospective only it could not have impacted upon his earlier decision. Regarding the Convention argument, he found that this too was dependent on a conclusion that the 2003 Act had retrospective effect which, based on the decision in *Dublin City Council v. Fennell* [2005] I.E.S.C. 33, he ruled it did not. As the new system of civil registration had not existed at the time, the introduction of the Civil Registration Act, 2004 was also of no significance in terms of that judgment.

[8] Accordingly, Dr. Foy's arguments on these remitted points were unsuccessful. The sole question which remains for this Court to consider is whether the High Court, in adopting the *Corbett* test erred in law.

Background to the Case

[9] For a detailed account of the facts, background to the case and the medical evidence presented in submissions, I refer to the compassionate, comprehensive and considered judgments of McKechnie J. in the High Court. Nevertheless, there are some aspects of the facts that I wish here to note.

[10] Dr. Foy was one of a large family of seven children and has five brothers and one sister. According to the evidence presented, Dr. Foy was at all times raised and treated as a boy by his family. In discussing his childhood, Dr. Foy notes that he was very different from his brothers and conscious of the clothes he wore, of his sense of femininity, and of his interest in and attraction to the clothes of his younger sister. He described a secret world: one of recurring dreams where he desired to act, look like and be feminine. According to Dr. Foy these feelings have always been part of his sense of self. Dr. Foy noted the occasion of his First Holy Communion as an instance which caused acute distress as he was part of the boys' group and was required to dress accordingly. Dr. Foy found this period of his life very stressful and has very little recall of this time. His Communion caused a crisis: a conflict between his subject identity and the identity objectively assigned to him, and resolved his internal identity as a girl. He recalls using harmless household items to fulfil this need to express his identity, for example wearing a towel as if it were a skirt. Such incidents he now considers as moments of true expression of himself. Throughout the remainder of his co-educational primary schooling he reported envying the freedom of the girls in the class to openly express their identities. He was frequently on his own and had little, if any interest, in boyish activities.

[11] Once he began secondary school as a boarder in Clongowes Wood College in the early 1960s he was considered by some classmates to be gay and others treated him in a manner he described as "gentlemanly". He had no close friends and described that time in his life as walking on a tightrope as his feelings regarding his gender identity continued. Again he reports experiencing an "in world" and an "out world" and reports cross dressing during holiday time in the early morning or late evening when it was safe to do so.

[12] It was in his mid-teens that Dr. Foy began consciously and deliberately to question his identity. He explored certain books which became available to him for information, yet this heightened his confusion. For example, in Hadfield on *Childhood and Adolescence* the word "transsexual" was defined by reference to the section on "sexual deviancy", which created in him a huge guilt complex. Thus Dr. Foy was left in a constant state of questioning his identity; whether he would ever recover from his unidentified condition; whether he was the oldest person in the world to experience this conflict; and so on.

[13] At University College Dublin where he studied Pre-Med and subsequently Dentistry, Dr. Foy had increased access to books to facilitate his research into his condition but he could not uncover much concrete information, apart from a book written by journalist Jan Morris which discussed the availability of gender reassignment surgeries in Casablanca. None of the material available provided the appellant with the information he sought: a thorough explanation of exactly what a transsexual person is. He was a member of the College's Musical Society but no other details from his undergraduate career were presented.

[14] Dr. Foy began to practise as a dentist in 1972. There was little information about his life during this time in the evidence from the High Court. No elaboration was given regarding dissonance between his inner life and his outward life. Nor was there any information about the persistence of his cross-dressing practices or otherwise. It was confirmed that he had a non-sexual relationship with a woman prior to meeting Mrs. Foy and had proposed marriage to that woman.

[15] While he worked as a dentist in Mullingar in the early 1970s, Dr. Foy maintained an active membership of a local musical society. It was there that he met Ann Naughton, the future Mrs. Foy, in 1975. A courtship ensued and the couple became engaged at Christmas 1976 and were married on 28th September, 1977. The birth of their daughters followed quickly: Jennifer on 16th August, 1978 and Claire on 18th September, 1980. In 1982/3 Dr. Foy was hospitalised due to a physical condition affecting his leg and was generally unwell. Towards the end of 1983 in November or December he first went to work in Saudi

Arabia for a two year period, returning home at quarterly intervals for a few weeks. When he renewed his contract the entire family joined him for seven or eight months after which they all returned to Ireland.

[16] Sometime in 1982, Dr. Foy became increasingly concerned by the conflict between his inner sense of femininity and his outer male persona such that he became severely depressed and consulted a psychiatrist. The stress caused by attempting to conform to his social role as a man, a husband and a father while attempting to reconcile his internal sense of himself as woman caused deep and profound unhappiness which manifested in a number of stress-related physical complaints. He told Mrs. Foy that he was a transvestite and enjoyed wearing female clothing. She responded that neither she nor the children would have anything to do with such activity, were not to see him so dressed and ordered that he never mention this to her again.

[17] In 1989, Dr. Foy was referred by a colleague to see another psychiatrist Dr. Wilson. He in turn referred her to Dr. Frank O'Donoghue who was the most experienced doctor at the time in this area of medicine in the country. Following a series of meetings, Dr. Foy was diagnosed as a transsexual and underwent gender assignment surgery in 1992. These interventions were medically successful and she now lives her life as a woman. I refer to my colleague McKechnie J.'s detailed accounts of the medical treatment undergone by Dr. Foy in his 2002 judgment from the High Court. I do not repeat them here as they are irrelevant to the core question before this court.

[18] In terms of Dr. Foy's private and family life it is noteworthy that in the summer of 1989 Dr. Foy told Mrs. Foy that he was taking female hormones. Understandably, Mrs. Foy was shocked at this disclosure. Naturally she wished to discuss this matter, but despite many attempts to do so, Dr. Foy did not engage with her on this topic. Following on from the initial consultation with Dr. O'Donoghue, both Dr. and Mrs. Foy attended joint and separate consultations. In was in the private consultation with Dr. O'Donoghue that Mrs. Foy was informed of the condition of transsexualism, of Dr. Foy's likely diagnosis and various treatment options up to and including surgery. Mrs. Foy was in utter shock and total disbelief. From the perspective of their family life, matters disintegrated from that point on with Dr. Foy vacating the family home in April 1990. Proceedings were set in train and were settled in the Circuit Court on 13th December 1991. Dr. Foy consented to the order for judicial separation with Mrs. Foy being granted sole custody of their children. Access arrangements were agreed, subject to certain terms and conditions. In October 1993, a barring order was obtained against Dr. Foy which was confirmed by the Circuit Court on 20th May, 1994. The order of 1994 also prohibited Dr. Foy any access to the children and directed that she transfer her interest in the family home into the sole name of Mrs. Foy. An appeal to the High Court was dismissed in October 1994. Dr. Foy continues to feel aggrieved at these orders. The facts of the case illustrate that there are no winners here. The inherent societal pressure that Dr. Foy felt in attempting to conform to acceptable notions of gender identity, gender expression and family has resulted in a situation where the entire Foy family has been bruised. The adversarial nature of the law as it attempts to resolve familial disputes can only have aggravated an already delicate situation.

Legal Gender Determination

[19] The test for determination of legal gender as set out in *Corbett* contains both biological and temporal aspects. It is resolved based on the congruence of the chromosomes, gonads and genitals at birth. The test was developed by Ormrod J. in the High Court of England and Wales in 1970 in the context of nullity proceedings. The plaintiff in the case (the husband) argued that the marriage of the parties was invalid as the respondent had been born, and registered at birth as male. Consequently, under *Hyde v. Hyde* [1866] L.R. 1 P. & D. 130, it could not be considered a valid marriage as the parties were of the same gender.

[20] In reaching this decision, Ormrod J. heard extensive evidence from the medical experts and noted the difference in opinion as to the aetiology or causation of transsexuality between the experts:-

> "[Some experts] regard it at present as a psychological disorder arising after birth, probably as a result of some, as yet unspecified, experiences. The alternative view is that there may be an organic basis for the condition."

[21] Studies on the latter proposition had been conducted only on immature rats and other animals by that time. Consequently, Ormrod J. was of the opinion that any application of that work to the human being was purely speculative. Thus he found that this second theory had "nothing to contribute to the solution of the present case." He went on to note that the medical experts agreed on four criteria for assessing the sex of an individual: chromosomal, gonadal, genital and psychological. Some of the experts, he noted, would add a fifth criterion: the hormonal factor. Such criteria, he remarked, had been evolved by doctors to systemise medical knowledge and to assist unfortunate patients who suffer either physically or psychologically from sexual abnormalities. However, he stated that "[t]hese [psychological and hormonal] criteria are, of course, relevant to, but do not necessarily decide, the legal basis of sex determination." Consequently he determined that, given the current state of scientific knowledge, at that time, the relevant criteria were the first three criteria as outlined above. The test, as developed by Ormrod J., is entrenched in scientific understandings from the 1970s and cannot and does not account for scientific, or indeed social, developments in the intervening years. I find myself pondering the potential stymieing effect of a legal test shackled to a specific moment in the evolution of scientific knowledge.

[22] In the High Court hearings on the instant case, Dr. Foy, in advancing an argument that scientific knowledge had developed in the 30 years since *Corbett* was decided, adduced medical evidence from Professor Gooren that male and female brains differ and that the size and shape of the hypothalamus in a male-to-female transsexual is the same as that to be found in "normal" females and smaller than that found in "normal" males. Thus Professor Gooren concluded that there is a neuro-scientific basis to transsexuality, and therefore it should be considered as a form of intersex condition. This argument did not find favour with the Court. McKechnie J. found that there were limitations with the studies Professor Gooren conducted and consequently there were difficulties with the conclusion he arrived at and the extrapolation made from that conclusion. He found that the scientific community was still debating the basis for transgender identity. McKechnie J. concluded that it was "insufficient to establish the existence of brain differentiation as a marker of sex and, accordingly, I do not believe that this court in such circumstances could give to it the legal recognition which is sought." Consequently, it was found that the *Corbett* test represents the law in Ireland on this matter.

[23] In ascertaining whether this was a correct interpretation of the law, it seems to me that we must consider how the information for noting sex in the Register of Births is ascertained.

How Gender is Determined for the Purposes of Recording Births in the Register of Births in Practice

[24] The Registration of Births and Deaths (Ireland) Act, 1863, as amended, established the scheme which governed the registration of births at the time when the birth of Dr. Foy was recorded. Under s. 1 of the Births and Deaths Registration Act (Ireland), 1880, certain individuals, known as qualified informants, are required to inform the Registrar General, or his officials, of the birth of a child within 42 days of said event. Such qualified informants include the father and mother of the child, the occupier of the house where the child was born, each person present at the birth and any person having charge of the child. In providing this information, the qualified informant must complete the required details as set out in Form A including the sex of the child. Neither the legislation, nor Form A, provides precise instruction as to how the sex of the child is to be determined other than that it must be recorded as male or female (although this specificity regarding gender was deleted by Schedule 1 to the Registration of Births Act, 1996 and was not reinstated in the first schedule to the Civil Registration Act, 2004). In the absence of such guidance, some means of determining the sex of a child must be identified. Consequently, a practice has developed to use biological criteria, or more accurately the appearance of the genitalia, as determinative.

[25] As outlined in the 2002 judgment, Dr. Foy was the only person who gave evidence regarding the first 30 years of his life. It was noted in the judgment that his mother registered his birth and recorded his sex as male based on the appearance of his external genitalia. No evidence was presented regarding the nature of the chromosomal or gonadal aspects of his body at that time. As is clear, from the discussion above, for the *Corbett* test to apply the congruence of these three criteria at the moment of birth must be ascertained. From the evidence it does not appear, nor does it usually happen, that the congruence of all the relevant criteria was assessed at the moment of birth or prior to the registration of the birth.

[26] In his *Corbett* judgment, Ormrod J. recognised that a person might have incongruent criteria where a biological intersex condition exists. On that basis he found that in cases of incongruence, the genital criterion should be determinative. In this way he confirms the presumption that genital appearance can establish legal gender.

[27] The presumption that genital appearance can be determinative of gender was challenged before the High Court of England and Wales in the case of *W v. W* [2001] 1 F.L.R. 324. The applicant in that case sought a decree of nullity on the basis that the respondent (wife) was not female at the date of the marriage. Mrs. W was an intersex individual. Evidence was presented that Mrs. W had been born with indeterminative genitalia and, as her father had a preference for a son, her birth was registered as that of a boy. In applying the *Corbett* test to the facts before him Charles J. found that Mrs. W had XY chromosomes, her gonadal sex was likely male, and that prior to her gender reassignment surgery her genitals were ambiguous. In considering whether the flap of skin was a micro-penis or an enlarged clitoris he found that it would "fall on the male side of the line". On a strict application of the test Mrs. W ought to be classified as a male and her marriage annulled. However, further medical evidence attested that Mrs. W experienced spontaneous breast growth and Dr. Conway, the consultant endocrinologist providing expert testimony, diagnosed her as having Partial Androgen Insensitivity Syndrome (PAIS). Additionally she self-identified as a woman and had been socially accepted as a woman by others. Charles J. then moved to consider the expanded *Corbett* test for application in cases lacking the necessary congruence. He found that preferring the genital criterion as determinative would preserve a finding that Mrs. W was male. Consequently, Charles J. concluded that to apply the *Corbett* test to the case before him would be "an incorrect application". He accepted the diagnosis of PAIS and the opinion that had she been born today she would have been assigned the female gender at birth by the medical profession. Thus he found Mrs. W to be a woman for the purposes of marriage. The decision of Charles J. in *W* suggests that despite its widespread acceptance the *Corbett* test, and its extension in the case of ambiguity, does not always enable the determination of legal gender.

[28] For most people, the note on the register of births as regards the recording of their sex is based on a *prima facie* presumption that the outward appearance of their genitals will conform to the subsequent development of their gender identities. As was held by McKechnie J., the function of the register of births is not to establish the present legal identity of an individual but rather to record matters as they were on a particular day. Of course, in focusing so tightly on the purpose for which the register was created, my colleague neatly avoids confronting the reality that its practical utility goes beyond that limited function. The birth certificate, although not designed to be such, has in the absence of any other method become the mechanism by which legal identity is ascertained. It is necessary to produce a birth certificate in order to access other documents which serve secondarily as certificates of identification such a driving licences and passports. Nonetheless, the vast majority of the population do not contest the sex of record by asserting an alternative gender for the purposes of legal recognition. Consequently, the law proceeds in its interactions with an individual on the basis of the presumption that, where it becomes legally significant the sex recorded on the birth certificate represents the gender of legal recognition. As is evident from *W*, this is a rebuttable presumption. Thus, consideration must be paid to the question of what can rebut this presumption. In other words, what is the test to be applied to the determination of the gender of an individual for legal purposes?

Legal Tests for Determination of Legal Gender

The Biological Temporal Test

[29] The *Corbett* test represents one possibility for the determination of gender for legal purposes. This test consists of two aspects, the biological congruence aspect and the temporal aspect of the moment of birth as determinative. As discussed, in practice the information required to satisfy this test is rarely obtained prior to an entry being made on the register. Despite the prioritisation of the moment of birth as a core element of this test, the *prima facie* presumption as to sex based on the appearance of the genitalia at birth is only upheld or displaced at the later date when the *Corbett* test is applied retrospectively. The *W* case highlights the limits of the test—it cannot properly account for situations where the required congruence is not present.

The Harmonisation Test

[**30**] A different test was proposed two years prior to *Corbett* in *Re Anonymous* 293 N.Y.S. 2d. 834 (1968) when the question of whether to legally recognise the preferred gender identity of a post-operative transsexual woman arose before the New York City Civil Court. The Court stated that "any difficulty presented herein is not so much in the nature of the problem itself, but in trying to apply, perhaps inadequately, static rules of law to situations … which perhaps merit new rules and/or progressive legislation." The Court held that where there is disharmony between the psychological gender and the anatomical sex as a person ages the anatomical sex is determinative. Where that dissonance has been harmonised, either with or without medical intervention, the social gender of the individual should reflect the harmonised status and be recognised by the law. Additionally, Pecora J. stated that there was a serious question of whether to deny the petitioner relief (namely the alteration of her birth certificate to reflect her newly acquired gender) would amount to a violation of her human rights. Thus the Court recognised the harmonisation of the petitioner's psychological gender identity and post-surgical anatomical sex as determinative of her legal gender.

[**31**] *Re Anonymous* was cited with approval by the Superior Court of New Jersey, Appellate Division in *M.T. v. J.T.* 140 N.J. Super. 77 (1976) which also took this second, harmonisation, approach to the determination of legal sex. The plaintiff was a male-to-female transsexual who was seeking an order of maintenance from her ex-husband. The respondent asserted that M.T. had been born a male, therefore the marriage was void and he was not liable for maintenance payments. The Court examined *Corbett* as the only case which had previously considered the legal status of transsexuals as regards marriage. The Court considered that the decision in *Corbett* had been incorrectly reached. The *Corbett* court, it was found, viewed sex and gender as disparate phenomena and its conclusion was rooted in the premise that a "true sex" must be ascertained by biological criteria. The *M.T.* Court found that if the anatomical sex of a transsexual is made to conform to the psychological gender then legal recognition of gender must be governed by the congruence of these standards.

Right Based Test

[**32**] A final approach to the question of how legal gender ought to be determined was developed by the European Court of Human Rights. From the first time the question as to how legal gender ought to be determined arose before that Court in *Van Oosterwijck v. Belguim* (1980) 3 E.H.R.R. 557, the Court acknowledged the existence of a right to legal recognition of one's preferred identity is a general principle of law. In that particular case it

was not vindicated due to the failure to exhaust domestic remedies. In his partly concurring judgment, the Belgian Judge Gansof Van Der Meersch stated that:-

> "A man or woman who is unable to obtain recognition of his or her sexual identity, an aspect of status which is inseparable from his or her person will be unable to play his or her full role in society. As has been said, the right to such recognition is a general principle of law."

[33] Support for the vindication of a right to recognition of preferred gender continued to be manifest throughout the dissenting judgments of the Strasbourg Court on this matter. It should be noted that in these cases the majority consistently found that there was no violation of the article 8 right to respect for one's private and family life due to the lack of consensus on the issue and the consequent margin of appreciation afforded to each state. In *Cossey v. United Kingdom* (1990) 13 E.H.R.R. 622 Martens J., dissenting, cited approvingly the approach adopted by the New Jersey Superior Court in *M.T. v. J.T.* He criticised the majority decision in cases such as *Rees v. United Kingdom* (1986) 9 E.H.R.R. 56 for focusing on biological and medical technicalities to the detriment of the essential principles at stake:-

> "The principle which is basic in human rights and which underlies the various specific rights spelled out in the Convention is respect for human dignity and human freedom. Human dignity and human freedom imply that a man should be free to shape himself and his fate in the way that he deems best fits his personality. A transsexual does use those very fundamental rights. He is prepared to shape himself and his fate."

[34] Martens J. stated that recognition of preferred gender was a request which the law should refuse only if it had "truly compelling reasons", and in the absence of such reasons, a refusal "can only be qualified as cruel" and is inconsistent with the principles of privacy and human dignity.

[35] In *Sheffield & Horsham v. United Kingdom* (1999) 27 E.H.R.R. 163 the Strasbourg Court found that due to the margin of appreciation on the issue there was no positive obligation on the UK to legally recognise the acquired genders of the applicants. The Court reiterated its caution from *Rees* that this area of the law would have to be kept under review. In his concurring opinion Freeland J. warned that "continued inaction on the part of the respondent State, taken together with further developments elsewhere, could well tilt the balance in the other direction." In their joint dissenting opinion Judges Bernhardt, Thór Vilhjálmsson, Spielmann, Palm, Wildhaber, Makarczyk and Voicu noted the recent scientific developments in the area and found that these were of secondary importance: "Respect for privacy rights should not, as the legislative and societal trends referred to above demonstrate, depend on exact science." I find myself in agreement with these judges that while science can be a useful tool to explain and understand the facts of a case we cannot permit it to become a tourniquet which strangles legal developments, and access to fundamental human rights in particular.

[36] In his judgment Van Dijk J., found that the core of this case involved the issue of the fundamental right to self-determination. He stated that this right is not expressly enunciated in the E.C.H.R., but:-

> "is at the basis of several of the rights laid down therein, especially the right to liberty under Article 5 and the right to respect for private life under Article 8. Moreover, it is a

vital element of the "inherent dignity" which, according to the Preamble to the Universal Declaration of Human Rights, constitutes the foundation of freedom, justice and peace in the world."

[**37**] As was noted above, it was shortly after the 2002 judgment was handed down in this case that the Strasbourg Court found in *Goodwin* that the growing consensus and "unmistakable trend" among Contracting States towards legal recognition of the acquired gender of transsexuals had the effect that the UK could no longer claim that the matter fell within its margin of appreciation. The Court found unanimously that the failure of the UK to recognise the applicant's acquired gender breached her rights under Article 8:-

> "[T]he very essence of the Convention is respect for human dignity and human freedom. Under Article 8 … the notion of personal autonomy is an important principle underlying the interpretation of its guarantees … In the twenty first century the right of transsexuals to personal development and to physical and moral security in the full sense enjoyed by others in society cannot be regarded as a matter of controversy … In short, the unsatisfactory situation in which post-operative transsexuals live in an intermediate zone as not quite one gender or the other is no longer sustainable."

Rebutting the Presumption that the Sex Recorded on the Register of Births Represents the Gender of Legal Recognition

[**38**] Having identified the possible approaches to the question of how the *prima facie* presumption based on genital appearance at birth might be rebutted, I now turn to consider which of them represents the legal test in this country.

[**39**] The *Corbett* congruence test has the initial advantage of being widely accepted across the common law world as authoritative on this issue. However, as seen from *W* it is not without its limits, such as its failure to encompass the non-congruent intersex body. Furthermore, as it purports to be effective from the moment of birth, it cannot account for the lived experience of those whose selves, whether physical or psychological, do not develop in the expected manner.

[**40**] Although *Corbett* was decided on the basis on the congruence test, Ormrod J. did go on to consider the question of whether there had been a valid consummation of the putative marriage. In examining the consummation of the marriage, he considered the decision of Lord Wilmer in *S. v. S. (otherwise W.) (No. 2)* [1963] 3 All E.R. 55 where a decree of nullity was declined on the basis that a woman who suffered a vaginal defect, which could be remedied by surgical intervention, was found to be capable of consummating her marriage. Lord Wilmer held that it was irrelevant whether the vagina was artificially enlarged or indeed wholly artificial, the salient point was that:-

> "In either case full penetration can be achieved, and there is thus complete union between the two bodies. … In such circumstances I do not see why intercourse by means of such a vagina should not be regarded as amounting to "vera copula"…"

[**41**] Ormrod J. in *Corbett* found this statement to be obiter and therefore not binding. It is, the Court found, its essential heterosexual nature that distinguishes the marital

relationship from all others. Therefore any intercourse between the parties in the *Corbett* case is unnatural:-

> "When such a cavity has been constructed in a male, the difference between sexual intercourse using it, and anal or intra-crural intercourse is, in my judgment, to be measured in centimetres."

From this statement it is evident that the Court was concerned about homosexuality and that to rule that the Corbett marriage was valid might permit the legitimacy of homosexual marriage.

[42] The *M.T.* harmonisation test has its attractions. This approach appears to give priority to an individual's preferred gender identity and to publicly, and legally, validate that sense of self. Yet, on closer examination the decision is not as simple as it initially seems. I note the emphasis in the judgment on the fact that M.T. was a post-operative trans woman. Given the great attention the Court placed on ascertaining that M.T. could no longer function sexually as a man and that her acquired vagina could function as a site of heterosexual intercourse I cannot help but wonder if recognition would have been denied her had this not been clarified.

[43] The decisions in both the *Corbett* and *M.T.* cases can be compared as both were concerned with the sexual performance of the parties. Mrs Corbett's body was found to be incapable of marital consummation as a woman. Similarly in *M.T.* the applicant only fully achieves harmonisation when her body can function effectively as a site of heterosexual intercourse to the satisfaction of her partner. Conceiving of gender in this manner is to reduce the lived experience of individuals to their functionality of their genitalia. Considered from this perspective, neither approach respects the privacy nor the dignity of the person. Both approaches are preoccupied with intercourse and whether it can be classified as heterosexual or homosexual. I am reminded of the statement by Griffin J. in *McGee v. A.G.* [1974] I.R. 284 that invasion of the "sacred precincts of the marital bedroom" is repulsive to the notions of privacy surrounding the marital relationship. It seems to me that a fixed focus on the functionality of a person's genitals is equally repugnant to respecting that person's inherent human dignity.

[44] The approach of the Strasbourg Court is based on the inherent dignity of individuals. Under the Preamble to the 1937 Constitution the promotion of the dignity and freedom of the individual is assured. The courts have consistently stated that the dignity of an individual is a value to be pursued: *Re. Article 26 Offences Against the State (Amendment Bill)* [1940] I.T. 470 and *Re. Philip Clarke* [1950] I.R. 235. As my esteemed college, Justice Denham (as she then was) stated in *Re. A Ward of Court* [1996] 2 I.R. 79:-

> "An unspecified right under the Constitution to all persons as human persons is dignity—to be treated with dignity."

[45] McKechnie J. in his 2002 judgment noted that:-

> "The evidence in this case, irrespective of legal outcome, shows, without dispute or debate, that [gender identity disorder] is an established and recognised condition, that present or hoped for societal status is entirely foreign to its existence, that such condition is not influenced by sex orientation or driven by sexual pleasure and that those inflicted

suffer greatly, usually for long periods, in relative isolation and frequently without understanding. Any person, reasonable in view and tolerance, would be horrified at the mockery, derision, and downright abuse which such individuals have to endure."

[**46**] Section 2(1) of the European Convention on Human Rights Act, 2003 states that:-

"In interpreting and applying any statutory provision or rule of law, a court shall, in so far as is possible, subject to the rules of law relating to such interpretation and application, do so in a manner compatible with the State's obligations under the Convention provisions."

[**47**] In light of this obligation, I find that in ascertaining the test for legal gender recognition I must do so in manner which best respects the dignity of the appellant. Consequently, I find that the rights based approach, grounded in a respect for the self-determination and dignity of the person is the correct one.

Application of the Test to the Facts

[**48**] On that basis, I accept Dr. Foy's assertion that the presumption that the sex recorded on the register of births represents her self-identified gender is rebutted. It is clear from an analysis of the facts that Dr. Foy struggled throughout her childhood, adolescence and marriage attempting to live as a man. The tension between her inner and outer life manifested in physical ill-health and stress induced hospitalisations on a number of occasions. Her struggles did not end with her physical transition as her family life disintegrated completely, her marriage ended and she lost all access to her children as a result of the court orders following her judicial separation from Mrs. Foy. I find that Dr. Foy has, as suggested by Martens J. in *Cossey*, shaped herself in the way that she deems best fits her personality. To refuse legal recognition of her preferred identity as female would not be consistent with the obligation on this court to respect her inherent human dignity. Consequently, I find that Dr. Foy should be legally recognised as a woman.

[**49**] I also find that this rebuttal of the presumption of legal gender can be prospective only. To find otherwise would be to potentially imperil actions done while the presumed sex was the gender of legal recognition. Any claim to retrospectivity would introduce such levels of uncertainty into the law that no person could engage in even the simplest of legal actions without actively asserting their gender of legal recognition.

Impact on the Notice Parties

[**50**] Thus, I turn to consider the situation of the notice parties and what impact such a finding has on their situation. The notice parties, being the daughters of Dr. and Mrs. Foy, are concerned that any decision of this Court might negatively impact upon their status and, notwithstanding the judicial separation of their parents, strip them of the special Constitutional protections they currently enjoy as members of a family based on marriage.

[**51**] Mrs. Foy has not sought to annul the marriage. Rather, Dr. Foy consented to a judicial separation on the 13th December, 1991 and divorce proceedings are now underway. Nonetheless, I find that a review of the law on nullity can assist in the clarification as to the legal status of the notice parties.

[52] According to the law on nullity, the defining moment when assessing the validity or otherwise of the marriage is the moment at which the marriage occurs: *Napier v. Napier* [1915] Probate 184. No subsequent event can render a valid marriage invalid; see *A.B. v. N.C.* [2006] I.E.H.C. 127. Therefore, a marriage validly contracted by two parties who presented as, and were legally recognised as, being of opposite genders at the moment of marriage does not transform into a same sex marriage upon the legal recognition of the preferred gender of one spouse. Neither is the status of the notice parties in any way disturbed by recognition of the preferred gender of Dr. Foy.

Reliefs

[53] In terms of the reliefs sought by the plaintiff, I find that the High Court applied the incorrect test for the determination of legal gender, and overrule that aspect of the decision. What impact does this have on the question of whether the Registrar General acted *ultra vires* in refusing to amend the record of Dr. Foy's birth on the Register of Births?

[54] I accept and agree with the finding of McKechnie J., that the record on the Register of Births is merely a historical document recording particular facts on a particular day—it is a "snapshot" of a moment in time. This register is not an identity document nor is it the official *curriculum vitae* of events of legal import for a person. Significant events subsequent to the birth of a person, for example marriage or death are not recorded on the Register by way of annotation. S. 27 of the Births and Deaths Registration Act (Ireland), 1880 permits alteration of the register by reason of "clerical errors" or "errors of substance" by way of marginal annotation. No error was made in the recording of the sex of the appellant as male as that represented the best information available at the time the record was completed. Neither is it a "mistake" within the meaning of the Civil Registration Act, 2004 and thus the power to rectify mistakes contained in sections 63 and 64 of the 2004 Act are also not applicable.

[55] Thus I find myself with very limited options by which to affect a meaningful resolution for the appellant resulting from my findings. In the absence of some mechanism whereby an official record can be made of a successful rebuttal of the presumption of gender flowing from the record in the Register of Births I find that the most useful mechanism available to me is the possibility of issuing a Declaration of Incompatibility under s.5 of the European Convention on Human Rights Act, 2003. While such a Declaration would not disturb the validity of any existing law it is, nonetheless, a valuable tool. It will oblige the Taoiseach to lay the order identifying the incompatibility before both Houses of the Oireachtas within 21 sitting days. It will also enable the appellant to make an application under s.5(4) of the 2003 Act to the Government, through the Attorney General, for an *ex gratia* payment. Such a Declaration may also have implications for the exercise of court discretion regarding the costs of the proceedings.

[56] I close by reiterating the call made by my colleague Mr Justice McKechnie in his 2002 judgment when he urged the Oireachtas to review the matter of the legal recognition of gender urgently. Now, some seven years later, this matter is even more vital.

29

Commentary on *Barnes v Belfast City Council*

FIONA COOKE[1]

It may not be readily apparent to readers why a volume on feminist judging would include a case that generated a public outcry following the destruction of a pet dog by Belfast City Council under Northern Ireland's version of the much derided dangerous dog legislation. This perhaps reflects the somewhat contested relationship between feminist and animal studies. As Paolo Cavalieri observes, 'the intellectual history of the women's movement is marked by disassociation from nonhumans … what prevails in feminist theory is a negative attitude toward nonhumans and their status'.[2] This negative attitude has often been replicated in feminist legal theory, and at times has resulted in feminist scholars seeking to distance themselves from animals in order to stake their own claims to being human,[3] or more commonly simply overlooking or downplaying the issue of harm to nonhuman animals.[4] Yet, as Catherine MacKinnon has argued powerfully, there are many commonalities between the harms that the legal system has perpetrated (or failed to remedy) in the cases of both women and nonhuman animals:

> [B]oth animals and women have been socially configured as property … specifically for possession and use. Less widely observed, both women and animals have been status objects to be acquired and paraded by men to raise men's status among men, as well as used for labor and breeding and pleasure and ease … Both women and animals are seen as needing to be subdued and controlled. Both are imagined as dangerously powerful so must be kept powerless if not locked up and kept down in place, and killed when they step out of line…[5]

[1] With many thanks to the editors for their comments.

[2] Paola Cavalieri, 'Consequences of Humanism, or, Advocating What?' in Marianne DeKoven and Michael Lundblad (eds), *Species Matters: Human Advocacy and Cultural Theory* (New York, Columbia University Press, 2012) 58–59.

[3] Interestingly, while women have been particularly prominent in animal activist and welfare campaigns—see, for instance, Coral Lansbury, *The Old Brown Dog: Women, Workers and Vivisection in Edwardian England* (Madison, WI, University of Wisconsin Press, 1985)—feminist theory generally has been less accommodating of animals. Thus, Donovan and Adams note that the most common feminist position on the question of animal status is to reject links between feminism and animal ethics—Josephine Donovan and Carol Adams (eds), *The Feminist Care Tradition in Animal Ethics* (New York, Columbia University Press, 2007) 7. On feminist legal theory see Marie Fox, 'Re-thinking Kinship: Law's Construction of the Animal Body' (2004) 57 *Current Legal Problems* 464–86; Catharine MacKinnon, *Are Women Human?* (Cambridge, MA, Harvard University Press, 2006).

[4] Marie Fox, 'Exposing Harm: The Erasure of Animal Bodies in Health Care Law' in Sheila McLean (ed), *First Do No Harm: Law, Ethics and Healthcare* (Aldershot, Ashgate, 2006).

[5] Catharine MacKinnon, 'Of Mice and Men: a Feminist Fragment on Animal Rights' in Cass Sunstein, and Martha Nussbaum (eds), *Animal Rights: Current Debates and New Directions* (New York, Oxford University Press, 2004).

The case of *Barnes v Belfast City Council*[6] is a story of a dog alleged to be dangerous, who is seized from his home, locked up and ultimately killed as a result of his appearance. The case demonstrates vividly the consequences for animals of being designated as property.[7] It illustrates how, to an even greater extent than occurs in cases involving women, animals—in this case a dog named Lennox—who should be central figures in legal cases that concern them, effectively disappear as law discounts their interests. Furthermore, configured purely as property, their vital role as family members is simply erased by a legal system that fails to acknowledge the lived experience or relational interests of animals, or to recognise the possibility of inter-species relationships that are equally valuable to the humans involved. It is highly unlikely that an intersectional theory that recognises species as a salient characteristic[8] can be accommodated by a legal system premised on the idea that animals are property. However, this feminist judgment shows how, even within the confines of a much criticised legislative regime, it remains possible for judges to fashion a better outcome for nonhuman animals and those humans with whom their lives are enmeshed. Moreover, as outlined below, *Barnes v Belfast City Council* is of interest even to feminist lawyers who would repudiate the connections between women and animals, since it demonstrates how easily women's voices and expertise can be discounted in favour of what is deemed to be a more authoritative male testimony.

The Facts

Lennox, thought by his owner, Caroline Barnes, to be an American Bulldog/Labrador cross-breed, was seized by dog wardens employed by Belfast City Council during a visit to her home. He had been reported to the dog warden as having the appearance of a 'dangerous' dog,[9] as outlined under article 25(a) and article 25A(70) of the Dogs (NI) Order 1983 (SI 764/83) (as amended by the Dangerous Dogs (Northern Ireland) Act 1991 (DD(NI)A)). In April 2011, Lennox was formally identified by Mr Peter Tallack, a specialist in dangerous dog identification, as a Pit Bull Terrier type, and Ms Barnes accepted this. As a consequence of this identification, a Destruction Order was placed on Lennox.

Broadly speaking, legislation adopts two different approaches to regulating dogs alleged to be dangerous. The first approach addresses incidents of aggression in individual dogs, whilst the second specifies breeds or 'types' of dogs considered to be inherently dangerous. This second type of legislative approach is often referred to as Breed-Specific Legislation (BSL) and is the focus of this case. The Pit Bull Terrier is the type most often identified in the UK under BSL. There is a huge media interest in these dogs, which typically construes them as 'status' or weapon dogs. Thus, as Lennox had already been identified as a Pit Bull Terrier type, this may arguably have influenced the judgments in the case, due to preconceptions of the breed and their owners. As Reg Graycar points out, judicial

[6] *Barnes and Belfast City Council* [2011] NICty 3.

[7] See generally, Gary Francione, *Animals, Property and the Law* (Philadelphia, PA, Temple University Press, 1995).

[8] Maneesha Dechka, 'Toward a Postcolonial, Posthumanist Feminist Theory: Centralizing Race and Culture in Feminist Work on Nonhuman Animals' (2012) 27 *Hypatia* 527–45.

[9] 'Dogs bred for fighting'.

common sense and intuitions based on societal assumptions and their own experience often significantly affect the process of judging,[10] and such assumptions may well have coloured the original judgment.

Having accepted that Lennox was of type, Ms Barnes appealed against the decision to destroy him. Because the identification of a Pit Bull Terrier type is based almost exclusively on physical characteristics, as contained in a 1977 American Dog Breeders Association article,[11] it is very difficult to challenge a decision based on a finding that dog conforms to certain physical standards.[12]

Consequently, it is rare for an appeal to be brought regarding a dog who has been 'typed'. The county court judge, Rodgers J, stated that the court was bound by 'clear and uncompromising terms' in the 1991 legislation to order the destruction of a dog of prohibited type, despite agreement by two experienced behaviourists acting as expert witnesses that Lennox could return home without posing a risk to public safety. The Court of Appeal dismissed the appeal and Lennox was destroyed.[13] The differences between the original county court judgment and Marie Fox's feminist judgment are largely dictated by the following three issues: their different approaches to the interpretation of the law, their contrasting evaluation of the expert testimony, and the differing ways they understand Lennox and his behaviour. Fox J's alternative approach to interpreting the law enables her to reach the conclusion that Lennox could be returned to his family.

This case fuelled a huge 'Save Lennox' campaign,[14] with a number of highly established and well-respected professionals becoming involved in the media furor[15] surrounding Lennox's case. He became a 'pawn in a political game'.[16] In consequence, footage of the behavioural assessments produced for the court was released, and several press interviews held with those involved. The campaign and the resulting publicity offer an insight into the impact of this case on public perceptions of dangerous dogs legislation, 'status' dogs and ownership choices, as well as providing further detail for analysis of this case. A perfunctory 'Google search' for 'Pit Bulls' reveals images mainly of strong men holding large, powerful dogs, often pulling towards the camera. These connotations pervade the 'Pit Bull' image and potentially create a predetermined image of the type of person who owns (or could 'handle') such a dog.[17] The potential for media depictions of Pit Bull types to affect judgments about the threat posed by such dogs, and who would be capable of managing them, arises here. Suffice to say that these images and articles do not portray an average pet owner, and are far removed from the reality of the relationship between Lennox and Caroline Barnes. Fundamentally, the case emphasises the flaws inherent in dangerous dog legislation, which discriminates on the basis of appearance and is not based on appropriate evidence as to public safety.

[10] Reg Graycar, 'The Gender of Judgments: An Introduction' in Margaret Thornton (ed), *Public and Private: Feminist Legal Debates* (Melbourne, Oxford University Press, 1995) 262–82.

[11] *Pit Bull Gazette*, vol 1, issue 3, 1977.

[12] *R v Knightsbridge Crown Court, ex parte Dunne; Brock v DPP* [1993] 4 All ER 491.

[13] *Barnes v Belfast City Council* [2012] NICA 19.

[14] See www.savelennox.co.uk/ (last accessed 27 July 2015).

[15] eg video footage of assessments was released, such as a partial clip of David Ryan's assessment. Available at www.youtube.com/watch?v=A72yVQEsqMU (last accessed 28 July 2015).

[16] Victoria Stilwell, 'How the legal system failed Lennox', https://positively.com/victorias-blog/how-the-legal-system-failed-lennox/ (last accessed 30 July 2015).

[17] See also Maria Kaspersson, 'On Treating the Symptoms and not the Cause: Reflections on the Dangerous Dogs Act' (2008) *Papers from the British Criminology Conference* 205–25.

Interpreting the Law

Dangerous dogs legislation is extremely controversial across the UK and Ireland. The regime in the Republic of Ireland is radically different from that in the UK, and presents different yet equally problematic issues,[18] including the fact that over 10 'types' are identified as requiring a lead and muzzle in public places,[19] and exemptions take a different form.

The UK law has been branded 'not fit for purpose'[20] and 'a failure',[21] following enactment caused by a 'knee-jerk reaction'[22] to a number of tragic incidents involving dogs and children in the late 1980s and early 1990s. Initially, the law was 'draconian',[23] requiring any dog identified as type to be destroyed. In damning evidence to the Northern Ireland Assembly on reform proposals in 2010, Veterinary Northern Ireland commented:

> The 1991 order refers to dogs of the Pit Bull Terrier type … There is no such breed of dog, and as a result its interpretation is impossible. The vet profession worldwide, backed by veterinary behaviourists is totally opposed to any attempt to classify dangerous dogs according to breed … no evidence exists that the currently listed 'dangerous' breeds in DDA 1991 … show an increased frequency of biting behaviour as compared to other breeds.[24]

It is not possible to ascertain type by conducting a DNA test.[25] A DNA test would have the advantage of allowing specific identification of a breed, whereas at present any crosses that result in a dog conforming to type can be subject to this legislation. However, deploying DNA tests would not address the principal fault of this legislation, which is its attempt to assess the risk dogs pose by their physical type rather than their behaviour.[26]

To compound the complexity of the dangerous dogs legislation, in Northern Ireland the type-specific legislation was grafted onto the Dogs (Northern Ireland) Order 1983. Section 25 of the DD(NI)A applies to 'dogs bred for fighting'. Specific regulations and requirements

[18] Control of Dogs Regulations 1998 (SI 442/1998).

[19] Art 5.

[20] 'Bark but no bite: Dangerous Dogs Act in spotlight as attacks rise', *Guardian*, 18 January 2012, at: www.theguardian.com/uk/2012/jan/18/dangerous-dogs-in-spotlight (last, accessed July 2012).

[21] David Joyce, 'Children & People Killed & Injured in Dog Attacks', paper presented at the Public Policy Exchange Symposium, *Clamping Down on Dangerous Dogs: Protecting the Public and Promoting More Responsible Pet Ownership* (London, 2014).

[22] As described by Lord Redesdale in discussion; Dog Control Bill, (HL) 2nd Reading, 24 April 2009, vol 709, col 1689.

[23] Rose LJ in *Bates v DPP* (1993) 157 JP 1004.

[24] Des Thompson, Northern Ireland Assembly: Report on the Dogs (Amendment) Bill, 2010–2011. See http://niassembly.gov.uk/assembly-business/committees/agriculture-and-rural-development/archive/archive-committee-reports/session-2010-2011/report-on-the-dogs-amendment-bill/ (last accessed 30 July 2015).

[25] Dog Law, 'Dangerous dogs (pit bull types): Section 1 & 4B Dangerous Dogs Act 1991' (2015) www.doglaw.co.uk/pitbull.php (last accessed 30 July 2015).

[26] Some commentators have depicted this as a form of 'canine racism'—eg Karyn Grey, 'Breed-Specific Legislation Revisited: Canine Racism or the Answer to Florida's Dog Control Problem?' (2002-3) 27 *Nova Law Review* 415–18. As with the feminist judgment in this volume by Julie McCandless in *A and B (by C)* (ch 30), the *Barnes* case highlights the problematic nature of classification systems based on appearance. Additionally, of course, feminist legal scholars have long pointed out the negative consequences for women of the societal tendency to judge women on their appearance, and how women are impacted much more significantly than men by aesthetic judgements. See, eg, Deborah Rhodes, *The Beauty Bias: The Injustice of Appearance in Life and Law* (New York, Oxford University Press, 2011).

were created for two types alleged to be inherently dangerous under the DD(NI)A—Pit Bull Terrier and Japanese Tosa types. Restrictions are placed on management, ownership, breeding and sale of these dogs,[27] with the aim of eradicating them. In practice, the vast majority of cases under this legislation concern Pit Bull Terrier types. The intrinsic value of the dog, and consequently whether or not he or she should live or die, is therefore decided solely on appearance.

In England, Wales and Scotland, a provision for exemption from compulsory destruction was made by amendments in 1997,[28] by way of the Index of Exempted Dogs, which allows destruction to be avoided if the dog is considered by the court not to pose a risk to public safety.[29] A similar provision was introduced in Northern Ireland only in 2001,[30] while provisions to establish a similar Index were not enacted until 2011.[31]

Crucially, in their judgments, both Rodgers J and later Girvan LJ, who delivered the judgment of the NICA, omitted any reference to the Dogs (Amendment) Act (Northern Ireland) 2001 (DAA(NI)), and therefore the possibility of placing Lennox on the Index of Exempted Dogs. Hence, Rodgers J relied upon only two of the three provisions that actually constitute the law applicable to this case. By drawing on the DAA(NI) 2001, Fox J, in rewriting the county court judgment, is able to conclude that Lennox should be exempted. Rodgers J noted that although the section amending Article 25C of the Dogs Order appears to be permissive, stating that the court '*may* order the destruction' of a dog subject to the statutory prohibition, that discretion was limited by the further stipulation that the court '*shall* do so unless satisfied that the dog will not be a danger to the public' (emphasis added). He then proceeded to make the rather curious remark that the opportunity to place dogs on the Index of Exempted Dogs in England and Wales 'is not the case in Northern Ireland where local authorities have no facilities to use Exemption certificates' (para 8). However, this begs the question of the purpose of the Northern Ireland Assembly in passing a law to permit exemption if no mechanism was provided to put it into practice.[32] The judge's statement also betrays his misunderstanding of the complex statutory framework in Northern Ireland and the fact that the 2001 Act did permit him to make an exemption order—an oversight that the Northern Ireland Court of Appeal also failed to rectify.

To the extent that the judge considered the intention of the legislature at all, this came only in the penultimate paragraph of his judgment, where he noted:

> Before coming to the decision in this case it is important to remember the purpose of the Dangerous Dogs legislation. The issue is public safety and it is the duty of the court to put public safety above anything. (para 36)

In prioritising this somewhat vague notion of public safety—undoubtedly a key aim of this body of legislation as a whole—Rodgers J overlooked other subsidiary aims of

[27] Ss 25(A)(2) and (3).

[28] Dangerous Dogs (Amendment) Act 1997.

[29] Stringent requirements are imposed on keepers: Gov.UK, Controlling your dog in public, at www.gov.uk/control-dog-public/banned-dogs (last accessed 1 July 2015).

[30] Dogs (Amendment) Act (Northern Ireland) 2001.

[31] Dogs (Amendment) Act (Northern Ireland) 2011.

[32] For discussion see at http://niassembly.gov.uk/assembly-business/committees/agriculture-and-rural-development/archive/archive-committee-reports/session-2010-2011/report-on-the-dogs-amendment-bill/ (last accessed 19 July 2015).

the amending legislation. Crucially, he ignored the fact that some of the 2001 and 2011 amendments were expressly designed to ameliorate the lack of discretion previously allowed to courts.[33] Rodgers J also ruled that local authorities in Northern Ireland had no facilities to issue an exemption certificate under Section5(4) of the 2011 Act. However, as Fox J points out in her judgment, the courts had already been granted this power by the 2001 Act, although no structure to implement it was established prior to 2011. Her recognition of the potential for Lennox to be placed on the Exempted Index gives her the opportunity to avoid a destruction order, and allows for a different assessment of the evidence as to temperament.

Dangerous Dogs legislation conflicts with usual criminal law requirements for evidence provision, as it reverses the burden of proof in a departure from the standard expectation that the prosecution have a case to prove. This unusual legal position was challenged as a breach of human rights, but the European Commission of Human Rights ruled out the challenge.[34] Thus, 'if it is alleged by the prosecution that a dog is of type, it shall be presumed that it is such a dog',[35] and the owner of an alleged type dog will be required to prove otherwise.[36] This typically results in the employment of expert witnesses who are experienced in identifying dogs of type—in this case Mr Peter Tallack, an ex-police officer with many years' experience identifying such dogs. Where temperament is relevant in assessing whether the dog poses a risk to the public and may therefore be considered for exemption, expert witnesses in dog behaviour may be consulted. In this case behavioural experts (Mr David Ryan and Ms Sarah Fisher) were called only on Ms Barnes' behalf. Ms Lightfoot, the dog warden, also expressed her views on Lennox's behaviour. I will not explore her testimony further since she was not a court expert and her final testimony was not considered in depth by Rodgers J, except to reference her opinion as to Lennox's 'dangerousness', which was not supported by the behavioural experts' testimonies.

Evaluating the Expert Evidence

My own experience as a professional behaviourist, often working with behaviourally challenging large Bull breeds in complex and welfare-compromised environments, leaves me concerned about the potential for behavioural expertise and knowledge to be misconstrued and taken out of context in the legal setting. By contrast, a key feature of feminist judging is attentiveness to the context in which the subjects of the legal case find themselves.[37] In Lennox's case, he had been uprooted from his familiar environment and placed in kennels from May 2010 until he was euthanised in July 2012. The kennel environment

[33] See further www.niassembly.gov.uk/assembly-business/official-report/committee-minutes-of-evidence/session-2010-2011/october-2010/dogs-amendment-bill-veterinary-northern-ireland/ (last accessed 18 July 2015).

[34] *Bates v UK* [1996] EHRLR 312.

[35] Dangerous Dogs Act 1991(DDA), s 5(5).

[36] DDA, s 1.

[37] See, eg, Rosemary Hunter, 'Can *Feminist* Judges Make a Difference?' (2008) 15 *International Journal of the Legal Profession* 7–36.

creates at least some welfare compromise for dogs,[38] with specific compromises for seized dogs.[39] In fact, there have been cases where seized dogs have been released in Northern Ireland yet subsequently euthanised due to the long-term psychological consequences of such confinement.[40] Lennox's welfare compromise is likely to have been exacerbated by his general anxiety,[41] as well as by a seeming neck injury and other sores noted by Ms Fisher.[42] The potential impact of pain or illness on behaviour is widely acknowledged,[43] hence the emphasis on Lennox's health in this case. Lennox was prescribed Amixytrolene for 'depression', suggesting recognition by Belfast City Council of a compromised psychological state. Fox J's judgment displays a greater attentiveness to the circumstances in which Lennox finds himself, highlighting his likely health problems and the impact they may have had on his welfare, whereas these are only fleetingly referred to in Roger's judgment, despite their being crucial to providing a full overview.

Mr Tallack and Mr Ryan were both previously police dog handlers. Although Mr Ryan pursued additional avenues in order to develop his expertise (acquiring professional qualifications in animal behaviour science), his testimony was not considered to be as authoritative as that of Mr Tallack in the original county court ruling. I would also argue that Mr Ryan's testimony is fundamentally misunderstood, in that Rodgers J aligns it with that of Mr Tallack, even though Mr Ryan states that Lennox would be suitable to return home, whilst Mr Tallack states otherwise.

Ms Fisher's expertise is widely acknowledged, yet Rodgers J does not appear to recognise this. In a highly gendered way her greater expertise than that of Mr Tallack in the behavioural profession is downplayed and disregarded. Rodgers J comments that 'unfortunately Ms Fisher has very little experience of Pit Bull Terrier type dogs'.[44] He then reiterates her 'lack of experience of these powerful dogs'.[45] Fox J's judgment omits this negative comment on Ms Fisher's expertise, recognising that Pit Bull Terrier types can be assessed by suitably qualified professionals.

The conflicting expert evidence is treated very differently by the two judgments. In Rodger J's judgment the highly prejudicial account of Lennox offered by Mr Tallack's evidence is outlined first and treated as authoritative. It serves to cast Lennox as dangerous and unpredictable. In contrast to his opinion of Mr Tallack, Rodger J is highly critical of Ms Fisher and positions her as an outlier amongst the witnesses, notwithstanding the fact that she and Mr Ryan agree that Lennox would not pose a danger to public safety if managed properly by his family. Mr Ryan's expert opinion aligned more closely in outcome with

[38] Elly Hiby, Nicola Rooney and John Bradshaw, 'Behavioural and physiological responses of dogs entering rehoming kennels' (2006) 89 *Physiological Behaviour* 385–91.

[39] RSPCA and Chartered Institute of Environmental Health, 'The welfare of seized dogs in kennels: A guide to good practice', at http://politicalanimal.org.uk/wp-content/uploads/2015/04/RSPCA-Guide-The-welfare-of-seized-dogs-in-kennels.compressed.pdf (last accessed 12 July 2015).

[40] eg Missey, see www.ddawatch.co.uk/in_memory.html (last accessed 2 June 2015).

[41] See *Barnes and Belfast City Council* [2011] NICty 3, para 27.

[42] Victoria Stilwell, 'Positively' Podcast, at http://positively.com/2011/10/10/positively-podcast-episode-201/ (last accessed 12 July 2015).

[43] Association of Pet Behaviour Counsellors: The APBC and the veterinary profession, at www.apbc.org.uk/help/vet (accessed 30 July 2015).

[44] *Barnes and Belfast City Council* [2011] NICty 3, para 21.

[45] ibid.

Ms Fisher than Mr Tallack. Fox J recognises this and emphasises the expertise of the witnesses in their field, in contrast to Rodgers J, who aligns the statement of Mr Ryan with that of Mr Tallack. Strikingly, Rodgers J undermines Ms Fisher's credibility by stating that 'This picture she portrays of the dog flies in the face of every other witness, even the Appellant'.[46]

The complexity of the evidence presented, and the need to have an understanding of behavioural science in order to apply it effectively, is evident when considering the arguments presented by the expert witnesses. The downplaying by Rodgers J of the evidence given by Ms Fisher, in comparison to the weight accorded this testimony in Fox J's judgment, raises questions as to the consideration of evidence by the judge. In this regard Schullera et al studied the impact of expert witness testimony on jury decisions in a simulated civil trial about an antitrust price-fixing agreement. They systematically varied the gender of the expert and the complexity of the testimony given, to examine whether these factors would impact judicial views of the authority of testimony. Their study demonstrates that the gender of an expert witness is used as a heuristic cue to evaluate the evidence presented by that expert: 'It was expected that the male expert would be more persuasive than the female expert, but only when the testimony presented was complex. As predicted, this interaction was revealed across a range of dependent measures.'[47] As highlighted in Fox J's judgment, the complexity of the law itself, coupled with the intrinsic complications of integrating behavioural science with it, meant that the expert testimony presented was difficult to evaluate. As Stillwell points out, someone 'who is unqualified to analyze dog behavior, can easily and mistakenly draw incorrect conclusions regarding the severity, motivation for, and circumstances surrounding such behavior'.[48]

Presentation of Evidence

A number of legal scholars have shown that how a judge structures his or her account of the facts and evidence can influence the outcome of cases.[49] This too is borne out by the contrast in the judgments. Thus Fox J reverses the order in which the evidence is given so that the more positive assessment of Lennox comes first. She also highlights that two of the three experts before the court recommend that Lennox can be returned to his family. This highlights how it is Mr Tallack who is the sole expert not in agreement with the possibility of returning Lennox to his family under appropriate management.

Fox J also contextualises the expert evidence by emphasising the difficulties of assessing a dog in a situation where he is, as the expert testimony noted, under stress. In contrast Rodgers J is dismissive, noting that 'what troubles me about [Ms Fisher's] evidence was

[46] ibid, para 34.

[47] Regina Schullera, Deborah Terry and Blake McKimmiec, 'The Impact of Expert Testimony on Jurors' Decisions: Gender of the Expert and Testimony Complexity' (2005) 35(6) *Journal of Applied Social Psychology* 1266–80.

[48] Victoria Stilwell, 'How the legal system failed Lennox', at: https://positively.com/victorias-blog/how-the-legal-system-failed-lennox/ (last accessed 30 July 2015).

[49] See, eg, Donald Nicolson, 'Telling Tales: Gender Discrimination, Gender Construction and Battered Women Who Kill' (1995) 3 *Feminist Legal Studies* 185–206; Jo Winter, 'The Truth Will Out? The Role of Judicial Advocacy and Gender in Verdict Construction' (2002) 11 *Social and Legal Studies* 343–67.

that she saw nothing at all to concern her in the dog's behaviour'.[50] By acknowledging Lennox's potential trauma at finding himself in kennels and by highlighting the fact that he has harmed no one, Fox J is able to portray Ms Fisher's expert evidence as more credible before the court.

How the Judgments Construct Lennox

This section examines two issues: first, the differing terminology the two judgments use; and, secondly, how they construct Lennox very differently—in the original as property (or indeed a weapon) and in the feminist version as a family member.

The Importance of Terminology

Feminist legal scholars have highlighted the importance of judges' adopting gender neutral language in order to communicate effectively to their various audiences, including other judges, lawyers, students and the public.[51] Language has been shown to be equally important in colouring our attitudes towards animals.[52] In this regard the feminist judgment deploys language markedly different from the original. In the original judgment, Rodgers J consistently depersonalises Lennox and treats him as an item of property. In law, of course, dogs are property, which is an obstacle to assigning them 'morally significant interests'.[53] The judge's detachment from and objectification of Lennox allows him to treat Lennox as a piece of property. Lacking in interests and separated from his family, I would suggest that this facilitates the ultimate decision to end Lennox's life. Significantly, Rodgers J refers to Lennox as 'the dog' or 'it' throughout the case, while in contrast Fox J names Lennox and refers to him as 'he' throughout.[54]

The role of Lennox as a family pet and the relationships he formed within his family are not referenced in Rodger J's judgement. Although Lennox became the subject of this case due to his appearance, consideration of his behaviour is clearly more relevant to ascertaining whether he poses a risk to the public. Yet Rodger J's judgment fails to take account of the years he spent living as a family pet. Fox J, by contrast, shows how throughout his life Lennox had never actually harmed anyone, and that appropriate management techniques had been employed by the appellant to ensure that he was safely controlled.

[50] *Barnes and Belfast City Council* [2011] NICty 3, para 34.

[51] See, eg, Leslie Rose, 'The Supreme Court and Gender-Neutral Language: Setting the Standard or Lagging Behind?' (2010) 17 *Duke Journal of Gender, Law and Policy* 81–199.

[52] Arran Stibbe, 'Language, Power and the Social Construction of Animals' (2001) 9(2) *Society & Animals* 145–61; Joan Dunayer, *Animal Equality: Language and Liberation* (Derwood, MD, Ryce Publishing, 2001).

[53] Gary Francione, 'Animals-Property or Persons?' (2004) *Rutgers Law School (Newark) Faculty Papers*, Working Paper 21, at http://law.bepress.com/rutgersnewarklwps/art21 (last accessed 30 July 2015).

[54] Though naming animals does not produce uniformly positive outcomes for them: 'Cecil the lion was doomed from the moment he got his name.' (*Guardian*, 29 July 2015, at http://www.theguardian.com/environment/shortcuts/2015/jul/29/cecil-the-lion-doomed-name (last accessed 29 July 2015)).

Lennox as a Family Member

In the feminist judgment Lennox is to some extent constructed as a family member embedded in a network of relationships. Fox J's judgment draws attention to Lennox's background, to his relationship with Ms Barnes' young daughter, Brooke, and to the responsible ownership of Ms Barnes. Her approach fits with a body of research showing that many people consider their pets to be part of the family.[55] Charles and Davies found that respondents in their mass observation study included their pets as 'part of their kinship networks'.[56]

Such considerations and the central role of Lennox in this case are virtually disregarded in Rodger J's judgement. There is little reference to Lennox's six years in the home prior to the events leading to the court case; but his role as a family member is highlighted in Fox J's judgment. The evidence provided in this case and in the media coverage suggests that Lennox was regarded as a family member by his owners. Although he is legally considered property, Lennox's principal value to his family is as a much loved companion. As noted above, the role of 'type' dogs as portrayed in the media may have served to undercut the understanding of Lennox as a family pet. A combination of popular views of status dogs[57] and the construction in law of Lennox as property, may have contributed to Rodger J's perception of him as a weapon, particularly in light of the testimony of Mr Tallack.

This understanding of type dogs is widely acknowledged,[58] with the designation 'dangerous dog' in itself generating a particular view of a dog, even one assessed as temperamentally sound. Thus, the perception of Lennox as a family member living within a web of relationships is overridden by stereotypes not only of what this dog represents, but of the type of person who chooses to own such a dog. The potential harm to the family of the loss of a valued family member is not considered by Rodgers J. Even when his decision is communicated, there is no recognition of the impact this may have on those who will grieve for a companion, although the level of grief caused by the loss of a pet indicates that 'the human–animal bond'[59] is that of the level of a primary relationship.

Rodger J's judgment gives scant credit to the actions of Ms Barnes. To the relatively brief extent that her role is addressed, she is cast as irresponsible and disingenuous. Thus, the fact that she takes action such as muzzling Lennox is used to exemplify his potential risk to public safety, rather than portraying her as a responsible owner. Yet use of a muzzle is often considered to be an aspect of responsible dog ownership.[60] Nevertheless, Rodgers J references this as a concern, whereas Fox J uses this action to credit the responsible actions

[55] James Serpell, *In the company of animals: a study of human-animal relationships*, 1st edn 1986 (Cambridge University Press, 1996).

[56] Nickie Charles and Charlotte Aull Davies, 'My Family and Other Animals: Pets as Kin' (2008) 13(5) *Sociological Research Online* 4, at www.socresonline.org.uk/13/5/4.html (last accessed 29 July 2015).

[57] Gordon Hughes, Jenny Maher and Claire Lawson, *Research Project Report: Status dogs, young people and criminalisation: towards a preventative strategy* (RSPCA and Cardiff University, 2011).

[58] Simon Harding, 'Bling with Bite' (2013) 173 *Veterinary Record* 261–63.

[59] Marie Jose Enders-Slegers, 'The meaning of companion animals: qualitative analysis of the life histories of elderly cat and dog owners' in Anthony Podberscek, Elizabeth Paul and James Serpell (eds), *Companion animals and us: exploring the relationships between people and pets* (Cambridge, Cambridge University Press, 2000) 237–56.

[60] The Company of Animals, 'Muzzles are frequently used by responsible owners', at http://companyofanimals.co.uk/brands/baskerville-muzzles (accessed 30 July 2015).

of Ms Barnes and acknowledge that this method of management had hitherto ensured that Lennox remained part of his family without coming to the attention of the authorities for aggressive behaviour.

Conclusion

Whereas Rodgers J dismissed the appeal on the basis that he would find it 'very difficult' to be satisfied on the balance of probabilities that 'the dog will not be a danger to the public', and that he did not believe that 'it would be practical or possible to put restraints on the ownership of this dog that would bring it within the statutory test',[61] Fox J concludes that there is little evidence on a balance of probabilities that Lennox poses a danger and stresses the responsible actions of the owner.

As well as reaching different outcomes, the judgments exhibit differing levels of awareness of how problematic the dangerous dogs legislation is. The troublesome nature of the legislation is apparent throughout the above discussion as regards the aims of the legislation, its terms and the capacity for effective implementation. Although these problems afflict dangerous dogs legislation throughout the UK, they are particularly acute in Northern Ireland, as demonstrated by the lack of implementation of the Exemption Index structure. The feminist judgment demonstrates that even when faced with such flawed legislation, it is open to judges to reach different conclusions if they carefully evaluate the facts and the evidence as to threats to public safety. It shows how it is possible to mitigate the draconian nature of the 1991 legislation and place Lennox on the Exemption Index. Such judicial creativity and empathy does not, however, eradicate the need for effective reform of the unnecessarily complex and ineffective law that allows animals to be seized and potentially destroyed merely due to their appearance.

The reasoning underpinning the feminist judgment allows the professional roles of the expert witnesses to be evaluated effectively, and the evidence provided to be accorded appropriate weight with regard to their professional qualifications and expertise. Fox J also highlights the individuality of Lennox within this case, enabling his role as a family companion to be acknowledged within the context of the judgment.

The use of language by Rodgers J that depersonalises Lennox emphasises the situational objectification of Lennox. Through use of language that accords subjectivity to Lennox and a different weighting of the expert witness evidence, Fox J identifies key aspects of Lennox's character, creating space to recognise Lennox's role as a valued companion. Consequently, the feminist judgment preserves relationships that are downplayed and at times erased within the judgment of Rodgers J. The feminist approach places Lennox at the centre of the case,[62] generating a different outcome. The ruling by Fox J is therefore more in line with a feminist approach premised on care and relationality,[63] which allows her to reach the conclusion that Lennox should not be euthanised but should be returned to his family.

[61] *Barnes and Belfast City Council* [2011] NICty 3, para 37.

[62] See also Mary Donnelly's feminist judgment in this collection, ch 20.

[63] Josephine Donovan and Carol Adams (eds), *Beyond Animal Rights: a Feminist Caring Ethics for the Treatment of Animals* (New York, Continuum, 1996).

Citation No. [2011] NICty 3 [delivered 30/09/2011]

IN THE COUNTY COURT FOR DIVISION OF BELFAST

CAROLINE BARNES

(Appellant)

and

BELFAST CITY COUNCIL

(Respondent)

Her Honour Judge Fox*

Application

1. This case came before the County Court on an Appeal by Caroline Barnes ("the Appellant") against a decision in Belfast Magistrates' Court which convicted her of keeping a dog a Pit Bull Terrier Type contrary to Article 25A(1) of the Dogs (Northern Ireland) Order 1983 as amended by the Dangerous Dogs (NI) Order 1991. As a result it was ordered that the Appellant's dog, Lennox, be destroyed.

Facts of case

2. On 11 May 2010 dog wardens from the Respondent Council went to the Appellant's home, following a call from a colleague who indicated that there appeared to be a Pit Bull Terrier at the home of the Appellant Ms Barnes. First, Ms Lightfoot—a council dog warden with almost 10 years of experience—called at the house and enquired about the dog. She was refused entry by Ms Barnes' partner, and later returned accompanied by a police officer and two other dog warden colleagues—Sian Wilson and John Templeman. On this occasion the Appellant allowed Ms Lightfoot to examine Lennox, her six year old pet dog. Ms Barnes explained that Lennox had a problem with stress and that he was bad with strangers. Surrounded by these strangers in the kitchen of his home, Ms Barnes muzzled Lennox and held onto him. However, according to the testimony of Ms Lightfoot and her two colleagues, Lennox eventually struck Ms Lightfoot on the head with his muzzle, knocking her back, although she suffered no injury. There was absolutely no indication that Lennox had ever bitten anyone and Ms Barnes denied that she knew that he was a Pit Bull Terrier. However she finally acceded to the dog wardens seizing Lennox, and walked him out of the house to their vehicle.

3. Ms Barnes was charged with being the keeper of a type of dog known as a Pit Bull Terrier contrary to article 25(a) and article 25A(70) of the Dogs (NI) Order 1983 as amended

* I would like to thank the editors for their comments on an earlier version and to acknowledge the helpful feedback from participants at the Dublin workshop, particularly Rosemary Hunter. The writing of this feminist judgment was also informed by information on the case available via the 'Save Lennox' campaign website (www.savelennox.co.uk) and Victoria Stilwell's website (https://positively.com).

by the Dangerous Dogs (NI) Order 1991. Through her counsel she accepted that Lennox was a dog of the type known as a Pit Bull Terrier and was convicted of the offence by the learned District Judge (Magistrates' Courts) siting at Belfast on 15 April 2011. The judge ruled that since Lennox was accepted to be a Pit Bull Terrier type, he had no discretion regarding Lennox's fate and therefore ordered that Lennox had be to destroyed (at para 6).

4. The Appellant now appeals against that decision

The Law

5. The relevant offence is contained in four separate legislative provisions, which are the Dogs (NI) Order 1983 as amended by the Dangerous Dogs (NI) Order 1991, Dogs (Amendment) Act (Northern Ireland) 2001 and the recently enacted Dogs (Amendment) Act (NI) Order 2011. In the interests of clarity I set out these somewhat convoluted provisions at some length. They provide as follows:-

6. Article 25A Dogs (NI) Order 1983 (as amended by the 1991 Order):

(1) This Article applies to
(a) any dog of the type known as the Pit Bull Terrier ...
(2) No person shall –
(a) breed, or breed from, a dog to which this Article applies;
(b) sell or exchange such a dog or offer, advertise or expose such a dog as a gift;
(c) make or offer to make a gift of such a dog or advertise or expose such a dog as a gift;
(d) cause or permit such a dog of which he is the keeper or of which he is for the time being in charge to be in a public place unless the dog is muzzled and kept on a lead; or
(e) abandon such a dog of which he is the keeper or, being the keeper or for the time being in charge of such a dog, permit it to stray.
(3) After 30 November 1991 no person shall have a dog to which this Article applied in his possession or custody except –
(a) in pursuance of a power of seizure conferred by this Order; or
(b) in accordance with an order for its destruction made under this Order;

...

7. Article 5 of the 1991 Order:
(1) Article 33 of the Dogs Order (power of court to order destruction of dogs) shall have effect subject to the following provisions of this Article.
(2) After paragraph (1) there shall be inserted the following paragraphs –
(1A) Where a person is convicted of an offence under Article 25A, the court shall make an order directing the dog in respect of which the offence was committed to be destroyed.

8. Section 1(3) of the Dogs (Amendment) Act (Northern Ireland) 2001 amends section 25C of the Dogs Order 1983 by inserting the following provision:

Article 33 (1A) Where a person is convicted of an offence under article 25A [dogs bred for fighting, including Pit Bull types] or of an offence under an order under Article 25B, ["other specially dangerous dogs"] the court may *make an order directing the dog in respect of which the offence was committed to be destroyed and shall do unless the court is satisfied that the dog will not be a danger to the public*" (*emphasis added*).

9. Finally section 5 of the 2011 Act has recently further amended the Dogs Order and also contains the key phrase, outlined above, from the 2001 legislation:

> *5(1) Article 25C of the Dogs Order (seizure of dangerous dogs) is amended as follows.*
>
> *(2) In paragraph 3 for sub-paragraphs (a) and (b) substitute "the district judges (magistrates' courts) may order the destruction of the dog and shall do so unless satisfied that the dog will not be a danger to the public"*
>
> *After paragraph (3) insert –*
>
> *"(4) If –*
>
> *(a) the dog is one to which Article 25A applies*
> *(b) the district judge (magistrates' court) does not order the destruction of the dog under paragraph (3), and*
> *(c) the dog is subject to the prohibition in Article 25A(3), the district judge (magistrates' court) shall order that unless the dog is exempted from the prohibition in Article 25A(3) within the period of two months beginning with the date of the order, the dog shall be destroyed".*

10. As will be apparent, the legislative regime governing destruction of dangerous dogs in this jurisdiction is highly complex because of the interaction of the four statutes cited above. Following a Minister's review and public consultation on dog control legislation in 2009–10, the Northern Ireland Assembly took the decision not to repeal and replace the existing legislation. It concluded that the best option was to "amend the Dogs Order where necessary to implement the key policy proposals, developed by the Minister's Review. This was considered to be a proportionate response to the ongoing problems identified by the Review" (Northern Ireland Assembly, 'Dogs (Amendment) Bill: Explanatory and Financial Memorandum' EFM 20-09, para 15). Given the extensive criticism leveled at the legislation throughout the process by the veterinary profession, district councils and others this decision was perhaps to be regretted.

11. While the 2011 Act was not in force at the time that Lennox was originally seized, it is helpful to refer to the explanatory notes which accompany it, since they shed light on the interpretation of section 1(3) of the Dogs (Amendment) Act (Northern Ireland) 2001, for which no accompanying explanatory notes were issued. The wording of section 1(3) is, however, identical to the corresponding provision in section 5(2) of the 2011 Act, and given that the life of a much loved family pet is at stake it is important to be clear about the law, given the complexity of the provisions outline above. Paragraph 8 of those explanatory notes states:

> Under Article 25A(5) of the Dogs Order dogs of a type normally prohibited by Article 25A may in certain circumstances be exempted from the prohibition. One of the amendments made by the Dogs (Amendment) Act (Northern Ireland) 2001 was that where a person was convicted of an offence under Article 25A (that is ... having possession of a dog of a prohibited type) the court could make an order directing that the dog in

respect of which the offence was committing could be destroyed, but also could exercise a discretion not to make such an order if satisfied that the dog would not be a danger to the public.

Thus the explanatory notes issued in 2011 are clear that the 2001 amendments granted discretion to the court to exempt from destruction a dog who was deemed not to present a danger to the public.

12. These explanatory notes also make it clear that section 5 of the 2011 Act was designed simply to clear up an anomaly generated by the discretion in the 2001 legislation. The 2001 legislation had indicated that "a dog of a type normally prohibited under Article 25A might escape being made subject to a destruction order". However paradoxically such a dog might also continue to be prohibited if no exemption order "was sought or gained in respect of that dog". To address this anomaly, the 2011 Act inserted a requirement for the court to make a contingent destruction order to be exercised where no exemption order is sought within two months of the court order exempting the dog.

13. These explanatory notes are helpful in indicating that, as a result of the 2001 amendments, the key question in considering whether an exemption order could be granted in respect of a prohibited type of dog is whether the court is satisfied that the dog concerned would not be a danger to the public.

The Issue

14. Lennox has been in the custody of the Respondents since May 2010 awaiting the outcome of legal proceedings. He is now six years old. It is worth noting that in the period of approximately 16 months he has spent in kennels he has been denied any contact with his family with whom he lived for five years. Since Ms Barnes now accepts that Lennox is a Pit Bull type, the sole issue for this court is to determine whether he should be destroyed as a result of Ms Barnes' conviction for keeping a prohibited type under Article 25A of the Dogs Order 1983 as amended. Under article 33 ((1A)) of the Order (inserted by section 1(3) of the Dogs (Amendment) Act 2001) I am directed that a destruction order should be made, unless I am satisfied that Lennox will not be a danger to the public.

The Expert Evidence

15. In determining the issue of whether Lennox presents a danger to the public the court heard from two expert witnesses, one from each side. We also heard, as part of the expert witness evidence given by Ms Barnes' current expert witness the views of an expert who had previously acted for her.

16. Ms Barnes' current expert, Sarah Fisher, is an experienced and highly respected dog trainer and counsellor of dogs. She lectures extensively, broadcasts and is the author of several books on the subject of dog behaviour. She is also a TTouch practitioner (the Tellington TTouch is an internationally-recognised approach to animal handling, training and rehabilitation, developed by Linda Tellington, which equips its practitioners with expertise in canine physiology). Ms Fisher examined Lennox in August 2011. She raised concerns about Lennox's care and health while in the Respondent's custody. As is common for dogs subjected to long stays in kennels, Ms Fisher noted that Lennox had been

diagnosed as suffering from stress and depression while in kennels, although he was now responding to medication (Amitriptyline) to treat his depression. She also raises the possibility of other health problems, noting that when she examined him his ears were not level and that there was a change in the lay of his coat over the Atlas in line with the nuchal ligament that is present between T1 and C2 vertebrae. To her this suggested tension, or problems with the soft tissue in his neck, which in her opinion required further investigation by a veterinary surgeon. Ms Fisher noted that Amitriptyline may also be prescribed for the treatment of chronic pain and testified that such pain may have the effect of making a dog more than usually difficult to handle. In addition, she observed that newly forming scabs were present on Lennox's flanks and that there was blood around the nail beds on his right hind paw.

17. Ms Fisher's session with Lennox was recorded, so that the court has had the benefit of viewing the recording as well as hearing Ms Fisher's evidence. She said that Lennox was brought in a van to the inspection. She opened one rear door of the van in order to observe Lennox and said that he was clearly distressed. The recording shows that in her careful examination Ms Fisher spent almost eighteen minutes interacting with Lennox before he alighted from the van. She testified that at no stage was he aggressive, even when she established eye contact with him. She believed that the dog wanted to stay with Ms Lightfoot, the dog warden, who had been charged with looking after him while in the Respondent's custody. She stated that Lennox had clearly established a very good relationship with her and that consequently Ms Lightfoot accompanied Ms Fisher while she walked him on the lead.

18. During the assessment Ms Fisher deployed various strategies to test Lennox; these included using a 'clicker' to see if the clicking sounds would upset him, stopping Lennox from going where he wanted to go and withholding food. She observed that Lennox constantly looked for reassurance from Ms Lightfoot, but that he nevertheless did whatever she asked of him. Also, when she let the lead slip on two occasions Lennox simply walked up to the two people with her and went around their legs. Nor did he react when a man happened to walk through the yard where the assessment was being conducted.

19. Part of Ms Fisher's evidence related to an examination carried out by the expert behaviouralist who had previously acted for the Appellant—David Ryan. Ms Fisher watched a recording of an assessment which Mr Ryan conducted on Lennox on 15 March 2010. One purpose of that assessment was to measure Lennox in order to ascertain whether he conformed to the type known as a Pit Bull Terrier. It is now no longer necessary to call evidence on that matter at this hearing as the Appellant now accepts that Lennox is a Pit Bull Terrier type. Mr Ryan also carried out tests to see how Lennox would react in different situations. All went well until he reached over Lennox to attach a lead to his collar. At this, point according to his written report which was available to the court, "in one movement he lunged towards me, growled, barked and snapped". Importantly, however, Lennox did not bite Mr Ryan, who acknowledges that he could have done so had he wanted.

20. Mr Ryan concluded that, notwithstanding the snapping incident, Lennox should be returned to his family. He added, however, that he should be kept muzzled, walked on a lead in public places and kept in a secure enclosure. Mr Ryan also noted that Lennox lacked confidence, probably inherently, which made it difficult for him to cope with novel experiences

and new people. As a result the move to kennels would have proven more traumatic for Lennox than for most dogs.

21. Commenting on the video of Mr Ryan's interaction with Lennox, Ms Fisher observed that the dog exhibited anxiety with Mr Ryan and obviously did not relate to him. She also stressed that it was significant that Mr Ryan was not bitten, although Lennox had had the opportunity to do so.

22. Ms Fisher concluded that Lennox was a well behaved dog, who was not hyperactive and was a real pleasure to deal with.

23. The court also heard from Peter Tallack who gave evidence for the respondent. Mr Tallack is not a trained dog behaviouralist. However, he has been in the Metropolitan Police for thirty years, including twenty-six years of service as a Dog Handler. He is therefore highly experienced in working with police dogs. He said that he then became directly involved in Dangerous Dogs Act cases and has been an instructor on courses dealing with Dangerous Dogs.

24. Mr Tallack came to Belfast on two occasions to examine Lennox. The first of these visits was three weeks after Lennox was taken into the custody of the Respondent. His objective on this occasion was to ascertain whether Lennox conformed to the type known as a Pit Bull Terrier, but as we have seen that has now been conceded by the Appellant and is no longer an issue. Mr Tallack returned to Belfast on 4 November 2010 to carry out a further assessment of Lennox. The assessment was not recorded. Mr Tallack was clear in his evidence that it is a myth that all Pit Bull Terriers are aggressive. In fact, he stated that most of these dogs are docile around humans as their training has always been centred on fighting against other dogs, not humans.

25. Mr Tallack testified that physically Lennox was a typical example of a Pit Bull Terrier and was very strong. However, he stated that in his view Lennox was different from other Pit Bull Terriers he had encountered in that all his body language was aggressive. Having formed this opinion, Mr Tallack used a rigid pole to keep Lennox at bay. At the end of the assessment session he took Lennox back to his kennel. He turned to leave the kennel, at which point he momentarily lost eye contact with Lennox, who suddenly attacked him, leaping from a lying position to head height in one movement without any warning. As Mr Tallack had closed the kennel door a moment before this he was unhurt.

26. Mr Tallack stated that, in his view, Lennox was a dangerous example of the Pit Bull type, and that he believed Lennox to have a severe personality defect. He further stated that he believed that Lennox has a problem with strangers and that in his view it is not possible to determine when Lennox will feel under stress. He agreed that a temperament test only shows the position on the day that it is undertaken. However, his main concern was that Lennox had been able to go so quickly from a lying position to the height of the head of a standing man.

27. In court Mr Tallack watched a DVD recording of the visit by the Appellant's expert witness, Ms Fisher, to assess Lennox. He commented rather unfavourably on her methods of assessment, which he believed failed to put Lennox under any stress. He also said that Ms

Fisher seemed not to establish any rapport with Lennox, despite the cheese treats that she fed him throughout his assessment. Moreover, he was critical of the fact that she did not stop Lennox biting his lead, which he said was a strong warning sign, although he failed to specify what it warned of.

28. Ms Fisher rejected these criticisms of her methods and Mr Tallack's view that she had simply walked around giving Lennox food. She was clear that the food was not used as a bribe, and stated that no amount of food can disguise aggressive behaviour. Since in her view giving food to a dog with aggressive issues can be extremely dangerous, she indicated that she would not have fed a dog she deemed to be aggressive. Rather, the food was used in order to monitor what was happening with Lennox on an emotional and physical level throughout her assessment of him. She also took issue with Mr Tallack's view that lead biting was a bad sign and that she should have prevented him from doing that, noting that while Lennox does rag on the lead it is very self-controlled.

29. Mr Tallack concluded by stating his opinion that Lennox is an accident waiting to happen and that he is a mature dog fixed in his attitudes.

Consideration

30. It will be apparent that in the evidence the court had heard that there is little agreement between the parties. In assessing the relevant weight to be accorded to this conflicting expert evidence on the dog's dangerousness, it is therefore important to set them in the context of Lennox's overall behaviour. It is also necessary to recognise the circumstances in which these assessments are undertaken, which, as all three experts acknowledge, are extremely artificial situations which can only indicate the dog's temperament at that particular time.

31. In assessing the credibility of the conflicting evidence offered to the court I was impressed by the evidence of Ms Fisher. It was also extremely helpful that she had her assistant record her evaluation of Lennox, so that it could be seen by the court. Ms Fisher is one of the UK's leading experts in the field of canine behaviour and also a TTouch practitioner which means that she has expertise in canine physiology. She has seventeen years of experience of lecturing, filming, writing about and working with various dog breeds in the UK, other European jurisdictions, South Africa and the United States. She undertakes work with dogs in many different situations—companion dogs, working dogs, assistance dogs and shelter dogs. Ms Fisher acknowledges that Lennox has a difficulty with strangers, but concludes that with careful handling he is "polite, friendly and appropriate with excellent social skills" and "a wonderful family dog". She concluded that he could safely be returned to his family.

32. The documentary evidence of Mr Ryan, who is also a trained dog behaviouralist, was also recorded. He too was supportive of the return of Lennox to his owners. Notwithstanding his description of how the dog at one point lunged at him without warning, in the remainder of his long assessment Lennox allowed himself to be handled and teased by Mr Ryan—a complete stranger—without reaction.

33. The Respondent's expert, Mr Tallack, is a highly experienced police dog handler, but unlike Ms Fisher and Mr Ryan he is not a trained dog behaviouralist. Moreover, his expe-

rience of working with police dogs means that his experience with bull breeds has been limited. His subsequent work on dangerous dogs cases has largely focused on assessing their conformity with the Pit Bull type rather than assessing their temperament and behaviour. Unfortunately Mr Tallack did not record his interactions with Lennox, so the court was unable to witness his assessment. However on his own account he did not feel able to walk Lennox on a lead or to touch him and kept him at bay with a pole, which must have limited his ability to build any kind of rapport with the dog. He testified that upon being returned to his kennel Lennox attempted to attack his head and did so without warning, and with great speed and agility. Mr Tallack's conclusion was therefore that Lennox is a very dangerous dog.

34. Similarly Ms Lightfoot, who has been a dog warden for ten years, has considerable experience of working with dogs, but is not a trained dog behaviouralist. She gave evidence that Lennox lunged at her (while muzzled) when she first saw him in the kitchen of the Appellant's home. As regards his behaviour while in the Respondent's custody, her testimony was that having spent time with him he was one of the most aggressive and unpredictable dogs that she had encountered. This, however, seems somewhat at odds with Ms Fisher's evidence that Lennox appeared to have formed a close relationship with Ms Lightfoot while in kennels.

My Judgment

35. Faced with this conflicting evidence I turn now to the law. Article 25C of the Dogs Order 1983 appears to be permissive, stating that the court "may order the destruction" of a dog subject to the statutory prohibition. It then goes on to make the further stipulation that the court "shall do so unless satisfied that the dog will not be a danger to the public". As noted above, the explanatory notes issued to accompany the 2011 Act expressly state that "under Article 25A(5) of the Dogs Order (as amended) dogs of a type normally prohibited by Article 25A may be in certain circumstances be exempted from the prohibition."

36. It is, of course, important to remember that the primary purpose of the dangerous dogs legislation (and particularly the amendments introduced by the Dangerous Dogs (NI) Order 1991) was to protect the public from attack or fear of attack by a dog, particularly a large strong dog of a type bred for fighting, and to ensure public safety.

37. However, I am also bound to consider that this legislation has attracted extensive criticism and that the amendment introduced by the Dogs (Amendment) Act (Northern Ireland) 2001 was expressly designed to ameliorate the lack of discretion previously allowed to courts. This amendment thus mitigated the harshness of the 1991 Order which left courts with no option but to order the destruction of dogs of a prohibited type. Indeed the magistrates' court which originally heard this case seemed to feel compelled to destroy dogs of a prohibited type

38. In deciding whether I should exercise the discretion afforded me by the 2001 Act to issue an exemption order provided I am satisfied that Lennox does not constitute a danger to the public, I take the following factors into account:-

39. First, and perhaps most importantly, there is no evidence before this court that Lennox has in fact ever bitten anyone. No complaint has been made about his behavior by any

member of the public. For five years, notwithstanding his anxiety about new situations and coming into contact with new people, Lennox lived with the Barnes family as a much loved family pet, who had formed a particularly close bond with Ms Barnes' daughter Brooke, who is registered disabled as a result of severe asthma. Brooke was twelve years old at the time that Lennox was seized and removed from his family and had formed a close bond with him since she was seven years of age.

40. In court, Ms Lightfoot, the Council dog warden, stated that Lennox had not bitten while in the Respondent's custody. This evidence is significant given that Lennox has been kept in isolated conditions in his kennel, lacking proper exercise and adequate socialization. He has been diagnosed by a veterinary surgeon to be suffering from depression and has been prescribed medication. Ms Fisher's evidence suggests that he may have experienced other health problems, including chronic neck pain, which could impact on his behaviour, and yet he has not attacked anyone. Nor is there any evidence to suggest that Lennox ever harmed anyone during the five years he spent in the care of his family. Given the considerable publicity which this case has attracted it is highly likely that had he done so someone would have come forward by now.

41. Secondly, in stressful situations where Lennox had the opportunity to bite, he in fact showed good bite inhibition. Thus, on the two occasions when he lunged at witnesses—i.e. while being assessed by Mr Tallack and Mr Ryan each of whom was a complete stranger to him—he refrained from biting, notwithstanding the stressful circumstances in which he found himself. There was also evidence Lennox lunged at Ms Lightfoot in the kitchen of Ms Barnes' home, but at that stage he was securely muzzled, and thus unable to bite.

42. In summary, therefore, in the sixteen months since Lennox was seized and removed from his family home he has on three occasions lunged at a person who was a complete stranger to him, but on none of these occasions has he actually bitten. It is also worth noting that although Ms Fisher was also a complete stranger to Lennox, by taking a short time to gain his confidence she was able to walk and handle him without incident. By contrast Mr Tallack conceded that "the circumstances in which Lennox is being examined are not ideal" and on his own account of his interaction with Lennox this would seem to have been a confrontational experience.

43. Assessing the conflicting expert testimony in the context of Lennox's behaviour over his six year plus lifespan, both while in the care of the Appellant and in the custody of the Respondent I have concluded that it is appropriate to place greater weight on the evidence of Ms Fisher and Mr Ryan, who are trained and experienced experts in dog behaviour, and who both agree that Lennox may safely be returned home.

44. On the balance of probabilities, therefore, and provided that appropriate measures are taken by those responsible for Lennox, which I am confident they will be, I am "satisfied that the dog will not be a danger to the public" and should therefore be exempted from destruction.

45. I would just add that it is regrettable that Lennox appears to have been seized purely on the basis that he looked like a Pit Bull type rather than because he posed any danger to the public, and his case and the considerable costs it has imposed on the tax payer point to the need for a reconsideration of breed specific legislation. In this particular case a dog who

had harmed no one and generated no public complaint, was removed from his family and kept in less than optimum conditions in kennels for well over a year. In addition to being financed by the tax payer, this action caused considerable distress to Lennox and his family.

46. I conclude by considering the measures that need to be taken to minimize any small risk that Lennox may pose. Ms Barnes, who is a former veterinary nurse with extensive experience of caring for dogs, has shown herself to be a responsible dog owner. Prior to being seized by the Respondents under the Dogs Order Lennox was neutered, licensed, microchipped, insured and DNA registered. He was not allowed to wander and was walked on a lead. Indeed ironically the licence fee was paid to the very council which has sought to destroy him. Given her history as a responsible dog owner, I therefore believe that the Appellant, Ms Barnes, will comply with the exemption conditions along these lines which are now in place under the 2011 Act and that she will ensure that he is kept in an enclosure from which he is unable to escape. She is well aware of Lennox's inability to cope with strangers. She has experience in training and keeping dogs and I am confident that she will ensure that Lennox will be kept under control when he is returned to her care and will not pose a threat to the public.

47. Accordingly I allow the appeal.

30

Commentary on *A and B (by C) v A (Health and Social Services Trust)*

MARIAN DUGGAN

Introduction

This case involves twins, who were born via IVF treatment using donor sperm in Northern Ireland. Their mother and father had requested sperm from a 'Caucasian' donor to ensure any resultant children would appear as racially 'matched'. The clinic's oversight meant that sperm was administered from a 'Caucasian (Cape Coloured)' donor, thus South African in origin with a background comprising white, black and Malay heritage.[1] The children were born with a different and darker skin colour from their parents, and different skin colour from each other. The basis of the children's legal claim was that while growing up in Northern Ireland, they had been subjected to 'abusive and derogatory comment' about their skin colour and their mother's implied infidelity. This had led them to question their relationship to their parents and each other, causing emotional upset. The children also expressed concerns over their future prospects as a result of the racial hostility to which they were exposed.[2]

This case may seem like an odd selection for a feminist judgment as it does not obviously raise issues of gendered harm, stereotypes or injustice on which feminist analyses of tort law have traditionally focused.[3] It is also a troubling case for feminist analysis, as underpinning the children's complaint is the assumption that they were entitled to inherit and benefit from their parents' Whiteness,[4] raising important questions pertaining to power and privilege associated with the intersection of perceived racial characteristics and family structure.

[1] For a history of the term 'Caucasian' and its problematic associations with Whiteness, see Nell Irvin Painter, *The History of White People* (New York, WW Norton and Company Inc, 2010, reprint edition), 72–90.

[2] The case was heard at the High Court and the Court of Appeal, with Gillen J and Girvan LJ delivering judgment in *A and B (by C, their mother and next friend) v A (Health and Social Services Trust)* [2010] NIQB 108 and *A and B (by C, their mother and next friend) v A (Health and Social Services Trust)* [2011] NICA 28 respectively. Morgan LCJ and Sir John Sheil sat with Girvan LJ, but as per the vast majority of Northern Ireland Court of Appeal decisions, no concurring or dissenting judgments were delivered and the presiding judge delivered the 'one voice' judgment of the court. The feminist judgment is a replacement Court of Appeal decision.

[3] Janice Richardson and Erika Rackley (eds), *Feminist Perspectives on Tort Law* (Abingdon, Routledge, 2012).

[4] Ruth Frankenberg, *The Social Construction of Whiteness: White Women, Race Matters* (Minneapolis, MN, University of Minnesota Press, 1993).

Such assumptions tend to be ripe for feminist and critical race theory critique,[5] prompting the dilemma of how best to respond to the distress and disadvantage experienced as a result of such disruptions. In her feminist judgment Julie McCandless is explicit about her discomfort with the children's claim. However, by foregrounding the children's concerns and experiences, she delivers a judgment that tackles, rather than overlooks, the culturally specific factors of racism and identity in Northern Ireland. In doing so, she challenges the 'colour blind'[6] approach in the original judgments, as well as the judicial individualisation of racism in Northern Ireland to a 'misguided'[7] and 'boorish'[8] minority. While perhaps not asking the 'woman question',[9] this feminist judgment asks the 'power question' in an attempt to rectify the judicial silence in the original judgment on the complexities and operation of racism and structural inequality in society.

Unpacking Racism in Northern Ireland

'Race' is a socially constructed concept that has underpinned—and continues to underpin—significant levels of material persecution based on (mis)interpretations of lesser worth, citizenship and ability.[10] This case poses uncomfortable questions that both illustrate and engage with issues of race and racism in Northern Irish society, as well as the law's limited role in ameliorating the effects of racism. The children's alleged emotional upset was caused by comments illustrating the differences in the family's skin colour: while distressing, this does not ordinarily constitute 'harm' in a legally actionable sense, regardless

[5] Patricia Hill Collins, 'It's All in the Family: Intersections of Gender, Race and Nation' (1998) 13(3) *Hypatia* 62–82. Indeed, a recent legal case in Ohio involving a white lesbian couple and the mistaken use of sperm from a black, rather than a white, donor has been heavily criticised by eminent critical race theorist, Patricia Collins, who framed the case as a 'wrongful birth' action against a 'black child'. Available at www.thenation.com/article/value-whiteness/ (last accessed 25August 2015).

[6] The literature on 'colour blindness' relates predominantly to the US (see, eg, Michael Brown, Martin Camoy, Elliott Currie, Troy Duster, David Oppenheimer, Marjorie Schultz and David Wellman, *Whitewashing Race: The Myth of a Color-Blind Society* (Berkeley, CA, University of California Press, 2003)), with some studies countenancing Britain (see Amy Ansell, *New Right, New Racism: Race and Reaction in the United States and Britain* (New York, New York University Press, 1997) and James Rhodes, 'Revisiting the 2001 Riots: New Labour and the Rise of "Colour Blind Racism"' (2009) 14(5) *Sociological Research Online*, at www.socresonline.org.uk/14/5/3.html. For a related analysis of how the rise of 'post-sectarian' and 'good relations' discourses following the Good Friday/ Belfast Agreement have allowed the Northern Ireland state to hide its incapacity to address rising racism and sectarianism, see Robbie McVeigh and Bill Rolston, 'From Good Friday to Good Relations: sectarianism, racism and the Northern Ireland state' (2007) 48(4) *Race & Class* 1–23.

[7] Gillen J in *A and B (by C, their mother and next friend) v A (Health and Social Services Trust)* [2010] NIQB 108, para 24.

[8] Girvan LJ in *A and B (by C, their mother and next friend) v A (Health and Social Services Trust)* [2011] NICA 28, para 10. On the connection between a state's commitment to neo-liberal policies and the incumbent emphasis on the individual to a corresponding reduction of focus on structural racism and inequality, see David Goldberg, *The Threat of Race: Reflections on Racial Neoliberalism* (Hoboken, NJ, Wiley-Blackwell, 2009).

[9] Defined by Rosemary Hunter as one of the techniques of feminist judging: Rosemary Hunter, 'Can *Feminist* Judges Make a Difference?' (2008) 15 *International Journal of the Legal Profession* 7–36.

[10] For a critical consideration of the relationship between nature and culture in ideas about race, see Peter Wade, *Race, Nature and Culture* (London, Pluto Press, 2002). On race as social construction, see David Goldberg, *Racist Culture: Philosophy and the Politics of Meaning* (Oxford, Blackwell, 1993); and Goldberg, above n 8.

of the past, present and perceived potential impact on the applicant. In his original judgment, Gillen J rejected the children's argument that the clinic owed them a duty of care, and reasoned that if he was wrong on this point, the children had been born 'normal and healthy' and therefore had not suffered any legally recognisable harm. He ventured that to compensate them financially would be to allow the children to grow up believing that their skin colour meant that they were somehow inherently 'damaged'.[11]

Gillen J therefore does not find the clinic at 'fault' for the children's emotional distress; yet it was the clinic's error that resulted in the children's being exposed to repeated racist victimisation from individuals that caused concern for their futures. Awarding damages for having the 'wrong' colour of skin is clearly neither desirable nor an effective way in which to address the structural issues informing what is right or wrong. However, Gillen J occupies a site of significant racial (as well as social) privilege; it is perhaps this that informs his comparisons of the children's skin colour to hair and eye colour or intelligence, belying the potential impacts of racism in society.

The children's experiences are reflected by research into racism in schools in Northern Ireland, which found that three-quarters (75 per cent) of children from ethnic minority groups had experienced derogatory racist name calling.[12] A significant number (42 per cent) of minority ethnic 16-year-old students reported having been victims of 'racist bullying or harassment' in their school, which can impede academic progress and have a significantly detrimental effect on a victim's economic future. The situation appears to fare just as badly in the workplace, with the report suggesting that racism had supplanted traditional cross-community sectarianism as the main reason for employees being harassed, bullied or threatened in their places of work.[13] Therefore, McCandless LJ is right to question the judicial failure in the original judgments to expand on the societal source of the racism suffered by the children, and the possible longevity of this impact on their wellbeing.

In drawing attention to the operation of racial and other inequalities, McCandless LJ reveals the feminist judgment to be a broader commentary on social relations and justice, and takes the opportunity to consider the role of law—however limited—in ameliorating prejudice and disadvantage. The rewritten judgment also foregrounds the children's concerns in a manner reflective of feminist values in recognising the individual as an expert in his or her own experience, particularly when faced with a counter-narrative that represents the dominant race, class and status.[14] McCandless LJ's invocation of 'the history of structural racism' evident in Northern Ireland importantly addresses the real implications of inequality, unfairness, distress or prejudice incurred by the children (and their parents). A fuller examination of this proves integral to understanding the cultural dynamics of the case.

[11] *A and B (by C)*, above n 7, para 24.

[12] Robbie McVeigh and An Dúchán, *The Next Stephen Lawrence? Racist Violence and Criminal Justice in Northern Ireland*, Research Report for the Northern Ireland Council for Ethnic Minorities (2005).

[13] ibid.

[14] This approach borrows from the tradition of feminist standpoint theory: Sandra Harding (ed), *The Feminist Standpoint Theory Reader* (New York and London, Routledge, 2004). For critical and reflective discussions, see Susan Hekman, 'Truth and Method: Feminist Standpoint Theory Revisited' (1997) 2(2) *Signs* 341–65; and Sandra Harding, 'Standpoint Theories: Productively Controversial' (2009) 24(4) *Hypatia* 192–200.

The Impact of Northern Ireland's Cultural Dynamics

Even if you do not see yourself in a box, others may put you there and close the lid.[15]

At the time of the original ruling, Northern Ireland was over a dozen years into the peace process, which signalled an end to the worst of the previous three decades of cross-community sectarian conflict.[16] Rapid changes occurred within a short period of time, particularly with respect to increasingly visible cultural diversity and difference, as urban areas such as Belfast became popular for economic migrants seeking to resettle in the UK. However, Gillen J's comment about Northern Ireland's 'multicultural' nature[17] is somewhat ambitious, given that just 1.8 per cent of the population (32,400 people) belonged to an ethnic minority group in 2011, double the number recorded in 2001 (0.8 per cent).[18]

These cultural changes were not always met with accepting attitudes; several high-profile incidents motivated by racial hostility, particularly against members of the Roma community in 2008,[19] led to Northern Ireland's being branded the 'hate crime capital of Europe' and 'race hate capital of UK' in the media,[20] casting doubt on the supposed inclusivity of the 'new' purportedly 'post-conflict' and 'post-sectarian' Northern Ireland. Surveys on racial integration have unsurprisingly indicated that the majority of people believe that minority ethnic communities face 'a lot' of prejudice in Northern Ireland, and an awareness that racial prejudice had increased, rather than abated, over time.[21] These perceptions correlate with official data showing that reports of racially motivated incidents have increased annually.[22] However, just 12 out of 13,655 hate-motivated offences reported to the police between 2008 and 2012 resulted in a successful prosecution.[23] Therefore, whilst it is true to suggest that the children's genes did not render them 'victims' at the hands of the clinic, the clinic's error had indeed put them at greater risk of victimisation from wider society.

[15] Edna Longley, 'Multi-Culturalism and Northern Ireland: Making Differences Fruitful' in Edna Longley and Declan Kiberd, *Multi-Culturalism: The View from Two Irelands* (Cork, Cork University Press, 2001) 2.

[16] This sectarian conflict, known as 'The Troubles', overshadowed other areas of cultural development at a time in history when, elsewhere in the UK, civil rights movements were gaining traction in connection with race relations, sexual minorities and women's equality. As a result, the primacy of ameliorating Northern Ireland's pressing sectarian problem meant that addressing other forms of prejudice—such as racism, sexism or homophobia—featured far lower down on the hierarchy of need.

[17] *A and B (by C)*, above n 7, 23.

[18] Northern Ireland Census, *Key Statistics Summary Report* (2011), at www.nisra.gov.uk/archive/census/2011/results/key-statistics/summary-report.pdf (last accessed 24 June 2015).

[19] 'Romanians leave Northern Ireland after attacks', *BBC News*, 23 June 2009, at http://news.bbc.co.uk/1/hi/8114234.stm (last accessed 24 June 2015).

[20] 'Two racist attacks are taking place every day in Northern Ireland—with fears Belfast is rapidly becoming the race hate capital of the UK', *Belfast Telegraph*, 21 April 2014, at www.belfasttelegraph.co.uk/news/northern-ireland/two-racist-attacks-every-day-in-northern-irelands-racehate-crime-surge-30202329.html (last accessed 24 June 2015).

[21] *Northern Ireland Life and Times Survey* dataset, at www.ark.ac.uk/nilt/results/mineth.html (last accessed 24 June 2015).

[22] Datasets made available by the Police Service of Northern Ireland indicated an increase of 36% to 1,132 incidents and 51% to 796 crimes in the 12 months to June 2014, at www.psni.police.uk/index/updates/updates_statistics/updates_hate_motivation_statistics.htm (last accessed 24 June 2015).

[23] ibid.

Montague and Shirlow have described the growth in racist hate crimes in Northern Ireland as often being 'a crude way of "defending" resources coupled with notions of protecting community identity from the "outsider"'.[24] Identity hostility has evidently extended beyond the sectarian divide; the past experiences and future fears expressed in this case may be linked to racism rather than sectarianism, but one cannot be condoned/eradicated only for an alternative to take its place.[25] As traditional sectarian tensions abate, it appears that space has opened up in which other forms of targeted prejudice are recognised.[26] The traditionally Christian-inspired cultural conservatism informing Northern Irish politics and society—poignantly captured by Girvan LJ reciting a psalm at the start of the original Court of Appeal judgment[27]—has also been a contributing factor in the stagnation of socio-legal progress, such as ensuring equality and rights for racial, religious and sexual minorities, and implementing full legal protection from (and redress for) discrimination, persecution and victimisation. This case offered a significant—but missed—opportunity for judges in Northern Ireland to develop the common law in the context of addressing the harms that emanate from identity-based persecution. While the feminist judgment embraces the novelty of the case to develop the legal principles pertaining to substandard fertility treatment, Gillen J and Girvan LJ firmly operated within the law as given,[28] to include a keen deference to Parliament and a straightforward application of 'wrongful birth' precedents to a case that quite simply was not about a wrongful birth.

Situating the Feminist Perspective

Feminism has long been critical of the power of law to effect progressive social change,[29] and the dilemmas presented by this case are similarly present in other areas of law designed to countenance racial prejudice and victimisation. For example, 'hate crimes' and their related legislation are subjective in nature, situating the perception of harm and motive with the *victim*. Taking this stance, the children's experiences—and fears—are valid but, if addressed accordingly, emulate the problems inherent in 'hate crime' legislation—namely, that laws seek to punish the *individual* rather than address broader issues in *society*. An important feminist question to be asked of McCandless LJ's judgment is whether it achieves a better outcome not just for the individual claimants, but also for wider society through development of the law?

[24] Richard Montague and Peter Shirlow, *Challenging Racism: Ending Hate* (2010), at www.qub.ac.uk/research-centres/isctsj/filestore/Filetoupload, 472425, en.pdf (last accessed 24 June 2015).

[25] Marian Duggan, 'Sectarianism and Hate Crime in Northern Ireland' in Nathan Hall, Abbee Corb, Paul Giannasi and John Grieve (eds), *The International Handbook on Hate Crime* (Abingdon, Routledge, 2014) 117–28.

[26] Marian Duggan, *Queering Conflict: Examining Lesbian and Gay Experiences of Homophobia in Northern Ireland* (Farnham, Ashgate, 2012).

[27] *A and B (by C)*, above n 8, 1.

[28] See further Stephen Livingstone, 'And Justice for All? The Judiciary and the Legal Profession in Transition' in Colin Harvey (ed), *Human Rights, Equality and Democratic Renewal in Northern Ireland* (Oxford, Hart Publishing, 2001) 131–61.

[29] Carol Smart, *The Power of Law* (London, Routledge, 1989).

In not holding the clinic fully liable for the emotional distress and disadvantage experienced by the children, the feminist judgment in part reaches the same outcome as the original. However, McCandless LJ deploys significantly different reasoning in reaching this conclusion. First, she holds that a duty of care was owed by the clinic to the children because of their interconnected interests in their parents' treatment. In doing so, she lends judicial support to the feminist-inspired concept of relational autonomy.[30] This seems to be particularly important given the reproductive and familial context of the case.[31] Secondly, she subverts judicial reliance on policy-based reasoning that is underpinned by abstract 'reasonable man'[32] assumptions by rejecting the 'healthy child' exemption to the normal principles of recovery,[33]and instead developing policy-based reasoning around societal accountability for inequality and class-based injury. Here, she takes inspiration from feminist scholarship that problematises the conventional tort idea of individualised and privatised injury, as well as the dichotomised demarcation between private and public law spheres.[34] While the feminist judgment does insist on holding the clinic accountable for its careless treatment by ordering the payment of a conventional award of £15,000, it also points to the responsibility of public authorities in Northern Ireland to take positive action to ameliorate the effects of racism in society. The possibility of a conventional award was rejected in the original judgments on the basis that the children had not suffered any loss or damage. By teasing out the children's relational interests in having their parents' treatment preferences upheld, McCandless LJ retells their story in a way that refuses to dismiss their distress and lived experiences. She also gives judicial notice to feminist critiques of previous conventional awards in cases involving reproduction, by making clear the different context in which this award is granted, that is, not as a pale substitute for an award of full damages that would otherwise have been recoverable 'but for' a policy-based exception to the usual rules of recovery.[35] Rather, the award is ordered here in acknowledgement of the substandard treatment and as a way of helping to make the children's lives better.

An alternative feminist approach could reasonably have seen the complete dismissal of the children's claim on the basis that it is impossible for conventional tort law doctrine to countenance class-based injury,[36] or that to award monetary compensation in the circumstances would be to shore up patriarchal ideas about inheritance, race and family

[30] Jennifer Nedelsky, 'Reconceiving Autonomy: Sources, Thoughts and Possibilities' (1989) 1 *Yale Journal of Law and Feminism* 7–36. On the use of relational autonomy in a judgment about refusal of life-saving medical treatment, see ch 20 in this collection by Claire Murray (commentary) and Mary Donnelly (feminist judgment).

[31] For an application of relational autonomy to family law, see Jonathan Herring, *Relational Autonomy and Family Law* (London, SpringerBriefs in Law, 2014).

[32] Leslie Bender, 'A Lawyer's Primer on Feminist Theory and Tort' (1988) 38 *Journal of Legal Education* 3.

[33] *McFarlane and another v Tayside Health Board* [1999] UKHL 50; *Rees v Darlington Memorial Hospital NHS Trust* [2003] UKHL 52. See Nicolette Priaulx, *The harm paradox: tort law and the unwanted child in an era of choice* (London, Routledge-Cavendish, 2007).

[34] Adrian Howe, 'The Problem of Privatized Injuries: Feminist Strategies for Litigation' in Martha Fineman and Nancy Thomadsen (eds), *At the Boundaries of Law: Feminism and Legal Theory* (New York, Routledge, 1991) 148–68; Leslie Bender, 'Feminist (Re)Torts: Thoughts on the Liability Crisis, Mass Torts, Power, and Responsibilities' (1990) 39(4) *Duke Law Journal* 848, 864–72.

[35] Nicolette Priaulx, 'Damages for the "unwanted" child: time for a rethink?' (2005) 73(4) *Medico-Legal Journal* 152–63.

[36] See further Regina Graycar, 'A Feminist Adjudication Process: Is There Such a Thing?' in Ulrike Schultz and Gisela Shaw (eds), *Gender and Judging* (Oxford, Hart Publishing, 2013) 436–57.

structures.[37] While McCandless LJ appears to accept such critiques in her judgment, she reasons that to so reject the children's claim entirely would be to attack a 'symptom' of patriarchy rather than its root causes. Her approach is marked by sensitivity towards the prevalence of 'family secrets' in the context of reproduction and fertility treatment.[38] This is perhaps controversial in a national context haunted by the brutality of what James Smith has conceptualised as 'an architecture of containment', whereby state institutions 'concealed' marginalised citizens, typically 'fallen women' who transgressed social mores and dominant morality.[39] A criticism that could therefore be levied at the feminist judgment is that it smacks of 'keeping up appearances' in order to ensure the cultural primacy of the biological family,[40] akin to the political refusal to extend abortion provision in Northern Ireland while hundreds of Northern Irish women travel abroad each year for pregnancy termination.[41] However, McCandless LJ's concern with family secrets and 'passing' does not seem motivated by shame or containment discourses; rather she acknowledges the family's interests in having the parents' legitimate expectations upheld in a reproductive context where people must necessarily articulate choices and preferences that often go unspoken. In doing so, she hints at an alternative way in which this case could have been argued by counsel; that of the clinic's interfering with the privacy interests of both the children and the parents.[42]

[37] See Hill Collins, above n 5.

[38] Carol Smart, *Personal Life* (Cambridge, Polity Press, 2007); Petra Nordqvist and Carol Smart, *Relative Strangers: Family life, genes and donor conception* (Basingstoke, Palgrave Macmillan, 2014).

[39] James Smith, *Ireland's Magdalen Laundries and the Nation's Architecture of Containment* (Notre Dame, IN, University of Notre Dame Press, 2007). Smith writes in the specific national context of Ireland rather than Northern Ireland, but it seems likely that the women incarcerated in Magdalene Laundry institutions in Northern Ireland shared experiences similar to those of women in Ireland: see www.amnesty.org.uk/sites/default/files/doc_23218.pdf (last accessed 25 August 2015). The Historical Institutional Abuse Inquiry currently taking place in Northern Ireland is only taking evidence from persons who were under 18 when they were in a residential institution, precluding many women who would have been incarcerated in Magdalene Laundries or similar institutions: www.hiainquiry.org/ (last accessed 25 August 2015).

[40] Martha Fineman, *The Neutered Mother, The Sexual Family and Other Twentieth Century Tragedies* (Oxford, Routledge, 1995); Alison Diduck, *Law's Families* (London, LexisNexis, 2003); Julie McCandless and Sally Sheldon, 'The Human Fertilisation and Embryology Act (2008) and the Tenacity of the Sexual Family Form' (2010) 73(2) *Modern Law Review* 175–207.

[41] Ann Rossiter, *Ireland's Hidden Diaspora: The Abortion Trail and the Making of a London-Irish Underground, 1980–2000* (London, IASC Publishing, 2009).

[42] This argument was not developed in the feminist judgment as it was not introduced by counsel. While appellate courts can introduce new matters of law, they must restrict their decision to arguments that have been presented. On framing the case in terms of privacy, see Sally Sheldon, 'Only Skin Deep? The harm of being born a different colour to one's parents' (2011) 19(4) *Medical Law Review* 657–68.

A and B (by C, their mother and next friend) v A (Health and Social Services Trust)

[2011] NICA 28

QUEEN'S BENCH DIVISION
GILLEN J
13 OCTOBER 2010

COURT OF APPEAL
MORGAN LCJ, McCANDLESS LJ, SIR JOHN SHEIL
9 MARCH, 24 JUNE 2011

24 June 2011. The following judgment of the court was delivered.

McCANDLESS LJ.*

INTRODUCTION

[**1**] At the heart of this case are a family who have suffered distress following negligent treatment at a licensed fertility clinic. The clinic operates under the auspices of the respondent Health and Social Services Trust. The appellants, A and B, are the children of the family; twins, now aged almost sixteen. They were eleven years old when the proceedings began in October 2006. The issue is whether they can recover damages against the clinic.

[**2**] The family's distress follows from the clinic's careless selection of donor sperm for the mother's IVF treatment. The parents are both White and, in line with accepted clinical practice at the time of treatment—and indeed, formal guidance from the Regulator, the Human Fertilisation and Embryology Authority (HFEA)—they requested that the mother's eggs be inseminated with sperm from a donor classified as 'Caucasian' so that any children born through her IVF treatment would, with all probability, appear racially similar. Instead, and unbeknownst to the parents, sperm from a donor classified as 'Caucasian (Cape Coloured)' was used. As a result, the children have different and darker skin colour from their parents. Their skin colour is also markedly different from each other.

[**3**] As a result, the children allege in their statement of claim that they have suffered distress and emotional upset following abusive and derogatory comments from other children and adults. These comments have been about their difference in appearance from each other, and from their parents. Some comments were racially abusive. They further assert that their quality of life has been adversely affected and that they may suffer future loss and damage. Finally, if either twin goes on to have a genetically related child with a mixed race partner, any child born to them is likely to be of different skin colour than either parent.

* I would like to thank Máiréad Enright, Sarah Keenan and Sally Sheldon for their very helpful comments on earlier versions of this judgment, as well as Antony Blackburn-Starza for discussing his doctoral research with me.

[**4**] At the High Court, my colleague Girvan J dismissed the claim in its entirety.

SIGNIFICANCE OF THE CASE

[**5**] The points raised in this case are novel and important. There are few cases pertaining to negligence in this context, and indeed, this is the first action to be brought by children conceived through negligent treatment. The case therefore provides a valuable opportunity for an appellate court to publicly consider, clarify and question the legal principles in this area, in contrast to the more usual 'out of court' settlements following substandard care or treatment provision.

[**6**] The case is also significant because the appellants' emotional distress emerges from a situation that no court in this jurisdiction—and possibly no other jurisdiction—has yet considered in the context of a negligence claim: that to be born a different skin colour from your parent(s) and sibling(s), and to receive racist and other derogatory abuse because of these differences, constitutes legally actionable harm against a negligent provider of fertility services whose carelessness caused you to be so born. This is not only a novel question but also a deeply uncomfortable and difficult one, for it simultaneously relies on and challenges racism in society. Gillen J, in determining that the appellants "do not carry the seal of another person's fault" [28], articulated something that I do not think he intended; for it is potentially problematic to attribute the distress that the appellants have suffered to the 'fault' of any one person, when the reality is that the mistake only matters because of the pervasiveness of racism in society. I have found it difficult to consider these important issues of public policy and accountability in the context of a negligence claim, the strictures of which petition me to individualise fault. While it seems important to hold the clinic accountable for substandard treatment, whether this can or should translate into damages for emotional distress because of racist and other derogatory abuse is far from straightforward.

DISTINGUISHING WRONGFUL LIFE AND WRONGFUL BIRTH CASES

[**7**] That the claim comes from the children, rather than the parents, signifies it as what has become known in legal terms as a 'wrongful life' claim i.e. where a child alleges that, but for the defendant's negligence, she would not have been born and, hence, the harm she now suffers would have been avoided. The last time a claim like this was considered in this jurisdiction was almost thirty years ago by the English Court of Appeal in *McKay v Essex Area Health Authority* [1982] QB 1166. *McKay* determined that disabled children can have no reasonable cause of action in 'wrongful entry into life' claims following negligent pre-natal screening which failed to diagnose the cause of the injury. This was on the policy basis that the alternative was non-existence by affording the mother an opportunity to terminate her pregnancy. The framing of such actions as being about existence *per se* has been heavily criticised on the basis that it fails to capture the reality of the issue, which is that the claimant is alive and suffering because of another's negligence (JK Mason (2007) *The Troubled Pregnancy: Legal Rights and Wrongs in Pregnancy* (Cambridge University Press)). This policy decision to prohibit such claims means that justice becomes highly elusive for child claimants who must bear the brunt of the consequences of substandard treatment without any possibility of recovery of damages. A few courts have permitted wrongful life

claims, reasoning that a claimant can be both benefitted (born) and harmed (injured) at the same time (*Curlender v Bio-Science Laboratories* 106 Cal App 3d 811 (1980)) or that an award of damages would appeal to justice in helping the claimant lead a more bearable life (*Leids Universitair Medisch Centrum v Kelly Molenaar*, no C03/206, RvdW 2005, 42 (18 March 2005)). However, despite powerful dissenting judgments which frame the actions as being about 'wrongful suffering' (Kirby J in *Harriton v Stephens* [2006] HCA 15), the development of the law in most jurisdictions has proceeded along the same lines as *McKay*. While an appropriate time may yet come for *McKay* to be reconsidered, the case before us does not present such an opportunity. The preponderance of analogous authority makes it impossible to contend that the *McKay* decision was given *per incuriam*. The reality that potentially unjust doctrine reinforces itself—because cases in other jurisdictions have relied heavily on *McKay* in their reasoning—does not go unnoticed by this court.

[**8**] Gillen J did not consider the applicability of *McKay* to the present case and neither counsel for the appellants or the respondent have referred to it in their arguments. However, given that *McKay* is still good law and could potentially bar a negligence claim such as this from proceeding, I will make clear how the case before us is distinguishable.

[**9**] In *McKay* the child, Mary, was born disabled because her mother, Jacinta, contracted rubella during her pregnancy, which the defendant doctor negligently failed to diagnose. Ultimately the rubella, rather than the negligent diagnosis, caused the child's dreadful injuries. This was why Mary had no claim under the Congenital Disabilities (Civil Liability) Act 1976, which imposes liability when a careless action of a defendant causes a child to be born with disabilities. In Mary's case, the negligence meant that her mother continued with her pregnancy, when she might otherwise have not, had the diagnosis been correct. In the case before us, the respondent's negligence—the incorrect selection of donor sperm—is the *direct* cause of the children being born mixed-race instead of White, as their parents intended. While different—presumably White—children would have been born had the respondent not been negligent, the appellant children's suffering stems directly from the respondent's careless actions. It is not the case that the respondent's negligence deprived the appellants' mother of an opportunity to terminate her pregnancy; and indeed, even if the respondent's mistake had come to light during their mother's pregnancy, a termination would not have been available to her in this jurisdiction given the restrictive conditions in which abortion is legally available in Northern Ireland.

[**10**] For these reasons, the appellants' claim is distinguished from *McKay* and is therefore permitted as a free-standing action, rather than only being arguable through a proxy 'wrongful birth', or some other, claim by their parents. To allow a free-standing action from the children is important as it means that the ability to recover damages is not reliant on an action from the parents that effectively requires them to portray their children as a burden; something which most, if not all, parents would find objectionable.

[**11**] So that the children's claim can be considered on its own terms, I also want to make clear how it is distinguishable from precedent relating to wrongful birth claims from parents. In *McFarlane and another v Tayside Health Board* [1999] UKHL 50, the House of Lords determined that the parent(s) of an unintended but healthy child may no longer recover damages for the child's upkeep from a negligent defendant. This exception to the ordinary

principles of recovery for negligence was reaffirmed in a subsequent wrongful birth case of *Rees v Darlington Memorial Hospital NHS Trust* [2003] UKHL 52. Gillen J interpreted these cases to mean that as a matter of legal policy, no damages may be recovered where a child is born healthy and without disability or impairment [21]. For whatever reason, counsel for the appellants presented no arguments to the contrary. However, and with respect, to interpret the ratio of these cases so widely would mean that the common law would be forever fossilised. The law would be unable to develop incrementally in response to new forms of damage, for all future cases involving healthy children would simply be barred, even where they suffer from some novel type of personal injury or loss. This cannot be what the House of Lords intended.

[**12**] While the children in this case are healthy, their claim is substantively different from the claims in *McFarlane* and *Rees*, which were claims from parent(s) for the upkeep of their unintended child, where the defendant's carelessness caused the child to be born. In the case before us, the parents sought medical treatment in order to help them try and have children, rather than prevent conception and pregnancy. The context of fertility treatment, and the reproductive choices which it makes explicit, renders the appellants' parents' situation very different from Laura and George McFarlane—who sought to avoid the birth of a fifth child which they felt they could not afford—and Karina Rees—who sought to avoid having children at all because of her own physical disabilities. As the appellants' parents have negotiated settlement out of court with the respondent trust, we do not know if a legal claim from them against the respondent trust would have been successful, given the fertility treatment, as opposed to sterilisation context. However, what we do know is that the case before us is a claim from children—not parents—in relation to their emotional distress—not existence *per se*—which they would not have suffered had the respondent not been careless. They are not seeking to recover for their lifetime's upkeep, and although it is unclear precisely what level of damages they do seek should their claim be successful, their counsel's argument that they are at least entitled to a conventional award, as was permitted in *Rees* (£15,000), signals something more modest. For these reasons, I determine that the present case is distinguishable from *McFarlane* and *Rees* and that the policy exception developed in these cases does not prevent the children from having an arguable case.

DUTY OF CARE

[**13**] Whether a duty of care exists on given facts is a question of law. For a claimant to be owed a duty of care by the defendant there must be sufficient proximity of relationship between the parties and the damage must be reasonably foreseeable (*Donoghue v Stevenson* [1932] AC 562; *Caparo Industries Plc v Dickman* [1990] 2 AC 605). In this case, we must determine whether the clinic owed the children a duty of care not to harm them. Gillen J framed the question to be asked as: 'Was there a duty owed to the cells that the eggs would not be so fertilised?' [14] and concluded that it would be inappropriate for a first instance judge to vest human cells with the relevant status for a duty of care to be owed. He determined that this was an issue for Parliament as it would involve the court venturing 'into the complexities of the creation of life involving a unique physical and scientific process' [14].

[**14**] With respect, the court is not being asked whether fertility clinics owe duties to human reproductive cells—for such would be absurd—but rather, whether they owe a duty

of care to the children born from the treatment services that they provide. Such duty is clearly owed. As counsel for the appellants quite rightly submitted at trial, the respondent is a provider of fertility treatment; the very purpose of which is to help patients conceive and have children. The duty, therefore, is not properly reflected in the summoning of an image of a cluster of cells, but must instead be considered in the broader context of the purpose of the service and the class of persons countenanced through the provision.

[**15**] Support for this position can be derived from both statute and the common law. There is legislative direction relating to the establishment of a duty of care in the context of fertility treatment. The Human Fertilisation and Embryology Act 1990 inserted section 1A into the Congenital Disabilities (Civil Liabilities) Act 1976. The effect of this provision is to extend liability under the 1976 Act to injuries suffered as a result of fertility treatment because of, for example, negligent storage of gametes or embryos, or, as in this case their negligent selection. Gillen J correctly states that the 1976 Act does not apply to the children in this case given that they have suffered no congenital disability as a result of the clinic's negligence. However, the 1976 Act does afford for the possibility of recognising that fertility practitioners owe a duty of care to children born through the provision of fertility treatment. I cannot agree with Gillen J that the 1976 Act 'settled' [10] the question of when 'a foetus' has sufficient status to be owed a duty of care. This is for two reasons. First, the 1976 Act did not establish any duty of care towards foetuses. A foetus does not have legal standing to make a claim, whether in negligence or some other area of law. Instead, the 1976 Act afforded such standing to children born with a congenital disability because of an 'occurrence' which affected either parent's ability to have a non-disabled child, or affected the mother during pregnancy. The claim is brought against the person responsible for the occurrence. Section 1A extends this provision to encompass negligently provided fertility treatment. If, following such an occurrence, a woman terminated her pregnancy because foetal abnormalities were detected in pre-natal screening—an option that I note is not available to women in Northern Ireland unlike women in Great Britain and many other jurisdictions—there would be no possibility of a claim under the 1976 Act, because no child suffering injury would be born. Second, it would be overly rigid to conclude that, in limiting this provision to cases involving congenital disability, Parliament was signaling its intent to forever limit the scope of the duty so that only children born with congenital disabilities could recover damages. It is credible that the type of case before us was simply not contemplated by Parliamentarians in the process of reforming a piece of legislation designed to deal with the consequences of congenital disability, and originally enacted before the dawn of IVF and at a time when donor insemination was only beginning to be accepted as routine clinical practice. In this court's view the 1976 Act does not preclude courts from incrementally developing the common law in the face of novel situations such as the appellants' claim; healthy children alleging a different type of harm following negligent fertility treatment.

[**16**] What is more helpful to consider is when the 1976 Act countenances the existence of a duty between the providers of fertility treatment and the children born from the treatment, so that we can draw parallels to the present novel situation. Section 1A(2) makes clear that the 'defendant' will be answerable to the child if he or she was liable in tort to one or both of the parents. For the purposes of this section it does not matter whether or not the parents have suffered any actionable injury. All that needs to be made out is that a duty of

care was owed to the parents of any child making a claim against the defendants. In the case of fertility treatment, as with other medical treatments, this is straightforward.

[**17**] The common law also signals the existence of a duty of care. *Burton v Islington HA* [1992] EWCA Civ 2 decided that a duty of care can 'crystallise' at birth, for it is at birth that the child sustains injuries as a living person. As with the 1976 Act, this ruling related to the specific context of congenital disability caused by pre-natal—rather than pre-implantation—injury caused by the defendant. However, the principle established in relation to when a duty of care exists is likewise instructive. This case also appropriately limits any duty on the part of the respondent clinic to children that are born and suffer harm as a result of negligently provided treatment, allaying Gillen J's concern that he would be establishing a duty of care between fertility providers and human cells. Such a development would indeed be concerning, for extending legal duties in this way would attribute the same legal personality to cells, embryos and foetuses as living persons; rather than it being clear that legal rights of action only come into existence at birth (*Re MB* [1997] EWCA Civ 3093). However, that is not what the court is being asked to determine in this case. The actual question is much more limited: do the appellant children have sufficient status to be owed a duty of care by the respondent clinic?

[**18**] The respondent clearly owed the children's parents a duty of care to provide treatment that did not fall below the requisite standard. This court therefore determines that the respondent owed the appellants a duty of care to avoid acts or omissions that would be likely to harm them. The reproductive nature of the treatment provided by the respondent means that the relationships involved fall squarely within the well-established 'neighbourhood' paradigm.

BREACH OF DUTY

[**19**] In October 2003 the respondent sent a letter to the appellants' parents detailing the mistake that had been made in the careless selection of donor sperm. This letter detailed the potential effects of using sperm from a 'Caucasian (Cape Coloured)' donor and confirmed that the usual clinical practice would be that only sperm from a 'Caucasian' donor would be used in treatment as this was what had been agreed with the parents. In using the wrong sperm the respondent's actions fell below the reasonably expected standard of care in the provision of fertility treatment. For avoidance of doubt, and because this issue was not specifically addressed by the High Court, the effects of using sperm from a 'Caucasian (Cape Coloured)' donor were either known, or should reasonably have been known, by the respondent. This is not a case where scientific evidence has come to light since the mistake was made. Nor is it a case where it fell within the parameters of reasonable clinical practice for the respondent to use sperm from a donor other than a 'Caucasian' donor. This is because, and as the evidence makes clear, the use of sperm from only a 'Caucasian' donor was a crucial component of the parents' consent to the mother's IVF treatment.

[**20**] I conclude that this is sufficient to establish breach of duty for the purposes of the appellants' claim. However, I offer further reasons as to why this violation of the appellants' parents' consent to treatment means that the respondent's actions fell below the reasonably expected standard of care towards the appellants.

[**21**] Reproductive technology and genetic screening allow for selections which we might not otherwise be able to make. For example, pre-implantation genetic diagnosis (PGD) can be used to select embryos which are not affected with a particular genetic condition, or embryos of a particular sex. Fertility treatment also makes explicit preferences that we do not necessarily articulate in other reproductive contexts. If the appellants' parents had been able to have children who were genetically related to both of them it seems unlikely that they would at any stage have had to articulate their preference of having a racially similar child. However, the need for donor sperm in their treatment meant that this preference had to be expressed. It is important to note that this was not done in a regulatory vacuum. The regulatory framework gives guidance on certain preferences. In relation to the sex selection of embryos, guidance in the Regulator's Code of Practice, and since 2008 the legislation itself (Human Fertilisation and Embryology Act 1990 (as amended), Schedule 2 para 1ZB), only permits such for medical reasons, as opposed to those that are regarded as non-medical or social. The racial matching of gamete donors and prospective parents is not referred to in the legislation, but the Code of Practice gives guidance to fertility clinics. At the time of the appellant parents' treatment—1995—the Code of Practice stated the following:

> "When selecting donated gametes for treatment, centres should take into account each prospective parent's preferences in relation to the general physical characteristics of the donor which can be matched in accordance with good clinical practice." (3.20, Code of Practice, 2nd Edition, revised June 1993)

At the time of the relevant treatment, 'good clinical practice' included racial matching, as confirmed by the new wording of the revised Code of Practice of December 1995 (a few months after the treatment):

> "When selecting donated gametes for treatment, centres should take into account each prospective parent's preferences in relation to the general physical characteristics of the donor. This does not allow the prospective parents to choose, for social reasons alone, a donor of a different ethnic origin(s) from themselves." (3.22, Code of Practice, 3rd Edition, revised December 1995)

[**22**] We may agree or disagree with this guidance. But for the purposes of this claim it is important because it makes clear that the appellants' parents would have had strong expectations that their preference would be upheld, given the regulatory framework. For sake of clarity, the respondent's carelessness is not covered by the warning in the guidance that any attempt at matching physical characteristics cannot be guaranteed for this is clearly referring to the fact that genes are far from determinative, whether in relation to physical, or indeed other, characteristics. The appellant children were not born mixed race because of genetic variation: they were born mixed race because the respondent carelessly used the wrong donor sperm. It is for this reason that I must disagree with Gillen J who gave considerable weight to the argument presented by counsel for the respondent—that because we are all the product of a mixed gene pool, variations and random mutations are ever possible—in determining that the appellant children could have no legitimate expectation to be born with certain racial characteristics.

[**23**] Finally, the appellants' parents would have been offered counselling on the basis of receiving treatment using donor sperm from a 'Caucasian' donor only. In the Human Fertilisation and Embryology Act 1990 there is a statutory requirement that fertility clinics provide patients with suitable opportunities for counselling before any treatment takes place (section 13(6); Schedule 3 para 3(1)a). This means that although counselling is not compulsory for fertility patients an opportunity for counselling must be provided by licensed clinics. The Code of Practice draws particular attention to what is known as 'Implications Counselling' (see sections 6.10-6.15 of the 2nd edition, which was the version in place at the time of the appellants' parents' treatment) whereby counsellors should invite patients to consider, *inter alia*, 'the implications of the procedure for themselves, their family and social circle, and any resultant children' (section 6.10(b)) and where treatment will involve the use of donated gametes, 'their perceptions of the needs of the child throughout his or her child hood and adolescence' (section 6.12(b)). We do not know in this case whether the appellants' parents availed of this counselling. However, it is clear that the statutory framework signals the importance of affording fertility patients an opportunity to think through the consequences of possible fertility treatment, not just for their own benefit, but for the benefit of existing and future familial relationships. This reflects the reality that any breach of duty relating to the mistaken use of donor sperm is interconnected: as well as interfering with the parents' autonomy to make reproductive decisions, it has a broader impact on the family and personal life of children born from the fertility treatment, as well as on existing family members such as older siblings and grandparents. Gillen J was of the opinion that the appellant children could have no legitimate expectation other than to be born healthy and well [34]. I disagree on this point. As children born from legally regulated fertility treatment, the appellants are entitled to expect that factors crucial to their parents' consent to fertility treatment should have been upheld by the respondent. This is because these factors have a fundamental and interconnected impact on their personal and familial existence in the world.

[**24**] This means that the duty of care owed to the appellant children by the respondent was clearly breached.

LOSS AND DAMAGE

[**25**] The court must next address whether the appellants have suffered any legally recognisable loss and damage. Here, the court is not considering in general terms whether it is harmful for there to be racial difference between family members, or whether it is harmful to receive racist and other derogatory abuse because of one's skin colour. Nor is it considering whether it is inherently harmful to be born a particular race. It must consider a much more specific question as to whether the appellant children have suffered legally recognisable harm because of the frustration of their parents' gamete donor preference by the respondent.

[**26**] I lay the question out in precise terms as the appellant children's claim seems incorrectly framed in the High Court judgment, particularly in the determination that because the children have been born healthy they cannot have suffered any legal harm. Race and racial discrimination are difficult and sensitive issues and Gillen J has been

studious in making clear that racial or ethnic discrimination in society is wrong [23]. On this point I agree. He has also been careful to make clear that to be born a particular race does not equate with being born 'damaged' or disabled [23–24]. This is also correct. However, with respect, the conflation of these general issues with the children's claim has resulted in an inappropriate framing of their case, which is actually about whether they have suffered harm because of the respondent's carelessness. In a rush to dissuade the children from seeing themselves as 'victims' because of the respondent's carelessness, my colleague has failed to give adequate emphasis to both the role of the clinic in bringing this situation about and the specific circumstances which the children and family find themselves in. He also, unfortunately, minimises the impact that the children's skin colour has, and will continue to have, on their life.

[**27**] However, while I disagree with much of Gillen J's judgment, the question of whether the children have suffered legally recognisable harm is a difficult one, and without the benefit of my colleague's initial judgment, I might have found it even more so. In reaching a decision, it is important for this court, as a public forum, to give an appropriate account of the difficulties that the children have experienced and are likely to continue to experience.

[**28**] The children have received abuse for two main reasons: first, because their skin colour marks them as racially different from their parents and each other in a way that draws into question the assumed legitimacy of their family unit; and second, because their skin colour does not confer White privilege in a racist society. If the case before us involved non-White parents having a White child, when their preference was for a racially similar child, the issue of racist abuse—as opposed to familial dissimilarity—would likely be very different in their situation, if it was an issue at all. While Gillen J draws our attention to the principles which underlie multi-culturalism and the cruelty of members of society who would levy racist and other abuse at the appellant children, it would be unfortunate for a court to give the impression that racism was purely down to individual meanness and the crass behaviour of a minority in society who do not abide by the values of multi-culturalism. Given the often invisible and pervasive systems and structures which confer racial dominance on some members of society and not others, the values of multi-culturalism remain elusive and aspirational, rather than in any sense real. Northern Ireland is no exception here and we are increasingly seeing divisions, intolerance and violence being practised in terms of racial, as much as sectarian and other political difference (Paul Connolly (2002) *'Race' and Racism in Northern Ireland: A Review of the Research Evidence*, Equality Directorate of OFMDFM). While racism can manifest in exceptional, dramatic and often violent ways, it is important to remember that it is also present in ordinary and everyday life; and for some, it may well be saturating. The challenge for a non-White person of dealing with racism in a society where almost 98% of the population identify as White in the national census—whether White-British, White-Irish or White-Other—is not to be underestimated.

[**29**] To not be White in Northern Ireland is a very visible thing indeed and the appellant children's experiences may be compounded by the fact their parents and wider family network—which as far as I know all identify as White—will be unlikely to have faced similar challenges and may therefore find it difficult to provide support and guidance; however

loved the children are and however well-meaning the actions of their parents and other relatives. Furthermore, the challenge of being racially different from their parents may be further exacerbated by the fact that their parents never set out to create or raise children who were racially different from them. This family's situation is therefore in contrast to mixed-race couples who have genetic offspring, or families where a child is adopted or fostered by a parent or parents who are a different race: in the former, the child reflects the 'mixing' of the parents' genetic material, while in the latter, the parent(s) make a deliberate decision to raise—rather than avoid raising—a child who is not a genetic reflection of them. Likewise, a couple or an individual may, for whatever reason, not select a gamete donor who is racially similar. In these examples, the parent(s) may feel better equipped and prepared to cope and support their children through any incumbent challenges, in contrast to the appellants' parents who were concerned that only sperm from a 'Caucasian' donor would be used in the mother's IVF treatment.

[**30**] As such, the distress that these children have experienced is simultaneously indicative of the wider ills and prejudices in society and particular to their family circumstances. Although race and racism are social constructs, they are understood in a way that materially connects to ancestry and inheritance. Racial markers such as skin colour have long been conceptualised in terms of 'blood' and are seen as fairly rigidly determined by nuclear DNA. Yet the 'genetics' of race are clearly socially constructed, for although these children are mixed-race, they will be regarded in society as non-White and potentially also as 'not from' Northern Ireland. In seeking to ensure that only sperm from a racially matched donor was used, the appellants' parents were trying to ensure that their family would 'pass' in society as genetically related. Of this, they must surely have been conscious given the widespread stigma that is attached to male-factor infertility. At the time of the mother's IVF treatment donor anonymity was a cultural and clinical norm and fertility treatment was not as routine and familiar as it may seem today. Secrecy around the use of donated gametes was—and still is—common. I do not know if the appellants' parents were also conscious of trying to pass on racial privilege to their children. The thought they were may make many of us feel uncomfortable; yet our discomfort seems misplaced given the regulatory framework within which they indicated their preference and as against the backdrop of racial privilege being passed on every day in human reproduction. Likewise, to criticise these parents for wanting to 'pass' as a genetically related family when so many other families are afforded less or no cultural legitimacy or legal recognition, seems to attack a symptom rather than a cause of the privileging of certain types of family structure in society. It seems therefore right to have sympathy with this family's predicament, while at the same time being attentive to the broader political structures which inform our sympathy. The material consequences of oppressive hierarchies in society are not as easy to escape as some might like to believe.

[**31**] On one level, because the distress suffered by the appellant children is both general and particular to their family situation, it is reasonable to conclude that their distress has been caused by the respondent; for if the respondent had not been careless, the children would not be suffering as they are (the 'but for' test of causation: *Barnett v Chelsea and Kensington Hospital* [1968] 1 All ER 193 (HL)). To experience derogatory abuse because of the colour of their skin and the assumed lack of relatedness to their parents and each other is also a reasonably foreseeable consequence of the respondent's carelessness (*Wagon*

Mound (No 1) [1961] 1 All ER 404 (PC)). A legal wrong has therefore been done against the appellant children and it would seem just for our system of civil liability to hold the respondent accountable for its carelessness. However, three factors prevent me from making this finding.

[**32**] First, the issue of causation is not as straightforward as indicated above. While it is clear that the respondent's carelessness caused the children to be born with the skin colour they have, their distress is simultaneously caused by the wider prejudices and structures of society. So while I have no doubt that the children's situation causes them difficulty and emotional distress—along with their parents—it seems neither appropriate nor proportionate to hold the respondent trust entirely liable for the consequences of societal inequality.

[**33**] Second, I find that it would be contrary to public policy to require the respondent to compensate the appellants for the emotional distress they have experienced, for to do so risks individualising the responsibility of dealing with racism and other inequalities in society. Compensation through our civil liability system is heavily individualised, given that it rests on individual litigants identifying fault against defendants. It redistributes the costs associated with injury—whether caused intentionally or by omission—amongst a limited pool of persons. Other systems are possible, but the current system is what the courts must operate under, and such does not countenance compensation for the general effects of structural inequalities. While similar arguments can clearly be made in terms of compensating claimants for disabilities, we can point more directly to the costs of medical and other care, treatment and equipment that a person with disabilities may require, whether to survive on a day to day basis, or to partake generally in societal activities or earn a living. Nor should anything in this judgment be taken to indicate that there is not a need for society to become more accommodating of disability. However, while a person's skin colour is a physical characteristic, there is nothing physically determinative of a non-White person having higher living costs, or experiencing discrimination or racist violence. Instead, such happens because of societal prejudice and in my view courts should be wary of signalling individual defendants such as fertility clinics, rather than our public authorities, as primarily responsible for ameliorating the harms caused by inequality and prejudice. These issues must be addressed by our public institutions and measures put in place to address the very real, often saturating effects of racism, sexism, class prejudice, homophobia and the myriad of other intersecting inequalities that make some lives more difficult than others. Indeed, the existence of such structural inequality is why section 75 of the Northern Ireland Act 1998 puts in place statutory duties which aim to encourage public authorities to address inequalities in the work and functions that they carry out, at least with respect to 'equality of opportunity'—which of course is a more limited aim than fully ameliorating the harms of structural inequality.

[**34**] In making this policy determination I have sought to resist the familiar reasoning that this is what 'right thinking people' or the 'common man on the Clapham omnibus' might think fair or reasonable, for I doubt either would want to find themselves in this family's predicament or walk in the appellant children's shoes. Instead, my decision is based on where I think the responsibility lies for making the appellant children's lives more bearable.

[**35**] Finally, I think the appellants' claim for damages must fail because emotional distress is not actionable damage, however upsetting and real this distress may be. Negligence claims tend to derive from actionable loss—such as physical or psychiatric injury—rather than loss of preference, which results in difficult or upsetting circumstances for the person or persons affected. This court has already made clear how the respondent's frustration of the appellants' parents' gamete donor preference was a relational obligation to the appellants. However, while claimants can now recover for pure psychiatric injury—as opposed to psychiatric harm only being recoverable if accompanied by physical injury—the claimant must suffer from a recognised psychiatric injury, of which emotional distress or upset, as well as fear and grief, does not qualify: *Grieves v FT Everard & Sons* [2007] UKHL 39; *White v Chief Constable of South Yorkshire Police* [1999] 1 All ER 1. No evidence has been presented to indicate that the appellant children are suffering from a recognised psychiatric illness, however distressed they may feel at the abuse that has been directed towards them and their family. I have also heard no arguments from counsel to advance the proposition that the appellants' emotional distress should constitute legally recognisable harm in the context of this novel scenario. This will be because such is very difficult, for even in those jurisdictions which permit claims for negligently inflicted emotional distress, some criteria or restriction other than reasonable foreseeability of the damage must also be satisfied, such as the distress being directly associated with: 1) a physical injury negligently inflicted on the victim; 2) defamation of the victim; or 3) witnessing an injury caused to others.

[**36**] Even if the appellant children were suffering from recognised psychiatric illness—and we should not rule out the possibility that they may go on to suffer from psychiatric illness because of their distress—their claim would still be difficult to make out given the 'patchwork quilt of distinctions' that is the law on the recovery for pure psychiatric harm (per Lord Steyn in *White*, at 500). For example, the conventional starting point of a claimant having to categorise themselves as a primary or secondary victim is nonsensical for the appellants in this case, for they would have to argue that they are primary victims who are suffering psychiatric injury because their skin colour is a physical injury (*Alcock v Chief Constable of South Yorkshire Police* [1992] 4 All ER 907 (HL)). It would be erroneous and problematic for any court to determine that to be born a particular race constitutes physical injury, as this would distract from the reality that racist abuse is levied on the basis of socially constructed difference; however material in its effect. To Gillen J's perceptive comment that claims for personal injuries, loss or damage do not fit easily into situations which relate to human reproduction [19], I would add that neither do claims for emotional distress or psychiatric injury (see also: Law Commission (1998) *Report on Liability for Psychiatric Illness*).

[**37**] For these three reasons, the appellants' claim that they have suffered legally compensable loss or damage connected to the respondent's breach must fail. The final issue for the court to consider is whether the appellants may be entitled to what has become known as a conventional award.

CONVENTIONAL AWARD

[**38**] Gillen J rejected the appellants' counsel's argument that the children should be awarded a conventional award in recognition of the legal wrong done by the fertility clinic,

in accordance with the conventional award given to Katrina Rees in *Rees*, as well as a series of other modern negligence cases such as *Chester v Afshar* [2004] UKHL 41 and *Fairchild v Glenhaven Funeral Services Ltd* [2002] UKHL 22. Counsel argued that this litany of cases represents a modern legal policy that where a wrong has been done a remedy will be provided. Gillen J was of the opinion that while there was merit in the argument that the appellants' parents had a legitimate expectation frustrated by the respondent's carelessness, no such argument could extend to the children [33–34]. As indicated above, this court has found that the children were owed a duty of care by the respondent and that this duty included respecting their parents' gamete donor preference, given the relational impact of this preference on the entire family and the regulatory strictures in which their decision was made and supported by the respondent. The appellants therefore had a legitimate expectation that their mother's IVF treatment should have proceeded in accordance with the wishes of their parents. I therefore disagree with Gillen J that the children cannot be entitled to a conventional award.

[**39**] While there is much merit in the argument that conventional awards are a less than satisfactory means of compensating claimants whose action would otherwise have succeeded had it not been for policy departures from the usual principles of recovery (Nicolette Priaulx (2005) 'Damages for the "unwanted" child: time for a rethink?' *Medico-Legal Journal* 73(4), pp 152–163), the development of conventional awards does provide a route into compensating claimants for a loss of preference or autonomy when the conventional categorisations of damage—as deriving from actionable loss—simply do not countenance a novel case, but where some compensation seems just. So while counsel should be wary of shying away from challenging and creative legal arguments—for the development of the common law relies on such—and short circuiting to arguments for a conventional award for their clients in an effort to secure 'at least' some compensation, there is scope for a conventional award to recognise an interference with personal rights and autonomy that is not otherwise contemplated by conventional doctrine. Due to the carelessness of the respondent, the appellant children have faced, and will continue to face difficulty. While the cause of that difficulty is wider than the respondent's negligence, it is clear that they would not be suffering had the fertility clinic not been careless. A modest conventional award of the amount permitted in *Rees* (£15,000) goes some way to acknowledging that wrong and the court, as a public institution, encouraging accountability for substandard treatment which relates to the expectations that legally regulated fertility clinics generate. The children and their parents may well incur costs in accessing counselling or support networks to help them with their distress. While other legal avenues for redress will be open to the appellant children should they find themselves victims of discrimination or a racially motivated hate crime, such are far from perfect and will once again require individual litigation. It seems fair, just and reasonable that the respondent should in some way contribute to these potential burdens by providing the appellants with a modest, but life changing amount of compensation.

[**40**] The court orders that the appellants are each entitled to a conventional award payment of £15,000 from the respondent.

PRIVACY ARGUMENT

[**41**] I was surprised not to hear any argument from counsel pertaining to the privacy interests of the children under Article 8 of the European Convention of Human Rights, given that the actions of the respondent Trust have clearly impacted on the privacy of this family unit. Such may have been a valuable line of argumentation.

GLOSSARY OF TERMS

Anglo-Irish Agreement	Agreement between the Government of the United Kingdom of Great Britain and Northern Ireland and the Government of Ireland 15 November 1995
An Post	Irish Postal Service
An t-Ard Chláraitheoir	Registrar General
Belfast Agreement/Good Friday Agreement	Agreement between the Government of the United Kingdom of Great Britain and Northern Ireland and the Government of Ireland 10 April 1998
Bunreacht na hÉireann	Irish Constitution
Conradh na Gaeilge	Gaelic League
Comhaltas Ceoltóirí Éireann	Society of Musicians of Ireland
Cóir	Justice (social Catholic, conservative Eurosceptic lobby group, founded to campaign against the Treaty of Lisbon 2007)
Dáil Éireann	Irish Assembly (Lower House)
Éire	Ireland
Fianna Fáil	Irish political party
Fine Gael	Irish political party
garda	Irish Police Officer (plural: gardaí)
An Garda Síochána (Garda)	Irish Police Force
Irish Free State	Official name Irish State (1922–37)
Mná na hÉireann	Women of Ireland
Oifig	Office
Oireachtas	Parliament
Saorstát Éireann	Irish Free State
Seanad Éireann	Irish Senate (Upper House)
Stormont	Northern Ireland Assembly
Sunningdale Agreement	Communiqué between Ireland and the United Kingdom of Great Britain and Northern Ireland on Council of Ireland December 1973
Tánaiste	Deputy Prime Minister of Ireland
Taoiseach	Prime Minister of Ireland
The Troubles	Period of sectarian violence (1966–98)

INDEX

www.ingramcontent.com/pod-product-compliance
Ingram Content Group UK Ltd.
Pitfield, Milton Keynes, MK11 3LW, UK
UKHW051448290926
15471UKWH00008B/1088

9 781849 465748